THE
CAMBRIDGE
MODERN HISTORY

CAMBRIDGE
UNIVERSITY PRESS
LONDON: Fetter Lane

New York
The Macmillan Co.

Bombay, Calcutta and
Madras
Macmillan and Co., Ltd.

Toronto
The Macmillan Co. of
Canada, Ltd.

Tokyo
Maruzen-Kabushiki-Kaisha

THE
CAMBRIDGE
MODERN HISTORY

PLANNED BY

THE LATE LORD ACTON LL.D.

EDITED BY

SIR A. W. WARD LITT.D.

SIR G. W. PROTHERO LITT.D.

SIR STANLEY LEATHES M.A., C.B.

VOLUME VI

THE EIGHTEENTH CENTURY

NEW YORK: THE MACMILLAN COMPANY
CAMBRIDGE, ENGLAND: AT THE UNIVERSITY PRESS

1925

First Edition 1909

Second Impression (corrected) 1925

PRINTED IN GREAT BRITAIN

PREFACE.

THE present volume covers a section of time falling far short of that implied by the literal meaning of the word. But it seems hardly necessary to defend the use of the term " the Eighteenth Century," as denoting a period of Modern History with characteristics peculiar to itself and exhibiting a more or less self-consistent development of its own. We have accordingly, without doing much violence to ordinary usage, restricted the application of the term to the years reaching from the Peace of Utrecht and the supplementary pacifications to the outbreak of the French Revolution. Moreover, the original design of this work has made it necessary, not only to discuss in the volume dealing with the Revolution itself those earlier aspects of the political and social condition of France and of her administrative and financial system, as well as those new currents of philosophical thought and literary effort, which have to be taken into account in tracing its origin; but also to devote a large part of another volume, concerned with the history of the United States, to a narrative of the War of Independence and an examination of its causes. It has therefore been our desire to avoid whatever recurrence to these topics was not needed in order to make clear the course of European history, and of the history of particular States, within the limits deliberately chosen from the outset for the present volume.

Nevertheless, as it seems to us, these limits may be justly designated "natural"; in other words, they are prescribed by the nature of the subject, and not only by our desire to adhere, in essential matters, to the original scheme of this *History*. In the political annals of Europe, and of those other parts of the world whose progress was directly affected by that of the European States, a new epoch unmistakably begins with the Peace of Utrecht, which is our starting-point, though, strictly speaking, that settlement can be called definitive only after the Treaties of 1725 had confirmed those of 1713, 1714 and 1718. A solution had at last been found for the great problem of the partition of the Spanish inheritance between the Houses of Habsburg and Bourbon, and at the same time for that of the Balance of Power which had long been, to all intents and purposes, identical with the question of their historic rivalry. During the whole of this epoch, down to the outbreak of the French Revolutionary Wars, the Utrecht Treaties (if this name may be given to the whole group) remained the established basis of the relations between the European Powers. The Quadruple Alliance of 1718 and the Anglo-Spanish War of 1719 enforced the Utrecht policy with not less rapidity than success; nor can there be any doubt but that, in its broad results, the foreign policy of Stanhope and Dubois, and the long pacific *entente* between England and France under Walpole and Fleury, were alike in thorough consonance with the system carried through, notwithstanding so many obstacles, at Utrecht. The eighteenth century witnessed repeated departures from that system, and successive interruptions of the Peace of Europe caused by a series of wars extending from that of the Polish to that of the Bavarian Succession; but, with certain exceptions, the several Congresses which met in turn to bring about the conclusion of these wars reestablished that Peace without great difficulty on the general basis of the Utrecht arrangements. The most signal exception was the appropriation of Silesia by Prussia in the War of the Austrian Succession, and the maintenance of that conquest after the tremendous struggle of the Seven Years' War; but it should be pointed out that the House of Austria had laid itself open to such a loss when it had sought to settle its succession by means of a series of treaties negotiated separately between itself and the other European Powers, instead of by seeking to bring about a common agreement between them. The escheat of Lorraine to France—an event of even greater moment for the destinies of Europe than the transfer of Silesia to Prussia—was an event stipulated by treaty a generation before it came to pass; but it was none the less a contravention of the Utrecht settlement, destined to avenge itself bitterly upon both the Powers which were the true principals in the bargain— upon Austria as well as upon France.

In eastern Europe, a new epoch begins after the Moslem advance had been finally driven back at the gates of Vienna. The Turkish Power henceforth virtually stood on the defensive against the European Powers;

and the Eastern Question became, what it has since remained, the problem of restricting—perhaps ending—the dominion of the Turks in Europe. The Turkish Wars of the eighteenth century ceased to exercise any direct influence upon the general course of European affairs after the Peace of Passarowitz had reduced the limits of the Turkish empire, even as compared with those assigned to it at Carlowitz. Henceforth, it was no longer in Austria, but in Russia, that the Porte found its most determined foe, against whose advance it had to stand on the defensive both before and after the new ambition of Joseph II had fallen in with the plans inherited by Catharine II from Peter the Great. That the Eastern Question was not solved in this century, was due to the complications and jealousies of Western rather than Eastern politics, and specially to the fact that the Eastern Powers were pre-occupied by their Polish schemes. The intervention of Russia in the concerns of Poland, facilitated by the unpatriotic selfishness of native partisanship, gave Frederick II his chance of pressing on a series of annexations which he regarded as indispensable to the security of the Prussian monarchy. Austria felt herself obliged to follow suit; and the First Partition of Poland, by which the Republic was shorn of nearly one-third of its territory, proved the first step towards a consummation not less subversive of the paramount authority of public law in Europe than the French Revolutionary propaganda itself. But of the story of the Partitions of Poland only the opening chapter properly apper-tains to our present volume.

Among the principal European Powers, Great Britain is found, at the outset of our period, and during by far the greater part of its course, exercising an influence upon European public affairs such as she was again to exercise, and then for a shorter time, only at the close of the Napoleonic Wars. The primary cause of this influence is to be sought in the leading part which Great Britain had played, through the armed forces which she had sent forth or equipped, and by the way in which they had been led to victory, in the great Spanish Succession War; but that she maintained her political position so long was due to further reasons, which it is part of the task of this volume to discuss. The traditions of a free parliamentary government prevailed in England more potently than ever before; but they were no longer associated, as they had been during most of the preceding century, with a mutability of political system for which this nation had become proverbial. The "principles of 1688" as formulated by Locke, to the origins of whose political philosophy a separate section is devoted in this volume, had become, in Sir Leslie Stephen's words, "the political bible of the eighteenth century"; and they remained such till the French Revolution changed both scope and method of modern political thought. To the strength of constitutional, aided by that of dynastic, stability— for Jacobitism had ceased to be a political force even before its final effort—was added the stimulating influence of a well-considered foreign policy far removed from insularity, and already conscious of the demands of a world-empire. The power of Great Britain was already expanding into that of a British empire extending from the East Indies to the New World; and British enterprise was depriving Dutch and French rivals of most of their share of the field, as it had of old aimed at driving out the Spaniards and drove them out again when, after the close of Ferdinand I's prudent reign, they had once more begun to aspire to a revival of their old colonial power. Thus, under Chatham's inspiring guidance, and in alliance with a King after Chatham's own heart, Great Britain's star rose to an unprecedented height. Meanwhile the "sister island" long remained down-trodden; nor was it till the close of our period that Irish loyalty, in a season of danger to the empire, led to a relaxation of some of the disabilities imposed upon the country, and even obtained for it a transitory legislative independence. Before this, Great Britain had to confront the rebellion of her American colonies, the armed intervention of France and Spain, and the armed neutrality of Russia and her allies. Some of the noblest representatives of English parliamentary statesmanship had sought to withstand the coercive legislation which had given rise to the colonial crisis; and its termination was thus made easier. No general view of the history of Great Britain during this period would be complete which should leave out of sight the religious condition of its inhabitants. Without the renewal of its religious life from within, no soundness of mind or muscle could have arrested the decay into which, in the middle of the eighteenth century, factiousness, frivolity, and vice seemed to be hurrying large sections of the population.

While, until towards the close of this period the power and influence of Great Britain steadily progressed, and even in the Peace of Versailles (1783) her losses, with the one great exception of the insurgent colonies, were relatively small and in respect of her colonial cessions to Spain were morally more than compensated by her retention of Gibraltar, the European prestige as well as the maritime and colonial power of France no less manifestly declined. Her struggle with Great Britain for naval and colonial supremacy was decided in the course of a stirring series of conflicts, treated partly in the chapter on the *Conquest of Canada* which finds its proper place in our seventh volume, partly in the portion of the present volume which offers a connected account of Indian history from the days of the Moghul empire to those of the rule of Warren Hastings, the first Governor-General of India. The failure of the policy of Louis XV (which was far from being always the policy of his Ministers) must be ascribed, partly to the personal shortcomings of the sovereign himself and some of those whom he trusted in Court or camp, partly and chiefly to the excessive strain put upon the resources of France by the efforts which she made simultaneously in the European conflict and in the struggle for supremacy beyond seas. Whether the "reversal of alliances" in the middle of the century, which on the part of France implied a renunciation of her ancient policy of antagonism to the House of Habsburg, was in itself irrational and inopportune, or whether its breakdown was due to the conduct, rather than the conception, of the new "system," there can at least be no reason for regarding that breakdown as the result of internal rottenness in a State whose administration was in many respects un-surpassed, or a people whose inborn vigour was, under the guidance of genius, to shake the world.

To no Government was the superiority of French administrative methods better known than to that of the great Prussian King, and by none was it more openly acknowledged. To Frederick II his father had bequeathed the sinews of war in the shape of an army incomparably disciplined and a well-filled treasury; and thus he was enabled to put into execution his design, conceived with unexampled audacity and carried out with wonderful determination, of raising his poor and straggling kingdom to the position of a great European Power. The story of this achievement will be found narrated in this volume without the distortions of either apotheosis or apology; and, where the views of historical scholars differ as to the immediate motives of Frederick the Great's action, room has been found for an expression of this difference. Alike when he first invaded Silesia, and when he fell upon his Saxon neighbour, as when he thwarted the dynastic ambition of Joseph II on behalf of the Princes of the Empire, Frederick the Great's plan of action lay clear before his eyes both in war and in peace; and it was one from which the State that through him had taken its place among the chief motive forces of European political life could not swerve with impunity. For a time it seemed as if his successor were, without any strain upon the military and financial resources of a State of mettle so proved, to add fresh laurels to those of the great King; and the politically effete Dutch oligarchy collapsed among its canals and counting-houses, when, in 1787, a Prussian force invaded the Low Countries to vindicate the honour of the House of Orange.

To the history of the Austrian Netherlands—down to the time of their complete alienation from a Government whose intentions with regard to them they with reason suspected, and for whose domestic reforms they had nothing but distaste—attention is directed elsewhere in this volume, in which it has been sought to include some notice of every European State whose progress or decline affected the general course of European history. In that course there has not often been a time when the several members of the European family were less disposed to acknowledge among them any principle of unity or paramount authority; and the system of a concert of Powers was still in an imperfectly developed stage of recognition or acceptance. Religious differences had almost (though not quite) ceased to count; and the diplomacy of each State, or of each dynasty, was single-mindedly confined to the advance of its particular interests. The Austrian dominions had been kept together by the ceaseless anxiety of Charles VI for the maintenance of their cohesion; nor was it on the accession of Maria Theresa permanently disturbed except by the loss of a single province. Once again, and more seriously, imperilled by the ambition of Joseph II, whose miscalculations of season and method should not be allowed to detract from the honour due to the nobility and humanity of his purpose, the power of the House of Habsburg held out, as it was to hold out for many a generation afterwards, though the Imperial Crown still worn by its chief seemed to have become little more than a highly respectable ornament. Russia, diplomatically speaking a member of the family of European States only from the Treaty of Amsterdam (1717) onwards, virtually decided the issue of the greatest continental struggle of the eighteenth century—the Seven Years' War—and, under the rule of the "most political woman" that any century (unless it be that of Semiramis) has produced, appeared ready to arbitrate in the still more critical conflict of the French Revolutionary War. The northern neighbours of Russia had sunk into Powers of the second and third rank—Sweden paralysed by the selfish contests of rival oligarchical factions; Denmark under an absolute monarchy tempered by ministerial wisdom or endangered by ministerial rashness. In the south, Spain under her first Bourbon King, after a passing effort towards better things, sank back into the condition of misrule and bankruptcy in which she had been left by her last Habsburg sovereign. And though, under the second Bourbon King, a further fraction of her former Italian dominions, which Philip V's ambitious consort had succeeded in recovering as a Spanish appanage, was restored to the dynasty, it was not till the reign of Charles III that Spain seemed for a time about to assume a place among the progressive States of Europe. But neither the reforms of Florida Blanca and his colleagues, nor even the expulsion of the Jesuits, which here and in Portugal seemed more astounding than it did in contemporary France, could change the economic condition of the nation; and the foreign policy of Spain, after finally settling down into a willingness to fulfil the obligations of the Bourbon Family Compact by means of which Choiseul had hoped to revive the political ascendancy of France, ended in a peace which left Gibraltar still in British hands. In Italy, the Papacy passed out of the tenure of an adversary of the Bourbons and a friend of the Jesuits into that of a pontiff pledged to the overthrow of the Order. But neither the Papacy nor any other Italian Government exercised any considerable influence upon the course of European politics; and it was only the mutual jealousy of foreign Powers that stayed the immediate downfall of Venice and Genoa as independent States. Switzerland, though largely dependent upon France through her unhappy foreign-service system, contrived to preserve her so-called neutrality and, amidst an endless succession of "class-wars," her existing political institutions, till the advent of the French Revolution.

The intellectual note of the "eighteenth century" is that of "enlightenment"—in other words, the self-confident revolt of the trained human intellect against tradition for tradition's sake, and against whatever that intellect holds to be superstition or prejudice. In the great majority of European States, which had passed through the stage of the diminution of oligarchies, based on the rights and liberties of particular classes, and were under strong monarchical rule, it was unavoidable that enlightenment, if it asserted itself at all, should prevail through the authority of a benevolent despotism; but, as the example of English society in the eighteenth century shows, there was no exclusive connexion between the methods of despotism and the principles of enlightenment. Of the enlightened absolute monarchy of the period examples will be found in many of the chapters succeeding each other in the present volume—from great historical figures like those of Catharine II and Frederick II, and above all that of Joseph II, the true protagonist of the *Aufklärung*, to lesser potentates or their Ministers—Charles III in Parma and the Two Sicilies, and his reforming Administration in Spain, Leopold II, more especially as Grand Duke of Tuscany, and the Bernstorffs and the unfortunate Struensee in Denmark. But an age of despots, whether it be also an age of enlightenment or not, must always exhibit both sides of the medal; and thus we find here, on the obverse, a prince whose ambition it is, like that of Frederick the Great, to be nothing more than the first servant of a State upon all of whose members rests the same duty of self-devotion to the welfare of the whole; and on the reverse—Sardanapalus in the shape of Louis XV. It was Goethe, born in the middle of the eighteenth century, who drew this latter parallel, while at the same time reverencing no type of humanity so highly as that of conscious beneficence to the world around it. And, as the commentator who recalls these traits in Goethe reminds us, it was he again who with unerring finger pointed to the most signal weaknesses in the century from which he came forth—its contempt for true originality, its lack of compassion for failure, and its impatience at the inevitably slow process of historic growth.

In issuing the present volume at a rather later date than we had intended, we desire to tender an apology to those of our contributors who had some time ago sent in the chapters written by them, and who may have been inconvenienced by the delay in publication. In no instance had any of the contributions to this volume reached us more punctually, or been prepared for publication with greater care and completeness, than the three chapters written by the late Mr Robert Nisbet Bain, Assistant Librarian at the British Museum, whose lamented death occurred after this Preface was already in type. Mr Bain was one of the contributors selected by Lord Acton at the inception of the present work, as a historical writer who had few rivals in his intimacy with the languages and the historical literature of northern and eastern Europe; and, as our readers are aware, this *History* is deeply indebted to him for the ample share he has taken in its production.

We wish to express our obligations to Mr J. F. Chance, who, besides contributing an important section with its bibliography, has permitted us the free use of a comprehensive Bibliography compiled by him for the political history of Europe during a considerable part of the period covered by this volume. We have also to thank Mr H. G. Aldis, of Peterhouse and the University Library, for the compilation of the Index and for other services rendered in connexion with this volume, Professor H. J. Foxwell for help in connexion with chapter VI, Miss A. D. Greenwood for drawing up the Chronological Table, and Mr A. T. Bartholomew, of Peterhouse and the University Library, for aid in the matter of the Bibliographies.

A. W. W.
G. W. P.
S. L.

May, 1909.

TABLE OF CONTENTS.

CHAPTER I.

GREAT BRITAIN UNDER GEORGE I.

(1) THE HANOVERIAN SUCCESSION.

By A. W. WARD, Litt.D., F.B.A., Master of Peterhouse.

(2) THE FOREIGN POLICY OF GEORGE I.
(1714–21.)

By J. F. CHANCE, M.A., Trinity College.

CHAPTER II.

THE AGE OF WALPOLE AND THE PELHAMS.

By H. W. V. Temperley, M.A., Fellow and Assistant Tutor of Peterhouse.

(1)

CHAPTER III.

JACOBITISM AND THE UNION.

By C. Sanford Terry, M.A., Clare College, Burnett-Fletcher
Professor of History in the University of Aberdeen.

CHAPTER IV.

THE BOURBON GOVERNMENTS IN FRANCE AND SPAIN. I.

(1714–26.)

By EDWARD ARMSTRONG, M.A., F.B.A., Fellow, Bursar, and
Lecturer in Modern History, Queen's College, Oxford.

CHAPTER V.

THE BOURBON GOVERNMENTS IN FRANCE AND SPAIN. II.
(1727–46.)

By Edward Armstrong, M.A., F.B.A.

CHAPTER VI.

FINANCIAL EXPERIMENTS AND COLONIAL DEVELOPMENT.

By E. A. Benians, M.A., Fellow of St John's College.

CHAPTER VII.

POLAND UNDER THE SAXON KINGS.

By the late R. Nisbet Bain, Assistant Librarian, British Museum.

CHAPTER VIII.

THE WAR OF THE AUSTRIAN SUCCESSION.

(1) The Pragmatic Sanction.

By C. T. Atkinson, M.A., Fellow of Exeter College, formerly Demy of Magdalen College, Oxford.

(2) Prussia under Frederick William I.

By Dr Emil Daniels.

(3) The War.

By C. T. Atkinson, M.A.

CHAPTER IX.

THE SEVEN YEARS' WAR.

By Dr EMIL DANIELS.

CHAPTER X.

RUSSIA UNDER ANNE AND ELIZABETH.

By the late R. NISBET BAIN.

CHAPTER XI.

THE REVERSAL OF ALLIANCES AND THE FAMILY COMPACT.

By JEAN LEMOINE.

CHAPTER XII.

SPAIN AND PORTUGAL.

(1746–94.)

By the Rev. George Edmundson, M.A., formerly Fellow
and Tutor of Brasenose College, Oxford.

(1) Spain under Ferdinand VI and Charles III.

(2) PORTUGAL.

(1750–93.)

(3) BRAZIL.

(SEVENTEENTH AND EIGHTEENTH CENTURIES.)

CHAPTER XIII.

GREAT BRITAIN.

(1756–93.)

(1) WILLIAM PITT THE ELDER.

By Dr WOLFGANG MICHAEL, Professor of History in the
University of Freiburg-im-Breisgau.

(2) The King's Friends.

By J. M. Rigg, Inspector of Manuscripts under the Historical Manuscripts Commission.

(3) The Years of Peace, and the Rise of the Younger Pitt.

(1782–93.)

By Martin J. Griffin, LL.D., C.M.G., Parliamentary Librarian of Canada.

CHAPTER XIV.

IRELAND IN THE EIGHTEENTH CENTURY.

By Robert Dunlop, M.A., Victoria University.

CHAPTER XV.

INDIA.

(1) THE MOGHUL EMPIRE.

By the Right Hon. Sir ALFRED COMYN LYALL, K.C.B., G.C.I.E., F.B.A., LL.D., Honorary Fellow of King's College.

Contents.

(2) The English and French in India.

(1720–63.)

By P. E. Roberts, B.A., late Scholar of Worcester College, Oxford.

(3) Clive and Warren Hastings.

By P. E. Roberts.

CHAPTER XVI.

ITALY AND THE PAPACY.

By Mrs H. M. Vernon.

CHAPTER XVII.

SWITZERLAND FROM THE TREATY OF AARAU TO THE FRENCH REVOLUTION.

By Professor J. J. Schollenberger, University of Zurich.

CHAPTER XVIII.

JOSEPH II.

By Professor Eugène Hubert, University of Liége.

CHAPTER XIX.

CATHARINE II.

By Dr Otto Hötzsch, Professor in the Royal Academy, Posen.

CHAPTER XX.

FREDERICK THE GREAT AND HIS SUCCESSOR.

(1) HOME AND FOREIGN POLICY.

(1763–97.)

By Dr EMIL DANIELS.

(2) POLAND AND PRUSSIA.

(1763–91.)

By Professor Dr OTTO HÖTZSCH.

CHAPTER XXI.

DENMARK UNDER THE BERNSTORFFS AND STRUENSEE.

By W. F. REDDAWAY, M.A., Fellow of King's College, Censor of Non-Collegiate Students.

CHAPTER XXII.

THE HATS AND CAPS AND GUSTAVUS III.

(1721–92.)

By the late R. NISBET BAIN.

CHAPTER XXIII.

ENGLISH POLITICAL PHILOSOPHY IN THE SEVENTEENTH AND EIGHTEENTH CENTURIES.

By ARTHUR LIONEL SMITH, M.A., Jowett Fellow and Tutor of Balliol College, Oxford.

CHAPTER XXIV.

THE ROMANTIC MOVEMENT IN EUROPEAN LITERATURE.

By C. E. Vaughan, M.A., Balliol College, Oxford, Professor of English Literature in the University of Leeds.

LIST OF BIBLIOGRAPHIES.

CHAPTER I.

GREAT BRITAIN UNDER GEORGE I.

(1) THE HANOVERIAN SUCCESSION.

HAPPILY for England, the Hanoverian Succession was, so far as the predominant partner in the Union was concerned, accomplished without bloodshed; and, happily for the continental Powers of Europe, they were not drawn into a direct settlement by arms of the question of the British Succession, as they previously had been in the case of the Spanish, and afterwards were in that of the Austrian. This result was by no means reached as a matter of course, or in accordance with common expectation; it was due to a combination of causes, among which not the least effective lay in the sagacity and self-control shown by the members of the House of Hanover in the crisis of its fortunes.

Without again going over ground covered as part of English and European history in a previous volume, it may be convenient to note briefly the principal phases through which the question of the Hanoverian —or, as it may from first to last be called with perfect propriety, that of the Protestant—Succession in England passed, before, after long years of incubation, that Succession became, with a suddenness more startling to contemporaries than to later observers, an accomplished fact. This summary may furnish a suitable occasion for recalling the personalities of those members of the Hanoverian dynasty who were immediately concerned in the transactions preceding its actual occupation of the English throne, and of some of the counsellors and agents with whose aid the goal of their labours was attained. And it may be permissible to add a word as to the antecedents of a House about whose earlier history the English people knew little and cared less, but which was never truer to its past than when it assumed the inheritance of a great future.

In the critical year 1688 Sophia, the youngest daughter of the Princess Elizabeth of England who during the long years of her exile continued to call herself Queen of Bohemia, was fifty-eight years of age; she was thus senior by eight years to Louis XIV, whom accordingly she was, as she says, always accustomed to regard as "a young man." She had been married for thirty years to Ernest Augustus, the youngest of the four brother Dukes who in their generation represented the Lüneburg branch of the House of Brunswick, and whose territories included Lüneburg-Celle and Calenberg-Göttingen. In 1662 Ernest Augustus, in accordance with the alternating arrangement made in the Peace of Westphalia, became Bishop of Osnabrück, and in 1679 he succeeded to the rule of the principality of Calenberg (Hanover). His and Sophia's eldest son, George Lewis (afterwards King George I) was in 1688 a man of twenty-eight years of age, to whom a son, George Augustus (afterwards George II) and a daughter (afterwards Queen of Prussia) had already been born. Besides George Lewis, five younger sons and a daughter (Sophia Charlotte, afterwards the first Queen of Prussia) were living to Sophia and her husband in 1688. Thus her family was numerous; nor were her husband's prospects of territorial dominion less promising.

The historic grandeur of the House of Guelf dates from a very remote past; and the laborious investigation of its antiquities which at this very time was being commenced by Leibniz (though, so far as is known, this was the only research conducted by him which ever engaged the attention of the future George I) could have possessed only a very academic interest for Englishmen. What had been left of the vast possessions of Henry the Lion, or had been added to the remnant by his descendants, had been partitioned and repartitioned by them on innumerable occasions. Towards the end of the sixteenth century the efforts of the Princes of the House of Guelf had raised it to a position of importance and influence at least equal to that of any other princely family in northern Germany; but the two main, or Brunswick and Lüneburg, branches, which had separated in the thirteenth century, were never actually reunited, and even the dominions of the Lüneburg branch were never united as a single inheritance. Although of the five elder brothers of Duke George, who in the latter part of the Thirty Years' War so signally asserted the position of his House, four in succession held undivided sway over the territories which formed their joint inheritance, on his death in 1641 his will established an exception to the principles of unity of government as well as of indivisibility of territory formerly observed by the Lüneburg Dukes. Calenberg (Hanover), where he had ruled independently of his brothers since 1636, was to remain separated from the more important Lüneburg-Celle; while the principle of primogeniture was only to be applied so far as to give the eldest brother the right of choice between the two divisions. In obedience to this rule, the eldest of Duke George's four sons, Christian Lewis, after first holding sway at Hanover, succeeded his uncle Frederick at Celle in 1648. On his death, without children, in 1665, the second brother, George William, who had ruled at Hanover, succeeded to Celle, where he carried on the government till his own death in 1705, having been followed at Hanover by his younger brother John Frederick (Leibniz' Roman Catholic patron), who ruled there till he died, leaving only two daughters, in 1679. In that year came the turn of the youngest brother, Ernest Augustus, the Bishop of Osnabrück, Sophia's husband, who now succeeded at Hanover, from which his line took the name generally used in England.

But before this long-delayed rise took place in the fortunes of the pair, a more important advance had been prepared. Ernest Augustus' elder brother George William (who had himself been at one time affianced to Sophia, then a poor Palatine princess at her brother's Court in Heidelberg) had long since gone back from his undertaking to remain unmarried during the lifetime of Ernest Augustus and his consort, and thus to secure to them or their offspring the succession in Celle. In 1676 he married the daughter of a Poitevin nobleman, Eleonora d'Olbreuse, who had already borne to him several children. Only the eldest of these, Sophia Dorothea, who had been legitimised five years before her mother's marriage, survived; and the right of any issue from that marriage to succeed to George William's inheritance during the survival of any descendant of Ernest Augustus was expressly barred. But the marriage of Sophia Dorothea to Ernest Augustus' eldest son, George Lewis, in 1682, followed by the birth in 1683 and 1687 of the two children already mentioned, furnished a final safeguard that the union of Celle-Lüneburg and Calenberg-Göttingen would ultimately be carried out. And thus in 1683 the imperial sanction was obtained for the testament "set up" by Ernest Augustus (*i.e.* promulgated by him in his lifetime), which established in all the dominions of the line the twofold principle of indivisibility and succession by primogeniture.

The marriage of George Lewis and Sophia ended in infidelity on both sides and in a sentence of divorce (1694); and the rest of her life (which lasted thirty-three years longer) was spent by the unhappy Princess in custody at Ahlden. The proclamation of primogeniture was bitterly resented by the younger sons of Duke Ernest Augustus, and one of them, Prince Maximilian, contrived a plot (with some dangerous ramifications), on the discovery of which (1691) he was exiled, and his chief agent put to death. But the unity of the dominions of the Brunswick-Lüneburg line was now assured, and, although it was not actually accomplished till the death of George William of Celle in 1705, a sufficient basis had been secured for the protracted efforts of Ernest Augustus to bring about his recognition as an Elector of the Empire. In December, 1692, he actually obtained investiture as such from the Emperor; but his admission into the Electoral College took sixteen more years of negotiation; so that it was not till 1708 that George Lewis, who had succeeded to his father ten years before, reached this consummation.

The electoral investiture accorded to the House of Brunswick-Lüneburg was the avowed reward of the services which it had rendered to the Empire and the House of Austria during the whole of the period between the Peace of Westphalia and the crisis of 1688. In the early part of this period the foreign policy of that House was chiefly intent upon preventing France and Sweden from breaking through the limits within which the Peace of Westphalia had sought to confine them. The Triple Alliance (1668) in some measure shifted the relations between the leading European Powers; and, for a time, the goodwill of the Brunswick-Lüneburg Dukes was solicited—and not by means of fair words only—by both France and her adversaries. But, in 1672, the policy of George William of Celle was, by the advice of his Minister von Schütz, definitively emancipated from French influence; and both he and his brother Ernest Augustus were now gradually gained over to the political system devised by George Frederick of Waldeck and adopted by William of Orange. A loyal adherence to the House of Austria was henceforth the guiding principle of the policy consistently pursued by the two brothers, and by Ernest Augustus' son and grandson, both before and after the accession of the former of these to the English throne, and was handed down by a series of trusted advisers, from the elder Schütz to his son-in-law Andreas Gottlieb von Bernstorff, and from Bernstorff to Münchhausen.

The Treaty of 1674, by which all the Brunswick-Lüneburg Dukes except John Frederick of Hanover (whose death, five years later, ended this schism in the politics of the House) joined the coalition against France, bound them to furnish 15,000 men, in addition to 2000 maintained at their own cost, in return for subsidies paid by the States General, Spain and the Emperor; and in August, 1675, the Brunswick-Lüneburgers under their Princes gained the brilliant victory of the Bridge of Conz. They then returned home to protect the dominions of the House against the Swedes; but of this enemy a sufficient account was given by the Great Elector of Brandenburg, between whose dynasty and its Brunswick-Lüneburg kinsmen relations of intimacy and of jealousy alternated in rapid succession. When, after the Peace of Nymegen (1679), the chief anxiety of the House of Austria was the Turkish peril, Prince George Lewis and the Hanoverian Life-guards rendered important service at the siege of Vienna (September, 1683), and he and four of his brothers took an active part in several campaigns against the Turks (the importance of which for the Empire has often been underrated) both in Hungary, where in 1685 George Lewis particularly distinguished himself at the taking of Neuhäusel, and in the Morea; two of the Princes laid down their lives in these conflicts. When, partly in consequence of the Imperialist successes in the East, the armies of France invaded the Empire in the West, Celle and Hanover joined in the Magdeburg Conference (October, 1688), and contributed to the forces which secured the middle Rhine 8000 men under the command of Ernest Augustus, George Lewis taking an active part in the operations.

Such was, in bare outline, what may be called the political record of the House of Hanover at the time of the English Revolutionary settlement of 1688–9. Curiously enough, the House which had rendered and was prepared to render excellent service in the struggle against the political predominance of France—of which struggle the accession of William and Mary might justly be called an incident—was in the persons of its reigning Dukes ardently attached to French modes of life and thought. By a combination of military discipline with an easygoing freedom of thought they had been trained to habits of mind in better accord with the conditions of benevolent despotism than with those of a steady regard for constitutional rights and liberties. These tendencies were united to a love of social dissipations of which Venice, a favourite resort of the Brunswick-Lüneburg Dukes, long remained the most fashionable scene; but George Lewis, though, like his father and uncle before him, a lover of licence, was from first to last as little French in his tastes as he was in his politics; and his wife's French blood did not tend to soften his antipathy to her nationality. The descendant of the Stewarts, through whom the House of Hanover had become connected with the royal family of England, differed entirely in her intellectual tastes and principles of conduct from her husband and her eldest son, but she was not less alien to the principles than they to the ideals and usages of recent English politics. Accustomed at once to a free view of life and to a frank and cheerful acceptance of its responsibilities, high-spirited and courageous, but in nothing more shrewd than in her self-knowledge, the Electress Sophia (as she was already called) was, like her sister Elizabeth and her brother Charles Lewis, Elector Palatine, the friend of philosophers—and at least in so far herself a philosopher that she could shape her course according to principles transparently clear and definite, and sufficient to enable her to meet with unbroken serenity the varied troubles of more than fourscore years. Inasmuch as throughout her life the question of the form of religious faith professed by princes as well as by peoples was still a very important factor in politics, it seems strange that neither then nor afterwards should the confessional position of the House of Hanover have been very clearly understood in England. The Electress Sophia (though as a child she had been accustomed to attend the services of the Church of England at her mother's Court) had been brought up as a Calvinist, and adhered through life, in no half-hearted way, to that "religion"; but the Elector and his family were steady Lutherans. Neither in them, nor most certainly in her, was there a trace of bigotry or intolerance; and, while detestation of Popery was part of her nature as well as of her training, she not only was quite ready to do what was expected of her in the way of Protestant conformity, but sympathised cordially with those schemes of religious reunion which were among the noblest aspirations of the greatest minds of the age—of Leibniz above all.

As there was a great deal of piety in Sophia's heart, she could not but take as she did a continuous interest both in the dynasty from which her mother sprang and in the country with which its connexion remained unsevered. In her girlhood there had been some passing talk of her becoming the bride of the banished Charles II; and, in 1681, the design of marrying her eldest son to Princess Anne of England was approved by William of Orange, though it does not seem to have been favoured by Sophia herself. As it came to nothing, George Lewis was not to anticipate Monmouth as a Protestant candidate for the English throne. When the Revolution of 1688 was at hand, Ernest Augustus displayed no eagerness such as was shown by most of the German Protestant Princes, including his own elder brother and notably the Elector of Brandenburg, to associate himself with the English project of William of Orange; and his consort manifested sympathy with her kinsman James II, though the statement that she supported his appeal to the Emperor for mediation cannot be proved. At no time would she listen to the doubts cast upon the genuineness of the birth of the Prince of Wales. But her own position in the matter of the succession to the English throne she neither did nor could ignore. When the Declaration of Right, which settled the Crown, after William and Mary, upon the posterity of Mary, then on Anne and her posterity, and then on the posterity of William was, in 1689, turned into the Bill of Rights, the additional proviso was inserted that no person in connexion with the Church of Rome or married to a member of it should be capable of inheriting or possessing the Crown. By this clause, it has been calculated, the eventual claims to the succession of nearly threescore persons were taken away. In the Lords, Bishop Burnet by the King's desire proposed, and carried without opposition, an amendment naming the Duchess Sophia and her descendants as next in the succession; but it was rejected in the Commons, on the ground of its injustice to claimants nearer in descent who might have become Protestants in the interval. As a matter of fact, the birth of the Duke of Gloucester in the midst of the discussion (July 24, 1689) removed one reason for pressing on the amendment; but, whatever the reason why the Government gave way, Sophia's name was not mentioned in the Bill or in the Scottish Claim of Rights. The whole transaction had, as she warmly acknowledged, revealed the goodwill of King William towards the Hanoverian Succession, and this goodwill he steadily maintained. He cannot, as has been supposed, have seriously favoured the pretensions of the House of Savoy-Carignan, in the absence of any assurance of a change of religion in that quarter; and in any case those pretensions would have been relegated into limbo, when, in 1696, Savoy deserted the Grand Alliance.

In general it may be said that the policy of the House of Hanover as to the Succession in the years which ensued was one of waiting— patiently on the part of the Electress Sophia, and with something very like indifference on the part of her son. Her consciousness of the uncertainties of fortune at her time of life suffices to account for her tranquillity; George Lewis never cared to conceal his dislike of the possibilities before him, though he would at any time have made it give way to his sense of duty towards his dynasty. The English throne seemed to many of his contemporaries the most uncertain of royal seats, and the English nation the very exemplar of mutability. Though a British envoy extraordinary was from 1689 accredited to Hanover and Celle among other north German Courts, that of Hanover was during the last decade of the century almost absorbed in its own intimate troubles and immediate ambitions. The electoral dignity, which as has been seen was not acknowledged by the Electors of the Empire at large before two of them—Saxony and Brandenburg—had each compassed a royal crown, had been secured from the Emperor by means of the *Kurtractat* of 1692, by which the new Elector under- took to furnish a force of 6000 men for service against the Turks, and, should this be no longer required, against the French, as well as to support the Habsburg interest both in coming imperial elections and in the matter of the Spanish Succession. It may be truly said that George Lewis was as cordially interested in what his dynasty gave as in what it took; and even the additional importance which the prospect of the English Succession gave to his House he would seem to have chiefly valued because it enabled him to take a prominent part in military operations. After he had succeeded his father at Hanover in 1698, not only did he and his uncle at Celle join the Grand Alliance reknit by William III, but they obliged their kinsmen at Wolfenbüttel to throw up their alliance with France. When the War of the Spanish Succession broke out, Hanover and Celle placed under Marlborough's command more than 10,000 troops, which fought with distinction at Blenheim and elsewhere, though (as the Electress Sophia complained) no notice was taken of them in the gazettes; and, after George Lewis had (in 1705) become ruler of the entire dominions of his House, he asserted himself by strongly opposing the first suggestions of a pacification (1706); and his most cherished ambition was fulfilled when (1707) he was appointed to the command of the army of the Rhine. It was his misfortune, not his fault, that in this position he was unable to accomplish any military results of much importance.

Meanwhile, in England the death of Queen Mary (1694) could hardly fail to bring the Succession question forward again. In 1696, the Brandenburg scheme of a marriage between Princess Louisa Dorothea and King William III had come to nothing; and, in 1698, he paid a visit to Celle and its neighbourhood, during which his conversations with the (now Dowager) Electress Sophia and her clever sister-in-law at Celle beyond a doubt revived his interest in the Hanoverian Succession. But neither he nor English politicians had just then much time to occupy themselves with the question, which only became one of general interest when the death of the young Duke of Gloucester (August 7, 1700) left no life between the Electress Sophia and the throne but that of Queen Anne herself.

In the course of the autumn the Electress Sophia paid a visit to King William at the Loo, in which she was accompanied by her daughter the Electress of Brandenburg and her grandson the young Electoral Prince (afterwards King Frederick William I of Prussia). Curiously enough, the idea seems to have crossed King William's mind of placing this young Prince (whose father had claims upon the King's own inheritance as Prince of Orange) in the position left vacant by the Duke of Gloucester—though, as is pointed out by Onslow, he never had it in his power to nominate any one to the English throne; and the Brandenburg (soon to become the Prussian) Court was quite awake to what, as it seemed, might happen. So late as 1699 the Elector Frederick III's sagacious Minister Fuchs was pressing his master "to aim at the English throne." The episode is curious; but there is no reason for assuming, either that a letter written by the Electress Sophia to Stepney shortly before her visit to the Loo was really "Jacobite" in intention, or that at their meeting the Electress, by opposing the wishes of William III, led him to turn his thoughts to the rival electoral House.

Already in January, 1701, it was known that a new Act of Settlement would be proposed by the Crown to Parliament, in which the Electress Sophia and her descendants would be named; and, notwithstanding the rumours of intrigues in which Marlborough was believed to be involved, an excessive display of zeal on the part of the indefatigable Leibniz, and a protest on behalf of Duchess Anna Maria of Savoy, the Act which in default of issue of the Princess Anne or King William settled the English Crown upon "the most excellent Princess Sophia and the heirs of her body, being Protestants," on June 12, 1701, received the royal assent. On August 14, the Earl of Macclesfield, with the voluble Toland in his train, arrived at Hanover, to present a copy of the Act of Succession to the Electress, and to bring the Garter to the Elector. They were treated with much honour, but more significant is the fact, long concealed, that the Committee of the Calenberg Estates secretly furnished the Hanoverian legation in London with a sum of 300,000 dollars for any unforeseen emergency. At an interview which King William immediately afterwards had at the Loo with George William of Celle, he promised to try to obtain an annual income for the Electress from Parliament, and to invite her and the Electoral Prince to England in the coming spring.

That spring William III never saw, and during the whole of his successor's reign no part of the obviously appropriate arrangement suggested by him was carried out. In the last days of August, 1701, the new Grand Alliance against France was concluded; and a few days later, by the deathbed of King James II, his son was recognised by Louis XIV as successor to the English Crown. The "indignity" (the word is Bentley's) filled all England with wrath; and, beyond all doubt, the magnanimous action of Louis XIV helped to bring about, if it did not actually cause, the insertion in the final form of the instrument of the Grand Alliance a provision binding the contracting Powers not to conclude peace with France until the King of England should have received satisfaction for the grave insult implied in the recognition by the King of France of the "pretended Prince of Wales" as his father's successor on the English throne. The War of the Spanish Succession thus, in a sense, became a war of the English Succession also; and, though during its earlier years the victories of the Allies added, as it has been happily expressed, a guarantee of their own, no sooner were conditions of peace under discussion than this clause could not but again come to the front. Those interested in the Hanoverian Succession could then hardly fail to ask themselves in what way it would be advanced— or peradventure endangered—by the conditions proposed for the peace itself. Meanwhile, in January, 1702, was passed, together with an Act attainting the Pretender, the Abjuration Act, which made it obligatory to abjure him and to swear fidelity to the King and his heirs according to the Act of Settlement. Somewhat ominously, the clause making this oath obligatory was carried in the Commons only by a single vote.

Shortly afterwards (March 8) King William died; and a period, in some respects obscure, began in the history of the Hanoverian Succession, which extended over thirteen further weary years. But this obscurity was due neither to the conduct of the heiress presumptive of the English throne nor to that of her son. The Electress Sophia continued to remain true to herself and to the line of conduct which her judgment had marked out for her, in her conduct towards the English Crown and Parliament, and in her daily intercourse with friends and well-wishers, sincere or insincere. Occasionally her tranquil interest in a drama of which she scarcely expected to see the *dénouement* was quickened into some measure of precaution, as when (in June, 1703) she signed three forms for the Hanoverian envoy extraordinary in London (Baron Ludwig Justus von Schütz), authorising him to claim the throne on her behalf in the event of the Queen's death; but, while she at no time concealed her conviction as to what would be the appropriate way of recognising her position, she made no demand, and still less allowed herself to be seduced into manœuvres or intrigues with any English party or individual politician. Her eldest son only gradually, and never quite completely, suppressed his reluctance to move in the matter; but, while plainly resolved to do nothing prematurely, he was as a matter of duty towards the interests of his House and of the Empire resolved to use all due means of preparing and, when the time came, of asserting a claim not of his own seeking, but now interwoven with the whole political situation of Europe in which he had become an important factor. That he now saw matters in this way was largely due to Andreas Gottlieb von Bernstorff, since 1705 (on the death of George William of Celle, whose affairs he had directed for more than a quarter of a century) George Lewis' chief political adviser (with the title of Prime Minister from 1709), and his confidential adviser long after the Elector's accession to the English throne, until his own political downfall in 1720. Bernstorff's training was that of a territorial or particularist statesman; and in the earlier part of his career his jealousy of the Danish and more especially of the Brandenburg Government seemed to be the guiding principle of his policy. These tendencies, and his personal connexion with Mecklenburg, he never forgot or repressed; but he had a great grasp of affairs as well as singular acuteness of insight; and the charges of venality brought against him were largely if not wholly attributable to spite. Of the policy which he in a great measure inspired more will be said hereafter.

The darkness in which the progress of the Succession question in these years is shrouded is, of course, mainly caused by the insincere and tortuous conduct of Queen Anne, her Ministers and the political parties out of whose jealousies and ambitions the inner history of the reign evolved itself. Their proceedings, and the motives by which they must be concluded to have been actuated, have been discussed, in their relation to the fallen Stewarts and to the general progress of affairs in other passages of this work; here it only remains to note their direct bearing upon the Succession which according to Act of Parliament was to follow, should the Queen die without leaving any descendants of her own.

Queen Anne—no longer hopeful of issue, and from October, 1708, a widow—very naturally felt a certain measure of sympathy for her half-brother as to the genuineness of whose birth she had at first been so demonstratively sceptical. But the really dominant motive of her behaviour (a few unavoidable civilities apart) in the matter of the Hanoverian Succession, was a deep, not to say a superstitious, aversion from the whole topic and its associations. In the earlier years of her reign she did nothing in recognition of the " Princess Sophia's " claims beyond ordering the insertion of her name in the liturgy. She would at no time hear of carrying out King William's intention of inviting the Electress Sophia and the Electoral Prince to England, or grant a specific title to the former; nor would she approve of an annual income for the heiress to the Crown sanctioned by Parliament. Sophia on the other hand declined to entertain the idea of a private allowance from the Civil List, which would merely oblige her to surround herself with expensive English servants. The Electoral Prince was created Duke of Cambridge, and Knight of the Garter like his father—and that was all. Coolness thus came to be returned for coolness; and it was only in the last four years of the Queen's reign that the relations between her and the old Electress assumed a friendlier aspect—till at last the explosion came.

With the English political leaders and factions the Electress and, till nearly the last, her son forbore from entering into intimate relations. To Marlborough they were alike attracted, and he was always ready with judicious advice; but he was not the man to mortgage his future by identifying himself with either side, more especially so long as he was the first man in the State and controlled the action of the Queen. But on the other side there was equal caution. At what date he offered to the House of Hanover a loan of £20,000, in return for a blank commission signed by the Electress confirming him in the command of both army and navy, is uncertain; on the other hand, when in 1710 it was expected that the new Ministers proposed to offer the chief command in the field to George Lewis in Marlborough's place, the Elector had, notwithstanding his military ambition, made up his mind to decline it. Godolphin was less accessible; he was always suspected of partiality for the House of Stewart, with which he is known to have been in communication; and for the royal assent to the Scottish Act of Security (1704), which seriously endangered the Hanoverian Succession beyond the Border, he was mainly responsible. The Whigs proper could not but consistently maintain the principle of the Hanoverian Succession except in a moment of factious aberration (Sophia said that they would always be for it "so long as it suited their purpose"); but it was not till a discontinuance of the War became an integral part of the Ministerial policy that the Elector began to take special thought of securing the support of the party in the matter of the Succession. To the Tories—whether or not of the so-called "Hanover" section which upheld the Succession—the behaviour of both the Electress and the Elector always remained frank and courteous; and even the duplicity of the game played, first by Oxford and then more persistently and for a time more audaciously by Bolingbroke, though perfectly well known to Sophia and to her son, was met by them with an unruffled front.

Thus, the main incidents in the history of the Succession in Queen Anne's reign may be very rapidly reviewed. In 1704–5, when party relations in England were much confused, and Buckingham and Rochester were in correspondence with the Electress Sophia, the "High-flier" section of the Tories, headed by Rochester, sought to assert their power by means of an address urging that the Electress should be invited to take up her residence in England. The address was thrown out in the Lords (November, 1705), the Whigs voting against it; but their leaders adroitly seized the occasion to introduce two Bills, which signified a real step forward in the interests of the Hanoverian Succession—the Naturalisation Bill, which made an Englishwoman of the heiress to the throne, and the Regency Bill, which empowered her to appoint twenty-one

Lords Justices, who, in addition to the great officers of the Crown, were to carry on the government of the country in the event of her absence from it at the time of the Queen's death. The Earl of Halifax was appointed to announce the passing of these Bills at Hanover; but it cannot have been very agreeable to his personal feelings that the Electress struck his name with six others out of the list submitted to her, or acceptable to his Whig principles that she insisted to him on the hereditary character of her right to the throne.

In 1708, when the death of Prince George of Denmark had removed the last possibility of further issue from the Queen, the Whigs were fully established in power; but the Electress was by no means thrown off her balance by the enthusiasm of her Whig visitors at Herrenhausen, and the Elector was much out of humour at the lack of confidence shown to him in connexion with the conduct of the War. But a more critical period soon drew near, and it was not without reason that the Elector went out of his way to remonstrate with Queen Anne on the Ministerial changes reported as imminent in the early part of 1710. After these changes had been actually accomplished, Earl Rivers was sent to Hanover by the Queen to explain her view of them, and made a favourable impression. In December the Electoral Prince was installed Knight of the Garter by proxy—somewhat tardily, as he had been invested with the insignia of the Order some four years earlier. In 1710—a few months before, in May, 1711, Harley became Lord Treasurer with the title of Earl of Oxford—Hans Caspar von Bothmer, Hanoverian Minister plenipotentiary at the Hague, arrived at the Court of St James, to take the place of the envoy Schütz (who had died in the previous February). Bothmer, who was more directly and effectively instrumental than any other man in bringing about the Hanoverian Succession, had, like Bernstorff, been originally in the service of George William of Celle, and had when Minister at the imperial Court been sent as a plenipotentiary to the Peace of Ryswyk. He had acquired the complete confidence of the electoral family and of the Electress Sophia in particular, whose letters show her appreciation of his great ability, except as the executant of feminine commissions. He had been active in the electoral interest already at the Hague whither he returned for part of 1711; and both here and in London, which he again quitted for a time to act as plenipotentiary at Utrecht, he laboured incessantly in the main task of his life. He failed indeed to secure the goodwill of the Queen, to whom his very presence was a memento of the future to which she desired to shut her eyes, or of her Ministers—Bolingbroke declared that, notwithstanding his air of coldness and caution, he was "the most inveterate party-man" of his day—but he was praised by the Electress for being on friendly terms with both parties, without compromising himself with either. His management of the funds placed at his disposal appears to have been discreet and well-proportioned; some peers were to be had cheap. When the crisis came, he rose to the full height of the situation, and for a moment commanded it, assuming even such a responsibility as that of the destruction of the Queen's private little packet of papers. When all was happily over, and his services had been acknowledged by his being made a Count of the Empire, he remained for some time in active service, retaining his post of the Elector's Minister to the Court where the Elector was now King. But as the influence of Bernstorff rose to its height that of Bothmer, whose views began to diverge from his, waned, and he supported Stanhope against Bernstorff in some of the transactions which preceded the fall of the latter in 1720—a fact which shows the term "Hanoverian Junta" to be hardly more accurate than the expression "Stanhope's German Ministry." Bothmer died in 1732, leaving large estates in Mecklenburg.

Bothmer had made it clear from the first that in matters of European policy, and in the question of war or peace with France in particular, his master was by no means disposed to fall in tamely with the system of the Queen and her Ministers. Already, when, in the autumn of 1711, Rivers paid a second visit to Hanover, and his customary assurances of the Queen's benevolent intentions were met by the Electress with the observation that it seemed to her quite natural that "the Queen should be more in favour of her brother than of us," the real object of his mission broke down on the Elector's steady refusal to declare himself in favour of the British overtures of peace to France. In November, 1711, Bothmer, who had returned to London with fresh credentials, brought with him a memorandum against the conclusion of peace which in England was ascribed to Whig influence, but which as a matter of fact developed principles of action of far more importance to the Elector than the interests of any English party-principles, and from his point of view dominating the question of the Succession itself. Both sides were now competing for the goodwill of the electoral House. When, in January, 1712, the Whigs through the Duke of Devonshire proposed to give the Duke of Cambridge precedence over other peers, the Ministry at once overbid them by rapidly carrying an Act securing precedence to the entire electoral family. Oxford sent his kinsman Thomas Harley to Hanover to present a copy of this Act, and to utilise the opportunity for laying, if possible, the belligerent spirit which possessed the Elector. But Bothmer still pressed his master's point of view, presenting a letter from him to the Queen on February 14.

At Utrecht, whither Bothmer soon repaired to watch the progress of the peace negotiations, the policy of the Elector was in many respects deliberately calculated to thwart that of the English Ministry. More significant, however, than even his wish to continue the Dutch Barrier Treaty and to promote a good understanding between the Dutch and imperial Governments, was the order given by him to General von Bülow, the commander of his contingent in the Low Countries, to pass

from under the command of Ormond, Marlborough's successor, and to
unite with the imperial troops under Prince Eugene, on the day on
which Ormond should conclude a truce with the French (July).   There
was no difference of opinion as to the mention in the Treaty of Peace of
the Hanoverian Succession; but the addition, suggested by Leibniz, of a
clause securing to the Elector and one or more members of his family a
residence and annual income in England, was never seriously entertained.
As an Estate of the Empire the Elector of course withheld his signature
from the Peace.

  After Bothmer's recall Baron Thomas von Grote, who belonged
to a family distinguished in the service of the Elector's House, was
sent to London (December, 1712).   His instructions were drawn up by
Jean de Robethon, a Hanoverian official of French Huguenot descent,
who has been justly described as the very soul of George I's diplomatic
chancery, and who continued in favour so long as Bernstorff maintained his ascendancy in the counsels of his Prince.   Grote carried with
him, besides elaborate instructions from both Elector and Electress,
lists of the best friends of the House of Hanover in England, most
of whom were Whigs; but he was also told to make friends with
the clergy.   He found no opportunity of urging the establishment for
the Electress, the provision of which would have furnished the best
proof of the sincerity of the Queen's and Oxford's professions, and in
February, 1713, sent home to Hanover a very gloomy account of the
situation.   The hopes of the friends of the Succession in England were,
for reasons which it is not very easy to assign, once more sinking.   It
is idle to ascribe the fact to the "unpopularity" of a House practically
unknown to all but a few English men and women.   The Electress had
offended nobody, and, so long as the War had continued, the Elector
had been a faithful and a zealous ally.   But it was the time when both
Oxford and Bolingbroke, whose mutual rivalry was becoming more
intense, were seeking to intrigue with Berwick and the Jacobites at
Paris, and trying to accommodate their attitude at home to the wishes
of the Queen, which seemed by no means to point towards Hanover;
Bolingbroke not only going further than Oxford in his overtures to the
Jacobites, but occasionally treating the Elector's envoy with insolent
brusqueness.   In March, 1713, Grote died; and in the same month
Oxford, who could never continue long without trimming, appears to have
sent his useful kinsman to make the customary meaningless declarations
at Hanover.   The Whigs were anxious that the Elector should force the
situation, and at the same time exercise an influence upon the elections
that were to follow on the dissolution of Parliament in July, by sending
over a member of his family, preferably the Electoral Prince, who in the
new Parliament would as a matter of course take his seat in the Lords.
Bothmer favoured the step, but Bernstorff was unluckily ill, and in his
absence the Elector decided against sending his son—whom for reasons

which have been guessed but cannot be determined he cordially detested. Thus, though Parliament was duly dissolved in July—the Queen in her closing speech ominously omitting the usual friendly reference to the Hanoverian Succession—nothing was done; while the Whigs were so enraged at the conduct of the Ministry as to be ready to tamper with the Union with Scotland, provided nothing else could be done to secure the Hanoverian Succession in that kingdom. Thus matters stood, when in September, 1713, Baron Georg Wilhelm Helvig von Schütz (a nephew of Bernstorff) arrived in London as Hanoverian envoy. It may be noted that he was expressly instructed to abstain from any sort of interference in British affairs.

The new Parliament assembled (February, 1714) without either any representative of the Hanoverian family, or (as Berwick had suggested) the Pretender, putting in an appearance. But the situation had become more strained than ever, more especially when, in the last days of 1713, the Queen had fallen ill. Had things then come to a crisis, it would, owing to the great age of the Electress, and the unwillingness of the Elector to take a step in advance, have found the Whigs and the friends of the Succession at large ill prepared to meet it. Their best security lay in the fact of Oxford and Bolingbroke's perfectly clear perception that, while it would at any time have been impossible to persuade the Queen to summon the Pretender to London, it would have been madness to bring him into England from Scotland; and that, so long as he refused to cease to be a Roman Catholic, he had no chance of the English throne. On the other hand, Bolingbroke was convinced that a German Prince such as George Lewis could never permanently occupy the English throne. But, now that the chance had gone by, Oxford lost himself in renewed duplicities which revealed only too clearly his uncertainty of mind. At one moment, he proposed to alter the Regency Act, so as to give to the Electress Sophia the nomination of the entire body of Regents—which would have enabled Parliament, if so disposed, to rescind the Act altogether. At another, he invited Parliament to declare it treasonable to introduce foreign troops into the country—a prohibition which might have been worked either against the Pretender or against the House of Hanover. Thus the feeling that Ministers were allowing things to drift—possibly into disturbance and civil war—operated in favour of the only interest in which there was certainty of purpose; and in the early months of 1714 Tories as well as Whigs, clergy as well as laity, began to lay themselves at the feet of the electoral House. Though in the new House of Commons the Tories outnumbered the Whigs by at least two to one, a large section of the former party, the so-called "Hanover Tories," had made up their minds in favour of the Protestant Succession. In April, Oxford himself thought it well to make another of his "hedging" movements; and Thomas Harley appeared at Hanover once more, with a bland enquiry on the part of the Queen as to whether anything could be done to further the Hanover Succession, and the old offer of a private pension for the Electress; but without a word as to a member of the electoral family coming to England. Harley brought back with him a reply, dated May 7, pointing out the desirableness of a parliamentary income for the Electress, and of the sojourn in England of a member of the electoral family (the Electoral Prince being probably intended).

In the meantime it became known that the action of the Elector's Minister in London had with quite unexpected suddenness transformed the situation. In the ordinary course of things the Electoral Prince would as Duke of Cambridge have received his writ of summons to attend the House of Lords like any other English peer; but Lord Chancellor Harcourt, being like his Ministerial colleagues afraid of nothing so much as of offending the Queen, had indefinitely delayed its issue. Schütz had become very uneasy, when he received a letter from the old Electress requesting him to inform the Lord Chancellor of the great astonishment at Hanover caused by the fact that the writ had not yet been sent to the Prince. "As he (the Lord Chancellor) has always been friendly to me...I think that he will not consider it objectionable *que vous* le *lui demandiez et la raison*." Schütz could hardly conclude otherwise than that he was desired to demand the writ as well as the reason for its having been withheld; and the Whig leaders, to whom he showed the Electress' letter, took the same view. He therefore asked for the writ from the Lord Chancellor, who replied that it was quite ready, but that, the custom not being for peers to demand their writs except when present in London, he would mention the matter to the Queen.

When, on April 26, Schütz made it known that he had carried out the instructions of the Electress, the effect was electrical. Marlborough, Townshend, and Cadogan expressed their delight at the envoy's action; Bothmer wrote from the Hague in the same strain; and at Hanover, where Leibniz' exultation was unbounded, it was thought that the opportunity should be seized, and the Electoral Prince sent to London at once. But the Elector demurred—most fortunately, for Queen Anne was deeply angered at the action of his envoy. At first she was for refusing the writ, and Bolingbroke dared to be of the same opinion. But the Cabinet decided that the demand could not be refused, and on April 27 the writ was handed to Schütz by the Chancellor. The envoy was, however, speedily advised by Oxford not to show himself at Court, and was soon formally prohibited from appearing there. On May 2 he took his departure, leaving the Resident, Kreyenberg, to carry on diplomatic business. On Schütz' arrival at Hanover the Elector, in pretended displeasure, refused to receive him, and told Thomas Harley who was on the eve of returning to London that the envoy had acted without orders from his sovereign.

The Elector and his mother, had they really been afraid of any action on the part of the Queen, would not have despatched to her by

Thomas Harley the very outspoken memorandum of May 7 mentioned above; and the Electress' account of the whole matter to Leibniz was perfectly cool. But the letters in which Queen Anne—or Bolingbroke, who held her pen—expressed her annoyance to the Electress, the Elector, and the Electoral Prince, were—especially the first-named—couched in terms of intolerable arrogance and violent menace. When they were, with the exception of the letter to the Elector, surreptitiously published by a Whig scribe (whom Bolingbroke immediately clapped into prison) the mistake made by the Queen was at once patent; and Oxford seems at once to have ceased intriguing for the Stewart cause and to have begun protesting at Hanover. Bolingbroke could think of nothing better than to seek to implicate his rival in the demand for the writ.

But the Queen's letters had another effect. They arrived at Hanover on June 5, and on the 6th the missive to the Electress Sophia was delivered to her at Herrenhausen. On the evening of the 8th, when walking in her beloved gardens, she was suddenly overtaken by death. Since the arrival of the letters, she had never lost her self-control or even her high spirit; but the shock had been too severe for her aged frame. On her death the Elector at once took the threads of the conjuncture into his own hands, addressing a conciliatory letter to the Queen and once more sending over Bothmer, furnished with full instructions for the event of her death. Whatever secret orders Bothmer may have had for his dealings with the Whigs, he was told to avoid all appearance of partisanship and took with him a letter to Oxford, insisting on the advisability of the presence in England of a member of the electoral family. On the part of Queen Anne, however, her relative the Tory Earl of Clarendon was sent over to Hanover with instructions to place a negative upon the proposals of the memorandum of May 7.

The events which now took place in England have already been narrated in this *History*. No sooner had Oxford been dismissed from office (July 27) than he at once offered Bothmer to keep him confidentially *au courant* with Bolingbroke's proceedings. Yet the Elector was of course completely in the dark as to whether Bolingbroke, at last in possession of full power, intended in the event of the Queen's death to risk a *coup d'état* on his own account or to ask for the aid which Louis XIV had promised to give. The Elector was determined at least not to be taken by surprise. He promptly caused a fresh instrument of Regency, comprising his own nominations, to be prepared (Marlborough's name being left out from this, whether or not only because he happened not to be in England); while at home he received assurances of support from his nephew Frederick William I of Prussia and other German Princes. With the Whig project of an outbreak during the Queen's life the Elector had no concern.

Then came the startling news of Queen Anne's illness, and of her death. The Elector's commission of Regents (in which 13 of his 18 nominations were Whigs) was opened, and he was proclaimed King on the day of the Queen's death (August 1) in London, and again a few days later there as well as in Edinburgh and Dublin. King George I, who received the news informally on August 6, and formally three days later, though he kept up a correspondence with Bothmer, gave no sign of his intentions as to English affairs before leaving Hanover. But Bolingbroke was dismissed from office, Townshend taking his place on the day of the King's departure (August 31). After spending a fortnight at the Hague, George I arrived at Greenwich on September 18, and two days later held his entry into London. It was now made quite manifest that he had elected to break completely with the late Queen's Government. He took no notice of Ormond or Harcourt on landing; and, when next morning Oxford (who during the Queen's fatal illness had been at the pains of sending an express messenger to summon the Elector immediately to London) kissed hands, he was received in silence. Bolingbroke, though as yet he kept a bold front, had absented himself on both occasions. His day was over. The King's action was confirmed by the elections for the new Parliament, which assembled on March 15, 1715, and in which the Whigs commanded a large English majority, while of the Scottish seats the Jacobites, then on the eve of a rising, had only been able to secure an insignificant fraction.

Bothmer's vigilance and the Elector's self-contained but intrepid conduct had triumphed; but Fortune had had her hand in the game. The Queen's illness had taken Bolingbroke by surprise, though not in the sense that he would in any case have joined with the Hotspurs of his party in proclaiming the Pretender. And the rapid close of that illness in death had prevented the Elector from responding to Oxford's summons, as, there is reason to think, he might have done in apprehension of immediate Jacobite action. Had he come while Queen Anne lived, tumult and bloodshed might have followed; and, though resolute in action, George might not have proved the man to conjure the furies of civil discord—perhaps of civil war. For the nation's trust in the new dynasty was still a thing of the future; and the consensus of all but the extreme factions in Church and State to accept it was no guarantee that this acceptance would prove enduring. Had the Electress Sophia, the heiress presumptive of the British throne during so many years, been called to it in her earlier days, she might conceivably have attained to something of the popularity which has surrounded more than one English female sovereign; for none of our Queens has surpassed her in intellectual clearness and courage, in geniality of disposition, and in loyalty of soul. But in her son, who mounted the throne in her stead, there was little to attract, though there was much to command respect; for he was cast in a manly mould, and veracity and trustworthiness were inborn in his nature. He had given abundant proof of military ability and courage, and he was fond of the pastimes which in his day commended themselves to his class. On the other hand, he was too old to shake off the absolutist habits of thought and conduct which had long become incompatible with the conditions of English political life; and he was wholly devoid of literary or scientific tastes—quite the last man to have considered that the union of Great Britain and Hanover represented in his person was "the union of Leibniz with Newton." Fortunately for the King's fame, he took Handel again into favour (out of which he had fallen for doing honour to the Peace of Utrecht, or for some other reason) almost immediately after his accession to the English throne. For the rest, it is well known that, while his mother spoke English as well as Dutch with perfect ease, the new King of England never acquired the English tongue; in return it is doubtful whether more than one of the leading English statesmen of his reign could speak to him in his own language. It may have been partly due to George I's ignorance of the English tongue that he dropped the habit of presiding at Cabinet Council meetings (though, of course, continuing to preside at Privy Councils)—and that, as was unavoidable, he resorted instead to private consultations with advisers whom he could uniformly understand, and who could understand him in return.

George I, unhappily, brought no consort to England, and the cloud of scandal which enveloped the story of his past married life did him much harm with many besides his son, with whom he was ostensibly on better terms since the death of the old Electress. The Prince of Wales resembled his father in his military ambition and absolutist convictions; but to him as a younger man wider hopes attached themselves, and to the intelligence and charm of his Princess prejudice alone could fail to succumb. Instead of a wife, the King brought with him a mistress, in accordance with the almost imperative fashion of the day. The legend that Countess Melusina von der Schulenburg (afterwards Duchess of Kendal) had a rival in Baroness Sophia Charlotte von Kielmannsegge (afterwards Countess of Darlington), the daughter of Countess von Platen, who had been the mistress of King George's father, Ernest Augustus, can be traced back to the malicious pen of the Margravine Wilhelmina of Baireuth; as a matter of fact George I acknowledged and honoured his half-sister as such. For the rest, though the style of the Hanoverian Court, magnificent under Ernest Augustus and Sophia, had become less ceremonious and restrained under George Lewis, it had not much to learn in the way of refinement from that of St James.

Of the political counsellors who accompanied George I to England, or whom, like Bothmer, he found awaiting him there, something has already been said; and of their advice and its effects note will be taken in another section. Possessed as they were of their Prince's well-earned confidence, the continuance of their influence depended on himself alone, and on his and their power of shaping in new conditions the foreign policy of which he would never change the main purposes, and of which his succession to the throne of Great Britain had always seemed nothing more than an important incident. With Bernstorff and Robethon, no other Hanoverian councillors of much mark came to England. Baron Friedrich Wilhelm von Schlitz-Görtz, who was in the Elector's suite and bore the reputation of a *grand seigneur* as well as of a valuable official, returned to Hanover as head of the electoral Chamber of Finance. Jobst Hermann von Ilten, under both Ernest Augustus and George Lewis one of the most capable servants of the electoral Government, remained behind to preside over it at Hanover, where he died in 1730. Among other trusted followers of the King were Baron von Kielmannsegge, whose Mastership of the Horse gave much offence in England; and Privy Councillor Johann Ludwig von Fabrice (a son of Weipart Ludwig, who held a high judicial office at Celle)—it was either in his arms, or, more probably, in those of his brother, Chamberlain Friedrich Ernst, that George I died. In the course of the reign, Philip von Hattorf, a man of great ability and tact, was Hanoverian Minister in attendance—an office which soon became one of high importance.

No account can be given here of the adjustments made on the accession of George I between the administrative systems of his kingdom and his electorate; but it is worth pointing out that the Hanoverian Chancery in London was at no time a branch of the Foreign Office, but always concerned with purely Hanoverian business. For the rest, the prohibitory clause of the Act of Settlement as to the employment of foreigners in civil or military offices, and as to the granting of pensions to them, was observed in the spirit as well as in the letter; and while it is not easy to find even isolated cases in which Germans were admitted under George I into the service of the British Administration, the very few pensions granted to others than Englishmen or Englishwomen were of a wholly exceptional nature.

The title of the new dynasty was (notwithstanding what the Electress Sophia thought) parliamentary in its essence as well as in its basis, and therefore implied the assurance of a rule which, if only for the sake of the rulers, might be, whatever their own traditions, depended on to respect the principles and the practice of parliamentary government. But the Succession was not merely an incident in the conflict of English political parties. It was something more, and as such of vital importance to the national life and history. The Hanoverian was the Protestant Succession, both by Act of Parliament and by the whole history of the process of its accomplishment. The House of Hanover as represented by the Elector had adhered staunchly to the Protestant traditions of both his father's and his mother's line, while many of the members of both had fallen away from them. The attempt made in England both before and after the accession of George I to depreciate, as it were, the quality of Hanoverian Protestantism, by emphasising or exaggerating differences between it and that of the Church of England, had to be met by a great deal of unavoidable argument. But, if it took time to convince the beneficiaries of the Schism Act, that the Tories—and the Jacobite Tories in particular—could claim no monopoly in the protection of the rights of the Protestant Church of England, on the other hand the goodwill of the English Nonconformist body was very effectually assured to the Hanoverian dynasty; and their attachment was won for a sovereign who approved, and with the traditions and principles implanted in him could not but approve, the proposed abrogation of the Test and Corporation Acts. Elsewhere it will be shown that in Scotland the results of the Succession were on this head even more complete; for with the rising of 1715 episcopalian Jacobitism ceased to have any significance as a political force. But in England, without the drawing of a sword from its scabbard, the will of the nation had been vindicated, and a new security gained, as to that which the nation as a whole held most dear.

(2) THE FOREIGN POLICY OF GEORGE I.

(1714–21.)

The first years of the reign of George I form, in the history of European politics, a period of transition from old principles and conditions to new. The necessity of combination against France passing out of date, a novel alliance ensues between that Power and Great Britain. Spain is roused to new life. On the conclusion of the long war in the north, the European circle is forced open to admit the new-born Empire of Russia, while the Swedish yoke is broken. For Prussia her new King marks out the path which is to lead her to dispute ultimately with Austria the hegemony of Germany. Holland and Turkey pass, with Sweden, from the front rank among the Powers. Europe in 1721 is not the Europe of 1714.

Great Britain was first of all concerned to establish firmly the Protestant Succession. But her sovereign had a second preoccupation: to secure for his electorate the Swedish provinces of Bremen and Verden —the former, at the time of his accession, occupied by Denmark. For both these objects the support of the Emperor, while France remained hostile, was absolutely necessary; and, to obtain it, George was willing to connive at Austrian expansion in Italy. But, when the Triple Alliance, as shown below, had secured him in England against "James III," and in Hanover against the Northern Powers, the old principle of the Balance of Power, that principle which aimed at peace and produced constant war, resumed its sway. The danger, however, to Europe was no longer from France, but from Austria and Spain. To settle the affairs of the south, and so to remove that danger, Stanhope devised the plan which developed into the Quadruple Alliance of 1718. Disagreement between Austria and Great Britain marked the negotiation of this compact, and grew greater during the execution of its provisions. One cause of this was the accord reached in 1719 by Great Britain and Hanover with Prussia, the product of French interest and French influence. Alliance with Prussia meant alienation from Austria; but it was the necessary preliminary to George's pacification of the north.

The circumstances in which George I ascended the throne of Great Britain necessitated the recall of the Whig party to power. There were at this period two Secretaries of State for Foreign Affairs, charged with the direction of the two "provinces," into which foreign countries were, for convenience, grouped. Their authority was nominally coordinate, but the business of the two departments was always intermingled, and in practice the stronger Minister prevailed. The two men chosen by George for the charge had little in common but high principle. Charles, Viscount Townshend, secretary for the Northern province and head of the Ministry, was a moderate Whig of excellent record and sufficient but not dominating importance. He was chosen, probably, for these reasons. His colleague for the Southern province, General (afterwards Earl) Stanhope, imported into state affairs the energy and dash which had marked his conduct in the field. He was an accomplished diplomatist and linguist, who could undertake embassies to foreign capitals in person; a man of wide views and with a fine conception of the part proper to be played in Europe by Great Britain. During his lifetime he was the real Minister for Foreign Affairs, even while temporarily occupying another office.

But, during the earlier part of the reign, it was not the Whig leaders only who directed foreign policy. George had always with him in London the Hanoverian Ministers previously noticed, whose tried fidelity he repaid with complete confidence. To Bernstorff English Ministers deferred as to a recognised authority on European politics, while foreign representatives resorted to him preferentially. The interests of Hanover were by him consistently placed in the forefront. He appreciated the danger threatening them from the rise of Prussia, and insisted upon the necessity of maintaining the old devotion of the House of Brunswick to the Emperor. His influence was strongest after the Whig schism at the beginning of 1717 had removed from the Ministry his principal opponents, Townshend and Robert Walpole.

George himself took the keenest personal interest in European politics, and Whig tradition accorded with his desire that Great Britain should once more take an active part in them. The first consideration determining her action was the renewed hostility of France. For nearly two years a fresh outbreak of war was thought likely and at times even desirable, the principal subjects in dispute being the protection afforded by Louis XIV to the Pretender, and the evasion of that article of the Treaty of Utrecht which stipulated the dismantling of Dunkirk, by the preparation of a new war-port at Mardyk, hardby. It appeared to be of the first importance to revive the alliance with the United Provinces and the Emperor, which the Peace of Utrecht had destroyed. To George and his Hanoverian Ministers such views were entirely congenial; their Government had always been the most steadfast in Germany in loyalty to the Emperor and the most zealous in the war with France; and its close relations with the Hague were unimpaired.

On George's accession the breach with Holland closed, indeed, of itself. But the Emperor could not readily forget the betrayal, as he deemed it, of 1712. And with the Dutch he was at special issue about their so-called Barrier—the line of fortresses in what were now the Austrian Netherlands, which, as has been seen in a previous volume, they had the right to garrison. That right Charles VI obstinately repudiated. George was readily accepted as mediator in the dispute by both sides, and appointed General Cadogan to conduct the mediation at Antwerp; but all that could be obtained at Vienna in regard to a renewal of alliance with Great Britain, although Stanhope repaired thither in person, was the expression of a desire for it, after the Emperor's demands in regard to the Netherlands should have been satisfied. Cadogan, however, sent to Vienna in February, 1715, had the boldness to represent how, in England, Stanhope's failure had inspired the belief that the Emperor was engaged in negotiations of a wide-reaching character with France; and Charles thereupon declared himself faithful to the old system, conceding also the three points about the Barrier which it was the object of Cadogan's mission to carry. Yet it was not till the prospect of the Jacobite rebellion reduced the British Government even to entreaties, that a solution in this matter was reached. A Barrier Treaty was signed at Antwerp by the representatives of the three Powers on November 15, 1715. But its provisions remained inoperative for three years, nor could a reconciliation between Austria and Holland be carried further.

In the north the situation was as follows. The occupation of the Swedish duchy of Bremen and its fortress-capital Stade by the Danes in 1712, following upon the failure of the Neutrality Convention of 1710 and the threats of Charles XII, had finally decided George, though hitherto reckoned the principal ally of Charles in Christian Europe, to turn against him, and he had entered into negotiations with Frederick IV of Denmark and Frederick William I of Prussia for the division of the Swedish provinces in Germany among themselves, his own share to be the duchy of Bremen and the principality of Verden. But, the Danes refusing to give up what they had won, and the demands of Hanover upon Prussia being too great, the negotiations bore no fruit until it was known that Charles was about to return from Turkey. Then, George

concluded with Frederick William a "punctation" for a convention
(November 11, 1714), which appointed the permanent possession of
Bremen and Verden to Hanover and that of Stettin and its district,
also Swedish property, to Prussia.   Negotiations during the winter
between Frederick William and Charles, who had returned to Stralsund,
having proved fruitless, war broke out between them in April, 1715.
And, Denmark now consenting to receive the north-western portion of
Swedish Pomerania (*Vorpommern*), and a sum of money from Hanover,
in exchange for Bremen, treaties between the three Powers were shortly
concluded, distributing the Swedish provinces in Germany among them.
That Hanover should possess Bremen and Verden was agreeable enough
to the merchants of Great Britain ; for greater commercial advantages
might be expected from the rule of George than from that of either
Sweden or Denmark.

The part allotted to George under the treaties was nominal, namely,
to prevent aid from coming to Stralsund, while besieged by the Danes
and Prussians, from other German States or from France.   He did not
actually declare war against Sweden till Stade had been given up to him
in October.   But the real service demanded from and explicitly promised
by him was, that the British squadron proceeding to the Baltic for the
protection of trade should prevent the relief of Stralsund by sea.   It was
the commercial interests of Great Britain which made this service possible.

After Peter the Great had conquered from Sweden the eastern ports
of the Baltic, Charles XII had prohibited all trade to them.   This trade
was of essential importance to the Maritime Powers, because only from
the Baltic could a sufficient supply of materials for ship-building at this
time be obtained.   The damage done by the Swedish privateers, even
while Charles remained in Turkey, was sufficient to provoke the pacific
Ministry of Queen Anne to equip a small squadron for the Baltic—
a useless demonstration, since the ships dared not pass the Sound, and
only by grace of the Swedes were permitted to return home.   Charles,
when he came back, increased the stringency of his prohibition.   In
February, 1715, he issued an Ordinance of Privateers, which, in the words
of the British resident at Stockholm, rendered it impossible for a
merchant-ship to enter the Baltic without being made a prize.   Great
Britain and the United Provinces thereupon agreed to send a joint fleet
thither to convoy the traders.   But the instructions given to Sir John
Norris, the British Admiral, authorised him, beyond protecting commerce,
to make reprisals upon Swedish shipping, if opportunity offered ; and
George gave his allies to understand that this power would permit an
attack upon the Swedish fleet, if it were encountered.   Circumstances
prevented this consummation, in spite of urgent personal appeals to
Norris from the King of Prussia ; and vehement complaints came in
consequence from Berlin and Copenhagen.   As a compromise, Norris
was ordered to leave behind him, on his return, eight ships to act in

conjunction with the Danish fleet—the first definite act of hostility towards Sweden on the part of Great Britain.   When Stralsund fell, Charles XII escaped miraculously to Sweden, falsifying the hopes which had been placed upon his death.   And thus, at the beginning of 1716, King George found himself confronted by rebellion at home, and an unconquerable enemy abroad.

On the other hand there was a prospect of improved relations with France and Spain.   Louis XIV had been succeeded in September, 1715, by the boy-king, Louis XV.   The next heir, Philip V of Spain, though he had renounced his right to the succession, disclaimed the validity of the renunciation.   In defiance of his pretensions his cousin, Philip Duke of Orleans, had seized the Regency.   Confronted by powerful opposition at home, Orleans was driven to seek allies abroad.   Overtures which he made to the Dutch Government were a principal cause of its resoluteness in resisting the Emperor's demands in the matter of the Barrier.   With George, his near relative on their mothers' side, he had exchanged strong assurances of friendship already during the last year of Louis XIV, and though these were suspended on the outbreak of the Jacobite rebellion, they were renewed on its suppression.   On the part of Spain, previously not less hostile than France, a new policy was begun by Alberoni, the obscure minister of Parma at Madrid, who was beginning to rule the country through the new Parmesan Queen.   With the consent of the sovereigns, and in opposition to the views of the Spanish Ministers, he offered a commercial treaty of the most favourable character.   It was signed on December 14, 1715, and was followed in May by a revision of the *Asiento*, which allowed Great Britain to export negroes to the Spanish Indies.   The provisions of the treaty were not, indeed, carried out; after it was signed, oppression of British trade continued as before.   Alberoni's intention would seem to have been to quiet England, in order to get rid of opposition on her part to his Italian schemes; for his objective was the replacement of Austrian rule in Italy by Spanish.

But the Austrian alliance was far more important to George than any advantages which Spain could offer.   And, on his side, the Emperor was realising that he could not carry out his designs upon Sicily without the aid of a British fleet.   The Spanish treaty disturbed Vienna for a while, as also did another British treaty with Holland, renewing former treaties of alliance and commerce, concluded on February 6, 1716.   But at length the Treaty of Westminster was signed by the two Powers on May 25 (O.S.).   The peculiarly phrased second article stipulated the mutual protection and maintenance of the kingdoms, provinces and rights actually enjoyed, and the defence, if either party were attacked, both of these possessions and of such as might be acquired by mutual consent during the continuance of the treaty.   The parties to it being Great Britain and the Emperor only, it could not extend, formally, to the new acquisitions of Hanover in the north; but this subject had been

CH. I.

brought forward in the negotiations, and much in regard to it was implied.

Definite overtures from the Regent Orleans were again made in March. In June he sent his confidant, the Abbé Dubois, to the Hague, to confer personally with Stanhope, then travelling with the King to Hanover. But George and his advisers were not at this time anxious to come to the proposed understanding; and they insisted upon the demolition of the works at Mardyk, and the expulsion of the Pretender and his adherents from France, as preliminary conditions. The interviews were not, however, without fruit; they were accompanied by negotiations in London, and were followed by a yet more secret visit of Dubois to Hanover in August. As the result, a preliminary convention was signed; and on October 11 Dubois took his departure, in order to complete a treaty with Great Britain and Holland at the Hague.

This outcome was principally due to developments in the north. The plan of war against Sweden in this year (1716) had taken the form of a Russo-Danish invasion from Zealand, while a joint British, Danish and Russian fleet blockaded the Swedish in its harbours. Pending the completion of the Danish preparations, the Russian force intended for the attack took up quarters in Mecklenburg. Its doings there, and the support which Peter the Great gave to Duke Charles Leopold of Mecklenburg-Schwerin, as described in a previous volume, roused the violent resentment of Bernstorff and other Mecklenburgers in the service of Hanover and Denmark; and the good relations established between Peter and George by their Treaty of Greifswald of October, 1715, were seriously impaired. And when, on September 17, all being at last ready for the invasion, Peter suddenly declared that the season was too late, and showed his intention of quartering his troops again in Mecklenburg for the winter, an all but open hostility supervened; while in England jealousy of Peter's rising power and the fear of his supremacy in the Baltic increased from day to day. Furthermore, the gravest anxiety was aroused by the doings of Charles XII. The belief obtained that his invasion of Norway was but preliminary to a descent upon Scotland from its ports. He left the remonstrances addressed to him through Sir John Norris simply unanswered. In July, Baron Görtz, whose enthusiasm and resource alone made it possible for Charles to carry on the war, arrived in Holland, the principal object of his mission being to raise money for his master's service, in order to procure for him ships and sailors. He was suspected of secret negotiations with the Jacobites, and his doings confirmed the belief that Charles intended to take revenge upon George in Great Britain—a revenge the justice of which was recognised. Under these circumstances, anxiety to conclude the alliance with France had replaced the former lukewarmness. Orders were sent to the British envoys at the Hague (October 9) to sign a preliminary treaty with France only, if the Dutch were not ready to join in it. Later, the anxiety was increased. Görtz was found to be approaching the Russian Ministers at the Hague and communicating with Paris. It began to be believed that a great league in the interests of the Pretender was in course of formation. Peter proceeding to Holland in December, George refused to meet him on his way, and rejected the conciliatory proposals of Russian envoys sent to Hanover.

The completion of Dubois' work was delayed by several causes. Full powers for the British envoys, Horatio Walpole and Lord Cadogan, had to be obtained from England; and these were twice objected to by Dubois as not in strict form. The Dutch Ministers were not satisfied with the terms of the convention, and were bound, besides, by a resolution of the States General, not to enter into alliance with France, unless a treaty with the Emperor could be concluded at the same time. Nor could the Pretender be expelled from France, because he lay dangerously ill at Avignon. At length, however, a treaty was signed by Great Britain and France on November 28, and on January 4, 1717, there was substituted for it one signed by the three Powers. This "Triple Alliance" brought the accord between Great Britain and France designed at Utrecht into real existence. Great Britain need no longer seek to restore the Grand Alliance, nor France encourage the Pretender. The security of the House of Orleans in France and of that of Hanover in England became a mutual interest. France could enjoy the repose of which she stood so urgently in need. Together, George and the Regent could direct the affairs of Europe. The alliance between them was genuine and proved lasting.

For the delays at the Hague Townshend was held responsible, undeservedly. But he had differed from the King and Stanhope in their recent policy, and there were other reasons for the royal disfavour. He was relieved of his office, and shortly, as is detailed elsewhere, the Ministry was reconstituted, with Stanhope at its head. His ideas on foreign policy agreeing in the main with those of his German colleagues, their influence rose to its height.

George returned to England at the end of January. Immediately was put into execution an act which awaited his coming. The Swedish envoy, Count Gyllenborg, was arrested, and his papers seized. Görtz also was arrested in Holland, and kept in prison till August. The so-called conspiracy was published to the world. It is probable that, but for the Whig schism at home, war with Sweden might have been declared. Charles XII, when the news reached him, retorted by putting the British resident at Stockholm under arrest and forbidding his Dutch colleague the Court. In the course of the summer the quarrel was arranged by the interposition of the Regent, and though the settlement was little to George's satisfaction, he was obliged to accept it, owing to growing discontent in Holland. But, before its terms could be carried out, Görtz was released by the independent action of the States of Gelderland; and,

CH. I.

instead of being sent back to Sweden, as had been intended, he was left free to pursue his schemes in Holland and Germany.

In May Peter the Great visited Paris. His proposals of alliance with France only resulted, as has been seen in a previous volume, in a colourless treaty of friendship between France, Russia and Prussia, signed on August 15 at Amsterdam, which admitted French mediation in the north and put an end to the payment of French subsidies to Sweden on the expiration of the existing treaty. One consequence of the negotiations was the withdrawal of the Russian troops from Mecklenburg.

A British squadron again visited the Baltic this year. The principal instructions given to Sir George Byng, who was in command, were to prevent a Swedish descent on the British coasts. He would, with the Danish fleet, have assaulted Karlskrona, had not the help of a land-force been required. A Swedish frigate was attacked and destroyed. Furthermore, trade with Sweden was prohibited, in order that the country might be reduced by famine. This measure, however, recoiled upon its authors; for the Dutch, whose Baltic trade was twice as great as the British, declined, in spite of all possible persuasion, to follow suit, and British merchants saw their trade cut off only to benefit their chief rivals. Frederick IV of Denmark also prohibited trade to Sweden, but failed in his attempt to conclude treaties with Great Britain and Hanover for the prosecution of the war.

Final negotiations with Peter the Great took place at Amsterdam in August. They were conducted by his old acquaintances, Sir John Norris and Charles Whitworth, the latter, perhaps, the ablest of British representatives abroad. But the aim on both sides seems to have been less to arrive at an understanding than to discover intentions. The conferences led to nothing. In fact, both George and Peter were now separately engaged in private peace negotiations with Sweden. These had been opened by George in the spring through Landgrave Charles of Hesse-Cassel (whose eldest son had married Ulrica Eleonora, sister of Charles XII), and through the Regent's envoy, Count de La Marck. Then, while his British Ministers were busy at Amsterdam, George arranged very secret conferences between his Hanoverian Councillor, Weipart Ludwig von Fabrice (Fabricius), and Count Vellingk, the Swedish governor of Bremen. The negotiations failed, for the cession of Bremen and Verden was refused. But early in 1718 Fabrice's son, Friedrich Ernst, in the service of the Duke of Holstein-Gottorp, who, after acting as intermediary between his father and Vellingk had been summoned to England in great secrecy, was sent on a private mission to Sweden. On Peter's side there were conferences with the Swedish resident at the Hague and others, and with Görtz after his release. In consequence, Görtz was accorded Russian and Prussian passports to return to Sweden through those countries. Evading certain British cruisers on the look-out for him, he arrived safely at Lund, the bearer of proposals which led to the Åland conferences of the following year.   His doings gave King George special anxiety, on account of events of the first importance, which had happened in the south.

All this time, Alberoni had been quietly but unceasingly at work on the regeneration of Spain.   He had succeeded in creating a fleet, and in August, 1717, suddenly put the weapons which he had forged to their trial-stroke.   A Spanish expedition sailed from Barcelona for Cagliari; and by the end of November all Sardinia, then belonging to the Emperor, was in Philip's hands.   Austria, having no ships, could not retaliate without the aid of a British fleet.   But the Emperor's demand that a fleet should be sent, in accordance with the Treaty of Westminster, was met by the reply that nothing could be done while he remained at issue with Holland, the British Government being well aware that the nation would not submit to see its Spanish and West Indian commerce imperilled, unless the Dutch undertook an equal risk.   Friendly expostulations were made at Madrid; but Alberoni, who was supposed to lay value on the friendship of England, unexpectedly proved defiant.

The Treaty of Westminster, indeed, and the Triple Alliance were antagonistic to each other.   The latter was as little relished at Vienna as the former had been at Paris.   But now the two were to be combined in a great scheme which had for its object the settlement of affairs in southern Europe.   Charles VI was not only still at war with Philip V of Spain, and claimed his crown, but was bent on depriving the House of Savoy of its recent gains in Sicily and the Milanese, and on succeeding to the dominions of the expiring dynasties of the Medici in Tuscany and the Farnesi in Parma and Piacenza.   Philip V, besides claiming the succession in France, aimed at the recovery of the old possessions of Spain in Italy.   The "Plan," as it was called, confirmed and confined him in Spain, gave Sicily to the Emperor and Sardinia to Savoy in exchange, and settled the succession in Tuscany and Parma and Piacenza upon the Duke of Parma's great-nephews, the sons of Philip V by his second marriage.   Such a settlement, it was thought, would at once set limits to Spanish and Austrian ambition, and secure the position of the House of Orleans in France and of that of Brunswick in Great Britain and in Hanover.

The Plan had been opened in November, 1716, at Vienna and pursued in conferences at Hanover with the Austrian envoy, Baron von Penterriedter.   On his way back to England, Stanhope communicated it to Dubois at the Hague.   But the Emperor refused to renounce either his Spanish claims, or his designs against Savoy; and negotiations halted until the news arrived of the invasion of Sardinia.   Meanwhile, efforts on Alberoni's part to conciliate the Regent, aided by the strong influence of the Spanish party at Paris and by increased jealousy of Austria consequent upon Prince Eugene's great victory at Belgrade, all but brought about an alliance between Spain and France.   To prevent this, and to

CH. I.

keep his master in the right path, Dubois, who was in London, came
back hurriedly to Paris at the end of November. His arguments prevailed, and the Regent definitely rejected Alberoni's overtures.

Besides ships for the Mediterranean, the Emperor urgently needed
money. In 1716, after the Turks had conquered the Morea from Venice
and had advanced into Dalmatia, he was compelled by his treaty
engagements and by the danger which threatened Hungary to declare
war upon them. Its course brought fresh laurels to Prince Eugene;
but it cost much money, and detained on the Turkish frontier armies
that were wanted in Italy. Although this War was specially excepted
from the Treaty of Westminster, George was ready to provide funds,
on condition that the Belgian ports should be forbidden to furnish
transport vessels to the Swedes or give protection to their privateers, and
that all Jacobites should be expelled from the Emperor's dominions upon
request—these demands to be embodied in an additional secret article
to the Treaty of Westminster. In return, Great Britain was to find
£130,000, nominally in satisfaction of arrears from the Spanish War.
Though the Emperor long held out against the mention of the Pretender
by name, in the end the article was signed, in December, 1717. In order
that the concessions might not appear to have been bought, it was
antedated September 1. The money was paid in January.

Meanwhile, a new project for the Plan had been handed to Penterriedter
in London (November 23). Although he expressed doubts as to its
being worth while for him to remain in England, he was in February,
1718, ordered to renew the conferences. But the British Government
thought it better to transfer them to Vienna, and sent thither the able
Swiss diplomatist, Luke Schaub, with a draft for a treaty between Great
Britain, France, Austria and Holland—the " Quadruple Alliance."

But a new complication now appeared. Charles VI had entered into
negotiation with the King of Sicily (Victor Amadeus II of Savoy). The
Prince of Piedmont was to marry an Austrian Archduchess, and Italian
questions were to be settled by a separate agreement. Schaub's proposals
were rebuffed, and it seemed as though all would fail. He and his
fellow-countryman, St Saphorin, the British Minister at Vienna, were
therefore surprised, when on April 4 they were informed that the
Emperor would accept the treaty in its main points. Discussions,
however, dragged on for seven further weeks before reference could be
made to Paris. At the beginning of April Stanhope resumed the
office of a Secretary of State, while the very capable James Craggs (the
younger) took the place which had been unsuitably filled by Addison.

To endeavour to persuade the Spaniards to accept the Plan, the
Regent sent the Marquis de Nancré to Madrid in March. But Alberoni
had schemes now on foot beyond conquest in Italy : nothing less than to
combine Sweden, Russia and Prussia, when they had concluded the peace
expected, and France too, if the Regent's Government could be upset, in

a great league to oust George I from the British throne in favour of James III. Spanish emissaries were busy in Holland trying to buy ships and munitions of war, and in the north. Overtures too were made to the Transylvanian Prince, Francis II Rákóczy, formerly leader of the insurrection in Hungary, inviting him to raise fresh difficulties for the Emperor there. On the news of naval preparations in England, Alberoni threatened to seize British ships and merchandise in Spain. When the terms proposed were handed to him they were indignantly refused. He declined even to consider the restoration of Gibraltar, offered as the price of commercial concessions and peace.

Schaub was back in Paris on June 18, but found the situation altered; the French were now unwilling to enter into the treaty. Proceeding to London, he found Dubois, who had returned thither, in despair. It was decided as a last hope to send Stanhope in person to Paris. He arrived there with Schaub on June 29, and learnt that another Spanish armament had sailed from Barcelona.

It was now, after much resistance, resolved to draw up an ultimatum to the Emperor, in the form of a convention between France and Great Britain. But when the convention was ready, the president of the Council of Foreign Affairs, Marshal d'Huxelles, refused to take the responsibility of signing it, or at least its secret articles, which provided for compulsion upon Spain and Savoy, if required. In this emergency Stanhope proposed to submit the convention to the whole Council of Regency, and, due preparatory measures having been taken, the bold stroke succeeded. It was signed on July 18, and Charles VI accepting it, the Quadruple Alliance was at last concluded in London as between Great Britain, France and Austria, on August 2, 1718. In part a treaty of mutual defence and guarantee, it also dictated to Spain and Savoy the terms, in substance, originally proposed. While to Stanhope should be given the chief credit of success both in the conception and execution of the Plan, it must be allowed that he could hardly have achieved it, but for the special influence enjoyed at Vienna by the Court of Hanover.

The Dutch Republic was a party to the Quadruple Alliance in nothing but name. The British Government made the greatest efforts to obtain the accession of the States General; but there was always a strong party in Holland objecting, in the interests of trade, to war under any circumstances. Grand Pensionary Heinsius had been able for many years to stem its arguments, upholding the traditions of the Stadholders; but he was now old and ailing, and there was no man to take his place. The efforts of the British envoys failed, even when they seemed to be successful. At first the Dutch required from France and Austria conditions extraneous to the Spanish question. When these had with difficulty been obtained for them by King George, they found other pretexts for evasion. A resolution to accede was adopted by the States General at the end of January, 1719; but, when the time for signature came, it was found that the powers provided did not extend to the essential secret articles. On a like occasion, in June, the cunning insertion of a word or two was held to render the accession valueless. And, though, on December 16, 1719, it was resolved to sign, after an interval of three months for the exertion of good offices, without reserve, the signature was still withheld.

William III had made the Hague the political centre of Europe. The enforcement of the doctrine of peace at any price by a minority of merchants, enabled to do so by the formalities of the constitution, forfeited that high position. Perhaps their policy was necessary, for the Republic was almost bankrupt. The United Provinces fell to the second rank among the Powers. The date of the death of Heinsius, August 3, 1720, may be taken to mark this fall.

Shortly before the Quadruple Alliance was signed, the Turkish War ended. George all along had watched its course with anxiety, for it grievously weakened his ally. The victory of Belgrade (August 16, 1717) was hailed in England as a success of the greatest consequence, affecting both north and south. Immediately thereon George offered his mediation. The Dutch followed suit, and a congress was opened at Passarowitz. The first exorbitant demands of the Emperor were reduced under the pressure of the Italian crisis, but Austria gained greatly. The prestige of the Peace, signed July 21, 1718, accrued to George, whose plenipotentiary, Sir Robert Sutton, had carried it through with little aid from his Dutch colleague, Count Colyer. With the Quadruple Alliance and the Turkish mediation, George's European ascendancy reached its zenith. He assumed the position, says Ranke, which William III held after the Peace of Ryswyk, with the French alliance to boot.

The destination of the Spanish armament which sailed from Barcelona in June, 1718, was Sicily. Palermo and the greater part of the island were rapidly conquered with the willing aid of the inhabitants. Hereupon, however, in compliance with the Emperor's demands, a British fleet appeared in the Mediterranean; and Colonel Stanhope at Madrid was ordered to use firm language to Alberoni, in regard both to the oppression of commerce and to the prosecution of the war.

Admiral Sir George Byng, after changing garrisons in Minorca, sailed straight for Naples. Here he learnt that Messina was partly taken, that the citadel must fall unless assistance could be sent, and, further, that the King of Sicily had expressed his desire to join the Quadruple Alliance, and asked for help. If Messina fell, the Spaniards would have a secure port from which to transfer their army to Calabria. Byng was instructed to prevent a Spanish invasion of Italy, or of Sicily with that object, by force, if negotiation failed. He proceeded, at the request of the Austrian Viceroy, to act accordingly. Arrived at Messina, he found that the Spanish fleet had retreated before him down the Straits. Landing an Austrian force, which he brought with him, at Reggio, he sent to request the Marquis de Lede to agree to a suspension of arms, pending receipt of further instructions. This being refused, he started in pursuit of the fleet, and on August 11 utterly destroyed it off Cape Passaro. That he had done right, he learnt from instructions received later, ordering him not to content himself with driving the fleet away with the loss of a ship or two, but to annihilate it.

Great Britain was not at war with Spain; her fleet acted as auxiliary to the Emperor. Diplomatic relations were not broken off for some months. Stanhope himself arrived at Madrid the day after the battle had been fought. He could effect nothing; Alberoni curtly intimated that Byng might carry out his instructions. The news of the capture of the town of Messina and the arrival of a large sum of money from America fortified Philip's resolution. When the news of Cape Passaro came, early in September, orders were issued to seize all British ships and merchandise in Spanish ports, as had been threatened. Byng was ordered to make, in return, the severest reprisals.

One result of the attack on Sicily was the submission of Victor Amadeus. After vain efforts on his part to obtain better terms, his plenipotentiaries acceded to the Quadruple Alliance in London on November 8. In exchange for his title of King of Sicily he received that of King of Sardinia.

Alberoni would not submit. His Italian enterprise frustrated, he turned to attack Great Britain and France. Feigning conciliation, he set on foot a plot against the Regent. The Spanish ambassador at Paris, Prince Cellamare, concerted it with the Court of the most active of the malcontents, the Duchess of Maine. Their doings were known, or at least discovered when matured; Cellamare was conducted to the frontier, the other conspirators imprisoned. On Great Britain Alberoni's attack was overt. The Atlantic ports of Spain resounded with the equipment of a second Armada. To meet the danger, the British Government got ready every available ship and arranged for the help of Dutch, French, and other soldiers and sailors. Parliament by a large majority authorised a declaration of war on December 17 (O.S.). And, in consequence of the strong reaction against Spain at Paris, resulting from the Cellamare conspiracy, the Regent was enabled to carry out his promise of like action, although the Quadruple Alliance only obliged France to furnish subsidies. France declared war against Spain on January 9, 1719.

Alberoni's scheme comprised a Swedish descent on Scotland and an attack by Sweden and Russia upon Hanover, in combination with the Spanish invasion of England. It was fully believed that Charles XII had concluded the peace with Peter the Great which would render this possible; indeed, on September 6, 1718, the latter actually signed a treaty for a joint invasion of Germany. In self-defence George, as Elector, concluded with Austria and Saxony the Treaty of Vienna of January 5, 1719. It engaged the parties to mutual defence and to offensive diversion into

neighbouring countries of the enemy. This provision could, in the case
of Hanover, only apply to Brandenburg or Mecklenburg, and, indeed,
the treaty was directed against Prussia as well as against the dreaded
Tsar, and was so understood at Berlin.   Its chief object was to prevent
the passage of Russian troops through Poland into Germany.

The year 1718 had in the north been devoted to negotiation.
Fabrice arrived at Lund at the end of February, and, when nothing was
heard from him, was followed by another emissary, Schrader, conveyed
to Sweden on a British man-of-war.   Fabrice saw Görtz and Charles
himself, and believed that he had obtained acceptable terms.   The
negotiation was purely Hanoverian ; it was kept as secret as possible
from the English Ministers, though confided to Count de La Marck.
Nothing came of it; Charles would not cede Bremen and Verden; George
was in a sufficiently strong position to be able to await events.   Sir John
Norris, instructed as Byng had been in the previous year, conducted a
squadron to the Baltic to act as he had done.   Meanwhile, Peter was
occupied with the conferences at the Åland Isles.   Four times Görtz
repaired thither ; three times he brought back proposals which Charles
rejected.   On his last return, at the end of November, he learnt that a
British envoy was going to St Petersburg.   He then decided to support
the plan of Chancellor Müllern for peace with Hanover.   But on
December 11 Charles XII met his fate at Frederikshald, and three
months later Görtz perished on the scaffold.

The mission to St Petersburg was the consequence of amicable
assurances given by the Russian resident in London.   In the place of
Sir John Norris, who had been appointed to it, but evaded the task,
it was undertaken by Captain James Jefferyes, who had been with
Charles XII at Poltawa, and accredited to him at Bender and in
Stralsund.   Jefferyes found that the Russian professions were illusory ;
all that was presented to him was a draft of the defensive treaty
proposed and rejected in 1716.   Instead of a desire for amity, he could
only report extensive armaments by sea and land.

With the death of Charles XII, the hopes of Alberoni and the
Jacobites from this quarter vanished into air.   So great was the relief in
England that Craggs saw in the catastrophe the hand of Providence.
But the new Spanish Armada sailed, only to be defeated, even more
conclusively than the old, by the elements.   Violent storms dispersed it
before it ever reached English waters.   A separate force, which landed
in the Western Highlands, was easily mastered.   Later, a French army
entered Spain.   Philip V could not believe that it would fight against
the next heir to the French throne, or the Duke of Berwick conduct it
against the interests of his brother.   He tried seduction, but failed ; nor
had he troops fit to oppose the French ; the army that should have
defended Spain was locked up in Sicily.   Fuenterrabia and San Sebastian
fell ; Catalonia was then invaded ; an English expedition under Lord

Cobham captured Vigo. These successes did not end the war, but they decided the fate of Alberoni, against whom, rather than against Spain, it was waged. Philip and his Queen protracted it, but its author had to bear the blame of its failure. In December he was dismissed by a palace intrigue promoted by his own patron, Francis Duke of Parma.

Before submitting to peace, Philip demanded extravagant concessions. His prospects were now brighter: the French army had been obliged to retire from Catalonia; the Marquis de Lede was holding out well in Sicily; a private settlement with Austria was possible. But Great Britain and France insisted upon accession to the Quadruple Alliance without reserve, before further terms could be discussed. In January, Philip reduced his demands to the restoration of the places taken— including Gibraltar—and the occupation of the Italian duchies by Spanish troops and their complete independence of the Emperor, as conditions for the evacuation of Sicily and Sardinia. But he was still met with firmness; and at length his ambassador at the Hague signed the Quadruple Alliance on February 17, 1720.

By this time George had almost completed that pacification of the north, which the support of the Regent enabled him to carry out. When, after the death of Charles XII, it became obligatory on Sweden to make peace, and in the first place either with Hanover or Russia, George's plan was that Hanover, Denmark, and Prussia, in return for the cession to them of the Swedish provinces in Germany, should combine with the Emperor and the King of Poland to force the Tsar to restore his conquests on the eastern coast of the Baltic. But the Powers concerned had different views. Sweden was ready to make peace with Russia, if Peter would restore Livonia and the Port of Reval as well as Finland. Denmark was for prosecuting the war to its extremity, in order to win back provinces in Sweden lost sixty years before. Frederick William of Prussia was closely allied with Peter, and was resolved upon maintaining the alliance. Finally, France insisted that Sweden must preserve a footing in the Empire, in order that her voice might be used, as of old, against the supremacy of Austria. The Regent advocated, as a first step, a reconciliation between Hanover and Prussia.

Bernstorff, ever loyal to the Emperor, threw the whole weight of his authority against this suggestion, but was overruled; the French alliance was indispensable. The Regent's policy was accepted; Whitworth was sent back to his old post at Berlin to conduct negotiations for treaties with Great Britain and Hanover. These were protracted for three months by difficulties of Hanoverian origin, and by Frederick William's hatred of the King of Poland, whom George desired to include in the latter treaty. Twice Stanhope and the French ambassador, Count Senneterre, fought pitched battles with Bernstorff at Hanover, and were victorious. In spite of the angry reluctance of Frederick William, continued to the end, the treaties were forced upon him. They were signed on August 14, 1719. The Hanoverian treaty guaranteed Bremen and Verden to Hanover, and Stettin and its district to Prussia.

In the meantime the young Lord Carteret, ambassador from Great Britain, and Colonel Adolphus Frederick von Bassewitz on the part of Hanover, had been busy at Stockholm. Under the pressure of the simultaneous Russian and Danish invasions, the Swedes signed a convention ceding Bremen and Verden (July 22). This was received at Hanover on August 5, but contained nothing about a cession of Stettin, Carteret having been forbidden to make any mention of this. In order that the cession might appear to have been agreed upon at Berlin before the Swedish convention reached Hanover, the Prussian treaties were antedated by ten days. A clause providing for it was sent to Stockholm to be inserted in the British treaty.

The main condition for the cession of Bremen and Verden was that the British squadron, now at Copenhagen, should proceed up the Baltic to protect Sweden from the Russian attack. But the Russian men-of-war were twice as many as the British, and might be reinforced by those of Denmark. Not until Prussia had been secured and other ships had arrived, was Sir John Norris allowed to sail. Anxiety was expressed that he might meet with the Russian fleet and destroy it, as the best possible service to his country. But it was already safe at Reval, and the galleys could not be reached among the northern shallows. The news of Norris' sailing, however, enabled Carteret to obtain the reluctant cession of Stettin; the preliminary convention with Great Britain embodying it and confirming that with Hanover was signed on August 29. Carteret's success was due less, perhaps, to his great diplomatic talents than to lavish bribery of the Swedish senators. Essential, too, was the promise of British and French subsidies. The first of the latter, obtained by George's influence, was brought to Stockholm by the French envoy, Campredon, at the end of August.

Norris stayed on in Stockholm waters till November. Threatening letters, pressing mediation on the Tsar, were sent to the Åland Isles, but unceremoniously returned. Final treaties with Hanover and Great Britain were signed on November 20, 1719 and February 1, 1720, the latter binding Great Britain to aid Sweden against Russia. On that day also the Swedish plenipotentiaries signed, and Carteret and Campredon, as mediators, accepted a treaty between Sweden and Prussia. They adopted this course in order that the *Riksdag*, about to meet, might not interfere. The Prussian envoy, Knyphausen, could not sign, being bound by orders from home on minor points. But the King of Prussia was persuaded to accept the treaty. A preliminary convention with the King of Poland was signed on January 18.

There remained the peace with Denmark; but to bring this to a conclusion seemed impossible. The Danes were throughout as insistent on their full demands as the Swedes were determined on yielding nothing.

With great difficulty an armistice had been forced upon Denmark as from October 30. When after six months it lapsed, little progress had been made. Frederick IV, in the end, was driven from his position, not by the threats of George, but by the action of the Emperor in taking up the cause of the dispossessed Duke of Holstein-Gottorp. It appeared that, if he persisted, Denmark might even lose Schleswig. By May, 1720, disputes were narrowed down to the amount of money to be paid by Sweden for the restoration of Stralsund and Rügen. On June 14 Carteret accepted, as before, terms signed by the Swedes alone. With these he repaired to Frederiksborg, and persuaded the King of Denmark to accept them (July 3). All that Denmark obtained by her ten years' war was a payment of 600,000 crowns, the abolition of the Swedish exemption from the Sound dues, and British and French guarantees for the retention of her conquest of Gottorpian Schleswig.

Besides George's plan of peace there was his plan of war, and this failed utterly. No Power would join him in offensive action against Peter the Great. British squadrons again entered the Baltic in 1720 and 1721, but they could not attack the Russian ports, or even prevent fresh incursions. The men-of-war could not penetrate among the rocks and islands to the north of Stockholm; when four Swedish frigates made the attempt, they ran aground and were destroyed. Already in October, 1720, George advised the new King of Sweden (Frederick I) to conclude with the Tsar on what terms he could. He offered £20,000 for distribution among the senators, and a subsidy of £100,000, if the cost of another expedition to the Baltic could be saved. But the Swedes held him to his engagements, and were consequently forced to accept the Peace of Nystad (September 10, 1721). Peter the Great kept all the coast from Finland to Courland, and Sweden passed finally from her high estate.

While Great Britain was thus working in accord with France both in north and south, her relations with the Emperor were changing for the worse. He resented King George's alliance with Prussia and the disposal of provinces in Germany without reference to himself. In the attacks which were being made upon Protestant liberties in the Palatinate and elsewhere his sympathy was with Rome, while George and Frederick William were strenuous in their defence. It was believed that the Pretender's bride, Clementina Sobieska, had escaped from Innsbruck with the connivance of the imperial Court. The Spanish party at Vienna, headed by the "favourite," Count Althan, and supported by the papal Court and by that of Turin, was employing every means to subvert the policy of the Quadruple Alliance. The Piedmont marriage mentioned above was again in contemplation, and Charles was only dissuaded from its accomplishment by George's personal appeals. And, lastly, there was the question of the succession to the Italian duchies. Strictly speaking, Spain not having acceded to the Quadruple Alliance within the allotted term of three months, the Queen of Spain's sons had forfeited those " expectatives," as they were termed.   Charles VI claimed them, but his allies resisted the claim, demanding an extension of the term of grace.   The Dutch insisted on this as a condition of their accession to the Quadruple Alliance. It came to be believed at Vienna that France and Great Britain were prompting these delays for the sake of conciliating the Duke of Parma, who, on the other hand, was looked upon by the Emperor as his principal opponent in Italy.   In the end, a convention was signed on November 18, 1719, obliging Spain to accede within three months, or forfeit the expectatives.   The Emperor was forced to submit by his inability to expel the Spaniards from Sicily and Sardinia without the aid of a British fleet, and by his want of money.

Spain, as has been seen, acceded within the term.   But now Great Britain and France, unanimous during the War, disputed the conditions of the Peace.   The principal subject of their quarrel was Gibraltar.   The Regent supposed that the offer of the restoration of the fortress, made before the war, still held good, and pledged himself to it.   Both George and Stanhope approved, the latter more than once expressing the opinion that possession of the place was a burden to England rather than an advantage.   But the suggestion was met in Parliament by so violent an outburst of resentment that he was glad to let the subject fall, fearing a formal resolution to the contrary.   Furthermore, the vigilant Lord Stair at Paris, always suspicious of the Regent's good intentions, was sending alarming reports of military and naval preparations, and of favour shown to the Jacobites.   George went so far as to fit out a squadron for defence against France, under pretext of danger in the Mediterranean.   The strain was increased by the conduct of Law, described elsewhere in this volume.   Dubois, his personal antagonist, strove earnestly for the maintenance of good relations, yet so critical was the situation in March, 1720, that Stanhope had to repair to Paris a second time that year.   Stair, who had attacked Law violently, had to be recalled.   Stanhope's arguments were fortunately supported by the discovery, or belief, of the Regent that Philip V was playing him false. It was agreed to send special envoys to Spain to treat conjointly. Moreover, the unsoundness of Law's System, as it had now been developed, was becoming evident.   So greatly had its success been previously feared, that Stanhope wrote that if it took root, as appeared probable, the Emperor, Great Britain and Holland, even with Prussia on their side, would not be able to stand against France ; and Stair's last service at Paris was to demonstrate to the Regent that it must be abandoned. Sir Robert Sutton, who replaced him in June, adopted a different line of conduct.   He showed confidence, instead of withholding it. Having investigated the reports of French armaments, he declared his belief that they were unfounded.   Yet, in July, Craggs detailed to him a list of grounds of suspicion still entertained, and the French ambassador was informed of the real reason for the equipment of the squadron of defence. But at the end of the month George decided that it might be laid up, and the autumn saw a restoration of amity. The case against Law was quietly but firmly pressed; in December he was dismissed from his employments. Great Britain and France could now pursue amicably the consummation which both desired, reconciliation with Spain. It was decided to refer the question of Gibraltar and other matters in dispute to the Congress appointed to meet at Cambray, though it seemed desirable to arrive at an accord upon them in advance, in order to oblige the Emperor to adhere to his engagements. Stanhope held out to Spain the definite expectation that Gibraltar would be restored, after the Government should have extricated itself from the difficulties due to the failure of the South Sea Company.

By this time the Emperor was looked upon at the English Court almost as an enemy. Bernstorff, still faithful to him, had lost his credit— the result of his opposition to the Prussian alliance and of Court intrigues consequent upon the reconciliation of George with the Prince of Wales, and promoted by Walpole, his determined enemy, whom the South Sea catastrophe called to power. George and Frederick William not only refused to send plenipotentiaries to the Congress of Brunswick—that shadowy Congress which had been sitting in form for the settlement of northern affairs since 1712—but dissuaded the King of Sweden from doing so. The Emperor persisted in refusing to invest the King of Prussia with Stettin; and the refusal obliged George to decline for the present the investiture of Bremen and Verden. Protests addressed to Vienna against the impolicy of driving Prussia, possibly, to raise a storm within the Empire, were in vain. Further, the homeless Duke of Holstein-Gottorp, having repaired to Vienna, was favourably received there, and, through him, an approximation ensued between Austria and Russia. In November, 1720, Cadogan was recalled from Vienna in anger, and St Saphorin was ordered to speak no more about northern affairs.

On March 27, 1721, a treaty was signed at Madrid between Spain and France. It was a treaty of mutual defence and guarantee, the King of France promising his most pressing offices for the restoration of Gibraltar and for the regulation of questions concerning the Italian duchies. Stanhope had died on February 16, but his policy was pursued by his successors under the direction of the King, who wrote to Philip promising to restore Gibraltar, in return for certain concessions, so soon as the consent of Parliament could be obtained. On June 13, the Treaty of Madrid was extended to include Great Britain. There followed the betrothals of the Infanta of Spain to Louis XV, and of the Regent's eldest daughter to the Prince of Asturias. A new system of European politics was set on foot. At the beginning of Walpole's term of power the conduct of foreign policy by Townshend and Carteret was based on a grouping of Great Britain, France, Spain and Prussia against the Emperor and the Tsar.

CH. I.

CHAPTER II.

THE AGE OF WALPOLE AND THE PELHAMS.

(1)

CHATEAUBRIAND once caustically declared that the Revolution of 1688, which Englishmen termed the "glorious," would be more fitly entitled the "useful." This epigram is less applicable to the age of William and Anne than to that of Walpole. Under William and Anne the wars, the conspiracies, the executions, the victories, remind us that we are still, in some sort, in a heroic age; under Walpole idealism or self-sacrifice is absent, the scene reveals few great events or great figures. His period is one of peace, uneventful, almost undisturbed; its chief crisis was due to stock-jobbing, its chief disputes are about currency and excise, its chief victories those of commerce, its type, if not its hero, a business man. The age has changed; the claims of rival merchants, not the sermons of rival preachers, are the incentives to strife; to the wars for religious or political rights succeed the wars of dynastic or commercial ambition. The tyranny of ideas, which had caused the religious contentions of the seventeenth century, yields to the tyranny of facts and materialism, which causes the political strife of the eighteenth. England, exhausted by two generations of civil strife, at length learns to acquiesce patiently in a dynasty that is foreign, in rulers who are opportunist and uninspiring, and in standards that are low. No one, indeed, will deny that the age of Walpole brought many benefits to England—a long peace which enabled her to recover from effort and overstrain, to garner the spoils won for her by the diplomacy of William and by the sword of Marlborough, to fill her coffers with gold and to cover the sea with her ships. Few ages have been more useful to England in the narrowest sense, few more materially prosperous; yet few have been less productive in the nobler and more ideal elements of national life. We are only saved from describing the age in the words which Porson once applied to an individual—as "mercantile and mean beyond merchandise and meanness," by the reflexion that the age of Sunderland, of the second George, and of Walpole is also that of Berkeley, of Wesley, and of Pitt.

The period opens, perhaps a little too characteristically, with the hideous scandals of the South Sea Bubble. This gigantic crisis of stock-jobbing, which is described elsewhere, was perhaps less serious for England than was the national decadence to which it called attention. The politicians had revealed their widespread corruption, directors and business men their unscrupulous greed, and the public, as a whole, hardly appeared in a better light. The fury which it showed in its pursuit and punishment of the directors, was little less discreditable than its previous avarice and credulity. In the midst of this turmoil, persecuted directors, hard-pressed politicians, and a public thirsting for their blood, alike turned for salvation or counsel to the shrewd and experienced statesman, who had once been First Lord of the Treasury, but who since April, 1720, had held the quite insignificant post of Paymaster of the Forces. Walpole, as the one prominent man in the Ministry responsible for the disaster who had disbelieved in the success of the Bubble, was therefore the only politician to improve his reputation by its failure. As a private individual he had profited largely from the credulity of the public at the time of the Bubble; he was now to profit yet more from it as a statesman. The universal recognition of his business ability, of his massive common sense, of his political moderation, marked him out as the one man fit to cope with the disaster and to minimise its ill-effects. His plan for restoring the tottering credit of the nation was accepted by Parliament, and its success secured him in power. He had indeed no rivals to fear or to face among the Ministers; Earl Stanhope and the two Craggs were dead; Aislabie was in the Tower; Sunderland and Charles Stanhope, though acquitted by Parliament, had not been absolved by the nation. Feeling his unpopularity to be insuperable, Sunderland resigned in 1722, and Walpole succeeded him in office as First Lord of the Treasury, becoming also Chancellor of the Exchequer (April, 1722). As Townshend—Walpole's brother-in-law—had already (February) become Principal Secretary for Foreign Affairs, Walpole found it easy to grasp the chief power in the State. So long as he agreed with Townshend, he needed only the favour of his sovereign, in order to remain supreme.

In some respects the character of George the First—as of his son— has been wronged, for, though their standard of private conduct may have in some respects been low and their view of human nature not high, they had genuine merits. Each showed a judicious patronage towards learning both in England and in Hanover, and, though they have been accused of despising the arts, few of their English subjects had so genuine a love for music, or showed so good a taste in appreciating it. With regard to their public conduct, it can hardly be denied that they were in many ways superior to the average English politician of the age. Each did his best to stop the infamous traffic and sale of commissions in the army and something to check the prevalent political corruption. With little knowledge of English ways and much innate aversion from

constitutional government, they both consented to be directed by
their English Ministers, and honestly observed the bargain between
themselves and the English people.   It is true that their foreign policy
sometimes showed an intelligible bias towards Hanoverian interests; but
this defect was more than balanced by their avoidance of vexatious
interference in domestic policy, and by the zeal with which they laboured
to compose differences between rival religious sects and rival political
factions.   The safe mediocrity of the first two Georges was indeed their
salvation, for it induced the English people to avoid pressing further a
conflict between Crown and people, which could only have endangered
the one and demoralised the other.   Great as were the restrictions
imposed upon the sovereign's power, his influence was still real, and
might have been dangerous, if unscrupulously used.   Eighteenth century
statesmen were so deeply conscious of this fact that they continually
suspect or accuse one another of intriguing in the closet, or of trying to
catch the ear of the King; Walpole spent hours daily in the boudoir
of Queen Caroline, telling her what policy he desired George II to
pursue; and to the same King's mistress, Lady Yarmouth, Pitt actually
submitted his military plans and the proposed list of his administration.
Such facts draw the curtain aside, and show but too clearly the influence
of court intrigue and of the King's will on the determination of public
policy, and on the rise and fall of Ministries.

Though Anne and the third George did not hesitate to make full
use of their opportunities, the authority of the two first Georges was
exercised with less frequency and effect by reason of their ignorance of
English parliamentary methods.   Nevertheless, in his relations with his
sovereign Walpole was anything but the autocrat that fancy has often
supposed.   In 1725, he reluctantly yielded to the royal will and permitted the recall of Bolingbroke to England; in 1728, he only secured
his power over the new King, George II, by obtaining for him the
substantial gratuity of an additional £100,000 yearly for the Civil List.
Subsequently, the favour of the able and enlightened Queen Caroline
assured Walpole's supremacy over the mind of George II; but her death
in 1737 brought about a visible decline of his influence, which contributed,
in some degree, to his subsequent fall.

If Walpole sometimes found it hard to win over his sovereign, still
less easy did he find it to prevail on his colleagues in the Cabinet or on
his party in the House.   More will be said below as to the working
of party government in this period.   Here it is enough to say that,
though Walpole ruled long, and though his majority was sometimes
large, his tenure of office was never so secure as to enable him to persist
in an unpopular course.   On many occasions, he bowed before a storm of
popular abuse, which was sometimes as fleeting as it was violent, and the
usual cause of his surrender was instability, not of conviction, but of
position.   From a Minister, who felt himself so unsafe during each one

of his twenty years of rule, bold initiative and far-reaching reform could not come. A careful stewardship of the national resources, an unwearied energy in promoting English industry and commerce, a good-natured tolerance of rival political and religious opinions, so long as they were not too extreme—these were the elements of that Walpolian system, which carried out the Revolution of 1688 to its logical conclusion, by developing the power of Parliament and assuring the Protestant Succession.

Bolingbroke had thought that England would never submit to be governed by a German; and the quiet acceptance of an uninspiring ruler by a proud and patriotic people, accustomed to kings of marked personality, is one of the wonders of English history. The character and policy of George I, the scheme of alliances which he reared to prevent interference from abroad, the errors of the Jacobites which enabled his Ministers to preserve his *régime* at home—all these have been discussed elsewhere. Here, it is needful to touch upon the difficulties of that energetic clique of Whig oligarchs, who had selected a king for themselves and who had to force their choice on the reluctant masses of the English people. The body of James II lay in state in the Church of the Faubourg St Jacques, unburied and surrounded by flaming tapers, awaiting the day when the Jacobites could lay it to rest in English earth. They had some justification for their hope, for the sentiment for the exiled Stewarts was always strong and often dangerous during the first fifteen years of the new dynasty. Even after the suppression of the Earl of Mar's rising in 1715 and the conclusion of the French Alliance of 1717, contemporaries thought that George I sat, not on a throne, but on a rocking-chair. The Septennial Act (1717), that extraordinary exercise of power by which the existing Parliament extended its term to seven years, can only be justified, as it was obviously prompted, by fear of Jacobite interference. In 1718 the Bishop of Salisbury quarrelled with his Dean and Chapter, on the ground that their singing "By the waters of Babylon" as an anthem was a sign of their attachment to the King over the water. In 1721 *Floridante*, an opera in which a rightful heir is restored to his own after misfortunes, was received in London with thunders of applause, not all intended for the composer, even though he happened to be Handel. More significant perhaps than any ebullitions of popular feeling is the fact that most prominent statesmen, even Walpole himself, deemed it prudent to indulge in secret, if not always sincere, correspondence with the exiled Stewart. That the Hanoverian Succession became infinitely more secure during Walpole's tenure of office was, in no small degree, due to his policy of cautious temporising, and to his deliberate conviction that, the less he harassed people with new taxes or new laws, the more likely would they be to acquiesce in a new dynasty. *Tranquilla non movere* was his motto and his policy; and for the moment it could claim an unusual justification. The country gentry—so powerfully represented in Parliament— were the most important class attached to the Stewarts, and the most

CH. II.

innately conservative section of the community; and they could only be conciliated by the absence of innovation. Hence, though the statute book during this period is barren, its sterility was more productive of genuine result than have been some periods of legislative fertility. Old abuses and a new dynasty alike remained unchanged, and Walpole tolerated the one to secure the other.

Even in religious policy Walpole suffered his personal views to be determined by his political necessities. After the discovery of the not very transparent Jacobite treason of Francis Atterbury, Bishop of Rochester (1721–2), Walpole exacted a special tax from the Catholics to the extent of £100,000, on the ground that they had disturbed the country, and must therefore pay an indemnity. Here, the desire of securing a round sum in a manner agreeable to the majority of his countrymen overpowered his love of justice and his notions of policy, for the Exchequer's gain was the dynasty's loss. But there is no more reason to doubt the genuine religious tolerance of Walpole than that of the Georges, and the efforts of King and Minister were mainly instrumental in securing alleviation for the Dissenters. By the Indemnity Acts, passed annually from 1727 onwards, Nonconformists, except Catholics, Jews, and Quakers, were practically relieved from the civil disabilities which a score of oppressive Acts had imposed. But Walpole's zeal for religious tolerance, as might be expected, was more practical than theoretical. When measures were brought forward in Parliament for the more complete relief of Dissenters (1730, 1734, 1739), he wavered and temporised. He received meetings of Dissenters in private, sympathised, held out hopes, and expressed desires; but he would risk neither his parliamentary majority nor his personal credit in trying to secure measures of full legal tolerance for Dissenters from a house full of country squires, to whom the high church parson was not only a fellow believer but a brother sportsman.

Political considerations and the need of defending the Ministry entered even into Walpole's dealings with the financial world, that world which he best understood and where he was best loved. "No man," all Lombard Street admitted, "had his equal in figures"; and this admission was the more remarkable, since some of his best-known financial schemes were not entirely original. Nevertheless, Walpole was able to kindle in merchants some of that enthusiasm which Carteret was to inspire in diplomatists, and Pitt in the people as a whole. He gauged their wishes with perfect accuracy and knew that the moneyed classes must be reconciled to the new dynasty by administrative activity, just as the country gentry were to be won by legislative sloth. The squire wanted the old laws and the old taxes to remain; the merchant wanted new trade regulations, new bounties for his exports, and new tariffs against his foreign rivals. Walpole was as ready to comply with the one as with the other, and the most cautious of legislators became the most daring of financiers. England had possessed great finance Ministers in Burghley, Montagu, and Godolphin; but no man before Walpole had ever so comprehensively grasped the whole economic system of England or had so decisively left his impress upon it.   From the very moment of his accession to office we note a thorough change and improvement in every department of national finance.   His earliest financial scheme marked the character of future effort, for his plan for the settlement of the South Sea Company (in which he persisted despite great opposition) eventually succeeded.   He brought the Bank of England and the East India Company to the rescue of the South Sea Company, and provided eventually for the sale or redemption of about a quarter of its stock.   It was impossible to restore the South Sea Company to complete health, but Walpole kept it alive by cordials from the Sinking Fund until it gained convalescence.

In pure finance the Sinking Fund is at once Walpole's chief achievement, and the chief illustration of the political difficulties which hampered his financial reforms.   During his first tenure of the Treasury, in the years 1716–7, he had devised a scheme for reducing the National Debt, by the formation of an annual sinking fund for the purpose of paying it off in instalments.   There was to be a general reduction of interest on the various types of national securities (averaging six to five per cent.), and the surplus thus gained was to be formed into a sinking fund for the annual reduction of the debt.   There is no indication that Walpole intended this surplus to accumulate at compound interest; and the comparison between his sinking fund and that of the younger Pitt is not to Walpole's disadvantage.   His sinking fund scheme was actually introduced by him after he had resigned office in 1717.   Its principle was extended in 1727, when he further reduced the interest on the various types of national securities (five to four per cent. average), and thereby raised the contribution to the sinking fund to an average of about a million a year.   The sinking fund contributed directly to debt reduction, indirectly to the stability of public credit.   Unfortunately, it formed a convenient fund to be appropriated or raided in case of necessity.   Thus, for instance, when in 1728 Walpole granted George II one hundred thousand pounds more for the Civil List than had been allotted to George I, this addition was to be annually charged on the sinking fund. This particular instance of a raid on the sinking fund is not to Walpole's credit, for there can be no doubt that it was connected with his desire to ingratiate himself with the new King.   A still worse, though an unimportant, instance of appropriation, occurred in 1729, when the sum of £4200 (which thieves had stolen from the Exchequer) was made good from the sinking fund.   Other arrangements for diverting the sinking fund, between 1733 and 1737, are also not very defensible, and incurred the weighty censure of Adam Smith.   Moreover, the genuine fear with which the increase of the debt was then regarded, which pictured it as a vampire sucking away the life of the State, as a fell disease slowly subduing its victim, makes these attacks on the sinking fund even less creditable than they would seem to-day. What was intended to be a cash reserve was treated as if it were a Fortunatus' purse. But the matter cannot be settled wholly on economic grounds, for the annual sinking fund surplus was an almost irresistible temptation to a Minister like Walpole, who was unwilling to risk an insecure position by imposing new taxes. The only other way of getting money except by new taxes was by raising new loans; but the sinking fund had been intended to prevent national loans, and direct appropriation from it might avoid a loan altogether. Such seems to have been the argument, and it is one which makes Walpole the victim rather than the dupe of circumstance. It should be remembered, however, to his credit that, while he sometimes robbed the sinking fund to avoid raising a loan, he never raised a loan without devoting some part of it to pay off that part of the National Debt, which bore the highest rate of interest.

If Walpole had been asked for his ideal of a golden year in finance, he would probably have answered "a year with the sinking fund at a million and the land tax at a shilling." The land tax was a lucrative direct tax; but, if he ventured to raise it, Walpole risked the alienation of the country gentry, and, not improbably, his own overthrow, or even that of the dynasty. All his efforts could not prevent the land tax from standing at an annual average of two shillings, though he got it down to a shilling in 1732–3. Probably with the same view of not irritating the Stewart-loving squires, Walpole never proposed a reassessment of the land tax, though such a measure was obviously in the interests of the National Exchequer and an act of justice to particular districts. The land tax was borne chiefly by the gentry; but indirect taxation of the moneyed classes likewise yielded good results. As Walpole said in his coarse, humorous way, the landed gentry resembled the hog, squealing whenever you laid hands on him, while the merchants were like a sheep, yielding its wool silently. Excise and customs were the two blades which shore away the commercial fleece. Walpole recognised that the fleece would be the richer if he could devise effectual checks upon smuggling. The severest laws and penalties were enacted in vain, for reasons which are not far to seek. No one who is acquainted with the traditions of Romney Marsh, or of the Welsh or Cornish coasts, can think that either Revenue officers or regulations availed against old traditions, excellent opportunities, and the cooperation of whole country-sides in the extensive industry of smuggling. The chaos was inde-scribable; the regulations were waste paper; the Exchequer must have lost hundreds of thousands yearly. Walpole's only chance of reducing the smuggling was either to lessen the huge customs duties on tea, coffee, and wine, or to replace these duties by excises, which should be chargeable on the commodities sold for home consumption. In 1724, he introduced an excise in the place of customs duties on tea and coffee;

but, though the result increased the revenue, he was very cautious about extending the principle.   In 1732, he revived the excise on salt, and on March 14, 1733, he opened his famous Excise Scheme in the House of Commons.   It simply consisted in the imposition of an excise on wine and tobacco, which was to be levied on the goods after they had been placed in English warehouses, in order that the chief possibilities of smuggling might be prevented.   Besides this, there was a further plan of allowing all raw materials to receive a drawback on reexportation, and thus make London a "free port" and the market of the world.   This scheme, he contended, would increase the revenue and benefit the honest trader at the expense of the smuggler.

There had been ominous mutterings already; now there were loud cries of indignation.   Pulteney led the opposition in the Commons, denouncing the excise as a monster, as injurious to liberty, as the greatest exercise of arbitrary power ever attempted by a tyrant.   A vast mob surged round Westminster Hall, penetrated to the Court of Requests and the Lobby, howled insults at the Ministers, and tried to tear Walpole from his carriage as he left St Stephen's.   Pamphlets of the coarsest abuse and the wildest imagination abounded; mobs paraded the streets; Walpole was burnt in effigy in dozens of bonfires.   People saw in imagination the tyrannical excise officers entering the Englishman's castle, and beheld Magna Carta trampled beneath the feet of merciless uniformed bureaucrats.   Jacobites openly spoke of the return of the Stewart; Whigs whispered that they would resist excise officers by force of arms.   Though the Venetian ambassador wrote that the pension list was increasing, Walpole's majorities diminished, the tables in the Commons were weighed down with petitions, Ministerial speakers were hissed and abused in the lobbies, howled down when they rose to speak in the Commons.   Queen Caroline feared for the loyalty of the army and the safety of the dynasty, and gave a tearful consent to the abandonment of the Bill.   After the session of April 10, Walpole announced this decision in a short speech to a private meeting of his supporters—" This dance, it will no further go."   The words disguised his emotion, and observers noted that his voice trembled and that his eyes filled with tears.   The abandonment of a cherished scheme of finance probably meant as much to this coarse-fibred man as the failure of a negotiation to Carteret, or the loss of a regiment to Pitt.

That Walpole, cautious and placable, would not persist in a scheme which threatened him, that he refused to "enforce taxes at the price of blood," is not surprising.   The whole course of this movement illustrates the strange and feverish agitations which sometimes suddenly gripped the English people during this century, disorganising policies, changing Ministries, and making England's Governments a proverb for fickleness and an object of pity to foreign diplomats.   But the Sacheverell agitation, the South Sea Bubble, the outcry against Wood's Halfpence, the

CH. II.

Jenkins' Ear frenzy, the Porteous riots—all these are, to some extent, more intelligible than the tempest which raged over the excise. It is a commonplace among modern historians that there was nothing in the actual scheme to cause alarm, that the measures proposed were at once just and practicable, and that, half a century later, they were, in large part, adopted by the younger Pitt without protest from anybody and with an enormous resultant gain to the revenue. But the circumstances of the time must be considered—the genuine hatred of unjustifiable state interference that existed among all parties, the real belief in the rights of liberty and property in their narrow and individualistic sense. Moreover Walpole's actions and utterances on the excise question looked somewhat equivocal; before 1732, he seems to have supported the principle of an excise on salt, because it imposed a small duty on a necessary which all could pay; in 1733, he seems to have advocated the excise on wine and tobacco, on the ground that these were luxuries on which a few paid. That the agitation was, in a large measure, fictitious, that the Opposition arguments were due partly to pure malice, and partly to impure self-interest, ought not to obscure the fact that Walpole's actions gave cause for suspicion. Why, asked his opponents, why did he revive the salt excise and reduce the land tax to a shilling in 1732, unless he had in contemplation a scheme of general excise for 1733? In introducing the excise scheme, he declared roundly that he had no intention of extending the excise to articles such as bread or common necessaries, and that no such scheme as a general excise had ever entered his head. That posterity accepts his assurances without question is not necessarily a reason why contemporaries should have shown the same recognition and confidence.

After the failure of the great Excise Scheme, Walpole seems to have lost interest, as well he might, in the essentially internal problems of trade and finance. The regulation of internal industry, the inspections to secure purity of goods, and the like, fell into some disuse in his later years, and he made no serious attempt to better the condition of industrial or agricultural workers. Indeed, the masters were supreme in the Commons, and Walpole would never have imperilled his own interests for the workers, against whom various Acts prohibiting combination were passed in this period. It may be urged that this epoch was the golden age of English agriculture, that the rate of industrial wages, relative to that in other times, has seldom stood higher, and that the worst evils of the capitalised industrial system were still to come. There can be little doubt, moreover, that Walpole genuinely believed the development of capitalism to be the source of all wealth and the remedy for all evils. Agriculture, manufactures and commerce, in this view, could be best improved by capitalistic development, for, as nothing else so quickly increased the sum total of national wealth, nothing else could provide so effectual or so speedy a remedy for poverty, unemployment, in a word for all economic ills. Hence the Corn Bounty Act of 1690, which had encouraged the capitalistic landowner at the expense of the yeoman, was now supplemented by bounties on exported manufactures, which gave advantage to the merchant with the large purse over the merchant with the small.

Mercantilism—of which Walpole was a convinced disciple—assumed that the State should stimulate national wealth, to the best of its ability. An export bounty had already been applied to corn by the Corn Bounty Act of 1689, and there had been a few export bounties upon manufactures; but these were now extended as a matter of general principle. Bounties and encouragements given to English-made gunpowder, worked silk, sailcloth, and refined sugar, attest the wide and diverse range of his efforts. Characteristically, he made no change in the bounties affecting the landed gentry, but bent all his energies to assisting the commercial classes. But with Walpole, as with all true mercantilists, it was not enough to bring the State to the assistance of those industries which most obviously increased national wealth: it was necessary to encourage and support others, which increased national power.

Bounties were given on whale fisheries in Greenland and on herring busses in the North Sea; subsidies flowed out to great trading companies in Africa, in the Baltic, or in the Levant, to encourage our sailors to seek distant seas, and to create a large commercial marine as a reserve from which the royal navy could be indefinitely increased. Under Walpole, the navy itself was not only kept up at its full standard, but the number of ships was even increased, though its administration left much to be desired. It is worthy of note that, except in cases where the object was purely to increase national power, Walpole seems to have granted bounties, drawbacks, and the like, not with the view of protecting infant industries at home, but in order to enable well-grown industries to capture foreign trade. Such a policy flowed necessarily from the ideas of the age; for, as the tariff wall was supposed to be high enough to enable England to retain her internal trade, an increase to her external trade was the only way of adding to the store of national wealth. Thus it was on commerce, that, as the King's Speech of 1721 put it, "the riches and grandeur of this nation chiefly depended."

Every effort was used to develop commerce, and to secure a favourable balance of trade—attempts which often began in commercial and ended in actual warfare, for the tariff-war was often the precursor of the trade-war, and, where the duty failed, the sword might succeed. The Methuen Treaty with Portugal in 1703, the commercial clauses of the Peace of Utrecht in 1713, were universally regarded as concessions to English trade which only arms, or the threat of arms, could have extorted. Much as Walpole himself loved peace, he was at one time ready to go to war with the Emperor, unless he abolished the Ostend Company—which threatened a formidable rivalry with England's East India Company.

The balance of trade actually became as great a fetish as the balance of power, and demanded from its votaries as many sacrifices and as much blood. In 1721, the King's Speech referred to the necessity of securing a "favourable balance of trade" by increasing our commerce. It proposed, as the most effectual means towards this end, to facilitate the import of foreign raw materials and the export of home manufactures. In accordance with this principle, the export duties, which had weighed heavily on the development of our external trade, were almost entirely swept away, with the exception of that upon white woollen cloth. At the same time and on the same principle, while import duties on manufactures were rigidly maintained or even raised, those on raw materials were almost totally abolished. Walpole was far too wise not to understand that a too rigid system of monopoly defeats itself, and that his repeal of duties on incoming raw materials would allow a far freer circulation to capital and to trade.

The great aim of Walpole's policy, whether we look to his tariffs against foreign or his bounties on home manufactures, was to secure a favourable balance of trade. Mercantilists held that, in commercial dealings between two countries, one nation invariably got the best of the bargain. The balance between the imports and exports of England to Holland, in the years 1720–2 for example, indicated according to the figures that England had gained £1,526,682 in the three years. It was believed that a good deal of this amount had passed in hard gold to England, though the figures were in any case somewhat dubious, and important factors were entirely omitted from consideration. The chief defect of the theory was that each particular country was isolated, and treated as an economic island: thus, in the case of a country like Holland, through which German goods filtered, England's tariff for Dutch goods remained intact because the balance was favourable to her, whereas the German share in effecting that result was entirely ignored. The rigidity with which this theory of balance of trade was held at this time, is of great importance, because it helps to explain the great and increasing attention which England paid to her plantations and colonies. The course of trade, as well as of empire, set westward. Joshua Gee, the most popular mercantilist writer of the age, corrected the official figures from the best evidence, and showed that, in reality, the trade balance from the Continent obstinately inclined against England. In her colonies the case was otherwise; they are, wrote Horace Walpole the elder, a wise and experienced statesman, "the source of all our riches, and preserve the balance of trade in our favour, for I don't know where we have it but by the means of our colonies"; and this conclusion found general acceptance. Investments of colonial money in English concerns, and the like, together with actual cash remittances, were probably the real cause of this favourable balance, but no means, whether by legislation or regulation, were left untried to produce it.

A scheme clearly floated in Sir Robert Walpole's head, of making a self-sufficing empire, to which the colonies would supply raw materials and the mother country manufactures. The bargain was not entirely unequal. It is true that the British merchant got Parliament to forbid the colonies to manufacture those articles which threatened to compete with his own manufactures. Such prohibitions were extended during this period to copper smelting (1722) and the manufacture of hats (1732); but, insomuch as the colonies were as yet chiefly agricultural, these measures seem to have caused comparatively little grievance till 1750. In the period 1720–50, certain commodities—tobacco, indigo, dyeing woods, rice, molasses, sugar, furs, copper ore—were "enumerated," *i.e.* were not allowed to be exported from the colonies, except to England and the other colonies. In passing through England they were obliged to pay duties; and this burden, together with the restriction to English markets, reacted unfavourably on colonial manufactures. At the same time there was some return for this injustice—bounties were given on many materials which the colonies produced, various exceptions were made and relaxations permitted. In 1721, in order that England's naval stores might be obtained from the colonies rather than from the Baltic, bounties were given on various kinds of naval materials which the colonies might supply, and all their hemp, timber and lumber were allowed to come in duty free. To encourage the colonial fishing industries, salt was allowed to be imported from any part of Europe directly to Pennsylvania (1727) and to New York (1730). In 1729 the rice of Carolina, which had hitherto, as an "enumerated" commodity, been forced to touch at an English port and pay a duty, was allowed to proceed direct to any part of Europe south of Cape Finisterre, subject to the payment in Great Britain of the amount equal to English duties less the drawback. The principle was also extended to the new colony of Georgia in 1735, with the result that the colonial growers speedily ousted the rice of India and of Egypt from Mediterranean markets. In 1739 the same principle was applied to sugar from the colonies with a corresponding increase to their sugar trade with southern Europe. Meanwhile, the English manufacturer rubbed his hands, the greater the wealth of the colonists through the sale of raw materials, the more would they be obliged to purchase of the English manufacturers. The preamble to the Rice Act of 1729 expressed this conception in a somewhat nobler way, by declaring that the prosperity of the colony must be considered as well as that of the mother country.

The scheme of a self-sufficing economic empire—which appears in this period—is of peculiar interest. The policy which put it into execution afterwards brought upon itself the denunciation of Adam Smith, on the ground that there had been an entire sacrifice of colonial interests to those of the mother country. Indeed, it can hardly be denied that the object of the policy was to procure a "favourable balance" to England, whatever might happen to colonial trade, and that, in this sense, the policy was really adverse to the colonies. But, when that balance was once secured, encouragements could be really given to the colonies. The economic interests of the colonies were, therefore, in some degree, subordinated to those of the mother country; but they were not absolutely disregarded. The encouragements given to colonial raw material were a direct gain to the colonial producers, to English manufacturers only an indirect one. Again, in certain cases, as in the prohibition of tobacco-growing in England and Ireland, the home producers were sacrificed to the interests of planters in Virginia and Maryland. In addition, the Navigation Act of 1662 forced all foreign goods from Asia, Africa, or America to be imported in bottoms that were British—a designation which covered colonial as well as English ships. Under the influence of this Act and designation many of the colonies, especially those of New England, had created veritable commercial fleets of their own. Thus, in this respect, they benefited largely as against the foreigner; and their gain from the shipping and the bounties was a great compensation for the loss occasioned by the restrictions on certain colonial manufactures. It is difficult to estimate that loss, because, as was inevitable, a vast illicit trade sprang up, which was systematically connived at by the mother country, and, in those good easy days, a kind-hearted Government at home and tolerant officials in the colonies often did away with much actual injustice.

Nevertheless, the theoretical grievance remained; and, when any dispute between the interests of colony and mother country came up for public settlement, it was not the latter who suffered. For instance, though encouragement was given to colonial raw sugar, a high duty was placed against their refined sugar for the benefit of the sugar refineries of England proper. Again, in 1733, the British sugar colonies petitioned Parliament, because the New England colonies were importing sugar and other commodities from the French and Dutch sugar isles, to the detriment of the British colonial sugar trade. Parliament contained many persons with interests or estates in British West Indian islands, not so many with a stake in New England; accordingly, it replied by the famous "Molasses Act," imposing heavy duties on foreign sugar, rum and molasses imported into British plantations. The preamble falsely stated that her sugar isles were the mainstay of England's commerce, but, even if they were, their chief industry was not in sugar but in slaves. Had the "Molasses Act" ever been seriously enforced, the economic grievances of New England would have been heavy; fortunately, its application was lax, and the cloud, for the moment, passed. Nevertheless, the Act made it clear that, when the interests of colonies and mother country formally conflicted, those of the former had to give way. The economic grievances under which the colonies laboured at this time were probably not as yet serious, except in theory; until 1750 the prohibitions on colonial manufactures caused comparatively little inconvenience; the Molasses Act was inoperative, the bounties and the Navigation Acts favoured the colonies. It would seem that the various restrictions were felt but slightly in communities that were primarily agricultural, and whose political self-consciousness was immature. It was not the presence of oppression, but the absence of foresight, which was the evil; *tranquilla non movere* was perhaps a policy for Old England—it was hardly such for New. The industrial developments and the increase of population, which were completely transforming the more northerly American colonies, were putting the old colonial system out of date; and the policy of drift served for the moment, though it was fatal for the future. Moreover, colonial grievances were aggravated by the fact that the French treated their colonies with more insight and sympathy, and deferred more obviously to their trade interests. During this period a judicious spirit of moderation, shown by the various concessions in bounties and the like, the connivance at the irregular trade, appeased colonial discontent; but there were not wanting signs of that intense resentment of a grievance, always in theory acute, and destined to become, in no distant hour, a deep cause of that internecine strife which tore asunder the Anglo-Saxon race.

Such was the Colonial System as Walpole left it; but our view of it would be incomplete, if we did not anticipate the developments which took place after his fall. It was evident that the demands of English and colonial merchants must sometimes conflict, and that, as one side had the ear of Parliament and the other had not, the latter must suffer. No Minister in the eighteenth century found it easy to resist parliamentary supporters, and only the utmost amount of prudence, or of far-seeing statesmanship, could have averted this result. Unfortunately, neither was at hand in the crucial year 1750, which is a milestone in colonial policy. In that year, English ironmasters clamoured against the colonial competition, and Henry Pelham decided to appease them by an Act, exactly as Walpole had appeased English capitalists, with West Indian interests, by the Molasses Act of 1733. The Colonial Manufactures Prohibition Act of 1750 sternly forbade the manufacture of bar or pig-iron in the American colonies, and provided for the abolition of colonial slitting-mills, tilt-hammers, and iron furnaces. The measure was to be rendered palatable by the granting of a preference to colonial raw iron as against continental, *i.e.* by the removal of duties on colonial bar and pig-iron, though these duties were retained on iron from the Baltic and elsewhere. But the concession was useless; the preamble of the Act announced that the production of raw iron was to be encouraged in the colonies, and its working prohibited, in each case for the benefit of the English manufacturer. This conception—familiar to English statesmen and statutes—was now at last brought home to the colonies, for, while earlier Acts had either been inoperative or had caused little practical grievance, the new Act was effective and obnoxious from the beginning. The old Acts had applied to young countries primarily agricultural, and rich only in raw materials; the new Act bore hardly on countries which were beginning to be industrial; and it was unfortunate that Puritan New England was now the home of colonial industry, as it had always been of colonial independence. It was easy to put out a New Englander's furnace, but the act lit a smouldering fire in his heart, for he now realised—in his own case and for the first time—that the commercial interests of a colony must be sacrificed to those of the mother land, and arguments as to the tyranny of tariffs easily led a Puritan community on to arguments about the tyranny of kings.

In his speech in 1749 Pelham declared himself a foe to monopoly and a disbeliever in the efficacy of human regulation to stay the currents of labour or of trade. His successors were to find that, while it is hard to check economic movements, it is easy to arouse political, and that the date 1750, which marks the beginning of industrial strife between Old and New England, is, in its way, as significant as 1783, which marks the close of military conflict. There is no indication that Pelham realised that colonial policy was entering on a new phase, and the Molasses Act is an apparent anticipation of the Colonial Manufactures Prohibition Act. The wisdom, which refused to enforce the one, and the energy, which made the other practicable, are characteristic of Walpole and Pelham. Neither had the genius and imagination to see the dawn of the new day; but, at least, Walpole was not responsible for the more portentous change in policy.

Politically, the colonies had few grievances to allege until 1750, for most of them were governed on principles more liberal than any known or practised elsewhere. Newcastle, otherwise energetic enough, was justly accused by the elder Horace Walpole of neglect of colonial business, though his attention to it was greater than has sometimes been supposed. Sir Robert Walpole contented himself with economic interference, and is said to have waved aside the not infrequent suggestion for taxing the colonies with this sentence of shrewd and homely wisdom: " I have Old England set against me for taxes, do you think I will have New England likewise?" Outside Downing Street, there were signs that the importance of colonial politics was increasing, that the conception of colonies as the local branches of a central business firm was giving way before ideas less mercantile and more political. Colonial particularism grew; local patriotism stirred; possession of vast trade was ceasing to be the one source of colonial pride or existence; pride of territory or of race was beginning. England herself witnessed Berkeley's great scheme for planting a spiritual Utopia in the Bermudas, and beheld the dream, whose ideal was to provide a money-ridden empire with a conscience, end with a present of books to a poverty-stricken library. About the time (1732) when the failure of Berkeley's scheme was announced, the new colony of Georgia was founded, on a scheme which appealed more to the aspirations of the patriot than to the desires of the business man. The scheme, in brief, was a charitable device for settling poor emigrants in a new land; it was started by private charity and aided by contributions from the state exchequer. There wanted not noble patrons of the Georgian plantation, and the King himself had smiled upon Berkeley's plan; but Walpole was indifferent, if not actually hostile, to both, and his delay in paying Berkeley the sums promised by the Treasury certainly wrecked the Bermudas venture. For the gentle religious idealism of Berkeley was almost as suspect to this genial materialist, as were any political schemes which looked for economic support to the State and to the future instead of to shareholders. It would be wrong to deny that the conception of an empire, based on an economic unity, floated before England's vision as before that of France; but Walpole conceived that unity, in the main, as resting on the broad interests of the mother land, while the French conception implied a bond of mutual benefit and obligation. Walpole recognised what appeared to be, the French what ought to have been, the facts; neither saw the facts as they really were. Walpole's aim was mainly economic, and his calculations were therefore too short—the French mainly political and their calculations therefore too long; in the one case the ideals were too low, in the other too high. Both schemes ended in disaster; but Walpole was nearer to the facts, and hence, when the catastrophe came, France lost all, and England only half, of the North American continent.

Walpole's economic policy, though everywhere defeated and marred by political considerations, has nevertheless a remarkable unity and harmony of aim. The Sinking Fund, which was to redeem the National Debt; the excise policy, which was to destroy smuggling; the colonial policy, which was to unite the Empire—all these achieved useful results, though political necessities sadly restricted and hampered their operation. Elsewhere, Walpole had a freer hand, and won such decisive success in his policy of encouragements to English trade, of placing tariffs on foreign manufactures and taking duties off foreign raw materials, that he might claim to be the first of financiers, if the evidence either of figures or contemporaries could pass without criticism. Walpole had produced a system which was a model of balance and consistency; he had imposed his bounties and prohibitions for short periods, and had made constant revision and adaptation of the tariff the very essence of his policy. Unhappily, the system was never simple, and its increasing elaboration and complexity prevented speedy revision, and annually increased the strength of the vested interests concerned. Under his successors, Walpole's system fared badly: bounties, once imposed to develop living, remained to prolong the agonies of dying, trades; prohibitions formerly effective became meaningless; the empiricism of one age had become the dogmatism of the next, with the result that contradiction, confusion, obsolescence reigned everywhere. Under these conditions, the system which Walpole had fathered encountered the most brilliant and destructive criticism that economic science has known.

Adam Smith's attacks on the Mercantilist System require some qualification, for they fail to do justice to the ideals and objects which it pursued, nor do they recognise that, because that system had ceased to be of service in 1776, it was not necessarily an anachronism under Walpole. Adam Smith undoubtedly proved that the system was not the easiest way of increasing national wealth; but Walpole would have replied that, none the less, it was the easiest and perhaps the only way to secure national power and wealth at the same time. Adam Smith rightly contended that colonial trade had been overdeveloped to the detriment of foreign; but this view marked a revolution in economic theory, so that a practical business man like Walpole may be excused for acquiescing in a view almost universal even among theorists in his own day. So long as the balance of trade was a fetish, it was only reasonable to develop trade with the colonies, where that balance could be regulated so as to be especially favourable to the mother land.

On the more purely economic side, however, some aspects of Walpole's policy are open to severe criticism, even after every allowance has been made. Thus, for example, the production of corn was encouraged by bounty to the detriment of turnip and grass cultivation, and at the expense of the small farmer; in other cases, one industry was selected for encouragement, without regard being paid to the fact that such forcing might have a bad effect on other industries indirectly associated with it. An industry—like a country—was regarded as an economic island, with results often serious in each case. Such measures, however erroneous in theory, were still more erroneous in fact; and the criticism of the practical man would be more severe than that of the theorist. The main evil of the system, however, was that it tended to monopoly, and monopoly always has its victims and its penalties; but Walpole's resolute insistence on the principle that raw materials from foreign lands should enter English ports duty free prevented the price exacted from being higher. His errors resulted from a too complete adoption of mercantilist theory, which made him as much the idol of contemporaries as it has rendered him the target of subsequent criticism. But, after every deduction has been made, when we regard the immense range and scale of his achievement, he must be deemed worthy to rank beside the great financier at the beginning, and the great financier at the close, of his century. It is an irony in which Swift would have delighted that the white staff of Lord High Treasurer, bestowed thrice during the eighteenth century, was never grasped by the hand either of Montagu, of Walpole, or of Pitt, whose supreme financial talents most justly entitled them to that reward.

During the early years of his government, Walpole exercised comparatively little influence over foreign policy, though he kept a watchful eye from the Treasury on subsidies and commercial negotiations. For our purpose, England's foreign policy begins in the early twenties, when Townshend was First Foreign Secretary, and when the diplomatic world was yawning over the Congress of Cambray. England was still reaping the fruits of her French alliance of 1717, which, combined with a resolute diplomacy, had given her German ruler, in the years that followed, a diplomatic position no less commanding than that which her Dutch "Deliverer" had enjoyed. George I had mediated between Emperor and Sultan in 1718, and had been the arbiter of the Baltic in 1721; at the Congress of Cambray, summoned for 1722, he seemed about to settle the affairs of Habsburg and Spanish Bourbon, as he had settled those of Turkey and Sweden, and to become the universal pacificator of Europe. Unfortunately, George I's resemblance to William III was now to cease, and, after giving the law to the east and to the north, he was to suffer a diplomatic defeat in the west. English diplomatists thought that the beginning of the Congress of Cambray was too dull—they discovered that its end was too exciting. Under the influence of the fiery Elisabeth Farnese, Queen of Spain, who blamed England and France for the endless delays of the Congress, Spain and the Emperor drew together; and these two disputants, for whose reconciliation France and her ally Great Britain had, in the end, laboured, made a formal agreement to unite against the peacemakers. The Treaty of Peace signed at Vienna by Austrian and Spanish representatives on April 30, 1725, announced to the world the reconciliation of the two quondam rivals, and, as a consequence, the dissolution of the Congress and the discomfiture of France and of England. George I, formerly the arbiter of Europe, found his projects dissolved in air, and himself threatened by a positive danger. He had only the dubious friendship of France on which to rely, and an Austro-Spanish combination might have to be met in the field.

The chief aspects of the Vienna Treaties are described elsewhere, but their English side concerns us here. The Treaty of Peace of April 30 had announced that Spain had accepted the Pragmatic Sanction (thus guaranteeing the complete succession to the Austrian possessions of the Emperor's daughter, Maria Theresa). Two supplementary and secret Treaties, of Alliance and Commerce respectively, signed on May 1, bound the Emperor Charles VI, in return, to use his good offices to induce England to surrender Gibraltar and Minorca to Spain, and engaged the Spanish Government to encourage and assist the Emperor in developing the commerce of the Austrian Netherlands, and in promoting the Ostend Company, a corporation already licensed with a view to trading in the East Indies. These provisions were alarming enough; but the sense of danger was increased by a further, and most secret, agreement between the two Powers (November 5, 1725), which provided, in certain eventualities, for marriages between two Austrian Archduchesses and two Spanish Infants. A secret article arranged for a partition of French territory between the Habsburg and the Spanish Bourbon, in case they defeated France in war. English diplomats persisted in thinking (quite incorrectly) that there was another secret clause arranging for the joint support of James Edward's claims to the English Crown. English popular opinion was thoroughly alarmed, as a passage in a pamphlet published near this date shows : " The Archduchesses are destined to the Infants of Spain, and such a Power arising from this conjunction, as in all probability may make the rest of Europe tremble." Clearly, the wedding-bells of Austria and Spain were the passing-bells for England and for France. The Peace of Utrecht, which had asserted the balance of power by separating the Crowns of France and Spain, would have been in vain, if Europe was to be overshadowed by a Spanish-Austrian alliance, and threatened by a union of the forces of the two monarchies. In that case the balance of power was overthrown once more. France saw Austria and Spain dominating Italy, and their armies on the road to Paris ; England beheld Spanish fleets ravaging the coast of Scotland, and Austrian merchantmen sailing up the Hooghly. A common danger threatened the allies of 1717, which only resolution could meet. It was necessary to face the Austro-Spanish danger ; and, though French diplomacy was wavering, Townshend was not the man to hesitate. The substance of the secret articles had filtered through to the British public, and England, touched in her pride by the Gibraltar, in her pocket by the Ostend, article, was ready to support her Minister.

The instructions issued by Townshend to Stanhope at Madrid on June 28 (O.S.), 1725, after the Emperor had formally announced his wish to mediate between England and Spain on the subject of Gibraltar, mark the proud and resolute character of his policy. " The Imperialists are thoroughly sensible of the great fondness the Parliament and even the whole nation have for Gibraltar; they likewise know that by our laws and Constitution the Crown cannot yield to any foreign Power whatsoever any part of his dominions without consent of Parliament, and that Gibraltar being yielded to Great Britain, by the Treaty of Utrecht, is as much annexed to the Crown as Ireland, or any part of England ; they are also convinced, that even the bare proposing the delivering up this place to the Parliament will put the King's affairs into the utmost confusion, and therefore are sure the King is not to be prevailed upon to mention it to them. They are in like manner persuaded that all the discerning men in England are at this juncture so irritated with the slights, and indignities that have been put upon the King's mediation by the Crown of Spain and the injuries done the nation by the Treaty of Commerce, lately concluded by Spain with the Emperor at Vienna, in which amongst other things, there are so many manifest favours and partialities shown to the Ostend Company, that they are firmly persuaded if they could by their dexterity throw in, at this time, the affair of Gibraltar it would raise such a flame in the nation as would certainly bring things to the greatest extremities between the two Crowns, and this is beyond all dispute, the point at which the Emperor does at present drive." It is difficult to read this passage without perceiving that it vibrates with a national and patriotic feeling rare indeed in this age.

But, though Townshend relied on national feeling to support him, he was not blind to the further necessity of dynastic alliances. So early as February 4, 1725, when the Austro-Spanish union was first suspected, Newcastle, the Second Secretary of State, had suggested that it could be countered by a league of Northern Powers, a policy which Townshend now adopted in full. Proceeding to the Continent, he signed the Alliance of Hanover (or Herrenhausen; September 3, 1725) between England, France and Prussia, in order to provide guarantees of mutual defence, to arrange for the destruction of the Ostend Company, and to form a union which should balance the overwhelming predominance of the Austro-Spanish alliance. Frederick William I of Prussia showed duplicity, and, after hesitating for about a year, finally retired altogether from the Hanover Alliance and made an agreement at Wusterhausen with the Emperor (October 12, 1726). But, by a lavish use of bribes and subsidies which caused growls from Walpole at the Treasury, the complicated network of a vast alliance was gradually woven together. Imposing demonstrations were made to impress the smaller Powers; French troops were massed on the Rhine; English fleets paraded up and down the Channel, the Spanish coast, the Baltic, and the Caribbean Sea. Sweden and Denmark came into the Alliance; the Landgrave of Hesse-Cassel and other smaller German Princes were also swept into the net. In 1727 Europe was an armed camp. France had raised nearly 100,000 additional troops, Holland 30,000, Denmark and Sweden were prepared to contribute handsomely. On the sea France and England were enormously superior, and, though on the land the Emperor and Spain had the predominance in mere numbers, the treasury of the former was wholly empty, that of the latter wofully bare. An alliance more formidable, because more united, than that which had defeated Louis XIV and Philip V was now facing this same Philip and his new Imperial ally, and, as the main architect of the first structure had been William III, so the main contriver of the second was Townshend.

The need of disbursing large sums for Townshend's subsidies and bribes seems to have awakened Walpole, who from this time forward exercised considerable influence in foreign affairs. Townshend resented his interference, and there were many quarrels before the final one of 1730. The strength and use of the Alliance were soon tested, for Spain (to whom Townshend's alliances and despatches must have been alike objectionable) declared war against England in February, 1727. The value of Townshend's diplomacy was speedily revealed, for the Emperor was far too impressed with the power of the counter-combination to join his ally. Gibraltar endured a languid siege; but the chief interest lay in the stopping of the Spanish treasure fleet. If Spain could get home her usual amount of bullion, she might bribe her Imperial ally into action. To prevent this eventuality, Admiral Hosier had been blockading Porto-bello in the West Indies so early as September, 1726; and in 1727 Sir Charles Wager cruised up and down the Spanish coast for the same purpose. They did not succeed in stopping the treasure fleet; but the Spaniards managed to bring only a small part of the usual supply of bullion into Cadiz. Since there was no decisive action at sea, and as each belligerent had a pacific and timorous ally on her flank urging her to peace, an accommodation was soon reached. Hostilities were suspended at the end of 1727, not very much to the taste of the English people—"it's like God's peace; it's both long in coming and passes all understanding," wrote a witty lady to Lord Carlisle; in fact, there supervened, as usual, tedious delays, solemn trifling, and ineffective congresses. This time a settlement was ultimately arranged, owing to the sudden interference of Elisabeth Farnese, whose policy was always unconventional and some-times, as in this case, highly effective. In December, 1728, Elisabeth had learnt that the project of Austrian marriages was ruled out on the Austrian side. She was furious, and determined on revenge. In 1725 she had rejected the friendship of France and Great Britain for that of the Emperor; now, in her bitter anger, she reversed the process. On November 9, 1729, the representatives of England, France, and Spain signed at Seville a Treaty, which they agreed to force on the Emperor. The two allies, neatly profiting by Elisabeth's anger against the Emperor, induced Spain to grant, for the first time, a frank and ungrudging recognition of the full consequences of the Treaty of Utrecht, in so far as it secured commercial advantages to England and to France, and the English possession of Gibraltar. In return, England and France promised to aid in the introduction of Spanish garrisons into Tuscany and Parma. These stipulations, together with the suppression of the Ostend Company, were eventually ratified by the Emperor in the ("Second") Treaty of Vienna (July 22, 1731). This agreement marks the culminating point of the union between England and France, and the greatest material advantage derived by the former from that alliance: namely, the final abolition of the Ostend Company.

The Treaty of Seville is a landmark in the history of diplomacy, more decisive and important than the *Pacte de famille* of 1733. It marks the breakdown of one new combination—the Austro-Spanish Alliance, and the beginning of the collapse of another—the Franco-British. The confusion introduced by the Peace of Utrecht was beginning to dis-appear, and events were gradually reverting to the European System at the beginning of the eighteenth century—that of a union between France and Spain, opposed by the combination of England, Holland, and the Emperor. Townshend, who had specially favoured friendship with France and had looked coldly on the Emperor, was dismissed in 1730; and, from 1731 onwards, the estrangement between England and France becomes evident and decisive. When historical writers speak of the " Hundred Years' War between England and France on the sea," which lasted from the days of the third William to those of the third George, they omit the interlude of fourteen years (1717–31), when England and France were not only at peace but in alliance. During this period there was a real chance that the two nations, by careful avoidance of difficulties and by joint pressure upon Spain, might pursue lines of territorial expansion and commercial development, which ran close to one another, but never intersected. When England began to draw back from this alliance, her position was fundamentally altered, and the old forces, hitherto suspended in their action, began again to exert their influence.

A new age now opens for English diplomacy : national influences strengthen, dynastic ones weaken. The place of the resolute, adroit Townshend with his eye ever on the least movement among the Princes of Germany, is taken by the fussy, impulsive Newcastle, with his ear carefully trained to public opinion in England. Hanover, King George, and the Balance of Power fall in importance ; the South Sea Company, the West Indies and the Balance of Trade rise. Newcastle, now Principal Secretary, was without steadiness though not without insight ; but he was steadied by William Stanhope (Lord Harrington), whose skill in negotiating the Treaty of Seville had been rewarded by a peerage and the seals of the second Secretaryship of State. Behind the pair stood Walpole, whose calm judgment, shrewd wisdom, and increased prestige now gave him an influence in foreign affairs, to which he had never before attained. Both by predilection and by the pressure of the forces behind them— popular, commercial, parliamentary—Newcastle and Stanhope were driven to the new policy which Townshend had denounced with his last diplomatic breath. That policy was one of accommodation with the Emperor, an accommodation which was bound eventually to provoke French hostility. It is by no means certain that they were wrong in the new move ; but the balance of probability seems against them. The Emperor proved to be restless, impotent, and unstable ; England's danger in estranging France was that she might in consequence turn to Spain. A Franco-Spanish Alliance was really far more dangerous to England's position in the New World than an Austro-Spanish combination against her could have been. The joint action of England and France had secured the English commercial privileges in the New World in 1729 ; when France and England were at enmity, it seemed as if France and Spain might settle the future of the New World by friendly arrangement or alliance. When Spain gravitated towards France, England could rely only upon the Emperor—an ally whose power, interest and authority were purely territorial—and had consequently to face in the New World the combined fleets of the two strongest naval Powers except herself. The danger was at once real and new, for it was only gradually that English diplomatists began to perceive and to fear that their country might fall prostrate before the House of Bourbon—an issue which the genius of the elder Pitt averted, but which came to pass in 1783. The true point of departure, which rendered this combination possible, was taken in the momentous decisions of the English Cabinet during the years 1731 to 1733 —decisions in which the voice of Newcastle and the hand of Walpole are specially to be discerned. At first, the consequences of the separation from France were not realised. The sturdy good sense of Walpole did not penetrate deep into the future : it saw clearly that the French alliance might mean continental entanglements and campaigns on the Rhine; but it did not perceive that combination with the Emperor, though perhaps less dangerous in this direction, would not be of much real value to England when the question was one of supremacy in the Caribbean Sea or the Indian Ocean ; or that the abandonment of direct interference in the Old World did not secure uninterrupted expansion in the New.

No better example of the benefits of non-interference in the affairs of the Old World could have been supplied than when, in 1733, England deliberately refused to take part in the War of the Polish Succession, waged between Russia and the Emperor against France and Spain. England's view is put tersely enough by Newcastle in a Memorial written not long after November 1, 1733. "They [the English Ministers] were apprehensive of being involved in a War, on account of the Polish Election, in which neither his Majesty nor the [Dutch] States were, either by interest or engagements, at all concerned." As a matter of strict fact, his Majesty was very much "concerned" both in and about the Polish Election, for the Emperor had offered him a command on the Rhine, and the martial little monarch was burning to wear his Oudenarde coat and display his military valour in a campaign against the French. But his Majesty's Ministers thought otherwise, and Walpole was the most urgently pacific of them all. His policy won the day, and his famous boast to Queen Caroline, that fifty thousand men had been killed in Europe that year (1734) and not one Englishman, marks the nobler side of his enthusiasm for peace. Other considerations, however, drove home the humanitarian argument for peace ; the Whig advocates of liberty were not particularly desirous of military glory ; reduction of the army and withdrawal from the Continent were not less popular with those who liked to flout Hanover, than were the increase of the fleet and of enmity towards Spain congenial to the passions of Protestantism and the interests of commerce. The English Ministers and people had alike decided to disregard the Polish War. That Russian troops and Russian diplomacy made their first appearance in western Europe, that Don Carlos' Garibaldi-like conquest of Naples meant the substitution of Spanish influence for German in southern Italy, or that the conquest of Lorraine opened one more French gate into Germany—all these changes affected the balance of power, indeed, but not sufficiently to cause England's interference.

Very serious differences had already arisen between England and

Spain; they were naturally not lessened by a war in which England took no part, except by showing a diplomatic bias in favour of the Emperor. It was, however, of unspeakable importance to her that French and Spanish Bourbons drew together, for their union might disturb England's commerce, and threaten the New World where her favourable trade balance was assured. On March 22, 1733, Newcastle wrote to Earl Waldegrave, British ambassador at Paris, that "French Ministers...will give the worst turn they are able to the conduct of England towards Spain, in order to create a breach or at least a coldness between us." His foresight was justified: the prospect of war drew France and Spain closer together, and the breach between Spain and England was completed by the signing of the Treaty of the Escurial (November 7, 1733). This famous Treaty, usually called the first of the three *Pactes de famille*, was signed amid precautions of the most extraordinary secrecy; nevertheless, its substance, or even its full provisions, were known to Newcastle in February, 1734. It began by describing the union between the two branches of the House of Bourbon as eternal and irrevocable; France engaged to provide an army of 40,000 at need, and agreed to help Spain to recover Gibraltar; and Spain, in her turn, consented to abrogate, on the first favourable opportunity, the special commercial advantages given to England by the Treaty of Utrecht. Such was the famous *Pacte de famille*, further discussed elsewhere, and often described as the main origin and cause of that Franco-Spanish alliance which was to be so prominent in continental diplomacy until it produced the humiliations undergone by England in 1783. But such an estimate of this treaty is based on the words of the document, rather than on the intentions of its signatories. The Treaty between Spain and France in 1721 contained the words "eternal and irrevocable union," and, within four years, the two countries were the bitterest of foes. In a precisely similar way and in about the same period of time, the eternity and irrevocability of the union in 1733 was dissolved. The truth is that the importance of the Bourbon Alliance in 1743, 1761, and 1783 has caused the same importance to be attributed to that of 1733. Family connexions did not always win the day even in the eighteenth century, when weighed in the balance with what rulers considered to be their own or their country's interest; and within four years Louis XV was to illustrate this truth very strongly in his attitude towards Spain. The *Pacte de famille*, accordingly, is interesting rather as indicating the unconscious tendency of events than as the definite starting-point of an epoch in foreign policy. If any such definite starting-point is to be found, it must be fixed either in 1730, when the tendencies, which drew France and England definitely apart, were first manifested; or in 1743, when the tendencies, which drew France and Spain definitely together, exercised a commanding force. In any case, the *Pacte de famille* of 1733 must not be regarded as the mainspring of the future policy of France and Spain.

CH. II.

England and Spain had rarely been without disputes in the past; and, though the Treaty of Seville in 1729 had improved matters, the Commission—appointed in connexion with it to settle disputes between the two Powers—had made little headway. The grievances of both sides centred round the South Sea Company, which was to inflict no less political than financial misfortune upon England. By the Treaty of Utrecht the South Sea Company had acquired from Spain the very valuable privilege of the *Asiento*, or contract for supplying the annual quota of negroes imported from Africa to work the plantations of Spanish America. Their further privilege of sending annually one large trading ship to the Spanish possessions had been grossly abused, and a large illicit trade had sprung up, partly under cover, partly independently, of the South Sea Company. Smugglers plied between the Spanish possessions and Jamaica with great frequency. Spain replied by sending out ships as *guarda-costas* to arrest and punish smugglers. These *guarda-costas* seem, on occasion, to have behaved with needless brutality, as in the case of the *Rebecca* (1731), when the famous Jenkins was forcibly deprived of that ear, the display of which subsequently occasioned much sympathy in the House of Commons and did something to cause the war. In any case, a number of vessels were wrongly seized and confiscated on the plea of carrying smuggled goods—in some cases, because Spanish privateers were masquerading under the guise of *guarda-costas*; in others, because Spanish governors readily winked at a practice profitable to themselves. But the brutalities and the grievances were not wholly of Spanish origin; if there were Spanish privateers off the coast of Jamaica, there were English off Havana and Honduras. If Jenkins lost his ear and some other captains their goods, Spanish shipowners had suffered in their turn; if Englishmen had been seen working in irons in the harbour of Havana, Spaniards had been publicly sold as slaves in the British colonies. To these facts popular fancy in both countries had stitched a rich embroidery of fiction, so that, in England, it was believed that hundreds of sailors were rotting in Spanish dungeons; in Spain, that an English captain had made a certain noble Spaniard cut off and devour his own nose.

In truth both sides had real grievances; the English Government, however, complained most vigorously as to various outrages, especially that of Jenkins' ear, but without satisfactory result. Patiño—the chief Minister of Spain from 1726 to 1736—was not very compliant, and Spanish diplomacy always moved slowly. Even with the best will in the world, it was extremely difficult to control quasi-independent Spanish governors at the other side of the Atlantic, who, for their part, found it equally impossible to line their coasts with troops to check smuggling, or to prevent an occasional Spanish privateer from raiding an English ship. The truth seems to be that, despite the Spanish *guarda-costas*, the illicit trade went on with undiminished vigour. This fact is at once

Spain's defence and England's condemnation. Even if England had more injuries of which to complain, she had continued the illicit trade[1]. What was the use of Patiño punishing Spanish governors, if English smugglers continued to deprive Spanish trade of real sources of material wealth? The value of the smuggling trade was the real key to England's secret desire to maintain it, and Spain's open resolution to suppress it. Unpublished records show clearly that England made far less effort to suppress her illicit trade with Spanish America, than did either France or the Dutch Republic. Such action must have been particularly annoying to a commercially minded Minister like Patiño, who wished to revive the trade of Spain, and who knew that Walpole himself showed especial and increasing severity towards all smugglers on English coasts. With these causes for irritation, it can hardly be surprising that Patiño should have kept a map of Gibraltar open on his table; that war should be said to have been, in 1732, only averted by the bad health of King Philip; or that Newcastle should be found writing to Keene on June 29, 1733, that "such enormities for the future" (as some of the late outrages) "...could not fail of bringing on a war between the two nations."

It is a singular commentary on the *Pacte de famille* that within a very short time from its signature Anglo-Spanish relations actually improved. During 1737, the Spanish Court was on exceedingly bad terms with the French, and their relations with England improved in a corresponding ratio. The scene was again changed towards the close of the year, when Newcastle grew impatient at the Spanish disregard of his petitions and, under pressure from West Indian merchants, made formal demands for reparation to various English vessels and seamen. The popular voice began to be heard on both sides, Spaniards complaining of the outrages and insolence of the heretical English dogs, Englishmen dreaming of the days of the "great Eliza," and the short way Drake and Ralegh had with the tyrants who flayed Indians alive and put Protestants to the rack. Public opinion was somewhat divided in Spain; in England it was united and the agitation grew rapidly to be serious under the influence of a rabid Protestantism and of a raucous patriotism. In 1738, the hope that war would be averted rested solely with the Ministers of the respective countries, for the peoples had already announced their views. After Patiño's death in 1736, his place had been taken by La Quadra (subsequently Marquis of Villarias), stubborn and obstinate, full of true Spanish pride, and yet a mere tool in the hands of Elisabeth Farnese, whose fiery temperament was no longer

---

[1] It should be noticed that there were two kinds of illicit trade: first, the smuggling in connexion with the *Asiento* and the annual ship sent to Spanish America, which was engineered, or connived at, by the South Sea Company; secondly, the smuggling carried on by interlopers from the British West Indies and from British America. In the last resort, the British Government appear to have been willing to suppress the latter practice. With their tenderness towards the South Sea Company, it is unlikely that they would ever have consented to repress the former.

curbed by a great Minister.   On the English side was Benjamin Keene, ambassador at Madrid, a resolute diplomatist, and yet easy in his ways, and one who knew how to make himself liked by the Spanish royalties; Walpole, anxious as always for peace, and Newcastle too prone to give way to popular clamour.   Unfortunately the latter was not decreasing in England, for the South Sea Company was busy trumpeting its grievances. There were the old quarrels about the *Asiento*, smuggling, and the right of search on suspicion of smuggled goods exercised by Spaniards over English vessels; and fresh disputes about the frontiers of Georgia and the British right to cut logwood in Honduras had come to the front. These might well have been settled, had there not been a general impression among Englishmen that their Government was supine and inclined to truckle to Spain; "The crowd must not be suffered to know, that many tuns of logwood, and even the ears, or even the life of a man (whatever compassion he deserves) are not worth a general war."   Parliament met raging in March, 1738.   Jenkins presented his ear and his grievances at the bar of the Commons; violent speeches were made—Pulteney breathing defiance, the young Pitt declaring our trade and our honour to be at stake, the Prince of Wales looking down sympathetically from the gallery; and violent resolutions were within an ace of being passed.

The British Ministers had neither been as pacific nor as idle as journalistic charity implied.   On March 2 (O.S.), Newcastle had instructed Keene that the British Government intended to issue letters of reprisal on Spanish vessels.   On March 30 (O.S.), Captain Clinton, "Commander-in-chief in and about the Mediterranean," was ordered to proceed to Minorca with his squadron.   La Quadra was indignant, and sent haughty letters to Keene; but the resolutions of Parliament and the anger of the British public undoubtedly impressed while they irritated him.   On May 9 (O.S.), the British Government ordered a reinforcement to the Mediterranean, and placed Admiral Haddock in command.   On May 18 (O.S.) Keene transmitted a violent letter from La Quadra, but informed Newcastle that the Spanish Minister had verbally expressed his sovereign's desire for an amicable settlement of outstanding differences. This commendation came just in time to avert war; the violence of the letter was set on one side by the British Government, and arrangements were made to accept the verbal overture.   Negotiations, already put in hand between the British Ministers and the Spanish ambassador in London, Sir Thomas Fitzgerald (Don Geraldino), were now pushed forward.   England owed Spain a debt of £180,000 at this time, while she claimed from Spain £343,277 for damages to English vessels and the like, so that, on the balance, Spain owed her about £160,000.   After a great deal of haggling, it was provisionally arranged that, in return for a speedy payment, Spain should pay £95,000 as a discharge for all debts. This arrangement was finally embodied in the Convention of the Pardo, signed by Keene and La Quadra on January 14 (N.S.), 1739, with the addition that Spain should pay the money in four months after ratifications were exchanged. Concessions had been made on both sides; Spain, by agreeing to pay the £95,000, acknowledged what she had never acknowledged before, that wrongs had been inflicted on British vessels; England, by abating her terms, admitted that some of her claims for injured vessels might have been too large. Neither can there be any doubt but that the Convention was intended on both sides as preliminary to a genuine settlement of all outstanding grievances, on which a Commission was appointed to sit. This is proved by the fact that Spain proceeded immediately to disarm her fleet and disband her regiments, and that Newcastle actually wrote to Keene on January 26 (O.S.) to suggest the possibility of an Anglo-Spanish alliance.

Unfortunately for the intentions of Ministers, a number of most delicate negotiations remained to be adjusted, and unhappily this had to be done just at the time when English public opinion was expressing its disapproval of the Convention. But this was not the only difficulty. The South Sea Company and their claims had been left out of the Convention by La Quadra for separate settlement. The King of Spain claimed £68,000 as a fourth share of the profits from voyages of the annual ship trading in Spanish waters; this sum the South Sea Company were unwilling to pay, because, as they alleged, the King of Spain owed them thrice as much for damages to their ships, though they refused to produce their accounts on this head. It was unfortunate that Keene was not only British ambassador, but agent for the South Sea Company, for he thus spoke with two voices, as a diplomatist with responsibility, and as a merchant angry at the loss of goods and desirous of driving a hard bargain. In private, he complained of the unreasonableness of the South Sea Company, and thought them foolish, and even dishonest. The quarrel between the South Sea Company and the Spanish King, which ended on May 6 (O.S.) by the latter's declaration that he would revoke the *Asiento*, unless the £68,000 were paid to him at once, contributed greatly to aggravate the situation.

When the news of the Convention arrived, a storm of abuse broke out in the Press. One quotation from a pamphlet may serve to typify many: " Jack English truly makes a fine figure and is of great weight in the balance of power, when he is forced to come cringing up to a Convention." Amid much violence and dwindling majorities, the Convention was ratified by both Houses in February, 1739. But the clamour had not missed its effect. Newcastle—ever willing to give way to popular feeling—was thoroughly frightened. " We must yield to the times," he wrote on February 24 to Lord Hardwicke, and Keene was instructed to press Spain to abandon the " right of search." Whatever intention Newcastle had of yielding to the current of popular feeling, after this display of it the South Sea Company had no idea of yielding to the King of Spain. La Quadra, like a true Spanish Grandee, was inexpressibly disgusted by the violence of both company and of public, and Keene soon experienced a new hauteur and defiance in his tone. Walpole was, however, still desirous of peace, and Spain, being disarmed, was not anxious for war. But, if there was any possibility of a pacific solution, it was now removed by the action of the British Ministry. On January 29 (O.S.), 1739, orders had been sent to Admiral Haddock to recall his fleet from the Mediterranean and "forthwith to repair to England." In February, the British Government became anxious, partly because it feared that the public clamour might produce war, partly because their information led them to suspect that a secret alliance of France and Spain was on the point of being signed. At any rate, the Admiralty records show that, on March 10, the January orders were revoked, and that Haddock was commanded to remain at Gibraltar. In some way, which is not discoverable, the Spaniards came to suspect the fact that these counter-orders had been issued, though Newcastle denied (falsely) that there were any, and instructed Keene to that effect. La Quadra naturally regarded this strange counter-order as a menace, to which Keene's bland innocence only added mystery. On May 8 (O.S.) Newcastle wrote to Keene that he was certain that some sort of alliance had taken place between France and Spain, and that, therefore, the fleet must remain at Gibraltar. On May 15 (O.S.), at the conference of Commissioners, Keene was officially informed that the £95,000 (due the day before) would not be paid, unless the counter-orders to Haddock were revoked. Keene was smooth-spoken, and replied that this matter was not within his competence; but the time was past when fair answers would turn away wrath, for each party had obviously reached a point from which it was impossible to recede. Spain had no intention of paying the £95,000, being very short of money and fearing that war would break out immediately; Newcastle did not mean to recall Haddock's fleet, because then Gibraltar and Minorca would be defenceless. La Quadra justly suspected Newcastle of issuing counter-orders to the fleet; Newcastle unjustly suspected Spain of having made an alliance with France against England. On June 14 (O.S.) Newcastle wrote to Keene to decline any further conferences with the Spanish Commissioners, and henceforth war became only a question of time and opportunity. In August Keene was recalled from Madrid, and at length, on October 19, the King's heralds passed through the City to Temple Bar and proclaimed that war with Spain had begun. The Prince of Wales, in the Rose Tavern hard by, drank to the success of the War against Papists, and the church bells rang merrily out from the steeples.

Every reader of English history knows how passionately Walpole regretted the War, and of his bitter epigram when he heard the bells ringing for joy; and every sympathy must be extended to a reluctance as sincere as it was humane. The War, which owed so much to the hot-headed young Prince, and the frenzied crowd, was not, however, indefensible on the grounds of national self-interest, though it certainly was on those of justice and right. Walpole thought that we should gain by peace and an accommodation with Spain; Newcastle was partly driven to war by his information as to a Franco-Spanish alliance. The public thought it better to fight Spain so long as she stood alone; and, as a matter of fact, the public instinct was right and Newcastle's information was wrong. Whatever causes of suspicion there might be, no actual agreement between France and Spain existed at this time, except the inoperative *Pacte de famille.*

Fleury, in France, loved peace as genuinely as Walpole, but, unlike him, had made genuine sacrifices at the shrine of his idol by allowing the French fleet to dwindle. Fleury saw that it was not in accordance with French interests to help Spain against England, until the French fleet was better able to defend her commerce. Hence, to the no small amazement and delight of Newcastle, France remained neutral, until the War of the Austrian Succession, as related elsewhere, forced her to engage in the struggle, and converted the existing strife in American waters into a struggle for the mastery of the sea, which carried with it supremacy in the West and the East Indies, and the dominion over the whole continent of North America. Whether South America was to remain Spanish, whether North America was to become English or French—these were the great questions first raised in 1738 and 1742. The raising of them forms the first act of a great drama, which extends over ninety years and only closes with the proclamation of the Monroe doctrine by the United States and with Canning's recognition of the Spanish-American Republics in 1823.

Two great events of the period—namely, the securing of the Hanoverian Succession, and the development of England's commercial greatness—have already been noted in this chapter. The third great event—the less obvious and perceptible development of England's parliamentary system—can only be briefly summarised. Walpole's position was throughout insecure, depending on delicate balances, on obscure negotiations and skilful combinations between groups, for the homogeneity of the Cabinet and of the party in office were alike imperfectly recognised. After the accession of George I, the avowed Jacobites gradually sank into a minority, the dualistic party system broke up, the great dividing lines between Whig and Tory became blurred and confused. The struggles under Walpole were not between two distinct parties with different views of prerogative, but between a Ministry and an Opposition, holding the same views as to the advantages of office. The members, no longer divided into parties, were separated into groups, and this disunion was increased by the growth of corruption and by undue influence at elections. By these means many constituencies, especially borough ones, fell entirely under the control of a few persons. These "boroughmongers," as they were called, appointed their own candidates to seats in Parliament, and called on them to resign when they disagreed with their views. Hence Walpole found himself ruling not over a large compact party, but over a number of patrons, each of whom possessed a large parliamentary following. Under these circumstances, the individual views of a powerful patron might be of great importance ; for example, the defection of the arch "boroughmonger" Newcastle would have meant a loss of near fifty votes to the Government. To adapt a happy comparison, the difficulties of Walpole might be likened to those of Charles Edward ; he had to deal with a number of proud and resolute chiefs—powerful, because they had many followers who slavishly obeyed them ; dangerous, because their personal quarrels threatened to make the execution of united movements impossible.

A relative independence of patrons and boroughmongers was secured to the First Lord of the Treasury by his control of the place-holders under the Crown. So long as the King and the First Lord agreed, at least a hundred members of Parliament depended absolutely on the Minister for their places, and a further number could be secured by a more indirect patronage. The place-holders were not always a source of strength, for they did not desire to lose their places ; and, when a Minister grew unpopular, his majorities fell because the place-holders were anxious to make terms with a possible successor to the First Lord's officership, and therefore either abstained from voting, or attacked the Government. Hence a Minister with a large majority was not secure, and a Minister with a falling majority was doomed, unless he took drastic measures. The history of the Excise Bill well illustrates this point. Walpole's majorities fell from 100 to 16, upon which he dropped the Bill. But he struck hard against the place-holders, who had tried to make fair weather with the Opposition. Chesterfield, Stair, Cobham, the Duke of Bolton, and a crowd of lesser victims, suffered loss of place or regiment. The system was very bad, and, in depriving officers of their commissions, Walpole undoubtedly went too far. But, in the imperfect state of parliamentary discipline, it would seem that indirect bribery at any rate was a necessity. The only alternative was parliamentary reform, which would have enabled electors to check members' corruption ; but hardly anyone thought of this remedy, and, in any case, legislative innovation was not in Walpole's line. Direct bribery has been proved against him in a few cases, but the evidence suggests that it was not common, and most of Walpole's "corruption" consisted in the use of indirect means of securing party allegiance which every parliamentary leader employs. The scale on which it prevailed was far too large, but the influence of the Crown had been regularly employed by the Minister since the days of William III. Onslow, who had every reason for knowing, said that it was Sunderland who extended and systematised corruption. Walpole did little or nothing to check the system; but he did not carry it further—here at least the policy of *tranquilla non movere* showed its good side. The Secret Committee of Enquiry (which consisted, with two exceptions, of political opponents) failed to produce evidence against him of an impressive character. It is usually forgotten that the officials of the Secret Service Fund (out of which direct bribes would be paid) refused to give evidence to the Committee; but there is not much reason to suppose that an unusual amount of money went in this way. After Walpole's fall, parliamentary corruption greatly increased under the Ministries of Wilmington and Pelham, though they contained several men who had frequently stigmatised Walpole as the master and origin of all such practices.

During the early twenties, the Opposition groups were so divided, and Walpole's prestige so great, that his task was simple. But, after Bolingbroke's return to England in 1725, Walpole's difficulties grew; he had done his best to form a homogeneous Cabinet and a compact Ministerial party, and Bolingbroke replied by forming a compact Opposition, which should comprehend not only Tories but malcontent Whigs. The Jacobites he threw over altogether, and formed the basis of his homogeneous Opposition by calling for a national party of " Patriots." His project succeeded, and he was eventually joined by Whigs out of office like Pulteney and Carteret, by Tories like Sir William Wyndham, and, later, by young enthusiasts like George Lyttelton and his friend William Pitt. After the party was formed, the public remained to be won; and for this purpose a journal, *The Craftsman*, was started on December 5, 1726, to which Pulteney and Bolingbroke alike contributed. It ran for ten years, and was remarkable for its immense effect upon public opinion. Bolingbroke's invective was terrific, his declamations against corruption popular, his designation of Walpole as the " brazen image the king had set up "—and the like—amusing. It was in vain that the Government subsidised pamphleteers, that Walpole even took the pen himself— " railers on one side, writers on the other," said Swift.

The first great victory of the Opposition over Walpole was the abandonment of the Excise Bill (1733), due to the fury into which they had lashed the public. In the next year Pulteney denounced Walpole in Parliament, under a transparent disguise, as the plunderer of the nation; Walpole replied, in a strain of extraordinary bitterness, denouncing Bolingbroke, in the same manner, as having gained over persons of fine parts and as having moved the whole Opposition to Jacobitism, and warning them that he had betrayed every master he ever served. In 1735 Bolingbroke and Pulteney quarrelled, with the result that the former practically retired from active politics. *The Patriot King* (written 1738, published 1749) continued the influence which a ready wit, an unscrupulous courage, and a golden eloquence had never failed to exercise upon a generation to whom all three qualities were dear.

CH. II.

In 1737 Frederick, Prince of Wales, joined the ranks of the Opposition, and thus redeemed it from the charge of Jacobitism, which had been Walpole's chief weapon against its members.   The disputes with Spain in 1738–9 gave the Opposition their chance, and landed Walpole in a war of which he never pretended to approve.   The gleam of success at its opening, when Vernon took Portobello (1739), was followed by a series of thoroughly mismanaged operations, which offered a glorious opportunity to an Opposition destitute alike of mercy or scruple.   In 1741, Walpole was fiercely attacked on the ground that the Constitution abhorred the idea of a Prime Minister, which office he had assumed.   The charge seems to have meant that he aimed at being sole Minister or Mayor of the Palace, and had used the royal authority to override the rest of the Cabinet.   It was a singular irony that, a year or two before, his colleagues had forced him into a war which he detested, and that they had continued to overrule him in directing its operations. The charge was fantastic, and the attack failed, Walpole being supported by a large majority.   But the end was not far off; the debates had shown that Walpole was the enemy for whose blood the Opposition thirsted, and Newcastle was not unwilling to make terms with them by throwing his colleague to the wolves.   In February, 1742, after debates of extraordinary heat and violence, Walpole was defeated on a petition relating to a disputed election at Chippenham.   The "Robinocracy" was at an end, and Walpole resigned, taking to himself the earldom of Orford.

Few English Ministers have ruled so long as Walpole, few have shown such contemptuous indifference to criticism, or suffered so much from its influence on posterity.   The facts as to his corruption have already been made clear; and, though he did well for himself, for his family and his friends, it is preposterous to describe him as the plunderer of his country or to speak of the "True Sinking Fund" as the "bottomless pocket of Robin."   After twenty years the corruption of Parliament was no worse, the general state of the finances infinitely better, than when he became Premier.   As a Minister of finance and commerce his genius is unquestionable; his claims to the same tribute in other directions are dubious.   He had a shrewd insight into mankind, especially into their weaknesses, and much tact and skill in the management of men or of parties.   His firm grasp of practical politics enabled him to see and to develop the principle that Ministries must be homogeneous and parties united—services of which the importance can hardly be overemphasised; but he did not shrink from depriving political opponents of military posts, or from appropriating the Sinking Fund—actions which alike demoralised public life.   Onslow touches another side of him, when he calls him "the best man from the goodness of his heart…to live with, and to live under, of any great man I ever knew."   Even Bolingbroke wrote of him that his "greatest enemies have allowed him to my knowledge the virtues of good nature and generosity."   But, unfortunately, Walpole's easy good nature was the complement, perhaps the result, of an easy virtue; he seldom failed to ridicule high aspirations, and seems genuinely to have suspected noble enthusiasms. There is indeed a certain large simplicity in his utterance, a magnanimity in his indifference to calumny and in his freedom from cant, which wins admiration. But he wanted, wrote Chesterfield, a certain elevation that is necessary both for great good or great mischief, and he was not the man to die for a cause, or to live for an ideal. One who had assailed him in his declining years was now to show that there were other ways of governing England than by lulling her to sleep, other ways of dealing with corruption than by sneering at virtue, and another way to popularity than that of following the people's wishes.

The chief interest of the years 1742–57, otherwise barren in our internal history, lies in the fact that they describe the gradual rise to power of the most extraordinary genius of the age. The early career of William Pitt was not always creditable to him; his oratory was impassioned, but theatrical; and his violence against Walpole was not by any means uninspired by self-interest. On the fall of Walpole, Newcastle and his brother, Henry Pelham (who was Paymaster of the Forces), opened the Cabinet door wide enough to admit Pulteney (Lord Bath) and Carteret, but remorselessly slammed it upon Pitt. Meanwhile Carteret, with the King's favour to back him, launched England into the turmoil of continental warfare (1743). Pitt wreaked his vengeance on the Ministry by stigmatising Carteret as a Minister who had drunk of the potion "causing men to forget their country." His attacks, though immeasurably violent, were not absurd, he had never been acquainted with official secrets from the inside, and throughout his speeches on the Spanish War of 1739 and on the Continental War of 1743–4 ran a sound vein of strategy, and a genuine, if not quite accurate, apprehension that British and colonial interests were being sacrificed to those of Hanover— "the despicable electorate." Throughout them can be discerned, together with an ardent ambition and a boundless love of fame, the yearnings of a lofty spirit and the glow of an unquenchable patriotism. Pitt's eloquence from the Opposition benches, and Newcastle's intrigues in the Cabinet, finally drove the high-minded but unbalanced Carteret (now Earl Granville) from office (November, 1744). As Henry Pelham had already in July, 1743, succeeded to the First Lordship of the Treasury on the death of the amiable cipher—the Earl of Wilmington, who had held it since February, 1742—the Newcastle interest became supreme. But there was now a new force to be reckoned with, for Pitt's oratory could not be withstood in the Commons. In 1745, it was, for the first time, employed on behalf of the Government, and Newcastle and Pelham, hoping to silence Pitt by office, prayed the King to admit him to the Ministry. George II was inexorable; he had never forgiven the attacks upon Carteret or the sarcasms about Dettingen. When the King definitely refused this request, Newcastle, Pelham and the other Ministers took the rather unpatriotic step of resigning in a body (February 10, 1746), just at the height of the agitation caused by Charles Edward's successes in Scotland. The King sent for Lords Bath and Granville, who formed a Ministry which lasted forty-eight hours. "Bounce went all the project into shivers," wrote a well-informed contemporary, "like the vessel in the *Alchymist,* when they are on the brink of the Philosopher's Stone." Granville retired, laughing at the whole *fiasco* as an excellent joke, and the King sulkily capitulated; Pitt became Joint Vice-Treasurer for Ireland and (May 6) Paymaster-General. This incident has sometimes been claimed as the definite precedent for the establishment of the joint responsibility of the Ministry. It is difficult to view it altogether as such; in this case some of the resignations were calculated, some spontaneous, and later history shows several instances in which the principle has been ignored that Ministers ought to resign in a body. The incident of 1746 is less important because it asserted a principle in the Constitution than because it admitted a man into the Ministry.

From 1746 to 1754 the land had rest from party bickerings; Pelham, the head of the Ministry, was a sort of lesser Walpole, an excellent financier, and a shrewd and amiable party leader. His Ministry witnessed the Reform of the Calendar (1751) and the foundation of the British Museum (1753), but for neither of these measures can he claim the chief credit; the reduction of the National Debt and the prohibition of the right to manufacture certain articles in the colonies (elsewhere described) are measures more truly his, and give Pelham, in the one case a genuine, in the other a sinister, renown. In 1748—at the end of the war—the National Debt stood at near eighty millions; Pelham, imitating Walpole's measures of 1717 and 1727, reduced the rate of interest on it to three per cent. average, and the gain to the Treasury was substantial. The unfunded Debt was paid off, the Sinking Fund (sadly depleted of late) was replenished, credit soothed, and the merchant world flattered. Pelham has been praised for his careful stewardship and for his economic reform in all departments; but this praise requires qualification. Genuine love of economy, in the main, prevailed; in particular, a reduction of the army and navy was carried by him, despite bitter fraternal opposition from Newcastle. His discouragement of payment of subsidies, on the grand scale, to foreign Princes, for the use of their armies, is balanced by an encouragement of payments to members of Parliament for the use of their votes: subsidy treaties were fewer, pensions more numerous. This, however, is not the most serious charge against his conduct of affairs: after all, the demands of the English place-hunter were not too excessive a burden on the Treasury under Pelham, while his measures towards American manufactures began to place a heavy strain on the loyalty of the empire. A reduction of the

National Debt, an increase of the Pension List, and a diminution of colonial loyalty—these are the main features of Pelham's Ministry, and the ultimate logic of the policy of *tranquilla non movere*. Pelham's errors were due to the fact that he had too faithfully followed Walpole, at a time when his master's policy was becoming more and more antiquated. The new age was not to be one of peace, indolence, and materialism, but of war, adventure, and idealism ; and for inspiration it was to turn—not to a shrewd and cautious financier, but to a passionate orator, who struck chords to which Pelham was deaf, and followed ideals to which he was blind.

Pelham's death in March, 1754, left his brother, the hasty and fickle Newcastle, to succeed him at the vacant Treasury. The Duke foolishly appointed Sir Thomas Robinson (afterwards Lord Grantham)—a diplomatist quite fresh to party politics—leader in the Commons, and tried to manage everything himself from the Lords. Unlike Pelham, he could not command respect from his subordinates ; and Pitt and Henry Fox openly ridiculed their nominal leader in the Commons, and their real leader in the Lords. After agonies and distractions of no common kind, even Newcastle recognised the inevitable, dismissed Pitt, and won over the war party by offering Fox a seat in the Cabinet (April, 1755). But he soon found himself weaker than ever, for a crisis was at hand, war was inevitable, subsidy treaties must come before the Commons, and there Pitt was supreme. Pitt was finally dismissed from office in November, 1755, after he had not only ridiculed but vehemently denounced Newcastle. His language in private was equally contemptuous, and, in a secret interview with Newcastle on December 22, 1755, he belaboured him with all the force of his eloquence, rejecting all his terms. In November, Robinson had been succeeded by Fox as Secretary of State ; but even he could not face Pitt's invective in the Commons, and at last, after having been in office for a generation, Newcastle resigned (November, 1756). A short-lived Ministry, under the Duke of Devonshire as nominal head with Pitt as guiding spirit, endured from 1756 to April, 1757. It took vigorous measures and won much outside popularity, as was shown by the shower of gold boxes with which patriotic corporations veiled the fall of Pitt. After eleven weeks' interregnum, Lord Hardwicke, the sage and veteran Chancellor, brought about an accommodation between Pitt and Newcastle (June 11, 1757). Newcastle had the largest following, Pitt the most commanding voice, in the Commons ; and the one neutralised the other. Pitt sought power, Newcastle office, for its own sake, and the compromise of a coalition Ministry enabled each to win his desire. But Pitt, though the greatest, was not the only man in the Government ; the diverse talents of Granville, of Anson, of Fox, of Ligonier, and of Hardwicke, contributed largely to make the Ministry of 1757 the most glorious and successful in English annals.

Though Pitt had been greatly aided by his popularity outside

CH. II.

Parliament in the period immediately preceding 1757, it is wholly inaccurate to say that he ascended to power on the shoulders of the people. He owed his early rise to his parliamentary success, which had been established by conventional means. At first he had been supported by the influence of connexion, by the help of the Lytteltons and the Cobhams, by the favour of the Prince of Wales. Later, he had been aided by the Grenville interest, and by certain intrigues with Lady Yarmouth, George II's reigning mistress, which were of an unusually degrading character. In the sense that the people directly aided a statesman in rising to power, Pitt—the friend of peers, of a royal mistress and of a prince—was less truly their choice than Walpole, who had been but a plain country squire. In 1720, the popular voice had called for him far more loudly than it had called for Pitt in 1746, and his bluff manners, coarse accent, and homely acquaintances, never ceased to distress patrician taste. Pitt's influence from connexion had been strengthened by his influence in the House of Commons and by office, before the people began definitely to support him. Despite some equivocal actions due to an exorbitant ambition, his hatred of corruption was sincere, his objects were pure and patriotic. His genuine moral enthusiasm, joined to extraordinary powers of oratory, made him resistless in the Commons, and eventually forced Ministers of that day, always insecure, to make terms with him. But, though Pitt had secured power by oratory in the Commons and influence with boroughmongers, he was the last man to despise popularity. He thought himself called to office in 1757, " in some sort by the voice of the people," and he understood how to kindle their enthusiasm, though he was not afraid, on occasion, of resisting them. Of his powers as a great war Minister, of his deep knowledge of foreign politics, of the needs of England's commerce, and of the wishes of her colonies, no mention has to be made here. It is sufficient to say that, for the first time in this period, England possessed a Minister with the majority which Carteret, and the ideals which Walpole, had lacked. The heroic age had come again, and a dominating figure was not wanting to it. His oft-quoted utterance that he alone could save his country was no arrogant boast at this moment, for Pitt's actions support these haughty words. His matchless energy, no longer confined to empty invective, was at length to be translated into action, and was to awaken the admiration alike of generals and admirals, parliament and people, in the crisis of the world struggle which gave England her empire.

(2)

The earlier half of the eighteenth century in England is an age of materialism, a period of dim ideals, of expiring hopes; before the middle of the century its character was transformed, there appeared a movement headed by a mighty leader, who brought forth water from the rocks to make a barren land live again. Dropping allegory, we can recognise in English institutions, in English ideals, in the English philosophy of this age, the same practical materialism, the same hard rationalism, the same unreasonable self-complacency. Reason dominated alike the intellect, the will, and the passions; politics were self-interested, poetry didactic, philosophy critical and objective. Generalisations such as these are but rough approximations, for no age is without its individual protests and rebels, without men who seek to dam or to divert the streams of tendency. Of these men, Chatham among politicians, Thomson among poets, Berkeley among philosophers, Law among divines, all derived new thoughts, evoked new harmonies, or caught new inspirations from the age. But more important than any of these in universality of influence and in range of achievement were John Wesley and the religious revival to which he gave his name and his life.

The history of thought and action—always closely interwoven—in this age is inextricably intertwined. The framework of the national life appears to be entirely political, the civil revolution of 1688 has vanquished the religious revolution of 1642. Even the most abstract of thinkers and the most unworldly of clerics have a mundane and secular stamp upon them; even Butler is a courtier, even Leibniz is a wit. Religious, social, and literary influences show but as the tiny satellites of a political planet, to which they owe their warmth and their light. When, in 1727, Caroline, Princess of Wales, became the Queen of George II, all these political influences were intensified, for the Court became the chief centre not only of power, but of learning. She loved at all times to surround herself with learned men—profound theologians like Butler and Berkeley, deep-read divines like Clarke and Potter, wide-minded philosophers like Leibniz, cultured Deists like Chesterfield. The Queen's interest in theology and the Establishment was keen; but it was primarily intellectual. She loved theological arguments rather than good works, and valued divines for depth of learning or subtlety of metaphysic rather than for fervour of piety. Deism—never popular with the masses or the country gentry—had immense vogue at Court; and it implied a vague monotheism for the educated few, with a very definite dogmatic system for the ignorant many. The notion that it was necessary to preserve the Establishment in order to secure the obedience of the vulgar was accepted by Walpole, who confessed himself a sceptic in private, while publicly proclaiming his adherence to the Church, and by Bolingbroke, who outdid him alike in the secret fervour of his freethinking and in the open passion of his orthodoxy. When Bolingbroke and Walpole agreed on a principle, it is hardly rash to conclude that the governing classes as a whole acquiesced in it. Nothing, indeed, could be worse for a religion or a Church than a public adherence to its forms and a private ridiculing of its substance by a large proportion of the governing class. They might almost consider themselves as beings of another race and religion; the classics had taught them their creed of isolation and their doctrine of Deism, and the weeping classical nymphs and cupids who support Latin inscriptions on their tombs in many a church are true witnesses to their half-unconscious adherence to the ideals of Greece and of Rome. A Roman noble of the age of Horace, with his vast estates, his nominal adherence to Augustan morality, and his playful hesitance between rival philosophies, is, indeed, no inapt prototype of his English brother in the age of Walpole, with his broad acres, his lip-service to the Establishment, and his benevolent neutrality between rival religions. Such a society was perfectly self-sufficient and perfectly self-contained, and, had not new and mighty influences arisen to overthrow class barriers, the chasm between the few and the many might have given birth to revolution.

The danger to orthodoxy was, not that its precepts were ceasing to be avowed, but that they were ceasing to be believed among the upper class; and it was unfortunate that the Establishment, at the moment when it was most open to attack, had provided for its defence only in the least adequate way. Pluralism and indolence were frequent among the clergy; the age was active only in religious controversy, and the generation between 1710 and 1740 witnessed works of real importance by such men as Clarke, Butler, Berkeley, Wake, and Warburton. But the controversies were in the main barren and dusty, and were handled in too arid and hard a fashion to win the recognition of posterity; there is a fine harvest of wit, of learning and of intellect, a rank crop of abuse, partisanship, and acrimony, and an utter dearth of moderation and sympathy. Noble exceptions are to be found in men like Law and Butler; but even these seem to have viewed controversy or religious meditation rather as comforting to themselves than for the sake of its immediate benefit to the world. Despairing of the general attitude towards religion, they walled themselves up in an intellectual city, where they could exert but little influence on the general run of men. With lesser and baser men, controversial theology served not spiritual but worldly interests, and a clever religious tract or sermon availed as much for ecclesiastical, as did a smart pamphlet for political, promotions. The famous Sacheverell trial is the most important instance of the way in which ecclesiastical controversies shifted into partisan politics, and the Non-Jurors, the Bangorian, and a score of other controversies, are more typical if less striking examples. The process of secularisation is apparent in other directions. Political considerations dominated ecclesiastical patronage and behaviour; and, while the Church became more and more political, the State became less and less religious. Episcopal politicians forgot their fervour in the presence of the cultured sceptics of the Court, and learnt the mundane lessons of corruption and venality from the place-hunters of Parliament.

Among the parochial clergy, as a whole, there was a frequent reaction against episcopal dominance, which had in it the symptoms of a healthy revival. In the country parishes there were, indeed, a number of too worldly clergy. Smollett spoke of "rosy sons of the Church," who quaffed too much ale in ingle corners; Cowper of "cassocked huntsmen," who set horse and hound before parish; and, in general, Georgian wits made the parson as much of a butt as ever Elizabethans did the friar. But satire is not history, and there is evidence that many country parishes were well served by their incumbents. The habits of the town clergy gave the satirist more justification for his wit; for they were often indolent and worldly, their sermons were often directed only to the refined understanding, the presence of the "unsavoury multitude" was sometimes resented or discouraged. When a popular preacher brought the poor flooding into his church, the wealthier members fled, locking their pews behind them to keep out the poor, the churchwardens would cut off the lights, and the pulpit be illumined by a solitary candle in the hand of the preacher. Such was the recorded experience of William Romaine, lecturer at St George's, Hanover Square, and at St Dunstan's, Fleet Street—a man of blameless life and devoted character. Even if this incident is not typical, it is difficult to ignore the force of the opinions held by serious men as to the conduct and usefulness of the Episcopal Bench, of Chesterfield's solemn private warning to his son that it was a vulgar error to regard clergymen as necessarily hypocrites—or of Voltaire's published assertion that England was the most irreligious of countries.

If we were to rely upon the amount of churchbuilding under Anne, the number of charity schools founded both by Church and Chapel, and the amount of poor-relief subscribed by voluntary effort under the Georges, we might think the age not deficient in religious vitality. But the deficiencies in religious force, at any rate in the early Georgian period, are attested by witnesses more powerful than statistics. Butler and Berkeley both publicly confessed—with melancholy and sorrow—the too common indifference to religion and the general ridicule of clergymen, and betrayed signs of this conviction in their works. Butler's *Analogy* and his theory of Probabilism exhibit religion on its last line of defence —he appeals to reason and common sense, and substitutes the proof by induction and the external senses for the proof from internal conviction and faith. Berkeley's practical efforts to create a religious imperialism in his Bermuda Scheme met (as told above) with a disastrous check from the indifference of the age; and his theoretical attempts to recreate the imagination by proclaiming the reality of ideas, were in large measure a reaction from contact with too materialistic an age. One virtue—a rare virtue indeed—this age possessed, that of tolerance. Clergy whose opinions approached Deism were not inhibited from preaching; controversies which led to advocacy of quasi-scepticism were not openly suppressed; and the bands of ecclesiastical discipline and political control were often amiably relaxed. That there was a real advance towards the greatest of religious blessings—respect for the individual conscience—was due at least in part to indolence, and yet more to political considerations; but the notion that persecution for religious opinions was bad in itself undoubtedly gained ground at the same time. Thus, in 1753, the Bishops showed real zeal in supporting the Act for the Naturalisation of Jews, and only capitulated to the furious outburst of indignation from the lower clergy and the mob, which secured the repeal of the Act in 1754.

The religious and social condition of the masses under the two Georges is the severest condemnation of the religious life of the period. The masses were ignorant and brutalised, and their numbers and demoralisation rapidly increased. The medieval corporations in town or city were powerless to cope with the growing evils of industrial life; the Government pandered to mob passions by public executions or by unworthy concessions to mob violence, and insulted humanity by the brutal ferocity of its criminal code. A governing class, intent only on pleasure or politics, a Church occupied chiefly with patronage and controversy, were now to feel the force of a great religious wave which was to beat on every wall of privilege.

The real ulcer of the age lay in its uncompromising individualism, and in the inadequacy of existing social organisations to cope with those evils. Political and religious institutions had crystallised into a species of hereditary or privileged oligarchy, into an officialdom which, though not entirely exclusive or unsympathetic, seemed incapable of change or advance. That nothing but reform from the outside would avail to alter the existing system, had already been demonstrated by the politics of the age. Its most characteristic decisions—Sacheverell's acquittal, the rejection of Wood's Halfpence, and of the Excise Bill—owed much, if not everything, to the stormy outbursts of national feeling or of mob violence. So, again, the most effective attempts at church reform were to come from without; for it was only an outside organisation, unaffected by existing institutions, which could break free from the traditions of stagnation and appeal to the vast mass of the people. This unconscious tendency is exhibited by the number of religious societies, which anticipated the work of Wesley by sixty years. So early as 1678, small societies, composed of orthodox Churchmen, sought by intimate religious intercourse "to quicken each other's affections towards spiritual things." All these societies were primarily formed by men who sought to save their own souls, and it marks a serious reaction against the selfish individualism of the age, that they were all eventually directed towards saving the bodies and souls of others, to relieving unemployment, to promoting education, or providing for the needs of the poor. During the first thirty years of the century their numbers increased, and they became an active and important religious force; but, by the middle of the century, their vitality gradually sank, though they had borne a brave witness for religious idealism at a time of need. All these societies were, without exception, composed of members of the Established Church; but official prelacy chilled, if it did not disavow, them. Anything that savoured of originality, of indecorous fervour, was an object of alarm and suspicion, and was denounced as "enthusiasm[1]." If this was the attitude of church dignitaries towards movements and associations which were unquestionably orthodox, it is no wonder that they showed more hostility to the movements heralded by such men as Griffith Jones, George Whitefield, and John Wesley.

The Welsh Revival of the period beginning with 1735 (which was due, in large part, to Griffith Jones) is a singular, and an almost exact, anticipation of Methodism. Griffith Jones experienced a spiritual conversion about the same time as Whitefield, and was moved to preach the tidings to others. All the signs of intense emotion, which Wesley and Whitefield were to awake in thousands of meetings at a later date, were present among the congregations of Griffith Jones, and of his fellow-evangelists, whom he raised up and trained. His organising skill was manifested in the foundation of a system of circulating schools, and in general the Welsh Revival is of great importance, because it foreshadows most of the peculiar developments of Methodism, and because it marks the beginning of an even more formidable secession from the Establishment than that which Methodism brought about in England.

As the Welsh Revival anticipates one aspect of Methodism, the early writings of William Law (whom John Wesley at one time " took for an oracle") foreshadow another. Indeed, the deepest source of religious inspiration in the eighteenth century seems to be reached in this passage in his *Serious Call to a Devout and Holy Life*: "If, therefore, persons of either sex...desirous of perfection, should unite themselves into little societies, professing voluntary poverty, virginity, retirement, and devotion, that some might be relieved by their charities, and all be blessed with their prayers, and benefited by their example;...such persons would be, so far from being chargeable with any superstition, or blind devotion, that they might justly be said to restore that piety, which was the boast and glory of the Church, when its greatest saints were alive."

The revival of religion in England will always remain linked with the names of George Whitefield and John Wesley, each an ordained clergyman of the Church of England, and each, despite himself, the

---

[1] The use of the word "enthusiasm" in the sense of "fanaticism" in the eighteenth century is singularly characteristic of the age. Any ill-regulated impulse came under this head, and it was a favourite term for discrediting an opponent, especially a religious one. [In an age when political stability was the chief aim of society, and when the clergy figured as a kind of spiritual police, the use of the term is intelligible. Any irresponsible movement might be a political danger; and hence Wesley warns his followers, and Chatham cautions his nephew, against giving way to enthusiasm.]

founder of a sect in separation from it. They were closely associated with each other; each admired the other's gifts and loved his friendship; but—except for their earnest piety—no two men were ever more dissimilar. Whitefield was the first religious preacher of his age, an unexampled orator, impetuous and earnest, emotional rather than thoughtful, a revolutionary who broke through old forms before he realised the consequences of his action. John Wesley was of another type; he was a great preacher, but a far greater organiser; his nature was the reverse of sentimental; his cold, keen intellect contrasts with the warm impulsiveness of Whitefield, as did his dislike of mysticism (for all his dependence on superstition), his hatred of irregularities, his appreciation of scholarship, order, and refinement. The respective evolution of the two great branches of Methodism—Calvinistic and Wesleyan—harmonises closely with the character and views of these two men. Whitefield is ever in the van, leading forlorn hopes or exploring new continents; Wesley is more slow and calculating, advancing oftener along trodden paths, reaping from fields already sown, and, for that reason, making his influence the more enduring and momentous.

The origin of Methodism is ascribed to the year 1729, when the name was bestowed on a small society at Oxford of whom the best known were Charles Wesley, his elder brother, John, and Whitefield, who joined in 1733. The society, though it differed little from the preceding private religious societies, encountered such scorn and abuse at Oxford that even Whitefield confesses to having often visited the Wesleys in secret. Private prayer, religious communings with one another, visitation of the sick, of the poor, and of criminals in gaols: these were the aims of the society and the cause of the ridicule to which it was exposed. By the end of 1737, when Whitefield started for America, he had not only experienced a spiritual conversion whose effects on his life were to be permanent, but had already become a very famous preacher. The two Wesleys (John and Charles) had preceded him to Georgia (October, 1735) in the brave hope of converting the "poor heathen" in America. On the voyage, John Wesley came into contact with some pious Germans; on his return to England (after a not very successful ministry in Georgia) he encountered the Moravian preacher Peter Böhler, whose earnest simplicity produced a spiritual revolution in him (May, 1738), and induced him to journey to Herrnhut, where for three months he studied Moravian principles at their fountain-head. His career, up to this point, as he frequently assures us, had been principally marked by a desire to save his own soul. Henceforward, he was assured of his own salvation, but "felt his heart burn within him" to tell his message to other men; and he soon found an opportunity for doing this on a scale unknown to the religious life of the age. At Oxford, Whitefield tells us, "the Wesleys were the first who openly desired to confess Christ"; but, in 1739, says John

Wesley, it was Whitefield who reconciled "myself...to this strange way of preaching in the fields."

Whitefield was anxious to go to America, but wished to find someone to continue his work at Bristol, where he had excited extraordinary enthusiasm by preaching in the fields among the colliers of Kingswood. These men—hitherto the most neglected and degraded of humanity—had shown real signs of amendment under Whitefield's charge, who now persuaded the hesitating John Wesley to undertake their care. While Whitefield was sailing to Georgia, John Wesley "proclaimed in the highways the glad tidings of salvation, speaking from a little eminence in a ground adjoining to the city (Bristol), to about three thousand people." From this day, April 2, 1739, may be reckoned a new era in the religious history of England; for her greatest religious leader between Cromwell and Newman had found his way to the hearts of her people.

To narrate in detail the further experiences of Wesley and Whitefield is impossible, but a few words may indicate their influence, their methods, and their triumphs. Both were consumed by a burning desire to save souls, to go on "spiritual huntings" for the welfare of all mankind; and, since the days of St Francis Xavier, none had journeyed so far or toiled so earnestly to win the fame of Evangelists. These devoted men travelled five thousand miles a year, rode fetlock-deep in snow or mud on English roads, journeyed wearily afoot over trackless Scotch moors or by blazed paths in American forests, and shrank from no toil and no danger in order to preach their personal Gospel. Wesley traversed the British Isles from North Scotland to Land's End (not forgetting Man and the Scilly Isles), whilst Whitefield was more often seen in America than in England. Unimagined numbers in two hemispheres must have listened to their words, for each was accustomed to preach twenty times a week, and to audiences that were claimed to have sometimes reached to thirty thousand. At first they endeavoured to preach in churches; but, when incumbents forbade them, they took to preaching in the fields, now speaking on a bare hillside, now in a gaol, now in a back street in a crowded city, now on a village green, now from a tombstone in a churchyard, now even on the roof of a pigstye. Nothing deterred them or lessened their congregations. Wesley preferred to preach at five in the morning, without ever lacking auditors at that time, any more than when he preached in the evening in the open during torrents of rain, his face illumined by lightning-flashes. They feared the fury of mobs even less than that of the elements, and stood unmoved when crowds rushed on them, now impelled by sectarian bitterness, now drawn by mere curiosity, now merely riotous and drunken. Often the preacher was struck with stones, jostled or crushed by the crowd, his clothes torn, his body bruised, his face battered with blows; often, again, his fearless demeanour awed a hostile crowd into silence, and then into shamefaced reverence. As the sermon progressed, the crowd underwent extraordinary emotions, some shouting out boastfully that they were kings, others confessing themselves sinners; yet others burst into songs of thanksgiving and praise, writhed in convulsions, foaming at the mouth, or dropped down motionless as dead. Results such as these were produced by the sermons of both men; but the effects of Whitefield's oratory were sometimes even more extraordinary. Despite Dr Johnson's sneer, Whitefield was able to impress the educated; he won admiration from so complete a technical master of rhetoric as Garrick; he carried away such convinced worldlings as Pulteney and Chesterfield; and, when he addressed a less cultured audience, thousands were sometimes bathed in tears, while the fainting and the convulsed were carried away like the " wounded from a battlefield." His farewell sermon in America on September 29, 1770, spoken with a premonition of coming death, "I go, I go to a rest prepared; my sun has arisen"—has no parallel and no equal for immediate effect in the clerical oratory of modern times.

That enormous influence may be exerted by a great orator on an audience highstrung by an appeal to its deepest emotions is a familiar fact in spiritual psychology, and Whitefield is only remarkable for the degree of emotional response which his preaching produced. Wesley, not the equal of Whitefield as an orator, could exercise in the intimate circle of his friends, in small meetings of committees, on the conference of his preachers as a whole, an influence perhaps more remarkable and certainly more unique. None of his followers questioned his decisions, and, even if he sought (and he very seldom sought) to devolve some of his authority, they persisted in referring everything to him. This faculty of commanding obedience, of awaking inspiration, and his general aspect of imperious tyrannic strength, has induced a not very apt comparison between him and two of the greatest of statesmen. Wesley was deficient in imaginative power, and in his creative genius and capacity for organisation he resembles Loyola or Colbert far more than Chatham or Richelieu. It is strange that a man, whose objects were so disinterested, lofty and pure, should have had so firm a grasp of the realities of life, of business, finance, and administration. Wherever Whitefield passed he left memories of overwhelming passion and eloquence, wherever Wesley passed he left more enduring memorials in the shape of schools, mission-rooms, meeting-places, and unions for prayer, for charity, and for self-help. Not one of his creations was original; but he lent a new meaning and force to them all, especially to the class meeting, the most peculiar and characteristic feature of Methodism. A vast organisation of lay preachers—constructed on a system acknowledged to be a model for ecclesiastical institutions—is the most remarkable result of his work; and to this more than anything else is due the fact that it has endured, and that the waves of religious emotion were not lost in space.

The relations of Whitefield and Wesley to the Establishment have an interest and a pathos rarely equalled; for the one seceder left it only with the greatest sorrow, and the other always denied that he had left it at all. The general attitude and character of Whitefield, his utter scorn of conventions, his generous rashness, his serious doctrinal differences with the orthodox theology, make it impossible to suppose that he could have permanently remained in a Church so wedded to tradition and the existing order of things. The case of Wesley is very different; much of the atmosphere and doctrine of the Church of England was congenial to him, and, during his later years, hostility towards him so declined that many clergymen allowed him to preach in churches from which they had once excluded him. This fact suggests that a separation, though probable, was not inevitable. Such a separation was certainly not directly sought by either Wesley or by the established hierarchy, which never took any collective action against him. It was, indeed, rather their indifference to the institutions which he was creating than their active opposition which had so large a share in producing separation. Wesley's lay preachers were very carefully supervised by him, were distinctly limited in their functions, and rigorously subjected to those of the ordained clergy, who cast in their lot with Methodism. Had more care been taken to regularise this institution of lay preachers, as might have been the case had there been an English episcopate in America, separation might have been averted. As it was, the lay preachers felt bound to trespass on the functions and influence of the incumbents of parishes, whenever these proved hostile, or the bishops indifferent; and they thus supplied the strongest material incentive to separation. An organisation external to the Church, having failed to reform, was logically bound to abandon, it.

Wesley had created an *imperium in imperio,* and had caused a contest between two different kinds of organisation within the limits of one Church. But, paradoxically enough, this was not the most powerful cause of separation, for the spirit is more important than the letter and the form. Wesley's whole spiritual development was, in reality, a slow emancipation from the conventions and organisations which history and tradition had furnished to the Establishment. Wesley's father had bequeathed to his son a passionate devotion to the Church, but the son's spiritual awakening had taught him the relative unimportance of forms and rules— in comparison with direct spiritual appeals. Even in his early days he had declared that power could be given to a presbyter to act as a bishop over the souls of men, and in his unrivalled religious experience he beheld simple appeals to faith working apparently miraculous changes in hundreds of men. It is therefore small wonder that he gradually began to cast aside his old love of order, regularity and form, and sought to judge everything by its simple apparent worth as an instrument of righteousness. Lord Acton has placed the crucial date in this spiritual transformation at December 1, 1767, and Wesley's journal of that day shows clearly (though almost unconsciously) that he had begun to conceive salvation as outside the Church, that he desired a return to the simplicity of evangelical days, and to the "plain word, He that feareth God, and worketh righteousness, is accepted with Him." Henceforth, more than ever, his lay organisation was to him the heart and soul of his religion, the ecclesiastical one the mere frame and body of it. He who thinks on the real significance of things will place the act of separation in 1767 rather than 1784.

Thus the two strongest motives of separation were present and working towards fissure, the external difficulty of reconciling two opposed organisations, and Wesley's inward spiritual conviction that righteousness lay in the heart of man rather than in the mechanism of his faith. During the sixties his lay preachers began to administer the sacrament, and, finally, in 1784, Wesley, taking on himself the episcopal function (there being still no bishop in America), ordained ministers to that continent, and shortly afterwards also to Scotland. No Church which holds strongly to episcopal ordination could suffer this, and the highest legal authority of the eighteenth century pronounced that "ordination meant separation." Wesley—with a logic consistent with this spiritual position—refused to admit that a mere external act could thus affect his spiritual relations to the Church.

On Wesley's death (March 2, 1791) his followers speedily acknowledged a separation which the majority of them both approved and desired. Wesley during his last years had stood almost alone in his desire to preserve the union, and, with an amiable inconsistency, had never shown more outward devotion to the Establishment than in the years after 1767. Perhaps an extract from his journal (of January 2, 1748), when he was refused the sacrament at Epworth, where his father had once been rector, may typify, as in allegory, his personal attitude on the whole question of his relations with the Establishment: "How wise a God is our God! There could not have been so fit a place under heaven, where this should befall me first as my father's house, the place of my nativity, and the very place where, 'according to the straitest sect of our religion,' I had so long 'lived a Pharisee'! It was also fit, in the highest degree, that he who repelled me from that very table, where I had myself so often distributed the bread of life, should be one who owed his all in this world to the tender love which my father had shown to his, as well as personally to himself."

All the great changes of the eighteenth century, religious or social, political or industrial, profoundly as they differed in character, were similar in that they were produced by a resolute minority of men, pessimistic as to the past and present, and optimistic as to the future. Hence, they had no hesitation in applying unsparing criticism to existing conditions, or in constructing ideal plans for future ages; and this fact accounts alike for their extraordinary triumphs and equally extraordinary failures. The men who produced the religious revival in England were really only three—Whitefield the orator, John Wesley the organiser, and Charles Wesley the poet of the movement. All of them were profoundly impressed with the blackness and despair of the past and the present, all hoped, desired, and believed that the future would be rich in promise, that their triumphs would be great, and the sway of their gospel irresistible. As in all other cases, their achievement fell far short of their ideal; but they effected a transformation at once so sudden in its appearance and so far-reaching in its effect, that what would have been a marvel in any age appears a miracle in this.

No great personality in this age came into such vivid and direct contact with the masses as John Wesley; hence, his general social and political influence is of more importance than is usual with religious leaders. He was, indeed, too much a child of his age—in some of its faults—not to exercise great influence upon it, and the unworldly part of his character is strangely mingled with a singular practical shrewdness. For instance, his politics were very definitely partisan; but he had a strange independence of outlook. The King in his coronation robes excited in him no awe, and was described by him as swathed in ermine blankets, adorned with a huge heap of borrowed hair, and with glittering baubles; the nobles were triflers unaware of their latter end; the lawyers were dishonest and self-seeking; British landlords in Ireland were absentees, careless of their tenants, and working for the depopulation of the country; the Slave Trade (which even Chatham defended) was that "execrable sum of all villainies." It may surprise anyone who reads these opinions in his journal to discover that his general views were strongly conservative, and that he was not only a Tory, but even supposed to support the Divine Right of Kings. He never ceased to denounce all disobedience to the law and to the sovereign; his condemnation descended upon Jacobites and American Revolutionists; and his fiercest invective was poured upon the smugglers and wreckers of Cornwall. As he never had the slightest fear or reserve in proclaiming his views, and as he appealed most particularly to the poor and ignorant, his influence must have contributed most powerfully towards preserving the existing frame of society, especially when the shocks of the French Revolution were already being felt. Dissenters of other kinds were inclined to favour the Revolution; from the first, Wesleyans met it with rigid hostility—an attitude of which it is difficult to exaggerate the national importance. The teaching of the one man who had really stirred the masses in the middle of the century went all towards allaying their excitement at its close, and the Duke of Wellington found no better soldiers than those that were Methodists.

The general influence of Wesley was far less happy. He was descended from a stern and heroic race, and inherited a singular fervour and sense of duty, as well as a curious hardness and rigour. Some of these faults he was never able to conquer, and his denunciations of harmless gaieties and of art show some inconsistency, exceptional narrowness, and a curious Puritanism. He advocated card-playing, but denounced dancing and ordinary pleasures; desired toleration, but refused to extend it to Catholics; had some enlightened views on education, but wished to establish schools where there should be no vacations, and universities where there should be lectures for every day in the year. All these singular eccentricities (which were of no very amiable kind) were due to his defects in imaginative vision, which could not break entirely free from the trammels of tradition and environment.

The religious effect—which Wesley produced upon the Establishment—was neither obvious nor immediate. Religious thought, instead of growing more liberal, became more narrow, controversy more embittered and sterile; and we pass from the philosophic temper and literary grace of Butler and Law to the dreary aridities of Paley. Religious life in the Establishment underwent no immediate marked improvement; rather— by reaction against Wesleyanism—it deteriorated. It became even more formal and less emotional, and the worship of decorum and etiquette was more pronounced than ever—even Butler telling Whitefield that pretending to be inspired by the Holy Ghost was "a horrid thing, a very horrid thing." None the less, the leaven was slowly penetrating, and the Wesleyan emotional influence worked within as well as without the Establishment. The Evangelical movement, which began about 1780, and which profoundly influenced every side of the national life, was mainly an adaptation of Wesley's methods and ideas by men who remained inside the pale of the Establishment; and his direct influence is apparent in many of the Evangelical aims, especially in their noble desire to abolish the Slave Trade, and in their general humanitarian impulses.

On the general religious life of the country, so far as it lay outside the Establishment, both Whitefield and Wesley made the profoundest impression, and the followers of both—counted by thousands at their deaths—are now reckoned by millions. Not only the Church of England, but the Dissenting bodies likewise, had been affected by the prevailing materialism and stagnation of the age. Methodism mediated between the two religious bodies, brought them more into harmony with one another, and gave to each the breath of a new and invigorating life. Congregationalism, like the Establishment, had worked by old methods, and had leaned too near the doctrines of religious individualism. Wesley and Whitefield changed all this, when they showed an astonished world that souls could be won in the hedges and the byways, and that the people, who had displayed a remarkable susceptibility to political, made a still further response to religious, agitators. Introspection—the value of knowing one's own soul aright—the blessedness of religious certainty and conviction—all these came with a rush of force and passion to untaught minds and untutored impulses. To the upper classes, in part over-educated and in part unspiritual, Wesleyanism never ceased to be something of a mystery. Wesley was thought an actor by Horace Walpole, whose class as a whole despised " enthusiasm," and loathed a movement which sought to raise the " common wretches" above their station.

Whitefield and Wesley had to face the formidable hostility of many members of the upper class; but, on the other hand, the unconventionality of their methods aided their success among the poor. Bolingbroke— when the House of Lords was closed to him—spoke no more in public; Wesley, when the churches were shut, preached in the fields. As the medieval scholastic thinker anticipated the modern democratic philosopher, so the eighteenth century field-preacher may claim to have foreshadowed the modern platform speech and mass meeting. The whole population of a remote village or country town, where strangers were very rare, came out to hear the far-travelled preacher, and were under the spell of excitement before he had uttered a word. The disorder thus occasioned affords a poor and partial excuse for the severity which induced magistrates to press, fine, or imprison offending preachers. The mob in many towns—with a less calculating brutality— enabled Wesleyans (like Anglicans and Jesuits in other days) to claim the title of martyrs, though in this case they only beat, stoned, flogged, or flung them into water. In a brutalised age the spectacle of men— and even of delicate women—willing to endure these cruelties for the sake of their faith, must have been impressive enough. Indeed, the real reason of the success of Methodism was that its teachers, and especially its chief leader, were ready to endure anything to bring home the glad conviction of salvation to all minds. In the most intellectual of ages, it is the glory of Methodism to have appealed to the heart, and to have restored emotion—not always indeed the best kind of emotion— to its rightful place in religion. Such an effect as this upon a people may not be weighed in the statistical balance or measured with the numerical rod.

Wesleyanism was partly Puritanical in its effects, and opposed outbursts of emotion except when they followed certain recognised channels. Hence, it was generally unfavourable to art and literature— with one conspicuous exception. Many of its converts were hymn-writers, who expressed themselves in words as simple and touching as their thoughts, and of these far the greatest was Charles Wesley the brother of John. His hymns—besides being something new in eighteenth century literature—are the purest revelation of its religious feeling, and embody, far more fitly than any recorded words of Whitefield or Wesley, the truest and tenderest aspects of Methodism. Hymns like *Jesu, Lover of my Soul* are worth all the histories that have ever been written, as a revelation of the true power of Methodism, and teach us the secret, which brought men—degraded and brutalised beyond expression—to listen to John Wesley, as if he were a prophet of God, and to Whitefield as though he were an angel from Heaven.

CHAPTER III.

JACOBITISM AND THE UNION.

In an earlier volume the history of Scotland has been followed to the point at which her political fusion with England in 1707 promised identity of activity based upon uniformity of interest and outlook. In fact, the half-century that followed the Union tested its reality and permanence almost to the breaking-point. The Union of 1603 had produced a similar crisis. Menacing the distinctive Protestantism adopted by Scotland as most consonant with her national temperament, it excited opposition in a true sense national. The Union of 1707 eventually satisfied the commercial ambitions to satisfy which Scotland had sacrificed her separate political entity and had placed her Church, by association with the southern Establishment, in danger of a renewal of the Stewart policy of harmonisation. The magnitude of the sacrifice, together with the failure of the Union at once to yield the anticipated results, again stimulated national sentiment. But, as the century proceeded, the danger of nationalism repeating the menace of the Covenant vanished—a result due less to a dulling of sentimental retrospect, than to a recognition that Protestantism itself was involved in the permanence of the Union. Had Jacobitism raised a Protestant banner, the conflict between sentiment and material interests must have been acute. But it presented itself in the guise of the Counter-Reformation: France and Spain stood behind it: its Pretenders were pensioners of the Vatican, and the last of its titular kings was a Cardinal of the Roman Church. Jacobitism depended also upon other forces which may be termed reactionary, inasmuch as Celticism and Stewartism were practically synonymous. Hence, a cause which offered to rally Scottish nationalism furnished the most convincing reason for the Union's continuance, and provoked measures which completed it by extending to the Highlands social and political systems which for centuries the Lowlands and England had followed in common.

The Act of Union took effect on May 1, 1707. Anticipating it, and taking advantage of a tariff lower in Scotland than in England, Scottish merchants had warehoused imports, particularly French wines and spirits, in readiness to launch them lucratively into England after May 1. The House of Commons (April 7, 1707) passed a measure to prohibit the speculative traffic, and though the Lords did not proceed with the Bill, Scottish resentment was not appeased. The tardy payment of the "equivalent" also caused annoyance. It was payable on May 1, 1707, but did not reach Edinburgh until the following August 5. The fact that only £100,000, roughly one-quarter of the amount, was in specie and the remainder in Exchequer bills roused suspicion. But the prompt and easy conversion of the bills, and the restitution of the capital of the ill-fated "Company of Scotland trading to Africa and the Indies," restored confidence in England's intention to observe the conditions of the Union. The adjustment of Scotland's fiscal system to that of England had been provided for in the sixth article of the Act. The Scottish farmers of the Customs and Excise were replaced by two mixed Commissions, while the adjustment of the Excise to English measures and methods of collection confirmed apprehension that the Union would entail upon Scotland a contribution to the Exchequer out of proportion to her resources. Smuggling elevated itself forthwith to the plane of patriotism. Side by side with irritating fiscal innovations, and to a large extent to support them, the institution of Justices of the Peace, whose functions had been defined in a Scottish Act of 1661, was revived as from September 2 or 16, 1707, according as the locality was south or north of the Tay, with the powers conferred by English pre-Union Acts of Parliament. The abolition of the Scottish Privy Council as from May 1, 1708, which passed (February 13, 1708) in the form of an "Act for rendering the Union of the Two Kingdoms more entire and complete," deepened the popular impression of the Union as the surrender of Scotland's independence and sovereignty, and was protested against as an infringement of the treaty, since the powers vested by the Act in Justices of the Peace were held to trespass upon the heritable jurisdictions confirmed in the twentieth article. A Court of Exchequer in Scotland was constituted as from May 1, 1708 (6 Anne, cap. 26).

Events in Scotland had been followed closely at Saint-Germain, where the titular James III and VIII resided. Without the strenuous qualities of his son Charles Edward, James was eager to attempt the recovery of the kingdoms his father had lost, and France's fortunes in the War of the Spanish Succession inclined Louis to stimulate James' adherents to activity. In August, 1705, his agent, Colonel Nathaniel Hooke, arrived in Scotland. Louis professed lively interest in the maintenance of Scottish autonomy. But Jacobitism for the moment preferred to remain passive, at least until sympathy took material shape. Marlborough's victory at Ramillies, Eugene's at Turin, and the progress of the Archduke Charles in Spain, revived Louis' scheme to exploit Jacobitism: Hooke again arrived in Scotland, in April, 1707, shortly before the Union came into effect. He found the party divided as to

CH. III.

the wisdom of a resort to arms. The Duke of Hamilton, who had received Hooke in 1705, now pleaded illness as an excuse for refusing an interview. He intimated that a rising would be futile unless James secured a considerable party in England, and was liberally supported by French troops. Hooke's instructions (March 9, 1707), however, were to commit Louis to no conditions. From Ker of Kersland he received an egregious assurance that a supply of gunpowder, James' presence, and his undertaking to secure the Protestant religion, would bring out 5000 Cameronians and 8000 "other Presbyterians." Hooke, in his own words, "now thought only of rendering the design more general," approached the Duke of Atholl's section of the party, and obtained from them an engagement (May 7, 1707) to raise 30,000 horse and foot to march into England with James upon his arrival. The strength of the force to accompany the Prince was left to Louis' discretion; 8000 men were asked for in the event of his landing near the English border. Arms, money, and officers were requested, and James was urged to denounce the Catholic policy of his father. Hooke returned forthwith to France to report the result of his mission.

James' arrival in Scotland was looked for in August, 1707. The opportunity was favourable; for, though the secret of Hooke's negotiations had passed to the Government through Ker of Kersland, no measures had been taken to meet the threatened rebellion. The castles of Stirling, Blackness, and Dumbarton had but three barrels of powder between them: the guns of the last two fortresses were either unmounted or unserviceable: in Edinburgh Castle the "equivalent" was feebly guarded: and the Earl of Leven, commanding-in-chief, could muster only 1500 "almost naked" troops. Not until January, 1708, however, were James' adherents informed that Louis XIV, influenced, according to Saint-Simon, by Madame de Maintenon, had resolved to place troops at their disposal. On February 29 Charles Fleming was sent from Saint-Germain to announce the French expedition as on the point of sailing, and to arrange a service of signals and pilots in preparation for its arrival in the Firth of Forth. On March 1 James drafted a proclamation "to his good people of his ancient kingdom of Scotland." He reminded them that "Usurpations have always been fatal and ruinous to the liberty of Scotland," and promised to annul the Union, to sanction an Act of Oblivion, to maintain Protestants in the free exercise of their religion, and to submit "differences about Church government" to a Scottish Parliament for settlement. On March 7 James left Saint-Germain for Dunkirk, where a fleet of five men-of-war with transports under Count de Forbin, and an expeditionary force of six regiments and the Irish corps, numbering 5100 in all, under Marshal de Matignon (Count de Gacé), had assembled. The expedition had been planned to start on March 11; but James inopportunely developed measles, and was barely convalescent when Forbin loosed anchor on March 17. Closely pursued by Sir George

Byng, Forbin made the Firth of Forth at nightfall on March 23 (March 12, O.S.). The following day Byng hove in sight. Forbin's signals were not answered from the shore: Byng threatened an engagement. The French therefore dashed for the open sea and coasted northward. James importunately demanded to be put on shore, but Forbin refused in view of Byng's close pursuit. On April 7 (March 27, O.S.), after a stormy passage and with only nine ships in company, James returned to Dunkirk.

Three months after James' abortive attempt, a general election (June 17, 1708) gave Scotland her first opportunity of sending to Parliament members elected by the constituencies. The election raised important constitutional questions. Two shires (Aberdeen and Linlithgow) returned a peer's eldest son. In accordance with the practice of the Scottish Parliament the Commons (December 3, 1708) declared them ineligible, and ordered (December 6) new elections in both counties. In the election of the sixteen representative peers Queensberry's vote was challenged on the ground that he was also a peer of Great Britain. The votes of the few Scottish peers who were peers of England prior to the Union were also objected to, and minor irregularities were alleged to disqualify the votes of others. Upon the petition of four defeated candidates the Lords conducted an enquiry, and ruled (January 21, 1709) that a Scottish peer advanced to a post-Union peerage of Great Britain was not entitled to vote in his own name or as a proxy at the election of the representatives of his order. When two years later Hamilton was created Duke of Brandon in the peerage of Great Britain, apprehension of an enlargement of Scotland's influence in the Upper House caused the Lords to resolve (December 20, 1711), by 57 to 52 votes, that Scottish peers created peers of Great Britain after the Union were unable to sit in the latter capacity. A majority of the Scottish representatives condemned the resolution as a violation of the Union and as reducing their order "to a worse condition, in some respects, than the meanest or most criminal of subjects." The Queen sent a message to the Lords on the matter (January 17, 1712); but the order was not reversed until June 6, 1782.

The French attempt of 1708 was followed by the arrest of suspected sympathisers. Hamilton's opportune agreement with the Whigs procured the release of all but five, who had drawn together under arms in Stirlingshire in anticipation of James' landing. They were indicted for High Treason at Edinburgh, but were discharged (November 22, 1708) upon a verdict of "not proven." The verdict suggested that the Scottish law of treason required adjustment to the English code. On March 28, 1709, an "Act for improving the Union of the Two Kingdoms" reached the Commons from the Lords. It enacted (as from July 1, 1709) that crimes regarded as High Treason by the law of England should be regarded as such in Scotland; transferred the jurisdiction of the High

CH. III.

Court of Justiciary over such offences to special Commissions of Oyer and Terminer, and established identical penalties for both countries. In the Commons the measure was opposed by the Scottish members, but was carried (April 9, 1709) with two amendments. By the first, estates in land were declared non-forfeitable for treason beyond a single life. By the second, the names of witnesses for the prosecution and a copy of the indictment were to be submitted to the accused ten days before his trial. With the addition of a clause providing that the amendments should not come into force until the death of the Pretender and the completion of three years of the reign of the Queen's successor, the measure became law (April 21, 1709).

The Scottish Church meanwhile had reason to consider the conditions of the Union disregarded. Such of the episcopal clergy as had qualified under the "Act concerning the Church" of July 16, 1695, were excluded from Church Courts and ordinations, but were free to conduct public worship in their own way. Others, more numerous, were debarred by an earlier Act (June 28, 1695) from administering the rites of marriage and baptism, but (provided they had taken the Oath of Allegiance, and the Assurance) were not expressly forbidden to minister in conventicles. Their public ministrations were tolerated by connivance, not by law. English Protestant nonconformists enjoyed security of worship under the Act of 1689. It had been foreseen that, although Scottish nonconformity was riddled with Jacobitism, the Union would make it difficult to withhold from it a legal status; since, apart from the plea of symmetry, the Union drew the two episcopal communions into more intimate relations. The English Book of Common Prayer was increasingly adopted in Scotland, where episcopal worship was as yet non-liturgical, and the General Assembly (April 21, 1707) passed an Act condemning "set forms." The order was challenged by James Greenshields, an episcopal minister. In 1709 he opened a chapel in Edinburgh and used the Book of Common Prayer. Summoned by the Presbytery for "presuming without authority to exercise the office of the holy ministry," he exhibited his letters of ordination by the Bishop of Ross in 1694, proved that he had taken the oaths, and denied the Presbytery's jurisdiction over him. The Presbytery, contending that he was "within their bounds," suspended him for introducing a form of worship "contrary to the purity and uniformity of the Church established by law," and on September 15, 1709, the magistrates convicted him for continued contumacy. He remained in prison for seven months, and twice appealed unsuccessfully to the Court of Session. On February 13, 1710, he entered an appeal in the House of Lords, and obtained (March 1, 1711) a verdict reversing the decision of the Courts below.

Greenshields' case corrected the claim of the General Assembly to exercise national jurisdiction, and was exploited to capture the sympathy of English episcopacy for the sister communion in Scotland. On

March 3, 1712, the royal assent was given to a Bill securing Scottish episcopal nonconformists in the exercise of public worship and use of the English liturgy, and repealing the Scottish Act of June 28, 1695. The Bill passed the Commons (February 7, 1712) by 152 to 17 votes. In the Lords, though the Commission of Assembly was heard by counsel (February 13), their proposal that abjuration of the Pretender should be required from tolerated episcopalians was extended to the Established clergy as well. The former, provided they had taken the oaths and produced letters of ordination from a Protestant Bishop, were given liberty to conduct public worship, marriages, and baptisms. Tolerated episcopacy was objectionable to Presbyterianism, but the Abjuration Oath was trebly offensive. It submitted the Church to Erastian discipline : imposed a test and thereby infringed the liberty which the Union had guaranteed to the Establishment : and bound the subscriber to maintain the succession " as the same is and stands settled " by the Act of 1701 (12 and 13 William III, cap. 2), which required the sovereign to " join in communion with the Church of England." Scottish Protestantism resented a demand to maintain the exclusive claims of the other Establishment, and the Government did not venture to force the oath upon ministers who refused to take it. In 1715 (1 Geo. I, stat. 2, cap. 13) the oath was redrafted with verbal alterations which allowed the subscriber to hold himself non-committed to the conditions of the Act of 1701. In 1719 (5 Geo. I, cap. 29) reference to that Act was omitted altogether from the oath.

Ten days after the Toleration Act received the royal assent, the Commons gave leave (March 13, 1712) to introduce a Bill " to restore the patrons to their ancient rights of presenting Ministers to the churches vacant in Scotland." The measure commended itself to episcopal and Jacobite patrons as a means to exclude ultra-Presbyterians from the pulpits of the Church. But Jacobitism failed to capture them. On the contrary, the moderatism which the Act encouraged contributed to consolidate the Union. Patronal appointment to church livings had been twice abolished, in 1649 and 1690. The latter Act offered patrons compulsory compensation for renunciation of their right of presentment: vested the patronage of country benefices in the elders and Protestant heritors, and of town benefices in the heritors and magistrates. The new Act, which passed the Commons on April 7, 1712, restored to such patrons as had not taken advantage of the Act of 1690 the patronage of benefices in their gift after May 1, 1712, provided they had taken the oaths and were purged of suspicion of Popery : conveyed to the particular presbytery the patronage of a benefice to which the patron failed to nominate within six months of a vacancy occurring : and reserved to the Crown the presentation to benefices in the gift of the Bishops before the abolition of Episcopacy in 1689. Notwithstanding a petition of the Commission of Assembly, representing the measure as violating the rights of which the Church was possessed at the Union, the Act received the royal assent on May 22, 1712. On the same date was repealed part of the Scottish "Act discharging the Yule Vacance" (1690). The Court of Session and inferior judicatories were now bidden to observe the Christmas vacation from December 20 to January 10 inclusive yearly, a vexatious attempt to adjust Scottish to English practice. This amending Act was repealed three years later (September 21, 1715).

Since 1707 the United Parliament, in which Scotland's representation was fractional, had passed Acts running counter in varying degrees to principles which Scotland as an independent kingdom had deliberately adopted. A measure of another character excited a demand for repeal of the Union itself. By Article XIV of the treaty Scottish malt was exempt from duty "during this present war." Although on May 9, 1713, the Queen informed Parliament that the treaty with France had been signed, peace with Spain had not been concluded formally. The point was seized as a pretext for opposition to a proposal (May 18) to subject Scottish malt to a sixpenny duty per bushel, uniform with the English rate. The Bill passed the Commons (May 22) with a majority of 197 to 57 votes, the Scottish members opposing it as an infraction of the terms of the Union, and as imposing a duty beyond what Scottish malt was able to bear. Two of their number, with Argyll and Mar from the Lords, waited upon the Queen (May 26) to represent that a motion for the dissolution of the Union was contemplated. Anne's timid hope "to make all things easy" did not discourage a campaign of somewhat inflated protest. On June 1, the Earl of Findlater in the Lords moved for leave to introduce a Bill to dissolve the Union. He instanced the quashing of the Scottish Privy Council, the Treason Act, the barring of the peerage of Great Britain against Scottish nobles, and the threatened malt duty as grievances which justified disruption. Mar seconded, and Argyll and the Whigs supported, the motion, chiefly as a tactical move against the Tories. Findlater's motion was lost only by four votes. Its single result was that the duty on Scottish malt, though agreed to by the Lords (June 8), was suspended until 1724, when the proposal was revived in another form.

In the last Parliament of Queen Anne, which assembled on February 16, 1714, the Queen's recent illness focused attention upon the crisis threatened by her death. The Queen was petitioned to demand James' removal from Bar-le-Duc in Lorraine, whither the Treaty of Utrecht had driven him. A proclamation (June 23) offered £5000—increased in August to £100,000—for his apprehension should he attempt to land in Great Britain. Both Bolingbroke and Oxford had been in touch with him since the autumn of 1712. But James imposed conditions which made it futile to act in his behalf. Rejecting Oxford's advice, he declared (March 13, 1714) his resolution neither to change nor to dissemble his religion. To Cardinal Gualterio, his agent at Rome, he expressed himself at the same time with similar emphasis.

The premature death of the Queen in her forty-ninth year (August 1, 1714) disappointed the vague hopes of James founded upon her affection for him. The English Tories feared to move for a Roman Catholic claimant, and preferred to assume that a Hanoverian dynasty would immediately collapse. The European situation also was discouraging. The Hanoverian Succession had been recognised in the Utrecht pacification, and there was for the moment no disposition in any quarter to disturb it. Clement XI, intent upon the eastern assault of Islam rather than upon the problematical chances of a western crusade, refused (August, 1714) to approach the European Courts in James' behalf. With difficulty James' appeal (March, 1715) drew a subsidy of 30,000 crowns from the Vatican. From the Emperor James received a clear rebuff; and efforts made in 1714 and 1715 to secure the hand of the Emperor's sister, or that of one of his nieces, daughters of the late Emperor Joseph, or of the daughter of Charles Philip of Neuburg (brother of the Elector Palatine), failed to ensure to the Pretender a backing from Catholic Germany. An appeal to Charles XII of Sweden (July, 1715) promised better results. A Swedish descent upon Newcastle was planned, and 50,000 crowns were transmitted by James to support it. But in spite of Denmark's cession of Bremen to Hanover, Charles refused (August 3) to take action. Most discouraging of all was the attitude of France. A loan of 100,000 crowns was obtained upon Louis' guarantee, and no objection was offered to the purchase of arms and secret preparations in James' behalf. But Louis refused (February, 1715) to take any course which would prejudice the maintenance of peace; and, despite James' protest (July, 1715), Berwick's services were denied him. The death of Louis (September 1, 1715) handed over France to the Duke of Orleans, who held it more vital to exclude the Spanish Bourbons from the French succession than to encourage a Stewart restoration in England. On December 6 the Irish officers in the French service were forbidden to proceed to Scotland. Spain was as cautious as France, and James was surprised (December 12, 1715) at receiving so much as a subsidy.

In these disheartening circumstances James countered George I's accession with no more effectual measure than a proclamation (August 29, 1714) asserting his hereditary right. But the vindictive spirit of the Whig Parliament brought him adherents whose attachment so far had been secret. Early in April, 1715, Bolingbroke fled to Paris. On June 10 the Commons resolved to impeach him; and, there being no longer need for caution, he accepted (July) the seals as James' Secretary of State. The Duke of Ormond, whose impeachment the Commons voted on June 21, and Mar, whose professions of loyalty failed to gain George's favour, remained in England to concert measures. Their plans were marked by the ineptitude inseparable from Jacobite enterprise. About July 15, a verbal communication from England determined James, without consulting Berwick, Bolingbroke, or Torcy, the French Foreign Minister, to appoint July 31 for a rising and to give it the encouragement of his presence. Shortly before his proposed departure (July 28) from Bar, James received a joint report from Mar and Ormond, representing that unless an army accompanied him a general insurrection was impracticable. On August 3 Bolingbroke therefore conveyed to James the unanimous opinion of Berwick, Torcy, and himself that the situation was not ripe for action. Ten days later (August 2, O. S.) Mar boarded a collier in the Thames and sailed to Scotland. Before he reached his destination, Ormond had taken flight and was in Paris.

Mar arrived at his Castle of Kildrummy in Aberdeenshire on August 20, 1715. Berwick's accusation of collusion between James and Mar to force the situation must be dismissed: but Mar cannot escape censure for precipitately plunging Scotland into civil war. Before he left London he was aware that James had cancelled his order for an immediate rising, and the Prince's instructions only empowered him to take the field in "the last extremity." On September 6 he raised the standard at Braemar. The ceremony was repeated at Aberdeen by the Earl Marischal, at Dunkeld by the Marquis of Tullibardine, at Gordon Castle by the Marquis of Huntly, at Brechin by the Earl of Panmure, at Montrose by the Earl of Southesk, at Dundee by the titular Viscount of Dundee, and at Inverness by William Mackintosh of Borlum. The Jacobites of Perth mastered the town (September 18) and proclaimed James there also. A plot to seize Edinburgh Castle had all but succeeded (September 8). On September 28 Mar entered Perth. By October 9 the accession of Farquharsons, Atholl Highlanders, Robertsons of Struan, Gordons, Breadalbane's Campbells, Mackintoshes, Drummonds, and Lowland contingents, brought Mar's strength to 6000 foot and about 600 horse. In the west, Macdonalds, Macleans, Macgregors, and Glenmoriston Grants were in arms to harass the Campbell country. In the south, on both sides of the border, the Jacobites were stirring: James was proclaimed at Warkworth on October 9, and at Lochmaben on October 13.

Meanwhile the Government showed none of the lethargy of 1708. On July 20, 1715, the royal assent was given to an "Act for preventing tumults," which obliged an assemblage of twelve or more persons to disperse upon proclamation by a single magistrate. On July 23 the Habeas Corpus Act was suspended; and, a month later (August 30), the royal assent was given to an Act which decreed the penalties of High Treason against owners and occupiers of land in Scotland supporting the Pretender by acts committed in or out of the country; the loyal vassals of a rebellious superior were converted into tenants of the Crown; his

loyal tenants and tacksmen were released for two years from paying
rent; the lands of a rebellious vassal reverted to his loyal superior;
collusive settlements made since August 1, 1714, were declared void;
and from September 1, 1715, until January 23, 1716, the Commissioners
of Justiciary were empowered to summon suspected persons of Scottish
domicile to Edinburgh or elsewhere to find bail for their peaceable
behaviour. About September 8 a camp was formed at Stirling to secure
the fords of the Forth. The Duke of Argyll, commanding-in-chief, set
out thither from Edinburgh on September 16, and found himself at the
head of some 1800 men. Reinforcements were ordered from Ireland;
and the United Provinces were called upon under treaty obligations
to furnish eight regiments of foot and one of horse, 6000 in all.
Parliament had already (July 25 and 26) sanctioned the raising of
7000 horse and foot and the calling-up of half-pay officers. An addition of 6000 men to the fleet was also agreed to (August 11). In
Scotland Argyll's appeal for volunteers met with a loyal response on the
part of Edinburgh, Glasgow, and the towns of the south and south-west.
On September 28, the Earl of Sutherland arrived at Dunrobin to raise
the loyal northern clans; and, about October 6, Argyll's brother, the
Earl of Islay, was sent into the west to rally the Campbells.

In spite of his numerical superiority, Mar remained inactive at
Perth. His commission (September 7, 1715) as Commander-in-chief
reached him on October 6; and the capture at Burntisland (October 2)
of arms and powder destined for Sutherland partially stocked his empty
magazines. But he preferred to play a waiting game until James'
arrival, and meanwhile to implicate English Jacobitism. In the first
week of October the coast towns of Fife and their shipping were
secured. On October 12 Mackintosh of Borlum, embarking detachments at Pittenweem, Crail, Elie, and other ports, crossed to North
Berwick with about 1100 men. On Mar's western front the appearance
of Macdonalds and others before Inveraray (October 19) threatened an
enveloping movement which would make Argyll's situation precarious.
But the withdrawal of the clans from before Inveraray (October 25)
destroyed the symmetry of Mar's tactical design, and Mackintosh
imperilled the execution of his mission by a dash upon Edinburgh
(October 14). He was within a mile of the city when the arrival
of Argyll, and the militant posture of the citizens, caused him to
take shelter in Leith fort. On the following morning (October 15)
Argyll summoned Mackintosh to surrender; but, having no artillery, he
withdrew to make preparations for dislodging the insurgents next day.
Before daybreak (October 16) Mackintosh transferred his force to Seton
Castle. A few hours later Mar, apprised of his subordinate's situation,
advanced upon Stirling, thereby compelling Argyll's return. A week
later (October 22) Mackintosh joined the Northumberland and Galloway
insurgents at Kelso.

Three weeks of inaction followed Mar's return to Perth (October 18). His feint upon Stirling might have become a general advance but for Argyll's timely reinforcement and the failure of the clans in the west. On October 25 they retired from before Inveraray towards Strathfillan. Thence, reinforced by the Camerons and Stewarts of Appin, who had refused to appear against Inveraray, they marched to join Mar, and encamped at Auchterarder about November 1. In number they were about 2500. A week later Seaforth's Mackenzies, Sir Donald Macdonald of Sleat's following, and others, in all about 2000, arrived at Perth. Mar's levies were now complete, and a general advance against Argyll was resolved upon (November 9). Assuming incorrectly that Argyll would not move from Stirling, Mar on November 10 marched from Perth, about 8000 strong, horse and foot, with eleven cannon, indifferently supplied with powder and ammunition. On November 12 the clans, marching in advance, were a little beyond Ardoch when Mar learnt that Argyll was already between him and Dunblane. Mar hastened up his main body, and that night the whole army encamped at Kinbuck.

Late in October Argyll had received the reinforcements summoned from Ireland. Upon the news of Mar's advance from Perth, he resolved to give him battle in front of Dunblane; for the slopes of the Ochils favoured the operations of cavalry, and Argyll doubted the ability of his small numbers to hold the Forth river-front, especially as frost threatened to make the fords passable. On November 12 he marched from Stirling and encamped before Dunblane, his right resting on Sheriffmuir. His army numbered eight battalions of foot and five regiments of horse, in all about 3000, with six three-pounders. Before sunrise on the 13th Mar advanced from Kinbuck. Argyll's position, sloping from his right on Sheriffmuir towards Dunblane, drew the Highlanders' attack on his left centre. Mar's horse bungled in taking their position, and further weakened the force opposed to Argyll's right. At the first onrush the Highlanders drove back Argyll's left upon Dunblane, while the Duke, commanding in person on his right, scattered and pursued the force opposed to him to beyond Kinbuck. Those of Mar's army who had neither joined in the pursuit to Dunblane nor had been scattered by Argyll's right drew up on the hill of Kippendavie and confronted Argyll upon his return. But neither side ventured to renew the attack, and towards evening both withdrew, Argyll to Dunblane, Mar towards Perth. Mar's timidity in refusing to engage Argyll's right, wearied by pursuit, left the battle indecisive. As it was, Argyll lost about one-fifth of his army killed, wounded, or captured.

Almost simultaneously with Sheriffmuir, two disasters elsewhere rendered James' cause hopeless even before he embarked for Scotland. Seaforth had left a garrison in Inverness, after driving off Sutherland's force of Mackays, Rosses, and Munroes. On November 5 Simon Fraser of Beaufort, intent upon securing the Government's favour and the

Lovat title, arrived in the north. Except those of his name who had marched to Perth—who also deserted Mar (November 10) upon news of Beaufort's arrival—the clan rallied to him. At the head of a force of Frasers, Forbeses, and Rosses he drove the Jacobite garrison from Inverness on November 10, after heading off Macdonald of Keppoch, who was marching ostensibly to its relief. Sutherland joined Beaufort a few days later (November 15), and the control of the north passed conclusively to the Government.

In England the prospects of a Jacobite rising were extinguished by Forster's surrender at Preston on November 14. On October 22, at Kelso, the Galloway Jacobites under Kenmure, Nithsdale, Carnwath and Wintoun had joined Mackintosh of Borlum and the Northumberland contingent under Thomas Forster, Derwentwater, and Widdrington. Their combined force, ten troops of horse and six regiments of foot, numbered less than 2000 men. The Scots urged a junction with the clans in Strathfillan and an attack upon Argyll's rear while Mar assailed his front. The English desired to encourage the Jacobites of Lancashire by marching thither. The appearance of Lieutenant-General George Carpenter and three regiments of horse at Wooler (October 27) forced the insurgents to a resolution, and in spite of protests, desertions, and even mutiny on the part of the Highland foot, the march into Lancashire was agreed to (October 29) and began forthwith. Advancing through Jedburgh, Hawick and Langholm, the force crossed the Esk (November 1) and entered England. Forster, whose Protestantism was his only recommendation to a place of prominence, assumed the chief command under Mar's commission. On his advance to Penrith on the 2nd, the insurgents scattered a force of militia without striking a blow, and, after a day's halt at Appleby, entered Kendal on the 5th. In Lancashire the Jacobite gentry showed a disposition to join them ; and at Lancaster, where they continued from the 7th to the 9th, they captured six cannon. Encouraged by assurances of a welcome in Manchester, Forster pushed on his cavalry to Preston on the 9th, and his foot entered the town on the following day. On the 11th Major-General Wills reached Wigan from Manchester with six regiments of horse and the Cameronian foot. Forster took no measures to impede his advance. Upon his arrival at the Ribble, about midday on the 12th, Wills found the bridge giving access to Preston unguarded. Within the town the insurgents had erected four barricades. Wills ordered an immediate assault ; it was stubbornly met and at nightfall was abandoned. Next morning (November 13) Carpenter came up with three regiments of horse. The insurgents were trapped ; resistance, however prolonged, could not avert ultimate surrender ; to break cover with nine regiments of horse in pursuit would be madness, and Forster acted sensibly in proposing surrender. Terms were refused ; and early on the 14th the insurgents, 1500 in number, laid down their arms.

CH. III.

Six weeks after Sheriffmuir, the loss of Inverness, and the Preston surrender, James arrived in Scotland to head a beaten cause. Other discouragements had failed to deter his coming. France had not been stirred to more active sympathy, and Berwick (November 3) decisively refused to serve James as Captain-General. Ormond, who on October 24 left Paris to raise the south and west of England, found his plans betrayed, and the persons and places he designed to employ arrested or alert. Before November 8 he returned to St Malo. On November 27 he again sailed for Cornwall, but returned by December 12 without having effected anything. Meanwhile James, chafing at inaction, had set out from Lorraine for the coast. He reached St Malo on November 8, and designed to sail thence to Dunstaffnage. But, the wind remaining contrary, he set out on December 2 overland to Dunkirk, to take ship for the east coast of Scotland. Three weeks later (December 27 or 28) he sailed; on January 2, 1716 (December 22, 1715, O.S.) he landed at Peterhead.

Since Sheriffmuir Mar's position at Perth had steadily deteriorated. Keppoch brought his clan; but the Highlanders deserted in large numbers, and Seaforth, who returned to the north after the battle, made his submission to Sutherland. On January 9, 1716, James made a public entrance into Perth. His arrival did not improve the situation, though he appointed January 23 for his coronation. Huntly, who left Perth before James' arrival, and Seaforth, who again took arms, were unable to restore the position in the north. On the other hand Argyll was incomparably stronger: he had recovered Burntisland (December 19, 1715) and other Fifeshire ports: reinforcements, including the Dutch contingent, joined him; and, soon after James' arrival, he was at the head of 9000 horse and foot and a powerful artillery train. His failure to push the campaign to a conclusion had roused suspicion; and, upon emphatic instructions from Townshend (January 10, 1716), he began his advance in a season exceptionally severe. On January 24 he reconnoitred towards Auchterarder. Undecided whether to retreat or give battle, Mar took futile measures to hinder Argyll's advance. On the 25th the clans burnt Auchterarder and Blackford; by the 29th Crieff, Dunning, Muthill, and Dalreoch had been dealt with similarly. On the 29th Argyll advanced in force from Stirling, along roads cleared of snow in advance, and on the 30th halted at Auchterarder. Within Perth all was confusion. The Highlanders were impatient for battle; the cautious proposed to withdraw to more advantageous ground; Mar himself was bent upon abandoning a hopeless enterprise. On the 30th it was resolved to retreat, and early on the 31st the army withdrew towards Montrose. Argyll hotly pressed the pursuit. On February 4 his vanguard was at Arbroath. James was at Montrose on the same day. He had written (February 3) to the French Regent to beg for succours, and to assure him of the vitality of his cause. But an alarm of Argyll's advance from Arbroath compelled James to consider his safety. A ship, named the *Forerunner*, was in Montrose harbour. On the 4th James went on board, accompanied by Mar, leaving General Alexander Gordon of Auchintoul to command the retreating army, and a farewell letter to his adherents representing his departure as necessary to promote " a more happy juncture for our mutual delivery." On February 21 (February 10, O.S.) James landed at Gravelines. Scotland he never saw again. Gordon led his troops to Aberdeen, thence to Badenoch, and from Ruthven on February 15 petitioned Argyll for clemency. By July the leaders had made their escape to France.

Severe punishment was dealt out to those who had placed the Union and the Hanoverian Succession in jeopardy. On March 6, 1716, an Act empowered the withdrawal of persons in custody for High Treason (committed before the previous January 23) from the shire in which the crime had occurred for trial before special Commissions of Oyer and Terminer. Of those made prisoners in England, 738 were transported; 53 died in prison; 57 (including Derwentwater and Kenmure) were executed. Derwentwater, Widdrington, Nithsdale, Carnwath, Kenmure, Nairne, Wintoun, Forster, Mackintosh of Borlum, Mar, Tullibardine, Linlithgow, Drummond, Marischal, Seaforth, Southesk, and Panmure were attainted. The policy of a later date was adumbrated in an Act (June 26, 1716) which forbade the inhabitants (except peers and commoners qualified to exercise the parliamentary franchise) of all counties north of the Forth and Clyde estuaries (except Fife, Clackmannan and Kinross) to carry arms on or after November 1, 1716, and empowered the Lords Lieutenant to appoint centres for the surrender of arms, and to pay the full value of their forfeited weapons to those who had remained loyal in the late rebellion. The Act also directed that after August 1, 1717, the claim of a superior upon his tenants for " hosting, hunting, watching, and warding" should be commuted in money. But in this, and in the attempt to disarm them, the Act had little effect upon the clans most deeply tinged with Jacobitism. The rebellion had revealed another menace to the established Government. While Mar was at Perth, in his rear episcopacy frankly avowed itself Jacobite. Over 200 loyal clergy, according to Wodrow, had been ousted from their pulpits. Their places were taken by episcopal nonjurors, who as a body, while accepting the liberty conferred by the Toleration Act of 1712, had been careless to fulfil the conditions upon which it was granted. Episcopacy paid the penalty for the manifestation of its political bias. By an Act of 1719 (5 Geo. I, cap. 29) nonjuring ministers were forbidden to conduct public worship where more than eight persons, not being members of a single household, were present.

For a generation after the '15 the Union was not seriously assailed. Jacobitism never again rallied the forces which Mar controlled so inefficiently. As the material benefits of the Union were recognised, the

Lowlands were tempted to break away from the separatists; and the Stewart cause found support chiefly among the clans, who correctly interpreted the Act of 1716 as the beginning of a determined attack upon their distinctive polity. Jacobitism was further weakened by the cessation of intimate relations with France. James, excluded from France and Lorraine, arrived at Avignon on April 2, 1716. Driven thence (February 6, 1717) by the Triple Alliance, he crossed the Alps to Italy, and accepted a hospitality which identified his cause with the Papacy and confirmed the conviction that his restoration would endanger the Protestant settlement.

Yet the European situation produced two crises of which with indifferent success Jacobitism sought to take advantage. Sweden, as shown in a previous chapter, viewed the Triple Alliance (January, 1717) as a formidable obstacle to her recovery of Bremen and Verden. Jacobite intrigues with Charles XII, abortive in 1715, were accordingly renewed in 1716 through Görtz. The scheme contemplated coincident insurrections in England and Scotland. Baron Sparre, Swedish Minister in Paris, was in communication with James; and Count Gyllenborg, representing Sweden at the Court of St James', was in touch with the English Jacobites, who subscribed over £30,000. Stanhope got wind of the intrigue, and on January 29, 1717, exposed it to the Privy Council. Gyllenborg was arrested; his papers were impounded; and Görtz was seized in Holland at the request of Great Britain. Both were released soon after, and the sole result of the plot was the prohibition of commerce with Sweden (February 28, 1717), and the postponement to the end of the parliamentary session of an Act of Pardon (July 15, 1717) covering the recent crisis.

France being now allied with Great Britain, and all hope of Sweden's help having been dashed by the death of Charles XII (November 30, 1718), every direction whence Jacobitism could draw support seemed closed. Opportunely Alberoni offered the resources of Spain. Resolved to free Italy from the Imperial yoke which the Treaty of Utrecht had laid upon her, Alberoni viewed Great Britain, doubly pledged to enforce that treaty by the Triple Alliance and the Treaty of Westminster (May, 1716) and withal a maritime Power, as the most serious obstacle in his path. After Byng's destruction of the Spanish fleet off Cape Passaro on August 11, 1718, the Cardinal—he owed his hat (July 12, 1717) to James' interest at Rome—turned to the Jacobites to avenge frustrated projects. In November, 1718, the Duke of Ormond was summoned from Paris to Spain. Alberoni undertook to send him to England with 4000 foot, 1000 horse, besides artillery, and with two months' pay for the force. He agreed also to equip a small expedition for Scotland, and Ormond invited (December 8) the Earl Marischal from Paris to take charge of it. Of these motions in his behalf James received information on January 26, 1719, with an intimation that Alberoni deemed it advisable

for him either to accompany or to follow the English expedition. A fortnight later (February 8) James left Rome, embarked at Nettuno, and on
March 9 landed at Rosas in Catalonia, whence he proceeded to Madrid.
Meanwhile, after a month's delay, the Spanish fleet, consisting of five
men-of-war and twenty-two transports with 5000 men on board, sailed
from Cadiz (March 7).   Ormond since February 24 had been waiting to
join it at Corunna.   But it met the fate of an earlier Armada.   On
March 29, when about fifty leagues west of Cape Finisterre, a violent
storm scattered the vessels to such sheltering ports as they could reach.
In August, finding that Philip V would make no further effort in his
behalf, James sailed to Italy and his marriage (September 1, 1719) with
Maria Clementina, grand-daughter of John Sobieski, the warrior-king of
Poland.

Once more Scotland was invited single-handed to uphold the Stewart
cause.   On March 8, 1719, the Earl Marischal sailed from Pasajes with
two frigates bearing arms, money, 288 rank and file and 19 officers of
Don Pedro de Castro's regiment of foot.   The Earl's brother, the future
Marshal Keith in the Prussian service, had already (February 19, 1719) set
out from Madrid to engage the Jacobite exiles in France.   With Seaforth,
Tullibardine, and Colin Campbell of Glendaruel, he sailed from Havre
on March 19.   By March 24 (April 4, N.S.) they reached the Lewis,
and a week later (March 30) joined Marischal's frigates at Stornoway.
The two parties differed regarding the course to pursue.   Marischal
advocated the immediate seizure of Inverness; Tullibardine thought it
folly to take action until Ormond's landing in England was announced.
The decision rested with Tullibardine, who exhibited a commission
as commander-in-chief from James.   Marischal, however, refused to
part with the control of the Spanish frigates.   On April 4 the three
vessels sailed to Gairloch.   Upon a rumour that Ormond was in England,
Glendaruel was despatched to rouse the clans.   On the 13th the ships
anchored off Ellandonan, a rocky island, crowned by the castle of the
Mackenzies of Kintail, at the forking of Loch Alsh into Lochs Long and
Duich.   Arms and ammunition were landed and the Spaniards formed
a camp.   The rumour of Ormond's landing had not been confirmed;
without that assurance the Lowland Jacobites would not rise; Glendaruel
returned with a similar message from the clans.   By the 20th Clanranald,
Lochiel, Mackinnon, and Chisholm of Strathglass arrived, and a council
of war was held.   The majority favoured Fabian tactics.   Marischal,
who still urged an immediate stroke against Inverness, suspected that
Tullibardine intended to reembark, and despatched the two frigates to
Spain on the 30th.   On May 4 news of the dispersal of Ormond's fleet
arrived, and five days later three British men-of-war entered Loch Alsh.
On the 10th they compelled the surrender of Ellandonan, its garrison,
arms, and ammunition.   There was no course open to Tullibardine save
to withdraw.   On the 13th he skirted Loch Long towards Glen Elchaig,

CH. III.

and thence marched to the Croe at the head of Loch Duich. Inaccurate news arrived, that the Spanish fleet was repaired and on the point of sailing. Tullibardine thereupon (May 21) sent an urgent summons to the clans. With about 1100 men—Mackenzies, Camerons, Macgregors, Mackinnons, and the Spaniards—Tullibardine on June 9 took position in the Pass of Glenshiel, whither Major-General Wightman with 986 foot (including 136 Munro Highlanders), 120 horse and 4 cohorns, was advancing from Fort Augustus. On the 10th he appeared, shelled the insurgents' position, and after a stubborn resistance put them to flight. On the following day the Spaniards surrendered, and the rising was at an end.

One by one every ally of Jacobitism had been detached. France and the Channel had been secured by the Triple Alliance. The Quadruple Alliance secured Austria. The Treaty of Stockholm (November 20, 1719) gained Sweden's support for the Hanoverian dynasty and closed the Baltic. Finally, Spain's adhesion to the Quadruple Alliance (January 26, 1720) closed the Mediterranean to Jacobite enterprise and relegated James to Italy and isolation. His domestic troubles, and the small repute of those who controlled his affairs after Mar's supersession in 1724, filled his Scottish partisans with dismay. George II's accession passed unchallenged, and Lockhart of Carnwath in 1728 regarded James' cause as one which "must in process of time be totally forgot." None could discern in the youthful Prince Charles Edward (born December 31, 1720) the champion who was to resuscitate it.

In 1719, Jacobitism was dormant; but the unpopularity of the Union was not encouraged to diminish. The Peerage Bill could be regarded as a violation of the Union inasmuch as it substituted twenty-five hereditary for the sixteen representative peers elected by their order. In the Lords, where the measure passed (November 30, 1719), the Scottish peers welcomed a proposal to convert their elective into a hereditary status, and, on broader grounds, supported it as freeing them from the influence of English political parties. In the Commons the Bill was lost (December 8, 1719) by 269 to 177 votes. Vastly more unpopular was a proposal in the Commons (December 10, 1724) affecting Scottish beer and ale. The resolution of 1713 to impose a duty on Scottish malt had never been acted upon. In order to balance the immunity which Scotland had enjoyed, it was now proposed to levy an additional excise of sixpence per barrel on Scottish beer and ale, and to withhold from Scotland the bounty that England enjoyed on the export of grain. Considerable clamour was raised against a proposal which was declared to violate the Union's promise of fiscal uniformity, and a threepenny duty on malt, being half of the English duty, was substituted. In its new form the impost was not less unpopular. An inaccurate statement was put abroad, that the Convention of Royal Burghs encouraged non-payment of the duty; and, on June 24, 1725, Captain Bushell and two companies of infantry were drafted into Glasgow to support the excise officials in valuing the maltsters' stock. They were received with shouts of " No malt tax"; the Guard-house was locked against them; and the mob gutted the house of their Member of Parliament, Daniel Campbell. On the 25th, encouraged by the inactivity of the soldiery, the rioters stoned them and drew a volley. Bushell thereupon sought safety in Dumbarton Castle, and informed General Wade at Edinburgh of his predicament. On July 10 the General, with the Lord Advocate (Duncan Forbes of Culloden) and a considerable force of horse and foot, entered Glasgow. Four men and one woman implicated in the riot were sentenced, the former to whipping and transportation, the woman to the pillory. Glasgow was fined £6080 to make good Campbell's losses. The Duke of Roxburghe, suspected of sympathy with the demonstrators, was removed from the Scottish Secretaryship (August, 1725).

While the Lowlands were in a ferment, measures were being taken to settle the Highlands. Wade reported (December 10, 1724) that the Disarming Act of 1716 had failed in effect. The loyal clans, numbered at 10,000 men, had more or less obeyed the injunction to disarm; the disloyal, 12,000 in number, as Wade estimated, had surrendered old and useless arms, their effective weapons remaining hidden and within reach. Wade therefore recommended (April, 1725) that the disarming of the clans should be prosecuted vigorously, that six Highland companies should be raised, an armed barque launched upon Loch Ness, and forts and barracks provided at Inverness (Fort George) and Cillachiumein (Fort Augustus). On May 31, 1725, a new Disarming Act received the royal assent. The surrender of arms in the shires scheduled in the Act of 1716 was ordered under the penalty of forcible enlistment for military service in the colonies; women concealing arms were liable to two years' imprisonment and a fine not exceeding £100; peers, their sons, and commoners qualified to vote for or sit as Members of Parliament, were exempt from the Act. The disarmament of the disaffected clans was undertaken systematically by Wade, but, as the future proved, not effectually. Fort George and Fort Augustus were built, and from Inverness to Fort William, and from Stirling to Inverness, military roads were constructed. The Highland Watch, or police, had been disbanded after the '15. Six companies were now raised, and in 1739 were embodied as a regiment of the Line, the 42nd (Black Watch). It was the good fortune of England to enlist the commercial ambition of the Lowlands and the military aptitude of the Highlands in behalf of an Empire which both had entered reluctantly.

At the moment when Parliament was considering the pacification of the Highlands, the trustees of the estates forfeited after the '15 presented their final report. By an Act of June 26, 1716, a Commission had been constituted to ascertain the extent and value of the property of persons who had been attainted since June 29, 1715; and a further

CH. III.

Act (March 21, 1718) vested the forfeited estates in trustees, to be sold to Protestant purchasers for the public use and to provide a capital sum not exceeding £20,000 for the erection of schools in the Highlands. The operations of the trustees terminated on June 26, 1724; and on April 17, 1725, their final report was presented to Parliament. Of thirty-nine Scottish estates vested in them they had sold thirty-four, and had paid over to the Receiver-General £295,926. 14*s*. 9*d*., debited to the extent of £234,517. 13*s*. 7*d*. due to creditors of the estates, and leaving a meagre balance of £61,409. 1*s*. 2*d*. which was further diminished by the expenses of the trust and by grants to the widows and relatives of forfeited proprietors. Only £27,616. 10*s*. had been remitted to the Treasury; and the unsold estates were entrusted (13 Geo. I, cap. 28) to the Scottish Court of Exchequer to be sold and applied according to the directions of the Act of 1718.

Scott has immortalised an event of 1736—a year otherwise memorable in the history of the Scottish Establishment for the publication of their *Judicial Testimony* by Ebenezer Erskine and his associates, the beginning of a movement which developed leisurely towards Voluntaryism. On April 14, 1736, Andrew Wilson, a smuggler, was hanged at Edinburgh for robbing the Customs. His case roused sympathy; his sentence was excessive in relation to an offence which the general community held venial, if not praiseworthy; and at their public churching before the execution Wilson had aided the escape of his confederate in the crime. An attempt to rescue him at the gallows was anticipated, and precautions were taken. Seventy of the City Guard, under Captain John Porteous, were on duty round the scaffold; a detachment of the 23rd foot was stationed close by. The execution was not interrupted; but, after it, the mob stoned the guards and cut down Wilson's body. The guards replied with promiscuous shooting; six persons were killed and about twenty were wounded. Public indignation was intense; and, three months later (July 5), Porteous was arraigned on a charge of murder. Conflicting evidence was offered, both as to his having fired upon the crowd himself, and as to his having ordered his men to fire. He was found guilty, however, and his execution was appointed for the following September 8. Porteous petitioned the Queen, in the King's absence, and obtained a respite till October 20. It was suspected that respite was preliminary to pardon; and on the eve of the day originally appointed for his execution Porteous was dragged from the Tolbooth by a mob and was hanged on a dyer's pole in the Grass-market. The outrage roused lengthy debates in the Lords, who on May 13, 1737, passed a Bill to imprison and incapacitate the Provost of Edinburgh from municipal office, to remove the gates from the Nether Bow of the city, and to disband the City Guard. In the Commons the Bill was severely criticised and barely survived. In the form in which it received the royal assent (June 21, 1737), it imposed upon Edinburgh a fine of

£2000 in behalf of Porteous' widow (who accepted £1500 in full payment), and disabled the Provost from holding magisterial office. Scottish nationalism was roused by the measure; the Church was inflamed by a supplementary and futile Act (June 21, 1737), ordering the clergy on the first Sunday of each month for one year to summon the persons implicated in Porteous' death to surrender themselves.

When Walpole declared war upon Spain (October 19, 1739), and the death of the Emperor Charles VI, a year later, opened a wider warfare, the common interests of France and Great Britain had isolated the Pretender in Italy for more than twenty years. But the crisis created by the Emperor's death caused France and Great Britain to drift apart; while the fall of Walpole (February 2, 1742) and the death of Cardinal Fleury (January 29, 1743) surrendered both countries to warlike influences. So soon as war with Spain seemed imminent, and Walpole's position precarious, Jacobite intrigues were set on foot. Francis Sempill, the son of an officer in the French service and resident in Paris, and William Macgregor (or Drummond) of Balhaldie, were employed to solicit France. From July, 1739, when the storm clouds were lowering, Sempill acted as the secret channel of communication between James at Rome and the cautious Fleury. Balhaldie visited the latter in the spring of 1740 and returned to Scotland with vague and verbal promises. To watch the situation, an "Association" was formed, whose members were Lovat (angling for a dukedom), Lochiel, the Earl of Traquair, his brother John Stewart, Lord John Drummond, Sir James Campbell of Auchinbreck, and the titular Duke of Perth. Balhaldie again visited France with a signed assurance (March 13, 1741) of their readiness to resort to arms, and with a list of Scottish partisans whose names, according to John Murray of Broughton (acting since about August, 1740, as James' correspondent in Scotland), he used with uncommon freedom. Though Balhaldie asserted a French expedition to be imminent, Fleury was cautious and undecided. In December, 1742, Balhaldie announced a French descent for the following spring, and the Associators were directed to have everything in readiness. But France was not yet in earnest; and the intrigue lapsed with Fleury's death. The Cardinal had confided to Amelot, the Foreign Minister, that he was in communication with James. To Amelot, therefore, Sempill and Balhaldie turned.

Amelot satisfied himself that the Scottish Jacobites were ready to take arms. They on their part were sceptical as to Balhaldie's representation of France's attitude. In February, 1743, Murray of Broughton went over to Paris, where he received from Amelot only a vague assurance of Louis' support "as soon as the situation of his affairs would permit." Circumstances hastened that eventuality. Breaking his neutrality, George II placed himself at the head of a Pragmatic Army in the Netherlands, and fought the French at Dettingen (June 27, 1743).

CH. III.

Amelot thereupon awaited only an assurance of the party's vitality in England to commit himself, and sent over an agent to make enquiries. Taken in hand by Balhaldie and others whose object was to bluster France into action, Amelot's agent returned in October, 1743, with eulogistic reports of the strength of English Jacobitism. Amelot hesitated no longer. On November 13, 1743, he told Sempill that France was prepared to strike for James' restoration. Louis informed Philip of Spain to that effect on December 10, 1743; and, a week later (December 17), Balhaldie reached Rome with the news. James' correspondence (December 4, 1743) proves that he already discerned an opportunity for sending his elder son from Italy. With the connivance of Cardinal Aquaviva, Spanish Protector at the Vatican, and of de Tencin, representative there of the Knights of Malta, Charles left Rome secretly on January 9, 1744, landed at Antibes on the 23rd, and reached Paris by February 10. He carried a commission (December 23, 1743) to act as Regent in his father's behalf. The Prince's presence in France was likely to be, and actually proved, embarrassing. Amelot declared Charles' departure from Rome to have taken place without the knowledge or connivance of France. The Vatican likewise remained uninvolved. James, in fact, was anxious to have some personal share in any attempt on his behalf, but chiefly to seize the opportunity for affording Charles the chance of the action for which he longed and the experience which he needed.

On November 15, 1743, orders were given to prepare transports to convey the French expeditionary force. Early in December they concentrated at Dunkirk, 38 in number, to embark Maurice de Saxe and a force numbering 9274 infantry, 622 dragoons, 133 gunners, and six twelve-pounders. A fleet of 22 sail of the line under Count de Roquefeuil assembled at Brest. It was intended to launch the expedition early in January, 1744; but the English Jacobites advised the postponement of the attempt until February, by which time the members of the party in Parliament could withdraw to the provinces. The arrival of Charles in France made it necessary to strike before the British Ministry could avert a danger whose proportions were now revealed. On February 2 Saxe was instructed, on the arrival of an escorting convoy under Admiral de Barailh, to land in the Thames and occupy London. Roquefeuil set sail from Brest on the 6th, to clear the Channel. Barailh parted company with him off the Isle of Wight on the 28th, and reached Dunkirk by March 3. Meanwhile Admiral Norris and a powerful fleet appeared in the Downs; and the news from England suggested that Balhaldie and Sempill had exaggerated everything except the number of troops available to oppose a landing. On March 6, Argenson instructed Saxe that the expedition was indefinitely postponed, and the equinoctial gales enabled the French Government to retire plausibly from an enterprise already regretted. A violent tempest on the night of March 6–7 drove on shore eleven transports and damaged others. A second storm, on the 11th, inflicted further losses. On the same day Saxe was informed that the enterprise was abandoned. Jacobitism looked vainly to France until the clans under Prince Charles had proved the vitality of the Stewart cause.

Meanwhile Charles remained in France. Louis rejected Great Britain's demand for his expulsion; but the Prince received neither official courtesies nor the hospitality of Versailles. In September, 1744, Murray of Broughton visited him in Paris. He found him full of exaggerated ideas of the latent loyalty which would spring into life if he appeared among his father's subjects, and longing to be himself in action. If, as he had declared to Sempill (March 15, 1744), he withdrew without achieving something, his party would hold him inheritor of the ill-fortune of his father and grandfather, and would forsake a cause persistently unfortunate. He therefore informed Murray that, even though he were unattended, he would come to Scotland in the summer of 1745. Murray thereupon returned to Edinburgh, and founded the "Buck Club" to organise the party. Excepting the Duke of Perth, all concurred as to the rashness of the Prince's resolve. Early in 1745, a representation to that effect was entrusted to Traquair for Charles; though Lochiel, Glengarry, Clanranald, Keppoch, Glencoe, Stewart of Ardshiel, and other members of the Club declared their readiness in any circumstances to give proof of their loyalty. Traquair's despatch never reached the Prince, nor did Young Glengarry with a later message. Charles would certainly have been deterred by neither. The news of the battle of Fontenoy (May 11, 1745) conveyed to him an absurdly ill-informed impression of the precarious footing of his Hanoverian rival; and he forthwith despatched Sir Hector Maclean of Duart to Scotland to announce his imminent arrival. On such haphazard foundations was raised the last Jacobite effort. With Charles chiefly rests the blame for its rashness.

For months Charles had been preparing for his enterprise. He had procured nearly £4000, arms, and ammunition. Anthony Walsh, a Nantes shipowner, lent him the frigate *Du Teillay*, 18 guns. Walter Rutledge, an Irish merchant in Dunkirk, provided her escort, the war frigate *Elizabeth*, 60 guns. James was ignorant of Charles' project: the Prince's letter (June 12, 1745) announcing it was intentionally not despatched to Rome until Charles was on his way to Scotland. On July 2, Charles embarked on the *Du Teillay* at Bonne Anse, at the mouth of the Loire. He was accompanied by Tullibardine (titular Duke of Atholl), Sir John Macdonald (an officer in the French service), Æneas Macdonald (a Paris banker), Francis Strickland, who had been Charles' companion on his Italian tour eight years before, Colonel O'Sulivan, his former Governor (Sir Thomas Sheridan), and George Kelly—the "Seven Men of Moidart." On July 13, in the roads of Belle Isle, the *Du Teillay* was joined by the *Elizabeth*. The two vessels set sail for Scotland on the 15th. On the 20th, before rounding Land's End, the *Elizabeth* was engaged by H.M.S. *Lion,* and returned to Brest in a shattered condition. The *Du Teillay* proceeded alone, and on July 23 (August 3, N. S.), at Eriska in the Outer Hebrides, Charles first trod Scottish soil. On July 25 the *Du Teillay* crossed to the mainland and anchored in Loch-na-Nuagh. In spite of Charles' meagre following, Lochiel, Keppoch, Glencoe, Clanranald, Glengarry, and Stewart of Ardshiel agreed to bring out their clans. Like Marischal in 1719, Charles resolved to force a campaign by sacrificing the means of retreat. On August 8 the *Du Teillay* weighed anchor for France, bearing an appeal to Louis XV for assistance. Ten days later (August 19) Charles raised the standard in Glenfinnan at the head of Loch Shiel, and by the 27th commanded a little over 2000 men, of whom more than half were Macdonalds.

Meanwhile, the Government had proclaimed (August 1) a reward of £30,000 for Charles' capture; and Sir John Cope, commanding in Scotland, prepared to act vigorously with the unpromising material at his disposal. The military establishment in Scotland consisted of three-and-a-half battalions of infantry and two regiments of horse: all, save one regiment of foot (Guise's, the 6th), being either newly raised or inexperienced in active warfare. Leaving Gardiner's horse (13th Hussars) at Stirling and Hamilton's (14th Hussars) at Leith, Cope advanced from Stirling with twenty-five companies of foot (August 20). His objective was Fort Augustus; but, finding the clans in position to contest the Pass of Corryarrack, he changed his route and pushed on to Inverness (August 29). The south lay open to Charles, and thither he marched. On September 4 he entered Perth, and was joined by the Duke of Perth (Lord James Drummond) with 200 of his clan, and a contingent of Robertsons and Macgregors. More important was the accession of Lord George Murray, a man of military ability to whom, with Perth, Charles committed the command of his army. Lord George had taken part in the '15 and '19; but his recent relations with the Government, the sanity of his judgment, and his refusal to countenance enterprises patently futile, gained him the suspicion of Charles and of the Irish dare-alls whom Charles chiefly trusted. His inability to subordinate his judgment to the Prince's inexperience drew upon him, when the adventure was ended, ungenerous accusations of treachery. On September 11 the southward march was resumed, a proposal to meet Cope, hurrying to Aberdeen and his transports, having been wisely rejected. The Forth, so obstinately held by Argyll in 1715, was crossed at Frew without opposition on the 13th, Gardiner's regiment falling back on Falkirk and Coltbridge, where Hamilton's joined it. On the 16th Charles halted at Gray's Mill, two miles from Edinburgh, and summoned the city. The Provost, Archibald Stewart, was irresolute; the volunteers who had been enrolled disbanded in the crisis of danger; the dragoons again turned tail—

the "canter o' Colt-Brig." Cope's arrival from Aberdeen was imminent; the Provost therefore manœuvred for time. But in the small hours of the 17th the Camerons rushed the Nether Bow, and seized the guard-house and the gates. At noon Charles entered the city. James VIII was proclaimed forthwith, and Holyrood, after more than sixty years, again housed a royal Stewart.

Striking as was Charles' occupation of Edinburgh, his march through the Lowlands revealed how firm a hold the Union had secured. The squadrons which the Lowland gentry provided in 1715 were represented now by a single troop of 36 horse, the "Perthshire squadron." The Highland infantry still numbered few more than 2000, many of whom carried guns of dangerous antiquity, Lochaber axes, pitchforks, and scythe-blades mounted on poles. Edinburgh was requisitioned for arms, ammunition, tents, and shoes for naked feet. On September 18 Lord Nairne, with 700 Atholl and 300 of Menzies of Shian's men, joined Charles. The reinforcement was opportune; for, on the 17th, Cope disembarked at Dunbar and, on the 19th, advancing towards Edinburgh, encamped westward of Haddington. Charles, on the 20th, led his army from Duddingston. He expected to engage near Musselburgh; but, learning that Cope was at Tranent, he ascended Carberry Hill, associated now for a third time with the fortunes of the Stewarts. Cope, a little over 2000 strong, lay on the sea-ward plain below, a broad ditch intervening. The night passed, with the two armies half-a-mile apart. Before sunrise on the 21st, the Highlanders descended and hurled themselves on Cope's left flank, almost before he had time to re-form. In fifteen minutes the battle was over: six guns and Cope's military chest were the prize of the victors.

For a month after his victory Charles remained inactive at Edinburgh. The protest against the Union in his father's proclamation had roused little response. But Charles, like his father, viewed Scotland as the stepping-stone to an English restoration, and France was relied on as accessory. On August 11, 1745, James wrote to Louis XV to place his younger son Henry at the disposal of France. A fortnight later Henry (August 29) left Rome for France. A scheme of Maurepas (October 13) to convey him with 10,000 French troops to England came to nothing; but on October 14 the Marquis d'Eguilles arrived at Edinburgh with instructions (September 24, 1745) as Louis' secret ambassador to Charles. Money, arms, and six four-pounders also arrived, and on October 24 Argenson signed the secret Treaty of Fontainebleau, binding Louis to render Charles assistance. Encouraged by these marks of French interest, Charles resolved to rouse his English adherents. His proposal to advance upon Newcastle was strongly opposed by Lord George and others, who were incredulous of the effect which Charles anticipated from his appearance in England. They objected that, if his adherents there were in earnest, they ought not to need the encouragement of his presence;

while, if a French landing in England was imminent, as was asserted, it was sounder strategy to draw off English troops to Scotland. As a compromise Lord George proposed an advance into Cumberland, where the ground was more suitable for the Highlanders, and Charles reluctantly agreed.

On October 31 Charles marched from Edinburgh upon an enterprise bravely executed, but as futile in result as Mackintosh's a generation earlier. Since Cope's defeat, the Prince had received reinforcements. Mackinnons, Macphersons, Ogilvies, Gordons, and Grants of Glenmoriston swelled his infantry; Elcho, Balmerinoch, Pitsligo, Kilmarnock, and Murray of Broughton commanded five troops of horse. Charles marched to the border with 5000 foot, 500 horse, and 13 guns. On November 8 he crossed the Esk, his force lessened by about 1000 through desertion. On the 15th, Carlisle and its castle capitulated after a two days' siege; Wade, who marched from Newcastle on the 16th, got no further than Hexham, the roads being impassable. Cope's successor, Lieutenant-General Handasyde, had already reached Edinburgh (November 14), with two regiments of foot and Hamilton's and Gardiner's dragoons. In the south, Sir John Ligonier was massing an army about Lichfield, of which the Duke of Cumberland took command later (November 27). In these circumstances Charles' council agreed (November 18) to advance into Lancashire, and rouse the west of England before Cumberland and Wade could unite. At Preston, where (November 26) the Prince received his first enthusiastic welcome in England, the Highlanders were marched across the Ribble to dispel the sombre memory of that stream as the terminus of earlier invasions in 1648 and 1715. Manchester (November 29) surpassed Preston in the vigour of its welcome, and about 200 recruits were formed into the Manchester Regiment under Francis Townley. Charles was elated: " his conversation that night at table was, in what manner he should enter London, on horseback or afoot, and in what dress "—he had marched from Scotland on foot, and in the Highland habit. His officers did not share his elation, and retreat was already discussed among them. It was resolved, however, to march to Derby, so as to avert any complaint that England had not been encouraged to rise or France to send troops. Advancing on December 1, Charles' cavalry was speedily in touch with the outposts of Cumberland, whose army, over 10,000 strong, rested on Newcastle-under-Lyne, Stafford, Lichfield, and Coventry. Wade, who had set out from Newcastle on November 24, was advancing through Yorkshire; a third army was forming on Finchley Common. On December 4 Charles entered Derby. On the next morning, Lord George and other officers waited upon him with a reasoned refusal to advance further. Three armies were in the field against them; they had entered England to encourage the English to rise, and to support a French landing; but the country had not risen, and had given no encouragement

to suppose it would do so, while a French landing seemed equally remote.
Mindful of the disasters which had attended similar endeavours in 1648
and 1715, they refused to force upon England a king whom she had
given no sign of desiring. Charles protested angrily, though it is
patent that a further advance must ultimately have proved futile. On
December 6 the retreat began. Cumberland's cavalry and Wade's horse
under Oglethorpe followed in close pursuit. At Lancaster (December 13)
a proposal to give battle to Cumberland was abandoned; and, after
fighting a rearguard action on the 18th at Clifton, near Penrith, the
whole army on the 20th crossed the Esk into Scotland. Ten days later
(December 30), Cumberland compelled the surrender of the Manchester
regiment which Charles had senselessly left behind in Carlisle, and the
winter campaign ended.

From December 27, 1745, to January 3, 1746, Charles and his army
rested at Glasgow after eight weeks of almost continuous marching.
During his absence the position in Scotland had improved in his favour.
On November 22, 1745, Lord John Drummond had arrived from France
with 700 of the Royal Scots and Irish regiments, and six heavy field-guns.
His arrival put out of action the Dutch auxiliaries, who before their
arrival in England were on parole not to fight against French colours.
In the north, Lord Lewis Gordon had raised a force of 800 Gordons,
Farquharsons, and Moir of Stonywood's men, and at Inverurie repulsed
(December 23) Loudoun's attempt to recover Aberdeenshire. The
Frasers had at length come out, and, after an unsuccessful attempt upon
Fort Augustus (December 3), marched to Perth, where, before the end
of the year, detachments of Mackintoshes and other clans were assembled,
to the number of 2400. Charles had at his disposal a total force of
8000 men and 19 guns.

While Cumberland was in England to confront the threatened
French landing, and Hawley, superseding Handasyde, was bringing up
Wade's command from Newcastle, Charles evacuated Glasgow (January 3,
1746). Stirling surrendered on the 7th, and trenches were opened
(January 16) before the castle. Hawley had already advanced from
Edinburgh and on the 14th was at Linlithgow. Charles proposed to
engage him near Bannockburn; but, on the 17th, Hawley not advancing,
the clans surprised him at Falkirk, and after an indiscriminate engagement reminiscent of Sheriffmuir, put him to flight with the loss of his
camp and seven guns. Jacobitism had won its last victory. Charles
returned to the siege of Stirling Castle, and, a week later, Cumberland
took over and reinforced Hawley's demoralised army at Edinburgh.
Charles was anxious to meet him and confident of the issue; but Lord
George and the principal chiefs advised a retreat. They alleged
(January 29) the desertion of a " vast number" since the recent battle,
and urged withdrawal to the Highlands, whence in the spring the clans
would draw together in greater strength. Other motives inspired their

communication. Possessed of extraordinary driving power, and making no
demand upon his men that he would not obey himself, Charles inherited
the rashness of his grandfather and the obstinacy of Charles I. To the
Stewart belief in inspired ability he added a masterful self-reliance which
encouraged courtiers and looked askance on advisers. After his disappointment at Derby he declared his intention to act without consulting
his council, and fulfilled his threat till the eve of Culloden. The Scots
also resented the Prince's reliance on his companions from France, who
had little at stake in the country which provided them with adventure,
rather than on the men who gave him the army he commanded. Nor
did the abrupt transition from the dull stagnation of Italy to the keen
activity of high adventure tend to encourage the qualities of tact and
judgment in which he was by nature lacking.

On February 1 the army crossed the Forth in confusion, and with
the sacrifice of heavy guns and ammunition. Charles and the clans
retreated along Wade's road to Inverness; Lord George with the horse
and the French auxiliaries followed the coast to Aberdeen. The Prince's
immediate object was to dissipate Loudoun's force in the north, reduce
the Government's forts in the Highlands, and secure the coast route
along which Cumberland would probably advance. After an ineffectual
attempt to surprise Charles at Moy Hall (February 16), Loudoun
abandoned Inverness and withdrew into Sutherlandshire. Fort George
surrendered on February 20, and Fort Augustus about March 1. Fort
William offered a prolonged resistance, and the siege was raised on April 3.
Since it was important to keep open a route to the Lowlands, Lord
George appeared (March 17) before Blair Castle, into which Cumberland
had put a garrison. Lord Crawford and the Hessians moved to its
relief. Failing to entice them into the Pass of Killiecrankie, Lord
George abandoned his investment of Blair on April 2 and rejoined the
Prince. Meanwhile, Cumberland had been heavily reinforced. On
February 8, 500 Hessian foot arrived at Leith to replace the Dutch.
Settling them at Perth to secure the south against Charles' possible
return by Wade's road, Cumberland advanced along the coast and on
April 11 united his columns at Cullen—15 battalions of foot, 3 regiments of horse, and Highland auxiliaries, in all 8811 strong. Charles
awaited him at Culloden, with a shrunken force of 6700 foot and 240
horse. A mismanaged attempt to surprise Cumberland at Nairn during
the night of the 15th brought the army back to Culloden tired and
famished. Not more than about 5000 were present in the ranks when
Cumberland a few hours later (April 16) opened the engagement with
his artillery. Some of the clans charged heroically, but in vain, against
regiments schooled by the experience of Cope's and Hawley's disasters.
No measures had been concerted for a rendezvous in case of defeat, and
the Prince thought only upon escape. After five months of wandering,
hardship borne heroically, and experience of loyal devotion, the French

frigate *L'Heureux* bore him on September 20, 1746, from Loch-na-Nuagh to France, whence the Treaty of Aix-la-Chapelle (1748) expelled him. His later disreputable life, and his brother's acceptance of a Cardinal's hat (July 3, 1747), extinguished Jacobitism as a national force. In February, 1800, the Cardinal received a pension from George III; and George IV contributed to Canova's monument in St Peter's to the joint memory of James and his two sons, of whom the Cardinal, the younger, died on July 13, 1807.

The Jacobite assault upon the Union and Protestant settlement invited severe reprisals. On May 24, 1746, Cumberland established himself at Fort Augustus; the soldiery swept the glens of the disaffected clans; the Campbells were let loose upon Appin, Loudoun's Highland companies upon Badenoch and Lochaber; those found with arms were summarily shot; houses whose inmates had absconded were burnt; their cattle were raided. After Cumberland vacated (July 18) his command the storm of vengeance slackened. Of those indicted at Carlisle, York, and Southwark for rebellion, 73 paid the death penalty. Kilmarnock, Balmerinoch, Cromarty (August 1, 1746) and Lovat (March 19, 1747) were found guilty of treason by their peers, and, excepting Cromarty, were executed. An Act of Attainder was passed (June 4, 1746) against Lords Kellie, Strathallan, Pitsligo, and forty others. A year later (June 17, 1747), the estates of those attainted were forfeited to the Crown; their revenues to be applied to "civilising" the Highlands and Islands. Friction such as that which had arisen with the trustees of the Act of 1718 was avoided by vesting the administration of the forfeited properties solely in the Scottish Court of Exchequer. The rental of the 46 forfeited estates amounted to £16,285. 17s. 7d., the personality to £19,345. 14s. 4d. But creditors advanced claims amounting to £277,127. 4s. 8d., and on February 28, 1752, the Exchequer reported that the estates had yielded nothing to the Treasury. The Act, in fact, was leniently interpreted, and permanently affected few families; though the Lovat, Cromarty, Barrisdale, and Lord John Drummond's estates were annexed to the Crown (March 26, 1752).

The Scottish episcopalians had refrained from overt expressions of Jacobite sympathy such as had come from them in 1715: but they remained non-juring. James' patronage of their hierarchy further prejudiced them; and many of their meeting-houses had been burnt during Cumberland's campaign. On August 12, 1746, the royal assent was given to an Act which empowered the local authorities to close meeting-houses attended by five or more persons whose minister had failed to take the oaths by September 1, 1746; disfranchised and disqualified for a seat in Parliament peers and commoners who had attended an unlicensed meeting-house more than once within the year preceding an election; and condemned unlicensed officiating ministers to six months' imprisonment for the first, and transportation for life for a second offence. The Scottish episcopate being deeply suspect, ordinations by an English or Irish Bishop were alone recognised. By a later Act (May 13, 1748) ministers who had been ordained by a Scottish Bishop and had qualified before September 1, 1746, were expressly debarred (as from September 29, 1748) from a continuation of their licenses. The deaths of James (January 1, 1766) and of Charles (January 31, 1788) enabled episcopacy to purge itself of Jacobitism: but it was not even partially relieved from the penal laws pressing upon it until the Act of June 15, 1792.

In dress, tongue, and polity the Highlands stood apart—the "barbarous part of the island, hitherto a noxious load upon the whole," as a Scotsman described them in 1747. The Union of 1707 represented a compact between two races whose political institutions, differing in particulars, were traceable to a common origin. But, if the Union was to cover both kingdoms, the Highlands needed to be purged of characteristics which made one half of Scotland foreign to the other. A policy of harmonisation was therefore attempted. The first of the legislative measures to this end was a Disarming Act (August 12, 1746), that of 1725 having expired. While reenacting the procedure whereby to procure surrender of arms, the Act differed from its predecessor in two particulars. It offered a fine of £15 sterling alternative to military service in America for those convicted of bearing arms—a concession likely to relieve few. The second point of difference concerned all. Under penalty of imprisonment for six months for the first, and transportation for seven years for a second offence, it was forbidden from August 1, 1747, to man or boy in Scotland (the King's forces excepted) to wear "the plaid, philebeg or little kilt, trowse, shoulder-belts, tartan or party-coloured plaid or stuff for great-coats or for upper coats." The period of grace proved inadequate and was extended (landowners and their sons excepted) to August 1, 1748 (20 Geo. II, cap. 51), and eventually to December 25, 1748, for the plaid and kilt, and to August 1, 1749, for the other proscribed habiliments, under penalty of enforced enlistment (21 Geo. II, cap. 34).

More deep-reaching in purpose were legislative measures which removed survivals of feudalism long since discarded in England, where jurisdictions dangerously interfering between the Crown and its subjects had been abolished. In Scotland the provincial administration of justice in the Lowlands was still the heritable privilege of individuals, and its exercise a source of emolument. In the Highlands tenure "in ward" permitted the chiefs to require the military service of their tenants, and prevailed in spite of the license granted by the Disarming Act of 1716 to commute the claim for money. Two Bills were framed for the abolition of these survivals of medievalism; and, on June 17, 1747, both received the royal assent. The first abolished (from March 25, 1748) all heritable offices of justiciary, regalities, baillieships, constabularies (the High Constable of Scotland excepted), sheriffships, stewartries, and vested them in the Crown. The Courts of Barony were restricted to jurisdiction in minor charges of assault involving a maximum penalty of £1 sterling or one month's imprisonment, and to civil causes where the debt or damages at issue (the recovery of rent excepted) did not exceed £2 sterling. Compensation was offered to the owners and officials of the forfeited jurisdictions, who were directed to enter their claims in the Court of Session before November 11, 1747. Claims were recorded by 161 claimants in respect of 250 heritable or life jurisdictions and 15 dependent clerkships. Of the former offices 117, and of the latter 9, were allowed and were commuted for £152,037. 12s. 2d., considerably less than one-third of the total amount (£583,090. 16s. 8d.) demanded. The second Act abolished tenure "in ward" from March 25, 1748. Tenures "in ward" of the Crown were converted into tenures "in blanch," and of superiors below the Crown into tenures "in feu," the amount of the feu-duty or rent being left to agreement according to a rule to be laid down by the Court of Session.

The legislation of 1747, concluding a long series of enactments "for rendering the Union of the two Kingdoms more complete," was accompanied by an Act of Pardon (June 17, 1747) for offences committed before June 15, 1747. From its operation exiles who on that date were in the service of the Pretender, France, or Spain; estates forfeited and persons attainted before June 15, 1747; and those concerned in the late rebellion and in the intrigues which (since July 1, 1742) had prepared the way for it, were excepted. The Macgregor clan and 87 persons were expressly barred. Ample opportunity remained for further vengeance; but the law claimed only one more victim, Archibald Cameron, implicated in the hare-brained Elibank Plot, who was executed on June 7, 1753, under the Attainder of 1746. With the Elibank Plot, serious only by reason of Frederick the Great's suspected connivance, Jacobitism as an active force expired. It had failed as an effective national movement in protest against the Union. It had failed as a weapon in the hand of European Powers, who, employing it for their own ends, had the opportunity to impede Great Britain in the attainment of her own. Freed from the incubus of civil commotion, Scotland realised the material prosperity which had tempted her adherence to the Union. England, on her part, benefited not merely by the conversion of a suspicious neighbour, but obtained a valuable partner in the development of Greater Britain, the most signal creation of the century in which the permanence of Great Britain was for a time in jeopardy.

CHAPTER IV.

THE BOURBON GOVERNMENTS IN FRANCE AND SPAIN. I.
(1714–26.)

ABSOLUTE to the end as Louis XIV had been, a single day sufficed to annul the testamentary provisions of the dead hand. The problem of the Regency during his great-grandson's minority was the main pre-occupation of the old King's last year. He loved his bastard, the Duke of Maine, and disliked the character of his nephew, the Duke of Orleans; but he was too scrupulous wholly to ignore the claim of the latter. The Regency was assigned to Orleans, tied down by a cooptative Council, which controlled patronage; to Maine was confided the guardianship of the child-King, and the command of the household troops. This, hoped Louis, would secure his great-grandson's safety, his son's prestige, and the satisfaction of his nephew's reasonable expectations.

On September 1, 1715, the King died; by the evening of September 2 the Regent was as powerful as he cared to be. The *coup d'état*, sudden as it seemed, had been sedulously prepared. Orleans had long lived in dissipation and disgrace. He was suspected of clearing the path to ultimate succession by poisoning all who stood before him; his un-questionable vices debarred him from decent society. Such energy as his mistresses and champagne suppers left him he wasted on what were regarded as frivolous pursuits—painting, music, carving, and chemistry. Yet in Italy and Spain he had shown marked ability both as strategist and administrator; his liberality of thought and freedom from prejudice well suited a new age. The short stout figure, the bad eyesight, the contrast of black hair and a complexion fiery from excess, were redeemed by a pleasant, open face, an easy dignity, an irresistible gaiety. He never lost his rapid insight into men, especially into their weaknesses. The more he promised, the readier were his petitioners to believe.

Orleans cared little for power, and would have gladly been left alone. But disgraced men are often sensitive of their honour, and at this one crisis he displayed the courage, the resource, the reserve of power which intelligent idlers take long to lose—and the Regent was only forty-two. Thus, then, he had wormed the dead King's testament out of Chancellor

Voisin, had bought the colonels of the household troops by cash, the political and military magnates by promises of office, the princes of the blood by the humiliation of the bastards, the higher nobility by expectations of an oligarchical constitution, the *Parlement* by hopes of restored prerogatives. He could rally round him persecuted Jansenists and Quietists, all those who writhed under the austerity of the Maintenon repression, all who wished France rid of Jesuits.

The *Parlement* was summoned for the morrow of the King's death. In direct contravention of the testament, Orleans appeared unaccompanied by Louis XV. His speech consisted of an imaginative embroidery on his uncle's last wishes, and an attractive programme. He claimed the right to command the royal guards, to nominate or dismiss members of the Council of Regency, to monopolise royal patronage. Harmony was only marred by an altercation with the Duke of Maine, and even this turned to the Regent's advantage, for Maine refused the guardianship if deprived of the command of the household. The Spanish ambassador, Cellamare, had instructions to create a party and present a protest, claiming the Regency for his master. The party was unformed, and the protest remained unread. Ten days later the proceedings were confirmed in a *lit de justice*, in the presence of the grave and feeble child-King of four, who raised and replaced his cap as he was told. The Regent's success was popular in Paris. The people felt the load of discipline removed, and believed that the burden of taxation would be lightened. They admired the sudden courage, the unexpected ability, of the long calumniated debauchee. There was, perhaps, a generous reaction in his favour. He had, writes Lemontey, the merit of having tired out the satirist and the scandal-monger.

The Regent's triumph necessarily affected European politics, and especially the relations of France and Spain. But for the Treaty of Utrecht, Philip V came before Orleans, as being Louis XIV's direct descendant. He had indeed most solemnly renounced his claims to the French Crown, but in his supersensitive conscience self-interest disguised itself as duty, whose call could loose the binding power of oaths. Orleans had fought bravely for him in Italy and Spain; but he was too popular and independent to please the inept, shrinking King, and had been recalled to France. Stories of plots to replace and even to poison Philip created an atmosphere of horror and suspicion. Everywhere Orleans seemed to stand just before or behind him. He blocked the way to the French throne, and trod upon his heels in the succession to the Spanish. Political grievances were aggravated by the personal contrast between the sociable, liberal Orleans, lax in morals and cynical about religion, and the proud, morbid Philip, obsessed by the dignity of kingship, absorbed in marital duties and pietistic practices. Before Louis XIV's death the rivals had been formally reconciled, and Orleans bore no malice; but Philip brooded on his wrongs, and the clash became inevitable.

CH. IV.

Philip V had now been for nine months married to his second wife, Elisabeth Farnese of Parma. This girl, undistinguished by beauty, education, or experience, had on her entry into Spain given proof of the masterful temper, which for thirty years kept Europe in unrest. Madame des Ursins had been sent by Louis XIV as *Camarera Mayor* to the late Queen. Since then, save for a temporary recall, she had ruled King, Queen and Government. Philip's new bride had been her choice. Nevertheless, on the very stairs of the wayside inn where she first met Madame des Ursins, Elisabeth picked a quarrel, and despatched her shivering over the snowy mountains to the frontier. By next morning Philip was his wife's slave for life. This strange consort had been suggested on the day of the late Queen's funeral by the Parmesan agent Giulio Alberoni, son of a gardener at Piacenza. He, too, had urged her to rid herself of a rival influence, and thus he naturally became the new Queen's confidential adviser. While Alberoni controlled the ante-chamber, Elisabeth's nurse, Laura Pescatori, commanded the back-stairs. There was already a powerful Italian party composed of Philip's adherents from the lost provinces, and this now gained consistency.

The aim of the Italo-Spanish Government was the undoing of the Treaty of Utrecht. The immediate object was to secure for Elisabeth the successions to Parma and Piacenza, at present occupied by her uncle and stepfather, Francesco Farnese, and to Tuscany by virtue of her descent from the Medici, who in the male line seemed drawing towards extinction. A substantial wedge would thus be thrust in between the Austrian possessions in northern and southern Italy. The motive was strongly personal. It seemed probable either that Philip would die early, or that the Spanish Court would be a nursery of Princes. The fate of a Queen Dowager was a suttee of impecunious ennui, while it was not the custom, as in France, to parcel out royal domain among younger sons. Italy therefore must provide a retreat for Elisabeth and portions for her children. Such a project dovetailed into Alberoni's dearest interests—his typical Italian love for his own little State, and his passion for Italian liberation from the Austrian. The Duke of Parma was peculiarly exposed to Imperial buffetings; and, even before Elisabeth's marriage, was the only Italian Power prepared to run some risk for national independence.

Such then was the situation when Orleans became Regent. Being himself the creation of the Treaty of Utrecht, he would naturally defend its provisions, while Philip must sooner or later adopt the offensive, in pursuance of either his own aims or his Queen's. Unfortunately these were incompatible. If he could frankly have accepted the territorial rearrangement, he might more safely have intervened in France, or, if he had honestly abandoned his French claims, he might have won support from France in Italy. Insistence on both aims involved twofold infraction of the treaties. For success in Italy the favour or neutrality of the Western Powers was essential. Alberoni hoped to have secured

England by the favourable commercial treaty of December, 1715.   He had no belief in the Pretender's success: his intention was to go behind the rival dynasties, and propitiate the nation and the Parliament.   But George I, tied tightly by his German interests to the Emperor, made in June, 1716, a defensive alliance with Charles VI.

The Regent and Alberoni had been well disposed towards each other, for the latter had contributed to the outward reconciliation with Philip V. In alarm at the Anglo-Austrian treaty Orleans turned definitely towards Spain.   Here he took his first false step by identifying the objects of the Italian party with Philip's French ambitions.   He instructed his envoy, Louville, to divide and overthrow this party.   Alberoni had recently contrived the dismissal of its ostensible chief, Cardinal Giudice, and now controlled the Government.   Divining Louville's instructions, he refused him a royal audience.   In this he, in turn, overstepped the mark, for Orleans, flouted by Spain, was thrown back on England.

Genuine friendship between France and England was difficult indeed. The Whig Government was traditionally anti-French, while all French sympathies were with the Stewarts.   Orleans himself had no prejudices against the Protestant establishment, no sympathy with the decorous dulness of the Pretender's Court.   The aristocratic constitutionalism of Hanoverian England attracted him ; his disgrace had given him distaste for the war, perhaps even a fellow-feeling for the enemy.   The Orleanist and Hanoverian dynasties were secured by the selfsame treaty.   But the Regent was easily led, and his Council was anti-English and pro-Stewart. Alliance even with the Emperor would have been less unpopular, and Philip V's hostility both to Orleans and Charles VI gave hopes of this, until they were damped by demands for Strassburg and Alsace.

The isolation of France gave the Regent's humblest but cleverest adviser, his old tutor Dubois, his opportunity.   Dubois supplied backbone for his master's flexible volitions, and led him to the Triple Alliance of January, 1717, elsewhere explained.   Doubt remained whether the Triple would become a Quadruple Alliance by inclusion of the Emperor or Philip V, with both of whom England, which held the key of the situation, had recently made treaties.   A general pacification was impossible, while sanguine Neapolitan exiles predominated at Madrid, and Catalan refugees had influence at Vienna.

Alberoni, meanwhile, was feverishly reforming Spain.   He pared away ineffective elements in the services, ships useless in the fighting line, superfluous officers of rank.   The bureaucracy was reduced, waste and corruption in financial departments severely controlled.   Along the Spanish sea-board fortresses, arsenals, and shipbuilding yards were rising. Above all Alberoni relied on colonial revival, and was untiring in improving communications, and regularising trade.   That Spain might not have only a market but products to sell therein, and so retain the precious metals perpetually drained abroad, he stimulated native manufactures.

CH. IV.

The improvements ascribed to him might seem exaggerations but for Stanhope's evidence that no power could resist Spain after a few years more of such advance. These few years were not vouchsafed. Alberoni had prayed for five, wherein to organise resources and equip armaments; he had at most two before his hand was forced.

Aggressive as Spain now became, it was not without provocation. No sooner had Sicily been granted to Savoy than the Emperor intrigued for its possession. His scheme was in flagrant contradiction to the treaties. It was one thing that Sicily should be held by a weak Power with little or no marine, another that it should serve the Emperor's intelligent naval and commercial projects, and directly menace Spain's Mediterranean coast line. To Spain, moreover, had been conceded the reversion to Sicily in default of the House of Savoy. She was therefore not unreasonable in forestalling a policy unjust to herself and destructive of recent treaties. The Austro-Turkish War expedited the opening of hostilities. It would be perilous to wait till Austria's victories set her arms free for Italy. Alberoni's promise to the Pope of a squadron to cooperate with Venice against the infidel provided a pretext for mobilisation, while rupture was provoked by the insolent arrest of Cardinal Molinés, the new Inquisitor-General, by Austrian officials in Lombardy. Alberoni privately threw the blame on the stupid octogenarian Cardinal. He was scarcely ready for war, and was awaiting a Cardinal's hat, his reward for reopening friendly relations with the Papacy which his French predecessors had suspended. The Inquisitor's arrest, however, acted powerfully upon Philip's pugnacity, and Alberoni, securing his hat, had no sufficient motive for postponement.

Alberoni, by seizing Sardinia, deprived Charles VI of the equivalent which was to be granted to Victor Amadeus for Sicily. It was, moreover, a convenient half-way house to the Spanish fortress of Porto Longone in Elba, and a stepping-stone for Tuscany. This easy success and the fluttering anxiety of the Western Powers encouraged the bolder move on Sicily. Both islands were old possessions of Aragon, older than the union with Castile or the conquest of Granada or Navarre, of Naples or Milan. Their character was more Spanish than Italian, and Spanish rule was infinitely less unpopular than Austrian or Savoyard. It was argued that, as they were not parts of Italy, their occupation was no infringement of treaties. To the last moment the Powers doubted whether Spain was acting as Victor Amadeus' ally or enemy: he was treating both at Vienna and Madrid.

The landing of Spanish troops near Palermo on July 1, 1718, settled the conclusion of the Quadruple Alliance. Savoy acceded to it, and Spain was completely isolated. Alberoni's hopes had been placed on France and Holland, and, indeed, Dubois had with the utmost difficulty kept Orleans true to England. On the night of August 10–11 an English squadron, acting as the Emperor's auxiliary, destroyed the Spanish fleet, laden with troops and unprepared for action, off Cape Passaro. Alberoni was now reduced to his more fanciful expedients, to risings of provincial malcontents and disaffected legitimists against the Regent, attacks on Charles VI by the Tsar and Prussia, and a landing in England by the King of Sweden, combined with an expedition from Spain. But Alberoni's tools all broke in his hand. Charles XII was killed; the Tsar remained inactive; the Turks were forced to the Peace of Passarowitz. The dramatic disclosure of the Duchess of Maine's intrigues with the Spanish envoy Cellamare, who was totally incredulous as to their utility, gave Orleans the much needed pretext for declaring war in January, 1719. England had already done so in December.

French armies invaded Spain from the west and the east of the Pyrenees, and in the disaffected north-western provinces made rapid progress. The considerable expedition which sailed for England under Ormond was wrecked off Finisterre. The new arsenals at Vigo and Ferrol were destroyed by English ships aided by French soldiers. Alberoni clutched, as a last straw, at the preparations for a Breton revolt. But the auxiliary Spanish squadron was blockaded by the English in Corunna; and, when it reached Santander in November instead of September the Admiral refused to sail. The best Spanish troops, locked up in Sicily without hope of reinforcement, won a brilliant victory over the Austrians at Franca Villa, but in October held little more than Palermo. Peace was essential, and Alberoni knew it. The combination against Spain was turning into a conspiracy against himself, in which France and England, the King and Queen of Spain, and even the Duke of Parma, all took a part. On December 15, 1719, Philip condemned him to immediate banishment. He took refuge in Genoese territory at Sestri Levante, and afterwards lay hid in Austrian Lombardy; whence, on Clement XI's death, he travelled in disguise to Rome to take part in the Conclave.

Alberoni was the scapegoat who bore with him the sins of all whom he had served, or whom he had opposed. But memory is an optimist, and whenever the Spanish Court was in difficulty there were schemes for his recall. Elisabeth confessed as late as 1743 that he was a great minister, and that she might have pardoned him but for the King's dislike. As a diplomatist Alberoni was over-subtle and over-sanguine, not sufficiently patient and too hot-tempered. He lacked the sense of the relative possibilities which opportunities offered. But for Italy he had genuine patriotism, and for Spain a sense of duty. If he was an adventurer, self-interest was not his strongest motive. His chief personal aim was the cardinalate, because this alone gave him adequate security, and the status which enabled him to control the government of a foreign country. But it was also of value for Spanish and Parmesan interests. Without any administrative training he believed in his own power of revival and reform. His results were considerable, nor did they quite die with him. He had given a stimulus to Spanish-American trade, and

CH. IV.

prestige to Spanish arms, in spite of their reverses. From the first he had realised the value of Patiño, who was to be the greatest Spanish minister of the century. The story of the Triple and Quadruple Alliances is that of a duel between the sons of a French chemist and an Italian gardener, between scientific opportunism and constructive imagination. Dubois won; but, within Alberoni's life-time or soon after, the greater part of his Italian projects found fulfilment.

The pretensions of Philip V delayed his accession to the Quadruple Alliance until January 26, 1720. Sardinia was transferred to Victor Amadeus, and Sicily to Charles VI. Philip renewed his renunciation of the French Crown, and recognised the Emperor's claim to the Italian provinces which he now occupied. Charles VI, less honest, continued to thwart the succession of a Spanish prince to Tuscany and Parma. Relations between Spain and France grew closer, and on March 27, 1721, a formal alliance was concluded, which England joined in June. France had ceded all places captured in the war, including Pensacola, to which much importance was assigned. George I, not to be behindhand in generosity, wrote that he would take the first opportunity of surrendering Gibraltar. England and France resolved to press in concert the claims of Spain at the coming Congress of Cambray.

Disquietude was still caused by rumours that Philip V was negotiating the marriage of the Infants with Austrian Archduchesses, an expedient suggested by Alberoni. He gave the lie to these reports by suddenly offering the Infanta's hand to Louis XV, and by the yet more surprising proposal that his own heir should marry the Regent's daughter, Mademoiselle de Montpensier. The princesses were exchanged on January 9, 1722. A year later Mademoiselle de Beaujolais followed her sister to Spain as *fiancée* of Elisabeth's eldest son Don Carlos. Philip's motives are to be found in his intended abdication. He wished to leave his children securely guarded by French protection. The Angevin claims to the French succession would at least be realised in his daughter's line. Should Louis XV die before a son was born, the Infanta might be strong enough to overthrow the Orleanist succession in her father's or her brother's favour. The marriage of the Regent's daughter with Don Carlos would secure French support for Elisabeth's Italian schemes. For Orleans the prospects were yet more brilliant. Don Luis and his father were, said Schaub, as like as two drops of water, both in body and mind, so that the prince would let himself be governed by his wife, who would prevent him from disputing the Orleanist claims to the French throne. The Regent's influence would prevail in Spain, while in France the Opposition would receive its *coup de grâce*.

Orleans could now stand without Hanoverian support. An Orleanist Family Compact might even have forestalled those of the later Bourbons. England feared this French predominance at Madrid, and her ambassador, Colonel Stanhope, watched the Pretender's partisans. The policy of Dubois seemed to be veering towards the Vatican. Death came to England's aid. Dubois died in August, 1723. When, in December, the Regent was struck down, the family alliance was imperilled. It is said that Philip showed unseemly pleasure at the death of his old rival and new connexion. He could never forget his own forsworn claims to France or his ridiculous fears of poison.

The hopes of reform which Orleans had inspired were not fulfilled. With all a drunkard's optimism, he probably himself mistook a programme of promises for a scheme of government. Though he worked laboriously to redeem his pledges, excess had weakened the power of continuous will and consecutive thought. Even the art of pleasing needs perpetual pains. Brave enough for momentary action, Orleans had not the courage of his convictions, nor always the convictions. Yet failure was mainly due to his heritage of national debt. But for this his honesty of intention, his liberal instincts, and quickness of vision might have carried him creditably through his short lease of power. His first measures were auspicious. The establishment of the young King in the Tuileries propitiated the capital. Taxes were lowered, and the army reduced by 25,000 men, who were settled on uncultivated lands. The *Parlement* recovered its ancient right of remonstrance. Immensely popular was the release of persecuted Jansenists from the Bastille; yet Orleans would not curry favour by counter-persecution of the Jesuits.

The Council of Regency included almost all those whom Louis XIV had nominated. Orleans, perhaps imprudently, gratified the faithful Saint-Simon's darling wish by adopting the late Duke of Burgundy's scheme for departmental Councils, to lessen governmental centralisation, and provide scope for the more ambitious or industrious nobility. Louis XIV had condemned the project as incompatible with the French character. It was, indeed, exotic, imported from Spain at the moment when she had substituted the French absolutist plan for this very system, whereby the nobles had dominated the bureaucracy. After all, the idea had its merits. Men were looking in all directions for relief from the strain of absolutism. An elaborate representation of the Parisian and provincial law Courts had been suggested, and also a revival of the Estates General. Nobody, however, believed in the utility of Estates General, and few besides lawyers admired the *Parlements*. France was in no danger of reverting to feudalism, and it might be worth while to raise the nobility from the worthlessness to which absolutism had condemned it, by opening a career in the national Councils.

Seven departmental Councils were created, finding a point of contact in the Council of Regency, where their presidents had a deliberative voice. Saint-Simon wished membership to be confined to the greater nobles, but Orleans must find place for the more intelligent of his *roués*, while he knew that between ignorance and indolence, pride and pleasure, little practical work would be accomplished without leaven from the industrious and experienced bureaucracy. It was a clumsy expedient, intended mainly to win temporary support. Yet, perhaps, the fault of failure lay neither with Saint-Simon, nor Orleans, nor the Councils themselves, but with the immemorial preference for being governed rather than for governing.

Upon Noailles, president of the Council of Finance, fell the burden of the accumulating debt. Fertile in expedients as he was, they were but palliatives for the State, though deadly enough for the capitalists of the late reign. His final proposal was the least possible or palatable for a young Government—severe economy for fifteen years. Then Law found his opportunity, and on the foundations of his bank and his modestly capitalised Mississippi Company reared the fantastic edifice of credit, which, in the architect's own metaphor, reached its seven storeys— a height too stupendous for the sound but slight substructure, which was built for three. The phenomenal success and startling failure of Law's System, which is discussed more fully elsewhere, affected, not only the character of French society, but the Government's popularity and policy. For a time the Regency seemed the realisation of the age of gold, or, better still, of appreciated paper; but, when the crash came, the Government had to bear the blame of the nation's speculative craze. The violent measures which forced those who had realised their holdings at high prices to disgorge gratified the populace for the moment, but added to the area of discontent. The collapse, moreover, coincided with the outbreak of plague which between June and December, 1720, destroyed one-third of the inhabitants of Marseilles. Aix, Arles, Avignon, and Toulon suffered scarcely less, and the scourge reached the northern provinces, though in a mitigated and sporadic form. At the close of the disastrous year Rennes, the capital of Britanny, was burnt to the ground. " Fire at Rennes: Plague in Provence: Ruin of Paris" are three headings of the chapter of Barbier's memoirs which deals with a single black month.

The Liberalism of the Regency was short-lived. There was an inevitable, if unconscious, return to the irresponsible absolutism, which, when at its best, had suited the national temperament. Liberalism, moreover, is apt to be absolutist, when once its own ideals of liberty are questioned. Orleans had imagined that the sources of danger would be reactionary. the claims, that is, of Louis XIV's legitimised sons, or of his grandson, Philip V. He soon, however, discovered perilous progressive possibilities Each of these dangers had, speaking roughly, its ecclesiastical aspect. Jesuitism allied itself with the old monarchical party, Jansenism with the new aspirations. Thus the incidents of the Regency are blows struck alternately or coincidently at both forms of Opposition, until the Government became outwardly as absolute as that of Louis XIV himself.

The Duke of Maine sat still under his first affront; but the Duchess, a tiny elf-like sprite of mischief, converted her *salon* into a hot-bed of intrigue, unaware that her infantile airs and calculated cajoleries were watchfully observed. Orleans would have left matters alone; he liked Maine's brother, the Count of Toulouse, and was considerate, if unfaithful, towards his own wife, their sister. But he was pushed by Bourbon and other princes of the blood, and by the Dukes, who posed as successors of the old Peers of France. The nobility in general resented the pretensions of the Peers, and supported Maine and Toulouse. When Orleans forbade their assemblies, they protested before the *Parlement* that the status of the legitimised Princes could only be altered by the King when of age, or by the Estates General. Orleans was annoyed or alarmed into action, and the Council deprived the Princes of the right of succession and most of the prerogatives of blood royal. The edict was registered in *Parlement* with hesitation. It had little sympathy with the Bastards, but was at issue with the Peers on the portentous problem when and whether the President and the Peers should respectively raise their hats. There were symptoms therefore of a struggle of classes, which the Regency seemed too weak to stifle.

The friendship of the Regent and the *Parlement* was soon over. The latter hoped by refusing to register Edicts to establish a veto on legislation. No King had tolerated this claim, and Orleans declined to prejudice a minor's rights. He braced himself for the conflict by replacing his original triumvirate of ministers by a second. The liberal, widely read Noailles, who could argue for and against his own effervescent fads and freaks on successive days, gave place to Law, whom the *Parlement* from the first opposed. D'Aguesseau, an honourable and learned lawyer with Jansenist proclivities, was too favourable to the *Parlement*, whereas a Chancellor's mission was to uphold the Crown's residuary jurisdiction against the delegated authority of the Courts. His successor, d'Argenson, late Minister of Police, was a foe of lawyers and Jansenists, courageous and industrious, tempering an iron fist by a witty tongue, a finished student of the weaknesses of French mankind. Finally, to the surprise of all, Marshal d'Huxelles, Minister for Foreign Affairs, gave place to the Abbé Dubois, to whose private character gossip has been, perhaps, unfairly spiteful, but who was gifted with the priceless qualities of persistence and persuasion.

Orleans provoked the conflict by registering an edict for remintage in the *Cour des Monnaies* instead of in the *Parlement*, which retaliated by forbidding the manufacture and issue of the coinage (June, 1718). It attacked Law by ordering the exclusion of naturalised aliens from state finance. Justice was almost suspended, but the Mint worked quietly under the protection of fixed bayonets. Pickets watched the circulation of the coinage in the markets; muskets rattled on the pavement outside the *Parlement's* printing-press. A flood of atrocious libels against Orleans poured forth from legal circles and from the Duchess of Maine's coterie. The accidental discovery of the *Memoirs* of Cardinal de Retz had caused indescribable sensation. The Fronde had returned with the old combination of prince and lawyer against the Crown.

If the lawyers had read history aright, they might have realised their powerlessness. The insignificant Dubois sufficed to shatter the combination. On August 20 he arrived, having concluded the Quadruple Alliance. Six days later, in a *lit de justice*, the Bastards were reduced to their rank as Dukes and Peers, though Toulouse was granted his prerogatives for life. The *Parlement* lost its right of remonstrance, and was degraded to the position held under Louis XIV's humiliating ordinance of 1667. Two Presidents and a Councillor, who had been among the noisiest, were exiled. The Duchess of Maine plunged wildly into the plot for Philip V, which, though named after Cellamare, was recognised as hers. This was the final ruin of her cause, for it gave Orleans the justification for the Spanish War.

More serious than these Parisian troubles was the threatened revolt of Britanny, for which the Government was wholly to blame. The relation of this province to France under the treaties of union was almost federal. The Breton Estates of 1717 were within their rights in refusing to vote the subsidy without enquiry into provincial finances. The Government replied by dismissal of the Estates, levy of tax by edict, illegal garrison, and arrest of members of the nobility and the *Parlement* who protested. In 1718 the imposition of a toll on wine was a formal breach of the Act of Union. The *Parlement* of Rennes forbade the levy; the Governor made wholesale arrests; and the nobles formed an association for resistance.

This organisation had no connexion with the Cellamare conspiracy, which was over by the close of 1718, whereas the Bretons only armed in the following spring. Two nobles, acting on their own initiative, brought in June, 1719, a promise of Spanish aid. If the Bretons had struck at once, they might have caused serious embarrassment, especially as the Poitevin gentry felt some sympathy. The delay of the Spanish auxiliaries gave time for the conspiracy to leak out. In September, troops were poured into Britanny, and a penal commission established. The leaders were executed in person or in effigy, and the province was treated as a conquest. The suppression of the last genuine provincial liberties in France must be debited to the Regency. Another step towards absolutism was the dismissal of the Departmental Councils, which were replaced by the old Secretarial system. The *Parlement* had a fresh flicker of courage on the first symptoms of Law's collapse, which entailed d'Aguesseau's reinstatement, in order to conciliate public opinion. But the Regent went yet further than Louis XIV, and exiled the Courts to Pontoise for some six months.

The Council of Regency, next, lost such independence as it possessed —a loss resulting from the gain of a cardinalship by Dubois. For four years the purple was his aim, and he enlisted such heterogeneous allies as George I and the Pretender, the Emperor and Philip V. As an intermediate step, English influence helped him to the archbishopric of Cambray. Clement XI was never to be brought to fulfil his promise of a hat; but the agents of Dubois, headed by Cardinal de Rohan, contributed largely to Innocent XIII's election, and in July, 1721, Dubois obtained the hat, which is said to have cost France eight million francs. The political object was soon apparent. Rohan on his return was admitted to the Council. His claim to precedence led to the withdrawal of the Dukes and Chancellor d'Aguesseau. But Rohan was merely the warming-pan for Dubois, who now became a member and the Council's ruling spirit. An all-powerful Ministry was thus prepared for the cessation of the Regency on the King's majority. There was, however, a personal factor which might prove dangerous. Louis XV seemed attached to his governor, Villeroi, who somewhat posed as a leader of opposition to Orleans. Personal monarchy might after all be restored for Villeroi's benefit. The Regent forced a quarrel upon the old Marshal, trapped him, and sent him far from Court. Fleury, who was the King's tutor, affected to retire, but Orleans could not dispense with the one man who had the boy's confidence. A little note from Louis brought the tutor back from his mock hiding-place.

Dubois now received the title of First Minister, and the Regency might safely end. The King was consecrated at Rheims; and, on February 16, 1723, the Regent came to the royal bedside to resign his office, telling the boy of thirteen that he was now absolute ruler of the State. The character of the Government remained unchanged. Orleans was President of the Council. Dubois, aping Richelieu, monopolised patronage, accumulated benefices, presided over the assembly of the Clergy, took his seat in the Academy. His vanity was laughable, but his administration not injudicious. The good humour of Orleans tempered his outbursts of passion, and his tendency to persecute the Jansenists. Ultramontanism was advancing step by step with absolutism. Dubois without scruple threw his weight on the side of Rome, and the Bull *Unigenitus* was accepted by the Grand Council: its registration was the price paid by the *Parlement* for release from its exile at Pontoise.

Dubois had not long to live. It is said that his enemies in the Ministry deliberately killed him, by plying his insatiable brain with business. He died on August 10, 1723, leaving an evil reputation in an age peculiarly debased. Yet there have been respectable ministers in virtuous epochs who could be better spared. Every venomous pen in France poisoned the memory of Dubois, but a heavy fall in Mississippi Stock has been called his funeral panegyric. Orleans became First Minister, but the work was beyond his failing powers. On December 2 he was sitting before the fire with the Duchess of Falari, awaiting the King's commands, when the apoplexy of which he had been forewarned struck him down. He fell with his head upon the knees of this frail and luckless beauty of his set—a fitting ending.

The liberal hopes, constitutional and religious, with which the Regency had opened ended in disillusion. The period is remembered for little else than an overflow of sensualism and gigantic financial failure. Yet the colours may be unduly dark. The flaunting vice of a clique is often represented as a natural reaction against the austerity of Louis XIV's later years. And, again, the examples of Orleans and his eldest daughter are made responsible for an epidemic of drink and lust. This view is, however, too favourable to the French society of the age, and too hard upon the Regency. The most flagrant sins and the most notorious sinners existed without disguise under the Maintenon *régime*. Orleans himself had been only one of many notable offenders. The change was less one of nature than of pose. The scandals of the Regency were the outcome of fashion rather than of passion. Men hitherto respectable appeared drunk in public, and paraded their mistresses, as a concession to their social standing. Great ladies surrendered themselves to the Duke of Richelieu, not because they were enamoured of his silly oval face or brutal impudence, but because their reputation in the smart set depended on their being the heroines of his anecdotes of his *bonnes fortunes*.

The open vices of Orleans and his daughters doubtless contributed to the prevailing shamelessness of sin; but he was hardly popular enough to lead the fashion, and he had some scruples. When the King was taken to Versailles, the Regent kept his own mistresses at a distance. He had not the brutality of members of the Houses of Bourbon and Conti; he treated with respect his indolent, worthless wife, who, as his mother said, ruined his life, and brought her children to the gutter from neglect. In the reliable memoirs the vilest stories relate, not to Orleans, but to other princes; it would be uncritical to credit the farrago of lustful libels concocted for political consumption by the Duchess of Maine's coterie. He was, writes Saint-Simon, bored with himself from birth. He sought relief in wine and witty women; vice with him was neither passion nor fashion, but the tiresome habit of a tired man.

The example of the princes was followed by the dukes, by such of the nobility as came in contact with society, by lawyers and financiers. As in the sixteenth century young widows flocked to Paris to find husbands, so in the eighteenth they crowded thither to seek lovers. In Court circles, and far below them, the marriage tie was a mere slip-knot. Judicial separation came into use. It was as easy, wrote Madame, to cast off a wife or a husband as a mistress or a lover; only among the lower classes did married love still linger. Morality suffered by the passion for the stage. Actors and actresses, singers and dancers became the rage. The masked balls at the Opera, a prominent feature of the Regency, were the usual source of seduction, as in the case of the Regent's son, who afterwards scrambled from the quagmire to the heights of propriety. Gambling was stimulated by the speculative mania of Law's period. The King was infected while still a boy, while the Regent's daughter, Mademoiselle de Valois, on her leisurely journey to marry the Prince of Modena, carried the taint into the provinces. Suicide naturally became a vogue, and was dramatically performed, as when a young actress destroyed herself in her paint, her beauty-spots, and her flesh-coloured stockings, or a nobleman plunged into the Seine, with sword in one hand, and gold-headed cane in the other.

It may be doubted whether France was really impoverished by the crash of Law's System, although she suffered much temporary inconvenience. It was noticed at the time that the money taken from Peter's pocket was put into that of Paul. The result was a redistribution of wealth, and a consequent shaking-up of classes, for all speculated, and success became the standard of repute. The cook in diamonds who was recognised at an Opera ball doubtless made a genteel match. Nobles who disdained to take a direct part in commerce were without shame as shareholders in joint-stock undertakings, just as, under the Second Empire, leaders of fashion contributed capital to the great Parisian shops. Country gentlemen, who at the close of Louis XIV's reign could not meet their mortgage interest, in the palmy days of the System paid off their mortgages, and left their property unencumbered. Agriculture throve, not merely owing to peace, but to the rise of prices during the speculative period, which benefited landlord, peasant-proprietor, and labourer for wage. The rapid growth of Paris was no unmixed advantage, but a permanent boon was her closer intercourse with the great seaports. Always the capital of pleasure, she was henceforth also the capital of commerce. Her material necessities and the very shock of speculation quickened the inert population of the central provinces.

Orleans, like the equally abused Napoleon III, did much to revive provincial France. During his short career he is said to have done more road-making than Louis XIV in his long reign, while the slower construction of canals owed to him at least the plans. The Regent was, for his day, a free trader, removing inter-provincial restrictions, encouraging untrammelled commerce with and between the colonies, allowing a more liberal export trade to foreign countries. The admixture of banished salt-smugglers and the sweepings of gaols and hospitals with innocent girls seized by press-gangs and industrious Swiss and German emigrants, was not a promising foundation for a colony, and yet New Orleans has perpetuated the Regent's name. The settlement of the Mauritius and the fortification of the Île Royale off Newfoundland bore witness to French activity in southern and northern seas.

France under the Regency benefited by a breathing-space from the baleful governance of women. The English might be ruled by women, scornfully said Madame, but it did not suit the French. Of all the

Regent's mistresses not one had political influence. When Madame de Sabran pressed him, he took her to a mirror and asked if politics were fit for such a pretty face. In all his drunken bouts he never revealed state secrets. His intoxication was, perhaps, rather that of the weak head than of the sot. The first glass of champagne set his tongue wagging with such blasphemous indecency that his presence at his wife's table became impossible. Yet he could cut off, as it were, connexion of tongue and brain, and drink never obtained complete mastery of his reason.

The Duke of Chartres was too young to succeed his father as First Minister, and it was therefore impossible to ignore the Duke of Bourbon. Fleury proposed him to the King, and the silent boy nodded assent. Orleans and Dubois were soon regretted, for once more a woman was at the helm. The big-boned, one-eyed, brutal Bourbon was the bond-slave of the aerial sylph-like beauty and engaging mock-modesty of his mistress, Madame de Prie. Being too stupid for practical administration, he took as working partner Pâris Duverney, youngest of the four sons of a Dauphinois innkeeper, who had made fortunes by army contracts, and then fattened on the national bankruptcy of the Regency. Pâris was a capable agent, with some ingenuity in meeting emergencies, no scruple as to means, and no outlook on the future. This trio now governed France.

Six weeks after the Regent's death Spain had its counterpart sensation. On January 10, 1724, Philip V announced his abdication. This was no sudden freak, for in 1721 the King and Queen had bound themselves to retirement by solemn oaths, which were annually renewed. Philip's religious mania was the real cause, though contemporaries attributed his action to a belief that abdication would facilitate succession to the French Crown. The site chosen for spiritual preparation was the gorgeous palace of San Ildefonso, constructed in a clearing of the dense Segovian forest, and surrounded with snow mountains "of a very hideous aspect." The sums squandered on the palace and its gardens had been torture to Alberoni; the approach thereto was martyrdom for elderly ambassadors.

The close of Philip's first reign is a convenient stage at which to take stock of the character of Spanish administration, and of the personal influences of King and Queen. A complete contrast to France of the Regency was Philip V's Spain, governed from the low four-post marriage bed, four feet in width. Here each morning the King and Queen in their dressing-jackets received their Chief Secretary, who wrote his instructions, while Philip read despatches and Elisabeth worked and commented. The Queen's will had become her husband's law, yet not without humouring and watching, for Philip, though irresolute, was prejudiced, and indolence was balanced by self-conceit. He must therefore be coaxed to assimilate her likes and dislikes, to imagine her suggestions to be his own ideas. If once she lost touch of the drift of his mind, if once another influence gained the mastery, her game was lost. Thus the eternal *tête-à-tête* was as necessary to Elisabeth as to Philip, whose uxoriousness was as sensuous as the Regent's infidelities. Never for a night did she sleep from his side ; never for a day had she time to herself, save the fifteen minutes when she donned her shoes and stockings, or the weekly hour in which Philip received the report of the Council of Castile.

On his wife Philip depended for appropriate replies when giving audience, while he shifted from foot to foot, or poised himself upon his heels ; a pluck at her gown would warn her that he wished the interviewer gone. Elisabeth must walk at his side during his three rounds at mall, applaud the good strokes, and explain away the bad. With confinement approaching or just past, she must jolt over rough roads in the seven-windowed chariot to sit for silent hours on rush-bottom chairs in the shelter, past which the game was ultimately driven, and from which King and Queen fired shot for shot. For Philip Elisabeth must abandon her favourite amusements, her cards, and the music in which she excelled. Balls were forbidden as alien to Spanish character and conducive to impropriety, yet a Court dance was occasionally permitted. Here her husband and her step-sons were Elisabeth's only partners. Fortunately Don Luis danced as divinely as herself ; Saint-Simon alleges that, could the Opera but engage them, the price of stalls would rise. In meat and drink alone the Queen allowed herself some independence. She was not content with the soup, poultry, and invariable loin of veal which formed the King's daily dinner, preferred champagne to his burgundy, and, in spite of his wishes, could not break herself of snuff.

The tragic monotony of such a life might well have proved fatal to reason or morality. Elisabeth was saved by natural high spirits, by absence of self-consciousness, by growing mental activity. Above all, her passion for her children's advancement became all absorbing. Thus, notwithstanding outward constraint, she was never without excitement. She doubtless enjoyed the hot temper, which ambassadors politely described as vivacity, and which had no slight results on European politics. Sometimes it was natural, sometimes assumed, but the outbursts were short and sharp, and anger soon yielded to her own sense of humour or her husband's gentleness. Some of the envoys whom she handled most roughly liked her best ; and, indeed, her cheerfulness, her lack of affectation, her natural conversational gifts must have been a relief in eighteenth century Court life. Yet her political *début* was not promising. Her mode of life, added to some innate indolence, prevented any possibility of study. The daily experience of royal audiences taught her in time to judge of men and measures ; but the process was very slow. Hampered by Philip's presence, she could never talk freely to ambassadors or ministers. Unpopularity made her suspicious, and thus in early days she was subject to misconceptions, rejecting straightforward criticism and counsel for the crooked approaches of adventurers. Spaniards respected Philip, but disliked Elisabeth. They resented her marriage as a *mésalliance*, and were further alienated by her favour for Alberoni. She made no concealment of returning this dislike. She was tolerant towards Philip's personal Spanish friends and French followers, but her sympathies were with the Italian party, to which were attached the Flemings, and to some extent the Irish. An *entourage* of exiles is a sorry school of politics.

Alberoni's fall left Spain virtually without government. Grimaldo was as yet little more than confidential secretary. He seemed destined to be a stop-gap. His loyalty and patriotism, capacity and experience, qualified him to steer the State more than once through the groundswells which followed squalls. Ambassadors laughed at, but liked, the bourgeois Biscayan, who boasted of noble Italian origin. He was fair and fat as a Fleming, with bright blue eyes and a clever, kindly face ; his small hands pressed upon a portly paunch emphasised his arguments or compliments by appropriate gesticulations of their elastic fingers. The bribes accepted by him to gratify his grasping wife did not affect his policy.

Of constitutional machinery little was left. Alberoni's French predecessors paved the way towards absolutism by introducing the French secretarial system, with four Ministers for Foreign Affairs, Marine and Indies, War, and Ecclesiastical and Judicial Affairs, and an Intendant-General of Finance. Alberoni had reduced these five to three by accumulation of offices. They referred matters for discussion to the ancient Councils of Castile, Finance, the Indies, War, and the Military Orders. On their report the King decided, after consultation with his confessor and the Queen. Alberoni discredited the once influential Council of State. The Castilian Cortes were almost as defunct as the French Estates General. The liberties of Navarre, Aragon, Valencia, and Catalonia had been engulfed by the cataclysm of civil war.

For personal monarchy Philip's personality was singularly unfitted. He could never make up his mind, and, indeed, had little mind to make up, though what judgment he retained was sometimes sound. The illness of 1718, which ranged from dropsy to dementia, left its traces. For a superstitious man it was unfortunate that his shirts and sheets should emit phosphorescent light, even when manufactured by the holiest nuns, and tended by the Queen's own nurse. Saint-Simon found him in 1720 sadly altered. His chin projected at almost right angles from his face ; his feet knocked each other in his hurried walk, while his knees were twelve inches apart. He had a sawny manner and a drawling voice. His clothes did little to set him off, for he wore his brown serge suits to rags. Conscience was Philip's curse. Besides confessing twice a day, he would summon his confessors at all hours of day or night. In vain they urged that duty had superior claims to conscience. His only obvious merit was a certain dignity, which Louis XIV's descendants found it hard to lose. Nevertheless those who knew Philip the more closely loved him best. That he retained, without a breath of scandal, the affection of his ill-nurtured, ill-regulated Queen, amid an epidemic of matrimonial infidelity, must be placed to the credit of both consorts.

Spain was jubilant over the accession of Luis, a Spanish-born King, but the experiment proved a dismal failure. It was easier for Philip and Elisabeth to lay aside their crowns than their habit of command. They kept with them Grimaldo, whose creatures, interspersed with nonentities, filled the young King's Council, while its secretary, Orendayn, had been successively his page and clerk. "In every petty matter," wrote the Venetian envoy Bragadin, "the oracle was consulted at San Ildefonso: it might be said that the royal title was at Madrid, its essence at San Ildefonso." Luis, a youth of sixteen, was unfitted for power by shyness, indolence, and preference for servants' society. His Queen had from her first arrival scandalised the Court by her gross vulgarity, her pronounced dislike for Elisabeth, and her unveiled contempt for Luis. On her promotion sulkiness yielded to high spirits; her gluttony and indelicacy passed all bounds. Spanish prudery was shocked by a Queen who scoured the royal gardens in her night-gown, or was rescued in such costume from the heights of a ladder by an indiscreet French officer. Luis placed her under restraint by way of punishment; but the tactful French ambassador, Tessé, contrived a temporary reconciliation.

On August 31, 1724, Luis died of small-pox, commending to his father his girl-wife, who had made atonement by her courage in nursing him, when others held aloof. Everyone hoped that she would die of the penalty which her unusual devotion entailed, but she recovered, and found recompense in wilder licence. She was but fourteen, but in wisdom, till her dying day, she never aged.

By the Act of Abdication the Crown should have passed to Ferdinand, who was not quite twelve. The nobility desired a long minority which might restore its influence. The confessor Bermudez implored Philip to keep his oath, and a committee of theologians opined that he should at most govern till Ferdinand was of age. But Philip was moved to resumption by Elisabeth's tears, her nurse's objurgations, and Tessé's arguments and entreaties. The Council of Castile recommended this, though with hesitation, some members thinking that Philip's absolutism should be limited. Tessé cleverly suggested an appeal to the Pope, in the person of his Nuncio, Aldobrandini, who naturally gave the desired reply. Philip was King again. For Tessé Philip's resumption was a triumph for French influence. The President of Castile and others of the national party were disgraced. Grimaldo, who was thought to have English sympathies, offered passive resistance to dismissal; but Orendayn was pushed up to an independent position beside him. Nevertheless, while the old ambassador was pluming himself, this very Orendayn

had signed the instructions for a diplomatic revolution, which was
nothing less than the reconversion of Spain from a Bourbon to a Habsburg
Power. Success would ultimately have entailed the substitution of a
personal union between Spain and Austria, based on descent through
female lines from Charles V, for that between France and Spain under
a male descendant of Louis XIV, which had latterly been Europe's
bugbear.

The cause of this was the inconclusiveness of the Congress of
Cambray (1724–5), the occasion the failure to set France and England
against the Emperor. It was becoming clear that Charles VI had no
intention of fulfilling his engagements as to Don Carlos' admitted
eventual rights to Tuscany and Parma. The Grand Duke, Giovanni
Gastone de' Medici, resenting alien interference, upheld the claims of
his sister, the Electress Palatine Maria Anna Louisa, while a party in
the State desired the revival of the Republic on the extinction of the
male line. Siena was held under a different title, since Cosimo I had
received it as a fief of the Spanish Crown. Both Charles VI and Philip V
now claimed its suzerainty. The Duke of Parma was devoted to his niece
Elisabeth, and saw in Carlos the founder of a great Farnese State. To
ensure his succession, he prevented his own brother Antonio from
marrying. Thus the Emperor's policy was to encourage the Grand Duke's
resistance to the terms of the Quadruple Alliance, to stimulate Antonio's
matrimonial instincts, and to humiliate Francesco Farnese. Pretending
that the eventual investiture granted to Carlos already made Parma an
imperial fief, he levied contributions and marched troops across the State.
On these questions the mediatory Powers leant towards Spain, England
being the more pronounced, because she wished Spanish attention
diverted from Gibraltar, and had a private quarrel with Charles VI over
the Indian trade of his flourishing Ostend Company.

Elisabeth, impatient with the shuttlecocks of the Congress, sent
a clever Sicilian, the Marquis of Monteleone, on a secret mission to
Versailles and London to demand that the Swiss garrisons proposed
at the Congress should at once escort Don Carlos to Italy among his
future subjects. This overstepped the terms of the Quadruple Alliance,
and meant war with Charles VI, to which Bourbon was absolutely opposed. England was more ready to take drastic measures, but Elisabeth,
to conciliate her husband, had to combine Spanish with Italian interests,
and requested the fulfilment of the promise to restore Gibraltar. This
was sufficient to make the mission an absurdity, and to court refusal.

The refusal irritated Philip as profoundly as Elisabeth, and "in no
more time than it took to drive from Madrid to the Pardo" they
determined to approach the Emperor. The idea was not new; it had
been Alberoni's last suggestion, and under Luis had found favour with
the old Spanish party, at heart devoted to the Habsburgs. The desire
was, at that time, to oust both French and Italian influences by marrying

Ferdinand to an Archduchess. On the other hand Francesco Farnese, who engineered the Italian party, had foreseen the necessity of some such scheme, if France and England refused adequate protection. His envoy, the Marquis Scotti, was during Luis I's reign sounded by a certain Ripperdá, and discussed the project with Elisabeth in the autumn of 1724. Now that she seriously adopted it, her own sons, Carlos and Philip, aged respectively eight and four, slipped into Ferdinand's place. The eldest Archduchess, Maria Theresa, was now seven.

The mission was now entrusted to Jan Willem Ripperdá, a native of Groningen, but professedly of Castilian origin. Born a Catholic, he had become a Protestant to qualify himself for the Dutch public service. While deputy for his province in the States General he had had communications with Prince Eugene and Sinzendorff. A knowledge of economics made him of service in the Treaty of Utrecht. Sent as envoy to Spain in 1715, he subordinated Dutch interests to Spanish. The States General, highly dissatisfied, recalled him, but he returned to Spain, was naturalised, and reverted to Catholicism. Alberoni employed him in commercial matters, and a post in the cloth factory at Guadalajara, in which Elisabeth was interested, may have brought him to her notice. Ever since 1721, when he actually wrote to Sinzendorff, his brain was full of an Austrian alliance. He was now probably chosen because he was obscure, and could be disavowed, while he had the knowledge of foreign languages which most Spaniards lacked; Grimaldo, for instance, could not easily speak French.

Ripperdá's instructions divide themselves into two sections—those which regarded the fortunes of Elisabeth's children, and those which were meant to satisfy Philip and the nation. Carlos should marry Maria Theresa and ultimately receive the German territories of the Habsburgs. He should be educated in Vienna, and in due course be elected King of the Romans. His present *fiancée*, Mademoiselle de Beaujolais, might be transferred to his half-brother Ferdinand. For Philip was intended the second Archduchess with Milan, the Two Sicilies, Tuscany, and Parma. The Austrian Netherlands should return to Spain, or else be conferred on Philip with reversion alike of them, Milan, and the Two Sicilies to Spain, whereas that of Tuscany and Parma should be granted to Carlos. Charles VI was expected to buy Sardinia from Savoy by a slice of Milanese territory, and restore it to Philip V, obtaining also Gibraltar and Minorca from England. Should the Emperor insist on the indivisibility of his possessions as provided by his Pragmatic Sanction, Ripperdá might yield, and make sure of the two marriages. The whole of the Habsburg dominions, with the exception of the Netherlands as a sop for Philip, would then pass to Carlos, who, in view of Ferdinand's weak health, might easily inherit Spain.

The bribe wherewith to tempt the Emperor was the promise of

Spanish aid against the Turk and the Protestant Princes, the privileges of the most favoured nation in the Peninsula, and an opening for the Ostend Company in the Indies. Outstanding disputes relating to the Golden Fleece, the titles of Charles and Philip, the restoration of the Emperor's Spanish partisans and the King's Flemish and Italian followers could be amicably settled. From a matchmaker's standpoint Carlos was superior to Francis of Lorraine, hitherto intended for Maria Theresa, especially with regard to Italy. Italy and the Ostend Company were, indeed, Charles VI's chief interests. The religious motive, moreover, which had almost disappeared from politics, began to reassert itself. The projected alliance had a distinctly Catholic complexion ; it had the Pope's favour, and was intended to result in a Catholic restoration in England.

The first stage in Ripperdá's mysterious negotiations in Vienna did not reach far. Of the three members of the Secret Committee, the two more conservative, Princes Eugene and Starhemberg, were entirely opposed to the more sensational clauses, and even Sinzendorff, though deeply interested in the Ostend Company, concurred. Ripperdá could only extract a guarantee of the terms of the Quadruple Alliance, a commercial treaty, and a mere defensive alliance, which would free Austria from isolation, and protect her Italian possessions and her merchant ships. The Emperor merely promised not to oppose the restoration of Gibraltar and Minorca by friendly arrangement; as to the marriages—the Spanish Court must rely on his good intentions. These conditions were despatched by Ripperdá on March 9, 1725, and would certainly have been disavowed but for the startling news which reached the Spanish Court upon that very day, announcing the return of the Infanta.

Most good Frenchmen resented the postponement of their King's marriage. The Infanta was under seven, and her physical development was slow, whereas Louis was a well-grown youth of fifteen. Strong as he was, his intemperate passion for hunting occasionally caused violent illnesses. His death without heirs would open possibilities of civil war. Bourbon had every reason for alarm. His hated rival, the Duke of Orleans, was heir presumptive, and his projected marriage with a Princess of Baden was believed to aim at English and German support. Louis himself was obviously indifferent to the pretty, prattling child. There was no time to lose, for Bourbon had promised that the betrothal should take place when the Infanta was seven. The young King's dangerous illness in 1725 hastened the decision to break the engagement. Tessé, as being a personal friend of Philip and Elisabeth, was recalled, and the task of breaking the news was imposed upon the Abbé de Livry, a subordinate diplomat. The King and Queen received him with dignified anger, and refused his letters. Livry and all French Consuls were ordered to leave within twenty-four hours. Luis I's widow and her sister were, by way of reprisal, sent home to France. The fabric reared by the Regent fell with a crash. Troops marched towards the frontier, and the two nations were on the brink of war.

The rupture with France made the fortune of Ripperdá. Philip V accepted the Austrian proposals: the treaty of peace, the commercial treaty, and the defensive alliance were signed at Vienna by April 30 and May 1, 1725. The news was received with jubilation in Madrid, where Frenchmen were stoned in the street. Orendayn was created Marquis de La Paz, Ripperdá Duke and Grandee of the First Class. Philip for the first time in twenty years allowed a bull-fight. Yet, when the terms of the treaties became known, a revulsion of feeling set in against a convention so one-sided.

The Powers were seriously disturbed; they could no longer patronise the Emperor at the expense of Spain, nor assume the protection of Spain against the Emperor. English and Dutch merchants saw their privileges extended to the Emperor's subjects, while the Spanish fleet was pledged to defend the Ostend Company against their piratical attacks. Stanhope was assured that the treaties with England would be respected, if Gibraltar were immediately restored. Ripperdá's wild boasts of George I's dethronement and the dismemberment of France contributed to the nervous fear of a revived Habsburg predominance. The result was the Alliance of Hanover (September 3, 1725) between France, England, and Prussia. It was professedly defensive only, but it provided for the maintenance of the balance of power, threatened by the supposed engagement of Don Carlos and Maria Theresa.

Nothing could have suited Ripperdá better than the Alliance of Hanover. Austria was isolated, threatened on every frontier; Spain was her only possible ally. Thus, at length, the Emperor promised that two of his three daughters should marry Carlos and Philip, and that, if he himself should die before Maria Theresa became marriageable, she should wed Carlos. These engagements were embodied in a most secret treaty, providing in case of war for the conquest by Austria of the Franco-Belgic provinces, Franche Comté, the Three Bishoprics, Alsace, and Strassburg, while the Spanish share should be Roussillon, Cerdagne, and Navarre, together with Gibraltar and Minorca. Austria was pledged to find the men, and Spain the money. The Imperial Government greatly disliked the matrimonial clauses; but there were many loopholes. Charles VI, being young and strong, might easily have a son. Much might happen before Maria Theresa was of age to marry. An escape, moreover, was provided by a clause that the whole treaty should be voided by failure to execute any single item. Meanwhile, Spanish subsidies would be invaluable for buying support in Germany, and the Ostend Company was the Emperor's pet plaything. Ripperdá's blatant vulgarity was only tolerated, because commercial projects were the fashion, and even Prince Eugene believed him to possess unusual financial knowledge.

CH. IV.

The treaty was not so secret but that its contents were soon bruited abroad—with something beyond its contents, for the English Government had information that it included a clause for a Stewart restoration, which was false.

Ripperdá left Vienna on November 8, 1725, and hurried, booted and spurred, to the royal presence with his treaty. He persuaded the King and Queen that the Emperor wished him to be universal Minister. Grimaldo and Orendayn were elbowed out of office; even the Council of Castile was thrust into a corner, and grace and justice were in Ripperdá's sole hands. Castelar, the clever Minister of War, and Don José de Patiño, his yet abler brother, were dislodged on the pretext of missions to Venice and Brussels. But Grimaldo pressed his hands a little more tightly on his waist, and Castelar and Patiño dawdled over their preparations.

Elisabeth probably hoped to compass her ends by the confusion of a general war. Ripperdá knew that war was impossible for Spain. He strove alternately to cajole, bully, and divide the members of the hostile alliance. Alberoni's schemes for the resuscitation of Spain were revived as in a nightmare; faint, feverish efforts were made to fortify the northern outposts, to raise the army to war strength, to equip a squadron to protect Havana. A Stewart restoration became an integral part of Ripperdá's plans. The Duke of Wharton, with his bottle and his pipe, was invited to Madrid to reinforce the more respectable Jacobite leaders, the Duke of Liria, Marshal Berwick's son, and the Duke of Ormond. Alliance with Russia replaced the hopes which Alberoni had reposed on Sweden. The presence of Russian ships in Spanish waters caused actual alarm in England. Ripperdá believed that war would be here unpopular; but supplies were cheerfully voted; three squadrons were commissioned, and before long Admiral Hosier was peaceably blockading the treasure-fleet in Portobello harbour. In vain the Emperor was urged to invite the Pretender to the Netherlands, and escort him thence to England. Charles VI showed no interest in Stewart restoration, and to and fro off Ostend were cruising the English frigates.

The arrival of the Emperor's ambassador, Marshal Königsegg, was the beginning of Ripperdá's end. The Imperial Government was determined not to fight, but equally resolved to handle the subsidies, which alone made fighting possible. Königsegg exposed the falsehood of the promises which Ripperdá attributed to the Emperor, and discovered the virtual bankruptcy of Spain. Lying had carried the adventurer far in the field of diplomacy, but was inadequate as a permanent principle of administration. There were stormy scenes, in which the handsome, contemptuous aristocrat had the upper hand. Elisabeth herself fell under Königsegg's influence, and she throughout had been Ripperdá's sole support. He was dismissed suddenly, but kindly, with a pension. Panic-stricken, he took refuge in the English embassy, where Stanhope read his papers, and elicited a farrago of facts and fancies. From the embassy he was forcibly removed, and imprisoned for two years at Segovia, whence a sentimental maid-servant contrived his escape. He settled later in Morocco, but the contemporary tales of his adventures, military, political, amorous, and religious, are now discredited. It is natural to compare Ripperdá with Alberoni ; but the Dutchman does not stand on the same plane with the Parmesan, who possessed the real talent for administration which the former lacked. Alberoni in hours of difficulty was always regretted, but never Ripperdá. The Italian gardener's son was more of a gentleman than the Groningen baron. It was only upon two women, the Empress and the Queen, that Ripperdá had imposed.

The fall of Ripperdá was closely followed by that of Bourbon, whose clumsiness had made the Dutchman's temporary fortune. It never occurred to Bourbon that it was easier to dismiss the Infanta than to find a substitute. The essentials were that the princess chosen should be healthy, well-made, and not too powerful or intelligent to be independent of Bourbon and his mistress. One hundred marriageable princesses were scheduled, and then sifted down to seventeen. These comprised Bourbon's two sisters, two daughters of the Prince of Wales, two of Peter the Great, a daughter and two nieces of the King of Prussia, four other Germans, a Modenese, a Portuguese, a Dane, and a Lorrainer. A further scrutiny was survived by Bourbon's sisters and the English Princesses only. Fleury warned Bourbon that, if Louis disliked the selected sister, the failure would be debited to him, and so too the war which would certainly result from Philip's accentuated anger. Thus in January, 1726, George I was sounded, the only condition being that his grand-daughter must become a Catholic. To Bourbon's astonishment, the English Government was opposed to the conversion of the Princess.

The idea was now ventilated of a confidential mission to Germany to examine all the Princesses in that nursery garden of Queens. Suddenly, it occurred to Bourbon to transfer to the King the lady for whom he had been himself proposing. This was Maria Leszczynska, daughter of Stanislaus, lately King of Poland, now a French pensioner living the simplest of lives at Weissembourg. She was twenty-one, and her portrait, painted for Bourbon, was pleasing. Madame de Prie had sanctioned the match with Bourbon, because Maria was insignificant. Now, her lover's marriage would be postponed, and the future Queen would owe her splendid position to herself. The Council consented, and so, with much joy, did Stanislaus. Peter the Great's widow then proposed that Louis XV should marry her daughter Elizabeth, who was beautiful, clever, and theologically amenable. Both Bourbon and Orleans had previously rejected her for themselves, as being too low-born on her mother's side, and as probably inheriting her father's temper. Russia, indeed, would support French interests in Poland, Germany, and Italy ; but Bourbon feared that England would be alienated, and Madame de Prie objected to so formidable a rival.

Thus the marriage with the Polish Princess, the strangest that French King ever made, was performed by proxy at Strassburg, and consummated at Fontainebleau on September 5, 1725. This beggar maid, who brought no dowry and no political connexion, but merely the certainty of complications in eastern Europe, was the butt for pasquinades; but her tact and kindliness were soon to blunt their edge. She justified the main object of her selection. After bearing three daughters, she gave birth in 1729 to an heir, the father of Louis XVI.

War with Spain was now threatening France, and this was attributed to Bourbon's blunders. Every act of his government had reflected his brutality or stupidity. The two planks of its rickety platform had been fiscalism and ultramontanism. Dubois had at least been economical; Bourbon and his mistress were more extravagant than Orleans and his harem, and that too at the State's expense. To meet deficits, Duverney had revived the universal income tax of 2 per cent., and had, for the last time in French history, levied the old feudal due of *joyeux avènement.* The clergy had protested in full session against the breach of their immunity, the *Parlement* against registration of financial edicts in a *lit de justice.* Bad harvests aggravated discontent. Bread riots broke out in Normandy; other provinces were controlled by bands of women armed with pitchforks, who prevented the levy of the taxes. Paris was only saved from revolution by extravagant measures for feeding the populace. Yet the French people was so long-suffering that Bourbon's government might have lasted indefinitely, had he respectfully treated the mild old tutor, whose influence over Louis was popularly ascribed to magic. Bourbon tried to eliminate Fleury, as Orleans had rid himself of Villeroi. By a preconcerted arrangement with the Queen he detained the King from his invariable interview with his tutor. Fleury sent in his resignation and retired. The King withdrew to the innermost recess of the palace, and there sat and sulked until a gentleman-in-waiting ventured to intrude, and suggest that Fleury should be recalled. Bourbon returned an ungracious message, which proved the signal of his own dismissal. On June 11, 1726, the King rode out, begging the Minister not to wait supper for his return. Immediately afterwards Bourbon received an order to retire to Chantilly. His mistress was exiled to her Norman property, where she shortly died. Duverney, who had done his best in an impossible situation, was lodged in the Bastille.

In France, as in Spain, the sudden fall of the First Minister marks the close of a distinctive period. The provisional administrations of Orleans and Bourbon were now to be replaced by the long, uniform ministry of Fleury. In Spain, though the Queen remained throughout the dominant factor, the reign of foreign adventurers was over. For the future, however wild might be her dreams, their workaday execution was controlled by normal, national Ministers.

CHAPTER V.

THE BOURBON GOVERNMENTS IN FRANCE AND SPAIN. II.
(1727-46.)

THE Austro-Spanish Alliance seemed only strengthened by Ripperdá's disgrace. Stanhope clamoured at the violation of his embassy; war with England seemed certain, and Spain must cling to her Imperial ally. Königsegg became, wrote Stanhope, the idol of their Catholic Majesties. Spaniards chafed at his escutcheon, which proclaimed the Emperor's title to the Spanish Crown, and at his team of mules driven through Madrid in defiance of the bye-laws. But Elisabeth cared little for Spanish opinion. For her personal ends she would use the Austrian, as she had used the Italian and the Dutchman. She had, moreover, never met a personality so imposing, so endowed alike with military and diplomatic graces. Königsegg became the fount of honour, while ministers obediently brought their portfolios to his rooms. Orendayn was merely his instrument. Philip submitted to the dismissal of Grimaldo, and of his confessor Bermudez, who had handed him a letter from Fleury behind Elisabeth's back. His soul was in charge of Father Clarke, formerly Königsegg's confessor, a Scottish Jacobite who could scarce speak French; his body in that of the Irish Jacobite, Dr Higgins.

In Jacobite circles at Madrid the fall of the Hanoverians was thought imminent. The Duke of Liria was sent as the first Spanish ambassador to Russia to arrange a descent upon the English coast. The siege of Gibraltar was opened, and the South Sea ship, *Prince Frederick*, embargoed. The treasure-fleet slipped past Admiral Wager; Patiño was buying and building ships, and crimping fishermen. Yet war was not declared, and the trend in Spain was really towards peace. There was disaffection in Aragon, discontent in the trenches before Gibraltar, disgust at the subsidies for Austria and at the alien confessor. Patiño, knowing Spain's weakness, was furtively corresponding with Stanhope; the Infant Ferdinand made no secret of his opposition to the Austrian Alliance. Above all Charles VI and Prince Eugene were averse from war, for Spain could give no adequate protection to the Ostend Company, while Eugene had no belief in the capture of Gibraltar.

Bourbon's fall, just four weeks after that of Ripperdá, made reconciliation between France and Spain more possible. Early in 1727 Philip V expected Louis XV to die, and he resolved to make a bid for the succession. He chose as his agent the Abbé Montgon, an amateur diplomatist, whose pretentious piety had appealed to him during his retreat at San Ildefonso. Montgon was instructed to win the clergy, the *Parlements*, the nobles, and above all the House of Bourbon. He was ordered not to unbosom himself to Fleury, as being opportunist if not Orleanist, nor to Morville, Minister for Foreign Affairs, as being Anglophil. His papers included a proclamation for the *Parlement* of Paris, a scheme for a Council of Regency, and for the supervision of the Queen's possible confinement. Montgon's disguises and mystifications were worthy of comic opera, but the results had some importance. Bourbon flung himself into the Legitimist movement against the hated Orleans succession. Philip's party gained consistency among nobles and lawyers, and found support with the Marshals, Villars and d'Huxelles. But the decisive result was the unexpected. Fleury at the very first interview picked Montgon's brain. Truly or falsely, he then declared himself in favour of Philip's succession, and opened a confidential correspondence with Elisabeth. The Queen was assured that the Emperor never intended his daughters for her sons, and that he was raking up Imperial pretensions to the Italian duchies. Simultaneously, Fleury negotiated at Vienna for a general peace, and Charles VI pressed a more pacific policy on Spain. The siege of Gibraltar made no progress, while the death-bill daily rose. Elisabeth cooled towards Königsegg, and Patiño closed the purse-strings, so that the proud ambassador could pay neither his servants nor his tradesmen. The Emperor agreed to suspend the Ostend Company for seven years, pending legal enquiry. Spain engaged to abandon the siege of Gibraltar, restore the *Prince Frederick*, and remove the embargo on the cargoes of the treasure-fleet which belonged to foreign consignees. The Preliminaries were signed at Paris on May 31, 1727, by representatives of France, England, the Emperor, and the States General. As there was no Spanish minister in France, a duplicate was executed at Vienna on June 13, here lacking an English signatory. Hence this compact is called the Preliminaries either of Paris or Vienna.

Elisabeth smarted under her dynastic disappointments and the humiliating concessions to England. Philip's melancholia was so obstinate that he had appointed her as Regent. Reconciliation with France was therefore doubly welcome. On the birth of Don Luis, Louis XV wrote a friendly letter, and she sent a warm reply. Diplomatic relations were renewed, and the Count of Rothembourg, a strong and plausible Legitimist, arrived at Madrid. This entailed formal intercourse with England also. The new envoy was Benjamin Keene, who, as agent for the South Sea Company and Consul-General, had fathomed the peculiarities of Spanish politics. His energies were, however, confined to solitary walks in the royal garden, for Elisabeth flared up at the very name of England. She angrily showed Rothembourg George I's letter promising Gibraltar, sarcastically asking if it were a forgery. The English people also and their new King, George II, were dangerously bellicose. Wager cruised off Cadiz, and Hosier was instructed to chase the galleons. To provide the sinews of war, which at the close of 1727 seemed inevitable, Elisabeth ordered a levy of 25 per cent. on foreign merchandise in the treasure-fleet. Yet Patiño, when asked if Spain's resources could bear a war, returned a melancholy negative. In Italy the outlook was unpromising. The Grand Duke of Tuscany intrigued against the claims of Don Carlos. Antonio Farnese, under Imperial pressure, abandoned his celibate comforts for marriage with Henrietta of Modena, in the hope of a successor. It proved impossible to move Fleury from the English alliance, and thus Spain was isolated at the moment when Philip was carried to the Pardo desperately ill. Elisabeth had protested that Gibraltar was her only care, but her Italian interests won the day. The Convention of the Pardo (March 6, 1728) confirmed the Preliminaries with trifling modifications. The European Congress of Soissons could begin its work.

If Preliminaries were tedious, Congresses were leisurely; they gave the Powers plenty of time in which to reconsider their position. Fleury's task was the most difficult. He was no religious Liberal like Orleans; he could not but have visions of a union of the Catholic Powers, of a lasting peace upon the Continent as the result of reconciliation between Bourbon and Habsburg, of the consequent revival of French commerce at the expense of the Maritime Powers. But he saw no element of permanence in the Spanish-Austrian alliance, which depended on the caprice or fortunes of Elisabeth. Should the Empress die, and the Emperor marry again, Elisabeth would have no further interest in the alliance. Should Philip die or abdicate, and Ferdinand succeed, the alliance would vanish of itself. A breach between Spain and Austria could only be a matter of time, and then France must make her choice. If she chose Austria, Spain with her American trade would be thrown into the arms of England; if she selected Spain, there would be a fresh coalition of the Empire with the Maritime Powers, which had previously proved too strong for the Bourbon Courts. Fleury therefore elected to cleave to the alliance of Hanover, and break up that of Spain and Austria, while honestly striving for European peace.

The situation of England was somewhat simpler. She must re-capture the Spanish-American trade by peace or war, but the alternative must be rapidly decided, for she was undergoing the expense of war without its plunder. There was danger from a coalition of Austria, Russia, Poland, and Prussia, which had early deserted the alliance of Hanover, or again from a family alliance of the Bourbon Courts. The growing influence of the new Foreign Minister, Chauvelin, was regarded with suspicion, and the British ambassador, Horatio Walpole, had to throw the whole weight of long-standing influence upon Fleury to keep him true. The Emperor's chief aim was to enjoy the benefit of time by postponing a definite answer either on the subject of his daughters' marriage, or on the succession of Don Carlos to the Italian duchies. If, meanwhile, fair words could procure Spanish subsidies, so much the better; if not, it was Königsegg's creditors who mainly suffered.

Political problems depended largely upon personal accidents. It seemed impossible that Philip V should live or recover reason. He had a mania for abdication, and actually smuggled through to the Council a letter of renunciation, which Elisabeth was only just in time to recover. His malady took forms aggressive or absurd. He would scratch his wife, pommel Patiño, and bite himself. At one moment he fancied himself a frog, at another a corpse. Usually the most pious of men, he now had fits of irreligious mania, rejecting his confessor's ministrations and the sacrament. Yet if the Queen ventured to talk politics in his presence, he became inconveniently sane. Envoys and statesmen began to worship the rising sun in Ferdinand, and Elisabeth wisely gave him his proper position, which his tact and kindliness deserved. Yet his health was so bad, and he was so painfully conscious of it, that excessive adulation was unwise. The progeny of the Parmesan princess was far healthier than the Savoyard's, and behind the valetudinarian Ferdinand was the bonny figure of Don Carlos.

While politics seemed to centre in the Spanish sick-room, the pustules which had troubled Louis XV in the hunt and the Council Chamber were diagnosed as small-pox. Philip, as usual, assumed that the youth was going to die. He was now in fancy no longer corpse or frog, but King of France: in France he could eat, drink, and not be poisoned. He would march on Toulouse, have himself proclaimed Regent by its *Parlement*, and then move on Paris. He empowered Fleury to act in his name. At Madrid Louis XV was long believed to be dead. Even when the news of his convalescence arrived, excitement scarcely subsided. But, after bearing three daughters, Maria Leszczynska was on September 4, 1729, delivered of a son, and the *ignis fatuus* of Philip's hopes was at length extinguished.

Less fortunate than the two Kings, the Emperor's youngest daughter died, and Elisabeth concluded that the remaining sisters would marry her two eldest sons. Charles VI's scrupulous conscience, however, admitted the argument that circumstances alter cases, and that arrangements made for three daughters must be modified in the face of two. Hatred for the Emperor now replaced Elisabeth's detestation for England. Not the cession of Gibraltar but the establishment of Don Carlos became the touchstone. She insisted on Spanish garrisons for the duchies instead of Swiss. The English Government, to make Gibraltar safe by Italian concessions which cost it nothing, extorted Fleury's reluctant assent. In

October Stanhope arrived in Spain; and on November 9 the Treaty of Seville was signed. English trade was restored to its former footing, the privileges of the Ostend Company were cancelled, Gibraltar was ignored. The succession of Don Carlos was secured by the guarantee of the allies of Hanover, and the presence of Spanish garrisons. The Emperor's reply was to pour troops into Italy, and to recall Königsegg.

Fleury did not intend to fight. He threw away the fruits of the much desired family reconciliation by irresolution, which was partly constitutional, partly the growing result of age. To this must be added the incompatibility of temper between Elisabeth and himself, which long embarrassed both French and Spanish envoys. Chauvelin, whose influence was increasing, was resolute enough, but he lacked tact. His scheme for a resettlement of Italy, which should exclude Austria, and establish a balance between Savoy, Venice, the Papacy, and Don Carlos, was as yet visionary. England, more practical, insisted on immediate satisfaction for Spain. Tension increased between the Bourbon Courts, and at length Castelar, sent as envoy extraordinary to Paris, declared the Treaty of Seville annulled (January, 1731).

For England meanwhile a decisive settlement was essential. In Spanish-American waters *guarda-costas* were at open war with contrabandists and professedly peaceful English and Anglo-American merchantmen. Now it was that the Spaniards cut off the celebrated ear of Captain Jenkins, and that an English man-of-war had a four hours' fight to protect its convoy. The boundaries of Georgia and the encroachment of logwood cutters in Campeachy Bay were also subjects of angry correspondence. In Spain English merchants and sailors were subjected to annoyance from the Inquisition, from excisemen, press-gangs, and quartermasters. Products of English colonies were prohibited, and new imposts illegally exacted. Ships provisioning Gibraltar were overhauled, and works actually commenced against the fortress. Fortunately Patiño was now predominant, and worked in harmony with Keene, who knew that faults were not all on the Spanish side. But Philip was dangerously excited about Gibraltar, and Patiño professed that he would sooner face drawn bayonets than broach this topic. England and France negotiated behind each other's backs both at Seville and Vienna, but England, thanks to her ambassadors Keene and Thomas Robinson, was the better served.

The crisis came with Antonio Farnese's death. His widow believed herself to be with child, but diplomatists were sceptical. Charles VI occupied Parma nominally on behalf of Don Carlos. The Maritime Powers offered to guarantee his Pragmatic Sanction, and in return he made the Treaty of Vienna (March 16, 1731), to which Spain in July acceded. Spanish troops were to be introduced even if the widowed Duchess' problematical child should be a boy. The Imperial investiture was to precede possession of the duchies by Don Carlos. Spain confirmed the terms of the Quadruple Alliance and of the Treaty of Vienna of June 7, 1725. Curiously enough the Spanish signatory was the Duke of Liria, who had left Spain to provoke a Russian attack on England.

It only remained for Don Carlos to take possession. He travelled by land to Antibes, creating a favourable impression by his expansive gaiety, his anxiety to learn, his industry in mechanical employments. He was his mother's son, an Italian and no Spaniard. Elisabeth could not look at her other children without tears starting to her eyes. He was welcomed by Admiral Wager, who had escorted the Spanish squadron and the transports which conveyed the much disputed garrisons. Don Carlos landed at Leghorn on December 7, 1731, at night, and passed through illuminated streets to the cathedral. In March, 1732, he made his formal entry into Florence, and was afterwards installed in his capital of Parma. Fleury professed that, as other people were satisfied, France was content. The only discordant note in European harmony proceeded from Pope Clement XII, who declared the installation illegal and claimed Parma as a lapsed fief.

Elisabeth's set purpose had outlasted two unsuccessful wars. She had worn down the resistance of the Powers, disregarded the preferences of her husband, scorned the protests of the Pope. Her aims were personal —a principality for her son, a possible retreat for her own widowhood. Yet to her was due the fresh prestige of Spain, which had regained a foothold in Italy, and thereby became once more a European Power. She had thrown open to the Bourbons the preserves which all French dynasties had coveted, had thrust an Italian principality between the German possessions in the north and in the south, with sufficient power to make itself fresh elbow-room. Everything, wrote the Tuscan historian Galuzzi, presaged immediate revolution. The medal struck for Don Carlos had for its device a lady with a lily in her hand, and for its legend *Spes publica.* For Italians this was an augury of liberation.

From the arrival of Don Carlos in Tuscany until the War of the Polish Succession Spain seemed to set her sails for every course in turn. The immediate object of France was to gain Spanish support against the ratification of the Pragmatic Sanction. But Elisabeth bore no gratitude towards France, nor would she needlessly irritate the Emperor, upon whom her son's comfort in Italy depended. The mutual aversion between herself and Fleury became apparent. To Rothembourg, who asked when she would cease to abuse the Cardinal, she replied truthfully, "Not till he is dead." Fleury had no strong leaning towards England; but the necessity for recuperation and distaste for decisive measures led him to propitiate the Maritime Powers. Peace was his end and aim; even later, when harrying the Habsburg in Poland, Germany, and Italy, he never quite lost his hold on the dogs of war. On the other hand, Elisabeth's further ambitions could only be realised by war. She scorned an academic alliance; she must have a fighting friendship. Both King and Queen wished to break up the Treaty of Utrecht and the Quadruple Alliance, and throw their fragments into the melting-pot. They kept proposing a close family alliance, annulling all previous treaties up to and including that of Ryswyk. Such a prospect appalled Fleury, for it implied cancellation of Philip's renunciations, and consequent war with Europe. Patiño himself realised that a family alliance would ultimately produce a rupture with England, and this he meant to avoid until he had nursed the navy to maturity.

Philip and Elisabeth were pugnacious, and the atmosphere electrical, when the Powers were agitated by the gathering of a large Spanish expeditionary force. Memories of Alberoni suggested Naples and Sicily as the objective, while English fears centred on Gibraltar and Port Mahon. The storm broke upon the African coast. Oran was taken by surprise, and all Spain was jubilant. Moors, however, have a pillow-like rebound. Aided by warlike Algerians and even Turkish regulars they swarmed round Oran and Ceuta. Loss of life was great, and among those killed was the heroic commander, Santa Cruz, the King and Queen's especial friend, and the mainstay of the pro-English party. It was once more proved that it was useless to scratch at the North African seaboard. Doubtless, however, Philip V's Government, like that of Ferdinand in 1511, meant Africa to be the "jumping-off place" for Italy. Spain mobilised, though not without suspicion, and started the later Italian war with *cadres*, military and naval, comparatively complete.

English cannon were unfortunately discovered at Oran, and powder was shipped by English subjects at Gibraltar to the Moors besieging Ceuta. This added to the irritation caused by the increasing enterprise of smugglers, the high-handed measures of English admirals, and the captious claims of the South Sea Company. Just as the Spanish people was exasperated with England, Elisabeth was losing patience with the Emperor. Her son pressed for permission to occupy the duchies while still under age, and for immediate instead of eventual investiture. Charles VI, annoyed at the oath to Don Carlos taken by the Florentine Senate, rudely refused. Upon this Don Carlos made a formal entry into Parma, and assumed the unauthorised title of Grand Prince of Tuscany. Elisabeth would at once have allied with France, if she had thought that France would fight. Her ambitions rose to ideas of Milan for her son, and Naples and Sicily for Spain. At the close of autumn (1732) the Bourbon Powers were drawing towards a family alliance. Patiño strove to delay it by impossible demands, but was forced to abandon them; in January, 1733, Liria was recalled from Vienna. George II then intervened, and, to please the English King, Charles VI granted the dispensation of age, and immediate investiture, if Don Carlos would drop the title of Grand Prince. Elisabeth was so grateful that peace seemed assured, when, on February 1, Augustus II of Poland inopportunely died.

The succession to Poland was of absolutely no moment to Spain, and of not much more to France. " Must we," plaintively asked Fleury, " ruin the King to aid his father-in-law?" His hesitation encouraged Elisabeth to propose the election of one of her own sons. Her real resolve was, however, to attack the Emperor, if she were convinced that Fleury meant to go to war for Stanislaus; but this he would not commit to writing. Another difficulty was her detestation for Charles Emmanuel, whose house she prophetically regarded as her own descendants' most dangerous rival. France had already offered him the whole of the Milanese, on condition that he should cede Savoy to herself; but Elisabeth insisted that Cremona and Lodi should be given to Don Carlos. When Charles Emmanuel claimed Mantua as a set-off to these, Elisabeth rejoined that Mantua was the key of Italy and must be in her son's keeping. This remained the stumbling-block throughout, preventing any alliance of Spain with Savoy.

In August, 1733, news reached Paris that Russian troops had entered Poland, and Stanislaus set out for Warsaw. War was certain, and this must eventually bring to its slow conclusion a Bourbon family alliance. On September 26 France signed the Treaty of Turin with Charles Emmanuel, offensive and defensive as against the Emperor. He was promised the whole State of Milan, with its boundaries as fixed when Charles V bestowed it upon his son. Don Carlos should receive Naples, Sicily, and the curious little State called the Presidi—the Sienese ports which had been retained by Philip II, when he granted Siena as a Spanish fief to Cosimo de' Medici. The Spanish Government mistrusted this treaty, especially as all mention of Mantua was omitted. Philip V refused assent to Charles Emmanuel's claim to the supreme military command, while Louis XV declined to regard Spanish captain-generals as equal in rank to French marshals. A compromise was made by the appointment of Villars, whose age and prestige gave him an admitted precedence. France declared war against Charles VI on October 10; and, ten days later, Philip, though protesting against the Treaty of Turin, gave the order for embarkation. On November 7 France and Spain signed the Treaty of the Escurial. The two Kings pledged themselves and their posterity to eternal friendship. They guaranteed each other's possessions in Europe and without. To Don Carlos were secured Parma and Piacenza, the reversion to Tuscany, and, subject to the terms of the Treaty of Turin, all conquests made in Italy. Louis XV would aid Spain if attacked by England, and promised his good offices for the restoration of Gibraltar; the two Powers were mutually to enjoy the commercial privileges of the most favoured nation, and the abuses of English con-trabandism in the Indies were to be checked. The Kings engaged not to negotiate separately on the Pragmatic Sanction, or on the election of Francis of Lorraine as King of the Romans, or to lay down arms save by common assent. All previous treaties were annulled, except in relation to mutual trade—"All earlier treaties made between France and Spain, and between their majesties and other Powers, shall no longer have effect between France and Spain." These few words cancelled the obligations of the Treaty of Utrecht and all subsequent engagements. This high-sounding and far-reaching treaty was broken almost as easily as signed, but it has importance as being the first of the three " Family Compacts."

Meanwhile in Italy war went merrily enough. The old year saw the Milanese cleared of Austrians, and Villars was in touch with the Spanish general, Montemar. But the incompleteness of diplomatic unity began to obtrude itself. The task assigned to Montemar was to guard the Po, and prevent an Austrian descent by the eastward Alpine passes. Charles Emmanuel refused to bridge the river, as a means of communication with Montemar, unless the Treaty of Turin were signed. Montemar was therefore ordered to abandon concerted action, and to proceed to the conquest of Naples. But for this withdrawal and Charles Emmanuel's sulks the weak Mantuan garrison must have surrendered, for exceptionally dry weather had neutralised the protection of the marshes.

Don Carlos and Montemar justified the new Spanish plan of campaign. Marching southwards in February they obtained right of passage through the Papal States, and crossed the Neapolitan frontier on March 26, 1734. Public opinion at once declared itself for Don Carlos. On April 5 Naples tendered its submission : by May 10 all its forts were taken, and he made his entry. The viceroy, Visconti, left garrisons in Capua and Gaeta, and withdrew to Bari, hoping to receive reinforcements from Trieste. But Montemar was on his heels, and on May 25 destroyed his army at Bitonto. By August Capua, defended by Traun, alone held for Charles VI. Sicily also clamoured to be free from Austria. Montemar sailed for Palermo, and Marsillac for Messina. Town and country welcomed them. Peasantry hemmed in the scattered Austrian detachments, while the citadels of Messina, Trapani, and Syracuse alone offered serious resistance. Montemar was free to lead his victorious army northwards.

Montemar's departure had reduced the Franco-Sardinian forces to the defensive. Their duty was to guard the States of Milan and Parma, and prevent the Austrians from slipping round their right flank to Ferrara, and thence gaining the great southern high-road. Villars, indeed, would have advanced to the Adige, blocked the Brenner, and destroyed Mantua at leisure. In this he was baulked by Charles Emmanuel's refusal to lend artillery, and his own Government's fear of a general engagement. Even for the defensive his forces were inadequate. The Austrians on May 2 crossed the Po near Borgoforte, cut Villars off from communication with Modena and Ferrara, whence he drew his supplies, and forced him back on the Oglio. The friction with Charles Emmanuel became intolerable, and he asked for his recall, leaving Coigni, an officer of only moderate ability, in command. The old Marshal never saw France again ; for, three weeks after leaving the front, he died at Turin. The Austrian objective was now Parma, for which they twice made a spring. The first attempt was checked by Maillebois near the ducal palace at Colorno, the second by a hard-won French victory under the walls of Parma, in which the Austrian general, Mercy, was killed (June 29). Coigni and the King then resolved to drive the Austrians north of the Po by seizing Borgoforte, but Königsegg, acting with great dash, surprised the French camp, and forced Coigni back on Guastalla. Here on September 19 another French victory was won, as fruitless as that of Parma. In spite of defeats the strategical superiority was with the Austrians; Maillebois had to retire hurriedly from before Mirandola, and Coigni abandoned the Oglio for the Adda, leaving the territories of Cremona, Parma, and Piacenza open to the enterprising enemy.

The campaign of 1735 opened with Montemar's appearance in Lombardy. To prevent his taking command as senior officer to Coigni, Marshal Noailles, who was also a Captain-General of Spain, was sent to Italy. Late in May French, Spaniards, and Sardinians, acting at length in concert, drove the Austrians down the Po, crossed the Mincio and Adige, and turned the enemy out of Italy. Montemar offered to besiege Mantua with his Spaniards, if the French and Sardinians, aided by his cavalry, would cover him from a return of the Austrians. Charles Emmanuel refused to do anything at all, unless Philip V would sign the Treaty of Turin. While the Generals were wrangling, the astounding news arrived that France had signed preliminaries of peace; and Noailles was ordered to conclude an armistice. So clumsy were the orders that they did not include the Spaniards. Montemar, on Noailles' advice, withdrew south of the Po, with the Austrians in pursuit. He might have been crushed, had not Noailles stretched his instructions, and secured his inclusion in the armistice. As it was, he fell back, not without loss, on Parma—a cruel termination to his brilliant career.

The Spaniards had throughout shown the best military qualities of the three armies, alike in the field and in the siege and storm of fortresses, and had been the most effectively supported by their Government. The French had fought well in defensive actions forced upon them; but their discipline was bad, and the Spaniards expressed contempt for troops which spent their time in pulling off women's rings and plundering their allies' orchards. Villars and Noailles were both checked by diplomacy at home; but the main cause for comparative failure was the selfish obstinacy of Charles Emmanuel, who would neither fight a decisive battle nor lend his artillery for a siege.

On the part of France the War had been half-hearted, disliked by Fleury, and unpopular with the nation. A low marriage, it was thought, had dragged the country into needless war. Fleury was disgusted by his inability to reconcile Spain and Sardinia. He feared that Charles Emmanuel might be bribed by Milan to change sides and evict the Bourbons from Italy. Elisabeth was suspected of still hankering after an archduchess, and of intriguing at Vienna, while the intimacy of

Patiño and Keene was nervously watched. Elisabeth, half in fun, had prophesied to Rothembourg the end of the War—"France will have some check or other, and one fine day we shall be told that you have been obliged to make peace." The envoy slily replied that European gossip reported that Charles VI would resort to a daughter's marriage to end the War. "The old refrain," rejoined Elisabeth; "we are not so keen for a girl without a dower; they can be found anywhere."

Though peace came as a surprise, it had been long in the air. In February, 1735, the Maritime Powers had offered their mediation. Their main proposal was an exchange between the Emperor and Don Carlos of Naples and Sicily for Parma, Piacenza, and the reversion to Tuscany. At this Philip and Elisabeth were deeply offended, and would not hear of peace. It seemed possible that England might enforce peace by siding with the Emperor. On occasion of a trifling dispute between Spain and Portugal an English squadron sailed for Lisbon, while a French fleet prepared to protect Cadiz. Nevertheless, tension between France and Spain increased. Elisabeth would have none of the French marriages proposed by Fleury: a scalded cat, she exclaimed, fears cold water. In despair of reconciling Spain to peace, Fleury negotiated behind her back. At a very secret conference in the suburbs of Vienna the Preliminaries were drafted. They corresponded in most respects with the proposals of the Maritime Powers. The French Government, assuming that Francis of Lorraine would marry Maria Theresa, and ultimately be elected Emperor, declared that an Emperor holding Lorraine and Bar would be a standing menace to French security. It was agreed, therefore, that Stanislaus, renouncing his claim to Poland, should be indemnified by these duchies, which should revert to France upon his death. To the Duke of Lorraine, thus dispossessed, the succession to Tuscany was assigned, and to the Emperor Parma and Piacenza. The share proposed by the Maritime Powers for Charles Emmanuel was slightly decreased, and that of Don Carlos increased. The former should have Tortona and either Novara or Vigevano instead of both, while the latter should receive the Presidi in addition to Naples and Sicily. France promised her guarantee to the Pragmatic Sanction, and on October 3, 1735, the Preliminaries were signed, to Fleury's unfeigned delight.

Spain acceded in principle to the Preliminaries of Vienna in February, 1736, with less difficulty than had been expected. Yet the ensuing treaty of November 18, 1738, lacked the assent of both Spain and Naples, and it was not until June 28, 1739, that they became parties to it. Even then the guarantee of Charles VI's Pragmatic Sanction (discussed elsewhere) was withheld. Several causes contributed to this delay. France and Spain were not wholly fortunate in their respective envoys. La Mina, who went to Paris in August, 1736, was a known opponent of French policy, and a scathing critic of French campaigning. Clever and self-confident, he fought point by point, while his sarcastic despatches strengthened Spanish resistance by their exposure of Fleury's weakness. He reported moreover that the French Government had an unduly intimate knowledge of affairs at the Spanish Court. It appeared that the French ambassador Vaulgrenant was in the habit of entering the royal apartments when the King and Queen were out, of actually sitting in the royal chair and rummaging all papers not under lock and key. He was consequently recalled in April, 1738; but his successor, Champeaux, a mere commercial agent, made matters worse by forwarding the most disgraceful libels on Philip and Elisabeth. The new Minister, La Quadra, was no genius, but he was an expert at opening sealed letters, and had discovered Champeaux' cypher. Thus, until the phlegmatic and conciliatory La Marck reached Spain, ambassadors had been rather a hindrance than a help.

A more prominent rock of offence was the marriage of Don Carlos. The French Government wished to engage him to a French princess. But the oldest was scarcely ten, and he was eager for a wife, that within a year he might have an heir as a Christmas present for his mother. Elisabeth in vain tried for Maria Theresa's sister, and Don Carlos then chose Maria Amalia, daughter of the Saxon King of Poland, the successful rival of Stanislaus. This seemed an intentional insult to the French Court, and it is surprising that the irritation so soon subsided. The sweet-tempered Queen, who, on hearing the news, had spoken with unusual acerbity, at length told La Mina that, though it would be improper to congratulate, she wished the young couple every happiness. There was consolation too in the proposals for a marriage between the Dauphin and the Infanta, on which Fleury had set his heart. The boy sent a pretty picture of himself, drawn by his own hand, which won the heart of the parents as well as of the little girl. The negotiations, however, were in October, 1737, abandoned, to be resumed a year later.

Another cause of delay had been the death of Patiño on November 3, 1736, followed on February 20, 1737, by the disgrace of Chauvelin. Patiño was succeeded by La Quadra, a mere head-clerk without initiative; nor had Chauvelin's substitute, Amelot, much greater push. Fleury's main wish was to win Austria to peace, and this could only be at the expense of Spain. The immediate cession of Lorraine to Stanislaus had been a point of paramount importance, since it was thought dangerous to wait for its evacuation by the Duke until the Grand Duke of Tuscany should die. This point was secured; and Francis of Lorraine was pensioned from March, 1737, till July 9, when Tuscany fell in. It was also of consequence that the family property within the duchy of Lorraine should follow the fortunes of the State. This implied a similar absorption of the allodial possessions of Elisabeth in Parma and Tuscany. Her very natural opposition to surrendering her patrimony was the main difficulty in the final conclusion of the Treaty of Vienna.

Peace in Europe gave breathing space for war in American waters—

war perhaps inevitable in the end, but which tact and patience might have indefinitely postponed. The practical grievances on either side have been already mentioned, but these were not all. Spanish economists, such as Ulloa and Ustariz, were enamoured of the protective theory, which was the apparent fountain-head of English and Dutch wealth. Her exclusive colonial market had been of little use to Spain, when she had no manufacture and no trade. It was otherwise when, under the nursing of Alberoni, Patiño, and Campillo, production and commerce had been created simultaneously with the instruments of defence. The commercial privileges contained in the *Asiento* treaty were a recognition of the Spanish theory by England for a definite consideration. This consideration was grossly abused, and the Spanish-American officials were rough-handed in their remedies. The English nation, feeling itself practically in the wrong, strove to put itself theoretically in the right by denying the Right of Search—a theory which it was the first to denounce when against the national interests. Religion came to the aid of economics, and in the literature of the time Papist and *guarda-costa* were almost convertible terms. But for economic pedantry and public-house Protestantism the two nations might perhaps not have come to blows. Smuggling, logwood-cutting, and vague colonial boundaries were matters of course to those who were practically concerned in them.

Spain had every pretext for a war, and yet she did not want it. It was not a King's war, nor a nation's war, nor even a Queen's war. On the English side Robert Walpole at home and Keene in Spain strove hard for peace. But Walpole's prayer for peace caused the Opposition to howl for war, and Jenkins became the war-cry of the hour. The Convention of January, 1739, by which Spain agreed to pay an indemnity less an off-set for damage done to her fleet in the battle of Cape Passaro, appeared to exorcise the peril. Unfortunately, two questions remained unsettled. Admiral Haddock's fleet, which had deeply wounded national pride by cruising off southern Spain, was not recalled; while Philip V refused to include in the Convention the debt due by the South Sea Company to himself. The Company had been, as Keene believed, short-sighted and dishonest from the first; it now pretended that it was an act of patriotism to withhold the accounts stipulated by the contract with the King, who was himself a partner.

Throughout the negotiations preceding the English War Fleury's policy had been characteristic. He blew on the live coals, and yet wished to stay a general conflagration. If Spanish attention could be diverted westwards, Elisabeth might cease to harass him on Italian topics. Thus he stiffened the resistance to England, stimulating La Mina by the sight of an English map of America with the greater part, so to speak, coloured red. Yet when war became imminent, he made the sensible proposal that England should withdraw her fleet from Gibraltar, and Spain pay the sums agreed. La Marck had successfully negotiated the

CH. V.

marriage of the Infant Philip with Louise-Elisabeth, which took place on October 25, 1739. Both Courts wished for a yet closer union; but, while Spain was bent on a political alliance for common action against England, France bargained for a commercial treaty as the *quid pro quo*. As monopoly of her markets was the real cause of the English War, Spain hesitated to open the door to the teeming produce of the French West Indies. Public opinion in France concerned itself little with commercial details, and was all in favour of joining hands against the hated English. La Mina became the most popular man in Paris; even tradesmen shut their eyes to the growing length of his accounts. At length the impulsive soldier presumed too far, and, forcing himself upon Louis, denounced Fleury's huckstering policy. The impassive King coldly referred him to his Minister, and La Mina's recall was the result. His successor, Campo Florido, a subtle, unscrupulous Italian, was better suited to wheedle concessions out of Fleury. The two Governments came very near agreement. Fleury declared himself content, if Spain would admit the sugar and coffee, which were not grown in the Spanish colonies. He was twitted by Campo Florido with drinking Levantine coffee himself, and palming off the inferior French article on Spain. At this moment, to Philip's delight, Fleury ordered a fleet to American waters, not indeed to attack the English, but to protect Spanish America from unjust aggression. This generous action was, however, only meant to sweeten the bitter draught which followed. The French Minister suddenly declared that both treaties, political and commercial, must be suspended, lest Bourbon ambition should alarm all Europe. France and Spain seemed as far as ever from alliance, when on October 20, 1740, at the close of a week's illness the Emperor died.

Sudden as it was, Charles VI's death found the Spanish Court prepared. Philip at once laid claim to all the hereditary possessions of the Habsburgs on the plea of an alleged arrangement between Charles V and Ferdinand; but his real aim was to secure the Italian provinces. Fleury was implored to plunge into war, or at least to give Spain a free hand in Italy. Timid by temperament, and irresolute from physical decay, he was not to be hurried into a definite policy. He had none of the bellicose humours of the Spanish Court; he would be content if the Imperial dignity passed from the House of Habsburg. When, at length, his hand was forced by Frederick II's attack upon Silesia, his design was that, as France acted in support of Prussia in Germany, so Spain in her Italian campaign should combine with Savoy. On this combination, and on the neutrality of Tuscany, which had been the equivalent for Lorraine, he continued to insist. But Tuscany was Elisabeth's chief desire, and she rightly dreaded the aggrandisement of Savoy. Fleury himself prophesied that one day a King of Sardinia would use all his power to eject the Bourbons from Italy; but he thought the Savoyard alliance indispensable at the present emergency. The interchange of compliments, however, became unusually warm. The new French ambassador to Spain, Vauréal, Bishop of Rennes, was the Cardinal's intimate friend, and Fleury assured him that his attachment for Elisabeth was lively and tender, though he afterwards refused to believe that he had used such warm expressions.

In view of French hesitation Spain determined to act alone. La Quadra, now Marquis of Villarias, was supplanted by the more strenuous Campillo, Patiño's best pupil, who absorbed the ministries of Finance, War, Marine and the Indies, while he poached on the foreign correspondence of Villarias. The Infant, to whom his father surrendered his rights in Lombardy, journeyed to Antibes; and Spanish troops poured through Languedoc into Provence. Montemar had already in December, 1741, landed a division at Orbitello, where it was joined by the Neapolitans. Nevertheless the Infant's prospects were not so rosy as had been his brother's in 1733. Charles Emmanuel had then been a lukewarm colleague—he was now a hesitating enemy, protecting Milan and Parma for Maria Theresa. In the former war England had been neutral; now a Mediterranean war gave a new opening to the sea power, which she utilised with effect.

The naval and military operations of France and Spain belong to other chapters; but they are closely interwoven with political relations. On January 29, 1743, when clouds hung heavily over the Alps, and the sky in Germany was at its blackest, Fleury died. Within three months his death was followed by that of his very opposite, the energetic Campillo. In neither country had these deaths any immediate effect. Amelot for fifteen months faltered in Fleury's footsteps, while Campillo had a worthy successor in Ensenada, who had all the activity of forty years, and the experience of campaigns in Africa, Naples and Savoy. The ill-success of the Franco-Spanish arms in Germany and Italy at length induced Spain to treat for an alliance with Charles Emmanuel. This seemed in September, 1743, to be practically concluded, when his treaty with Maria Theresa was suddenly made known. The counterblow was the Second, and more important, Family Compact of Fontainebleau (October 25, 1743). This professed to be imperishable; but, as d'Argenson later said, it was the fleeting fruit of ill-temper, and as burdensome to France as it was impossible of execution. The Infant was to be Duke of Milan, while Elisabeth should receive Parma and Piacenza for her life. The only territorial gains for which France stipulated were Exilles and Fenestrelles, ceded to Savoy by the Treaty of Utrecht. France had refused to declare war upon England; yet England became the first objective of the new alliance. In the latter part of 1743, Louis XV and Philip V made a personal and secret engagement to restore the Pretender. Troops were drafted to Dunkirk, which the Brest and Rochefort squadrons were to convoy to England in January, 1744, without declaration of war: meanwhile the combined French and Spanish fleets

CH. V.

would attack Admiral Mathews from Toulon. Exiles are of all friends the most embarrassing. Success depended on surprise; yet Charles Edward, who was persistently dogged by English spies, courted publicity by leaving Rome for Antibes. England demanded explanations; France, in reply, ordered Admiral de Court to attack Mathews off Hyères in conjunction with the Spanish admiral Navarro. De Court's cowardice or incompetence left the Spaniards to bear the brunt of a well-fought but disastrous action, which resulted in a honeymoon quarrel between France and Spain, the presage of divorce. Public feeling in Spain, always at heart adverse to France, was dangerously roused, in spite of the French Government's generous apologies.

Outwardly the Family Compact was in December, 1744, cemented by the marriage of the Infanta Maria Theresa to the Dauphin. Yet a disintegrating force was already in operation, for the Marquis d'Argenson, brother of the War Minister, had the portfolio of Foreign Affairs. Talents, industry and patriotism would have fitted him for constructive statesmanship, had he not been a philosopher and sentimentalist. He invented political formulae, and staked their success on the honour of Charles Emmanuel and Frederick II. Chauvelin's wish for an Italy free of all barbarians, German or Spanish, was now developed into an Utopian federation of four monarchies and two republics, and Charles Emmanuel as its sword and shield. For Spain d'Argenson had intense disdain and dislike. Elisabeth's chimerical schemes disturbed European peace, and thwarted his darling project. His prejudices were confirmed by exaggerated reports of Spain's military and financial weakness, supplied by Vauréal who also detested Elisabeth's personality.

French and Spanish generals were acting in greater harmony than their Governments. The brilliant campaign of 1745 was due to the adoption of the Spanish plan, and in great measure to the ability of the Spanish general Gages. In September Parma and Piacenza were won, and for a few months Elisabeth was actually sovereign of her Italian home. The Infant then made a triumphal entry into Milan. If only its huge unwieldy fortress, and the citadel of Alessandria, could be coaxed or starved into surrender, the aims of the Family Compact were secured. This was the moment chosen by d'Argenson to realise his Utopia. Since April he had negotiated with Charles Emmanuel behind the back of Spain. Her Italian ambitions had become the main obstacle to his wholesome desire for peace, for when in September Maria Theresa's husband was elected Emperor France had no sufficient motive left for war. Nothing, however, could excuse the manner of his negotiations, concerted with Louis XV alone, without the knowledge of his colleagues or of Spain.

Charles Emmanuel was no Utopian, and d'Argenson had to discard his visionary map of Italy for an unromantic partition of Lombardy, assigning to the King of Sardinia the duchy of Milan, which the Family

Compact had reserved for the Infant. Even these terms were only wrung from Charles Emmanuel on Christmas night, when the Infant was actually in Milan, and the citadel of Alessandria on the point of falling. The condition was an immediate armistice, but, as this could scarcely be granted without the knowledge of Spain, d'Argenson privately instructed Maillebois to act purely on the defensive. On January 25, Vauréal divulged the disgraceful treaty to Philip V, adding that failure to accept it within two days would entail the withdrawal of the French troops. It was falsely represented that the overtures had proceeded from Charles Emmanuel, whereas Louis XV had taken the initiative. Philip V was righteously indignant. It was easy to show that the situation was far more favourable than at the date of the Family Compact, and that the increase of the Sardinian State was more dangerous to both Bourbon Powers than the retention of part of Lombardy by Austria; and the Duke of Huescar was sent as envoy extraordinary to France to remonstrate against the treaty.

On the day on which Huescar reached Paris d'Argenson granted a half-hearted armistice which failed to satisfy Charles Emmanuel. He had concentrated his troops within striking distance, while his enemies were scattered over a too extended line. He pounced upon Asti, raised the siege of Alessandria, and forced the Infant to evacuate Milan. A fortnight in March had lost all the gains of the preceding year. Disaster convinced Louis XV that he had treated Spain shabbily. He ordered Maillebois to place himself at the Infant's disposal, while Noailles was sent to Madrid to undo d'Argenson's machinations, and effect a family reconciliation. The courteous old nobleman was received by Philip as a former comrade in arms, and clinched success by virulent abuse of d'Argenson. He returned to France to concert measures for the next campaign, for which the time indeed was ripe. On June 15 the Infant attacked the Austrian lines at Piacenza, and was beaten. His mother's little State was lost by this the last battle of his father's reign. On the afternoon of July 9, 1746, Philip V broke a blood-vessel, and died.

France had been absolutely ruled for seventeen years by a very old ecclesiastic of no striking ability, no political experience, and little fixity of purpose. But there are periods when negative qualities make for statesmanship, and, indeed, foreigners sometimes regarded Fleury's administration as a golden age. The Cardinal was at once hard and soft, anxious not to offend, but difficult to browbeat or circumvent. More tenacious of office than of principles, he ought to have resisted royal pressure in the Polish war, and popular clamour in the Austrian. The former brought France no credit, the latter little but shame; but Fleury had wanted neither. France was in fact impatient of the rest cure which he prescribed, and which she truly needed. Perhaps he allowed the *régime* to last too long; the national fibres became relaxed; material well-being resulted in moral flabbiness, of which coming conflicts were to give conspicuous proof.

Fleury was unfortunate in living just a few years too long, for his senile vitality became tiresome. Wonder when a statesman is going to die merges in the wish that he should do so quickly. His most positive quality was economy, untainted by avarice. Fleury, wrote Voltaire, understood nothing whatever about any financial question, but exacted rigorous economy from subordinate ministers; incapable of being an office-clerk, he was capable of governing the State. Though he at once abolished the two per cent. tax and reduced the *taille*, receipts rose rapidly. An end was put once for all to the wild fluctuations of the coinage, which of itself gave stability to commerce. Administration mainly consisted in doing nothing. This suited the more energetic elements of France: the larger cities grew apace; Paris became yearly wealthier and more luxurious. The colonies, less fidgeted by government control than usual, had never been so prosperous; the wealth of the French Sugar Islands far surpassed that of other nations' colonies. A powerful mercantile marine developed, which was, however, destined to fall a prey to England, owing to Fleury's lack of interest in the navy. "There goes the French fleet!" rudely exclaimed Lord Waldegrave, as he watched the pleasure-boats pass under the Parisian bridges.

In the backward provinces, where the people were used to being drilled, the *laissez faire* system had unfortunate results. Prosperity depended upon local weather. The peasantry were said to be eating grass in Anjou and Poitou, while elsewhere there was abundance. The famine in Paris during 1740 and 1741 was discreditable to the Government. The transport system collapsed, and grain was double as dear in Paris as in Languedoc. The temper of the people was, indeed, dangerous at this time, and Fleury's carriage was mobbed. The Bishop of Chartres wrote hotly that famine would be followed by plague, which would not confine itself to the lower orders. A law was passed to send back the needy poor who were overcrowding Paris to their provincial parishes; but it was asked how they were to get there, and where live when there. Fleury's efforts to improve communications took the form of the royal *corvée*, which forced the peasantry near the high-roads to employ time, horses and carts on betterments which profited distant towns, but not small cultivators who consumed what they grew. Rapid transit injures intermediate districts, which live on the traveller's inconveniences.

Of internal events under Fleury's administration the most striking was the sudden disgrace of Chauvelin, his ablest minister, who was generally given the credit of the acquisition of Lorraine. His rise had been equally rapid. The public was surprised when he succeeded d'Arménonville as Keeper of the Seals on d'Aguesseau's return to Court. He at once became Minister of Foreign Affairs, and then Fleury's adjunct. Henceforward he worked with the King and the Cardinal, or in Fleury's absence with the King. Chauvelin had married a very rich *bourgeoise*; he knew much about everything, and had boundless energy and ambition. It was rumoured that, if his wife died, he would take orders and become a Cardinal, in order to succeed Fleury. He appeared to be Fleury's *alter ego*; together they had taken part in every step which led to the Peace of Vienna; his disgrace in February, 1737, was a mystery which has never been explained.

If Chauvelin was guilty of any actual fault, it probably consisted in secret negotiations with Spain, encouraging resistance to Fleury's peace policy, from which his own views were gradually diverging. He was harking back to the traditions of Louis XIV's reign, to hostility with Austria and England, and consequent friendship with Spain, whereas Fleury's desire for peace insensibly led him towards the policy of the Regency. It was rumoured that the Emperor and England pressed for Chauvelin's removal. Personal reasons no doubt contributed. The Minister was unmannerly to subordinates, and his colleagues hated him. His strident voice and vulgar laugh were disagreeable to the King. Fleury himself, tenacious of the power which he could no longer efficiently wield, was jealous of the one Minister of sufficient calibre to succeed him. In the ensuing war Chauvelin's capacity was greatly missed; but on Fleury's death he ruined his chance of restoration by presenting to Louis XV a scathing criticism of the Cardinal's administration.

A contrast to the sudden split with Chauvelin was Fleury's dragging dispute with the *Parlement*, which originated in the Jansenist controversy. After Bourbon's fall the persecution of Huguenots slackened. They could only be politically dangerous in a war affecting southern France. In the War of the Austrian Succession Fleury expressed some nervousness as to this, giving it as a reason for non-intervention in Italy. The Jansenists were a source of peril much nearer home. Whole Parisian parishes, the backbone of Ultramontanism in the Wars of Religion, were now Jansenist from the priests downwards, and hostile to the Government which accepted the Bull *Unigenitus*. Some of the nobility and most of the wealthy *bourgeoisie* were covert or overt Jansenists. The party had ample funds, and its charities nursed political support.

In the *Parlement* a large majority was, if not Jansenist, Erastian, and opposed to the Government's Ultramontanism. The quarrel, taking shape in 1730, reached its climax in 1732. The original combatants were the *Parlement* and the Ultramontane Bishops, who found support in the Council, and finally in the King. The Government signally failed to win the Advocates, but somewhat weakened the solidarity between the senior members who constituted the *Grande Chambre*, and the hot-blooded juniors of the *Enquêtes* and *Requêtes*. Nevertheless the *Parlement* showed exemplary courage in face of the pettish violence of the Crown. In August, 1732, Louis XV withdrew from it the *Appel comme d'abus*, the most effective weapon of the State against church encroachment.

Three-fourths of the *Enquêtes* and *Requêtes* were exiled to the four quarters of France. Then Fleury, frightened at his own audacity, showed the white feather. The order was suspended, the exiles reinstated. For once the lawyers won a notable victory, and it was well deserved.

Society under Louis XV lacked a centre, for there was virtually no Court. The King, ever restless, wandered round from Versailles to his hunting lodges, or the luxurious house of his greatest friend, the Countess of Toulouse, at Rambouillet. His life was absolutely idle, devoted at first to his dogs and horses, and afterwards shared by them and his mistresses. He had been carefully brought up after an external, Pharisaic fashion : his confessions were written out, and corrected by Fleury, as if they were exercises. " The young King," wrote Madame in 1717, " has a nice face and plenty of sense, but is a bad-hearted child. He loves nobody except his old governess, takes dislike to people without any reason whatever, and already likes to say biting things." " They let him do everything," she elsewhere writes, " for fear he should fall ill ; I am convinced that, if he were punished, he would not fly into such passions." Louis retained his fear of Hell, and, absolute as he became, never regarded himself as having a divine right to sin. He would gloomily refer to rheumatism in his arm as a befitting reminder of his adultery, and was morbidly disturbed by deaths. On public occasions the silent, impassive youth gave the impression of stupidity. His abilities, however, were good. He was a mathematician and mechanician, and even in state affairs had sound judgment. In intimate society he was talkative and amusing, and wrote scurrilous *chansons* with the worst. This love for friendly, natural society led to the abandonment of state functions, to the elaboration of *petits appartemens*, and to the long, late suppers, where champagne loosed his tongue.

The craving for amusement probably caused Louis XV's first lapses into the sensuality which later became a habit. The Queen, with all her pretty little accomplishments and love for anecdotes, was not amusing. Neither of the two sisters, Madame de Mailly and Madame de Vintimille, who were the King's first mistresses, was young or pretty ; but both were gay and companionable. Contemporaries seem agreed that Louis was pushed into the first connexion, partly perhaps for political reasons. The Countess of Toulouse, herself virtuous, and the best of his friends, is credited with this intrigue. No one foresaw the horrible future ; the public was disposed to approve, thinking that Louis might become less a wild man of the woods, and be weaned from the excessive exercise which had more than once endangered his life. Even Fleury is said to have welcomed Madame de Mailly, but was horrified at the extension of the King's affections to two, if not three, younger sisters. He had, however, indulged his pupil so long that he had lost the practice of contradiction and reproach. He did not even persuade Louis to behave with decency towards his Queen ; Madame de Pompadour first taught him the externals of gentlemanly behaviour.

There were still respectable circles in high places, such as those of the Dukes of Noailles and Luynes; but general society leaves an impression of vulgar decadence. The abuses in the faster set are peculiarly modern. A young married Prince of the Blood vies with a middle-aged Dutch Jew for the favours of an opera-singer. A Duke of Nevers marries a comedy actress, lately mistress of an elderly financier. Ladies of rank make passionate love to the tenor of the season. Enormous fortunes made by doubtful means facilitated intermarriage between blue blood and the underbred. A successful speculator's widow was besieged by young sprigs of nobility. The banquets of *parvenu* millionaires formed the model for those of royalty itself. Decadence was far from delicate, for the best society was often drunk. Everyone strove to be amusing, and, to judge from the rage for tediously indecent *chansons*, usually failed. Even Montesquieu first made his reputation by frivolities. The prevailing degeneracy early affected the army. "That French nobility and soldiery," said Philip V to Tessé in 1724, "which formerly made war on Europe, seems now the captive of the young ladies of the opera, of the soft life of music and good cheer." One noble colonel led his men to steal a neighbouring regiment's flag; another outraged a lady's-maid, because her mistress had refused to bow to his hostess. Ugly stories came back from the Italian war, and Frederick II described the French troops under Maillebois by an unprintable dissyllable.

To literature the social and intellectual *laissez faire* was probably beneficial, encouraging the development of the divergent talents of Voltaire and Montesquieu, of Rousseau and Diderot. The contrast with contemporary Spain is curious. Here intellectual activity followed the French models of half a century before, taking corporate and not individualistic shapes. It was the age of cooperative intellectual labour, of the Spanish Academy and its Dictionary, the Royal Academy of History, the Academy of Medicine. In literature, as in foreign policy and constitutional machinery, Philip V's Spain looked backwards to Louis XIV's France.

Philip V's reign to the end was really that of Elisabeth, and the comparison must lie not between Louis XV and his uncle, but between Fleury and the Queen, between the inexperienced priest and the half-educated woman, the gentle old humourist and the vivacious termagant. The advantage was not wholly on Fleury's side. Elisabeth knew what she wanted, and got much of it. Spaniards disliked herself and her policy, but she nevertheless acted as a disagreeable tonic to the nation, imparting the vigour which France lamentably lacked. Spain created a fleet which was not afraid to fight the English; her infantry, wrote a French agent, was inadequately clothed, but its spirit was higher than that of other armies. In the field the Spaniards were well led by Montemar, La Mina, and above all by the Walloon Gages, the ablest officer who fought in either of the Italian wars. Nor must Eslava, the gallant defender of Cartagena de las Indias in 1741, be forgotten.

CH. V.

Elisabeth is usually too exclusively associated with the adventurous careers of Alberoni and Ripperdá. These Ministers only covered the twelve first years of her reign, before she had gained political experience. During the last twenty years the *régime* of the foreigner and the adventurer is over. It may be said that Alberoni was her master, Patiño her collaborator, while, after his death, she was mistress. The administration of Spain by Spaniards began with Patiño. Though he was born in Milan and educated in Italy, he was of Spanish extraction, and his interests were Spanish. Keene was right in saying that his death left a gap difficult to fill, and Elisabeth knew it. La Quadra was only her chief clerk, but an excellent specimen of his class, honest, faithful, sensible, and industrious. Her good heart regretted the necessity of his displacement; but when the storm arose she had to choose a more skilful pilot in Campillo, and, after his early death, in Ensenada, the two best of Patiño's pupils. These three statesmen were no mere politicians, but administrators with practical knowledge of military and naval organisation, of finance and provincial government. Thus they had real creative power, and compare favourably with other European ministers. To Elisabeth is due the credit of their appointment. She supported Patiño even against her husband, who so hated him that he drew a curtain whenever the Minister came to transact business. In diplomacy Castelar, Montijo, La Mina, and Campo Florido were all on a level with the abler diplomatists of the day.

Philip V's Court, as that of Louis XV, was never the centre of society. For four years, indeed, its seat was in southern Spain. The immediate occasion of removal was the double marriage of Ferdinand and his sister with Barbara and Joseph of Portugal. After the wedding ceremonies at Badajoz in January, 1729, Seville became the King's headquarters, whence a long visit was paid to Granada, and frequent excursions were made to Cadiz. Madrid, which had no trade, became "little more than a corpse"; but Cadiz, under Patiño's stirring influence, was really the centre of what life there was in Spain. Philip's health showed little improvement. Either he would only give himself and his wife three hours of rest, or else he lay in bed for weeks, his eyes fixed, his finger in his mouth, or his lips moving vehemently, but without sound. Often he refused to be shaved, to have his hair brushed, or his nails cut. He wore his trousers till they dropped off; when his valet tired of mending them, he would borrow silk from his wife's maids, and essay the task himself. Fits of violence were not uncommon. Once, when the Duke of Arco tried to save Elisabeth from Philip's fists, the King threw the gallant soldier to the ground.

Augustus II's death had a most healthful effect on Philip. The Court moved northwards, and life at Aranjuez and San Ildefonso resumed a more or less normal course. Elisabeth, whose figure began to unfit her for active exercise, provided indoor amusements, making her children act drawing-room plays, and curing Philip of his dislike for music by the importation of Farinelli. For some three-thousand nights this incomparable falsetto sang the same five songs to the infatuated King, who howled them after him song by song, or repeated the whole selection till the small hours. On the whole Philip was never so much master of himself as in his last five years; during the crisis of the Franco-Sardinian treaty (January, 1746), he played, perhaps for the first time, the leading part.

Elisabeth's character never changed. She outlived Philip by twenty years, and till the end the quality which visitors ascribed to her was vivacity. Her reputation unfortunately rests mainly on the full despatches of French ambassadors. Noailles complained that the fault of all French envoys was their ignorance of Spain—it may be added, of the Italian character. Thus it is that Keene on the one hand and the Venetian ambassadors on the other are often the safer guides. Elisabeth was a thorough Italian, practical, material, and natural. She had the passionate family sentiment of the Italians—"You would get impatient," she cried to the professedly celibate Bishop of Rennes, "if you had a large family to provide for." She thought that she ought to have everything that she desired, and that this everything was possible. The defects of her early education could never be corrected. Sitting on a stool the livelong day in front of her husband's armchair, she could only pick up knowledge at random from ministers and ambassadors. She acted on impulse rather than reason, but impulse sometimes possesses a spirit of divination. In both the wars of Polish and Austrian Succession she prophesied that French professions of eternal friendship would end in the secret surrender of Spanish interests. She divined truly that the Savoyard and not the Austrian was to be the real enemy of the Italian Bourbons. In foreseeing that the Savoyard dynasty, then hated by all Italy alike, would one day become the national leader, d'Argenson was more prophetic.

Elisabeth's career must be misjudged if viewed from a solely Spanish, and not Italo-Spanish, standpoint. In wresting Italian provinces from Spain the Treaty of Utrecht had dealt less hardly with Spain than with Italy. The evils of Austrian domination were indisputable, and Montesquieu stated in 1729 that Spanish reoccupation was the only remedy. To put her own Italian children in the place of the foreigner was no ignoble ambition for an Italian mother. The enthusiastic welcome of Don Carlos in Naples and Sicily, and of Don Philip in Parma and Milan, proved that her efforts were appreciated. Tuscany bitterly resented its alienation to Lorraine. Even for Spain, if she was ever to be more than a mere peninsular power, this renewed connexion with Italy offered prospects. It was, after all, a return to the policy of her cleverest and most successful King, Ferdinand the Catholic.

CH. V.

CHAPTER VI.

FINANCIAL EXPERIMENTS AND COLONIAL DEVELOPMENT.

THE intensity of national rivalries in the seventeenth century stimulated enquiry into the foundations of national power. It was easy to see that behind power lay wealth; and, though the time was not then ripe for a systematic study of "the nature and causes of the wealth of nations," economic writers already argued that wealth depended on numbers of people, their continuous employment, and an influx of treasure to give life to industry. Thus it was that the competition for commerce, by means of which the raw materials of many industries were obtained, their finished products exchanged, and supplies of the precious metals procured, and for colonies, with the commerce to which they gave birth, waxed keener and keener, and contributed to cause the long War of the Spanish Succession. That War marked only one stage in a struggle for commercial and colonial opportunities prolonged throughout the century; but it bequeathed to England and France a heritage of financial problems, in the solution of which both countries ventured on daring experiments, and encountered immense disasters. The story of these experiments forms an episode, though, in some respects, an isolated episode, in colonial history; for, while they had their root in, and drew their character from, the ambitions and theories which governed commercial and colonial policy, their influence on the course of events was not commensurate with their intrinsic interest, nor with the resounding effects which their failure at the moment produced.

In 1715 France, with her rich resources, seemed on the brink of ruin. Since the death of Colbert the standing debt had been increased to a gigantic height. By its side was a huge floating debt. The Government was without credit; it raised loans only at a ruinous cost; its promissory notes, *billets d'état*, circulated at a quarter of their face value, and much revenue was pledged for two years ahead. Agriculture, commerce, and industry struggled beneath usurious rates of interest and the accumulating burden of taxation. Recovery along the traditional lines of French finance opened a long and dreary vista. In the circumstances, bankruptcy was boldly proposed as a royal road to solvency, but from considerations of honesty and policy was reluctantly rejected, and more defensible, though scarcely less arbitrary, means were adopted, to deprive the financiers who had battened on the necessities of the State of a part of their ill-gotten gains. But such measures did not increase a declining revenue, nor facilitate the raising of funds by an embarrassed Government; and France cried out for a great statesman to give her relief.

There was one man whom the situation did not appal, but who saw in it the opportunity of realising a life's ambition, and of putting to the test certain theories of national wealth and progress which he had developed into a system. This was the celebrated John Law, already well known to the Regent Orleans and to the principal Courts of Europe for his personal attractions, brilliant intellect, and mastery of finance. The son of a goldsmith in Edinburgh, he had gained an experience of banking in his father's business, which he had much enlarged by a study of the banks of London, Amsterdam, and Genoa. Calculation was to him an absorbing passion, and though he had lived a roving life, and was said to have built up a fortune by gambling and speculation, he was far from being a mere adventurer. Ambitious, sanguine and disinterested, with a clear and penetrating mind, and a grasp of economic principles far in advance of his time, he longed to give his theories a practical application, believing that he had found a secret more potent in its influence on the destinies of nations than the discovery of the Indies with all their silver and gold. But conservative and impoverished Courts would not stake their fortunes on his principles. In vain he appealed to the Emperor, the Duke of Savoy, the Parliament of Scotland, the English Government, the Ministers of Louis XIV. His overtures were always refused. For years he watched the downward course of France, until, the accession of his friend the Duke of Orleans to the Regency seeming to open a new opportunity, he hurried to Paris to offer his services to the French Government and people. His ardent mind bridged with a single idea the gulf between national bankruptcy and prosperity; and, under the guidance of his System, he believed that France might mount at one bound to such a preeminence of wealth and power in Europe as no nation had ever possessed.

Economics, or at least finance, he maintained, was a science, resting on fundamental principles, and capable of supporting a coherent system of policy. The troubles of France were due to financial mismanagement, to the unscientific policy pursued. France had all the resources of wealth and power—a favourable geographical position, fertile soil, pleasant climate, an industrious and active population—and her prosperity ought to be apparent in the increasing numbers of her people, in magazines well stocked with home and foreign goods, and in the cheerfulness, courage, and good nurture of her working classes. But France had neglected her industry and trade, on which population and commodities

depended.   Now, he argued (and here we reach the point of departure
of the System), "trade depends on money."   What the blood is to the
body, that, he believed, money is to the State, the animating force which
gives life and vigour to every part.   "The best law without money
cannot employ the people, improve the product, or advance manufacture
and trade."   The first difficulty, then, to be overcome in the economic
regeneration of France was "the great scarcity of money"; and the
centre of the problem was to adopt such a kind of money that the supply
could easily be equalised with the demand.   In this respect the precious
metals failed, for, in spite of their many useful qualities, they were too
difficult and costly to procure.   Banks had been "the best method yet
practised for the increase of money," since by the circulation of their
credit they had multiplied money on a basis of gold and silver.   But
while they suggested a solution, they had not attained it.   The industries
of a country demanded more money than any bank yet established had
been able to supply.   Banks must therefore work on new principles; and
in his proposals to the Scottish Parliament, Law had suggested that the
banks should issue notes secured, not on the precious metals, but on land.
He did not suppose that indefinite quantities of money could be circulated, or that the mere increase of money was in itself an enrichment of
a country; but he believed that, in most countries at the time, and
particularly in France, the supply of money was much less than the
demand or need for it, and very much less than the demand would be if
trade and industry revived.   He appears also to have believed that an
inconvertible paper-money would circulate, so soon as the people became
familiarised with the conveniences of paper, provided that it were not
over-issued; and, if this paper were supplied by the King on his credit,
he was confident that it would not be over-issued, because the King
would never be so unwise as to ruin his own credit and destroy the
prosperity he was creating.   Hence he concluded that paper, or, in other
words, credit—the credit of the State—could serve as money.   At the
centre of affairs, under the royal control, would be a great state bank,
drawing into itself all the specie in the country, and supplying credit
money—symbols of transmission—which were all that was required
in commerce and industry, in far greater quantities than the specie
received; increasing or diminishing the quantity as circumstances dictated;
in its sovereign wisdom never over-issuing; and thus satisfying without
trouble and cost the great need of money in accordance with the sure
principle of equalising demand and supply.   No longer, then, would
money be withdrawn from circulation and hoarded.   Who would hoard
paper?   Who would need to hoard when scarcity of money was never to
be feared?   But what if the people were reluctant to use state notes in
the place of gold and silver?   On this problem Law's views oscillated.
In 1716 confidence was a plant of slow growth, and the acceptance of the
notes must be voluntary.   In 1720 circumstances, and with them his

opinions, had changed; the King must use his absolute power to compel the circulation of the notes; legal compulsion created confidence.

To ensure a supply of money proportionate to the demands of industry was perhaps Law's dominant idea; but, beyond this, the System involved far-reaching changes in the economic organisation of the State. Law conceived of the nation as a whole, whose members, though rendering different services and holding different stations, ought to have a common interest in the national prosperity. But, looking round, he saw on all sides class struggling against class, and no consciousness of a common interest. He saw a Government that burdened the people with oppressive taxation, and shackled industry with needless restriction, to the detriment of its own and its subjects' revenues; a class of capitalists whose gains depended on the distresses of their country, who stifled commerce with usurious interest; an official hierarchy, ridiculously large, doubling the weight of taxation by their numbers and their corruption; many small companies struggling with inadequate capital to hold their own in the competition of foreign commerce; a labouring class, "the more necessary part" of the State, unemployed and poverty-stricken. Was it impossible to create a conception of a united interest and compel all to serve it? Could not the national forces be combined, and the striving of individual men and classes be laid to rest, in some great scheme of cooperation, some giant consolidation of existing enterprises, which, without destroying individual activity in certain spheres, would unite competing groups and provide the strength for vaster undertakings? Law believed that the System could achieve this. A company could be formed to which the Government should grant all the commercial and financial privileges then farmed by various bodies; in which the creditors of the State should receive shares in exchange for their debts; and in which the public should be induced to invest their savings. The one great organisation would control the foreign commerce of France, develop the magnificent resources of her colonial empire, reorganise her fiscal system, and, if necessary, exercise a controlling influence on domestic producers; by consolidation with the state bank it would unite the money and trading powers, so that the stream of money should flow straight into the fields of commerce; by swallowing up all existing associations, and thus engrossing all large capitals and sources of revenue, it would enable the French nation to trade as a unit, and "compel all subjects to find their fortunes only in the happiness and opulence of the whole kingdom." Thus would be reared a giant trust, broad-based as France, wide-reaching as the realms of commerce and finance. No foreign rival could withstand such an institution, and English and Dutch would be swept from the seas. Within the State the old conditions would be completely transformed. Jarring interests would be harmonised, for all would be concerned in the general prosperity. No more would the nation lie stricken at the feet of the money-lender, whose power would be abased.

The Government, so far from living by loans, would find abundant means in the growing wealth of the country, and would itself finance industry and develop the resources of France. The standing debt would be abolished, and the capitalist, instead of preying on his country, would look to the gains of commerce for his reward. No more would there be unemployment, for usury would be extinguished and industry and commerce would not be starved for want of capital. Restrictions on industry would be removed and the fiscal administration remodelled. The nobility would be lifted out of the morass of debt in which they were involved, and the peasantry, instead of being impoverished by taxation and unemployment, would profit by a reviving agriculture and lighter burdens. Thus, with abundance of money, a reorganised commerce, interests harmonised, a united France would become " the mistress of commerce and the arbiter of Europe." Such was the glowing vision which Law conjured up.

The foundations of the System were laid with difficulty. The Regent, though convinced himself that Law's proposals were practicable, was not strong enough to secure their immediate acceptance. The Council, advised by leading merchants and financiers, disliked experiment and distrusted Law. Facile and persuasive, he argued his case in memoranda and letters, and modified his scheme until he asked simply permission to establish at his own risk a bank, to be worked on the strictest lines, confident that it would succeed, and prove the starting-point of the mighty financial revolution he designed. Founded in May, 1716, as a bank of discount and deposit, with the right to issue notes, the Bank quickly achieved a conspicuous success. Its notes were welcomed, for they were payable on demand, and represented not the *livre tournois*, whose value was liable to sudden fluctuation, but a fixed weight of gold. Its recognised utility enabled the Regent to extend its privileges. In April, 1717, its notes were made receivable for taxes, and the provincial collectors, much against their will, were ordered to use them in making their remittances to Paris.

Law's second creation was a commercial company. In the last quarter of the seventeenth century intrepid adventurers marked out in North America a new sphere for French enterprise, the great central basin of the continent watered by the Mississippi. An influential merchant, Antoine Crozat, enjoyed in 1717 the monopoly of its commerce, with little profit to himself or the country. Law's genius perceived that this great region must be capable of immense development; and he asked and obtained permission to take over Crozat's monopoly, and to float a company for the commerce and colonisation of Louisiana. Thus, in August, 1717, the Company of the West came into being, endowed with liberal privileges, and possessing a nominal capital of a hundred million *livres*. But France had seen too many schemes of colonisation bear no fruit, to regard with enthusiasm an enterprise over which the past history of Louisiana, and of other commercial companies favoured with state patronage cast a shadow of doubt. Moreover, the capital, like the capital of the bank, was subscribed in *billets d'état*, and was thus invested, not in Louisiana, but in the state debt, leaving only the interest available for use. None the less, Law could congratulate himself on the success he had achieved. The two great organs of the System, the Bank and the Company, had been established—it remained only to extend their functions and influence until they fulfilled the promises he had made and achieved the regeneration of France.

In 1718 the *Parlement*, always the enemy of the System, after a severe struggle with the Regent, in the course of which it attacked both the Bank and Law, suffered defeat and humiliation, and the way was thrown open for fresh advances. In December the Bank was made a royal bank, and its notes became legal tender throughout the kingdom, though from this time they represented only current coin. Their circulation, continually growing with experience of their utility and confidence in their value, was now quickened by the voice of the law. Gold and notes alone, which meant in practice chiefly notes, were henceforth to be used in large payments; and, in expectation of the increased demand for notes, branches of the Bank were established in five of the principal towns. Thus the acceptability of the notes was diminished, while at the same time new facilities were opened for multiplying the quantity, since the dangerous power of creating money rested virtually in the hands of the Regent.

The extension of the Company next occupied the mind of Law. It was necessary to enlarge its operations and increase its profits, in order to attract the capital of the investor. The manufacture and sale of tobacco was a state farm, whose term was just expiring. It was obviously of advantage to the Company to acquire a monopoly which would benefit its colonial plantations; and Law accordingly offered more than double the two million *livres* which had previously been paid. He followed this up in December, 1718, by purchasing the privileges and property of the Company of Senegal. These measures exercised a stimulating influence on the fortunes of the Company whose shares began to rise. The following year Law prepared for vaster operations. In May, the East India Company and its off-shoot the China Company, neither of which was prospering, and in July, the Company of Africa, which traded with the Barbary States, yielded up their rights to the Company of the West, which henceforward took the name of the Company of the Indies. In 1720, the last two independent commercial associations, the Company of San Domingo and the Guinea Company, shared the same destiny. In order to take advantage of the opportunities thus multiplied, the Company required to raise new capital. The public, which had neglected the Company of the West, had been profoundly impressed by the great transactions which had brought into being the Company of the Indies. Law was thus able to issue 50,000 shares of 500 *livres* each, at a premium of 50 *livres*, and to add the condition that four of the original shares of the Company of the West, called *mères*, must be presented in purchasing a *fille*, or share in the Company of the Indies. As subscriptions were payable in twenty monthly instalments, a great impetus was given to speculation, for which an unrestricted issue of notes gave every facility; and the price of the shares mounted with great rapidity. In July (1719) the Company bought the right of coinage for nine years—a profitable right for which fifty million *livres* was promised. Another issue of 50,000 shares, *petites filles*, followed this new bargain. The price was 1000 *livres*, the price of the existing shares, and four *mères* and one *fille* had to be presented by each subscriber for a *petite fille*. At the same time Law boldly announced that from the beginning of 1720 two dividends of 6 per cent. would be paid annually. The promise fed the fires of speculation; though it was very doubtful whether the tobacco monopoly, the profits of the mint and of commerce, and the interest payable by the State could yield the sum that would be required. Law, however, had other sources of revenue in view. The farms of the indirect taxes were in the hands of the brothers Pâris, powerful financiers, who, copying Law's methods, had organised a company known as the Anti-System, which proved a formidable rival of the Company of the Indies. In August, 1719, Law, outbidding the Anti-System, secured these farms for fifty-two million *livres* a year, and struck down his opponents. To them were added the general receipts from direct taxation, hitherto collected by Receivers-General in each generality, so that the whole fiscal administration was united under a single control. The reforms that followed cannot be particularised here, but they constitute one of the chief triumphs of the System. No sub-farms were created; taxation was simplified, and some oppressive taxes removed; the Receivers-General were abolished; and by various measures greater order, unity, and economy were introduced into this branch of government.

It was in return for these last concessions that Law attempted the greatest of his financial operations. One by one he had dealt with the worst evils that afflicted France—the scarcity of money, the floating debt, the paralysis of foreign commerce, the costly and oppressive fiscal system—he now approached the problem of the standing debt. The System had made money cheap. Everywhere debtors were gaining. The *seigneurs* were clearing off their mortgages. The moment had come for the State also to liquidate its debt, whose very existence represented a dominance of private over public interest. So Law maintained; and he therefore proposed that the Company should lend the Government fifteen hundred million *livres* at 3 per cent., with which to pay off the *rentes*-holders. Both parties were to gain—the creditors of the State would find a more profitable investment in the shares of the Company, while the Government would reduce the rate of interest on the public debt by 1 per cent. Immense financial transactions followed. In four successive issues Law placed upon the market 324,000 shares of 500 *livres* at a price of 5000 *livres* each. The bank poured out notes to meet the demands of speculation, and the public rushed in and bought the new shares. Their price leaped up and excitement reached fever pitch. It was only with difficulty and loss that the *rentes*-holders made the exchange of their rights from the State to the Company. For months there continued a madness of speculation which has never been surpassed. The price of a share was raised to 12,000 *livres*. Fabulous fortunes were realised by unknown and low-born men. Foreigners crowded into Paris, and all classes were mingled in the *mêlée* of the Rue Quincampoix. A new and vulgar passion seemed to have asserted its intrusive presence, and amidst the excitement men observed a luxury and a depravation of manners that contrasted strangely with the severities in which the late reign had closed. In such a tumult of extravagant anticipation the System reached its zenith. Under its auspices real things had been done, and fruitful enterprises set on foot; but they were not represented by the milliards of paper values with which a cosmopolitan throng gambled in the Rue Quincampoix. By conjuring up prospects of gain, Law had awakened the interest and cupidity of the nation, which took his vision for a reality, and bought and sold the wealth which he imagined.

Law had now reached the summit of his fame and power. He was honoured and courted on all sides. The fashionable world crowded to his levees, dukes and peers waited in his ante-room. Lady Mary Wortley Montagu, passing through France in 1718, found to her delight "an Englishman (at least a Briton) absolute in Paris." Foreign Governments sought his good offices. From Germany, England and Italy came proposals for the marriage of his children; from Edinburgh the freedom of the city in a gold box. He was made a member of the Academy of Sciences, and, in January, 1720, after becoming a convert to the Catholic faith, Controller-General; in March the title of Superintendent of Finance was revived and conferred on him. But the inevitable reaction was at hand. A share of 500 *livres* could not be maintained at 12,000 by a dividend of 12 per cent.; and shrewd men had begun to realise and invest in real property. The shares showed signs of falling; and, as speculation ceased, the evil effects of the inflated currency made themselves felt. The System was threatened by a severe financial crisis, from which there could be no escape. Uncertain what might happen were confidence seriously disturbed, Law embarked on a heroic struggle against irresistible forces, and burdened the System with the impossible task of maintaining the price of the share and preventing the depreciation of the note. It is impossible here to do more than summarise the fruitless efforts by which he prolonged the agony throughout 1720, without staving off a collapse wherein Bank, Company, and System were involved in common ruin. He declared a dividend of 40 per cent., and took measures designed to stimulate the circulation of the notes, which were becoming suspect in commerce. In February the Bank and Company were united—perhaps the two struggling swimmers might support each other. But the effect of this measure, intended apparently to maintain the credit of the note, was rather to sacrifice the credit of the share. In March the price of the share was fixed at 9000 *livres*, and shares and notes were made interchangeable in this ratio at the Bank. The use of specie was virtually proscribed, and large quantities were confiscated. The Rue Quincampoix was closed, and speculators were dispersed by the sabres of the police. But notes still flowed from the bank presses in an unending stream. More desperate remedies seemed to be required, and in May, on the ground that the notes and shares were over-valued in relation to specie and commodities, it was ordered that by gradual stages their value should be reduced to one-half. With this the credit of the note was utterly destroyed, and panic complete and universal reigned. A confused period followed. The edict was revoked, and Law was superseded, though, with great courage, he remained in France throughout the year and, fertile as ever in expedients, exerted himself to save the institutions he had founded. But confidence could not be restored, and various attempts to call in a part of the notes issued proved unavailing. The enemies of the System closed in upon it. In October the Bank was abolished and the use of specie permitted; in December Law went into exile, while the *Parlement* returned from it. Early in 1721 the Company was deprived of many of its privileges, and a severe inquisition made into all the debts of the System. The creditors were divided into five classes and received compensation according to the apparent justice of their claims. The inquisition ended, the mighty mass of records that had been collected was deposited in a huge iron cage and burned in the Bank court.

Not so easily could the memories of Law's work be obliterated or its influence for good and evil undone. He had struck the note of a more liberal commercial and industrial policy. He had simplified taxation, removed oppressive duties, broken down provincial customs-barriers, recalled emigrants, and improved means of communication by building roads and cutting canals. He had introduced fruitful ideas into commerce and administration, had laboured hard to promote the colonisation of Louisiana, and had turned the attention of France once more towards maritime and colonial enterprise. In addition, he had relieved the State of a part of its debt, and enabled many of the *seigneurs* to free themselves. The price of this was the widespread ruin, the violent redistribution of wealth which the rise and fall of the System caused, and the reaction that followed in its train, wherein the benefits of most of his reforms were lost. The Bank was not reestablished; but the Company, protected by powerful friends, weathered the violences of the liquidation, recovered some of its former privileges, and, though never very prosperous, survived until 1769.

From the retreat of exile, his eyes turned on France, in vain hope to be recalled, Law watched the dissolution of his work. Invincible optimist as he was, his faith in his principles remained unshaken. He confessed that he had moved too fast, but attributed the failure to unexpected events which had compelled a departure from his plans. Montesquieu visited him at Venice, where he died in 1729, and found him still the same man, still absorbed in projects, still calculating values. It is no longer necessary to add that he was no charlatan. He was, in fact, a great man, and of his disinterestedness and integrity there can be no question. Ambition actuated him; and, playing ever high, he staked and lost his name and fortune on his System. In character he exhibited the rare combination of the audacious and brilliant theorist with the cool-headed man of action. His mind, solely absorbed in economics, was, in some respects, typical of the commercial spirit of his time; yet, in his sympathy and care for the masses of the people, he rose above its harder manifestations, and joined hands with later thinkers. No doubt prudence ought to have restrained him from the attempt to revolutionise the financial system of a nation in a few brief months; but a sanguine temper urged him along untrodden paths, whose pitfalls experience had not then revealed. He brought disaster on France; yet he deserved better of her than exile, spoliation, and calumny.

It was not a mere coincidence that events, in some respects similar to those just narrated, were happening at the same time on the other side of the Channel. England, like France, was burdened with a heavy debt, and her Government also turned, not for the first occasion, to a commercial company for aid, and secured financial assistance by the concession of trading privileges. But the South Sea Company and its scheme cannot altogether be compared with the Company of the Indies and the System. The sustained and scientific effort of Law to remodel the economic life of France has an originality and a scope far beyond the attempt made in England to lighten a financial burden and to develop a trade with South America. The same cupidity, the same infatuation contributed to the failure of both; but the Bubble, inspired by fewer ideas than the System, and less vast in its ambitions, was also less fearful in the ruin that it wrought. The South Sea Company owed its origin to a measure of Harley's for the improvement of the public credit. In 1710 there existed a floating debt of more than nine millions sterling, for the repayment of which no provision had been made. Harley offered to incorporate the proprietors of this debt as a chartered company with a monopoly of the trade to Spanish America, for which it was expected that considerable facilities would be granted in the Treaty of Peace then being negotiated. The rumoured wealth of the Spanish Indies gave to the proposal a singular fascination, and the Company was formed. It was forbidden to transact banking business, or to send vessels into Eastern waters, but it was to have the exclusive right of trade with Spanish America, and to be permitted to make discoveries and plant settlements within the territorial limits assigned. Its privileges were to be perpetual, but the debt, on which the Government guaranteed an interest of 6 per cent., was to be redeemable at one year's notice after 1716.

That the Company thus founded never took a conspicuous place in the annals of our trade and empire, but had a chequered and unprosperous career, and sank into an inglorious decline, was due, not to defects in the scheme or to lack of energy, but principally to want of opportunity. It never enjoyed any real prospect of developing commerce with the Spanish possessions, or of planting colonies in South America, and the enlargement of its trading privileges which it was led to expect was afterwards refused. The concessions secured by the Treaty of Utrecht proved very slender, and were hedged about with qualifications which much diminished their utility. In addition to the famous *Asiento*, Great Britain received permission to send for thirty years an annual vessel of 500 tons burden (Spanish measure) to trade at certain specified ports. Both of these rights were chiefly valued for the more profitable contraband trade which they made possible. Troubles gathered thick round the American trade in its infancy. Unexpected delays, obstacles, charges, and confiscations by Spanish officials, for which no redress could be obtained, diminished its profits ; and, on the outbreak of war in 1718, the Spanish Government seized the effects of the Company, contrary to the original agreement. The Directors, however, had achieved some success and profit by certain financial transactions which they had undertaken on behalf of the Government ; and they were thus encouraged to put forward the great scheme which has given to the Company its principal fame.

Their proposal, after some of its more grandiose features had been removed in consultation with Ministers, was that the Company should take over thirty-one millions of unconverted debt, consisting chiefly of irredeemable annuities, by purchase from the proprietors or by subscription into their capital stock. The gain to the State was large and evident. An immense debt would be converted into a redeemable form, while the interest upon it was to be reduced from five to four per cent. after 1727, and in addition, the Directors offered to pay £3,500,000 as the price of the contract. The Government accepted the scheme; but the House of Commons, persuaded that taking over debt was a very profitable operation, determined " as it were to set the nation to auction," with the result that the Bank outbid the Company. The Directors hereupon increased their offer to £7,500,000. This competition, carried far beyond the bounds of prudence, was fatal to a doubtful scheme. The Company's stock could never be worth the high price to which it would have to be raised before the transaction could be successfully completed, and the project should have been still-born. But, unfortunately, people were deceived by the arts and the rashness of the Directors, with the extraordinary consequence that "the more the South Sea Company were to pay to the public, the higher did their stock rise upon it"; and, before the South Sea Act had passed through Parliament, where it was opposed by Walpole and others, the price of the stock had risen above 300. Before proceeding to deal with the annuitants, the Directors issued two money subscriptions, the first at 300, the second at 400, which were eagerly bought. They then proposed what were, in the circumstances, favourable terms for the exchange of the annuities, of which considerably more than one-half were immediately subscribed, some having been deposited at the South Sea House before any announcement had been made. The price of the stock rose at a prodigious rate, though with strange and violent fluctuations; the Directors lent out money freely on subscription receipts and the bankers treated them "as good as land security." In the conditions that prevailed, these facilities stimulated speculation until the course of events became "ungovernable." The Directors yielded to the clamour for a third money subscription, and sold five millions of stock at 1000. In August, 1720, they received a second subscription of the irredeemables.

But the South Sea Company did not monopolise the interest of the public. It was the giant bubble in a sea of bubbles. During the preceding two or three years many projects of various kinds—industrial, commercial, and financial—had been advertised; and in the fever of excitement which attended the great operations of the South Sea Company, their number multiplied with astonishing rapidity. Every day saw new schemes put forward by enterprising stockbrokers who took small deposits. The majority at least bore rational titles, and related to fisheries, insurance, colonisation, land improvement, or the establishment of some manufacture, though a few were purely fantastic, and one audacious thief sounded the depth of public credulity with "a certain...design, which will hereafter be promulgated," and found it bottomless. Neither promoter nor subscriber as a rule expected that a business would be set on foot; both wished to gain by speculating in the shares created. Many of these smaller companies received the support of distinguished names. The Prince of Wales became a Governor of the Welsh Copper Company, in spite of the protests of Walpole, and gained £40,000, before a remonstrance from the judges induced him to resign his lucrative position. Amid scenes of great excitement the shares were hawked in Change Alley. At milliners' and haberdashers' shops, or in taverns and coffee-houses, ladies and gentlemen met their brokers. Innumerable transactions took place, and much money changed hands. People who had made profits in the smaller ventures hastened to invest them in the older and greater companies, whose shares rose to an unprecedented height. The Hudson's Bay Company, anxious to improve the occasion, prepared to create additional shares for sale to the public. "The very bank became a bubble," and lent out money on its own stock. The Government remained, in Aislabie's words, "only spectators of this melancholy scheme"—unable to control the Company from whom such hard terms had been exacted.

The great majority of the Bubble Companies had no legal status, being neither partnerships nor chartered bodies; and the South Sea Directors, believing their existence prejudicial to the rise of South Sea stock, procured a writ against some of them by name and against the others in general. The writ struck consternation on the crowd of operators in Change Alley. The projectors disappeared, and the orgy of speculation suddenly ceased. But prudent men had doubted for some time the soundness of the Company's own policy; and the extraordinary collapse of the smaller bubbles, with the consequent ruin of many people, spread distrust far and wide, and the price of the stock fell rapidly. The Directors sought to sustain it by lavish promises of dividends, but a more calculating spirit had succeeded to the frenzy of expectation, and men no longer believed that dividends of thirty and fifty per cent. were possible. By September 20 the stock had fallen to 410, whence it rose for a moment to 675 on the rumour that the Bank was coming to the assistance of the Company, only to fall again with greater rapidity, when the negotiations with the Bank failed, to 175 by the end of the month. Passion had subsided, and the great delusion was at an end. Thousands of people of all classes now found that, in a moment of infatuation, they had been beguiled into surrendering a substance to grasp a shadow, and that they were ruined.

In the general confusion and recrimination Walpole found himself summoned by common consent to propose a remedy. It was no easy matter to mitigate the vindictive spirit of the Commons, and turn their energies towards practical measures for the restoration of public credit and the relief of those who had suffered. Believing that the South Sea scheme, for all the evils that it had entailed, had achieved a great public end, by transforming the irredeemable annuities into a redeemable debt bearing a lower rate of interest, he wished to "rely on the main foundation" that the contracts made with the Company should be left untouched. When this had been agreed, he proposed that 18 millions of South Sea stock should be engrafted into the stocks of the Bank and the East India Company; that unsold South Sea stock, of which there remained some 14 millions, should be distributed amongst the existing proprietors as a dividend; and that money subscribers should be relieved from further payments. In addition part (afterwards increased to the whole) of the sum promised by the Company to the nation was to be remitted. The proposals were accepted by Parliament, but the engraftment of the 18 millions of stock, owing to the opposition of the other two Companies concerned, was never carried out.

Meanwhile, the Commons proceeded with punitive measures. In

January, 1721, a committee was appointed to examine the manner in which the South Sea Act had been executed. Its report exposed "a scene of iniquity and corruption." The Company's books would not bear examination. Some had been destroyed or secreted. Knight, the cashier, had disappeared with the register called the green book; in others "false and fictitious entries," "entries with blanks," "entries with rasures and alterations" were discovered. A fictitious stock of £574,000 had been disposed of before the South Sea Act was passed, and "no mention made of the name of any person whatsoever to whom the stock is supposed to be sold." It had helped to promote the Bill. The Directors had laid themselves open to charges of illegality, corruption, and favouritism; and some members of the Government appeared to have been accomplices. Aislabie, the Craggs', father and son, Charles Stanhope, and Sunderland were all accused of having used their position to make profit from the scheme. The House of Commons, carried away by the passions of the moment, acted with great severity and little discrimination and confiscated the greater part of the estates of the Directors, as well as of Aislabie and the elder Craggs. Walpole moderated as far as he could the fierceness of the outburst. He defended Stanhope, who was acquitted by a majority of three, "which put the town in a flame"; intervened on behalf of Aislabie, who was expelled the House and committed to the Tower, and saved his old rival Sunderland, and with him the Whig administration. The Craggs', father and son, dying suddenly, escaped condemnation—against the younger little had been proved. Thus the Bubble mania ended. There had been a widespread overturning of fortunes, many innocent people had suffered severely, and the collapse of credit injured industry and trade in all parts of the country. But the nation had gained in having achieved its ends; and a few more prescient individuals, who sold their stock at the right moment, reaped immense fortunes.

The subsequent history of the Company may be briefly outlined. In 1722 it was permitted to sell four millions of its stock to the Bank, and in the following year to divide the remainder, nearly 34 millions, into two equal parts, the one to be annuity, the other trading stock. For eight years it made a courageous effort to revive the Greenland whale-fishery, but without success. Nor did its American trade prosper. As early as 1732, the surrender of the *Asiento* and of the annual ship for an equivalent was seriously discussed; but the irregular trade connected with these rights was considered too valuable to the nation. However, the next year, the Company obtained permission to transform three-quarters of its trading stock into new annuity stock, clear of all trading risk; and at last, in 1750, in exchange for £100,000 from the Spanish Government, they abandoned, for the remaining four years of their term, the concessions obtained at Utrecht, and an end was put to a trade which, "without any substantial benefit to Great

Britain, had given insuperable umbrage to the Court of Madrid." The surrender virtually terminated the commercial history of the Company, though its exclusive privileges were not taken away until 1807. In 1853 the remaining South Sea annuities were either redeemed or converted into other government stock.

"National power and wealth," wrote Law, "consists in numbers of people and magazines of home and foreign goods. These depend on trade...." The statement may serve as a terse expression of the economic faith and ambition of the early eighteenth century. It explains the concentration on commercial and industrial expansion, to which both the Bubble mania in England and the System in France bore witness. It explains moreover the colonial policy of the older nations. They still regarded the new lands as plantations, sources whence raw materials were obtained, markets under control, playing their part in general history by the services they rendered to their mother States; and remained blind or indifferent to the significance of the great development these lands were undergoing. Thus trade increased and flourished; but, save in the case of the French, colonising energy waned. Between 1713 and the outbreak of the American War few new colonies were planted; and in the history of maritime exploration, there is little to record from the voyages of Dampier to those of Cook and his French and English contemporaries. To the eagerness of the sixteenth century, and the enthusiasm of the seventeenth, had succeeded, with more knowledge, a more calculating spirit and more definite aims. It seemed better to develop existing fields of colonisation than to compass sea and land to find new. With fewer fresh beginnings there was less unavailing effort; and, save that the long rivalry of French and English proceeded to its conclusion, less wasting strife amongst the nations for the ownership of territory. By 1713, their various spheres of action had been largely determined, either by treaty, or by the surer arbitration of impregnable possession. In the East, Dutch, English, and French divided almost the whole of the trade; and, in 1731, the Emperor Charles VI's endeavour to obtain a share for the merchants of the Austrian Netherlands by the foundation of the Ostend East India Company, was finally defeated by their united diplomatic efforts. The political significance of this transaction is described elsewhere. But, though colonial progress rested principally on the foundations already laid, it did not slacken. The young societies of the New World grew rich and strong, enlarged their borders, and found in their own vigorous life the impetus which the overflowing enterprise of Europe, now concentrated in narrower channels, had formerly provided. Only a few words need here be said as to their expansion, since it resulted in the founding of new States and a complete transformation of the colonial world, which are described in later volumes.

On the continent of North America the great problem of the eighteenth century was, who should colonise the vast interior—the English, firmly planted on the Atlantic plains, or the French, strongly posted on the St Lawrence? In favour of the French were their prior possession, ease of access and unflagging and brilliant ambition. But they fought against insuperable odds. It was population and wealth that were to tell, and the adventurous enterprise of their leaders was fruitless when not backed by the strength of the colonist. Louisiana, indeed, had struggled painfully into existence, and Canada, in spite of an unfavourable climate and soil and the dangerous navigation of the St Lawrence, had made real progress. At a time when kings had ceased to study Canadian censuses, and the hopes of France were turned towards the Mississippi, a French-Canadian people was coming into being. But in this competition the English had completely distanced their opponents. In the growth of their population, the success of their agriculture, and the activity of their commerce, England's Atlantic colonies had more than realised the promise of the preceding century, and already discerning eyes caught a glimpse of a marvellous future. Rich and populous, these colonies craved wider boundaries, and threatened to overflow into the Ohio Valley. Nor was their strength that of wealth alone. They were fully developed societies. Their self-government was a reality; only in industry and commerce did they suffer the control of the mother country, and in commerce her regulations were systematically evaded. They enjoyed a substantial race unity, and though local patriotism was strong—for differences of religion and of economic conditions had caused striking diversities in their development—they were not unconscious of common interests or of a common destiny. Thus economic strength seemed to be pitted against imperial imagination; but, while the issue was still doubtful, the fortunes of war over a wider field transferred the French North American possessions to the English Crown.

In Central and South America the distribution of power remained unchanged. No further Teutonic encroachments disturbed the Latin nations in the security of their vast dominions; save where, in Central America, the persistence of the logwood-cutters established a right which, recognised and amplified in treaties, led to the foundation of the British colony of Honduras. The Spanish Government still continued, but with no greater success, a vain struggle to monopolise the commerce of its empire; and the strange spectacle was presented of colonist, foreigner, and official combining to defeat the regulations and policy of the mother country. Mexico and Peru cried out for freer trade; and Dutch, English, French, and Danish smugglers bought or forced an entrance for their goods. Several islands in the West Indies flourished on this contraband, and Buenos Ayres became a great city. In the latter half of the century, by cautious and leisurely steps, Spain relaxed her restrictions, to the great advantage of her colonies, but without removing the sense of grievance which her policy had excited. The progress of Brazil continued, and the southern provinces much increased in wealth and importance. The discovery of gold and then of diamonds brought settlers and commerce. Rio de Janeiro became a busier port than Bahia, though the wealth of the country still rested on sugar and coffee plantations rather than on minerals.

These great developments and their consequences form the chief features of colonial history during the eighteenth century. In the earliest arenas of colonisation, the West Indies and the African coast, such changes were not possible. Nature fixed narrow limits to the economic progress of small islands, and hence also to their capacity of self-defence and their political outlook. And progress was not only limited, it was also uncertain and fluctuating. Where fertile land was to be had, thither men hurried; and the growth of an island community might be rapid in the extreme; but, wasteful methods of cultivation exhausting the soil, the fortunes of most islands, after a brief period of prosperity, declined to a certain normal level, varying according to their advantages and the competition of other islands. Thus supremacy shifted from one to another. Throughout the West Indies the principal industry was the cultivation of sugar. Cocoa, indigo, cotton, and coffee plantations also existed; but the exports of these commodities could not compare in value with that of sugar—and only in the Bermudas and Bahamas, which were comparatively neglected, were other industries more important. Yet the anxieties of sugar cultivation were great. A large capital had to be sunk in land, buildings, and stock, and serious risks of loss by hurricane, slave revolt, or capture at sea to be faced; though, on the other hand, could be set the sure market at a high price, and the large returns of a good season. From the English islands the greater part of the crop was exported to the mother country; the remainder, together with rum and molasses, to the English colonies on the mainland, in exchange for horses, lumber, and provisions, since few of the islands were entirely self-sufficing in their food supplies. Many of the proprietors were absentees, and much of the capital invested was raised in England, especially in the case of the Windward Islands. As sugar production extended, so also did the slavery system. The large plantation displaced the small freehold, and the negro ousted the white workman. Almost everywhere the African population out-numbered, and was generally many times greater than, the European. The social order took the form of a planter aristocracy resting on slave labour, and the white middle class either disappeared or lost in status. Hence arose societies fragile in their structure, limited in their development, and cruel in their laws. The governing class, exposed to constant danger of an upheaval in the ranks of industry below, protected itself by stringent and heartless legislation. On the plantations the slaves appear to have been generally overworked. It was not the climate, but the system, which decimated the black population, and rendered its natural increase so small that an immense annual importation was necessary to maintain its numbers. Yet the negro was not incapable of freedom, any more than he was of brutal retaliation. The Maroons of Jamaica, hardy descendants of Spanish slaves, or of fugitives from English masters, gave an example, before the day of Toussaint L'Ouverture, of black communities able to assert and maintain their independence. The Government of the island, unable to extirpate these troublesome bands, had been compelled to guarantee their freedom and assign them reserves of land. Thus, in much which represents the triumph of civilisation over barbarism, the development of the West Indies was slow. In days of struggle and experiment it was no wonder that life was restless, and the progress of the arts small. But the eighteenth century saw little amelioration of these evils. Nature offered no fairer scene of colonisation than the islands in the Caribbean Sea, but nowhere were manners more unbridled, slavery crueller, and the higher interests of civilisation more completely neglected. Commerce, lawful and unlawful —the sugar trade, the logwood trade, the negro trade, the contraband trade—governed all things. Buccaneering indeed had ceased; but piracy, mean and cruel, continued. Desperate men still infested the seas, giving little quarter and receiving less. Slave conspiracies and revolts darkened the annals of most years. The evils were partly a result of political and economic insecurity, and partly of a spirit of commercial exploitation unrestrained in the interests of the general social welfare.

The rivalry of French and English showed itself as conspicuously in the West Indies as on the mainland. After 1713 both Powers turned their attention to the Windward Islands. But their claims collided, and for years little was done, since each prevented the other from making settlements. The pressure of population, the impetus of progress, and the attractions of such islands as St Lucia, Grenada, and St Vincent were, however, certain to break down this policy of mutual exclusion. A partition was necessary, and fortunately for England, one was made in 1763, at the close of a war in which she had achieved a decisive success. France received St Lucia; England, Grenada and St Vincent as well as Tobago and Dominica, and new fields of colonisation were thus laid open. But the relative position of the different Powers depended on the development of the islands which they owned as well as on the acquisition of new territory. In this respect the French had an advantage. Their islands were larger than those of other Powers, with the exception of the Spanish, and their policy was wiser. In the English islands taxation was heavier, and trade was more restricted than in the French, while the refining industry was discouraged by a high duty on refined sugar imported into the mother country. In addition, the French were more successful in the management of the negro, who, under better treatment, was found more orderly, sensible, and honest. It was generally said that the energy of the English had declined, and they certainly suffered from a want of great leaders. In Jamaica much good land lay unoccupied, and, though this remained the most populous and richest of the English islands, its progress had disappointed expectations. Both from a military and a commercial point of view its central position rendered it of great value to the English, and Kingston was a home of all West Indian trades. In the Leeward Islands there was little change. The occupation of the Windward Islands proceeded slowly after 1763. Tobago, which suffered endless vicissitudes of fortune, was ceded to the French in 1783, though afterwards recovered. Barbados remained throughout the century an inviolate fortress of British power, and exhibited more of the order and decency of civilisation than was to be found elsewhere in the West Indies. Of the political life of the English islands little needs to be said. In 1764 the Government of Grenada was formed, including also the islands of Tobago, St Lucia, and, for a time, Dominica, though Dominica in 1770 received a separate Governor. All the islands enjoyed self-government, and on the whole their relations with the mother country were good. They had grievances; they complained that the Governor was sent to make what he could of them, that the civil establishment was too expensive, and that heavy taxation handicapped them in competition with the French islands; but they were probably not unconscious that their interests were carefully regarded in England, and that the mother country bore the burden of their defence, which the condition of their militia did little to lighten.

In the West Indies the activity of French and English always contrasted strongly with the receding energy of the Spaniards, as did their policy of colonisation with the commercial policy of Dutch and Danes. Thus the stream of progress scarcely touched the Spanish islands. Porto Rico remained a penal settlement, and in Trinidad the cocoa plantations went into decay. Nor did sugar cultivation yet usurp the upper hand in Cuba, where the whites still outnumbered the blacks, and the small freeholder held his ground. The Danes in 1733 bought Santa Cruz from the French, but the progress of their islands was for a long time fettered by the control of an exclusive company. The Dutch owned but a "rock or two," St Eustatius and Curaçoa with Oruba and Buen Ayre; but frugality, diligence, and concentration on business brought them wealth. The trade of Curaçoa always flourished, and in war time it was "the common emporium of the West Indies." On the mainland, by persistent industry, they established sugar plantations on the banks of the Berbice, the Essequibo, and, in 1745, of the Demerara also; whose courses they followed far into the interior in pursuit of the Indian trade.

The price of the rapid colonisation of North America was partly paid by Africa, which still lay under the blighting influence of the slave trade. On the west coast a line of forts and factories, planted at the mouths of small streams or on adjoining islands, and much coming and going of vessels, bringing in the varieties of manufactures required, and bearing away their human cargoes, represented the principal activity of Europe. No Power sought territorial dominion, or attempted exploration and settlement. The primitive civilisations of the interior offered little opportunity for general commerce, and though there was a Gum Coast, a Grain Coast, an Ivory Coast, and a Gold Coast, and these commodities and also redwood were obtained in small quantities, almost everywhere it was the negro traffic which dominated. From Cape Blanco in the north to the Portuguese settlement of Loanda in the south, over a distance of 1300 leagues, the slave trader ranged. In Senegambia control passed into the hands of the English; the Windward Coast was a Portuguese sphere; on the Gold Coast the trade belonged chiefly to the English and Dutch; further south chiefly to the French and Dutch, and south of the Congo to the Portuguese again, who from here worked across the continent to their possessions on the east coast. It is difficult to estimate accurately the volume of a trade which fluctuated from year to year, but certainly it underwent a continual expansion down to the time of the American War, when it had probably attained its largest dimensions. The growth of the sugar islands, the cultivation of tobacco in Virginia and of rice and cotton in the Carolinas, the development of the Spanish mines, the increasing needs of Brazil, where Pombal made the freedom of the Indians a reality, all contributed to enlarge the demand for negroes, until, in occasional years towards the end of the century, the total export from Africa might exceed 100,000, though the annual average was certainly very much less. The English alone, at a low estimate, carried over two million negroes to America in the period between 1680 and 1786. They generally enjoyed the largest share of the trade, but no one of the colonising nations kept its hands entirely clean. All saw in it "the chief and fundamental support" of their American plantations. The Portuguese drew their slaves from a wider field than the other Powers, from East as well as West Africa; and they had in Brazil an immense market, whose nearness diminished the losses of the Atlantic journey, or Middle Passage, as it was called. The French took a prominent part, until at the end of the century they were driven from the seas; so did the Dutch, who in 1791 owned fifteen of the forty stations on the Guinea Coast, and the New Englanders and Danes also had a share. The encouragement and control of the trade received the most careful attention of the English Government; and the African Company was described as "the most beneficial to this island of all the Companies that ever were formed by our merchants." A business destined in the course of time to be prohibited by law seemed in the eighteenth century so important for the development of our manufactures, shipping, and plantations as to receive, not only national regulation and protection, but also a national subsidy. In 1730 Parliament granted the African Company £10,000 a year towards the maintenance of its forts and factories, for the ten per cent. on their exports to Africa paid by private traders had lapsed in 1712, and the Company could no longer bear its burdens unaided. But the Company did not recover, and at last Parliament, fearing the injurious results of a declining negro trade, intervened, and in 1750 wound up the old Company and substituted a Regulated Company, subject to the control of a managing committee and including all merchants trading to Africa, to which the annual grant was continued. This was the third distinct system on which the African trade had been organised.

It was impossible that such extensive traffic in the human species by the foremost nations of the world should continue indefinitely. Even in an age which did not lend an attentive ear to human suffering, the horrors of the Middle Passage, and the fearful mortality of the negroes in the process of acclimatisation and under the rigours of the plantation system, excited protest; and when, in the latter part of the century, with the progress of the Evangelical party, a strong humanitarian sentiment gained ground in England, a movement was begun which, gradually accumulating strength from various quarters, assembled some of the most distinguished men of the day to battle against the commercial interests involved. In 1787 was formed the famous committee for the abolition of the trade, whereon sat many members of the Society of Friends, long to the front in this fight; Granville Sharp, who had procured Lord Mansfield's decision in 1772, putting an end to slavery in England; Clarkson, who as a Cambridge graduate had written a memorable thesis against slavery; and Wilberforce. But the fear of injuring the country's shipping and colonial trade, and the belief that other nations would continue the business, even if Great Britain abandoned it, long prevented any change; and it was the Regent of Denmark who led the way in 1792 by prohibiting the trade in Danish possessions from 1802; nor was it until 1807 that in England and the United States Acts of abolition were passed. Meanwhile, other events were changing the relations of Europe and Africa. In 1795 Mungo Park made his first great journey of exploration for the African Association. Moreover in 1787 the Sierra Leone Company was founded; certain philanthropists fathered and the Government supported a scheme for returning the emancipated negro to the land of his origin, and for opening the continent to a more civilised commerce than that which had hitherto darkened its history.

There was one part of Africa which lay outside the sphere of this desolating traffic. In the Cape Colony, which had remained a possession of the Dutch East India Company, settlement had been extended, and, as a result of peculiar geographical and political conditions and a mixture of races, a new national type had come into being. The Dutch formed the predominant element, but the French Huguenots, who came to Africa at the end of the seventeenth century, and the Germans, who arrived in considerable numbers after the middle of the eighteenth, had also contributed. In 1791 the European population numbered about 15,000 with 17,000 slaves. The white colonists could be divided into three groups, whose interests were somewhat separate: the trading classes of Cape Town, the corn and wine farmers of the adjoining country, and the graziers. The latter had penetrated into the interior. Silently dispersing over the country—their ranches far apart—they had carried the bounds of settlement north almost to the Orange river, and east to the Great Fish river, where they had come at last into collision with the Kosa Kaffirs, then advancing along the eastern margin of the continent. They formed the Boer people, whose character, fashioned in circumstances of isolation, hardship and simplicity, was to exert so strong an influence on the course of South African history. No foreign Power interfered with a colony which seemed to have only the slenderest resources, and which was in fact a continual source of expense; but its life was troubled by the economic oppression almost everywhere associated with company control. The Dutch saw the Cape as part of a wider dominion, and failing to reconcile the problem of local self-government with that of imperial development, they ruled it autocratically. A governor, who was usually seeking promotion to some more lucrative post, advised by a council of officers, shared with a financial minister, the Independent Fiscal, the responsibilities of administration. Representative institutions were wanting, though local boards for the settlement of small disputes sustained in some degree the spirit and form of local liberty, and, in addition, burgher councillors sat in the High Court of Justice. The selfishness of the Company's rule, especially in the last quarter of the century, and the corrupt practices of its officials, at last provoked a section of the colonists to resistance; but, in the midst of their struggle for a greater economic and political freedom, the Revolutionary Wars began, and the colony passed into the hands of the English.

The signs of change visible in Africa were but a faint reflexion of the greater changes taking place or threatening on the other side of the Atlantic. For the colonial world an epoch was ending, and a period of great and violent transformation had begun. In North America the English colonies, easily alienated at the last, wrested their independence from the mother country, and resisting the inclination to division, united to form a powerful State. In the West Indies, incapable of so great an effort and so wide an outlook, voices of sympathy were raised. In San Domingo a negro republic made itself free. In South America the hold of Spain on her vast dominions was loosed at last, and they broke up into a group of States. About the same time, Brazil repudiated the authority of Portugal. All the great colonising Powers shared the same fate—their offspring threw off their control. With one mind, the young nations rose up and condemned the old colonial system. The South African farmer and the New England merchant, the Creole of Peru and the emancipated negro, all were animated by the same spirit. So universal was the movement that it seemed like a normal and inevitable development. It seemed as though the life of a colony naturally progressed through certain stages to this final issue—first, the distant voyage, the perilous exploration, the clash with aboriginal peoples, the long and painful struggle with nature; then, the young society, embodying the civilisation and arts of the mother country, with its useful commerce and its nursery of political posts; and, after that, the growth of its own characteristics and the increasing sense of power and self-interest, to be disregarded and stifled as long as possible, but sure to lead on to the last act of separation and self-assertion. Certainly, the Governments of Europe were not unconscious that this might be the end of all their efforts, and France and Spain denied to their colonies the political life which might hasten its coming. England to a great extent neglected possibilities and waited to deal with facts. But all alike were helpless in face of so great an issue, and saw no alternative line of colonial evolution. In this sphere the political ideas of the eighteenth century seemed to be exhausted. To develop imperial commerce had become a less urgent problem than to foster the sense of a common loyalty in mother country and colony; but no nation proved capable of adaptation to the new conditions, and no adequate imperial policy was anywhere formulated. The conceptions of the Old World lagged behind the facts of the New. Where communities of white men had established themselves and grown strong, political ambition and self-consciousness were sure to make their appearance, and such communities would not rest satisfied with a limited economic freedom and a subordinate political status. With interests and character of their own, they would not remain the appendages of greater Powers, mere counters in the game of European preeminence. Either the nature of the relations must change or the bonds be broken. And, since the mother country offered at best nothing more than a commercial treaty, whose terms were settled wholly by herself, the colonists gave play to a more youthful and vigorous imagination, and saw in an independent national being a more attractive vision. Looking back, then, on the attitude of Europe to her colonies, with little elasticity, imagination, or sympathy, and also on the character of those colonies themselves, strong, sensitive, and aspiring, the dissolution of their union awakens no surprise. If it was possible " to found a great empire for the sole purpose of raising up a people of customers," it was not for this alone that it could be maintained. Thus the old colonial system collapsed, and an epoch of colonial history ended in obstinate and fluctuating war, in furious excesses, or in peaceful and silent transition.

CHAPTER VII.

POLAND UNDER THE SAXON KINGS.

OF the eighteen competitors for the throne of Poland vacant in 1696 by the death of John III, Sobieski, the most notable were the Austrian candidate, the Królewicz, or Crown Prince, James Sobieski ; the Prussian candidate, Margrave Lewis William of Baden-Baden ; Frederick Augustus, Elector of Saxony ; and Prince Henri of Condé and Prince Louis of Conti, successively supported by France. The chances of James Sobieski, on the whole the most suitable candidate, were ruined by the hostile intrigues of his own mother the Queen Dowager, Maria Casimiria, and the jealousy of all the other native candidates. The Margrave of Baden, ill supported, retired betimes from the contest which finally resolved itself into a duel between the Elector of Saxony and the Prince of Conti. At first the Elector was regarded by nobody as a serious candidate ; but his prospects brightened after he had publicly abjured Protestantism for Catholicism at the crisis of the struggle. He also had a longer and better administered purse than that of the French Minister in Poland, Abbé de Polignac ; but his chief advantage lay in the fact that all the neighbouring Powers preferred to see a German rather than a Frenchman or a Pole on the Polish throne. Tsar Peter even went so far as to threaten the Polish Senate with an invasion if they dared to choose a Frenchman. Nevertheless, the Prince of Conti was elected King of Poland by a considerable majority. It was only as the nominee of a minority, and consequently without possessing any legal status, that Frederick Augustus, at the head of a well-disciplined Saxon army which had been patiently awaiting the issue of events close to the Polish frontier, drove out the lawful sovereign. On September 16 he was crowned at Cracow as Augustus II ; but his title was not generally recognised in Poland till nearly two years later.

The determination of the new King to transform, and if possible abolish, the hopelessly vicious Constitution which was the source of all the calamities of Poland, furnishes the key to the right interpretation of the events of this unlucky reign. Augustus judged, rightly enough, that the presence in the country of a permanent and devoted regular army was the only means whereby a *coup d'état* could be effected. The Poles, always preternaturally wary of the least movement on the part of an enterprising ruler, had, indeed, already bound his hands to some extent, by insisting, energetically, on the withdrawal from the kingdom proper of all the forces of Augustus except a body-guard of 1200 men. But they had no objection to his maintaining an army corps of 7000 in the grand duchy of Lithuania, and with this, for a time, Augustus had to be content.

During the last years of the reign of John III Lithuania had suffered from chronic anarchy, due mainly to the tyranny and violence of the great House of Sapieha which preyed upon its neighbours, lay and clerical. Casimir Sapieha, Grand Hetman of Lithuania, in a private quarrel with the Bishop of Vilna, had devastated the whole diocese and burnt dozens of churches and hundreds of manor houses. Twice, in 1693 and 1695, John III had been forced to summon Sapieha to answer for his misdeeds before the one tribunal he could not ignore—the sovereign Diet. On both occasions the partisans of Sapieha had succeeded in "exploding[1]" the Diet before it had time to consider the case. In other words, that palladium of individual liberty, the *liberum veto*, had sunk so low that its principal use was to shelter high-placed felons from the pursuit of justice. In 1700 the insupportable misrule of the Sapiehas provoked an insurrection of all the other Lithuanian nobles against them, and, with the assistance of the Saxon troops, they were finally subdued, deprived of all their honours and dignities and expelled the country. A few months later, however, they were back again in the track of the victorious armies of Charles XII. Subsequently they became the chief supporters of the new King, Stanislaus Leszczynski, whom Charles placed upon the Polish throne.

After the removal of the Sapiehas, Augustus found a fresh justification for the continuance of his Saxons in Lithuania, and in Poland also, in the obligations of the great Northern War, of which he was one of the principal promoters. The details of that momentous episode, more especially its influence upon European politics, have already been set forth in this *History*. It only remains to be added that, as regards Poland, this war was an unmitigated disaster. The Republic had emerged from the most terrible of the cataclysms of the sixteenth and seventeenth centuries, not unscathed indeed, but at least morally chastened and stimulated. The stress of calamity had invariably rekindled the old martial spirit of the *Szlachta* (gentry), and, even in the darkest hours, evoked national heroes and deliverers. But the ten years' war which terminated with the collapse of Charles XII at Poltawa had no such salutary after-effect. It produced not a single eminent Polish captain, not a single valiant Polish soldier. Again and again, thousands of

---

[1] *I.e.* abruptly terminating it by the "*nie pozwalam*" (I protest) of a single deputy, instead of letting it run out its term, which was generally fixed beforehand.

ornamental Polish cavalry fled before mere handfuls of Swedish and even of Russian troops. Still worse, the war left Polish society more demoralised than it had ever been before. For the first time in Polish history the spirit of the nation languished hopelessly, the natural elasticity of the most mercurial of nations seemed broken, its wonderful recuperative energy seemed at last to be exhausted. Politically, too, Poland gained nothing by this war. Its immediate result was a degrading dependence on the Tsar, who still further increased his influence in the country by constantly mediating between Augustus and his mutinous subjects. The desperate efforts of the King Elector to shake off this galling yoke, culminating in the defensive alliance concluded at Vienna on January 5, 1719, with the Emperor Charles VI and George I of England against "any enemy whatsoever," with obvious reference to Russia, were frustrated by the helplessness of the Polish Diet, which, instead of cooperating with the Saxon Government, allowed itself, notably in 1719 and 1720, to be "exploded" by Russian hirelings. During the ensuing ten years of peace and material prosperity, the leading men in Poland, sunk in apathy and inertia, regarded with indifference the presence and the depredations of their Muscovite "auxiliaries," and at the same time rejected every opportunity of concluding favourable alliances, in nervous apprehension of exciting fresh wars and complications. Absolute neutrality in any circumstances was now the political maxim of the *Sejm* (Diet). In the last years of his reign Augustus endeavoured to form a Saxon party in Poland itself, with the view of securing the succession to his son Frederick Augustus. To disarm foreign adversaries he, at the same time, meditated a partition of Poland between Austria, Prussia, and himself, whereby the bulk of the territory of the Republic was to be erected into an hereditary monarchy under the rule of the Saxon House. Nefarious as this project undoubtedly was, it might, nevertheless, have been the saving of Poland, if only it could have been carried out. But all the schemes and intrigues of Augustus were suddenly cut short by his death (February 1, 1733).

The leading man in Poland on the death of Augustus II was the Primate and *Interrex*, Theodore Potocki, a devoted adherent of Stanislaus Leszczynski. He was upright, conscientious, and a true patriot, but too old to fight effectually for freedom, and, besides, circumstances were against him. His first steps were to dissolve the Diet; disperse the body-guard of the late King; order the Saxon auxiliaries to quit Poland; and put small corps of observation along the Austrian and Prussian frontiers. He found active supporters in the French ambassador, Count Monti, in the great Lithuanian family of Czartoryski, and above all in the Palatine of Mazovia, Stanislaus Poniatowski, the one really capable statesman Poland then possessed, who had served Charles XII's *protégé*, King Stanislaus, with zeal and ability thirty years before, and was now ready to sacrifice everything for him once more. It was to France that Potocki and Poniatowski looked for help, nor was France slow to champion a cause that was peculiarly her own. For the first time since her eclipse at the Peace of Utrecht, she saw before her an opportunity of recovering her hegemony on the continent. It had ever been her interest, as the arch-enemy of the Habsburgs, to environ the Empire with actual or contingent foes. Her ideal system, so far as it concerned eastern Europe, was a hostile combination of Sweden, Poland, and Turkey against the common foe. With the father-in-law of the French King on the Polish throne (Marie Leszczynska, the daughter of Stanislaus, had been married to Louis XV on September 5, 1725), a first step would have been taken towards the reestablishment of French influence on the continent. As a preliminary measure, 4,000,000 *livres* of secret-service money were despatched from Versailles to Warsaw for bribing purposes, and Monti succeeded in gaining over to the cause of Stanislaus the influential Palatine of Lublin, Adam Tarlo. In a circular letter, addressed to all its representatives abroad, the French Government formally declared that, as the Court of Vienna, by massing troops on the Silesian frontier, had sufficiently revealed its intention of destroying the liberties of Poland by interfering with the free election of her King, his Most Christian Majesty could not regard with indifference the political extinction of a Power to whom he was bound by all the ties of honour and friendship, but would do his utmost to protect her against her enemies. On May 8, 1733, the Interrex summoned a preliminary or "convocation" Diet to Warsaw. The temper of the assembly was unmistakably hostile to any foreign candidate. Indeed, many of its members declared they would rather see a gipsy on the throne than another German. It was finally resolved that none but a native Pole, who was a Catholic and married to a Catholic, should be elected. But, when the Diet was called upon by the Primate solemnly to swear to observe its own resolutions, not a few deputies began to raise objections or make reservations, while others quitted the Diet determined to protest against all its proceedings on the first opportunity. Thus the chronic and incurable divisions of the Republic encouraged the Powers opposed to the election of Stanislaus plausibly to come forward as the champions of a free election, with the certainty of finding partisans among the Poles themselves.

When the tidings of the death of Augustus II reached St Petersburg, a grand national council was summoned, at which it was agreed unanimously that the interests of Russia would not permit her to recognise Stanislaus Leszczynski, or indeed any person dependent directly on France (and therefore, indirectly, on Turkey and Sweden also) as a candidate for the Polish throne. Thereupon, a menacing letter was addressed to the Polish Primate demanding that the name of Stanislaus should be struck off the list of candidates, and Count Carl Gustaf Löwenwolde was sent to Warsaw to reinforce his brother, Count Frederick Casimir, the actual Russian resident at the Polish capital. The two Ministers, accompanied by the envoys of Austria and Prussia, lost no time in waiting upon the Archbishop; but Potocki was not to be intimidated and their interference only led to a sharp altercation. Immediately afterwards, the Interrex summoned an elective Diet, which assembled at Praga, a suburb of Warsaw, on August 26, 1733.

The protest of Russia and Austria had been bold and resolute; but they were hampered at the outset by a peculiar difficulty: they had no alternative candidate of their own to offer. Stanislaus Leszczynski was the only native Pole who had the slightest chance of being elected King. It was therefore necessary to look abroad for a candidate. The Infant Emmanuel of Portugal, who had visited Russia in 1731, as a suitor for the hand of the Empress Anne, was at first proposed by the Court of Vienna; but his father would not consent to his nomination, and, ultimately, both Russia and Austria agreed to support the pretensions of the Elector of Saxony, the late King's son. Hitherto, indeed, Frederick Augustus had been regarded at Vienna with no friendly eye. He was suspected of leaning too much upon France as his father had done before him, and he had always steadily opposed the Pragmatic Sanction; but, when it became evident that none other but the Saxon faction was strong enough to oppose Stanislaus, all objections on the part of the two Courts ceased, and Löwenwolde concluded a treaty with the Elector (August 14, 1733), whereby he acceded to the Pragmatic Sanction, contracted a treaty of mutual defence and guarantee with Russia and Austria, and promised to keep inviolate the Constitution of the Polish Republic. Eighteen regiments of Russian infantry and ten of cavalry were then sent to the frontier, to be ready, at a moment's notice, to enter Poland.

But the march of events had been so rapid that it had now become necessary not merely to direct, but to reverse, the decision of the Polish nation. Nine days after the assembling of the *Sejm*, the vast majority of whose members remained faithful to the Primate, it issued a manifesto (September 4) solemnly cursing all who should assist or welcome the Muscovites. On the 9th, Stanislaus himself arrived at Warsaw, having travelled through central Europe disguised as a coachman. On the following day 60,000 armed and mounted noblemen assembled on the field of election. For eight hours the aged Interrex, after disregarding as irregular a protest from some 3000 malcontents, who were observing the proceedings from the opposite side of the Vistula, proceeded on horseback through the drenching rain, from group to group, asking all the deputies in turn whom they would have for their King, and greeted everywhere with shouts of: "Long live King Stanislaus!" Finally, after making another vain appeal to the patriotism of the malcontent minority, the Primate solemnly pronounced Stanislaus the duly elected King of Poland; while the minority retired to Wongrowa, whence they issued a counter-manifesto, declaring the election null and void.

Thus Stanislaus had been elected King of Poland for the second time; but his tenure of that perilous office was to be even briefer than it had been before. Immediately after his election, he issued a proclamation ordering a *levée en masse* of the gentry; but, having no forces ready at hand to support him (the Polish regular army existing only on paper), he was obliged, twelve days after his election, to leave the defenceless capital, and shut himself up in Danzig with the Primate, Poniatowski, the Czartoryskis, and the French and Swedish envoys. A week later (September 30), General Peter Lacy, at the head of a Russian army, appeared on the right bank of the Vistula.

Lacy was speedily joined by the Polish malcontents, who formed (October 6), under his protection, what they called "a general confederation," though it consisted of only 15 senators and 500 of the *Szlachta*. This phantom of a Diet forthwith proclaimed the Elector of Saxony King of Poland, under the title of Augustus III, amidst loud acclamations. The Empress Anne had hoped to terminate the Polish difficulty in a single campaign, but the hope had soon to be abandoned. Almost the whole of Poland was in favour of Stanislaus, the country swarmed with his partisans, while he himself lay in the strong fortress of Danzig, awaiting the arrival of the promised succour from France. He knew his countrymen too well to expect any material help from their guerilla bands, and his past experience had taught him that the invasion of Saxony was the only way to make Augustus relinquish Poland. He looked to Louis XV to do for him now what Charles XII had done for him five and twenty years before. Failing this, he felt that all was lost. "I shall be compelled to return to France if the King does not occupy Saxony," he wrote to his daughter Queen Marie. On the other hand it was of paramount importance to Russia that Stanislaus should be driven, as speedily as possible, from Danzig, whither help could readily be conveyed to him by sea. Accordingly, at the end of 1733, Lacy was ordered to invest and reduce the place without delay. But it soon became evident that the difficulty of the enterprise had been vastly underrated. After leaving garrisons at Warsaw, Thorn (which he captured on his way) and some other places, Lacy, on sitting down before Danzig, found that his army had dwindled to 12,000 men, whom he was obliged to distribute over an area of two leagues swarming with more than 50,000 hostile guerillas, while the numerous artillery of the Danzigers, well served by French and Swedish gunners, did great execution. All through the winter the siege dragged on, and no impression seemed to have been made upon the fortress. On March 17, 1734, Lacy was superseded by Marshal Münnich, who brought with him considerable reinforcements. On the 19th, a strongly fortified redoubt called "Scotland" was captured; but for the next fortnight the siege languished as the Marshal had no field-pieces with him but 8-pounders, and the King of Prussia refused to allow any artillery to be conveyed through his dominions to the besiegers.

At one time an actual rupture with Prussia was feared. Münnich is said to have threatened that he would pay a visit to Berlin when he had done with Danzig. He actually wrote to the Empress that Stanislaus had bought over Frederick William and that the latter was about "to mediate" at the head of an army corps. At last the arrival of some mortars from Saxony enabled Münnich to capture Fort Sommerschanz which cut Danzig off from Weichselmünde, its port at the mouth of the Vistula (May 6-7); but a subsequent attempt to storm the strong redoubt Hagelburg, the key of the whole position, was repulsed with the loss of 120 officers and 2000 men (May 9-10). On May 20, the long-expected French fleet appeared in the roads and disembarked 2400 men under the command of Brigadier La Motte Pérouse. A week later, they made a gallant attempt to force the Russian entrenchments, but were repulsed and forced to take refuge behind the cannon of Weichselmünde. This encounter is memorable as being the first occasion on which French and Russians crossed swords. On June 10, the Russian fleet, under Admiral Gordon, brought Münnich the siege artillery, the want of which had so seriously hampered his operations, and at the same time vigorously bombarded La Motte's little army till it was forced to surrender and was conveyed to St Petersburg on board the Russian fleet. Two days after the capture of the French army, the fortress of Weichselmünde also surrendered. The loss of its port decided the fate of Danzig. On June 30 the city capitulated unconditionally after sustaining a siege of 135 days, which cost the besiegers 8000 men. The Primate, Monti, and Poniatowski were arrested. King Stanislaus, disguised as a peasant, had contrived to escape two days before.

Even after the fall of Danzig the embers of war continued to smoulder in Poland for nearly twelve months longer. The fugitive Stanislaus issued, in August, from Königsberg, a manifesto to his partisans, urging them to form a confederation on his behalf; and it was formed accordingly at Dzikowa, under the presidency of Adam Tarlo, and sent an envoy, Ozarowsky, to Paris to urge France to invade Saxony with at least 40,000 men, the confederates promising to cooperate simultaneously on the side of Silesia. In the Ukraine, too, Count Nicholas Potocki kept on foot a motley host of 50,000 men and entered into negotiations with the pretender to the throne of Transylvania, Francis Rákóczy II. But nothing came of these isolated and therefore impotent efforts. France was ill disposed to waste any more men and money on a patently unserviceable ally, more particularly as she had found ample compensation for her reverses on the Vistula in the triumphs of herself and her allies in Lombardy and on the Rhine. The desertion of France sealed the fate of the Stanislausian faction in Poland. The Primate and Adam Tarlo submitted to Augustus; Stanislaus signed his abdication (January 26, 1736); and the Diet which met at Warsaw (June 25) completed the pacification of the Republic, the new King swearing to withdraw his Saxon and Muscovite auxiliaries within 40 days, and proclaim a general amnesty.

The new King was, in every respect, the antithesis of his alert, jovial and dissolute father. His character has been admirably symbolised in the famous picture which represents the portly Prince, enveloped in a luxurious dressing-gown, reclining in an easy chair and holding in his lap a tea-cup and saucer. Pious, pacific, and thoroughly domesticated, nothing but his one passion, a love of the chase, was ever able to tear him from the seclusion of his family circle, while a constitutional sluggishness compelled him to leave everything in the nature of business to Ministers who virtually ruled in his name. Thus, in Saxony, during the greater part of this thirty years' reign, Count Heinrich von Brühl held absolute sway, while in Poland the Czartoryski family—"the Family" as, from its immense influence and political predominance, it was generally called by contemporaries—endeavoured to rally round it the most enlightened and progressive elements of the nation.

The Czartoryskis were of very ancient lineage. They had held princely rank as early as the fifteenth century and were akin to the royal House of Jagello which had ruled Poland from 1384 to 1572. It was only in the middle of the seventeenth century, however, that they had risen to political eminence in the person of Florian Czartoryski, who became Primate of Poland during the brief and troubled reign of Michael Wisniowiecki (1669–73). At the beginning of the eighteenth century the fortunes of the family were completely reestablished, partly by the patronage of Augustus II, who exalted them at the expense of the wealthier aristocracy, but principally through the ability of two brothers, Prince Michael, who became Grand Chancellor of Lithuania, and was henceforth known as "the Prince Chancellor," and his brother Prince Augustus, Palatine of Russia (*i.e.* the Polish province of "Red Russia"), generally called "the Prince Palatine." These two brothers agreed with each other in all things, politics included, so absolutely that they must be regarded as a single personality rather than two separate individuals. The eminently capable Prince Chancellor was the statesman of "the Family," and as such was always deferred to without question, while his brother the Prince Palatine, who had served with distinction in the Turkish wars of the close of the seventeenth century, and been decorated for valour by Prince Eugene on the smoking bastions of Belgrade, was its military celebrity. The marriage in early life of the latter with the fabulously wealthy Pani Sieniawska, the last survivor and sole heiress of the united possessions of the Sieniawski and Denhof families, finally placed the Czartoryskis on a level with the mightiest magnates in Poland.

The focus of the influence of the Czartoryskis was Pulawy, their mansion in Volhynia, which became as famous in Polish as Holland House was in English politics, and in nearly the same period. Again and again, Pulawy is gratefully described by contemporaries as a "refuge for learning," "an oasis in a desert of savagery." During three generations it became a training-school of pedagogues, organisers, and reformers. The most promising youths in Poland, quite irrespective of rank and birth, were diligently sought for in the most out-of-the-way places and brought to Pulawy to be educated for the service of their country. The most advanced foreign scholars and philosophers were consulted as to the best curriculum to be adopted for the students there assembled. It was the Czartoryskis who encouraged and assisted the great educational reformer Stanislaus Konarski, 1700–73 (himself a pupil of a still earlier pioneer of enlightenment, the ex-King Stanislaus, whose little Court at Nancy was, for native Poles at any rate, the first nursery of the new ideas), to establish his *Collegia nobilium* in Poland. Indeed, it may truly be said that of the writers on political and social subjects who abounded in Poland during the latter part of the eighteenth century everyone owed something to the generous and intelligent assistance of this noble House.

The real aim and explanation, however, of all the efforts of the Czartoryskis was the reform of the Polish Constitution, which they rightly regarded as the indispensable preliminary of any permanent improvement in the condition of the country. To educate, and thereby transform, public opinion, was the first step towards the realisation of this noble ambition. It was not enough that the new, saving ideas should be introduced by books and pamphlets—a new social atmosphere was to be created in which these ideas might expand and multiply. A new generation, full of courage and free from prejudice, was to be trained up to furnish the protagonists of the new ideas.

When the time came to translate these ideas into action in the field of politics, the Czartoryskis, at first, looked for assistance to the Saxon Court, where, from 1733 to 1753, their credit was very great. They won the friendship of Brühl by obtaining, though not without great difficulty, an "*indigenat*" or patent of nobility and naturalisation for his family in Poland; and, in return for this extremely lucrative privilege, which opened the door to all manner of honours and dignities, Brühl, so far as he was able, supported their programme of reform. The period of comparative tranquillity which immediately succeeded the Peace of Aix-la-Chapelle (1748) seemed to favour their views. Two advantageous matrimonial alliances (the marriage of Augustus III's daughter, Mary Josepha, to the Dauphin Louis, son of Marie Leszczynska, and that of his son Frederick Christian to Maria Antonia Walpurgis, daughter of the Emperor Charles VII) had greatly elated the Saxon Court, and induced the King to promise to assist the Czartoryskis to abolish the *liberum veto* at the very least. Even when the Court of Vienna, which was first consulted on the subject, advised strongly against the attempt for fear of irritating Russia and Prussia, Brühl and the Czartoryskis still persisted in their efforts to remedy this scandalous abuse. All their efforts in this direction were frustrated, however, by the determined opposition of the reactionaries, headed by the powerful Potocki family who, having many ancient grievances against the Czartoryskis, deliberately exploded every Diet favourable to them, and nullified all their confederations by counter-confederations. Then the Saxon Court, fearful of losing Poland altogether, refused to assist the Czartoryskis any further; whereupon they broke with Brühl, and began to look elsewhere for assistance. They now proposed to dethrone the useless Augustus III with the aid of Russia, to whom, in the first instance, they appealed through Kayserling, the Russian minister at Warsaw, for help to reform the Polish Constitution, promising, in return, to recognise the Russian imperial title adopted by Peter the Great and his successors—a thing the Republic had, hitherto, steadily refused to do. There is no reason whatever to question the *bona fides*, or the patriotism of the Czartoryskis on this occasion. But that they should seriously have believed that Russia would consent to strengthen and rehabilitate her ancient enemy (for that is what their appeal amounted to) is the most cogent proof of their political short-sightedness. During the hurly-burly of the Seven Years' War they could do nothing. Throughout that miserable period the Polish Republic was treated by all the belligerents as if it did not exist. There was not even a pretence of respecting its neutrality. Russians, Prussians, and Austrians marched up and down its territory, fought their battles in it and black-mailed it indiscriminately without the slightest intention of offering any sort of compensation. All that the Czartoryskis did during these years was to plot industriously against Augustus III. In 1755 they sent their nephew Stanislaus Poniatowski to St Petersburg in the suite of the English ambassador, Sir Charles Hanbury Williams, in the hope that he might gain a diplomatic footing in the Russian capital. The handsome young fellow won the heart of the impressionable Grand Duchess Catharine and, in 1757, through her influence, was accredited Polish ambassador to Russia, from which post he was ignominiously dismissed, a few months later, by the Empress Elizabeth, for intriguing against her during her illness. Obviously, the object of this somewhat mysterious mission was to cultivate the friendship of the aspiring little Grand Duchess who, four years later, was to mount the Russian throne, in such a sensational manner, as Catharine II. Immediately after her elevation, the Czartoryskis formally applied to her for an auxiliary corps; but the new Empress, whose own situation, for some months after her accession, was somewhat precarious, declined to interfere in Polish affairs till after the death of Augustus III. That event took place on October 5, 1763; whereupon the Czartoryskis immediately resumed their appeal to the Russian Empress. The result of their overtures has been elsewhere recorded.

CHAPTER VIII.

THE WAR OF THE AUSTRIAN SUCCESSION.

(1) THE PRAGMATIC SANCTION.

THE great struggle for the Spanish Succession was barely over before another succession problem began to occupy the Foreign Ministries of Europe. Like their Spanish cousins, the Austrian Habsburgs found themselves threatened with a failure of male heirs; and, to meet this possibility, Leopold I in 1703 had made definite regulations (*pactum mutuae successionis*) by which, in default of male heirs, females should succeed, with the special proviso that the daughters of Archduke Joseph were to take precedence of those of his brother Charles. But, after 1711 Joseph's sudden death had placed Charles on the Imperial throne, this arrangement was altered in April, 1713; and by a secret family law, known hereafter as the "Pragmatic Sanction," Charles gave his own daughters priority over his brother's, and at the same time insisted strongly on the indivisibility of the Habsburg dominions—a principle now first adopted. In making this change the Emperor was well within his rights, and circumstances had changed since 1703, when the renewed establishment of separate branches of the family at Vienna and at Madrid had seemed probable. Moreover, Joseph's daughters could hardly claim former Spanish provinces like Milan and the Netherlands over which their father had never ruled.

It was not till the marriage of Joseph's elder daughter, Archduchess Maria Josepha, to the Electoral Prince of Saxony (1719), that the question became prominent. Several children had been born to the Emperor, but only daughters had survived. Charles therefore exacted from his niece a formal renunciation of her claims, and a similar pledge was given by her sister, Maria Amalia, when she married Charles Albert of Bavaria (1722). Moreover, the Emperor set about obtaining the formal recognition of the Pragmatic Sanction from the Estates of his various dominions, a process begun with Upper and Lower Austria in 1720 and completed by the adhesion of the Austrian Netherlands in 1724 —even Hungary, though after some demur, giving her recognition in 1722.

This was an important step gained; but to secure the recognition of the European Powers was far more necessary, and by this object the foreign policy of Charles VI was henceforward dominated.

Curiously enough, the first guarantor of the Pragmatic Sanction was Philip V, Charles' successful rival in Spain.   On hostile terms with England and Holland, separated from France by dynastic pretensions, Spain found in the Ostend Company a bond with the Emperor, whose efforts to shake off the restrictions imposed on the commerce of the Netherlands and to obtain a share in the lucrative East Indian trade had embroiled him with the Maritime Powers.   Among the stipulations of the League of Vienna (May, 1725) was Spain's recognition of the Pragmatic Sanction; and the adhesions which the League subsequently received increased the number of guarantors.   Russia (August, 1726) was the next; and, before the end of 1726 Prussia (October), Mainz and the four Wittelsbach Electors, Charles Albert of Bavaria, his brother Clement Augustus of Cologne, and their cousins Charles Philip of the Palatinate and Francis Lewis of Trier, had joined the League.   However, though Bavaria's support was thus obtained, the somewhat unnatural Austro-Spanish alliance soon collapsed without having effected anything.   Charles Albert, regarding himself as thereby absolved from his pledge, with the assistance of the Elector Palatine Charles Philip and the Elector of Saxony, vigorously opposed the Emperor's efforts to obtain the guarantee of the Diet.   This, however, was obtained in January, 1732, Frederick William of Prussia lending the Emperor his support, while in the same year Denmark became a guarantor, Cologne having renewed its guarantee in 1731   Long before this, however, Elisabeth Farnese, distrusting the Emperor's sincerity and seeing no prospect of the proposed marriages between her sons and Charles' daughters ever taking place, had come to terms with the Maritime Powers and France, concluding in November, 1729, the Treaty of Seville, by which, in return for a guarantee of Parma and Tuscany to Don Carlos, she withdrew the concessions promised to the Ostend Company.   To this the Emperor would not agree; and in 1730 war again seemed imminent, when Walpole, by promising to guarantee the Pragmatic Sanction, induced Charles VI to give way.   The Second Treaty of Vienna (March 16, 1731) sacrificed the trade of the Netherlands to the needs of the Habsburg dynasty and to the jealousy between England and Holland, though France refused to follow her allies in guaranteeing the Pragmatic Sanction, declaring that to do so would be as bad as the loss of three battles.

A year later, the opening of the Polish Succession question afforded Charles an opportunity of disposing of the most formidable of his daughter's rivals.   To win Austria's support in his candidature for the Polish throne, the Elector of Saxony (Frederick Augustus II, who became King Augustus III of Poland) abandoned his wife's claims and recognised the Pragmatic Sanction (1733).   But, as the result of her intervention in Poland, Austria became involved in a war with France and her Spanish and Sardinian allies, which went against her both on the Rhine and in Italy. To purchase the peace which was finally signed on November 8, 1738, she had to cede the Two Sicilies to Don Carlos and to agree to the annexation of Lorraine to France, the dispossessed Duke, Francis Stephen, receiving as compensation Tuscany and the hand of Maria Theresa. At this heavy price Charles secured from Fleury an ominously guarded recognition of the Pragmatic Sanction, Sardinia giving her guarantee in February, 1739, when she acceded to the peace, an example which Spain and Naples followed later in the year.

Charles had thus attained his object: with the exceptions of Bavaria and the Palatinate, the Powers of Europe were pledged to support Maria Theresa's accession, though their assent had been dearly bought. Judging by the way in which the majority of the guarantors afterwards treated their solemn obligations, these concessions would seem to have been made in vain; yet, indirectly, Maria Theresa's case was strengthened, when she could appeal to the treaties her assailants had broken: their faithlessness makes their greed all the more conspicuous and has enlisted on her side the sympathy of posterity, though in her own day it only helped to secure her the not altogether disinterested support of England and the neutrality of the Turks. But, if Charles VI can be justified of his efforts to secure Maria Theresa from molestation by her neighbours, it is less easy to refute another charge brought against him—of having neglected the warning usually attributed to Eugene, that a strong army and a full treasury would be the best guarantees. In 1740 Austria had neither. Part of the price paid for the Russian alliance of 1726 had been a promise of assistance in Russia's wars with Turkey; and Austria's share in the Russo-Turkish War of 1736–9 had served to aggravate her internal disorders and difficulties, already serious enough after the misfortunes of the War of the Polish Succession. Apart from costing her Belgrade and the other cessions made to her at Passarowitz, the Russo-Turkish War left Austria in a sad plight. The evils normally arising from her lack of unity and cohesion, her obsolete and inefficient administrative system, her embarrassed finances, and her medieval social organisation, were aggravated by the inevitable consequences of unsuccessful wars. The Treasury was all but empty; the revenues had dwindled to half the income of 1733; while expenditure and indebtedness had increased, and the taxes, at once oppressive and unproductive, were causing widespread discontent. The army, demoralised by defeat, with its principal leaders discredited, its ranks depleted to half their paper strength, urgently needed reorganisation and reforms which the financial situation forbade. The provinces enjoyed a local autonomy which, though little more than a survival of feudal and oligarchical privileges, yet was strong enough to make the control of the central government weak and ineffective. As the immediate future was to show, provincialism was

CH. VIII.

stronger than patriotism, even in the "hereditary dominions" themselves. Hungary, indeed, was a source of anxiety : discontent was prevalent ; an insurrection was feared, and no trust could be placed in the inhabitants. Moreover, even Austria itself was not free from disloyalty ; the Bavarian claim had many partisans ; and lack of zeal for the dynasty and of readiness to make sacrifices on its behalf was only too general

Yet the dynasty was almost the only link between the three groups into which it is natural to divide the Habsburg possessions—the Austrian, including Styria, Carinthia, Carniola, Tyrol, and scattered fragments of Swabia ; the Bohemian, with which went Moravia and Silesia ; and Hungary, with Croatia and Transylvania. Each of these had its own Chancery, its own quite independent administrative, judicial, and financial systems. There was not even a federal union between them and, apart from the dynasty, the only institutions common to all three groups and to the outlying possessions in Italy and the Netherlands were the "State Conference," a council composed of the principal Ministers, the War Council (*Hofkriegsrath*) and the Treasury (*Hofkammer*). But the control of the War Council over the army was considerably limited by the difficulty of obtaining adequate contributions from the provincial Estates, and efficiency in administration was made almost impossible. Nor was there in the Conference at the time of Charles VI's death (October 20, 1740) any man of real capacity as an administrator or with any of the qualities of a great statesman, and able to make good use of such authority and influence as the Conference possessed. The inexperienced girl on whom the succession devolved found among her father's ministers only septuagenarians who had long outlived the days of their usefulness. Sinzendorff, the Chancellor who acted as President of the Conference, had experience but no vigour or decision : selfish and indolent as he was, neither his character nor attainments inspired confidence, and his implicit belief in the sincerity of Fleury's professions shows to how little purpose he had studied foreign affairs. Kinsky, the Chancellor of Bohemia, and Joseph Harrach, President of the War Council from 1738 to 1763, lacked capacity and strength ; and, though Gundacker Starhemberg, who had charge of the finances, was honest and patriotic, with an honourable record of good service, he was long past his prime. Bartenstein, Secretary to the Conference, enjoyed the distinction of being only fifty-one and had some of the vigour so conspicuously lacking to his colleagues ; but he was conceited and opinionated, apt to lose sight of main issues in a mass of detail, and as much at fault as Sinzendorff in his appreciation of the European situation. In the early years of Maria Theresa's reign Bartenstein's undoubted talents and capacity for hard work made him the adviser on whom she most relied ; but, as experience exposed his shortcomings, his influence and authority declined. Indeed, at the outset of her rule Maria Theresa had really to rely on herself alone : the husband she loved so dearly proved neither a pillar of strength

in council nor a capable commander in the field; and, though in the end
the Austrian army produced some admirable officers, it was not till after
the war that any Minister of more than mediocrity appeared.   Indeed,
though Charles VI had not been a strong or successful ruler, though he
had done little to check abuses or effect the reforms of which he realised
the need, though his foreign policy had been ambitious, ill-counselled
and disastrous in its results, though he was inferior both in capacity and
character to his successor, the peculiar circumstances of the moment
made his death as inopportune as possible.   Austria's most malevolent
enemy could hardly have selected for her a more unpromising situation
at home and abroad in which to be confronted with a disputed succession.

(2)   PRUSSIA UNDER FREDERICK WILLIAM I.

Frederick William I ascended the throne of Prussia on February 25,
1713, at the age of twenty-four.   His father and mother had maintained a Court of great magnificence; but Frederick William had
inherited Queen Sophia Charlotte's good sense without her love of refinement and of tasteful splendour.   Immediately on his accession he cut
down the expenditure of the Court so that it scarcely exceeded the
establishment of a wealthy private gentleman.   This decision on the
part of the new sovereign almost completely ruined the arts and crafts
of the capital, and several artists of real eminence were compelled
to seek a livelihood in other countries.   These rigid economies, which
were carried into all the departments of State, increased the yearly
revenues of the Crown so considerably, that it was practicable to raise
the infantry from 38 to 50 battalions, and the cavalry from 53 to 60
squadrons.

The Great Elector had evolved a model postal organisation, the
benefits of which extended far beyond the disjointed Prussian State.
This postal system of the seventeenth and eighteenth centuries operated
like the railway system of the nineteenth; and Justus Möser, one of
the greatest political economists of Germany in the eighteenth century,
maintains that the postal system had extraordinary results and in many
respects transformed the condition of the world.   The young King took
all the more interest in this department because it yielded 137,000
thalers (£20,000) a year to the exchequer, sufficient for the maintenance
of six or seven battalions.   On one of his early morning walks Frederick
William I noticed that the postmaster of Potsdam kept the carrier of
the night mail from Hamburg waiting in the street vainly knocking at
his closed door.   The King drove the postmaster out of bed with his
cane, and cashiered him, apologising to the mail-carrier that the King of
Prussia had such remiss servants.

CH. VIII.

Frederick William had himself learnt obedience when as Crown Prince he had served under Eugene and Marlborough at Malplaquet. The King looked up with admiration to his best general, Prince Leopold of Anhalt, who was then thirty-seven years of age, and hoped with the accession of his youthful friend to be called upon to take the lead in political and military affairs. But, when he attempted to put himself forward, he was very distinctly sent about his business. "Tell the Prince of Anhalt"—so runs one of the first letters written by Frederick William as King—"that I am the Finance Minister and the Field-Marshal of the King of Prussia; this will keep the King of Prussia on his legs."

Soon after the Prussian Crown had passed to Frederick William I European affairs took a turn which allowed Prussia to secure an important territorial acquisition. The Northern War was still in progress. The representatives of Charles XII (who was away in Turkey), together with Tsar Peter and his allies, offered Stettin to King Frederick William I. Frederick William's grandfather, the Great Elector, had all his life carried on a heroic but ineffectual struggle to wrest Stettin, the port of Berlin, from Sweden. Under King Frederick William I Prussian troops seized the emporium at the mouth of the Oder without firing a shot; the sole requirement was the payment of 400,000 *thalers* (£60,000) to the Tsar and his allies; and the financial transaction was made possible by the melting down of the royal plate and other economies. But this quite exceptionally favourable diplomatic situation did not continue. Russia, indeed, by the Treaty of Havelberg (May, 1718) guaranteed Stettin to the King of Prussia, who in his turn guaranteed to Tsar Peter the acquisition of Ingria and Esthonia, and in certain circumstances also that of Livonia. So far her intimate relations with Russia were advantageous to Prussia; but Peter I next aimed at making himself master of Mecklenburg. At that point he was opposed by a counter-alliance formed between England, Hanover, Saxony and the Emperor. What if Imperial troops set forth to march from Silesia to Mecklenburg, and Frederick William I, protesting his alliance with Russia, prohibited their transit? In that contingency Austria, Saxony, and Hanover, who had all watched with the keenest envy the strengthening of the Prussian army, bound themselves to make war upon Frederick William. The Hanoverian Ministry in particular took up a very hostile attitude towards the rising House of Brandenburg, and even contemplated a partition of Prussia between Hanover, Saxony, and Austria. A Hungarian named Clement, who was at the time paying a secret visit to Berlin as an agent of Saxony, reported that he had heard bitter complaints how no acceptable posts were now bestowed on anyone but officers, and how all other persons, especially men of learning, were passed over, and even well-earned pensions had been cancelled. Clement concluded that the King of Prussia was not so powerful as it appeared.

The discontent generally prevailing, and particularly among business people and officials, and even in the army, notwithstanding its enormous privileges, would, in Clement's opinion, make it an easy matter to stir up a rebellion against Frederick William I. At Court it was considered that the King's most distinguished general, the Prince of Anhalt, would with the help of officers devoted to him be capable of dethroning the King, if Germany were convulsed by a breach on the part of Prussia with the Emperor and England—capable of the deeds of a Marius and a Sulla, as Frederick the Great in his *History* writes of the victor of Turin, the founder of the Prussian infantry.

The antagonism between Great Britain and Russia was constantly growing. In 1719 a British squadron sailed to the Baltic. At the same time Stanhope, the English Prime Minister, went to Berlin to turn Frederick William from his alliance with Peter and draw him over to the side of England. But, though Frederick William acquiesced in Stanhope's remark that the English had a fine fleet and he a fine army, and that these two forces ought to cooperate, he very judiciously decided not to take part in an English attack on Livonia. All the Powers were soliciting the friendship of Prussia; and in 1720, when the danger of a general outbreak of war was past, the Berlin Cabinet by the intervention of England and with the connivance of Russia obtained the definite cession of Stettin by Sweden.

In spite of his physical strength, King Frederick William was subject even in his earlier years to severe attacks of illness. At the beginning of 1722 the thought of death possessed his mind, although he was only thirty-four years of age. At that time he drew up directions for the ten year old Crown Prince, in which he gave an account of his own reign and pointed out to his son the lines he was to follow. "I am at peace with Almighty God," Frederick William wrote in this so-called testament. "Since my twentieth year I have put my whole trust in God; I have continually besought Him mercifully to hear me, and He has always heard my prayer." Rulers, the King continues, who have God before their eyes, and do not keep mistresses, will be abundantly blessed. His successor is to order himself thus, and plays, operas, ballets, masquerades, and fancy balls are therefore not to be tolerated, nor excess in eating and drinking, for all such things are ungodly and of the Devil. So far the King speaks as might a British Puritan; but the resemblance ceases when he comes to deal with the standing army, and threatens to withdraw his parental blessing from his son if he should reduce the military expenditure. Should the Crown Prince do this, may there come upon him " the curse which God laid on Pharaoh: may your fate be that of Absalom !" Later passages of this document continually revert to the army and bid the King's successor be indefatigable in his care and discipline of the troops, now that the King himself has made the Prussian army and artillery equal in fighting strength to those of any other European Power.

"You must yourself alone superintend the revenue and keep the supreme command of the army firmly in your own hands....Officers and officials must know that you hold the purse-strings." For the first six weeks of his reign the King's successor must, following his own example, devote himself entirely to the study of the budget; he should then reduce all official salaries by about 25 per cent., but on no account reduce the income of the army. In a year's time he may begin to raise again the salaries of those who are doing their duty. But, he adds, "you must *work* as I have always done; a ruler who wishes to rule honourably must attend to all his affairs himself, for rulers are ordained for work and not for idle, effeminate lives such as, alas, are led by most great people."

The King deals next with economic conditions, which, like all his contemporaries, he judges from the point of view of mercantilist theories. "If the country is thickly populated, that is true wealth." Small towns must be founded where they are wanting. Industries, more especially the manufacture of cloth and woollen goods, are to be encouraged everywhere by the Government. "Then you will see how your revenues increase and your land prospers!" The French refugees settled there had first taught the Prussians to become manufacturers in important branches of industry. "A country without industries is a human body without life, a dead country, which is always poor and wretched and never prospers....Therefore I beg you, my dear successor, maintain the industries, protect them and tend their growth, establishing them wherever possible throughout the country." Warnings followed against listening to flatterers, and ignoring the corruption still prevalent among Prussian officials, and the successor is exhorted to pay all salaries promptly, to contract no government loans, but every year to pay 500,000 *thalers* (£75,000) into the treasury. Every year he is to travel through all the provinces to see for himself that everything is in perfect order. In religious matters, the chief thing is to build churches and schools. The Reformed Church and the Lutherans must not be allowed to quarrel, and only a limited freedom is to be granted to the clergy, because everyone of them would like to be Pope. The Catholics are to be tolerated, but not the Jesuits, nor foreign Jews wishing to immigrate.

"My dear successor will think and say: 'Why did not my late father himself do everything as stated here?' When my late father died in 1713, I found the province of Prussia almost at its last gasp with plague and murrain, most of the domains mortgaged, all of which I have redeemed, and the finances in such a plight that bankruptcy was imminent, the army in so bad a way and so low in numbers that its shortcomings baffle description. It is assuredly a masterly achievement to have in nine years, by 1722, brought law and order once more as I have done into all the affairs of State....The Elector Frederick William (the Great Elector) brought prosperity and advancement to our House; my father secured to it royal rank; I have regulated the country and the army; your task, my dear successor, is to keep up what your forefathers have begun and to win the territories claimed by us, which belong to our House by the laws of God and men. Pray to God, and never begin an unjust war; but never relinquish what is justly yours."

This memorable testament proves how unjust was the opinion formerly prevalent in Europe and among historians that Frederick William I was nothing more than a barbarian with the ideas and gifts of a sergeant. This conception has doubtless some truth in it, but there is equally good reason for the verdict of Theodor von Schön, himself an eminent reformer in the days of Stein and Hardenberg, who described Frederick William I as "Prussia's greatest King in respect of domestic policy."

The political situation changed completely soon after the acquisition of Stettin by Prussia. Though Russia and Great Britain were still enemies, the latter Power and Austria were no longer allies but bitter opponents, on account of the Ostend Company. A joint attack on Hanover by the Austrians and Russians was threatening. Once again, as had been the case a few years before, the King of Prussia held a geographically central position between the Great Powers whose encounter seemed imminent. After considerable hesitation the Prussian sovereign decided to support Austria; and at the close of 1728 a defensive alliance was concluded between the two Powers at Berlin.

Besides France, Prussia was at this time the only civilised country in which an absolute form of government had been completely established. But it was a convincing proof of Frederick William's great force of character that between 1713 and 1740 the material resources of Prussia were placed at the service of the Government in a far fuller measure than had ever been secured by the French Crown. To the Cabinets of Europe it was a mystery how the sovereign of a poor barren State like Prussia was able in 1729 to maintain a standing army of nearly 70,000 men. Added to this, there was a well-filled treasury. Two hundred years ago a State so organised was a Great Power, even though its population hardly exceeded two millions.

The change in the balance of power in Germany brought about by the rise of Prussia was extremely unwelcome to George I and to George II, who succeeded about this time (1727), in their capacity of Electors of Hanover. On the other hand the Whigs, who dominated the public life of England, had strong leanings towards Prussia; and their leaders complained that the Court was neglecting a Power whose strength had quite recently doubled. International diplomacy had become so much alive to the consolidation of Prussia's position as a Great Power that, when early in 1730 the English were discussing a plan of campaign with their French allies, they abandoned the idea of an invasion of Silesia, which could not but have injuriously affected Frederick William's kingdom. Instead of this expedition against Silesia, it was resolved that French troops should join with the forces of several German Princes at Heilbronn, and thence march through southern Germany, to attack the Emperor in Bohemia.

King Frederick William was, not without reason, proud that his internal reforms had given him sufficient strength to be able to prohibit foreign nations from fighting their battles on North German soil. "It is no mere boast," he said, "that I have won honour for the House of Brandenburg. All my life long I have never sought alliances, nor made advances to a foreign Power. My maxim is to injure no one, but not to let myself be slighted." Yet, at the same time, his self-consciousness as to his achievements in the sphere of foreign policy was not justified to its full extent. His strength lay entirely in his home policy; in his foreign relations he felt insecure—and rightly so, for he lacked both sufficient mental training and the inborn gift of perception which would have made it possible for him to understand the great affairs of the world.

In 1730 Sir Charles Hotham arrived at the Prussian Court as British envoy extraordinary to conclude the negotiations which had been pending five years for the marriage of Prince Frederick, who had in the meantime become Prince of Wales, with Princess Wilhelmina, eldest daughter of the King. But his instructions went still further. He was to propose a further marriage, between the eighteen year old Prussian Crown Prince and an English princess. Queen Sophia Dorothea, herself an English princess, and her children, were strongly in favour of Hotham's proposals. But a powerful party at the Court opposed this fresh connexion between the Houses of Brandenburg and Hanover. At the head of this party was General von Grumbkow, the King's chief support in his military administration, and financial and commercial policy. Grumbkow belonged to the "Tobacco College," as it was called, a party of gentlemen in favour with the King who met regularly in the evening to smoke and drink beer—practices considered very vulgar by contemporary European society. Other frequenters of the "Tobacco College" were Prince Leopold of Anhalt-Dessau and the Emperor's ambassador, Field-Marshal Count Seckendorf, a Protestant, who played a curious double *rôle* at Berlin as friend of the King and representative of the Emperor, but took advantage of his position with an unscrupulousness beyond ordinary diplomatic subtlety. Among these associates Frederick William allowed himself the utmost unconstraint; unsuspicious and docile as he was, he thus afforded his generals and officials frequent opportunities for influencing him and gaining him over to their selfish ends. But the Court at large was likewise full of intrigues.

Grumbkow and Seckendorf, who were both working in the Imperial interests, had enlisted the services of the Prussian resident in London, Reichenbach, for a very base transaction. Reichenbach was in correspondence with Seckendorf, whom he kept informed as to every incident in England connected with the marriages; and, worse still, Reichenbach allowed Grumbkow to decide for him of what the King should be apprised. He made his reports precisely as the powerful Minister directed. Thus the King was deceived, for he took as true and authentic what Reichenbach wrote or Grumbkow transmitted. The three never tired of representing to the King that England was urging this double marriage, in order that the little kingdom of Prussia, having detached itself from the Empire, might be made into an English province. Frederick William I was not, like his successor, master of the art of oscillating between the Powers. Frederick the Great owed his successes almost as much to negotiation as to the sword; his father, who was not a whit less eager for the acquisition of territory, did not know how to lead up to it diplomatically. Frederick William's servants and friends in the pay of the Court of Vienna scored a success, when, Hotham having ventured to show the King an intercepted letter by which Grumbkow was compromised, the unaccountable monarch was incensed, not with Grumbkow, but with Hotham, and subjected him to a violent scene. Hotham, who was a proud man, took his departure without soliciting a farewell audience.

As the testament of 1722 proves, King Frederick William I detested loose habits of life; but in other respects he was unable to control himself. Every man and woman in Berlin to the best of their power avoided coming across a sovereign who would strike out blindly with his stick, threatening that he would compel his subjects "in Russian fashion" to observe his edicts. He was on very unfortunate terms with his eldest son, the Crown Prince Frederick, who in 1730 was eighteen years of age. The son had a quite different nature from the father's and obeyed him very unwillingly, showing by his scornful defiance that he felt himself mentally the King's superior. In return, Frederick William boxed the Crown Prince's ears in the presence of the household, of the officers of the Crown Prince's regiment, of the generals—in short, of everybody. Frederick William I was quite convinced that his son, whom he had detected in youthful excesses and whose taste for French culture seemed to him sheer idleness, would on succeeding to the Crown do everything forbidden to him in the testament of 1722; and that his own death would be followed by the rise in Prussia of a luxurious Court and a costly *régime* of mistresses, accompanied by a reduction of military expenditure. In short, Frederick William anticipated with the accession of his son the ruin of all that he had called into life and the abandonment of all the methods of his home government. The conflict between the monarch and his heir also extended to matters of religion. Frederick William adhered with all the zeal of a bigot to certain narrow dogmatic conceptions, which Frederick contradicted with witty effrontery. Regarding the Crown Prince as certain to bring about the moral ruin of the young

Prussian State, the King on one occasion went so far as to say, after administering a few of his usual cuffs, that, had he been treated so by his father, he would have shot himself, but that Frederick had no sense of honour, and would put up with anything.

The unhappy Prince now formed a rash resolve to escape from his tormentor, taking flight by way of France to England. He applied for aid to Sir Charles Hotham and his *attaché* Guy Dickens; but they refused it and discouraged the whole plan. Nevertheless, when on a journey with his father to the south-west of Germany, Frederick made every preparation for escaping across the Rhine into France. But at the last moment, at Mannheim, one of the pages of the Crown Prince, who was involved in the plan of escape, threw himself at the King's feet and disclosed everything. Frederick's chief accomplice had been Lieutenant Hans Hermann von Katte, a young man of good family, rather older than the Prince. Most of the aristocracy detested the institutions of absolutism; "Court and army teem with unrest," wrote Grumbkow. The young officer, though barely of age, was pronounced guilty of high treason, and, after having been for weeks threatened with torture, was finally beheaded at Cüstrin; the Crown Prince, who was kept a close prisoner in the fortress, being obliged to witness the execution from the window of his prison (November 6). Frederick William's pitiless action was universally condemned abroad, particularly in England; but Frederick William defiantly bade his ambassador in London state that if a hundred thousand Kattes made their appearance he would have every one of them beheaded. "He would have the English know that he would suffer no rule beside his own." Frederick William for a time had serious thoughts of compelling the prisoner at Cüstrin to renounce his birthright, and of transferring the succession to the Crown to his second son; but, as a matter of course, he soon had to relinquish any intentions of the kind. It was, however, very slowly and with the utmost reluctance that he submitted to the necessity of resuming normal family relations with the Crown Prince. For the next few years the relations between father and son were rather less stormy; but the Crown Prince still had so much cause to tremble before the passion of Frederick William that he often desired his father's death.

The King was greatly incensed against England because the members of the British diplomatic service had not given information of the Crown Prince's plan of escape, though they had not furthered it. Confidently expecting the Austro-English war to break out shortly, he declared: "I shall not desert the Emperor, even if everything goes to the dogs. I will joyfully use my army, my country, my money, and my blood for the downfall of England." In one of the most elaborate memoranda extant from Frederick William's hand he writes that he wishes his relations in London every happiness, "provided it be not at my expense and intended to upset the whole of my organisation, which is a stone of offence to these Anglo-Hanoverian gentlemen. My organisation, *c'est la pierre de touche*."

France was at this time reckoned to be maintaining land forces to the extent of 160,000 regular troops; the Russian army was estimated at 130,000 men, the Austrian at from 80,000 to 100,000. Frederick William, with little over two million subjects, raised the Prussian army to a total of 80,000. At his accession, in 1713, before the close of the War of the Spanish Succession, the Prussian army was only 38,000 strong, about equal to the forces of the Kings of Sardinia and of Saxony and Poland respectively, and, like the troops of these sovereigns, could only be maintained by means of subsidies from the Western Powers. Since such payments were only made in time of war, the Prussian army, under both the Great Elector and Frederick I, was invariably almost entirely disbanded on the conclusion of peace. Frederick William I, at that time the only real autocrat in the civilised world besides the King of France, followed the example of France in creating a large standing army which could be maintained from his State's own resources in time of peace and during a certain number of campaigns. In proportion to the population and wealth of the two countries, the Prussian army was immeasurably stronger than the French. Consequently, it was no easy task for the King of Prussia to supply the human material for his new military creation. He cherished the prejudice that only tall men were fit to be soldiers. Besides, in his army the troops were treated much as his own son had been. Whereas in France the punishment of flogging was never inflicted on soldiers and in England its application was surrounded by protective provisions, in the Prussian army flogging was as freely used as in the Russian. According to the King's notions the stick was an indispensable implement of military education. After his visit to King George I at Hanover in 1725, he wrote to Leopold of Dessau in high commendation of the impressive appearance and the many fine qualities of the Hanoverian troops, but added: "What in my opinion is wanting is subordination; they do their duty because they delight in it, not from a sense of subordination, for scarcely a blow can be dealt any man among them under pain of the King's displeasure. Every private soldier knows this, and yet the army is in good order; which greatly surprises me."

At the King's accession there was no conscription in Prussia. The army was recruited by voluntary enlistment, partly from within the Prussian monarchy, partly from the rest of Germany, and to a considerable extent also from nationalities speaking their own languages. As in other countries, too, when voluntary enlistment yielded insufficient numbers, it gave place to impressment. There is probably no doubt that this system has never been resorted to in any country so extensively and so recklessly as in Prussia and in the petty States of Germany, which through fear of Prussia had to submit to the misdeeds of Frederick William's recruiting-officers. It was simply kidnapping accompanied by bloodshed—a sort of slave-hunting. In the Rhenish and Westphalian possessions of the House of Brandenburg, which consisted of a number of enclaves, young men could easily escape across the border when pursued by a recruiting-officer. Accordingly there was here a wholesale emigration of young men; and townsmen and peasants alike were left without serving-men. In the compact eastern territories the majority of the young men could not elude the recruiting-officer by emigrating, so that by force or by stratagem large numbers could be impressed. King Frederick William I was a very devout man; but his recruiting-officers were allowed to take the congregations at Sunday service by surprise and carry off the biggest and strongest young men. The total of the standing army was so enormous compared to that of the population, and the methods of recruiting so harsh, that in many parts of the country there soon began to be scarcity of labour for tillage and for the harvesting of crops. As a result, nobility and peasants made common cause against the recruiting-officers, and expelled them by force. The Estates and the magistrates expressed apprehension lest the proceeds from the land-tax should diminish, trade decline, and with it the revenue accruing from the excise. These representations by the authorities produced some impression on the King; for it was the taxes alone that enabled him to maintain the army.

Frederick William I's views as to the treatment of the recruits won by earnest-money, or by force and cunning, were quite reasonable in theory. He demanded of his officers that a young soldier should be taught everything without railing and abuse, so that a man might not turn sullen and timid at the very outset. Neither was a recruit to be beaten or otherwise ill-treated, particularly if he was of a nationality other than German. But these wise provisions of the regulations remained a dead letter in the practice of the service. Frederick William cared rather more effectively for the comfort of the soldiers than for their humane treatment; but a good deal of what was intended for the troops was embezzled by the officers, many of whom were still very corrupt.

Soon after his accession, the King issued an edict declaring that, according alike to the natural and the divine order of things, the young men of both town and country were bound to serve him with their lives. But among the Prussian middle classes the edict met with almost universal disapproval. According to the conceptions of humanity then current, it was impossible that public opinion should be in favour of universal conscription, when discipline was so barbarously enforced in the army, that during the reign of Frederick William I there were no fewer than 30,000 desertions, and this in spite of the brutal penalty of flogging through the line. Moreover, in the King's eyes it was of secondary importance whether the captains, whose duties included recruiting, made up the *cadres* of their companies by voluntary enlistment, impressment or conscription, provided only the prescribed number were obtained.   At the end of Frederick William's reign half the army, 40,000 men, consisted of foreigners, while the other 40,000 were drawn from home.   Voluntary enlistment and impressment had been gradually almost entirely abandoned for the native element in the army, for these were costly methods and inconvenient to manage.   But, without any cooperation on the part of the King, the captains found a way by which they gradually succeeded in making conscription acceptable to the population.   Eligible lads were already in their tenth year entered on the list of recruits for their "canton" (the particular district appropriated to every single regiment for recruiting purposes).   They were given a bunch of red feathers to wear in their hats, and a pass certifying leave of absence, and had to take the military oath after their confirmation. In this way these *Enrollirte* (enrolled) were familiarised from childhood with the thought of having some day or other to follow the drum; while landowners and parents had time to prepare for the falling off in labour.   In this manner, not as prescribed by the King but as the result of habit, the edict of universal conscription was in course of time realised so far as the social and economic conditions of the age permitted.   Very important exemptions from the obligation of service were allowed; but they were not strictly enough formulated to protect the middle classes entirely against the imposition of military service. Through this loophole most abuses crept in, since the officers liberated " enrolled " persons from conscription for a money payment, and sold to soldiers on active service their discharges.   Frederick William was aware how widespread was this extortionary practice among his officers.   Just as Napoleon I organised in France the system of substitution along with universal conscription, so the practice of buying out of the service existed under Frederick William I, but in a very crude form.   Frederick William manifestly did not proclaim universal conscription on account of the ideal advantages attaching to a national army, but only because he required an expedient for filling up the regiments when voluntary enlistment and impressment appeared inadequate for this purpose.

The discipline inculcated in the troops alike by the King and by Prince Leopold was the strictest then in existence anywhere.   It can be stated with absolute certainty that an army so sternly disciplined had not been seen in Europe since the Roman centurion and his rod had vanished from the pages of history.   The Prussian regulations prescribed that a soldier who on or off duty abused his superior officer should be rigorously flogged through the line; in the case of a man on duty, a single word was sufficient to incur this barbarous penalty.   A soldier who resisted his superior officer or threatened him was shot without further ado.   On the parade grounds at Potsdam where the King drilled his own regiment, the "Giant Guard," and at Halle, where Prince Leopold's regiment was garrisoned, the men were drilled with incredible perseverance and success. The Prince of Dessau spoke with justifiable pride of that "marvel, the Prussian infantry." Their perfection was least of all due to the much-vaunted iron ramrod which Leopold introduced into the Prussian army. The strength of Frederick William's battalions lay rather in the combination of discipline and mobility imparted to them by infinitely laborious exercises. The troops had been accustomed by the use of the stick to such absolute obedience that, even amid a rain of bullets, they would act with machine-like precision and carry out calmly and surely the elaborate evolutions commanded.

In 1809 Napoleon wrote to Alexander of Russia that, when they should have jointly forced England to make peace, they might do Europe the service of abolishing the system of enormous standing armies begun by Prussia. This statement of the French Emperor's is a little biassed, as Louis XIV's was the first standing army of any dimensions raised since the days of classical antiquity. But it is, nevertheless, true that, in proportion to the population and wealth of Prussia, the army of Frederick William I was of enormous size. The military Powers of to-day oblige at most $1\frac{1}{4}$ per cent. of the population to serve in the army. Frederick William's standing army amounted to nearly 4 per cent. during the three months of the year in which the soldiers on leave (whose numbers at other times were no doubt very large) were called in.

The royal Commander-in-chief of this exorbitantly large army was not completely dominated by the dynastic point of view which still prevailed in the European Courts. He called himself a Republican, thereby implying his belief in the idea of the State as the true rule of conduct for all sovereigns. Putting the genuineness of his religious feelings to a practical test, Frederick William worked for the good of his subjects in a way which indirectly became a pattern for a whole generation of princes. His father's schooling, which was so repugnant to him, taught the Crown Prince the virtue of application so especially prized by the royal taskmaster. The father wished to pass for a Republican, and the son designated himself "the chief servant of the State." Following the example of Frederick the Great, numerous German Princes applied themselves diligently to the political work which their predecessors had neglected. Thus the condition of Germany benefited largely through the change in the spirit of the government introduced by Frederick William I.

Yet never had a Republican less respect than King Frederick William for the freedom of his fellow-men. From the nobility he exacted without any question of exemption that compulsory service which he could only partially enforce with the people at large. He required all able-bodied noblemen to serve as officers till their physical powers were virtually exhausted. The *Landräthe* in the several provinces had to send in lists of the young nobles between the ages of twelve and eighteen; whereupon, without more ado, royal orders were issued as to which youths from each district were to enter the *Cadettenhaus* (military school) at Berlin. The Great Elector had broken the political power of the feudal Estates, and Frederick William turned them into an army-service nobility, who learned, besides military discipline, that self-subordination in public matters was a sacred duty.   Hitherto, the young nobles of the various territories which happened to be subject to the House of Brandenburg had been quite as ready to take military service under alien governments as under their own.   Thus, the East Prussian nobility liked to serve in the Polish or Danish army, that of Cleves in the Dutch.   But, now that the whole nobility of the Prussian monarchy was forced to undergo conscription, the King gained for his huge army a supply of officers both numerous and of high quality.

Where the aristocracy resisted this compulsory service, Frederick William resorted without hesitation to dragonnades and kidnapping of children.   A certain Herr von Kleist of Zeblin in Eastern Pomerania would not let his son enter the regiment of his district; and a widow, Frau von Below, refused to direct her son, who was away in Poland, to do the same.   The King thereupon ordered the commander of the regiment to quarter a corporal and twelve men on the property of these two persons until they sent in their sons.   In East Prussia boys of good family were carried off by the soldiery from their fathers' houses and sent under escort in bands of 18 or 20 to Berlin, where they were placed in the military school.   Peter the Great had in like manner compelled the Russian provincial gentry to serve as officers.   The Kings of France did not dare to go to such lengths.

In Prussia the officers of the army were the ruling caste, like the priests in other countries.   The King insisted on the fact that he stood on a far more intimate personal footing with the officers than with the rest of his subjects.   Following his example, the officers treated the official classes, the learned professions, and the upper middle classes generally, with a contempt and at times a brutality which rendered the position of these classes uncomfortable and insecure.   Prussia was a polity of officers. Their numbers were enormous, their service monotonous and very rarely interrupted by periods of leave.   The nobility might console themselves for the loss of their freedom by the fact that, in the main, they made up the whole of this officers' polity.

Frederick William was not only the organiser of the Prussian army, but also the founder of Prussian finance, without a judicious and firm settlement of which a military State could not have been called into life. He created the royal Treasure proper.   Prussia was not, like England, France and Holland, in a position to raise war loans; the subjects of the House of Brandenburg were too poor to advance large sums; and foreign countries, generally speaking, refused to give credit. Frederick William gradually amassed 10,000,000 *thalers* (£1,500,000) in the royal treasury, in order not to be dependent in the event of war upon subsidies from the Western Powers, as were the other German Princes, Austria and Russia—one and all. The yearly revenue of the Prussian State amounted at the King's death to 7,000,000 *thalers* (£1,050,000). Now, the United Kingdom in 1905 had an income of about £140,000,000 ; hence the ready money which lay in the vaults of the castle in Berlin meant practically what a reserve of £200,000,000 in gold would mean to the British Government of to-day. No other country in the eighteenth century possessed an institution combining fiscal and political uses in so peculiar a fashion. To the Treasury belonged also the silver plate procured by Frederick William to the value of 600,000 *thalers* (£90,000), after the inherited silver plate had been melted down and the proceeds used for the acquisition of Stettin.

In those days a very great deal of the fixed capital in Prussia belonged to the Crown. Even at the outset of the reign of Frederick William I a quarter, if not a third, of the peasant vassals consisted of peasants bound to the royal domains. In order to increase the profits from these domains and generally to raise the population of the kingdom which was still remarkably small, Frederick William organised immigration on a large scale. East Prussia and the Mark Brandenburg were the provinces which offered the greatest scope to foreign settlers. In 1713 the population of East Prussia was estimated at some 400,000 ; under Frederick William more than 30,000 new colonists came in, of whom by far the larger proportion hailed from more highly civilised countries, some of them bringing money with them. There were south Germans and west Germans, as well as Swiss. The nucleus of the immigration was formed by 15,000 Protestants from Salzburg, who had been compelled by Archbishop Firmian to emigrate. The other colonists whom King Frederick William secured were also to some extent victims of religious intolerance ; but there were likewise many who left their homes for economic and other material reasons. The King made use of the Dutch Press and other journalistic agencies to win over the less stable element in any country within reach. Allowances for the journey, remission of taxes, timber for building, grants of money, exemption from military service, and every other imaginable privilege were promised—and good land to boot. But, in reality, the King took good care not to establish the immigrants on fertile soil. This he put into the hands of native Prussian tenants of the Crown possessed of capital, to whom six-year leases only were granted, so that on the expiration of this short term the rent might be raised whenever possible. Inferior land on the domains was for the most part allotted to the impecunious among the colonists ; if they were hard-working and managed well, the money advanced by the King soon yielded a very good interest, often 10 to 12 per cent.

It was no doubt the fiscal point of view which predominated when this civilising movement was set on foot. The immediate object was to open up the resources of East Prussia so that the land might be able to contribute more towards the army. A report from the Board of Domains of East Prussia to the King states that the establishment of the Swiss in that province had occasioned no great outlay ; for the horses, oxen and cows supplied to them as an advance in the King's name had been charged to them at five to six *thalers,* whereas they had cost on an average about three *thalers.* Hence it came about that many of the settlers who had been attracted by the King's promises bitterly repented their coming, the more so as the effects of this fiscal policy were further aggravated by corruption in official circles. Frederick William would on no account permit dissatisfied colonists to emigrate again ; in fact, he punished attempts on the part of settlers to get away from their new homes almost as severely as military desertion. But, despite all distressing accompaniments, the resettlement of East Prussia remains a most praiseworthy proceeding. The province, which lay on the borders of European civilisation, was raised to a higher plane by the colonists, who were mentally and morally superior to the original inhabitants. The King, who never succeeded in raising the revenue to more than seven million *thalers* a year, is proved to have expended at least three millions, possibly much more, on the resettlement of East Prussia. It was a very difficult matter to transplant thirty thousand country people with south and west German customs to a distant province of widely different character and devastated by pestilence, and to settle them so that they gradually became acclimatised and raised the native population to their own level. The whole movement was personally organised by Frederick William, who visited East Prussia on six different occasions for this purpose ; in accordance with his general practice of constantly travelling through his State.

The King managed the Crown lands as a farming enthusiast manages his estate. The farmers-general, to whom he let the several domains for six years each, administered police and justice on feudal principles over the " subjects " of the domain. The fees accruing to them from these prerogatives were taken into account when fixing the rental. So the masters had a very keen moral sense when it came to punishing all misdemeanours of the country people ; and the fines imposed on the peasants were far from light, whether for disobedience and remissness in bearing the feudal burdens or for disorderly conduct and bad language.

The King was cautious in espousing the cause of the distressed peasantry. No contemporary Prince had a greater sense of his duties as a monarch towards the lower classes ; but Frederick William was anything but sentimental, and with him fiscal considerations almost always predominated. It was not only the peasant who suffered on this account, but the nobleman and the burgher likewise. Thanks to their privileged position, the farmers-general could carry on breweries and public-houses under the most favourable business conditions, so as to compete unduly with similar industries on *Rittergüter* (knights' manorial estates) or in towns. By the extension or introduction of *Mühlenzwang*, as it was called, the peasants, whether or not belonging to the domain, were compelled by law to have their corn ground in the domain mill, whether they had been previously in the habit of using the landlord's mill, or hand-mills, as the custom was in backward East Prussia.

By a drastically maintained policy of this kind the King during his reign of twenty-seven years raised the income from the domains from 1,500,000 to 3,300,000 *thalers*. A host of civil suits decided by arbitrary administration of justice in a manner advantageous to the Treasury had contributed to this very large increase.

At the end of the reign of Frederick William I the Crown lands yielded, as stated, 3,300,000 *thalers*; the taxes 3,600,000. This taxation, in Prussia as on the Continent generally, was borne by the burgher and peasant classes, the nobility being for the most part exempt. In East Prussia alone was this privilege denied the nobles; but they resorted to fraud and bribery. They paid no higher tax for their richest acre of land than for their poorest, and kept no cattle in order to shift the burden of the cattle-tax upon the shoulders of the peasantry, which, being held in bondage, must work for the feudal lords. Any deficiency in the domestic economy of the landlords was made good by demanding an excessive amount of forced labour from the peasants. Much land belonging to the nobles was not taxed at all. The King completely overthrew this system. The newly introduced General Hide Tax (*Generalhufenschoss*) imposed on a large number of the East Prussian noblemen six times more taxes than they had hitherto paid; fully 34,681 hides of land belonging to the nobility, the existence of which had been kept secret by the owners, were entered on the tax roll. The increase in revenue was considerable enough to allow of the formation of three or four battalions. But, at the same time, owners of moderate and small properties were sensibly relieved. This was most essential, if the process of absorption of peasant proprietors by the big landowners was to be stopped. While in Western Pomerania, under Swedish rule, and in Mecklenburg the class of peasant proprietors—living, it is true, as bondmen, but on their own homesteads—almost entirely disappeared, a class of landless labourers taking their place, Frederick William I, and still more his son Frederick II, successfully laboured to preserve the peasant proprietor in their dominions. In East Prussia not only the reform of taxation but the settlement of 32,000 foreign country-folk decidedly contributed to securing for the province a tolerably fair apportionment of the rural landed property.

Both these Prussian Kings could not but be pronounced opponents of an excessive growth of large estates, because rural depopulation was compatible neither with the cantonment system nor with the system of taxation which in the rest of the kingdom left the nobility untaxed and in East Prussia still favoured this above other classes. "*Tout le pays sera ruiné,*" the spokesman of the East Prussian nobility declared, in opposition to the King, in the course of an attack on the General Hide Tax. Frederick William replied that it was not the land that would be ruined, but the authority of the *Junkers*; the King's sovereignty he would maintain "like a *rocher de bronce.*"

Measured by the standard of the French peasant class of that day, the social and economic level of the rustic population of Prussia remained, notwithstanding, very low. The peasants on the Crown lands, who were better off than those on the estates of the nobility, were often subjected to forced labour for the Contractor-General for four or more days a week. Then, besides other feudal burdens, there was the specially heavy obligation on all peasants to provide teams at the marches and reviews of the troops, and to supply straw for the camp. To mitigate these impositions, Frederick William instituted in particular districts "March and Burden (*Molestien*) Funds" which were to be supplied by the Estates, not by the Crown; but these afforded nothing like complete relief. Characteristic of the position of the smaller rural landowners is the principle laid down by the royal Domains Commission in Lithuania, that a peasant on the Crown lands having an annual net income of 55 *thalers* cash should keep 20 and hand over the rest to the King. The subjects of the nobility were, as has been seen, in a considerably worse plight. It is therefore no wonder that the substitution of agricultural labourers for peasant proprietors progressed, although, as has been seen, in a large portion of the kingdom effective restrictions were put on this movement which were harmful to the community and unwelcome to the Crown. The French peasants were in almost every respect better off than the Prussian ; for most of them there was nothing beyond remnants of feudalism left to bear, and they were constantly acquiring more land.

The urban excise, established by the Great Elector as the financial corner-stone of monarchical authority, had not been introduced in any part of the monarchy except the Mark Brandenburg, Pomerania, and Magdeburg, when Frederick William came to the throne. He extended it to East Prussia and the wealthy districts round Halberstadt and Bielefeld. In the country round Hamm and Crefeld there was a special form of excise, which treated least effectively those dutiable articles which happened to be the most valuable. The King exchanged this relatively unproductive system for that in force in Brandenburg. He likewise procured fresh receipts by extending the monopoly on salt, introduced by the Great Elector, to almost the entire State. His system of taxation was most successful, as he increased the proceeds of taxation from 2,500,000 *thalers* to 3,600,000.

One of the most powerful levers worked by the King for raising his revenues was the reform of the provincial administration. He adopted the principle of never stationing an official in his native province. The Pomeranian, the Brandenburg, and the East Prussian officials and likewise those from Magdeburg, Halberstadt, Ravensberg, Mark, and Cleves had, in place of a local patriotism, to cherish the interests of the Prussian State, which this King had been the first ruler of the House of Brandenburg to make a reality. Under the stern control of Frederick William I a growing proportion of the official class learnt honesty—and they all learnt obedience.

Furthermore, the King completely transformed the organisation of the government authorities. When he came to the throne, there were working side by side in Berlin a General Directory of Finance (*Generalfinanzdirectorium*), which managed the receipts from the Crown lands, and a Chief War Commissariat (*Oberkriegskommissariat*), into whose chest the taxes flowed. This historic dualism held good in the provinces likewise, where the Crown lands pertained to the boards of finance, and the taxes to the commissariat offices. Frederick William merged these two branches of the administration in one, in order to put an end to the constant friction between them. In Berlin the General Directory (*Generaldirectorium*) was established as a central administrative department; in the provinces Chambers of War and Domains (*Kriegs- und Domänenkammern*) were formed. This organisation, instituted in 1723, remained practically unchanged until the extinction of the old Kingdom of Prussia in 1807. It formed the nucleus of a bureaucracy which was the finest in the world after the French, and in the end outstripped its prototype. The General Directory was divided into four departments, to each of which belonged a Minister and four or five head officials of the Treasury (*Finanzräthe*).

The King ordained that the members of the General Directory, the Ministers and Councillors, were not to be expected to be distinguished by special departmental knowledge. Rather, these officials were all alike to be well informed as to the whole of the affairs of the public administration. But, in the case of the provincial administrative bodies, Frederick William I was inclined to allow greater scope for specialisation to the War and Domains Offices, and the several Councillors of War (*Kriegsräthe*) were each to devote himself to a particular branch of the administration.

But it is impossible here to enter into all the details of importance in the changes which the Prussian administration underwent under Frederick William I. Only as to the Councillors of Taxes (*Steuerräthe*) and their functions a word must be said. The Councillor of Taxes was a Commissioner from the War and Domains Office, who administered six to twelve small and moderate-sized towns, while large towns had each a separate Councillor. The Councillors of Taxes took rank after the Councillors of the War and Domains Offices (*Kriegsräthe*), and were generally chosen from among the officials of the Military Commissariat Department.

At the outset of his reign Frederick William I encountered a corrupt, oligarchical municipal government, resembling that which the Municipal Reform Bill of 1835 amended in England. Frederick William cleansed the municipalities of much of their ancient corruption; but at the same time he almost completely destroyed the self-government of the towns. The town councils lost the right of cooptation. They might, it is true, send in to the Government a list of nominations whenever there was a vacancy on the council; but neither the War and Domains Offices nor the General Directory took much notice of such lists, and they created only such people burgomasters and councillors as were in the Government's judgment capable, honest, and submissive. The municipalities also might no longer collect their own taxes. If the municipal revenues were not sufficient for the maintenance of street pavements, fire brigades, fountains, roads, bridges, etc., in the condition prescribed by the regulations of the General Directory and of the War and Domains Office, the latter body voted a special grant for the purpose out of the urban excise.

At this point the supremacy of the Councillor of Taxes began. The municipal budget was under his control; not a *groschen* might be spent either in accordance with the regular budget or beyond it without his knowledge. Town councillors were mostly holders of state appointments who also served the commune; but, even if the War and Domains Office allowed a few councillors to be taken from the merchant class or some other independent calling, the municipal authorities counted for nothing at all as against the all-powerful Councillor of Taxes. He had a hand in everything. He closely superintended the management of the municipal property and urged on the city-fathers, who were, generally speaking, slow to move in economic matters, the draining of marshes and the building of mills, and the construction of brick-yards and sheep-runs on land belonging to the municipality.

As the income from an important government tax like the urban excise depended upon the general prosperity of the community in which it was raised, the Councillor of Taxes had a far wider sphere of influence. He controlled weights and measures, and superintended the watch kept over building materials and food-stuffs; the duties on bread, meat, and beer had to be adjusted in his presence; he had to see that good beer was brewed; that thatches and shingle roofs were replaced by tiles, and draw-wells by pumps.

It was the Councillor of Taxes, not the town council, who suggested to the War and Domains Office which persons should be appointed as municipal recorders, treasurers, secretaries and other civic officers, when vacancies occurred. For an inefficient municipal administration would have been detrimental to the royal finances, not merely to those of the municipality. Again, in the narrow conditions of life which then obtained in the towns of Prussia, it seemed to be most important from an economical point of view that not merely office-holders but, so far as possible, all the citizens should lead moral lives. Otherwise, to begin with, there was a danger of a rise in the charges for poor relief. This state of things made the Councillor of Taxes the moral censor of the whole population of the town. He summoned before him persons who were leading notoriously wicked lives, admonished them in the presence of the municipal authorities, and depicted to them in glaring hues pauperism as the inevitable result of their sins. He was authorised to banish from the town incorrigible ne'er-do-weels, and under certain circumstances even to sentence them to imprisonment with hard labour. Nor was it by any means only the morality and industry of the proletariat which were taken in charge by the commissioner of the War and Domains Office; he also concerned himself with the way in which the work at the *Rathhaus* was distributed—whether the city-fathers and officials were faithfully observing the rules, or whether they were being lazy and imbibing too much beer and spirits.

The advancement of commerce and manufactures was one of the chief duties of this representative of the Crown and of Providence. He must endeavour to attract capitalists and manufacturers to the town. He was commanded to manage the guilds and to encourage industries. In the Prussia of Frederick William I these latter were subjected to government inspection, on the principle introduced by Colbert in France. The cloth-weavers were told how they were to clean, card, and dress the wool, and any shortcomings in any part of the technical process were notified by the inspectors for punishment to the revenue official, who had to see that there were proper fulling-mills, that the cloth-workers possessed good modern appliances, and that there were proper arrangements for dyeing. This state socialism even went so far as to impose upon the Councillor of Taxes the duty of finding employers and constant occupation for the home-workers among the weavers, and of settling the scale of wages in consultation with both parties.

This paternal supervision on the part of the Councillor of Taxes extended to all other industries. Mercantilism met the needs of the age, notwithstanding the crudeness which marked that economic theory; and beyond doubt many services were rendered from an economic point of view by the Prussian Councillor of Taxes. In particular the stimulus given to cloth-weaving under his auspices was of lasting benefit to the textile industries of Prussia. The close diplomatic relations between Prussia and Russia noted above enabled the "Russian Company" in Berlin to supersede the English contractors of army-cloth for the Tsar's dominions; and for many years the stuffs used for the uniforms of the Russian army were woven in the Electoral and the New Mark. The needy Mark Brandenburg received more than 1,600,000 *thalers* for these fabrics, though they were thick and heavy and not to be compared in quality with the soft English materials; so that the "Russian Company" had to be wound up when a coolness set in in the diplomatic relations between Berlin and St Petersburg, and the English textile trade regained the

Russian market. But in the meantime the cloth manufacture in Brandenburg had, over and above the money earned, made technical progress which was not lost, and there had been an enduring gain of commercial insight. The cloth-weaving industry of the Mark survived the loss of the Russian market and flourished anew.

Altogether the economic advance of the country was unmistakable, though slow—for statistics from which it is sought to deduce a great rise of prosperity in reality prove nothing. A mercantilist commercial policy pursued by a monarch with common sense and energy perhaps suited Germany even better than France, because the national decline of the seventeenth century had crippled the enterprise of the German middle class, formerly so alert. Not only was the progress of this policy carefully regulated from above, but it also received pecuniary aid. The rigid economy adopted by Frederick William in the interests of the army did not deter him from making great outlays for productive purposes. It has already been stated that at least three million *thalers* were spent on the resettlement of East Prussia. More than two millions (£300,000) were divided among the several provinces for municipal improvements. If a town suffered heavy damages by fire, or by any other serious calamity, which if not allayed, must entail an appreciable abatement of the royal taxes, the King would with well-considered generosity open his purse. He left a specially fine memorial of himself in the Havelland, where he drained the marshy region of the Luch, employing military labour for the purpose. Thirty-five square miles were reclaimed for cultivation, after several large canals, numerous trenches, and more than thirty dikes of considerable size had been constructed.

The statement that Frederick William made large pecuniary grants to the subjects of the Crown for his own well-understood advantage, does not imply that the King incurred these heavy expenses without including, as a secondary consideration, the furtherance of the well-being of the people committed to him by God. Many as were the faults attaching to his character, his piety was sincere, deep, and at the same time practical. In the testament of 1722 the necessity for founding schools is mentioned in the same breath with the obligation on the Prussian Government to build churches. It was this ecclesiasticism (to use the word in no invidious sense) which gave rise to Frederick William's edict introducing universal compulsory education. But the Prussian State was not yet ripe for so sweeping a reform. The edict decreed that the cost of the compulsory primary schools was to be borne by the parents with assistance from the various communities. In this period the large wealthy States of western Europe contributed nothing towards elementary schools, and did not concern themselves at all with this serious problem. If Frederick William I's edict bore but scanty fruit, nevertheless more was done under his rule for the education of the masses than under any other contemporary sovereign.

In everything which this eminently practical monarch seriously undertook, he was favoured by fortune, so far as internal policy was concerned. His ecclesiastical policy also proved successful. He wielded a power over his clergy even more absolute than that in the hands of the King of France. With the help of the University of Halle, he used this supremacy to win over the Protestant clergy of his kingdom to pietistic views. The Pietists were the only party in the Protestant Church of Germany at that time which was not torpid but full of life and productivity. Methodism, which was akin to it and which sprang up almost contemporaneously in England, was rejected by the Established Church of that country. The English Church accordingly fell into a state of apathy which lasted for a century, while in Prussia Protestantism continued active and spread its vivifying spirit among adherents of the same form of faith far beyond the boundaries of the Prussian monarchy.

Political equality was not enjoyed by religious minorities of that day in any European State; and in the dominions of the House of Brandenburg the Catholics were not on an equality with the Protestants. But the King, if a keen Protestant, was a practical man; he had Catholic officers and soldiers, and treated his Papist subjects in general so well that Rome, which at that period indeed could make no great claims, was satisfied with him. Of course, in a State so rigorously absolutist as that of Frederick William I there could be no question of liberty for the Church, whether Catholics, Lutherans, or members of the Reformed Church were in question. The King would have liked to effect a union of the two Protestant confessions. He considered it a step in that direction to forbid the Reformed ministers to preach on predestination, while the Lutheran clergy were prohibited from chanting in Latin, or introducing any music or the use of lighted candles on the altar, during the consecration of the elements in the Eucharist. They had also to give up surplices, stoles, eucharistic vestments, and the elevation of the Sacrament, and were no longer allowed to pronounce the benediction, crucifix in hand, at the close of the service. In these innovations the King encountered passive resistance, and he died in the midst of this difficulty before he had been able to come to a settlement with the clerical Opposition. Otherwise, the clergy as a class rendered absolute obedience to him. The submissiveness of the Prussian ministers in all political matters was further increased by the doctrines of Spener and Francke, both of whom considered that the mission of the clergy consisted almost exclusively in fostering the spiritual life and in charity.

King Frederick William I was only fifty-one years of age when he died, on May 31, 1740. He was ill-satisfied with the results of his reign, because all the Cabinets of Europe denied his claims to the duchy of Berg. Everyone ridiculed the soldier-king, who was constantly preparing for war and never fought. The Austrians thought that half these Prussian soldiers, trained by profuse thrashings, would desert when it came to war. It was not for the last time that the world under-estimated the strength which Prussia had been quietly building up.

Despite all the repellent traits in his character and in that of a polity of officers formed in his image, Frederick William remains a historical figure of the greatest importance. He, and he alone, created the means by which his son raised Prussia to the level of a Great Power. If Frederick William succeeded in laying the foundations for the development which was to follow, he owed his great and lasting achievements to his earnest piety, unsullied reputation, and eminently practical ability, and to a steadfast diligence which the pleasures of life were unable to turn aside from the strait path of duty. Last but not least, we must remember his scrupulous economy. The economy practised by him would have been superfluous in other countries; but the King of Prussia, a small and poor State, felt that he must carry the exercise of this virtue so far, that when writing he used to put on over-sleeves to save the expensive cloth of his uniform. The King was so absolutely possessed by this idea as to feel that, if his object were to be attained, he must turn every *thaler* over three times before spending it.

Ranke rightly observes that Prussia might have advanced on other lines than those laid down by Frederick William I. As a matter of fact, Prussia, more than any other State in the world's history, is what her great Kings have made her. After the death of Frederick William I, when the various classes paid homage to the new sovereign, they combined with this solemn act the expression of countless grievances and of the ill-concealed wish that almost everything that had been accomplished might be annulled. The tone of the officers was not much more amicable than that of the civilian population. The most distinguished of Frederick II's military subjects, Field-Marshal Schwerin, informed the young King that he regarded as indispensable a more or less complete return to the system of feudal estates abolished by the Great Elector two to three generations earlier. But Frederick II was much more of an autocrat than his father. He staunchly upheld the unpopular institutions of Frederick William I. Further, on the Prussian people, or rather on the collection of German-speaking peoples united by chance under the House of Brandenburg, he imposed two fresh obligations—the one in respect of home policy, the other in respect of foreign. The former was a realisation of the ideas of the *Aufklärung*; the latter the enforcement of the hereditary rights belonging to the House of Brandenburg over a part of Silesia. Public opinion in Prussia was indifferent to the Silesian claims of the dynasty, and detested the Voltairean innovations. But the King had absolute power. He ordered the abolition of torture and took other important measures in the spirit of the *Aufklärung*; and on the sudden death of Charles VI of Austria on October 20, 1740, after fruitless negotiations with the Court of Vienna, the Prussian army advanced into Silesia.

CH. VIII.

15—2

(3) THE WAR.

Had Maria Theresa merely been confronted with the problems of internal reform which Charles VI had not attempted, or attempted only to relinquish, her task would have been formidable enough. But that was by no means all: the chief perils lay in the possibility that her neighbours might see in the embarrassments of Austria a chance of profit. The desperate efforts of Charles VI to induce the Powers of Europe to guarantee the Pragmatic Sanction are some indication of the danger. The succession of a woman, especially in the unsatisfactory condition of the Habsburg dominions, was sure to be the signal for the putting forward of claims which Charles VI had endeavoured to meet in advance. As has been pointed out, the most formidable claims were those of the husbands of Joseph I's daughters, Charles Albert of Bavaria and Frederick Augustus II of Saxony. Those of Spain and Sardinia were less serious, and only caused anxiety because of the danger of a combination of claimants against the ill-prepared Habsburg State. Those of petty principalities like Würtemberg were not deserving of serious consideration. But it was not only from possible claimants that Charles VI had sought to obtain guarantees: Powers only indirectly interested in the question had been induced to give their pledges also; and it was really more important to see what line Russia and France and the Maritime Powers would adopt, for if they adhered to their guarantees it was unlikely that any of the rival claimants would endeavour to press their claims. Spain was already engaged in war with England; Sardinia might fish in troubled waters, but would hardly venture to disturb an unruffled pool; Saxony actually promised to help in putting the Pragmatic Sanction into force; and, though the Elector of Bavaria declined to acknowledge Maria Theresa's succession and laid claim to the Habsburg territories, he could not dispose of a force strong enough to push his claims unaided. Indeed, at first it almost seemed that Maria Theresa was to have an unexpectedly easy accession. England and the United Provinces, Pope Benedict XIV and the Republic of Venice, all acknowledged her as the lawful heiress of the Habsburg lands; and, though the death (October 28, 1740) of the Tsarina Anna Ivanovna and the consequent changes at St Petersburg deprived Maria Theresa of the help which she might have expected from Russia had Anna lived, nothing was to be feared from that quarter. The new King in Prussia, Frederick II, sent most friendly letters, containing not merely a formal recognition of Maria Theresa but an unsolicited offer of military help in case of need—conduct which effectually concealed his real intentions and made his subsequent action all the more outrageous. France did not, it is true, give any formal or definite acknowledgment, though Fleury spoke in the most reassuring manner to the Austrian ambassador at Paris, Prince Liechtenstein, ascribing the delay over the recognition to the need for research into the proper ceremonial to be observed. Thus it was only Bavaria whose attitude could be called hostile; and the claim advanced by the Elector in virtue of his descent from Anna, daughter of Ferdinand I, to whose representatives her father was alleged to have promised the succession in case of failure of his male heirs, was confuted by the production of the authentic will, showing that the contingency actually contemplated was the failure of legitimate heirs.

But, while Bavaria had claims, without the force to render them serious, another Power had a force so strong as to lend weight to claims which would not otherwise have been taken into account. Prussia's pretensions to the Silesian duchies of Brieg, Liegnitz, Jägerndorf and Wohlau were mainly important as a cloak under which to attempt to conceal the ambition and rapacity by which Frederick II was actuated. The falseness of his friendly professions had barely been suspected at Vienna, before it was published to the world by the invasion of Silesia by Prussian troops, 30,000 of whom crossed the frontier on December 16, 1740. They found the province quite unprepared to meet this unexpected attack. The troops quartered in it were much below even its peace establishment of 13,000, and could only throw themselves into the fortresses of Brieg, Glatz, Glogau, and Neisse, letting the Prussians overrun and take possession of the rest of the province, while the capital, Breslau, hastened to come to terms with the invader.

Simultaneously with his invasion of Silesia Frederick had despatched Baron Götter to Vienna to offer Maria Theresa the disposal of his vote at the coming Imperial election and armed assistance against her enemies, if she would satisfy his claims on Silesia. Maria Theresa, enraged by this effrontery, and by the mendacious proclamation in which Frederick represented to the inhabitants of Silesia that he was acting with her approval and in her interests, would not listen to Sinzendorff and other timid advocates of surrender; she at once set about collecting an army with which to expel the invaders from Silesia, and appealed to the guarantors of the Pragmatic Sanction for assistance against this unprovoked aggression. But only England showed any disposition to fulfil her obligations: elsewhere Frederick found imitators. Augustus III, after much haggling, withdrew his recognition, alleging objections to the appointment of Francis Stephen as co-Regent with Maria Theresa. Spain, Sardinia, and Bavaria prepared to push their claims; and, while Fleury continued to profess friendly intentions, there were among the counsellors of Louis XV many who urged their sovereign to put a finishing touch to the work of Richelieu and Louis XIV by seizing this opportunity of destroying the Power whose dangerous predominance his predecessors had resisted and reduced. An offer of a defensive alliance put forward by Frederick at the same time that he invaded Silesia found favour at Versailles; and, though no agreement was at once reached—for Frederick promptly raised his terms—France came gradually round to the side of Austria's enemies. It was decided that Marshal Belleisle should be sent on a special mission to Germany, to win over the Spiritual Electors to the side of Charles Albert of Bavaria and to arrange for Franco-Prussian cooperation in a personal interview with Frederick (March, 1741).

Meanwhile, the Austrian force charged with the recovery of Silesia was collecting on the frontier; but its mobilisation was greatly delayed by manifold defects in the military administration and by the lack of money which was mainly responsible for these shortcomings. Before Marshal Neipperg took the field (March 29), Frederick had been able to storm Glogau (March 9) and to reduce Ottmachau and other minor fortresses. But Frederick had not yet realised the importance of concentration: his troops, scattered to a dangerous degree, must have been caught and beaten in detail, but for Neipperg's blindness to his opportunities. Frederick himself at Jägerndorf had barely 4000 men with him; and, though he was fortunate enough to be able to rally 10,000 more under Kalckstein at Steinau on April 6 and to pick up the blockaders of Brieg on the 9th, if Neipperg had used his numerous and excellent cavalry properly, the King might easily have been crushed before he could have effected these junctions. As it was, the Prussians had to relinquish their blockades of Brieg and Neisse; and Neipperg was actually seven miles nearer Breslau than was Frederick on the morning of April 10, the day on which the armies met near the village of Mollwitz. Had the Prussian infantry's fighting capacities been of the same order as their monarch's strategy, Mollwitz would hardly claim to rank among decisive battles. Yet such it was; for, although the Austrian cavalry, superior in numbers and in quality, promptly routed the Prussian horsemen and drove them and Frederick with them headlong from the field, when the victorious troopers turned on the Prussian infantry, repeated charges on the flank and rear failed to break the steady ranks. Meanwhile, the Austrian infantry had advanced but could make no head against the superior artillery opposed to them and the rapidity of fire which their iron ramrods allowed the Prussians to maintain, and before long Neipperg's whole army was retreating in disorder on Neisse.

In the history of tactics Mollwitz is remarkable as one of the first victories of infantry over cavalry, of the combined musket and bayonet over the *arme blanche*. It was due mainly to the admirable training and fire-discipline established by Frederick William I, and it took the military profession by surprise. Its immediate results were insignificant. The defeat of the Prussian cavalry prevented any pursuit; and Neipperg, retiring to Neisse, took up his position there and maintained it all through the summer, Frederick making no effort to attack him, though he resumed the investment of Brieg which fell on May 4. Indeed, Mollwitz did not seem to have brought Frederick any nearer the direct conquest of Silesia: it was only its political results which made it decisive. Europe had been watching Silesia, and the Austrian defeat promised an easy victim to those who had hesitated to strike because they did not feel certain of success. If Maria Theresa could not oust Frederick from Silesia, how could she hope to resist a cooperative robbery?

Even before Mollwitz France was all but resolved on adopting the cause of Bavaria: Belleisle's influence was now predominant, and Fleury was only restrained from warmly advocating intervention by his natural irresolution and timidity and by jealousy of the supporters of the proposal. On March 10 Belleisle set out on his journey, in the course of which he was able to secure for Bavaria the support of the Spiritual Electors, though Mainz and Trier had hitherto shown themselves well disposed to Francis Stephen's candidature. At Dresden he was less successful, for Augustus III was jealous of his Bavarian brother-in-law, hated and distrusted Prussia, and was anxious to come to terms with Maria Theresa, could he induce her to make some concessions in Bohemia. Nor was Belleisle's first interview with Frederick, at Brieg about the end of April, any more satisfactory. Frederick was not anxious for French intervention and, while determined to keep Silesia, would have preferred to come to terms with Austria on that basis. But, although England (hoping to arrange a combination of Austria, Hanover, Saxony, and Prussia on the lines of the "Grand Alliance" of William III's day) sought to induce Maria Theresa to conquer her resentment and to secure Frederick's aid against Bavaria and France, not even Mollwitz could shake the Queen. Rather than make concessions to Frederick, she offered to the Bourbons substantial gains in the Netherlands, and even made overtures to Bavaria; but her offers were rejected, and on the last day of July Charles Albert began hostilities by seizing Passau. He was able to do this, because on May 18 the Treaty of Nymphenburg had assured him the active assistance of France, while by Belleisle's mediation a compact had been made with Spain (May 28) for the partition of the Habsburg heritage. Moreover, Frederick, finding Maria Theresa deaf to the counsels of England and prudence, fell back on his alternative and concluded, on June 5, a treaty at Breslau. By this France guaranteed to him Breslau and Lower Silesia, in return for his promise to vote for Charles Albert and his renunciation of all claims on Jülich and Berg in favour of the Sulzbach line of the Wittelsbachs (the representatives of the other partner in the Jülich-Cleves partition of 1666), a pledge which helped to secure for the Bavarians the support of the Elector Palatine.

It was on September 11 that Charles Albert's forces, 50,000 strong, two-thirds of them French "auxiliaries," began their advance down the Danube. Upper Austria proved an easy prey; few troops were at hand to defend it; Bavarian partisans were numerous; and the whole province submitted with discreditable readiness, nobility and officials exhibiting a culpable negligence if not actual disaffection. Vienna was in the gravest peril. Its fortifications and garrison were weak, its population panic-stricken; and, though Maria Theresa's dramatic appeal to Hungarian loyalty had met with a success which justified her confidence as much as it surprised her Ministers, the succours promised from this quarter were not yet in the field. So urgent was the extremity that Maria Theresa had reluctantly to agree to the conclusion by English mediation of the secret Convention of Klein-Schnellendorf (October 9) by which she gave up Lower Silesia, including Neisse, which was to be surrendered to the Prussians after a mock siege. At this heavy price, Prussia's neutrality was secured and Neipperg's army set free.

But Klein-Schnellendorf would have been too late to save Vienna, had Charles Albert been a strategist. When Neipperg left Neisse (October 16) the Bavarians, despite a quite unjustifiable delay of three weeks at Linz (September 14—October 5), were within a few marches of the ill-prepared Austrian capital. But from St Pölten, which he reached on October 21, the Elector suddenly turned back and, crossing the Danube at Mauthausen (October 24), directed his march into Bohemia. Military justification for this step he could not plead; he could gain nothing in Bohemia that he might not have secured by taking Vienna—the only possible explanation is that he could not trust his allies and feared they would forestall him by seizing Bohemia for themselves. He had certainly good reason for distrusting Frederick, and Augustus III, who after much vacillation had finally been persuaded by Belleisle to join the coalition against Maria Theresa (September 19), certainly hoped for part of Bohemia; but the move not only carried Charles Albert away from Vienna, the critical point where success might be assured, when the city was absolutely at his mercy—it also exposed Bavaria to a counter-stroke.

For the moment, however, all went well with the Bavarian cause. The appearance on the Lower Rhine of another French army under Marshal Maillebois had deprived Maria Theresa of the promised assistance of George II, who found himself forced by the peril which thus threatened Hanover to agree to become neutral (September 27). Bohemia, like Silesia and Upper Austria, was but poorly provided with troops; the fortifications of Prague were in bad repair, and the Bohemian nobility somewhat disaffected. Moreover, Neipperg's movements were so slow that Charles Albert was able to join a French reinforcement which entered Bavaria by Amberg, and to unite under the walls of Prague with the 20,000 Saxons under Rutowski (November 23), without any interference by the tardy Austrians. At the instigation of Maurice de Saxe an assault was at once made on Prague (November 25) with complete success, the Austrians being still fifty miles to the southward. As after Mollwitz, the fall of Prague was followed by a dead-lock, the Bavarians and their allies making no effort to drive the Austrians from the strong position near Neuhaus to which they had retired, while they were content to keep the main army of their enemies in check and so to cover operations in progress elsewhere.

One of the measures adopted by Maria Theresa to provide for the defence of her capital had been to recall 10,000 men from her Italian possessions. These, it is true, were likely to be attacked before long by Spain and Naples; but for the moment the troops could be spared, and their arrival at Vienna (December) provided a backbone of regulars for the wild irregulars whom the Hungarian "insurrection" was placing at Maria Theresa's disposal. Under the competent leadership of Count Khevenhüller and his able subordinate Bärenklau, this force took the offensive with complete success (December 31). The 10,000 men whom Charles Albert had left to hold Upper Austria were surrounded in Linz and forced to capitulate (January 24, 1742), after an attempt at relief by the Bavarian general Törring had been foiled at Scharding (January 17), and the Hungarian levies overran Bavaria in all directions. There was no little irony in the coincidence that on the day of the surrender of Linz the Diet at Frankfort elected Charles Albert to the vacant Imperial throne, and that, while the new Emperor was being solemnly crowned as Charles VII, Munich was capitulating to avoid being plundered (February 12). Törring had to retire on Ingolstadt, one of the very few places in Bavaria which had not passed into Khevenhüller's hands before the end of February. But, once again, the course of events was changed by what was happening elsewhere.

Frederick II had had good reasons for making the Convention of Klein-Schnellendorf: after ten months' campaigning his army sorely needed rest, and to obtain Neisse without the labours of a siege was a great advantage. But it is probable that Frederick made the Convention with the full intention of breaking it when he had profited by it, and found this course convenient. The insincerity of his attempts to throw on Austria the responsibility for the failure to keep the Convention a secret may be gathered from the treaty for the partition of Maria Theresa's territories which he concluded with Bavaria and her allies on October 31; and before Khevenhüller crossed the Enns the Prussians had invaded Moravia and (December 26) captured Olmütz. There for the moment they rested; but in February Frederick took the field again in person, pushing forward to Brünn and laying siege to that town, while his raiding parties penetrated almost so far as Vienna. In this operation Frederick had counted on the assistance of his allies; but only the Saxons gave him any active support—for neither Charles Albert nor Marshal de Broglie, now in command of the French "auxiliaries," approved of the invasion of Moravia, being anxious to relieve the pressure on Bavaria by an advance due south. Furious at the inaction of his allies, Frederick found the resistance of Brünn more than he could overcome with the means at his disposal, while the Hungarian light cavalry operated very briskly against his communications with Silesia. Thus, no sooner had the Austrian main army left Tabor for Znaim (April 1) than Frederick abandoned his attempt on Moravia, moving across into

Bohemia, instead of retiring on Silesia. The only effect of his attack on Moravia had been that Khevenhüller had had to detach some 10,000 men to Bohemia, which brought his own operations to a standstill. Thus reinforced, Charles of Lorraine proceeded to take the offensive against the French, hoping to bring de Broglie to action before he could be joined by further reenforcements from France. Partly to secure this junction, partly to ensure his own retreat if necessary, for his army was in a bad condition, de Broglie had just detached 10,000 men to secure Eger; and between his left and the Prussians at Chrudim there was a gap into which the Austrians proposed to thrust themselves. But, when on May 12 the Austrian vanguard reached Czaslau, about two-thirds of the way from Znaim to Prague, it found the Prussians moving westward, evidently to hinder the Austrian manœuvre, instead of retiring northward over the Elbe, as had been expected. On this, Prince Charles resolved to seek an action with the Prussians. Had he moved with greater speed, he might have caught Frederick at a disadvantage, for on the morning of May 16 there was a considerable space between the King, who was with his vanguard, and the main body, which was at Podhorzan. But an unnecessary halt of twelve hours at Ronnow and the miscarriage of a night-march, by which he sought to surprise the Prussian main body, deprived Charles of his chance; while, though in the earlier stages of the action in which he engaged between Czaslau and Chotusitz on May 17 the Austrian commander gained some advantage, the balance was soon redressed by the return of Frederick and his division from Kuttenberg. When Frederick arrived, the Austrian cavalry, as at Mollwitz though with greater difficulty, had routed the Prussian horse and was chasing it off the field, while the opposing centres, composed in each case of infantry, were hotly engaged round Chotusitz. Seeing the left flank of the Austrian infantry exposed by the absence of their cavalry, he hurled his division on this critical point; and his success decided the day. The Austrians withdrew in good order, though they had suffered 7000 casualties, about a quarter of their force. The Prussians, out of about equal numbers, lost 5000 all told; their cavalry, though beaten, had done better than at Mollwitz; but so had the Austrian infantry, and Frederick made no attempt to follow up his success. Indeed, he even remained inactive while the Austrians, after effecting a junction with the corps under Lobkowitz at Budweis, resumed the move against the French. Outnumbered by over two to one and in bad condition generally, the French were somewhat easily driven in on Prague, suffering several minor defeats and heavy losses. The garrisons left by them at Frauenberg, Pisek, and Pilsen surrendered at once; and by the end of June the remnants of the French invaders of Bohemia were cooped up in Prague, their communications with their friends in Bavaria having been severed by the fall of Pilsen.

Frederick's inaction is easily explained. He had fought Chotusitz

for political not for military objects, and he had gained his end.
Chotusitz added the necessary weight to the arguments of the English
envoys, who were as usual seeking to persuade Maria Theresa to come
to terms with Prussia.   All Frederick wanted was the definite cession of
the territory surrendered to him at Klein-Schnellendorf.   He had the
less compunction about deserting his allies, because he attributed to
them the failure of his invasion of Moravia.   Moreover, the substitution
for Walpole's of a Ministry in which foreign affairs were entrusted to
Carteret promised a more active intervention of England on Maria
Theresa's behalf, and increased his desire for peace.   And, for the
moment, Maria Theresa was more eager for revenge on France and Bavaria
than intent on prosecuting the attempt to recover Silesia, which, to judge
from Chotusitz, was likely to prove a formidable undertaking.   Accordingly, after some hesitation, it was decided to accept Frederick's overtures,
and on June 13 the Preliminaries of Breslau ceded to him Upper and
Lower Silesia, including Glatz, but excluding Tetschen and Troppau.
Six weeks later, a definitive peace was concluded at Berlin (July 28);
whereupon Saxony also withdrew from the anti-Austrian coalition, having
merely ruined her army and her finances by her effort to plunder Austria.

Prussia and Saxony thus disposed of, Maria Theresa proceeded to
frame schemes for compensating herself for Silesia by annexing Bavaria,
provision being made for the Elector at the expense of France.   Her
immediate object was to compel de Broglie and his army to surrender at
discretion, a humiliation France was not less keen to avoid.   Diplomatic
measures failing, since Maria Theresa promptly rejected all Fleury's
overtures, the French Ministry had to utilise the army under Maillebois
which had hitherto been keeping George II in check by threatening
Hanover; for, though Harcourt's French corps and the Bavarians had
gained ground against Khevenhüller after he had had to detach
troops to Bohemia, they were not strong enough to effect the relief of
Prague unaided.   In August, therefore, Maillebois started for Bohemia,
and on September 27 was joined at Bramahof in the Upper Palatinate
by the French corps from Bavaria, which had moved north to meet him,
Khevenhüller moving parallel and joining the Austrian main body at
Hayd.   Charles of Lorraine, on hearing of Maillebois' march, had moved
out to oppose his advance, leaving Lobkowitz and 10,000 irregulars
to blockade Prague.   A battle seemed imminent, but none occurred.
Maillebois, after some manœuvring, came to the conclusion that the
relief was beyond his powers, and decided (October 10) to retire into
Bavaria to take up winter-quarters.   Charles of Lorraine, content to
have foiled the attempted relief, made no effort to bring Maillebois to
action and moved southward to the Danube parallel with him.   Meanwhile, de Broglie had not taken advantage of the chance of escaping from
Prague afforded by Maillebois' move; to get away would have been easy,
for Lobkowitz and his irregulars maintained a most inefficient blockade;

CH. VIII.

but the French commander was unwilling to acknowledge the failure of the invasion of Bohemia by abandoning Prague, and still hoped for relief. On the retreat of Maillebois the investment was resumed, just after de Broglie himself had left the town (October 27) to replace Maillebois in command of the French army about to winter in Bavaria. That electorate was once again in Charles Albert's hands. After Khevenhüller's departure (September), Bärenklau had been unable to hold his ground against Seckendorf's 15,000 Bavarians, and the Austrians had recoiled behind the Inn, though holding on to Passau, round which town and Scharding their main army took up winter-quarters (November), the French being at Straubing, the Bavarians at Braunau.

The chief military event of the winter of 1742–3 was Belleisle's famous retreat from Prague. Finding relief hopeless, he managed to force his way out by the Beraun valley to Eger, which he reached on December 27, after great hardships and heavy losses. Chevert, left behind in Prague with 6000 men unfit for the toils of the march, was able by a threat of destroying the town to obtain a capitulation with the honours of war from Lobkowitz (January 21), whose interests in the town caused him to grant these extraordinarily easy terms, for which and for permitting Belleisle's escape he was deservedly blamed. But, though Belleisle and his army had escaped, all Bohemia except Eger was again in Maria Theresa's hands; and, if she had had to relinquish Silesia, she had fair reason to hope to obtain some compensation for that loss in the coming year.

1742 had also seen the theatre of war extended to Italy. On the death of Charles VI Elisabeth Farnese had seen a chance of establishing yet another branch of her dynasty in Italy; and, though Charles Emmanuel of Sardinia, jealous of Bourbon aggrandisement, preferred assisting Maria Theresa—for a consideration—to joining the Bourbons in attacking Lombardy, King Charles III of the Two Sicilies prepared to assist his mother. But he was not ready to move alone; and, as the bulk of the Spanish fleet had gone to the West Indies, the English Mediterranean squadron under Haddock was greatly superior to Navarro's ships in Cadiz. Thus it seemed as if the Milanese might escape attack. The decision as to whether this should be lay with France, and Maria Theresa begged Fleury to refuse the Spaniards passage to Italy by land. But this he would not do, and when, Haddock having had to withdraw to Gibraltar to refit, Navarro put to sea (November) and made for Barcelona, the Toulon squadron under de Court came out and assisted him to escort a Spanish army to Orbitello in Tuscany, Haddock who was outnumbered by two to one and unwilling to precipitate a breach with France, offering no opposition. A Neapolitan contingent joined the Spaniards; and, though operations had to be deferred till the spring of 1742, Maria Theresa found her Italian possessions in peril. To save them she had to come to terms, somewhat distrustfully, with the "Prussia of Italy."

Charles Emmanuel's action in throwing in his lot with Austria was dictated by no higher motive than self-interest. He carried on simultaneous negotiations with both parties and decided to support Austria, because he feared the Bourbons more and could get better terms from Maria Theresa, though the alliance of February 1, 1742, left the question of concessions to be settled later, and was mainly concerned with military cooperation. Thanks to the help thus secured and to his own energy and resolution, Traun was able to ward off the Bourbon menace, actually taking (June 28) the capital of their ally the Duke of Modena and causing the Spanish-Neapolitan army to fall back in order to avoid an action. Moreover, in August the Neapolitans were recalled, an English squadron having appeared off Naples and threatened to bombard that city unless Charles III at once withdrew from the coalition. This was only one of the services rendered to the allied cause by the English fleet, now reinforced and under a zealous and active officer, Mathews, who forced the Franco-Spanish squadrons to withdraw into Toulon and cut off sea communications between Italy and Spain. In August a second Spanish army under Don Philip invaded Savoy, having been allowed a passage across France; but it was repulsed from Piedmont (September), and, though the invasion called off Charles Emmanuel from the Papal States, which caused Traun also to retire into the Legations, an attempt of the Spaniards to follow him up ended disastrously for them at Campo Santo (February 8, 1743).

One result of the advent of the Carteret-Pelham administration to power had been the despatch to Belgium of some 16,000 British troops (May, 1742), all that Walpole's neglect of the army had left available. This force, though reinforced by a Hanoverian contingent, had remained inactive, a project put forward by Lord Stair for an invasion of France being rejected by George II, who still posed as being at peace with France and only a mere auxiliary of Maria Theresa. For 1743, the Austrians were anxious to get King George and this "Pragmatic Army" into Germany; and, as George was anything but unwilling, the middle of February saw the British and their auxiliaries starting on their move up the Rhine. By May 6 Stair's headquarters were on the Main; but, just as it seemed that he was in a position to repeat Marlborough's stroke of 1704 and push across to Bavaria to catch the French corps there between two fires, George directed him to suspend the march. Thus the advantage gained was thrown away, and the sole effect of the move was to increase de Broglie's desire to be gone from Bavaria. His relations with his Bavarian colleague were greatly strained; his army was in no condition to resume hostilities, and, when early in May Charles of Lorraine took the offensive, de Broglie left the Bavarians to their own resources, and, evacuating Straubing and Ratisbon, retired up the Danube to Ingolstadt. Thence, on June 23, he fell back to Donauwörth and, though reinforced by 10,000 men from France, continued his retreat to the Rhine, where he posted his forces round Strassburg and Colmar. Deprived of French assistance, the Bavarians could not resist Charles of Lorraine, who cut off a corps, 6000 strong, at Simbach and forced it to surrender on May 9, stormed Dingolfing (May 19), and Deggendorf (27), pushed out a detachment which reoccupied Munich on June 9, and finally forced Seckendorf and the relics of the Bavarian army to conclude a capitulation at Nieder-Schönfeld, which allowed his troops to retire into Franconia and become neutralised, but left Bavaria in Austrian hands. Braunau, Ingolstadt, and a few other fortresses held out; but by the end of September they had all fallen.

This success in Bavaria promised well for the recovery of Alsace and Lorraine; and Maria Theresa's prospects were further improved by the victory won by the Pragmatic Army at Dettingen on June 27. George II's delay on the Main had not merely thrown away a good chance of intercepting de Broglie's retreat, but it had given time for the collection of a fresh army under de Noailles, which crossed the Rhine near Worms (May 25) and proceeded to plant itself between the Pragmatic Army and Bavaria. Encouraged by George's hesitation, the French pushed closer to the Main; and their cavalry, crossing to the northern bank of the river, so hampered the foraging operations of the Allies and curtailed their collection of supplies that the Pragmatic Army found it necessary to fall back from Aschaffenburg to its magazines and reinforcements at Hanau. It ought never to have got through, for de Noailles had it at a grave disadvantage, hemmed in between river and mountains, with enemies in flank, front and rear. But the rashness of a French subordinate officer and the splendid fighting capacity of the British and Hanoverian infantry gave George a victory which he neither deserved nor knew how to utilise. Instead of following up his success, he remained inactive at Hanau till August 10; and, when at last a joint attack on Alsace by the Pragmatic Army and the Austrians was arranged, the former force only crossed the Rhine at Mainz to relapse into inactivity at Worms (August 29—September 24). Charles of Lorraine was more enterprising; but, being repulsed in an attempt to cross at Breisach (September 3) and finding his allies inactive, he took up winter-quarters betimes in Austrian Swabia.

Diplomatic necessities may to some extent explain the failure of the Pragmatic Army to utilise its opportunities both before and after Dettingen. The old fiction that England and France were still at peace had not yet been abandoned, though Carteret was endeavouring to build up a strong coalition against France. To that end he wished to detach Bavaria from France and to reconcile Maria Theresa with the Emperor, who was then to assist in the recovery of Alsace and Lorraine. However, Maria Theresa was reluctant to relinquish Bavaria till she had some other "equivalent" for Silesia, and the "Project of Hanau" broke down, though Carteret was successful in concluding a definite treaty with

Sardinia at Worms (September 13) by which Charles Emmanuel was pledged to assist in the expulsion of the Bourbons from Italy. The conclusion of this treaty, moreover, committed Maria Theresa to a policy of hostility to France, one result of which was to provoke in that country a reaction in favour of the war. France was heartily sick of the German campaign; but the threat to Alsace and Lorraine, and the hope of making acquisitions in the Netherlands which would retrieve Belleisle's failure in Germany, seemed to have aroused even Louis himself. The recent death of Fleury (January 29, 1743) had removed that Minister's hesitation and indecision out of the path of the "forward party," while Amelot's place as Foreign Minister had been taken by de Tencin, who concurred with de Noailles and Richelieu in advocating active measures. Thus, within six weeks of the Treaty of Worms, the Bourbon counter-blast was issued (October 25) in the shape of the Treaty of Fontainebleau, the so-called "Second Family Compact." This pledged France to help Spain in the recovery of Gibraltar and Minorca, to recognise Don Philip's rights on the Milanese, Parma, and Piacenza, and to declare formal war on England and on Austria (March 15 and April 26).

But before the formal declaration of war important collisions had taken place. Cardinal de Tencin's schemes included a vigorous offensive in Italy, as a prelude to which the blockade established by Mathews over Toulon must be raised, and an invasion of England on behalf of the exiled Stewarts, to which end de Roquefeuil's Brest fleet was to escort 15,000 troops across from Dunkirk. But when de Roquefeuil had crept cautiously up Channel to Dungeness (February 23), he found Norris and the Channel Fleet in his way, and only escaped an action against superior numbers by reason of a sudden and violent gale, which enabled him to regain Brest without a fight. The invasion project was accordingly abandoned, its only effect having been to detain in the Channel ships which would otherwise have reinforced Mathews. That admiral had meanwhile fought his notorious action with the Franco-Spanish fleet off Toulon (February 22, N.S.), in which, thanks mainly to obscure and imperfectly understood signals, the British attack miscarried altogether and resulted in a drawn battle not very unlike a defeat. But, despite this and the plentiful crop of Courts-martial to which it gave rise—Mathews himself being tried and cashiered on a technicality, while Lestock, his second-in-command and the principal culprit, escaped—the battle did not give the Franco-Spanish fleet the command of the Mediterranean, but only opened their communications with Italy for a couple of months, after which Mathews returned to the Gulf of Genoa and forbade passage between Spain and Italy.

As their principal objective in 1744 the French had selected the Netherlands, and their first operations in that quarter quite recalled the triumphs of Louis XIV. A well-equipped army of 80,000 men, skilfully directed by Count Maurice de Saxe (the brilliant son of Augustus II of

Poland and Aurora von Königsmarck), had little difficulty in overrunning West Flanders, for Dutch neglect had left the "Barrier" fortresses in an almost indefensible condition and the Allies had no field army capable of interfering.　They were at odds among themselves, and it was not till after a diversion elsewhere had called off 25,000 men from Flanders and reduced Saxe to the defensive that they at last took the field (July). Even then nothing was done; the Dutch were very lukewarm and still pretended they were not at war with France; Austria sent but few troops, leaving the defence of the Netherlands to the Maritime Powers; and Wade, the British commander, an adherent of false principles of strategy, would not attack the strong defensive position taken up by Saxe on the Lys and failed to dislodge him by an aimless and feeble move against Lille.　Thus the arrival of winter found Saxe still in possession of Menin, Courtrai, Ypres, and the other conquests made earlier in the year.

The diversion which had checked the conquest of Flanders was the Austrian invasion of Alsace.　On June 30 Charles of Lorraine and Traun forced the passage of the Rhine at Germersheim, and Coigni had to retire by Haguenau on Strassburg, leaving the route into Lorraine open.　But, before the Austrians, as usual somewhat deliberate and cautious, could follow up this advantage news arrived that on August 7 an ultimatum from Berlin had reached Vienna, and that the invaders of Alsace must return to defend Bohemia against yet another Prussian attack.　On August 24 the Austrians recrossed the Rhine and, marching with an altogether unusual celerity, in a month stood at Waldmünchen on the borders of Bohemia.

Frederick's action was the natural outcome of the policy he had pursued since the Peace of Berlin.　Never quite comfortable in Silesia, fearing that if successful elsewhere Maria Theresa would sooner or later turn her arms against Prussia, he had been negotiating and scheming all through 1743, encouraging Charles VII not to come to terms with Austria, trying to embitter the Tsarina against Maria Theresa and even seeking to rouse up the Turks.　In May, 1744, his efforts had taken shape in the Union of Frankfort, by which Prussia, Hesse-Cassel, and the Elector Palatine bound themselves together to secure the restoration of Charles Albert to his hereditary dominions, the maintenance of the Emperor in his rights and of the Imperial Constitution, and the reestablishment of peace in Germany.　It is impossible to attach much credit to Frederick's championship of the Imperial Constitution when it is noticed that this Union was promptly guaranteed by France, and that an additional compact with Charles Albert promised Frederick extensive gains in Bohemia.　The net effect of it all was the ruin of the Austrian attempt to recover Alsace and Lorraine, lost respectively to the Empire in 1648 and 1738.

Frederick's invasion of Bohemia opened successfully.　On August 15 his columns crossed the Saxon frontier; on September 2 they joined a corps from Silesia under the walls of Prague, and on the 16th that city had to capitulate. Hereupon, Frederick advanced towards the south-west, hoping to intercept the Austrians returning from the Rhine and to catch them between his force and the French, whom he somewhat rashly imagined to be in close pursuit of them, whereas in reality the French had turned aside to besiege (September 18) and take (November 24) Freiburg in Breisgau, and only a small corps had accompanied the Imperial army, now under Seckendorf, to Bavaria. Thus Frederick's rash advance brought him into some peril. His communications with Prague were threatened; for the Bohemian peasantry and Hungarian irregulars swarmed round his camp, while before him was a superior force under Traun, now reinforced by Batthyány and 20,000 Austrians from Bavaria, which he was not strong enough to attack. He had to retire from Budweis to the Sasawa and thence across the Elbe (November 9). But he could not carry out his intention of wintering on that river; for Traun, who had been joined by 20,000 Saxons on October 22, crossed it also (November 19), severed him from Prague, and forced him to beat a disastrous and costly retreat to Silesia, the garrison of Prague having to do the same. Traun might congratulate himself on having completely out-manœuvred Frederick, though he was perhaps overcautious in not forcing a pitched battle on the exhausted and demoralised Prussians. The only effects of Frederick's move, besides his loss of probably 20,000 men, were to relieve France; to allow Seckendorf to recover Bavaria once more, the Austrians retiring behind the Inn in face of superior numbers; and to intensify the hatred and distrust with which Maria Theresa regarded him, as the man who had treacherously robbed her of Silesia and had now spoilt a promising chance of securing an equivalent. For, while Bavaria had again been lost, her hopes of recovering Naples had been disappointed. Nothing had been done to follow up the success of Campo Santo, largely through the obstruction of Charles Emmanuel; but Lobkowitz, who had taken Traun's place in October, 1743, had driven the Spaniards back from the Pesaro to Velletri on the borders of Naples (May—June, 1744), where the Neapolitans had joined them; and he was hoping to raise the numerous Neapolitan partisans of Austria against Charles III, when the news of a fresh Franco-Spanish attack on Piedmont caused the return home of the Sardinian contingent, and compelled Lobkowitz to retire to the Adriatic and to take up winter-quarters on the lower Po (November). Piedmont, meanwhile, had been delivered from its assailants by Leutrum, whose stubborn defence of Coni lasted till winter forced them to withdraw.

Before operations were resumed in the spring, one important event materially altered the situation. On January 20, 1745, the death of Charles Albert left the Empire without an Emperor, and gave a finishing blow to the Franco-Bavarian alliance, already somewhat strained. The new Elector, Maximilian Joseph, was a mere youth, and there was no prospect of his reviving his father's pretensions to the Imperial throne which had not much benefited Charles Albert or his Bavarian subjects. Seckendorf was anxious for peace with Austria; and, when in March Batthyány suddenly fell upon the scattered French and Bavarians with complete success, once again giving Maria Theresa possession of the electorate, the Bavarian authorities hastened to conclude the Treaty of Füssen, by which Maximilian Joseph recovered his electorate on renouncing all claims upon the Austrian dominions, pledging his vote to Francis Stephen, and becoming neutral. Hesse-Cassel and Würtemberg promptly acceded to the Treaty; and, with the Ecclesiastical Electors again on her side, George II's vote at her disposal, and Augustus of Poland deaf to the efforts of France and Frederick II to induce him to stand for the Empire, Maria Theresa could look forward to the gratification of one of her desires, her husband's election as Emperor.

To her other great object, the recovery of Silesia, she was, however, no nearer. In January, 1745, an attempt to follow up the Prussian retreat proved a failure; and, by the time (end of May) that the Austrians were ready to attempt something more serious than the raids and forays by their light troops which had kept the Prussians busy but secured no real advantage, the Prussians had had time to refit and to recover their *moral.* Conducted without much skill or vigour, the Austrian invasion of Silesia met with an abrupt and effective repulse at Hohenfriedberg (June 4), which Frederick followed up by invading Bohemia. But the Austrians rallied in a strong position at Königgrätz, which Frederick did not venture to attack (July), though he maintained his ground at Chlum on the Elbe for a couple of months, despite the vigorous attacks of the Austrian light troops on his communications. However, when their capture of Neustadt (September 16) cut him off from Glatz, he found himself so straitened for supplies that he had to fall back towards Silesia by the Schatzlar Pass. The Austrians pursued, profiting by his delay at Straudenz to get between him and the Pass, and followed up this success by attacking his camp at Sohr at daybreak (September 30). The Prussians were undoubtedly surprised, and, had not the Austrian attack been delivered with excessive regard to orderly procedure, things might have gone ill with Frederick. However, he rallied his men and, concentrating all available force against a hill which commanded his right, managed to snatch a victory that allowed him to withdraw unmolested to Silesia.

Shortly before this, Frederick had concluded an important treaty with George II, who was for special reasons extremely anxious to end the Silesian wars and so set free the main army of Austria to defend the Netherlands. There things were going badly with the Allies. Saxe had, thanks to the failure of the Dutch to cooperate, repulsed Cumberland at Fontenoy (May 11, 1745), when the Allies' new Commander-in-chief endeavoured to relieve Tournay; Tournay had fallen after a discreditably short defence (May 22); Ghent had been surprised and stormed by Löwendahl (July 11). Moreover, the Jacobite insurrection in Scotland (July) had compelled Cumberland to send back to England, in the first instance, ten battalions of the infantry whom only Dutch misconduct had robbed of victory at Fontenoy, and then almost the whole of his troops. In their absence, Saxe had a series of easy conquests in Flanders, including Ostend, the English base; for the Dutch garrisons made but a feeble defence, and the bulk of the Austrian forces were in Bohemia or posted round Frankfort-on-Main to protect the Imperial election against Conti and the French army on the Rhine. Indeed, George feared that the French might move against his beloved Hanover, now entirely exposed to their attacks. Frederick, too, in great straits for money and very nervous lest success should crown Maria Theresa's efforts to include Russia in her offensive alliance with Saxony against Prussia, was anxious for any peace which would guarantee him possession of Silesia. This was the precise effect of the Convention of Hanover of August 26: Frederick bound himself not to vote against Francis Stephen, and the two Powers guaranteed each other's possessions, Maria Theresa being offered the opportunity of acceding to the treaty within six weeks. Her wrath at the offer and the faithlessness of her ally King George was natural enough; and she pushed on her plans for the combined attack in which Russia and Saxony were to cooperate, at the same time seeking to come to terms with France. Her proposals, which made over to France the greater part of her conquests in the Netherlands in return for peace and the recognition of the election of Francis Stephen as Emperor (September 12), were better than France was to obtain at Aix-la-Chapelle; but Louis XV's appetite for military glory had been aroused by Saxe's successes, and his Foreign Minister, d'Argenson, clung with more conviction than justification to the Prussian alliance. Hence the offers were rejected, and d'Argenson devoted his efforts to inducing Charles Emmanuel to desert Maria Theresa.

The course of affairs had taken an unfavourable turn for Austria in Italy. Here the adhesion of Genoa to the Bourbons had opened the Riviera route for the junction of the Spaniards and Neapolitans with the Franco-Spanish force hitherto engaged against Piedmont; and in July their joint forces, 70,000 strong, moved north across the Apennines, driving the much weaker Austro-Sardinians back before them to Bassignano. The numerical superiority of the Bourbon forces allowed of the Duke of Modena being detached against the Milanese. He took Piacenza (August 6), Parma, and Modena, thus threatening the communications of the Austrians with Tyrol and causing them to retire eastward. Left isolated at Bassignano, the Sardinians were severely defeated by the French (September 27); and the end of the campaigning season found all southern Piedmont in the hands of Marshal Maillebois, and the Milanese in the possession of his Spanish colleague, Gages. The

Habsburgs seemed about to be expelled from Italy, and d'Argenson's overtures to Charles Emmanuel were favourably received. But neither the peril of the Netherlands nor that of Italy could alter Maria Theresa's determination to make another effort to recover Silesia. Undeterred even by the withdrawal of Russia at the eleventh hour, she launched her armies again at Frederick in November, hoping by a move into Lusatia to push in between Silesia and Berlin. But a check at Gross-Hennersdorf (November 24) was enough to defeat the move; and simultaneously a Prussian force under the elder Leopold of Anhalt-Dessau advanced up the Elbe against Dresden. To save the Saxon capital, Charles of Lorraine moved thither by Aussig and Pirna, while Frederick marched across Lusatia to succour his lieutenant. Had the Austrians moved a little faster, Leopold might have been crushed; but, as usual, Charles of Lorraine was slow, and on December 15 the "Old Dessauer" gained a complete victory at Kesselsdorf over the Austro-Saxon army, which was endeavouring to cover Dresden. This victory was decisive. Dresden capitulated (December 18); Augustus III acceded to the Convention of Hanover (December 22); and Maria Theresa found herself with no alternative but to come to terms with Frederick, since England threatened to discontinue all subsidies if she remained obstinate, while France rejected all her overtures. On December 25, the Treaty of Dresden definitely ceded Silesia and Glatz to Frederick, who in return guaranteed the Pragmatic Sanction so far as it related to Germany, acknowledged Francis I as Emperor, and thus finally withdrew from the War of the Austrian Succession, alone among Maria Theresa's enemies gaining any substantial share of her dominions. For this success he had to thank, in the first place, the army which his father had raised and trained, the treasure which his father had collected, and the absolute power bequeathed to him by his ancestors. Secondly, gratitude was due from him to France, Bavaria and all the other enemies of Austria, whom he had joined and deserted with equal readiness as it suited his convenience. At the last moment, when he was nearly at the end of his resources and could ill have supported another campaign, he had derived important indirect assistance from the Scottish rising. But, above all, it was his own resourcefulness and resolution, his promptitude to perceive and profit by the necessities of friend and foe, his energy, determination, and daring, which had given him the coveted prize.

If the peril threatening her Italian possessions had contributed to force Maria Theresa into giving a reluctant assent to the Peace of Dresden, she was at least to have the satisfaction of accomplishing her purpose in Italy itself. Charles Emmanuel had probably been sincere enough in accepting d'Argenson's overtures, for, though his severely practical mind was not deluded by the French statesman's favourite but quite premature project for the federation of Italy, he had no intention of sacrificing his dominions for the sake of his Austrian ally, and might have come to

terms, had not the rivalry of Sardinia and Spain for the possession of
Lombardy proved an insuperable obstacle to agreement. Elisabeth
Farnese's refusal to accept d'Argenson's draft treaty of December 25
caused a dead-lock; and, though d'Argenson, still hoping to win her
consent, agreed to an armistice with Sardinia on February 17, that
concession was only used by Charles Emmanuel to gain time for
Maria Theresa to despatch to Italy a considerable portion of the forces
set free by her peace with Prussia. Maillebois, lulled into a false
security by a belief that the armistice was but the prelude to peace,
was thus completely surprised when, in March, 1746, Charles Emmanuel
threw off the mask. Eleven French battalions were forced to surrender
at Asti (March 8), and the siege of the citadel of Alessandria had
to be raised; while, on the approach of the Austrian reinforcements,
the Spaniards evacuated Milan (March 19) and fell back to Parma,
full of anger against the idealist d'Argenson for allowing Charles
Emmanuel to delude him. But Don Philip could not maintain
himself long at Parma; and, though Maillebois hastened to his aid,
their joint attack on the Austrian position at Piacenza (June 16)
was disastrously repulsed. This left them in an awkward position, for
Maillebois' move eastward from Novi had exposed his communications
to the Sardinians, who seized the Stradella Pass and cut him off from
Genoa. From this plight the Bourbon forces were only extricated by
the daring of Maillebois, who struck boldly at the Milanese, drawing
the Austro-Sardinians after him, and then, recrossing the Po near
Piacenza (August 10), broke through to Tortona (August 14); whence
by Novi and Savona he made his way back to France (September 17),
abandoning Genoa to the Austrians, to whom it had to submit (September 6). Masters of this important city, and with their Sardinian
ally no longer in peril, the Austrians would have preferred to renew their
attempt on Naples, had not England, with whose Mediterranean fleet
they were again in touch, insisted on their invading Provence. The
expedition was, however, brought to an abrupt conclusion by an insurrection at Genoa (December 5–10), which expelled the Austrian garrison
from the town and compelled the invaders to recross the Var (February 2,
1747) in order to undertake its reduction. In this task they were aided by
the English squadron; but the Genoese held out stubbornly, and Belleisle,
by attacking Piedmont through the Col d'Assiette, drew off the Sardinian
contingent of the besieging force and so raised the siege (June); though
the invaders of Piedmont were repulsed with heavy loss from Exilles
(July 19) and driven back to Dauphiné. With this the war in Italy
practically came to an end, though in 1748 the Austrians had renewed
the siege of Genoa when the conclusion of peace stopped operations.
Thanks to her own energy and courage, and to the assistance of Sardinia
by land and of England at sea, the Italian campaigns had left Maria
Theresa not merely with undiminished territories but in possession of

those of Modena also. That at the peace she had to give up this acquisition, and also to sacrifice Parma and Piacenza, was due to the turn the war had taken elsewhere. Italy had to pay the debts of Flanders.

Maurice de Saxe was not the man to miss the opportunity given him by Cumberland's recall. No sooner had frost made the ground hard enough for troops to move, than he dashed at Brussels and, after a three weeks' siege (January 30—February 20, 1746), forced it to surrender. Its fall was followed by that of Louvain and several other places, and the effect of the blow was seen when Holland hastened to send Wassenaer to Paris to negotiate a peace. The Dutch had never been enthusiastic for the war, and it would have been easy for France to close their ports to England by allowing Holland to become neutral, in which case, with Ostend lost, it would have been difficult for the English and Austrians to cooperate. But d'Argenson sought instead to arrange a general peace, for which England and Austria were not disposed. Cumberland's decisive victory at Culloden (April 16) and the Austrian successes in Italy improved the prospects and raised the demands of the Allies, and the whole negotiation broke down.

If France was not about to detach Holland from her allies by a separate peace, the obvious step to take was to make the United Provinces, as the point where the Allies would concentrate, the objective of the next campaign. Saxe urged this strongly; but political considerations—the wish not to provoke anti-French feeling among the Dutch or to imperil the negotiations—caused his scheme to be overruled in favour of the strategically less sound plan of a reduction of the eastern Netherlands. Saxe therefore, after forcing the Allies to retire from the Demer into Holland (May), detached Clermont to besiege Antwerp, himself covering the operation. Meanwhile, Conti's army, about 25,000 strong, was brought down from the Rhine and began operations by besieging Mons. It could be thus utilised with safety, because all the efforts of Maria Theresa and England to build up a coalition among the minor States of Germany had proved futile. Bavaria hired out 6000 troops to the Maritime Powers; but the Elector Palatine and Würtemberg were friendly to France, the Spiritual Electors merely cared to keep the war out of their borders, and the promise of the French envoy at Ratisbon that France would respect the neutrality of the Empire removed all chance of operations on the middle Rhine.

By the beginning of July a fairly respectable allied force had been concentrated at Breda, including a few English regiments, 6000 Hessians no longer wanted in Scotland, and considerable reinforcements from Austria under Charles of Lorraine. On July 17 the Allies took the field, moving south-eastward by Hasselt to relieve Charleroi, which Conti was now besieging, Mons having fallen on July 11. Antwerp too had fallen (May 31), and Saxe was free to move; but, as Conti continued his siege instead of joining the Marshal as directed, he could not check their move, and only the unexpectedly speedy fall of Charleroi (August 1) extricated Conti from a position of some peril. When Charleroi fell the Allies had just reached the Mehaigne, whence they pushed on to the Orneau, taking post to cover Namur. Saxe, with over 80,000 men to their 60,000, managed to cramp them into a narrow space in which they were greatly straitened for supplies, while his numerical superiority forbade them to attack. Later in August, the capture of Huy threatened Lorraine's communications and compelled him to retire east of the Meuse; whereupon Saxe besieged and (September 21) took Namur. Thence the French moved on Liége, on which town Lorraine also recoiled, standing at bay with his left resting on Liége while his right stretched to the river Jaar, the front being strengthened by the villages of Roucoux, Varoux and Liers. Here, on October 11, Saxe attacked the Allies. A well-contested struggle followed, in which the Dutch infantry somewhat retrieved the reputation tarnished at Fontenoy, while the British and Hessians were only ousted from the villages after a stubborn resistance which cost the French many casualties. What decided the action was the surrender of Liége, which turned the Allied left and compelled them to retire. However, they got off in good order, Saxe making no effort to follow up his victory. The campaign thus ended with the middle Meuse in his hands and only Maestricht left to cover Holland. The failure of the Allies to hold their own is mainly to be ascribed to their numerical inferiority, due to preoccupations elsewhere, the bulk of the Austrians being in Italy while the Highlands still absorbed most of the British, 6000 of whom, moreover, though available for Flanders, were wasted on an abortive attack upon the Breton port of Lorient (September).

For 1747 the Allies determined on a great effort, collecting over 90,000 men, more than half of whom were Austrians and about a sixth British, while Cumberland took the place of Charles of Lorraine in the command. However, when in February he attempted a dash on Antwerp, lack of transport ruined the design. Saxe, almost without quitting his winter-quarters, was able to hold him in check while a detached corps under his capable lieutenant, Löwendahl, took Sluys and Cadsand and secured the mouth of the Scheldt. Indeed, so negligent and unprepared were the Dutch that only the timely arrival of some British regiments prevented Löwendahl from adding Zeeland to his conquests (April— May). This attack on the territory of Holland marked the final abandonment of d'Argenson's policy of sparing the United Provinces; for Louis had dismissed the discredited Foreign Minister (January), and now announced that he intended to invade the United Provinces in revenge for the shelter and assistance they had given to his enemies. One result of this, predicted indeed by d'Argenson, was a movement in favour of the Orange party, culminating in the election of William of Nassau-Dillenburg as Captain-General and Stadholder (May); but this revolution was mainly important from its political bearing and cannot be alleged to have increased the military strength of the Allies.

After various unsuccessful efforts to entice Saxe from his strong position between Malines and Louvain, Cumberland suddenly set off south-eastward (June 26), hoping to fall on a detached corps under Clermont which was operating along the Meuse. But Saxe was too quick for him, and a brilliant forced march enabled the French to forestall Cumberland in occupying the Herdeeren heights just to the south-westward of Maestricht (July 1). The Allies thereupon took post on a lower ridge nearer Maestricht, the Austrians on the right, the Dutch in the centre, the British and their auxiliaries on the left, holding the fortified villages of Lauffeldt and Vlytingen. Here, on July 2, Saxe attacked them. Trusting to the proverbial immobility of the Austrians, he massed his forces on his right to attack the villages around which an even and desperate contest waged, the posts being several times carried but as often retaken. Indeed, Cumberland's left and centre were actually advancing to follow up a repulse of the French infantry when Saxe launched his cavalry at them to give the broken battalions time to rally. At the critical moment the Dutch gave way completely, leaving a gap in the line into which Saxe hastened to pour his reserves, while their flight threw the Hessians and some British regiments into disorder and paralysed Cumberland's advance. The Austrians, who were at last coming up to his assistance, halted; the French infantry rallied and again carried Lauffeldt; and Cumberland had no alternative but to retire on Maestricht, General Ligonier and the British cavalry sacrificing themselves to secure the unmolested retreat of their infantry. The French losses had been so heavy that Saxe did not venture to besiege Maestricht, which the Allies continued to cover; but they could not prevent him from detaching Löwendahl against the strong fortress of Bergen-op-Zoom, which he stormed on September 16, the Dutch defence once again proving half-hearted. With Bergen nearly all Dutch Brabant passed into French hands, and the campaign closed with gloomy prospects for the Allies. When the ruler of the Netherlands neglected their defence in order to prosecute her designs on Italy, while Holland was almost as lukewarm in the cause as she was inefficient, there was little inducement for England to continue a war in which her expenses were very heavy and her gains quite insignificant. Though Commodore Warren's squadron and 4000 New England militia had captured Cape Breton (June, 1745) the French had taken Madras (September, 1746), and had only been beaten off just in time from Fort St David (1747) by Commodore Griffin. Again, the victories of Anson (May 3, 1747) and Hawke (October 14) in the Bay of Biscay had prevented French reinforcements from reaching Canada and the East and West Indies, and had successfully reestablished England's naval position and reputation; but they did not do more than balance Saxe's successes.

But, if England and Holland were ready for peace, so were their adversaries. The death of Philip V (July 9, 1746) had diminished the influence of Elisabeth Farnese, whose aspirations were not shared by her pacifically-disposed step-son Ferdinand VI; while the recovery of naval supremacy by England was making itself felt in France through the heavy sufferings of the French mercantile marine, which was almost swept from the seas, with disastrous results to the French finances.

Thus, when the Congress of Aix-la-Chapelle met (March, 1748) only Maria Theresa, who had at last secured a promise of Russian assistance, was anxious to continue the War. Enraged at finding the Maritime Powers resolved on peace, she once again had recourse to separate negotiations with France; but, though Kaunitz really believed that this time success was his, France was negotiating with England and Holland at the same time and preferred to come to terms with them (April 30, 1748). Several months of complicated negotiations followed; but, finally, on October 18, a definite treaty was concluded between England, Holland, and France; Spain adhering to it two days later; and before the end of November Austria and Sardinia had given their reluctant assent. Unwilling as Charles Emmanuel was to resign Finale to Genoa and Piacenza to Don Philip, he was powerless without English subsidies; and, while Maria Theresa could bring no pressure to bear on England she could do nothing in Italy without the Sardinian army and the English fleet.

The principal provisions of the Peace of Aix-la-Chapelle were those which guaranteed Silesia and Glatz to Frederick II, the only combatant who gained appreciably by the contest which his greed and the opportunity of Charles VI's death had provoked. Charles Emmanuel had to content himself with the recovery of Savoy and Nice, and with securing another strip of Lombardy which brought his eastern frontier to the Ticino. Don Philip secured Parma and Piacenza, with the proviso (cancelled, however, in 1752) that he should resign them to Austria, if he ever succeeded his brother at Naples. Otherwise, the Treaty provided for a return to the conditions prevailing before the War. France evacuated the Austrian Netherlands and Madras, recognised George II as King of England, agreed to respect the Hanoverian Succession, to expel the Pretender, and to dismantle Dunkirk. England reluctantly gave up Cape Breton, " the people's darling acquisition," but received a pledge that Spain would fulfil the commercial concessions promised at Utrecht. The Duke of Modena regained his dominions; while, despite Maria Theresa's protests, the Barrier fortresses were again committed to the proved inefficiency of the Dutch garrisons. Finally, the Pragmatic Sanction was guaranteed, except as regarded Silesia and Parma and Piacenza, while Francis I was recognised as Emperor.

That after eight years of war no greater changes should have been made is in itself sufficiently characteristic of the nature of the struggle and of the indecisiveness of the result. In some respects, indeed, the War may be regarded as having achieved something definite. The strife between Habsburgs and Bourbons concerning Italy came to an end, while the territorial settlement of Italy was substantially unaltered till the Revolution. The acquisition of Silesia by Prussia has endured unchanged, if not unchallenged. The Jacobites ceased to be a factor of any importance in European politics. For the rest, the Peace merely marks a stage in the rise of Sardinia, in the decline of the power and importance of the United Provinces, in the relaxation of the old alliance between Austria and the Maritime Powers, and in the intervention of Russia in western Europe—factors none of them altogether new, but all destined to develop further. The struggle for maritime supremacy was, like the Silesian question, left unsettled.

The repeated faithlessness of Frederick II filled Maria Theresa with distrustful uneasiness lest a suitable opportunity might be similarly used, while desire for revenge was an additional incentive to putting her house in order with a view to a renewal of the struggle. But, while Austria had suffered in territory, it may be questioned whether this loss was not satisfactorily balanced by other gains. Hungary was no longer a cause for anxiety, but for the future was a source of strength; the War had done much to weld together the Austrian dominions; Maria Theresa's unfailing courage and determination had appealed to the best instincts of her subjects and awakened in them a fervid loyalty which none of her predecessors had ever aroused; the Austrian army had been greatly improved; Bavaria and Saxony, no longer rivals, were now faithful allies; and the drawing closer of the alliance with Russia had strengthened Maria Theresa's position. France, on the other hand, had assisted to place Don Philip on the throne of Parma and to secure Silesia for Frederick; yet these were but poor returns for her efforts and sacrifices. Fontenoy and Lauffeldt had retrieved the disgrace of Dettingen and Bohemia—but to have been Frederick's catspaw was of little benefit to Louis XV. The attempt to partition the Habsburg dominions had failed, and France had even lost control of her old clients in south-western Germany, such as Bavaria. Nor had she gained any success in the struggle with England; her enemy had not only retrieved a bad start, but had been able to wring from her the restoration of the provinces which her armies had overrun; while the War had served to purge the British navy of the ill-effects of peace and neglect, and had brought to the front many of the men—such as Hawke and Anson— who were to carry to a triumphant end the struggle whose renewal was only a matter of time. For, like the rivals for Silesia, England and France had suspended hostilities, not because they had abandoned their ambitions, but because they had exhausted their resources.

CHAPTER IX.

THE SEVEN YEARS' WAR.

On January 16, 1756, Frederick II of Prussia signed with England the Convention of Westminster, one of the most important treaties in the whole history of European diplomacy. England had been at war with France since 1755, and the King of Prussia in this Convention guaranteed the neutrality of Hanover. Thus the French, who had for many years been united with Prussia in a defensive alliance, found themselves prevented by their Prussian ally from seizing the German possessions of George II. The Ministers at Versailles viewed this clause in a much more hostile spirit than Frederick had anticipated; and they forthwith, on May 17, 1756, concluded with the Empress Maria Theresa, the sworn foe of the King of Prussia, the Treaty of Versailles. This was a purely defensive treaty, and not designed in any way to open up to the French the forbidden road to Hanover. It simply placed France in an advantageous position, should her former ally at Potsdam put forth plans which she might feel obliged to thwart at any cost.

The suspicion of the French that Frederick II meditated upsetting the European balance of power was perfectly well founded. The territorial configuration of what was then the kingdom of Prussia must have seemed intolerable to a monarch like Frederick the Great, the more so that the Prussian monarchy included some of the most barren districts of Germany. Four years earlier, when Frederick had believed himself to be at the point of death, he had drawn up a political testament for his successor. There were three territories which, according to this last will and testament, the King deemed it desirable to acquire by conquest, namely, the electorate of Saxony, Polish West Prussia, and Swedish Pomerania; but of these three Frederick regarded Electoral Saxony as by far the most important and urgent acquisition, because it would enable its Prussian conqueror to readjust the shapeless formation of his State, besides adding wealth, manufacturing industries, and civilisation. In the spirit of the " cabinet policy " of the times, Frederick II intended that the Elector of Saxony should be compensated by Bohemia, which was to be wrested from the House of Habsburg, the irreconcilable rival of the House of Brandenburg.

CH. IX.

It is true that Austria, in this very year 1756, protected herself, as will be related at length in a later chapter, by the Treaty of Versailles just mentioned; but it only bound France to come to the aid of Austria with 24,000 men or a yearly subsidy of 4,200,000 *gulden* (£400,000), in the event of her being subjected to attack. The King of Prussia did not believe that the French, involved as they were in a war with England, would make any sacrifice for Austria beyond what was entailed by their treaty obligations. That Spain would assist Maria Theresa with money seemed to him out of the question. Since 1748 a defensive alliance had existed between Austria and Russia against Prussia, but Frederick reckoned that the Empress could depend even less on her Russian than on her French allies. St Petersburg was, it is true, as little inclined as Versailles to allow the King of Prussia to establish his supremacy on the Continent by further conquests, nevertheless, Russia appeared to be an uncertain prop for Austria to lean on. The Empress Elizabeth had been repeatedly ill: Peter, her heir to the throne, was among the most fervent admirers of Frederick, and Russia's leading statesman, the Chancellor Bestuzheff, was in the pay of England.

The French diplomatists were never tired of urging the King of Prussia to abandon the alliance with George II; and Frederick, who met their representations in a friendly spirit, could easily have taken this step without breaking his word, for the Convention of Westminster stipulated for no fixed term. But all the negotiations between Frederick and the French led to the same insurmountable point of difference. The precise nature of the gift desired by the King, in return for his leaving Hanover open to the French, he did not disclose, waiting for the French on their side to break silence—for they must assuredly know that his ambition was very far from being satisfied. The Ministers on the Seine, however, regarded a fresh extension of the Prussian dominions and the amputation of a second limb from the Austrian monarchy as an overthrow of the Peace of Westphalia. Any such revolution the Court of Versailles resolved to oppose, no matter at what cost; and, if its defensive alliance with Austria did not prove sufficient for the purpose, it was ready to proceed to greater lengths. As the King of Prussia unfortunately could not be induced to break off his relations with Great Britain, the French Ministers intimated to the Austrian ambassador at Versailles, Count Starhemberg, their readiness to accept in principle the offensive alliance against Prussia for which the Court of Vienna had long been agitating.

Count Kaunitz, Maria Theresa's Chancellor of State, urged the offensive alliance against Prussia, not solely with the object of reconquering Silesia, but because he knew that Frederick was only waiting for the most favourable opportunity to mutilate the Austrian monarchy a second time. Desirous of forestalling such an enterprise at a convenient season for Austria, Kaunitz believed that the hour had now

come. In March, 1756, he informed the Russian Court that France
was prepared to enter into an offensive Coalition against Prussia, and
enquired whether, in the case of Russia intending to join it, the Tsarina's
troops would perhaps be able to march even before the year (1756) was
out.   In reply, the Russian Ministry signified their readiness to send an
army into the field against Prussia at so early a date as August, 1756.
Russia was absolutely in earnest in this intention; and the army designed
to encounter Frederick was without loss of time moved towards the
western frontier of the Tsar's dominions.   But scarcely had the Russian
marching columns been set in motion, when a serious crisis occurred in
the Franco-Austrian negotiations at Versailles.   On May 22, 1756, Kaunitz
wrote to the Austrian ambassador at St Petersburg, Count Esterházy,
that Frederick II " was exhausting himself with lavish caresses on the
French."   The Treaty of Versailles, he said, afforded no absolute protection to Austria against the contingency of Prussia and France renewing
their alliance.   Meanwhile, Russia ought to desist from provocative war
preparations, and so far as possible to disarm.   At St Petersburg, the
march of the Russian forces was instantly countermanded; but a
Russian Note dated June 10 reproached the Viennese Court in terms of
no little irritation for forcing the Tsarina's Government to issue the
unnecessary orders.

It was an unpleasant surprise for Frederick to find that English
influence and gold had no effect in restraining the Court of St
Petersburg from hostility to Prussia.   But it seemed to him of greater
importance that he now had the pretext for war which he needed in
face of England, and indeed of the world.   An English courier who, on
his way from St Petersburg to London, passed through Berlin, related
that he had seen all the roads in Livonia full of soldiers, and that
170,000 regulars and 70,000 Cossacks were marching against Prussia.
Frederick, hereupon, began immediately to make preparations for war
on his side.   On June 25, he informed his ambassador in Vienna that
he began to regard war as inevitable.   To his sister Wilhelmina at
Baireuth he wrote about the same time: "We have one foot in the
stirrup, and I think the other will soon follow."   Notwithstanding the
countermanding of the Russian advance, Frederick's preparations were
continued till more than half the Prussian army was mobilised.   It can
be shown that political and not military motives lay at the root of this
semi-mobilisation: some of the cross- and counter-marches for which
orders were given at the time had no object but that of sounding an
alarm in order to force Austria into warlike measures which might
furnish to Prussia an excuse for attacking.   For, as a matter of fact, it
is out of the question that Frederick should have felt himself menaced.
He knew, of course, that something was in progress against him, but he
also knew that he had no reason for apprehending within measurable
time the conclusion of an offensive alliance against Prussia.   From certain

documents, the contents of which the Saxon government clerk Menzel was bribed to betray to the King, it came out that in St Petersburg English and French influences were still contending.

As the King of Prussia, notwithstanding, was making preparations for war, the Empress Maria Theresa's private secretary, Baron Koch, urged Kaunitz to permit a few military precautions to be taken against a Prussian surprise; and Field-Marshal Browne, who held the command in Bohemia, attempted to influence the Chancellor in the same direction. But Kaunitz would not listen to the suggestions of these dignitaries. Premature preparations for war, he observed, might spoil everything, inasmuch as the negotiations with France did not yet inspire sufficient confidence. As he took care to explain, the ultimate purpose imputed by the Protestant party in the Empire to the Convention of Westminster was the establishment of a Protestant Germanic Empire with the House of Brandenburg at its head. The French, like everyone else in that age, believed that the era of religious warfare had not yet finally closed, and credited Frederick with the design of reopening it. Thus, the Convention which had united Prussia, England, Hanover, Hesse, and Brunswick, was at Versailles regarded in the light of a Protestant league. The truth was that nothing was further from the mind of the sceptic of Sanssouci than the wish to pose as the champion of Protestantism in Germany. Such weapons, he wrote once to d'Argens, were obsolete; no one, not even women, could any longer be roused to fanatical enthusiasm on behalf of Luther or Calvin. For all this, the King was anxious to conquer, in addition to Saxony, the territory of the Bishop of Hildesheim and, in general, to secularise the ecclesiastical States of northern Germany. He believed that he did not need for this object the assistance of religious ideas, but that he could rely on the material power of his absolute Crown.

The diplomatic adviser of Madame de Pompadour, Abbé Bernis, gave Count Starhemberg to understand that, if Austria met the preparations of Prussia with the necessary counter-measures, France would not hold her responsible for the consequences. The Court of Vienna, without quite trusting the Abbé's promise, now began to place its army on a war footing. Hereupon, the King of Prussia, on July 18, enquired at Vienna whether the Empress' preparations were directed against himself. When the relations between two great Powers once pass into this stage, there is never much hope of successful negotiation; and the *pourparlers* between the King and the Empress proved fruitless.

On August 29, 1756, the Prussian army moved into Saxony. Frederick called upon the Elector Frederick Augustus II to become his ally. At the outset, so the neighbour whom he had suddenly invaded was informed by Frederick, appearances might be against him; but, on his honour, he would regard the Elector's interests as sacred, if he would join with Prussia against Austria. To an envoy from Frederick Augustus the King declared : "If fortune favours me, the Elector will not only be amply compensated for everything, but I shall take as much thought for his interests as for my own." Frederick Augustus, however, declined to take advantage of this unscrupulous assignment of the Bohemian jewel in Maria Theresa's Crown, and retired into his kingdom of Poland. The small Saxon army was shut up by the Prussians in the entrenched camp of Pirna. Field-Marshal Browne hereupon advanced to the relief of Saxony; and Frederick fell in with his troops on October 1, at Lobositz, in Bohemian territory not far from the Saxon frontier.

The King of Prussia had pushed on his forces with so much *élan* that they assumed the offensive even before he had positively issued his command to attack. A thick mist prevented him from reconnoitring. When the sky cleared, he perceived that Browne's position was un-assailable—a prelude to many other events of a like nature during the course of the war, inasmuch as the enemies of Frederick nearly always sought and found their strength in a defensive attitude. With swift resolve the King stopped the battle, which could only be done with heavy losses. His opponent, satisfied to have got off so lightly, left the battle-field to the Prussians and retreated to the other side of the Eger. Frederick could not deny that the Austrians had fought very well; but, all the same, they dared not take effective measures for the relief of the Saxons, it having as yet been impossible to concentrate the military forces levied in the different parts of the widely extended and clumsily administered Empire, and, owing to want of money, still unfurnished with the necessary war material. Thus, on October 16, the Saxons were compelled to capitulate at Pirna; and about 19,000 men were made prisoners. By an unscrupulous use of the resources of Saxony, Frederick increased the army which he had in the field up to 148,000 men.

The necessity for this was all the greater because the whole continent of Europe united to withstand the overthrow of the balance of power by a fresh important aggrandisement of Prussia. Not only Austria, Russia, and France, but the Germanic Empire and Sweden, resolved to take arms against the disturber of the peace. The constitution of armies and the general conditions of life in the eighteenth century involved, as a rule, the necessity of avoiding winter campaigns. Accordingly, after entering Bohemia, the King evacuated it again and let his army take up winter-quarters in Saxony and Silesia. Frederick's opponents, too, undertook no strategical movement against him during the unfavourable season of the year; but they used the interval for the completion of their preparations. During the winter (1756–7) 133,000 Austrians took up their quarters in Bohemia and Moravia, whereas only 114,000 Prussians were encamped in Silesia and Saxony. The King of Prussia did not consider this numerical disproportion as dangerous in itself, inasmuch as he had the fullest confidence in the superior quality of his troops. He wrote to his heir apparent: "If you can oppose 75,000 men to 100,000 of the enemy, you must be content." However, he had in addition to look for the arrival, in the coming summer, of the Russian army, to meet which he had only a single corps under arms in East Prussia. France, moreover, had promised her allies to send an army into northern Germany, and to direct the operations of part of it, reinforced by the army of the Empire, against Magdeburg, the most important military centre of the Prussian monarchy. Frederick resolved, instead of remaining inactive till the Austrian, French, and Imperial troops bore down on him, to defeat the Austrians before the French came up.

In the latter half of April the season seemed to him far enough advanced for military operations on a larger scale. Starting from Lusatia and Silesia, he invaded Bohemia with over 100,000 men. His strategical object was the capture of the great magazines erected by the Austrians in northern Bohemia as a basis for their offensive action against Saxony and Silesia. If the Prussians succeeded in seizing these magazines, the King might fearlessly detach large bodies of troops for movements against the French; inasmuch as the Austrians without their supplies would be unable to march.

Frederick's plan of campaign was extremely hazardous. The Prussians had to penetrate into a hostile country in three widely separated columns, between which the Austrians were in command of the inner line of operations. Moreover, a mountain barrier had to be passed which could be defended by means of a few troops; and the Prussians had to begin by zing the magazines containing the supplies on which they were to live. The worst, however, was that through treachery the Court of Vienna had got wind of the intended Prussian operation. The Austrians still had time to concentrate their 115,000 men scattered through northern Bohemia, with every prospect of inflicting a defeat on the 100,000 Prussians invading the country at different points. But to the Empress' generals the plan ascribed to the King of Prussia appeared so reckless that they would not believe the traitors who announced it, and ignored their information although it was correct even in the details. Field-Marshal Browne, too, seemed perfectly unconcerned, and declared that no danger existed of a Prussian attack. He even proceeded to inspect once more all the Austrian stations, and praised what he saw of the disposition—or rather, scattered distribution—of the forces. Thus the Austrians were everywhere in a condition of distraction and imperfect readiness, when they were surprised and systematically attacked by the enemy. Nowhere could they offer any successful resistance, but on the contrary, were obliged at all points to retreat hurriedly and in disorder, abandoning their magazines in the western and central parts of northern Bohemia.

The two best generals of the Prussian army, Winterfeldt and Schwerin, would have prosecuted the plan of campaign with even more audacity than the King, if they could have had their way. The three Prussian columns which accomplished the invasion of Bohemia came from Saxony, Lusatia and over the Riesengebirge. The commander of the last of these columns, the septuagenarian Field-Marshal Schwerin, seconded by Winterfeldt, asked the King's permission to push on to Königgrätz and Pardubitz, where lay the largest of the Austrian magazines. But Frederick, not thinking himself strong enough to extend his operations so far, refused, and commanded Schwerin to join him to the north of Prague. He would be satisfied if the enemy's magazines in Jungbunzlau, Aussig, Budin, Lobositz, Leitmeritz, and Teplitz came under his control. A success of the kind would paralyse the Austrian offensive plans for months; but, if he aimed at more, his plan might be undone by the superior strength of the Austrians. Here we recognise the true strategical genius of Frederick the Great. He laid his plan of campaign with such boldness that his opponents were quite unable to grasp his audacity; nevertheless, he always kept in view the necessity of modifying his schemes, of bridling his imagination, and of limiting himself to the attainable.

King Frederick, as well as Schwerin and Winterfeldt, expected that the Austrians would not be forced out of Bohemia by mere manœuvres, but that they would give the Prussians an opportunity of engaging in a considerable combat, perhaps a great battle. To such an event the King and his generals looked forward with self-confidence and delight. The Austrian army was now under the command of the brother of the Emperor Francis I, Prince Charles of Lorraine, who was making ready for battle in the fortress of Prague. On May 1 and 2 the Austrians crossed over from the left to the right bank of the Moldau and took up their position, to the east of Prague, on the slopes of the Ziskaberg and Taborberg. At the same time King Frederick advanced at the head of the column from Saxony to the White Hill (Weisse Berg). Marshal Schwerin was posted with the Silesian and Lusatian columns opposite Brandeis on the right bank of the Elbe. If, therefore, the Prussian forces were to take the shortest way for uniting in face of the Austrian, a part of them would have to cross the Moldau, and another the Elbe.

Prince Charles of Lorraine wrote to the Empress Maria Theresa that, instead of undertaking so daring a manœuvre, Frederick seemed to him much more likely to draw the two columns under Marshal Schwerin in a great curve towards him by way of Melnik, and then by a second great curve encircle the Austrian position and cross the Moldau above Prague. Prince Charles hoped to gain a very significant advantage from the very leisurely manœuvre which he expected on the part of his adversary; for the strong division under Serbelloni, numbering 37,000 men, which had covered the magazines by Pardubitz and Königgrätz against Schwerin, was now approaching Prague from the east. If he could join forces with Serbelloni, Prince Charles would have at his disposal a fighting army of nearly 100,000 men, while the fortress of Prague was occupied by 13,000. But Frederick and Schwerin had a force of only 64,000, because more than 30,000 Prussians were obliged to stay behind on the left bank of the Moldau to cover the line of communication with the bases of the army. With 100,000 against 64,000 combatants, the Prince of Lorraine might reckon on gaining the victory; but he underrated the resolution and mobility of his opponent. On May 5, Frederick crossed the Moldau near Selz, an hour's distance from Prague—in face, that is, of the Austrian front. The most favourable opportunity thus offered itself to Prince Charles of punishing the King of Prussia's temerity. The transit of Frederick's 20,000 men across the Moldau lasted the whole day; and it was not till the middle of the night that the heavy artillery reached the camp. To the King's intense uneasiness, Schwerin's 44,000 men were still not on the spot; he had, indeed, crossed the Elbe on May 4 near Brandeis, but on the 5th, notwithstanding the King's orders, he had not ventured to march to the Moldau, because a false alarm led him to fear the approach of the 61,000 Austrians in the neighbourhood of Prague. Thus, had Prince Charles cared to look, he might on the 5th have discovered the Prussian forces in a condition of dislocation. But he lacked the swift resolve and energy requisite for dealing with so terrible an enemy; moreover, he had no confidence in the quality of his troops; and, finally, he was without personal authority over his subordinate generals. After Frederick had spent the whole of May 5 waiting for Schwerin, he issued an order in the evening that the Field-Marshal was to join him by means of a night march. Consequently, on the morning of May 6 the junction of the 64,000 Prussians took place in front of the 61,000 Austrians. The King now determined to attack instantly. A direct attack on the Austrian position being impossible, the only thing that remained to be done was to turn the enemy's right wing, where the ground offered no particular difficulty to the attacking force. Schwerin's tired troops were obliged to execute a long flank march through morasses, into which the men often sank up to their armpits; only the best-drilled infantry of the day could have overcome such hardships, and overcome them rapidly.

The battle began at ten o'clock with a cavalry engagement on the extreme left wing of the Prussians. In cavalry they had decidedly the numerical superiority (17,000 against 13,000 Austrians). On the other hand, the Austrian infantry was slightly superior in numbers to the Prussian (48,600 against 47,000). For hours the squadrons continued the attack without producing any decisive effect. Meanwhile, Schwerin had ordered the first divisions of the Prussian infantry which had come up to attack without waiting for the arrival of the rest. First, the grenadier brigade, then Schwerin's regiment and Fouqué's, advanced, without returning the Austrian fire, shouldering their guns; but the onslaught failed, and the regiments fled. The venerable Field-Marshal dismounted, snatched a flag, and addressed the troops. He was struck by five case-shot balls, and fell.

Opposite, on the Austrian side, the battalions moved resolutely forward to follow up their success. They were addressed by Field-Marshal Browne, till a Prussian cannon-ball shattered his leg, and he, too, fell mortally wounded. About the same time, Prince Charles of Lorraine was seized by a fit of cramp, just as he beheld his squadrons succumbing at last to the enemy's assault, and remained unconscious till the end of the battle. Thus the Austrian army found itself leaderless, no other general taking over the command. The battle on the Austrian side was continued as a purely defensive action—and this invariably means defeat. After the Prussian infantry had gradually deployed, the King and the other generals directed their special attention to the gap in the enemy's line of battle occasioned by the advance of Marshal Browne's battalions. Taking instant and energetic advantage of the opportunity offered them, the Prussians poured through the enemy's dislocated order of battle; and, outflanked by the victorious Prussian cavalry, and broken asunder by the Prussian infantry, the Austrian army took refuge within the fortifications of Prague. It was not quite four o'clock in the afternoon when the last shots were fired. 9000 out of 61,000 Austrians lay dead or wounded on the field; of 64,000 Prussians 14,000 were killed or wounded. Among his losses, which weighed heavily upon him as the ruler of a small country without allies in the field, Frederick would find it specially hard to make good that of his 400 officers who had fallen. "The pillars of the Prussian infantry," he wrote, "have been swept away."

After the victory of their comrades on the right bank of the Moldau, the body of over 30,000 Prussians which had remained behind on the left bank, to cover the original contact between the army and its magazines, and which was stationed on the White Hill under the command of Marshal Keith, now closed in on Prague from the "Kleine Seite," and prevented the beaten Austrian army from retreating to the left bank of the river. The main Prussian force invested the city on the opposite bank. The statement has been frequently, but quite erroneously, made, that it was a premeditated plan of Frederick's to drive his enemies after conquering them in battle, into Prague, and there force them to capitulate. When he marched against the Austrians, the position of the majority of Prince Charles' troops faced to the north, and they had an assured line of retreat towards the south behind the Sasawa. Not till Frederick found himself compelled, much against his will, to make so wide a circuit of the Austrian army, did Prince Charles' front come to face towards the east. Thus the bulk of the defeated army was left no choice but to seek refuge in Prague; in the direction of the Sasawa only a fragment of the Austrian force could escape.

46,000 Austrians, inclusive of the garrison, were now shut up in Prague. Their capitulation could only be brought to pass by starving them out; and the place contained provisions enough to last for eight weeks. But Frederick's original plan of campaign had been based on the idea that by the middle of May he would have finished operations in Bohemia. Now, the siege of Prague threatened to detain him till far into July and so to oblige him to postpone for the same length of time his march against the French. Moreover, the danger threatening from the latter was constantly on the increase. After the battle of Prague Louis XV had ordained that, besides the army which was to march against Hanover and Magdeburg, another was to be formed to give direct assistance to Maria Theresa in Bohemia. And what if the Hanoverians now resolved to declare themselves neutral in the Anglo-French War? The King of Prussia thought it not altogether improbable that George II, as Elector of Hanover, might engage in some such ingenious course of political manœuvring; in which case Prussia would have to contend single-handed against the onslaught of the whole military strength of France. Frederick felt that he dare not put off taking action against the French any longer than the middle of June, unless he wished to drive Hanover into a declaration of neutrality. But where was he to obtain troops for the purpose? He had at the most 85,000 men in Bohemia, with which force he had to invest Prague with its garrison of 46,000 Austrians, guard his military communications, and keep in check Serbelloni's division.

In the command of this division Field-Marshal Count Daun was substituted for the not very capable Serbelloni. Daun's personal influence proved to be such that he was able to extinguish in his troops (which had gradually increased to 54,000) all fear of the victorious Prussians and to inspire them with self-confidence. He was confronted by a Prussian corps under the command of the Duke of Bevern, which covered the main army before Prague under the command of the King. As Bevern's division was numerically weak, the hope gradually took possession of its Austrian adversaries that Daun would defeat Bevern and thus relieve the army in Prague. Maria Theresa sent explicit orders to the Field-Marshal to risk a battle, pledging her honour as Empress that she would not lay the blame on him if the result of the action was unfortunate. Thus Daun sought an opportunity for giving battle—with the excessive caution characteristic of him, but with true warlike ardour beneath his self-restraint. Such being the situation, it became an absolute necessity for the King of Prussia to wage another battle. If he defeated Daun, he could detach troops against the French, without foregoing the capture of Prague. At the head of a detachment taken from the investing force, Frederick effected a junction with Bevern, whose numbers now reached 33,000. With these forces the King hoped to defeat Daun's 54,000, who, on June 18, had drawn up on the heights between Kolin and Planian. The strength of the Prussian cavalry fell, in proportion, the least short of the enemy's; its main body was, as at Prague, commanded by General von Ziethen; 14,000 Prussian horsemen were opposed to 19,000, and only 19,000 Prussian foot to 35,000 Austrian.

On marching from their camp towards the Austrian position, Frederick's troops had, after a short night's rest, to accomplish a difficult march of four or five hours' duration. Although it was still quite early in the day, a sultry heat lay on the fields, which were overgrown with corn, and proved a great hindrance to the forward march of the Prussians. The King allowed his weary army a three hours' halt immediately in face of Daun's centre. The Austrians found themselves again, as at Prague, in a very strong defensive position which could only be attacked by turning their right wing. It was nearly one o'clock in the afternoon when there was a sudden renewal of life among the Prussians; and at two o'clock the battle began. Frederick's generals made some mistakes, such as may occur in every battle, and had been much more marked in that of Prague. The King afterwards accused himself of having erred in not personally reconnoitring the ground on the enemy's right wing. But, whatever errors there may have been in their leadership the Prussians, in spite of these, continued for hours to advance victoriously. About four o'clock, Daun saw his right wing heavily pressed and, as it seemed, hopelessly overwhelmed. But, according to the tribute paid him by Frederick in his *History of the Seven Years' War*, Daun was a "great general." He was, in truth, a second Fabius Cunctator—one of those tough and circumspect strategists whom Frederick the Great, with his just insight into the age's methods of carrying on war, valued so highly. Against the furious onslaught of the greatest captain and the best army in Europe, he defended himself steadfastly, infusing into his troops something of his own calm energy. Thus, in the end, the force of the Prussians' onslaught was broken by the great numerical superiority of their opponents. When the Austrians in their turn advanced to attack the exhausted Prussians, they obtained a complete victory. The Prussian army was all but destroyed, losing 13,000 out of 33,000 men. Of 19,000 foot but 7000 rallied round the flag. Again, as at Prague, 400 officers, the flower of the Prussian nobility, lay dead on the field. Twenty-two colours fell into the enemy's hands. If we can imagine Daun, with his great strategical ability, transported from the eighteenth into the nineteenth century, conducting war according to the rules of the later period, in all probability the Prussian army would have been entirely wiped out. But the military methods of the *ancien régime* made the pursuit of a routed army exceedingly difficult; and Frederick the Great himself accomplished very little in this branch of military operations. Daun attempted no kind of pursuit.

King Frederick, quitting his defeated troops, rode through the night by by-ways in the direction of the Prussian camp before Prague, accompanied by only two or three of his body-guard and a few hussars. Except for brief intervals, he had been in the saddle for thirty-six hours, when on the afternoon of the day after the battle, half-dead from exhaustion, he reached the besieging army before Prague. The reproach maliciously brought against him by his own brother Prince Henry (for Frederick was loved by few among those nearest to him): "Phaethon is fallen…Phaethon took good care of himself and withdrew before the loss of the battle was quite decided," was entirely unmerited. His place after the defeat was not at the head of his beaten forces, when another could lead them from the field as well as he could, but with the main army before Prague, where he had to superintend the now unavoidable raising of the siege. "In spite of the great disaster of the 18th, I decamped from Prague to-day with drums and fifes in the most defiant attitude," wrote the King on June 20 to Prince Maurice of Dessau, the commander of the beaten troops at Kolin. "In this misfortune we must do all we possibly can by our determined demeanour to retrieve matters. My heart is lacerated; but I am not cast down and shall seek the very first opportunity of obliterating this reverse." First of all, however, not only had the siege of Prague to be raised, but the whole of Bohemia evacuated. Severely damaged by the skilful manœuvres of the Austrians, the Prussian army retired over the mountains of the frontier back into Lusatia. Owing to their losses on Bohemian soil, the King's forces had melted to one-half of their original strength. Nevertheless, King Frederick sought a fresh battle with the Austrians, who were pushing into Lusatia after the retiring Prussians. But Prince Charles and Daun encamped themselves at Zittau, which was as impregnable as the position at Lobositz. Here they stood from July 24 till August 25. The King of Prussia almost despaired of finding any weak point at which to attack the Austrians, while the French, Russians, Swedes, and the army of the Empire were now advancing. France, especially, displayed in her defence of Saxony a vigour which Frederick had not expected. Louis XV not only sent a second army into Germany, but concluded on May 1, 1757, a second Treaty of Versailles, in which the yearly subsidies paid to the Court of Vienna were raised to twelve million *gulden* (£1,200,000). Thus Maria Theresa was enabled on her side to pay subsidies to Russia.

While Frederick waited with feverish impatience for an opportunity of forcing the Austrians encamped at Zittau to a battle, he composed an *Apology*, to be made public in the event of his being struck down. This document, preserved in the Prussian Archives, was first printed in 1856. In it the King expresses his bitter repentance that he had ever begun the war. "How could I foresee that France would send 150,000 men into the Empire? How could I foresee that the Empire would take part in the struggle, that Sweden would mix herself up in this war, that France would subsidise Russia?"

The main army of the French, 110,000 strong, was commanded by Marshal d'Estrées. On the other side, the Duke of Cumberland was at the head of 45,000 Hanoverians, Hessians, and Brunswickers. The forces contributed by these three small States went under the suggestive title of the "Army of Observation." The Hanoverian Ministers thought that a good Hanoverian had as much reason to fear the heavy hand of Prussia as that of the French. Moreover, England was indisposed to make any great financial sacrifices for the sake of the Hanoverian army, public opinion in that country fearing that the money of the British taxpayer would be misappropriated for purely dynastic interests. On these grounds the Hanoverians had really very little inclination to take part in the war. But Hanover's whole position was too exposed for the electoral Ministers to succeed in achieving its neutralisation, which Austria and France were seeking to bring about. Willing or unwilling, Hanover was bound to fight. On July 26 a battle took place at Hastenbeck between Marshal d'Estrées and the Duke of Cumberland, who was beaten and fell back behind the guns of the fortress of Stade on the North Sea. On September 10 he concluded with Marshal d'Estrées' successor, the Duke of Richelieu, the Convention of Klosterzeven, which meant the disbanding of the Army of Observation. There seemed now nothing to prevent the French from taking up their winter-quarters on the lower and middle Elbe and besieging Magdeburg in the course of the next campaign. "If the French get to Magdeburg," said the King of Prussia, "I am lost." Already Richelieu was being invited by the Swedes to cooperate with them. Frederick's defeat at Kolin had encouraged the Stockholm Government to move 17,000 men into Prussian Pomerania on September 13. Frederick was afraid that this body of troops, to which at present he had virtually none to oppose, would also take part in the siege of Magdeburg. Another consequence of the defeat of the Prussians was that the Estates of the Empire now ventured to assemble their contingents at Fürth in Franconia. Gradually they gathered together here something like 32,000 Imperial soldiery under Prince Joseph of Saxe-Hildburghausen. They marched into Thuringia and on September 17 joined at Eisenach 24,000 French under the Prince of Soubise—that second army, which Louis XV had sent after the battle of Prague, to give direct aid to the Austrian forces.

Frederick now decided to march at once against the French, without waiting to fight the Austrians. He indulged the hope that, when the French in their turn had lost a battle, they would help Prussia to obtain peace on a *status quo ante bellum* basis. Indirect overtures of this kind had, it is true, been made by him to the Court of Versailles, and had been emphatically rejected; but he had other reasons, of a diplomatic nature, for being specially anxious to obtain a victory over the French army. In England there was a strong feeling against the ratification of the Convention of Klosterzeven. Pitt and other Ministers were beginning to familiarise themselves with the idea that heavy British subsidies must be granted to the Hanoverians. The mere fact of Frederick's march into Thuringia with 28,000 men to meet Soubise and Hildburghausen materially strengthened this current of feeling in London. Frederick left the Duke of Bevern with 41,000 men behind in Lusatia, to oppose the Prince of Lorraine at the head of not less than 112,000. Charles, counselled by Daun, won Lusatia from his opponents by a series of manœuvres, and occupied it with a strong corps of 22,000 men under General von Marschall. Bevern's army was driven back into Silesia and stationed itself at Breslau, thus leaving the greater part of the province to the Austrians, who detached a column for the investment of Schweidnitz. In one of the minor combats of this manœuvring warfare Lieutenant-General von Winterfeldt, the most competent general in the Prussian army and a personal friend of the King, fell, near Görlitz, on September 7.

Meanwhile, on August 11, the Russians had crossed the frontier of East Prussia at Stallupönen. The Russian Commander-in-chief, Field-Marshal General Count Aprakin, advanced with his forces to the Pregel, intending to march along that river on Königsberg. In obedience to precise orders from the King, the venerable Prussian Commander-in-chief, Field-Marshal Lehwaldt, attacked the Russian army. He did so very much against his will, as the Russians were much stronger than he was. In the battle fought on August 30 at Gross-Jägerndorf, on the left bank of the river Pregel, the Prussians suffered a severe defeat. But, to the indescribable amazement of the defeated army, it was found, a few days after the action, that Aprakin not only refrained from following up his victory, but had actually retreated. The Russian general, like Lehwaldt an old man, had been greatly impressed by the coolness and discipline with which the Prussian infantry had manœuvred under hostile fire. He declared to his subordinate generals that Lehwaldt's forces were numerous enough to be able to hold several positions against Russian attack for a considerable time, while the Russian army could not keep the field any longer. In fact, the Russians melted away like snow in the sun, for their incapable commissariat kept them intolerably short of supplies and the ordinary necessaries of life. For this reason Aprakin began to evacuate Prussia on September 9. In the middle of May the Russians had entered Poland 88,000 strong. When, early in November, they had evacuated East Prussia except Memel and had taken up their winter-quarters in Polish territory, Aprakin had under him scarcely more than 30,000 or 40,000 combatants fit for service.

In the middle of September Frederick marched from Lusatia into Thuringia, to meet the armies of the Empire and of Soubise. But the Princes of Soubise and Hildburghausen, like the Austrian generals, avoided a decisive combat by concentrating at Eisenach, at the extreme western limit of Thuringia. On September 10 the Convention of Klosterzeven was signed by the Duke of Richelieu, who then, without waiting for its ratification and the promised disbandment of the Army of Observation, moved with 94 battalions and 106 squadrons from the lower Aller on Magdeburg. Threatened on his right flank by so powerful a force, the King of Prussia found it impossible to continue operations against Soubise. He detached 7000 of his 28,000 men to march under Prince Ferdinand of Brunswick into the neighbourhood of Halberstadt, in order to cover this district against Richelieu's advance column.

While Richelieu marched on Magdeburg, the Austrian General Marschall had accomplished in Lusatia a manœuvre which amounted to a considerable diversion in favour of Soubise. He ordered Field-Marshal Lieutenant Hadik to march towards the Elbe, so that Dresden, Torgau and Wittenberg appeared to be threatened. In addition, Hadik's hussars and Croats made a series of raids into the Mark Brandenburg. In view of Hadik's movements, which might even result in an attempt upon Berlin, Frederick divided his forces once more, sending a detachment of 8000 men under Prince Maurice of Dessau to Torgau, to cover the Elbe fortresses in Saxony and the Mark Brandenburg. In consequence, only 13,000 men remained to the King at Erfurt. With this handful of troops Frederick, from September 14 to 28, opposed the vastly superior forces of the " Combined Army," as the troops of Soubise and Hildburghausen were officially designated, while they held their impregnable position at Eisenach with stubborn tenacity.

They only ventured on a single reconnoitring expedition in the direction of Gotha; and this was attended with unfortunate results for those troops of the Combined Army which took part in it. The Prussian Major-General von Seydlitz, who at the age of thirty-six had proved himself in the last Bohemian campaign the ablest cavalry general in the Prussian army, at the head of 1900 dragoons and hussars, surprised 9500 of the enemy and put them to an ignominious flight, in which their losses were heavy. Here the extraordinary deficiencies from which the Combined Army suffered for the first time made themselves evident. Nevertheless, the preponderance of the enemy's numbers seemed certain to overpower the King. During the fortnight in which he was encamped near Erfurt he was absolutely at a loss as to how he should continue operations. Even at the time of the battle of Kolin, he had entertained the idea of suicide. Now, this temptation presented itself more strongly than ever, and he protested that princes of the eighteenth century would not let themselves be outshone by republicans of antiquity like Brutus and Cato in loftiness of soul.

In truth, the war seemed irretrievably lost for Prussia. Frederick had written to his Minister of Foreign Affairs, Count Finkenstein, that, if the main army of the French hurled itself in good earnest on the duchy of Magdeburg, he would need 40,000 more men than he had to escape annihilation. And at that moment, the French main army was

CH. IX.

actually advancing on Magdeburg, something like 60,000 strong. Prince Ferdinand of Brunswick with his 7000 was of course much too weak to offer resistance; he withdrew behind the Bode, leaving the rich district of Halberstadt exposed to the French. They had long since occupied the Rhenish and Westphalian possessions of Prussia; while the Austrians had overrun Lusatia and Silesia, and appropriated the resources of those provinces to their own uses. From Lusatia Austrian, and from Pomerania Swedish, raids laid the Mark Brandenburg under contribution—for 17,000 Swedes had occupied the whole of Prussian Pomerania with the exception of the fortress of Stettin.

And now Frederick was driven to the decision of leaving a great part of his country open to the enemy. He sent an order on September 29 to Field-Marshal Lehwaldt to evacuate East Prussia with his force of 29,000 men, and to march on Stettin. Lehwaldt's army was to be used for a winter campaign, which the King intended to open in December against French and Swedes.

Thus East Prussia was lost soon after it had been freed from the invasion of Aprakin. In January, 1758, the Russians took possession of the defenceless province, which they did not evacuate again till the conclusion of peace. For the rest, Frederick hesitated as to whether in the winter he should attack the French on the Elbe or the Austrians in Silesia. He negotiated with Marshal Richelieu for a truce to last till May, 1758, and to be also extended to the Swedes. Thus he hoped to obtain a free hand against Austria; but in other respects the truce could not but be of enormous disadvantage to him. George II was still hesitating as to whether he should ratify the Convention of Klosterzeven, the Army of Observation remaining meanwhile, undisbanded, in the environs of Stade. He informed his Hanoverian Ministers that he was disposed to refuse the ratification, if the King of Prussia obtained a military success and thus proved himself able to hold his own. But if, instead of this, an arrangement was accepted by Frederick which would strengthen the position of the French in Hanover, the effect on George could only be that despair and mistrust would take absolute possession of his mind; and he would then very probably, in his capacity of Elector, consent to an understanding with the conqueror of his German dominions.

Now, France, since the Convention of Klosterzeven, had already been negotiating with the Landgrave of Hesse and the Duke of Brunswick as to proposals for taking the 17,000 Hessians and Brunswickers, at present in English, into French pay. The Duke of Mecklenburg-Schwerin, whose country, like the Elector of Saxony's, Frederick wanted to annex, had been the ally of France since the beginning of the war. He now offered the Cabinet of Versailles to transfer 6000 men into the pay of France and to cede to the Most Christian King the fortress of Domitz, on the Elbe, which, if in the enemy's hand, would block the trade-communication of

Frederick's subjects with Hamburg. In this way another severe blow would be struck at the prosperity of the Prussian monarchy. But, above all, Mecklenburg formed the connecting territorial link between the army of Richelieu and the Swedish corps in Prussian Pomerania. The French intended to unite, for the campaign of 1758, Hessians, Brunswickers, Mecklenburgers, and Swedes, into an army 40,000 strong. This would have been a Protestant army, while already there were in the field against Frederick two Roman Catholic armies and one Orthodox, besides the army of the Empire, made up of a mixture of Catholics and Protestants. These five armies would certainly have crushed the King. Every day his hopes sank lower. "We are doomed," he said; "but I shall fall sword in hand."

He drew back slightly before the advances of the Princes of Soubise and Hildburghausen to positions near Buttelstedt and Buttstädt, north of Weimar, and here stood still for another twelve days, without knowing what to do next. Frederick's slight backward move had been intended as a trap for Hildburghausen, whom he believed to be incautious enough to follow him and lay himself open to the danger of a defeat. In fact, Hildburghausen did urge Soubise to risk a battle. The army of the Empire was composed in motley fashion of contingents supplied by numerous small dynasts. This had not hindered Marlborough and Eugene from winning partly by means of the army of the Empire the battle of Höchstädt; but in their day English and Dutch subsidies had helped to establish that army on a satisfactory footing. At present, in consequence of lack of money, such intolerable conditions prevailed among the Imperial troops that Hildburghausen despaired of being able to keep his forces together for long, and therefore impatiently sought a decision by battle. Soubise had no thought of acquiescing in the wishes of his colleague. The strategical genius of the King and the incomparable quality of his troops would in all probability turn the scale in a pitched battle, while, on the other hand, the allies would doubtless annihilate their opponents, whom they were encompassing on all sides, if they conducted a judiciously planned war of manœuvres against them. Soubise therefore showed extreme caution as he followed the retiring enemy, and ventured no further than Gotha with the bulk of his army. "When I advance," wrote the King of Prussia, "the enemy fly; when I fall back, they follow me, but always keeping well out of reach of shot. Should I leave these parts and, for instance, seek an encounter with Richelieu in his pride somewhere near Halberstadt, he would behave in the same fashion, and the enemy hereabouts, for the moment as immovable as statues, would soon come to life and nail me down somewhere near Magdeburg. If I fall back on Lusatia, they will take my magazines at Leipzig and Torgau and march straightway on Berlin. These moves cannot go on much longer; the game must shortly come to an end one way or the other." Prince Henry and Voltaire reminded him that other kings before him had purchased peace and self-preservation by cessions of territory; but his answer was:

> "*Pour moi, menacé du naufrage,*
> *Je dois, en affrontant l'orage,*
> *Penser, vivre et mourir en roi.*"

The King had spent nearly a month in the neighbourhood of Erfurt and Weimar, trying to force Soubise' corps and the Imperial army into fighting, when the news was announced that the Austrians were marching from Lusatia to Berlin. Reports were contradictory as to their strength. If it was the whole of Marschall's corps, the suspicion was unavoidable that Sweden had part and lot in the enterprise. Frederick was in the direst distress. Berlin contained invaluable resources for the defence of Prussia—the arsenal, the foundry, the manufactory of arms, the powder magazines, and the cloth factories. "Ah! dear brother, how happy are the dead!" the King wrote to Prince Henry. Then, with tremendous energy, he took his counter-measures. He not only wished to protect his capital, but hoped that the blow which the French had given him no opportunity of striking might now fall on Marschall's column. The Prince of Anhalt's detachment, which covered the magazines of Leipzig and Torgau, was despatched from Weissenfels on the Saale by means of quite extraordinary marches to the eastern side of Berlin. Prince Ferdinand was ordered to lead his troops from Magdeburg to the western side of the capital. The King himself moved with the main army from Buttstädt, and drove his breathless companies on towards the south side of Berlin. "We must," he said, "get these people into our power, alive or dead." But once more he had been merely fighting the air. Not until his forces had advanced close on Berlin did it become known that it was not Marschall's column at all, but merely a skirmishing party of 3500 men under Count Hadik, which had entered Berlin and, after levying contributions, had speedily departed. The enormous losses suffered by the King's forces on the march had served no purpose.

Frederick hereupon formed the design of tracking the Austrians in Lusatia and Silesia, regarding his operations against the French and the Imperial army as finally wrecked. Then came the announcement that Soubise had advanced to the Saale, and that Hildburghausen had actually crossed this river and was trying to get possession of Leipzig. The King's hopes of forcing the Combined Army into action revived, and he moved his troops, instead of on Görlitz, towards Leipzig. The army of the Empire retreated very hurriedly behind the Saale, and the King of Prussia's forces pushed on over the river in pursuit. During the operations in Thuringia the numbers of the Prussian battalions and squadrons had, through the influx of the autumn recruiting contingents, been restored up to their normal height; but during a period of eight weeks the counter- and cross-marches in Thuringia, Saxony,

Magdeburg and Brandenburg had been unceasing, and, in consequence of the superhuman hardships endured, the full battalions, consisting of about 840 men, had again already shrunk to an average of 600. Still, the whole force was held together by the iron Prussian discipline.

Quite different conditions prevailed in the French army, where neither officers nor soldiers observed discipline, although revolutionary ideas proper had not yet penetrated among the troops. The worst evil, and the root of all the rest, was the insubordination of the generals. It was precisely in the highest spheres of the army that the personal weakness of Louis XV, and the disorganised state of his government, had produced the utmost disorder—in fact, a kind of anarchy. The generals called every field-marshal who held the reins firmly a "despot," and yielded him a doubtful obedience. They were full of jealousy among themselves; each believing that in battle his fellow would leave him in the lurch. If Soubise had been perfectly master of his troops, he would not have made a stand before the King of Prussia, but have moved a couple of days' marches to the rear, in the same way as six weeks before he had withdrawn twenty battalions of his advance-guard from Erfurt to Eisenach on Frederick's advance from Lusatia to Erfurt. A procedure of this sort had been prescribed to him from Versailles, and Frederick, as has been seen, was apprehensive of it. But an army is a complicated and sensitive piece of mechanism. Marching to and fro demands more sacrifices from troops than a pitched battle; and for a long time the French had been grumbling at the interminable marches which led to no decisive result. The French army was without an equal in Europe, in so far as alone of all the armies of the globe it had abolished the punishment of flogging; nowhere was the common soldier so humanely treated, or his honour so generously considered. The French ambulance, too, was unequalled for efficiency. The system of drill was theoretically the same as the Prussian. In personal bravery the French soldier was unsurpassed. All the technique, the materials of war, etc., were first-rate. The commissariat, in spite of corruption, was without a superior as to ability and resource. Even Soubise, whom critical history was formerly wont to deride as the inventor of a sauce highly appreciated by *gourmets*, has by later research been proved to have been no insignificant commander. Hitherto, he had carried out his plan of operations consistently. But now he no longer had his troops in hand. They were eager to occupy winter-quarters, and resented being subjected by him to the hardships of a retreat, instead of his bringing the campaign to a quick and glorious close by a battle in the fine old French style. Least of all would tolerate a backward movement the twenty battalions and eighteen squadrons which Lieutenant-General the Duke of Broglie had just brought up from the Richelieu division of the army! These troops had already shown the utmost exasperation when carrying out the march from Halberstadt into Thuringia, as they had reckoned on going into winter-quarters without further delay. In the French camp, it had come to this: that the general in command obeyed the army, not the army the commander. Soubise halted near the left bank of the Saale and occupied a strong position not far from Mücheln. The King of Prussia led his army against this position; but, discovering in time that it was too strong, ordered a retreat and encamped himself opposite the French at Rossbach. He knew that his adversaries, through lack of the necessaries of life, would soon be compelled to abandon their impregnable position and either advance against him or retire upon their magazines. In the latter case, he hoped to force their rear-guard to a combat on the march. On the other side, Soubise was still unwilling to offer battle; his plan was to outflank the encampment at Rossbach on the left and thus threaten the Prussian communication with Weissenfels. The Prince hoped that Frederick would then voluntarily beat a retreat. When the Prussians had been thus manœuvred away from the Saale, Soubise would, directed by his Minister, take up winter-quarters behind this river.

To carry out these operations, Soubise began his march on November 5, not earlier than 11.30 in the morning. Frederick therefore could not attack on the same day if the French posted themselves opposite the left wing of the Prussian lines, on the heights of Obschütz. The army with which Soubise began his flank march on that fateful November 5 consisted of 30,000 French troops and 11,000 of the army of the Empire. Of the latter not less than 7000 were disbanded quite at the beginning of the battle—a fact which may be verified from the list of casualties on this day; they are therefore not included in the statistics concerning the action given in the present narrative, for only 34,000 of the Combined Army were reckoned on the battle-field as actual combatants. King Frederick had with him 22,000 men. Soubise' troops were eager for battle, their spirits having been raised by Frederick's retreat on the previous day.

When the King of Prussia became aware that the enemy was marching upon his left flank, he had no thought of retreating over the Saale in accordance with the expectations of the French generals. But he had just as little intention of venturing to attack the enemy on the heights of Obschütz. It was indeed not behind the Saale, but on Merseburg, that he arranged to fall back. It is generally stated that this was a feigned retreat, a mere stratagem; but such is not the fact. Cut off from Weissenfels by Soubise' flank march, the King of Prussia intended to make Merseburg the base of his operations. To the victor of Gotha, General von Seydlitz, was assigned the command of the larger part of the Prussian cavalry, with special orders to block the road to Merseburg. He was the youngest cavalry general present with the army.

It was about half-past two o'clock in the afternoon when the French perceived that the King of Prussia was falling back. They had now reached the goal of their advance and were on the heights of Obschütz.

But, as Soubise saw that the Prussians were retiring, he resolved to avail himself of the advantageous opportunity offered and to attack Frederick's rear-guard. After the French had once committed the cardinal mistake of lingering in the neighbourhood of the Saale, one can scarcely blame Soubise for this decision. For, if the King of Prussia had made up his mind to give battle, the French on their side were obliged to accept it either on this or some other day. So the Combined Army continued their march beyond Obschütz and descended into the wide trough of land which extends from that village to the north. The King of Prussia saw the enemy come down from the Obschütz heights, and at once gave up the movement to Merseburg—for the ardently desired chance of battle had come. The Prussian army were ordered to deploy. The undulating country behind Reichhardtswerben hid from the French the forward march of the Prussians; and their cavalry, advancing first, surprised and attacked the cavalry of the Combined Army, which had not yet deployed. The squadrons of Seydlitz maintained their advantage, but with some difficulty, as the enemy stood his ground for quite half-an-hour, so that the French infantry gained time for their deployment.

Soubise has been condemned as a careless general, of the superficial, frivolous, *grand seigneur* type, because he allowed himself to be surprised. But Frederick the Great was himself surprised at Hochkirch. So far from being guilty of carelessness, Soubise, on the contrary, exhibited an excess of anxiety. Already on the march from Mücheln to Obschütz he had feared being attacked, and, to protect the left wing of his marching columns, had left behind detached bodies of troops—eleven battalions of French and Croats, twelve good French squadrons and three of Austrian hussars, the last under no less important a leader than Laudon. These fifteen squadrons might, if used at the right point, have decided the day to the disadvantage of Seydlitz. Nothing better illustrates the difference between Soubise and Frederick than that the latter, on withdrawing towards Merseburg, had only left behind to watch those detachments a quite insignificant force—a single battalion against eleven, seven squadrons against fifteen.

It was chiefly through squandering his cavalry that Soubise lost the battle. According to the tactics and armaments of those times, cavalry was the most effective of the three engines of warfare. Soubise had 5500 horse, Frederick 5000. But, owing to the wrong dispositions of the French Commander-in-chief, his slight numerical superiority was changed at a critical moment into a pronounced inferiority; 3800 of the Combined Army were attacked and beaten by Seydlitz' 4600 men. General von Seydlitz had his squadrons so firmly in hand that, after defeating the enemy's cavalry, he was able to lead them in good order against the right wing of the French infantry. His success in this manœuvre won for Seydlitz imperishable laurels. Even Prussian troops did not always understand how to make best use of their victory. But

Seydlitz possessed the power of maintaining strict discipline in his whole force, from the major-generals down to the common soldier. He would not permit the pursuit of the enemy's cavalry to be continued longer than to the point at which the French squadrons were rendered harmless; then, his whole thirty-eight squadrons wheeled round to the right and attacked the French infantry and artillery. The Prussian cavalry dominating the plain, the French artillery was prevented by fear of the enemy's horsemen from falling into position. Consequently, the Prussian artillery, little embarrassed by fire from the French guns, was free to direct its own mainly on the enemy's infantry: which it did with excellent effect. The Prussian cannonade and cavalry charges shattered the French infantry so rapidly and so completely that Frederick's battalions, by that time deployed and advancing, found little left for them to do. Only about seven battalions of the Prussian line of battle fired a series of charges; this sufficed to rout the entire French foot. The whole action lasted only a single hour.

The Prussian losses amounted to not more than 550 men. Those of the French army were far greater, reaching about 7000 men, though certainly not beyond what a great military Power like France could bear without being shaken in the slightest degree. Nor did the French at Rossbach forfeit their old reputation for bravery. One company of the Piedmont regiment was nearly wiped out by Prussian grape-shot. Of the 3800 cavalry which fought against Seydlitz not fewer than 1000 were killed or wounded. But the insubordination of the army which had forced the Prince of Soubise, against his will, to stay in the region of the Saale was notorious and evident. Even on the battle-field there was among the French forces much disorder, want of guidance, and disagreement. In any case, Europe, to its astonishment, recognised that the French army was no longer what it had been. Nowhere was the impression thus created stronger than in London. Pitt breathed more freely, and the old King seemed to have recovered his youth—it was long since he had seemed to be in such spirits. The ratification of the Convention of Klosterzeven and the disbandment of the army at Stade were now definitely refused. In 1757 the British Parliament had reluctantly voted £164,000 for the Army of Observation; the grant made in 1758 amounted to £1,200,000. As Pitt expressed it in the Lower House, the Army of Observation was to become an "Army of Operations." That the Minister was able to obtain money from the representatives of the English people for the unpopular Hanoverian war, was one of the most important consequences of the battle of Rossbach. It may be noted here in anticipation that the allied "Army of Operations," which was now commanded by Prince Ferdinand of Brunswick, drove and kept the French out of Germany. The Court of Versailles despatched armies of continuously increasing size against the allies, because the defeat of Prince Ferdinand was the preliminary condition of the participation of France in the military operations against Frederick. For France the maintenance of the system established by the Peace of Westphalia in Germany depended on the overthrow of the King of Prussia. Besides, the war which the French were carrying on at the same time with England had gradually, both at sea and in countries across the sea, taken a turn unfavourable to France. The French were threatened with the loss of their colonies. All the greater was their desire to secure the Austrian Netherlands, which Austria had promised to make over to France, if Silesia was reconquered for the House of Habsburg. Once before, at the Peace of Aix-la-Chapelle in 1748, her colonies had been restored to France on condition that she evacuated so much of Belgium as had been conquered by a French army. For these reasons, the Court of Versailles, during the whole Seven Years' War from first to last, made the greatest possible sacrifices for the sake of the continental war. But Ferdinand of Brunswick intercepted all these blows. The French vanish almost entirely out of the sphere of Frederick the Great's military struggles; and, on this account, they will not be mentioned again in the course of the present chapter, except in the way of a single cursory reference.

Such were the indirect results of the battle of Rossbach; the direct consisted in the retreat of the Combined Army towards the Main and the interior of Franconia; so that Frederick's magazines in Leipzig, Wittenberg, Torgau, Dresden, and elsewhere, were no longer threatened. The King was now at liberty to march into Silesia against the Austrians without having any fears for his rear. In Silesia, at the time of the battle of Rossbach, 43,000 Austrians under General Nadasdy were laying siege to Schweidnitz, while 60,000 under Prince Charles and Daun protected the besieging lines. The Duke of Bevern, who was stationed in face of them with an army which had, particularly by desertions, melted down from 41,000 to 28,000 men, was urged by Frederick to take advantage of the division in the Austrian forces in order to attack them. But Bevern was no more a great general than Lehwaldt. He hesitated over the attack, till Schweidnitz, on November 11, capitulated, six days after the battle of Rossbach. The fortress, which had been newly built after the King's own ideas, had been held for seven weeks against 43,000 Austrians; nevertheless, the defence had not been conducted with much energy, and within the garrison treachery and desertion played into the hands of the besiegers. The fall of Schweidnitz cost King Frederick 7000 men, about the same number as the French had lost at Rossbach, not counting the losses of the Imperial army. Moreover, Nadasdy seized in Schweidnitz sufficient provisions to keep 88,000 men for two months, and helped himself to a war-exchequer containing 330,000 *thalers*—in the then financial condition of the King of Prussia a sum of considerable weight in the balance. After the capture of Schweidnitz almost all the Austrian forces united and marched on Breslau.

Bevern had now to contend against 83,000 Austrians instead of 60,000. On November 22, the Prince of Lorraine and Daun forced their way over the Lohe, and the battle of Breslau was lost by the small Prussian army. In moderately good order the Prussians retreated through the town of Breslau to the opposite bank of the Oder, where their general was during a reconnaissance taken prisoner by Croats.

His successor, General von Kyau, retreated with the army towards Glogau and thus left Breslau exposed. This retreat of Kyau's was a grave error. The danger of the cautious and slow-moving Austrians effecting the transit of the Oder was lessened by the fact that the victors of Rossbach had already advanced as far as Görlitz. With a rapidity of which in those days only Prussian troops seemed capable, the King's army marched on to Breslau. In spite, however, of Frederick's threats and exhortations to his generals, the governor of Breslau, the aged General von Lestwitz, capitulated without offering any resistance. The garrison was granted a free conduct to Glogau; but most of the non-commissioned officers and nearly all the privates had deserted so soon as the Austrians had entered the city, so that all ten battalions simply ceased to exist. Before this the Duke of Bevern's regiments had already been weakened to an extraordinary degree by desertion. Of the 13,000 men who, before the battle of Breslau, figured in the official list of Bevern's army as lost, 6000 were marked as deserters. Such were the feelings pervading the Prussian as well as the Austrian army in consequence of the system of the press-gang, the brutal treatment of the men, and their indifference to the despotic governments for which they were forced to spill their blood. A notable exception among the German troops of that period were the 14,000 men whom Frederick led from Thuringia into Silesia. Full advantage had been taken of the many opportunities of desertion offered by the cross- and counter-marches of September and October, when no supplies were furnished from the magazines; but the soldiery were billeted on the population, and those who remained might be trusted. Another force, of an ideal kind, operated in Frederick's favour. The belief in Luther and Calvin in Germany had not died out so completely as the King supposed; and this was the reason why the defeat of the French was hailed with jubilation by all German Protestants. For in the French army at this time—not more than a generation before the Revolution—the traditions of Catholic intolerance were still so alive, that Soubise' soldiers frequently desecrated the altars and chalices of the Protestant churches. Even among the cool and calculating frequenters of the Paris Exchange a fear was expressed, that the King of Prussia might play the deliverer in a war of religion and thus attain the headship of Germany. But a consummation of this kind suited neither the spirit of the times nor the personality of a Voltairean like Frederick. Anyhow, the aureole which surrounded the head of the victor of Rossbach had the effect of inducing a few thousand soldiers to find their way into his camp—in part deserters at the capitulation of Breslau, in part stragglers from the garrison of Schweidnitz, who had made their escape out of Austrian custody on the way to Bohemia. Every sort of reinforcement was a valuable gain for Frederick, who had to face a tremendous task.

Prince Charles of Lorraine and Daun marched against the King of Prussia with the object of gaining a position on the Katzbach. Here Schweidnitz could be covered. With the support of this fortress and of Liegnitz, which they manned and strengthened, the Austrians might now venture to take up their winter-quarters in Silesia. But it behoved the Austrian generals, from the outset, to observe the utmost caution, as against a foe so eager to strike and so mobile, although they believed him to be still on the other side of the Katzbach. They therefore, on December 4, occupied the fortified camp at Leuthen, where their forces numbered 55,000 men. Here Prince Charles and Daun learned to their amazement that the King of Prussia had crossed the Katzbach some time before, and was now at Neumarkt. In reality, he was even nearer, stationed immediately in front of the Austrians. After the junction of troops from Thuringia with the forces that had carried out the precipitate retreat to Glogau, he had under him more than 40,000 men. Prince Charles and Daun could be in no doubt that they would be attacked the next day.

At sunrise on December 5, the Prussians were on the move and marched upon the right flank of the Austrians, who had not time to dispose themselves calmly in order of battle. In the army of Prince Charles and Daun several battalions were not to be entirely trusted—to begin with, ten Bavarian battalions, for in those days a bitter antagonism obtained between Bavaria and Austria; further, fourteen battalions of Würtembergers, who hated their ruler, the ally of Austria, as the tyrannical oppressor of the Estates of his duchy, and passionately venerated the conqueror of Rossbach as the champion of German Protestantism. The Austrian generals placed these Bavarian and Würtemberg battalions on the left wing of their line of battle.

Frederick advanced against the right wing, in the direction of Borne; but by means of a personal reconnaissance he convinced himself of the extreme difficulty of attacking his adversaries' right wing, owing to the unevenness of the ground. The left Austrian wing had taken up a still more favourable position, and seemed almost unassailable. But Frederick's keen eye observed a weak point in the left wing of Prince Charles' position; and, with swift resolve, he led his army past the enemy's front (at a distance of not more than 4000 paces) to the point at which he had espied this flaw. Thus the attack of the Prussian infantry fell directly on the Würtembergers; and eleven out of their fourteen battalions at once fled, leaving behind only a few killed and wounded. The advance to the front, by General Nadasdy's orders, of some Austrian regiments

only increased the prevailing confusion—Austrians, Bavarians, Würtembergers, the whole of the infantry of Nadasdy's division, were routed.
The main body of Prince Charles' and Daun's forces was still intact.
But the right Austrian wing, which now had no enemy in front of it,
was obliged to make a very wide wheeling movement in order to be able
to take part in the combat. The training of the Austrian infantry was
not careful enough to enable it to carry out so complicated a manœuvre in
good order. It closed in towards the centre, where the regiments were
massed in so narrow a space that they were incapable of action, and in
parts stood nearly a hundred deep. The execution done by the heavy
Prussian artillery, which was numerically superior to the Austrian, was
proportionately effective. Nevertheless, the Prussians did not win their
victory with ease. Slow and immobile in the matter of tactics, and
strategically devoted to the system of the defensive pure and simple, the
Austrian army, within the limits of this same system, developed a notable
tenacity. Of 40,000 Prussians over 6000 were killed or wounded in a
combat lasting not more than four hours. But the Austrian losses were
enormous. In prisoners alone they lost 22,000 men. Moreover, Breslau,
with a garrison of 18,000 men, surrendered at discretion. Later, the
same fate befell the Austrians in Schweidnitz. All in all, out of the
90,000 Austrians in Lower Silesia, 55,000 were killed or taken prisoners.
The defeat was nothing short of a catastrophe.

Had Frederick the Great had modern armies at his command, he
would now have marched on Vienna and there dictated terms of peace.
Instead of this, it was high time for him to occupy winter-quarters.
Through the winter, operations on the Prussian side were confined to
Pomerania. Here the Swedes not only retired before the army of
Field-Marshal Lehwaldt, whose forces were greatly superior, beyond the
Prussian frontier, but they also evacuated Swedish Pomerania as far as
Stralsund and the island of Rügen. The Prussians were only prevented
from occupying these points by lack of a fleet: moreover, they could
now raise war contributions in Swedish Pomerania and Mecklenburg, and
impress recruits. In Mecklenburg they gathered into the service 4000,
no insignificant aid for the small Prussian State, threatened by nearly
the whole continent of Europe. The King summoned all his energies
and worked hard to render his army complete for the coming campaign.
It was not possible to cover expenses by raising taxes, for in this despotic
State the taxes on the unprivileged classes were so high in times of peace
that to put any abnormal strain on the taxation of that part of the
population was out of the question. To tax the privileged classes would
not have been compatible with the spirit of the King's internal policy.
In this dilemma Frederick took refuge in the debasement of the coinage,
and in paying his officials in paper instead of cash. Thus, in 1758, as in
1757, 150,000 Prussian troops were again put into the field. The Austrian
army, on the other hand, had shrunk from 133,000 to 85,000 men. In 1757

the King of Prussia had directed his attack against Bohemia rather than Moravia, which he would have preferred, but which lay too far east to enable him to send detachments thence against the French. When, at the end of April, 1758, Frederick opened his new campaign, Ferdinand of Brunswick was trying to come up with the French on the further side of the Rhine, across which the bulk of their military forces had been driven back. Frederick, who had now nothing more to fear from the French, had to prepare to meet, about midsummer, the Russian army in the Mark Brandenburg and Silesia. The interval he judiciously proposed to employ in an expedition into Moravia. Here lay Olmütz, the only important fortress which the Austrians held against Prussia; moreover, Moravia bordered on Hungary, where, by taking Olmütz, the King of Prussia hoped to stir up a rebellion among the Protestants. Field-Marshal Daun, who after the defeat of Prince Charles at Leuthen had succeeded him as Commander-in-chief of the Austrian army, had concentrated his forces in Bohemia and expected to be attacked there, when he heard that the Prussians were marching on Olmütz. He now led his army straightway into Moravia, and encamped on May 24 in an unassailable position at Gewitsch, two good days' march from Olmütz. His forces consisted of about 70,000 men; those of Frederick before Olmütz were not more numerous, for the Prussians had to present a three-sided front. Prince Henry of Prussia covered Saxony with 35,000 men against General Serbelloni in western Bohemia, where the army of the Empire was stationed in conjunction with one corps of Austrians. Serbelloni, if he liked, could also avail himself of a Saxon corps at Linz, 10,000 strong, composed of men on whom Frederick had forced the military oath and who had then deserted from the Prussian army. These Saxons were marching into France, where the Government had taken them into pay. On the other hand, Soubise' army was expected in Austria, having started from the Main in June, 30,000 strong, for western Bohemia. France having increased her subsidies to Sweden for the coming year, the Swedish army in Germany was to be raised from 20,000 to 30,000.

For the present, 22,000 Prussians blockaded Stralsund, commanded by General-Lieutenant von Dohna, successor to Field-Marshal Lehwaldt. Nevertheless Dohna's army was not destined to act alone against Sweden, but also against Russia. The command of the armies of the Tsar, like that of Maria Theresa's, had changed. The aged Aprakin was being tried by Court-martial for evacuating East Prussia, and Lieutenant-General Fermor, who had been appointed to the command in his stead, had, after reoccupying East Prussia, advanced with 32,000 men on Polish West Prussia. He had reinforcements in prospect, and was negotiating with the Swedes for joint action in Brandenburg and Pomerania. King Frederick, pressed by adversaries in so many quarters, could, as has been already mentioned, only muster 70,000 before Olmütz—a very inadequate force; for the fortress had to be invested, the trenches occupied, and the besieging lines covered against Daun. The inferiority of the Prussians in numbers prevented the King of Prussia, who never forgot Kolin, from attempting to attack Daun in battle. He preferred to take up a position south-west of Olmütz near Prossnitz, where within three hours he could collect upwards of 30,000 men. If Daun wished to relieve Olmütz by fighting, he would be obliged to attack Frederick at Prossnitz. This, however, was not at present contemplated by the Austrian general, who knew that Frederick's genius and the mobility of the Prussian infantry would give them an overwhelming advantage in a pitched battle, and who looked out for other means of relieving Olmütz. In the meantime he calmly and conscientiously drilled his very numerous recruits at Gewitsch. The Prussians invested Olmütz on May 8, but only succeeded in opening their first parallel on the 28th. The great lapse of time between these two proceedings was attributed to the army's heavy besieging wagons being retarded by the badness of the roads. Olmütz was a good fortress of the second class, occupied by a garrison of 9000 men under General von Marschall, an elderly but vigorous commandant.

The King of Prussia affirmed that his engineers made many grave blunders during the siege; and it was nearly five weeks before the third parallel was finished, while several successful skirmishes on the part of the besieged had achieved a partial destruction of the earthworks. Added to this, the ammunition and supplies of the besieging batteries gave out. A convoy of 4000 wagons was being brought to meet the need from Neisse to the army; but near the pass of Domstädtl General Laudon, who here made himself a name in the world's history, attacked the convoy on June 30. The Austrians were not much stronger in numbers than the 13,000 Prussians who escorted the convoy, but the latter had covered a march of forty miles with wagon-trains. The Austrians, on the contrary, had at their disposal the Croat light infantry, which seemed created on purpose for such enterprises and was far superior to the corresponding Prussian arm, the so-called "free battalions." These Croat troops were, as Frederick the Great told the British Major-General Yorke, the best in the Austrian army, which he, as a rule, estimated highly; and they were very loyal to their flag; they never deserted, and their mobility was irrepressible. For the attack on the Neisse convoy 2500 Croats were detached. Thus the combat at Domstädtl was lost by the Prussians, who were obliged to blow up their wagons in case they should fall into the enemy's hand. Of the gunpowder, cannon-balls, and supplies of various sorts, nothing reached the besiegers at Olmütz.

"*Convoi attaqué, convoi battu,*" said Frederick the Great, quoting an old military proverb, and he reproached no one for the mishap at Domstädtl. But the blockade of Olmütz was wrecked and had to be immediately raised. The Prussian army turned from Moravia into Bohemia. Its baggage was enormous. Besides dragging with it its siege-train, it had 2000 sick and wounded—altogether 4000 wagons, which, stretched out on a single road, made a line forty miles in length, like the convoy of Domstädtl. The King of Prussia, in order to cover his train of wagons, was obliged to split his army. In order to effect his purpose, he detached three divisions of 8000 men, and temporarily broke up his army into two halves, one of which marched in front, the other behind, the baggage. This arrangement afforded the Austrians an uncommonly favourable opportunity for attack. But, owing to Daun's infinite caution, the Prussians arrived after a twelve days' march at Königgrätz without any losses worth mentioning. Here the King could relieve himself of his baggage. General Fouqué conducted it to Glatz by way of Nachod, where he then took up his own position to cover the conveyance of provisions into the King's camp. In addition, Frederick resorted to a way of feeding his troops which, in a peculiar way, struck a medium between the requisition and magazine systems. As July had come and the corn was ripe in the fields, the soldiers were made to thresh, prepare, and clean the grain and deliver it at the bakery. Each regiment was allotted a certain number of bushels which it had to deliver, and immediately after the delivery the corn was ground and made into bread. The King had now 40,000 men in hand for combat; while Daun had at his disposal 50,000 regular troops and 20,000 irregular, who, generally speaking, did not count in a pitched battle. Avoiding a battle, Daun took up a strong position, opposite the enemy lying at Königgrätz, at Chlum, which he fortified artistically with redoubts and barricades. The King of Prussia, after remaining a fortnight at Königgrätz without getting a chance of battle, was, when July drew to its end, compelled to leave Bohemia, as he had left Moravia, without obtaining any result; in 1757, and in 1758, offensive action against Austria had come to nothing.

Action against Russia could no longer be postponed, for General Fermor was now encamped with his main army at Meseritz, on the frontier between what was then the kingdom of Poland (to whose territory Russia had free access) and the Neumark of Brandenburg. "A terrible time of trial for our poor family and all who call themselves Prussians...," Frederick, on evacuating Bohemia, wrote to Prince Henry. "But in spite of all that passes within me I put the best outward face on a bad business, and try so far as I can not to discourage those whom it is my duty as a general to inspire with hope and generous self-confidence." Fermor advanced into Brandenburg with 50,000 men and marched on Cüstrin, an important arsenal at the confluence of the Oder with the Warthe. Dohna's army had meanwhile given up the blockade of Stralsund in order to stop the way of the Russians. Thus the Swedes were free. The internal condition of the Scandinavian kingdoms made it impossible that they could put into the field the 30,000 men promised by them. A corps of 16,000 Swedes still continued to occupy Prussian Pomerania and Mecklenburg, commanded by General-Lieutenant Count Hamilton, a Scotchman by birth. On August 23 there arrived at Hamilton's headquarters at Friedland in Mecklenburg-Strelitz a Swedish officer attached to the Russian headquarters. He was escorted by Cossacks, and his coming was entirely unexpected by the Swedes. He brought despatches from Fermor in which Hamilton was informed that the Russians were bombarding Cüstrin, and that a detached corps under General Rumyantseff had occupied Schwedt. By means of the bridge there across the Oder, Hamilton's 16,000 men and the 12,000 belonging to Rumyantseff were to unite, according to Fermor's intentions. Hamilton acquiesced in the designs of his Russian colleague; the Swedish troops evacuated Pomerania and Mecklenburg-Strelitz as far as the Uckermark and marched on Schwedt, taking Prenzlau by the way. Cüstrin was not gravely imperilled, because the Russians had with them no siege appliances. Their bombardment left the fortifications unaffected. All the same, the town with the arsenal and a large magazine of corn was burnt; and such losses of material of war were grave disasters for Prussia in her actual condition. The barbarous ravages committed by the Russians, especially by the Cossacks and Calmucks, in the open towns and plains of the Neumark, were also injurious to Frederick from a military point of view. The financial position of the Prussian monarchy was becoming critical. Before the expedition into Moravia Frederick had very unwillingly concluded a subsidy treaty with England. After Rossbach and Leuthen, he was again in hopes of annexing Saxony; but he hampered himself in the achievement of this political end, by making the Prussian State financially dependent on another Great Power. While still in camp at Olmütz, Frederick had written to his ambassador in London that he trusted that for the present year he would not require to draw subsidies. Now, no choice was left him but to draw the first £200,000.

The bulk of his Silesian army was left by the King stationed at Kloster-Grüssau in Lower Silesia against Daun, while he gave over the supreme command to Margrave Charles of Brandenburg-Schwedt, attaching to him as tactical adviser Field-Marshal Keith. He himself led a corps on Cüstrin, the men being subjected to exertions as excessive as those of their cross- and counter-marchings in the autumn of 1757. Especially the last forced marches through the deep sandy soil of the Mark reduced the infantry to a state of utter exhaustion. On August 22, the King's corps united with General Dohna's army at Gorgast, west of Cüstrin. On the 23rd the Oder was crossed, the barrier which separated the Prussian forces from the Russian army besieging Cüstrin. Already Prussian hussars came in contact with Russian dragoons and Cossacks and scattered them right and left. Fermor raised the siege of Cüstrin, but refused to retreat. Moreover, owing to the unwieldy nature of the Russian troops, it would have been scarcely possible for him to escape Frederick, who was anxious for battle. He succeeded, however, in finding a defensive position almost as strong as those selected by Daun with so masterly a discrimination. Fermor, in posting his army behind the Mietzel, the swampy banks of which are only passable in certain places, rendered his front and flanks safe from attack. "I wish that the King would attack me here," said he to General Count Saint-André, who was attached to the Russian headquarters as Austrian military adviser; "I should beat him." Frederick had written quite to the same effect a few days earlier to his sister, the Princess Amalia: "I am not afraid in the least of this ragged crew, but only of the streams and swamps amongst which they can hide." Unable to attack the enemy either in front or flank, he had to turn them completely in order to force them to battle. For Fermor's position, as Frederick ascertained, was less unapproachable in its rear.

On August 25, at half-past three in the morning, having drawn up his army, he crossed the Mietzel with it close to the Neudamm mill by the Kersten bridge, and marched through the thinly-wooded pine forest of Massin. Thence the Prussians emerged 40,000 strong on to the undulating plain of Zorndorf, where the Russians stood in about the same strength. After the battle the King of Prussia told his reader, de Katt, that the Russians might have managed so as to have attacked his marching columns as they came undeployed out of the swampy wood. But such manœuvres presupposed a resolution in the leader and a mobility in the troops in which the Russians were, like the Austrians, altogether lacking. When the Cossacks announced to Fermor that the enemy obviously intended to reach the rear of the Russian position by the wood of Massin, Fermor ordered the army to turn right about face. How little the Russian general had calculated on the possibility of his opponent's daring to turn him is shown by the fact that he had directed some of his heavy baggage to take up a position at Gross-Kamin, close to Batzlow, where the Prussian army came out of the wood. Considering the enormous importance of the provision wagon in the age of the magazine system, the taking of Fermor's baggage would in itself alone have signified a victory for the Prussian army over the Russian.

But the King, who was weak in infantry, believed at this critical moment that he could not afford to detach any troops in the direction of Gross-Kamin. The escort of the Russian baggage was, it is true, not numerous; but they had built a battery and thrown up earthworks. Furthermore, 2000 Cossacks under Major-General Jefremoff, coming from Landsberg on the Warthe, were in full march on Gross-Kamin, where indeed they only arrived on the evening of the day of the battle. At any rate, Frederick left the Russian baggage on the left untouched, and marched on Fermor's army, which, after reversing its position, no

CH. IX.

longer had a safe line of retreat. For the swamps of the Mietzel, which in the eighteenth century were not even passable by single pedestrians, were now in rear of the Russians instead of in their front. Fermor himself had destroyed the bridges at Kutzdorf and Chuartschen, because, according to his opinion, the lower Mietzel formed the enemy's line of advance. That in reality his own line of retreat would be across that river in consequence of the bold evolutions of his formidable foe, had been as little foreseen by him as had the danger to his baggage-train at Gross-Kamin. Had Frederick succeeded in actually carrying out his masterly plan of battle, his success would have been even more complete than it had been at Leuthen; the entire hostile army must have been cut off and annihilated. And he needed, too, to gain a second crushing victory; for the distressful situation of the autumn of 1757 had returned. Not only were the Russians and Swedes in the Mark, but Laudon as well, who, with the greater part of a detachment of some 8000 men, was stationed at Cottbus on the Spree. The Hungarian hussars, desirous of coming into touch with the Russians, made raids throughout the south-eastern Mark and the adjoining districts of Silesia, levying contributions everywhere. Though the excesses they committed were not to be compared with the atrocities of the Cossacks and Calmucks, they were bad enough to excite the anger of Daun and the Austrian officers. The Austrian army was now also encamped on Prussian territory, at Görlitz in Lusatia. Daun had already for several weeks thought of leading the main Austrian army by way of Cottbus to Berlin, so soon as the King of Prussia marched against the Russians.

On the morning of August 25, a burning hot day, Frederick rode forth at the head of the eight battalions which composed his advance-guard. The Prussian army carried out a flank march past the whole length of the Russian front, now facing south, and wheeled into order of battle between Zorndorf and Wilkersdorf. The King's plan was to attack with his left wing, which marched up behind Zorndorf, the enemy's right. The Prussian right wing, made weaker than the left, was to remain in abeyance; while Fermor had expected the reverse tactics: namely, that he would be attacked on his left wing while the Prussian left remained stationary, so as to cover a possible Prussian retreat on Cüstrin. But Frederick, in projecting his plan of battle, had not thought in the least of the precautions imputed to him by Fermor, and was far less intent on preserving at all costs his communication with Cüstrin than on directing his attack to the weakest spot in the Russian position. Even in the contingency of his losing the battle and his connexion with Cüstrin, a line of retreat was open to him through the forest of Massin infinitely superior to Fermor's background of Mietzel quagmires.

Fermor's error led to considerable mistakes in his dispositions. The heavy artillery made a much weaker show on the Russian than on the

Prussian side, Fermor having only 60 heavy guns, Frederick 117. When the Russian general thought that his left wing would be attacked, he massed nearly the whole of his heavy artillery there; while Frederick distributed his heavy guns equally along both wings. The right Russian wing, which Frederick intended to attack, suffered terribly, being under fire for two whole hours from heavy guns, to which it could only respond by means of the light regimental cannon. The attack of the Prussian infantry followed at 11 o'clock, after the battalions had been on the move since about 4 a.m. in the glaring heat of the sun.

Even after Frederick had by his turning movement frustrated Fermor's plan of battle, the Russians still had an excellent defensive position. At Prague, and especially at Leuthen, the Prussian infantry had been able to outflank the enemy's; but at Zorndorf such a manœuvre was not to be thought of. The Russian infantry lay against the Zabergrund, a ravine which at that time was so swampy that, though cavalry might possibly get through it, it was impassable for infantry. The King of Prussia therefore ordered the left wing of his infantry to make a frontal attack. Herein lay the Achilles-heel of Frederick's scheme of battle. The King, who spoke contemptuously of the Russian army as tag, rag, and bobtail, was severely undeceived on this head at Zorndorf. The Russians fought very well, although they had been most terribly handled by the opening cannonade of the Prussian heavy artillery; but they had a powerful reserve of regimental cannon which were very skilfully used, and inflicted fearful losses on the Prussian infantry when it had come close enough.

Shortly before the battle Fermor had informed his troops that the method of the Prussian infantry consisted in insolently advancing and beginning to fire before they reached the proper distance; which habit should be courageously met, by relying on the effect of the artillery and of reasonable infantry fire at the correct distance. These instructions were applied with so much success that the attacking Prussian infantry began to waver. Hitherto, it had not been supported by the cavalry of Frederick's left wing; half of which had been placed behind the infantry. The other half, consisting of thirty-one squadrons, on the opposite side of the Zabergrund, where Seydlitz was in command, could not think of taking the ravine so long as the Russian infantry were close to it. Accordingly, Seydlitz' instructions forbade his making the attempt till the Prussian infantry should have shattered the battalions of the right Russian wing. But, instead of being shattered, they pressed on victoriously, mastered the heavy batteries of the left Prussian wing, and reduced its infantry to such a state of demoralisation that only the vigorous intervention of the cavalry posted behind the infantry saved the left wing of the Prussian infantry from a complete rout. These advances, which Fermor personally commanded on his right wing, were supported at enormous sacrifices by the badly-horsed Russian cavalry. The Prussians utterly outnumbered their adversaries in this arm; for, all in all, 12,000 Prussian fought against 3000 Russian horse—the 3000 Cossacks being of no real significance in a pitched battle.

After the victorious advance of the Russian right wing had put an end to its contact with the Zabergrund, Seydlitz could cross the defile. He did so in good order, and fell on the enemy's flank. The infantry of the Russian right wing and its handful of squadrons found themselves involved in defeat, and fled in the same state of demoralisation which had taken possession earlier of the Prussian battalions. But there remained a distinct numerical difference, to the disadvantage of the Prussians. Of their thirty-eight battalions, twenty-three were routed; of the Russian fifty-seven, only about eighteen; for one-half only of the exposed Russian wing had been included in the combat, while the other had not gone forward with the rest, but had remained quietly in its original position of defence. The reason was that, in the middle of the right Russian wing, lay a second watery swamp, called the Galgengrund. Those of Fermor's battalions which had not advanced with the rest now stood on the other side of this ravine, in close contiguity with it and unbroken. For Seydlitz' squadrons to capture the defile and to take the Russian infantry in flank was out of the question. This would have required a frontal attack by Prussian infantry; but the infantry of the Prussian left wing was now *hors de combat*.

In a word, the King's assault had been beaten off, and his plan of battle absolutely wrecked. His features revealed his anxiety, when, at one o'clock in the afternoon, he rode from the beaten left wing of his line of battle to the right. Maurice of Anhalt-Dessau, fearing that the sight of the King's clouded, brooding countenance might discourage the troops, wheeled round with assumed hilarity, waved his hat and exclaimed, "Victoria!" The troops joined in the cheer, and the English ambassador, Andrew Mitchell, who was present with the King of Prussia, credulously expressed his congratulations to the sovereign. The King listened to him politely and exhibited perfect composure; but, when they had ridden on, he said to Mitchell: "My good friend, things are going badly with the left wing. I shall put them straight; but do not follow me." Then he ordered the right wing, which hitherto had been inactive, to charge. It was a desperate resolve, for the Russian left wing was much better protected against a turning movement than the right. It leant on the village of Zicher and a series of woods, where neither cavalry nor infantry, fighting in the stiff linear formation of the eighteenth century, could penetrate. The frontal attack of the Prussian battalions was repulsed with much slaughter by the guns and regimental cannon of the Russians; and the handful of Russian cavalry made as brilliant charges as their comrades had made on the right wing. Thus the disorganisation of the right wing of the Prussian infantry was complete. The King, like Field-Marshal Schwerin at Prague, seized a flag, but his heroism was unavailing; the men refused to be taken under fire again. The commander-in-chief of the left Russian wing was Browne, a Jacobite emigrant from Ireland, and the uncle of the Austrian Field-Marshal Browne who fell at Prague. He made the same pardonable blunder in tactics which Fermor had committed as commander on the right. Instead of, after the repulse of the hostile infantry, using exclusively his cavalry, small though it was in numbers, for rapid pushes, success misled him into sending his infantry also to charge in the open plain, where the King of Prussia, to paralyse the onslaught of Browne's battalions, massed almost his whole cavalry, the bulk of Seydlitz' squadrons included. The combat now again took a turn in Frederick's favour; but the defensive advantages of Fermor's position were still not exhausted. As the right wing of the Russian battle line was traversed by the Galgengrund, so the left was cut into two parts by the Doppelgrund. Of the twenty-two battalions on the Russian left wing, again only a portion had assumed the offensive; those which had remained on the right of the Doppelgrund had not been scattered by Seydlitz' cavalry, and were able to arrest its victorious advance, thanks to the difficult lie of the Doppelgrund itself.

The battle had begun at 9 o'clock in the forenoon, and only at nightfall did it stop, without having been decided. The losses on both sides reached an enormous height. Of 40,000 Prussians (according to published lists) 10,000 were killed or wounded, including over 300 officers. Yet these numbers are perhaps not altogether trustworthy, as there are indications that there may have been as many as 15,000 or 16,000 Prussians killed or wounded. For a small country like Prussia, such sacrifices were irreparable; a large empire like Russia was better able to bear losses of officers and men, even if more considerable than those of the Prussians. Fermor withdrew his forces for the night towards the Mietzel, near Kutzdorf; the swampy ravines mentioned above separated the combatants. On the morning of August 26, Russian forces again crossed the Zabergrund and appeared on the heights of Zorndorf. Bearing with them the light baggage of the Russian army, they formed the vanguard of Fermor's retreat, which he wished to take the direction of Gross-Kamin, where lay his heavy baggage. The King of Prussia, noticing this forward movement, hoped to find an opportunity for a fresh encounter; for he was bitterly disappointed by the result of the day of battle. He personally reconnoitred the enemy's change of position at Zorndorf; and his passionate eagerness led him all too near his opponents' lines, so that he and his small cavalry escort were suddenly subjected to a lively cannonade from a hidden Russian battery. By a miracle the King escaped unhurt.

For the rest, a repetition of the Prussian attack was not to be thought of seriously. The immense hardships and losses undergone by Frederick's troops reduced them to a condition as disorganised as that of

Fermor's. King Frederick was even without sufficient troops fit for action to seize Fermor's heavy baggage at Gross-Kamin; and Brigadier Kokoschkin, who was in command there, was able to get into communication with the Russian army by way of Wilkersdorf and Zorndorf. Several messages from Kokoschkin to Fermor told how severely the Prussian army had suffered; and the Cossacks proved it by capturing many Prussian soldiers. Thus encouraged, Fermor set out at 2 o'clock on the morning of August 27 to march past Frederick's left flank to Gross-Kamin; though the Russian artillery had lost nearly all their horses or had to give them up for the transport of the wounded. Prussian historical accounts, generally so extremely severe in their criticism of Fermor, seem unable to praise sufficiently his masterly execution of this daring flank march. But, in truth, another fact is far more remarkable, namely, that on a fine August day between four and nine in the forenoon, a Russian army could march past Frederick the Great without being attacked. The Russians had an open plain over which to move, as the French had at Rossbach, and they were so slow about it, that to cover a distance of five miles they took quite seven hours. The Prussian army, even two days after the battle of Zorndorf, was still, as it were, paralysed. Fermor ordered his heavy baggage-train from Gross-Kamin to Landsberg on the Warthe, whither he intended to continue his retreat. This time the King of Prussia sent a detachment to deal the enemy a blow such as he had himself received at Domstädtl in Moravia. "This is their richest magazine," the King wrote to Maurice of Anhalt; "they have supplies for months on the wagons. If I burn them, the army must retire head over heels, and I shall be certainly rid of it. To effect this I have laid a plan and I will do everything I can to carry it out; that will be better than a battle." The last part of this sentence must, of course, not be interpreted too literally. On the morning of Zorndorf the King could, if he had liked, have taken the Russian baggage without a battle. Now, the enterprise failed because the detached troops came upon Rumyantseff's corps, which Fermor, after the action at Zorndorf, had recalled from Schwedt and ordered to proceed, together with his heavy baggage, to Landsberg on the Warthe. Hither the Russian main army also directed its march on August 31 from Gross-Kamin.

The King of Prussia followed the retreating enemy, looking out for an opportunity to attack him; but Fermor exposed no weak spots, and, failing these, Frederick felt he was not strong enough for a conflict, just as already on the 27th he had evaded risking a renewal of the battle. Unmolested, the Russian main army and its heavy baggage-train effected their junction with Rumyantseff's division, which was unweakened by fighting, at Landsberg on the Warthe. Frederick, after a violent inward struggle, was forced to acknowledge himself unable to achieve anything decisive against the Russians, and resolved on a return to the southern theatre of war, where Daun's operations were beginning to become dangerous. The King's mood was one of extreme irritation; in spite of the enormous losses undergone by his infantry, he was far from being satisfied by their efforts at Zorndorf. He wrote to Prince Henry, who was covering Saxony against the army of the Empire and the Austrians, that he had better inculcate discipline into his battalions: "N.B. Teach them to respect the stick." The King's march, again accomplished with extraordinary rapidity, was directed to Dresden, for the capture of which Daun had wished to use the time of Frederick's absence. But, as the latter united with Prince Henry just at the right moment, the Austrian attack on the Saxon capital was averted.

At the same time, however, the King of Prussia learned that the Swedes had advanced from Prenzlau to Neu-Ruppin. Though, after Zorndorf, General Hamilton could hardly hope that Fermor would hold out to him a helping hand, he was not discouraged, but led his troops into the heart of the Mark and threatened the capital. Frederick had to detach immediately, from the body of troops which he had brought from Landsberg to Dresden, eight battalions and five squadrons for Berlin. "Our infantry regiments are becoming postillions and couriers," Frederick wrote to his brother. Before the Russian invasion of the Mark, the King had confronted his Russian and Swedish opponents with, in all, twenty battalions and thirty-five squadrons. Now, he was obliged to divide, between General Dohna against the Russians and General Wedell against the Swedes, twenty-nine battalions and forty squadrons. The King expected that at least Dohna would succeed in manœuvring Fermor back across the frontier of the Polish kingdom, which was quite close to Landsberg. But even this modest success was not achieved, Fermor remained the greater part of September stationed at Landsberg and reorganised his army with the help of Rumyantseff's fresh troops. From Poland came the Russian sinews of war, stores, and substitutes for a part of the artillery lost at Zorndorf. Fermor, now again capable of undertaking operations, determined to stay on in the dominions of the King of Prussia and marched into Eastern Pomerania, where he remained during the whole of October. Although he failed in capturing the strongly fortified port of Kolberg, the Russian troops disquieted the whole of Eastern Pomerania and the Neumark; nor was it till November that they evacuated the former and withdrew into their Polish and East Prussian winter-quarters. Meanwhile the Swedes devoured the King's resources in Prussian Pomerania, in the Uckermark, and partly even in the Neumark. During the whole of September, October, and November, Hamilton's troops had to be fed by the King's dominions before they retreated into Swedish Pomerania and took up their winter-quarters there.

A review of the results of the battle of Zorndorf leaves no doubt that Frederick would have acted more to his own advantage if on the fateful August 25 he had contented himself with carrying off the

CH. IX.

Russian heavy baggage, instead of aiming at the higher goal of crushing the hostile forces. But it would have been at variance with a great genius like Frederick's to act with that sort of moderation, even though Prince Henry of Prussia, after his fashion one of King Frederick's ablest generals, was wont to exhibit it. The extraordinary force of Frederick's character is not fully understood till it is realised what had during his operations against the Russians been his general conception of his situation. A few days before the battle of Zorndorf he had been of opinion that Laudon would extend his invasion through Brandenburg to Berlin. The destruction of the treasure and public buildings of Berlin would be so heavy a loss, that on the evening of the day of battle, Frederick had meditated marching on the next morning with a division of his army to Guben, thence to cover the capital against Laudon and Daun. For the King thought it possible that the whole main Austrian army might advance on Berlin. When he saw, on the morning after the battle, how completely disorganised the Prussian army was in all its divisions, he abandoned the march to Guben. Instead, he impressed upon the Margrave of Brandenburg-Schwedt, whom he had left behind with the Prussian main army in Lower Silesia, the necessity of opposing Daun's invasion of the Mark by taking up suitable defensive positions till he was himself able to hurry to the rescue. The following was, accordingly, the situation of the King of Prussia immediately before the battle of Zorndorf. Not only was the very nucleus of his power attacked by the Russians and Swedes, but he further believed that the Austrians were encircling him on all sides and endangering his possession of his own capital. At such a crisis, he ventured, in the rage of despair—"with the passion of a desperate gambler," it was said in Prince Henry's *entourage*—upon attacking the army of Fermor in its unassailable position at Zorndorf.

In reality, Daun had given up the idea of a march on Berlin and, as has been related, had turned against Dresden. The absence of the King lasted from August 1 till September 10; but, before Daun had undertaken any serious enterprise against Prince Henry, Frederick was back again and had united with his brother. Margrave Charles also moved towards Dresden with his main army. There were now 80,000 Prussians in the environs of that town under the personal command of the King. Opposite them were encamped 75,000 Austrians and 15,000 of the Imperial troops, so that Frederick and his opponents were about equal in strength. No wonder, then, that the King wrote to Prince Henry that it would be the salvation of the Prussians if Daun received peremptory orders to attempt some engagement. But Daun did just the contrary of what Frederick wished. He hid himself in the camp of Stolpen, east of Dresden, among woods, bog, and mountains, where the King dared not attack him. From September 5 till October 5, Daun persisted in holding out at Stolpen, while Frederick was consumed with impatience.   Meanwhile, Russians and Swedes had ravaged a great part of the Mark Brandenburg and Pomerania. Further, the Austrians, soon after Frederick's withdrawal from Olmütz, had penetrated into Upper Silesia, where they blockaded the fortresses of Neisse and Kosel, and during the whole of August and September were a burden on the country.   Moreover, their numbers were increased, by the division commanded by Quarter - Master - General Harsch, hitherto stationed in Bohemia, and other troops, amounting in all to about 30,000 men.   On October 5, Harsch laid siege to Neisse; on St Theresa's day (October 15) he hoped to begin the bombardment. After Neisse, Kosel was to be bombarded, the capture of which place would complete the Austrian reconquest of Upper Silesia.   " Were it not for the *point d'honneur*," wrote the King in profound depression to Prince Henry, "I should long ago have done what I often spoke to you of doing last year.   Now, you and I are bound to practise patience; meanwhile, life is passing, and, when all things are weighed and considered, what has it been but care, trouble, sorrow and tribulation? Was it worth the trouble to be born?"   In this mood the King of Prussia set out on the march to relieve Neisse.   The Prussians, who had started on September 26, found their way barred at Hochkirch on October 10 by Daun.   The position in which the Austrian Field-Marshal embarrassed Frederick was as impregnable as that of Stolpen had been.   The King determined to turn the Austrian right; but the manœuvre had to be postponed for four days, as a supply of bread was momentarily expected from the Dresden magazine.   Meanwhile, the Prussians encamped close to the enemy, without sufficient support for their right wing, in order to lighten their intended flanking march. The King's attention was called by his generals to the exposure; but he ignored the timely warnings.   Daun had pushed on a corps under the Prince of Baden-Durlach in the direction of Görlitz, whither the King intended to march after receiving his provisions.   Frederick hoped to be able to surprise this detachment, if he retained touch with the enemy's main army.   Instead of this, however, he was himself surprised.   On October 14, at 5 o'clock in the morning, the exposed right wing of the Prussians was attacked unawares by the Austrians, whose movements were concealed by a thick fog.   Frederick did not succeed in asserting the superior quality of his troops, because the tactical units of his army, roused out of sleep, and in disorder, had not time for any close formation enabling them to act together.   In spite of the efforts of the King, who exposed himself to the fire of the Austrian guns till a horse was wounded under him, there was on the Prussian side a general confused attempt at dispersion.   Maurice of Anhalt, in the vain endeavour to form a manageable order of battle, was severely wounded. James Keith, of old a combatant for the Pretender in Scotland, met his death as a Prussian Field-Marshal from an Austrian cannon-ball.   The youngest brother of the Queen of Prussia, Prince Francis of Brunswick, also fell.

The struggle surged hither and thither for five hours. Then, the fog cleared and the sun shone brightly on the field of battle, strewn by 15,000 dead and wounded. Frederick recognised that the Austrians, by advancing in accordance with a well thought-out plan which the various divisions of troops had combined to realise, had won an advantage which it was impossible to make good. He therefore ordered a retreat to the heights of Doberschütz, near Bautzen, four miles from the battle-field. It was accomplished with such calmness and precision that the Austrians praised in the liveliest terms a manœuvre of which they said that no army but the Prussian was tactically capable. The defeated side left the victors the greater part of their baggage, thirty flags and standards, and a hundred and two guns. A great many battalions were so shrunk in numbers that one might almost speak of annihilation. While the King drew upon eight battalions belonging to Prince Henry's army to repair in some measure his losses, he impressed upon the Prince not to send any Silesian battalions. Zorndorf and Hochkirch had somewhat paled the nimbus of Rossbach. It was to be feared that Silesian soldiers, knowing every stock and stone of their native province, might desert in too great quantities. Such was the character of European armies before the French Revolution.

The next evening, the King appeared to his reader, de Katt, depressed, not to say profoundly dispirited. "I can end the tragedy when I choose," he said in a low voice. Then he showed the reader the *Apology for Suicide* which he had composed in the autumn of the previous year, and the poison which he had long carried about with him. Daun wrote to Harsch, that he would now guarantee the King of Prussia's failing to relieve Neisse. The Austrian general intended to throw himself again and again in the way of the enemy, in an impregnable position on the long road from Bautzen to Neisse. But Frederick, undaunted by his defeat, marched secretly past Daun's right flank and got ahead of the astounded Austrian general in the direction of Görlitz.

Several Prussian historians dispute the fact that Frederick made a mistake in encamping at Hochkirch, where he was surprised. They maintain that he had no choice if he was to steal a march on Daun in reaching Neisse. The real facts of the case contradict this view, for after the battle of Hochkirch the King of Prussia encamped at Doberschütz, which lay somewhat further back, and was perfectly secure against surprise; and from this position he accomplished without much difficulty the feat of stealing a march upon the enemy. As a matter of fact, he had selected the perilous position of Hochkirch, not at all on account of Neisse, but because he wanted to be near the corps of the Prince of Baden-Durlach, in order to surprise and scatter it. The more unfavourable the course of the campaign proved, the more indomitable became the King's eagerness to achieve successes. This wild impulse sprang from the depths of the soul of this mighty warrior; at other times the source of his triumphs, it had at Hochkirch carried him into foolhardiness.

Daun was never foolhardy. After the Prussian army had reached Görlitz before him, he felt convinced that the race to Neisse could not possibly be brought to an end without Frederick sooner or later meeting the Austrians on ground not absolutely favourable to them. Daun explained to his generals assembled in a Council of War, that, should Frederick then seize the opportunity for a battle and defeat the Austrian army, the forces of the Empress would have no certain line of retreat, and a second edition of the battle of Leuthen (which God forbid!) would be scarcely avoidable. The result of these considerations on the Austrian side was the raising of the siege of Neisse. Soon afterwards both sides retired into winter-quarters. The anti-Prussian coalition could boast no positive success, but the campaign of 1758, like that of 1757, had effected a very significant reduction of the King of Prussia's resources, and his strength was being visibly exhausted. Instead of 150,000 men, as in the last two campaigns, Frederick was in 1759 only able to confront his enemies with 110,000. Contrariwise, the Austrians had recovered from the enormous losses of the year 1757. While in 1758 they could put only 85,000 men in the field, they opened operations in 1759 with 120,000. The King of Prussia was once more eager to find Daun ready for battle. But the latter again entrenched himself in impregnable places— at first at Münchengrätz in Bohemia, then at Marklissa in Upper Lusatia. He was waiting for the Russians.

The end of June arrived before the slowly-moving Russian forces had concentrated. The Empress Elizabeth had given her army a new Commander-in-chief in the person of General Soltikoff; against whom Frederick now determined to direct his first great blow. Dohna's army marched from Landsberg on the Warthe to Thorn in Polish West Prussia, in order to capture the magazines placed in this and other West Prussian towns, and forming the base of the Russian army. The King attached to the staff of Dohna, whom he regarded as but moderately gifted, his own adjutant, General von Wobersnow, with instructions that it was Dohna's duty to consider all Wobersnow's suggestions as if they came from the King himself. But Frederick had difficulty in finding men among his generals able to satisfy his exorbitant claims upon them. On June 29 the Russians completed their concentration at Posen, while the Prussians gave up the march to Thorn as impracticable, and retreated. For the second time there followed a Russian invasion of the Mark Brandenburg. On July 20, 40,000 Russians were at Züllichau, where 27,000 Prussians confronted them. The King was violently incensed by the proceedings of his generals. He abused Wobersnow, saying that he was a mediocre commander, who could not have led the army worse if he had been drunk; that he had committed every blunder conceivable in war, and that the story of his campaign deserved to be printed as a warning example for all the generals of posterity. He then transferred the chief command of the army at Züllichau to Lieutenant-General von Wedell, promoting him over the heads of four older Lieutenant-Generals, and impressing upon these officers that Wedell's position in the army at Züllichau was to be that of a "dictator in Roman times."

But Wedell, too, failed to fulfil the hopes set on him by the King of Prussia. On July 23 he attacked the 40,000 Russians with his 27,000 men near the village of Kay, and was completely beaten. One-fourth of the Prussian army lay dead on the field of battle; the implacable King, roused to fury by the disaster, scolded his brave soldiers as a set of rascals. At the head of a division, he quitted the camp at Schmottseifen where he had faced Daun entrenched at Marklissa, and had sought an opportunity of battle with passionate impatience. Prince Henry stayed behind at Schmottseifen as Commander-in-chief.

There was one distinct point of difference between the situation of 1759 and that of the previous year, when the King had also advanced against Daun in Lusatia with a corps of Dohna's army. Daun, who lay at Lauban, had once more sent Laudon ahead to try to get into touch with the Russians; but this time with 18,000 instead of 8000 men. At Priebus Hadik joined forces with Laudon at the head of a second corps of 17,000 men. Frederick himself described as "frightful and cruel" the marches which his troops had to make, to cut off the progress of the two Austrian corps to Frankfort on the Oder, whither Soltikoff had proceeded. For six nights the King never slept. As a matter of fact, Hadik's corps was pushed away from the Russians and obliged to move in the direction of Spremberg; but in this position, from a dangerous proximity, it threatened Berlin, which Hadik had entered in 1757. Above all, Laudon emerged unchallenged, and effected a junction with the Russians at Kunersdorf, which is situated on the Oder quite close to Frankfort. At that time Daun was between Rothenburg and Priebus, near to the south-eastern frontier of the Mark Brandenburg, and not very far from Schiedlow on the Oder, where Soltikoff had promised to cross the river and join hands with his Austrian ally. Such was the critical condition of things, when Frederick attacked the Russians at Kunersdorf on August 12. He had 43,000 men, the Russians and Austrians 53,000 regulars, and 15,000 Cossacks and Croatians. Although these irregular forces played only an insignificant part in the action, the numerical superiority of the Russians and Austrians was very considerable—otherwise than at Zorndorf. The King of Prussia was confronted by a general of the first rank, in the person of Laudon. Moreover, the Russian position was once more incomparable.

The King of Prussia's attempt to storm this position resulted in one of the most horrible massacres recorded in history. Of 43,000 Prussians 19,000 lay dead or wounded on the field, that is to say, not much less than half. But the hills, swamps, and ravines which Soltikoff and Laudon defended could not be forced by the Prussians. Finally, a cavalry charge undertaken at the right moment by Laudon routed the Prussian army, already tired to death after a fifteen hours' exposure to the scorching heat of the sun. Frederick's heroic example could not avert the catastrophe. "The King," wrote a Westphalian private after the battle to his people at home, "was always at the front crying, 'Boys, don't desert me'; and at last he took a flag from Prince Henry's regiment and said, 'Whoever is a brave soldier, let him follow me!'" Two horses were shot under Frederick. He would have met his death from a bullet, if it had not flattened and glanced off the gold snuff-box in his pocket. He was one of the last to leave the battle-field. With eyes fixed, and half-stunned, he exclaimed: "Cannot some damned bullet hit me?" Close behind him Cossacks galloped in pursuit. He believed that he was doomed; but the gallantry of his life-guardsmen just succeeded in rescuing him; and he took up his headquarters in the castle of Reitwein on the opposite bank of the Oder. Here he transferred his command to Lieutenant-General von Finck, "because I am attacked by serious illness," so runs the order. In his instructions to the new Commander-in-chief, Frederick says: "General von Finck's commission is a heavy one. The unfortunate army which I give over to him is no longer in a condition to defeat the Russians. Hadik will hasten on to Berlin, perhaps Laudon also. If General Finck overtakes them, he will have the Russians in his rear; if he stays on the Oder, Hadik will be upon him on this side of the river." The King proceeds to mention that he has nominated Prince Henry Generalissimo and that the army is to swear fealty to the young heir to the throne, Prince Frederick William; and then he concludes: "If there had been any resource remaining, I should have held out." What all this signified is explained in a letter of the same date to his Foreign Minister von Finkenstein, which runs: "It is a cruel blow, and I cannot survive it. The consequences of the affair are worse than the affair itself. I have no resources left, and, to speak the truth, I consider all is lost. I shall not outlive the ruin of my fatherland. Adieu for ever!" Thus it would seem that the King thought that the hour had come at last to commit the act which had been in his mind more or less for over two years; believing that Soltikoff and Daun would, at least approximately, turn the victory of Kunersdorf to account with the energy which he was himself accustomed to display in the waging of war. But the Russian and Austrian generals showed themselves incapable of any such resolute action; and, perceiving this not very long after his defeat, Frederick pulled himself together with his usual elasticity, and carried on the struggle.

Still, in his momentary condition of weakness he could not prevent

CH. IX.

Dresden from falling into the hands of the Austrians. This was a heavy loss, not only from a military but from a political point of view. For at that time England and Prussia were meditating diplomatic steps towards a general peace. Frederick had mastered his despair sufficiently to hope that he might claim Saxony when terms of peace were negotiated. His desire to become possessed of the electorate was so ardent, that, at a pinch, he would have given East Prussia for it to the Russians and his Rhenish possessions to the French. Hence, after reorganising his forces as best he could, Frederick with the utmost energy prosecuted operations against Daun, who was in any case to be compelled to evacuate Dresden and take up winter-quarters in Bohemia. But this rash method of conducting a campaign brought a further terrible misfortune upon the Prussians. Finck, who had been ordered to Daun's rear with 15,000 men, was cut off at Maxen, and his whole corps captured (November 21).

During the unlucky campaign of 1759, the King of Prussia's provinces and the electorate of Saxony had been obliged to support the Russians and Austrians. After the battle of Kunersdorf the Swedes, too, were again encamped in western Pomerania and the Uckermark, and the troops of the Empire temporarily in Saxony. Despite the great weakening of his resources, Frederick brought together for the campaign of 1760 about 100,000 men—that is, 50,000 fewer combatants than in 1757 and 1758, but still an astounding result of organisation, even in the opinion of his enemies. They had placed in the field 223,000 combatants as against his 100,000. Their first strategical object was Silesia, the province which had suffered least, so that from it the King drew his chief supplies of money and recruits.

The Silesian campaign of 1760 began with a severe reverse for the Prussian troops. On June 23 General Fouqué's corps of 11,000 men, which guarded the passes into Silesia near Landshut, was attacked by vastly superior numbers, and, after heroic resistance, entirely annihilated. On July 26, the important Silesian fortress of Glatz capitulated, after a siege by Laudon of only fifteen days. In the heart of Silesia, at Liegnitz, gathered 90,000 Austrians, while on the opposite bank of the Oder 50,000 Russians advanced as far as Breslau. Soltikoff, at Auras, ordered bridges to be thrown across the Oder, and a Russian corps of 20,000 men passed the river. Its commander, Chernuisheff, had orders to pin down Prince Henry, who covered Breslau; in the meantime the 90,000 Austrians were to attack the King of Prussia who, with 30,000 men, was stationed at Liegnitz. On August 15 this attack took place. Laudon's corps succeeded in surprising Frederick. But neither did the much-tried King's wonderful presence of mind forsake him, nor did the Prussian infantry fail to give proof of that mobility which had already triumphed so repeatedly on the battle-field. This time, Frederick's adversaries had not the advantage of a strong defensive

position, but attacked the Prussians on the march, as the French had
been attacked at Rossbach. The Austrians were beaten and lost 4000
prisoners and 83 cannon. After the many reverses sustained by the
Prussian army, the moral significance for the King of the victory at
Liegnitz could not be overestimated. Since Zorndorf he had often
criticised with bitter severity the deterioration of his infantry. It was
a fact that the ranks of the Prussian army were filled with young
inexperienced soldiers. They had been thinned by the loss, at Maxen, of
about eighteen battalions, and thirty-five squadrons. The deficiency of
officers had been even more imperfectly supplied than that of men. The
war had played havoc with the Prussian nobility to such a degree, that
boys of fifteen and even fourteen were taken from the schools to be
trained as cadets, and, much to the King's disgust, to serve as officers.
Frederick's free criticism of his troops, sometimes just, but much oftener
exaggerated and unfair, had become known in the enemy's camp ; and,
after a whole Prussian corps had surrendered their arms at Maxen, without
firing a shot, Europe thought that the beginning of the moral break-up
of Frederick's army was in sight. But the day of Liegnitz put an end to
all such misapprehensions. The troops of Frederick the Great remained,
first and last, superior in quality to the Austrians and Russians. The
privates of the Prussian army consisted of mercenaries, enlisted as
voluntary recruits or pressed, partly natives, partly foreigners, with the
addition of rude peasant serfs who had been levied by conscription ; and
these were kept together by the merciless application of the stick. But,
besides these, there was a third and nobler element among the Prussian
soldiery. After the battle of Liegnitz, Frederick spoke to a veteran of
the Anhalt regiment, and praised the behaviour of the troops. The
veteran replied : "What else could we do ? We are fighting for you,
for our religion, and our fatherland." Tears came into the King's
eyes, and afterwards, when he narrated the incident, he was again
overcome with emotion. In accordance with these ideals, which animated
a section of Frederick's soldiers, the army which, fifty years after the
Seven Years' War, lay ingloriously crushed at Napoleon's feet, was
reorganised, and, by blending modern ideas with Friderician traditions,
has since marched from victory to victory. To the battle of Liegnitz
was due a new feeling of personal trust between the King and his
officers, amongst whom had arisen a rather dangerous spirit of opposition, encouraged by Prince Henry. But from a material point of view
the victory did very little to improve Prussian affairs. The Austrians
and Russians remained in Silesia, and drained the resources of that
province, which the war had hitherto but slightly affected. A second
Russian corps and the Swedes ravaged Pomerania. The whole of Saxony
was occupied by Austrian and Imperial troops, together with the adjacent
old Prussian territory of Halle, a wealthy district, where large contributions were raised. A serious invasion of the Mark Brandenburg followed

in the autumn. The army of the Empire advanced as far as Treuen-brietzen, and the Swedes had reached the Uckermark. The Russian main army occupied the Neumark, 40,000 Russians and Austrians entering the undefended city of Berlin. Here a contribution of two million *thalers* was raised—a sum, the significance of which for Prussia at that time will be clear when it is realised that Frederick was drawing from England not more than four and a half million *thalers* (£670,000) in yearly subsidies, and that without this sum he could not have carried on his campaigns. Berlin was in the hands of the Austrians and Russians from October 9 to 13, when the advance of the King from Silesia set it free, though he was forced to allow the invaders of his capital to retreat unmolested.

Next, he was obliged to march into Saxony, where Daun had taken up a position on the Siptitzer hills near Torgau, from which the Austrians disputed his possession of the electorate. The Siptitzer hills were regarded as impregnable, and on November 3 Daun accepted a battle. He had 50,000 combatants, Frederick 44,000. The King of Prussia's plan of battle was the boldest that he had ever conceived. The Prussian army fought in two sections, which, separated by a wide interval, were out of touch with each other. The one half, personally commanded by the King, attacked Daun's front; the other, under General von Ziethen, assaulted his rear. During the whole combat the King fearlessly faced the enemy's fire. His pages and the officers of his suite were for the most part wounded, and three horses were shot under him. A shell struck him on the chest. He fell swooning, but soon recovered himself: "*Ce n'est rien,*" he said, and continued to hold the command.

The dislocation of Frederick's troops remained unpunished because the Austrians, according to their traditions, would not depart from the defensive. They would finally have been beaten; indeed, had they been attacked simultaneously in front and rear, they must have been annihilated, had but Ziethen brought as much energy to bear on the combat as did the King. The latter, however, had no generals at his command able to execute an independent commission with the highest degree of strategical effectiveness. The Austrians, feeling themselves somewhat hard pressed in their rear, maintained sufficient order to be able to retreat under cover of the darkness. Crossing the Elbe, to the right of their position, they evacuated the whole of Saxony, except Dresden. Owing to linear tactics (implying the fighting of infantry in close battle-array) nearly all the battles of the Seven Years' War were attended by great loss of life, and Torgau cost the Prussian army more than thirty-three and a third per cent. of their numbers. The grumbling of his troops had already reached the King's ears. Already after the battle of Kunersdorf he had written that he stood more in fear of his own soldiers than of the enemy; he now forbade his adjutants, under threats of stringent punishment, to make known the real figures of the Torgau losses. The Austrians had lost somewhat less than the Prussians, but among their losses were 7000 prisoners; 30 standards and 46 guns were also left behind by Daun in the enemy's hands. The profound moral depression which Torgau and Liegnitz had produced in the Austrian camp in some measure compensated Frederick for the severe material losses of the campaign. He still had money, though, no doubt, he resorted to means of filling his war chests which affected injuriously the well-being of his subjects. The coinage was more unscrupulously debased. For example, when the gold (in which form British subsidies were paid) came to Berlin, there was added to it so strong an alloy of copper that one million was converted into two—a depreciation of value like that effected under Septimius Severus at the beginning of the iron age of the Roman Empire.

But even such extreme and desperate measures failed any longer to sustain the King of Prussia; in the campaign of 1761 his powers deserted him. Laudon, who commanded an Austrian army in Silesia, accomplished a junction with the Russians at Liegnitz, the scene of his former defeat. Frederick, who was commanding in person in Silesia, and had tried in vain to prevent the juncture of Laudon with the Russians, could for the moment only think of acting on the defensive. He had 55,000 men, his opponent at least twice as many. On August 20 the King of Prussia occupied the entrenched position of Bunzelwitz. Laudon and Field-Marshal Buturlin, who had succeeded Soltikoff in command of the Russian army, dared not attack the trenches of Bunzelwitz, but on October 16 Laudon conquered Schweidnitz in addition to Glatz, which had been in Austrian hands since the last campaign. This new acquisition made it possible for the Austrians to take up their winter-quarters in Silesia. In Saxony also the King's supplies for the most part came to a stop. In November Field-Marshal Daun and the Imperial army had dislodged Prince Henry from the extensive territory west of Freiberg on the Mulde. Freiberg, Chemnitz, Zeitz, Naumburg on the Saale, and many other productive parts of the electorate now supplied the Austrians, instead of, as hitherto, the Prussians, with recruits, provisions and money.

While the Austrians were able to take up their winter-quarters for the first time in Silesia and western Saxony, the Russians were able to do the same in Pomerania. On December 16 Kolberg capitulated to a Russian corps which had been detached for Pomerania. Thus the Russians had now, in the heart of Frederick's monarchy, a harbour which kept their fleet in communication with Russia and with their great magazine at Pillau, where were hoarded the supplies which flowed in from the resources of East Prussia to strengthen the Russian sinews of war. Even before Kolberg had fallen, the King of Prussia wrote to d'Argens: "Every bundle of straw, every transport of recruits, every consignment of money, all that reaches me, is, or becomes a favour on the part of my enemies, or a proof of their negligence, for they could, as a matter of fact, take everything. Here in Silesia, every fortress stands at the disposal of the enemy. Stettin, Cüstrin, and Berlin itself are open to the Russians to deal with at their pleasure. In Saxony, Daun's first move, so to speak, throws my brother back over the Elbe....If fortune continues to treat me so mercilessly I shall undoubtedly succumb. Only she can deliver me from my present situation!"

Frederick the Great's most trustworthy political friend, William Pitt, had, six months before this, begun to doubt the King of Prussia's ability to hold out, and advised him, as Voltaire and Prince Henry had formerly done, to purchase peace by cession of territory. Pitt now quitted the British Cabinet. Bute's Ministry, disapproving the eagerness for war which had characterised Pitt's policy, based its own programme on the restoration of universal peace; and Bute was of opinion that it was the King of Prussia's duty to contribute to the ending of the European war by some sacrifice of territory to his enemies. The King was to be forced to do this by the withdrawal of his British subsidies. Frederick believed that, in the present chaos of his financial affairs, he would be absolutely unable to dispense with English money. That Maria Theresa was also in desperate financial straits, and obliged to undertake a considerable reduction of her army in the middle of the war, made no essential difference, from Frederick's point of view, in his own hopeless position. All Europe now called upon him to renounce the idea that he could preserve the integrity of the Prussian State. He had not the means for sustaining himself in the coming campaign. Probably, if he had been ready to cede even the county of Glatz, he would have been granted a peace. But he determined that not a village under his rule should be lost to the State; rather would he take his own life. If, he wrote to d'Argens, he could not use Caesar's *Commentaries* as his guide, he intended to follow Cato.

Among Frederick's calculations in August, 1756, when he had regarded the general situation as propitious to his venturing on an invasion of Saxony, had been the surmise that the days of the Empress Elizabeth were numbered. But the Tsarina lived five years and a half longer than Frederick, and with him every European diplomatist, had thought probable. Not till January 5, 1762 (N.S.), did Peter the Great's daughter die, of a haemorrhage, in the fifty-third year of her age. This event brought about an immediate and complete revulsion in the political state of the world. On May 5, 1762, Elizabeth's nephew and successor, Peter III, who was not of quite sound intellect, concluded a peace with the King of Prussia, with whom his aunt had, on public grounds, been irreconcilably at war. East Prussia and eastern Pomerania were evacuated by the Russians, so that the resources of those districts could be employed for the immediately imminent campaign against the Austrians. Sweden, following Russia's example, also made peace with the King of Prussia. The agreement was signed on May 22. The great diplomatic and military change, which had come so unexpectedly, was accomplished with most extraordinary speed. On June 16 the new Tsar entered into an offensive alliance with Frederick against Austria, and ordered that 20,000 Russians should reinforce the Prussian army in Silesia. By June 30 the Russian reinforcement under General Chernuisheff had already crossed the Oder, and formed a junction with the forces of Frederick the Great at Auras. Hereupon, Daun was beaten at Burkersdorf on July 21, and driven back from Schweidnitz, which he was covering. At Burkersdorf Frederick was once more able to demonstrate that, although deprived of English subsidies, he was able to put into the field an army capable of manœuvring in the best style. Daun made yet one more attempt to save the besieged fortress of Schweidnitz. His advance led to the combat of Reichenbach on August 16. The Austrian outflanking movement was frustrated by the vigilance of Frederick, who, mounted on his roan Caesar, came up at a quick gallop at the head of a regiment of Brown Hussars, to take part in the fight.

Schweidnitz capitulated on October 9. On the 29th of the same month, Prince Henry, who was commanding on the subsidiary theatre of war in Saxony, at Freiberg defeated with an army of 24,000 men an equal number of Austrians, supported by 15,000 troops of the army of the Empire. The battle of Freiberg is the only great action of the Seven Years' War in which the Prussian troops were victorious when not under the personal command of Frederick. Unsatisfactory as were the relations between the two brothers, Frederick never acted with more royal wisdom than when he frankly expressed to himself and others his sense of Prince Henry's great services to the State. " He is the single Prussian general," said the King, " who has committed no blunder."

Meanwhile, a rupture had taken place in the Prussian alliance with Russia, caused by the assassination of Peter III. But, though the new Russian sovereign, Catharine II, recalled the reinforcements under Chernuisheff, she did not reenter the coalition against the King of Prussia. The Austrians, without the aid of the Russians, and with only the Imperial troops to help them, could not crush the Prussian army. To Maria Theresa's distress, this had been evident enough at Freiberg, where the Prussians had lost only 1045 men in all, whereas the Austrians had lost 3385 in prisoners alone, not counting those of the Imperial troops that had been made prisoners. The French also saw clearly that, after the withdrawal of Russia from the coalition, there was no hope of regaining Silesia for the Austrians, and so securing the Netherlands for themselves. On November 3 the French diplomatists signed at Fontainebleau the preliminaries of a peace with England, which imposed on France enormous cessions in North America and India, without giving her any compensation in Europe. Prussia and France had fought against each other at Rossbach, although war had never been formally declared between them. Thus, no peace was signed now between Louis XV and Frederick, though hostilities ceased *de facto*. The French evacuated the Rhenish possessions of the King of Prussia, which they had occupied—Cleves, Gelders, and Mörs.

On February 15, 1763, Austria and Saxony likewise concluded a peace with Prussia at Hubertusburg, a castle used as a shooting-lodge by the Elector of Saxony. King Frederick, to the last, clung with passionate longing to the idea of acquiring Saxony. Even when negotiating terms of peace with Russia, he was willing to give up East Prussia to the Tsar, Peter III, in exchange for the transference of the electorate of Saxony to the House of Brandenburg. But, in view of the issue of the War, there could be no question of any such transaction. The King was obliged to be content with the return of Glatz by the Austrians, who had held it for two years and a half. The basis on which peace was concluded was the *status quo ante bellum*.

Frederick, though only fifty-one years of age, returned to his capital an old man; from that time forward the Berliners dubbed him "Old Fritz." There was not much humour for hero-worship among those with whom Frederick came in personal contact; but all Europe, friend and foe alike, were at one in the conviction that a greater Prince had never sat on a throne. For all that, the King had certainly failed in achieving the political object of the war. Prussia remained small, uncultured, and broken up. The world found it hard to believe that so puny a "Great Power" could have any future before it.

CHAPTER X.

RUSSIA UNDER ANNE AND ELIZABETH.

THE government of Anne (whose accession has been described in a previous volume), prudent, beneficial, and even glorious, as it proved to be, was undoubtedly severe, and became at last universally unpopular. The causes of this unpopularity are to be sought in the character of the Empress and the peculiar circumstances under which she ascended the throne. Anna Ivanovna was in her seven and thirtieth year when, in 1730, she came to Russia. Her natural parts, if not brilliant, were at least sound; but a worse than indifferent education, and a life-long series of petty vexations and humiliations had dwarfed her intelligence and soured her disposition. Her past had not been happy, and she was very uneasy about the future. Her earliest experience of the Russian nobility had been anything but agreeable. They had showed a dangerous disposition to limit, or, at any rate, to define her prerogatives. It was only the energetic intervention of the Guards that had saved the monarchy. Suspicious and resentful, Anne felt that she could never trust the Russian gentry with power. She felt that she must surround her throne with persons entirely devoted to her interests, and these persons, from the nature of the case, could only be foreigners—Germans, Livonians, Courlanders. The chief of these was the favourite Ernst Johann Bühren, or Biren, the grandson of a groom who had risen in the service of Duke Jakob III of Courland. Biren had supplanted Count Peter Bestuzheff in the good graces of Anne while she was still only Duchess of Courland. Handsome and insinuating, with sense enough to conceal his ignorance and roughness beneath a bluff *bonhomie*, his influence over his mistress was paramount and permanent. On the accession of the new Empress, honours and riches were heaped upon him. At her coronation (May 19, 1730) he was made Grand Chamberlain and a Count of the Empire. During the latter years of the reign, Biren's power and riches increased enormously. His apartments in the palace adjoined those of the Empress; his liveries, furniture, and equipages were scarcely inferior to her own. Half the bribes intended for the Russian Court passed into his coffers. He had estates in Livonia,

Courland, Siberia, and the Ukraine. A special department of State looked after his brood mares and stallions. His riding-school was one of the sights of the Russian capital. The magnificence of his plate astonished the French ambassador, and the diamonds of his Duchess (a Fräulein von Treiden) were the envy of princes. The climax of this wondrous elevation was reached when, in the course of 1737, the Estates of Courland, under considerable pressure, elected Ernst Johann their reigning Duke. Henceforth his Most Serene Highness received all the honours due to sovereigns and, together with his consort, took his seat at the imperial table.

Another Livonian, Carl Gustaf Löwenwolde, was created a Count and made Grand Marshal of her Majesty's household; while his brother, Reinhold, a few months later, was (September 30) nominated Colonel of the newly raised regiment of foot-guards, consisting of 2000 gentlemen, mostly Livonians, henceforth known as the Ismailovski regiment, from Ismailovo, the Empress' favourite summer residence near Moscow. The all-important post of Commander-in-chief was (in 1732) bestowed upon yet another foreigner, the great engineer and contractor of the famous Ladoga canal, Burkhard Christoph von Münnich, who had entered the service of Peter the Great in 1721 and became, in rapid succession, War Minister, Field-Marshal, a Count, and Governor of St Petersburg. Foreign affairs remained in the capable hands of a fifth German, Count Osterman, whom everyone now regarded as indispensable.

Thus the principle of Anne's government was a reversal of the patriotic golden rule of Peter the Great: natives first, aliens afterwards. For the first time in her history, Russia was now dominated by foreigners. It must be admitted that, to some extent at least, the Russians themselves were to blame for this unnatural state of things. No sooner had the controlling hand of Peter been withdrawn than his pupils began to quarrel among themselves, and their mutual jealousies and hatreds had ended in the extermination of the Russian party. Menshikoff had ruined Tolstoi, the Dolgorukis and the Galitsins had ruined Menshikoff, Yaguzhinski had destroyed the Dolgorukis and the Galitsins, and now Yaguzhinski himself, the sole survivor of the little band of capable native statesmen whom Peter the Great had left behind him, was honourably exiled by being accredited as Russian ambassador to Berlin, to prevent him from interfering with Osterman. The cruel persecution of the Dolgorukis and the Galitsins in 1732, and again in 1738–9, carried on chiefly to allay Biren's craven fears of purely imaginary conspiracies, exasperated the Russian gentry still more against the German tyranny; but it is only just to add that the unpopularity of Anne's rule was due quite as much to its rigorous enforcement of order and discipline as to its cruel unfairness to the great Boyar families. The policy of the two preceding reigns had been purposely and consistently easy-going; and, although such laxity had been injurious to the State in many ways, it had made Catharine I and Peter II extremely popular.   Under Anne things were very different. The reins of government that had hung so slackly before were now drawn tight, and the nation winced beneath the change.   The overdue contributions from the small proprietors and peasantry were exacted to the last *copeck*; the soldiery were again compelled to labour in many arduous public works; both the army and the navy were thoroughly over-hauled and placed once more on an effective war footing; every symptom of insubordination was sternly suppressed ; everything like carelessness was severely punished.   It was an additional grievance that the Court had moved to St Petersburg, where the Russian magnates, far away from their estates, found life excessively costly and inconvenient.

Anne, it must also be added, for all her vindictiveness towards individuals, seems really to have endeavoured to do her duty towards her subjects in the mass.   She was, as a rule at any rate, prudent, careful, and conscientious.   She had a natural turn for business; loved order and method ; took some pains to get at the truth of matters ; and was always ready to consult people more experienced in affairs than herself, notably Osterman and Münnich, both of them men of extraordinary talent, who—even the patriots could not deny this— devoted all their energy to promote the honour and glory of their adopted country.   At the very beginning of the reign, shortly after the restoration of the Administrative Senate, Osterman persuaded Anne to establish an inner Council, or Cabinet, of three persons only (the Grand Chancellor, Count Golovkin, Prince Alexis Cherkaski, both of them nonentities, and Osterman himself), which was presided over by the Empress and acted as the sole intermediary between her Majesty and all the Departments of State.   Established ostensibly for the prompter despatch of business, it enabled Osterman, at the same time, to shake off troublesome rivals, and certainly gave him a free hand in his own special Department of Foreign Affairs, which he thoroughly understood.

The pivot of Osterman's political "system" was the Austrian alliance, of which he was the original promoter and the most devoted champion. France, on the other hand, he regarded with ineradicable suspicion.   In 1732 he persuaded the Cabinet to reject the offer of an alliance made by Louis XV, through Magnan, his *chargé d'affaires* at St Petersburg, on con-dition that Russia supported the candidature of the French King's father-in-law, Stanislaus Leszczynski, for the Polish throne on the next vacancy. It would be far better, Osterman urged on this occasion, to bring about a league between the three Black Eagles to protect the White Eagle.   When, after the death of Augustus II, Stanislaus was actually elected King of Poland, Osterman, with the aid of Austria, drove him out and procured the election of Augustus III.   He also accelerated the pace of the negotiations which ultimately concluded the War of the Polish Succession, by despatching Peter Lacy at the head of 20,000 men to unite with the Imperial forces on the banks of the Neckar—the first appearance of

CH. X.

a Muscovite army in central Europe. The French Court endeavoured to counter this blow by promoting a rupture between Russia and the Porte. There were many grounds for a quarrel between the two Powers— such as the perennial dispute about the ownership of the Kabardine district and the territories of the Kuban Tartars; the repeated violation of undisputed Russian territory by Tartar hordes; and, finally, the Polish question, in which Turkey was deeply interested. The French ambassador at the Porte, Marquis de Villeneuve, used every effort to induce the Sultan to declare war against the Russian Empress during the War of the Polish Succession. Had the Porte been able to attack Russia in 1733, that Power would have been placed in a very critical position. Fortunately, the effects of Villeneuve's intrigues were balanced by the crushing defeats inflicted upon the Turks at this very time by Kuli Khan in the interminable Persian War. Till the Persian difficulty had been disposed of, the Turk was inclined to leave Russia alone; but, in the meantime, the Court of St Petersburg, now triumphant in Poland, was tempted to reopen the Eastern question on its own account. Ivan Neplyneff, the exceedingly well-informed Russian ambassador at the Porte, began to urge his Government "to fall upon these barbarians" while they were still suffering from the effects of their reverses, and represented the whole Ottoman empire as tottering to its fall. Towards the end of 1735 the arguments of Neplyneff prevailed. Osterman counselled immediate war, and, after the cooperation of Austria had been secured, the Empress was won over to his opinion. A definitive treaty with Kuli Khan, in the vain hope of whose active assistance the Russian troops evacuated Peter the Great's Persian conquests, Derbend, Baku, and Svyesti Krest, was the first step. Circumstances were favourable, and everything promised success. The treasury was full, the army in an excellent condition, no interference was to be anticipated from any foreign Power. Accordingly, a formal declaration of war, drawn up by the Russian Vice-Chancellor, was despatched to the Grand Vizier; and, on July 23, 1735, Münnich received orders to proceed at once from the Vistula to the Don.

The Turkish War of 1736–9 marks the beginning of that systematic struggle on the part of Russia to recover her natural and legitimate southern boundaries, which was to last throughout the eighteenth century, finally succeeding after the expenditure of millions of lives and an incalculable quantity of treasure. The possession of the shores of the Euxine and the circumjacent tracts was as necessary to the complete and normal development of the Russian Empire as was the possession of the recently acquired shores of the Baltic. Again, these regions, infested as they were by the innumerable predatory tribes dependent on the Porte, were a standing danger to the Russian Government. Moreover, even as late as the middle of the eighteenth century, Turkey had the entire control of the five great rivers—the Dniester, the

Bug, the Dnieper, the Don, and the Kuban—that drain southern Russia
and, consequently, could control, and even suspend at will, no inconsiderable portion of her neighbour's commerce.   The most powerful vassal of
the Sultan in these parts was the Khan of the Crimea, who, from his
capital at Bagchaserai, ruled over all the scattered Tartar hordes from
the Dnieper to the Don.   The Crimea at this time was very rich.   The
Steppes poured the inexhaustible wealth of their flocks and herds into
it, and the trade between the peninsula and Turkey was enormous.
Kosloff, the chief port on its western side, exported 200,000 head of cattle
and an incalculable quantity of grain to Stambul every year, while the
still more prosperous Kaffa on the east coast was, perhaps, the largest
slave-mart in the world.   Hitherto the Crimea had been generally
regarded as impregnable.   On the land side the lines of Perekop, a
deep trench, five-and-twenty fathoms broad, defended by an earthen
wall eight fathoms high, and nearly five English miles long, protected
the narrow isthmus which united the peninsula to the mainland, while
the fortress of Azoff, at the head of the sea of the same name, commanded the Delta of the Don, and was thought a sufficient defence
against any attack from the north-east.   In order to keep out the
Tartars from Central Russia, and, at the same time, to form a base for
future operations against them, Peter the Great had conceived the
gigantic project of connecting the rivers Dnieper and Donetz by a chain
of fortifications a hundred leagues in length, to which he proposed to
give the name of the lines of the Ukraine.   The work began in 1731,
six years after the Emperor's death, and, completed in 1738, only
partially fulfilled its double purpose.   The ground covered was too
extensive to be adequately guarded.   The forts were placed so far apart
that the Tartars were able to pass and repass the lines continually,
despite all the efforts of the Russians.   Nevertheless, this system of
fortification was to prove an invaluable *point d'appui* for armies operating
against the Turks; and here, in the early autumn of 1735, Marshal
Münnich arrived for the purpose of collecting his forces.

The plan of campaign, as finally arranged by Münnich with his
colleague and fellow Marshal Peter Lacy, was as follows.   The enemy was
to be attacked from all sides simultaneously, Münnich invading the Crimea
while Lacy besieged Azoff.   So soon as Münnich had stormed the lines
of Perekop, he was to detach 12,000 against the fortress of Kinburn on
Dnieper to prevent the Budjak Tartars from crossing that river by way
of Ochakoff, whilst Lacy, after capturing Azoff, was to hasten to the
support of Münnich's army.   On April 20, 1736, Münnich began his
march across the steppes to Perekop.   His army, including the Cossacks,
numbered 57,000 men.   For 330 miles his way lay through a wilderness.   The first brush with the Tartars, at Chernaya Dolina, was so easily
repulsed that for the rest of the campaign these nomads were treated as a
negligible quantity.   So long as the army encountered them in square

formation, with the field artillery at the corners and in the centre, and the Cossacks inside guarding the baggage with their long lances, the hordes were found to be comparatively harmless. The Russian progress was very slow, however, owing to the enormous amount of its impedimenta. There was not a single town in the whole region; so that every necessary, even to firewood and water, had to be provided beforehand. Incredible as it may sound, we are assured by a reliable eye-witness that Münnich never entered upon a campaign without dragging at least 80,000 wagons after him.

On May 15, Münnich arrived at the lines of Perekop. On the evening of May 19 its central fortress, Or-Kapi, feebly defended by Janizaries and other Turkish regulars, was captured by assault, and the wealthy town of Perekop behind it was abandoned to pillage. From Perekop the Russians, who now began to suffer severely from dysentery and other diseases, advanced upon Kosloff, which was abandoned by the enemy on their approach (June 5). On the 17th the Crimean capital, Bagchaserai, was captured by the Cossacks, after a sharp fight which cost them 300 men. Münnich's further progress was arrested by a dangerous mutiny in his own army, which compelled him to return first to Perekop and thence to the lines of the Ukraine. Lacy, meanwhile, had been equally successful before Azoff, though there he had encountered a far stouter resistance than his brother Marshal had met with anywhere in the Crimea. The garrison consisted of picked men; and the Seraskier inflicted so much damage upon the besiegers that, after a seven weeks' siege, they allowed him and his garrison to march out with all the honours of war (June 30). Then, on hearing that Münnich had already quitted the Crimea for the Ukraine, Lacy followed his example.

The campaign of 1736 had been very costly to the Russians. Münnich alone had lost no fewer than 30,000 men out of a total of 57,000, and of these not more than 2000 had fallen in action. At Court, people naturally began to ask what was the use of a campaign in which half the army had been thrown away for next to nothing. Nevertheless, dissatisfied as she was with Münnich, the Empress could not afford to lose him; and, glad as the Russian Ministers would have been to see an honourable end put to the war (especially in view of the consistent ill-success of their Austrian ally on the Danube), they were, to quote the English envoy at St Petersburg, Claudius Rondeau, "ashamed to own it after all the great things they had proposed to do." Their hopes, too, were revived by the assurances of the new Russian resident at Stambul, Vishnyakoff, that everything in Turkey was in the utmost confusion, and that the slightest disaster would bring the crumbling edifice to the ground.

At the end of April, 1737, Münnich took the field for the second time. His army now consisted of 70,000 men, and he was supported by two officers of great ability, General James Francis Keith, who had entered the Russian service as a Major-General in 1728, and Alexander Rumyantseff. Münnich's objective was Ochakoff, the ancient Axiake, situated at the confluence of the Dnieper and Bug. It was by far the most considerable place in these parts, and was defended by 20,000 of the best troops in Turkey under the leadership of the valiant Seraskier Tiagya. On June 29, the Russians crossed the Bug, and, after forming into three huge squares, followed the course of the river till they reached the fortress (July 10). The failure of the field artillery to arrive at the set time at first embarrassed Münnich seriously; but the gallant conduct of Keith (whom the grateful Empress raised to the rank of Lieutenant-General besides sending him a present of 10,000 *roubles*), together with an impetuous dash of the Cossacks at the very moment when an explosion of the largest powder magazine in the fortress had entombed 6000 of the defenders, brought about the unexpected capture of the stronghold. The carnage, however, was terrible. Seventeen thousand Turks perished on the walls or in the ditches, while in the final assault the Russians lost 3000, the proportion of officers killed being enormous. The remainder of the campaign was comparatively uneventful. Towards the end of August Münnich brought back 46,000 men to the lines of the Ukraine. In the late autumn the Turks made a determined effort to recapture Ochakoff, but were repulsed from its walls with the loss of 20,000 killed and wounded.

A Peace Congress, which assembled (1737–8) at the little frontier town of Nemiroff, having proved abortive, owing, chiefly, to the exorbitance of the Russian demands, the war had to be resumed. The campaign of 1738 was entirely barren. Münnich had intended to invade the Danubian Principalities; but an outbreak of plague paralysed his operations. Indeed, in this campaign, he lost more men, horses and bullocks than in any other. Lacy was, from similar causes, equally unfortunate in the Crimea.

In the spring of 1738 the allies, weary of the war, accepted the mediation of France. But the Turks, elated by their recent victories in Hungary, and relieved from all pressure from the east (Kuli Khan, who in 1736 had ascended the Persian throne under the name of Nadir Shah, having, in the meantime, turned his arms against the Great Moghul), refused acceptance of the very moderate terms now offered by the Empress Anne, who would have been content with Azoff and its district. It was clear, therefore, to the Russian Cabinet that another campaign must be fought. It was resolved to cooperate, this time, energetically with the Austrians by invading Moldavia and proceeding to invest the fortress of Chocim on Dniester. At the end of May, 1739, Münnich quitted the Ukraine with an army 65,000 strong. On August 27, he defeated the Turks at the relatively bloodless battle of Stavuchanak, the Russians losing only 70 men during an action which lasted twelve hours, while the Turks left no more than 1000 dead on the field. The next day, Münnich advanced with all his siege artillery against Chocim, which surrendered unconditionally at the first summons, the tidings of Stavuchanak having created a panic in the garrison. On September 9 and 10 Münnich crossed the Pruth. On the 19th he entered Jassy in triumph, and reported that the principality of Moldavia had "solemnly submitted to the Empress of all Russia." The same evening he received from Prince Lobkowitz, the Austrian Commander-in-chief, "the miserable and crushing" notification of the Peace of Belgrade, whereby Austria sacrificed all the fruits of the Peace of Passarowitz. Disgusted as the Russian Ministers were with the conduct of their ally, they knew it was impossible to continue the struggle single-handed. Münnich was therefore recalled, and peace negotiations with the Porte were opened simultaneously at Paris and Stambul under the mediation of France. Finally, by the Treaty of Constantinople, 1739, Russia was forced to sacrifice all her conquests except Azoff and its district, while Azoff itself had to be dismantled. On this occasion the Porte was induced to change the old title "Muscovy" into "Russia," but refused to concede the imperial title to the Russian Empress.

Nevertheless, despite its seemingly meagre results, much more had been gained by this five years' war than was, at first sight, apparent. Münnich had, at least, dissipated the illusion of Ottoman invincibility. The Tartar hordes might still, for a time, continue to be a plague, but they had ceased for ever to be a terror to Russia. Again, Russia's signal and unexpected successes on the steppe had immensely increased her prestige in Europe. The progress of the Russian arms had been followed with intense interest both at London and Paris. Horace Walpole, in acknowledging the receipt of Münnich's map of the Crimea from Rondeau in 1736, remarked that the eyes of all the world were fixed upon the lines of Perekop. A year later, Rondeau himself observed of Russia, with some apprehension, that "this Court begins to have a great deal to say in the affairs of Europe." Cardinal Fleury was even more disturbed. "Russia in respect to the equilibrium of the north," he wrote, in his secret instructions to the Marquis de La Chétardie, the new French ambassador at St Petersburg, "has mounted to too high a degree of power and its union with the House of Austria is extremely dangerous." Indeed, after the Peace of Belgrade, the Russian alliance alone gave to Austria so much as the semblance of independence. The obvious way to render this alliance unserviceable to the Emperor was to involve Russia in hostilities with some other Power. Sweden which, even now, was, chiefly from her geographical position, of more account in the European concert than either Prussia or Holland, was regarded by the Court of Versailles as the instrument most useful for its purposes, especially after the rise at Stockholm, about this time, of the warlike Hat party, described below. Instigated by France, whose ample subsidies, paid three years in advance, replenished their empty coffers, the Hats in 1738 indulged in a series of warlike demonstrations, designed to provoke Russia to a rupture. A fleet was equipped; troops were massed in Finland; and Baron Malcolm Sinclaire, a member of the Secret Committee of the Swedish Diet, undertook to deliver despatches to the Turkish commandant at Chocim and secretly investigate the condition of the Russian army as he passed through Poland. When, at the suggestion of Michael Bestuzheff, the Russian Minister at Stockholm, Sinclaire was "suppressed"—in other words intercepted, robbed and murdered on his return from Chocim—war between Russia and Sweden seemed inevitable; but the bellicose humour of the Hats diminished sensibly after Osterman had made peace with the Porte.

The Empress Anne had been more perturbed than her Ministers by the Swedish complication, as Peterhof, where she resided during the summer of 1740, was within easy reach of a Swedish fleet. But all her alarms were forgotten when, in August of the same year, she held in her arms at the font the eagerly expected heir to the throne. This little Prince was the first-born of the Princess of Mecklenburg-Schwerin, the Empress' niece, whom on the death of the girl's mother (her own favourite sister Catharine Ivanovna) she had adopted. From the first, Anne had determined that this young Princess (who, in 1733, was received into the Greek Church, changing her German name of Elizabeth Catharine Christina to that of Anna Leopoldovna) should be the mother of the future Tsar; and in July, 1739, Anna Leopoldovna was married to the youthful Prince Antony Ulric of Brunswick-Wolfenbüttel, who was brought to Russia for that express purpose and educated there at the Empress' cost. Only six weeks after the birth of the child the Empress (October 16), while at table, had a fit of apoplexy and was removed insensible to her own room. On her death-bed, at Biren's urgent request, though greatly against her own better judgment, she appointed him Regent during the minority of her great-nephew, who was proclaimed immediately after her death as Ivan VI.

Anne died on October 17, 1740. Three weeks later the ex-Regent was on his way to Siberia in consequence of a smart little *coup d'état* organised by Marshal Münnich, who thereupon proclaimed the mother of the baby Emperor Regent, while he assumed all real power with the title of "Premier-Minister." By the ukase of February 8, 1741, Osterman, who had been ousted by Münnich, was reinstated in the direction of foreign affairs by the Regent, who had begun to dread the restlessness of the Marshal. Münnich, in great dudgeon, and believing himself to be indispensable, hereupon sent in his resignation (March 14), which, to his chagrin, was accepted on the same afternoon. "Count Osterman," wrote La Chétardie to his Court shortly afterwards, "has never been so great or so powerful as he is now. It is not too much to say that he is Tsar of all Russia."

The new Government had scarce been constituted, when it was confronted by a political event of the first importance, the outbreak of the War, or rather Wars, of the Austrian Succession. The necessity, from the French point of view, of fettering Russia, Maria Theresa's one ally, now became urgent. Again, the French influence was exerted to the uttermost in Sweden, and this time successfully. At the beginning of August, 1741, Sweden declared war against Russia, and invaded Finland. To embarrass the Russian Government still further, a domestic revolution in Russia itself was simultaneously planned by La Chétardie with the object of placing the Tsesarevna Elizabeth on the throne. The immediate object of this manœuvre was to get rid of Osterman, the one statesman in Europe who had guaranteed the Pragmatic Sanction with the deliberate intention of defending it. The sudden irruption of the young King of Prussia into Silesia, the defection of France, and the treachery of Saxony, had taken him by surprise. Old as he was in statecraft, he had not calculated upon such a cynical disregard of the most solemn treaties. He stigmatised the invasion of Silesia as "an ugly business"; and, when he was informed officially of the partition treaty whereby the Elector of Saxony was to receive Upper Silesia, Lower Austria, and Moravia, with the title of King of Moravia, he sarcastically enquired whether this was the way in which Saxony meant to manifest the devotion she had always professed for the House of Austria. He shrewdly suspected that the Moravian scheme must, inevitably, bring along with it a surrender by the Elector of Saxony of the Polish Crown to Stanislaus Leszczynski, the French King's father-in-law, in which case the interests of Russia would be directly menaced. He sent a strong note of remonstrance to the King of Prussia, and assured the Courts of the Hague and St James' of his readiness to concur in any just measures for preserving the integrity of the Austrian dominions. For the present, however, he was prevented from sending any assistance to the hard-pressed Queen of Hungary by the Swedish War with which the French Government had saddled him. Nevertheless, the Swedish declaration had found him not unprepared. More than 100,000 of the best Russian troops were already under arms in Finland, and Marshal Lacy's victory at Vilmanstrand, at the end of August, relieved the old statesman of all fears from without. The French ambassador, profoundly depressed by this unexpected triumph of the Russian arms, was even disposed to abandon, or at least postpone, the second part of his scheme, a *coup d'état* in favour of Elizabeth Petrovna. "An outbreak, the success of which can never be morally certain, especially now that the Swedes are not in a position to lend a hand would, prudently considered, be very difficult to bring about, unless it could be substantially backed up"—such was his official report on December 6, 1741. In the preceding night Elizabeth, without any help from without, had overthrown the existing Government in a couple of hours. As a matter of fact, beyond lending Elizabeth 2000 ducats instead of the 15,000 demanded by her, La Chétardie took no part in the actual *coup d'état*.

Elizabeth Petrovna was born on December 18, 1709, on the day of her father's triumphal entry into his capital after the victory of Poltawa. From her earliest years the child delighted everyone by her extraordinary beauty and vivacity. She was still one of the handsomest women in Europe; and even six years later Lord Hyndford described her as " worthy of the admiration of all the world." Her natural parts were excellent; but her education had been both imperfect and desultory. On the death of her mother, and the departure from Russia, three months later, of her beloved sister Anne, Duchess of Holstein-Gottorp (1727), the Princess, at the age of 18, was left pretty much to herself. As her father's daughter, she was obnoxious to the Dolgorukis, who kept her away from the Court during the reign of Peter II. Robust and athletic, she delighted in field-sports, hunting, and violent exercise; but she had inherited much of her father's sensual temperament; and her life in the congenial environment of Moscow had been far from edifying. During the reign of her cousin Anne, Elizabeth effaced herself as much as possible, well aware that the Empress, of whom she stood in some awe, regarded her as a possible supplanter. She never seems to have thought of asserting her rights to the throne till the idea was suggested to her by La Chétardie and his Swedish colleague, Nolcken, who communicated with her through her French physician Armand Lestocq. Frequent collisions with the Regent, Anna Leopoldovna, whom she despised, and with Osterman, whom she hated for setting her aside in favour of aliens and foreigners, though he owed everything himself to her father and mother, first awakened her ambition; but her natural indolence was very difficult to overcome. Not till December 5, 1741, when the Guards quartered in the capital, on whom Elizabeth principally relied, were ordered to hold themselves in readiness to proceed to the seat of war, did she take the decisive step. That night a hurried and anxious conference of her partisans, foremost among whom were Lestocq, her chamberlain Michael Vorontsoff, her favourite and future husband, the Cossack, Alexis Razumoffsky, and Alexander and Peter Shuvaloff, two of the gentlemen of her household, was held at her house. The result of their deliberations was that Elizabeth buckled on a cuirass, armed herself with a demi-pike, and, proceeding to the barracks of the Guards, won them over by a spirited harangue at two o'clock in the morning. Then, at the head of a regiment of the Preobrazhensk Grenadiers, she sledged, over the snow, to the Winter Palace, where the Regent lay sleeping in absolute security, arresting all her real or suspected adversaries, including Osterman and Münnich, on her way. The Regent, aroused from her slumbers by Elizabeth herself, submitted quietly and was conveyed to Elizabeth's sledge. The baby Tsar and his little sister followed behind on a second sledge. In less than an hour, bloodlessly and noiselessly, the revolution had been accomplished. Even so late as eight o'clock the next morning, very few people in the city were aware that, during the night, Elizabeth

Petrovna had been raised to her father's throne on the shoulders of the Preobrazhensk Grenadiers.

Thus, at the age of three and thirty, this naturally indolent and self-indulgent woman, with little knowledge and no previous training or experience of affairs, was suddenly placed at the head of a vast empire at one of the most critical periods of its existence. La Chétardie had already expressed his conviction that Elizabeth, once on the throne, would banish all foreigners, however able, give her entire confidence to necessarily ignorant Russians, retire to her well-beloved Moscow, let the fleet rot, and utterly neglect St Petersburg and "the conquered provinces," as the Baltic seaboard was still called. Unfortunately for his calculations, La Chétardie, while exaggerating the defects, had ignored the good qualities, of the new Empress. For, with all her short-comings, Elizabeth was no ordinary woman. Her possession of the sovereign gift of choosing and using able counsellors, her unusually sound and keen judgment, and her bluff but essentially business-like joviality, again and again recall Peter the Great. What to her impatient contemporaries often seemed irresolution or sluggishness, was, generally, suspense of judgment in exceptionally difficult circumstances, and her ultimate decision was generally correct. If to this it is added that the welfare of her beloved country always lay nearest to her heart, and that she was ever ready to sacrifice the prejudices of the woman to the duties of the sovereign, we shall recognise, at once, that Russia did well at this crisis to place her destinies in the hands of Elizabeth Petrovna.

It is true that, as La Chétardie had predicted, almost the first act of Elizabeth was to disgrace and exile all the foreigners who had held sway during the last two reigns. Osterman could expect little mercy from a Princess whom all his life long he had consistently neglected and despised. Elizabeth had often declared that she would one day teach "that petty little secretary" his proper place. She was now as good as her word. Osterman was charged with having contributed to the elevation of the Empress Anne by his cabals, and with having suppressed the will of Catharine I in favour of her eldest daughter. He replied, with dignity, that all he had ever done had been for the good of the State. His principal fellow-victim, Münnich, was accused of having wasted his men during the Crimean campaigns. He referred to his own despatches in justification of his conduct, and declared that the only thing in the past he really regretted was having neglected to hang Prince Nikita Trubetskoy, the President of the Tribunal actually trying him, for malversation of funds while serving under him as chief of the commissariat. Osterman, Münnich, and four other fallen dignitaries, were condemned to death; but their sentences were commuted on the scaffold to life-long banishment in Siberia. Osterman died at Berezoff six years later. Münnich was sent to Pelim, to reside in the very house which he had himself designed for the reception of Biren, whom, by a singular irony of fate, he chanced to encounter in the midst of the frozen wilderness, posting hope-fully back to all that his rival, Münnich, was leaving behind him.

The best justification of Elizabeth for thus abruptly extinguishing the illustrious foreigners who had done so much to build up the Russian Empire was that she placed at the head of affairs a native Russian statesman whom, personally, she greatly disliked, but whose genius and experience she rightly judged to be indispensable to Russia at that particular moment. This was Alexis Bestuzheff, the youngest and most precocious of Peter the Great's "fledglings," who had begun his diplo-matic career at the early age of nineteen, when he served as second Russian plenipotentiary at the Congress of Utrecht. From 1717 to 1720 he had occupied the honourable but peculiar post of Hanoverian Minister at St Petersburg, subsequently representing Russia at Copenhagen from 1721 till the death of Peter I. For the next fifteen years, for some inexplicable reason, he fell into the background. Towards the end of the reign of Anne, however, Biren recalled him to Russia to counter-balance the influence of Osterman ; but he fell with his patron, and only reemerged from the obscurity of disgrace on the accession of Elizabeth. He drew up the first ukase of the new Empress, and at the end of the year 1741 was made Vice-Chancellor.

It is difficult to diagnose the character of this sinister and elusive statesman. He seems to have been a moody, taciturn hypochondriac, full of wiles and ruses, preferring to work silently and subterraneously. Inordinate love of power was certainly his ruling passion, and he hugged it the more closely as he had had to bide his time till he was nearly fifty. He was a man who remorselessly crushed his innumerable enemies ; yet, in justice, it must be added that his enemies were also, for the most part, those of his country, and that nothing could turn him a hair's breadth from the policy which he considered to be best suited to the interests of the State. This true policy he alone, for a long time, of all his contemporaries, had the wisdom to discern and the courage to pursue. Bestuzheff's most serious fault as a diplomatist was that he put far too much temper and obstinacy into his undertakings. His prejudices were always invincible. On the other hand, he was quite fearless.

The first care of the new Empress, after abolishing the Cabinet system which had prevailed during the reigns of the two Annes, and reconstituting the Administrative Senate, as it had been under Peter the Great, was to compose her quarrel with Sweden. As already indicated, the sudden collapse of Sweden had come as a disagreeable surprise to the Court of Versailles. To baulk Russia of the fruits of her triumph, by obtaining the best possible terms for discomfited Sweden, was now the main object of the French diplomatists in the north. La Chétardie was accordingly instructed to offer the mediation of France, and to use all his efforts for cajoling the new Empress into an abandonment of her rights of conquest. In February, 1742, therefore, he suggested to Elizabeth, at a private interview, that the victorious Russians should sacrifice something for the benefit of the vanquished Swedes in order to satisfy the honour of France! The Empress, very pertinently, enquired what opinion her own subjects would be likely to have of her, if she so little regarded the memory of her illustrious father as to cede provinces won by him at the cost of so much Russian blood and treasure? Bestuzheff, to whom the Frenchman next applied, roundly declared that no negotiations with Sweden could be thought of except on a *uti possidetis* basis. " I should deserve to lose my head on the block," he concluded, " if I counselled her Imperial Majesty to cede a single inch of territory." At a subsequent council it was decided to decline the French offer of mediation, and prosecute the Swedish war with vigour. By the end of 1742 the whole of Finland was in the hands of the Russians. On January 23, 1743, direct negotiations between the two Powers were opened at Åbo; and, on August 17, peace was concluded, Sweden ceding to Russia all the southern part of Finland east of the river Kymmene, including the fortresses of Vilmanstrand and Fredrikshamm. Bestuzheff would have held out for the whole grand duchy; but the Empress overruled him. Even so this was a great blow to France. La Chétardie, perceiving that he was no longer of any use at St Petersburg, obtained his letters of recall, and quitted Russia (July, 1742).

The French Government had discovered that nothing was to be hoped from Russia, so long as Bestuzheff held the direction of foreign affairs. To overthrow him as speedily as possible, therefore, now became the primary object of the Court of Versailles and its allies. This determination to rid the league which proposed to partition the Habsburg dominions of the obnoxious Minister is the only clue to the unravelling of that intricate web of intrigue and counter-intrigue which has made the seven first years of the reign of Elizabeth Petrovna such a diplomatic puzzle. Bestuzheff, like Osterman before him, was on principle opposed to France, as the natural antagonist of Russia in Turkey, Poland and Sweden, where the interests of the two States were diametrically opposed to each other. Like Osterman, therefore, he leant upon the Austrian alliance. But the policy of the alert and enterprising Bestuzheff had a far wider range than that of the slow and cautious Osterman. Starting from the assumption that the norm of Russia's proper policy at this period was hostility to France, he insisted that all her enemies must necessarily be the friends, and all her friends the enemies, of Russia. The most active ally of France, the aggressive King of Prussia, was especially to be guarded against, whereas the friendship of Great Britain, the secular antagonist of France, must be sedulously cultivated. Bestuzheff consequently aimed at a combination of all the enemies of France and Prussia which, in the first instance, was to take the form of a quadruple alliance between

Russia, Austria, Great Britain and Saxony. Here, however, he was on dangerously slippery ground, where a single stumble might mean irretrievable ruin; for the representatives of the three Powers whom he wished to bring into line with Russia had all been active and ardent supporters of Anna Leopoldovna, and as such had done their best to keep Elizabeth from the throne altogether. Of this the Empress was, by this time, well aware. Her antipathies, therefore, were very naturally directed against those Powers which had been her adversaries while she was only Tsesarevna; and it required some courage on the part of Bestuzheff to defend a policy which, indispensable as it might be, was abhorrent to his sovereign for strong personal reasons. Moreover, the intimate personal friends of the Empress, headed by Lestocq, all of them extremely jealous of the superior talents and rising influence of Bestuzheff, were now in the pay of France and Prussia, and ready, at the bidding of the French chargé d'affaires, d'Allion, to embark in any project for overthrowing the philo-Austrian Vice-Chancellor. The expedient finally adopted was a bogus conspiracy alleged to be on foot for the purpose of replacing on the throne Prince Ivan (who, since the revolution, had been detained, provisionally, with his parents, at the fortress of Dunamünde)—a conspiracy which, very ingeniously, was made to include most of Elizabeth's former rivals at her cousin's Court, such as Natalia Lopukhina and the Countess Anna Garielevna, consort of Michael Bestuzheff, the Vice-Chancellor's elder brother. The former Austrian ambassador, Marquis de Botta, was alleged to be the chief promoter of the affair. This trumped-up conspiracy was "miraculously discovered" by Lestocq and burst upon the Empress in August, 1743. After a rigid inquisition of twenty-five days, during which every variety of torture was freely employed against the accused, " the terrible plot," says the new English Minister, Sir Cyril Wych, "was found to be little more than the ill-considered discourses of a couple of spiteful passionate women." Nevertheless, the two ladies principally concerned had their tongues publicly torn out before being sent to Siberia; and the Russian ambassador at Vienna was instructed to demand Botta's condign punishment. This was done at a special audience; whereupon Maria Theresa, with her usual spirit, declared that she would never admit the validity of extorted evidence, and issued a manifesto to all the Great Powers defending Botta and accusing the Russian Court of rank injustice.

Thus Lestocq, or rather the anti-Austrian League of which he was the tool, had succeeded in mutually estranging the Courts of St Petersburg and Vienna; and the result of the "Lopukhina trial" was hailed as a great diplomatic victory at Paris. But the caballers had failed to bring Bestuzheff to the block or even "to drive him into some obscure hole in the country," as d'Allion had confidently predicted they would. At the very crisis of his peril, when his own sister-in-law was implicated, the Empress, always equitable when not frightened into ferocity, had privately

CH. X.

assured the Vice-Chancellor that her confidence in him was unabated and that not a hair of his head should be touched. But Bestuzheff had now a still more formidable antagonist to encounter in Frederick II of Prussia.

From the very beginning of his reign Frederick had regarded Russia as his most formidable neighbour, especially as being the ally of his inveterate enemy the Queen of Hungary. So early as June 1, 1743, he wrote to Mardefeld, his Minister at St Petersburg: "I should never think of lightly provoking Russia; on the contrary, there is nothing in the world I would not do, in order always to be on good terms with that Empire." A few months later, the neutrality, at least, of Russia had become of vital importance to him. Alarmed for Silesia by the Austrian victories in the course of 1743, he resolved to make sure of his newly-won possessions by attacking the Queen of Hungary a second time, before she had time to attack him. But how would Russia take this fresh and unprovoked aggression? That was the question upon which everything else depended. Fortunately the "Botta conspiracy" provided him with an opportunity of ingratiating himself with the Russian Empress. He wrote an autograph letter to Elizabeth, expressing his horror at the plot against her sacred person, and ostentatiously demanded of the Court of Vienna that Botta, who had been transferred from St Petersburg to Berlin, should instantly be recalled. Elizabeth could not refrain from showing her gratification. But Bestuzheff had yet to be got rid of. "I cannot repeat too often," wrote the King of Prussia to Mardefeld (January 25, 1744), "that until that man has been rendered harmless, I can never reckon upon the friendship of the Empress." And again (February 29), "it is absolutely necessary to oust the Vice-Chancellor. So long as he is in office he will cause me a thousand chagrins." Frederick's chief tool at St Petersburg at this time was Princess Elizabeth of Anhalt-Zerbst, who, in February, 1744, had brought her daughter Sophia Augusta Frederica to Russia (received into the Russian Church under the name of Catharine Alexievna on July 8, 1744) to be educated there and ultimately married to the Empress' nephew and heir, Grand Duke Peter. Bestuzheff, in pursuance of his political system, would have preferred Princess Mary of Saxony, but was overruled by the Prussian party, who advisedly represented to the Empress that the daughter of a petty German House would be far more manageable, and far less dangerous to orthodoxy, than a bigoted Catholic like the Saxon Princess. The elder Zerbst Princess very willingly united with all the other enemies of Bestuzheff, including Mardefeld and La Chétardie, now back at his post again, to overthrow him. But Bestuzheff more than held his own against this fresh combination, and in June, 1744, Frederick urged Mardefeld to change his tactics and attempt to bribe the Vice-Chancellor. He was authorised to spend as much as 500,000 crowns for the purpose. Then, trusting to the *savoir-faire* of Mardefeld and the potent influence of the bank-notes, Frederick, at the end of August, threw off the mask and invaded Bohemia at the head of 60,000 men. By the end of September his troops had occupied the whole kingdom.

In the extremity of her distress, Maria Theresa sent a special envoy, Count Rosenberg, to St Petersburg, to express her horror at Botta's alleged misconduct, and placed herself and her fortunes unreservedly in the hands of her imperial sister. For two months Elizabeth hesitated while the anti-Bestuzheff clique did all in its power to prevent any assistance being sent to the distressed Queen of Hungary. But Bestuzheff was now growing stronger and stronger every day. By the aid of his secretary, Goldbach, he had succeeded in unravelling La Chétardie's cipher correspondence and furnished the Empress with extracts alluding in the most disparaging terms to herself. These Bestuzheff accompanied by elucidatory comments. Furious at the treachery of the ever gallant and deferential Marquis, the Empress immediately dictated to Bestuzheff a memorandum commanding La Chétardie to quit her capital within 24 hours. On June 17, 1744, he was escorted to the frontier. Six weeks later Elizabeth identified herself emphatically with the anti-French policy of her Minister by promoting him to the rank of Grand Chancellor. Bestuzheff now energetically represented to the Empress the necessity of interfering in the quarrel between Frederick II and the Queen of Hungary. He described the King of Prussia as a restless agitator, whose character was made up of fraud and violence. He had violated the Treaty of Breslau; he was secretly stirring up Turkey against Russia; he had impudently used neutral Saxon territory as a stepping-stone to Bohemia; he had procured the dissolution of the Grodno Diet to prevent the discovery of his anti-Russian intrigues, thus aiming a direct blow at the supremacy which Russia had enjoyed in Poland ever since the days of Peter the Great. The balance of power in Europe should be restored instantly, and at any cost, by reducing Frederick to his proper place.

These representations, all of them substantially correct, profoundly impressed the Empress. In the beginning of 1745 she gave a clear proof of her reconciliation with Austria by bluntly refusing Frederick a succour of 6000 men, though bound by her last defensive treaty with Prussia to assist him. Bestuzheff then submitted to the British Government an intervention project, which was rejected as too onerous and exorbitant; while Frederick, thoroughly alarmed, offered Bestuzheff 100,000 crowns, if he would acquiesce in Prussia's appropriating another slice of Silesia, an offer which the Russian Chancellor haughtily rejected Frederick's subsequent declaration of war against Saxony greatly agitated the Russian Court; and three successive Ministerial councils (August— September, 1745), inspired by Bestuzheff, unanimously advised an armed intervention. Elizabeth thereupon signed an ukase commanding that the 60,000 men stationed in Esthonia and Livonia should at once advance into Courland, so as to be nearer the Prussian frontier and ready for any emergency. A manifesto was also addressed to the King of Prussia, warning him that Russia would consider herself bound to assist Saxony if invaded by him. But nothing came of it all. Bestuzheff relied for the success of his plan on British subsidies; but the British Cabinet, having already secured the safety of Hanover by a secret understanding with the King of Prussia, had resolved upon neutrality. A subsequent proposal (January 6, 1746) that, if the Maritime Powers would advance to Russia a subsidy of six millions, she would at once place 100,000 men in the field and end the German war in a single campaign, was likewise rejected by Great Britain.

Bestuzheff had been unable to prevent the conclusion of the Peace of Dresden, December 25, 1745; yet the menacing attitude of the Russian Chancellor had contributed to make the King of Prussia, despite his recent victories, moderate his demands. Moreover, Frederick now played into Bestuzheff's hands by indulging in one of those foolish jests for which he had so often to pay dear. Before departing for Saxony, he had requested the mediation of both Russia and Turkey, at the same time remarking with a sneer, at a public reception, that, in his opinion, the mediation of a Turk was every whit as good as the mediation of a Greek. Elizabeth, promptly informed of this, was wounded in her tenderest point. That she, the devout mother of all the Orthodox, should be placed in the same category with the successor of the False Prophet revolted her, and her sentiments towards "the Nadir Shah of Berlin," as she called the King of Prussia, completely changed. Henceforth political antagonism and private pique combined to make her the most determined adversary of Frederick II.

The political triumph of the Austrian party at St Petersburg is to be dated from the conclusion of the defensive alliance of June 2, 1745, whereby each of the contracting parties agreed to aid the other, within three months of being attacked, with 30,000 men or, in case Prussia was the aggressor, with 60,000. Frederick saw in this compact a veiled plan for attacking him on the first opportunity, and in the course of the same summer formed another plot to overthrow Bestuzheff, which only recoiled on the heads of its promoters in St Petersburg. Bestuzheff's subsequent endeavours to round off his system by contracting an alliance with Great Britain was partially realised by the Treaty of St Petersburg (December 9, 1747). The victories of Maurice de Saxe in the Austrian Netherlands, and the consequent danger to Holland, were the causes of the somewhat belated *rapprochement*. By the terms of this Treaty, the Empress, besides agreeing to hold a corps of observation, 30,000 strong, on the Courland frontier, at the disposal of Great Britain for £100,000 a year, engaged to despatch Prince Vasily Repnin with another corps of 30,000 to the Rhine, on condition that £300,000 a year was paid for these troops by England and Holland, four months in advance. The tidings of the approach of Repnin's army sufficed to induce France to accelerate the peace negotiations, and, on April 30, 1748, a preliminary convention was signed between the Court of Versailles and the Maritime Powers at Aix-la-Chapelle.

Never yet had Russia stood so high in the estimation of Europe as in the autumn of 1748; and she owed her commanding position entirely to the tenacity of purpose of the Grand Chancellor. In the face of apparently insurmountable obstacles, Bestuzheff had honourably extracted his country from the Swedish imbroglio; reconciled his imperial mistress with the Courts of London and Vienna; reestablished friendly relations with these Powers; freed Russia from the yoke of foreign influence; compelled both Prussia and France to abate their pretensions in the very hour of their victory; and, finally, isolated the restless, perturbing King of Prussia by environing him with hostile alliances.

The seven years which succeeded the War of the Austrian Succession were little more than an armed truce between apprehensive and dissatisfied adversaries—an indispensable breathing-space between a past contest which everyone felt to have been inconclusive, and a future contest which everyone knew to be inevitable. Both the Peace of Aix-la-Chapelle and that of Breslau had been forced from without upon active belligerents. In the first case, the unexpected intervention of Russia had arrested the triumphal progress of the French armies; in the second, the sudden desertion of England had compelled Austria to surrender Silesia to the King of Prussia. The consequences of these prematurely suppressed hostilities were an unnatural tension between the various European Powers, a loosening of time-honoured alliances, and a cautious groping after newer and surer combinations. But Frederick was uneasy in the midst of his triumphs, and, far from diminishing his armaments after the war was over, prudently increased them. He had, indeed, nothing to fear at present from exhausted Austria; but the attitude of Russia continued as menacing as ever. In the autumn of 1750, Frederick, incensed beyond measure by an imperial rescript issued by Bestuzheff ordering all Russian subjects natives of the Baltic Provinces actually in the Prussian service to return to their homes, deliberately insulted the Russian resident at Berlin, Gross, who was thereupon recalled (October 25), and diplomatic intercourse between the two countries was suspended.

All this time Bestuzheff had been doing his utmost to promote his favourite project of a strong Anglo-Russian alliance with the object of "still further clipping the wings of the King of Prussia." But the Empress, who throughout these protracted negotiations exhibited a truer political instinct than her Chancellor, was by no means disposed to tie her own hands in order to oblige England. She perceived clearly, what Bestuzheff did not or would not recognise, that the interests of the two States at this period were too divergent to admit of any alliance profitable to Russia being formed between them. For more than three years all the arguments of the Chancellor were powerless to move her. At last, on September 19, 1755, a new convention was signed at St Petersburg between Great Britain and Russia, whereby the latter Power engaged to furnish, in case of war, an auxiliary corps of 30,000 for a diversion against Prussia, in return for an annual subsidy from Great Britain of £500,000. When, however, two months later, the ratification of this treaty was in question, Elizabeth still hesitated to set her hand to it. She suspected, not without reason, that the English Government would require a large proportion of the Russian contingent to fight their own battles on the Rhine, or in the Low Countries, and she was not disposed to direct her troops thither. Finally, on February 1, 1756, the ratifications were added; but the Empress never forgave Bestuzheff for the vehemence and petulance by means of which he had forced her hand. Yet the treaty which it had taken years to negotiate was already waste paper. A fortnight before the exchange of the ratifications an event had occurred at the other end of Europe which shattered all the cunning combinations of the Russian Chancellor, completely changed the complexion of foreign politics, and precipitated a general European war.

Frederick had been beforehand with his adversaries. Recognising the fact that decadent France could no longer be profitable to him, and alarmed by the rumours of the impending negotiations between Great Britain and Russia, he calculated that the chances, on the whole, were in favour of the superior usefulness of an English alliance, and (January 16, 1756) signed the Treaty of Westminster with Great Britain, whereby the two contracting Powers agreed to unite their forces to oppose the entry into or the passage through Germany, of the troops of any other foreign Power. The Treaty of Westminster precipitated the conclusion of the Franco-Austrian *rapprochement* which the Austrian Chancellor Kaunitz had been long preparing. On May 1, 1756, a defensive alliance, directed against Prussia, was formed at Versailles between the French and Austrian Governments. To this treaty Russia, Sweden, and Saxony were to be invited to accede.

The position of the Russian Chancellor was now truly pitiable. He had expended all his energy in carrying through an alliance with Great Britain which was now only so much waste paper. He had repeatedly declared that Prussia could never unite with Great Britain, or Austria with France, and now both these alleged impossibilities had actually taken place. No wonder that the Empress lost all confidence in him, especially as he still clung obstinately to a past condition of things, and refused to bow to the inexorable logic of accomplished facts. He was well aware that, if Great Britain could no longer be counted upon for help against Prussia, the assistance of France would be indispensable; yet so inextinguishable was his hatred of France that he could not reconcile himself to the idea of an alliance with that Power in any circumstances. Consequently, his whole policy, henceforth, became purely obstructive and therefore purely mischievous.

The course of events in Russia demonstrated that his influence was already gone. At the second sitting (February 22, 1756) of the newly established "Ministerial Conference," a permanent and paramount Department of State formed early in 1756, to advise the Empress on all matters relating to foreign affairs, Elizabeth decided that England's treaty with Prussia had nullified all the existing Anglo-Russian conventions. At its third session (March 14), the Conference determined to invite the Courts of Versailles, Vienna and Stockholm to cooperate with Russia "to reduce the King of Prussia within proper limits so that he might no longer be a danger to the German Empire," thus anticipating by nearly two months the Treaty of Versailles. It then decreed that the army should be mobilised forthwith, so as to spur Austria on to more rapid action. The Austrian ambassador at St Petersburg was, at the same time, instructed to inform his Court that the Russian Empress was ready to conclude a definite treaty with France whenever invited to do so. After this the inclusion of Russia in the grand alliance against Prussia was only a matter of time.

On December 31, 1756, the Russian Empress formally acceded to the Treaty of Versailles, at the same time binding herself, by a secret article, to assist France if attacked by England in Europe; France at the same time contracting a corresponding secret obligation to give Russia pecuniary assistance in the event of her being attacked by Turkey. The secret articles of the Versailles Treaty of May 1, as between France and Austria, were not, however, communicated to the Court of St Petersburg.

It is certain that at this crisis of his life the King of Prussia was by no means so well-informed as usual. Not till towards the end of June did he suspect the existence of the Franco-Russian understanding, and, till the end of August, he flattered himself that British influence would prove stronger than Austrian at St Petersburg. He was also mistaken, or misinformed, as to the relative attitudes of Russia and Austria. He was, for instance, under the false impression that Austria was urging on Russia against him, but that the latter Power was not prepared and would postpone an invasion till the following spring; whereas, in reality, it was Russia who was urging on dilatory and timorous Austria. At the beginning of June Frederick learnt from the Hague that Russia had definitely renounced her obligations towards England. Early in July he told Mitchell, the English envoy at Berlin, that Russia was lost to them; and on August 29, 1756, he invaded Saxony. The Seven Years' War had begun. It is beyond the scope of the present chapter to enter into the details of the struggle. Here only the salient facts, so far as they affected the policy of Russia and the general situation, can be very briefly adumbrated.

The lack of good generals, due to the neglect, during the last three reigns, of Peter the Great's golden rule of forming a school of native generals by carefully training promising young Russian officers beneath the eye of intelligent and experienced foreigners, was the cause of Russia's inefficiency in the field during the first two campaigns. In 1757 the Russian Commander-in-chief, Stephen Aprakin, accidentally gained the battle of Gross-Jägerndorf (August 29), one of the most casual victories on record, through the sheer courage of raw troops suddenly attacked by an enemy whom they were marching to outflank. During the rest of the campaign Aprakin did nothing at all but march and counter-march.

The great political event of the year 1757 was the resumption of diplomatic relations between Russia and France. In the middle of June Michael Bestuzheff, the elder brother of the Russian Chancellor, was accredited to Paris; and, simultaneously, the new French ambassador, Paul de l'Hôpital, Marquis de Châteauneuf, arrived at St Petersburg at the head of an extremely brilliant suite. His charming manners, ready wit, and truly patrician liberality made him a *persona gratissima* at the Russian Court; and, in conjunction with the new Austrian ambassador, Prince Nicholas Esterházy, he carried everything before him. It was through their influence that Aprakin and his friend the Chancellor Bestuzheff were arrested, early in 1758, on a charge of conspiring with the Grand Duchess Catharine and her friends to recall the army from the field and hold it in readiness to support a projected *coup d'état* in case of the death of the Empress, who on September 19, 1757, had had a slight apoplectic fit after attending mass at the parish church of Tsarskoe Selo. Bestuzheff's enemies had instantly connected the illness of the Empress with the almost simultaneous retreat of the army; though we now know for certain that the two events were totally unconnected. The retreat of the army had been ordered by an unanimous council of war, held a full fortnight previously to the Empress' seizure; while it is obvious that the Chancellor, especially in his own very critical position, had no object whatever in saving his old enemy the King of Prussia. Bestuzheff succeeded in clearing himself completely of all the charges brought against him; but the Empress, while accepting his innocence and refusing to allow him to be put to torture, showed she had lost all confidence in him by depriving him of all his offices and dignities and expelling him from the Court. He was succeeded as Grand Chancellor by Michael Vorontsoff, an honest man of excellent intentions but mediocre abilities.

The campaign of 1758 was a repetition of the campaign of 1757. After occupying the whole of East Prussia, Aprakin's successor, General Count William Fermor, a pupil of Münnich and Lacy, on August 25, defeated Frederick at Zorndorf, one of the most murderous engagements of modern times. But Fermor was incapable of making any use of his victory, even after being strongly reinforced; and at the beginning of October, he retired behind the Vistula.

Fermor seems only to have been saved from the fate of Aprakin by the growing conviction of the Empress and her Ministers that the Court of Vienna was sacrificing the Russian troops to its own particular interests. There can be no doubt that very little assistance was rendered by the Austrians to the Russians during the last campaign, and the apologetic tone adopted by Maria Theresa seems to show that Elizabeth had just cause for complaint. The Empress Queen pleaded as an excuse for her own remissness the failure of the Court of Versailles to fulfil its obligations to Austria. France, she said, instead of despatching the promised auxiliary corps of 30—40,000 men to Austria's hereditary domains, had wasted her strength in a fruitless struggle with England-Hanover. There were, she added, symptoms of growing weakness in the French monarchy. Several times since the beginning of the year, France had complained that the burden of the war was growing intolerable and expressed a desire for peace. Elizabeth's reply was both dignified and determined; but it also shows that the French influence at St Petersburg was at this time paramount. She protested that France had taken a more active part in the war than any other member of the league, and had, besides, the additional merit of bringing Sweden into it. The alleged infirmity of the French monarchy, assuming it to exist, was but an additional reason for assisting it more strenuously, and not allowing it to be sacrificed to England and Prussia. The Russian Empress opined that the war must be prosecuted till the Most High had blessed the righteous arms of the Allies with decisive success, and abated the pride and self-sufficiency of the King of Prussia.

Towards the end of the year, the hands of the Russian Empress were strengthened by the accession to power in France of a new and vigorous Minister of Foreign Affairs who fully shared her sentiments in the person of the Duc de Choiseul. The first act of the new Minister was to notify Michael Bestuzheff that pacific overtures had been made to Great Britain through the Danish Court with the object of isolating the King of Prussia, but that the English Ministers had steadily refused to separate their cause from his. Choiseul further informed the Russian ambassador that Louis XV had given his solemn word never to make peace without the consent of his Allies. Alexis Galitsin's despatches from London were, naturally, less satisfactory than Michael Bestuzheff's from Versailles. He reported "a fanatical enthusiasm of the whole nation for the King of Prussia," and a determination on the part of the English Ministers to make Prussia the leading German Power on the Continent instead of Austria. The damage done by Frederick II to the French monarchy was, no doubt, at the bottom of England's respect for him.

The increasing financial difficulties of the Russian Government in 1759, prevented the army from taking the field till April; and, on May 19, the incurably sluggish Fermor was superseded by Count Peter Soltikoff, an officer who hitherto had been mainly occupied in drilling the militia of the Ukraine. Frederick II communicated this new appointment to his brother Prince Henry with more than his usual caustic acerbity. "Fermor," he wrote, "has received by way of appendage one Soltikoff, who is said to be more imbecile than anything in the clodhopper way which Russia has yet produced." Within three weeks this "clodhopper" was to reduce the King of Prussia to the last extremity.

Although suddenly pitted against the most redoubtable captain of the age without having ever before commanded an army in the field, Soltikoff seems to have accepted his tremendous responsibilities without the slightest hesitation. On July 9, he reached headquarters; on July 23, he defeated, near Kay, the Prussian general Wedell, who had attempted to prevent his junction with the Austrians; early in August he united with Laudon at Frankfort on Oder; and, on August 12, the allies annihilated the army of the King of Prussia at Kunersdorf. Frederick was only saved from death or captivity, in the general stampede, by the devotion of Rittmeister Prittwitz and forty hussars. Late the same evening, 3000 repentant fugitives rallied to his standard, the sole remnant of a host of 48,000 men. Mortal indeed had been the hug of the "bears of the Holy Roman Empire," as he himself dubbed the Russians at the end of the year, when he had in a measure recovered from the shock of "that horrible catastrophe."

"Your Imperial Majesty must not be surprised at our serious casualties," wrote the triumphant Soltikoff to the Empress on the following day, "for you know that the King of Prussia always sells victory dearly. Another such victory, your Majesty, and I shall be obliged myself to plod staff in hand to St Petersburg with the joyful tidings, for lack of messengers." Soltikoff received the marshal's *bâton* from his own sovereign, and a diamond-ring, a jewelled snuff-box and 5000 ducats from Maria Theresa. His health was also drunk, "in imperial Tokay," at a grand banquet given at Versailles by Michael Bestuzheff in honour of the event, at which Choiseul and eighty of the most distinguished men in France were present. Nor were these rejoicings at all exaggerated. At that moment the ruin of the King of Prussia seemed imminent and inevitable; and, as is related elsewhere, for the first time in his life he despaired. At the urgent request of Frederick, Pitt at once made pacific overtures to Russia on behalf of Prussia and proposed a peace congress, to be held at the Hague. Not till December 12 did the Russian Empress deliver her reply to these pacific overtures. She declared that she and her allies were equally desirous of peace, but of a peace that should be honourable, durable, and profitable. Such a peace, she opined, would be impossible if things were allowed to remain on the same footing as they were before the war. After this, it was plain to the British Ministers that no more could be said at present, and that the war must proceed.

Frederick was, indeed, only saved from instant destruction by the violent dissensions between Soltikoff and the Austrian Commander-in-chief, Count Daun, who refused to take orders from each other, and thus wasted all the fruits of Kunersdorf. Moreover, Soltikoff was so elated by his astounding victories that he even refused to submit to the behests of his own Court. In spite of repeated and urgent orders to follow up his successes without delay, he absolutely refused to remain in Silesia a day longer than October 15, "as the preservation of my army ought to be my primary consideration." At the beginning of November he deliberately marched off to his magazines at Posen.

It is not too much to say that, from the end of 1759 to the end of 1761, the unshakable firmness of the Russian Empress was the one constraining political force which held together the heterogeneous, incessantly changing elements of the anti-Prussian combination, and prevented it from collapsing before the shock of disaster. From the Russian point of view, Elizabeth's greatness as a ruler consists in her steady appreciation of Russian interests, and her determination to promote and consolidate them at all hazards. She insisted throughout that the King of Prussia must be rendered harmless to his neighbours for the future, and that the only way to bring this about was to curtail his dominions and reduce him to the rank of an Elector. Russia's share of his partitioned dominions was to be the province already in her possession—Ducal Prussia as it was then called—certainly a very moderate compensation for her preponderating success and enormous sacrifices. On January 1, 1760, the Empress told Esterházy that she meant to continue the war in conjunction with her allies, even if she were compelled to sell all her diamonds and half her wearing apparel; but she also declared that the time had now come when Russia should be formally guaranteed the possession of her conquest, Ducal Prussia. The Court of Vienna was greatly perturbed. Maria Theresa was well aware that France would never consent to the aggrandisement of Russia; yet she herself was in such absolute need of the succour of the Russian troops that she was obliged to yield to the insistence of Elizabeth. Accordingly, on April 1, 1760, fresh conventions were signed between Austria and Russia, providing for the continuation of the war and the annexation of Ducal Prussia to Russia. When Louis XV categorically refused to accept these conventions in their existing form, and compelled Maria Theresa to strike out the article relating to Ducal Prussia, the Empress Queen added to the conventions so amended a secret clause, never communicated to the Court of Versailles, virtually reinserting the cancelled article. The British Ministers were not less apprehensive than were the Ministers of France lest Russia should claim any territorial compensation from Frederick II; for, in view of the unyielding disposition of the King of Prussia, such a claim meant the indefinite prolongation of the war, or,

CH. X.

which was even worse and far more probable, the speedy and complete collapse of the Prussian monarchy.

Frederick himself has told us that in 1760 the Russians had only to step forward in order to give him the *coup de grâce*. Elizabeth was equally well aware of this, and the New Year was not three days old when she summoned Soltikoff to the capital to draw up a plan of campaign. The plan he finally submitted was simplicity itself. It may best be described as an ingenious method of avoiding a general engagement at all hazards, and keeping out of harm's way as much as possible. He was curtly informed that Russia's obligations to her allies demanded a more aggressive, adventurous strategy, and reminded that after the experience of Kunersdorf there was no longer any reason to be afraid " of hazarding our army in an engagement with the King of Prussia, however desperate and bloody." Elizabeth's own plan was that Soltikoff should proceed at once to Silesia to cooperate there with Laudon, who had, at her particular request, been appointed to an independent command on the Oder, and was there holding Prince Henry of Prussia in check, while Daun, with another Austrian army, stood face to face with Frederick in Saxony. Before quitting Posen for Silesia Soltikoff was also instructed to detach 15,000 men, to besiege for the second time the maritime fortress of Kolberg, as a first step towards conquering Pomerania. Soltikoff set out for the army early in the spring; and nothing but captious criticisms, dolorous grumblings, and perplexing accounts of insignificant skirmishes, was heard of or from him for the next three months. His absurd caution more than neutralised the victories of Laudon at Landshut and Glatz, and the mere intelligence of the battle of Liegnitz drove him back into Polish territory. Simultaneous reports from General Chernuisheff informed the Empress that the whole army was in an anarchical condition and that the Commander-in-chief could do nothing but wring his hands and shed tears. It was now evident that Soltikoff's mind had become unhinged by his responsibilities. He was accordingly superseded, in the beginning of September, by the senior officer in the service, Field-Marshal Alexander Buturlin, who led the army back behind the Vistula. The closing incidents of this campaign were the occupation of Berlin (October 9–12) by Chernuisheff and Todtleben, which caused great rejoicings at St Petersburg and helped to refill the depleted Russian Treasury, the contributions levied amounting to 1,000,000 *thalers*, and the second siege of Kolberg, which proved to be an expensive failure.

If France and Austria had only with the utmost difficulty been persuaded to continue the War at the end of 1759, it may be imagined with what feelings they faced the prospect of another campaign at the end of 1760. Even in Russia itself there was now a very general desire for peace. The customary New Year illuminations in front of the Winter Palace at St Petersburg gave eloquent expression to this desire.

The principal transparency represented a winged genius (the New Year) with a gift in his hand, in the shape of a laurel wreath intertwined with an olive-branch, standing upon captured standards, cannon, and other military trophies, with the keys of Berlin in front of him. The contemporary Russian gazettes also emphasised the rumour that " Our most gracious Sovereign has expressly stated that the sole object of the glorious triumph of her arms is the restoration and the maintenance of peace." But peace was only obtainable by fresh exertions; these required plenty of money; and where was the money to come from? The new Commander-in-chief had demanded a minimum of 2,031,000 *roubles* (about £457,000) for putting the army on a war footing, but only about three-quarters of that amount was available.

And there was yet another difficulty. The allies of Russia were fast approaching the limits of their endurance, and were becoming clamorous for peace. On January 22, 1761, the new French ambassador at St Petersburg, the Baron de Breteuil, presented a despatch to the Russian Chancellor to the effect that the King of France, by reason of the condition of his dominions, absolutely desired peace, especially as the King of Prussia, being at the end of his resources, would now doubtless listen to any reasonable propositions. On the following day the Austrian ambassador delivered a memorandum to the same effect. In her reply of February 12, Elizabeth declared that she would not consent to any pacific overtures until the original object of the League, " the essential and permanent crippling of the King of Prussia," had been accomplished. Even if Austria could not get back all she had a right to, she should at least retain possession of her actual conquests in Silesia. The King of Poland should also be compensated for the inhuman devastation of his lands by the duchy of Magdeburg and all the Prussian possessions in Lusatia. Sweden's Pomeranian frontier should also be "advantageously rectified." Russia demanded nothing for herself besides Ducal Prussia, or, in default thereof, adequate compensation elsewhere " from her loyal allies." This reply was accompanied by a letter from Elizabeth to Maria Theresa rebuking the Court of Vienna for its want of candour in negotiating with France behind the back of Russia, and threatening, in case of any repetition of such a violation of treaties, to treat with the King of Prussia directly and independently. Elizabeth declared, however, that she was not averse from a peace congress sitting while the war still went on, though she was firmly opposed to anything like a truce as being likely to be "extremely useful to the King of Prussia." To these propositions the allies yielded after some debate. A fresh Russian note, at the beginning of May, laid it down as an imperative necessity that France should leave America and the Indies alone for a time and concentrate all her efforts on the Continent. Thus Russia was assuming the lead in continental affairs, not only in arms but in diplomacy also.

The equally uncompromising attitudes of Russia and Prussia rendered another campaign inevitable; and, despite the leisurely strategy of the Russians, it was to result most disastrously for Frederick. Moreover, in the autumn of 1761 Pitt, his zealous friend, had been compelled to retire from the Cabinet, and Great Britain, shortly afterwards, had embarked in a war with Spain, so that, as Galitsin, the Russian ambassador at London, shrewdly observed, she had no more money to waste on the King of Prussia. Nor could he even dare to reckon, as heretofore, on the sluggishness of the foes he feared the most —"the bears of the Holy Roman Empire." The timid incompetency of the first four Russian commanders-in-chief had materially simplified his strategy. They had moved with mechanical deliberation to the wire-pulling of a council of civilians 1000 miles off; they had sustained, stubbornly but unintelligently, the impact of any enemy that might happen to cut across their line of march; and they had been amazed after the engagement to discover, sometimes, that they had won a great victory without being aware of it. But they had never taken any steps to follow up their purely fortuitous triumphs and, at the slightest rumour of danger, at the slightest suspicion of scarcity, they had retreated to their *depôts* behind the Vistula. But now there were ominous indications that even in the Russian ranks the lessons of a five years' warfare were beginning to produce good scholars. Foreign military experts already spoke highly of Zachary Chernuisheff, who had so brilliantly cooperated with Laudon in the capture of Schweidnitz, while the talents of young Peter Rumyantseff, the victor of Kolberg, who had sent the keys of that stubborn fortress to the Empress as a Christmas gift, were universally recognised. There could be little doubt that Rumyantseff would be the next Russian Commander-in-chief, and it was equally certain that his strategy would be of a very different order to the strategy of his predecessors. Frederick was indeed in evil case and his correspondence at this period is a melancholy reflexion of his despair. But a fortnight after he had informed Finkenstein of his determination to seek a soldier's death on the first opportunity, and thus remove the chief obstacle to a peace for want of which Prussia was perishing, he received the tidings of the death of the Russian Empress who had expired on January 5, 1762—and he knew he was saved. "*Morta la bestia, morto il veneno*," he wrote to Knyphausen on January 22, 1762. The first act of Elizabeth's nephew and successor, Peter III, a fanatical worshipper of Frederick, was to reverse the whole policy of his aunt, grant the King of Prussia peace on his own terms (May 5), and to contract a regular defensive alliance with "the King my master"—even going the length of placing at Frederick's disposal Chernuisheff's army as an auxiliary corps against the Austrians. This shameful and unpatriotic subserviency contributed not a little to the overthrow of Peter III, a few months later (July 9); but the change came too late to modify the situation. Despite her enormous expenditure of blood and money, Russia gained nothing except prestige from her participation in the Seven Years' War.

CHAPTER XI.

THE REVERSAL OF ALLIANCES AND
THE FAMILY COMPACT.

Upon the death of Cardinal Fleury in January, 1743, it might have been expected that the King of France, following the precedent set by his great-grandfather at the death of Cardinal Mazarin, would resolve to take into his own hands the practical direction of affairs. But, if Louis XV had as keen a sense as Louis XIV of the prerogatives of the royal dignity, and was equally jealous for his authority, he had neither the same devotion to labour, nor the same lofty conception of his duty. He was known on more than one occasion to grieve over the sorrows of his people; yet he lacked not only the will to carry out the necessary reforms, but the mere strength to look them in the face. Indolent to the point of lethargy, he reigned without governing, suffering himself to be led by his Ministers even while he distrusted them. Above all, in the matter of foreign policy, he had his own ideas, tastes, and preferences; but these he expressed half-heartedly, keeping silence as to whatever he felt most deeply; he had, too, his own agents, his own policy, which served more than once to paralyse or thwart official diplomacy. These agents and this policy formed the "King's Secret," famous by reason rather of the mystery surrounding it than of the importance of the transactions it covered, or of the influence it exercised upon the politics of France and of Europe.

The death of Fleury marks, nevertheless, a date of importance in the history of the reign. Although he did not boast the title of Chief Minister, the Cardinal had been the real possessor of power, and when he died no one was capable either of influencing the King's mind with equal authority, or of inducing the Government to follow any consistent course. "Never," writes one of the Ministers of this period, d'Argenson, "have the Ministers been so deeply at variance as now. Each one is equally master in his own department....If they are in harmony, it is by chance—the King is never responsible for their agreement. The least of the departments is as independent, in its own sphere, as the greatest; and it is the constant effort of each to persuade the King that on it his greatness and glory depend. Such mutual jealousy on the part of his viziers would be an advantage to a Prince who should administer, over-rule all others, and make plans freely on his own account. But, instead of those realities, what reigns over us is a *vacuum*....All the measures taken for the good of the State are at cross purposes one with another."

Towards the end of the Seven Years' War, there was, it is true, one Minister, the Duc de Choiseul, who, rather through his versatility than through any statesmanlike qualities, succeeded in maintaining for a time a position of acknowledged superiority in the direction of state affairs. But neither his intellectual suppleness nor his patriotic activity, was capable of maintaining him in power. As his rise had been mainly due to the favour of a royal mistress (Mme de Pompadour), so his fall was caused by the resentment of another (Mme Du Barry), whose goodwill he had supposed his past services entitled him to treat with disdain.

The external influence needed to dominate the weak character of the King, without in any way affronting his acute sense of his own authority, not being supplied by his Ministers or by the members of the royal family, was contributed by the ladies of his Court. Among the earlier favourites, Mme de Mailly had all the modesty and the disinterestedness of Mlle de La Vallière; her two sisters, Mme de Vintimille and Mme de Châteauroux, showed a strong determination to arouse the King from his apathy and to turn his activities in the direction of politics and of war; but their period of favour was too short for them to produce any serious effect: the influence of the royal mistresses in the direction of affairs began in reality with Mme de Pompadour.

Jeanne-Antoinette Poisson—the daughter of a wine-merchant's clerk who had been hung in effigy, and the wife of an official concerned in the collection of the revenue, Lenormant d'Étiolles—had been brought up in the express and avowed hope of winning the King's favour. She was presented at Court in 1745, and created Marquise de Pompadour a few months later. She had from the first won the King's heart by a com-bination of qualities which made her one of the most fascinating women in the kingdom; and, by the skill with which she could amuse or divert a monarch who was a prey to incessant *ennui*, she succeeded in maintaining her influence. Although it had not been her desire to take any part in politics, she was not slow to perceive that in no other way could she make her power permanent. She had at first to encounter strenuous opposition, on account of her humble birth; and the resentment thus roused in her reacted more than once upon the choice she made, when she disposed, after the manner of a queen, of the highest offices of State. Her appointments, partly for this reason, were not invariably happy: again and again, at critical moments, certain Ministers and generals owed their nomination simply to the place which they held in the favourite's regard. Nor was this all-powerful influence limited to the nomination of men to fill the public employments and offices, but it was also of the greatest weight in the whole direction of political affairs. Throughout this portion of the reign, the whole of the political life of France is dominated by her foreign policy, which reacts upon her military and naval institutions, and which leads to the loss of her colonies, the disorder of her finances, and an entire change in public feeling. With a review of this policy the present chapter may therefore appropriately begin.

The War of the Austrian Succession, undertaken by Cardinal Fleury ostensibly in order to continue the traditional policy of France, of which the aim was the overthrow of the House of Austria, continued after the Cardinal's death, having had no other result than to establish more firmly upon her throne the Empress Maria Theresa. The struggle was still carried on for several years, although the contending parties had lost sight of its original object. The endeavours of France, which since 1745 had been concentrated upon Flanders and the Netherlands, had led to a series of important successes: victories had been won at Fontenoy in 1745, at Roucoux in 1746, at Lauffeldt in 1747; and Bergen-op-Zoom was taken in 1748. France from this time forward could accept—could even impose—peace; and it was accordingly signed at Aix-la-Chapelle in 1748.

In the conclusion of this treaty, Louis XV displayed some chivalrous inclinations. He had declared that he wished to make peace not after the fashion of a merchant, but like a King. His plenipotentiary, Saint-Sévérin, was accordingly not slow in coming to an agreement with his English colleague Lord Sandwich, and the preliminaries of peace between France and England were signed on April 30. The establishment of friendly relations with Austria, represented by Kaunitz, was a more protracted affair, and the general peace was not concluded until October 18 and subsequent dates. So far as France was concerned, the conditions agreed upon in this Treaty were not in proportion either with the sacrifices entailed by a long war, or with the successes she had gained during the later campaigns. The King of France restored all the fortresses captured by his forces in the Netherlands and in Italy. In America, he regained possession of Louisburg and Cape Breton. There was no determination of boundaries between French and English possessions in America, the only stipulation being that matters should be restored to their original footing, and that the frontiers should remain as determined by the Treaty of Utrecht. But England obtained the demolition of the coast defences of Dunkirk and the exclusion of the Stewarts from the realm of France.

The Peace of Aix-la-Chapelle, which the imagination of Louis XV had for a moment pictured as destined, thanks to his moderation, to be a perpetual peace, was to be short-lived. Between France and England, above all, there were rivalries of every description, which could not fail to provoke a further conflict. The essential cause of this jealousy was the struggle for supremacy on the sea and in the colonies—the two being indissolubly linked together. On the one hand, England was eager to profit by the advantage already gained and to prevent her rival from reorganising her maritime power. In France, besides the discontent created by the terms of the Treaty of Aix-la-Chapelle, there was clear comprehension of the fact that a strong navy was necessary to protect the merchant-service and the colonial trade; and a strong impetus was thus given to naval reform, while at the same time praiseworthy efforts were made to restore order in the financial department. In 1754, a Minister belonging to the reform party, Machault d'Arnouville, an ex-Controller-General of finance, was placed at the head of the navy, and began at once to plan the organisation of an imposing force. The value of his endeavours was about to be proved by the Minorcan expedition of 1756, when he was overthrown by a political intrigue.

The ink was scarcely dry on the Treaty of Peace, when the permanent causes of antagonism between France and England found fresh fuel and natural opportunities for breaking forth anew, in the daily conflicts between the colonies of the two countries, at all their points of mutual contact. These conflicts had been incessant from the first; but, while in India they were confined to struggles between rival Companies, in the New World they were becoming more rancorous from day to day; and, aggravated as they were by the greed of the Companies or of the settlers, on the one hand, and by the ambition of the military commanders, on the other, they could not fail to provoke more and more serious armed encounters and to challenge the efforts of both military commanders and diplomatists on both sides. The Treaty of Aix-la-Chapelle had left undecided the question of the boundaries of the English and French colonies. This indecision was the more to be regretted, since, between the possessions of the two countries stretched vast territories occupied by the Indians—territories to which neither side could put forth claims that were not highly contentious, resting on the right of discovery, treaties with the natives, or concessions granted to particular Companies.

The early difficulties of the years 1750 to 1754 are described elsewhere. The first blood having been drawn near Fort Duquesne in June, 1754, the two sides made open preparation for a sustained conflict. However, a special commission, called the Boundary Commission, had been appointed by the two Governments to settle these differences; its chief task being to determine the boundaries in North America and to decide the question of ownership of the islands St Vincent, Tobago, and St Lucia. Its work was begun in 1750 and continued until the rupture between the two Powers in July, 1755. But, notwithstanding the competence of the commissioners, no practical result was gained by their deliberations; and, in proportion as matters grew more serious in America, it became more and more apparent that there must be direct negotiations between the two Governments. These were begun in July, 1754, and were continued in Paris and at Versailles by Rouillé, the new Minister of Foreign Affairs, and Lord Albemarle, British ambassador in France, until the sudden death of the latter at the end of the year 1754. In January, 1755, they were reopened in London, between the Duke of Newcastle and the French ambassador, Mirepoix. Beneath an appearance of friendliness, expressing itself by repeated presents to Mme de Pompadour, the attitude of the English Minister, supported by the wishes of Parliament and by the demands of the colonies, was resolute to the last degree. The same cannot be said of the French diplomatist. Mirepoix was severely judged by his contemporaries, even in France, and there was for a moment some thought of reinforcing him by a colleague. But, though he was rather a soldier than a diplomatist, his frank and loyal—at times even ingenuous—disposition accommodating itself with difficulty to duplicity and finesse, his task was certainly far from easy. Not only had he to take into account the secret action of the King and Mme de Pompadour, which was not always in agreement with that of Rouillé, but that Minister himself, though conscientious and honourable, lacked breadth of view and initiative, and was, partly by his own fault, partly by the force of circumstances, entirely destitute of authority. When in February, 1755, the differences between the claims of the two countries in the matter of the boundaries were intensified, Rouillé still had recourse to dilatory methods, sending to Mirepoix lengthy monographs on the rights of France, and proposing to refer to the Boundary Commission the enquiry into the disputed points. Hereupon, as related elsewhere, Major-General Braddock was sent to America to support the English claim by force of arms; and, in the following April, Admiral Boscawen sailed, with secret instructions to intercept the French convoys bound for America. While Rouillé was still hoping to convert the English Ministry to his opinions, the news reached London, on July 15, that Boscawen's fleet had seized the French frigates *Leys* and *Aleide*. The negotiations were at once broken off, and a few days later Mirepoix was recalled. Nevertheless, many long months were still to pass before the opening of hostilities. This irresolution and evasion on the part of France, in a situation admitting of only one issue, is explained by the inferiority of the French naval forces, and by the desire on the part of the King and Mme de Pompadour to keep the peace at all costs. Hence the endeavours of the French Government to shift the whole blame on to the shoulders of their adversary by calling on all Europe to witness their own peaceful intentions, and further, since the struggle could not continue to be confined to the two countries, the desire to win for France as many allies, or at least to secure the neutrality of as many Powers, as possible. Strangely enough, in this race for alliances, England displayed the greatest eagerness. Her first step was to secure a friendly neutrality on the part of Spain, which the unskilful policy of the Duc de Duras failed to win over to the side of France. In Russia, the British envoy, Sir Charles Hanbury Williams, after overcoming countless difficulties by means of lavish liberality, at last succeeded in concluding a defensive treaty, which was signed in September, 1755.

But the efforts of British diplomacy were directed chiefly towards Austria. If public opinion in England was indifferent to continental affairs, the same could not be said of the English King, George II, whose hereditary possessions in Hanover needed to be protected from any sudden attack on the part of France. Austria, England's ally in the last war, was ready and willing to help in the defence of Hanover, but on condition that the British subsidies should be sufficient to enable her at the same time to renew her conflict with the King of Prussia. The conferences on this question, after being prolonged for months, came to nothing. England thus found herself, at the end of 1755, isolated in Europe, deprived of the help of Austria, and with but little hope of any change favourable to her in the policy of Prussia.

During this period, the behaviour of France presented a most amazing spectacle of irresolution. The Minister of War, d'Argenson, had at first proposed to extend the struggle to the Continent, and to secure in Hanover and the Netherlands compensation for the losses which France could not fail to suffer in the colonies. But this plan, after being discountenanced by Machault, the Minister of Marine, was speedily relinquished in consequence of the opposition of Mme de Pompadour, who feared that a continental war might estrange the King from her, and of Louis XV himself, who still hoped for a friendly understanding with England. Secret negotiations were carried on during the closing months of 1755, until the moment when the declarations of the English Ministry in Parliament put an end to all hope of a friendly arrangement. The Treaty between France and Prussia, the most important of her allies, expired in May, 1756. During the months following on the cessation of negotiations between England and France, Frederick had been constantly urging his ally to resolve upon decided action; but the Court of Versailles had shown no alacrity in profiting by this friendly attitude. Not only had they apparently resolved not to carry the war into Europe, but they imagined that any haste in concluding a fresh treaty with Frederick II would render the latter still more exacting. The Duc de Nivernais, charged with an extraordinary mission to Berlin in August, 1755, did not enter upon his duties there until the beginning of January, 1756. During this time, events were following one another in rapid succession, as the outcome of several months of conferences. Frederick II, whose principal care it was to secure himself against possible attack on the part of Austria and Russia, signed with England on January 16, 1756, the Treaty of Westminster, whereby the two signatory Powers obtained a guarantee of the security of their dominions, both agreeing to take up arms against any Power which should encroach upon Germanic territory. The Duc de Nivernais arrived at Potsdam at the very moment when this arrangement was on the point of conclusion; and, notwithstanding his evident desire that the previous relations between Prussia and France should be maintained, he could do nothing but inform his Government of this decisive event.

This sudden change of policy on the part of Frederick II, although it had been made known for some time past, produced at the Court of Versailles, where up to the last moment it was regarded as incredible, a proportionately violent impulse of vexation and wrath. In these circumstances, the negotiations between France and Austria, begun some time previously, were carried on with increased eagerness. Austria had now for several years shown a disposition to a *rapprochement*: this was the master-thought of Kaunitz, who at that time, with the full confidence of the Empress, directed the policy of Austria. Intellectual, eloquent to the point of taking pleasure in hearing himself talk, and gifted with a marvellous memory, Kaunitz had kept this design before the Council of the Empire since the year 1749, without finding a single voice to second him. When, at the end of 1750, he was appointed ambassador at Paris, he employed himself in laying the foundations of his plan; but, in face of the protestations of a loyal adherence to the Prussian alliance, which were at the time in vogue in France, he could do nothing beyond establishing personal relations, which were in the end to prove of use. When, in 1753, he became Chancellor of the Empire, he was succeeded in Paris by Count von Starhemberg; but explicit negotiations were delayed until the latter part of the year 1755. In view of the refusal of England to enter into a league against Prussia, an important council had been held at Vienna on August 19 and 21, which resulted in a decision to lay certain proposals before the French Court. Mme de Pompadour was mentioned by Kaunitz to Starhemberg, as likely to prove the best intermediary with the King. Abbé de Bernis, formerly French ambassador at Venice, who enjoyed the confidence of the Marquise, was taken into the secret, and played thenceforth the principal part in the whole affair. The first meeting took place at Sèvres on September 3, when Louis XV lent a friendly ear to the Austrian proposals, which were soon submitted, not only to Bernis, but to a Committee composed of Rouillé, Abbé de la Ville, his chief clerk, and Machault. However, the first negotiations, without touching the real point at issue, turned only upon a question of reciprocal neutrality, France refusing to enter upon any engagement hostile to Frederick II, and Austria being unwilling to take any steps against Hanover. But, when at the end of January, 1756, the news of the Anglo-Prussian Treaty reached Paris, the views of the French Ministry underwent a considerable modification; and, after fresh conferences extending over several months, the two Powers, recognising that the time was not yet ripe for a general offensive treaty, came to a preliminary agreement, which was practically only the preface to such a treaty, and was signed on May 1, 1756. This compact, known as the Treaty of Versailles, comprised a convention of neutrality, a defensive alliance, and a secret convention in five articles. Under the first of these heads, the Empress bound herself to observe absolute neutrality in the war between England and France, and the King of France, on his side, promised to respect the Austrian Netherlands and other States belonging to the Empress. By the agreement of union and defensive alliance, the two contracting parties guaranteed to each other the security and reciprocal defence of their possessions in Europe, and mutually promised an auxiliary force of 24,000 men, in the case of either being attacked. Finally, by the secret convention, Austria signified her willingness to intervene, in case a Power allied to England should invade the territory of His Most Christian Majesty; and the King of France gave a similar promise.

Thus was completed that diplomatic evolution which has been called by the well-known name of the "Reversal of Alliances." A close examination of the conditions under which this transaction took place, shows that, except in the case of Austria, which from the first had a clear view of the object to be attained, circumstances had as much to do with the new arrangement as had the enlightened and deliberate resolve of the personages responsible for it. So far, however, as France was concerned, the shifting of the bases of her policy must be allowed to have corresponded to certain tendencies and conceptions which, though still not fully realised by those who entertained them, were far from new. Louis XV had long been painfully conscious of the comparison which was being drawn between himself and Frederick II—owing to the contrast between his own indolence and the activity of the Prussian sovereign, and to the witticisms which Frederick permitted himself at his royal brother's expense; moreover, as a *dévot* (notwithstanding his immoralities) Louis was pained by his alliance with a Protestant monarch, who, though privately a sceptic, was capable of protecting, and defending in case of need, the interests of his religion. Conversely, in the same line of thought everything attracted Louis XV to the Court of Vienna—" the similarity of etiquette and of religious policy, the prestige of the Imperial dignity, the tone, the ceremonial, nay, the very proceedings, the actual circumlocutions, of the Empress' Court"—and many cognate considerations. The cause of this shifting of the bases of French diplomacy must be sought in the King far more than in Mme de Pompadour. It has been alleged that, provoked by the jests and sarcasms of the King of Prussia, she was responsible for the Austrian alliance, and that the Empress of Austria wrote her an autograph letter conveying her thanks; but Maria Theresa always denied most emphatically that such a correspondence had ever taken place, and it seems that the idea originated in some confusion with the letter written by Kaunitz to Mme de Pompadour in consequence of the treaty of May 1. But, great as was the enthusiasm for the Austrian cause displayed by the favourite after that date, and in spite of her emphatic demand to be credited with it, the indications of direct intervention on her part in the preceding negotiations are proportionately scanty. And as for the Ministry—apart from Bernis, who was indeed an ardent adherent of this alliance, but had no longer any official status—though the defection of the King of Prussia had seriously shaken their previous convictions, they would never have ventured to propose, on their own initiative, so radical a change of policy.

The new Treaty contained the germ of most of the military and diplomatic events which were to follow. This is not intended to imply that in itself it was contrary to the interests of France and to a reasoned policy on her part. Since the days when Richelieu had laid it down as a fundamental maxim of French politics that the House of Austria must be brought low, great changes had taken place on the other side of the Rhine; but the French Government, in seeking at the Court of Vienna a substitute for the Prussian alliance that had come to a sudden end, had hurried into concessions of the most dangerous order. While Austria, admirably safeguarded by Kaunitz and Starhemberg, derived unquestionable advantages from the new combination, in "changing the most important of the continental Powers from an enemy into a friend, in freeing herself from anxiety as to her distant possessions in the Netherlands, and in recovering her freedom of action against the King of Prussia"—France, on the other hand, not only made it impossible for herself to obtain in the Netherlands any indemnification for her losses in the colonies, but transformed an ally of yesterday, who had desired nothing but to remain neutral, into an enemy of to-morrow. Of these extraordinary concessions on the part of France, which the later treaties were to aggravate to a still more remarkable degree, there can be only two explanations: the desire to take vengeance on the King of Prussia for his recent action, and the fear of a coalition against France of the three continental Powers, Prussia, Austria, and Russia. But, as a matter of fact, such a coalition, of which England had indeed dreamed for a moment in 1755, could never be formed, so long as those three Powers were kept apart by unconquerable jealousies.

The Treaty of May 1, 1756, was at first interpreted, throughout Europe, as certain to ensure peace on the Continent. After negotiations had been suspended for several months, France and England at last entered upon open hostilities, in Acadia (from which country the Acadians were driven out), and in the Mediterranean, where a body of troops commanded by Marshal Richelieu seized the island of Minorca. War was at last declared by England and France, but the King of Prussia was uneasy about the coalition which the Court of Vienna was preparing against him. In signing the subsidy treaty with England, in 1755, Russia, whose sovereign was entirely devoted to the interests of

Austria, had stipulated, by a *note secrétissime*, that the diversion in favour of England, provided for in the treaty, could only be understood of an attack upon the possessions of the King of Prussia. This essential detail, which made the Anglo-Russian agreement thenceforth valueless to himself, was not certainly known by Frederick until June, 1756, when he was apprised of it by Mitchell, the new British ambassador at his Court. He learnt at the same time through Knyphausen, his ambassador in Paris, that negotiations were still being carried on between the Court of Vienna and the Courts of Versailles and Russia, and through various emissaries that Austria was beginning to place her army on a war footing. It has been related elsewhere, how Frederick addressed to the Empress Maria Theresa an ultimatum as to her armaments and warlike intentions, and how then, without even waiting for her reply, he invaded Saxony and forced the Saxon troops encamped at Pirna to capitulate.

This sudden intervention on the part of Frederick II was destined to work a radical change in the position of affairs and to open a new era in European warfare. The immediate result was the rupture between France and Prussia. So soon as the news of the unexpected invasion of Saxony was known at Versailles, the Dauphiness Marie-Josèphe, daughter of the Elector, had burst into a torrent of complaints and demanded with tears the help of the King on behalf of her family; the lack of consideration shown by Frederick for the Count de Broglie, French ambassador in Saxony, and the active measures of Starhemberg did the rest. Count de Valori, French ambassador at Berlin, was recalled by a despatch of October 19: Knyphausen, the Prussian ambassador in France, was not ordered to quit his post till the beginning of November.

The second result of the invasion of Saxony was that it gave a fresh direction to the negotiations between France and Austria. These negotiations had been carried on throughout the summer at Paris or at Compiègne, and our chief source of knowledge respecting them consists in the despatches of Starhemberg to Kaunitz. On the side of France, Bernis continued to be the most earnest promoter of the transaction: Mme de Pompadour showed scarcely less enthusiasm, and multiplied her interviews with the Austrian ambassador. "She told me," writes Starhemberg, "that she would see me in private whenever I wished; that I must speak with her often, use perfect frankness, and, above all, lose no time." But the irresolution of Rouillé and the opposition of d'Argenson had still to be reckoned with; above all, the deep discrepancy between the claims of Austria and the demands of France, must be removed. At the end of August, 1756, and a few days before the invasion of Saxony, France consented to include among the objects of the agreement in course of negotiation the recovery of Silesia out of the hands of Prussia, promising assistance in money as well as an auxiliary force of 30,000 men. She further agreed not to make any separate peace with England, and undertook to maintain a considerable army to keep watch on the Rhine. Austria, in exchange for these benefits, contented herself with agreeing to the surrender of the Austrian Netherlands to the Infant Philip, in exchange for his Italian possessions, and to the cession to France of certain frontier towns. Kaunitz accordingly could not refrain from expressing his satisfaction with this arrangement, and he wrote thus to Mme de Pompadour: "The instructions of Count de Starhemberg, the equity and superior discernment by which I know the King to be distinguished, and your indefatigable zeal for his true interests...lead me to hope that we shall shortly bring to perfection the greatest achievement for which any European Cabinet has ever been responsible."

The intervention of the King of Prussia in Saxony changed the immediate purpose of the negotiations. Before proceeding further with the preparation of a second treaty, Austria demanded of France that the former agreement should be carried out, and notably that the auxiliary force provided by the convention of May 1, 1756, should be sent at once. The reply was at first entirely satisfactory; but, while the Court of Vienna demanded the despatch of these troops to Moravia, the French Government recommended operations against the principality of Jülich or against Hanover, and Marshal de Belleisle, though favourable to the Austrian alliance, likewise, for military reasons, opposed the Austrian project. As the prolongation of these disputes made the despatch of the troops impossible, Marshal d'Estrées was sent to Vienna to prepare a plan of campaign for the year 1757. Meanwhile, domestic incidents mentioned below—the struggle against the *Parlement*, Damiens' attempt upon the life of the King, and the important Ministerial changes which ensued in the course of the winter of 1756–7—contributed to retard the negotiations for the second treaty. This treaty, known to history as the Second Treaty of Versailles, was at last signed on May 1, 1757, exactly a year later than the earlier agreement. It comprised a preliminary clause, 32 principal and 10 separate articles, and provided that France, over and above the 24,000 auxiliaries prescribed by the defensive treaty, was to furnish the Austrian armies with 10,000 German soldiers, equip 105,000 men of her own, and pay to Austria an annual subsidy of twelve million florins. France obtained in exchange merely the possession of certain frontier towns of the Netherlands, Mons, Ypres, Furnes, Ostend, and Nieuport: the rest of the Austrian Netherlands was assigned to the Infant Don Philip, in exchange for the Italian duchies, which reverted to the Empress. The two Powers further promised not to lay down their arms until the King of Prussia should have been forced to relinquish Silesia and the county of Glatz in favour of Austria, and Magdeburg and Halberstadt in favour of Sweden. As a set-off to this, Austria, without actually entering upon an agreement hostile to England, merely promised her good offices in preserving Minorca for France when peace should be made, and in putting an end to the stipulations bearing on the fortifications of Dunkirk.

For several months previously, the coalition against Prussia had gained strength from another quarter by the alliance of Russia and Austria. In spite of the opposing influence of the Grand Chancellor, Bestuzheff, and the Grand Duchess Catharine, who were entirely devoted to England, and of the Grand Duke Paul, whose partisanship for the King of Prussia amounted to fanaticism, the Tsarina Elizabeth, inspired by an inveterate hatred of Frederick II, no sooner learnt of the Anglo-Prussian agreement of January 16, 1756, than she showed herself entirely ready to renew the former treaties with Austria. The chief difficulty which had to be encountered in these negotiations consisted in the attitude of France. The truth was that Russia only displayed readiness to undertake the war on condition of an enlargement of her dominions, notably at the expense of Prussia and of Poland, while the traditional policy of France, agreeing in this particular with the private policy of Louis XV, had two objects to secure in the East: namely, to prevent any extension of the dominions of Russia, and to watch with jealous care over the independence of Poland. It is well known that one of the chief objects of the private policy of Louis XV was to smooth the way to the throne of Poland for the Prince de Conti. At last, thanks to the modifications introduced by Austria, these contentions were happily evaded, and the French Government, while consenting to the stationing of Russian troops upon Polish territory, actually intervened in Poland to quiet the national susceptibility. This difficulty settled, the conferences were soon brought to a conclusion by the Convention of February 2, 1757, which confirmed the compact of 1746, the two Empresses promising not to lay down their arms until Silesia and the county of Glatz had been recovered and Prussia finally enfeebled. Meanwhile, conferences were still in progress between Prussia and England on both diplomatic and military questions, neither side displaying any great confidence. The change of Ministers in England, the anxiety of King George to preserve the neutrality of Hanover, and the negotiations with Vienna carried on by him up to the last moment with this end in view, had made a sinister impression upon Frederick II. However, at the end of the winter he had succeeded in obtaining the appointment of the Duke of Cumberland, well known for his hatred of France, to command the "Army of Observation" levied with his approval.

The Great Powers having now definitely chosen their sides, the struggle was to continue for seven years, at once in Europe, in Asia and in America; but it would be an entire mistake to suppose that the combinations thus formed were destined to continue unaltered. The unforeseen course of events provoked, on more than one occasion, an attempt to evade a promise given, or to conclude a separate treaty of peace. The first of such attempts took place between Austria and

France at the end of 1757. It has been related how after the French successes at Hastenbeck and the capitulation of the Duke of Cumberland at Klosterzeven, Soubise had been defeated by Frederick at Rossbach, and how, on their part, the Austrians, after being vanquished at Prague and victorious at Kolin, had eventually been utterly routed at Leuthen. These disasters had produced considerable discouragement at Vienna, and above all at Versailles. Bernis, who in his private letters to Choiseul, the new French ambassador at Vienna, displays a very pessimistic disposition, enlarged upon the difficulty of adhering to all the promises made by France, and suggested the idea of negotiations for peace. An indignant reply on the part of Kaunitz, an eloquent piece of special pleading from Maria Theresa, and the strenuous efforts of Starhemberg, conquered the hesitation of the French Court, and Louis XV, in the instructions sent to Choiseul after a council held on February 8, proclaimed himself a whole-hearted adherent of the alliance, and ready to satisfy all its conditions during the forthcoming campaign—namely, the payment of the subsidies, the upkeep of his army in Germany, and the promise not to conclude any separate treaty of peace with the King of Prussia.

The chivalrous response of Louis XV, though it had triumphed over the opposition of Bernis, who was before all else a courtier, had not in the slightest degree changed his personal convictions, which were only still further strengthened in the course of the campaign of 1758 and the reverses by which it was marked. Bernis, the chief promoter of the Austrian alliance, in proportion as the confidence displayed by him before the outbreak of the war had been precipitate, now showed himself discouraged, and a prey to nervous indecision. Once more he pictured in the most life-like colours to the Court of Vienna the financial distress of France, and proposed that the subsidies should be reduced, and peace negotiations set on foot. When he met with resistance on the part of Kaunitz and Maria Theresa, he finally proposed to Mme de Pompadour that Choiseul should act as his collaborator. After much hesitation, the King went beyond the wishes of his Minister, and sent him, on December 13, notification of banishment. Among the principal causes of his disgrace were the coldness which he had for some time displayed towards Mme de Pompadour, his too evident desire to play the part of Chief Minister, and the fact that he had more than once exceeded the wishes and the instructions of the King.

The Duc de Choiseul, who succeeded Bernis as Minister of Foreign Affairs, after having played a distinguished part during the War of the Austrian Succession, and shown much ability as ambassador at Rome and at Vienna, entered the Council with the support of Mme de Pompadour. He had originally won her favour by sacrificing to her a relative of his own, Mme de Choiseul Romanes, who had been in passing distinguished by Louis XV. Being raised by the King not long

CH. XI.

afterwards to the dignity of duke and of peer, he was not slow to accept the part of Chief Minister, for which he was indeed well qualified by nature. At once courtier and statesman, with the gift of combining pleasure with business, he succeeded in giving a perceptible impulse to the wheels of government, and displayed as much consistency in forming his projects as perseverance in carrying them into effect.

By way of marking his happy advent, Choiseul threw over the negotiations which had been carried on by Bernis, more or less secretly, with the object of coming to an understanding with England and Prussia through the medium of Spain. He affirmed the resolution of France to continue hostilities, and not to separate her cause from that of Austria. By the Third Treaty of Versailles, which bore the official date of December 30 and 31, 1758, although the signatures were not affixed until March, 1759, and ratifications were not exchanged until May of the same year, France undertook the continued maintenance of 100,000 fighting-men in Germany and the payment of the Saxon and Swedish corps. Mme de Pompadour was equally emphatic. "She is so far from any thought of peace," writes Starhemberg to Kaunitz on September 26, 1759, "that I have never found her so resolute and so clear-headed." The witticisms with which Frederick II continued to assail Louis XV and his mistress were, again, largely responsible for the warlike inclinations displayed by the French Court. It must not however be hence concluded that Choiseul accepted without reserve the consequences of the Austrian alliance. His language and his actions from this time forward bear witness to his having considered that alliance rather as a necessity imposed by the policy of the foregoing years, of which it was his business to get rid under the best possible conditions; they show, too, that he was from the first intent upon preparing a more and more intimate accord with Spain—an accord which was to be singularly assisted by the force of circumstances. (See *Addendum* after p. 837.)

The year 1759 was marked by several important events: chief among these, the disasters experienced by France in Canada (the loss of Quebec), and in Germany (her defeat at Minden); at home, the fall of credit and financial distress. In Spain, King Ferdinand was succeeded by Charles III, formerly King of the Two Sicilies, who was frankly in sympathy with France. The financial embarrassment in England, and the exhaustion of Prussia in the very midst of her victories, helped to impart manifest sincerity to the negotiations for peace now set on foot. These negotiations assumed the twofold form of proposals of mediation made by Spain to England, and declarations on the part of England and Prussia. From the moment of his accession, Charles III had displayed the most unmistakable desire to take an active share in the reestablishment of peace—less, indeed, by reason of his sympathy with France and resentment against England, than because an exclusive English maritime supremacy made him apprehensive for the Spanish possessions in the New World. But these tendencies, however skilfully encouraged by Choiseul and Osuna, French Minister at Madrid, were thwarted by the opposition of Pitt.

At the same time, proposals were made by England and Prussia, with the object of assembling a congress to treat for peace. Austria and Russia looked upon these propositions with suspicion, thinking that they detected in them a secret intention of sowing disunion and distrust between themselves; these two Powers, moreover, persisted in their desire to cling to the advantages they had gained over Frederick II. The proposals were taken more seriously by Choiseul, who sought to find in them an honourable means of putting an end to the maritime conflict between France and England. While the Bailli de Froulay was sent to Paris to act as an intermediary between Choiseul and Frederick II, a long conference was held at the Hague, early in 1760, between Yorke, on behalf of England, and Comte d'Affrey, representing France. Once more the efforts of France were brought to a standstill by the unacceptable terms imposed by Pitt, who laid it down as a preliminary condition that France should abandon her allies; but Choiseul had at least succeeded in persuading Russia and Austria to accept, though very reluctantly, the idea of a separate peace between France and England.

In spite of the obstacles encountered in England by the advocates of peace, Choiseul had no wish to cut himself off from that Power. During the series of alternate successes and reverses which marked the campaign of 1760 in Germany, the conferences were carried on, practically without interruption. At Vienna, Count de Choiseul, cousin of the Minister, was engaged in more than one stormy discussion with Kaunitz and Maria Theresa, who refused to accept the principle of private negotiations between France and England, and preferred the establishment of a general Congress. Choiseul appeared for a moment to be resigned to this last solution, and had even agreed to the despatch of plenipotentiaries to Augsburg; but the idea of this congress was to prove abortive, and the negotiations between France and England were now to assume a more active character, after the despatch, in the spring of 1761, of Hans Stanley to Paris and of Bussy to London, as plenipotentiaries of the two Powers. The bases of the negotiations had been fixed by the memorandum issued some weeks previously by Choiseul, which provided that each of the belligerents should retain the conquests made by him during the war; but the first difficulty arose when it became a question of deciding whether the conquests made by France in Germany came under that head. Many other difficulties retarded the negotiations: the quarrels about the fisheries in the New World, the possessions of England and France in the Indies, and the evacuation of Germany by the French troops; further, the opposition of Kaunitz, and above all, the introduction into the negotiations, at the instigation of Choiseul, of the question of the Spanish grievances.

CH. XI.

For many months, in truth, while the negotiations between France and England were being carried on, Choiseul had been holding with Spain certain conferences which were destined to bring about, under the name of the "Family Compact," a diplomatic event of equal importance with that "Reversal of Alliances" which had marked the beginning of the war.   Since his accession, the new King of Spain had not made any effort to conceal the signs of his sympathy with France. Under his influence, his advisers, and especially Wall, his Minister of Foreign Affairs, who had been quite recently a devoted partisan of England, had notably modified their attitude.   These new tendencies found another explanation in the discontent aroused in Spain by the action of England—the capture of Spanish vessels, on more than one occasion by the British squadrons, disputes about the right of fishing in the waters of Newfoundland carried on between England and the fishermen of Biscay and Guipuzcoa, and quarrels on the subject of the trade in logwood, had given rise to more and more vigorous protests on the part of the Spanish Cabinet.   These protests had invariably been met in London by an obvious determination to disregard them.   Osuna, the French Minister at Madrid, was consequently received with favour when he proposed, in the name of his Government, a project of offensive alliance against England (November, 1760); this project, which began, in the mind of Choiseul, at the time of his entry into the Cabinet, was supplemented by a close economic alliance between the two countries. Charles III showed great readiness to accept both proposals, only demanding time to put his colonies in a fit state for defence and to equip a fresh army and navy for Spain, before entering on the campaign.   But it was not long before the progress of the negotiations between France and England completely changed the aspect of affairs.   Charles III began to fear that peace between France and England might enable the latter country to steal a successful march on the Spanish possessions in the Philippines and the New World, and he soon showed himself most eager to come to an agreement.   The conditions proposed by Choiseul were accepted practically entire, and formed the principal bases of the treaties signed in Paris on August 15, 1761, and ratified at San Ildefonso on the 25th of the same month.   By the first of these treaties—known as the "Family Compact"—"any Power which shall become the enemy of the one or the other of the two Crowns" was declared the enemy of both ; the advantage of this protection was further extended to the King of the Two Sicilies and to the Infant Don Philip, Duke of Parma.   The aid to be furnished by each of the two Powers consisted of 12 ships of the line, 5 frigates and 24,000 men—a number which in certain contingencies might be reduced, for Spain, to 12,000.   The two Powers were not to treat for peace "save by mutual and common agreement and consent," and on the basis of an equitable balance of losses and gains.   In another section of the treaty the political and commercial relations were defined in the most liberal spirit: the Spaniards and Neapolitans were no longer to be accounted aliens in France, and the French were to benefit by similar advantages, having the right to dispose of all their property by will, donation, or any other method. Further items were: liberty of import and export for subjects of either Crown in the dominions of the other; equal treatment in the matter of trade, taxes, and navigation, and finally, union and friendly understanding between the representatives of the two Crowns in their attitude towards foreign Powers. The name of "Family Compact" was justified by the stipulation: "no other Power than those of this House (the House of Bourbon) shall be either invited or permitted to give adherence to this compact." As a matter of fact, the Princes reigning at Naples and at Parma joined this alliance shortly afterwards.

This Compact was supplemented by a secret Convention bearing the same date (August 15, 1761), whose principal stipulations were that Spain should undertake to declare war on May 1, 1762, if peace had not been concluded before that date; that France should from that time forward incorporate the complaints of Spain with her own grievances, and make no treaty on her own account, unless those grievances were remedied by it; and, finally, that Portugal should be compelled, if necessary by force, to embrace the cause of the two Powers.

The "Family Compact" thus comprised two divisions—the one relating to affairs of war, the other to politics and trade. We shall have occasion below to speak of the advantages and the importance of the latter division, which, for the rest, possessed by far the most enduring significance. The other was of far more doubtful value. Choiseul's great mistake was that he was deceived about the military resources of Spain. In 1761, the forces of France were too much exhausted, and those of Spain too little inured to the discipline of war, for the union of the two Powers to produce any essential change in the aspect of affairs. These errors on the part of Choiseul could not but react upon affairs both diplomatic and military. From the diplomatic point of view, Choiseul imagined that, by putting forward Spain in his negotiations with England, he would gain at the same time certain important advantages. Not only, however, did Pitt, who was better acquainted with Spanish affairs, refuse to follow this lead, but even the two negotiators themselves, Bussy and Stanley, were of opinion that the introduction of the Spanish grievances into the Franco-British conferences, though perhaps not amounting to a change in the substance of Pitt's ultimatum of July 25, 1761, at any rate made its terms more impracticable. We know the chief articles of this ultimatum: France was not to aid Maria Theresa except with the 24,000 men stipulated by the First Treaty of Versailles; while England might continue to assist the King of Prussia with all the resources at her disposal; the fortifications of Dunkirk were to be destroyed; and England was to keep all the colonies in her possession

CH. XI.

at the date of the signing of the Treaty. Choiseul replied to this ultimatum by the *"ultimatissimum"* of September 3, in which he accepted the principle of the demolition of the fortifications of Dunkirk, but demanded for France the unchallenged possession of the islands of St Pierre and Miquelon, and claimed satisfaction for the Spanish grievances. A deadlock had now been reached, and the commissioners were recalled.

In England, the fall of Pitt was hastened as much by his own intractability, his disagreements with his colleagues, particularly with Newcastle and Lord Bute, and the lack of sympathy displayed towards him by the new King, as by the rupture of the negotiations with France; but his disappearance from the Cabinet of St James' caused no essential modification in its policy. The cessation of the conferences with France was followed almost immediately by the rupture of relations with Spain, which had been growing more and more strained during the past months; at the end of December, 1761, the ambassadors were recalled, and war was declared by England on January 2, 1762.

This last phase of the War, which in the opinion of Choiseul and Charles III must decide the question of naval and colonial supremacy between England on the one hand and France and Spain on the other, was of short duration. The rapid opening of hostilities against Spain, recommended by Pitt, had the result which he had foreseen. The campaign of 1762 entailed upon France the loss of such possessions as she still had in the West Indies, the capture of Martinique and the islands of Grenada and St Vincent, while Spain lost Havana and the Philippines. Meanwhile, on the Continent, the death of Elizabeth and the accession of the Tsar Peter III to the throne of Russia marked a change of policy on the part of that country in favour of Prussia; and after Peter's death, at the end of a few months, the new Tsarina, Catharine II, showed herself disposed to remain neutral. The weariness and exhaustion of the belligerents led to a resumption of the conferences, and this time a decision was soon reached.

In accordance with the principle laid down by Choiseul, the negotiations were carried on by each country separately—Prussia being represented by Hertzberg, Austria by Frisch and Collenbach, Augustus III by Brühl—and the result was the Treaty of Hubertusburg, signed on February 15, 1763. This Treaty confirmed the *status quo* before the War, Frederick II retaining Silesia, and promising his voice in support of the election of Joseph, the eldest son of Maria Theresa, as King of the Romans, while the Elector of Saxony regained possession of all his dominions. Between France and England, negotiations were resumed after the despatch of the Duc de Nivernais to London and of the Duke of Bedford to Paris. The preliminaries were signed at Fontainebleau on November 3, 1762, and confirmed by the Treaty of Paris on February 10, 1763. By this Treaty France ceded to England the whole of Canada, and only retained, in the West Indies the island of St Lucia, in Senegal the island of Goree, and in India the five towns of Mahé, Pondicherry, Chandernagore, Karikal, and Yanaon; she further restored Minorca, and ceded Louisiana to Spain in exchange for Florida, which the latter Power made over to England.

This Treaty, which secured the maritime supremacy of England and the military prestige of Prussia, was called in France "the disgraceful peace." It did in fact signify for France the loss of her colonial empire, the annihilation of her navy and of the ruin of her finances; and the discontent created among all classes by so unparalleled a series of reverses was to prove a source of great trouble in the future. Before reviewing the efforts made by Choiseul, in the second period of his Ministry, to repair these disasters, we may briefly recall the principal events which had marked the domestic history of the country during the previous years.

Among the institutions which played a prominent part in the internal history of France in the eighteenth century, the *Parlement* holds the foremost place. At the very beginning of the reign of Louis XV, that body, by setting aside the will of the late King, had striven to take vengeance for the state of dependence in which it had been kept by Louis XIV. In the absence of the States General, which had not been convoked since 1614, the *Parlement* aspired to play a political part, and to transform its right of remonstrance into a real control over the proceedings of the royal power. The disputes constantly arising upon the subject of the Jansenists, who had become a political coterie, had furnished the *Parlement* with frequent opportunities of intervention. On several occasions its members had refused to sit, and had been sent into exile: the banishment to Pontoise in 1753 lasted for upwards of fifteen months. In 1755 it was engaged in a vigorous dispute with the Archbishop of Paris on the subject of the Jansenists and of the administration of the Sacraments. In 1756, the *Parlement* had to meet in the presence of the King, in order to be forced to adopt the edicts for extraordinary taxes issued at the beginning of the War; at the end of the year, resort was had to the same proceeding, and on this occasion several edicts were read, modifying the constitution of the *Parlement* and reducing its powers.

During the course of this struggle, on January 5, 1757, a fanatic, Jean-François Damiens, who had formerly been a domestic servant, stabbed the King with a knife as he was entering his carriage. The wound was slight; but profound emotion was excited at the Court. When the assassin was tried by the *Parlement*, a strange light was thrown upon the sentiments produced in the lower classes of society by their misery, and by the political and religious discussions of the time. The attempt of Damiens also had unforeseen consequences in another sphere of public life. In the first stress of his emotion, the

King had refused for several days to see Mme de Pompadour. From this it had been generally inferred that the favourite had fallen into lasting disgrace; and her return to favour resulted in the fall, at the very moment when the Seven Years' War was about to begin, of the two Ministers who had shown themselves most strenuously opposed to her influence, but who, on the other hand, were the most capable of ensuring satisfactory preparations for the War—d'Argenson and Machault.

The combined influence of the ill-feeling of the *Parlement* and the Jansenists, and of the opinions of the Philosophers, was responsible for the movement against the Jesuits, which began in France some years later, and resulted in the dissolution of their body. The animosity aroused by their ascendancy in the principal Catholic Courts of Europe, and by their interference in politics, which in Portugal brought about their expulsion, is described in another chapter of this volume. In France, the looked-for opportunity arose with the action brought by several merchants against Père Lavalette. This Jesuit had founded in Martinique a business house, which had at first prospered, but eventually failed, in consequence of the capture by the English of a number of vessels laden with cargo belonging to the concern. Some merchants of Marseilles, Lavalette's creditors, had brought a suit against the whole Order, as being responsible for the debts of its members. The Jesuits refused payment, on the ground that they had excluded Père Lavalette from their Order, and further invoked the principles of their constitution. They lost their case before the Consular tribunal of Marseilles, and before the *Parlement* of Paris; but the latter body, when an appeal " on the ground of abuse " was entered by the Attorney-General, undertook to examine the constitution of the Society. The result was that the King's subjects were forbidden to join it, and the Jesuits themselves interdicted from teaching. Meanwhile, several provincial *Parlements*, notably those of Rouen and Rennes, gave decisions against the Order. Under the pressure of public opinion and of the Philosophers, and following the advice of Choiseul, Louis XV disregarded the opposition of the Dauphin, a number of Bishops and the *dévot* party, and issued at last, in November, 1764, an edict enacting that " the Society should no longer exist in France; that its members should only be allowed to live in private in the King's dominions." Nine years later, in 1773, the abolition of the Society of Jesus was pronounced by Pope Clement XIV.

While Choiseul was thus satisfying the principles of the Philosophers and the ambitions of the *Parlements*, he was also engaged upon the reform of the army and of the navy, undertaking himself, from 1761 to 1766, the entire responsibility of those two departments, and leaving in the meantime the Ministry of Foreign Affairs to his cousin, the Duc de Choiseul-Praslin. In 1766, he again resumed the conduct of foreign affairs and entrusted his cousin with the management of the navy; but, as a matter of fact, it was at any given moment his opinion and his behaviour that inspired and dominated the entire policy of the Cabinet. With regard to the army, a preparatory military school was established at La Flèche to supplement the military school at Paris; the guns were thenceforth manufactured in the state factories; and, in 1765, the new system introduced by Gribeauval established the artillery corps— thenceforth distinct from the engineer corps—consisting of the first seven artillery regiments. As to the navy, the three arsenals already existing were supplemented by two more—Marseilles for galleys, and Lorient; by means of voluntary contributions, the fleet was increased by a certain number of vessels, and important works were set on foot at Brest. The Naval Academy was reorganised, and a new impetus given to scientific studies. But the indefatigable activity of Choiseul displayed itself above all in the department of politics and diplomacy, during the seven years (1763–70) which formed the latter portion of his Ministry.

During the last period of his career, the foreign policy of Choiseul displayed two chief tendencies: to annul the effects of the Treaty of Paris and to intervene in the Eastern question in favour of the old allies of France concerned in it—Sweden, Poland, and Turkey. Never had the qualities and defects of his character been more clearly marked than in his application of this policy. Of quick and resourceful intelligence, far-seeing at times to the point of divination, swift to conceive schemes which sometimes evinced a very real force, when it came to execution he was invariably inconsequent, thoughtless, and blundering, thus in a measure justifying the quip attributed to Louis XV: "he thinks himself a great Minister, and has nothing in his mind but a little phosphorus." These defects could not fail to have a sinister influence on his schemes. But he was in any case, from his very position as Chief Minister of such a King as Louis XV, foredoomed to disaster. All his efforts against England and in the East ended in war—a result which he foresaw and, far from dreading, almost welcomed; but Louis XV, especially in his later days, was incapable of following Choiseul in this redoubtable enterprise, and the foreign policy of the Minister inevitably ended in his downfall. That downfall was for him well-timed, in that his plans scarcely had to endure the test of being put into practice: it was ill-timed, in so far as it caused the results obtained to appear disproportionate to his efforts. Hence the different judgments passed by recent historians upon Choiseul—some honestly admiring his policy, and others seeing in him only a fanatic and a blunderer.

With regard, in the first instance, to his policy against England, he has been accused of failing to grasp the importance of the losses entailed by the Treaty of Paris. The assertion has been put into his mouth, that he had done the English a good turn by obliging them to distribute their strength all over the world, and he has been reproached for speaking disdainfully of the loss of Canada. His words were doubtless nothing more than the capricious utterance of a statesman trying to put a good face on a bad business; and his failure to appreciate the value of Canada was shared at that time by the English themselves. In any case, he had projects of reorganising the naval and colonial empire of France—projects summed up in his dream of supremacy in the two Mediterraneans—that of the old Continent, and the American Mediterranean (the Gulf of Mexico and the West Indian seas).

France owed to Choiseul the acquisition of Corsica in the western Mediterranean, which was controlled by the English forts of Gibraltar and Port Mahon. In 1755, a patriot, Paoli, raised the whole island against its Genoese masters, who, as is related elsewhere, were in 1756 forced to appeal for help to the French troops occupying the principal forts on the coast. In 1768, Choiseul induced Genoa to sell the island to France. Equilibrium was thus restored in the western Mediterranean, and Toulon and the coast of Provence were protected by advanced posts of first-class strength. The English Government, preoccupied by their disputes with the American colonists, realised too late the importance of the proceedings, when, in response to the protests of Paoli, the whole of the patriot party indirectly came to their aid. The Paolists defeated the first troops sent by Choiseul, but in May, 1769, Count de Vaux, thanks to his superior numbers, won the decisive victory of Pontenuovo. These proceedings bred in the Corsicans a bitter resentment against France, while the English chafed at their lost opportunity. Thus it came to pass that the island once more revolted under the leadership of Paoli (1790), and the English established there a naval fort threatening that of Toulon, until in course of time the ascendancy of Napoleon Bonaparte transformed the Corsicans into French patriots.

Perhaps an expedition sent by Choiseul against Tunis and Biserta— an expedition which was, moreover, premature and productive of no lasting results—need not be regarded as more than an incident in the long-standing quarrel between the inhabitants of Barbary and the Europeans. But, on the other hand, Choiseul in 1769 encouraged the French advance into Egypt, which was a station of first-class importance in the eastern Mediterranean, in contact with the seaports of the Levant, where the influence of France predominated, and at the same time affording an approach to India. Choiseul anticipated Bonaparte by cherishing the thought of Egypt as a French possession.

But, in the direction of the American Mediterranean, Choiseul had a yet more exalted aim. Ever since the Bourbon dynasty had placed Philip V upon the throne of Spain, France had dreamed of opening to French products that market, hitherto jealously barred to European importation. This traditional policy of France, interrupted by the Regent's anti-Spanish policy, and by the friendly relations between Spain and England signalised by the commercial treaty of 1750, reappeared when France and Spain came to an agreement, inspired by a common dread of the flourishing navy of England. Since 1758, Choiseul had employed on the drafting of an economic alliance a functionary established in Spain by the French since the reign of Philip V—the Agent-General of commerce and naval affairs, who combined the functions of a commercial attaché with those of a secret diplomatic agent, and whose part it was to guide and—when necessary—to take the place of the ambassador, in matters of trade. In 1758, this post was occupied by Abbé Beliardi, "the channel of communication between M. de Choiseul and M. d'Aranda." He set on foot a great commercial enquiry in Spain, from 1758 to 1763, concerned principally with Cadiz, the general market in the West Indian trade. The Family Compact of 1761 was, in certain of its bearings, an economic alliance. In 1763, after the War, Choiseul developed his views as to the method of turning that alliance to account. " I should like," he wrote to Louis XV, " all other alliances to be subordinated to this union." The object of France was to obtain from Charles III the opening of the Spanish Indies to her industrial products, and so to assist the economic development of Spain as to procure for herself a prosperous ally. From 1763 to 1766, negotiations for a commercial agreement were carried on; in 1765, Charles III reduced the export duties on Spanish products imported into America, which were principally French goods imported under the protection of Spain : these goods, becoming consequently cheaper, competed in America with the English contraband merchandise brought from Jamaica. Finally—most important of all—Choiseul hoped to form out of all that remained of the French empire in America—St Dominique, Martinique and Guiana—a colonial domain in the Gulf of Mexico and the West Indian seas. This domain was, under the protection of Spanish America, to make French influence supreme in the American Mediterranean and provide a means of taking away the trade of British America from the south ; it was, further, to serve as a market for French products destined for Spanish America, and would even make possible, in case of need, an attack upon Brazil, or the blocking of the road by which English contraband goods came from British Guiana to Peru. With this end in view, Choiseul took in hand the colonisation of French Guiana ; his attempt, however, was a dead failure, not through his own fault, but through that of d'Estaing, to whom he had entrusted the management of the scheme : and even then he still had the hope of obtaining from Spain a station in the Philippines, whence French commodities could be carried to the Pacific coast of Spanish America.

Such schemes could not fail to produce disquiet in England, on whom, however, Choiseul was eager to inflict a more direct injury. He judged, quite correctly, that the loss of Canada by France would lead to a rising in British America, now that they had no further need of the mother country as a point of resistance to the Canadians. So early as 1767, Choiseul foresaw this insurrection of the British settlers, and sent a secret agent, Kalb, to study the situation.   At first Kalb did not recognise any signs of a separatist movement, but presently he changed his opinion and urged Choiseul to take active steps.   But that Minister was no longer able to spare attention for America, and Kalb's reports left him unmoved.   Choiseul, whose fall in 1770 was due to a "plan of campaign against England," showed a prophetic belief in the inevitable rivalry to come between the revolted Americans and the English. Though, as has been seen, at times guilty of inconsequence or of blindness, in the question of the American Mediterranean he neverthe- less displayed amazing foresight, anticipating the ephemeral project of Napoleon I, in 1803, of constituting a French empire in America with the help of Louisiana and St Dominique—which project, it may be, in turn influenced Napoleon III's scheme of a French empire in Mexico.

We are now in a position to appreciate Talleyrand's description of Choiseul as "one of the most prophetically-minded men of our genera- tion."   It will also be seen that Pitt was right, when he said, in 1763, that England, by making peace with France, was offering her the oppor- tunity of reconstituting her navy and her colonies.   This reconstitution was the work of Choiseul.   But, as Captain Mahan has said, "In the naval development of a State, the regular action of a moneyed class, preponderant in the nation and free to act, is of more importance than the initiative of a despotic and temporary power."   Choiseul, so long as Louis XV left the government in his hands, had a certain influence on the reconstitution of the navy and the colonies of France: but Louis XV deprived him of this power, and from that moment the plans of Choiseul were destined to fall into oblivion.

The Eastern question was another of Choiseul's chief preoccupations. In the eighteenth century, France had three allies in eastern Europe— Sweden, Poland, and Turkey.   These three States had been falling into decadence since the end of the seventeenth century, while, in their place, Prussia, Austria, and Russia were coming into prominence.   Thus had sprung up the idea of a partition of each of the three declining Powers by their three rivals; and, in the time of Choiseul, Sweden was threatened with partition by Prussia, Russia, and Denmark, Poland by Prussia, Russia, and Austria, and Turkey by Russia and Austria. However, Prussia, Austria, and Russia were themselves divided by mutual jealousy and apprehension.   Frederick II of Prussia, since the Seven Years' War, had lived in mortal fear of the colossal and barbarous power of Russia, declaring her to be a "deadly neighbour and a peril to the whole of Europe."   He would fain have had the support of Austria, France, and England, in keeping in check Catharine II, to whom he preached the duty of moderation in her appetite for conquests. Catharine, on her side, declared to Potemkin that the Prussian alliance was "the most ignominious and intolerable thing in the whole world," and sought rather to make an ally of Austria.   That Power, which, now that Silesia was finally lost to it, nursed a permanent grudge against Prussia, had another ground for uneasiness in what has been called "the Greek project" of Catharine II—her desire, that is, of reuniting the Orthodox party in Russia with their kinsmen in the Balkan peninsula, and of establishing the Christian faith in Constantinople, by introducing there the supremacy of Russia. If Prussia, Austria, and Russia were divided, Sweden, Poland, and Turkey, which ought to have joined forces in their common danger, were similarly separated by a traditional hostility, and England, instead of supporting Turkey, was disposed to sacrifice that Power to Russian ambition. But France always took up the cause of the three Powers thus menaced. Though she had lost much of her authority in Europe by her reverses in the Seven Years' War, Choiseul reckoned on the help of his ally, Austria, against Russia and Prussia—a calculation which, in fact, lay at the root of his Eastern policy. But, unhappily, this was, like much of the official policy of France, not in accordance with the secret policy of the King. Louis XV distrusted Austria equally with Prussia and Russia, and the "King's Secret" consequently resisted any extension of Austrian influence in Turkey and above all in Poland. It cannot be denied that events were to prove the farsightedness of the "King's Secret" with regard to Austria, and the mistake of Choiseul on the same head. In any case, the opposition between the official diplomats and the secret agents of France deprived her Eastern policy of all definiteness and all efficacy.

The real danger for Sweden, Poland, and Turkey lay not so much in the sinister designs of their neighbours and the powerlessness of France as in the shortcomings of their internal organisation. They were feudal States—States, that is, without unity, without a centralised government, without any financial or military organisation—opposed to such modern States as Prussia and Austria were, and Russia was trying to be. At the end of the Seven Years' War, Russia, Prussia, and Austria, having gained no new territory in that War, fell to dreaming of compensation. The year 1762 saw the death of the King Augustus III of Poland, Elector of Saxony; and the election of a new King furnished an excellent pretext for foreign intervention. Consequently, Peter III of Russia and Frederick II of Prussia undertook, by a secret treaty, to maintain the Constitution of Poland—in other words, to perpetuate anarchy in that country. From 1763 onwards, in view of the defects of her Constitution, the situation of Poland became extremely grave. As for Turkey, she was then what she is now. The Mussulman Turk pitched his camp in the midst of infidel Slavs and Hellenes, whom he had neither absorbed nor converted; he did not govern them, for the Sultan despot, torpid in his seraglio, left the Pachas to act for him, and they had no other administrative system than that of "devouring the country." The Sultan's Christian subjects, too, were waking little by little to covet independence, and were no longer indifferent to the propaganda issued by Russia in favour of the project of rousing the Greeks to revolt.

Given the position of Sweden, Poland, and Turkey, what steps did Choiseul think fit to take? To save Sweden, he lectured the heir presumptive to the throne, Prince Gustavus, the son of King Adolphus Frederick, upon the dangers threatening his country. He thought that Turkey was strong enough in military force to save herself, and even to help in safeguarding Poland. Poland it was, above all, that Choiseul was planning to protect, and she was in truth the most severely menaced of the three. The first transaction demanding attention was the election of the successor of Augustus III. The candidate put forward by Prussia and Russia was Stanislaus Poniatowski, by birth a Polish noble, who was supported by the powerful family of the Czartoryskis, and a favourite of Catharine II. Choiseul and Austria had another candidate—Prince Xavier of Saxony, brother of the Dauphiness of France; and Choiseul reckoned on obtaining the intervention of Turkey in favour of his nominee. But Austria had no other motive in upholding the claims of a Saxon in Poland than that of gaining the vote of the Elector of Saxony in the election of Joseph II as King of the Romans; and, that election once made, Austria had no further interest in the question. Turkey declined to act, because Prussia and Russia assured her that the only desideratum was liberty in elections to the throne of Poland, and that to uphold Poniatowski was simply to support a true Pole. Finally, Xavier of Saxony offended the Primate of Poland, Lubienski, whose influence was very great. Choiseul, thus finding himself alone against Prussia and Russia, dared not state precisely the attitude of France. Some Russian troops entered Poland, and Stanislaus Poniatowski was elected (September, 1764). Choiseul's endeavour was now to screen Stanislaus from Russian influence, to the advantage of Austria and France. With this end in view, Choiseul sketched a plan of marriage between Stanislaus and an Archduchess of Austria; but the plan came to nothing, through the machinations of the "King's Secret" against Austria.

From 1766 onwards, Stanislaus and the Czartoryskis endeavoured to reform the Polish Constitution; while an opposition faction, formed by the adherents of Xavier of Saxony, but claiming the title of "national party," demanded the preservation of the old Constitution in every point. Matters were, however, upon the point of being arranged in the Diet by a reconciliation between the Czartoryskis and the national party, when the Russian ambassador, Repnin, brought the Russian soldiery to bear upon the Diet, and obliged it to repeal the laws against Dissidents, which pressed hard on the Greek Catholics, and restored the *liberum veto* in its unrestricted form (1768). By way of revenge, the nobles who were hostile to the Dissidents and to the Czartoryskis formed the Confederation of Bar. Choiseul espoused the cause of the Confederates; but public opinion in France, following the Philosophers, in whose eyes Catharine II appeared as the patroness of religious tolerance in Poland, pronounced

against them.   The support of Choiseul was given indirectly, by sending
to the Confederates certain officers, such as Dumouriez and Choisy, whose
record as adventurers would justify him in disowning them, in case of
need, and by gifts of money and ammunition.   But the Russian troops
penetrated further and further into Polish territory, and under the
pretext of helping the Dissidents drove out the Confederates of Bar.
Choiseul now urged Austria to give direct support to the Confederates,
and since the Russian troops, in pursuing their prey, violated Turkish
territory, the French ambassador in Constantinople, de Vergennes, persuaded the Sultan Mustafa to declare war against Russia (1768).

Upon this occasion also, the " King's Secret " baffled the effort made
by Choiseul to rouse Austria to arms, and the war dragged on in another
quarter between Turks and Russians, while in Poland the state of anarchy
increased.   Frederick II and Maria Theresa posted troops to keep a look-
out on the Polish frontier, and these troops, in particular the Austrians,
encroached little by little upon the Polish territory.   Prussia and
Austria were uneasy at Catharine's seizure of Poland, and Frederick II
wished to divert her attention to Sweden ; in certain interviews with
Joseph II of Austria at Neisse and Neustadt, he sought to devise ways of
keeping Russia in check.   And in the midst of all these complications and
intrigues, the idea already formulated in the seventeenth and the first half
of the eighteenth century was taking shape—the idea of a partition of
Poland which should satisfy the conflicting desires of her neighbours.

At this moment Catharine II, instigated by her favourite, Gregori
Orloff, who was himself inspired by the Greek Papazoglu, tried to carry
out her " Greek project " by sending into the Archipelago, by way of
the Mediterranean, a Russian fleet to rouse the Hellenes to revolt.
England favoured this scheme, in order to play a trick upon France
and her ally, Turkey ; and it was an English sailor, Elphinston, who
piloted the first Russian fleet that ever sailed the waters of the Levant.
The Turkish fleet was burnt at Tchesmé (in August, 1770), and the
Straits and Constantinople were only saved by the menaces of Baron
de Tott, an adventurer sent by Choiseul to the Sultan to play the
same part in Turkey as that played by Dumouriez, Choisy, and their
fellows, in Poland.   It was these advantages gained by Russia over the
Turks which determined Austria and Prussia to call upon the Tsarina to
check her advance on Constantinople, and to offer her indemnification in
Poland.   Before these consequences of the Russian cruise manifested themselves, France saw the fall of Choiseul from power, in December, 1770.

The fall of Choiseul was brought about partly by his foreign policy :
his naval and colonial policy was driving him into a war with England,
and his attitude in the Eastern question was also involving him in a war
with England and Russia.   These adventurous schemes " disturbed the
senile egoism of Louis XV."   The Minister was, moreover, the victim of
his domestic policy—in other words, of his concessions to the *Parlements*,

his lack of foresight in financial questions, and his quarrel with the *dévot* party at Court, together with the ill-will of the new favourite, Mme Du Barry.

The eternal conflict between the Crown and the *Parlements* was renewed in 1763–4, when the Government, in spite of the fact that peace had been concluded, sought to continue the taxes levied on account of the Seven Years' War. In Britanny, this conflict resulted in a coalition between the Estates of the province and the *Parlement* of Rennes, led by its Attorney-General, La Chalotais, against the Duc d'Aiguillon, the royal Governor of Britanny, whom the *Parlement* of Rennes, followed by that of Paris, undertook to subject to solemn censure. Thus the *Parlements* were setting on foot proceedings against a representative of the royal authority, while resisting the financial policy of the Crown. But the King could not allow himself to be set at defiance; and, moreover, the state coffers were empty. Choiseul had none of the qualities of an expert financier : he was too lofty a personage to interest himself in questions of statistics, and the successive Controllers-general whom he had chosen, Bertin and L'Averdy, had not succeeded in supplying the deficiencies of the Treasury. At any price, then, in 1769–70, the opposition of the *Parlements* to the authority and to the fiscal demands of the Crown must be overcome—and this had, in fact, been the cry of Maupéou, Chancellor since 1768, and Terray, appointed Controller-general in 1769. But Choiseul shrank from crushing the *Parlements*, because they had the support of public opinion, which it was ever his care to please ; and he forbore to give serious consideration to the attitude of Maupéou and Terray, because he believed himself at that juncture to be all-powerful. The death of the Dauphin had indeed freed him from his most powerful enemy, and that of Mme de Pompadour from a compromising patronage, and he had succeeded in marrying the new Dauphin, the heir presumptive, whose reign could not be long delayed, to Marie-Antoinette of Austria. But Maupéou and Terray had on their side the *dévot* party, lately headed by the deceased Dauphin, and now under the leadership of the Duc de La Vauguyon and Nicolay, Bishop of Verdun, and they could not forgive Choiseul for the fall of the Jesuits. This coalition was further strengthened by Mme Du Barry, whom Choiseul had been so ill-advised as to hold in contempt ; not that she was contemptible—Mme de Pompadour, his protectress, had scarcely been more powerful—but because the Minister believed Louis XV's attachment for her to be nothing more than a fleeting caprice. The Duc d'Aiguillon and Marshal Richelieu instructed Mme Du Barry to slander Choiseul in the King's hearing. The quarrel with the *Parlements* furnished the coalition with the opportunity of overthrowing that Minister. Between June and December, 1770, Maupéou insisted on forcing the King's will upon the *Parlements*, until that of Paris suspended its functions. The strike was brought to an end on December 20 by a royal injunction that the *Parlement* should resume its duties ; and on December 24 Choiseul was dismissed.

His fall came none too soon for his reputation. The ingenuous confidence of his foreign policy with regard to Austria, which he regarded in the light of an instrument for safeguarding Poland, marked him out for speedy disaster, while at home his compliance towards the *Parlements* and his laxity in financial matters could not long be allowed to continue. His fall relieved him of responsibility for the difficulties bequeathed by him to his successors, and he carried with him into retirement the reputation of a great statesman. That reputation was, indeed, in some measure exaggerated; for in spite of his magnificent designs in certain matters of foreign policy, he had often proved himself trifling, blundering, indiscreet; while at home, by the expulsion of the Jesuits, the upholders of absolute royalty, by the impunity accorded to the *Parlements* when they attacked that same royalty, and by his heedlessness in finance, he had contributed not a little towards the overthrow of that system of absolute monarchy of which he was, nevertheless, a partisan.

The new Minister of Foreign Affairs was the Duc d'Aiguillon, who, with Maupéou at the head of judicial affairs and Terray in charge of finance, formed the Ministry called by their contemporaries the Triumvirate. Public opinion was against them from the first, because the will of an unpopular King and his infamous favourite had put them in the place of the people's hero; and, inheriting difficulties which Choiseul himself would unquestionably have failed to solve, they were to find disasters at home and abroad, which he had rendered inevitable, laid to their account.

It was not in the power of d'Aiguillon to save Poland, who lost her frontier provinces to Prussia, Austria, and Russia, after their coalition in 1772. From 1770 to 1772, Catharine II, under pressure from Prussia and Austria, slackened in her hostility towards the Turks, and then granted them a truce. Prince Henry of Prussia familiarised the mind of Frederick II with the idea of a partition of Poland, and, in 1771, was sent by his brother to enforce this project upon Catharine II, who would have preferred to retain the monopoly of influence in Poland and to conquer Turkey, but dared not break with Prussia and Austria, now once more united. Austrian and Prussian troops now followed the example set by the Russians, and penetrated into Polish territory. Austria, however, still hesitated: she would have preferred, instead of being allotted a fragment of Poland, to deprive France of Alsace and Lorraine, or to recover Silesia from Frederick II, or to receive part of Turkey. But Frederick II forced her to adopt his views by inspiring her with a fear of Russia, exactly as he forced Russia to adopt them by making her afraid of Austria; and, after he had signed with Catharine II, on February 10, 1772, the First Treaty for the Partition of Poland, Austria, eight days later, signified her adherence to the treaty. France could not possibly oppose the division, abandoned as she was by her ally, Austria, and jealously watched by England. The "King's Secret," farsighted in its

distrust of Austria, was powerless to find any other solution, and
Louis XV, a prey to senile weakness, let his cherished policy fall to
pieces. D'Aiguillon, then, was not responsible for the ruin of Poland.
Nor would the saying, attributed without probability to Louis XV, that
"if Choiseul had been there, the partition would never have taken place,"
have been just in the mouth of a King who had excellent opportunities
for a fair assignment of the responsibilities in question.

During the same period, Sweden escaped the fate of Poland. The
Prince Royal of Sweden, Gustavus, summoned by Choiseul to France to
receive his advice, had arrived there at the end of 1770, after the fall of
the Minister. But the Duc de La Vrillière, who was taking the place of
d'Aiguillon till the latter should arrive, and the officials of the Foreign
Office, did what Choiseul would have done. Gustavus returned to
Sweden in 1771, with four million francs and Vergennes as his mentor.
When on his return he took up his duties as King, he received from
d'Aiguillon and Louis XV the same support as Choiseul had given him;
and he prepared a *coup d'état* against the Diet. Though England sent
to the Diet a copy of a letter in which Gustavus disclosed his plan to
Louis XV, the young King was too quick for the Senate, and the
Constitution of 1772, which reestablished absolutism at the expense of
the nobility, was followed, in 1773, by the renewal of the alliance
between Sweden and France. The partition of Poland and the renewal
of war with Turkey prevented Catharine II from putting any obstacle
in his way. In this affair d'Aiguillon had shown himself a worthy successor of Choiseul: it is true that he was helped by Sweden herself, and
by the diversion created in her favour by Poland and Turkey. As for
the Turks, Frederick II had incited the Tsarina to renew hostilities
against them; and they were eventually forced to sign the disad-
vantageous Treaty of Kutchuk-Kainardji, in July, 1774, some months
after the death of Louis XV. But d'Aiguillon was no more responsible
for her misfortunes than he had been for those of Poland.

The Chancellor Maupéou, for his part, had assigned himself the task
of consolidating the absolute monarchy by the destruction of the *Parlements*. In the night from January 21 to 22, 1771, the magistrates of
the *Parlement* of Paris were sentenced to exile and relieved of their
positions. Maupéou established a new *Parlement*, whose members were
nominated by him and were entirely devoid of political authority; the
jurisdiction of the old *Parlement* was mutilated by the institution of six
other Courts of justice, called Superior Councils. The other *Parlements*
and all the judicial tribunals suffered the same fate. Maupéou did away
with the sale of legal offices and made justice free to all; he wished,
further, to simplify legal procedure and to codify the laws. These
reforms in the administration of justice were applauded by the Philosophers; but public opinion was far from following them; and, in truth,
Maupéou had nobody to put in the place of the dismissed magistrates
except persons of damaged reputation, one of whom, Goëzman, was

convicted by Beaumarchais of having taken a bribe from him; while, again, the fact that Maupéou's *Parlements* were the creatures of a Minister and of a King who were alike detested, was not calculated to inspire confidence. Maupéou's *coup d'état*, instead of consolidating the royal authority, threatened its stability. What he really did was to cause an extraordinary effervescence; and, though this speedily subsided, the public did not forget the dialogue held between the *Parlements* and the King at the time of the *coup d'état*. That dialogue bore upon the respective rights of the Crown and the nation: the *Parlement* of Paris declared, for example, in 1763, that the French were "free men and not slaves"; in the same year, the *Cour des Aides* demanded that the States General should be convened, and the magistrates on all sides invoked "the right of resistance." Louis XV answered: "We hold our Crown from God alone. The right of making laws belongs to ourselves alone; we neither delegate it nor share it." Such language could not be forgotten.

Terray, for his part, freed from fear of the *Parlements*, asserted that the only way of paying the royal debts was to make a declaration of bankruptcy. This he accordingly did, silencing protest by the words, "The King is master." Bankruptcy was a usual proceeding for the State under the *ancien régime*; and even Colbert had recourse to it. But Terray at first neglected to employ the discreet formalities of his predecessors, and it was a matter of common knowledge that the money which he withheld from the creditors of the State went to Mme Du Barry. Public opinion was, in consequence, less quietly resigned to the fraudulent proceedings of the Government than it had been in the time of Colbert; and, by invoking the authority of the King as a cloak for his actions, Terray brought that authority into final discredit.

It will be seen that the Triumvirate, all things considered, deserved a better reputation than it obtained, but that it contributed equally with Choiseul to the dislocation of the *ancien régime*. The person of Louis XV served as a mark for the anger of all parties—that of Choiseul, who occupied the leisure afforded by his disgrace in writing memoirs, in which he spoke of the King as "impressionable wax," and blamed his cowardice and evil disposition; that of the intellectual spirits of the time, who compared the enlightened despotism of Frederick II, Catharine II, and Charles III of Spain with the paltry and hackneyed despotism of the King of France; that of the people of Paris, who in their turn attributed to Louis XV the "Treaty of Famine"—a vast wheat "corner" existing only in the popular imagination. It may be that, if the reign of the Triumvirate had lasted long, it would have finally disarmed all opposition; for there was no hatred of Louis XV in the rural population, or in parts of the country at a great distance from the capital, and his vices were not known outside Paris and the great towns. But the King died in 1774.

At the end of his reign—when Louis' egoism and slothfulness were causing the despotic system of government to become arbitrary, and the administration incoherent and mechanical, and when ample room was left for unjust practices based on the social privileges of the nobility and clergy—the popular cry in favour of reform was so insistent, that on every side the subordinates and subjects of the King tried on their own initiative to find some remedy for the existing abuses. The high officials, especially the *intendants*, offered every encouragement in their power in their several departments to industry, to commerce, to agriculture ; the nobility and ecclesiastics on their lands, the bishops in their dioceses did the same. The middle classes profited by this state of feeling to gratify their desire for wealth ; but, the richer they grew, the more they were exasperated by the obstacles put in the path of industry and commerce by superannuated institutions, by the privileges of the nobles and ecclesiastics in the matter of taxation ; and by "Gothic" laws such as the *coutumes*, dating from the Middle Ages, which regulated business transactions and were in flagrant contradiction to the commercial law which was taking shape by degrees. The protection given in high places to agriculture did indeed lighten the condition of the peasants, who ceased to be despised as such, now that the citizen class had begun to take an interest in them and to bring into fashion the love of nature and the pleasures of rustic life ; the peasant profited by this state of things to acquire land of his own, practising desperate economies within his own miserable income. But he always had just too little land to cultivate, and upon whatever he had there weighed always the heavy burden of the royal taxes and the rents due to the privileged classes. And, besides all this, the literature of the day, instinct with activity, with the spirit of propagandism and criticism, was spreading the ideas of the Philosophers and Economists, with the help of the learned provincial societies, of masonic lodges, of novelists, of letter-writers, of drawing-room gatherings. Welcomed by the nobles and ecclesiastics, these ideas robbed them of all confidence in the legitimacy of their privileges ; spreading among the well-read and ambitious commons, they encouraged them to claim a part in political life ; they sank deeply into the minds of the populations of the great towns ; and, if they came to a standstill before the ignorance of the unlettered country-folk, their echo awoke even in these a confused sense of the suffering and misery which pressed them down. Hence, when the day should come for the deserters from the ranks of the nobility, the Church, and the middle classes, to continue to lead the revolutionary movement, they were destined to have behind them the uncivilised mass of the people of the great towns and of the peasantry—an untamed and redoubtable force.

Louis XV thus died on the eve of a *beau tapage*. A saying has been attributed to him which evinces cynical clearsightedness and egoism : *Après moi le déluge.* In very truth, the "deluge" was not to be long delayed.

CHAPTER XII.

SPAIN AND PORTUGAL.
(1746–94.)

(1) SPAIN UNDER FERDINAND VI AND CHARLES III.

FERDINAND VI, the sole survivor of the four children of Philip V by his first wife, Louise of Savoy, ascended the throne of Spain on July 9, 1746. The long exercise of supreme power by Elisabeth Farnese was now replaced by that of the new Queen, Maria Barbara of Braganza, whose influence over her dull and indolent husband was very great. The King had many good qualities and virtues, but he was conscious of his lack of ability and was content to leave the administration of affairs, in the details of which he took no interest, in the hands of others more capable than himself. His Queen, to whom, though she was quite without personal charm, he was tenderly attached, had the stronger character, and the King rarely took any resolution except by her advice.

The immediate effect of the accession of Ferdinand was the relinquishment of the ambitious and warlike policy which had so often dragged Spain into hostilities for objects in which the country had little or no interest. The new King, however, treated his step-mother, who thenceforth lived in retirement at San Ildefonso, with kindliness and magnanimity, and introduced no violent changes into the conduct of affairs. The old Ministers of Philip V, Villarias and Ensenada, continued to hold office. The war still went on; but efforts were quickly made for bringing about a peaceful settlement. The Queen was Portuguese, and negotiations were privately set on foot through the Court at Lisbon with the British Government. Ferdinand wished to pursue a national policy, and no longer to allow the interests of Spain to be subordinated to dynastic and family ties. Villarias, the President of the Council of Castile, who, as Minister of Foreign Affairs, had shown strong French sympathies, was therefore replaced by Don José de Carvajal y Lancaster, a younger son of the Duke of Linares, and a descendant of John of Gaunt. Carvajal was a man of the strictest integrity, somewhat stiff and reserved in manners, experienced in affairs, and a sound and capable diplomatist. He was proud of his descent from the House of Lancaster and anxious to promote good relations with England. His colleague, Zeno Somodevilla, Marquis of Ensenada, who had in 1743 succeeded Campillo in the Ministries of Finance, of War, of Marine, and of the Indies, was a man of humble origin, but of the greatest industry and brilliant abilities, whose love of luxury and ostentation formed the strongest contrast to the almost austere simplicity of the aristocratic Carvajal. Ensenada was an adherent of the French alliance, so that the influence of the one nearly balanced that of the other. Side by side with the two statesmen were the two court favourites—Father Rabago, the Jesuit confessor of the King, and Carlo Broschi (Farinelli), the Neapolitan singer, whose lovely voice secured for him the same highly privileged position in the home life of Ferdinand and Barbara as it had in that of Philip and Elisabeth. Rabago aimed at the formation of a party independent of Carvajal and Ensenada, and was able to exercise a secret control over the very devout King's mind in moments of doubt and irresolution. Farinelli's influence, especially with the Queen, was so great that his favour was courted on all hands, even by Ministers of State and foreign ambassadors. But, amidst all the temptations that surrounded him, he remained honest, unassuming, and independent, and was content to give his services to his royal patrons in a spirit of disinterestedness.

One of the first steps of the new Government was the nomination of the Marquis de La Mina to the command of the Spanish forces in Italy, and the supersession of Generals Gages and Castelar. Mina found the Franco-Spanish army retreating from Piacenza before the victorious Austro-Piedmontese in a state of disorganisation. After halting at Genoa, he withdrew his forces into Provence, whither he was followed by the French under Maillebois. Genoa was left to its fate, and surrendered on September 15. Not content with this success, the allied armies, under the command of Charles Emmanuel and Count Browne, crossed the Var and invaded Provence. Their progress was however speedily arrested by the news that the Genoese had risen in revolt and expelled the Austrian garrison (December). Finding their enemies discouraged and hesitating, the Spaniards under Mina and the French, now commanded by Marshal Belleisle, assumed the offensive and advanced (February, 1747) along the western Riviera to the relief of Genoa, which was closely invested by the English fleet and an Austrian army. They were at length successful, and the blockade was raised (July 6). A fortnight later, an attempt of the French to force the pass of Assietta brought upon them a disastrous defeat at the hands of Charles Emmanuel (July 19) at Exilles. After this no serious operations were undertaken.

Meanwhile, the negotiations for a peaceful settlement were making headway. The brilliant successes of Marshal de Saxe in the Low Countries had alarmed the British Government. France, too, was anxious to terminate hostilities which had crippled her navy and

finances. The *pourparlers* between the Courts of St James' and of
Madrid carried on through the mediation of Portugal had led to an
understanding between them. The chief obstacle had been the question
of the establishment of Don Philip in Italy; but on this point Ferdinand
stood firm. He had no desire to have his half-brother, with his pronounced French leanings and intriguing temper, back in Spain. The
recognition of Philip as Duke not only of Parma and Piacenza, but also
of Guastalla, was ultimately conceded by the Treaty of Aix-la-Chapelle,
the preliminaries of which were signed (April 30, 1748) by France and
Great Britain, and which was definitely accepted by Spain six months
later (October 20). The commercial differences required separate treatment and raised questions of some delicacy between the British and
Spanish negotiators. Thanks, however, to the skill of Sir Benjamin
Keene, who was now for some years to exercise great influence at Madrid,
the Treaty of Aquisgran was signed (October 5, 1749), by which Great
Britain secured the confirmation of all the commercial immunities and
rights obtained by the earlier treaties, and undertook to renounce the
remaining term of the *Asiento* contract, accepting £100,000 as compensation to the South Sea Company for the loss of its privileges.

The years that followed were marked by the struggle between the
English and French Governments to secure the goodwill of Spain. The
Peace of Aix-la-Chapelle was felt to be little more than an armed truce,
and both Powers were anxious for the Spanish alliance in case of a fresh
outbreak of hostilities. Ferdinand and his Queen were alike in favour
of a peaceful policy, and of maintaining friendly relations with both the
rival Powers. In this policy they had the firm support of Carvajal. On
the other hand, Ensenada, who was jealous of the growing influence of
his colleague, worked incessantly in the interests of France, with the
object of securing a renewal of the "Family Compact" between the
Bourbon Kings. Madrid became thus for a succession of years a centre
of diplomatic scheming and intrigue, of which a wonderfully clear and
graphic account is given in the despatches of Keene. Ensenada's failure
to induce Ferdinand to entangle himself in a French alliance was largely
due to the sleepless vigilance and statesmanlike tact and address of
this eminent ambassador, whose exertions placed the relations between
England and Spain upon a more amicable footing than that on which
they had stood for more than half a century. The decline of the
influence of the Court of Versailles was conclusively shown by the Treaty
which, in spite of French opposition, was signed at Aranjuez (June 14,
1752) for securing the neutrality of Italy. All points of dispute with
regard to territorial rights in Italy were settled to the satisfaction of the
interested parties, with the solitary exception of the King of Naples.
Charles complained that it infringed his rights to the allodials in
Tuscany, and to the disposal of the Crown of Naples on his succession
to the Spanish throne, which he regarded as assured.

CH. XII.

He even went so far as to appeal to the French and English Governments for support against his half-brother, but without success. The defeat of the French party at Madrid was even more marked in the failure of the effort made to obtain the recall of the Spanish ambassador at the Court of St James', Richard Wall, who had done much to promote a good understanding between England and Spain, and was accused of having lent himself to intrigues hostile to France. Wall, an Irishman by birth, had early in life entered the Spanish service; his abilities had secured for him the patronage of Ensenada, and it was to this Minister that he owed his earliest diplomatic appointments. On the present occasion Wall was able successfully to disprove the charges against him, and was confirmed in his post at London.

The sudden death of Carvajal, on April 8, 1754, was a serious loss to Spain. It was feared that the inclinations of Ensenada, whose influence with the Queen was great, would ensure the triumph of the French party. Both Ferdinand and Barbara, however, were bent on the maintenance of peace, and dreaded the consequences of any tightening of the bonds with France. They were strengthened in their resolve not to permit any change of policy by the advice of the Duke of Huescar and the Count of Valparaiso, two prominent court officials and friends of Carvajal. Neither of them would accept the vacant ministry of Foreign Affairs; but, acting on the instigation of Keene, they suggested the fitness of Richard Wall for the post, and their counsel was accepted. But Ensenada, still intent upon embroiling Spain in hostilities with Great Britain, entered into secret negotiations with the Court of Versailles for a close alliance, and, in his capacity as Minister of the Indies, sent out orders to Havana for an expedition to be got ready for the expulsion of the English from their settlements on the Gulf of Mexico. He thus hoped to force the hand of his sovereign, relying upon the help of his friends Farinelli and Rabago. But the British Minister, Keene, whose vigilance had discovered these intrigues, took Wall and Huescar into his confidence, and furnished them with proofs of Ensenada's manœuvres, which they in their turn laid before the King. The Minister was suddenly arrested in the night of July 20, 1754, and, after being deprived of his offices, was sent into retirement at Granada. An inventory of his effects showed him to be possessed of immense wealth. He was, however, treated leniently, no proceedings were taken against him; and, though he was exiled, a pension was granted to him. Father Rabago was likewise exiled, on the charge of having fomented a rebellion of the Jesuits in Paraguay.

Ensenada, whatever his faults, deserved well of his country. Even the chief author of his downfall, Sir Benjamin Keene, speaks with unstinted admiration of his "perspicuous parts, extensive knowledge and activity in the transaction of business," and of the great services which had signalised his ministry. Among these may be mentioned his efforts to improve agriculture, to open out communication by means of canals and roads, to reopen the mines by revoking the prohibition on the exportation of precious metals subject to a small royalty, and to reform the system of taxation, by the abolition of the system of farming the taxes in Castile and by a scheme for replacing the hateful imposts known as *millónes* and *alcabalas* by a single tax (*contribución unica*) levied upon a valuation of income and property. At the time of his fall, this reform was under consideration. His most remarkable achievement was his reorganisation of the Spanish navy. The fortified harbour and arsenal at Ferrol was his creation, and all the other arsenals were enlarged and put in order. To effect this, he neglected the army; for his paramount aim was to enable Spain to hold her own against England at sea, and in the course of his administration he raised Spain both in number of vessels and in efficiency to a more formidable maritime position than she had held since the days of Philip II. He had also a large share in bringing about the conclusion of a Concordat with Pope Benedict XIV, which was signed on January 11, 1753. This instrument recognised unreservedly the royal right of patronage, save in the case of a small limited number of benefices, and settled other matters of controversy between the Papacy and the Spanish Crown.

The redistribution of offices which ensued upon the fall of Ensenada, and the appointment of Wall as successor to Carvajal, did not, as had been expected, effect any real change of policy. Ferdinand had firmly convinced himself that peace was necessary for the recuperation of Spain, and nothing could move him from his determination to remain neutral in the war which broke out between England and France in 1756. In this determination he could always reckon on the support of the new Minister for Foreign Affairs, who, though well-disposed to England, was anxious to act disinterestedly and impartially for the best interests of his adopted country. The capture of Minorca by the French (May, 1756) furnished both the belligerent Powers with an opportunity for making an appeal to Spanish patriotism. The French Government proposed an offensive and defensive alliance between the two Bourbon kingdoms, in which France should engage to cede Minorca and to aid the Spaniards by land and by sea in the recovery of Gibraltar. Keene was instructed by Pitt in a long confidential despatch (August 23, 1757) to use all his well-tried diplomatic skill and influence at the Court of Madrid to secure Spanish cooperation with Great Britain in the War, more especially in the recapture of Minorca. In return, the British Government actually offered to cede Gibraltar, besides giving full satisfaction to all Spanish complaints in the matter of privateering and of encroachments on the coast of Honduras. It was the last act of Keene, who died on December 15, 1757. From the first, his experience told him that the British offer was doomed to failure. Neither bribes nor entreaties, whether from London or from Versailles, could move Ferdinand from his fixed resolve not to be dragged into hostilities.

CH. XII.

In the pursuance of his pacific policy, Queen Barbara had given the King her fullest sympathy and support. Unfortunately, her health had been of late seriously impaired, and an attack of illness terminated fatally on August 27, 1758. The bonds of affection, which had so long united the royal pair, had grown with the lapse of time constantly stronger and closer, and now the loss of his wife had the most fatal effect upon the mind of Ferdinand. His mental powers had always been feeble, and he was subject to fits of hypochondria. He now completely secluded himself, refused to speak, and finally fell into a state of complete lunacy. After lingering on in this condition for some months, he died on August 10, 1759. Thus ended the reign of this well-intentioned prince who, though lacking all the qualities of a great ruler, was enabled nevertheless by his personal integrity, his prudence, his kindliness of temper, and his simplicity of life, to endear himself to his subjects and advance their welfare. He did much for the encouragement of learning and science. The proceedings of the Inquisition were greatly restricted, and public *autos-de-fé* abolished. Ferdinand could, moreover, boast that he had found the country's finances ruined and the navy in a state of decay, but that he left behind him a formidable fleet, and a balance of three millions sterling in the national treasury.

By the death of Ferdinand without issue the succession to the Spanish throne passed to his half-brother, Charles, King of Naples. The Queen Dowager, Elisabeth Farnese, by the will of the deceased monarch, became Regent until the arrival of Charles III. The first care of the new King was to negotiate with the Empress Queen and the King of Sardinia concerning the arrangements made by the Treaty of Aquisgran (1749), to which Charles had never acceded, by which Philip, Duke of Parma, was to succeed to the Crown of the Two Sicilies, and his duchies of Parma, Piacenza, and Guastalla to be shared between Austria and Sardinia. A speedy settlement was effected, for it was the interest of Austria at this juncture to conciliate the new ruler of Spain and the Indies; and the claims of Charles Emmanuel on Piacenza were compromised by a money payment. The eldest son of Charles III, Philip, had been imbecile from his birth; and he was now formally and publicly declared to be incapable of reigning. Charles, accordingly, designated his second son, Charles, to be Prince of the Asturias and heir to the Spanish throne, and he abdicated the Crown of Naples and the Two Sicilies in favour of his third son, Ferdinand, then eight years of age. This act accomplished, Charles III, accompanied by his Queen and family and escorted by a Spanish squadron, set sail for Barcelona from Naples, where during a reign of twenty-five years he had won the hearts of his Italian subjects. His reception on Spanish soil (October 17, 1759) was enthusiastic, and on December 9 he reached Madrid, where he met his mother again for the first time since his departure from Spain in 1731. It was soon clear, however, that neither he nor his wife,

Maria Amalia of Saxony, though they treated Elisabeth with respect and deference, had any intention of allowing her to exercise any influence in affairs, and she speedily withdrew into retirement at San Ildefonso. Three months after her state entry into the capital (July 13, 1760) Queen Amalia, who had been in bad health ever since her arrival in Spain, died. Her husband was deeply afflicted at his loss, and never married again.

The habits of King Charles were exceedingly methodical. He rose early and spent the morning in the transaction of business, making himself minutely and conscientiously familiar with the details of all affairs of State. He was not a man of striking ability; but his experience was already great, and he united great honesty of purpose and an inflexible regard for justice with a sincere desire to promote the well-being of his subjects. He combined deep piety with a keen interest in the advances of science and knowledge. The whole of his afternoons, whatever the weather, he occupied in hunting and shooting, in which he sought and found not merely amusement, but a healthful diversion from the pressure of state cares and an antidote to the constitutional melancholy which afflicted so many members of his family. Simple in his tastes and habits, and genial in manner, this robust and bronzed sportsman had all the qualities for winning the hearts of those with whom he was brought into contact. Charles governed indeed autocratically, but Spain had never been more in need of the firm hand of a benevolent and enlightened ruler. On his accession he made few changes in the *personnel* of the Government. He retained Wall in his post, and gave no office to Ensenada, though recalling him from exile. Farinelli was banished, and the Marquis of Squillaci, a Sicilian, was made Minister of War and Finance.

The beginning of the new reign was to be attended by misfortune. Charles never forgot that he was a Bourbon and cherished strong French sympathies. Moreover, the imperious action of the British admiral in 1742, and his threat to bombard Naples, had rankled in the King's memory. The Seven Years' War was now in mid course and in every part of the world the British arms, directed by the genius and energy of Pitt, were victorious over the French. Choiseul, of whose policy a connected account is given elsewhere, in the autumn of 1759 began to make overtures for peace and offered to submit certain disputed points to the arbitration of His Catholic Majesty. But Spain had herself grievances against England with regard to contraband, and settlements on the coast of Honduras, the searching of Spanish ships, and the claim of Spain to a share in the Newfoundland fisheries. The proposed mediation of the Spanish King was accordingly rejected by the British Government. The war went on still, disastrously for France. Meanwhile there was a continual exchange of friendly communications between the Courts of Versailles and Madrid, and the efforts of Choiseul were skilfully directed to persuading Charles that the triumph of England would spell danger to the Spanish dominion in South America, and that it was in the interest of Spain that the two countries should make common cause against a common foe. The refusal of Pitt to offer any satisfactory redress to the Spanish grievances gave added force to the representation of the French Minister. In the spring of 1761 matters came to a climax. The Marquis de Grimaldo, who had been ambassador at the Hague, was sent by Charles to Paris (February 11), with secret instructions to approach Choiseul with proposals for a renewal of the "Family Compact," and for the conclusion of an offensive and defensive alliance between France and Spain. The final result of their deliberations was the conclusion of two treaties, one permanent on the lines of those previously concluded between the sovereigns of the House of Bourbon, and known as the "Family Compact." (It was afterwards joined by the King of Naples and the Duke of Parma.) In the second, which was a secret convention, it was agreed that in the conditions on which France was willing to make peace should be included a settlement of the grievances of Spain against Great Britain, the King of Spain undertaking to declare war, should these overtures be rejected. Both the treaties, which have been more fully described elsewhere, were actually signed on August 15. Pitt had, however, already peremptorily declined to allow the disputes with Spain to be mixed up with the French negotiations, and, had he had his own way, would at once have summoned the King of Spain to withdraw his demands on pain of instant war. The retirement of Pitt and the accession of Lord Bute to power gave Charles III an opportunity of delaying, by a further exchange of notes and explanations, the inevitable hostilities until his naval and military preparations had been completed and the treasure ships from America had safely come to port. When this object had been attained, the categorical demand of the British Government as to the cause of the warlike preparations and of the existence of a treaty with France was met by a refusal to give any explanation. The British ambassador, Lord Bristol, left Madrid in December, 1761, and at the same time an embargo was laid by the Spanish Government on all British ships in Spanish ports. Ferdinand's prudent policy of neutrality was definitely abandoned, and Charles threw in his lot with Louis XV for a renewal of the struggle in which France had already suffered so many defeats.

One of the first steps taken by the allied Bourbon monarchs, in accordance with the terms of the secret treaty, was the sending of a joint note to Lisbon, requiring the King of Portugal to close his ports to the English and observe strict neutrality. The reply was a firm refusal. Hereupon, an army of 40,000 crossed the Portuguese frontier under the Marquis of Sarria, a general old in years but inexperienced in command, and proceeded to take possession of the country north of the

Douro. There was little serious resistance. Moncorvo, Braganza, and Miranda fell rapidly into the hands of the invaders. Lack of provisions stopped the advance on Oporto, and the news of the landing of 6000 English troops at Lisbon under the command of a distinguished German officer, Count Lippe, led to a change of plans. It was resolved to besiege Almeida, and to push on to Lisbon by the valley of the Tagus. Before Almeida, the Spaniards, now under the command of the Count of Aranda, were reinforced by a body of 8000 French. Nine days after the trenches had been opened, Almeida surrendered and Aranda now advanced with the intention of crossing the Tagus at Villavelha. He found that Lippe had entrenched himself with a strong British and Portuguese force at Abrantes, and had established fortified posts at Alvite and Niza, to prevent the Spanish general from effecting the passage of the river. Aranda succeeded in forcing the pass of Alvite and reaching Villavelha; but the strength of the position of Abrantes, and the vigilance of Burgoyne, who commanded the detachment at Niza, checked his further progress. The autumnal rains began to fall; and Aranda found it impossible to remain longer in a desolate and rugged country, with troops suffering heavily from disease and privations. He accordingly ingloriously withdrew his discouraged and diminished army into winter quarters at Alburquerque.

Meanwhile, two serious disasters had befallen the Spanish arms in the West and East Indies. Admiral Pocock appeared before Havana (June 6, 1762), in command of a British fleet of twenty-four ships of the line and ten frigates convoying a large number of transports. Every effort had been made to put Havana in a state of defence, and the Governor, Don Juan de Prado, was confident of his ability to hold his own. On June 8, 8000 British troops, commanded by Lord Albemarle, effected a landing on the coast without opposition, and then proceeded to lay siege to the Castle of Morro, the chief defence of the harbour of Havana. The garrison, led by a gallant naval officer, Don Luis Velasco, made a most determined defence; but, though the British force had suffered heavy losses through sickness, the vigour of its attack triumphed over all obstacles. The Castle of Morro was taken by assault (July 30) after a prolonged struggle in which Velasco himself fell. Prado, fearing the destruction of the town by bombardment, a few days later entered into negotiations for its surrender, and the capitulation was signed on August 13. This important success had cost the British 2910 men. Twelve ships of war were captured, and immense military and naval stores and treasure amounting to fifteen million dollars. On September 22 Admiral Cornish appeared before Manila with thirteen ships, and a force of 6000 men under General Draper effected a landing. After a fierce bombardment the town surrendered; and of an indemnity of four million dollars demanded from it more than half was secured, the Treasury of Madrid being left to pay the remainder—which was never

received. The only set-off to this series of misfortunes was the conquest
of the colony of Sacramento from the Portuguese.

Finding that Bute's Government was pacifically disposed, the Courts
of Versailles and Madrid, as has been related in another chapter, now
seriously entered upon negotiations for peace. The Spanish ambassador
at Paris, Grimaldo, was the representative of Charles III at the *pourparlers*. All parties being desirous for a cessation of hostilities, the
terms for a peaceful settlement of the many points in dispute were
arranged without much difficulty ; and the definitive Treaty was signed
on February 20, 1763. In return for the restoration of Havana and
Manila, Spain ceded Florida to Great Britain, and an important piece
of territory east and south-east of the Mississippi. The right to cut
logwood in Honduras was granted to British subjects but coupled with
the stipulation that all fortifications were to be rased. The claim of
fishery rights on the banks of Newfoundland was abandoned, Portugal
was evacuated, and the colony of Sacramento restored to the Portuguese.
By a private agreement Spain received Louisiana from France in
compensation for the loss of Florida.

The conclusion of peace was speedily followed by the retirement of
Wall. He had served his adopted country well, in spite of his dislike
both of the Family Compact and the War with England ; but he was
not a self-seeker or enamoured of office, and he now begged the King
to allow him to resign his post of Minister of Foreign Affairs on the
ground of failure of eyesight and other growing infirmities. Charles
assented most unwillingly and granted a substantial pension to the
retiring Minister. He was succeeded by the Marquis de Grimaldo, a
Genoese of noble extraction, who as ambassador at Versailles had been
one of the chief authors of the "Family Compact." Disputes quickly
arose with Great Britain about the privileges accorded to the English
settlers in Honduras, and war at one time seemed imminent. As,
however, it was not the wish of the King to be dragged into hostilities,
these questions were settled by concessions on both sides. The necessity
of a policy of reform at home aiming at a revival of the country from
the state of decay and lethargy into which it had for some time been
falling, had since his accession been continually present to the mind of
Charles. Squillaci was now to carry out the changes, which the King
considered necessary for the purpose; but this Minister, though experienced
in the management of affairs, and exceedingly industrious and exact,
was not a man of talent, of culture, or of tact ; and he showed a conspicuous disregard of the tenacious attachment of the Spanish people
to their traditional customs. Finding that the streets of the capital were
badly lighted, extremely filthy, and hardly safe for passers-by, Squillaci
had them cleansed and lighted ; and, not content with these measures,
he attempted to enforce a change in the national dress, on the ground
that the wide-brimmed hats and long cloaks generally worn were

favourable to the perpetration of crimes.   An edict was therefore issued
prohibiting the wearing of the Spanish *capas* and *sombreros*, and
enjoining the general use of the French style of dress (March, 1766).
The populace were already hostile to the Minister of Finance, to whose
measures they attributed a considerable rise that had taken place in
the price of provisions, and the attempt of the police to compel the
Madrileños to abandon the national costume aroused fierce opposition.
Resistance was secretly organised, and on Palm Sunday (March 23) it
broke out in open revolt.   At 4 o'clock in the afternoon of that day a
body of men, arrayed in the forbidden costume, openly challenged arrest,
and attacked the soldiers, who tried to seize them.   It was the signal
for a general rising.   With loud cries of "Long live the King; death
to Squillaci," the crowd made their way to the house of the obnoxious
Minister; but he had been warned in time and fled to one of the royal
palaces, his wife seeking refuge in a convent.   The house was gutted,
and the furniture thrown out of the windows and burnt.   The windows
of Grimaldo's house were likewise smashed.   At midnight the insurgents
dispersed, only to gather in still greater numbers on the morrow.   An
encounter then took place between them and a picket of the Walloon
Guards, who, on being assailed with stones, fired and killed and
wounded some of the populace.   Then the Guards were in turn attacked
and dispersed; those who were captured being murdered and their bodies
horribly mutilated.   All efforts to appease the tumult proving in vain,
Charles was at length compelled to appear in person on the balcony of
the palace, and to accede to the demands of the mob.   He promised to
dismiss Squillaci and appoint a Spaniard in his place, to revoke the
edict about the hats and capes, to reduce the price of provisions, and to
grant a general pardon.   Alarmed for his safety, the King with his
family secretly made his escape at night through the cellars of the
palace, and betook himself to Aranjuez.   Irritated at this seeming act
of treachery, the mob hereupon rose again and for two or three days
held Madrid in its power.   Not till the Governor had read a message
from the King undertaking to carry out his promise was tranquillity
restored.   Squillaci had followed Charles to Aranjuez; but on the 27th
he departed under charge of a military escort for Cartagena, whence
he sailed to Sicily.   Six years later he was appointed ambassador at
Venice.

The King's pride was deeply hurt by these occurrences, and it was
many months before he returned to Madrid.   Don Miguel Musquiz,
Squillaci's first secretary, was appointed Minister of Finance, and the
office of President of the Council of Castile was conferred upon the
Count of Aranda, with full powers for dealing with a state of affairs
that needed the firm hand of a strong and capable administrator.   He
proved himself to be the right man for the task.   By a rare combination
of tact and energy, order was speedily restored, the city was divided

into districts and thoroughly policed, vagabonds and idlers were expelled, and finally, on the petition of the representatives of the nobles, the *gremios* (trade gilds) and the Municipal Council, the concessions extorted from the King by the insurgents were revoked. The King, however, consented not to enforce the edict about dress except in the immediate vicinity of the Court, and at last, in the month of December, reentered his capital amidst the plaudits of the people. The death of the Queen Mother, Elisabeth Farnese, had taken place at San Ildefonso on July 10. Charles, though strongly attached to her, had never allowed her to exercise any political influence.

The year 1767 was marked by the expulsion of the Jesuits from Spain. The members of this Order had already been expelled from Portugal (1759) and from France (1764). Charles III, though extremely devout, had throughout his reign shown that in ecclesiastical no less than in civil affairs he was determined to be master in his own kingdom. Jesuit intrigues both in Spain and in Paraguay had prejudiced him against the Society, before a secret enquiry instituted by Aranda into the origin and causes of the Madrid outbreak laid the blame upon the Jesuits. Aranda was himself a Voltairean and an enemy of the Society, and there can be little doubt that he used his opportunity to persuade the King that the Jesuits were disloyal to their country and plotting against his own life. Charles was induced to determine upon the immediate expulsion of the Order from Spain; and the execution of the decree was entrusted to Aranda, who carried it out with the most extraordinary secrecy and success. Orders in the King's own hand were despatched to the Governor of each province, to be opened on April 2, those for the capital on March 31. The six colleges of the Jesuits in Madrid and its neighbourhood were simultaneously surrounded at midnight, the inmates summoned to the refectory, ordered to seat themselves in parties of ten in vehicles prepared for the purpose, and then conducted to some place on the sea coast, where frigates were ready to carry them to Italy. On April 2 similar orders were executed throughout Spain. No resistance was offered. After suffering untold hardships, the unhappy Jesuits were after three months on shipboard allowed to land at Cività Vecchia, and settled in various towns in the Papal States, a scanty pension being granted to them by the King for their maintenance. The expulsion of the Jesuits from Spanish America and especially from the flourishing missions of Paraguay would have been attended with great difficulty, had the Fathers opposed the royal orders. Trained to submission, they obeyed everywhere with the greatest fortitude and resignation. The sufferings of the South American Jesuits in their voyage to Italy were even more prolonged and more severe than those of their Spanish brethren.

The suppression of disorder and the overthrow of the power of the Jesuits left the King, who had never summoned the Cortes since they had taken the oath of fidelity to him on his accession, supreme and absolute in the State. He had never lost an opportunity of circumscribing the privileges of the clergy and the abuses of papal interference in his dominions, and had made the bishops to recognise his authority. He had not ventured to abolish the Inquisition; but he had forced this dreaded tribunal to submit its decrees against books to the approbation of the royal Council and to soften its penalties. Very few persons were put to death by sentence of the Inquisition between 1759 and 1788, and long before the latter date its power had been reduced to a mere shadow.

The cession by France of Louisiana to the west of the Mississippi in 1762 had been unwillingly accepted by Spain, and speedily became the cause of trouble. The Spanish Governor, Antonio de Ulloa, stirred up general discontent among the *habitants* at New Orleans by the restrictions imposed upon trade and by his general tactlessness and severity. An insurrection broke out in 1768, and a large force had to be despatched from Havana under General O'Reilly for its suppression. Meanwhile, the relations between the Spanish and British Governments continued to be strained. The extent of the contraband trade carried on by British subjects on the Mississippi, at Campeche, and other places on the Gulf of Mexico, and with the Spanish colonies generally, caused much friction. A further irritant was the question of the ransom of Manila, which Charles III obstinately refused to pay, while the British Ministers as persistently pressed for a settlement. A dispute about the Falkland Islands increased the soreness, and well-nigh led to an outbreak of hostilities between the two nations. Both Spain and Great Britain claimed the possession of these bleak and inhospitable islands (discovered by Captain Cowley in 1686), which were useless except as a station for whale and cod fishery. In 1766 an English settlement was made for this purpose and named Port Egmont. Four years later (1770), the news that an expedition sent by the Spanish Governor of Buenos Ayres had expelled the English from Port Egmont aroused general indignation in England, and a strong protest, with a demand for reparation, was lodged at the Court of Madrid. Aranda urged Charles not to yield; and both sides made preparations for war. Relying on the terms of the Family Compact, Charles caused urgent diplomatic representations to be made at Paris; but the finances of France were not in a condition to bear the burden of another war. In 1770, as related elsewhere, the influence of Madame Du Barry was supreme at Versailles, and Choiseul fell from power. Spain found herself isolated, and, her fleet being in no condition to face the sea-power of Great Britain single-handed, Charles was compelled to give way. An apology was made to the British Government; the Spanish forces were withdrawn from the Falklands, and the English settlers reinstated at Port Egmont. Aranda, on whom Charles threw part of the blame for the humiliating position in which he found himself, was appointed to the embassy at Paris, and was succeeded in the presidency of the Council of Castile by Don Manuel Ventura Figueroa (August, 1773).

In 1774 the Moors made an attack upon the Spanish fortresses of Melilla and Peñon de Velez on the African coast, but were driven off with loss. As it was known that the Dey of Algiers had been the instigator of this breach of the peace, Charles III determined to use his army and navy, which now had been by strenuous efforts reorganised and made effective, to destroy the power of this potentate and make himself master of the nest of pirates which had so long been a scourge to the Mediterranean. He chose as commander of the expeditionary force Alexander O'Reilly, who, after his success in suppressing the insurrection at New Orleans, had been entrusted with the task of reforming the organisation of the Spanish army on the model of that of Frederick the Great. A great effort was made. A fleet of 46 vessels of war conveying 22,000 men appeared before Algiers on July 1, 1775. After disembarking on the 7th, the troops, misled by a feigned retreat of the enemy, advanced towards the town, only to find themselves suddenly enveloped on both flanks by far superior forces. They were compelled to retreat in disorder and suffered heavy losses before O'Reilly was, with difficulty, able to reembark them. In this disastrous affair 27 officers and 500 soldiers were killed, 191 officers and 2088 soldiers wounded. Sixteen guns and all the stores that had been landed were abandoned. The lack of provisions making it impossible to remain in the bay, the whole armament returned to Alicante, bringing back the news of their disgrace. The utter collapse of this enterprise on which so many hopes had been placed caused deep disappointment and general indignation in Spain. O'Reilly barely escaped with his life from the fury of the populace, and was removed from his post at Madrid. Nor did Grimaldo escape a full share of the odium which fell upon O'Reilly. He offered his resignation to the King; but Charles, always staunch to those who served him well, refused to accept it. The Minister, however, had many enemies, among them the Prince of the Asturias; and at last the King reluctantly yielded to his desire for retirement (November 7, 1776). In February, 1777, Grimaldo left Madrid for Rome, where he had been appointed ambassador in the place of Don José Moñino, Count of Florida Blanca, whom the King by Grimaldo's own wish had nominated to succeed him as Minister.

Florida Blanca, who had already won distinction during his embassy at Rome, was able to begin his administration with a successful settlement of the long pending disputes with Portugal in South America concerning the colony of Sacramento and the question of boundaries generally. As to this question it will be sufficient to say here that, finding the English fully occupied by their difficulties with their own insurgent colonies in North America, the Spanish Government had determined to take advantage of the situation by despatching a strong force to the Rio Plata to put an end to the aggression of the Portuguese in that region, and to drive them away from their settlements on the north bank of the river. The despatch of an expeditionary force with 12 vessels of war conveying 9000 men was one of the last acts of Grimaldo's Ministry (November, 1776). After seizing the island of St Catharine, it took possession, almost without resistance, of the colony of Sacramento. At this very time Joseph I, King of Portugal, died (February 24, 1777). This event was the signal for the fall of Pombal, and the accession of Maria I, whose mother, Maria Victoria, the sister of Charles III, had been opposed for years to that Minister's policy. Florida Blanca thus found an opening for an accommodation, of which he skilfully availed himself. His proposals for the drawing up of a treaty of limits were favourably received, and the negotiations were conducted with such mutual goodwill that an agreement was signed at San Ildefonso, October 1, 1777, by Florida Blanca and the Portuguese plenipotentiary Francisco de Sousa Coutinho. By this so-called Preliminary Treaty of 1777 all the disputed boundary questions were regulated, but its importance was greatly augmented by means of a treaty of defensive alliance and amity concluded at the Pardo on March 24, 1778. This drawing together of the two neighbouring countries, so long alienated from each other, which was marked by a visit of a year's duration by the Queen Dowager of Portugal to her brother, was of especial value to Spain when on the eve of a new war with England.

On the outbreak of war between Great Britain and her North American colonies, France, having after some hesitation thrown in her lot with the rebels (March, 1778), made every possible effort to induce Charles III to seize so favourable an opportunity for drawing the sword against the hereditary enemy of the House of Bourbon. Aranda at Paris energetically supported a war policy. But Charles was more than doubtful. The consequences of the participation of Spain in the Seven Years' War had been disastrous, and he listened not unsympathetically to the plea urged by the British Government that it would be dangerous for his monarchy to support American colonists in armed revolt against their mother country. Florida Blanca, therefore, pursued a cautious and temporising course. Finally, at the beginning of 1779, Charles proffered his mediation. Since France required that the independence of the colonies should be recognised by England as a preliminary to the discussion of such a proposal, it was contemptuously rejected by the British Government, which declared that the right to treat with its own colonies without foreign interference was a first principle on which it must insist; and that any other course would be inconsistent with the national honour. Florida Blanca's specific plan was that a truce should be concluded between England and France, to which the colonies should agree; and that then the plenipotentiaries of the three parties and of the mediating

Power should meet at Madrid and enter into negotiations for a permanent peace. The reply of the British Ministry was that this proposal "seemed to proceed on every principle which had been disclaimed, and to contain every term which had been rejected." Charles had hoped that he might without war have obtained the concession of Gibraltar, as the price of his neutrality and mediation. As soon, however, as the unbending demeanour of the British Ministry convinced him that further diplomatic efforts were useless, he suddenly changed his attitude ; and, after despatching to Lord Weymouth, the Secretary of State, a long memorandum recounting at length all the grievances of Spain against Great Britain, he declared war (June, 1779).

Spain commenced hostilities in a more favourable position than on previous occasions. The recent alliance with Portugal meant security from attack both in Europe and in South America, and the closing of Portuguese ports to the English squadrons. The relations with the Moors were friendly. The Spanish people were filled with patriotic enthusiasm at the prospect of the recovery of Gibraltar and Minorca, and eagerly made voluntary offerings for the prosecution of the war. The combined Spanish and French navies had a great numerical superiority over the British, and the design was formed of landing a large force upon the Isle of Wight and striking at the very heart of the British power by the capture of the port and arsenal of Portsmouth. Never perhaps has England been in more serious danger of invasion than in July, 1779, when the combined Franco-Spanish fleet under Admirals d'Orvilliers and Cordoba appeared before Plymouth, while an army of 40,000 men lay encamped at Brest and Dunkirk, furnished with transports. The British fleet under Admiral Hardy numbered only 38 sail. How the Bourbon alliance failed in its ambitious enterprise has been told elsewhere. When the fleets returned to winter in Brest and Cadiz, their crews decimated by sickness, and without having achieved anything, except the capture of one British ship, the *Ardent* which had mistaken the enemy for her own fleet, there was grievous disappointment and heartburning.

The chief efforts of the Spanish Government were thenceforth centred on the capture of Gibraltar, which had already been closely invested by sea and land. So strict was the blockade that it was believed the garrison would soon be driven by hunger to capitulate. These hopes were frustrated by the brilliant exploit of Admiral Rodney, who in the depth of winter, with a relieving squadron of 28 ships, ran the gauntlet of the fleets at Brest, Ferrol, and Cadiz, succeeded in capturing a large convoy off Cape Finisterre, and then, near Trafalgar, destroyed a Spanish squadron under Admiral Langara (January 10, 1780), which had been prevented by the tempestuous weather from effecting a junction with the rest of the Spanish fleet under Cordoba. Out of nine ships of the line and two frigates only four escaped. In the teeth of the storms, which scattered his foes, Rodney now revictualled the fortress and then sailed to the West Indies.

In the following summer a gleam of success was to attend the Spanish marine. Two weakly guarded British convoys, one destined for the West, the other for the East Indies, were surprised at the Azores by a Spanish squadron and captured. Sixty transports and merchantmen, 1800 troops, and stores to the value of £2,000,000, were brought in triumph into Cadiz harbour. In America the Spaniards also achieved brilliant successes. Don Bernardo Galvez, Governor of Louisiana, aided by a Spanish squadron under Admiral José Solano, who brought with him a large force from Havana, made himself master of the course of the Mississippi, and then conquered Florida. Mobile was taken on March 14, 1780, and the capital, Pensacola, on May 10, 1781. During the same period the British were likewise expelled from their settlements on the Bay of Honduras.

The failure of the great expedition for the invasion of England in the summer of 1779 led to bickerings and disputes between the two allied Powers. The chief object for which Spain had plunged into hostilities was the recovery of Gibraltar, but in this the French showed little interest. In November Florida Blanca appears to have received indirectly, through Fernan Nunez, the Spanish envoy at Lisbon, information that the commander of a British squadron in the Tagus, Commodore Johnstone, had hinted that the British Government might be willing to purchase the friendship of Spain by the cession of Gibraltar. On such slight grounds a clandestine negotiation was set on foot. The agent was an Irish priest, Hussey by name, formerly chaplain to the Spanish embassy in London, who put himself in communication with Richard Cumberland, private secretary to Lord George Germain, Secretary of State for the Colonies. In his turn Cumberland conveyed to Lord North and Lord George Germain the confidential information that the Spanish Government in consideration of the restitution of Gibraltar would abandon the French alliance and give ample compensation. It was a critical moment both at home and abroad, for Rodney had not yet relieved Gibraltar, and the Ministers, without committing themselves to any definite proposal, determined to send Hussey back to Madrid, with a letter addressed to himself by Germain, and permitting him in perfectly general terms, should opportunities occur " of conversing with persons in high trust and office," to state " that any opening or overture on the part of Spain towards a pacification so essential to the interests of both Kingdoms...will be entertained with all possible sincerity and good faith." Gibraltar was not even mentioned. Hussey reached Madrid on December 29, 1779, and had a series of interviews with Florida Blanca. Finally, he returned with a letter in Florida Blanca's own hand, which had been approved by the King, together with confidential instructions. On January 29, the secret agent arrived once more in London, where the subject was discussed at four successive cabinet councils. The question of compensation, should Gibraltar be ceded as a condition of peace, was fully considered. In exchange for the coveted fortress was demanded the island of Porto Rico, and the fortress and territory of San Fernando de Omoa, an indemnity of £2,000,000 in addition to payment in full for all the stores and artillery, rupture with France, assistance to Great Britain in the reduction of the rebels to obedience, or at least a solemn engagement not to furnish succour to them. These conditions are interesting as showing the high value that was attached to the possession of Gibraltar. As a matter of fact, they were never submitted to the Spanish Government. In an interview, indeed, which was granted to Hussey, one of the Ministers, Lord Stormont, declared: " if Spain would lay before him the map of her empire, to take his choice of an equivalent, and three weeks to fix that choice, he should not be able in the period to find in all the dominions of Spain what in his judgment would balance the cession of Gibraltar"; and he was further informed that Lord North and all his colleagues disavowed having given Commodore Johnstone any authority for the statement advanced by him. Deeply chagrined Hussey betook himself to Cumberland, who, expressing his own willingness to go on a special mission from the Cabinet to Madrid, persuaded Hussey to write to the Spanish First Minister (February 13, 1780) that the British Ministers, while unwilling to assent to the cession of Gibraltar as an indispensable article of a treaty of peace, might be willing to treat upon the basis of the Treaty of Paris under the title of Exchange of Territory. In this letter Hussey went on to express his personal belief that, though he had no authority written or verbal for his assertion, the British would cede Gibraltar on terms. This letter, after being read by Lord George Germain and Lord Hillsborough, was sent, and, vague though it was, led to a continuance of negotiations, and finally to the sending of Cumberland on a confidential mission to Madrid. He resided there for eight months, and had frequent interviews with Florida Blanca. The Spanish Government, however, insisted on the cession of Gibraltar as a previous and indispensable article of peace; and an insuperable obstacle having thus been placed in the way of any favourable result, Cumberland was recalled.

While, however, these clandestine and abortive negotiations were proceeding, Florida Blanca had also been actively engaged in promoting friendly relations with Russia, and he lent his support to the action taken by Catharine II in forming that league of the neutral nations, headed by Russia, known as the Armed Neutrality, of which an account has been given elsewhere. He saw that it was a blow aimed at the naval power of Great Britain.

One effect of the Cumberland negotiations was, as was no doubt foreseen by Florida Blanca, to arouse the French Government through fear of being deserted by Spain to more vigorous cooperation in the

Mediterranean. A great joint expedition was secretly prepared for the capture of Minorca. The united fleets of 52 sail left Cadiz on July 22, 1781, and were followed by 63 transports conveying 8000 troops under the command of the Duke of Crillon. The British garrison, taken by surprise, withdrew into Fort St Philip, which was blockaded. A reinforcement of 4000 French troops was despatched from Toulon on October 16. But as General Murray, the British commander, despite the shortness of provisions, continued to hold out, Crillon determined at the beginning of the new year to turn the blockade into a regular siege. On January 6, a tremendous fire was opened from 150 pieces of heavy artillery, and a more formidable enemy than the besiegers, the scurvy, reduced the defenders to a mere handful of effectives. As no relief came, the Governor was compelled to capitulate, February 5, 1782, receiving most honourable terms.

Encouraged by this success, the allies resolved to prosecute the war with all possible vigour. A large armament was despatched across the Atlantic to complete the conquest of the West Indies. Island after island was captured, and hopes rose high that these successes would be crowned by wresting Jamaica from the hands of the British. The splendid victory, however, gained on April 12, 1782, by Rodney over the French fleet, restored British naval supremacy in western waters, and saved Jamaica from the threatened attack. To the still more determined attempt made to gain possession of Gibraltar, reference is made elsewhere. There is scarcely a more glorious page in the military annals of England than the defence of the "Rock" by Eliott and his unconquerable garrison. The utter failure of the grand attack of September 13, 1782, and the destruction of Chevalier d'Arçon's floating batteries, proved a crushing blow to Charles III, who had been led to believe in the certainty of success. Even the faint hope that lack of munitions and supplies might compel surrender was dissipated, when in tempestuous weather (October 10) Admiral Howe succeeded, by sheer superiority of seamanship, in eluding the far larger fleet under Admiral Cordoba, which was drawn up at the entrance of the Straits to dispute his passage, in bringing his transports safely into the harbour of the fortress, and in repassing the Straits without being forced to an engagement. This brilliant exploit rivalled that of Rodney in the first year of the siege.

Meanwhile, negotiations both direct and indirect had been in progress since the late spring of 1782 between Great Britain and the members of the hostile coalition. The negotiations of which Paris was the centre, and the French Minister Vergennes the active agent, it is unnecessary to follow here. The rapid changes of ministry in England during this period and the obstinate insistence of Charles III upon inadmissible conditions rendered a speedy settlement of the differences between Great Britain and Spain impossible. Their negotiations were carried on at

CH. XII.

Paris by the two ambassadors, Fitzherbert (afterwards Lord St Helens) and the Count of Aranda, and later (September) in London also whither de Rayneval, the confidential secretary of Vergennes, was sent over to treat directly with Lord Shelburne (now at the head of the Government) himself. The demands of Charles, who was elated by the successes of the Spanish arms in Florida and Honduras, and by the capture of Minorca, and who believed that Gibraltar was on the point of being taken, were exorbitant. He asked for the cession of Florida, all the British settlements on the Gulf of Mexico, the Bahamas, fishery rights on the shore of Newfoundland and, last and most important of all, he demanded Gibraltar. In compensation for Gibraltar and Minorca, he offered to hand over to Great Britain, Oran and Mazarquivir on the African coast. Aranda was instructed to say, "if England desires peace, this is the only means of procuring it: since the King, my master, from personal as well as political motives, is fully determined never to put a period to the present war, till he shall have acquired Gibraltar either by arms or by negotiation." But Shelburne, though ready for considerable concessions, well knew the exhausted condition of the Spanish treasury, and in the matter of Gibraltar he was immovable. His reply to Rayneval was not less explicit than the demand of the Spanish King: "Gibraltar being actually in the possession of George III cannot be a subject of discussion." Month after month, the defiant fortress continued to block the way to an understanding. Even the destruction of d'Arçon's floating batteries by Eliott's red-hot shot, and the subsequent revictualling of the garrison by Howe, failed to make King Charles withdraw his demand. Gibraltar he must have, though it should be at the cost of restoring to England all his conquests in America and the West Indies, with Porto Rico thrown in. But, whatever compensation Shelburne himself might have been ready to accept in lieu of "the Rock," English public opinion would not hear of its surrender. Faced by the coalition of North and Fox against his Ministry, Shelburne in self-defence had no choice but to stand firm. Spain ostensibly began to prepare for a renewal of hostilities; but the hopelessness of an attempt to fight Great Britain single-handed was no doubt apparent to Florida Blanca, and by him impressed upon the King. On November 23, the Minister wrote in a despatch to Aranda: "the King would like to know what considerable advantage Spain might derive from the treaty, if, for any reason, she made the sacrifice of desisting from such a claim," *i.e.* the cession of Gibraltar. Aranda gave Vergennes the despatch to read, and the French Minister at once informed Rayneval at London that Spain would abandon Gibraltar if she obtained Minorca and the two Floridas. Rayneval replied that peace could be obtained on these terms and Aranda thereupon, as Spanish plenipotentiary, gave his adhesion. Both Florida Blanca and Charles III declared that Aranda, in taking this decisive step, had exceeded his instructions; but he was the last man to have run the risk of his sovereign's displeasure for the sake of bringing about peace with England. The preliminary articles were signed, January 30, 1783. Possibly the Spanish Court hoped to revive the claim to Gibraltar at a later stage of the negotiations. The fall of the Shelburne Ministry (April, 1783), however, dissipated any such expectation, and in September the definitive treaty was concluded. Gibraltar remained British, and the two Floridas and Minorca passed into the hands of Charles III. Outwardly, therefore, Spain emerged from this arduous struggle with the fruits of victory; but it was purchased by the ruin of her fleet and the serious crippling of her finances.

Nor was this all. The consequences, which had been partly foreseen, of a policy which lent armed support to the revolt of the American colonies against their mother country, in due course followed. Insurrectionary tumults and risings took place in various parts of Spanish America and had to be put down by force. The rebellion in Peru under Tupac Amaru, a descendant of the Incas, assumed dangerous proportions. In a short time he found himself at the head of some 60,000 men, but without discipline and badly armed. He was defeated (March, 1781) by a Spanish force under Don Joseph de Valle, and was himself taken prisoner.

After the conclusion of peace, Charles III's efforts were steadily directed to an object which had so often before occupied the serious attention of the Spanish monarchy—the freeing of the Mediterranean from the Algerian and Tunisian piracies. His aim was to effect by treaty a result, which arms had failed to accomplish. An amicable understanding had already been reached with the Moors. Negotiations had been set on foot at Constantinople, which issued in a commercial treaty (December 24, 1782), and the way was opened for negotiations with Algiers, Tunis, and Tripoli. By a mixture of threats and bribery, and the influence of the Sultan and the Moorish emperor, the piratical Governments were at last persuaded to listen favourably to Florida Blanca's proposals. A treaty with Tripoli, similar to that with the Porte, was concluded (September, 1784). Algiers and Tunis were more obdurate; but both assented to arrangements on the same lines two years later (June, 1786). Piracy ceased, and the lands on the Mediterranean coast of Spain, now freed from the fear of raids and depredations, began to be cultivated and peopled. The bonds of friendship with Portugal, which had so happily subsisted since 1778, were further cemented by a double matrimonial alliance between the reigning Houses. In 1785 the Infant Don Gabriel, third son of Charles III, was married to Doña Mariana Victoria, daughter of Queen Maria, and Doña Carlota, eldest daughter of the Prince of the Asturias, to Dom John, second son of the Portuguese sovereign. Florida Blanca had during this period to contend against the enmity and obstructions of a powerful cabal, hostile to his measures of internal reform, headed by the Count of Aranda, who had now been recalled from the embassy at Paris. Wearied at last with long years of continuous labour, hurt by the bitterness of the attacks of his adversaries, and feeling himself in declining health, the Minister now (October 10, 1788) drew up a lengthy memoir or apology, for submission to the King, in which he gave a full account of the whole of his administration and concluded by asking his Majesty's permission on the ground of health to retire. But one of the most marked characteristics of Charles III was the immovable firmness of the support which throughout his life he always gave to those who had once won his confidence. He now refused to accept his Minister's proffered resignation, and removed from their posts two of his chief opponents, the Marquis of Rubi, Governor of Madrid, and General O'Reilly, the Minister of War.

This was one of the last acts of Charles. The deaths in rapid succession, from small-pox, of his daughter-in-law, Doña Mariana, of her infant, and then of Don Gabriel himself (October and November, 1788) were a great shock to him. Shortly afterwards the King fell ill of a fever, and he died on December 14, in the seventy-third year of his age. Of Charles it may in truth be said his faults were few, his virtues many. To assert of him that he was the most capable, intelligent, honest, and best-intentioned of all the kings who have ruled in Spain since the death of Philip II, would perhaps be in itself small praise. The best tribute to his memory is a survey, however brief, of the many reforms, administrative, material, economic and social for the public welfare, carried out or initiated under his auspices.

The Minister to whom the chief credit is due for the internal progress of Spain after the conclusion of the war with England is Florida Blanca. He seized the opportunity of the restoration of peace to push forward in every department of the national life the system of reform, which Patiño initiated and which Campillo, Ensenada, and Aranda had each of them striven, not altogether unsuccessfully, in spite of many prejudices and much opposition, to carry on. Florida Blanca was fortunate in having at his side so capable an adviser as Pedro Rodriguez, Count of Campomanes, jurist, historian, statesman, writer, and above all one of the leading authorities of his day on economic science. Campomanes, as President of the Council of Castile, gave his whole-hearted cooperation to the First Minister in putting into practical shape the projects of reform, which the King had at heart. Francis, Count de Cabarrus, a Frenchman by extraction, and Joseph de Galvez, Marquis de Sonora, the conqueror of Florida, also did excellent service in the departments of commerce and the Indies.

It is not possible to do more than indicate all that was accomplished for the advancement and prosperity of Spain by the efforts of these statesmen. To relieve the heavy burden of public indebtedness and to increase the revenue by a readjustment and reorganisation of the whole system of taxation was a pressing necessity. The foundation of the National Bank of St Charles, with a capital of 300,000,000 of reals (£3,593,750) in 1782 carried out chiefly by the financial skill of Cabarrus, did much to give stability to the credit of the State. In Catalonia the obnoxious duties known as the *bolla* and *plomos de ramos*, a charge of 15 per cent. on all articles manufactured and on all sales, were abolished. The corresponding duties in Castile and other parts of Spain—the *alcabalas* and *millónes*—which were exacted not merely on manufactures and fabrics, but upon all the necessities of life, were all greatly reduced—those on food products from 14 per cent. to 2, 3, and 4 per cent. In place of these oppressive charges there was at first imposed a single tax of 5 per cent. upon incomes, which it was afterwards found expedient to graduate, a reduction of one-half being allowed to those who resided on their own property. At the same time, all restrictions upon the commerce of the mother country with the colonies were gradually swept away. As a result of this policy, the export of home produce to America was speedily quintupled, and the imports from America were increased nine-fold. Every effort was also made to stimulate the prosperity of home industries. In 1783 a new tariff was brought into operation to check the import of foreign manufactures, and at the same time skilled artificers from abroad were introduced to teach the native workmen their craft. Thus the Government were enabled to start factories for glass-making, and porcelain, fine cloth, velvets, leathers, and other goods, and to create profitable occupations for large numbers of the people. Every possible encouragement was also given to agriculture and means of communication. The Canal of Aragon, planned in the time of the Emperor Charles V, was completed from Tadela to Saragossa, enabling a large extent of country that had passed out of cultivation to be irrigated. Other canals on a large scale—the Canal of Old Castile to connect Madrid with the Tagus, the Canal of Guadarama, and others of less importance—were begun, and likewise proved of great service for irrigation purposes. A practical school of agriculture was founded near Aranjuez. Attempts were made at afforesting the bare plateaux of Castile, and to establish colonies in waste lands in the north of Andalusia. A perfect network of new roads was constructed, and regular posting between the chief towns established. Hospitals, colleges, schools, philanthropic institutions, arose on every side. Mendicity was suppressed and punished, and vagabonds placed in houses of correction where they were compelled to work, while for the infirm and aged asylums were provided. The funds for these objects were largely derived from the confiscated property of the Jesuits and by charges made upon the revenues of the clergy for what was called "the pious fund" (*fondo pio beneficial*). Much was done for the codification and revision of the laws and for securing the prompt administration of justice. Many abuses were swept away ; a good police system secured order in the large towns; and the rapacity and extortion of officials checked. All these changes and reforms could not be effected without friction, or without opposition from those whose privileges or whose liberties were curtailed. But, on the whole, the result for good rivals that achieved in an equally short time in any other country; and in the history of Spain there is certainly no period which can compare with the reign of Charles III. Despite the wars against England, with their disastrous drain upon the finances of the country, the welfare and the prosperity of the kingdom continually advanced. It was an age at once of material and intellectual advance. The Universities became centres for the acquiring and the diffusion of knowledge, and scientific and literary societies were to be found in all the chief cities of the land. Unfortunately, the brighter days which seemed to be dawning for the Spanish people were not destined to endure. In an absolute monarchy very much depends upon the enlightenment and character of the monarch. With the accession of Charles IV the old evils attendant upon weakness and misrule were once more to reappear, and the destinies of the country to sink with the moral tone of its government.

(2) PORTUGAL.
(1750–93.)

John V died in 1750 after a long reign of 44 years, marked by peace and lavish expenditure. The incomings from the mines of Brazil had been very large; but they had been wasted in the erection of costly edifices and in a continual stream of donatives to Rome. As a reward for the religious zeal, which showed itself in this practical form, Dom John received from the Pope in 1748, the title of Most Faithful. During the last eight years of his life this King fell into a state of imbecility, and the government was carried on by a Regency. He was succeeded by his son Joseph I, who, though he was 36 years of age, had hitherto been allowed to take no part in the administration. He had no love of the details of business, and, though a man of some ability, was content to leave the practical work of government in the hands of his Ministers. He was fortunate in finding one capable of dealing with the difficult task of restoring prosperity and vigour to a country that had become impoverished, stagnant, well-nigh moribund. Sebastian Joseph de Carvalho e Mello, after filling the posts of ambassador at London and Vienna, had been summoned by the Queen Regent in 1750 to take the Secretaryship of Foreign Affairs. Before he arrived at Lisbon, Joseph had ascended the throne; but he was confirmed in his office by the new King, over whom he speedily acquired complete ascendancy.

Carvalho was already 51 years old; but, though he had had to wait so long for an opportunity for the exercise of his great abilities, he now began at once to display an energy, industry, and strength of character which won the King's unlimited confidence, and secured for the Minister, until Joseph's death in 1777, the exercise of absolute and autocratic power. There were no Cortes to dispute his predominance; but he had to encounter the opposition of the nobility and the Church in his efforts at reform, besides the prejudices of the people—and these were no slight obstacles. One of his first steps, in 1751, was to curb the power of the Inquisitor. A royal decree enacted that henceforth no *auto-de-fé* was to take place, or execution be carried out, without the approval of the Government. He set to work to put the defences of the country into a more satisfactory state, by putting aside an annual sum for the mainten-ance of the fortresses, and at the same time did his utmost to revive agriculture, and stimulate industries. The streets of Lisbon and other towns, which had been the scenes of licence and outrage, were efficiently policed, and offences were severely punished. The finances were re-organised, and great economies in expenditure effected. The condition of the colonies next occupied the Minister's attention. In June, 1755, a charter was issued incorporating a Company with special privileges for trading in Maranhão and Grand Pará; and this was followed by the establishment of the Pernambuco and Paraiba Companies. A decree was issued in the same month by which all the native Indians in Maranhão and Grand Pará were declared free; and Carvalho's brother, Francisco Xavier de Mendoça, was sent out as Governor to carry it into effect.

An awful catastrophe was to interrupt the course of these well meant efforts at reform. On the morning of All Saints' Day (November 1, 1755), a great earthquake laid Lisbon in ruins and caused the death of some 30,000 of its inhabitants. A terrible tidal wave, sweeping up the estuary of the Tagus, completed the destruction caused by the upheaving of the ground. The courage and energy displayed by Carvalho were extraordinary. Working day and night, visiting personally the scenes of devastation, he issued decree after decree in rapid succession, for the restoration of order, the tending of the wounded, the burial of the dead, the provision of necessary food. From this time forward, the trust reposed by the King in his Minister was practically unbounded. Under his care and supervision, the city rose from its ashes with handsome streets and squares, cleansed, improved, and embellished. The old feelings of amity between England and Portugal were greatly strength-ened by the munificent donation of £100,000 made by the British Government for the relief of the sufferers in the earthquake. In 1756, Carvalho was made First Minister, and all departments of administration were placed under his supreme control; while, on his nomination, he was succeeded as Secretary for Foreign Affairs by Luis da Cunha. The establishment of the Oporto Wine Company in September, 1756, which gave to the company the exclusive right of buying all the wines in a given district for a fixed price during a certain period after the vintage, was intended to benefit the quality of the wine and the growers. It gave, however, much umbrage to the English, who, through the trade privileges granted them under the Methuen Treaty of 1702, had been the almost exclusive consumers of these wines, and excited such discontent in Oporto that formidable riots broke out (February, 1757). These were suppressed with great severity.

Carvalho had two great obstacles in his path to absolute autocratic authority in the State—the powerful Order of the Jesuits and the nobility. He now set about the task of crushing them both. The conduct of the Jesuits in America furnished the pretext. The Jesuit missionaries in the seventeenth century had converted the Indians in the interior of Paraguay, and had formed a colony, consisting of 31 mission stations or *reductiones*, as they were called, which carried on a considerable trade and by its remoteness had become almost independent. In 1748, an agreement had been made between Spain and Portugal, by which the latter ceded the long-disputed territory known as Nova Colonia to Spain, in exchange for seven of the Paraguay *reductiones* adjacent to the Brazilian frontier. The attempt to carry out this compact was resisted by the Jesuits in 1754–5 by force of arms, and the *reductiones* had to be conquered by a difficult and costly campaign. The Jesuits, who had on the Amazon many mission stations, which were also centres of trade, likewise opposed, as much as they could, the operations of the Maranhão and Pará Company and the decree of 1755 for the freeing of the Indians. Hitherto, the Order had been powerful in Portugal and had exercised, through the royal confessors, great influence at Court. Joseph, however, placed himself entirely in his Minister's hands, and Carvalho determined to strike hard. The King's confessor, Moreira, was dismissed, and Jesuits were forbidden to approach the Court. Representations were made to the Pope as to the misdemeanours of the Order in America and elsewhere. Finally, on April 1, 1758, Benedict XIV nominated Cardinal Saldanha as Visitor and Reformer of the Society of Jesus in the dominions of His Most Faithful Majesty. By a decree dated May 15, 1758, the Visitor ordered the Jesuits to desist thenceforth from trading and commerce, and suspended them from preaching and confessing in his patriarchate.

The next blow fell on the nobility. On September 3, 1758, an attempt was made on the life of the King. He was fired at in his carriage and wounded. In the middle of December, some of the most influential members of the Portuguese aristocracy, the Marquis and Marchioness of Tavora and their two sons, the Duke of Aveiro, the Count of Atouguia, and others, were arrested as the authors of the crime. They were strong opponents of the Carvalho autocracy. A special tribunal was appointed to try them; they were condemned to death, and their property was confiscated. The sentence was carried out, on January 13, 1759, with cruel brutality. A great mystery surrounds this summary procedure. Whether the accused were innocent or guilty is one of those questions on which no positive opinion can be given.   Many people believed in their innocence; but Carvalho succeeded in persuading the King that the step he had taken was just and necessary, and as a reward for his services he was in June created Count of Oeyras.   The conviction of the Tavoras had meanwhile served as a pretext for further attacks upon the Jesuits.   On the ground of evidence found in the Tavora papers, Gabriel Malagrida, the confessor of the Marchioness, and eight other Jesuits were arrested.   The whole Society were accused of being the instigators of, and accomplices in, the crime.   On January 19, a decree was issued for the sequestration of all their estates; and this was followed, in September, by the expulsion of the Jesuits from Portugal and from the Portuguese possessions in Brazil and the East Indies.   Malagrida, a half-crazy enthusiast, was burnt alive as a heretic in 1764.

The Minister, having thus with a strong hand removed opposition from his path, was able to carry out his policy of reform without further let or hindrance.   His reign was a reign of terror; spies filled the land; the prisons were crowded; but all that a man could do for the welfare of his country was taken in hand by Carvalho, and carried out with an unsparing energy and an administrative capacity and resource that have rarely been surpassed in the annals of statesmanship.   He rebelled against the political and commercial dependence upon England to which Portugal had been reduced by the Methuen Treaty; but, when attacked by Spain in 1762, he was, as has been related elsewhere, ready to avail himself of British assistance in repelling the invasion.   After the campaign he retained the services of Count William of Lippe-Bückeburg to reorganise the Portuguese army and to train a force of 32,000 men on the Prussian model.   The fortresses were also repaired, and a respectable navy of thirteen ships of war and six frigates was created.   In 1769, an attempt attributed to the Jesuits was made upon Carvalho's life.   It was at this time that the King conferred upon him the title of Marquis of Pombal, by which he is best known to history.

To recount all the reforms of Pombal would occupy a larger space than is at our disposal.   A brief *résumé* must therefore suffice.   Mention has already been made of the commercial companies established by him. He did his utmost to offer facilities for an increase of trade between the mother country and her colonies, and by shutting out foreign imports he endeavoured to stimulate the growth of native manufactures and industries which he set on foot.   The distinctions between "old" and "new" Christians were swept away, and all Portuguese subjects were made eligible to serve in Church and State.   The system of internal administration was revolutionised, and a crowd of useless and costly petty officials were abolished in 1761 by a stroke of the pen.   The legal machinery was simplified and made more effective.   Education occupied a large share of the Minister's attention.   The expulsion of the Jesuits and the sequestration of their property necessitated the creation of fresh educational institutions, and also afforded the financial means for their establishment. The former Jesuit College at Lisbon was transformed into a College of Nobles under secular administration, and Pombal introduced into the University of Coimbra faculties for instruction in the Natural Sciences and the latest modern learning; while 837 elementary and secondary schools were scattered over the land. The ideas and projects of Pombal were in these matters far in advance of his time; unfortunately, they never had an opportunity to take root and acclimatise themselves, and the fall from power of the great Minister was a fatal blow to that revival of the prosperity and welfare of the Portuguese people on which he had spent his best efforts and energies during twenty-six years. The King died on February 24, 1777; and Pombal, who was now 77 years of age, at once fell into disgrace.

The new sovereign, Maria I, was married to her uncle, who now became King Consort as Pedro III. Both Maria and Pedro were weak and amiable, and disinclined to treat the aged Minister with harshness, but the Queen Mother, Mariana Victoria, resented his treatment of the Jesuits, and was bitterly incensed against Pombal because of an attempt that he had made to exclude females from the right of succession. Through her influence he was ejected from power, and would doubtless have incurred heavy penalties, but for his vindictive adversary's death (January, 1781). He was, however, banished to his estates, and died in 1782. One of Maria's first acts had been to release many great noblemen and others, whom Pombal had thrown into prison on various pretexts. The Court was therefore full of his bitter enemies; nevertheless, his policy of reform was not reversed. The Queen was well disposed, and efforts to promote agriculture and industry, and to advance the progress of education and learning, continued. The Royal Academy of Science was founded in 1779, and many judicial abuses were corrected. In all matters of administration the Queen placed herself in the hands of her confessor, Ignacio de San Caetano, the Grand Inquisitor, who, though a religious bigot, was on the whole an enlightened adviser.

In May, 1786, Pedro III died, and shortly afterwards his eldest son Dom José. The second son of Pedro and Maria, Dom John, who was married to Carlota Joaquina, grand-daughter of Charles III of Spain, now became heir to the throne. For some time the Queen had been showing signs of religious mania, and the death of Caetano, following closely upon that of Dom José, completely upset the balance of her mind, so that she became more and more unfit to discharge the duties of her office. She remained nominally sovereign until 1792, when Dom John took upon himself the administration of affairs. He was not, however, actually named Regent until 1799.

(3) BRAZIL.

(Seventeenth and Eighteenth Centuries.)

In the course of the sixteenth century the Portuguese had established themselves along the whole coast line of Brazil from the Rio de la Plata to the mouth of the Amazon. The country was divided into captaincies —hereditary grants of territory, covering about 50 leagues of the coast and extending to an indefinite distance inland. In 1548 the first Governor-General was appointed, with the seat of government at San Salvador (Bahia). Brazil was the first of the European settlements in America to attempt the cultivation of the soil; and, in particular, sugar plantations soon became a flourishing industry. In 1581, Philip II conquered Portugal; and Brazil passed under the dominion of the Spanish kings. The colony now suffered from the apathy and neglect of the new rulers, and, being especially vulnerable to attack by European freebooters, suffered much during the closing years of the sixteenth and earlier half of the seventeenth century from attacks by the enemies of the Spanish monarchy, English, French, and Dutch. The French established a settlement on the island of Marajo in 1612, but were expelled in 1618. The successful ejection of the foreign colonists (1648) led to the formation of the State of Maranhão-Pará. The Dutch during this same period planted a number of trading stations in the mouth of the Amazon and some way up its main stream, but were finally driven away (1606–24).

The formation of the Dutch West India Company, in 1621, led to serious efforts being made by Holland for the conquest of Brazil. San Salvador (Bahia) was captured in 1624 by a large Dutch armament, but was recaptured by a great expedition sent from Spain in the following year. In 1630, the Dutch directed their attack on the town of Olinda in Pernambuco and its port, the Reciff, which fell into their hands. Count Maurice of Nassau, appointed Governor-General in 1636, succeeded in establishing a great Dutch dominion stretching along the coast from the Rio San Francisco to Maranhão. He established friendly relations with the Portuguese settlers, and the colony prospered under his rule. Maurice retired in 1644; in the meantime, the disposition of the Portuguese towards their foreign conquerors had been changed by the successful revolt of the mother country against Spain in 1641, and the assumption of the Portuguese Crown by John IV. The Brazilian settlers rose against the Dutch, and gradually reconquered the territory that had been lost. Ill supported from home, the Dutch were finally driven out in 1654, when the Reciff, their last stronghold, was taken. From this time onwards, the Portuguese were able to set themselves to the task of the development of the enormous territory which had now, without further let or hindrance from foreign aggression, fallen into their hands.

The four centres of settlement in Brazil were Pernambuco, Bahia, Rio de Janeiro, and, in the interior, São Paulo on the central plateau. Of these the last, founded by the great Jesuit missionary Nobrega, in 1553, was the most vigorous and enterprising. The Paulistas intermarried frequently with the natives, and their descendants were noted for their daring activity in exploring the interior in search of gold. They penetrated as far as the Jesuit *reductiones* on the Parana, 1635, and into the districts to the north afterwards known as Minas Geraes, because of the gold that was found there. The first discovery of rich mines was made in 1670 near the head-waters of the San Francisco river and in 1690 at Sabará. Adventurers now flocked in, both from the sea-coast and Portugal, and considerable population grew up round the mines. At first, the mining laws were liberal, but afterwards more and more restrictions were imposed, export was forbidden, and one-fifth rigorously exacted as the King's share. A revolt of the *emboabas* or foreign immigrants broke out under a leader named Nunez Vianna, and was with difficulty subdued in 1709. A little later, there was a further rebellion in Pernambuco against the rapacity and corruption of the Portuguese Governors and officials, which was not put down without difficulty, many concessions having to be made to the settlers by the home authorities. In the north, the provinces of Pará, Maranhão and Ceará had in 1621 been united as the State of Maranhão and created a separate Governorship. This enormous stretch of territory included the mouths of the Amazon and the vast watershed of that river. For a long time the settlements were confined to the neighbourhood of the sea-coast, the seat of Government being the town of Pará. Only very slowly did any settlements rise on the Amazon or Rio Negro. The Jesuits, under the leadership of the famous Padre Antonio Vieira, established a number of mission stations in the interior, and at the end of the third decade of the eighteenth century they had made their way far up the river Solimões and Negro. They gathered the Indians together into villages, *aldeas*, and with their aid cultivated the soil and carried on a considerable commerce. Meanwhile the hunting for gold had led to discoveries on the head-waters of the Madeira and the Paraguay, and to the foundation of the two new provinces of Cuyabá and Matto Grosso. In 1729 came the further discovery of diamonds in northern Minas. So immense was the yield that it is said that, between 1730 and 1770, more than 5,000,000 *carats* were taken from the district. This output, unequalled in the world at that time, was a source of immense profit to the Portuguese Crown.

In the south events had not moved so smoothly. Spain had neglected to occupy the north bank of the Rio de la Plata, although she claimed its possession as falling to the west of the boundary between the Portuguese and Spanish spheres as defined by the Treaty of Tordesillas. But this district was also claimed by Portugal, in whose early maps this portion of the South American continent had been placed eight degrees to the eastward of its correct position. In 1680, the Portuguese planted a fort and settlement, called Colonia, right opposite Buenos Ayres. It was captured by the Spanish Governor; but it was restored by the influence of Louis XIV, and finally ceded definitely to Portugal by the Treaty of Utrecht. The Portuguese retained possession of this coveted outpost, which was valuable as a centre of clandestine trade, with one or two short intervals until 1777. In the years 1710–11, during the War of the Spanish Succession, two daring attacks were made on Rio de Janeiro by French expeditions. In the latter year it was captured by Admiral Duguay-Trouin, and had to pay a heavy ransom.

The importance of Colonia was greatly diminished by the founding, in 1726, of Montevideo; and in 1737 a Portuguese force was sent to capture it, but failed. It was at this time that the Portuguese, for the protection of their southern frontier, fortified the only entrance to the series of great lagoons which skirt this part of the coast. This fort was the beginning of the city of Rio Grande do Sul.

An effort was made, in 1750, to settle all disputed boundary claims between Spain and Portugal on the principle of *uti possidetis*, and it was arranged that seven of the Jesuit *reductiones* in the interior should be given in exchange for Colonia. But the Indians strenuously resisted this attempt to hand them over to new masters. Colonia was, accordingly, not surrendered, and in 1761 the outbreak of war in Europe reopened the whole question. A strong army despatched from Buenos Ayres took possession both of Colonia and Rio Grande (1763). By the Treaty of Paris Colonia was given back to Portugal, but Rio Grande was retained by the Spaniards. In this diplomatic surrender, however, the inhabitants refused to acquiesce. They carried on fierce guerilla warfare with the intruders, gained strength year by year, being aided by the Paulistas from the interior, and finally, in 1775, succeeded in recapturing the town of Rio Grande, and driving the Spaniards out of their conquests. When the news of these events reached Madrid a great expedition was despatched to recover the lost ground. Santa Catharina was taken, and preparations were made for an invasion of southern Brazil in force, when the resolve of Spain to join France in supporting the revolted American colonies against Great Britain led to a change of attitude towards Portugal. A treaty was signed at San Ildefonso in 1777, by which all disputed questions between the two Peninsular Powers with regard to their frontiers in South America were amicably settled.

The interval between these two treaties of 1750 and 1777 covered the period of the Ministry in Portugal of the Marquis of Pombal. At the time of his accession to office nothing could have been worse than the administrative and economic condition of Brazil. The policy of the mother country towards its great colony was narrow and restrictive. No trade was permitted except with Portugal, and this was hampered by manifold restrictions. Corruption among the officials, high and low, was

universal. Justice was an affair of bribery, and the industrial development of the country was at a standstill. The Brazilians were gradually
learning to regard Portugal as their enemy, and to nourish a deep feeling
of resentment against the treatment they received. For a time this
inimical attitude to all things Portuguese was changed to a more friendly
one by the energetic efforts of Pombal to reform abuses in Brazil as well
as at home. He did his utmost to encourage commerce, agriculture, and
industry. Corruption was sternly dealt with and suppressed. As has been
already told, charters were granted to trading companies. A decree
was issued in 1753 forbidding the enslaving of the Indians, and encouraging intermarriage with them. Lastly, in 1759, there came the order
for the expulsion of the Jesuits and the confiscation of their property.
Under Pombal's wise administration the revenue from the mines was greatly
increased, and, despite the hostilities in the south, commerce and prosperity began to make a real start in many parts of the country. With the
great Minister's fall this promise of better things speedily vanished. The
old abuses crept back and with them the desire for freedom from political
dependence on a distant and selfish mother country began to make headway among the more ardent spirits of the cultured class. It was fomented
by the declaration of independence of the United States, which set an
example, and gave an impulse, which was to bear fruit at a later date.
How the Portuguese royal family were compelled in 1807 to take refuge
at Rio, is related in another volume. It was an event which profoundly
affected the relations between the colony and the parent State, and caused
the severing of their political ties to be effected (in 1822) after a quite
different fashion in the case of Brazil from that of the armed revolts
which led to the establishment of the Spanish colonies as a series of
independent republics.

CHAPTER XIII.

GREAT BRITAIN.

(1756–93.)

(1) WILLIAM PITT THE ELDER.

The Seven Years' War, the military events of which have been recorded in other chapters of this work, brought about two results of universal historical significance. England, after her victories over France beyond the confines of Europe, now appears as unmistakably the foremost colonial Power. For America was wrested from the French and their power in India broken. The command of the seas lay in the hands of Great Britain, and even a Napoleon was not able to take it from her. Next, in the old world of Europe the little kingdom of Prussia had successfully held its own in the face of a strong coalition. Both of the old military Powers, France and Austria, had been its opponents in the field, and a few other States, Russia and Sweden, were ranged by their side. English help was mainly indirect and consisted, from the Prussian point of view, chiefly in occupying hostile activity at remote points and in supplying subsidies. Relying almost entirely on her own resources, Prussia carried on this struggle under her gifted King, who, with equal courage and tenacity, daring and prudence, overcame all dangers and proved to the world that Prussia's ambition to be counted among the Great Powers could no longer be arrested.

With England's share in bringing about these results the name of William Pitt is inseparably associated. In him the French recognised their most dangerous adversary. In the archives of the Foreign Office in Paris is a report of the year 1783 in which a government official points out the dangers that would arise for France if she should remain without sufficient warlike preparations on land and sea and confine herself to a passive attitude. "She will be what Lord Chatham wished her to be: a Power of secondary rank limited to the Continent of Europe." And Frederick the Great, who found his best ally in Pitt, calls him "a lofty spirit, a mind capable of vast designs, of steadfastness in carrying them into execution, and of inflexible fidelity to his own opinions, because he believed them to be for the good of his country which he loved."

When the War began, Pitt was already a man of forty-eight. His grandfather, Thomas Pitt, had been in the service first of the old, then of the new (combined) East India Company, though not above an occasional connexion with the "Interlopers"; and, by a bold and successful commercial career, he had attained to wealth and importance. Posterity has remembered him as "Diamond Pitt," because of the celebrated transactions (which occupied fifteen years of his life) concerned with the disposal of a diamond of unprecedented size and beauty, which he sold —greatly to his own advantage—to the Regent Orleans. He was one of the earliest of those "nabobs" who invested their imported riches in English estates and parliamentary seats.

Thomas' grandson, William Pitt, would probably have persisted in the military career which he had originally chosen in accordance with his own inclination and natural gifts, had he not been at an early date compelled by a gouty tendency in his constitution to relinquish a soldier's life. From 1735 he was a member of the House of Commons. He joined the party of the "Patriots" who gathered round the heir to the throne and whose intellectual head, though he remained excluded from Parliament, was Bolingbroke. Pitt grew up in Opposition. He helped to overthrow Walpole; he attacked Carteret; after he had been a member of the Pelham Ministry, though not in the Cabinet, he again went over to the Opposition in 1755, and until the outbreak of the War remained the most dangerous parliamentary adversary of the Government.

Pitt's strength was founded on his own personality, and not on powerful family connexions. From his first appearance in Parliament onwards he was accounted one of the best speakers. How his contemporaries were impressed by the flash of his eye, the music of his voice, the noble bearing of his tall figure—doubtless the outward dignity of his personal appearance was no less impressive, even when he rose in the House for the delivery of his great orations leaning on crutches and wrapped in bandages. It cannot be denied that the form of these speeches is superior to their substance; the energy of the delivery was more remarkable than the strength of the arguments. But, even so, he was possessed of the power of fascinating and convincing his hearers. "You don't know," Lord Cobham once observed, "Mr Pitt's talent of insinuation; in a very short quarter of an hour he can persuade any man of anything."

He presented himself on every occasion as the whole-hearted champion of nothing less than the true ideals of every Englishman: the interests of the nation, the Constitution, the privileges of Parliament, the honour of England. And, most assuredly, his whole nature was pervaded by the moral earnestness which was the keynote of his speeches. For, beyond all doubt, Pitt was a high-minded patriot; and, if

his ambition was bent for power, he was also impelled by the conviction
that no other could guide the helm of the State so safely as himself.
In the years of Opposition he had struggled against the great political
evils of the time, or at least against what his contemporaries regarded as
such. No one gave stronger expression to the indignation provoked by
Walpole's system of corruption than Pitt. And just as, a few years
after the accession of George I, the Jacobite Shippen declared the Speech
from the Throne fitter for the meridian of Germany than for that of
England, so, with not less animosity, Pitt, the Opposition leader, a few
decades later, asserted of the connexion of England with Hanover,
"that this great, this powerful, this formidable kingdom, is considered
only as a province to a despicable electorate," and adjured the House to
show "that, however the interest of Hanover has been preferred by the
Ministers, the Parliament pays no regard but to that of Great Britain."

When George II ascended the throne of Great Britain, Sir Robert
Walpole stood at the height of his power. At the death of that monarch
the affairs of the State were controlled by Pitt. The two men, as has
been already indicated in an earlier chapter, were wholly different in their
relations both to the Crown and Parliament. Walpole, it is aptly said,
was given to the people by the King, Pitt to the King by the people.
Walpole rose to power, and was supported by the King, as the most
capable man in the Whig party, which under the two first rulers of the
Hanoverian dynasty had the monopoly of political power. When the new
reign began in 1727, it rested with the sovereign whether Walpole should
go or stay. George II decided, after a short hesitation, for his father's
Minister, and Walpole remained. His highest aim being to maintain
himself in the monarch's favour, he was not less ready to please the King
in his foreign policy, by a punctilious consideration for the Hanoverian
electorate, than to satisfy his personal requirements. He drew his support
from above, from the Crown; but in order to secure his own rule, he
needed to retain the lasting cooperation of Parliament. By means
which would now be condemned, but which were then acquiesced in as
indispensable, he succeeded for a long while in mastering a very troublesome Opposition, and in keeping a majority without ever sinking to be
its tool. In fact the general sentiment declared his rule necessary for
the country. His system was the policy of peace and of the prosperity
which depends upon peace. He was not the originator of what had
become the leading principle of English politics since Utrecht—the
maintenance of peace and friendship with France—but he adopted it
and carried it out. He thus became the historical embodiment of this
principle; foreign policy always being accounted by him of secondary
importance, while his primary purpose was the development of finance,
commerce, and the colonies. Thus he condemned the Treaty of Hanover
of 1725, because it might lead to a great war, and always remained
disinclined to push matters to extremities. Herein he was, as we shall

see, the exact opposite of Pitt, the great war Minister, who was resolved to carry through the struggle to its final conclusion, and not to desist till victory had been won all along the line. When at last Walpole was obliged by the will of the nation to enter on a war against Spain, it was precisely this War which caused his fall. For he carried it on with an insufficient expenditure of force and with indifferent success; Parliament had little confidence in the bellicose achievements of his Ministry; and the actual successes won were not placed to his credit.

Walpole has been called the first Prime Minister in England; but his position still retained much of the traditions of earlier times. The Minister rules for the King and can, like him, change his political system. He leads Parliament and seeks to assure himself of its support; but he is not yet the choice of Parliament. William Pitt, on the contrary, is the first great representative of the new conception of the office of Minister. He had begun by joining in the Opposition against Walpole; but every complaint which he brought forward, after all, addressed itself rather to the system than to the man. In his later years Pitt came to esteem Walpole far more highly than he had done at first, and indeed to admire him. To understand Pitt, it will always be necessary to recall the Administration of Walpole and the contrast between the two great Ministers, though many years lay between their periods of office. In the course of this interval numerous men of talent appeared on the political scene, but no great genius dominated England. Carteret was a man of great intelligence and signally well acquainted with the problems of European politics. But, on the other hand, he was neither sufficiently familiar with the internal affairs of Great Britain (he had never sat in the House of Commons), nor had he a true insight into the rising importance of Britain beyond the seas, that is, of the colonies.

Still less deserving of praise is the Administration of the Pelhams, which, as has been seen, was conducted, quite in Walpole's way, by patronage and bribery. The younger, Henry, for some time First Lord of the Treasury, was certainly a clever business man, with a special gift for finance. The elder, the Duke of Newcastle, who sat in nearly every Cabinet through many decades, from the time of Walpole until after the great Ministry of the elder Pitt, was necessary to the Government on account of the number of votes of which he disposed, although his personal qualities in no way recommended him for great office in the State. But the long term of his activity in high place, his immense political experience, his familiarity with routine—all this gave him as a rule great weight within the Cabinet, and explains how he could be a valuable fellow-worker even for a man of genius like Pitt. Extremely self-confident, but with moderate powers of judgment, he had, besides the merits already mentioned, an immense personal capacity for work; he was certainly one of the most industrious Ministers whom England ever had. His business papers, which are now national property, contain, besides countless political despatches, often couched in a somewhat solemn long-winded style, large collections of various materials to aid him in finding his way; and yet historians are always dwelling, surely with some exaggeration, on his grotesque ignorance. His diligence, his loyalty, and his blameless personal conduct, make him by no means the most unattractive figure among the English Ministers of the eighteenth century. He had a gift for hard work, but no personal distinction; he was a man who under superior guidance was capable of rendering excellent service, but he was himself little fitted for the position of leader. Thus, for more than forty years, and under three English sovereigns, Newcastle filled high political offices; until, at last, weary of his many burdens and of his many adversaries, he retired, not without dignity, from public life.

In the great days of Pitt's Ministry, when England's position in the world had risen to so great a height, foreign policy occupied a much larger place than home affairs. Since the time of William III it had been assumed that England and France were adversaries, and in the formation of alliances it was only necessary to ask who would take the side of England and who that of France. It was also customary to find the Imperial Court, that is, the Austrian Power, in alliance with England or—as the traditional friendship between England and Holland had made it possible to say from the days of William III onwards—with the Maritime Powers. For the rivalry of the House of Habsburg with France was still older than that of England; it dated from the days of Charles V. The electorate of Brandenburg, too, which had now grown into the kingdom of Prussia, stood on the side of the opponents of France ever since the Great Elector had in 1672 hastened to succour Holland, when hard pressed by Louis XIV. Thus, the system of coalitions *pour contrebalancer la France*, as it was expressed in the diplomatic language of the time, was, in the eighteenth century, a familiar notion kept up all the more tenaciously because of a corresponding joint policy on the part of the kindred Bourbon Courts in France, Spain, and Italy. Temporary deviations from this Old System, as it was called, indeed occurred. In Walpole's time England on the whole maintained friendly relations with France. The year 1725 had seen the Powers of Europe grouped in unusual combinations in face of a threat of war—the Emperor and Spain on the one side, the Western Powers on the other; but this position appeared to politicians so unreasonable that 1725 came to be spoken of as "the mad year."

Thereafter, England and France once more stood opposed to each other, especially on account of their interests beyond sea; and in the War of the Austrian Succession the conflicting Powers of Europe were seen again in the familiar old grouping. Only in one case had a remarkable change been carried out. Prussia, under her young King Frederick, had entered upon a wholly new course of action, and her invasion of Silesia had been followed by a series of conflicts between herself and Austria. From the year 1740 onwards, the enmity of the two most powerful German States was as much taken for granted in European politics as was the old hostility between England and France; and whoever ignored it had to learn it to his own cost. Newcastle, in 1748, failed completely in his attempt to recall Prussia to her traditional place in the "Old System." An alliance between Prussia and Austria, said Frederick himself, is quite as inconceivable as a combination of fire and water.

In substance, the policy of Frederick from the end of the Second Silesian War had been directed to the maintenance of peace and the security of his own possessions. The chief import to him of the negotiations of 1748 and the conclusion of the Peace of Aix-la-Chapelle was that by this Treaty he obtained a European guarantee of his recent acquisition of Silesia. Feeling assured of the hate of Queen Maria Theresa, who had not given up the hope of reconquering Silesia, he for eight years sought to deprive her of the chance of renewing the contest under favourable conditions. But these years of diplomatic efforts for the maintenance of peace he afterwards himself regarded as having been wasted and fruitless; and, declaring the futility of his policy before the Seven Years' War to be a topic unworthy of the attention of historians, he left a lacuna in his own historical narrative of his reign.

Hereupon, it gradually became patent that the system of alliances maintained up to 1755—England and Austria on the one side, France and Prussia on the other—was no longer based on common interests, and that such was especially the case with regard to Austria and England. The English Ministers had in view the great colonial conflict with France, in which it must be decided whether America should belong to the English or to the French. The Austrian alliance was only important to England in a continental war in so far as it was calculated to keep in check the French land forces and to resist any attack by them on the Netherlands or on Hanover. But this concerned Austria far less than the new struggle against Prussia. Maria Theresa longed to crush and cripple the foe who had despoiled her of Silesia; in comparison with this the antagonism to the House of Bourbon had ceased to be of the same account as of old. And in a passage of arms with Frederick the English alliance could be of no great use.

Thus both parties began to look for more valuable allies. Already in 1749, soon after the Peace of Aix-la-Chapelle, the keen-witted Kaunitz had recommended his mistress to abandon her old policy. "Inasmuch as the loss of Silesia cannot be forgotten and the King of Prussia is to be regarded as the greatest, most formidable and implacable enemy of the illustrious Archducal House," and as little assistance against him could be hoped for from the Maritime Powers, Kaunitz recommended an alliance with France. The suggestion clashed too much with the accepted view to meet with sympathy at once. But, during the ensuing years which Kaunitz spent as ambassador at Paris, he certainly did not relinquish it; and as Chancellor he repeated (August 21, 1755) what he had said six years earlier as the youngest member of the Conference of State at Vienna—"It is certain that Prussia must be overthrown, if the illustrious Archducal House is to hold its own"—further pointing out that with Austria's present allies, the Maritime Powers, this goal would never be reached. France must be won. His endeavours were accordingly from this time onwards directed to bringing over France from the Prussian to the Austrian alliance. For the moment, however, the idea was too novel to the French Government; though it was quite ready to draw nearer to Austria, even to guarantee to her security against external attack, while in the case of an Anglo-French war Austria was, like Prussia, to stand aloof. But all this was to be included in the existing system; and the French had no intention of abandoning their alliance with Prussia.

But, at the same time, England and Prussia were preparing to approach each other. George II wished to secure Frederick the Great's army for the protection of his Hanoverian inheritance in the event of a French attack. Frederick, at first mistrustful, ceased to show himself indisposed to listen to these overtures, after he had been informed of the conclusion of an Anglo-Russian Treaty and had seen it carried into effect. From Russia and the Empress Elizabeth, who was unfriendly towards him, Frederick could hope for little good. But now the King thought that, if he were but in alliance with England, there would be nothing more to fear from her other ally Russia. In that event, Austria too, left to herself, would not venture upon a new conflict with Prussia.

The result of these calculations was the Anglo-Prussian Alliance— or, as it was called, the Convention of Westminster (January 16, 1756) —purchased, in the opinion of Pitt, by the sacrifice of British rights. Both the contracting sovereigns undertook to preserve peace and friendship with each other. Each was to prevent his allies from any hostile attempts upon the European territories of the other. Were a foreign Power, under any pretext, to move its troops into Germany, the two contracting parties were to join forces to meet them and to maintain tranquillity in Germany; for a guarantee of the neutrality of Germany was the explicit object of this treaty. Accordingly, on the present occasion the term "Germany," which was officially quite unknown, was employed instead of that of "the Roman Empire," in order not to involve Prussia in an undertaking to defend the Austrian Netherlands.

Both Powers were completely mistaken as to the effect of the new alliance. While they had wished to secure peace on the Continent, they brought about war. England and Prussia alike believed it possible to enter into the new alliance without dissolving their old ties. The result would have been a sort of general European fraternisation. But the age was predisposed to war, and herein lay the mistake of the political calculation. France, on the one hand, Austria and Russia on the other, felt themselves injured and repulsed by the Powers which had hitherto been their allies. They now found themselves quickly at one. The Convention of Westminster completed what Kaunitz' diplomacy could not of itself have brought about. It led to the alliance between Maria Theresa and Louis XV.

Yet the Convention of Westminster contained nothing by which France need have felt aggrieved. She had herself already declared that she did not wish to attack Hanover. She could not, therefore, regard as hostile to herself the obligation into which Prussia had entered to defend the electorate. It was not so much the conditions of the Treaty which caused annoyance in Paris as the secrecy with which it was concluded. Frederick tried conciliatory methods, and sought in sundry conversations to convince the French ambassador, the Duc de Nivernais, of the harmlessness of his Treaty with England. He affirmed that the new Treaty would change nothing in his relations with France. He regretted the haste with which he had been obliged to conclude it, insomuch that a previous communication to France would have been dangerous, indeed impossible. He even caused Nivernais to open in his presence the box containing the original documents of the Westminster Treaty which had just arrived, in order that the Frenchman might convince himself that there was nothing in them which he did not already know.

It was all to no purpose. The unpleasant impression was not to be effaced. The French Court could not pardon the King of Prussia for allying himself with England, the enemy of France, without having in any way first asked her permission. A ready hearing was now given to the Austrian overtures. The Imperial ambassador, Count Starhemberg, who was earnestly supported by the Marquise de Pompadour and by the Abbé Bernis, could, on February 27, inform Kaunitz that France had no opposition to offer, if Austria were, in alliance with Russia, to deprive the King of Prussia of his conquests, and that she held out hopes of subsidies for this object. Further than this, however, the Government of France did not go; and its consent to any notion of the dismemberment of Prussia was out of the question.

The Treaty of Versailles, which the two Powers signed on May 1, 1756, was, therefore, of a purely defensive nature. Austria declared that she wished to remain neutral in the Anglo-French wars and would renounce any defence of Hanover. In return, France promised her aid, in case Austria were attacked by Prussia or by the Porte. No threat was hereby intended to the peace of the Continent. King Frederick received the news of the Treaty of Versailles somewhat indifferently, and gave a polite answer to the French ambassador who informed him of it. The Court of St James', however, regarded the event with more concern.

Newcastle, never far-sighted, spoke of the unnatural alliance by which the Protestant Courts were especially threatened. Either a powerful counter-alliance must now be formed, or Europe would be given over to the supremacy of France. The remark shows Newcastle's curious under-valuation of the strength of England, whose marvellous expansion under Pitt no one, indeed, could have foreseen.

The Peace of Europe was in the end imperilled by the Treaty of Versailles, but only when it became the starting-point for agree-ments with an ulterior scope between the sovereigns of the Houses of Bourbon and Habsburg. Maria Theresa and Kaunitz had had no other intention from the beginning but to move on towards a joint war upon Prussia; and Louis XV and the woman who held sway at his side, the Marquise de Pompadour, were quite willing to be pressed into this course. The King's responsible advisers, the very men who but shortly before had been the most earnest partisans of Frederick the Great, acquiesced. In June, 1756, an agreement as to the most important points had been reached, although the Treaty of offensive alliance, towards which these efforts were directed, had not yet been finally drawn up. Both Powers were already agreed that Silesia should be restored to Austria, and Kaunitz also found the French Court well disposed towards his intention of despoiling the Prussian monarchy of other provinces, perhaps of dismembering it altogether. France would support the action of Austria with military and financial assistance. She would also make no separate peace with England. Austria was, however, to make over the Netherlands—but only after the conquest of Silesia—to the son-in-law of Louis XV, the Spanish Infant, Don Philip, in exchange for his Italian possessions; nor would she raise any objection if certain parts of the Netherlands should become directly incorporated with the French State.

Russia, too, was won over to Kaunitz' policy. The expectation that the Empress Elizabeth would submit to the Treaty of Westminster and remain the ally of England ended in disappointment. She cared for nothing beyond the attack on Prussia, and was quite ready to agree to the Austrian proposal that this attack should be supported by Russian troops. She was even ready to exceed the stipulated number of 60,000 or 70,000 men and to employ the whole of her forces by sea and land in the war against Prussia.

"Are you sure of the Russians?" the King of Prussia asked the new English ambassador, Sir Andrew Mitchell, on May 12, 1756. "The King, my master, thinks so," was the answer of the diplomatist, who shared the mistake under which his Government laboured. But to Frederick this was the key of the political situation of Europe. The Treaty of Versailles roused no fear in him, so long as English influence prevailed in Russia. From the beginning of June, however, news had reached him from different quarters which left him in no doubt that Russia was actually planning an attack on Prussia. Hereupon, he at once recognised the full extent of the danger. He now knew that the military preparations of Russia, which he was meant to believe, and had believed, were to be undertaken in the interest of England, were directed against himself. The situation appeared to him all the more serious, when he simultaneously learnt of an unusual concentration of Austrian troops in Bohemia. He resolved to be beforehand with his enemies. Certain recent historians have refused to be satisfied with the assumption, attested by Frederick's own words, that he now began the War himself only on account of the clear impossibility of preserving peace, and have adduced his political testament of 1752, in which he speaks of the necessity of extending his dominions, together with the timely commencement of Prussian preparations in 1756, as evidence that he had from the first intended to attack and, therefore, did not precipitate the War only as an act of self-defence: so that it would be rather a case of two attacking Powers, Prussia and Austria, clashing together. While unable to accept this hypothesis, or to enter fully here into the arguments for or against it, we may refer to the discussions which passed between England and Prussia during the critical weeks of the year 1756. It would be difficult to see how it could have been possible for the English Ministry to fail to detect any false play on the part of their ally. But, so far as we can see, they appear to have had no suspicion. On the contrary, however strongly they desired the maintenance of peace on the Continent, they unreservedly recognised the emergency which threatened Frederick. They candidly declared to Michell, the Prussian ambassador in London, as he states in his despatch to his King, "that His Majesty is not in the least to blame if he tries to forestall his enemies instead of waiting until they carried out their hostile intentions." And Frederick, on his side, declares to his English friends in the most emphatic manner that he has tried every means to maintain peace. His language rises to solemn heights when he calls on Heaven to witness that there is no other course by which he may hope to prevent the threatened destruction of his kingdom except that of forestalling his enemies. "If ever I had had the intention of injuring that Court and seeking a quarrel with them, I could have attacked them two months ago without giving them time to prepare for battle. God is my witness that I never thought of it." This is not the language of a guilty conscience, or, to be explicit, of a sovereign who is deceitfully betraying the confidence of his ally.

The English, at all events, believed the truth of his words. In any case, they had to accept the facts as they were. For now the double character of the approaching struggle was revealed. The maritime war and the struggle in distant parts of the world, for which they were prepared, would not be all: they were now forced into a continental war.

At the death of Henry Pelham in 1754 his brother, Newcastle, had, as has been seen, become First Lord of the Treasury and head of the Ministry.

But it was a weak and incompetent Government. Corruption and patronage, the supports with which it could not dispense, might, in times of peace, suffice for the management of the House of Commons. But they were not enough for solving the more difficult problems which the outbreak of war offered in both the New and the Old World. For this purpose creative ideas were needed, and Newcastle was not a man of creative ideas. It was soon recognised that the War had been as ill prepared as it was ill conducted. The loss of Minorca, and Admiral Byng's withdrawal (May 20, 1756), produced the most painful impression in England. A British admiral, after an indecisive action with an opponent nearly equal in strength to himself, had sailed away with his fleet and abandoned to the enemy the island he had been sent to defend. The Government was eagerly bent on laying the whole responsibility on Byng, who was certainly not free from blame. Nevertheless, the incident could not but tell unfavourably on their own position. Moreover, the sudden invasion of Saxony by the Prussian King amounted to another rebuff for the English Cabinet, which had quite recently been extolling the Westminster Convention as the infallible means of preserving peace on the Continent. News from America further embarrassed Newcastle's position. The fall of Fort Oswego (August, 1756) made it clear that the English were driven from the territory round the Great Lakes, and that no obstacle remained to prevent the French from establishing a connexion between their possessions on the St Lawrence and those on the Upper Ohio.

All these events rendered the position of the Cabinet untenable. Two of its most important members, Murray, now Lord Mansfield, and Henry Fox, withdrew from the Government. The people of England had lost confidence in this Ministry of mediocrities, and called for a deliverer in their need. At this crisis every eye must of necessity have turned to William Pitt, the man who for twenty years had been one of the most interesting personalities in the House of Commons, admired and respected by the people, feared by the Government ; the man who was never at a loss for the severest rebukes with which to visit the weaknesses and faults of the Ministers ; but who had hitherto not been granted an opportunity of proving his capabilities at the head of affairs. The use of his brilliant and unimpaired energies could no longer be denied to the State in its hour of stress.

George II recognised that he must give way to the general pressure and admit the great member of the Opposition into the Cabinet. The influence of Leicester House, the Court of the heir apparent, the recommendations of the King's most intimate counsellor, his mistress Lady Yarmouth—all worked together to force the reluctant sovereign to call in the dreaded Commoner. Personally, he expected little good from him : " Pitt will not do my business," the King is recorded to have said, presumably referring to the care for the interests of Hanover which always lay so near to his heart. But the crisis was serious, and for the first time in English history the sovereign found himself compelled to accept as principal Minister a politician personally odious to him.

When it had been decided to summon Pitt, the composition of the Cabinet still offered very great difficulties. Pitt declined to sit in the Cabinet under or even beside Newcastle; neither would he tolerate Henry Fox, or anyone else who might threaten his own predominance. His first concern was to take the entire direction of the War into his own hands. He consented to allow the office of First Lord of the Treasury, the occupant of which had ever since the time of Walpole been regarded as Prime Minister, to be held by the Duke of Devonshire, the head of one of the first families in the land. Pitt became one of the two Principal Secretaries of State. Newcastle, Hardwicke, Fox—indeed, all the leading names of the late Government—disappeared from the Cabinet. It was an attempt to compose an Administration of new men and with new principles, to carry on the Government without seeking to influence the elections, without patronage or corruption, and to apply no other standard but that of the interests of the nation.

The attempt failed. Pitt's first Ministry lasted no longer than four months (December, 1756 to April, 1757). But even in this first brief period it is unmistakable that Pitt's action was informed by a grand and unbroken impulse. We see him indefatigable in action, but at the same time always keeping in view the political situation and its needs as a whole, ever calculating and planning, reviewing the chances and dangers of impending struggles on the Continent and on the high seas, in America and in the West and the East Indies. We see him endeavouring, by means of more sympathetic forms of intercourse, to establish more friendly relations with the colonial Governments than had hitherto been customary—doubtless in the main with no other intention than that of stimulating the colonists to increased efforts for the objects of the War. We see him preparing and setting in motion the despatch of armies and fleets, while at the same time taking steps for the introduction of important measures concerned with the home affairs of the country. We see him directing *la haute politique*, successful in winning the personal confidence of his ally, the King of Prussia, and contriving to maintain peace with Bourbon Spain while maturing plans hostile to Bourbon France. Yet, for the present, we are still in the region of projects, attempts, designs only half begun—sufficiently significant for us to recognise *ex ungue leonem*, but not important enough in their actual effects and results to need further discussion at this point.

In spite of what he had already achieved, Pitt's position was not yet assured. It could not but be threatened, so soon as the national belief in him, which alone had raised him to power, began to waver. Such was the effect of the further developments connected with the case of Byng. The unfortunate Admiral, who had been responsible for the loss of Minorca, was condemned to death by Court-martial. The King was ready to yield to the demand of public opinion, merciless in a case of neglect of duty, which the Court declared this to be. But the Court itself had recommended mercy, inasmuch as the Admiral's conduct was attributable, not to cowardice or disaffection, but to an error of judgment. The King laid the sentence before the highest judges in the kingdom for revision, and they upheld it. The sovereign would now have been very glad if the Minister had advised the carrying out of the capital sentence. But Pitt recommended mercy; although, in view of the popular feeling, he did not absolutely insist upon this course. On March 14, 1757, Byng was shot.

When the question arose of the appointment of a Commander-in-chief for the Army of Observation established in Germany for the protection of Hanover, the Duke of Cumberland, the victor of Culloden, was proposed by the wish of the King of Prussia. George II was willing; but Cumberland, anxious for the security of his laurels, was apprehensive that the necessary military and financial support might not be afforded him under Pitt's Ministry. For Pitt, who was during these months suffering from gout, which plagued him throughout his life, seemed to the Duke to be a sick man, and moreover little interested in the conflict on the Continent. Cumberland, therefore, made Pitt's resignation the condition of his own acceptance of the command in Germany. For George II, however, all other considerations fell into the background when Hanover was in question. Marshal d'Estrées was marching towards the Lower Rhine, and Cumberland's departure could not be delayed. He demanded the dismissal of Pitt, and the King granted his wish (April 6, 1757). It is not correct to assert that Pitt was thrust from office by the opposition of the great Whig families. Only so much is true: that, without the support of those powerful groups, even Pitt with all his popularity was unable to form a strong Government, that is, one which would not fall to pieces in the face of adverse circumstances.

The interregnum of eleven weeks which elapsed between the first and the second Ministry of Pitt revealed to the world the fatal confusion among English parties. In the circumstances, no other result could follow except the return of William Pitt as the one man in whom the country could find its preserver in the hour of need. "I know that I can save this nation and that nobody else can," was Pitt's often quoted proud remark. Devonshire, still the nominal head of the Government, Newcastle, indispensable on account of his parliamentary following, the formidable orator Henry Fox, who was much more concerned with an ample official income than with the exercise of power, the aged Carteret (Granville), the famous jurist Lord Mansfield—all of them were summoned and treated with, before the King finally reached the conviction that he could form no Cabinet of which William Pitt was not the actual leader.

Thus was the Newcastle-Pitt Ministry formed, a kind of alliance between the great Whig nobility and its henchmen, and the great orator and statesman upheld by the people.   Newcastle, as First Lord of the Treasury, undertook the management of home affairs.   Pitt no longer refused to act with him, provided that he would place the national resources at his colleague's disposal for the purposes of foreign policy and the War. For in this sphere Pitt's rule was absolute.   Indeed, he was considered the actual head of the Government.   His personal influence in the Cabinet was greater than that due to his office.   Pitt again became merely one of the two Secretaries of State.   He took the Southern Department, which included the Romance nations as well as the Colonies.   The latter were especially important to Pitt at the time of the conflicts beyond sea.   Holdernesse, the Secretary of State for the North, willingly carried out Pitt's intentions.   Yet it was not Holdernesse, but Pitt, in whom Frederick the Great recognised the mainstay of his alliance with England.

In Pitt's mind, too, the sense of the importance of military affairs occupied a dominant place—possibly because of his brief period of service in the army.   He intended to be the supreme organiser of war, not only in diplomatic but also in military matters.   As to the Continental War, there was no difficulty on this head.   The Secretary for War (Lord Barrington) was controlled by the Secretaries of State.   But as to the Admiralty open dissensions took place between Newcastle and Pitt.   Pitt seems to have waived his original demand to keep in his own hands the correspondence with the commanders of the fleets, to the exclusion of the Admiralty.   The regular practice of his Ministry on this head conformed to custom; for before his time the admirals were accustomed to take their instructions direct from the Secretaries of State. No supersession of the Admiralty was implied by this procedure, since the instructions were approved by the Cabinet of which the First Lord of the Admiralty was a member; so that there was nothing unconstitutional in their reaching the Commander of the Fleet after being drafted by the Secretary of State and merely signed by three Admirals. Pitt was in the position of being sole author of these instructions, simply because the direction of the Cabinet lay entirely in his hands.   With perfect justice, therefore, he could declare in 1761 that he had never issued orders in disregard of the chiefs of other Departments.

Owing to Pitt's personal authority these other chiefs, his colleagues, wholly confined themselves to administrative work without decisively cooperating in the determination of policy.   In this way there was still employment enough for them.   The services, for instance, of Newcastle to the English nation in these four years 1757 to 1761 lie in the fact that as First Lord of the Treasury he skilfully and industriously supplied Pitt with the means for his conduct of the wars in progress in all parts of the world.   And Pitt was hard enough to please, and troubled himself little about the cost of his military expeditions.   The National Debt rose in these years from £70,000,000 to £150,000,000. That this was possible, that the credit of the country could bear such a strain, must be also placed to Pitt's account. The personal confidence of the nation in his policy provided the Government with the necessary capital. Under the Ministry of Bute confidence in the Government was wanting, and the public was no longer so willing as before to take up its loans.

Lord Chancellor Hardwicke called Pitt's Ministry "the strongest Administration that has been formed for many years." A modern author describes it as "an organisation for war which theoretically, at least, could scarcely be nearer perfection." Its methods and its achievements seemed to contemporaries equally wonderful. "There has been as much business done in the last ten days as in as many months before," wrote Newcastle himself, who in these words unintentionally pronounced the keenest criticism on the preceding Government, of which he had himself been the head.

The scale of the undertakings corresponded to this activity of action; the number of expeditions, of ships, of troops, was in keeping with the grandeur of the strategic conception, and with the consistency and the energy of its execution. That England, for the first time, carried on alone a maritime and colonial war with France without the assistance of Holland, seems to call for merely incidental mention. Everything else was subsidiary in Pitt's mind to the main offensive movement which was to take place in America. But to that end his other undertakings might very usefully contribute, as, for instance, demonstrations and attacks on the French coasts, and also the War in Germany, of which we shall speak presently. It would be enough if the French by these means were prevailed upon to break up their forces and induced to turn their attention from the scene on which the main issues would have to be decided.

The particular incidents of the struggle are narrated elsewhere. The results were nothing less, than that England became the first sea Power in the world, with whom contemporary France could no longer vie; that the Continent of North America became an Anglo-Saxon not a Romance dominion; that in the East Indies the power of England rose superior to that of France. The result of the War in Germany, too, the establishment of Prussia as a Great Power, is scarcely conceivable without the Ministry of Pitt. The present is not the place for narrating the campaigns of the Seven Years and the events which occurred on the widely-separated scenes of war. Our task is to indicate briefly the principles which guided the English Government and the aims which it pursued.

England's ally was King Frederick of Prussia. Let us see what England was to him, and he to her. The Treaty of Westminster brought the two Powers together. Their common enemy was France. But, besides her ally, every English Government was obliged also to consider Hanover, the source of the King's ancestry. However eagerly

Pitt had attacked the Hanoverian policy of the earlier Governments, he could not, when himself chief Minister, decline to provide the necessary protection for Hanover.   Already in his first Ministry he had brought about the return to Germany of the Hanoverian and Hessian troops which had been kept in England for protection against foreign invasions. Their departure was hailed with joy, and it was a popular step when Pitt, in the Speech from the Throne on September 2, 1756, caused the King to announce the formation of a national militia "planned and regulated with equal regard to the just rights of my crown and people." The return of the German troops was mentioned with the addition, "relying with pleasure on the spirit and zeal of my people in defence of my person and realm."   Part of the troops sent back were used for forming an army in western Germany, which was described as the Army of Observation, and destined, as was publicly stated in the royal Message of February 17, 1757, for the protection of his Majesty's electoral dominions, and to enable him to fulfil his engagements with the King of Prussia.

The Army of Observation, paid for by England, and commanded, in the first instance, by Cumberland, and later by Ferdinand of Brunswick, was a most important military instrument, which in the course of time was not less serviceable to the King of Prussia than to purely Anglo-Hanoverian interests.   Each of the two parties endeavoured to induce the other to strengthen the Army of Observation, to which, as a matter of fact, both Prussian and English troops belonged.   It must be recognised that Pitt, although the Continental War was never his prime interest, nevertheless did his utmost on its behalf.   He steadily endeavoured to strengthen still further the resistance offered to the enemy by his Prussian ally who had saved Hanover, as well as his own country, by his victory at Rossbach.   For this object, a special Treaty was signed on April 11, 1758, between England and Prussia, and renewed several times during the ensuing years.   The King of England pledged himself to maintain an army of 55,000 men (in other words, the "Army of Observation" which thus became permanent), and Frederick was further to receive a subsidy, which in the following year was to be reckoned at £670,000.   No negotiations or treaties with the enemy were to be undertaken except by both sovereigns jointly.

It was in this shape that the Anglo-Prussian alliance during the Seven Years' War assumed practical significance; for Pitt carried it no further.   In particular, he always deferred, and practically prevented, the fulfilment of one request which Frederick the Great repeatedly made for assistance on the part of England.   This was the intervention of an English fleet in the Baltic.   Frederick desired this movement as a demonstration against his enemies Russia and Sweden.   Communications were being made on the subject from 1756 onwards.   In 1757, Frederick begs that England will now, according to her promise, despatch a squadron to the Baltic, to keep Russia in check and prevent her "from harassing my Baltic Coasts with her ships and galleys." In May, 1757, the Prussian envoy in London is informed, in reply, that England will menace Russia with a squadron, should the latter appear likely to harass the Prussian coast. Frederick expresses his joy at the information, and adds his thanks to the Secretary of State, Lord Holdernesse, in the most complimentary terms. But the Russian fleet actually appeared in the Baltic without any English fleet being at hand. Memel was blockaded, troops were landed, villages burned down, the country was ravaged, and every kind of cruelty and horror perpetrated. Similarly, in the same year, the Swedes were able without let or hindrance to send reinforcements to their army in Pomerania, in order to advance against Prussia. Frederick had no better success during the campaign of 1758. The English ambassador, Mitchell, told him in February, 1758, that it would be impossible for England to provide the necessary number of ships for a demonstration in the Baltic, because the claims upon the naval strength of Great Britain were already so numerous in various and remote parts of the world. Intimations of this sort led King Frederick to reduce his demands, but without dropping them altogether. Even if not a "formidable" fleet, they might at least send him a "promenade" squadron, for the sake of the moral effect. At last he signed the Convention of April 11, 1758, without having received the promise of the Baltic fleet.

Whatever may have been the reason of the British Government's refusal, it was perfectly justified in laying stress on the enormous and diverse duties of its fleet in the War with France, and on the difficulty of sparing the additional ships, and, what was more, the complement of men required for an expedition into the Baltic. Moreover, if the King of Prussia desired a British squadron, in order to threaten his northern enemies, Russia and Sweden, this opened a new question for England, who was not at war with these Powers, and was particularly anxious not to disturb her trade with Russia. Again (although this reason was not confided to the Prussian King) the local conditions of the Baltic, and the inadequacy of the English navy for meeting the special difficulties which had to be overcome in navigating these waters, had a strong, perhaps a decisive, share in the English refusal of the Baltic fleet demanded by Frederick. In a word, then, the King of Prussia was denied the assistance which he so eagerly implored. Perhaps his heroism may be rated all the higher inasmuch as, thrown back now on his own military resources, he nevertheless parried the attacks of the enemies pressing round him. Nor is our estimate of it much lowered if we take into account the aid which England gave him by means of her subsidies and the maintenance of the Army of Observation.

No one recognised more frankly than Frederick the Great that Pitt was the inspiring force in England's conduct of the Continental War. He had at first watched the Minister's rise to power with suspicion, for Pitt had been described to him as a brilliant orator, but also as a fault-finder who carried no real weight. And, when the reports of his ambassador soon overflowed with praises of the new Minister, Frederick wrote reprovingly to him that his letters seemed written by "one of Mr Pitt's secretaries, rather than by an envoy of the King of Prussia." But before long there was no more enthusiastic eulogist of the British states-man than Frederick himself. And yet, as we have seen already, the interests of Frederick the Great, though straightforwardly upheld by Pitt, never occupied the central place in his political system. To him the struggle with France, on the sea and in the colonies, was of paramount importance. The memorable results achieved in this struggle, in America, in the East and West Indies, are related elsewhere. We must content ourselves with advancing certain general considerations as to the general aims and objects pursued by Pitt with regard to, and for the sake of, the colonies, which may be summed up as Pitt's colonial policy.

We turn, in the first instance, to the American Continent, as the theatre on which the greatest and most striking results were won, and which most clearly exhibits the operation of Pitt's own ideas. Leaving aside Spanish Central America, it was the English and French colonists, alike inspired by strong tendencies towards expansion, who sought to bring an ever larger proportion of the Continent within their grasp. The English occupied the greater part of the eastern coast; the French share consisted principally of two blocks of territory: namely, Canada, the region of the St Lawrence, and, in the widest meaning of the name, Louisiana, the valley of the Mississippi so far as its mouth. The natural course of development therefore was to unite the two blocks and thus form a French colonial empire, which should stretch from the mouth of the river St Lawrence across the region of the Great Lakes, down the course of the Ohio and of the Mississippi so far as the outlet of this mighty river into the Gulf of Mexico. But by this development the further expansion of the English colonies would be arrested. It is only necessary to review on the map the ring of territories by which the French strove to surround the English colonies on the east, and to push them back from the interior, in order to understand the threat, occasionally uttered on the French side, that the English would be driven into the sea.

The conditions under which the two European nations lived here in the New World were fundamentally different. The English, in a much smaller area, had a population about fifteen times as numerous as the French. But this numerical preponderance was amply counterbalanced by other circumstances unfavourable to the English. There was little or no cohesion among the several colonies, and it was all but impossible to induce them to take common action. They showed attachment and goodwill to the mother country, because it was in their interest to do so—but only just so far as such was actually the case. The French

possessions, consisting, except for a few centres that were beginning
to prosper, of a thin extended chain of outposts, were well protected
from a military point of view; but, being entirely a creation of the absolute
monarchy of France, they were administered thence on a perfectly uniform
system. In addition, the French were far more skilful than their rivals in
their policy towards the Indians; so that the half-savage tribes of the
Redskins usually stood in much greater numbers on the French side
than on the English.

In the Spanish and Austrian Wars of Succession, while France and
England had been at war in Europe, Frenchmen and Englishmen had
also been fighting each other in America. By the Peace of Utrecht
(1713), Nova Scotia and Newfoundland, important countries lying in
front of French Canada, were assigned to England. But the Peace of
Utrecht, as well as that of Aix-la-Chapelle (1748), contained several
ambiguities, as well as omissions, in the definitions of the boundaries and
rights of the two sides on the American Continent. The Peace of Aix-
la-Chapelle, as has been seen, produced disappointment in all quarters;
and in Paris the phrase was current: *bête comme la Paix.* An early
renewal of the War was looked upon as probable. In such cases, indeed,
the French were in the habit of thinking in the first instance of campaigns in the Netherlands and conflicts on the Upper or Lower Rhine.
" For with the French nation," says Ranke, "a land war is always more
popular than a sea war, as being associated with a greater number of
glorious memories." But, on the present occasion, there was no lack of
warning intimations of the dangers at hand beyond the confines of
Europe. The old Duc de Noailles, who had served under Louis XIV,
and who was now in the habit of submitting his garnered experiences in
long *exposés* to Louis XV, from 1748 onwards made the imminent
renewal of war with England almost the exclusive topic of his communications to the King. The fleet ought to be reconstructed and at
once provided with the organisation which it had in the days of the
great Colbert. Six thousand regular troops must be sent to the
colonies; " Your Majesty may reflect," he adds, as a modest admonition,
"that such a force would hardly be sufficient to garrison one of your
Flemish fortresses."

Still more significant is a report to be found in the present French
archives, drawn up so early as the year 1747 by a Ministerial official.
He, too, advocates the encouragement and strengthening of the colonies
in view of the danger of a new war, and refers with much point
to their want of both money and men, in order to recommend, in
the first instance, the immediate despatch of a few thousand settlers to
Louisiana. He concludes with a side glance, almost of alarm, at the disquieting development of England's trade and colonies, and at the dangers
which might threaten the position of France in Europe from the further
advance of the English in America. " They would rule the seas through

their fleets and the land through their wealth, and America would furnish them with the means of dictating to Europe." "France alone," he continues, "is in a position to prevent this catastrophe, and France must do so, for her own sake and that of all Europe."

In England, too, similar anxieties prevailed. From 1748 onwards, a new war seemed inevitable. It was keenly felt how much had been left insufficiently defined in the existing territorial relations beyond seas. The frontiers between British Nova Scotia and French Canada were still unsettled, and the imperfect delimitation between the more southern English colonies and the territories held by the French must inevitably give rise to fresh quarrels. In America itself hostilities, in fact, scarcely ceased between 1748 and 1756, that is, between the Peace of Aix-la-Chapelle and the renewal of war. During those years the French were engaged in constructing a chain of forts along the Ohio and Mississippi, and thus actually bringing about the long apprehended connexion between Canada and Louisiana, which implied the strategical enclosure of the English colonies by a long line of military stations from the mouth of the St Lawrence to that of the Mississippi.

On both sides of the Atlantic, during these years, it began to be clearly perceived among Englishmen that special measures were required for checking the threatening development of the French power. In point of fact, the issue only depended upon making effective use of the great existing numerical preponderance of the English colonists over the French. With this object a scheme was earnestly mooted, in America and in England, for a closer union between the English colonies. The Board of Trade in London had, on September 18, 1753, instructed the Governors of a number of the colonies to hold a joint conference with the tribe of Iroquois Indians, in order to keep them firm to their alliance with England. And, if possible, the colonies were to conclude an agreement among themselves with a similar object. The policy thus suggested by the Government in London with a view to the Indians became the origin of a much larger scheme. In a meeting held at Albany, in 1754, the representatives of all the colonies, convinced of the necessity of combining in self-defence, unanimously resolved to propose a scheme for a close political federation among themselves. This was drawn up instantly and accepted unanimously. It contemplated an executive for the United Colonies in the person of a President-General and a legislature to be called the Grand Council. The foremost place among the intellectual authors as well as among the draughtsmen of this scheme was taken by the distinguished man who afterwards came forward as the spokesman of the American colonies when united against England—Benjamin Franklin.

Before Franklin's scheme could be submitted to the Parliament of Great Britain, it was shattered by the unanimous opposition of all the colonial Assemblies. They were alarmed at the financial burden which a joint defence of the new Commonwealth would have laid upon them. But the Government of the mother country would hardly have approved the plan; for, though ardently desiring the awakening of a military temper in its American colonies, it had no wish to see them politically united, inasmuch as such a federation might easily lead to the severance of the colonies from the mother country—an event always dreaded in London.

The Board of Trade decided upon a colonial scheme of its own, according to which commissioners from all the Assemblies were to determine, in time of peace, the expenditure and measures needed for military purposes, in proportion to the capacities of the several colonies. The Crown was to name a Commander-in-chief for the whole of the colonial forces. And, in fact, a commissioner, Edward Braddock, was sent over, with two British regiments. For the rest, however, the scheme of the Board of Trade had as small a chance of realisation, in face of the independent attitude of the colonial Assemblies, as the more far-reaching ideas of Franklin. Not until twenty years later was the federation of the colonies brought about, through the enthusiasm aroused by the new ideals of freedom and independence in conflict with the mother country. Things had, however, changed by that time in America; and the French no longer held Canada. In the efforts to establish a federation before the Seven Years' War, military considerations and preparations for the conflict with France had the greatest share. A series of schemes was projected during these years for the same purpose, which aimed at levying an assessment, common to all, for the joint defence of the colonies— a kind of legislative enactment which could not be determined by the colonial Assemblies, but only by the Parliament at Westminster. The question of the equitableness of such a measure was, however, not yet decided, although it was already manifest that any such taxation by the British Parliament would call forth fierce resistance from the Americans. In other words, if already at this date, when the French were still threatening the rear of the English colonists, it was impossible to carry out such a taxation, though intended only for the purpose of military defence, there is no difficulty in understanding how the attempt of the mother country to effect it, when the danger from France had been removed, became the cause of the historic conflict which resulted in the assertion of American Independence.

In truth, the Government of the mother country had a difficult task before it when attempting to preserve harmonious relations with the colonists in America. This task became harder and harder, as during the course of the eighteenth century the colonists themselves, with a rapidly increasing population and steady economic advance, grew into a flourishing and powerful community. It must be remembered that here, as elsewhere, the principles of Mercantilism governed the system of administration, implying much control and coercion of the colonies by the mother country. The Navigation Acts of the seventeenth century were still in force, by which the foreign trade of the colonies was kept within narrow bounds; and there were corresponding restrictions on industry. The cardinal principle was the belief that the possession of colonies ought to be a source of revenue. On the other hand, the colonies already possessed a considerable share of self-government and legislation of their own. The Governors, as representatives of the King, often found their seats thorny, often played a rather ignominious part in the Assemblies, which, in the matter of military or financial contributions, treated their demands as importunate, and looked upon them as unwelcome police officials charged with the obstruction of industrial activity when it clashed with existing commercial laws. When, in the period from 1754 to 1756, the frequent Anglo-French strife in America developed into a war between the two nations, some of the colonies at first showed little inclination to break off their trade with the French in the *Hinterland*, and actually continued to supply them with materials of war. Naturally, the English Government intervened with a stringent prohibition, but whether with much effect is very doubtful. In any case, instead of stimulating patriotic enthusiasm, it caused much discontent among the colonists. Thus the unsatisfactory restrictions which England was obliged to lay on her colonists for military purposes made bad blood— and this at a time when, without hearty cooperation on the part of the colonies, there was no hope of a successful termination of the War.

Under the rule of Pitt, the scene entirely changes. He possessed the gift of engaging the confidence of the British subjects in the New World in the same measure as that of his countrymen at home in England, if indeed not in a still greater degree. His primary purpose was to reconcile the colonies and to bring about a ready cooperation on their part in the struggle which, after all, was carried on essentially in their interest. The repression of illicit commerce was only continued so far as this commerce directly interfered with military ends. Not until later, when the whole issue of the War depended on it, and when the French in the large West Indian islands could only hold out by means of the supplies which came to them from English sources, were the Governors instructed by Pitt, in a sharply worded circular (August 23, 1760), to ascertain exactly "the state of this dangerous and ignominious trade" and bring the culprits "to the most exemplary and condign punishment."

But Pitt's best way of winning the confidence of the colonies was his system of carrying on the War. For the traditional frontier war were substituted combined attacks on a grand scale by land and water, the successful cooperation of British regular troops and the American militia, of army and fleet, and the effective isolation of the French colonial possessions as regards all assistance from France by means of the command of the sea which England's victories had secured to her.

Thus a series of decisive blows were dealt—Louisburg 1758, Quebec 1759—which brought home to the colonists the joyful conviction that the final goal would be reached, and that they would be completely freed from their old enemies the French. And to this result they had themselves materially contributed.

But a still greater significance attaches to the fact that Pitt was able to induce the colonists themselves to take part in the War, when it was no longer a question of the French in their immediate vicinity but of those in far distant Louisiana and in the West Indies. In the conquests, some won, some planned, by Pitt in 1761, when he overstepped the customary programme of wars with France, the cooperation of the colonists on the American mainland played a decisive part.

So much as to the actual facts of the period of Pitt's great Ministry. In order to ascertain his conception of the relations between the mother country and the colonies, and the lines on which he might perhaps have developed them, had he remained longer in office, we are obliged to appeal to his later utterances. In his great speech of September 9, 1762, on the Preliminaries of the Peace of Paris, Pitt declared himself against the restoration of the great West Indian islands to France. Yet to retain them together with Canada would have necessitated a new colonial policy. How far Pitt would really have been in favour of this—practically a relinquishment of the Mercantile System—is uncertain. It seems warranted to assume that he had thought of materially lightening the economic burdens of the colonists, though certainly without granting to them complete freedom of trade. He would have been as little inclined to advocate the abolition of the Navigation Acts, or the removal of the control of economic conditions exercised by the Parliament at Westminster for the common good, as to champion the independence of the Americans. On the other hand, he protested energetically against their taxation by the English Parliament, and went so far towards conciliating them, during his short Ministerial service as Earl of Chatham under Grafton (1766–8), that he was called the "Father of America." And it is true that he had a full understanding of their complaints in the sixties and seventies. The rights of the Americans were among the favourite questions of which he never wearied during the course of his whole political career. Thus, there is ground for believing that he was not averse from a federal connexion between the mother country and the colonies. In 1766, he drew up the draft of a Ministry in which appears the new office of "Secretary of State for the American Department," and the holder of it was to be "Mr Pitt." He had further considered the idea of a representation of the colonies in Parliament, and among the Chatham papers a memorandum has been found on the number and the proportion of votes which should be assigned to the several colonies, although it is not quite certain how far this may have been a plan of Pitt's own. And, lastly, when on April 7, 1778, the death-stricken Lord Chatham by a final effort raised his voice to protest once more against the independence of America, what that voice expressed was not the self-will of a ruling people clinging to its sovereign power; rather, his speech may have sounded like the cry of a father who cannot bear that the children whom he has loved and reared to manhood should despise the paternal protection and seek to renounce him.

England now stood at the height of success, and William Pitt at the climax of his fame, for, by Englishmen and foreigners alike, the conquests won were regarded as being in reality his. The foremost minds of the age were agreed in their admiration of Pitt. "England," said Frederick the Great, "has long been in travail and has suffered a great deal to produce Mr Pitt, but she has certainly brought forth a Man." Voltaire, when about to put forth an edition of the works of the great Corneille, begged for the honour of being allowed to place the name of Mr Pitt at the head of his list of subscribers. A French nobleman who had fought against England in India and had been sent a prisoner to London declared that, since he had left Europe five years before, he had become "historically acquainted with but two men in this world, the King of Prussia and Mr Pitt." And yet the position of the great Minister was no longer the same as in the days of the victories in Canada and Bengal. On October 25, 1760, George II suddenly expired, at the age of nearly seventy-seven. He was succeeded by his grandson George III, a young man of twenty-two. The change of sovereign was in many respects of great importance. The young King was naturally born to an easier position than that of his two predecessors. They felt more at home in Hanover than in England, and their foreign policy too readily, and repeatedly, assumed a Hanoverian bias. In former days, the people had accepted the succession of the House of Brunswick-Lüneburg as a lesser evil than a Stewart Catholic reaction; but their hearts had not gone forth to meet the son of the Electress Sophia when he landed on English soil.

George III had been born and bred in England. The electoral hat of Brunswick-Lüneburg had fallen to him together with the crown of Great Britain, but his affections did not draw him across the sea to the home of his ancestors. He never visited Hanover. The world was to recognise that he was different from his predecessors. Entirely on his own impulse, he had added a sentence to his first Speech from the Throne. "Born and educated in this country, I glory in the name of Briton." In fact, the national mistrust of the first two Georges on account of Hanover had now, in so far as it was attached to the person of the monarch, definitively passed away. The Stewart Pretender had, in the meantime, forfeited all support in England, and the name of Jacobite lost its terrors for the Government.

And there were other points in which the new King differed from his predecessors. The period 1714 to 1760 had derived its characteristics from the rule of the Whigs. The King governed with them and through them. The sovereign himself was no longer so prominent as had been the case in the days of William III and Anne. More is heard of Townshend and Walpole, of Carteret and Pelham, than of George I and II; while the personal influence of the King sank completely into the background during the popular Ministry of Pitt, allied by marriage with the Grenvilles, one of the greatest of the Whig families.

The young George III was inspired by an ambition to rule in reality, and not merely bear the name of King. His mother, the widowed Princess of Wales, had imbued him with this conception, and her favourite, the Scotchman Lord Bute, had instructed him in the politics of the time with the same intention. Bute himself was a man of varied scientific acquirements and aesthetic interests, though scantily gifted for the conduct of public affairs. After the young King's accession he came forward to announce the royal views, almost as a kind of middleman between George III and his Ministers. Whether the King from the beginning felt the power and popularity of Pitt oppressive and sought to check it, can scarcely be ascertained. At all events, it was obvious that, so long as the War lasted, Pitt's genius could not be dispensed with. And, as the King at once showed himself inclined to peace, the thought cannot have been far from his mind that Pitt might be made no longer indispensable, and might perhaps even be removed. In his first speech to the Privy Council, shown to none of the Ministers beforehand, the King spoke of the " bloody and expensive War "—words which were considered by those who heard it as an invidious expression aimed at Pitt. The latter—though only by means of excited explanations lasting for hours—contrived to have the expression softened in the printed speech into " an expensive but just and necessary War." In the same speech the King had already spoken of the securing of an " honourable and lasting peace "—words which must have seemed still more objectionable to Pitt, in view of the impression they could not but create in Frederick the Great, since, according to the terms of alliance, neither of the allies was to conclude a peace without the other. He succeeded in inserting in the printed speech the words " in concert with our allies."

Almost too much honour is accorded to George III and Bute, when this little incident is treated as if two radically different systems of policy had here come into conflict. The King had no such definite programme; and his opposition was rather that of a dilettante in politics to a great statesman. Nothing can really be argued from the incident, except that Pitt's position under the young King was no longer so strong as under the old. This was made clearer in a few months, when Bute had to be admitted into the Cabinet, as Secretary of State, in the place of Holdernesse, who retired, possibly for this very purpose.

Though Pitt was resolved only to conclude a peace which should ensure the conquests of the War to England as permanent possessions, his hope of accomplishing this at some time late in the summer of 1761 seemed to have vanished again. The negotiations, which have been detailed elsewhere, had temporarily assumed a hopeful aspect. Pitt and Choiseul, the leading statesmen on the two sides of the Channel, were working to bring about an accommodation; but naturally the difficulties were not slight. The consideration of the allies on both sides was the first and permanent obstacle. So far as Prussia was concerned, Frederick had certainly every confidence in the proved friendship of Pitt; but now he began to be suspicious. He was willing that England should keep all her conquests; but he did not want, as he put it, to "pay the piper." In other words, he was determined not to sacrifice one foot of territory, notwithstanding the unfavourable position in which he found himself.

Nevertheless, it was not this which wrecked the negotiations, but the intervention of France in the Anglo-Spanish conflict. While Pitt mercilessly sought to utilise the English victories to the full for the humiliation of France, for the destruction of her commerce and fleet and the ruin of her colonial dominion, Choiseul was playing the game of diplomacy merely as a blind to his adversary, until he had secured an ally in the kindred Bourbon kingdom of Spain; then he would lay down the pen and take up the sword again.

Pitt saw through the scheme and recalled his agent Stanley from Paris. A new and powerful impulse now communicated itself to his own schemes. The crucial question is not whether he actually knew the details of the Bourbon "Family Compact" signed at Paris on August 15, before he took the decisive step—a point which is much debated—for he knew enough to convince him of the actual fact. He knew that France had pledged herself to conclude no peace without taking Spanish interests into consideration; he knew also that to go to war with England at this moment, before the expected Plate fleet from America had reached Cadiz, would be exceedingly inconvenient to Spain; he even knew that Spanish men-of-war had been sent out to convoy the *flota* safely home. This information convinced Pitt, not only that war with Spain was unavoidable, but also that it must be declared by England at once. It was on this head that the memorable disagreement arose in the Cabinet which ended in the resignation of Pitt.

The Minister had little difficulty in convincing his colleagues of the necessity of breaking off the negotiations at Paris and recalling Stanley. But now they declined to go any further with him. The majority would not consent to an immediate declaration of war against Spain. We are now fully informed from various sources as to the stormy Cabinet meetings of September 17, 18, and 19, 1761. Pitt laid before the Cabinet an intercepted letter from the Spanish envoy in Paris, which revealed everything. He showed, in an impressive speech, that the danger could only grow greater if Spain were to declare war herself in the following spring. There was at present but one House of Bourbon. The Spanish fleet must be regarded as a French fleet. "Spain is France, and France is Spain." The peace party in the Cabinet raised the objection that action could not be taken on the ground of an intercepted letter without a previous declaration of war, and that the attack of the Spanish fleet off Cape Passaro, in 1718, without such a declaration, still remained a cause of bitterness. Anson, the First Lord of the Admiralty, declared that the preparations necessary for the stroke which Pitt demanded could not be finished in time. And the conclusion reached was that it would be sufficient to present a protest at Madrid and demand explanations, and perhaps to make some advances towards settling the differences which embroiled England and Spain in Central America. Only Pitt's brother-in-law, Lord Temple, supported him in demanding the recall of Lord Bristol, the English ambassador at Madrid. Pitt and Temple drew up a protest to lay before the King. It exposed the aggressive and unexampled conduct of the Spanish Court, which aimed at producing a crisis in a conflict with England by causing the intervention of a Power at war with her, and this at a time when Spain was loudly proclaiming her friendliness to Great Britain. The King was therefore begged to order Bristol to hand in a declaration of war, and to return to England without taking a formal leave.

The King declined to receive the protest. He was already completely under the influence of Pitt's opponents in the Cabinet, who were led by his favourite, Lord Bute. We find the little coterie assembling at Devonshire House to concert, in secret meetings, the best tactics to be followed in their opposition to the powerful Minister. They were still alarmed at the possibility that Pitt might at this moment retire from the Cabinet and leave them to conduct the War without the genius which organised the fleets and armies of England. Nor could they altogether parry Pitt's argument for the necessity of an immediate war with Spain, that the Plate fleet had not yet reached Europe, and that the wealthy Spanish colonies could be attacked with good prospects of success, inasmuch as England was in command of the sea. But they did not flinch from their opinion, when Pitt made his retention of office conditional on the acceptance of his scheme. The personal attitude of the King was, moreover, of extreme importance. The Ministers came separately to him to give their advice. Pitt had his audience like the rest. But George was already estranged from him, and there is no doubt that the King's desire to free himself from the influence of the great Minister was an element of extreme importance in the whole struggle. Bute, too, appears in these proceedings quite as much in the character of the tool of an autocratic master as in that of the exponent of a policy whose consequences he was hardly able to grasp. How thoroughly he could rely upon the support of the sovereign if he opposed Pitt in the Cabinet is seen by a remark of Newcastle's on September 26: "the King seems every day more offended with Mr Pitt, and plainly wants to get rid of him at all events."

The situation was in no way altered by the arrival of Stanley and his verbal explanations, although they seemed to justify Pitt's contention completely. On October 2, the decisive sitting of the Cabinet took place, when for the last time the two sides had the opportunity of explaining their intentions. Pitt repeated his earlier statements; but he added with great dignity that he could not remain in office without possessing a real control, nor be responsible for a policy of which he had not the direction—old Lord Granville urging against him that, when a matter had once been submitted for the decision of the Cabinet, it was to be regarded as a Cabinet measure and not as that of a single Minister. In the entry which Burke made in his *Annual Register* for 1761, the different attitudes of the Ministers with regard to the constitutional question are indeed set in much sharper mutual contrast than is shown in the notes of those who were present. But, however little credit be attached to Burke's account, it at least shows clearly enough in what light the relations between the young King and the great Minister were popularly regarded. Pitt is reported to have said that he had been called to the Ministry by the voice of the people, and was answerable to them for his conduct, and that he would not remain in a position which laid upon him the responsibility for measures which he could no longer direct. Granville is stated to have replied: "I find the gentleman is determined to leave us, nor can I say I am sorry for it, since he would otherwise have certainly compelled us to leave him. But if he be resolved to assume the right of advising His Majesty and directing the operations of the war, to what purpose are we called to this Council? When he talks of being responsible to the people, he talks the language of the House of Commons, and forgets that at this Board he is only responsible to the King."

On October 5, 1761, William Pitt laid down the office which he had conducted so gloriously as to become the foremost man in England. His fall was an event of far greater moment than ordinarily belongs to the resignation of a Minister. No other could wield the tremendous power which he had possessed—neither Lord Egremont, his successor in office, nor Bute, the King's favourite, nor the King himself. For the confidence of the nation, which had been given to Pitt, could not be transferred with the office to another. Bute's fears that when Pitt left the Government he would take its popularity with him were by no means groundless. In the constitutional history of England this important fact is to be observed, that the first great statesman raised to power by the will of the people laid down his office voluntarily, not only because his colleagues did not agree with him in his policy, but also because government by the will of the people, which had been extorted from the monarchy in the last years of George II, was no longer possible under his successor. The rule of the Great Commoner is followed by George III's attempt at personal government, for which his Scottish favourite endeavoured to smooth the way.

To return to the year 1761: it was the struggle with Spain which led to the resignation of Pitt. If, then, convinced of the impossibility of avoiding war, he wished to forestall the attack of the enemy, wherein did his design differ from the action of Frederick the Great at the beginning of the war in 1756? Frederick, like Pitt, was decided by the strategical question—by the advantages to be derived from an immediate and well-aimed stroke against an enemy taken unawares. Only, the position in which these two great men, akin to each other in genius, found themselves was not identical. Frederick could conduct his policy as he liked in time of war and peace; he could mockingly dub Podewils, when that Minister proffered his warnings, *Monsieur de la timide politique*—for he was King. Pitt at the moment of the supreme crisis had to recognise the limits of his power.

Pitt's foresight was justified. The War with Spain became a fact. It provided fresh successes for the British fleets and armies, which are described below. England once more clearly proved her superiority in power over Spain. At the same time, it is as if the mighty impulse communicated to English warfare by Pitt had been still in action. Some of the operations which were being carried out had actually been prepared by him. The nation judged rightly in hailing him as the real conqueror. More especially, the conquest of Martinique and the smaller French islands in the sphere of the Antilles, even to the smallest, was to be looked upon as the accomplishment of Pitt's plans. The impression which all these events made in the world was tremendous. The Pope in Rome admiringly declared to an English Catholic that he knew no greater honour than that of being born an Englishman.

With these successes in warfare the conclusion of peace is signally out of keeping. Now, at last, the lack of the great personality no longer at the head of the State impresses itself upon the mind beyond all possibility of mistake. Pitt would never have submitted to either the terms or the form of the Peace. The form was that of a separate treaty, which England without her principal ally concluded with France and Spain. Pitt had assured Frederick the Great that England would always adhere to her alliance with Prussia; he was in the habit of repeatedly referring in his parliamentary speeches to the value of the Prussian alliance; and never had he done so more effectively than when in opposing the conclusion of peace he made use of the celebrated hyperbole: "America had been conquered in Germany." As to the actual terms of the Peace, victorious Great Britain amazed all sides by giving up voluntarily more of her conquests than seemed necessary for the sake of a permanent pacification. Pitt would have required a far greater share for England, and, if necessary, would have sought to force the enemy by fresh humiliations to submit to his demands. The course of the peace negotiations, which were eagerly taken up in 1762, is intimately connected with the internal politics of England, and is described in this connexion in the following section.

The good understanding between England and Prussia was not restored. In 1762, Newcastle and Bute had for the first time left unrenewed the Convention of April, 1758, which had hitherto been annual. They had at first been prepared to pay the subsidies; but it was precisely at this point that a difference of opinion arose between the two leading Ministers. Newcastle retired, and the King's favourite became the head of the Administration as First Lord of the Treasury. But it was no longer possible for Frederick to remain in alliance with the English Government, which had nothing to offer him but good advice—to the effect that he should make a sacrifice for the sake of peace, the very sacrifice which a world in arms had proved unable to wring from him.

It was not to the English alliance that Frederick was indebted for being at last able to extricate his State from the difficulties of the Seven Years' War without loss of territory and with great increase of prestige. He never forgot the treatment which he had experienced from the English Government in 1762. He declined the suggestion of an English alliance in 1773, in remembrance of " the indecent, I might almost say infamous, way in which England treated me at the last peace." The judgment of history will hardly be so severe. The eighteenth century is too full of treaties of peace concluded by one member of an alliance without the other for the instance of 1762 to appear utterly unprecedented. In any case, the English people resented the abandonment of the hero of Rossbach bitterly—almost more bitterly than the loss of so many valuable conquests. But how could it have been otherwise? How could such a Government as Bute's have been expected to uphold England's Prussian ally more energetically, when they actually gave back the most valuable portion of her own magnificent conquests? The question, which has recently been asked, whether England would have been able to maintain all these possessions without reorganising the relations between the mother country and the colonies, can no more affect our judgment of Bute's policy than the circumstance, so favourable to the English, that the French, after generously presenting Spain with the whole of Louisiana, had now retired completely from the Continent of America. As things then stood, the Peace seemed so out of proportion to the conquests won that, very soon after the event, Bute was stated to have been bribed by France—and the statement has been repeated up to the present day. At the time, in 1762, the indignation was great. Such a result was not what the nation, though certainly anxious for peace, had contemplated. Never had Pitt expressed more perfectly what was in the nation's heart than in the great speech which, on December 9, 1762, he delivered against the Preliminaries of the Peace. When he left the House, he was hailed in the street by the acclamations of the people. But, in the House itself, gross corruption had once again won the day. In the division on the Address, moved by Fox, which approved the signature of the Preliminaries, an enormous majority was in favour of the Address. Only sixty-five members voted against it. "The Ministers have had the numbers printed," wrote Horace Walpole; "if they had but put the names to them, the world would have known the names of the sixty-five who were not bribed." When the Princess of Wales heard the news of the acceptance of the Preliminaries she is said to have exclaimed, " Now my son is really King of England."

The settlement of the Peace was followed by the fall of the great Whig families. The day of the personal rule of King George III had come.

(2) THE KING'S FRIENDS.

It has been seen how the accession of George III was accompanied by the revival of aspirations and pretensions that had long been in abeyance. The Whigs had owed their ascendancy not merely to their wealth, capacity, and solidarity, but also—and in a principal degree— to the foreign character of the dynasty of which they were the mainstay. Their wealth was still enormous and secured them commensurate influence, but they were rent with schisms, and their disordered ranks contained no statesman of genius save William Pitt, while with George II the foreign character of the dynasty passed away. The new King could claim to be an Englishman born and bred, and as such entitled to the loyal allegiance of Whig, Tory, and Jacobite alike. It was open to him, were he so minded, to essay the realisation of the ideal set forth by Bolingbroke of the "Patriot King" governing through constitutional forms, but yet freely, as the head of the State, not as the puppet of a party.

Perhaps no King was ever inclined by nature to take a low view of his prerogative; and certainly George III's education had not been of a kind to impart any such bias. His father's death and his grandfather's neglect had left him to the guidance of a mother, Augusta, Princess of Wales, who was imbued with all the autocratic ideas of a petty German Court. She was never tired of exhorting her son to be a King; and her mentor and confidant, John Stewart, third Earl of Bute, having, so to speak, prerogative in his blood, was not the man to counteract her influence or to choose for the Prince instructors who would be likely to do so. The Prince therefore came to the throne with a mind made up to shake off the yoke of the Whig oligarchy, and form for himself a party which should secure him against the danger of ever again falling beneath their yoke. Such a party Bute, who on the accession was sworn of the Privy Council and admitted to the Cabinet, undertook to organise and to maintain in subservience; and the moment was peculiarly propitious, for the political equilibrium was unstable in the extreme.

CH. XIII.

Government by the collective Cabinet was still the pure theory of Whig constitutionalism, to which whatever savoured of a Prime Minister was abhorrent. Pitt, the strong man just now at the helm, was by consequence regarded with suspicion by such old Whigs as Devonshire, Hardwicke, Newcastle and Bedford, who stood or fell by the system of "general cabinet advice," and could not recognise a principal Minister as being more than their most trusted spokesman in the Closet. So soon as Pitt claimed to exercise a paramount, or anything approaching to a paramount, influence in the Cabinet, it was time to concert some new arrangement, and Newcastle and Hardwicke were excellently well qualified for such work.

To Bedford Pitt's policy was no less obnoxious than Pitt himself. He adhered to the Walpolean tradition of an *entente cordiale* with France, and was for making peace at almost any price. His connexion consisted of Marlborough and Lords Gower, Sandwich, and Weymouth, with Richard Rigby, an unscrupulous wire-puller recently appointed Master of the Irish Rolls. Hardwicke recognised that after the conquest of Canada England had nothing substantial to gain by a prolongation of hostilities. George Grenville, who had a private feud with Pitt and a small connexion of his own, which included Lords Egremont, Barrington, and Hillsborough, was ready to approve any honourable terms of peace, and to coalesce with whoever might be able to secure them. Newcastle and Anson took their cue from Hardwicke; Ligonier was no politician; Henry Fox was nothing else; and Halifax was pledged to no policy or faction. In short, except Temple, no Minister was prepared to give hearty support to Pitt's policy of pulverising the House of Bourbon, which might well seem quixotic to Mansfield and questionable even to Granville.

Outside the Ministry, Whiggism had no more typical representative than Charles Watson-Wentworth, second Marquis of Rockingham; while in Augustus Henry Fitzroy, third Duke of Grafton, and Charles Lennox, third Duke of Richmond, it was tempered by popular sympathies, and, in Grafton's case, by admiration for Pitt. Bute's immediate *entourage* consisted of his brother James Stewart Mackenzie, who had gained some trifling experience of affairs of State at the Court of Turin; Charles Jenkinson, a clerk in the Secretary of State's office, whom he made his private secretary; Gilbert, afterwards Sir Gilbert, Elliot, member for Selkirkshire; and Bubb Dodington, an old *habitué* of Leicester House. Jenkinson and Elliot were both men of some ability, and Dodington had a great capacity for small intrigue; but the favourite's most trusted adviser was the Sardinian Minister, Count de Viry, who acted as his intermediary in all important secret negotiations. In Lord Egmont, an Irish peer, the notorious Sir Francis Dashwood, and the Earl of Northumberland the Court might find Ministers *faute de mieux*; and in Jeremiah Dyson, Clerk of the House of Commons, it possessed a wire-puller all the more zealous for prerogative because he was a quite recent convert from republican principles.

The keynote of the new policy was struck in the Speech from the Throne which inaugurated the first parliamentary session of the new reign. The speech itself was drafted by Hardwicke in the tone of sobriety congenial to his temperament and training; but Bute took care that the King should interpolate with his own hand the flourish in which he gloried in the name of Briton. Two measures followed, the limitation of the Civil List to £800,000, and the exemption of judicial offices from defeasance on the demise of the Crown. These Acts were gratefully received by the people as an earnest of the young monarch's good intentions. The dignity of Chancellor was at the same time conferred on Lord Keeper Henley, soon afterwards created Earl of Northington.

On the eve of the dissolution of March 20, 1761, Bute was admitted by Newcastle to a sort of partnership in parliamentary patronage, which placed perhaps thirty or forty votes in the House of Commons at the disposal of the Crown. About the same time, George Grenville, of whom the Court had hopes, was accorded cabinet rank, retaining, however, his office of Treasurer of the Navy (February 11). Occasion was found in Legge's opposition to the proposed indemnification of Landgrave Frederick II of Hesse-Cassel for his losses in the recent campaign, to dismiss an able financier and put in his place Lord Barrington, the very type of respectable mediocrity (March 12). Gilbert Elliot was made a Lord of the Treasury. Holdernesse, Pitt's makeweight colleague in the Secretaries' office, was pensioned off, and the seals were transferred to Bute (March 25). Halifax surrendered the Board of Trade to a veteran placeman, Lord Sandys, and succeeded Bedford in the Irish viceroyalty. These changes were made with the cognisance and consent of Newcastle, Devonshire, Hardwicke, and Bedford, whose countenance of Bute gave great umbrage to Pitt. The elevation of Bubb Dodington to the peerage as Lord Melcombe secured a seat in the House of Commons for Dashwood. It was now that was formed the nucleus of the party which, as consisting of the avowed supporters of Prerogative, soon came to be known by the appropriate designation of "the King's Friends." About the same time, the seat vacated by Lord Fitzmaurice on his succession to the Irish earldom of Shelburne and the English barony of Wycombe was taken by Colonel Isaac Barré, a staunch Whig with a great command of rhetoric and a grudge against Pitt. The return for the Ayr boroughs of a versatile Scottish lawyer, Alexander Wedderburn, served to strengthen the Grenville group.

Bute, as has been related above, received the seals at a critical juncture. The outlook, dark as it was for Russia, was hardly less so for France; and in these circumstances Choiseul proposed a general pacification (March 27) and consented to lead the way by a separate negotiation. As was only to be expected, Pitt dallied with Choiseul's

CH. XIII.

proposals, while the reduction of Belle Isle and Dominica was in progress; and Choiseul in his turn fenced with Pitt until he had signed a new Family Compact (August 15). A month later Pitt ruptured the negotiation, and shortly afterwards he announced to the Cabinet the existence of a secret understanding between France and Spain, which he proposed to make a *casus belli*. Temple alone supported him, and after several stormy meetings he and Temple resigned (October). The seals of the Southern Department were thereupon given to Lord Egremont, and the Privy Seal to Bedford, who, however, had not the full confidence of the King and the inner Cabinet, which consisted of Bute, Egremont, and George Grenville. Natural as was Pitt's resentment, no less natural was the divergence of opinion which occasioned it. Choiseul's renewal of the Family Compact was a suspicious circumstance; but, however much Pitt may have gathered of the provisions of the Treaty, it remained unauthenticated, and so long as that was so, its existence could, in the cool judgment of statesmen less bellicose than Pitt, hardly warrant an immediate declaration of war. It was fairly arguable that the resources of diplomacy should first be exhausted.

The resources of such diplomacy as was employed on this occasion were, however, soon at an end. Disclosure of so much of the Family Compact as concerned British interests was demanded rather than requested of the Court of Madrid, which took the only course consistent with its dignity and haughtily refused the required information. In December the British ambassador, Lord Bristol, was recalled, and early in the following year war was declared. The Council was, however, to the last far from unanimous; Newcastle, Hardwicke, Bedford and Mansfield holding that there was no *casus belli*.

The course of the War proved on the whole disastrous to the House of Bourbon. The conquest of Martinique by Rear-Admiral Rodney and Major-General Monckton (February 12, 1762) was followed by the occupation of St Lucia, St Vincent, and Grenada. On September 18, the only recent French acquisition, St John's, Newfoundland, was recovered by Colonel Amherst. In Germany Prince Ferdinand of Brunswick, brilliantly seconded by the Marquis of Granby, defeated the united forces of Soubise and d'Estrées at Wilhelmsthal (June 24) and Lutternberg (July 23), and compelled the evacuation of Göttingen (August 16) and the surrender of Cassel (November 1). Nor was Spain much more fortunate. The army, 42,000 strong, which in May she threw across the frontier of Portugal, at first carried all before it; but the defence of the line of the Tagus was ably organised by the eminent artillerist Count William von der Lippe-Bückeburg, aided by Lord Loudoun, in command of a contingent of 7000 British, while Colonel Burgoyne adroitly surprised Valencia de Alcantara (August 27) and Villavelha (October 6). Havana, blockaded by nineteen sail of the line under Admiral Pocock and besieged by twelve thousand seasoned troops under Lord Albemarle, surrendered after an obstinate defence (August 12). In the East Indies the recent reduction of Pondicherry (January, 1761) made it possible to equip an expedition at Madras under Rear-Admiral Cornish and General Draper, which carried Manila by assault and held the Philippines to ransom (October, 1762). Unfortunately, however, the splendour of these feats of arms had its foil in the misguided policy of the Government. Bute saw in the alliance with Frederick the Great nothing but an obstacle to peace; and, being inexperienced, tactless, and none too scrupulous, he, upon the accession of Tsar Peter III, made to the Courts of St Petersburg and Vienna overtures of a kind to suggest a triple alliance for imposing peace on Bourbon and Hohenzollern alike. Upon the fairest construction, the policy was scarcely loyal, and it wore the appearance of downright treachery.

Kaunitz suspected a snare, and the Tsar was already pledged to Prussia. Bute's advances therefore met with a haughty repulse at both Courts; and Frederick, discovering what had happened, put the worst construction upon the British policy. His irritation was increased, when he learned that the British Government had determined to discontinue his subsidy and withdraw from the German War. Since the subsidy was contingent upon annual conventions which alone precluded the making a separate peace, its discontinuance was no positive breach of faith; but, as Frederick's position was still critical, such a *volte-face* at such a juncture was, to say the least of it, discreditable. The new policy, first mooted by Bedford, speedily gained the adhesion of George Grenville, but was stoutly resisted by Newcastle, Hardwicke, and Devonshire. Upon its definitive adoption by the Government, Newcastle, whom Bute had treated with studied indignity, resigned, and Devonshire and Hardwicke withdrew from the Council Board.

On May 26, 1762, the King gave the Treasury to Bute, who was also invested with the Garter. He was succeeded as Secretary by George Grenville, the Treasurership of the Navy being given to Barrington, and the Chancellorship of the Exchequer to Dashwood. Frederick, Lord North, eldest son of the Earl of Guilford, remained Junior Lord of the Treasury; and, on Anson's death (June 6), Halifax succeeded to the First Lordship of the Admiralty. Jeremiah Dyson became Secretary to the Treasury, and Charles Jenkinson Treasurer of the Ordnance Office. Lord Melcombe was admitted to the Cabinet; and honours were dispensed with a lavish hand to the supporters of the Court.

Meanwhile, the Family Compact had ceased to be regarded as an obstacle to peace. Occasion had been found for resuming negotiations with Choiseul upon a basis which included the Spanish claims. To ensure secrecy, the correspondence was for a time conducted through the medium of the Sardinian Ministers at London and Paris; but by May, 1762, the fact that the negotiation was pending had transpired. It was then formally notified to the Empress Queen, and in the course of the summer the matter was brought to a point at which it was ripe to be entrusted to plenipotentiaries. As such, in September, the Duc de Nivernais was accredited at London and the Duke of Bedford at Paris. Bedford, however, was not allowed a free hand, though, except the Spanish claims, there remained little to discuss. When the question of the exchange for Havana came on the tapis, there was much divergence of opinion in the Cabinet, and, though Florida was eventually insisted upon, George Grenville, the stoutest opponent of gratuitous concession, changed places at Bute's instance with Halifax and gave up the lead in the House of Commons to Henry Fox (October 14). A seat in the Cabinet was offered to Newcastle, in the hope of securing not only his but Hardwicke's and Devonshire's support for the peace, but was unceremoniously refused; and the three malcontent peers absented themselves from the Council summoned for the discussion of the final draft of the preliminaries, though all three had received the customary writs. In the circumstances the King regarded their absence as a personal affront, and took the first opportunity of denying Devonshire an audience. The Duke, in consequence, resigned the office of Lord Chamberlain (October 28), and the members of his family and his principal political connexions and friends followed suit. The King thereupon erased his name from the list of Privy Councillors, and deprived Newcastle, Rockingham, and Ashburnham of their Lord Lieutenancies.

The Preliminaries of the Peace were signed at Fontainebleau on November 3, 1762; but the Treaty was not made definitive until the virtual completion of the separate negotiation between Austria and Prussia. It was signed at Paris, with the accession of Portugal, on February 10, 1763, five days before the Peace of Hubertusburg. Thus, by two separate Treaties, the general pacification was at length effected.

During the final stage of the negotiation Bedford had been placed at a great disadvantage by the fact that the tenor of his instructions was perfectly known to Choiseul. Choiseul's informant was the Chevalier d'Éon, Nivernais' secretary, who by a discreditable artifice had got sight of the instructions and copied them. Bedford, however, believed that he had been betrayed by Bute, and on his return to England marked his resentment by resigning the Privy Seal and refusing the Presidency of the Council, vacant by the recent death of Granville.

By the Peace of Paris Great Britain, retaining Canada and Cape Breton, ceded to France the islets of St Pierre and Miquelon as an unfortified station for her fishermen, who were guaranteed their rights under the Treaty of Utrecht and accorded a circumscribed right of fishing within the Gulf of St Lawrence: the neutral islands were partitioned —St Vincent, Dominica, and Tobago falling to Great Britain, St Lucia to France, to which Great Britain ceded Martinique and Guadaloupe for Grenada and the Grenadines, in Africa the island of Goree for the Senegal Protectorate, and in Europe Belle Isle for Minorca. With Spain

Great Britain exchanged Havana for Florida, and agreed to dismantle her forts in the Bay of Honduras in return for a guarantee of a limited participation in the logwood trade, Spain totally renouncing her claim to participate in the Newfoundland fishery. As the westward limit of British dominion France and Spain accepted the line of the Mississippi from source to mouth, exclusive only of the New Orleans territory, which with western Louisiana France ceded to Spain by a separate convention. In the East Indies the *status quo* of 1749 was restored, except that France engaged to keep no army in Bengal and ceded Natal and Tapanuli in Sumatra to Great Britain. All other conquests were restored by the signatory Powers. France engaged to reduce the fortifications of Dunkirk to the condition stipulated by the Peace of Aix-la-Chapelle.

The discrepancy between the concessions which Great Britain made by this Peace and the terms which she was in a position to dictate was so glaring as to raise a suspicion that the country had been betrayed—a suspicion which, all things considered, cannot be characterised as entirely unreasonable. It is a significant fact that, after the battle of Wilhelmsthal, Bute wrote to Choiseul as to an ally, urging him to do his utmost to check Prince Ferdinand's advance. But, though the Peace was by no means such as the country was entitled to expect, it encountered, except on the part of Pitt, no determined opposition and was carried by majorities too large to be attributable wholly to corrupt influence. The country was weary of the War, and sullenly acquiesced in sacrifices which were speciously represented as essential to the durability of the Peace. The victory was crowned by a proscription of the Opposition, which did not cease until they had been stripped of most of the places of honour and profit which they held under the Crown, down to subordinate posts in the customs and excise departments.

The unpopularity of the Government was increased by their budget, which saddled the country with a loan of £7,000,000 and an excise duty on cider, leviable on the maker. The cider duty was still (as in Walpole's day) extremely obnoxious to the people, and was only carried after a severe struggle which reunited the Opposition. The odium which it brought upon the Government found peculiarly pungent expression in the *North Briton*, a journal edited by John Wilkes, member for Aylesbury. Bute felt his position to be intolerable, and lost no time in resigning (April 8). Dashwood, who followed suit, was consoled with the barony of Le Despencer; and about the same time Henry Fox, retaining the Pay Office, was created Lord Holland. The lead of the King's Friends in the House of Commons devolved upon Jenkinson.

There is no reason to seek for other explanation of Bute's retirement than lassitude and a desire to relieve the Government of the obloquy in which it was involved by his presence at its head. He continued for a while to enjoy the royal confidence, and selected as his successor George

CH. XIII.

Grenville, who united the seals of the Treasury and the Exchequer. The Admiralty was given to Sandwich. Charles Townshend, who had just succeeded Sandys at the Board of Trade, was displaced to make room for Shelburne (April 20). Stewart Mackenzie received the Privy Seal of Scotland. These arrangements, except the last, were, however, merely provisional. Bute contemplated an early reconstruction of the Administration, with Pitt as Secretary and some other First Lord of the Treasury than Grenville. He lost no time in sounding both Pitt and Bedford, but was encouraged by neither. On Egremont's sudden death (August 21) he renewed his overtures; and the King sent for Pitt (August 27). But it was in vain that he offered to place Temple at the Treasury; Pitt required the dismissal of all who had had a hand in the Peace. Bedford, however, whose son-in-law, Marlborough, was already Lord Privy Seal, at length accepted the Presidency of the Council, though only on condition that Bute retired from Court—a condition which Bute fulfilled in the letter by rusticating himself at Luton Hoo. Egremont's place was taken by Halifax, with Sandwich for his colleague, whom Egmont succeeded at the Admiralty. Shelburne, who had now cast in his lot with Pitt, resigned, and was succeeded by Hillsborough (September).

The Grenville-Bedford Administration compounded with France a claim for the maintenance of prisoners of war (April, 1765), but failed to recover the unpaid moiety (2,000,000 *pesos*) of the Manila ransom. It is chiefly memorable for the series of blunders by which it embroiled the Court and eventually the House of Commons with the country, the country with the American colonies, and itself with the Crown. On April 19, 1763, the session closed with a Speech from the Throne, in which the nation was congratulated on the Peace, and the Treaty of Hubertusburg was represented as a consequence of the Treaty of Paris. The Speech furnished the *North Briton* (No. 45, April 23) with matter for much free comment. In particular the passage concerning the Treaty of Hubertusburg was characterised as "the most abandoned instance of ministerial effrontery ever attempted to be imposed on mankind"; and more followed, amounting to an insinuation that the King had allowed himself to be made a party to a deliberate falsehood. George III keenly resented this licence, which, indeed, in the opinion of the law officers, constituted a seditious libel. As, however, evidence was wanting to convict the anonymous writer, the Secretaries of State issued warrants for the apprehension of the persons and papers of the authors, printers, and publishers of the libel. The warrants named two printers who had been in Wilkes' employ, but not Wilkes himself; and, as by common law a warrant must name all persons to be apprehended thereunder, and the Secretaries had no exceptional powers, neither warrant was valid against Wilkes. Nevertheless, on April 30, he was arrested in the vicinity of his house, which was entered, searched, and cleared of his papers. He was taken before the Secretaries, examined, and, notwithstanding that, on Lord Temple's application, his writ of *habeas corpus* had in the meantime been granted, he was committed close prisoner to the Tower. General warrants by Secretaries of State were not without precedent since the Revolution, and, on the return of the writ of *habeas corpus*, Sir Charles Pratt, Lord Chief Justice of the Common Pleas, refrained from pronouncing those issued in the present instance to be illegal, and discharged Wilkes on the ground of privilege of Parliament (May 6).

To the King it was intolerable that privilege of Parliament should stand between him and the object of his displeasure; and, as Parliament alone could determine the extent of its privilege, to Parliament he appealed. A message conveyed through George Grenville on the first day of the ensuing session (November 15) readily elicited from the House of Commons resolutions not only censuring the *North Briton*, No. 45, as a seditious libel and consigning it to the common hangman to be burned, but withdrawing the aegis of privilege from all who had been concerned in its production. Even Pitt joined in the censure on Wilkes and opposed the waiver of privilege on purely constitutional grounds. As, however, treason, felony, and breach of the peace were the only offences then recognised as ousting privilege of Parliament, its withdrawal even in the case of Wilkes was felt to be so serious an innovation as to demand the sanction of both Houses. A conference of Lords and Commons, managed on the part of the latter by Lord North, was accordingly held; and, though the Court triumphed, there was a goodly array of dissentients. The waiver was opposed by Shelburne with studied moderation, and with inflexible determination by Temple, who, with Grafton, Portland, Bristol, Devonshire, Scarborough, Bessborough, and ten other peers, entered a protest against it in the Journal of their House. Few constitutional lawyers to-day would be found to regret the abandonment of a privilege which was only valuable as a check upon prerogative; but the circumstances of the hour fully justified the strong stand made by the minority.

Matter for collateral proceedings against Wilkes was furnished by a pseudonymous production printed at his private press. Its contents consisted of a filthy parody of Pope's *Essay on Man*, entitled *An Essay on Woman*, with notes purporting to be by Bishop Warburton, and some blasphemous paraphrases of Christian hymns. Only a dozen copies of the work were in print, and there was no evidence that they had been circulated. One, however, had been procured from the compositors by Sandwich, on whose motion (November 15) the House of Lords voted the book a breach of privilege and a scandalous, obscene, and impious libel.

Wilkes, laid aside for a time by a wound received in a duel, coolly employed his convalescence in reprinting the *North Briton* at his private press. He then found himself menaced with two prosecutions for libel, one because of the *North Briton*, the other because of the *Essay on Woman*, and absconded to France. He was expelled the House of

Commons (January 19, 1764); and, having thereupon been found guilty before Lord Mansfield on both the charges of libel (February 21), and not appearing to receive judgment, he was outlawed (November 1). Popular feeling acclaimed Wilkes a patriot, and the dismissal of Temple from the Lord Lieutenancy of Buckinghamshire, of Shelburne from the post of aide-de-camp to the King, and of General Conway and Colonel Barré, who had supported the "patriot's" cause in the House of Commons, from their respective commands, served to intensify the public indignation. The burning of the obnoxious number of the *North Briton* caused a riot, and, though Mansfield by reserving the question of law for his own decision secured the conviction of the publisher, the pillory to which he was consigned proved a place of honour rather than of ignominy. Wood, the Under-Secretary who had superintended the seizure of Wilkes' papers, was cast in £1000 damages in an action instituted by Lord Temple in Wilkes' name (December 6, 1763); and cognate legal proceedings elicited from Mansfield himself a final determination of the illegality of general warrants (1765). An action against Halifax was delayed by legal chicane until the outlawry could be pleaded in bar, but was revived on the reversal of the outlawry, and resulted in a verdict for Wilkes with £4000 damages (November 10, 1769).

The American policy of the Government, which has been already discussed in an earlier volume, was dictated by no set purpose of subverting liberty; but its errors were none the less fatal because they sprang from nothing worse than defective insight and foresight. It proceeded on the principle, in itself plausible enough, that the colonies, delivered by the mother country from imminent peril of subjugation by the French, ought thenceforth to contribute to the cost of their defence and administration by some method more regular and remunerative than voluntary and occasional aids and the insignificant revenue from the Crown quitrents. It ignored the fact that, if the supplies which in times of emergency the colonial Assemblies were accustomed to grant, and the commercial intercourse which the Navigation Laws regulated in the supposed interest of the mother country, did not constitute an adequate compensation for her expenditure upon the colonies, no revenue which she could exact from them could possibly turn the scale in her favour, while the mere attempt to raise such a revenue, however small, by Act of Parliament could not but excite the resentment of a people singularly jealous of its liberties. The Government, however, was bent on trying this hazardous experiment, and, as the Opposition did not as yet concern itself seriously with America, the experiment was made without delay. The Sugar Act of 1733 (6 Geo. II, c. 13) was revised, reenacted without limit of duration, and converted from a merely commercial into a fiscal measure (4 Geo. III, c. 15); and the powers of the Admiralty Courts and executive were amplified, both for the enforcement of the Navigation

Laws and for the collection of the revenue. Pursuant to this Act, a Court of Vice-Admiralty was established for the whole of the colonies (May 18, 1764). The measure was peculiarly obnoxious to the colonists, because the Governors were entitled to one-third of the value of the forfeitures and had thus a substantial interest in enforcing the law. Complaint was also made that the Courts sat at places that caused great inconvenience to the parties. But this was not all. From the purview of the Navigation Acts bullion was expressly excluded; nevertheless, by some strange oversight, commodities bartered for bullion were not exempted from seizure. The authorities had hitherto refused to take advantage of this oversight, and had also relaxed the law with regard to Portuguese lemons and wines. All this was now altered. The bullion trade was treated as contraband; and the whole available naval force was commissioned for the enforcement of the law. The revenue officers, armed with "writs of assistance" from the superior Courts, obeyed their instructions to the letter, and, despite strenuous resistance, with such effect that the supply of bullion fell short. The stringency of this policy was increased by the inopportune demonetisation of bills of credit, which had hitherto circulated as legal tender. In these circumstances, it was scarcely to be wondered at that the colonists viewed the establishment in their midst of a standing army of twenty regiments rather as a menace to their liberties than as a means to their protection, and bitterly resented the requisitions served upon them for the provision of recruits. Their resentment was aggravated by the application to their business transactions of an elaborate system of stamp duties appropriated to the same account as the tariff, and enforceable by the same machinery.

The Stamp Act passed almost unopposed (March, 1765), and, indeed, could hardly have been opposed on strictly constitutional grounds. The delegated powers of the colonial Assemblies could not oust the authority of Parliament. The attempt made by Pitt at a later date to limit that authority in colonial matters fiscal to the imposition of "external" duties merely evinced his ignorance of the true incidence of taxation. Nor could the principle of no taxation without actual representation be maintained with logical consistency by any statesman not prepared for a radical reform of the British representative system. If the unenfranchised masses of Great Britain were to be regarded as virtually represented because they possessed the power of influencing the electorate and Parliament by money and agitation, the same might be said, though doubtless with a less degree of plausibility, of their kith and kin beyond the Atlantic.

Moreover, the same logic which made actual representation a condition precedent to taxation by Act of Parliament implied either the actual inclusion of the colonies within the British representative system or the concession to them of virtual independence. The former alternative was generally regarded on both sides of the Atlantic as impracticable, and only the stern logic of fact could be expected to reconcile the mother country to the latter. In truth, the issue between the colonies and the mother country was simpler and broader than it at first sight appeared. Nothing could be urged against the Stamp Act which was not in principle equally valid against the vexatious restrictions of the Navigation Laws; nothing short of complete autonomy could permanently satisfy the aspirations of the colonists; and the injudicious action of the British Government did but precipitate a struggle which in any case could not have been long deferred.

The Grenville-Bedford Administration went to pieces on a Bill for the constitution of a Regency in the event of the demise of the Crown during the minority of the Heir Apparent. It was a Ministerial measure, introduced in the House of Lords in response to a Royal Message in the spring of 1765. The Bill proposed to vest the Regency in the Queen or such other member of the royal family as the King should appoint, with such powers and advisers as were provided by the similar Act passed on the death of the King's father (24 Geo. II, c. 24). The ample discretion thus reserved to the sovereign by no means commended itself to the entire Cabinet. Bedford and the Secretaries of State suspected that the message which had determined the scheme had been inspired by Bute, and, by way of asserting their independence, attempted so to construe the term royal family as to exclude the Princess Mother from the Regency. The Princess had not been naturalised by Act of Parliament, and it was therefore contended that she was still an alien. This injurious quibble was summarily disposed of by Northington and Mansfield, who pointed out that she was naturalised by her marriage; and an opinion to the same effect was elicited from the *puisnés,* who were quite free from the suspicion of court influence. Richmond then moved (May 3), that the Queen, the Princess Mother, and lineal descendants of the late King resident in England, should be designated as eligible for the Regency. Halifax procured the King's sanction to an amendment which had the effect of excluding the Princess Mother. The amendment was carried; but the triumph of the cabal was only transient. The House of Commons inserted the Princess Mother's name; and, thus reamended, the Bill was returned to the House of Lords and passed into law (May 15). Nothing had, in fact, been further from the King's thoughts than to countenance such a slight to his mother, and he determined at all costs to deliver himself from Ministers whom he regarded as little better than traitors. To this end he opened, through Cumberland, negotiations with Pitt and Temple, on the one hand, and Newcastle and Rockingham, on the other. Pitt and Temple demanded in effect *carte blanche* as to men and measures. Lord Lyttelton, to whom the King then turned, would not take office without Pitt. The cabal threatened resignation. The King temporised; but the terms—the proscription of Bute and all his connexion and the Commandership-in-chief for Granby—on which the cabal insisted as the price of their retention of office, were more than he could brook, and, through Grafton, he renewed his overtures to Pitt. An arrangement seemed assured, when, suddenly, everything was upset by Temple's unexplained refusal of office. Probably, he nominated as colleagues persons obnoxious to Pitt, who was prepared neither to defer to Temple nor to dispense with him, and thus lost what proved to be his last chance of forming a homogeneous Administration. To the King no option remained but the recall of the old Whigs to power. Rockingham became First Lord of the Treasury with Newcastle as Privy Seal, William Dowdeswell, a man of ability, as Chancellor of the Exchequer, the aged Earl of Winchilsea as President of the Council, and the Earl of Dartmouth, a mere cipher, as President of the Board of Trade. At the same time the Pittite Grafton was associated with General Conway, a Rockingham Whig, in the Secretaries' office. Charles Townshend retained the Pay Office, in which he had just succeeded Lord Holland, Egmont the Admiralty, and Northington the Great Seal. Lord Chief Justice Pratt was raised to the peerage as Baron Camden; Charles Yorke, Lord Hardwicke's second son and intellectual successor, was reinstated in the office of Attorney-General which, pending the proceedings against Wilkes, he had resigned; and Lord George Sackville, to Pitt's intense disgust, was restored to the Privy Council, and appointed joint vice-treasurer of Ireland. The Privy Seal of Scotland was given to Lord Breadalbane.

In his private secretary Edmund Burke, member for Wendover, and Attorney-General Yorke, Rockingham had two mentors whose views on the American question had taken definite shape. Both acknowledged the competence of Parliament to legislate for the colonies in regard to all matters, and both regarded the Stamp Act as impolitic, and were therefore prepared to approve its repeal, provided this were accompanied by a measure affirming the limitless legislative authority of Parliament. Without such a measure there was, indeed, little chance of carrying the repeal; nor were Ministers by any means unanimous on the question. They therefore temporised, and allowed Parliament to adjourn for the Christmas recess without affording any clear indication of their policy. When the Houses reassembled (January 14, 1766), opinion was divided between the repeal, the modification, and the enforcement of the Stamp Act. In this difficulty, Ministers appealed to Pitt to come in and save them.

Pitt stipulated for the dismissal of Newcastle, the removal of Sackville from the Council, and "a transposition of offices," which was understood to mean the removal of Rockingham from the Treasury. Newcastle was patriotically willing to be sacrificed; but the King demurred, and the negotiation fell through. Meanwhile, Pitt pressed for the total repeal of the Stamp Act, on the fallacious ground of a natural right in the colonists to the exclusive regulation of their internal taxation; and in the House of Lords the same argument was used by Camden and Shelburne. Its refutation by Mansfield, who showed that no valid distinction could be drawn between an internal and an external tax, the incidence of both being upon the community at large, served to clear the issue. On the one hand, the plenitude of the sovereignty of Parliament, on the other, the futility of any mere modification of the Stamp Act, came to be generally recognised, and thus Yorke's policy was at length adopted. The omnipotence of Parliament was affirmed by a Declaratory Act and exemplified in practice by a Mutiny Act, which required the Provincial Assemblies to vote supplies for the housing and maintenance of troops. Compensation was voted to be due by the Provincial Assemblies to the sufferers by the recent disturbances, and the vote was made an instruction to the Colonial Governors. The Stamp Act was repealed, not without an indemnity to those who had incurred penalties through inability to comply with its provisions. The American tariff was materially lightened; the bullion trade was authorised; and Dominica and Jamaica were opened to foreign shipping. The Government also concluded a commercial treaty with Russia, adjusted with France the claims of holders of Canadian paper currency issued by the French Government before the Peace, and exacted from her a partial demolition of the fortifications of Dunkirk.

Notwithstanding strenuous opposition, the repeal of the Stamp Act was carried by a handsome majority (275 to 161) in the House of Commons, and by a substantial majority (34) in the House of Lords. The Administration was, however, already doomed. It held office by sufferance of Pitt and the King; and, mortified by his failure to obtain an allowance for his brothers and by the House of Commons' express condemnation of general warrants, the King determined to try once more the effect of a new deal of the political cards. Pitt already made no secret of his hostility to the party system as such, and was able through his friends Grafton and Northington to make his influence felt in the Closet; but, when offered office, he, according to his wont, demanded *carte blanche*, and it was not until both Grafton and Northington had resigned that the King was brought to accede to his terms (July 12). There was at first some talk of coalition with the existing Administration; but, as Pitt continued to proscribe Newcastle, this proved impossible. A coalition with the Bedford faction was equally out of the question; and Temple, to whom Pitt offered place, declined it, on learning that he was to have no share in the formation of the Cabinet.

Forced thus to rely on the magic of his personality to make good the lack of common principles, Pitt thereupon formed that ingenious and incongruous combination so happily described by Burke as a "tessellated pavement without cement." The Treasury was entrusted to the *poco-curante* capacity of Grafton, the Exchequer to the erratic genius of Charles Townshend. The Secretaries were Conway for the Northern, Shelburne for the Southern, Department. Pitt himself took the Privy Seal and a seat in the House of Lords as Earl of Chatham. Northington resigned the Great Seal to Camden and accepted the Presidency of the Council. Hillsborough was made President of the Board of Trade, with powers subordinate to Shelburne's. Granby was installed in the office, which had been long left vacant, of Commander-in-chief. Sir Charles Saunders succeeded Egmont at the Admiralty. Bute was propitiated by the restoration of the Privy Seal of Scotland to his brother and the grant of a ducal coronet to his family connexion, Northumberland. The Pay Office was divided between Lord North and George Cooke, member for Middlesex. James Grenville replaced Lord George Sackville as joint vice-treasurer of Ireland. Charles Yorke, whom Chatham could not forgive for having, as he conceived, trimmed in the Wilkes case, was succeeded as Attorney-General by William de Grey.

That this congeries of indifferent or mutually repellent atoms should have proved more than ephemeral is attributable solely to the potent influence which even in his eclipse emanated from its author. Chatham's peerage and insignificant office were rightly interpreted at home and abroad as symptoms of weakness, and in fact gout and hypochondria rendered his position in the Cabinet from first to last little more than nominal. Grafton and Conway, the one from indolence, the other from sheer irresolution, were unfit to act except under Chatham's guidance. Townshend, who owed his place to Grafton's interest and his admission to the Cabinet to Chatham's indisposition, was enamoured of a plan for raising a revenue from the colonies by external taxation. Shelburne and Camden were opposed to the reopening of the American question in any form; but Hillsborough, who supported Townshend, was not a subordinate whom Shelburne could readily control; Camden's influence was limited; and Northington was only desirous of ending his days in peace.

The Administration was hardly in office before it became necessary partially to reconstruct it. The dismissal of Lord Edgcumbe from the Treasurership of the Household to make way for one of Chatham's friends, John Shelley, led to the exodus of the remnant of Rockingham Whigs, with the single exception of Conway. Saunders was succeeded at the Admiralty by Sir Edward Hawke, with Jenkinson *vice* Keppel as Junior Lord.

In Europe the new Government commanded no confidence and inspired little respect. Frederick the Great denied to the Earl of Chatham the trust he had reposed in the Great Commoner. Spain met the claim on account of the Manila ransom with a counter-claim to exclusive possession of the Falkland Isles, on one of which a small British settlement, Port Egmont, had been established in 1765. Nor could Ministers rely on hearty support at home. Hitherto, the country gentlemen had sulkily acquiesced in a land tax of 4*s.* in the pound; now, led by Dowdeswell, they rose in revolt, and carried its reduction to 3*s.* (February 27, 1767). Meanwhile, the American question had assumed a new complexion. The colonists had ignored the Declaratory Act, while they received the repeal of the Stamp Act with professions of gratitude; but the suggestion of compensation for the sufferers by the riots, and the demand of supplies for the army, evoked a contrary spirit. The Assembly of Massachusetts Bay voted the compensation, but by the same Act granted a general pardon to the rioters (December 6, 1766). The Assembly of New York made provision for the quartering of the troops in a manner contrary to the Mutiny Act. The Privy Council annulled both Acts, the one as an usurpation of the royal prerogative, the other as inconsistent with the Charter of the Province. An Act of Parliament, as has been related elsewhere, suspended the legislative functions of the Assembly of New York until the provisions of the Mutiny Act should be complied with. These measures were essential to the maintenance of the authority of the Crown; but wanton offence was given to the colonists by the imposition of Townshend's port duties on glass, leads, pigments, teas, and paper.

Amid these manifold embarrassments, the Government essayed to grapple with the formidable problem which the prowess of Clive had forced upon their consideration, and which is discussed in another chapter. The immense extent and importance of the recent territorial acquisitions of the East India Company raised the question whether or how far such imperial dominion was consistent with the terms of the Company's Charter—a question upon which the Cabinet was far from unanimous. Chatham, Grafton, Shelburne and Camden construed the Charter strictly, claiming for the Crown the eminent domain in all the provinces in which the Company exercised a virtual sovereignty. Townshend, on the other hand, boldly claimed for the Company the prerogatives of an independent State, and carried Conway with him. The extravagance of the contention was patent; and Parliament, without expressly affirming, tacitly recognised the title of the Crown by leasing the new territories to the Company for two years at an annual rent of £400,000, and restricting the Company's dividend, in the meantime, to ten per cent. The measure, which was "managed" by Dyson and supported by the rest of the King's Friends, was carried, and was afterwards continued, with certain modifications, for five years.

Grafton's overtures to Rockingham for a reconstruction of the Administration upon a broad basis led to much consultation, but to no agreement either as to men or measures. The general feeling among the Opposition was that Chatham had better be allowed to "run himself aground." This deplorable decision paved the way for the ultimate triumph of the Court. On the premature death of Charles Townshend, the seals of the Exchequer were given to Lord North (September, 1767). About the same time, Viscount Townshend succeeded Lord Bristol in the Irish viceroyalty, and Jenkinson was transferred from the Admiralty to the Treasury Board. Grafton, acting upon a hint dropped by Chatham, now completely disabled, was at last resolved to detach, if possible, the Bedford group from the Opposition; and, though Bedford himself steadfastly refused office, he released his followers from their self-denying ordinance. The result was that Hillsborough was accorded the status of Colonial Secretary—a guarantee for an unconciliatory policy towards America; Conway yielded the seals to Weymouth, retaining however cabinet rank; Gower replaced Northington as President of the Council, and Rigby succeeded North in the Pay Office. To everybody's surprise, a new Solicitor-General was found in John Dunning, a stuff gownsman who had distinguished himself as counsel for Wilkes' printer, Dryden Leach.

Coalition Governments are apt to be weak, and weak Governments are apt to drift into war; but the Grafton Administration, as now patched up, was too divided even to drift. In the east of Europe, events were marching towards the dismemberment of Poland; in the south, the acquisition of Corsica by France was imminent. The Polish crisis was too remote to interest British statesmen seriously, and the Cabinet had thus no temptation to intervene otherwise than by friendly counsel; but the Corsican question, involving as it did the aggrandisement of France at the expense of a people which had long maintained a heroic struggle for independence, might easily have been so handled as to lead to a renewal of hostilities. That such was not the case was due rather to the impotence than to the prudence of the Government. Shelburne took a high tone; Grafton was lukewarm; the rest of the Cabinet were either indifferent or opposed to overt intervention. Thus, while Ministers debated, and privily furnished Paoli with arms (July, 1768), Choiseul made good his hold on the island.

On the American question the Government were no less divided. The Assembly of Massachusetts Bay which had taken the lead in organising resistance to the collection of Townshend's taxes was dissolved by Hillsborough's orders (July, 1768), but continued to sit under another name. The agitation grew and spread, and the turbulence of the populace was hardly restrained by military force. It began to be plain that the duties must either be remitted or levied at a cost disproportionate to their value. The Bedford section of the Cabinet demanded enforcement *coûte que coûte*; while Grafton, Camden, Shelburne, Conway, and Granby advised their repeal. Chatham, anticipating Shelburne's dismissal, and Shelburne, despairing of Chatham's recovery, resigned without concert about the same time (October 12, 19); and thus the cause of conciliation lost its most earnest advocates. Shelburne's place was taken by Weymouth, whom Rochford succeeded in the Northern Department; Bristol receiving the Privy Seal (October—November). At the close of the year, a place was found for Dyson at the Treasury Board. The struggle in the Cabinet terminated, on May 1, 1769, in a compromise—the repeal of the duties on paper, glass and colours, the rest being retained. Futile in itself, this act of grace was

CH. XIII.

communicated to the colonies by Hillsborough in a manner so offensive as to convert it into an affront. A league for the total exclusion of British goods from the colonies was organised and assumed formidable proportions.

Circumstances were hardly more favourable to a sound domestic policy than to a reasonable treatment of the colonies. Nevertheless, in the course of the years 1768–9 two important additions were made to the Statute Book. The *Nullum Tempus* Act abolished the ancient rule of law by which no lapse of time was pleadable in bar of a crown claim, and made sixty years' possession of landed estate an indefeasible title; and, as noted elsewhere, the Irish Octennial Act struck a blow at the corrupt oligarchy to which the fugitive or absentee Viceroys—with Townshend began the rule of residence—had been wont to farm out the government. In 1769 the Court gained a signal triumph by carrying an Act for discharge of the debts, amounting to £500,000, upon the Civil List without account given of the purposes for which the expenditure had been incurred.

Meanwhile, no small share of the attention of Parliament was absorbed by Wilkes. Early in 1768 he came back to England, and by the supineness of the Government was suffered to stand for Parliament at the general election. Returned for Middlesex (March 28), he surrendered to his outlawry in the King's Bench and was committed to the King's Bench prison (April 27). The vicinity of the gaol was soon thronged with a rabble of disorderly patriots. Their demonstrations daily increased in violence, and, on May 10, the Riot Act having been read, the mob was dispersed by the military not without loss of life. One of the soldiers was tried for murder, but was acquitted. Wilkes was subsequently relieved of the outlawry on a technical flaw, but was sentenced on the prior convictions to two consecutive terms of ten and twelve months' imprisonment, with a fine of £1000 and the obligation to give recognisances in £1000, with two sureties in £500 each, for his good behaviour for seven years after his discharge (June 18). The judgment was affirmed by the House of Lords on writ of error; a petition presented in Wilkes' behalf to the House of Commons was dismissed; and a stinging paragraph on the precautions taken by the Government in anticipation of the riot, which he had caused to be inserted in the *St James's Chronicle* (December 10, 1768), was voted a seditious libel, for which, in addition to his previous offences, he was again expelled the House (February 4, 1769). On his immediate reelection, the House annulled the return, and declared him "incapable of being elected to serve as a member in this present Parliament." Other returns were also annulled, and eventually the Court nominee, Colonel Luttrell, was declared duly elected, though he had been beaten at the polls, and the return was falsified accordingly (April 15).

The proceedings were technically defensible, for each branch of the legislature has exclusive cognisance of the capacity of its members. Nevertheless, they were totally repugnant to the spirit of the Constitution, and, if sanctioned by the acquiescence of the electorate, would have established a precedent of most dangerous consequence, capable indeed of indefinite abuse, even to the annihilation of free speech and the transformation of the House of Commons from a representative assembly into a close corporation perpetuating itself by ostracism and cooptation. It was, therefore, no spirit of faction, but a sober appreciation of the gravity of the crisis, which now prompted George Grenville to lay aside personal considerations, and to enter the lists as the champion of the man on whom not so many years before he had led the first attack. His cold, grave constitutionalism fell, however, unheeded on ears deafened by passion and subservience. Wilkes was known to be still in the last degree obnoxious to the King, and the King's Friends were now in the ascendant. Petitions were multiplied in vain. Their rejection at St Stephen's, as at St James', was a foregone conclusion; and, though constitutionalism gained an unexpected champion in Wedderburn, the shortsighted and suicidal arrogance of the majority found a specious apologist in the young member for Midhurst, Lord Holland's third son, Charles James Fox. By all this Wilkes, of course, gained vastly in popularity. A society organised by his friend Horne under the title of "Supporters of the Bill of Rights" canonised him as a patriot, and raised sufficient funds to set him free from pecuniary embarrassment on his discharge from prison.

In the *Letters of Junius* (1769–72), which, whoever may have been the scribe that turned their classic periods, represent perhaps more nearly the sympathies and antipathies of Lord Temple than those of any other statesman of the day, the Wilkes case naturally occupied a prominent place. One of them indeed amounted to nothing less than a direct arraignment of the King as the prime mover in the persecution of the "patriot," and as thus, in effect, the subverter of the Constitution. This licence, unparalleled since the appearance of the *North Briton,* No. 45, provoked a fresh attack upon the liberty of the Press. The letter had appeared in the *Public Advertiser* of December 19, 1769, and had been at once reprinted in the *London Museum* and the *Evening Post. Ex officio* informations were filed by Attorney-General De Grey in the Court of King's Bench against the printers and publishers of all three papers. In each case Lord Mansfield, in strict conformity with precedent, reserved for the Court the determination of the question of law; and, so instructed, the juries in one case acquitted, in another convicted, the defendants, while in the third (that of Woodfall, the original publisher) they returned an evasive verdict of "guilty of printing and publishing only" (June 13, 1770)—a form of words without legal import, upon which it was impossible to found a judgment. This conflict between judge and jury led to much discussion in the House of Lords; but Mansfield's ruling, though vigorously impugned by Camden (December 10), commanded the general assent of the legal profession, and continued to be followed by judges and disputed by juries, until the controversy was closed by legislative enactment in 1792 (32 Geo. III, c. 60, commonly known as Fox' Libel Act).

The crisis elicited from Burke a manifesto entitled *Thoughts on the Cause of the Present Discontents* (1770), in which he sought to deduce all the disorders of the body politic from one and the same source, the secret and insidious influence of the Court—as if the Whigs had been incapable of intrigue and quite unversed in the arts of corruption, and had not, by their jealousy of Chatham, their determination to adhere at any cost to the obsolete system of "general cabinet advice," and their own interminable dissensions, given the Court its opportunity. In discountenancing the popular cry for Triennial Parliaments, Burke was doubtless wise ; but there was more to be said for a Place Bill than he was prepared to acknowledge ; and, in finding his panacea in the revival of the old Whig *régime*, he gave no hint of the means by which this consummation was to be attained. His truest admirers must recognise that in this pamphlet the political sagacity of which his name has become a symbol is none too apparent ; but, as yet, statesmen of all schools, with the single exception of Chatham, lacked either the insight to perceive or the courage to proclaim that the defective, the all but illusory, representation of the people was the true cause of the confusions, and its reform the paramount need, of the State.

In Parliament, the campaign against the Court was opened in form by motions for the disfranchisement of revenue officers (too often mere placemen), an account of the debt on the Civil List (which was shrewdly suspected to have been incurred for corrupt purposes), and a scrutiny of the Pension List. Defeat was inevitable ; but the programme became an integral part of Whig policy and bore fruit in due season. The Opposition was led by Chatham, now completely recovered and at one not only with Temple and George Grenville but (by the death of Newcastle) with Rockingham. The agitation in favour of Wilkes was accordingly pressed with the utmost heat, even to the verge of provoking a conflict between the two Houses, while the King was plied with Remonstrances on the part of the City of London. The Remonstrances were treated with contempt, and the Government triumphed in the divisions ; but the dismissal of Camden, and the secession of Grafton, Granby, Bristol, and Dunning, left gaps which were hardly to be filled. For Granby no competent successor could be found, and the Commandership-in-chief was in consequence left in abeyance. The Privy Seal was given to Halifax (February 26, 1770). North, retaining the Exchequer, succeeded nominally to the Treasury, but remained in effect only finance Minister, the real direction of affairs being assumed by the King, whose most confidential advisers were Mansfield and Sir Gilbert Elliot, the Treasurer of the Navy. Dyson was also high in favour, and generally supposed to be the main channel of influence. Edward Thurlow, who might be trusted to serve the King's turn so long as pay and promotion were to be had, was made Solicitor-General. A lawyer of a similar type, Sir Fletcher Norton, who, however, proved a thorn in the side of the Court, was chosen Speaker of the House of Commons. Charles Yorke, importuned by the King to accept the Great Seal, yielded against his better judgment, and died within three days—as it was supposed, of shame and remorse that he should have deserted his party at such a crisis (January 20, 1770). The Seal was then put in commission; and eventually, Henry Bathurst, the least able of the Commissioners, was elected as Chancellor, being created, on January 24, 1771, Lord Apsley.

In regard to America, the Government carried the remission of the port duties a step further, retaining only that on tea as a badge of subjection. In the way of domestic legislation, the most important result of the session of 1770 was George Grenville's Act, by which election petitions were referred to Select Committees, a form of procedure only superseded by the transference of the jurisdiction to the Courts of Law in the reign of Queen Victoria. It proved to be its author's last, as it was certainly his most important, achievement : he died on November 13, 1770, and, by the consequent dissolution of his connexion, the Court gained a recruit in Henry Howard, Earl of Suffolk.

When Grenville passed away, Parliament was reassembling to discuss matter of more stirring interest than economic reform or the jurisdiction on election petitions. As has been related in an earlier chapter, a dispute with Spain about the possession of the Falkland Isles threatened war; and when Parliament met, the situation was so grave that nearly £1,500,000 was added to the naval estimates, and a fleet was collected at Spithead. The *Pacte de Famille*, however, disappointed expectation ; and Charles III, unprepared for a single-handed contest with Great Britain, disclaimed responsibility for the action of the Governor of Buenos Ayres, and consented (January 22, 1771) to restore Port Egmont, which had been occupied by the Spaniards. The restitution was made on September 16, 1772, but without either acknowledgment of the British right or reparation for the insult offered to the British flag; and the withdrawal of the British garrison followed so soon afterwards as to seem like a virtual recognition of the Spanish title. During the crisis Weymouth resigned, doubtless to mark his disapprobation of a pusillanimous policy. He was succeeded by Rochford, the Northern Seals being transferred to Sandwich.

By this affair the country suffered even more in purse than in pride. Of the extraordinary naval supply no account was ever given, and its due appropriation to the purposes for which it was voted would, as matters then stood, have been nothing short of a miracle. The corruption, from which no department of government remained free, was especially marked where wise economy was most of all necessary—in the Admiralty, and was here allowed to shelter itself under the pretext that the fluctuating exigencies of the service precluded strict account. Hence a ruinous proportion of the sums annually voted for the repair, construction, and equipment of ships, was absorbed by the rapacity of subordinate officials, whom their superiors were either unable or unwilling to expose or control. The mischief was the more serious because, the supply of oak having fallen short, not a few ships had been built of timber of inferior quality, and were already rotten; while France, with the advantage of a better school of naval architecture than the British, had made, and was still making, every exertion to place her navy upon such a footing as might enable her once more seriously to contest the empire of the sea. Hawke, who can hardly have been blind to the gravity of the situation, was by this time superannuated, and resigned (January 9, 1771). Sandwich was, for purely party reasons, appointed his successor—a man entirely without nautical experience, and far too much engrossed by his pleasures to concern himself with the disagreeable details of administration. The Northern Seals were given to Halifax and, on his death in the following June, to Suffolk, the vacant Privy Seal being transferred to Grafton. About the same time Thurlow was made Attorney-General, and Wedderburn, weary of opposition, succeeded him as Solicitor-General.

The sanction of Parliament to the Spanish Convention was not obtained without long and acrimonious debates, of which, when reported, Parliament had good reason to be ashamed. The publication of debates was still technically a breach of privilege, and the House of Commons on this occasion saw fit to resent it as such by citing the publishers to its bar. Default being made in appearance, one of the culprits was taken into custody by the Serjeant-at-arms, and the other two were arrested under a royal proclamation. All three arrests were made within the City of London, and without the concurrence of a City magistrate. As this involved a breach of the City Charter, Lord Mayor Brass Crosby, with the concurrence of Aldermen Wilkes and Oliver, discharged the prisoners, and committed the messenger by whom the Speaker's warrant had been executed to gaol. A citation to the bar of the House of Commons was evaded by Wilkes, on the ground that his incapacity placed him beyond its jurisdiction. Crosby and Oliver attended, but only to refuse submission, and be committed to the Tower (March 25, 27). There they were visited by Rockingham, Burke, and other leading Whigs; and, on the prorogation, they came forth to find their popularity enhanced and the cause for which they had contended virtually won. A privilege of a different nature was asserted in 1774. An alleged libel on the Speaker (in the *Public Advertiser* of February 11), being attributed on inconclusive evidence to John Horne (afterwards Horne Tooke), the House of Commons usurped the functions of a Court of justice, summoned and interrogated the compositors, and was defeated by their profession of total ignorance of the authorship of the libel.

The session of 1772 produced the Royal Marriage Act (12 Geo. III,

c. 11), by which descendants of the late King other than the issue of princesses married, or who should thereafter marry, into foreign families, were disabled from marrying without the King's consent, unless, being of the age of twenty-five years, they should give twelve months' notice to the Privy Council of their intention so to marry, and Parliament should not in the meantime disapprove the union.   The measure was occasioned by the marriage of the King's third brother, Henry Frederick, Duke of Cumberland, with Anne, sister of Colonel Luttrell (Wilkes' supplanter in the House of Commons), and widow of Christopher Horton, of Catton, Derbyshire.   Such an alliance was extremely distasteful to both the King and the Queen ; and the extent of the royal prerogative in regard to such matters had not as yet been precisely determined.   That it governed the marriages of the King's grandchildren had been decided during the long and embittered contest between George I and the Prince of Wales (1718); but there was no precedent in regard to collaterals, nor were the majority of the judges prepared to make one.   Thus, though in terms declaratory, the measure was in fact an innovation, and as such was resisted stoutly by Rockingham, Shelburne and Charles James Fox, who had made his *début* as a ministerialist.   Upon Cumberland's banishment from Court, his elder brother, William Henry, Duke of Gloucester, magnanimously avowed his own prior secret marriage with Maria, Countess Dowager Waldegrave, an illegitimate daughter of Sir Edward Walpole, and was likewise banished; nor was it until 1780 that the brothers were restored to favour.

The session of 1773 was almost exclusively devoted to Indian affairs, of which a connected account will be found in a subsequent chapter. By a complication of causes, chief among them the recklessness of the Directors and the rapacity of their servants, the East India Company had been brought to the verge of ruin.   Parliament met the Company's more pressing needs by a loan of £1,400,000 on no very onerous terms, while taking security for the better management of its affairs by Lord North's Regulating Act, which in effect remodelled its constitution, substituting for the annual election of the entire Court of Directors a rota so arranged that in the ordinary course there should never be more than six places to be filled at any one election.   The presidencies of Bombay and Madras were subordinated to that of Bengal, and the administration of the latter was vested in a Governor-General and Council of Four.   The Act constituted Warren Hastings the first Governor-General, and named his Council ; but the appointment and removal of succeeding Governors-General and their Councils were left to the unfettered discretion of the Court of Directors.   This measure, of which more is said below, encountered strong opposition on the part of the Whigs— two protests against it were entered in the Journal of the House of Lords—an opposition grounded partly on the abrogation of chartered rights, partly on the extension of the royal prerogative which it involved.

The reform which it effected was however salutary and amply justified the means. The Company's Charter had not contemplated the assumption of imperial dominion by a trading corporation. It would have been sheer superstition to have held it sacrosanct in circumstances so novel. The title of the Crown to the territorial acquisitions of the Company was incontestable, and might reasonably have been held to warrant changes far more drastic than those which the Act introduced. The degree of centralisation which it effected was indeed no more than was essential, and subsequent events unfortunately proved that its provisions against malpractices were none too stringent.

A minor measure of the session, consisting of a slight boon to the embarrassed Company, the remission of the home customs duty on their consignments of tea to America, proved productive of effects wholly unexpected and out of all proportion to its intrinsic importance. Since the tea could thus be offered at a reduced price and the American import duty was only 3*d.* per pound avoirdupois, it was feared in the colonies that the loyalty of the people to their non-importation restrictions would be severely strained by the new regulation. The emergency nerved the more fiery spirits to extraordinary measures; and, as is narrated in another volume, three of the Company's ships were boarded in Boston harbour by a party of armed men disguised as Mohawks, who discharged their cargoes into the sea. At New York a single cargo was landed under the guns of a ship of war, and was immediately secured under lock and key. From other ports the ships were sent home with their cargoes. The rebellious temper evinced by these proceedings evoked a correspondingly high spirit in the mother country. Opposition was for the time extinguished, and in the course of the year 1774 Parliament passed several stringent coercive measures. The further use of Boston Port was prohibited. The Charter of Massachusetts Bay was annulled, and provision was made for changing the venue within the colonies or to Great Britain, when needful in order to secure a fair trial of persons capitally prosecuted for acts done in enforcing the law. At the same time the province of Quebec was extended so as to include parts of the basins of the Ohio and Mississippi, and converted into a crown colony, the French population being conciliated by a guarantee of religious equality and their ancient laws and customs except in criminal cases. These measures converted Fox from a wavering supporter into a determined foe of the Government.

In the autumn, Parliament was dissolved, and the Opposition returned from the polls, a demoralised remnant of seventy-three members. Wilkes, now permitted to take his seat, distinguished himself by his zeal in behalf of the colonies, and by the well-considered plan for the redistribution of seats which he laid before Parliament on March 21, 1776. He failed, however, to make a sensible impression on the Ministerial cohorts. The need of Parliamentary Reform was as yet unrecognised by all parties, and, as has been shown elsewhere, the Government was intent on pacifying the colonies by a judicious mixture of cajolery and coercion. Thus, in 1775, Chatham's moderate proposals, the withdrawal of the troops from Boston, the suspension of the obnoxious Acts, the delegation of the exclusive right of taxation to the Assemblies, and the restriction of the powers of the Vice-Admiralty Courts to their ancient limits, were summarily rejected; and the defeat in the House of Commons of Burke's more logical scheme, which would have repealed what Chatham proposed to suspend, and secured the judges against removal except by the King in Council upon complaint by the Assemblies, Governors, Councils, or Houses of Representatives, but was otherwise substantially identical with that of Chatham, was a foregone conclusion. On the other hand, North's illusory concession of temporary immunity from taxation to those colonies which should place at the disposal of Parliament such supplies as Parliament should deem adequate was carried by a majority of the usual dimensions—to be decisively rejected by Congress. In the same session not only the external but the intercolonial trade of Massachusetts Bay, New Hampshire, Connecticut, Rhode Island, Providence Plantation, New Jersey, Pennsylvania, Maryland, Virginia, and South Carolina was placed under severe restriction, while the military and naval forces of the Crown available for the coercion of the colonies were augmented. By the Prohibitory Act (1776), the entire external commerce of the colonies was laid under interdict, removable at the discretion of the Crown. Ministers, however, remained without a concerted plan of action, while the colonial militia surprised the principal fortresses on the Canadian frontier, invested Boston, and at Lexington and Bunker Hill (April 19 and June 17, 1775) came into collision with the King's troops.

In November, 1775, Grafton, who had hoped against hope that hostilities might be averted, resigned, and was succeeded as Lord Privy Seal by Dartmouth, the office of Secretary for the Colonies (which had been transferred to him from Hillsborough in the autumn of 1772) being given to Lord George Germain, whose competence for administration was apparently inferred from his proved incapacity for military command. About the same time, Rochford retired on a pension, and was succeeded as Secretary of State by Weymouth. In opposition as in office, Grafton still clung to the hope that, even at the eleventh hour, an irreparable rupture with the colonies might be averted by a very simple expedient. The Government had turned a deaf ear to the petitions of Congress, the last, presented by Richard Penn, being contemptuously dismissed—largely, it would seem, through the influence of Mansfield. Congress could not be expected to persevere in an evidently futile procedure. But Congress might be invited to present a petition to the Peace Commissioners in America appointed under the Prohibitory Act, and hostilities might be suspended pending its consideration. Such a petition, if considered by the Commissioners in a conciliatory spirit, might prove the basis of an accommodation. Accordingly, on March 14,

CH. XIII.

1776, Grafton moved for an address to the Throne, praying that the necessary powers might be delegated to the Commissioners. The defeat of this motion, after a long and animated debate, marks the turning point in the struggle. It was followed by the Declaration of Independence (July 4), and the confederation of the Thirteen States.

Towards the close of the year Rockingham virtually seceded from Parliament, and carried a great part of his followers with him. Chatham was at that time once more disabled by ill health; nor was it until the summer of 1777 that he was sufficiently recovered to resume the lead of the Opposition. He retained much of his old power of declamation; but the strange inconsequence with which, while deprecating the continuance of hostilities, he set his face against the recognition of the independence of the colonies—his last speech was a vehement repudiation of that policy (April 7, 1778)—raises a doubt whether his return to power would not have been productive of more harm than good. It was vain to hope that after the treatment which they had received the "removal of accumulated grievances" would have sufficed to bring the colonies back to their allegiance. A nation had been born, and it would never abdicate its sovereign rights.

The effect of the Prohibitory Act was to drive the colonial trade into foreign ports. Holland especially profited by this clandestine traffic, of which the island of St Eustatius became a principal emporium, and to which a quasi-legal sanction was given by the connivance of the States General in a Treaty of Amity and Commerce, concluded, on September 4, 1778, between the city of Amsterdam and Congress. Nor was the reception accorded to the merchantmen denied to the privateers of the Americans. To check the depredations of the privateers, the British Government issued letters of marque in profusion, and deprived persons suspected of piracy in American waters of the benefit of the Habeas Corpus Act. The resources of the colonists on land were greatly underrated, and the possibility of foreign intervention was ignored. The first war loan amounted to no more than £5,500,000—with so light a heart did the Government enter on the contest. The loan rose in 1778 to £6,480,000, and in 1779 to £7,490,000. The additional taxation was on the whole raised judiciously, being for the most part laid on luxuries; but it was supplemented by drafts on the Sinking Fund. The most grievous error of the Government was their neglect of the navy, which at the outbreak of hostilities was so weak that the Channel Fleet was only maintained at its nominal strength by the inclusion of several unseaworthy hulks, while the squadron commanded by Lord Howe in American waters was not only inadequate for the maintenance of an effective blockade over any considerable extent of sea-board, but barely sufficed for the discharge of the duties subsidiary to the military operations which were the most important services at first demanded of it. The colonists kept up in the vicinity of their coasts a desultory warfare, which in 1777 John Paul

Jones carried into British waters. The nearest approach to a regular fleet which they possessed was annihilated by Sir George Collier in the Penobscot River on August 14, 1779. Meanwhile, however, a more formidable enemy had appeared on the scene.

By the Treaty of Paris (February 6, 1778), France and the United States entered into a defensive alliance, which was to become offensive in the event of war between France and Great Britain. The Treaty escaped the vigilance of the British ambassador, Lord Stormont, though Franklin's presence at Paris caused him some uneasiness, and the Government first heard of it from Grafton some days before its official communication.

To France and Spain the independence of the United States was a secondary, the conquest of the British possessions in the West Indies, the Gulf of Mexico, and the Mediterranean the primary, object. Nevertheless, Spain was only with difficulty induced to comply with the terms of the Family Compact, and did not join the alliance till after the rejection by the British Government of her proffered mediation (June 16, 1779). The rupture with France brought in its train a rupture with the Dutch. While giving harbourage to Paul Jones, the States General refused the succours which by the Treaty of Westminster (March 3–13, 1677–8) they were bound to furnish in the event of a Bourbon aggression, and allowed their merchantmen to carry into French ports cargoes of naval stores and timber suitable for the construction of ships of war. These cargoes were treated as contraband by the British Government, and some of the merchant ships were accordingly arrested. The States General joined the Armed Neutrality, and Great Britain, further exasperated by the discovery of the secret Treaty of Amity of 1778 between the city of Amsterdam and the American Congress, declared war against the Republic (December 20, 1780).

In undertaking the coercion of the American colonies George III had erred mainly through ignorance, believing that their militia could never cope with regular troops. Grafton's warning that the employment of German mercenaries " would only increase the disgrace and never effect his purpose " he received with unfeigned amazement. To the risk of foreign intervention he was blinded by the fixed idea that the House of Bourbon would never ally itself with insurgents. As the prospect darkened, he became less sanguine; but he still clung tenaciously to the hope of avoiding a formal concession of independence, and, cajolery having been tried and found wanting, he stooped to conciliation. So in 1778 the tea duty was repealed, and a Commission appointed (April 5) with authority to negotiate with Congress as a quasi-independent Power, and in the meantime to suspend obnoxious laws. A more homogeneous Commission might well have been chosen; but, even so, the time for such expedients had gone by for ever.

To his " friends " the King clave more closely than they to him. Germain resigned in a fit of the spleen (March 3), but unfortunately repented and resumed office. North was eager to make way for Chatham and lacked only the resolution to resign. Both before and after Chatham's death, overtures were made to several members of the Opposition for a coalition; but, as no material change of policy was purposed, the Whigs saw clearly that the real object of the King was merely to seduce as many of them as might serve to strengthen his tottering Administration, and with one consent held aloof. If anything had been needed to vindicate their sagacity, it would have been the transference of the Great Seal from Apsley, now Earl Bathurst (June 1, 1778), to Thurlow, the truculent and trumpet-tongued coryphaeus of the party of coercion, and the substitution for Barrington as Secretary at War of Jenkinson, the most subservient of courtiers (December 16). North, whose better judgment disapproved the prolongation of hostilities, was by this time so weary of office that only the lucrative sinecures of Warden of the Cinque Ports and Constable of Dover Castle reconciled him to the retention of it (June 4). Lord Suffolk, the shameless apologist of the employment of Redskin warriors against the colonists, was with difficulty persuaded to remain at his post until his death in March, 1779. To take his place, Stormont, a diplomatist of proved incapacity, was recalled from Paris (October). On the subsequent defection of Gower and Weymouth, Bathurst became President of the Council and the vacant Secretary's place was given to Hillsborough (November). These changes, with the appointment of Carlisle, now returned from America, to the Presidency of the Board of Trade, constituted a virtual reconstruction of the Administration.

In the House of Lords, Thurlow, who was joined in June, 1780, by Wedderburn (created Baron Loughborough), early established an ascendancy which would have reduced the Opposition to impotence, even had it not been paralysed by the reluctance of Shelburne and Camden to follow the lead of Rockingham in demanding the immediate recognition of the independence of the United States. In the House of Commons, the cause of Parliamentary Reform made some little progress. A Place Bill (for the disqualification of persons interested in government contracts not made at a public bidding), which had been summarily rejected on its first introduction by Sir Philip Jennings Clerke in 1778, was reintroduced in 1779 and defeated by a reduced majority.

The naval war opened inauspiciously for the British. Only twenty sail of the line and three frigates could at first be mustered for the defence of the Narrow Seas; and with this inadequate force Admiral Keppel sailed from Portsmouth on June 13, 1778. In the Bay of Biscay he captured some French frigates, and from their papers first learned the greatly superior strength of the fleet (thirty-two sail of the line with ten or twelve frigates) which lay off Brest under Admiral d'Orvilliers. This compelled him to return to Portsmouth for reinforcements, and it was only by dint of great exertions that he was at length able to encounter d'Orvilliers with a force approximately equal in regard to the mere number of ships, but otherwise decidedly inferior in material. The fleets engaged off Ouessant on July 27, but without decisive result; for, though at the close of the action the advantage rested with the British, the French made good their escape. For this failure Vice-Admiral Palliser was held responsible by public opinion, and Admiral Keppel by Vice-Admiral Palliser. Both officers were tried by Court-martial (1779) and acquitted, it being established that Palliser's ships were too damaged for pursuit; but upon Palliser rested the stigma of having brought an unfounded accusation against his superior officer.

A parliamentary enquiry into the administration of the navy, demanded in the House of Lords by Bristol, in the House of Commons by Fox, was stifled; but the emphatic testimony not only of Keppel but of Lord Howe, who had recently resigned his American command, to the deplorable condition of the service was sealed by their retirement from it, and their example was followed by other officers of distinction. Howe was not the man to be moved either by pique or by panic, nor had he thrown up his command without grave cause. With an inadequate force (nine sail of the line and a few frigates) he had been left to cope with a squadron of twelve sail of the line and several frigates of superior armament under Count d'Estaing. The French commander had sailed from Toulon on April 13, 1778, and had been delayed for some weeks in the Mediterranean. The Admiralty had had early intelligence of his movements, but had made no attempt to intercept him until his destination was accurately known (June); and the intercepting squadron under Vice-Admiral Byron had arrived too late and in an unseaworthy condition by no means wholly imputable to the tempestuous weather which it had encountered. In the meantime, Howe, apprised of d'Estaing's approach by one of his own frigates, had succeeded in barring the access to New York and Rhode Island alike, until a storm of unusual violence so shattered the French ships that they were compelled to take refuge in Boston harbour. That Rhode Island and New York had not fallen into the hands of the French was thus entirely due to the vigilance and resource of the British Admiral, aided by the chapter of accidents. It was this experience which had determined Howe to return to England, and retire from the service; nor did he change his mind until the fall of North's Administration.

In November d'Estaing, evading Byron's blockading squadron, sailed from Boston for the West Indies, where Bouillé, Governor of Martinique, had already reduced Dominica. D'Estaing, with his twelve sail of the line and 7000 troops, arrived just too late to prevent the capture of St Lucia by Rear-Admiral Barrington and Commodore Hotham, whose joint forces amounted to seven sail of the line with 5000 troops under Major-General Grant (December 14, 1778). The advent of Byron with ten sail of the line (January, 1779) gave the British a temporary superiority of strength, which was maintained until the end of June, when the arrival of reinforcements from Brest turned the scale in favour of the French. Byron, who had the chief command, was embarrassed by convoy duty, and failed to prevent the reduction of St Vincent (June 18) and Grenada (July 4) by d'Estaing. Worsted in a general action off St George, Grenada (July 6), the British commanders withdrew to St Christopher, and soon afterwards sailed for England. D'Estaing, after refitting at Cap François, mustered twenty ships of the line, with which he sailed to Savannah; but, being repulsed with great loss in the general assault on that place (October 9), returned to France.

On the eastern side of the Atlantic the conduct of the war reflected no credit on the Allies. The French recovered Senegal (January—February, 1779) but abandoned Goree to the British (May). They massed troops to the number of 60,000 in Normandy and Britanny, and were beaten in two attacks on Jersey (May, 1779 and January, 1781).

The Franco-Spanish fleet (sixty-six ships of the line) sailed up the Channel in the autumn of 1779 as far as Plymouth, but did not succeed in bringing on a general engagement with the British fleet, hardly more than half as strong, under Admiral Hardy. In the autumn of the following year it made a similar idle parade between Ouessant and the Scilly Isles. In the North Sea, the Dutch Rear-Admiral Zoutman tried conclusions with Vice-Admiral Hyde Parker off the Dogger Bank on August 5, 1781. The fleets seem to have been about on a par, for each commander had seven ships of the line, and, if four of the British ships were so old as hardly to be worked, it is probable that the Dutch were in no better plight. The contest was maintained with great courage and carnage for more than three hours, when it terminated, by reason of the shattered condition of the ships, without decided advantage on either side.

In the Mediterranean the British squadron at the outbreak of hostilities consisted of only one sixty-gun ship, three frigates and a sloop; nor was it reinforced in time to prevent the blockade of Gibraltar and Minorca. Port Mahon, gallantly defended by General Murray, was reduced by sickness and famine to capitulate (February 5, 1782). Gibraltar was more fortunate: to the ample relief convoyed from home by Admiral Rodney in command of thirty-six sail, of which twenty-two were of the line, were added five Spanish ships of the line and twelve Spanish provision ships captured *en route* off Capes Finisterre and St Vincent (January 8 and 16, 1780); and the subsequent reliefs by Vice-Admiral Darby in command of the "grand fleet" of twenty-eight sail of the line (April, 1781), and Lord Howe with thirty-four sail of the line (October, 1782), enabled General Eliott and his heroic garrison to defy the assaults of the enemy until the Peace.

During the years 1780–2 the West Indian and American stations were the theatre of operations of great interest. In March, 1780, a French fleet of twenty-two sail of the line under Guichen lay in Fort Royal Bay, Martinique, on the look-out for a Spanish fleet under Don José Solano ; the two commanders were to join their forces for the conquest of Jamaica and New York. They reckoned, however, without Admiral Rodney, who assumed the command in the Leeward Islands station towards the end of the month and, with, roughly speaking, a parity of force, fought three engagements with the French (April 17, May 15 and 19), by which he so crippled their fleet that, though the junction with the Spaniards was effected, its purpose was frustrated. Guichen, with the bulk of his fleet, sailed to Cadiz, while Solano put into Havana.

In July, 1780, the American station was guarded by only four sail of the line under Vice-Admiral Arbuthnot, and Rhode Island had been denuded of troops for the defence of New York. Arbuthnot was by no means a brilliant commander ; but in such circumstances it was hardly in his power to prevent the occupation of the island by Rochambeau's six thousand veterans, convoyed by seven sail of the line under Ternay. Reinforced by Rear-Admiral Graves with five sail of the line, he succeeded, by an action off Cape Henry (March 16, 1781) in frustrating a descent on the Chesapeake by des Touches, Ternay's successor in command ; but a tactical error, the reckless exposure of his van, seriously impaired the value of the victory. He was in consequence recalled, and the command devolved upon Graves.

In May, 1781, Don Bernardo Galvez, Governor of Louisiana, reduced Pensacola, and thereby recovered West Florida.

In the spring of 1781 Rodney occupied the Dutch West India Islands, a conquest as easy as lucrative, but which left the rest of the islands almost at the mercy of Count de Grasse, who succeeded Guichen in command of the French fleet. After defeating Rear-Admiral Hood, whom Rodney had detached in command of seventeen sail of the line to intercept him in the straits between St Lucia and Martinique (April 29), de Grasse reduced Tobago, and then, with his whole fleet of twenty-eight sail of the line, bore down upon the Chesapeake and occupied the Bay (August 30), before Hood and Graves were able to join their forces. The junction effected, the British commanders were able to oppose nineteen sail of the line to the twenty-four with which the French Admiral guarded the mouth of the Bay. The disparity of strength was, therefore, not so great as to preclude all chance of victory had the British ships been properly handled. Graves, however, for some as yet unexplained cause, failed ; and an indecisive engagement left his van so crippled that, upon the arrival of a squadron under Barras, which raised the French strength to thirty-six sail of the line, he lost no time in withdrawing to New York to refit ; and, before he could return to the Bay, Cornwallis had capitulated (October 19). Ill health had meanwhile compelled Rodney's return to England, and in his absence disaster followed disaster in the West Indies. Bouillé carried

St Eustatius by a *coup de main* (November 26), and, while Hood manœuvred brilliantly against de Grasse, reduced St Christopher (February 13,
1782). Nevis and Montserrat also fell into the hands of the French, and
Antigua, Barbados, and even Jamaica, were in imminent peril when
Rodney's advent changed the aspect of affairs. Collecting his entire force
of thirty-six sail of the line off Martinique, he waited until de Grasse
slipped out of Fort Royal Bay (April 8, 1782) with the view of joining
the Spanish squadron off Hayti, and, at once giving chase, came up
with him in the offing between Dominica and Guadaloupe. De Grasse
commanded thirty-five sail of the line, and most of his ships were of
larger size and heavier armament than the British; and it would seem
that he, therefore, at first supposed that he could defeat his pursuers in
detail. At any rate, on April 9 his rear offered battle to Rodney's van,
but with no result; and, when on the 12th de Grasse resumed the offensive, the engagement became general, and Rodney carried the day by the
then novel manœuvre of breaking the enemy's line. Shortly after sunset
de Grasse struck his flag, and surrendered to Hood. In all, eight ships
of the line were taken or destroyed: the rest made good their escape.
The victory was less complete than it might have been, had the pursuit
been pressed with due vigour; nevertheless, it completely demoralised the
enemy, and practically terminated the war in the West.

In the East the capitulation (October 17, 1778) of Pondicherry to
General Munro and Commodore Vernon was followed by the expulsion of
the French from Chandernagore, Mahé, and the rest of the settlements
in India, and by the reduction of the Dutch settlements at Negapatam
(November 13, 1781) and Trincomalee (January 11, 1782). The situation
was, however, materially changed by the appearance off the Coromandel
coast of a French squadron of twelve sail of the line under the able and
gallant Suffren, who, after a brush with a numerically superior force
under Commodore Johnstone off Porto Praya, Cape Verde Islands
(April 16, 1781), had outsailed the British commander and frustrated
his designs on the Cape of Good Hope. In the course of 1782,
Vice-Admiral Hughes and Suffren fought several desperate actions, off
Sadras (February 17), Providien (April 12), Cuddalore (July 6) and
Trincomalee, which Suffren had meanwhile reduced (September 3). In
all these battles the advantage rested with the French, notwithstanding
that after the first there was no great disparity of strength; nor did
reinforcements, which gave Hughes eighteen ships of the line to Suffren's
fifteen in a final engagement off Cuddalore (June 20, 1783) enable him
to gain a decisive victory over his brilliant adversary.

While the air was heavy with rumours of imminent French invasion,
two liberal measures of a quiet character were carried through Parliament. By Sir George Savile's Act (18 Geo. III, c. 60) such Catholics as
would take the oaths of allegiance and supremacy in a form specially
adapted to negative the supposed pretensions of their Church in matters

temporal were relieved from the penal statute (11 and 12 Will. III, c. 4)
by which they were debarred from inheriting or otherwise acquiring real
estate within England and Wales and, if officiating priests or schoolmasters, were liable to perpetual imprisonment. By a further Act,
English Protestant Dissenting Ministers were relieved from the subscription to the declaration of faith required by the Toleration Act (1 Will.
and Mary, c. 18). Meanwhile, as is narrated in another chapter, Ireland,
suffering the more acutely by the War because of the shackles set upon
her commerce by British monopolism, now at last bestirred herself, and
organised a volunteer force of 40,000 men, while demanding through her
Parliament the abolition of the entire system of vexatious restrictions
imposed on her, and shortened supply to a six months' Bill (November,
1779). Shelburne and Rockingham, though both but recent converts
to her cause, gave it the support at St Stephen's which the gravity of
the crisis demanded. North, who in the previous year had made a
trifling concession, surrendered at discretion, and thus, at one stroke,
Ireland achieved her commercial emancipation.

The movement for curtailing the corrupt influence of the Crown, on
the other hand, made but slow progress. The House of Commons, indeed,
on the motion of Dunning, ably supported by Sir Fletcher Norton,
affirmed the principle of a periodical scrutiny into the Civil List (April,
1780); but the Government had still strength enough to wreck
Burke's grand scheme for the reform of the civil and certain other establishments by the abolition of sinecures and other redundant offices, the
consolidation of such offices as overlapped one another, and the due
regulation of the system of payment (May 18). Sir Philip Jennings
Clerke's Contractors' Bill reached the House of Lords, but was thrown
out by the Thurlow-ridden majority, which also negatived motions by
Richmond and Shelburne for the revision of the Civil List, the extraordinary charges of the services, and the entire system of public finance
(December, 1779, and February, 1780).

Parliament, however, was no true index of the public mind. Reform,
economic and parliamentary, was eagerly discussed at county meetings,
in which Yorkshire and Middlesex led the way. Numerous petitions
for reform were presented at St Stephen's, and associations spread the
agitation throughout the country. Fox and Richmond headed the
movement, the latter declaring for annual Parliaments, manhood suffrage,
and electoral districts. In the midst of this ferment, a singular outbreak
of popular frenzy, originating in a tumultuous demonstration in support
of a petition presented at St Stephen's by Lord George Gordon for the
repeal of the recent Roman Catholic Relief Act, was suffered by the
culpable supineness of the Government to spread anarchy and arson
throughout a great part of the metropolis, and was only suppressed by
the military, not without considerable loss of life (June 2–8). These
outrages, nevertheless, strengthened the hands of the Government, whose

partisans were not slow to attribute them to the machinations of the Whigs. The Court, after some coquetting with Rockingham, gathered courage, and, further exhilarated by the tidings of the capture of Charleston, resolved on an appeal to the country. Parliament was accordingly dissolved (September 1) ; and the verdict of the polls gave the Government a fresh, albeit a very brief, lease of life. During the first session of the new Parliament the Opposition was powerless. The Dutch War, against which they did not fail to protest, was popular both in Parliament and in the country ; and a new war loan of £12,000,000, though raised on terms so extravagant as seriously to damage North's reputation, was nevertheless sanctioned. Burke reintroduced his Establishment Bill, and Clerke his Contractors' Bill, but neither measure was committed, and a Bill for the disfranchisement of revenue officers shared the same fate. Lord Sandwich's administration of the navy was attacked and defended with the usual success.

The session closed (July 18, 1781) without more important result in the way of domestic legislation than a measure validating marriages solemnised in good faith in places of worship unauthorised by the Marriage Act of 1751. In Ireland, under the genial sway of the new Viceroy, Lord Carlisle, the Separatist cause made rapid progress. Across the Atlantic, the capitulation of Yorktown (October 19) virtually settled the question of the independence of the United States.

When Parliament reassembled (November 27), the fate of the Administration was already sealed. The old high language was indeed still heard from the Throne; but Fox' amendment to the Address censuring Ministers collectively, and his subsequent arraignment of Sandwich in particular as primarily responsible for the naval reverses, were defeated by reduced majorities ; and, on Conway's motion for an Address deprecating the continuance of offensive operations in America, the majority fell to one (February 22, 1782). The motion was thereupon renewed and carried without a division (February 27). The Reply which the Address elicited from the Throne being ambiguous, a further motion denouncing as enemies to the country all who should contribute to the prolongation of offensive war in America was also carried without a division (March 4). All classes were now weary of the War; and, though a new loan of £13,500,000 was carried, a vote of censure moved by a typical Tory, Sir John Rous, was only negatived by a majority of nine (March 15). On the 20th, North anticipated its renewal by announcing that his Administration was no more.

(3) THE YEARS OF PEACE, AND THE RISE OF THE YOUNGER PITT.

(1782–93.)

When the last parliamentary struggle of Lord North was over (March 20, 1782), and the beaten Minister drove away, in his coach, from the House of Commons, with "the advantage of being in the secret," Lord Rockingham entered (March 27) into a troubled inheritance. All the omens were unfavourable. The King was ostentatiously hostile; "the fatal hour has come," he wrote; and he talked of retiring to Hanover. The Whig party were not yet a compact body. The new Minister was committed to an adventurous policy. He had always encouraged the ambitions of the Irish Nationalists; and Ireland, still unconciliated, was on the brink of rebellion. He had always opposed the influence of the Crown; and the King was disposed to make a struggle for what remained of historic prerogative. Rockingham had always advocated drastic measures of royal and administrative economy, and he was now to undertake the ever dangerous experiment of retrenchment. He had, throughout the rebellion in the colonies, been constant to the American cause, and the Americans were now in a position to dictate the dismemberment of the Empire. To carry out a consistent policy in all these cases was a difficult task. The troubles of forming an administration began early. A preliminary negotiation, through Lord Thurlow, begun on March 11, 1782, while North was still in office, ended unsuccessfully on March 18, because Rockingham wished to set out to the King the conditions of his acceptance of office, while the King wished him to take office unconditionally, and settle the terms afterwards. Meantime an ineffectual negotiation, not known at the time, had been tried by the King with Lords Shelburne and Gower. Both refused the white elephant of office, and Shelburne, knowing his own weakness, urged on the King the necessity of sending for Rockingham. The King, after hitherto persistently refusing even to see Rockingham, whom he disliked, at length conceded the point, and accepted the unwelcome terms proposed to him; on March 27 the new Minister kissed hands. Lord Rockingham was First Lord of the Treasury; Lord John Cavendish, Chancellor of the Exchequer; Lord Camden, President of Council; the Duke of Grafton, Lord Privy Seal; Lord Thurlow (as a concession to the King), Lord Chancellor; Lord Shelburne and Charles Fox, Joint Secretaries of State. Among the minor appointments was that of Edmund Burke, who was made Paymaster of the Forces—a well paid office which did not, however, admit him to the Cabinet. The omission was questioned by many contemporary critics, and condemned by many subsequent commentators, perhaps not very judiciously, as discreditable to a party which his genius did so much to adorn.

CH. XIII.

The demands which Rockingham had made upon the King, first through Thurlow and again through Shelburne, were chiefly these: the acknowledgment of American independence; the curtailment of the patronage and influence of the Crown; the disqualification of contractors from sitting in the House of Commons; the exclusion of the numerous revenue officers from the privilege of voting; the abolition of sinecure offices; and the introduction of a system of rigid economy into all the departments of the Government. The programme was sufficiently large and radical; but it included everything for which the opposition to North had contended. Every separate item had, however, in the eyes of the King, an obvious relation to his known wishes and to his suspected policy. That the King should have been reluctant to submit to the new *régime* was not unnatural. Its advent inflicted on him the chagrin of a personal defeat. Dunning, Fox, Burke, Rockingham himself, had, one and all, made themselves conspicuous as personal opponents of the King; nor had they refrained from insulting personal reflexions.

The affairs of Ireland were the first to which the attention of the Ministry was peremptorily called. Two Acts of ancient date stood in the way of Irish legislative independence. One was the Irish Act, 10 Henry VII, cap. 4, commonly called " Poynings' Law." By this Act, no Parliament could be held in Ireland without the consent of England having been first sought and obtained, and no legislation passed without the substance of it being first submitted to the King of England and his Council. This Act was obviously restrictive of legislative freedom, but the Viceroys had never enforced it rigorously. Moreover, if the Act limited the powers of a Parliament which never represented the people, it had some well-understood merits in restraining the Viceroys from acts of selfish tyranny. The other Act was 6 George I, cap. 5, a declaratory statute affirming the right of Great Britain to legislate for Ireland, and declaring that the Irish House of Lords had no right to judge of, affirm, or reverse, any judgment of the Irish Courts. The repeal of these Acts was the demand made upon the new Ministry. The Irish Parliament, which had temporarily adjourned over the Easter recess, met on April 16, by special summons from the Speaker, ordering every member to be in his place, " as he tended the rights of Ireland." All efforts, by Portland in Dublin and by Fox from Westminster, to effect a postponement or compromise failed. Grattan, as an amendment to the address, moved his declaration of rights, in a speech which has become part of the national literature. The amendment was carried without division, though not without debate. The demands to be made upon Great Britain were settled, and a short adjournment to May 4, and then to May 27, was arranged, in order to await the results from Westminster. At Westminster there was little delay. Fox, on April 8, while protesting against the abandonment of the supremacy of England over Ireland, promised an early and complete measure. On the 9th, he presented a message from the King, recommending the consideration of Irish affairs; and hereupon proposed that, as it was impossible to proceed on the little information before the House, reports should be received from the Executive in Ireland before further steps were taken. Shelburne, on the other hand, asserted in the Lords that there was no need for further documents: "he was sure that every noble lord" was fully acquainted with the circumstances. He also asserted that the Irish leaders had "blended moderation with their steadiness"—a fact which was not very apparent. The address to the King was carried in both Houses, on May 17. The Act of George I was repealed, the necessary communications being made to the Lord Lieutenant in Ireland in advance of the royal signature to the repealing Act. On the reassembling of the Irish Parliament on May 27, the concessions made at Westminster were announced. The sum of £100,000 was voted for the service of the British navy; and £50,000 was offered for the purchase of an estate for Grattan. An address was voted to the Viceroy; Poynings' Act was, without special mention, repealed by the Act 21 and 22 George III, cap. 47 (Irish) "to regulate the Manner of passing Bills"; and Ireland entered on the short period of legislative independence which was to last till the Union.

Meanwhile, other events were occupying the attention of Ministers in England. From the beginning, the new Ministry was but loosely united. Fox had declared, before the Ministry was fully formed, that he perceived there were two parties in it, one devoted to the King and one to the nation. Shelburne was, of course, the King's man, and Fox the man for the nation. The jealousy of Fox towards Shelburne was acute, and he watched his colleague with suspicious eyes. On April 28, he describes Shelburne as "ridiculously jealous of my encroachment on his department." And, again, "he affects the Minister more and more every day, and is, I believe, perfectly confident that the King intends to make him so. Provided we can stay in long enough to have given a good stout blow to the influence of the Crown, I do not think it much signifies how soon we go out after." Posterity, looking back with impartial eyes on the situation, and aware that there was Ireland to pacify, Europe and America to conciliate, and the resources of the kingdom to safeguard, can hardly agree that to accept office under the King, merely in order to undermine his prerogative and then leave the country to its fate in other hands, was an ambition worthy of a statesman. Nor was Shelburne free from blame. Having easier access to the King than his colleagues, he made use of it largely for the purpose of patronage. Dunning was created a peer without Rockingham's knowledge. Barré was rewarded with a pension. Fox complained to Grafton that he was constantly thwarted in the Cabinet; and he was always on the point of resigning. The measures of economy to which Ministers were committed were with difficulty accomplished. The plan having been submitted by a royal message, the address of thanks was made the vehicle of reluctant but effusive

CH. XIII.

compliments to the King; it was "the best of messages, from the best of Kings, to the best of people," said Burke; but he could not refrain from pointing out that the measure was one of his own suggestion. Shelburne, on the other hand, was very specific in declaring that the message was the personal act of the King, and by no means framed on the model of that which had been put forward on a previous occasion, *i.e.* by Burke. The saving to be effected was only £72,368 per annum— hardly enough to excite a tempest of popular gratitude. And, as it was, after all, to be applied to the payment of interest on the arrears of the King's Civil List (£296,000), a confused impression was left that there had been no saving at all, but only a little financial juggling for the benefit of the creditors of the Crown. Several parts of the scheme had to be given up. A number of sinecures remained untouched; one of these, the clerkship of the Pells, being, as was alleged by Horace Walpole, retained in order that Burke might confer it on his son. But something practical had been done. An Act was also passed to prevent revenue officers from voting; and another excluded contractors from sitting in the House of Commons. The resolution which had affirmed the disability of John Wilkes to sit in Parliament was expunged from the Journals. Thus, somewhat disheartened by concessions to Ireland, disappointed at the result of financial reforms, and divided by growing jealousies, the Ministers found themselves face to face with the imperative duty of deciding the question of peace or continued war, with France, Spain, Holland, and America.

It can hardly be said that they were negligent in negotiation. Fox, as Foreign Minister, had taken the subject seriously to heart. From the first, he set himself to secure the aid of the Empress Catharine II of Russia in negotiating peace with Holland, against which England had been carrying on war since 1780—when Holland, in violation of existing treaties, had joined the "Armed Neutrality," proceeding (in 1781) to recognise the independence of the American Colonies. His correspondence with Sir James Harris at St Petersburg shows how earnestly he sought to secure Russian cooperation: he even went the length of offering to bribe the officers of the imperial Court—a proposal discountenanced by Harris. The death of Rockingham and Fox' subsequent resignation prevented the negotiation from being carried to an issue; and, though the mediatorship of Russia and Prussia was more or less recognised in the conclusion of the Peace of 1783, it never was an important factor in the negotiations. Contemporaneously with the Russian negotiations, steps had been taken to negotiate with Franklin in Paris. From 1779, propositions had at various times been entertained, at Philadelphia and in London, tending to a peace, but nothing had come of them. A resolution in favour of peace had been carried in the House of Commons in 1781, and North had taken some steps in that direction. In 1782 an Act was passed to enable the King to conclude a peace or truce. On April 6, Shelburne sent to Franklin

Richard Oswald, as a man of "pacifical" disposition, "fully apprised of Lord Shelburne's mind." On April 8, Franklin reported to Shelburne his interview with Oswald and Vergennes, with the explanation that the object was for a "general peace." In this interview with Oswald, Franklin committed to his care a paper in which a proposal was made for the cession of Canada. On this point much discussion—not yet fully ended—has arisen. Oswald always asserted that Shelburne, of whose mind he was "fully apprised," entertained the proposition. On the other hand, it is obvious from the *Diplomatic Correspondence of the Revolution* (the sole first-hand authority for the proceedings from day to day) that Shelburne did not formally adopt the suggestion; that he replied unfavourably; and that he did not think it worth while to place it before his colleagues for consideration. North had initiated the proposal before his retirement by means of a private agent, in March, 1782, as appears from a letter of Rayneval to Franklin, dated April 13. The offer was known to Vergennes. Franklin naturally adopted the idea at the opening of the new negotiations. His first plan was, that by the sale of lands in Canada a fund could be raised to compensate the Loyalists, to whose claim Vergennes was favourably inclined. This plan Franklin soon abandoned; and he was afterwards hostile, throughout the negotiations, to all the Loyalist claims. On May 9, Thomas Grenville was sent to Paris by Fox, in whose new department of Foreign Affairs the negotiations for a general peace naturally lay. Grenville was always overmatched in negotiation by Franklin and Vergennes. His chief work was, in effect, to stimulate the jealousy of Fox against Shelburne and Oswald. Up to a certain point Vergennes and Franklin worked harmoniously. But a distrust had been growing in the mind of Adams and of Jay towards France. The French Minister was favourable to the claims of the Loyalists; and he was not eager to press the claims of the Americans to the fisheries and to the *hinterland* of colonial territory. According to Jay, the French Minister "did not play fair." Before the negotiations had proceeded to the point of an agreement as to terms, Lord Rockingham died, on July 1, 1782, and the whole chain of negotiation was temporarily broken.

The whole system of government in England was, in fact, broken. The party which had made it a principle to dictate to the Crown the choice of Ministers was now unable to choose a Minister. "The Crown," said Horace Walpole, "devolved upon the King of England on the death of Lord Rockingham." Fox was naturally the nominee of his friends. The Duke of Richmond was ambitious, but was too deeply pledged to drastic measures of Reform. Fox pressed on the King the nomination of the Duke of Portland. The King, however, had made up his mind. There was a momentary chance that Lord North might be recalled; but Pitt refused to serve under him. Shelburne was sent for. Fox, who had long been restive and resentful, passionately refused to

CH. XIII.

serve with Shelburne. He resigned, thinking that he would be followed by the whole Rockingham connexion. He was followed only by the Duke of Portland, Lord John Cavendish, Burke, and Sheridan. The Duke of Richmond remained at the Ordnance, and Viscount Keppel continued head of the Admiralty. Shelburne proceeded to fill up the vacant places. Lord Grantham and Thomas Townshend became Secretaries of State; Pitt became Chancellor of the Exchequer at twenty-three; and Lord Temple went to Ireland. Lord Camden remained President of Council, and Thurlow continued to be Chancellor. The Cabinet now consisted of seven Chathamite Whigs, two Rockingham Whigs, and two members, Grantham and Thurlow, who were not strictly of any party. The triumph of Shelburne seemed to be complete.

In the months which elapsed between July 11, 1782, when Shelburne became head of the Government, and December 5, when Parliament met, much was done. The peace negotiations were pushed to completion. The situation had changed somewhat in favour of Great Britain. On April 12, Admiral Rodney, who had been commissioned by North, had defeated the fleet of France in the West Indies. The Rockingham Administration had sent an order for his withdrawal; but the news of his victory reached England a day too late to stop the order. Thus, the Ministry were compelled to glorify and reward the man they had dismissed, and to take what credit they could for the victory they had not expected. If the state of affairs in America had been encouraging, Rodney's victory might have prolonged the contest. But all parties were weary of the war and desirous of peace. France was dismayed at the defeat of de Grasse, and reluctant to concede further financial aid to the Colonists. Spain was disheartened by the failure before Gibraltar. Holland was under pressure from Russia. The American leaders were in despair at the discontent of the people, the mutinous spirit of the army, and the lack of all material resources for carrying on the conflict. The American negotiators at Paris had come to the conclusion to make a separate peace. Franklin held out long against this conclusion; but an intercepted letter from Marbois, the French *chargé d'affaires* in America (March 13, 1782), advising Vergennes unfavourably to the American claims to the fisheries and the territory of the valley of the Mississippi and the Ohio, which was put before Franklin, precipitated an agreement among the negotiators. On November 30 provisional articles of peace between the Colonies and Great Britain were signed. On December 15 Vergennes wrote to Franklin a dignified protest against the signing of the articles without consultation with France, and contrary to the instructions from Congress. Franklin wrote a reply, apologising for the "indiscretion," but hoping that Vergennes would not permit the English Ministry to suppose they had divided America from France. On February 14, 1783, a cessation of arms was proclaimed by King George, and, on the 20th, a like proclamation was made by Congress.

On February 24, Shelburne resigned office, and the negotiations were again suspended.

The events which led to the resignation of Shelburne may be briefly related. Coming into office with a following which, pitted against the party of Fox and the party of North, left him in a minority, his continuance in office was from the first doubtful. From July to December he had had a free hand in the negotiations. When Parliament met on December 5, 1782, the elements of opposition, which had used the recess for the purpose of agitation and intrigue, began to unite. The King's Speech contained the announcement of the provisional peace, but referred to "so great a dismemberment of the Empire." On this point great differences of opinion were expressed by Ministers. Shelburne, in the Lords, declared that the grant of American independence was revocable, should there be no final general peace. Pitt, in the Commons, asserted (December 11) that the recognition could not be revoked in any case; and General Conway supported him. But the King interpreted his speech in the sense adopted by Shelburne; and the Opposition naturally made much of this conflict of statements. Pitt was, indeed, obliged to confess that he was mistaken. Ministers were, however, sustained by an overwhelming majority. On January 27, 1783, the preliminary articles of peace with France, Spain and America were tabled. The amendments moved by the Opposition were vehemently debated. Pitt's speech was not very successful, and in the course of it he made an attack on Sheridan's theatrical associations, which produced the famous retort about the "Angry Boy." The amendments were carried by 224 to 208, Ministers being left in a minority. In the course of the debate the coalition between Fox and North, which had been rumoured, became apparent. On February 21, Lord John Cavendish moved resolutions of censure on the Peace. Fox in his speech admitted the necessity of a coalition; but Pitt, with his vigour renewed, attacked it with immense spirit and "in the name of the public safety forbade the banns." The amendments were again carried by 224 to 208; and on the 24th Shelburne resigned. Events had dictated the resignation, apart from the vote of the House. Keppel had resigned; Richmond had refused to attend Council; Grafton had informed the King of his intention to retire; Camden had advised Shelburne to give up the struggle; and Temple was dissatisfied in Ireland. North and Fox had put aside personal ambitions, and agreed upon the Duke of Portland as their leader. The Duke had indeed been negotiating beforehand and had approached Richmond and Temple; but both refused. The King did not yield without a struggle, and importuned Shelburne, who vainly put forward Pitt. After a day or two of hesitation, during which he is said to have attended for a few hours at the Treasury and prepared a list of Ministers, Pitt finally abandoned the dangerous task. An appeal was made to North; but he was too deeply committed to Fox;

CH. XIII.

Lord Gower, too, was tried unsuccessfully. Some differences of opinion now arose between Fox and North as to the distribution of offices; but on April 1 the Ministry was completed. The Government consisted of the Duke of Portland, First Lord of the Treasury; Lord North, Home Secretary; Fox, Foreign Secretary; Lord John Cavendish, Chancellor of the Exchequer; Viscount Keppel, Admiralty; Viscount Townshend, Ordnance; Lord Stormont, President of Council; the Earl of Carlisle, Privy Seal; the Chancellorship was presently put into commission, as Thurlow was not acceptable. Burke returned to his Paymastership, somewhat dejected; Sheridan was made Treasurer of the Navy; Lord Northington went to Ireland, with William Wyndham as Secretary.

The business of the session was but little interrupted. An American Intercourse Bill was introduced, but not then pressed; but a Bill to remove restrictions on American trade was carried. An enquiry into the sufferings of the Loyalists was ordered, and certain Loyalist troops were placed on half-pay. The session closed on July 16, 1783. The new and memorable session opened on November 11. The King's Speech announced that definitive Treaties of Peace had been signed on September 2 and 3 with America and all the Allies, except Holland, with which Power preliminaries only had been settled. There was no debate. The terms had been discussed in detail during the various debates, from the accession of Shelburne in July, 1782, to the close on February 24, 1783. The negotiation of treaties of peace had not been favourable to the Ministry of 1713, or to the Ministry of 1763; and neither the Ministry of Shelburne, nor the Coalition, was to prove more fortunate. The Treaties now accepted were much the same as those all but concluded by Shelburne; though Fox in his speech of November 11, 1783, made the most of such changes as he had been able to secure in the definitive treaty with France. The main articles of the Treaties remained unaltered. France obtained certain rights of fishing and drying fish on the uninhabited coast of Newfoundland, and the islands of St Pierre and Miquelon were ceded to her. She also obtained St Lucia and Tobago; but Great Britain retained Dominica, Grenada, St Vincent, St Christopher, Nevis, and Montserrat. The French gained Senegal and Goree in Africa; the English retained Fort James and the river Gambia. The French regained their establishments in Orissa and Bengal, Pondicherry and Karikal, Mahé and Surat, with some trade advantages. The provisions of the Treaty of Utrecht (1713) were abrogated as to the demolition of Dunkirk. Spain was forced to abandon all hope of Gibraltar, but obtained Minorca. She also retained West, and Great Britain ceded East, Florida; while Spain conceded the right to cut logwood in the Bay of Honduras, and gave up Providence and the Bahamas. The terms with the United States were open to some of the objections which they called forth. The boundaries of the country were enlarged unduly; the fisheries concessions were too liberal; the provisions for the collection of debts due before the Peace were too easily evaded; and the conditions as to the Loyalists were (so far as the Americans were concerned) insincere and inoperative. The concessions to France in the Newfoundland Fisheries, abrogated by the War of 1812, but renewed at Ghent in 1814 in a curtailed form, became a source of infinite trouble and correspondence. But, as it was impossible to foresee the future, and as peace was necessary to all parties, special censure can hardly be passed on the negotiations of men who were politicians and not prophets. To all the parties to the negotiations the Treaties were welcome—to the American Colonies they were a godsend. The latest authoritative writer on the subject, Van Tyne, sums up the situation thus: "Disorganisation was seen everywhere—in politics, in finance, in the army. Peace came like a stroke of good fortune rather than a prize that was won. Congress (January 14, 1784) could hardly assemble a quorum to ratify the Treaty."

Other subjects were simultaneously coming to the front. The question of Reform was not a new one. In 1766, 1770 and 1771 Chatham had given it his eloquent and prophetic patronage. Alderman Sawbridge had been making annual propositions in its favour since 1771. In 1776, Wilkes had moved for leave for a Bill proposing extensive reforms in representation. In 1780, the Duke of Richmond had presented a measure for annual parliaments, universal suffrage and equal electoral districts. The Gordon riots had temporarily discredited all such efforts; and, at the close of the session of 1780, the King's Speech warned the people against "the hazard of innovation." On May 7, 1782, Pitt moved for a Committee. His proposal was rejected by only 161 to 141. A year later (May 7, 1783) he brought forward a definite scheme which caused a division amongst Ministers. Fox supported it; North opposed; Burke was so badly received that he declined to proceed; Dundas, who had opposed Pitt's first measure, supported his second; but the proposal was rejected. Pitt's popularity was, however, greatly increased by his action in this matter.

Meanwhile, under the preceding two Administrations as well as in that under the new Coalition, the affairs of India, of which an account is given in another chapter, loomed large through the mists of political agitation at home. Since 1773 Warren Hastings was Governor-General, and in 1780 the East India Company's Charter was to expire after three years' notice. In 1781 there were discussions between the Directors and Lord North as to terms of renewal. In the same year, complaints and petitions had reached London from India concerning the conduct of Hastings, whose many enemies now began to be active. In 1781 an Act was passed (21 Geo. III, cap. 65) extending the privileges of the Company till three years' notice after 1791, regulating the dividends, and giving the Government larger powers over the political affairs of the Company. On April 9, 1781, North moved the House into committee to consider the affairs of India. On April 30, a secret Committee was named to enquire into the war in the Carnatic. Burke and Fox wished the Committee to be public;

but secrecy was maintained. On December 4 the Secret Committee was empowered to add the Maratha War to the scope of their enquiry. In March, 1782, North was out of office, and the Rockingham Administration was in. On April 15 Dundas, Chairman of the Secret Committee, moved a series of resolutions condemning the mode in which the two wars had been conducted. On April 24 a resolution condemning Hastings for his relations with Chief Justice Impey was passed; and on May 3 an address for the recall of Impey was voted. On May 30 Dundas carried a motion for the recall of Hastings, but on July 1, 1782, Rockingham died; Shelburne succeeded; and the Court of Proprietors, taking advantage of the change of Ministers, assumed authority to rescind the order for the recall of Hastings, which, in obedience to the House of Commons, the Directors had made.

On April 1, 1783, the Coalition was in office, and the parliamentary session opened on November 11 following. Pitt and the Opposition pressed for Reform, especially in India. Fox' reply was his famous India Bill, said, on incomplete and unsatisfactory authority, to have been the composition of Burke. Its first reading took place on November 18, when, contrary to modern custom, it was debated. A young speaker, John Scott (who, as Lord Eldon, was afterwards to become so familiar a figure in English public life) indicated at the outset the point which was in the minds of all, and against which North had forewarned Fox, viz. the too obvious exclusion of the powers of the Crown in the appointments under the Bill—the Commissioners being in the first instance nominated *en bloc* by the House, without reference to the Crown, for a period fixed and certain, though after that period the Crown might appoint. Fox observed the point at once, and, while complimenting Scott, not quite fairly accused him of stating his opinion with "a good deal of positiveness." Pitt immediately enlarged the breach made by Scott, and said that "the accession of power which it must certainly bring to the Ministers of the day was not the least considerable" of the objections to the Bill. On the lines thus laid down the opposition was conducted[1]. Fox' measure consisted of two Bills: one referring to the administrative

---

[1] The use of the terms "Crown" and "Ministers" all through the debates requires some discrimination. It illustrates a then existing difference in political theory. Fox' Bill presented to the Crown a list of party nominations, made first in the House, and not submitted in the Closet. This was a limitation of the Crown's prerogative, on well understood Whig lines. The appointments were for four years certain. This gave the appointing Ministers, through the persons appointed by them, an enormous and increasing patronage, even if they went out of office. Many Opposition speakers referred to the increase of the power of "the Crown" when they really meant the power of the Ministers. Pitt always spoke against "the Ministers." Under Pitt's Bill the Crown had no more real power than under Fox', since Ministers would naturally prepare for the Crown the lists of nominees. The difference was in great measure a matter of procedure, qualified by the personal feeling of the King, who was, no doubt, willing to accept as constitutional advice from Pitt what he resented as Whig dictation from Fox.

body in England, the other to the administrative powers in India. Petitions against the Bills were presented by the Company, and by the Lord Mayor and Aldermen of London; and counsel were heard at the bar of the House. On December 1 Fox moved the House into committee on the Bill, and Burke delivered the first of his memorable speeches on India; it occupies seventy-four columns of the Parliamentary History. At half-past four on the morning of December 2 the motion to go into committee was carried by 217 to 103. The third reading was carried by as large a vote. The names of the seven Commissioners had now been inserted, and Fox, accompanied by a triumphant procession, carried the Bills to the Lords. Here the Bills were debated on December 9. The Opposition was led by Thurlow and Temple; the Bills were supported by Loughborough and Carlisle. In the course of the debate a newspaper article was read by the Duke of Richmond stating that Temple had had an audience of the King, who had given him to understand that the Bills were "in the highest degree disagreeable to his Majesty." Temple admitted that he had tendered his advice to his Majesty, but would say no more than that it had been unfriendly to the Bills. The fate of the measure was sealed. Temple had in fact been authorised by the King to declare to his friends that the measure was objectionable to him, and that he should count as enemies those who voted for it. On December 17 the commitment of the Bill was rejected by a majority of nineteen. The Prince of Wales, who had voted for the measure on the first vote, was absent on the occasion of the final division.

The Ministers did not immediately resign as was generally expected. The King had been waiting for his opportunity to dismiss them. Writing to Fox on September 3 concerning the signature of the definitive Treaties, he had used this curious expression: "In States as in men, where dislike has once arose I never expect to see cordiality." He was now to prove his own philosophy. Late at night on the 18th, the King sent to Fox and North for their seals, which were handed to Temple, who next day wrote letters of dismissal to the other Ministers. On the 19th Pitt kissed hands, and proceeded to form an Administration. He had some initial difficulties. Camden refused; Grafton refused; Lord Mahon refused. Gower, who had contemplated total retirement, came to Pitt's rescue and offered to serve. Temple acted strangely. He had plotted the overthrow of Ministers; had advised the King how to proceed; had carried the King's message to the Lords; had received the seals of the dismissed Ministers; and had accepted the office of Secretary of State on December 19. On the 21st he resigned. On the vexed question as to the reason for this step, Lord Stanhope comes to the conclusion that Temple had asked for, or had expected, a dukedom, and, being refused, withdrew from the side of Pitt and the King. He never again filled any public position. In the new Administration Shelburne was not invited to take any part. He accepted a marquisate, with the promise of a dukedom if the King changed his policy of retaining that rank for members of the royal family. The events of the next few years, which gradually drove Pitt into a leadership of Toryism, equally impelled Shelburne (Marquis of Lansdowne) into a more intimate connexion with the Whigs and a general agreement with Fox and the Opposition. In spite of all the refusals, Pitt's Ministry was rapidly formed. He was himself First Lord of the Treasury and Chancellor of the Exchequer; Earl Gower, President of Council; the Duke of Rutland, Privy Seal; Lord Sydney—after Temple's resignation—and the Marquis of Carmarthen, Secretaries of State; Lord Thurlow, Lord Chancellor; Viscount Howe became First Lord of the Admiralty; the Duke of Richmond, Master-General of the Ordnance; Dundas, Treasurer of the Navy. Of the seven Cabinet Ministers, only Pitt was in the House of Commons, where Dundas was his chief support. Rutland subsequently went to Ireland, and was succeeded by Gower, as Lord Privy Seal. When Pitt's writ was moved for, the motion was received with derision. The Opposition, counting on an easy and early victory, proceeded to take matters into their own hands. They voted it a high crime and misdemeanour to report the opinion of the King on any public measure—though North was forced to confess that he had never felt any of the royal influence so much condemned by his present allies. They addressed the Crown against a dissolution. They refused payment of any money not already voted, postponed the Mutiny Bill, and carried a motion of want of confidence.

On January 14, 1784, Pitt moved for leave to bring in his India Bill, and leave was granted; on the 23rd, the second reading was taken. The Bill, which is more fully described in a later chapter, differed materially from that of Fox. The royal prerogative in the appointments to the Board of Control was maintained. The Board was to go out of office with Ministers, not, as in Fox' Bill, to be continued for four years without reference to any change of Ministers. It was to have no patronage; and the Company was left in control of administration and trade in India. On the second reading it was thrown out, but only by the small majority of eight. Fox, at once, moved for leave to bring in another Bill, but demanded to know if the discussion was to be interrupted by dissolution. Pitt refused to reply. From this date (January 23, 1784) the contest against his Ministry was carried on with vehemence, both in the House and in the country. In the House, the result was remarkable. At first, the Opposition majorities were large; but the House gradually grew weary of the contest; the echoes of hostile public opinion became formidable; and the majorities diminished from fifty-four to forty-seven, to thirty-nine, to twelve, to seven, and on March 8 to one. This was the last struggle of the Coalition in Opposition. In February a negotiation had been set on foot for a union of the friends of Pitt and Fox in one Cabinet. Both the leaders professed a willingness to join on "equal" terms; but what was meant by "equality" was a point that could not be settled, and the negotiation failed. On March 24 Parliament was prorogued; and on the 25th it was dissolved. The Great Seal was stolen from the Lord Chancellor's house by some over-zealous enthusiast; but a new one was speedily procured, for the purpose of the dissolution. The result was now a foregone conclusion. The King's active aid, Pitt's popularity, the India Bill of Pitt, the mistakes of the Opposition, and their actual defeat in the Commons—all contributed to a great Ministerial victory. Over a hundred and sixty members lost their seats, the greater part belonging to the Opposition. The first divisions in the new House showed majorities of from 147 to 168 for Pitt.

While three Administrations had been discussing the affairs of India, that country had been the scene of disquieting events. Haidar Ali had, indeed, been defeated by Sir Eyre Coote at Porto Novo (July 1, 1781), and was now (December, 1782) dead; but he had been succeeded by his ambitious son, Tipu Sultan, who, supported by a French force, was pressing on the divided forces of the English. At sea, affairs had gone badly for England, as indeed they had from 1746. Admiral Hughes and Admiral Suffren had, during 1782, encountered each other in force on several occasions, on February 16 and 17, on April 12, and on July 4, with indecisive results. The fort of Trincomalee was taken by the French on August 31. On September 3, 1782, and on June 30, 1783, naval engagements resulted unsatisfactorily for the British side. Operations on land were not more encouraging. The British under General Meadows had indeed captured Bednore with a large treasure; but the army was dispersed in detachments. On April 9 Tipu appeared before Bednore and, after a heroic resistance, the English army was forced to surrender. When this bad news arrived, during the discussion of Fox' India Bill, a mistaken expectation was entertained that it would promote the speedy passing of the Bill. The Treaties of Peace of 1783 brought about the retirement of the French from the service of Tipu. Peace was finally made with him on March 11, 1784, on the basis of a restoration of conquests.

Pitt's new Parliament met on May 18, 1784. The Opposition protested at great length against the dissolution which had destroyed them. The Westminster election case was raised by Fox, who had been a successful candidate; but in whose favour the sheriff refused to make a return, on the ground that a scrutiny had been demanded. The case was heard at bar, and the sheriff was ordered to proceed promptly with the scrutiny. The legislation of the session was largely fiscal. The budget, which was passed, included many new taxes. The franking privilege was amended; a Bill for the suppression of smuggling was passed; and provision was made for the arrears of the Civil List (£60,000). An Act was passed for the repeal of the Act confiscating estates in Scotland. The East India Company was granted an Act for its temporary relief. Hereupon, the great measure of the session, Pitt's India Bill (24 Geo. III, cap. 25), was introduced. Following the lines laid down in his Bill of January 14, it provided for a Board of Control, consisting of a Secretary of State, the Chancellor of the Exchequer and three Privy Councillors, all to be nominated by the Crown. The Commander-in-chief was to be nominated by the Crown. Commercial affairs were to be left in the hands of the Company, which was also to nominate all the chief officials in India, under the veto of the Crown. A special judicial tribunal was created, by ballot of the Lords and the Commons, for the trial of offences under the Act. The process was complicated. In each session twenty-six or more Peers, and forty or more Commoners were chosen by ballot in each House. On a case arising for trial, three Judges were appointed, and before these the names of the Peers and Commoners were placed in a box and drawn out singly. When, after the power of challenge had been liberally exercised, four Peers and six Commoners had been allowed, then the trial was to proceed. The Bill was moved for on July 6; was read a first time on July 9; and the House went into committee after the second reading on July 16. It was finally carried in the Commons on July 28, and in the Lords on August 9. Fox, throughout the session, continued to refer to the superior merits of his own Bill; and Pitt not less constantly retorted as to the assault made on the rights of the Crown.

One of his earliest efforts, in accordance with his general policy of fiscal legislation, was to bring forward a measure of commercial freedom with Ireland. His propositions, eleven in number, adopted during the recess by a Commission appointed by him, were at first carried in Ireland. When, after a long debate at Westminster, and the increase of the number of the resolutions to twenty in order to satisfy English jealousies, they were again considered in Ireland, they were carried by so small a majority that the Irish Government thought it best to withdraw them. A great opportunity for enlarged free trade was thus abandoned. The Westminster scrutiny occupied the House of Commons during part of two sessions. Pitt's persistence in continuing the scrutiny was not sustained by the House. An Act was passed which limited polling to fifteen days, and provision was made for an early return by the sheriffs. On the whole, the session of 1785 was unfavourable to Ministers.

In the conflict of European opinion during the years 1781 to 1785, which is discussed at length elsewhere, and which Sir James Harris, who was sent to the Hague, reported (December 6, 1784) to be "the most critical since the outbreak of the Thirty Years' War," England remained neutral. It had been provoked by the attempt of the Emperor Joseph II to abrogate the Barrier Treaty of 1715, the conditions of which were guaranteed by Great Britain, and to obtain the free navigation of the Scheldt. In the Treaty of November 8, 1785, by which war was averted, though the Barrier Treaty was in effect broken, England took no part.

Parliament met in 1786 on January 4. One important event was Pitt's measure for the gradual reduction of the public debt by means of a sinking fund. It was brought forward on March 29, and was passed with little debate, though Sheridan moved resolutions which he did not press to a vote. The scheme had an encouraging, though fallacious, appearance. It stood the test of much financial criticism, however, and continued in favour till 1828, when, after an elaborate report from a Committee, it was abolished. Other measures were adopted in 1866 and 1875 which remain operative still. Article 18 of the Treaty of 1783 with France having provided for a Treaty of Commerce, Eden was commissioned by Pitt to negotiate; and a Treaty was signed on September 26, 1786. It provided for a large measure of Free Trade between France and her dependencies, and Great Britain and her colonies. A Treaty was also arranged with Spain by which British settlers were to abandon Spanish territory in South America, and the liberty of cutting logwood in the Bay of Honduras was enlarged. The great event of the session was the beginning of the series of charges against Hastings, which ended in his impeachment. On February 7 Burke brought up the resolutions of May 30, 1782, for the recall of Hastings, and demanded the correspondence of the Governor-General with the Directors. The motion was carried. On the 20th, when the Benares charge was urged, Pitt significantly declared his impartiality; Hastings demanded a hearing at the bar, and was heard on May 1, when he made a long and laboured defence. On June 13, this charge was formulated, when Pitt, to the surprise of Hastings and the House, conceded that the fine of £500,000 imposed on Chait Singh by Hastings was an extortion. This practically settled the question of the impeachment, though it was not formally resolved till the following session. When Parliament met in 1787, Sheridan brought forward the charge against Hastings relating to the Princesses of Oudh, in a speech made memorable by the praise bestowed on its eloquence alike by Fox and Pitt. The charge was duly reported, and, a special committee of managers having been appointed to conduct an impeachment before the Lords, Hastings was taken into custody, but released on bail. And thus was begun that trial which figures so largely in the history and literature of England. It lasted till 1795, and ended in the acquittal of the accused on every charge, leaving him triumphant and ruined. His fellow in the accusations, Sir Elijah Impey, was more fortunate. In December, 1787, charges were made against him relating to the affair of Nuncomar. He made a successful defence, and the charge was abandoned.

In 1787, another question which caused more than ordinary debate at the time and which has been much discussed since, was brought before the House of Commons. The Prince of Wales, who had become an active supporter of the Opposition and was especially the ally of Fox' personal party, had exceeded his liberal income and was deeply in debt. An appeal to Parliament for aid was his only hope. The King refused any assistance of his own, and Pitt was unwilling to proceed without the command of the King; " he had," he said, " no instructions upon the subject." The Prince's friends were divided in opinion, and some retired temporarily from attendance in Parliament. Alderman Newnham brought the subject forward on April 20, 1787. In the course of the debate a member alluded in a vague but significant way to the current rumour of the Prince's marriage to Mrs Fitzherbert. On April 30 Fox made a specific and formal denial of the marriage, alleging the direct authority of the Prince for this statement. In spite of a subsequent vague explanation by Sheridan, intended to shield the lady, the denial was accepted, and a generous provision was made for the Prince. The *bona fides* of Fox' statement has been the subject of dispute. It was based on a letter written by the Prince to him on December 11, 1785. Ten days after that date, the Prince was, however, duly married by a Church clergyman in the presence of witnesses. All London society was possessed of a secret which the principal parties took little care to keep; and Fox must have been familiar with all the gossip of the time. Yet in 1787, after the lapse of sixteen months, he used the Prince's letter of 1785 as his authority for a denial of the marriage. Lord Holland contends that Fox was deceived, and his friends alleged that he did not speak to the Prince for a year; but it is certain that he corresponded with him. Meanwhile, the Prince had confessed to Grey that he was married; and Fox, immediately after his denial, was informed of the marriage by Harris, who was in the house when the event took place, though not one of the actual witnesses. The Prince's letter of 1785 was a transparent prevarication, and can hardly have imposed on Fox, who for some time after his denial in 1787 absented himself from the House.

In 1788, the question of the Slave Trade, which had long been agitated in England, and as to which a Committee of the Privy Council had recently collected much information, was brought forward by William Wilberforce; but, owing to his illness, it fell to Pitt to introduce the subject in the House of Commons. The trade in slaves had been legalised by charters in 1631, 1633 and 1672; by Act of Parliament in 1698; by treaty in 1713, 1725 and 1748. In 1772 Lord Mansfield in a celebrated case declared it illegal in England. A humane agitation was started by Granville Sharp and continued by Clarkson, Zachary Macaulay and Wilberforce. And finally Pitt, on the absence of Wilberforce, through illness, took charge of the business in the House, though he reserved his own opinion till the next session.

On May 9, he moved a resolution which had the strong support of Fox. It was that the House would take the question into consideration in the following session. Fox, on this occasion, declared for total abolition. The resolution was agreed to, and at a later date a

Bill was introduced and passed. It was amended in the Lords; and the amendments not being accepted in the Commons, a Compromise Bill (28 Geo. III, cap. 54), prepared by Sir William Dolben, was passed. This compromise bill, for the regulation of the trade on more humane conditions, was made necessary by the fact that the Lords' amendments had made the original bill a Money Bill, which could not originate in the Lords. In this year a Committee of the House was, with Fox' support, also appointed (June 6) to enquire into the losses of the American Loyalists. The promises of the American negotiators in 1783 had not been fulfilled; the Loyalists had been driven from their homes and harshly persecuted; and Parliament was already pledged in their favour. Commissioners had been appointed in 1783 to investigate their claims, and a series of reports presented. Parliament now finally disposed of the business. In 1788, the Commissioners reported that they had examined in all sixteen hundred and eighty claims, and had allowed £1,887,548 for payment. Pitt's proposals were made with much care as to details. The amount allowed in liquidation of the entire class of claims was £3,033,091, of which £2,096,326 had already been paid. There remained only £936,765, which was paid. A loyal address was presented to the King at the conclusion of the payments, signed by the representatives of the Loyalists of all the old Colonies expressing their grateful thanks for his " most gracious and effectual recommendations of their claims to the just and generous consideration of Parliament."

The most important question that had hitherto occupied the attention of Parliament was now suddenly sprung upon public notice. The health of the King (December, 1788) became curiously disturbed. On October 20, at the levee, he gave obvious signs of derangement. Parliament having met on November 20, the Lords, after a short adjournment, appointed a Committee to examine the King's physicians, and another to search for precedents. The Commons on December 4 received the report of the physicians, which was, in substance, that his Majesty was seriously incapacitated, but that there was great probability of his recovery. A Committee of the Privy Council, of both parties (54 in all, of whom 24 were of the Opposition), had examined the physicians on the day before their report was considered in the Commons. The doctors now began to differ politically as well as professionally, thus adding to the difficulties of the situation. Fox, who had been abroad, now hurriedly returned. He at once put forward the right of the Prince of Wales to assume the Regency without restrictions. This gave the key-note to the debates which followed, and to the agitation which arose in the country. Pitt promptly proceeded to " unwhig the gentleman " by challenging the constitutionality of Fox' doctrine as to the Prince's right to the Regency without the consent of the two Houses. It was, he said, a revival of the doctrine of Divine Right, which a Whig leader should be the last to put forward. The debates in both Houses

CH. XIII.

showed curious developments of doctrine.   In the Lords, Thurlow made
his celebrated speech in which he said: " When I forget my King, may
my God forget me "—though it was well known that he was privately
pledged to advance the Prince's cause.   Fox went so far as to hint
that the Prince had the right to enforce his claim, and was refraining
only out of respect for the two Houses; while Pitt advocated with
vigour the theory of the right of the two Houses to settle the Regency
on such terms as they were pleased to dictate.   It was now a struggle
for office between the Ministers and the Opposition.   The known
alliance between the Prince and the Opposition made it certain that
as Regent he would call them to power.   This was so well understood
that the Duke of Portland had prepared a list of Ministers.   On
January 19, 1789, Pitt gave notice of resolutions involving a highly
restricted Regency.   The resolutions were carried; the Lords concurred;
and at a conference an address to the Prince was agreed upon.

The Prince, in his judicious reply, accepted the Regency " in conformity to the resolutions now communicated to me."   The hopes of
the Opposition now ran high.   Pitt was preparing to resume his legal
practice.   On February 3 a new session was opened by commission, and
on the 5th the Regency Bill was passed.   It provided that the Prince
should exercise the Regency during the King's illness; that the care of
the King's person should remain with the Queen; that no royal property
was to be alienated; that no office or pension should be granted save
during pleasure, nor any peerages created save in the royal family.   On
February 13, all the speculations of the politicians were confounded by
the sudden announcement of the King's recovery.

During the excitement in London the atmosphere of Dublin had also
been disturbed.   The Duke of Rutland, the young friend of Pitt, died
on October 24, 1787, and had been succeeded by the Marquis of
Buckingham.   The Irish Government began to lose strength, owing
to the expected change in England.   Grattan had been in London in the
company of Fox and the Prince.   He hurried to Dublin before matters
had reached a crisis, and, on the very day on which Pitt introduced
the Regency Bill, moved for an address to the Prince to take on himself
the unrestricted Regency of Ireland.   In vain it was pointed out that
it was necessary to wait for the action of the British Parliament,
so as to avoid differences in legislation.   When Pitt's Bill arrived, no
notice was taken of it.   Grattan's address was carried, and presented
to the Viceroy, who refused to touch or forward it.   A deputation was
appointed to carry it to the Prince in person.   When the deputation
arrived in London, the King had recovered.   Meanwhile, certain gentlemen and noblemen in Dublin, some of whom were in office, had signed
a round robin to oppose any Government that would disturb them for
voting for the Regency Bill.   The round robin was communicated to
the Viceroy, who, in due time, exacted a separate submission from each

of the signatories; dissolved their compact; dismissed some, purchased others; and so put an end to what was meant to be a formidable conspiracy. It was at this very time, while the royal authority was upheld and respected in England and the hands of the King's Ministers were strengthened, that the King of France and his Ministers were entering the rapids of revolution.

The session of 1789 in England reopened after a short adjournment on March 10. Addresses were passed concerning the King's recovery, without any protest save from Fox, who protested against an address to the Queen, and suggested rather one to the Prince of Wales. Two Treaties of much consequence—one with Holland (April 15, 1788), and one with Prussia (August 13, 1788)—were laid before Parliament. They provided for a defensive alliance in each case, for the supply of troops and for the security of each other's possessions. The independence of the United Provinces was specially guaranteed. Wilberforce again took up the question of the abolition of the Slave Trade, in a series of resolutions which had the support of Pitt and Fox. The debate was not concluded at the end of the session. In 1790 he moved for a Committee to take evidence, by which much time was lost. In 1791 he made another attempt, but his proposals were rejected by a large majority, and no further effort was made during the period covered by this chapter. In the session of 1790, which was opened by the King in person, the affair of Nootka Sound at once attracted attention. A message from the King conveyed the information that British ships had been seized by Spain while peacefully engaged in the fisheries at Nootka Sound. An address was presented; a million was voted; and the country expected war. During the recess, however, an arrangement was effected, and, when the late session opened on November 25, 1790, the King's Speech contained the announcement of peace. A convention had been signed (July 24) by which Spain released the British vessels, restored the lands and property seized, and agreed to give compensation. There was to be no further disturbance of the fisheries on either side; no illicit trade with Spanish settlements; and no British fishing within ten leagues of Spanish territory on the Pacific coast.

The revival of disturbances in India occasioned debate. In 1788 Tipu attacked the Rája of Travancore. British troops were sent to his aid, and Tipu was defeated. In 1791, Lord Cornwallis personally took command; but the campaign was not highly successful In 1792 Seringapatam was attacked, and Tipu's army defeated and dispersed. On February 24 a treaty of peace was made, Tipu ceding half his territories and paying an indemnity of £3,300,000. The Governor-General and General Meadows resigned their prize-money to the army. In 1793 the outbreak of war in Europe justified the British in assailing French possessions in India. Pondicherry was taken, and all the French possessions passed into the hands of the English. Lord Cornwallis hereupon returned to England. The debates of 1790 were spirited; but the Government, pledged by treaty to sustain the Rája of Travancore, held its own. In 1791, a Catholic Relief Bill (31 Geo. III, cap. 32) was passed in England, and like measures were passed in Ireland and for Scotland. The agitation for the relief of Roman Catholics had proceeded slowly. In 1771 and 1774, Irish Acts enabled Catholics to hold certain kinds of real estate, and to testify to their loyalty by an oath which was accepted at Rome. In 1778, an English Act relieved Catholics from penalties imposed by 7 William III, cap. 4. The Act of 1791 relieved Catholics, who took the oath of allegiance, from prohibitions relating to education, property and the practice of the law. It gave Catholic peers the right of access to the King, and permitted attendance at religious services and entry into religious Orders. In 1792, a similar Act was passed in the Irish Parliament; and, in 1793, an English Act extended the relief to Scotland.

In 1791, the long-deferred Bill for the better government of Quebec, described elsewhere, was introduced and passed. It was during the discussion on this Bill that the painful quarrel occurred between Burke and Fox, which separated their political fortunes for ever. The alienation between the two statesmen, due to social as well as to political causes, had been for some time in progress. The outbreak was occasioned by a misunderstanding. Early in the debate Fox had intimated an intention, or a wish, to leave the House till Burke should have ended the irrelevant portion of his speech dwelling on the French Revolution. When, at a later stage, Fox and some of his friends actually left the House—for the purpose of refreshment only—Burke, with a sensitiveness habitual to him, interpreted this as a deliberate attempt to discompose and insult him; his temper flared up; and the breach was beyond repair. The quarrel marked the long impending division of the Whig party into two hostile sections, securing the support of one of them to Pitt during the continuance of his Administration.

Events were now (1792) proceeding rapidly. On May 28 the King's message relating to war between Russia and Turkey produced acrimonious debates. His Majesty announced the failure of himself and his allies in an attempt to put an end to the war and recommended an increase in the naval forces, to give added weight to his representations. Shelburne, now Marquis of Lansdowne, emerged from retirement and took part against the Government. Grey brought forward, at the request of the Friends of the People, a notice of motion for Reform, which Pitt resisted on the ground that "this was not a time to make hazardous experiments." In January, 1792, the King had recommended the reduction of the army and navy. In the following December, he was compelled to ask for their increase in view of the state of affairs in France and on the Continent; and, as will be seen immediately, on February 3, 1793, France declared war. The Duke of Portland and his friends now supported Pitt, and Fox could only muster a minority of forty. Treaties were negotiated with Hesse-Cassel and Sardinia, in June, for the supply of troops, and a treaty of peace and commerce was negotiated with Russia. On August 17 Earl Gower was withdrawn from Paris, though he was instructed to use conciliatory language to the existing Government. The King's Speech had referred to the seditions which were rife in the kingdom. Disturbances, accompanied by treasonable declarations, had occurred in various quarters; and a profuse flow of disquieting pamphlets had proceeded from a number of societies which had arisen in Great Britain. The Society of the Bill of Rights (1765), the Society for Constitutional Information (1780), the Society for Commemorating the Revolution (1788), the Constitutional Society (1788), the London Corresponding Society (1791), and finally the Friends of the People (1792)—all had exercised an activity deemed to be dangerous. Representatives had been sent to France to express fraternal sympathy with the Revolution, and it was suspected that money and arms had been sent in return. Prosecutions were begun under the Alien Act (33 Geo. III, cap. 4) and the Traitorous Correspondence Act (33 Geo. III, cap. 27), which had been passed in succession to meet the case of these offences. Some prosecutions failed, some succeeded; many agitators, including Thomas Paine, went into exile. Against the propagandism of sedition the friends of order had not been idle. In 1790 Burke had published his *Reflections on the French Revolution,* a work which at once became popular, and which has since exercised a dominating influence over the opinions of a large part of civilised mankind. In reply, Mackintosh (afterwards Sir James) published his *Vindiciae Gallicae,* which also had a wide success as the most scholarly attempt to justify the Revolution. The author subsequently altered his views and confessed to Burke that in writing it he had been " the dupe of his own enthusiasm."

In France, in the meantime, things had, as is narrated elsewhere, been going from bad to worse; and in June, 1791, the abortive flight to Varennes deprived the royal family of their last hope. All the attempts of the European Powers—half-hearted as they were—to accomplish the safety of the royal House failed. The acceptance of the Constitution by Louis XVI weakened the hands of his allies, while the emigrant nobles formed an ineffectual army on the frontiers. He was forced to declare war against the Emperor in April, 1792; and, on January 21, 1793, the King was executed, and the gauntlet was thrown down to humanity.

The declaration of war against Great Britain and Holland on February 3, 1793, followed. Pitt entered on the war with reluctance; for he did not share the propagandist enthusiasm of Burke. In 1792, he had recommended the reduction of the army and navy, which had been increased in view of the Nootka Sound dispute with Spain in 1790 and the possible rupture with Russia in 1791. He expressed a confident hope of fifteen years of peace. So much was he disposed to think peace certain that, in 1792, he allowed himself to be led into the project of a coalition with Fox, to which Burke was opposed, but to which the Duke of Portland had given his assent. The negotiation failed. Lord Loughborough, the leading Whig lawyer, accepted the Great Seal from Pitt in 1793, and secured the adherence of Portland. From this time forward a large section of the Whig party, prominent among whom were Earls Spencer and Fitzwilliam, the Duke of Portland, Burke, and Wyndham, followed the lead of Pitt, who now entered on that tremendous conflict which was to be made glorious at sea at Trafalgar, and finally victorious on land at Waterloo. On February 12, 1793, he accepted the gage of battle in these memorable words: "It now remains to be seen whether, under Providence, the efforts of a free, brave, loyal and happy people, aided by their allies, will not be successful in checking the progress of a system, the principles of which, if not opposed, threaten the most fatal consequences to the tranquillity of this country, the security of its allies, the good order of every European Government, and the happiness of the whole human race."

CHAPTER XIV.

IRELAND IN THE EIGHTEENTH CENTURY.

With the eighteenth century we enter on an entirely new period of Irish history. The process of conquest and colonisation, that had been going on for centuries, had at last been completed, and Ireland lay helpless in the grasp of her stronger sister, England. This is the key-note of the situation. Of the land, more than three-fourths had passed into the hands of a relatively small body of English owners, and of the two and a quarter millions of inhabitants that composed its population nearly four-fifths had sunk into a state of bondage bordering on slavery. Excluded by the operation of the penal laws from all share in the government of the country, reduced socially to the level of outcasts, exposed to the tyranny of the informer and the oppression of their land-lords, steeped in poverty, and debarred the means of acquiring wealth, while their religion was proscribed, and the possibilities of education were denied them, and deprived, as they were shortly to be, of the last vestige of their political rights, by the restriction of the franchise to the Protestants, the Irish Roman Catholics were subject to conditions of life as deplorable as those of any class in Europe. Year by year, the exodus that had set in with the surrender of Limerick and was drawing off the best blood of the nation, to replenish the armies of France, Spain, and the Empire, went on without intermission. None but the old and feeble remained at home to fill the offices of hewers of wood and drawers of water for their masters. It is a sad picture, and the Irishman may well be forgiven who prefers to see in the laurels won by the Irish brigade on the battle-fields of Europe the real history of his country at this time, rather than in the gloom and torpor that reigned at home. But the picture has another and more important aspect. For it was in the gloom and misery of the period that the Irish nation had its birth. Modern Ireland, the Ireland with which Englishmen are most familiar, with its deep drawn lines of social demarcation, dates only from the extinction of the clan system. The process had been slow, and painful for England as for Ireland. But the end had come at last, and, in the common fate that had overtaken both clansmen and chieftains, the old obstacles that had presented an unsurmountable barrier in the past to a sense of nationality and to national action were removed. But the time for national action had passed away, or had not arrived; and it was perhaps rather a sense of a common religious belief than any conscious feeling of nationality that was to provide a basis for unity of action in the future. For the period covered by this chapter the history of Ireland means practically the history of the English colony in Ireland.

The creation of an English colony in Ireland was the result of deliberate policy on the part of English statesmen. In such a result they had seen the only hope of reducing Ireland, as the phrase went, to civility and good government, and at the same time of securing England from a hostile neighbour. The latter object had been the predominant one; and, now that the establishment of the colony had been accomplished, it remained to be seen whether the object of the policy pursued had been achieved.

In considering this question and in tracing the causes which led to the recognition by England of an independent Irish legislature, it must be borne steadily in mind that, in the opinion of every Englishman, the English colony in Ireland existed for the sake of England and not primarily for its own sake. Without this underlying idea the colony would never have been established at all. We have seen in an earlier chapter how, in the pursuance of this policy, the English Parliament had thought fit at different times to interfere directly in the internal affairs of Ireland, and in the interests of English manufacturers to suppress the Irish woollen industry. In doing so it believed itself to be acting entirely within its rights, and, in order to put the question, as it thought, once for all outside the sphere of discussion, it passed an Act in 1719 (6 Geo. I), divesting the Irish House of Lords of its power of judicature on appeals, and affirming its own power and authority to make laws binding on the people of Ireland. The assumption that lay at the bottom of its action did not pass unchallenged. In 1698, at the time of the woollen controversy, William Molyneux published his *Case of Ireland being bound by Acts of Parliament in England stated,* in which, with no little learning and great moderation, he argued that the English Parliament possessed no right to the claim it alleged. Molyneux' book was condemned by the English House of Commons as " of dangerous consequence to the Crown and Parliament of England," and several attempts were made to confute it. His argument possesses little more than an academic interest to-day; but it contained an idea that was destined to germinate and bear fruit in the future. " If," said he, " it be concluded that the Parliament of England may bind Ireland, it must also be allowed that the people of Ireland ought to have their representatives in the Parliament of England. And this, I believe, we should be willing enough to embrace; but this is an happiness we can hardly hope for." The idea of a legislative union was not a novel one. Cromwell had given practical expression to it, Sir William Petty had argued strongly in favour of it, and there exists among the state documents of the Revolution period a memorial to Government, by an anonymous writer, warmly advocating its adoption. Later, when the question of a union between England and Scotland was broached, Irish writers came forward to urge the adoption of a similar policy in regard to Ireland, petitions to the same effect were presented by the House of Commons in 1703 and 1707, and no one who has studied the question can doubt that a union with Ireland might have been carried at this time with less trouble than it was in the case of Scotland, and would have been attended with equal benefits to both partners. But commercial jealousy and indifference to Irish needs prevailed. The opportunity of effecting a union on a basis of a mutual understanding was lost; and, though the idea was more than once revived during the century, times had changed, great parliamentary interests had been formed, and a spirit of independence, not to say of antagonism, had been aroused, so that, when the Union was actually effected, this was done in opposition to the wish of Ireland, and entirely in the interests of England.

The immediate consequence of the refusal of English statesmen to take advantage of the situation was a visible estrangement on the part of the colonists and the formation of a so-called Irish Interest. This Irish Interest must not be confounded with what, for distinction's sake, must be called a native Interest. Its leaders were men of English descent and members of the Established Church, between whom and the Roman Catholic majority there was not only no feeling of sympathy, but one of intense hostility. Such an Irish Interest, as distinct from both an English and a native Interest, had always existed in Ireland. But it had never till the present time been a Protestant Interest also. Herein lay its strength, so far as England was concerned. Its weakness lay in its antagonism to the bulk of the nation. The Irish Interest had already made its influence felt in the first Parliament of William's reign, in the disputes as to the right of the House of Commons to originate Money Bills. But its terror of Roman Catholicism and its jealousy of Presbyterianism had crippled its independence of action, and in its resistance to the restrictions placed by England on the woollen industry it had been criminally remiss. Still, it was by no means powerless; and in 1701 it showed its indignation at the callous subordination of Irish to English interests by striking off £16,000 from the already overgrown Pension List. In Parliament its acknowledged leader was William King, Bishop of Derry, promoted, in 1702, to the archbishopric of Dublin. King was neither a Whig nor a Tory, but something of both. His position, to put it briefly, was that the Revolution had been made by, and in the interests of, the Church of England party. But he also held that in coming to Ireland the English colonists had forfeited none of their rights and privileges as Englishmen. They had their own Parliament and their own Church, and in civil and ecclesiastical matters they were independent of England. Holding this opinion, he offered a strenuous resistance to every attempt on the part of the English Ministry and the English Parliament to subordinate the Irish to the English Interest in the country. His view was dictated by his care for the Church. For he clearly recognised that the dignity and usefulness of the Church rested ultimately on the material prosperity of its members. Anything that went to weaken the Irish Interest weakened *pari passu* the welfare of the Irish Church. He was far from desiring to loosen the natural bonds that held the colony to England; but he saw that, if the colonists lost their position of independence, they would sooner or later join hands with the natives to the detriment of the Church.

The destruction of the woollen industry proved a deadly blow to the rising prosperity of the English colony in Ireland. Its effects were felt in all directions. In 1702 the poverty of the country was so great that it was feared that the court mourning for the death of William would exhaust its resources. The promise to encourage the linen manufacture, that had been made a pretext for the restrictions on the woollen trade, was left unfulfilled, or so fulfilled as to afford a maximum of advantage to England. To alleviate the misery, the House of Commons, in 1703, came to the unanimous resolution that " it would greatly conduce to the relief of the poor and the good of the kingdom, if the inhabitants thereof would use none other but the manufactures of this kingdom in their apparel and the furnishing of their houses." Similar resolutions were passed in 1705 and 1707; but fashion and necessity rendered them ineffective. Forced to adopt other measures, the Irish Parliament did what it could to promote the linen industry. The services of Louis Crommelin, a Huguenot refugee and an eminent specialist in the art of growing and weaving flax, were secured, spinning-schools were established, premiums awarded for the best linens, bounties on exports granted, and a linen Board appointed. By its exertions a flourishing linen trade was created in Ulster; but its progress was at first slow, and its benefits restricted to a narrow area; and it was at best an inadequate equivalent for the ruined woollen industry. Meanwhile, the poverty and wretchedness of the people increased daily. Finding no employment for their labours, thousands of artisans, chiefly Protestants, quitted the country. But emigration was only the beginning of the mischief. As the industrial resources of the country declined, the people were driven back more and more on to the soil for a subsistence. But the condition of things was not favourable to the development of a flourishing agricultural community. The soil of Ireland—the spoil of war and confiscation—was in the hands of men who, in their uncertainty whether a fresh revolution might not deprive them of their possessions, were only anxious to turn their lands as quickly as possible to account. The Catholic natives, whom the penal laws had reduced to a state of impotence, were driven off to the bogs and mountains, to make way for sheep and oxen. Wool growing, thanks to the contraband trade, was a profitable business, so too was cattle rearing for the provision trade. Little capital was wanted for either and the returns were quick. In the process, whole villages were depopulated and the country filled with crowds of strolling beggars. With English grain flooding the markets, there was no inducement to cultivate the soil. As the favourable leases that had been granted after the Revolution began to fall in about 1716, rents were raised, in some cases trebled, and clauses inserted in their renewals, restricting the area to be put under tillage. In Ulster, where the disabilities placed on the Presbyterians by the Sacramental Test aggravated matters, the consequences were most serious. Hundreds of intelligent and industrious farmers, finding it impossible to make a living and resenting the interference with their consciences, threw up their farms and left the country. Their places were taken by Catholic natives, who, being debarred by the penal laws from taking profitable leases, were willing to offer higher rents, in the hope of making a profit out of the grazing trade. As often as not the landlord was an absentee, whose only means of turning his lands to account was to grant long leases of between forty and sixty years to some Protestant middleman, who made a fortune out of the transaction, partly as grazier himself, partly by subletting the land at rack-rents to Catholic cottiers. As he in turn grew rich, he also employed a middleman; and so the process went on till at last there were sometimes as many as three, and even more, middlemen between the proprietor of the soil and the cultivator. The result can be easily imagined. Of agriculture, in the strict sense of the word, there was little to be seen. Here and there a field of wheat or oats could be discerned, sufficient to meet the wants of the farm. Otherwise, as far as the eye could reach, nothing but one wide stretch of pasture land, with only the lowing of oxen and the bleating of sheep to break the silence, and with nothing to relieve its monotony save the tumbled-down hut of the lonely herdsman. Where the land was too poor for profitable grazing, or where the necessities of the landlord required his presence, there the Irish cottier raised his cabin and cultivated the plot of potatoes, which were becoming more and more his staple food. Tied to the soil, with little incentive to work and no opportunity to accumulate capital, with starvation staring him daily in the face, he grew up to a wild, reckless existence. Marrying early, he filled his cabin with half-fed, naked children. If he could pay his landlord his rent, the parson his tithes, and the parish priest his dues, and withal manage to scrape together a scanty livelihood for himself, he was tolerably happy.

But for the country the existence of such a class was fraught with terrible danger. This was recognised by Parliament. In 1716, the House of Commons intervened with a resolution condemning the insertion of clauses in leases restricting tillage; public granaries were established and in 1727 an Act was passed, enjoining that five out of every hundred acres should be under the plough. Considerable efforts were made, notably by the Dublin Society, founded in 1731, to promote a more scientific system of farming and to develop the industrial resources of the country. But neither legislation nor philanthropic endeavour could provide a remedy for the evils consequent on the destruction of the woollen industry. In 1727, and again in 1740, Ireland was visited by famine which swept away thousands; but the demand for land remained unsatisfied, thus paving the way for Whiteboy and other agrarian disturbances, which were to follow at no very distant date.

With the sad evidences of the folly of the policy, that had brought Ireland to this pass, staring them in the face, a feeling of indignation against England naturally grew up in the breasts of men, who, though themselves of English origin, were deeply concerned in the welfare of the colony. Were their interests to be for ever subordinated to those of England? The arguments of Molyneux had passed unheeded; the authority of their own Parliament had been set at naught; their demand for a union had been rejected; their protests had been disregarded; and, to add insult to injury, whenever a pension had to be found, for which no justifiable reason could be alleged to the English Parliament, it was placed on the Irish Civil List. The feeling of indignation was all the more justifiable as nothing had occurred to reflect on the loyalty of the nation at large. Of Jacobitism there was not the slightest trace. In 1715, when England and Scotland were convulsed by rebellion, Ireland was perfectly tranquil. In fact, neither colonists nor natives desired to have anything more to do with the Stewarts. It was a comparatively trifling affair that brought the long smouldering discontent of the colonists to an open flame.

The monetary system of Ireland had long been in disorder. She had no mint of her own, which of itself was a serious disadvantage, and commercial stagnation and the constant drain of metal currency in the form of rents to absentee landlords had produced a deficiency of coin. In 1724 it was calculated that the entire metal currency amounted to no more than £400,000. To relieve the pressure, it was resolved to increase the number of copper coins. The proposal was reasonable enough; unfortunately, in putting it into execution two mistakes were committed. Instead of undertaking the business itself, Government granted a patent to coin to the Duchess of Kendal, one of the King's mistresses. This lady, who already enjoyed a pension of £3000 on the Irish list, sold her patent to an English iron-master of the name of Wood for £10,000. Jobs were the order of the day, and this one might have passed, had the amount of the proposed new copper coinage borne any reasonable proportion to the standard currency of the country. But to flood the country with £100,800 worth of halfpennies and farthings was a grave economic blunder. The subject was taken up by the only man capable, by his genius, authority, and literary ability, of adequately expressing the sentiments of the nation. Jonathan Swift had the misfortune, in his own opinion, to have been born in Dublin. He loathed the land of his birth, and to his last day he reviled the untoward fate that had banished him to Ireland as Dean of St Patrick's. To-day men call him an Irish patriot and link his name with those of Molyneux, Lucas, and Grattan. But he has no real claim to the title. It was not the pure flame of patriotism, but the scorching fire of indignation at the folly and stupidity of mankind, that inspired him now and then to break a lance for Ireland. He did not love the Irish; but, fortunately for Ireland, he hated the Whigs. The disastrous effects of the woollen legislation had not escaped his notice, and in 1720 he had come forward with a pamphlet urging the Irish to use Irish manufactures only. The printer of the pamphlet was prosecuted; but the indignation of the public at the partiality of the presiding judge, Chief Justice Whitshed, was so intense, that the prosecution had to be abandoned. When the news of Wood's patent became known it caused no little commotion in Dublin. Parliament addressed the Crown on the subject; petitions against it were presented by most of the city corporations, and resolutions condemning it were passed by the grand juries. Government consented to reduce the amount of the new coinage to £40,000; but the concession failed to pacify public opinion. In the midst of the excitement Swift put forth his *Drapier's Letters.* From the moment he took the matter in hand the agitation assumed a new and, for Government, a very serious character. From Wood and his patent Swift passed on to review the whole system of the English administration in Ireland. Taking up the same constitutional ground as Molyneux in regard to the claim to bind Ireland by English Acts of Parliament, but in language bolder than ever Molyneux had dared to use, he retorted that " in reason, all government without the consent of the governed is the very definition of slavery; but, in fact, eleven men well armed will certainly subdue a single man in his shirt." The argument went home. A prosecution was commenced against the author of the *Letters*; the Lord Lieutenant, the Duke of Grafton, was blamed for his remissness and recalled; and Lord Carteret was sent over for the express purpose of forcing the patent through. But the prosecution had to be abandoned and at Carteret's own suggestion the patent was revoked.

So far as the cause of the agitation was concerned, the matter was at an end. But the agitation itself had created quite a new situation in the relations between England and Ireland. Only five years had elapsed since the English Parliament had deliberately asserted its right to make laws binding on Ireland (6 Geo. I). The recent agitation had shown that the English colonists were not inclined to submit tamely to be thus deprived of their rights; and to Sir Robert Walpole it was clear that, if Ireland was not to break away from England, some system of government other than the rather lax one that had hitherto prevailed, would have to be adopted. Since the beginning of the century the administration of the country had rested nominally with the Lord Lieutenant, who, with the single exception of the Duke of Ormond, had always been an English nobleman. There had been a rapid succession in the office; but it was practically a sinecure, and the real business of government had been transacted by the Lords Justices, with the assistance of the Irish Privy Council. Though differing nominally as Whig and Tory, the Lords Justices had, with few exceptions, been Irishmen. This fact had considerably modified their political views, so that there was not a little truth in the remark that a Tory in Ireland would have made a good Whig in England. The same distinction was observable in the Irish Parliament. During the sixteenth and seventeenth centuries Parliaments had been of rare occurrence in Ireland; but after the Revolution the practice had grown up of summoning one every second year. The reason is to be found in the insufficiency of the hereditary revenue of the Crown for defraying the expenses of government. Parliament meeting regularly at constant intervals, the idea had sprung up, and was confirmed by practice, that only the death of the sovereign could effect a dissolution. In this way a seat in the House of Commons became, owing to the many privileges attached to it, a valuable property; while by the operation of the English Act (3 William and Mary, c. 2) rendering it compulsory on all members to take the Oath of Supremacy and subscribe the Declaration against Transubstantiation, it could only be held by a Protestant. Recognising their dependence on England, the Commons had at first shown no desire to pursue an independent policy; but, as the effects of commercial policy became apparent, a spirit of opposition, neither Whig nor Tory in character, but directly anti-English, began to assert itself.

Ireland, it had become clear to Walpole, was drifting from her moorings. To keep her in place it was of all things most necessary to strengthen the English Interest. It happened, fortunately for his plan, that, just at this moment (1724), the primacy fell vacant, by the death of Archbishop Lindesay. In the ordinary course of events, King should have succeeded; but King had identified himself too closely with the Irish Interest to be acceptable to Walpole, and in November Hugh Boulter, Bishop of Bristol, was created Archbishop of Armagh. As a man, a scholar and a bishop, Boulter was admirably qualified to adorn the station to which he was called; but it is rather as manager of Irish politics than as head of the Irish Church that he is remembered in history. His business, to put it briefly, was to break down the rising opposition to England, and, in the language of the day, to secure a quiet parliamentary session. His method of proceeding was simple enough. Whenever a vacancy occurred on the episcopal or the judicial bench, or in the revenue, the person recommended by him for promotion was either an Englishman or an Irishman of whose subserviency the Primate was fully assured. His task was all the easier as, apart from the means employed, his policy was distinctly calculated to benefit Ireland. Coming thither when the country was convulsed by Wood's patent, he at once recognised the necessity of its revocation; but he was no less convinced of the importance of reforming the currency. His plan for reducing the value of gold, to meet the rise in the price of silver, was economically unsound; but the credit of having attacked the problem, and of having, after long years of worry and trouble, succeeded, in a measure, in alleviating the financial distress of the country, cannot be denied him. He viewed with sorrow and regret the emigration that was draining Ireland of its industrious population; and it was mainly in consequence of his endeavours that the measure rendering it compulsory on landlords to set apart five out of every hundred acres for tillage was passed. At different times, when Ireland was visited by famine, he exerted himself to keep down the price of grain, and did all that lay in his power to mitigate the misery of the poor. As virtual head of the Government he must be held responsible for putting the last touches to the Penal Code, by an Act (1 Geo. II, c. 9), depriving the Catholics of the franchise, and by another Act (7 Geo. II, c. 5), completely excluding them from the legal profession. But his attitude towards the Catholics was not one of blind hatred. He warmly supported Dr Richardson's efforts to reach the Irish through their native language, and, if the proselytising principle of the Charter schools, of which he was an early and ardent promoter, strikes us to-day as radically mistaken, the institution was at least a reasonable attempt to substitute persuasion for persecution. But neither political ability, nor private generosity, nor a genuine interest in the spiritual welfare of the Irish could compensate for the fact that his aim in all things was to subordinate Irish interests to those of England. The pride, if not the virtue, of Irishmen was outraged by a state of affairs, in which subserviency to Government constituted the sole claim to office. This fact introduced a personal element into the character of parliamentary Opposition, which under King in the House of Lords, and the Brodricks, father and son, in the House of Commons, had worn a distinctly patriotic aspect. For, seeing themselves in danger of being excluded from all share in the Government, the great borough proprietors prepared to come to terms with the Primate, and, on condition of being allowed to monopolise all the lucrative offices of State, agreed to drop their opposition, and to secure for Government a permanent "quiet session." It was a disgraceful bargain and highly detrimental to public morality; but the Government of the "Undertakers" did not on the whole work badly. For, though it was mainly their own interests they had in view, still, as Irishmen, they had some care for the country, and Boulter was wise enough to hold the reins as slackly over them as was consistent with the promotion of the English Interest.

CH. XIV.

Thus, except for the chronic distress of the country, the years passed quietly away, and at Boulter's death in 1742, no objection was taken to his successor, Archbishop Hoadly, whose daughter had married the son of Speaker Boyle. Even the promotion of George Stone to the primacy on Hoadly's death in 1747 failed at first to disturb the general harmony. He was barely forty; but it seemed a sufficient explanation that he was the brother of the Duke of Newcastle's friend, the influential Under-Secretary of State, Andrew Stone, and besides had the reputation of being himself an able man. Of his ability there was no question—or, as it soon became clear, of his ambition. Unlike Boulter, who had been content to govern through the Undertakers, and Hoadly, who had allied himself with them, Stone was determined to govern independently of them. It was partly jealousy and ambition, partly a conviction that the government of the Undertakers was tending indirectly to weaken the English Interest, that led him to make the attempt. Provided he could divide them and build up a party of his own, he might reckon upon ruling alone. With this object, he entered into an alliance with the Ponsonby faction, in order to oust Boyle from the Speakership. The scheme was well laid; but Boyle was alive to his danger, and Parliament had no sooner met in 1751 than he opened a counter-attack on the Primate by preferring a charge of malversation against the Surveyor-General, Nevill. Stone was unable to prevent a resolution requiring Nevill to make good his defalcations under pain of being expelled the House; but he scored a success on a much more important point. In 1749 the revenue had shown a considerable surplus, which the Commons had assigned to the reduction of the National Debt. A similar surplus occurred in 1751. It was proposed to devote part of it to the same object; and heads of a Bill to that effect were transmitted to England. The Bill was returned thence as accepted, but with the addition of a preamble expressing the consent of the Crown to the course proposed. The object of this preamble, to insist on the right of the Crown to dispose of the surplus revenue, was observed and sharply criticised in the Irish House of Commons; but the Bill was allowed to pass. It was thought Stone would take the hint; but he showed no intention of coming to terms with the Opposition, and a memorial, personally presented to the King by the Earl of Kildare, protesting against the Money Bill as unconstitutional was treated with contempt. Accordingly, when Parliament reassembled in 1753, the attack on Government was renewed. This time Nevill's expulsion was carried into effect, and a Money Bill, with a preamble similar to that of 1751, was rejected by a majority of five. Government retaliated by suddenly proroguing Parliament, depriving four of the principal members of the Opposition of their offices, and seizing the surplus revenue by an Order under the King's sign-manual. These proceedings raised a storm of indignation in the country. The

Press teemed with pamphlets lampooning Government, and particularly the Primate, in the most outrageous fashion. The peace of the city was disturbed by tumults, not unattended with bloodshed, that recalled the days of Wood's Halfpence. Stone had to barricade himself from the mob; but he begged Ministers in England to stand firm. The Opposition, he insisted, was on its last legs: to yield was to sacrifice the English Interest in the country for ever. But George II thought otherwise, and determined to come to terms with the Speaker. The Lord Lieutenant, the Duke of Dorset, Stone's ally, was dismissed. A modus was easily arranged between his successor, the Marquis of Hartington, and the Opposition. Boyle was created Earl of Shannon with a yearly pension of £2000; Anthony Malone was compensated with the Chancellorship of the Exchequer; and the Earl of Bessborough was conciliated with a promise of the Speakership for his son John Ponsonby. Everybody, except Stone—and of course the nation—was satisfied. It was a scandalous business; but it answered its purpose of securing a quiet parliamentary session. On returning to England at the close of it, Hartington omitted Stone's name from the Commission of Government. The omission greatly mortified him; and, when, on the formation of the Pitt-Newcastle Ministry in 1757, the government of Ireland was entrusted to the Duke of Bedford, he went, for a time, into Opposition. But his power was no longer what it had been, and, having promised submission, he was again included in the Commission of Government. The attempt to break the Undertakers had failed. Things returned to their normal condition; and, when a French expedition, commanded by Thurot, effected a landing at Carrickfergus in 1760, all parties, including the Catholics, rallied to the support of Government. The danger was averted, and in 1761, when Bedford surrendered the sword of State to the Earl of Halifax, the political horizon appeared cloudless.

The eagerness with which the Catholics had come forward to testify to their loyalty, and the cordial reception given to their addresses, both by Parliament and Government, were specially hopeful signs of a better understanding between them and the Protestants. Of religious intolerance there was really very little on either side. The wave of free thought that was spreading over Europe and permeating its literature had not failed to affect Ireland. The fact, even if it was deplored by those who still clung to their old beliefs, was admitted on both sides. An atmosphere of scepticism was fatal to the Penal Code. What element of religious persecution there had been in it had long ceased to be operative. Among the Catholics themselves, the rapidly increasing number of conversions was significant of a relaxation of religious principle, and of a growing reluctance to sacrifice their material welfare to a mere point of theology. The prevailing spirit of indifference to religion did not escape the notice of John Wesley, during his frequent visits to Ireland at this time. He encountered very little direct

CH. XIV.

opposition; indeed, the Catholic peasantry flocked to hear him; but his preaching left no permanent mark on the religious life of the nation.

But, as religious differences sank into the background, a new problem suddenly started into prominence. It has been pointed out how, by the destruction of the woollen industry, the bulk of the population had been thrown back on the soil for its existence, and how, by the operation of the laws restricting commerce, a great impulse had been given to the conversion of arable into pasture land. Cork, the centre of the provision trade, was now in population and wealth the second city in the kingdom. The profits of the business were enormous, and, to supply it, Munster and the adjacent parts of Connaught and Leinster had been turned into one large pasture field. With an ever increasing demand for meat, the greater by reason of a murrain that had recently broken out amongst English cattle, rents rose to an average of £3 an acre, for fairly good land. Pasture was exempt from tithe, and, to all but the large graziers, the rents were prohibitive. To make room for more cattle, the peasantry were evicted from their holdings, and lands which were regarded as commons taken from them and enclosed. The distress entailed by these proceedings was extreme, and in their desperation the peasantry resorted to outrage and intimidation. Towards the close of 1761 bands of men, numbering sometimes two or three hundred, known at first as Levellers, but later as Whiteboys, from the white shirts they wore over their clothes, ranged the country during the long winter nights, tearing down enclosures, hamstringing cattle, and, according to their view, administering a sort of rude justice on their oppressors. Obnoxious landlords were warned against exacting excessive rents; but it was the tithe-proctor and tithe-farmer that chiefly felt the brunt of popular vengeance. It is said that no actual murders were committed; but there was a good deal of personal violence, and so widespread was the conspiracy, so swiftly and secretly did the Whiteboys work, that the arm of the law was paralysed over a large extent of the province. A number of individuals were, however, arrested and a special commission presided over by Chief Justice Sir Richard Aston, was sent down to restore order. A few persons were executed; but justice was tempered with mercy, and the blessings of a sorely-tried but grateful peasantry accompanied the Chief Justice on his departure. The movement was stifled; but nothing was done to remove the root of the disease, and, ever and anon, the peace of the province was disturbed by agrarian outrage. The fact that the Whiteboys were mostly, if not exclusively, Catholics threatened a revival of sectarian intolerance. It was said they were only waiting for French assistance to create another rebellion. But no evidence of such intention was forthcoming, and the argument lost its point entirely, when similar disturbances broke out, almost at the same time, amongst the Protestants in Ulster. In the case of the Oakboys' rising, which, starting near Armagh in 1763, spread rapidly over the adjacent counties, the grievances chiefly complained of were tithes and the iniquitous assessment of county rates, which threw the burden of road-making almost entirely on the tenant. The rising was disgraced by none of the fiendish outrages that marked the Whiteboys' insurrection, and was easily suppressed without much bloodshed; while the chief cause of it was speedily removed by a new and more equitable Road Act. More closely resembling the Whiteboys' insurrection was that of the Steelboys, some years later, in counties Down and Antrim. The rising was directly attributed to the exaction, by the Marquis of Donegal, of a heavy fine from his tenantry, as the condition of a renewal of their leases, at a time when a depression in the linen trade had reduced them to the direst extremities. The fact that they were industrious Presbyterians made no difference. Inability to meet the demand was followed by wholesale eviction and, as a natural result, by agrarian outrages hardly less atrocious than those of the Whiteboys. The insurrection was suppressed with difficulty; but nothing was done to remedy the evil; and the Steelboys, with their wives and families, left the country, to swell the ranks of England's enemies in America. It was calculated that in 1773 and the five preceding years Ulster was drained of one-fourth of its trading cash and of the same proportion of its manufacturing population.

These disturbances were full of significance for the future. At the time, however, the agrarian problem attracted less attention than the political. The parliamentary storm that had raged in 1753 had passed away; but its effects remained. Neither to the English Ministry nor to the little knot of independent county members in the Irish House of Commons was the victory of the Undertakers at all satisfactory. To the Ministry it had long been evident that the power of the Undertakers was inconsistent with the system of keeping Ireland in a position of subordination to England. For, however venal, they were nevertheless Irishmen, who agreed with the Patriots on many points, by raising which they could at any time seriously embarrass Government. Their recent victory had served to emphasise the danger and had led to a revival of the proposal for a union. But times had changed since Molyneux had modestly urged its adoption; and a mere rumour that Government was meditating such a step led to a serious riot in Dublin in 1759. A union, indeed, was not contemplated; but there was a growing feeling in England that, if the existing relations between the two countries were to be maintained, some change in the form of government had become inevitable. The general indignation aroused in Ireland by the political fiasco of 1753 had resulted in a demand for the shortening of the duration of Parliament, as a likely means of diminishing the importance of the Undertakers, by bringing them more under the control of their constituencies. It was warmly supported by the Patriots in the House of Commons. The general election that followed

CH. XIV.

the accession of George III had given them a leader of unquestioned ability in the person of Henry Flood; and hardly less important than Flood's election was that of Charles Lucas. Without Flood's ability and oratorical talent, Lucas was an earnest and honest politician. He had at an earlier period of his career come into open conflict with the Government owing to the persistency with which he had striven, as a Common Councillor, to reform the Dublin Corporation. To evade punishment he had gone into voluntary exile for several years; but his memory was cherished by the citizens of the metropolis; and, having secured a pardon, he was rewarded by being elected one of their representatives in Parliament. The interest excited by the proposal to limit the duration of Parliament completely dwarfed, for a time, the other items in the popular programme—a diminution of the Pension List, a Habeas Corpus Act, a Place Bill, the independence of the judicial bench, and the creation of a national militia. Accordingly, when Parliament met on October 22, 1761, the matter was at once brought forward by Lucas. Leave was given to bring in heads of a Bill limiting the duration of Parliament to seven years; but further than this the House declined to go, and a motion recommending it for transmission to England was rejected. The measure was in fact as thoroughly distasteful to the Undertakers as it was to Government. But resolutions flowed in from all sides warmly supporting it. Government and the Undertakers were in an awkward position, the latter particularly. For, though they clearly recognised that the measure was calculated to diminish their influence, they were fully alive to the danger of obstinately resisting public opinion. A way to secure its rejection, and, at the same time, to preserve their credit with the country was discovered. Knowing that the Bill was just as objectionable to Government they resolved to support it, and to throw the odium of its rejection on the Irish Privy Council. These tactics succeeded in 1763; but, supported by Flood, Lucas held his ground tenaciously, and in the following session (1765-6) the Bill was once more referred to the Council for transmission. To refuse a second time passed the courage of the Council, and in the firm expectation that the Bill would be, as it actually was, shelved in England, it was transmitted thither.

But, much as English Ministers disliked the measure, they disliked the Undertakers even more; and towards the close of the viceroyalty of the Earl of Northumberland, who had succeeded Halifax in 1763, a plan was formed to break their power, by enforcing continual residence in Ireland on the Lord Lieutenant. There was some difficulty in finding anyone willing to accept the office on these terms. Eventually Lord Townshend consented to make the experiment. To strengthen his hands against the Undertakers, he was authorised to hint at a concession of some points in the popular programme. Unfortunately, in opening Parliament in October, 1767, he allowed himself to suggest a Bill to secure the independence of the judges as in England. This was more than his colleagues in London intended. They returned the long desired Bill for limiting the duration of Parliament, altering it from seven to eight years, to meet the custom obtaining in Ireland of Parliament meeting only in alternate years, and not from any desire, as is generally stated, to secure its rejection; but they insisted on adding a clause to the Judges' Bill allowing of the removal of any judge on a joint address of both Houses of the English Parliament. It was a wholly unnecessary stipulation; but it emphasised the intention of Ministers to keep Ireland in a state of subjection to England; and, being so interpreted in Ireland, it completely destroyed the popularity that had accrued to Townshend, and enabled the Undertakers to gratify their resentment against the Octennial Bill by throwing out a Bill for an augmentation of the army. Townshend had some reason to complain of the way he had been treated, and the caricature drawn of him, with his hands tied and his mouth open, was doubtless very expressive of his feelings. But his irritation only intensified his resentment against the Undertakers, and, Parliament being immediately dissolved, he set to work resolutely to break their power. His policy, and the means he took to realise it, recalled the days of Boulter and Stone; but the Octennial Act had rendered his task of securing a majority by corruption infinitely more difficult than it had been to them. He was still engaged in preparing his plan of campaign when Parliament met in October, 1769. It was known that Government was anxious to pass the Augmentation Bill, and, though the country could ill afford the additional expense, there was a general inclination to acquiesce in the proposal. But this benevolent attitude changed to one of opposition, when Parliament was asked to consent to a Money Bill that had originated in the Privy Council. Nothing irritated Irishmen more than the interpretation which English Ministers persisted in placing on Poynings' Law. The right to control their purse was the last remnant of independence they possessed and they were unanimous not to surrender it. They readily granted the taxes demanded and even acquiesced in the measure to augment the army; but the Money Bill was rejected, on the ground that it had not originated with the Commons. Following the precedent established by Lord Sydney in 1692, Townshend brought the session to a sudden close. In his speech proroguing Parliament he protested against the construction placed by Parliament on Poynings' Law, and insisted on his protest being entered on the Journals of both Houses. But times had changed since the Commons had been willing to barter their freedom for a free hand against the Roman Catholics, and an order was passed by the House, forbidding the clerk to obey the injunction. The quarrel attracted considerable attention in England and an article in the *Public Advertiser*, calling on the English Parliament to vindicate its authority, and, if necessary, to interfere forcibly to suppress "the spirit of seditious obstinacy" in Ireland, exasperated public opinion there. A resolution curiously recalling the treatment of Molyneux' book by the English Parliament was passed by the Irish House of Commons, ordering the article to be burnt by the common hangman. It was observed that Townshend did not imitate Sydney in dissolving Parliament; but one prorogation succeeded another, and, in the meantime, the Lord Lieutenant steadily pursued his plan of purchasing a parliamentary majority. The Privy Council was remodelled; the Earl of Shannon, Speaker Ponsonby, and a crowd of minor placemen were removed from office; peerages were distributed with a liberal hand; places were multiplied, and, despite the promise of the Crown to the contrary, the Civil List was encumbered with additional pensions. The result was apparent when Parliament reassembled in February, 1771. An address, thanking the King for continuing Townshend in office was voted; but Ponsonby refused to present it, and a new Speaker was found in the person of Sexton Pery. The business of the session was transacted without difficulty; but outside Parliament the indignation with which the shameful traffic was regarded rose to fever heat. The public Press teemed with lampoons, in which neither the person, nor the character, nor the habits, of the Lord Lieutenant were spared. His administration was ridiculed, and he was himself held up to scorn as a second Sancho Panza, in a series of powerful letters, afterwards collected under the title of *Baratariana*. From being the most popular, Townshend had become the best hated, man in the kingdom, and the appointment of Earl Harcourt as his successor came as a relief both to him and the country.

But it was soon to appear that the change of Viceroy had brought no change of system with it. The majority which corruption had purchased corruption alone could maintain. To satisfy its supporters, Government strained its resources to the utmost. New taxes were imposed and fresh loans raised; but the ever increasing number of bankruptcies was a sure sign that the limits of taxation were being rapidly reached. Public indignation was not so loudly expressed as it had been in Townshend's time. Harcourt was not personally disliked; Lucas had died in 1771; Flood, with an exaggerated notion of his ability to influence Government, had accepted office; and Grattan, on whom his mantle had fallen, only entered Parliament in 1775. But the inability of the country to meet the expenses of government was unmistakable, and the fact that these expenses had been incurred in a time of peace, for the avowed purpose of maintaining a system directly hostile to Ireland, rendered the situation unbearable.

On opening Parliament in 1775, Harcourt announced the intention of Government to concede certain privileges to Irish vessels engaged in the Newfoundland fisheries, to allow Ireland to provide clothing for her own forces when abroad, and to grant a small bounty on flax-seed imported into the country. These concessions, he added, would, he hoped, "secure riches and prosperity to the people of Ireland." The unintentional irony of his words is not less remarkable than the utter inadequacy of the concessions to alleviate the distress of the country, which the outbreak of the war with America, by closing the only profitable market for Irish linens and entailing an embargo on the export of provisions, was every day rendering more acute. But Harcourt's attention was wholly directed to the business of managing Parliament. So far, he had been successful in eliciting from it a loyal address in response to the declaration of war, and in winning a reluctant consent to the withdrawal, for service abroad, of 4000 of the 12,000 troops designed for the defence of the country. But a dissolution was approaching, and he was not so sure of the future as he could have desired to be. In fact, the declaration of war against America had been received with very mingled feelings in Ireland. An amendment to the address, urging the adoption of conciliatory measures, had been rejected; but the amendment spoke the general sense of the people, especially of the Presbyterians in Ulster. That Ireland was suffering from much the same grievances as those which had led to the revolt of the colonies was the subject of general comment. The similarity was pointed out by the Americans themselves in an Address to the people of Ireland; and a voice had been raised in the Parliament of Great Britain, warning the Irish that, if the experiment of taxing the Americans without their consent was successful, their turn would come next. The danger was probably exaggerated; but the writer in the *Public Advertiser* did not stand alone in his opinion that England had the right to tax Ireland; and the refusal of Lord North to yield to Harcourt's request to refrain from certifying a Money Bill as a reason for summoning a new Parliament was a sufficient proof that the claim to legislate for Ireland was to be fully maintained[1].

Harcourt retired in November, 1776. To smooth the way for his successor, the Earl of Buckinghamshire, he had, in one day, created eighteen peers and advanced seven barons and five viscounts a step in the peerage. But public opinion was growing too strong to be held in check by such a travesty of government. The distress of the country was appalling. Trade was wholly at a standstill; rents could not be paid; warehouses had to be closed; every day money grew scarcer and bankruptcies more frequent. Thousands of hands were turned off, and in Dublin the streets swarmed with half-starving mechanics, whose sole means of subsistence was the half-pound of oat-meal doled out to them daily by charity. Things, in short, had reached a pass when, as Hussey Burgh put it, England would either have to support the country or concede her the means of supporting herself. When Parliament met in October, 1777, a motion to retrench expenses was brought forward by

---

[1] It should be remembered that cause had to be shown for the summoning an Irish Parliament, and that, before being submitted to it, all Bills had to be "certified" in England.

CH. XIV.

Grattan. The motion was rejected. But the fact that Government was forced shortly afterwards to borrow £50,000 from the Bank of England to pay the army left no doubt as to the seriousness of the situation. The necessity of removing some of the existing restrictions was admitted by the Ministry, and Bills were framed conceding to Ireland the privilege of exporting all her articles of produce, with the exception of wool and woollen goods, to the colonies in British vessels, and of importing all goods, except tobacco, directly from them ; permitting her to export her manufactured glass to all places, except Great Britain ; and abolishing the restrictions on the importation into Great Britain of cotton-yarn and sail-cloth. The proposals drew down a storm of angry protest from the manufacturers of Manchester, Liverpool, Glasgow, Stafford, and other places. " A foreign invasion," it was said, " could scarcely have excited a greater alarm." Government yielded to the pressure put upon it, and, of all the proposed benefits, only that of allowing Ireland to export her cotton-yarn and sail-cloth was conceded. The inadequacy of the concession caused great dissatisfaction in Ireland ; but there was no disposition to lay the blame on Government, and the conciliatory attitude adopted by Ministers towards the English Catholics at this time afforded the Irish Parliament an opportunity of testifying to its own liberality, by an Act relieving their Catholic countrymen of the chief social disabilities laid on them by the penal laws and conceding them the right to acquire land by taking leases for 999 years. It was a large and generous measure of relief, and, coming as a free gift from the Protestants, did more than anything else to strengthen that feeling of national identity, which showed itself in the subsequent struggle for free trade and legislative independence. But the selfishness of British manu-facturers in intercepting the boon intended by Government was deeply resented, and associations were formed pledging their members not to import or wear any article of British manufacture. The enthusiasm with which the movement was taken up by all ranks and classes of society, and its success, startled the nation into a sense of its own power. Buckingham-shire regarded the situation with apprehension. The people were still perfectly loyal ; but they were clearly in earnest, and, with the example of the colonies before them, there was no saying what might happen.

Since France had taken part in the War, the Channel swarmed with privateers. All external trade had ceased, and any day might witness an invasion. But, with a country practically denuded of troops, and with an empty treasury, Government could only look on in helpless inactivity. Its inability to respond to a call from Belfast for a small garrison to ward off an impending invasion brought matters to a crisis. Driven to depend on their own resources, the citizens of Belfast acted as though Government had been dissolved, and raised a volunteer corps for their own protection. From Belfast the movement spread rapidly. Every-where the local gentry put themselves at its head. The danger of

foreign invasion, the helplessness of Government, the novelty of the
thing itself, and the appeal it made to the military instincts of the
nation, conspired to render volunteering the most popular and formidable
movement the country had ever known. Though excluded, by their
inability to carry arms, from actively participating in it, the Catholics
showed their ardour in the cause by liberally subscribing for the purchase
of implements of war. Buckinghamshire, who had hailed the appearance
of the Volunteers with a sigh of relief, began to tremble for the consequences, when he saw how formidable they were becoming. He would
gladly have suppressed them; but this was out of his power, and to the
reproaches of his colleagues in London, he could only urge the necessity
of "temporising." Of politics there had at first been no sign; but it
was not long before the Lord Lieutenant observed a disposition, in
certain quarters, to turn the situation to political account. It could
hardly be otherwise. The Volunteers were to a man non-importers, and,
next to the safety of the country, which was now provided for, free
trade lay nearest their thoughts. As the time when Parliament was to
meet approached, members were urged by their constituencies to limit
supplies to six months, until the commercial grievances were redressed.
Buckinghamshire was alarmed at the direction things were taking; but
the Speech from the Throne showed no appreciation of the seriousness
of the situation. An equally colourless Address was proposed and
seconded. Rising to oppose it Grattan pronounced both speech and
address to be an insult to the common sense of the nation. The time
for such inanities had passed. Ireland was in a state of dire distress
and he moved that nothing could satisfy her but "a free export trade."
Hussey Burgh proposed "a free export and import," Flood "a free
trade" simply; and in this form the amended Address was carried
without a division. In his answer, the King announced his intention of
concurring in all measures which, on mature consideration, should be
thought conducive "to the general welfare of all his subjects." But the
position was too grave to permit of such ambiguous phrases. A few days
later a riot broke out in the "Liberties" at Dublin; members of Parliament
were forced to alight from their coaches and swear to vote for Free Trade
and a short (*i.e.* six months') Money Bill. The House of Commons passed
a resolution resenting this intrusion on their authority. But there was no
difference of opinion between them and the mob. It was proposed that,
in view of the distress of the country, it would be inexpedient to grant
any new taxes. The motion was carried by 170 to 47, and was followed
by another, limiting supplies to six months. The resolution was
supported by Hussey Burgh in words which electrified the House and
stirred the nation to its depths—"Talk not to me of peace," he said.
"It is not peace; but smothered war. England has sown her laws in
dragons' teeth, and they have sprung up armed men." The resolution
was carried by 138 to 100. The vote was one that Government could

not mistake; and on December 13, Lord North submitted three propositions to the British Parliament, repealing the laws prohibiting the export of Irish wool and woollen goods to any part of Europe, abolishing the restrictions placed on Irish glass, and admitting Ireland to all the advantages of the colonial trade on terms of an equality of taxes and customs. The non-importation agreements had effectually convinced English manufacturers that Ireland was their best market, and this time they offered no opposition. Bills based on the proposals were drawn up, and easily passed through Parliament.

The joy with which the concessions were received in Ireland was largely tinged with the reflexion that she had owed them more to her own exertions and the unsheathed swords of the Volunteers, than to the generosity of England. Would England abide by the agreement? The commercial concessions implied no renunciation, on her part, of her claim to legislate for Ireland. Would she not, when the opportunity offered, recall the boon, that had been so reluctantly granted? England was herself responsible for this distrust. The feeling of gratitude gave place to one of uncertainty. Nothing could satisfy Ireland except the recognition of her national independence. Of this feeling Grattan made himself the mouthpiece. It was only four years since he had entered Parliament; but his ability, patriotism, and eloquence had already won him a conspicuous position both inside and outside the House of Commons. Early in 1780, in replying to an address presenting him with the freedom of the Guild of Dublin Merchants, he announced his intention of raising, in the following session, the question of the legislative independence of the Irish Parliament. His decision alarmed Government, and even his own friends doubted its wisdom. Considering the excited state of the country and the determined attitude of the Volunteers, now fully 40,000 strong, there could be no question that the step he proposed to take would put Parliament in the dangerous position of either running counter to the wishes of the nation, or of presenting England with an ultimatum. The Duke of Leinster declared that he for one " had no idea of constitutional questions being forced by the bayonet." Lord Hillsborough, the Secretary of State, suggested his favourite plan of a legislative union. Buckinghamshire begged him not to mention the subject: the mere suggestion of such a plan would set Ireland on flame. For himself, he preferred to try to tune Parliament.

True to his promise, Grattan on April 19 submitted a motion to the House of Commons affirming the legislative independence of Parliament. His speech made a great impression on the House; and Government, feeling itself unable to meet it with a direct negative, moved the adjournment of the debate. The danger was tided over; but Buckinghamshire admitted to Hillsborough that, though many members were annoyed that the subject had been mooted, still the feeling was almost unanimous in its favour. Grattan expressed himself satisfied with the result. " No

British Minister will now, I should hope," he said, "be mad enough to attempt, nor servant of Government desperate enough to execute, nor Irish subject mean enough not to resist, by every means in his power, a British Act of Parliament." The hope was well grounded. Two cases of desertion from the army had recently occurred; but in both cases the magistrates refused to convict on the ground that, Ireland having no Mutiny Act of her own, the English Act could not be regarded as binding. To meet the difficulty, a Mutiny Bill was immediately introduced. The Bill placed Government in the awkward position of either having to admit the inadequacy of the English Act or losing control of the army. Buckinghamshire was urged, against his judgment, to resist it; but, despite his efforts, it passed and was transmitted to England. It was returned in August, with the omission of the words limiting its operation to one year. The indignation of the country was intense; but the Bill was passed. Corruption had accomplished what nothing else could effect. Congratulating himself on his master-stroke, Buckinghamshire brought the session as quickly as possible to a close, and handed over the sword to his successor, the Earl of Carlisle. The situation, so it seemed to Carlisle, was by no means hopeless. A threat of parliamentary reform had considerably strengthened Government, by attaching to it all those who, for personal reasons, dreaded any such measure. A small secret fund, Carlisle suggested, would greatly assist in keeping them steady. He had not miscalculated the situation. When Parliament met in October, 1781, a motion by Grattan for leave to introduce a limited Mutiny Bill was rejected by 177 to 33. He replied with a threat to appeal to the country, in a "formal instrument." A week or two later, he published his *Observations on the Mutiny Bill*, and on February 15, 1782, a Convention representing the Volunteers of Ulster met at Dungannon. Resolutions were passed in favour of a modification of Poynings' Law, a limited Mutiny Bill, the independence of the judicial bench, and a further relaxation of the laws against the Catholics. The moderation of the resolutions was not less significant because they represented the opinion of 80,000 men in arms. A week later, Grattan moved an address to the King, declaratory of the independence of the Irish legislature. "Do you," he said addressing the House, "hesitate to weary the ears of his Majesty with your solicitations, or do you wait till your country speaks to you in thunder?" But the House was not to be moved: a motion to adjourn the debate was carried by 137 to 68. Outside Parliament, however, the agitation gained in volume daily, and, encouraged by the addresses that flowed in from all quarters, Grattan gave notice of his intention to renew his declaration on April 16. His intention and the determined attitude of the country alarmed Carlisle, and on March 27 he wrote suggesting the advisability of repealing the Act of 6 George I.

But the credit or discredit of yielding was not to be his. Before his letter reached its destination, the Ministry of Lord North had fallen and a new Administration, under the Marquis of Rockingham, had been formed. On April 14 the new Lord Lieutenant, the Duke of Portland, arrived in Dublin. Ministers were known to be favourable to Ireland: two of them, Rockingham and Fox, were personal friends of Lord Charlemont. But neither Charlemont nor Grattan would consent to postpone the question, and on the day appointed the latter rose to make his promised motion. His opening words struck the key-note of the position. "I am now," he said, "to address a free people." To the nation in arms, to the Volunteers, they that day owed the independence of Parliament. And now having given a Parliament to the people, he hoped and doubted not that the Volunteers would retire and leave the people to Parliament. He moved to assure his Majesty that the Crown of Ireland was an imperial Crown, inseparably annexed to the Crown of Great Britain, but that the kingdom of Ireland was a distinct kingdom, with a Parliament of her own, the sole legislature thereof. Ministers were mortified to find that their good intentions counted for so little. But there was nothing for it but to yield with as much grace and promptitude as possible. In submitting the proposals of Government to the British Parliament, Fox said it was desired to "meet Ireland on her own terms and give her everything she wanted in the way she seemed to wish for." There was no opposition. A Bill repealing the statute of 6 George I was passed, and when the Irish Parliament reassembled, after a short adjournment, on May 27, Portland announced that the King was prepared to give his unconditional assent to a modification of Poynings' Law and a limitation of the Mutiny Act to two years. Grattan expressed his entire satisfaction. "I understand," he said, "that Great Britain gives up *in toto* every claim to authority over Ireland." As a token of gratitude, and to signify to the world that Ireland was prepared to stand or fall with England, the House of Commons, at his suggestion, voted £100,000 and 20,000 men for the support of the British navy. A Habeas Corpus Act had already become law; and, to crown the work of reconciliation, a measure was passed relieving the Catholics from some of the restraints placed on their education and the exercise of their religion. On July 27 Portland adjourned Parliament to September 24.

Ireland had apparently, in Fox' words, got all she wanted. But the very completeness of the surrender bewildered men. Ireland had too long been treated by England with injustice to be able at once to understand that this time she was being dealt with fairly. The concessions, it was true, were there; but they had been extorted from England in the hour of her extremity, and there was no guarantee that she would not, at some future time, recall them. England, it was said, was taking advantage of the "generous credulity" of Irishmen. Simple repeal was insufficient; England must be called upon to renounce expressly her claim to legislate for Ireland. Grattan poohpoohed the suggestion and asked ironically, what guarantee an express renunciation could afford? But he had lost the ear of the nation. The agitation grew from day to day; it was taken up by Flood; the Lawyers' Volunteer Corps declared in its favour; the culpable negligence shown in drafting two trade Bills wherein Ireland was tacitly included, the utterances of irresponsible politicians in England, and a decision given in the Court of King's Bench on an appeal from Ireland, furnished apparent proof of its necessity. In the midst of the controversy the Marquis of Rockingham died. His death led to a reconstruction of the Ministry under Shelburne, and in September Temple succeeded Portland as Lord Lieutenant. Though inclined at first to resent the clamour for Renunciation, the new Ministry acted with due regard to public faith, and at the earliest opportunity a Bill was passed to remove all doubts which had arisen or might arise as to the exclusive rights of the Parliament and Courts of Ireland in matters of legislation and judicature.

Ireland had obtained from England the acknowledgment of her legislative independence. The importance of the victory was exaggerated in both countries. To be sure, the English Parliament could no longer directly interfere in the affairs of Ireland; but her counsels were still controlled by English Ministers, wholly irresponsible to the Irish Parliament, and it was inevitable that whenever the interests of the Irish people clashed with the views of English Ministers, these should be tempted to have recourse to corruption, in order to tune Parliament to their pleasure. The only guarantee for the independence of Parliament was a reform of Parliament itself. This everybody in Ireland admitted. But how was it to be effected? No doubt, Ireland owed much to the Volunteers, and the Volunteers were in favour of Reform. But the feeling of annoyance at the political influence exercised by them was not confined to the corrupt element in the House of Commons, whose existence Reform menaced. There were many independent members, who agreed with Grattan that, having given a Parliament to the people, it was the duty of the Volunteers to retire and leave the people to Parliament. But it was Flood, the author of the Renunciation agitation, and not Grattan, who had the ear of the nation, and with Flood went Charlemont and that eccentric ornament of the Irish Church, Frederick Augustus Hervey, Earl of Bristol and Bishop of Derry. During the summer of 1783 resolutions in favour of Reform became of frequent occurrence, and at a general assembly of the Ulster Volunteers at Dungannon in September, it was resolved to issue invitations to the other provinces to join with them in sending delegates to a national convention to be held at Dublin on November 10 to discuss the question. Meanwhile, the government of Lord Shelburne had given way to the Coalition Ministry of the Duke of Portland, with North and Fox as joint Secretaries of State, and in June Lord Northington arrived in Dublin as Temple's successor. Parliament was dissolved shortly afterwards and a new one met on October 14. The general election had caused little alteration in its complexion, though it was said that a third of the open constituencies had found fresh representatives. The question of parliamentary reform had not been mooted when the Volunteer Convention met at Dublin on November 10. It was a thorny subject, and even in the Convention it seemed at first as if no satisfactory solution of the question would be arrived at. Finally, however, a plan was resolved upon, which, while preserving to Parliament its character as a Protestant assembly, would, by raising the franchise qualification, opening close boroughs, incapacitating holders of pensions from sitting in Parliament, compelling members, who accepted office, to seek reelection, and rendering bribery at elections a disqualification, have gone far to remove the most glaring abuses in the representation. Both Charlemont and the Bishop of Derry thought it unadvisable to present the measure to Parliament until the Convention dissolved and the general feeling of the country had been tested. But Flood would admit of no delay, and on the same day (November 29) he moved from his seat in the House of Commons for leave to bring in a Bill for the more equal representation of the people in Parliament. The Attorney-General, Yelverton, immediately rose to oppose the motion, on the ground that it was an attempt on the part of the Volunteers to overawe Parliament. This was the general line of argument; and, after a heated controversy, the motion was rejected by an overwhelming majority. Grattan, it is true, both spoke and voted in its favour; but his speech, as Northington rightly interpreted it, was not intended to hurt the Government. It is easy to find excuses for him; but his conduct at this critical moment, though personal motives account for it, can never be sufficiently deplored. With singular self-restraint, the Convention manifested no resentment at the brusque rejection of its proposals, and, after passing a loyal address to his Majesty, it quietly dissolved itself, on December 2.

From this moment, public interest in the subject began visibly to decline, and, though resolutions in favour of Reform still continued to be passed at Volunteer meetings, the consideration of questions more nearly affecting the material welfare of the country gradually forced it into the background of politics. Despite the commercial concessions of 1779, the trade of Ireland continued to languish. There were several reasons for this, due partly to the incapacity of Irish manufacturers, chiefly from lack of capital, to take full advantage of the colonial trade opened to them, but mainly to the prohibitive duties placed by England on all goods, except provisions and plain linens, imported from Ireland. Unable to participate in the English market, Irish manufacturers found it difficult to hold their own even in Ireland, owing to the merely nominal duties placed on English imports. Competition, it was insisted, was impossible unless they were provided with some sort of protection. There was a good deal of reason in the argument; and, early in 1784, the matter was brought before Parliament by Luke Gardiner. The distress prevailing among the manufacturers of the metropolis was, he said, too well known to members to require special proof. But the distress was not confined to Dublin. It extended to every manufacturing town and to every industry in the kingdom. The only remedy was the imposition of a light duty on imports, just sufficient to place Irish manufacturers on a level with their English competitors. The House, however, was unwilling to give any cause of offence to England and rejected the proposal. Gardiner, it was said, had mistaken the causes of the distress which were to be found rather in an inadequate supply of bread-stuffs than in industrial depression. To remedy this evil, the new Attorney-General, John Foster, gave notice of his intention to introduce a Bill to regulate the corn trade and to promote agriculture. The Bill (which provided for a system of bounties) passed rapidly through Parliament, and received the royal assent on May 14. It is said that Foster's Corn Laws altered the entire face of Ireland, and turned her from a purely grazing and corn-importing country into an agricultural and corn-producing land. It would be more correct to say that they enabled her to take advantage of the economic situation created by the extraordinary development, at this time, of England as a manufacturing country, and thus indirectly led to that result. But the effect of the Corn Laws was not immediate. Distress continued unabated, and the indignation at the rejection of the demand for Protection found vent in serious riots and the revival of non-importation agreements.

The Lord Lieutenant, the Duke of Rutland, who had succeeded Northington, when Pitt came into office on the downfall of the Coalition Ministry in December, 1783, proposed to adopt severe measures of repression. But Pitt, while agreeing that disorder ought to be checked with a firm hand, was anxious to treat Ireland with consideration. The recent constitutional changes had, in his opinion, undoubtedly weakened the connexion between the two countries. Perhaps a union would have been a better solution. But Ireland had preferred independence, and the account was closed. All the same, it was clear that her new acquisitions had not satisfied her. The demand for Protection, backed up by non-importation agreements, might be repressed for a time; but, sooner or later, it was bound to make itself heard. Could not the concession of the Channel Trade be made the basis of a commercial union? Pitt studied the problem long and seriously. On February 7, 1785, the Irish Secretary, Thomas Orde, submitted a plan calculated to put Ireland on the same commercial footing as England, on condition that, whenever the hereditary revenue in Ireland exceeded a sum which remained to be fixed, the surplus should be appropriated towards the support of the naval forces of the Empire. It was a large and statesmanlike plan, and its acceptance would, as Pitt himself said, have made "England and Ireland one country in effect, though for local concerns under distinct legislatures—one in the communication of advantages, and of course in the participation of burdens." But the condition stuck in the throat of the Irish Parliament. Experience had taught Irishmen how unwise it was to trust ministers with the public purse. The hereditary revenue amounted to £652,000 and it was steadily rising. It was proposed to amend the proposition by making the contribution contingent upon the establishment of a balance between revenue and expenditure in time of peace at £656,000. The amendment, much to Pitt's annoyance, when he heard of it, was accepted by Orde, and, in gratitude for the liberal treatment of Ireland, the Commons at once created a substantial surplus by voting new taxes to the amount of £140,000. On February 22, Pitt submitted the proposals to the English House of Commons. The whole mercantile influence of Lancashire and Yorkshire was thrown into the scale against them. Fox seized on the alteration made in them by the Irish Parliament, to prove that Ireland was being made the arbiter of English commercial interests. They were withdrawn, revised, and again submitted to the House on May 12. From eleven resolutions they had grown to twenty. Some of these affected patents, copyright in books, the rights of fishing, and the like; but they were mainly intended to meet the objection raised by Fox. To avoid the very hypothetical danger of Ireland becoming "the emporium of trade," an obligation was placed on the Irish Parliament to adopt, without delay or modification, all the navigation laws then in force in England, or that might be afterwards made by the British Parliament. With a tergiversation reflecting great discredit on him, Fox denounced the clause as an insidious attack on the Irish Constitution. He could not prevent the acceptance of the resolutions in England; but his words awakened the jealous fears of the Irish Parliament. A motion for leave to bring in a Bill based on them only escaped rejection by nineteen votes, and it was thereupon dropped. The news of its abandonment was hailed with general satisfaction, and that night Dublin was illuminated. It would, perhaps, have been better if the commercial treaty had never been proposed; but its rejection in the circumstances was most deplorable. The measure was one which, as Pitt admitted, sat very near his heart. Its withdrawal was regarded in Ireland as a great constitutional victory. Perhaps both sides overestimated its importance. But in linking the fortunes of Ireland to those of the Whig party in England Grattan and his friends made a great mistake. No one of course could see that the future was to belong to Pitt and not to Fox. At the time Fox' factiousness was regarded as patriotism and Pitt's statesmanship misrepresented as treachery. It was a misunderstanding fatal in its consequences for Ireland.

Meanwhile, the effect of Foster's Corn Laws was beginning to be felt in the increased prosperity of the country. There was still, however, considerable distress; and in 1786 there was a fresh outburst of agrarian crime in Munster. The cause of the disturbances was admitted to be the tithes. It was confessed that, so far from being able to pay them, the peasantry could find neither food nor clothing for themselves; but it was in vain that Grattan pleaded for remedial measures, which should ease the peasant and at the same time satisfy the clergy. Parliament refused to countenance what it regarded as an attack on private property, and armed Government with exceptional powers for the restoration of order. On the whole, however, as the Irish Chancellor, Lord Lifford, wrote, in August, 1788, to the Marquis of Buckingham (Earl Temple), who had been reappointed Viceroy on the death, in October, 1787, of the Duke of Rutland, the country had, in his long experience, never been quieter. But, even as he wrote, disquieting rumours arrived of the terrible misfortune that had befallen the King. By the beginning of November it was impossible to doubt the fact of his insanity. The situation created was unprecedented; but, as everybody agreed that a Regent would have to be appointed and that the only person who could be so appointed was the Prince of Wales, there seemed little room for a crisis. Unfortunately, the Prince's appointment meant a change of Ministry; this was the one fact that possessed any real interest; and for Ireland it was the all-important fact. If Fox succeeded to power, the young Constitution would be secured a free development, and the balance of power would be definitely shifted to the side of the Opposition. This was the opinion of Grattan and those who acted with him. That their calculations were well based, was evident from the practical unanimity with which the proposal to address the Prince of Wales to take upon himself the government of the kingdom during his Majesty's incapacity, was received in both Irish Houses. As Fitzgibbon ironically remarked, all the hangers-on of office had gone over to pay their devotions to the rising sun. On February 19, 1789, both Houses waited on the Lord Lieutenant to request him to transmit the Address. He refused point-blank. Whether he acted constitutionally may be doubted; but his refusal brought into prominence the weak point in the Irish Constitution, viz. the inability of Parliament to control the Administration. The difficulty was surmounted by the nomination of a Parliamentary Commission to present the Address personally. But, by the time the Commissioners reached London, the King had recovered his health. His recovery sealed the fate of the Irish Parliament. Pensioners and placemen, scenting danger, drifted back to their allegiance. To make it easier for them Government held out an amnesty to all who repented. Those who were too proud or too independent to accept it, were dismissed. Corruption once more became the order of the day. The end did not come immediately. The Irish Parliament had still ten years of sickly existence before it. But, even in 1789, the Union was a foregone conclusion. The boasted independence of the Irish Parliament had proved a sham. Its corruption was past dispute. It had refused to reform itself when the opportunity offered, and it was itself mainly responsible for its own fate.

CH. XIV.

CHAPTER XV.

INDIA.

(1) THE MOGHUL EMPIRE.

THE points of connexion between the histories of Europe and Asia, and the reciprocal influence, moral and material, exercised from time to time upon each other by the two continents, would provide an attractive subject of enquiry. It might begin with the Asiatic conquests of Alexander the Great, who founded an Eastern empire which, under his successors, spread Hellenic ideas and institutions throughout all the regions that had been subject to the great Iranian monarchy, from the Mediterranean beyond the Euphrates almost up to the confines of India. The changes that followed his campaigns were wide and lasting. For, although Alexander's empire was reft asunder by partition among his successors, yet the Macedonian Greeks seem to have long maintained their general ascendancy as a ruling race, held together by the ties of common nationality, political interest, and intellectual superiority, in the midst of a vast indigenous population. When the Romans took over from the Asiatic Greeks the dominion over the lands west of the Euphrates, their strong, organised administration enforced order and restrained barbarism for several centuries, and cleared the ground for planting Christianity. In the seventh century ensued an event of supreme historical importance, the rise of the Mohammadan Faith; and in the long conflict between Islam and Christianity the Greek empire at Constantinople was gradually dismembered; until the final triumph of the Osmanli Sultans swept out of western Asia both Christianity and civilisation. From the middle of the fourteenth century may be dated the extinction of all European dominion in Asia. During the next century the Asiatic continent was slowly recovering from the devastations of the Mongol hordes under Tamerlane, who had dispersed armies, broken up kingdoms, and uprooted all political landmarks from the Chinese Wall to the Hellespont. The records of that age contain little more than the rise and fall of ephemeral rulerships, alternately won and lost in the strife among fierce tribal confederacies;

but towards the close of the fifteenth century this confusion abates; and the period which follows, so far as it relates to India, is the subject of this section.

Erskine, in the introductory chapter of his History of the Moghul Empire under the first two Emperors, Bábar and Humáyun, takes the beginning of the sixteenth century as the era in which the kingdoms of Europe began to settle down into their permanent form of great compact States, absorbing the minor principalities and feudatories under their absolute sovereignty. Something of the same kind, he observes, happened at the same period, though to a different extent, in Asia, where the incoherent rulerships and minor States were largely obliterated and superseded by strong centralised monarchies. In a broad and general way the parallel drawn by Erskine is correct. Early in the sixteenth century the Osmanli Sultans at Constantinople were uniting under their authority Syria, Egypt, in fact all the Asiatic provinces of the Roman Empire; and by the middle of that century their despotism was at its climax of power and expansion. At the same epoch Persia became consolidated under the able dynasty of the Safevi Kings; and India fell under the sway of the Moghuls. And it is important to remark, furthermore, that this simultaneous rise of powerful military States in both continents produced interacting effects and consequences that may be clearly traced in the history of the period; for at no other time, perhaps, was the political situation in Europe more directly influenced by events in Asia. The collisions of rival monarchies, in the process of enlarging their realms and planting their dynasties, were felt in reverberation across the world from west to east. Throughout the long contest, in the sixteenth century, between France and the Empire of Charles V, the Franco-Turkish alliance weighed heavily in the scale against the House of Habsburg; it placed the Empire between an enemy on either flank. On the other hand the desolating invasions of Hungary by Suleiman the Great were checked by his Persian wars, which drew off and divided the Turkish armies; and towards the end of his reign the Sultan was so involved in hostilities against Shah Tamasp that he was compelled to make peace with the Emperor Ferdinand I; a diversion which probably saved eastern Europe from dire calamities, since the Imperial forces were no match for the Turk. In one of his letters from Constantinople, Busbecq, Ferdinand's ambassador, compares the patience, temperance, and fighting qualities of the Turkish soldiers with the licence and loose discipline of the Christian troops; and he declares that the result of a meeting between two such armies cannot be doubtful. "The only obstacle," he adds, "is Persia, whose position on his rear forces the invader to take precautions. The fear of Persia gives us a respite, but it is only for a time." At the same time, moreover, the consolidation of a powerful State under the Safevi dynasty had an important bearing upon the course of Asiatic as well as of European affairs. For, while on the west

CH. XV.

Persia was strong enough to embarrass the Osmanli Sultans; on the north-east the first Safevi King had been cooperating with Bábar, the future conqueror of India, against their common enemy, the Usbegs, had assisted him with an army to subdue the countries along the Oxus, and had made it possible for him to fix himself so firmly in Afghanistan, that he could eventually descend upon India. And indeed the first three Moghul Emperors were considerably indebted for the security of their north-western frontier beyond Afghanistan to their friendly relations with the Persian rulers, who were so constantly engaged in hostilities with the Turkish Sultans on their western side that they were very willing to avoid trouble in the regions between Persia and India.

From the eleventh century the whole region of upper India had been conquered by successive Mohammadan invaders, who descended through the mountain passes from central Asia to carve out their kingdoms on the rich plains below; and throughout the fifteenth century rival dynasties, in perpetual strife with each other, had fixed their headquarters in different parts of the country. In the north and west the territory had been parcelled out among the tribal chiefs from Afghanistan owing nominal allegiance to the Emperors at Delhi; until, about 1450, Sultan Behlol, of the Lodi clan, who had been raised to the throne by a powerful confederacy, imposed energetically his supremacy over the lesser Princes, and founded his dynasty. But early in the sixteenth century this kingdom was again threatened with disruption. The Afghan feudatories were hard to keep in subordination; and under the weak rule of Sultan Ibrahim Lodi they were falling into rebellion, conspiring and intriguing at home and abroad, and throwing off their allegiance to the Delhi sovereignty. Four considerable Mohammadan kingdoms had become independent in the west and south; while in central India the Hindu chiefs of the Rajput clans were gathering strength from the dissensions among the Mohammadan leaders, the enemies of their race and religion. None of these principalities, except the Rajput chiefships, had any root in the land or natural stability; though the Lodi Sultan still maintained predominance by a numerous army and the possession of ample revenues. The general condition of the country and of its government, distracted by internal commotions and the alarms of civil war, undoubtedly pointed towards impending changes, and offered a favourable opportunity for another foreign invasion.

Zahírruddin Mahmud Bábar was by descent a Khan of the Chagatáis, a clan which took its name from the son of the famous Mongolian conqueror Chingis Khan. Although in Bábar's day the word "Moghul" denoted a separate and hostile clan, it nevertheless became affixed by common use to the northern tribesmen whom he led into India, and to the dynasty that he founded there. He was born in 1483, the hereditary

chief of Ferghana, a petty principality beyond the Oxus. After fighting
from his earliest youth to maintain his birthright, he was compelled to
abandon it in 1504, when he turned his arms against Afghanistan; and
in the course of the next seven years he contended indefatigably against
many vicissitudes of fortune, until, by the aid of the Persian King, he
established himself at Kabul, where he became engaged in long and
indecisive contests with the unruly Afghan tribes. Between 1514 and
1523 he made four expeditions into India, upon the pretext of his right
to the throne by descent from Tamerlane; he laid hold, more or less
firmly, of the upper Punjab, and placed a garrison at Lahore. But his
fourth incursion had been disconcerted by a tribal outbreak in the
mountains behind him, which convinced him that no plans of permanently conquering India could succeed without a solid base of operations
in Afghanistan; so for the next two years he put all his strength into
the work of reducing Kandahar and the country adjacent, and of
repelling an inroad made by the Usbegs from the north.

When the highlands had been pacified and effectually overawed,
Bábar set out in 1525 upon his fifth and decisive expedition into India.
On his march he was joined by several Afghan nobles, malcontents and
refugees from the Lodi Government, who brought over to his side their
troops and local support; and with their reinforcements he advanced
against the far more numerous army of Sultan Ibrahim, who was encamped at Pániput. There, after a fierce encounter, he won a complete
victory. The Sultan was killed on the field; Bábar seized Delhi and
distributed the imperial treasury as prize-money to his followers; he
pushed on to Agra; and the capture of these two great cities gave him
possession of all the broad and fertile plains lying between and along the
upper streams of the Ganges and Jumna. The provinces east of the
Ganges made some resistance, which was soon overcome; but in the west,
beyond the Jumna river, a formidable confederacy was gathering against
him. The famous Rána Sanga of Oodipúr had mustered all the fighting force of the Rajput clans and was marching upon Agra with strong
contingents from some of the leading Afghan nobles, who had by this
time perceived that a Moghul Emperor, firmly seated on the Delhi
throne, would speedily make an end of their local independence. Bábar
set out from Agra to meet his antagonist near Biána, where he threw
up entrenchments. Both the Hindu and Mohammadan commanders
of the two armies were skilful and daring soldiers, well trained by
long experience of war. Bábar's north-countrymen had been disheartened, like Alexander's Macedonians, by the Indian climate; and
his captains were daunted by the multitude of the enemy; they pressed
him to retreat, and it was only by entreaty and exhortation that they
were persuaded to stake their fortunes upon another pitched battle.
The Rajput strength lay almost entirely in cavalry; they made a furious
onslaught upon Bábar's position; but they suffered heavily from his

CH. XV.

artillery, and when their charges slackened he threw his horsemen upon either flank, making a simultaneous advance against their centre, which broke up the Rajput army into irreparable confusion. Although they still fought desperately, they were thoroughly beaten. Some of the principal Rajput chiefs were slain; Rána Sanga, who escaped in the rout, died within a year; the broken clans fell back into their own country; and Bábar's victory, which extinguished all serious danger to his dominion, left him free to extend and confirm it in two or three successful campaigns during the few remaining years of his life. When he died, in 1530, his authority was supreme over almost the whole of the wide Indian plains from the Indus to the confines of Bengal—the region which has always been the seat of empire; while his son Humáyun held Afghanistan for him with the help of the Persians. Bábar's courage, perseverance, and indefatigable activity of mind and body, his adventurous and triumphant career, rank him among the foremost of those men, famous in the history of nations at this period, who created or completed Asiatic monarchies quite as splendid and powerful as any of the contemporary sovereignties in Europe. No other authentic autobiography has been written by an Oriental prince like the vivacious narrative in which Bábar has described his own habits and character, with the events of an adventurous life extending over not more than forty-eight years.

But the foundations of the new dominion were still unsettled; and the reign of Humáyun, the second Emperor, was speedily interrupted by revolts and grave misfortunes. Just as in Europe disputed successions were constantly kindling great wars, so, throughout the period of the Moghul empire, each Emperor, on his succession, had to fight for his throne. Primogeniture carried an acknowledged right of little use to those who were incapable of enforcing it; for in practice the demise of the Crown was determined by the ordeal of battle; and one potent cause of the strength and stability of the Moghul dynasty was that for more than a century the imperial title passed in this manner to the ablest representative of the family. Humáyun's succession was at once challenged by his brother, Kámrán, who advanced from Kabul and occupied the Punjab; and insurrections broke out in the eastern and southern provinces. The Emperor took the field with promptitude and vigour; but these simultaneous outbreaks diverted his forces and disconcerted his strategy. The heirs of the Lodi kingdom, which Bábar had destroyed, rallied their partisans among the Afghan nobles, the most formidable of whom was Sher Shah, an Afghan chief of real military genius, who had taken up arms on the south-east. Against these rebels Humáyun marched; but while he was engaged with them the independent King of Guzerat, Bahádur, began hostilities in the west; and, although Bahádur was defeated by the imperial army, he renewed the war later and carried it on until he died in 1537. Meanwhile Sher Shah, with whom the Emperor had at first contrived to make terms, had collected his forces, and was now advancing from Bengal upon Agra. Humáyun led out an army to meet him; but on the banks of the Ganges he suffered a crushing defeat (June, 1539), which completely ruined his cause. He fled northward into the Punjab, making vain attempts to rally adherents; while Sher Shah, who had now proclaimed himself Emperor, followed in pursuit, capturing both Humáyun's capitals, Agra and Delhi, until, finding the Punjab untenable, he took refuge in Afghanistan with his brother Kámrán, who at first joined forces with him, but subsequently deserted him. After wandering through Sinde and Beluchistan, the Emperor ended his flight in exile at the Court of the Persian King. Shah Tamasp, although his behaviour towards the fugitive Emperor was at first cold and haughty, eventually agreed to assist him with troops to recover the Afghan fortresses, on condition that Kandahar should be made over to Persia. So, in 1545, Humáyun crossed the border again into Afghanistan, where his brother Kámrán, who was ruling there independently, was by no means inclined to make way for him. Many partisans joined his standard; he seized Kandahar, and occupied Kabul; but for the next ten years he was entangled in long and hard campaigns, thwarted by revolts, conspiracies, reverses, and all the complications of a war in which the tribal chiefs had no scruple about changing sides; until finally he beat down resistance of every kind, destroyed Kámrán's party and drove him out of the country. Having thus reconquered the whole of Afghanistan and Kashmír, he prepared to descend upon India, where Sher Shah and his heirs had been reigning in his stead.

The moment was favourable for his enterprise. Sher Shah had been killed at the siege of Kalinjar in 1545; the rulership had fallen into feeble hands; and four rivals were competing for it. The whole kingdom was distracted by civil war and intestine confusion; the frontier garrisons had been withdrawn to take part in the contest for supremacy at the capital. Humáyun swept the upper Punjab clear of enemies, with little resistance from the disorganised and divided forces of the Afghan Sultans; he marched straight upon Delhi, dispersed an army that offered battle at Sirhind, occupied the capital, and replaced himself upon the imperial throne, after fourteen years of strenuous contention against hardship and adversity. Some desultory fighting ensued in the lower provinces; but Humáyun had securely established his authority when he died, from an accidental fall, within six months after his triumphant restoration.

To his son, Akbar Shah, who was thirteen years old at his father's death, Humáyun bequeathed an unfinished conquest, and a dominion which hardly extended beyond the Punjab and the districts round Delhi and Agra. In India, and even in Afghanistan, the Moghul power still represented little more than another successful invasion of Tartar hordes from beyond the Oxus; it had struck no roots into either country;

it was encompassed by rivals and insurgents. The preservation of Akbar's throne during his minority was due to the energy, in war and administration, of Bairam Khan, Humáyun's best general, who took charge of the government at Delhi, put down a serious rising in the Kabul highlands, and forced the adherents of the old reigning Afghan family in India to lay down their arms. When, however, Akbar assumed, in his eighteenth year, the supreme authority, he found means of ridding himself with politic ingratitude of a Minister who was inconveniently powerful and popular. The young Emperor lost no time in proving his eminent capacity. He struck right and left at rebels and enemies; he defeated the Afghan chiefs who had declared against him in the eastern provinces; he repelled an inroad led into the Punjab by his brother Mirza Hakím; and, having rapidly suppressed all opposition to his internal authority, he proceeded to organise his government and to push forward the boundaries of his empire. During the next twelve years the strongholds of the Rajput clans in central India were taken and garrisoned, and their chiefs brought under allegiance to his sovereignty. In western India Guzerat and Sinde were annexed; and the rich province of Bengal submitted after some tedious and troublesome campaigns. In the far north Kashmír was regained for the empire; and in 1582, when his brother Hakím again broke into the Punjab from Afghanistan, Akbar fell upon him with an army, drove him back and followed him into the mountains, pursued him to Kabul and restored the imperial jurisdiction over this most important frontier province. It is true that the unruly Afghan tribes were never completely pacified; but, so long as the important fortresses and the lines of communication were held by Moghul governors, they attempted no further control; and the recapture of Kandahar from the Persians in 1594 gave them sufficient mastery over the whole country. The death of Shah Tamasp had been followed by internal commotions in Persia, which removed for some time any fear of reprisals from that quarter; and the historian Ferishta remarks that Akbar's military dispositions "had raised a wall of disciplined valour" against enemies in the north.

It was not until he had thoroughly pacified upper India, overpowered the Rajput chiefs, and secured his position in Afghanistan, that Akbar, toward the close of his reign, undertook the subjugation of the independent kingdoms in the south. In 1586 his armies had invaded, with partial success, the region commonly called the Dekhan, which may be loosely described as extending from below the Vindhya range of hills as far southward as the Tungabhadra river. Some of the territory in the northern part of this region had been annexed; but the kingdom of Ahmednagar resisted effectually. In 1595, when fierce disputes broke out among claimants to the rulership, the imperial troops again attacked Ahmednagar, and were repulsed by the Queen Regent, Chánd Bibi, a princess whose high spirit and romantic intrepidity are famous in Indian tradition. But in 1599 the city was besieged by superior forces under Prince Murád, Akbar's son; and the kingdom became a dependency of the empire.

The realm of Akbar, at its full expansion, may be said to have had its north-western frontier on the Oxus and the confines of Persia, and to have included all upper and central India down to the Bay of Bengal on the south-east. To the south his sovereignty had shifting and ill-defined limits, for which the Godavery river may be taken as an approximate demarcation. Yet the tribes in Afghanistan had never been thoroughly tamed, while in southern India the principalities outside his jurisdiction were restless and hostile; so that at each extremity the Moghul empire was exposed to revolt or attack. This, however, is the normal situation of Asiatic rulerships, which have no fixed delimitation, and whose territories are continually expanding or contracting as the balance of their respective military power rises or falls.

Nevertheless, when Akbar died in 1605, after a reign that synchronises closely with the reign of the English Queen Elizabeth, he transmitted to his successor the best-ordered and richest empire of that time in Asia, divided and subdivided throughout into provinces and districts, with the rent-roll of each division carefully estimated and recorded, under minute regulations, for assessment of the land-tax. His revenue system was based upon a detailed measurement of the culturable area, an investigation of the average produce, and a limitation of the proportion to be demanded, in cash instead of in kind, by the State. The rent calculated upon these data was fixed for ten years. It is not to be supposed that this system was actually enforced in all the outlying tracts, or that the measurements were actually carried out everywhere. Yet, although Akbar's reforms fell into neglect during the wars and disorders of the later Emperors, his great administrative principle—that an equitable adjustment of the land revenue is the basis of good government in India— has been maintained as the ground-plan of all subsequent settlements between the State and the landowners or tenants up to the present day.

The fortunes of every hereditary dynasty, at critical epochs, depend on the chance of its producing a representative fitted to cope with the needs and emergencies of his time. The Emperor Akbar happened to be endowed with a remarkable combination of the qualities required by the situation of the Moghul empire at the moment when he came to the throne. He united high military ability with political genius; he could lead expeditions and suppress internal rebellion with skill and resolution; he understood the art of ruling; and his wise government quieted the people whom he subjected to his arms. The territories which he conquered were never lost again by him; they fell away through the misrule of his successors. He attached the Rajput chiefs to his family by matrimonial alliances; he strove to win the confidence of all classes of his subjects by tolerance and conciliation; he aimed at softening religious antipathies by the humanising influence of intellectual culture. He had been a man of war from his youth upward, overburdened with the affairs of a vast dominion; yet in his later years he became profoundly interested in theological speculation; his mind was powerfully drawn toward the abstruse philosophies of Brahmanism. The atmosphere of India, which has a decomposing effect on all positive creeds, fostered Akbar's innate propensity toward sceptical ideas, which carried him far above the easy indifference that is a marked feature in the general character of the Moghul Emperors before Aurungzeb. None of them were fanatics; they were better trained in arms than in articles of faith; they were foreigners ruling over an immense population, among whom the Hindu unbelievers far outnumbered the Mohammadans. The Emperor Bábar's memoirs show him to have been a jovial free-liver, who noted with a contrite heart his frequent wine-parties; and an anecdote told of his son Humáyun proves him to have been no austere Islamite. As this Emperor was riding with his brother they saw a dog defiling a Mohammadan tomb, whereupon the brother made the pious observation that the man buried there had been a notorious heretic. "Yes," replied Humáyun, "and the beast of a dog represents orthodoxy."

It may be remarked, generally, that the Mongolian or Turkish races have bred mighty conquerors, and have founded dynasties that are still ruling from Constantinople to Pekin; but that none of the great prophets or propagators of spiritual ideas has arisen from among them. Akbar stands alone among all their great temporal rulers as a philosophic autocrat, absorbed in formulating the doctrines of a new eclectic religion. He instituted a kind of metaphysical society, over which he presided in person, and in which he delighted in pitting against each other Persian mystics, Hindu pantheists, Christian missionaries, and orthodox Mohammadans. He even assumed by public edict the spiritual headship of his empire, and declared himself the first appellate judge of ecclesiastical questions. "Any opposition," said the edict, "on the part of subjects to such orders passed by His Majesty shall involve damnation in the world to come, and loss of religion and property in this life." The liturgy of the Divine Faith, as it was named, was a sort of Iranian sun-worship, embodying eclectic doctrines and the principle of universal tolerance. We may be reminded that the Roman Emperor Julian adopted, like Akbar, the sun as the image of all-pervading divinity; and that he also asserted supreme pontifical authority. In each instance the new theosophy disappeared at the death of its promulgator; for great religious revolutions are never inaugurated by temporal authority, but invariably begin among the people. Nothing, however, could demonstrate more clearly the strength of Akbar's government than the fact that he could take upon himself spiritual supremacy, and proclaim with impunity doctrines that subverted the fundamental law and the primary teaching of Islam. In no other Mohammadan kingdom could the sovereign have attempted such an enterprise without imminent peril to his throne. Akbar's political object was to provide some common ground upon which Hindus and Mohammadans might be brought nearer toward religious unity; though it is hardly necessary to add that no such *modus vivendi* has at any time been discovered.

The prudent and powerful government of Akbar had left the empire, at his decease, in complete internal tranquillity, with the exception of some temporary disturbances in Bengal. And as Prince Selim, who took the title of Jehángir on his accession, was the only surviving son, he had to contend against no serious opposition; for his own son Khusru, who raised a futile rebellion in the Punjab, was easily defeated and cast into prison. But in south-west India, which had never submitted patiently to the overlordship of the Moghuls, the inevitable troubles, recurrent during the whole period of their dynasty, soon began again. The kingdom of Ahmednagar, which Akbar had reduced to vassalship, was now entirely in the hands of the Abyssinian Málik Ambar, a Minister who had usurped all power, and whose fame as a soldier and statesman is still remembered. He founded a new capital at Aurungabad, and so effectively repulsed an army sent against him by the Emperor that he was left for some years unmolested. In 1617, however, when Málik Ambar's position had been weakened by the jealousy of rival factions, Prince Kharram (the future Emperor Shah Jehán) attacked him in great force, recovered some fortresses, and reduced him to submission; yet although Málik Ambar was again defeated in 1621, he was never finally overcome or dispossessed. It was in the time when these and other complications had brought Jehángir into central India that Sir Thomas Roe, the ambassador sent by James I to the Moghul Government, travelled up from Bombay to join the Emperor at Ajmir. His letters give a description of the country's condition, of the imperial Court and camp, and generally of the arbitrary ill-regulated administration, that throws much light on the actual state of India under this reign. The highways were most insecure for traffic or travel, though robbers and rebels were speedily executed when caught; and in outlying districts the central authority was little regarded by local chiefs or leaders of banditti. Nevertheless it was an empire of great wealth and might, maintaining a large army of various races from the revenues yielded by a vast territory. Sir Thomas Roe, who had free intercourse with some of the principal officials, writes that "in revenue the Moghul doubtless exceeds either Turk, Persian, or any Eastern prince; the sums I dare not name."

Thomas Coryate, who had travelled from Constantinople to India, and was at Ajmir with Roe, compares Jehángir's annual income with that of the Osmanli Sultan, and says that it was far greater; while

CH. XV.

Captain Richard Hawkins, who had been high in the imperial service, has given a detailed account of the immense quantity of gold and silver coin stored up in the treasury. The opulence and rude splendour of the Court, its superb ceremonial, the crowd of officials, the ambassadors from Persia, " Tartary," and all the minor States, independent or tributary, of India, the profusion of jewellery and gorgeous apparel, astonished these Englishmen; they contrast this outward grandeur with the barbarous methods of government—" an hundred naked men left slain in the fields for robbery," when the camp was shifted—they remark the mixture of greed and capricious generosity in Jehángir's dealings with the people. Sir Thomas Roe, who followed the Emperor's march out of Ajmir with his army and his retinue of nobles and functionaries, declares that the camp, when it was pitched, had a circuit of little less than twenty English miles. This included long rows of shops for the supply of the commissariat and traffic of all kinds, with a miscellaneous horde of camp-followers and hangers-on ; and, to Roe's wonder, the whole city of tents had been set up, he asserts, in four hours. In the midst of all the pride and pomp of his court Jehángir could be frank and convivial privately ; he enjoyed select wine-parties with his boon companions; he admitted Europeans to his table and to his service, and discoursed freely with them. How little religious prejudice was allowed to interfere with his statecraft may be judged by the fact that he commanded three of his nephews to embrace Christianity, with the object, as Captain Hawkins intimates, of disqualifying them from raising any troublesome claims to succeed him on the throne.

In 1611 the Emperor had married Nur Jehán, the daughter of a Persian who came to India in search of employment. On his way he fell into such destitution that he abandoned the child, just born, by the roadside in Afghanistan. She was saved by a merchant in some caravan, and was brought to Agra, where her beauty, as she grew up, captivated Prince Selim, the future Emperor Jehángir. She was first given in marriage to a Persian, whom she accompanied to his estate in Bengal, where the husband, conceiving himself to be insulted at an interview by the provincial governor, stabbed him, and was himself instantly slain. Jehángir, who was now on the throne, sent for the widow and married her. She rapidly obtained complete ascendancy over the Emperor ; her father was appointed Prime Minister; and thenceforward in all the politics of the reign she played a leading part with admirable courage, cleverness, and high-spirited fidelity to her consort in times of great danger. " Nur Jehán," Sir Thomas Roe notes, " fulfils the observation that in all actions of consequence a woman is not only always the ingredient, but commonly a principall drug of most virtue, not incapable of conducting business, nor herself void of wit and subtilitie." And he intimates that a discourse upon the *arcana imperii*, the inner politics of the capital, " would discover a Noble

Prince and an excellent wife, a faithful counsellor, a craftie step-mother, an ambitious sonne, a cunning Favorite—all reconciled by a patient King, whose heart was not understood by any of these." Nur Jehán steadily supported her step-son, Prince Kharram the heir-apparent, until her own daughter married Jehángir's youngest son, when she transferred all her influence to the promotion of his candidature for the succession. The result was that Prince Kharram (afterwards the Emperor Shah Jehán) took up arms, was defeated and pardoned, but rebelled again, and eventually fled into exile. She then planned the ruin of Mohabat Khan, Jehángir's best general, whose power and reputation might interfere with her designs. Mohabat obeyed a summons to the Emperor's camp, but instead of submitting to arrest he captured Jehángir in his tent by a night attack, foiled a desperate attempt made by Nur Jehán to rescue him, and carried both the Emperor and his wife, who had joined her husband in captivity, to Afghanistan. For the eventual recovery of his liberty and authority Jehángir was entirely indebted to Nur Jehán, who fomented discord and mutiny among Mohabat's troops, until a sudden and daring stratagem set him free. Mohabat escaped, to join Prince Kharram in the Dekhan; but, in 1627, Jehángir's death stopped the civil war; and the new Emperor, Shah Jehán, took formal possession of the throne without opposition. Nur Jehán withdrew into seclusion, and lived on for twenty years, treated always with liberality and singular consideration.

Jehángir, when he died in 1627, left his throne to be the prize, as usual, of the strongest competitor. His two sons Kharram and Shahryar at once took the field against each other; and Shahryar seized Lahore, but was speedily defeated before Kharram reached his capital at Agra, where he was proclaimed Emperor with the title of Shah Jehán, and his brother was before long put to death. The disturbances which invariably beset each new ruler of this extensive empire, with its ill-assorted provinces, and numerous recalcitrant feudatories, and its restless tribes, soon broke out. In the north an irruption of the Usbegs, who were besieging Kabul, had to be repelled. In the country west of the Jumna river a chief of the Bundela Rajputs threw off his allegiance, and was not reduced to submission without sharp fighting. Then Khan Jehán Lodi, an Afghan commander in the imperial service, a man of intractable temper, suspecting that the Court was plotting his destruction, marched away from Agra with his troops in open mutiny. They were pursued and overtaken by the imperial forces; but though he lost many men in an engagement, Khan Jehán made his way through the woods and wolds of central India into the kingdom of Ahmednagar at Bijapur. Shah Jehán followed in pursuit, but the approach of an imperial army threatened the independence of both kingdoms. The Regent of Ahmed-nagar joined the mutineers; and, though he lost a battle, the war spread, involving the Emperor in long and laborious campaigns. Bijapur

CH. XV.

was besieged by him in person, when its ruler laid waste all the surrounding country, which was also ravaged by the Moghuls. After much fruitless and exhausting warfare Bijapur and Golconda agreed to pay tribute; the kingdom of Ahmednagar was destroyed; and Shah Jehán returned to his capital; but it may be said that from this time forward the Dekhan was in a state of chronic turbulence and smouldering insurrection against the authority of the Moghul Emperors. From the first establishment of their dominion, these three kingdoms had formed a barrier that checked its extension southward by combination to resist encroachment, by harbouring dangerous rebels and mutinous generals, by harassing warfare in a distant and difficult country. Their league was now broken, and their strength materially diminished; but, since the control of the imperial sovereignty could never be enforced or maintained, the unsettlement and dilapidation of all this region increased. From this period may be dated the first appearance, on the political stage, of the Marathas, who fostered and propagated rebellion until it became an epidemic plague, which proved eventually fatal to the Moghul dynasty.

At the opposite extremity of the empire, in Afghanistan, Shah Jehán's affairs had at first been remarkably prosperous. The important frontier fortress of Kandahar was surrendered to him in 1637 by the Persian governor, who undertook to reconquer the Oxus provinces, Balkh and Badakshán, which had been overrun by the Usbegs. He soon found the northern tribes too strong for him; and Shah Jehán brought an army to Kabul for his support; but after some victories in the field the imperial troops, wearied out by incessant incursions from beyond the Oxus and surrounded by active indefatigable enemies, were withdrawn. The provinces were left in charge of an Usbeg prince, who had tendered his allegiance to the Moghul; and Aurungzeb, the Emperor's son, who had been left in command, lost the greater part of his army in a calamitous retreat through the Afghan passes. Meanwhile the Persians were preparing to recover Kandahar. In the winter of 1648 Shah Abbás invested the town with a powerful force. Aurungzeb marched under urgent orders from headquarters to relieve it; but the snow blocked the road from Kabul and India; and, in spite of great exertions, he could not reach the place in time to prevent its surrender. When at last he arrived, in the spring of 1649, the Persian garrison made an obstinate defence, much assisted by a Persian army which hovered round the besiegers and cut off supplies. Aurungzeb was compelled to retire, and in the following year he was equally unsuccessful. Three years later, the Emperor's eldest son, Dára Shekoh, renewed the siege with a fresh army. Four months were spent in unsuccessful assaults, ending with the repulse of a final and desperate attempt to take the fortress by storm. Whereupon Dára led back his troops, enfeebled by heavy losses and thoroughly discomfited, to India; and

Kandahar, the most important frontier fortress of the empire, passed irretrievably out of the possession of the Moghuls.

The hardship and disasters of Afghan warfare, and his failures before Kandahar, had probably convinced Aurungzeb that he could neither increase his military reputation nor advance his fortunes by campaigns in that region. He had since been transferred to the command of the armies on the empire's southern frontier, where he soon contrived to foment intrigues which produced hostilities with the kingdoms of Golconda and Bijapur. Against these adversaries, much less formidable than the northern tribes, his operations were successful; and meanwhile he could organise his troops, augment his power and personal influence, and await the turn of events at the capital. His opportunity came in 1657, when his father fell dangerously ill, and Dára Shekoh, his eldest brother, took charge of the government at Agra. Shah Jehán had four sons, all in the prime of life, accustomed to military command, ambitious and jealous with good reason of each other's ascendancy; they lost no time in marshalling their forces and asserting their respective claims. Prince Shujah, who was Viceroy in Bengal, advanced toward the capital with the troops in his province. Prince Morád, Viceroy in Guzerat, laid hands on the provincial treasures, and assumed the royal title. Aurungzeb assembled his troops for a march northward from the Dekhan; but his movements were marked by politic circumspection; he held back until Dára had defeated Shujah, and he prevailed upon Morád to make common cause with him. These two princes led their united army toward Agra; and Dára sallied out to encounter them at a short distance from the capital, with a much more numerous force. On Dára's side the furious onset of the Rajputs at one moment brought Aurungzeb into imminent peril; but Dára's elephant, on which he was conspicuously leading the frontal attack, was struck by a rocket and became so unmanageable that Dára was obliged to mount a horse. When his men lost sight of him the rumour flew about that he was killed; and as the death of their commander meant the extinction of the cause for which they were fighting, the whole army dispersed in general panic, leaving Aurungzeb and Morád completely victorious. Dára, escaping with some cavalry to Agra, continued his flight to Delhi; and the two princes occupied the capital, where Aurungzeb deprived his father of all authority by placing him in honourable confinement. His brother Morád, being of no further use, was thrown into prison, and executed some years later. From Delhi, Dára attempted to reach Afghanistan; but Aurungzeb's pursuit was so hot upon his track that he turned southward into Sinde, and after some circuitous journeying reappeared in Rajputana, where the powerful chief of Jodhpur, after at first supporting, was finally persuaded by Aurungzeb to desert him. At Ajmir he was again utterly defeated by Aurungzeb, and wandered about India, an unhappy fugitive, until he was betrayed into the hands of his brother, who immediately put him to death. Shah Jehán, after eight years' confinement as a state prisoner, ended his life in the palace at Agra.

It was in Shah Jehán's reign that the Moghul empire reached its climax of external magnificence. His retinue, his brilliant Court, the grand scale of his civil and military establishments, far surpassed anything that had been seen before or after him in India. Splendid edifices, unmatched for size and beauty in the Mohammadan world, still remain to commemorate his passion for architecture ; and he entirely rebuilt on a new site the city of Delhi, with its palace, marble halls, and the great mosque. His general administration has been so often praised that it must have been much superior to that of his predecessors ; and the historians of his time give him full credit for governing firmly and consistently, with a generous disposition toward his subjects, and praiseworthy solicitude for their welfare. But he was a despot, ruling with no system effectively organised for controlling the abuses, the corruption, and the tyranny of his subordinates. The letters of Bernier, a French physician, who arrived in India about the end of Shah Jehán's reign, and was for twelve years in the service of Aurungzeb, contrast the opulence and glory of the imperial capitals, the prodigal luxury of the grandees, the glittering brilliancy of the Court, with the miserable impoverishment of the peasants and artisans, and the squalid aspect of the outlying towns and villages. Commerce and agriculture were overburdened with capricious exactions, and depressed by the general insecurity of all property. The wealth of the whole country was sucked in from all parts of the empire to the great cities that were the centres of government, to provide for the maintenance of a huge army, to defray the cost of the imperial buildings, and to supply a vast outlay on the sumptuous establishments of the official nobility, and on the horde of adventurers and parasites by whom the Court was infested. Upon the expenditure which flowed out in these various channels from the public treasury the prosperity of such cities as Delhi and Agra so largely depended, that when the Emperor marched out with his army and all his high officers of state, he was followed by such a crowd of merchants and shopkeepers that the camp was, as Bernier observes, little less than a travelling capital.

After four years of intermittent warfare against rivals and insurgents Aurungzeb had effectually disposed of all resistance to his authority, and was undisputed lord of upper and central India, from the Himalaya mountains to the eastern and western sea-coasts. But further south, in the Indian peninsula, the independent Mohammadan kingdoms of Bijapur and Golconda still held out against the encroachments of their powerful neighbour ; though within their own territory they were now threatened by a new and dangerous uprising against their governments. This region of India is for the most part a country of flat-topped hills, fertile vales, and long tracts of scrubby woodlands and stony wolds, spreading, with broad interspaces of cultivated land, from the mountains on the west coast far inland. It was studded with forts on craggy steeps among deep ravines; and toward the sea the inner ranges were peopled by a rough and turbulent Hindu folk, never thoroughly tamed by the Mohammadan dynasties that had been overlords in this part of India from the fourteenth century. This region bore the ancient name Maharáshtra; its population, which was really a medley of different tribes and castes, was known in northern India by the indefinite designation of Maratha. The Maratha leaders had originally made their way forward by service under the Mohammadan Kings in their wars against the Moghuls; they obtained grants of land and the charge of troops; and, when these kingdoms were being gradually weakened and overpowered by the imperial armies, the Marathas rose to the front. About the middle of the seventeenth century their famous chief, Sivaji, had collected a force of disbanded soldiery, outlaws and plundering brigands, with which he seized some forts and districts belonging to Bijapur, and dispersed a large army sent against him, having assassinated its general, Afzal Khan, by treachery. The Bijapur King was obliged to make peace with him, and to leave him in possession of considerable territory; whereupon Sivaji laid the whole country round under contribution and pillage. In one of his raids he plundered Surat, to the great damage of the English merchants at that seaport: an exploit that greatly incensed Aurungzeb, who despatched a large army to punish him.

Nevertheless it was Aurungzeb's policy to conciliate such a troublesome rebel. Sivaji's submission was accepted; he went to Delhi, fled back to his own country, and was soon again capturing forts and laying waste the Moghul districts in open defiance of the Emperor's authority. During the next few years, while Aurungzeb was occupied by an insurrection in Afghanistan, where a calamitous reverse had for the time upset his government, the Maratha chief increased his fighting power and extended his possessions, harassing and despoiling Bijapur and Golconda. He had assumed a royal title, and had made an alliance with Golconda to resist the imperial armies sent to attack that kingdom, when he died in 1680. His son, Sambaji, continued desultory hostilities against the Moghuls, until he was captured and put to death by Aurungzeb. The confusion and disorder in southern India were now seriously endangering the empire's integrity on that side. The Marathas were capturing hill forts, gathering into freebooting companies under daring captains, and declaring themselves the champions of the Hindu race and religion against Mohammadan oppression. It has been alleged that the imperial generals purposely let the war run on instead of terminating it by vigorous operations, lest they should be transferred to much harder and more hazardous commands among the Afghan mountains. The Emperor determined to assume the personal command

CH. XV.

of his southern armies, but he had driven the leading chiefs into revolt
by acts of bigotry and perfidy; and when he invaded their country
they opposed him with a formidable combination that was not broken
up until two years' hard fighting had devastated their country and
compelled them to accept a treaty.   In 1683, however, he threw his
whole military force against them, determined to extinguish resistance
of every kind, to extirpate the Maratha bands, and to subjugate all this
region permanently.   One of his generals advanced upon Golconda,
pillaged the town and the royal treasury, and left the kingdom crippled
by intestinal disorders and general dilapidation.   Bijapur surrendered,
after a siege, to Aurungzeb, who imprisoned its King, annexed his
territory, and dismantled his fortress.   He then turned again on
Golconda, which was reduced and finally ruined.   The capture and
execution of Sambaji had at first intimidated the Marathas; but their
principal chiefs raised the standard of revolt in different places, collected
strong bands of marauders, levied blackmail on all the landholders,
proclaimed a religious war of Hindus against Mohammadans, and spread
anarchy throughout the country which had been disorganised by the
subversion of the two Mohammadan States.   The fall of those Governments had thrown out of employ a swarm of mercenaries, and had stirred
up and set free the elements of turbulence and riot among the armed
peasantry, so that any freebooting adventurer could recruit his free-
lances to harry the outposts and cut off the convoys of the Moghul
army, to seize a fort, overawe a district, and sequestrate the land
revenue for the support of his men.   They lived on the country and
impoverished the imperial treasury.   Meanwhile Aurungzeb and his
generals were pressing the main body of the Marathas and recapturing
some important fortresses; but although they struck some heavy blows
they could never cut the sinews of their active enemy; and to disperse a
compact force was only to break it up into guerilla bands.

It is clear that Aurungzeb's great enterprise—the conquest of south
India—was a political miscalculation as well as a military failure.   The
expansion of his empire proved fatal to its solidity; he had seized more
than he could hold; he was unable to enforce an unpopular despotism
over distant provinces, where the nature of the country favoured
defence, among a people whom his intolerance had provoked to
obstinate resistance.   His huge, unwieldy army, burdened with all the
furniture and followers of a camp that was also a Court, was gradually
worn down by the attacks of a diffuse and impalpable enemy.   Throughout the last twenty-four years of his long reign, from 1683 to 1707, the
Emperor was commander-in-chief of his forces in the field, contending
vigorously but vainly against the growing strength of the Maratha
hordes, which swarmed round him, as a contemporary annalist said, like
ants or locusts, ravaging his lands, appropriating his revenues, and
rackrenting the peasantry; while his finances were ruined by the drain of

excessive military expenditure, and his troops became disheartened and insubordinate. On his northern frontier the Afghan tribes were in perpetual revolt; in the south he had been caught in a quicksand of misfortunes. Yet he strove stubbornly against manifest adversity. Encompassed and pursued by his enemies, he retreated to Ahmednagar, where he died in his eighty-ninth year, having reigned just half a century. No two rulers could be less alike in character than Aurungzeb and Marcus Aurelius, yet one is reminded of the Roman Emperor expiring in his Pannonian camp after fourteen years of incessant frontier warfare, when the Parthians were threatening Syria and the barbarian tribes were tiring out his legions on the Danube.

In a letter which Aurungzeb dictated from his death-bed to his son he confessed that his enemies were many, but pleaded, "Whatever good or evil I have done, it was for you." Bernier, who knew him intimately, admits that Aurungzeb gained his throne by violent and terrible deeds, alleging in palliation of them the cruel necessity that compelled a royal prince at each demise of the Crown to fight for his own hand and win, or perish. And he concludes the history of this reign thus, "I am convinced that a little reflection on all that has been here written will induce my readers to regard Aurungzeb not as a barbarian, but as a man of great and rare genius, a statesman, and a grand monarch."

After Aurungzeb's death the empire fell into rapid decline, for the growth and multiplication of internal troubles disabled resistance to foreign aggression. The inevitable war of succession began at once. Of Aurungzeb's three sons the eldest, Bahádur Shah, was proclaimed Emperor in northern India, and seized Delhi; another strengthened himself in the south, while the third brother marched upon Agra. Both of them were defeated and slain by Bahádur Shah; but in central India the Rajput chiefs rose in rebellion, and the Punjab was overrun by the Sikhs, a fierce and fanatical sect of Hindus, whom Aurungzeb had put down with bigoted severity, and who broke out again fiercely after his death. Bahádur Shah stormed their stronghold and killed their leader; but he died at Lahore in 1711, having reigned barely five years. He was the last able ruler of his dynasty, one who might have stayed for a time the crash of a falling empire; and the flood-tide of insurrection was too strong for his incapable successors. Hitherto, as has been seen, each Emperor had been the able man of his family, chosen by the ordeal of battle. The process was now reversed; and henceforward Emperors were selected for their impotence; they were set up and pulled down by ambitious ministers or vicious favourites, whose intrigues and factions completed the disorganisation of the Government.

The closing annals of the Moghul dynasty record brief reigns with intervals of bloody tumult, rebellions, privy conspiracies and assassina-

tions.   The local governors and military commanders began to parcel
out their provinces into independent principalities.   Nizám-ul-Mulk,
the Viceroy of southern India, defeated the imperial armies, and founded
the present State of Haidarábád.   Oudh and Bengal were slipping out
of control; a band of Afghan adventurers settled down as chiefs of
Rohilkhand; and in western India Poona became the capital of a formidable Maratha confederacy, whose armies overran all the midlands, and
ravaged the plains around Agra and Delhi.   In the midst of all this havoc
and spoliation came news from without that Nádir Kuli Khan, who now
reigned by usurpation in Persia, had taken Kabul, and was invading
India.   With a great army he descended upon Peshávar, traversed the
Punjab, routed the imperial forces, gave up Delhi to pillage and massacre, and went back after rending from the Moghul all his provinces
west of the Indus.   This fatal blow at the empire's heart precipitated its
destruction; for the north-west frontier of India now lay open and
defenceless.   Within the next forty years the splendid dominion founded
by Bábar's conquests was completely demolished.   It was reduced to a
few districts near Delhi, along the Ganges and the Jumna rivers;
and the Moghul empire became a broken wreck, with a crowd of
plunderers quarrelling over its fragments.   In 1747, when Nádir Shah
was murdered in his camp, Ahmad Shah Abdali, an Afghan chief who
commanded a corps in the Persian army, rode off with his tribesmen to
their own country.   At Kandahar he was proclaimed King, and he
soon took advantage of the distracted condition of Persia and India to
make himself an independent ruler of Afghanistan, to invade the Punjab,
and to place his garrisons at Lahore.   In a second expedition he sacked
Delhi, and scoured the country as far as Agra, retiring to his mountains
when the summer heat spread sickness among his troops.   Then the
Maratha confederacy, now at the zenith of their power, sent a great
army northward, which drove out Ahmad Shah's garrisons, and swept
over the Punjab; but in the northern plains they met an adversary who
was more than their match.   For in 1759 Ahmad Shah came down
again upon India with all the fighting men of the Afghan tribes; he
marched along the skirts of the Himalayas until he crossed the Jumna
and placed himself in the rear of the Marathas, intercepting their communications.   The two armies met at Pániput, near Delhi, in the spring
of 1761, when the Marathas were routed with tremendous slaughter.
After this victory nothing opposed Ahmad Shah's conquest of all
northern India; nevertheless he returned again to his highlands, leaving
the dismantled provinces of the empire to be appropriated by the
various Powers that were now contending for ascendancy in India.   His
successors kept their hold upon the frontier districts of the Punjab and
upon Kashmír; until early in the nineteenth century the Afghans were
finally driven back into their mountains by the Sikhs.   Meanwhile, from
1765 to 1771, the titular Emperor Shah Álam had been living at Allahábád

under the protection of the English Government, which was now established in Bengal. He then found his way back to Delhi, where he was
no more than a puppet in the hands of the Marathas. Finally, in 1803,
when Lord Lake defeated the Marathas, and drove them out of Agra
and Delhi, all the territory from the Jumna river and the Himalayas south-
eastward to Bengal (except Oudh) passed by cession and conquest to
the British Government; and the Moghul Emperor's jurisdiction was
thenceforward circumscribed by the walls of his palace at Delhi. There
for the next fifty years he held his Court, a mere phantom of extinct
sovereignty, sitting crowned upon the ruins of a magnificent empire.

If, now, we take a rapid survey of the course and constitution of the
Moghul empire, we find that it differed in no material respect from the
ordinary type of Asiatic despotisms. As it began with foreign conquest,
with the subjugation of an immense population by a band of Mohammadan
invaders, the civil and military services were kept mainly in the hands of
Mohammadans—many of them foreigners—and were continually reinforced
from abroad. The Court, Bernier says, was no more than a miscellaneous
crowd of aliens—Usbegs, Persians, Arabs, and Turks, who filled almost
all the high offices. The recruiting of the army was managed by the
chief commanders, who imported great numbers of men from their own
country or tribe, from Persia, Afghanistan, and various other parts of
central Asia. Under this system the military forces of the empire
must have consisted very largely of foreign mercenaries, almost entirely
Mohammadan, excepting always the contingents of the Rajput chiefs; for
in India the Hindus so greatly outnumbered the Mohammadans that the
Emperors were obliged to rely principally upon men of their own faith.
The situation of a military autocrat necessitates enlistment of the best
fighting men wheresoever they can be found; and throughout Asia the
religious element is still a powerful bond of union and a pledge of
fidelity. It may be observed that even in Europe the national army,
which strictly excludes aliens, and takes no account of sectarian divisions
in the ranks, is a very modern institution. But foreign mercenaries are
radically untrustworthy; they are apt to change sides on emergencies,
or to desert a falling throne; and so, when the Moghul Emperors could
no longer command or maintain discipline, their troops looked round for
better leaders; the professional soldier went where he expected to win.

It is clear that in all governments of this type the mainspring is
irresistible authority in capable hands at the centre. So long as each
successive Emperor gained his throne, and held it against all challengers
by personal superiority, the sceptre passed to the fittest man of the
family. The capacity of the four Emperors who followed Bábar is
attested by the length of their respective reigns, which covered in aggre-
gate a hundred and forty-one years; for in Asia a long rule is of
necessity a strong rule; the Moghul empire depended entirely upon

CH. XV.

vigorous autocratic administration. It is a fact worth notice that the great towns of India seem never to have attained any municipal autonomy that might have given them weight in politics; they played no part in the civil wars. Many of the petty chiefs and large landholders preserved independence within their own domains and in outlying districts; but the practice of the Moghul government was to level all obstacles to arbitrary power. The nobility created by the Emperors was almost entirely official; it consisted mainly of high civil officers and of military commanders, who held lands on service-tenure, and could be dismissed at the sovereign's pleasure. Most of these *Omrah*, as they were called, were foreign adventurers, soldiers of fortune, or slaves and parasites whom the Emperor promoted or degraded capriciously. Another point to be observed is that in India the great religious corporations never had the influence that they have possessed in other Mohammadan kingdoms. In the Osmanli empire, for example, the *Ulema*, the expounders of the law of Islam, have always kept the Sultan in check; but in the general population of India their authority could have little support, and could be disregarded by the government. Throughout western Asia, up to the borders of India, the Mohammadans had established complete political and religious supremacy; their subjects were united under one religious law, which controlled and fortified the civil power. But in India a general conversion to Islam was impossible; and the Emperors could only rule by holding the balance between two great religious communities, always ready to take up arms against each other. The combined result of all these facts and circumstances was an inordinate centralisation of authority at the capitals, whereby the whole fabric became unstable and top-heavy; so that when this supreme authority passed into feeble hands the empire, loosened by internal revolt and battered by foreign enemies, toppled over into irremediable collapse.

Nevertheless a weak and ill-governed rulership may last long if it can resist foreign aggression; but this was a danger to which the Moghul empire was peculiarly exposed. We know that from the beginning of authentic history all Asiatic invaders of India have made their entry from the west and north-west. On no other side, in fact, was it possible for armies to traverse the lofty mountain ranges which separate the northern plains of India from central Asia: they can only reach India by a few passes through the highlands, or by a circuitous route across barren regions on the south-west. But for the conquest of India it was never sufficient to bring an army successfully through the passes; it was also essential that the invader should be able to keep them open behind him; and for this purpose it was necessary to begin by securing a base in Afghanistan to hold in strength the fortresses which cover the few practicable roads through the mountains, and to guard the narrow defiles opening upon the plains. Since the days of Alexander the unruly Afghan tribes have always risen on an army's flanks and rear, have harried the march, intercepted convoys, and attempted to cut off communications. The centre of this country may be roughly described as a huge oblong quadrilateral block of mountains. On the east its steep ranges overlook the Indian frontier. But on the north-western side of Afghanistan, beyond the mountain ranges, and toward the lower course of the Oxus river, the lands are comparatively level, sparsely populated, and easily accessible from Persia and central Asia. On the western side also, from Herat to Kandahar, the country is open, and traversable by armies; while southward is a sandy desert stretching down to Beluchistan. To invade Afghanistan from the north and west is much less difficult than to do so from the east, where whoever occupies the mountain quadrilateral holds the point of vantage, the key of the Indian gates, for attack or defence. No invader by land has found it possible to conquer and establish himself in India without keeping strong garrisons in Afghanistan; and so long as he was master of the highlands he could subdue the plains at his leisure.

But the next difficulty is to hold the mountains from a base in the plains; for whenever a successful conqueror has settled down in India—in a wide and wealthy region, where great armies can be maintained on an ample revenue—some fresh invasion from the west, or a tribal revolt, has threatened his position in Afghanistan. All the successors of the Emperor Akbar were worried and weakened by exhausting campaigns and frequent military reverses in the Afghan mountains, which diverted their forces and cramped their operations against rebels and rivals elsewhere; while beyond those mountains the necessity of defending a distant frontier on the Oxus or the Helmand river laid an intolerable strain on their military resources, locking up their best troops in the far north at times when they were entangled in the wars of southern India. The consolidation, in the sixteenth century, of Persia under the powerful Safevi dynasty had given them an enterprising neighbour who was constantly encroaching upon the debatable lands between the two empires. The loss of Kandahar in 1648 made a serious breach in their strategic frontier on this side; and during the seventeenth century the government at Delhi was continually losing ground in Afghanistan. In 1666 Shah Abbás led a great Persian army by Kandahar against Kabul. He died on the march, and his forces withdrew; but his inroad was the signal for a general revolt of the Afghan tribes from the Moghul authority. And finally, in the eighteenth century, when Nádir Shah expelled the Moghul governor from Kabul and seized all their territory west of the Indus river, the barriers that protected India from invasion were thereby completely destroyed; and the gates of India, which had been held for two hundred years by the Moghul dynasty, were irrecoverably lost, to the mortal injury of an enfeebled and sinking empire.

In Afghanistan, therefore, we have a striking example of a poor and barbarous country, whose situation and natural strength nevertheless gives it great political importance; for its strategical position may exercise a permanent influence over the fortunes of a rich and powerful dominion. The case has occurred more than once in history—the nearest parallel is with the position of Armenia between the Roman and Parthian empires during the first centuries of the Christian era. Of Armenia Tacitus writes that it has been of old an unsettled country from the character of its people and its geographical situation, bordering as it does upon the Roman provinces and stretching far into Media, lying between two great empires, constantly at strife with both of them, hating Rome and jealous of Parthia. *Mutatis mutandis,* we have here a description of Afghanistan.

In the annals of Asia the Moghul empire stood foremost in wealth, population, and power among the great States that attained their climax in that continent during the sixteenth century, though the Osmanli sultanate is of much more historical importance, because its capital and its richest provinces were in Europe. Yet the events and circumstances which followed and were produced by the dissolution of the Moghul empire are closely connected with modern history, and exercised a marked influence on the politics of Europe. Simultaneously with the decay and disruption of this mighty rulership a new dominion began to grow and spread in its place; and the rise of the British dominion in India has been the direct consequence of its predecessor's fall. The epoch marks a turning-point in the fortunes of both continents, for Asiatic dominion was receding in Europe; while European dominion was beginning its advance into Asia. From the fifteenth to the seventeenth century the armies of the Osmanli Sultans had been subjugating eastern Europe; but the defeat of the Turks before Vienna in 1683 stopped and gradually reversed the tide of invasion; and from the commencement of the eighteenth century may be dated a renewal, after many centuries, of the ancient rule of European Powers over Asiatic lands. Russia was taking her first steps beyond the Caspian; and the maritime nations of Europe had fixed their settlements on the Indian coast.

Nevertheless, between the empire that fell and the empire that rose in India during the eighteenth century there was complete dissimilarity—a clear contrast of original character, of historical antecedents, and in respect to the ways and means by which dominion was at first attained. There is no likeness whatever between the gradual acquisition of territory by a pacific trading company and the violent inroad of a Tartar horde from the mountains, or between the slow penetration of commerce and the upsetting of thrones by the sword. So long as the Moghul empire was vigorously governed, the Europeans at the seaports made no progress inland; they began to gain ground when the outlying provinces fell away from the central authority, leaving the sea-coast entirely undefended, for the Moghul empire had never maintained a navy. For ages the long sea-board of peninsular India had been safe-guarded by the wide ocean; but from the sixteenth century, when the armed fleets of Europe found their way across it, the ocean became a high-road for invaders instead of a barrier against them. One vital defect in the fighting strength of purely Asiatic States on the mainland is that they have never maintained effective naval armaments; a fact that is of fundamental importance in the modern history of Asia. It explains why European ships of war, or even armed traders, could seize ports and promontories, land troops, and take up stations whence they could eventually advance to annex the maritime provinces of India, which are singularly exposed to attack. The estuaries of the great rivers offer safe harbourage, and waterways for penetration inland; their streams are like great arteries branching out from the heart of India; the low-lying tracts along the coast are flat, fertile, inhabited by an unwarlike, industrious population. In these distant parts of the empire the control from the capitals had always been weak; it was entirely lost when disintegration set in at the centre; and the Moghul dynasty never conquered the extreme south of the Indian peninsula. Early in the eighteenth century the Marathas had seized all the territory adjacent to Bombay; in the south-east the Viceroy of the Dekhan was master in the districts surrounding Madras; in Bengal the local governor was shaking off the imperial authority. But none of these upstart ruler-ships, excepting the Marathas—who were quarrelling among themselves—had any solidity or cohesion. At such a period of political confusion the rapid success of foreign intruders, well furnished with disciplined troops and money, and holding undisputed command of the sea, is no matter for surprise. The Moghul empire perished because, at a period of great internal disorganisation, its frontiers on the sea and on the land were equally defenceless—the European was advancing from the coast, while the hordes of central Asia were pouring in through the mountains of Afghanistan.

(2) THE ENGLISH AND FRENCH IN INDIA.
(1720–63.)

In a former volume the history of Europeans in India has been brought down to the second decade of the eighteenth century. A very brief review must suffice for the next twenty-four years. It was for the English and French alike a period mainly of commercial prosperity and silent growth; but it by no means merits such neglect as it has sometimes received; and it is useful to bear in mind that by 1744, the starting-point of so many histories of the British in India, the Company had already existed for more than half of its allotted span of life.

The greatest danger that menaced the Company at home was that of being involved in the misfortunes of the South Sea Company. The frenzy of the "Bubble" caused a great inflation of their stock in 1720, and one of the measures adopted by Sir Robert Walpole to allay the panic was an obligation laid upon the East India Company to take over nine millions of South Sea stock. The Directors wisely consented to the "Ingraftment," as it was called. It was worth some sacrifice to lay the State under still further obligations to the Company. Prudence also urged them to bow before the storm of public opinion which was running so strongly, not only against the South Sea Company but all trading associations of any kind, that a motion was made in the Commons to disqualify Directors of such bodies from being elected to the House. The sacrifice however proved unnecessary. Walpole carried his Bill, but it was superseded by the Act for restoring public credit passed a few months later. The Ingraftment, though an abortive measure, had given him a much needed breathing space. The knowledge that the East India Company was prepared to come to the rescue helped to check the panic. Walpole was not ungrateful, and proved himself the staunch friend of the Company at a time when his patronage was of value. An Act of 1712 fixed 1733 as a date for the possible termination of the Company's privileges. A few years before that time the forces of opposition to the East India monopoly gathered once more to a head. But the movement never appears to have had much chance of success. It was more political than commercial in origin, the work of opponents of the great Minister rather than the spontaneous act of the mercantile interest. In February, 1730, a petition was presented to Parliament against the renewal of the Charter with an alternative plan for the management of the trade with India. It proved to be, as was said at the time, an old and thread-bare scheme. The familiar features of a regulated as opposed to a joint-stock company reappeared. The petitioners proposed to buy out the East India Company by raising the sum (£3,200,000) lent by them to the State, and were prepared to accept a lower interest. Duties were to be paid by the individual traders, who were made free of the Company, for the upkeep of forts and settlements in the East.

The East India Company were in no danger. With customary astuteness, Sir Robert Walpole had taken the sting out of the attack, before it was launched, by a private understanding with the Court of Directors. The only consideration likely to attract in Parliament the votes of those who were not already committed to the scheme was the prospect of providing supplies for the public needs. Walpole was able to announce that the Company were prepared to pay £200,000 to the State for a renewal of their charter, and to accept a lower interest on their loans to the Government for the future. The petition was rejected on the first hearing by a majority of 85, and the privileges of the Company were extended to 1766. The East India Company were thus entrenched, as events were to prove, from all assaults in the rear during the critical period of the wars with France.

In the East the chief feature is the gradual growth of the Company's settlements amid that rapid dissolution of Moghul power which has been described in the first section of this chapter. The heart of the empire decayed faster than the extremities. Bahádur Shah was followed on the imperial throne by a succession of incapable men, whose short and turbulent reigns were marked alike at their commencement and close by dismal periods of revolution and intrigue. Meanwhile, the great feudatories of the empire were busy founding for themselves independent kingdoms, till the stage was reached when, as it has been graphically put, the paramount power became a supremacy with which none of the other parties had any other relation but that of rebellion. The effects of the process of dissolution were not fully seen till the middle of the eighteenth century, and they synchronised with the years in which the English and the French came to open hostility in the East. That conflict not only determined which nation should oust the other, but indirectly revealed the fact that the native powers were destined to succumb before the Western invader.

The ring of semi-independent principalities round the decaying centre of the empire shielded for a time the European possessions from the forces of disruption and anarchy. Of the British settlements, Bombay felt the ill effects of Moghul weakness most acutely. The shores of the Arabian sea were exposed to the depredations of the corsair chief Angria, originally the admiral of the Maratha fleet, who was often found acting in conjunction with a band of European pirates having headquarters in Madagascar. Unsuccessful attacks were made upon Gheria, Angria's stronghold, in 1717, and again in 1720, when the Company's fleet was assisted by a powerful naval force. Angria died about 1730; but his sons succeeded to his lawless sovereignty, and this nest of pirates was only destroyed in 1756 by the combined efforts of Watson and Clive. From the land side the Presidency was constantly threatened by the advance northward of the Maratha armies. Successively, the English allied themselves with the Siddi, or Moghul admiral, against Angria, with one of Angria's sons against the other, with the Portuguese against the Peshwa, and finally in 1739 with the Peshwa himself.

The Presidency of Calcutta prospered on the commercial privileges granted them by the Court of Delhi in 1717. In 1706 the population was not more than ten or twelve thousand; but in 1735 it had risen to one hundred thousand, and the value of its annual trade was estimated at a million sterling. The Viceroys or Subahdars of Bengal, now practically independent of the Moghul empire, though apt to levy exactions occasionally on the prosperous aliens within their territory, lived on the whole at peace with them. Two strong rulers covered the period from

1702 till 1739, and the usurper who supplanted them reigned till 1756. In 1742 the Marathas were making their presence felt even in north-eastern India, and Hooghly was sacked by a plundering force. In alarm for their settlement, the English in the following year hastily constructed the famous "Ditch" in the outskirts of Calcutta. But the rich Gangetic valley—the commercial and political key of Hindustan—was never destined to pass beneath the sway of the great Hindu confederacy. This advance wave of their onset was flung back, and when the main flood swelled up a few years later, it dashed itself in vain against the now greatly strengthened bulwarks of British power.

In the latter years of the reign of Aurungzeb southern India, or the Dekhan, passed nominally under the sway of the Moghul empire. The country was divided into six *Subahs* or provinces, and the whole was governed by a Viceroy. One, perhaps the most important, of these *Subahs* was the Carnatic—the strip of land between the mountains and the sea extending south of the Kistna to the frontiers of Tanjore, containing within its limits both Madras and Pondicherry. Fortunately for the European settlements, both the greater political division of the Dekhan and the smaller subdivision of the Carnatic passed soon after the death of Aurungzeb into the hands of men who, being in general capacity above the level of Indian rulers, established their respective governments with elements of permanency. After many revolutions and counter-revolutions Nizám-ul-Mulk, the Viceroy of southern India, founded what was practically an independent kingdom at Haidarábád in 1723 and reigned till 1748. In the Carnatic a strong dynasty ruled from 1710 to 1740. Till the end of this period there was on the whole tranquillity in the province, though from time to time rumours of trouble from the Marathas reached the ears of the dwellers in the seaports. A long duel for supremacy in the Dekhan was being fought out between the Nizám and Baji Rao, one of the greatest of the Peshwas. The English in Madras watched the issue of the conflict with an intense and strained interest. Complimentary letters were despatched to Haidarábád when the fortunes of the Nizám were in the ascendant. The internal history of the Presidency is uneventful. The most notable Governor was James Macrae, a Scotchman, of Ayrshire, who carried out many valuable reforms in financial administration. In 1740 Dost Ali, the Nawáb of the Carnatic, was defeated and slain by the Marathas, and the horsemen of the victorious army rode almost up to the outskirts of Madras. It is therefore noticeable that about the same time the Maratha confederacy was impinging on all the British chief settlements in India.

When the Scotchman John Law became the guiding spirit of the French finances, Colbert's East India Company became entangled in his all-embracing system. It was incorporated in 1719 with the Company of the West, or Mississippi Company as it was generally called, which was formed to exploit Louisiana. The new body, known as the Company of the Indies, also absorbed the Senegal Company, the old Canada Company, the China Company, and the Companies of St Domingo and Guinea, thus forming one mammoth association with exclusive rights to the trade of France with the world outside Europe.   Not yet satisfied, Law proceeded to dower it with several state functions, the profits of the coinage, the control of the public debt and the monopoly of tobacco, and finally amalgamated it with his own creation the Royal Bank.   When this architectonic structure collapsed in ruins in 1720, the East India Company was reconstituted as the "Perpetual Company of the Indies" on its old basis and divested of all the special privileges granted by Law except the monopoly of tobacco.   True to the traditions of its foundation, the Company tended more and more to become a mere department of State. After 1723 the greater officials of the Company, the Directors and Inspectors, were nominated by the Crown, and the shareholders were only permitted to elect the Syndics, whose influence over the administration was very slight.   Frequent changes were made in the next few years; but gradually all real control passed into the hands of the King's Commissaries.   The most famous of these was Orry de Fulvy, brother of the Controller-General of Finance, who held office from 1733 to 1745. Under his rule the fortunes of the Company materially improved; but the bureaucratic control of even an enlightened state official was a very different thing from the driving force of a vigorous private enterprise. After 1723 fixed dividends were guaranteed by the Crown, irrespective of the profit or loss on the trade with India and derived mainly from the farm of tobacco.   For twenty years after 1725 the shareholders of the Company held no meeting, and they gradually sank into a body of *rentiers* with no incentive to activity or real interest in Eastern affairs, utterly unlike the strong and turbulent English Court of Proprietors, who so often challenged and overruled the policy of the Directors themselves.   The evils latent in the anomalous and artificial nature of the Company's finance and its weak dependence on state control were not apparent in the long period of peace that followed Cardinal Fleury's accession to power.   In India, the French extended their influence by the acquisition of Mahé (1725), and Karikal (1739).   Dupleix, from 1730, greatly developed the trade and importance of Chandernagore which had hitherto languished.   Benoît Dumas, Governor of Pondicherry from 1735 to 1741, increased the prestige of his country by his statesmanlike outlook on Indian politics.   When Dost Ali was slain by the Marathas, his family and that of his son-in-law, Chanda Sahib, took refuge in Pondicherry; and to the skill and address of Dumas was due that close connexion between the French and the royal Houses of southern India upon which the policy of Bussy and Dupleix was afterwards built up.

Though nominally at peace, England and France had been facing each other on European battle-fields since 1740, and at last in 1744 war between the two countries was openly declared.   The roar of French guns off Madras in 1746 announced the beginning of a new era in the East. During the War of the Spanish Succession thirty years before, various agreements for a local neutrality were made between many of the English, French and Dutch settlements in India; and, apart from some uneasiness as to the fate of incoming or outgoing ships, neither side seems to have feared aggression on the part of the other. The French therefore were only acting in accordance with tradition when in 1742 they made informal overtures to the English Company for the declaration of a general neutrality in the East. These proposals came to nothing, but the principle that peace or war between European nations necessarily involves peace or war between their distant possessions hardly yet received open recognition. Even during the War of the Austrian Succession a strict neutrality was observed between the French and English in Bengal; and in southern India after 1748 the principle, at least in so far as the maintenance of peace was in question, received a nominal rather than an actual observance.

It is often stated that in 1744 the French and English were equal in point of strength; but this is probably a misapprehension. From the outset the advantage in material resources was on the side of the English. They had, as shown in a former volume, a longer, more continuous, and more prosperous, history in the East behind them. Their trade exceeded that of the French several times in bulk, and the importance of this must not be underrated. The sounder the financial condition of the Company, the more easily would it support any initial losses in the war and the greater sacrifices would it be prepared to make in the conflict to restore its fallen fortunes. On the mainland of India itself the English had a greater number of settlements and they were strategically the better placed. They possessed three Presidencies, the French properly speaking only one, for Chandernagore was a mere dependency of Pondicherry and, even under the rule of Dupleix, never really rivalled Calcutta. Their other base of operations was at Mauritius, distant from one to two months' voyage. Climatic conditions had an important effect on the strategy of the Coromandel coast, where the duel between the two nations was destined to be fought out. For nearly four months in the year beginning from the end of October, when the monsoons were blowing, the sailing vessels of those days could not exist off that unsheltered shore, and the English port of refuge, Bombay, was nearer than the French station in Mauritius. Though the fall of Pondicherry would, and ultimately did, imply the end of French dominion in India, the capture of Madras had no such significance for Great Britain. It was a serious loss; but Calcutta and Bombay still remained. Bombay was the one Presidency which was never captured either by an Indian enemy or by Europeans. Occupying an isolated position, it had been obliged to defend itself as we have seen against relentless foes. It was the birthplace and chief seat of that famous force, the Indian navy, and was in reality stronger than either

Madras or Calcutta where long dependence on native governors had created a spirit of helplessness and inertia.

The conception that the opportunity afforded by a European war might be utilised to assert supremacy in India originated in the fertile brain of Mahé de Labourdonnais, a famous sea-captain and free-lance, who had been Governor of the Isles of France and Bourbon since 1735 and had founded the prosperity of those colonies by his enlightened and strenuous policy. He was in France in 1740; and, foreseeing the probability of war being declared with England in the near future, he planned a privateering expedition against British shipping in India. To this scheme he succeeded in winning the support of Maurepas, Minister of Marine, who obliged the East India Company rather against their will to provide ships for the fleet. He sailed from France in 1741, proposing to await in Mauritius the news of the outbreak of hostilities. But war was not declared till 1744, and meanwhile, in 1742, the Company, which had never looked with favour on the scheme, ordered him to send back the fleet to Europe. Labourdonnais obeyed, declaring that all his projects had vanished like a dream, and his annoyance was not lessened by the fact that, immediately after the fleet had started, he received another despatch cancelling the order and expressing the hope that he had ventured to disobey it. In the meantime the English, having got wind of Labourdonnais' designs, had sent a royal fleet to India under Commodore Barnet, and the command of the sea had temporarily passed to them. Barnet threatened Pondicherry; but Dupleix, who had been appointed Governor in 1741, appealed to the Nawáb of the Carnatic. The Nawáb warned the English that he could not permit fighting between the European nations under his protection. Labourdonnais had been ordered by the home Government to remain on the defensive, but with characteristic energy he had equipped and manned a fleet from the slender resources of the Isles of France. He next proposed to Dupleix, that he should prey on English East Indiamen by cruising between the Cape and St Helena; but Dupleix, who was the master mind throughout this period of preparation, persuaded him to attempt the capture of Madras, boldly disregarding the neutrality of the Nawáb to which he had himself appealed against the English. Labourdonnais' fleet was reinforced by the arrival of a squadron from France, and he left the Isles in March, 1746. His ships being dispersed and scattered by a terrible storm, he was forced to refit them off the coast of Madagascar. The British commander, Peyton, Barnet's successor, attempted to bar his passage to the Coromandel coast; but Labourdonnais beat him back off Negapatam and anchored in the Roads of Pondicherry at the end of June.

Hitherto Labourdonnais had acted with the greatest energy and vigour; but, having come within measurable distance of performing the task to which all his preparations had been directed, he showed a strange indecision. For six weeks he refused, on various pleas, to

CH. XV.

proceed to the siege of Madras, unless he received from Dupleix and the Council of Pondicherry a signed order to attack the town with an admission on their part that they took full responsibility whatever the issue might be. The authorities at Pondicherry would not commit themselves further than to a formal demand that he should either blockade Madras or pursue the British fleet. Both parties to the dispute evaded responsibility before the siege, both claimed it after the town had fallen. Labourdonnais' relations with Dupleix were soon strained to breaking point. The quarrel between the two men which was at bottom rather petty has often been dignified into a fundamental difference in tactics. They had been acquainted earlier in life and each seems to have contracted a certain dislike of the other. Labourdonnais in his Memoirs refers to the political schemes of Dupleix as brilliant chimeras, and when Dupleix heard of Labourdonnais' appointment to the governorship of the Isles he spoke contemptuously of the "*fariboles de cet évaporé.*" But in planning the attack on Madras the Governor-General seems to have put a strong curb on his private feelings, and the responsibility for the rupture between the two men must be laid chiefly at the door of Labourdonnais.

On September 2 he was at last induced to sail for Madras. This famous siege hardly deserved the name. The bombardment lasted several days; but not a single man was killed or wounded on the side of the French, and the only loss sustained by the English was due to the accidental bursting of one of their own shells. The Governor, Nicholas Morse, was a man of feeble character, and, though the garrison did not amount to more than three hundred men, a far longer defence was possible. Dupleix, after the capture, recorded the surprise of himself and Labourdonnais at the large quantities of stores and ammunition found in the place. The town was surrendered on September 10. Labourdonnais at once announced his victory to Dupleix, and in his first despatch declared that he had the English at his discretion. Two days later he alludes vaguely to a capitulation on terms, but that nothing definite was settled seems proved by the fact that he discusses with Dupleix, as though the question were still open, the alternative plans of ransoming the place, converting it into a French colony, or razing it to the ground. Finding that Dupleix claimed the right to decide upon the fate of the captured town and that he was unalterably opposed to the idea of a ransom, Labourdonnais hurried on negotiations and signed a convention to restore Madras for a sum of £420,000, claiming that he had given his word to the English to adopt this course from the very beginning. Dupleix, with admirable restraint, had tried reason, persuasion, and even entreaty, but all in vain. There followed a bitter quarrel into the sordid details of which it is unnecessary to enter. It would be hardly possible within a short space to give an exhaustive pronouncement on the complicated technical and legal points involved. In the natural course of events the final decision as to the fate of Madras rested with Dupleix as Governor-General of the French in India, though by his apparent unwillingness to accept full responsibility before the siege he had given Labourdonnais something of a pretext for demurring to his authority.   On the other hand Labourdonnais had invalidated, by his previous demand for definite instructions, the claim he now put forward to complete independence of the Pondicherry Council.   He frequently appealed to his commission of 1741, which however applied to a different set of facts.   As a recent French writer has pointed out, Orry, in laying an injunction upon him not to retain any place captured in the East, never for a moment foresaw his cooperation with Dupleix in an attack on Madras.   The plain duty of the two men was to work together amicably for the good of their country; but to this sacrifice of personal animosities to the dictates of patriotism, they, or at any rate Labourdonnais, proved unequal.   Throughout the dispute Dupleix was mainly in the right, and his obstinate colleague in the wrong.   There is strong reason for believing that Labourdonnais had received a large sum of money as a personal present from the English in Madras.   Culpable as such an action may appear, the admittedly low standard of the age in all such matters must be taken into account.   It is not always easy to draw the line which differentiates a complimentary gratuity or *douceur* from a bribe.   Most men at this time, at all events in India, deemed that they had a right to lay the foundations of a private fortune by their manipulation of public policy.   Labourdonnais had no doubt honestly persuaded himself that the course he preferred was the right one.   The whole incident of the quarrel with Dupleix may easily be magnified out of due proportion.   To say that it saved the English in India is utterly to exaggerate its significance. It affected the fate of a single Presidency, and that only for a few years. The Peace of Aix-la-Chapelle in 1748 settled the affairs of India over the heads of those who had played the chief part in them.   Till that date, Madras was retained by the French, as it would have been if Dupleix had succeeded in bending Labourdonnais to his will.   Had the two men been harmonious from the very first, they might possibly have directed an attack upon the English in Bengal, though Labourdonnais refused even to entertain the idea when suggested by Dupleix, on the ground that if his neutrality were violated the Moghul would drive the French for ever from Hindustan.   Dupleix never even succeeded in reducing Fort St David at his own doors.   Peyton's fleet still held the sea.   Fort William was hardly likely to yield as pusillanimously as Fort St George, while, even if it fell, the English would still remain possessed of Bombay.   In 1747, Boscawen was already on his way from England with a powerful fleet, and, if the French forces had been engaged before Calcutta when it arrived, Pondicherry itself would have been at his mercy.

While Labourdonnais and Dupleix were still fulminating at each

CH. XV.

other in protests and manifestos, the break-up of the monsoons cut the Gordian knot of their quarrel. The terrific gales that blew off the Coromandel coast in October, 1746, shattered Labourdonnais' fleet and forced him to make all sail for the Isles. Twelve hundred disciplined troops were left behind—the flower of the army which enabled Dupleix to defend Pondicherry and carry out his daring incursions into Dekhan politics.

After Labourdonnais' departure Dupleix cancelled the convention with the English on the plea that it had been signed by an insubordinate officer who had exceeded his powers. He laid siege to Fort St David; but the English were at last stung into offering a resistance worthy of their national reputation, and he met here with his first check. The arrival of Boscawen and Griffin with the most powerful fleet that had ever appeared on the Indian Ocean, including thirteen ships of the line, completely transformed the position of affairs. In August, 1748, Pondicherry was subjected to a severe siege—war in grim earnest unlike the farcical operations round Madras. The English lost over a thousand men; and, though their conduct of the operations is said to have shown great incapacity, the French defence was brilliantly directed and remains one of the most considerable achievements of Dupleix. The siege was raised early in October, seven days before the Peace was announced in India. By the Treaty of Aix-la-Chapelle Madras was given back to the English in exchange for Cape Breton. Thus ended the first round of the Anglo-French contest. Nominally, the *status quo* was restored; but to those who could look below the surface the position was wholly different. The old neutrality and security were gone by for ever. The sword once drawn, it could not again be sheathed till the issue had been fought out to the bitter end. Though their material gains were taken from them, the prestige of the French was greatly increased. They had captured the enemy's chief settlement on the Coromandel coast and repelled him from the walls of their own. Dupleix well knew how to make the most of such a success, and his emissaries celebrated the victory in every native Court. Contemporary Englishmen might speak slightingly of French pride and gasconade; but, though the element of vanity was not lacking in the character of Dupleix, his action masked a very subtle and formidable policy.

Both English and French were after 1748 left with larger forces in garrison than they had been accustomed to maintain. The recent war had given them a taste for campaigning, and opportunities for indulging it soon presented themselves. To the English belongs the credit or discredit of the first step. Tempted by the offer of Devicota, a port at the mouth of the Coleroon river, they interfered in a disputed succession in Tanjore. Their success was so moderate that they were under little temptation to repeat the experiment; but the principle received a far wider application at the hands of the French. Unable to rival the

English in trade, Dupleix turned his attention to political intrigue.
The residence of native royal families in Pondicherry since 1740 had
brought him into close relation with the ruling Houses of the Dekhan.
His thoroughly orientalised imagination luxuriated in the study of
their conflicting claims, dynastic revolutions and strange vicissitudes
of fortune.   The Nizám-ul-Mulk, the virtual overlord of southern
India, died after a long and prosperous reign in 1748, and the succession
was disputed among his sons.   Dupleix, with great daring, supported
the cause both of a claimant to the throne of the Dekhan and a pretender against Anwar-ud-din, the ruling Nawáb of the Carnatic.   His
candidate for the latter post was the famous Chanda Sahib, a connexion
by marriage of the older royal House that had been supplanted by
Anwar-ud-din in 1744.   Chanda Sahib was a man of considerable ability,
who seems to have realised that the future in India lay with the
Europeans and employed his leisure in studying the memoirs and
campaigns of Condé and Turenne.   The French had already come into
serious collision with Anwar-ud-din in 1746, by refusing to fulfil their
promise to hand over Madras to him when conquered from the English.
The striking success of the French in the fighting which ensued made
Dupleix realise with characteristic quickness and vividness that the
best native troops could set no barrier to the advance of disciplined
European armies.

At the battle of Ambur, 1749, Anwar-ud-din was defeated and slain.
The Carnatic passed under the control of the *protégé* of the French,
and he in gratitude made large territorial concessions to his European
allies.   Mozaffar Jang, the French candidate for the throne of the
Dekhan, was not so successful; he was vanquished and taken prisoner by
Nasir Jang, the ruling Prince, mainly through a mutiny of the French
officers, who forced their general to retreat in face of the enemy.   But from
what was apparently a desperate situation Dupleix extricated himself
with a coolness and serenity that were truly admirable.   The military
position was restored in 1750 by the storming of Gingi, a fortress
hitherto regarded as impregnable.   Nasir Jang was soon after assassinated; Mozaffar Jang was released, and was enthroned at Pondicherry
as ruler of the Dekhan.   Masulipatam and Divi were made over to
the French; and a vague and high-sounding title was conferred upon
Dupleix, who was hailed as Governor of southern India from the Kistna
to Cape Comorin.   It is often said that henceforward Dupleix ruled
absolutely over thirty millions of people and a country larger than
France; but, though the reputation of the French was now carried very
high and their indirect influence was very great, the truth fell considerably
short of this.   The misunderstanding has arisen, because the Oriental
language of compliment and hyperbole has been taken too literally.
Dupleix appears to have been endowed with an office of high honour
and rather vague functions, which gave him the right to nominate some

of the petty rulers of the Dekhan and conferred upon him the virtual control of the Carnatic. To attempt an exact definition of the theoretical jurisdictions of the native Powers in southern India at this time would be an unprofitable task ; but it may be noted that within the limits of the alleged grant were the kingdoms of Tanjore, Madura, and Mysore, which never openly acknowledged the suzerainty of the Nizám far less that of Dupleix. Even in the Carnatic, Chanda Sahib was nominal ruler till his death, though no doubt he occupied much the same position in relation to the French as the puppet Nawábs of Bengal did to the English after 1757. Dupleix claimed that Chanda Sahib was merely his deputy, and on his death was anxious, instead of appointing a successor, openly to assume the position himself. From this he was dissuaded at the time by the saner judgment of Bussy who, foreseeing, as Dupleix himself curiously seems to have failed to foresee, the relentless opposition of the English, warned him that he was seeking to pluck the fruit before it was ripe.

When the new ruler of Haidarábád left Pondicherry in January, 1751, Bussy at the head of a few hundred French troops marched with him to begin his wonderful and romantic career in the Dekhan. It was originally intended that he should return so soon as the Subahdar was established on his throne ; but Mozaffar Jang was killed in a skirmish a few days after their departure, and Bussy with a rather cynical opportunism set aside the dead man's infant son in favour of Salabat Jang (the brother of Nasir Jang), who was a prisoner in the camp, conducted him to Haidarábád, and remained there to defend him against all rivals.

So far the French policy had met with astonishing success. The grandiose conceptions and striking character of Dupleix had bewitched the Oriental mind. The English, dazed and sullen, looked on with a sort of helpless admiration and envy. But there was one exception to the tale of victory. Mohammad Ali, a connexion of the vanquished Anwarud-din, had fled for refuge into the strong fortress of Trichinopoly. At length, when they saw Dupleix, the real ruler of the Carnatic, and Bussy paramount at the Court of the Nizám, the English were forced to realise that the struggle was one of life or death, and they nerved themselves to assist the fugitive with money and men. Trichinopoly, with its rocky citadel dominating the great plain of the Carnatic, became henceforward the centre and rallying-point of all opposition to the French.

It is unnecessary to enter into the details of the confused struggle that followed. The position was extraordinarily complicated. Two Western nations, at peace with each other in Europe, waged war nominally as the allies of native Powers that were in reality their creatures and tools. At first, some attempt was made to uphold the legal fiction by an agreement that the English and French forces engaged on opposite sides should not discharge their muskets at one another ; but it was soon found impracticable to observe this curious rule of warfare, and all disguise was thrown aside. From time to time the other Powers of the Dekhan were drawn into the *mêlée*, either of necessity, to protect their territories from depredation, or voluntarily, in their desire to fish in troubled waters. The Rájas of Tanjore and Mysore, the Pathan Nawábs of Cuddapah, Savanore, and Kurnool appeared in arms now on one side now on the other, while the Marathas were always hovering near the field of strife, ready to take an unexpected and disconcerting hand in the game. There ensued kaleidoscopic changes of allegiance, dynastic intrigues, revolutions and counter-revolutions, while, ever moving to and fro in the confused picture, may be discerned the brilliant but somewhat sinister figure of the great Frenchman.

Dupleix reached the zenith of his fortunes in 1751. In the spring, Trichinopoly was desperately hard pressed; but Clive's famous seizure and defence of Arcot in the summer, and his victories at Arni and Coveripak in the autumn and winter, relieved the tension. The triumphal course of the French received a decided check in June, 1752, when Jacques-François Law was forced to surrender to Lawrence and Clive before Trichinopoly, and their ally Chanda Sahib, who had surrendered himself to the Tanjorean leader, was put to death. For the next two years hard and persistent fighting went on in the Dekhan, always tending to converge on the fortress that dominated the position. The French were never able to reduce it, and their consequent failure to extend their control completely over the Carnatic neutralised in great measure the dazzling success of Bussy in the Dekhan. Slowly and step by step the English gained the upper hand. Their grip upon the throat of their foe, at first spasmodic and feeble, increased in power and intensity, till the whole gorgeous fabric of French dominion was dragged down into the dust. France had no general in India who was a match for Clive and Lawrence, and of the excellent school of subordinate officers formed in the war, the Englishmen, Cope, Dalton and Kilpatrick, proved on the whole superior to Jacques-François Law, d'Auteuil, de Kerjean, and Mainville. It should be added that Saunders, the Governor of Madras, a man whose fame hardly accords with his deserts, by his cool, cautious and tenacious policy showed himself no mean antagonist to Dupleix.

In 1753 even Bussy's influence waned for a time, for he was forced to recruit his health by a retirement to Masulipatam. It is true that in the autumn he recovered his position at Court and won for France the important districts of the Northern Circars extending north of the Carnatic to the frontiers of Orissa; but the whole of southern India was so desolated by the war that for some time but little revenue could be raised from them. Gradually there grew up a divergence of policy between Bussy and Dupleix. Bussy was in favour of keeping peace with the English and of extending French influence rather from Haidarábád in the Dekhan than from Pondicherry in the Carnatic. Since 1752 he had repeatedly urged arguments in favour of a pacification and counselled Dupleix to withdraw, if possible, from the labyrinth in which he was plunged.

The truth was that the policy of Dupleix, ingenious and imaginative as it was, had broken down. His position in 1754 was wellnigh desperate. He had been beaten in the field; his troops were clamouring for pay; and his treasury was empty. He had been compelled himself to acknowledge the necessity for a respite, and a conference was held with the English at Sadras in December, 1753. It proved abortive, mainly because Dupleix once more raised his claim to be recognised as ruler of the Carnatic in his own person. Meanwhile, both the Companies in Europe were thoroughly alarmed at the warlike propensities of their representatives in India, and, on the initiative of the English, informal conferences to negotiate a peace were held in London, 1753–4, by the Duke of Newcastle and the Earl of Holdernesse, with Duvelaer, a Director of the French Company, and the Duc de Mirepoix, the French ambassador. The recall of Dupleix however was not, as the popular rumour of the time supposed, the direct outcome of a demand from the English Company accompanied by a reciprocal pledge to recall the Governor of Madras. It was already decided upon in France before the conference could be said to have begun. Silhouette, the King's Commissary, had long been opposed to the Governor-General whom he considered a turbulent and dangerous spirit. The news of Law's surrender at Trichinopoly caused widespread alarm in France, and seemed to justify the warnings and criticisms of Labourdonnais, whose Memoirs were just then being given to the world. To all these circumstances, and in great measure to the unwisdom of his own conduct, as will presently be seen, the supersession of Dupleix was really due. In the summer of 1753, Godeheu, a Director of the Company, was appointed King's Commissioner to settle affairs in India. He was to supersede Dupleix, and had even sealed orders to arrest him if he proved contumacious.

Landing in August, 1754, Godeheu concluded in October a suspension of arms for three months which was followed in January, 1755, by the publication of a provisional Treaty, to be valid only if ratified by the Companies at home. As a matter of fact, it was never formally ratified, owing to the outbreak of the Seven Years' War, which occurred before the necessary steps could be taken in Europe. In the Treaty both parties agreed to interfere no more in the disputes of native States and to renounce all Mohammadan dignities and governments. The right of each nation to various possessions was recognised and defined. Dupleix sailed for France in October, 1754.

Scorn and contempt have been poured by English and French writers alike on Godeheu for having surrendered the interests of his country, and on the administration of Louis XV for not having appreciated and supported Dupleix. Dupleix himself contended that when Godeheu arrived the position had already veered round in favour of the French, and that, with the reinforcements Godeheu brought with him, he might have recovered all the ground that had been lost. For this version of the facts, though it has been widely accepted, there is little evidence. Though he railed against his successor, Dupleix was forced to admit that he had no money to pay his army and that financially his whole condition was desperate. Both sides, for obvious reasons, exaggerated, in letters home, the strength of the enemy; but, probably, the French troops brought by Godeheu were in no sense a match for the war-worn veterans of the British army, and it is sometimes forgotten that, while negotiations were going on, an English squadron superior to any French force on the Indian seas was hovering round the coast. It was, indeed, the news of the arrival of this fleet which obliged Godeheu to moderate the higher terms for which he at first stood out. Contemporary English writers, many of whom were in India at the time, without exception considered that the Treaty was unduly favourable to the French. The Pondicherry Council, itself by no means predisposed to favour Godeheu, recorded an opinion that the Peace was the happiest thing that could happen to the Company, and expressed astonishment that the English should acquiesce in it, in view of the advantageous position they held. The Council declared that the English possessed at least 2500 men, 1150 of whom were soldiers of a royal regiment, powerful allies, and no lack of money; they themselves on the other hand had but 1500 troops —"*Dieu sçait quelles troupes*"—and were destitute alike of allies and cash.

The Peace indeed can hardly be termed a surrender at all, when it is remembered that Bussy was left undisturbed at Haidarábád with his army, and that, while the territorial possessions guaranteed to the English were assessed at a revenue of £100,000, those retained by the French were valued at eight times that amount. There is no need to postulate particular baseness of soul, or personal enmity, on the part of Godeheu. He was not a genius; but as a practical man he saw that something drastic had to be done. He loyally endeavoured to follow his instructions, brought about a settlement that at least stemmed the tide of disaster, and earned undying infamy for not achieving the impossible. His personal relations with the man he had been sent to supersede, though they had been friends in earlier years, could hardly be cordial; but that was at least as much the fault of Dupleix as his own.

Dupleix indeed was largely responsible for his own recall. He had treated the authorities at home in a way that no body of men could be expected to pardon. On more than one occasion he deliberately withheld important information, and, though he promptly informed them of his victories, he almost invariably omitted to report his defeats; his despatches, for instance, made no mention of Clive's capture and defence of Arcot. The truth ultimately reached the ears of the French Government, usually through English sources, and it is hardly surprising that

CH. XV.

in time a deep distrust was engendered of his whole policy.   Moreover, they had before them no clear account of what that policy was.   The view is baseless which represents Dupleix as dreaming of empire even when at Chandernagore, and formulating a definite plan to acquire dominion through political and dynastic intrigue.   He entered upon this path only in 1749, and it was not till 1753 that he fully realised the possibilities of his schemes and drew up a full statement for the information of the Company.   This despatch was not received in France till six months after Godeheu had sailed for India.   When it arrived, the Government reversed the order for the recall of Dupleix; but, before the news could reach him, he had already embarked for home.   Nor is it true to say that Dupleix was left unsupported.   In four years he received more than four thousand men.   He complained that these recruits were the scum of Paris and the sweepings of the gaols; but most of the English troops were originally drawn from similar sources, and it was only by constant warfare that they were welded into a capable fighting force.

But, above all, the Company at home had a right to be alarmed by his management of the finances.   They heard impressive accounts of territorial possessions and revenues made over to them by native Powers; but it would be a complete mistake to suppose that any appreciable amount of such sums filtered through to them.   While its servants were dealing with millions of rupees, the Company was rapidly approaching bankruptcy. Dupleix deliberately formulated the doctrine that, for the French at any rate, the trade with India was a failure, and that it was better to enter upon a career of conquest.   The question is how he raised the funds to maintain the costly operations of the war.   Recent research has disproved the legend, which his Memoirs supported, that he had accumulated immense riches at Chandernagore.   In 1741 when he was appointed to Pondicherry, his fortune on his own admission was not large enough for him to retire upon in comfort.   Indeed the largest private fortune would have gone but a little way to maintain his costly system of subsidised alliances.   From 1751 most of the revenues of the Carnatic passed through his hands; but they barely sufficed to finance the ruinous war against Mohammad Ali.   He advanced large sums from the grants and *jagirs* (revenues derived from land) made to him by native Princes, which he had only a very doubtful right to hold at all, and charged the loans to the account of the Company.   Now, if his efforts had been crowned with success, it is possible that at some future time the Company might have had large sums to receive; but the fatal flaw in his policy was that it did not prove to be self-supporting.   He staked everything on victory and he was defeated.   When Godeheu asked him for his assets he could only talk vaguely of revenues and grants, and hand over bonds signed by native rulers for large amounts which he had lent them.   Many of his creditors were obviously incapable of paying anything.   Others, who perhaps had it in their power, showed little inclination to do so, and it was not easy to see how pressure could be put upon them except at the cost of more fighting. In many cases the revenues from ceded territory existed only on paper and were never realised. The peasants had been ruined by the long war. The devastation in the Carnatic was terrible, and it was some time before the proper contributions were received even from the Northern Circars, the most valuable of the new acquisitions. Bussy's army was exceedingly costly; the rate of pay was princely, and the commander himself was said to have become one of the richest subjects in Europe.

The net result of it all was that in 1754 the treasury was empty, while in addition Dupleix claimed that the Company owed him more than thirty lakhs of rupees. When Dupleix demanded assignments on future revenues to satisfy his private claims on the Company, Godeheu, though he granted him a sufficient sum for his immediate needs, referred the whole matter to the authorities at home. Dupleix inveighed fiercely against him, but it is not easy to see what else he could have done. With all his great qualities, Dupleix had many serious defects of temperament. He was sanguine to the point of wilful blindness. Even the bold and enterprising Bussy was staggered at the magnitude and multiplicity of his plans. His refusal to recognise a defeat often carried him to an unlooked-for success, but sometimes turned a check into a disaster. He was lacking in the quality of restraint, the clear appreciation of what was practical, the power to withhold his hand, which was characteristic of his great rival, Lord Clive. In all his schemes there was something of the gambler's rashness, the gambler's desire to advance from success to success, staking at each throw the whole of his past gains. He seldom stopped to concentrate his forces or conserve his conquests. He was inclined to expect impossibilities from his military commanders, and, his enmity once roused, was relentless and unforgetting. Yet, with all necessary qualifications, he must still be regarded as one of the ablest Europeans that have ruled in the East. He did anticipate in many ways the policy and the methods that were to carry Great Britain to the overlordship of India. His defence of Pondicherry, the ascendancy he won with the native Powers, his faculty of impressing the Asiatic imagination, his dauntless demeanour in the face of danger, the almost superstitious dread he inspired in the English, all these things testify to his great capacity.

Dupleix returned to fulminate in memoirs and protests against the Company. He wrote an account of his life and actions from the standpoint of the past few years. Unintentionally perhaps in part, he antedated the conception of his political schemes. He represented the whole of his sojourn in India as a careful and logical preparation for the acquisition of dominion. Every fact was wrested to fit into the picture, every incident moulded to a preconceived theory. Dupleix has won for himself the sympathies of posterity, and the protests of Jacques-François

Law and Godeheu against his version of the facts have gone unheeded; but, the nearer we get to his own time, the less conviction do his writings seem to have carried even among those who were most hostile to the administration of Louis XV. Yet the treatment meted out to him was ungenerous in the extreme. In view of their own misfortunes, the Company could, perhaps, hardly be expected to pay in full the large claims he put forward; but he should have been voted a generous pension to pass his declining years in comfort. He had spent great sums without authorisation, it is true; but he might have kept them for himself as others did. If he erred, it was from no ignoble motive or despicable aim. The glory and honour of France were ever before his eyes. He was treated with cold neglect, his frantic protests went unheeded, and his lot was only preferable to that of Labourdonnais and Lally, whose rewards were the Bastille and the block.

Bussy maintained his position in the Dekhan till 1758, but like the English a few years later he found that in the anarchic condition of southern India his alliances with native Powers often placed him in embarrassing situations. In 1756, when before Savanore, he received a formal dismissal from the service of the Nizám, and began his retreat to Masulipatam with a predatory army of Marathas hanging on his rear. Turning upon his pursuers at Haidarábád, he seized a strong position close to the city, and effected a junction with Law, who had been marching to his relief. He was soon afterwards reconciled to Salabat Jang, but never quite recovered his former influence.

In the short interval between Godeheu's Peace and the commencement of renewed hostilities occurred the extraordinary series of events in Bengal which, breaking like a thunder-clap upon the easy-going serenity of the European settlements, temporarily ruined Calcutta, taught the English their full strength in the efforts they made to recover their position, put an end to the power of the native government, and terminated the political and military existence of the French and Dutch in north-eastern India. It will be convenient, however, to reserve these events for the next section, and to complete here the account of the Anglo-French struggle in the Carnatic. The declaration of the Seven Years' War in 1756 determined the French Government to strike a decisive blow at the British settlements. The attempt was a formidable one, and, had it been better timed or better led, the results to England might have been extremely serious. Count de Lally, son of an Irish refugee, who was placed in command, had distinguished himself on many European battle-fields, and played a considerable part in the Stewart rising of 1745. A brave soldier, a capable general, conscientious and incorruptible, he was yet one of the worst men that could have been selected for the post. Utterly without tact or pliability in dealing either with men or circumstances, he proved singularly incapable of adapting himself to the special conditions of Indian warfare. He fell out with de Leyrit, the Governor of Pondicherry, with d'Aché who commanded the fleet, and with Bussy who should have been his most zealous coadjutor. He was hot-tempered, harsh to his subordinates, and intolerant of advice. The expedition was a long record of misfortunes and blunders, and at every point the general's unhappy temperament exerted a baleful influence on the trend of events. The vanguard under de Soupire arrived in September, 1757; but the succeeding months were frittered away in unimportant operations. Lally, with the main body, only reached the coast of Coromandel in April, 1758, after a twelve months' voyage, by which time the English had already warded off the worst of the critical situation in Bengal. Nevertheless, the French for the moment possessed a superiority of force which, under happier circumstances, might have been employed with great effect. The English admiral, Pocock, though he inflicted severe loss on the main division of the French fleet in a drawn engagement off Negapatam, was unable to bar their passage to Pondicherry. An initial success was won by the prompt siege and capture of Fort St David, after a bombardment of eighteen days. The defence was feebly conducted, and earned the strong censure and bitterly expressed contempt of Clive, who was anxiously watching the course of events from Bengal. Lally's next objective was Madras; but some very fatal features, unhappily characteristic of French history in India, now made their appearance. There was a complete lack of cordial cooperation between the land and sea forces, and the civil and military authorities. The French admiral was cautious to excess, and to his spiritless efforts to second Lally the latter with justice attributed much of his failure. There was the usual want of money. The Governor of Pondicherry declared that he was almost totally destitute of funds to maintain the war. Lally retorted that, if this were true, it was solely due to the corruption and mismanagement of the Administration—a reply which, though it contained a lamentable amount of truth, did not smooth his path in the future. The only expedient for raising the necessary supplies appeared to be to demand from the Rája of Tanjore the payment of a bond for fifty-six lakhs of rupees that had come into the possession of the French. Marching on Tanjore, Lally bombarded the town for five days; but, as his ammunition failed, he was forced to retreat without the money and with a serious loss of prestige. D'Aché, after fighting another fierce engagement with the English off Coleroon, left the Coromandel coast for Mauritius, in spite of the most earnest remonstrances of Lally and the whole Pondicherry Council. The English henceforward held the command of the sea, and this fact alone made the blockade of an open port like Madras a hopeless undertaking. Yet in preparation for it, Lally summoned Bussy from his post at Haidarábád, an action which proved calamitous from every point of view. The Nizám was mortally offended, and French influence at his Court was now at an end. Bussy proved himself an unwilling colleague; and, though it was not easy to work harmoniously with Lally, he failed, in a task that was thoroughly uncongenial, to do justice to his great abilities. There was indeed a fundamental difference in the policy of the two men. Lally's aim was a concentration of all available force for an irresistible attack on the British possessions one by one, risking, as Clive said, the whole for the whole. Bussy, now as ever, clung to the dream, which he had done so much to realise, of French dominion built up on a system of native alliances and supported by a resident at the Nizám's Court, commanding an army of picked men. Conflans was left by Bussy in occupation of the Northern Circars; but he proved utterly unable to cope with the diversion in that quarter planned by Clive, who, in the midst of his multitudinous anxieties in Bengal, played a preponderating part in the defeat of France in southern India. Realising the assured superiority given to England by her supremacy upon the seas, he had definitely made up his mind that the days of French political power in India were numbered, though he stood alone in thinking so. While, therefore, he steadily refused, in the face of strong pressure, to jeopardise his work in Bengal by sending the Madras contingents back to that Presidency, he despatched Forde, one of his best officers, in October, 1758, with a picked force from Calcutta, to support a petty Rája who had rebelled against French domination in the Northern Circars. Forde defeated Conflans at Condore in December, 1758, and carried Masulipatam by storm in April of the following year. The French were finally driven from that part of India, and subsequently, in 1765, Clive obtained from the Emperor an imperial grant making over the Circars to the Company.

In the meantime, December, 1758, Lally advanced against Madras. The issue, as Clive confidently declared, was predestined from the outset. In the respite they had gained by the failure of the French attack on Tanjore, the English had provisioned and strengthened their fortress. The defence was ably conducted by Lawrence and Pigot; and on February 16 the sails of a British fleet were descried standing in towards the Roads. The French immediately abandoned the siege; but, though they had parried the assault of the enemy, it was some time before the English felt themselves strong enough to take the offensive. D'Aché made a feeble attempt to intervene from Mauritius, but after fighting another indecisive battle with Pocock retired finally from the scene. Lally, who was no mean tactician, prolonged his resistance for another two years, but was gradually isolated and beaten to his knees. The campaign at first went on languidly; but, in October, 1759, Eyre Coote took over the command of the English forces from the hands of the veteran Lawrence. The position of the French was now deplorable. They were absolutely without money. The troops were in a periodical state of open mutiny. In January, 1760, Coote decisively defeated Lally at Wandiwash, when Bussy was taken prisoner. While the beaten general stood on the defensive at Valdore, Coote, one by one, reduced the French fortresses in the Carnatic. His operations were checked for a time by a French alliance with Haidar Ali, the able usurper who had just established himself upon the throne of Mysore. But a Maratha invasion obliged him speedily to return to his own country, and Lally was at last beaten back within the walls of Pondicherry. The siege began in September; all hope of relief vanished with the appearance in the offing of a powerful British fleet; and in January, 1761, Lally was forced to surrender from lack of provisions.

The fall of Pondicherry was the end of French dominion in India. Lally was taken to England as a prisoner of war, but was released on parole to meet the charges made against him in France. After a trial lasting two years, though he had been guilty of nothing more serious than errors of judgment, he was made the scapegoat of the popular fury for the colonial losses of France in the Seven Years' War, and was beheaded. Ten years afterwards, this iniquitous sentence was formally reversed by decree of the King's Council. Pondicherry and the other French possessions were restored by the Peace of Paris in 1763, with their fortifications in ruins. Mohammad Ali was recognised as Nawáb of the Carnatic, and Salabat Jang as Subahdar of the Dekhan. Largely through the instrumentality of Clive, always the evil star of the French in India, two clauses had been inserted in the Treaty limiting the armed force they might maintain on the Coromandel coast and excluding them altogether from Bengal and the Northern Circars except in the capacity of merchants. Henceforth, all French settlements in India were the easy prey of British armies so soon as war had been declared in Europe. Pondicherry was once more captured in 1778 and restored by the Peace of Versailles in 1783, retaken in 1793, and, though nominally restored again at the Peace of Amiens in 1802, not finally given back till 1816. The one formidable attempt of France to regain her old ascendancy in 1781–3 will be narrated in its proper place. With that exception, her influence henceforward was only represented by diplomatic emissaries or military adventurers in the Courts and camps of native rulers. The glamour of her great traditions, the memory of her wonderful and short-lived span of power remained as a vague menace to haunt the path of British statesmen and prove a will o' the wisp to more than one opponent of British rule.

The French Company had its privileges suspended by a royal decree of August 13, 1769. The trade to India, subject to certain restrictions, was henceforth laid open, and the settlements in the East passed directly under the control of the Crown. French thought of the day was all against the maintenance of a trading body dependent upon a state-granted monopoly. The Government had commissioned Morellet, one of the ablest of the Physiocrats, to conduct an enquiry into their financial condition, and his verdict was one of condemnation. He was no doubt employed to make out a particular case; but in none of the contemporary replies that his pamphlet brought forth, though one was from the able pen of Necker, is any serious attempt found to discredit his chief facts. No sound economist can deny his main conclusions: that a commercial enterprise which is not self-supporting ought to be abandoned, and that there are infinitely more legitimate and more important uses to which the public revenue can be put than in maintaining a Company which is bankrupt if left to itself.

Assuredly not the least of the causes of England's success was the greater prosperity of her East India Company. According to Morellet the French Company entered upon the war in 1744 with resources and credit already seriously impaired. From that date the number of vessels returning from the Indies dropped to about a fourth of their previous number, while there seems to have been a complete cessation of capital sent from France. Though there was a slight improvement in this respect after the Peace of 1748, the downward tendency was rapidly accelerated after 1751. On the other hand, the commerce of the English throve during the war. After 1744 the number of vessels returning from India and the amount of imports actually increased. In the very year of the outbreak of the war the Company made a new loan to the Government of £1,000,000, in return for which their privileges were extended from 1766 to 1780.

The French Company was so closely connected with the Government that it was not immune from the lethargy and demoralisation which crept into all state departments during the reign of Louis XV. While much, therefore, of the responsibility for the loss of the Indian possessions of France must be laid on the Ministers of the King, it is only fair to bear in mind that the French Government had never been able to rely upon a strong and self-sustaining commercial interest. If it was in some measure responsible for the Company's fall, it had also been almost wholly responsible for its creation. The English East India Company at this time had no official connexion with the State, but many of its Directors sat in Parliament and were able to press its interests on the attention of the ministry. As a result, the Company was neither isolated from nor cramped by state interference, and until the latter end of the century was lifted above the turmoil of party politics.

To sum up, therefore, it may be said that England's success was due to a variety of causes—the greater commercial prosperity of her trade with India, her superiority in the hard hand to hand fighting in southern India, the severely practical genius of Lord Clive, her general ascendancy on the sea which became particularly marked during the Seven Years' War, the wealth and resources she was able to draw after 1757 from her occupation of Bengal, and, lastly, the greater vigour and capacity of her national Government, which, less entangled than that of France in European wars, had the leisure to direct its chief energies at a most critical time to the field of maritime and colonial expansion.

(3) CLIVE AND WARREN HASTINGS.

In the rich alluvial plain of Bengal, with its wide waterways, fertile fields, industrious, peaceful and pliant population, a European nation with resources drawn from a sea-borne commerce was destined, when the first steps had once been taken, to advance towards dominion more rapidly than elsewhere. Yet this fact was not at first apparent. Till past the middle of the eighteenth century the European settlements in Bengal were far more submissive than those in western and southern India to the overlordship of native Powers. They bowed before the majestic pretensions of the imperial Court of Delhi, even when the suzerainty of the Moghul had become a mere shadow. The War of the Austrian Succession ran its course without any outbreak of hostilities between Calcutta and Chandernagore. The dynastic wars that ensued on the Coromandel coast were brought to a close before the peace was even broken in Bengal. The chief settlements of the English, French and Dutch, all built within thirty miles of one another, pursued their avocations in peace without a thought of violating the traditional neutrality of the province, till the native Government itself drew the sword by its savage attack upon one of themselves.

The last strong Subahdar or Nawáb of Bengal, Ali Verdi Khan, who possessed a very shrewd insight into the real meaning of the English occupation, died in April, 1756. He was succeeded by Siráj-ud-daulá, a youth of about twenty years of age, weak, vicious, and a degenerate. Both the English and the French at this time, knowing that war was imminent between the two countries, were fortifying their respective settlements. The new Nawáb sent them orders to desist. The French succeeded in quieting his suspicions, but the English failed to make their peace with him. They had already incurred his displeasure by refusing to give up a fugitive of whom he was in quest, and by expelling, through some misunderstanding, the messenger who came to demand his surrender. Siráj-ud-daulá promptly determined to extirpate the English, who were recognised by his ablest advisers as the most formidable of the European nations. He seized the factory of Kasimbazar, and news soon reached Calcutta that he was in full march upon that settlement with an army variously estimated as consisting of 30,000 to 50,000 men. The European stations in Bengal at this time were weakly defended. In all of them long years of peace had brought about a similar condition of affairs. The forts had fallen into disrepair, warehouses, godowns, and luxurious private houses had grown up round the ramparts, blocking the fire of the guns and affording cover to an enemy. There had been mismanagement of funds in the past and failure to carry out the recommendations of military experts; but for this state of things, in Calcutta at any rate, responsibility lay far heavier on the Presidency than on the Company at

CH. XV.

home.   In Calcutta the regular European garrison did not amount to more than 260 men, and even that was double the French force at Chandernagore.   In spite of this, had the spirit of Clive animated the defence, a sturdy resistance might have been offered to the Nawáb's unwieldy army.   But the siege of Calcutta proved one of the least creditable episodes in the history of British India.   Drake, the Governor, was a weak man respected neither by his colleagues nor by the native inhabitants.   Holwell, the only man of ability on the Council, was personally unpopular.   The attack began on June 16.   On the 18th the women and children were embarked on the ships in the river, and the next day, in a moment of unpremeditated pusillanimity, Drake, the military commander of the garrison, and some others, followed them on board.   The abandoned garrison, having watched with mingled rage and astonishment the fleet drop down the river below the town, held out under Holwell for two days longer; but, as their frantic signals to the fleet to return met with no response, they were forced to surrender on June 20.   That night, by an act of stupid brutality, one hundred and forty-six English prisoners were thrust into the notorious Black Hole, or military punishment cell, of the fortress.   It was the hottest season of the Indian summer, and next morning, after suffering indescribable torments, but twenty-three miserable wretches, Holwell amongst them, crawled out alive.   For this atrocity the Nawáb was not personally responsible; but he showed a revolting callousness after the event, and made no attempt to punish the perpetrators.   Meanwhile, the fugitives from the siege, huddled together in misery and privation, their plight further embittered by mutual reproaches and recriminations, were awaiting relief at Fulta, twenty miles lower down the river.

When the news reached Fort St George, the authorities there after long discussion decided, in spite of the imminence of war with France, to make the recovery of Calcutta their first care.   It was fortunate for them that the year 1756 witnessed the temporary eclipse of Bussy's power in the Dekhan, for he was thus prevented from either attacking Madras when seriously depleted of troops, or marching to support the Nawáb of Bengal.   Clive, just returned from England to assume office as Governor of Fort St David, was placed at the head of the land forces, while Admiral Watson was in command of the fleet.   The expedition, which consisted of five men-of-war, carrying 900 European and 1500 native troops, started on October 16.   They reached the Hooghly after a difficult and tedious voyage, sailed boldly up the river, though without pilots—a difficult and hazardous feat of navigation—and relieved the fugitives at Fulta in December.   Calcutta was retaken on January 2, 1757, and Hooghly a week later.   Siráj-ud-daulá once more drew towards Calcutta with a large army.   After a sharp fight, in which a dense fog neutralised the generalship of Clive, the Nawáb agreed on February 9 to conclude an offensive and defensive alliance with the English.   The Company's forts and former privileges were restored, and permission was given them to coin money and fortify Calcutta.

Clive at this period had to direct his course with the greatest circumspection. The difficulties that faced him were tremendous. News having reached India that war was declared between England and France, he was receiving urgent calls from the Government of Madras to return with his army to that Presidency, and was obliged to take upon himself the serious responsibility of refusing the summons. His relations with Watson were far from cordial, and on one occasion, in a dispute as to the government of Calcutta after the recapture, the Admiral even threatened to open fire upon him. Watson was a brave, frank and able man; but as a King's officer he considered that his main duty was to act against the French, and he hardly cared to conceal his contempt for the Company's affairs. Clive's instinct told him that either Chandernagore must be captured or the French bound to inaction by a very stringent agreement. This, more than anything else, induced him to consent to a peace with Siráj-ud-daulá which otherwise could hardly have been considered satisfactory; it was essential before all things to have a breathing space. After some futile negotiations for a neutrality in which neither side was sincere, Chandernagore was attacked and forced to surrender. On land, Clive drove in the outposts and kept the garrison employed so as to prepare the way for the main attack by the fleet. The French made a gallant defence, two hundred of their small force being either killed or wounded; but they were quite unable to repel Watson's brilliant onslaught from the river. The English too suffered heavily, in the flagship every commissioned officer, except Watson himself and one other, was either killed or wounded. A considerable portion of the garrison escaped to join Jean Law, the French commander at Kasimbazar. Pursued over the Oudh boundary, Law in an adventurous march made his way to Lucknow and Delhi, and twice within the next two years aided the Moghul Emperor to invade Bengal, finally surrendering to the English with the honours of war in 1761.

Meanwhile, English relations with the Nawáb were in a most unsatisfactory state. Their demands upon him were constantly increasing as they gradually felt their strength. He had only been kept quiet during the attack on Chandernagore by the exercise of great adroitness on Clive's part. It was known that he was giving his protection to the French, and was eager for Bussy to bring his army from southern India to Bengal. Despairing of any firm settlement while Siráj-ud-daulá remained on the throne, the English, contrary to their original intentions, were driven to contemplate a renewal of the war. A revolution at Court was obviously imminent, for Siráj-ud-daulá had few friends, and to Clive and his colleagues it seemed better that they should seek to guide events than merely hope to profit by their issue. A conspiracy was arranged to dethrone the Nawáb and set in his place Mír Jafar,

CH. XV.

a great noble of his Court. At a critical point in the negotiations Omichand, an influential native employed as a go-between by the English, attempted to levy blackmail by demanding a disproportionate amount of the plunder expected to accrue to the conspirators, under threat of divulging the whole conspiracy. At the instigation of Clive, who considered that " art and policy were warrantable in defeating the purposes of such a villain," two drafts of the treaty with Mír Jafar were prepared. One, written on red paper, guaranteed to Omichand the sum he demanded, and was shown to him to quiet his suspicions. The other, which was ultimately signed by Mír Jafar, omitted this stipulation. The fictitious document was signed by Clive and the members of the Secret Committee; and, when Watson, who, as has been well said, played throughout the transaction the part of a disgusted spectator, refused to append his signature, Clive directed that it should be forged. The agreement with Mír Jafar ceded to the British all the privileges and rights which had been promised by Siráj-ud-daulá. Heavy compensation was exacted for the loss of Calcutta : one million sterling was to be paid to the Company, and half that sum to the European inhabitants. By a private arrangement large sums as gratuities were guaranteed to the members of Council and the Commander-in-chief; Clive was to receive in all £234,000 ; Watts, the resident at Murshidábád, £117,000 ; and others in proportion.

Meanwhile Siráj-ud-daulá, accompanied by the traitor Mír Jafar, had marched to the famous grove of Plassey with an army estimated at 50,000 men. Clive advanced northwards from Chandernagore. Before crossing the river which parted him from the enemy's position, he held a council of war to discuss the advisability of immediate action. He himself voted in the negative, and was supported by the majority of his officers. The minority, headed by Eyre Coote, were in favour of the bolder course. The Council was dismissed ; but, after an hour's solitary meditation, Clive announced that he had changed his mind and intended to fight. He crossed the river, June 22, and reached Plassey an hour after midnight. The next morning he drew up his small army, consisting of about 900 Europeans and 2300 other troops, behind an embankment which defended him from the enemy's artillery. The two armies began to cannonade each other soon after daybreak, and continued to do so till eleven o'clock, when a torrential downpour of rain caused the fire to slacken. At two o'clock the enemy, having been repulsed in a charge, showed signs of wavering, and Kilpatrick, in the temporary absence of Clive, ordered an advance. Clive, hastening up, at first reprimanded him severely; but, seeing that the enemy were in motion to evacuate the field, he ended by putting himself at the head of the charge. The Nawáb's army, realising that they were betrayed by Mír Jafar's contingent, which had taken no part in the action, and suspecting treachery on all sides, now streamed from their entrenchments in hopeless rout across the plain.

Such was the battle of Plassey, which set the seal on Clive's military fame and brought him his peerage, though he had fought many actions which more severely tested, and more signally proved, his powers of leadership. The English lost nineteen men killed in action, and the enemy not more than five hundred. It was not a battle but a panic, and there was hardly any fighting worth speaking of. The real key to Clive's strategy is to be found in the fact that he had determined not to attack the Nawáb's huge army with his tiny force, but to entrench himself till the conspirators openly showed their hand. He was disconcerted for a time by the ambiguous attitude of Mír Jafar, who seemed also to wait upon the event, or who had perhaps been shamed into inaction by the deluded Siráj-ud-daulá's last desperate and pathetic appeal to his honour. Clive's momentary anger, when Kilpatrick ordered the final advance, was due to his belief that his preconceived plan was imperilled. The utter demoralisation of the enemy gave him the victory sooner than he had dared to hope, and he was quick as always to see and profit by the sudden change of circumstances.

After the battle Mír Jafar, in spite of his equivocal attitude, was hailed by Clive as the new Nawáb of Bengal. Siráj-ud-daulá fell into the hands of Miran, Mír Jafar's worthless son, and was put to death. On the examination of the Nawáb's treasury at Murshidábád, it was found to contain only one and a half million sterling, while the total amount to be paid over to the English was £2,340,000. It was therefore arranged that the payments should be made by instalments. The wretched Omichand was at the same time enlightened as to the deception that had been practised on him.

After establishing Mír Jafar at Murshidábád and quelling several insurrections against his authority, Clive returned to Calcutta to find that a despatch had arrived from home for the appointment of a "rotation" Government. A Council of ten was nominated, of whom the four seniors were to preside in rotation for four months at a time. The despatch was written before the Directors had been fully informed of Plassey and its results. The Council accordingly decided to deviate from the instructions given, and offered the Presidency to Clive who after some hesitation accepted it. In January, 1759, he successfully defended Mír Jafar from a dangerous coalition between a rebellious son of the Emperor and the Nawáb Wazír of Oudh. It was in return for this service, on some rather indelicate prompting from Clive himself, that Mír Jafar made over to him the famous *jagir*, consisting of the rents paid by the East India Company for the districts held by them south of Calcutta and amounting to about £30,000 a year.

The extraordinary change in the status of the English affected their relations with the Dutch, who had always acquiesced willingly in the sovereignty of the Nawáb while he was an independent Prince, but who now discerned in the shadow of his throne the form of an old and hated

European rival. Above all, they rebelled against the right granted to the English to search all vessels in the Hooghly, and to monopolise the pilot service. Accordingly, after some secret correspondence with the Nawáb, in which he played a very equivocal part, they appeared in the Ganges with a strong armament. Clive believed that to allow another European nation to establish itself in force in Bengal was, in the unsettled state of the province, tantamount to a surrender of the whole position so hardly won. On the other hand, to offer armed resistance when there was peace between the two nations was no doubt an utterly lawless proceeding. Yet he did not shrink from this extreme step, declaring that a public man must sometimes act with a halter round his neck. The Dutch foolishly afforded him a plausible pretext by seizing some English merchant vessels. He promptly assailed them with all his strength; their seven ships were captured, and their land forces utterly defeated by Forde. The Dutch at Chinsura were forced to surrender, and were only permitted to retain their settlement in Bengal on terms that robbed their rivalry for the future of all terrors for the English.

Clive left India in February, 1760. To few subjects of the British Crown has it been given to accomplish a more wonderful task than the one he had compressed into the space of three years. The dynastic war in southern India had revealed in him a born leader of men and a tactician of high order; the revolution in Bengal justified his claim to the greater qualities of the strategist and the statesman. In 1756 the Company had been driven with contumely from their chief settlement. Clive not only reinstated them, but utterly transformed the whole position. From being the obsequious servants of the Nawáb the British became his masters. Their influence for all practical purposes was now supreme throughout Bengal, which in its wider signification included Behar and Orissa. Clive had captured the chief settlement of the French in that province, materially helped to ruin their power in the Dekhan, and reduced the Dutch to submission.

But the manner in which these brilliant results were achieved is more open to criticism. The whole episode of the war with Siráj-ud-daulá falls below the standard which a Western nation should observe in dealing with an alien civilisation. The English made a fatal mistake when, in the words of Watts, they determined to "play the game in the Oriental style." They were thus beguiled into a course of action from which they would probably have recoiled, had every step been clear from the beginning. The fact that Clive, whose natural instincts were all in favour of frankness, was driven to write a "soothing" letter to the Nawáb, long after he had decided to ruin him, is typical of the moral degeneration which had overtaken British policy. The incident of the fictitious treaty with Omichand and the forging of Admiral Watson's name is but a detail in a course of action that was stained throughout with dissimulation. The first false step was taken (it was no doubt easy to see this after the event) in meddling with a dynastic plot at all. It would have been far preferable to defeat Siráj-ud-daulá in open warfare and then set up a successor. But Clive and his colleagues did not realise the Nawáb's weakness, prompt action of some kind was necessary, and the supreme difficulty of the position extenuates their policy, even though forming no adequate defence of it.

The private arrangement with Mír Jafar for donations to individuals cannot be justified, even though there be taken into account the lower standard in all questions of public action and private profit which was then universally prevalent. Technically speaking, there was no breach of the law, for the regulation forbidding the receipt of presents from native Powers was not passed till 1765. But the fact that the Council concealed the transaction from the Court of Directors shows that their consciences were uneasy. A palliation was subsequently found in the meagre official salaries paid to the Company's servants at this time. It is true that nominally they were very low; but, with allowances and the permission to engage in private trade, the real remuneration was probably higher than that of the Indian civilian of to-day. The Directors, as subsequent events were to prove, had some reason for their contention that higher salaries would not exempt their servants from temptation. Verelst, under whose rule corruption reached such a terrible height, received in salary and commissions £23,000 a year, besides permission to trade on his own account—remuneration on an infinitely more magnificent scale, considering the territory over which he ruled, than that enjoyed by the Viceroy of all India.

Clive's own defence is well known. He declared that he considered presents not dishonourable when they were received from an independent Prince as the price of services rendered without detriment to the Company. But it can hardly be said that any real independence was left to a man in Mír Jafar's position, who was supported entirely by British arms. Clive also claimed to have informed the authorities at home that the Nawáb's generosity had made his fortune easy; but a vague and incidental statement of this kind could scarcely give an adequate idea of the huge sums involved, and, when the Directors disclaimed the intention of objecting to any gratuity made to individuals, they could have had no inkling that these gratuities nearly equalled the whole amount awarded to the Company itself for the loss of Calcutta.

The additional gift of the *jagir* was rendered the more invidious in that it consisted of the quit-rent which the Company was bound to pay to the Nawáb for their territorial possessions in Bengal. Clive was man of the world enough to know that his position as at once servant and landlord of the Company was an impossible one. The surprising thing is, not that the Directors should ultimately have withheld payment of this huge annuity, but that they should have acquiesced in it so long. There was sound sense in their contention that it was inadvisable for them to be tributary to their own servant. It is true that they played their part exceedingly ill; they allowed Clive to retain the *jagir* till they had begun to quarrel with him, and then endeavoured to withdraw it on purely technical grounds to which Clive could, and did, make a good technical reply.

A more serious charge against Clive is that he had, by accepting these presents, seriously impaired the stability of his own work. It is probably true that at the time of the arrangement with Mír Jafar the English believed his wealth to be boundless. The most ridiculous reports were current as to the contents of the treasury at Murshidábád, which were said to amount to £40,000,000. After Plassey the sum was found to be but a million and a half, while the total demands of the English, including both the sums that were avowed and those that were concealed, amounted to more than two and a quarter millions. Yet on this discovery no remission of any kind was granted. Mír Jafar was obliged to make assignations on his revenue and pledge his credit for years to come. The whole administration was crippled and could not be properly carried on, so that a part at least of the responsibility for the notorious misgovernment of Bengal during the next few years must be shifted to the shoulders of Clive and his colleagues. Eyre Coote and several members of the Council declared at the time of Mír Jafar's deposition that his want of money proceeded, not from any fault of his own, but from the distracted condition in which the country had been left after Clive's departure. Clive's famous statement before the Select Committee of Parliament in 1773, that, when he recollected the gold, silver, and jewels in the treasury at Murshidábád, he stood astonished at his own moderation, must be set side by side with the fact that the wealth there accumulated was found by himself at the time to be insufficient to meet even the first drafts of the new reign. At the parliamentary enquiry Clive was asked whether, at the time the *jagir* was granted, he knew that the Nawáb was surrounded by troops clamouring for pay. He answered, yes; but he added as some sort of explanation that it was the custom of the country to keep soldiers in arrears. Again, he was asked if he knew that the Nawáb's goods and furniture were publicly sold to pay the Company the sums stipulated in the treaty, and again he had to answer in the affirmative.

Clive's responsibility was, of course, much less than that of the men who, under Vansittart, Spencer, Verelst, and Cartier, lowered the honour and prestige of England in the East. They had not the palliations that he could put forward, and they developed the evil tendencies that were only latent in his acts. Clive could always discriminate between his own interest and that of the State. When they clashed, he never for a moment hesitated which to prefer. In attacking the Dutch at Chinsura he risked the loss of a large part of his private fortune, which had been entrusted to an agent in the Netherlands. But, as a responsible administrator, he should have realised that lesser men would fail to tread so nicely the difficult and dangerous path lying between the domains of public and private interest. To sum up—there was neither criminality nor corruption in the acceptance of these presents, but there was inexpediency to a very high degree, and Clive himself afterwards found his previous conduct something of a millstone round his neck in his last and noblest work, the purification and reform of the civil service of Bengal.

After his departure, Shah Álam, the new Moghul Emperor, invaded Bengal, but suffered defeat at the hands of Caillaud and Knox. During the campaign Mír Jafar's son was struck with lightning and killed. The Bengal Council seized the occasion to effect another revolution in the Government. They deposed Mír Jafar in favour of his son-in-law Mír Kasim, from whom they took gratuities to the amount of two hundred thousand pounds. A minority of the Council protested forcibly against this revolution, which they considered unnecessary and likely to cast an indelible stain upon the national character. It was really planned by Holwell, who temporarily succeeded Clive. Vansittart, the new Governor, was a man of good instincts but weak character, whose own account of his period of office presents a pathetic picture of a constant struggle with a recalcitrant and corrupt majority on the Council.

Mír Kasim was a man of a very different stamp from Mír Jafar. He possessed great administrative ability and honestly did his best to put the affairs of the province on a sound footing, and to meet his engagements with the English. He cleared off most of the encumbrances left by his predecessor, discharged his debt to the Company, reduced the numbers, while greatly increasing the efficiency, of his army, and so completely won the allegiance of his soldiers that they fought for him with a bravery and fidelity rarely experienced in the native armies of this period. His position however was untenable. In the end the ruthless extortions of the Bengal Council drove him to desperation and brought out all the latent savageness and cruelty of his nature. The English policy towards him was an unfortunate mixture of weak compliance and unrighteous severity. The only two men of real ability on the Council, Vansittart himself and young Warren Hastings, consistently supported and defended him up to the eve of the appeal to force, declaring that with very few exceptions they found his conduct irreproachable. Hastings announced that, but for the Nawáb's final acts of treachery and barbarity, which made it the duty of every Englishman to unite in support of the common cause, he would have resigned the Company's service as a protest against the treatment of Mír Kasim.

The question of the internal trade was a complicated one. By Surman's Firman granted in 1717, the Company were allowed to carry on their trade to and from Bengal free of duty. But this exemption applied only to imports and exports by sea. After 1756, the Company's servants began illegally to claim exemption for the private trade which they carried on for their own profit within the province itself, though their competitors, the native merchants, were still obliged to pay all imposts in full. Thus unfairly favoured, the English diverted more and more of the trade into their own hands or those of their native agents, and many of the factors made a profit by selling the Company's passes to native traders unconnected with the Company. While therefore the English obliged the Nawáb to pay them heavy subsidies for the support of their troops, they were at the same time lessening the customs duties from which his revenues were mainly derived, and impoverishing by unfair competition that portion of his subjects who would normally have paid the tax. Against this state of things Mír Kasim protested at first with dignity and moderation, then with increasing irritation. Vansittart and his supporter Warren Hastings, the two men who played an honourable part throughout in opposition to the corrupt majority on the Council, met the Nawáb in conference in 1762. They agreed that the English should pay duties at nine per cent. on their internal trade, an arrangement which, even so, left them in a remarkably favourable position as compared with their native rivals. It was stipulated that no use should be made of this agreement till Vansittart had laid it before the Council; but Mír Kasim by a fatal error began to act upon it at once. The Council promptly disowned the action of the Governor. They would probably have done so in any case; but they were furious when they heard that the Nawáb was acting as though Vansittart's assent was all-sufficient. Hastings solemnly warned them that they were making themselves the "lords and oppressors" of the country, but in vain. One of the most significant features of the business was that the Council were prepared to embroil the province and risk the loss of Bengal for a point in which the Company, as distinct from their servants, had no interest at all.

Mír Kasim now abolished, as he had a perfect right to do, all internal dues for two years, thus putting his own subjects on a level with the British. The Council immediately demanded that he should reverse the order, Vansittart and Hastings alone pointing out the extreme injustice of requiring the Nawáb to ruin his own subjects for the purpose of upholding the British monopoly. Mír Kasim was gradually driven into open war. So far he had acted with forbearance and moderation; but from this date he exhibits a rapid deterioration of character. Frequent collisions took place between his officers and the agents of the Company. In June, 1763, William Ellis, a man of quarrelsome and tactless ways, who had long been on bad terms with the Nawáb, seeing that war was imminent, forcibly took possession of the city of Patna, but was surrounded by the enemy and captured. All the up-country agencies were seized and dismantled. In July Mír Kasim was formally deposed. Mír Jafar was brought from his seclusion and once more placed upon the throne. He was made to grant all the commercial privileges claimed by the English, promise a large donation to the army, and, by a most iniquitous provision, indemnify the Company for the acts committed by the usurper in whose favour he had been formerly deposed. Mír Kasim was brilliantly defeated by Adams in two fiercely fought battles in 1763 and, after ordering the massacre of Ellis and his other prisoners at Patna, took refuge with Shuja-ud-daulá, the Nawáb Wazír of Oudh and the Emperor Shah Álam, who were now acting in conjunction. Munro, who had first to quell by drastic measures a dangerous sepoy mutiny, defeated their combined forces in 1764 at the battle of Buxar, in which the English lost over 800 men killed and wounded and the enemy left 2000 dead upon the field. This was the most important victory in India won by the English up to that time, and it laid Oudh and a great part of northern India at their feet. Soon afterwards the titular Emperor of Hindustan with his chief Minister, the Nawáb Wazír, made his submission to the victors.

Early in 1765 the Bengal Council once more effected a lucrative sale of the succession to the Nawábship. Mír Jafar died in February, and was succeeded by his second son. A new treaty was concluded, extending British influence in the administration and transferring all real control to a Deputy Nawáb who was largely dependent on the Council. In spite of the fact that all the modifications of the former compact were against the Nawáb's own interests, he was compelled to make handsome presents to the Governor and Council. The whole affair presented a stronger instance of compulsion than had yet occurred, and the scandal was intensified by the fact that, before the documents were signed, strict orders against receiving any gratuities from native Powers were received from home.

The transaction was hardly completed, when, in May, 1765, Clive arrived, with special powers to take up his second governorship of Bengal. It was now five years since he left India. In England his course had not been altogether smooth. Though he was hailed by Pitt as a "heaven-born general," the political honour bestowed upon him was limited to an Irish peerage. Clive himself considered it inadequate; but Ministers were probably influenced by the fact that he had been munificently rewarded by a native Power. He entered Parliament as member for Shrewsbury in 1761, and by a lavish purchase of rotten boroughs soon gathered round him a little band of supporters. He was consulted by the Government in the framing of the Indian clauses of the Treaty of Paris in 1763, but never seems to have won the complete confidence of either political party in England; and his main sphere of activity lay in the domestic politics of the East India Company. A certain opposition had grown up against him even in the Court of Directors, partly due to a dictatorial letter he had addressed to them from Bengal and partly to the fact that his suggestion to Pitt, in 1759, of state control over Indian possessions had leaked out. Three years after his return, the attempt already referred to was made to stop the payment of his *jagir*. At this point news arrived of the calamitous position of affairs in Bengal. The Court of Proprietors, who never faltered in their allegiance to him, at once demanded that he should be sent out to set matters right. The Directors gave way; Clive was appointed Governor and Commander-in-chief in Bengal; an arrangement was made by which he was to receive the *jagir* for ten years, or till his death if it fell within that period; and his chief partisan was elected Chairman of the Company. If the existing Bengal Council were found to be opposed to him on his landing, Clive was empowered to call into being a smaller committee of four nominated by himself, and together they were to assume all the functions of government.

Having arrived in India, Clive found that the military position had been completely retrieved by the victories of Adams and Munro. It remained for him to reform the internal administration and determine the future foreign relations of Bengal. His task in both directions was a difficult one. Demoralisation had spread through every branch of the service. Insubordination was rife both on the civil and the military establishment; waste, plunder, and recklessness were everywhere prevalent. No living man but Clive, with his vast Indian experience and his iron strength of will, could have stemmed the tide of corruption, and of all his other achievements none is comparable to the work, incomplete as it was in some respects, that he accomplished during his second term of office in Bengal. Finding it necessary at once to exercise the special powers with which he had been endowed, he nominated his Select Committee two days after his arrival, amid the pale faces of the original Council, sick with apprehension of the reckoning to come. Every man was made to take the covenant against the receipt of presents, and the evil system which allowed the Company's servants to escape the regular internal dues on their private trade was abolished. Clive himself was in favour of the total abolition of licensed trading and the substitution of salaries on a liberal scale; but, as the Court of Directors refused to adopt such a solution, he did his best to legalise and limit a practice of which he disapproved by allocating the profit of the salt monopoly, carefully regulated and graded, to the emolument of the Bengal staff. After two years the system was abolished by the Directors, who granted instead of it a commission on the gross revenues of the province. These reforms were not carried without the fiercest opposition. Three of the original Council were driven into resignation; one was expelled. The immense sums he had himself received after Plassey were naturally, though unfairly, quoted against Clive. To a certain extent his past now rose up against him, and his position would undoubtedly have been stronger, if he had been able to offer something better than the technical and legal defence, sound enough in its way, that in 1757 there was no order of the Court of Directors against the practice and that the circumstances of a revolution and a peaceful succession were very different. To an uneasy sense of a certain sting in the taunts of his opponents are probably to be attributed both the strength of Clive's language of condemnation and the continual assertion of his own disinterestedness, which are alien to modern taste.

Clive had next to regulate the Company's relations with the Emperor and his hereditary chief Minister, the Nawáb Wazír of Oudh. His settlement with the latter was the constructive part of his work that was destined to endure the longest. Shuja-ud-daulá was required to pay 50 lakhs of rupees as a war indemnity, and was restored to all his dominions except the districts of Kora and Allahábád. A defensive alliance was concluded with him, by which the Company engaged, on his being responsible for their pay and maintenance, to provide troops whenever he required them for the protection of his frontiers. Thus Oudh definitely assumed that condition of a "buffer" State, which it retained down to its annexation by Lord Dalhousie in 1856.

A more difficult problem was presented by Shah Álam, who, with the prestige of his high office joined to the disability of material poverty and destitution, was drifting like a derelict vessel, powerless for good yet potent for harm, on the stormy sea of Indian politics. Clive called upon the Emperor once more to confirm the Nawáb of Bengal in his office, and took over on behalf of the East India Company the *diwani* of the province, which he had refused when formerly offered in 1759. The duty of the *Diwan* was to collect and administer all the revenues, to defray the expenses of government, and, after setting aside funds for the support of the Nawáb, to remit the remainder to the imperial treasury at Delhi. On this occasion certain modifications were introduced. The Company were to pay the Nawáb of Bengal a fixed sum of 53 lakhs of rupees (reduced to 41 lakhs in 1766, and to 32 in 1769), to give the Emperor an annual subsidy of 26 lakhs, and make over to him the districts of Kora and Allahábád as a means of supporting his imperial dignity.

Theoretically, it is perhaps not easy to justify this curious solution of the problem, which was, indeed, described by a political opponent as a "monstrous heap of partial, arbitrary, political inconsistencies." Practically it is difficult to suggest a more feasible course. The arrangement was attacked from diametrically opposite standpoints, according as the critics gave their attention to the Emperor's high claims or his feeble resources. Clive was accused both of driving too hard a bargain and of having been needlessly generous. Was it really worth while, it was asked, to buoy up the sinking empire, or, if so, would it not have been better to march to Delhi, and conquer all Hindustan in the name of the Moghul? From these dazzling dreams Clive had the strength of will to turn away his eyes. He realised, none more clearly, that the path to dominion lay open. "It is scarcely hyperbole to say," he wrote, "that to-morrow the whole Moghul empire is in our power." But he nevertheless confined the territorial influence of the Company to the three provinces of Bengal, Behar, and Orissa. As events showed, he was mistaken in the idea that British expansion could be permanently limited; but that he was right in so limiting it at the time, is proved, so far as such things are capable of proof, by the fact that the thirteen years of Hastings' rule barely preserved the frontiers as Clive had fixed them against external enemies. Had the British grasped the glittering prize too soon, they might with weakened and scattered forces have been unable to withstand the Maratha onset in the next decade. Concentrated within the narrower lines, they were able to repel it, and Clive perhaps was building better than he knew when he deliberately stayed his hand.

The position in Bengal after the acquisition of the Diwani was a very complicated one. The Nawáb himself became a mere puppet and the pensioner of the Company. His deputy, with whom Clive now associated two colleagues, remained as the visible head of the executive, receiving from the English the expenses of administration and liable to be called to account by them for any gross abuse or scandal. The criminal jurisdiction was also left to him, while to the Company's servants belonged the control of the treasury and certain limited judicial powers in civil suits. But, even in their own department, the Bengal Council kept sedulously in the background, and till 1772 they transacted the revenue business through the agency of native collectors, though, to control these, English "supervisors" were appointed after 1769. Clive's famous "dual system" broke down badly in operation during the next seven years, and can only be commended in so far as it was a logical step to the open assumption of responsibility on the part of the Company carried out by Hastings in 1772, and the completion of his work by Lord Cornwallis in 1788. There was inherent in it a fatal divorce of power from responsibility which caused most of the old scandals and abuses speedily to make their reappearance. The avowed reason why Clive stopped short of assuming the full sovereignty was that to do so would have offended the susceptibilities of other European Powers; and this plea was considered adequate and valid by the highest authorities of his day. He may also, not improbably, have been influenced by the conviction that such a burden was too heavy to be placed upon the shoulders of the civilians of Bengal, till a new generation had grown up under better conditions of training and discipline.

Before he left Bengal, Clive found himself called upon to face a crisis which threatened to endanger all his achievements. He had been ordered to abolish the system of extra pay and allowances known as "double *batta*," which, at first exceptional, had grown to be the rule throughout the Bengal army. The abolition produced a mutiny of the officers, planned with great deliberation and a cynical indifference to the public interest or the claims of military allegiance thoroughly characteristic of the demoralised state of the presidency. Clive had already alienated the civil service to such an extent that an open social boycott was organised against him. He now found himself in danger of losing the power of the sword. In this fearful predicament he never faltered, and his supreme mastery over men was never better exemplified. The slightest sign of weakness would probably have brought upon him the fate that afterwards befell Lord Pigot, of being deposed and imprisoned by a combination of the civil and military officers. In a few days, by amazing promptness of action and pure inflexibility of will, he had shamed the mutineers into submission. It is in a crisis of this nature that Clive appears almost a Titanic figure. He matched all the resources of his wonderful personality against a rebellious Council, an army in open mutiny, a foreign position of extreme peril, and won the day.

Clive left India in January, 1767, weary and disillusioned. When all necessary qualifications have been made, he must be acknowledged to have accomplished a task that made even greater demands upon his courage and intellectual powers than the terrible crisis of 1756. He returned to find, within a few years, the national gratitude for his latest services almost obliterated by the censure, in some cases merited though most unhappily timed, now visited for the first time (for the facts were only just becoming known) on his earlier and less reputable transactions in Bengal. In view of the revelations made by the Parliamentary Committee of 1772, this result was probably inevitable. The attack on Clive is often attributed wholly to the baffled spite and mean revenge of the corrupt Bengal gang who thronged back to England, bent on exacting vengeance for their dismissal and disgrace. But, though it was certainly a monstrous perversion of justice that a man like Johnstone, whose criminality was tenfold greater than that of Clive, should have been allowed to direct the attack instead of being put upon his defence, it would still be unfair not to recognise that a section of his accusers were influenced by a more righteous motive—the desire to set in no doubtful light England's relations with her Eastern dependency.

Clive's great speech in 1773, when he stood at bay before a critical and unfriendly House, is eloquent alike of his weakness and his strength. He scorned to gloss over or extenuate a single one of his acts, but justified himself throughout. It has been well said of him, that he possessed a high sense of honour with little delicacy of sentiment. He declared that he might have brought back from India after his second period of office an immense fortune, infamously added to the one already secured. This was true, and it was thoroughly characteristic of Clive's frank, honest, rather coarse-fibred, mind that he should claim a merit for not having incurred infamy. Just as he would not go an inch beyond what was legally permissible, so he could not understand how it was blameworthy for a man to take the utmost that his position allowed. His standards in matters of personal profit and public duty were not particularly fastidious, though hardly lower than those of his age; but, such as they were, he never failed to act up to them. The House of Commons, with his famous apostrophe ringing in their ears, that when they came to decide upon his honour they should not forget their own, took perhaps the best possible course. They accepted a resolution declaratory of the fact that he had received definite sums from native Powers; but they rejected that part of the motion which seemed to reflect on his personal integrity, and they added in simple and eloquent words the famous rider which so worthily set the seal upon his fame, that "Robert, Lord Clive, did at the same time render great and meritorious services to his country."

In 1774 Clive, who had been a victim to insomnia and melancholia, took his own life. He was one of the greatest men, intellectually at any rate, that have represented England in the East. In the field or at the Council-table, he was the incarnation of energy. However complicated the problem that confronted him, his clear and eager mind, disentangling the issues and sifting the trivial from the essential, sprang confidently and unfalteringly to a decision. It was conceivable that he might decide wrongly. It was almost inconceivable that he should hesitate. In the difficult sphere of action in which his life was passed, he towers above all his contemporaries. He is as supreme in India prior to 1770, as is Warren Hastings from 1772 to 1785. Nothing is so great a tribute to his powers as the deference of his colleagues. In the earlier part of his career they seem with few exceptions to have acquiesced gladly in his masterful leading, and at the end, when he came as accuser and judge, to have been blasted with the breath of his displeasure.

Five years elapsed between Clive's departure and the assumption of office by Warren Hastings. The administration tended to fall back into the old evil grooves. Verelst and Cartier, though the former at any rate was a man of estimable private character, proved incapable of resisting the bad tendencies latent in the dual system. While its servants accumulated vast fortunes, the finances of the Company were far from prosperous, and Bengal itself, already plundered by corrupt native officials, was scourged by a terrible famine in 1769–70. A sinister commentary upon the administration of this time is afforded by the fact that though a third of the inhabitants of Bengal are said to have perished, the revenue collections of 1771 exceeded those of 1768, the year preceding the famine. The blame for the unscrupulous scramble for wealth could not now at any rate be put down to the parsimony of the Company at home. The commission on revenues paid to Verelst in two and a half years amounted to about £45,000; and in addition he had an official salary, with allowances, amounting to £4800. The rhetoric of Pitt and Burke hardly exaggerated the sinister effect on public life, both in India and at home, of these great fortunes, won so easily and by such questionable means.

In southern India there was a beginning of those complications which were destined to embarrass the course of Warren Hastings. Three Powers were striving for supremacy in the Dekhan—Mysore, Haidarábád, and the Marathas. The Council of Madras, unable or unwilling to regard the instructions from home that they should stand aloof from all political entanglements, plunged into a path of war and diplomacy which brought discredit upon the British name. It was only with great difficulty and by the payment of a stipulated tribute that they could prevail upon their ally, the Nizám of Haidarábád, to recognise the validity of the imperial grant which made over the Northern Circars to the English. In 1766 they concluded a treaty with the Nizám, by which they were drawn into an alliance with him and the Marathas against Haidar Ali. The Nizám proved faithless and leagued himself with the enemy; but their united forces were severely defeated at Changama and Trinomali (1767). In spite of the successes they had won, the English concluded another treaty with the Nizám, containing such ignominious terms that it received the sharpest censures from the Court of Directors. The war with Mysore was waged without skill or judgment, and Haidar Ali dictated peace on his own conditions in 1769, almost under the walls of Madras. The Peace laid an obligation upon Madras to aid the ruler of Mysore if attacked by another Power. This engagement the English were unable to fulfil when Mysore was invaded by a Maratha army in 1771, and they earned by their default the undying hate of a formidable and relentless foe.

In 1772 Warren Hastings became Governor of Fort William in Bengal. His Indian career had hitherto been creditable rather than brilliant, and he had passed through the most corrupt era of the Presidency with reputation unsullied. He held office, first as Governor, then as Governor-General, for thirteen years. The period was the most critical in the Eastern history of Great Britain. Political anarchy in India reached its acutest stage. Never were the anomalies in the Company's constitution more prominent, their control over their servants weaker, or their policy more fitful and spasmodic. At home there was often sharp divergence of opinion between the Courts of Directors and Proprietors, and the Company, thus divided against itself, was called upon to repel popular and Parliamentary attacks of a most formidable character. Under this accumulation of evils, British power in the East was shaken to its foundations; and the fame of Warren Hastings rests not upon victorious campaigns or any wide extension of the frontier, but upon the claim, moderately and with perfect justification put forward by himself, that he maintained the provinces of his immediate administration in a state of peace, plenty, and security, when every other member of the British Empire was involved in external war or civil tumult.

In internal affairs his administration forms the connecting link between those of Clive and Cornwallis. The period of misgovernment that succeeded 1765 condemned the "dual system." The Court of Directors now determined to "stand forth as *Diwan*," or in other words to collect and administer the revenues of the Province through the agency of their own servants, and they ordered Hastings to carry out this great reform. The Deputy Nawábs of Bengal and Behar were removed from office and prosecuted for peculation, though in both cases they were acquitted. The treasury was transferred from Murshidábád to Calcutta. Hastings, on a fresh succession, reduced the Nawáb's allowance from thirty-two to sixteen lakhs of rupees a year; though, thanks to a more economical administration and the abolition of sinecure offices, a larger net sum was actually received by the Prince. In 1772 a quinquennial settlement of the land revenue was introduced, and English officers, now first called collectors, were appointed to control large districts. These men had certain powers of civil jurisdiction, but the criminal Courts remained in native hands. In Calcutta two Courts of Appeal were established, the *Sadr Diwání Adálat* (Supreme Civil Court), presided over by the Governor-General and two members of Council till 1780, when the presidency was conferred by Hastings on Impey, and the *Nizámat Adálat* (Supreme Criminal Court), presided over by a native judge. The whole tendency of these fiscal, judicial, and agrarian reforms was in the direction of the solution afterwards effected by Cornwallis; and it is noticeable that Hastings was personally in favour of going further than the Court of Directors, believing that it was a mistake to maintain the jurisdiction of the Nawáb in criminal affairs.

Hastings had next to face the problem of preserving intact the frontiers of Bengal. Clive's solution had hitherto worked fairly well, but at this stage it utterly broke down. The Marathas, having recovered from the rout of Pániput in 1761, were hanging like a threatening cloud over Delhi, Oudh, and Rohilkhand. The puppet Emperor, who had been living at Allahábád on the revenues allotted him by the Company, accepted, in spite of earnest remonstrances from his English allies, the proposal of the hereditary foes of his House that they should place him upon the imperial throne. He entered Delhi in 1771 under an escort of Maratha horse, but found himself the mere tool and dupe of his patrons, who forced him within a year to make over to them the districts of Kora and Allahábád, which had been assigned to him by Clive. The English were confronted by an awkward dilemma. The Emperor was merely a "pageant of our own creation." To continue paying his allowance was equivalent to subsidising their bitterest enemies; to allow the Marathas to occupy the ceded districts in his name was to surrender the gate of Bengal. In such predicaments Hastings never hesitated.

He had a hearty contempt for formulas as distinct from facts, which in moments of peril often proved his salvation, though it occasionally led him into difficulties and embarrassments. He chose a solution which at once replenished the Company's treasury, and was adapted to the traditional Bengal policy of strengthening Oudh. He withheld the tribute to Shah Álam, which as a matter of fact had not been paid since the famine of 1769–70, and he restored Kora and Allahábád to the Nawáb of Oudh for a sum of fifty lakhs of rupees in addition to the pay of the Company's troops employed to garrison them. The spirit, if not the letter, of Clive's treaty undoubtedly implied that the Emperor received these gifts as being under British protection, and by all ordinary political rules Hastings was perfectly justified in maintaining that he had forfeited his right to hold them at all by transferring them to a third party.

When in September, 1773, Hastings met the Nawáb of Oudh in conference at Benares, he took the first step in a transaction which led him into deeper waters. Shuja-ud-daulá proposed that, in return for a large subsidy, the English should lend him troops to conquer Rohilkhand, the fertile tract of country lying north-west of Oudh along the base of the Himalayas. The country was peopled by Hindu peasants under the sway of the Rohillas, a Mohammadan clan of Afghan pedigree, forming a loose confederacy and acknowledging as their leader an able chief, Hafiz Rehmat Khan. Against this man the Nawáb of Oudh had a plausible claim for a large sum of money, alleged to have been promised him in return for assistance given to the Rohillas against the Marathas. Hastings saw at once the strategical advantage to be gained by carrying the frontier of his ally to the base of the Himalayas, nor was he uninfluenced by the chance of procuring a large sum for the Company's treasury, though he always maintained that this was merely a secondary inducement; but he realised, at this time at any rate, that there were other objections to the scheme, and he gave a somewhat reluctant assent to the proposal, hoping apparently that the need for intervention would never arise. In 1774, however, the Nawáb required that the bargain should be fulfilled. Attended by a British brigade under Champion, to whom fell all the hard campaigning, he invaded Rohilkhand. Hafiz Rehmat Khan was killed fighting gallantly at the head of his troops, and about twenty thousand Rohillas were banished from the country, which passed finally under the sway of Shuja-ud-daulá. The episode of the Rohilla War formed one of the most serious charges made against Hastings in Parliament, and the fiercest denunciations were launched against his whole policy in regard to it. He was accused of having violated the rights of nations, and bartered away for gold the lives and liberties of an inoffensive people. An unhistorical and romantic halo was cast by the gorgeous imagination of Burke round the origin of the Rohilla race. It has since been recognised that much of this criticism was beside the mark. The Rohillas had no ancient prescriptive right to the country which they ruled. They had only been established there for a quarter of a century, and their title was no better, though certainly it was no worse, than that of most of the States that had risen to power on Moghul decadence. The Nawáb of Oudh had, according to the standard of the day, a specious pretext for going to war, though it probably could not have borne a very close scrutiny. It is untrue that the military operations were marked by any circumstances of peculiar atrocity, and the complaints which Champion recorded against his allies were obviously due far more to jealousy of the plunder they acquired than to disinterested compassion for the lot of the conquered. Though the government of Oudh could hardly have been an improvement on that of Hafiz Rehmat Khan, who was a man of ability, it is improbable that the Hindu population were greatly affected by the change, and it is certain that Hastings did his best to prevent any excesses on the part of the Nawáb and his army. But, when all this is admitted, some serious objections to the policy still remain. It ran counter to the clear instructions of the Directors against interference in Indian warfare. Hastings was creating a dangerous precedent when he lent his ally a brigade of British troops, to be used at discretion against a people with whom the Company had no quarrel, and in his arguments and minutes on the subject there is plainly apparent a rather cynical disregard of every other consideration except political expediency.

The campaign in Rohilkhand was the last important event of Hastings' administration as Governor of Bengal. In 1774 his position and powers were materially altered by the Regulating Act of Lord North, passed the preceding year—the outcome of Parliament's first attempt to construct by statute a constitutional government for India. To some such interference on the part of the State, events had long been tending. In his famous letter to Pitt in 1759, Clive had suggested that the Crown should claim sovereignty over all the Company's possessions; but the great Minister, as was his wont when he did not see his way clearly, spoke on the matter "a little darkly," plainly showing his reluctance to raise so important a question. During the next twelve years men thronged back to England loaded with the wealth, and what was strongly suspected of being the plunder, of Bengal. The incursion of these "nabobs" with their lavish notions and orientalised habits into the aristocratic circles of the time is one of the most striking social phenomena of the eighteenth century. Contemporary memoirs and letters reveal the mingled contempt, envy, and hatred with which they were regarded. "We are Spaniards in our lust for gold," wrote Horace Walpole, "and Dutch in our delicacy of obtaining it." The East India Company, as Burke said, was a State in the disguise of a merchant, a great public office in the disguise of a counting-house, and political thinkers saw a dangerous anomaly in the growth of an Eastern empire, linked to the main fabric of British dominion only through the agents of a private company.	From 1766 Indian affairs were constantly before Parliament, and in 1767 a compromise on the question of sovereignty was accepted by both parties, in the arrangement that the Company should pay a yearly sum to the State of £400,000 for its territorial possessions. In 1772 two Parliamentary Committees (Select and Secret) conducted those exhaustive enquiries into East Indian affairs which led incidentally to the attack on Lord Clive.	It was shown that within the nine years 1757–66, £2,169,665 had been distributed by the Princes and natives of Bengal in presents to the Company's servants, exclusive of Clive's *jagir*, and that a further sum of £3,770,833 had been paid as compensation for losses incurred.	At intervals of a few months the committees issued voluminous reports, and the revelations there made, together with the Company's appeal for a public loan of a million and a half, indicating the breakdown of their finance, led many to the conclusion, as stated by Burgoyne, that, if sovereignty and law were not separated from trade, both India and Great Britain would be overwhelmed.	The divorce of trade from the other functions of the Company was not destined to be effected for many years; but the Regulating Act of Lord North attempted in a rather half-hearted way some differentiation between the executive and judicial functions in India, and an extension of state control over the Company both at home and abroad.	The Governor of Bengal was to become Governor-General of all the settlements.	He was to be advised by a Council of four, and was allowed a casting vote in the event of there being an equal division of opinion.	A Supreme Court of Judicature was to be established at Calcutta, consisting of a Chief Justice and three puisne judges.	All correspondence on civil government or military affairs was to be laid by the Directors before his Majesty's Ministers, and the constitution of the Company was largely remodelled on a more oligarchical basis.	The Act was a compromise throughout and intentionally vague in many of its provisions.	It did not openly assert the sovereignty of the British Crown in India, or invade the titular authority of the Nawáb of Bengal.	It appointed a Governor-General, but shackled him with a Council that might reduce him to impotence. It established a supreme Court of justice, but made no attempt accurately to define the field of its jurisdiction, specify the law which it was to administer, or draw a line of demarcation between its functions and those of the Council.

Warren Hastings was appointed the first Governor-General, and he was also the last to hold office under the terms of the Act.	The Councillors, Monson, Clavering, and Francis (Barwell was already in India), the Chief Justice Impey and his three colleagues, arrived in 1774.	The members of Council, always inspired by Philip Francis, began by quarrelling with the Governor-General over some absurd point of etiquette in their reception, and they followed this up by a general revision and condemnation of his policy. There followed six years of an administration which is probably unparalleled. Hastings governed in the face of a hostile majority and a relentless opposition directed, not from Press or platform outside, but from the other side of his own Council-table. Philip Francis, one of the ablest and most merciless of men, directed a stream of criticism, vindictive, subtle, and provocative, on every detail of the Governor-General's policy. Hastings had control of Indian affairs at a peculiarly critical time; but the struggle at the Council-board alone, where Barwell was his only supporter, would have fully taxed the powers of any other man. He could not even rely upon consistent support from home, and in 1777, when his own precipitation in offering resignation had given a handle to his enemies, he only retained his position by refusing to accept the order appointing General Clavering Governor-General. In view of the nerve-destroying ordeal to which he was subjected, it would be more than surprising if his career did not reveal some faults and mistakes. When every act was submitted to the same fierce attack, every motive called in question, the very boundaries of right and wrong must have tended to become blurred in the mind of the victim who, as he himself said, was enveloped in an atmosphere of "dark allusions, mysterious insinuations, bitter invective, and ironical reflections." By his savage vindictiveness, Francis utterly neutralised all that might have been salutary in his opposition. From 1774 to 1776, Hastings was almost uniformly outvoted in the Council. By the successive deaths of Monson and Clavering in 1776 and 1777, and the exercise of his casting vote, he regained control, and maintained it though with difficulty till 1780, when he disabled Francis in a duel. After the final departure of the latter in the same year, his position was somewhat easier, for, though his Council were not fully in accord with him, they were men of much smaller powers than their predecessors.

The Council began with a thorough-going condemnation of the Rohilla War. They recalled Hastings' agent from Lucknow and Champion's brigade from Rohilkhand. The Nawáb Wazír of Oudh died in 1775; and, in direct opposition to the traditional policy of strengthening British friendship with that State, they forced his successor to enter into new treaties, imposing upon him largely increased subsidies for the use of British troops, and supporting the claims of the late Nawáb's widow to a disproportionate share in his wealth and estates. The personal hostility of the Council reached its highest point in 1775, when Nuncomar, a native of high rank and great influence but of doubtful character, appeared at the Council-board with a charge against Hastings of having received a bribe. The accusation was eagerly welcomed by Francis, Monson, and Clavering, who, without waiting for proof, placed on record a minute that "there is no species of peculation from which the Honourable Governor-General has thought it reasonable to abstain." Warren Hastings firmly refused to be arraigned at his own

Council-table by a man of "so notoriously infamous" a character as Nuncomar. He probably felt that, with the untrustworthiness of native evidence and before a prejudiced Court, it might be difficult to prove his innocence, and he had good justification for resisting the high-handed and insulting procedure of his enemies on the Council. While the matter was still pending, Nuncomar was himself suddenly arrested on a charge of forgery unconnected with the case. He was brought to trial in due course, condemned to death, and executed. The charge against the Governor-General was dropped and never proceeded with.

It is unlikely that the fascinating mystery which broods over this famous episode will ever be entirely dispelled. The insinuation that Hastings and Impey deliberately planned the destruction of Nuncomar is now regarded as baseless. It is, at any rate, as Pitt declared, unsupported by a shadow of proof. The two men were by no means always on the best of terms, and the quarrel between the Supreme Court and the Council as to the limits of their respective jurisdictions had already begun. The charge originated in a natural way out of an old lawsuit that had been before the Courts for many years, and Impey appears to have tried the case patiently and fairly according to his lights. On the other hand the punishment of death was undoubtedly too severe. Though the point has been disputed, the best reading of the law is that the English code making forgery capital was not introduced into Bengal till some years after the alleged crime had been committed. However this might be, Nuncomar's case was preeminently one in which the discretionary power of the judges to relax the general severity of the law should have been exercised. There was therefore something very like a miscarriage of justice; but for this the Supreme Court, and not Hastings, was responsible, and the part played by the judges is quite capable of explanation without any necessity for suggesting a corrupt motive. Impey and his colleagues were intensely jealous of their privileges and rights. They had hardly been long enough in the country to appreciate the difference between English and Indian ideas of law. Their conduct in the case was quite on a par with their whole attitude till 1780, during which time they were constantly engaged in a high-handed and injudicious attempt to apply the practice of the Courts of Westminster to the native population of Bengal. They were absolutely conscientious and utterly wrong-headed. The Chief Justice seems seriously to have considered that it was his duty to check by a severe example the prevalence of the crime of forgery in Bengal, and that to grant any remission of sentence to Nuncomar would, in view of his great wealth, have brought upon the Supreme Court the charge of being open to corrupt influence. Whether or not Hastings, finding there was a legitimate handle against his enemy, and having a shrewd idea from his knowledge of Impey's character of what the issue would be, if he once set the train of events in motion, gave a hint to Nuncomar's accuser to press on his case at this particular juncture, admits of no exact proof or disproof. The coincidence in time was extraordinary, and it is likely enough that Hastings would have regarded such a method of defending himself as perfectly justifiable. When he was fighting with his back to the wall he was not, any more than his adversaries, inclined to be fastidious as to the weapons he employed. Not the least mysterious part of the episode is the fact that Francis and his colleagues made no attempt, as they might constitutionally have done, by petition or intercession, to obtain a reprieve. The reflexion is inevitably suggested that, realising they had gone too far, they were actually relieved to see their tool and coadjutor put out of the way. Francis himself at the time stigmatised the suggestion of any complicity between the judges and the Governor-General as " wholly unsupported and libellous," and only adopted the insinuation as his own a few months later. If there is anything sinister in Nuncomar's fate, it is not perhaps the darkest shadow that falls across the reputation of the Governor-General.

It is a curious point that Hastings never seems to have denied in so many words that he had received the sum mentioned by Nuncomar, and even his most strenuous defenders have acknowledged that there was probably some irregularity in the business which he was anxious to conceal. A few words may profitably here be said on the whole subject of his financial transactions. The charge of rapacity was, as Hastings himself averred, that of all others the most foreign to his nature. Yet it must be admitted that in matters where money was concerned he was, at best, inexcusably careless and extravagant, and he afforded Francis, who, to do him justice, was personally incorruptible, too many opportunities for damaging criticism. Hastings' life in retirement shows a constitutional inability to keep clear of debt, and in India the extraordinary difficulties of his position compelled him, or seemed to compel him, to act in a manner which looked highly suspicious to those who did not possess the key to his conduct. In the depressed state of the public finances, he appears to have considered that he was justified in accepting for the Company presents or *douceurs* offered to himself; and, to avoid objections from his Council, he occasionally retained them for considerable periods in his own possession. He dared, in fact, to risk his reputation for what he conceived to be the interests of his employers, and was thus sometimes proved to have seriously compromised his own future defence. Whether the equivocal course followed by Hastings was really necessary, is open to dispute. The Directors themselves did not think so, and it may be said at once that no modern administration would tolerate for a moment the extraordinary latitude in financial matters claimed by the Governor-General. He seems to have considered that so long as he could assure the Company that he had "the applause of his own breast," they had no cause to make any further demand upon him. Francis was often needlessly provocative; but he was right in demanding a more stringent method of control, and the severe terms in which the famous Eleventh Report of the Select Committee of 1783 commented on Hastings' whole system of account-keeping cannot be said to be unmerited. No one now believes that Hastings was personally corrupt; but the real proof of his integrity depends, not upon the formal defence offered at the Impeachment, which was technically weak, but on the moderate fortune that he brought back from India, and on the well-attested fact of his absolute cleanhandedness during his early years in Bengal, at a time of life when the prospect of wealth holds out its most dazzling attractions, and his opportunities of acquiring it were unlimited. Moreover, Hastings cannot in fairness be judged by the standard that would be applied to a modern representative of the Crown in India. To govern provinces and wage wars successfully is one thing, to do either or both at a financial profit is quite another—and yet this is what was expected of him. The Governor of Bengal was now called upon to deal with high and intricate political problems; but, as the representative not of the State but of a private commercial company, he was required, not less than when his duties were confined within the walls of a factory, to show a credit balance in the pages of his ledger.

In the affairs of his own province of Bengal, Hastings exercised, at least when able to dominate his Council, a direct control. In western and southern India, since he was usually only informed of the *fait accompli*, he was limited as a rule to the rather melancholy choice of trying to wrest a partial success from the conduct of policies he condemned, or the alternative, so distasteful to a British administrator, of disowning his subordinates. In 1775 the Bombay Government engaged by the Treaty of Surat to support a Pretender to the Peshwaship at Poona, on condition that Bassein and Salsette were ceded to them. Hastings was at one with his colleagues in denouncing the war that ensued as "impolitic, dangerous, unauthorised, and unjust"; but, as the Bombay authorities had actually occupied Salsette and involved themselves in military operations, in which they had won a certain amount of success at a heavy cost, he argued that they must be allowed to continue the war to a point whence they could extricate themselves without loss. He was opposed, however, by the majority of the Council, and an agent was sent from Calcutta to Poona, who concluded the Treaty of Purandhar, by which the English were allowed to retain possession of Salsette on abandoning the cause of their *protégé*. Neither Hastings nor the Directors were satisfied with the treaty, and in 1778 it was proposed to make a new alliance with the Pretender. It is questionable whether, in spite of obvious drawbacks, it would not have been better, even in 1775, to have reversed the Bombay policy. It is fairly certain that in agreeing to a renewal of the war Hastings, though he had the support of the home authorities, made a serious mistake. No man could do more justice in debate to a good cause than Philip Francis, though he seldom allowed himself the luxury of supporting one. In this instance, he by his able minutes and protests undoubtedly got the better of the Governor-General. The only argument advanced by Hastings that could justify the long and harassing warfare, which ended without gain to either side, was the danger of a European and Maratha alliance, suggested by the presence at Poona since 1777 of a French envoy. The military successes, Goddard's march across India and capture of Ahmadábád in 1780, and Popham's storm of Gwalior in the same year, were gained by Calcutta forces and what his enemies called the "frantic military exploits" of Hastings. The Bombay expedition only met with disaster, and its commander in 1779 was forced to sign the disgraceful Convention of Wargaon, which surrendered all the territorial possessions gained by the English in western India since 1765. The treaty was disowned by the civil authorities, and the war, chequered by victories and defeats, dragged on till 1782, when peace was made by the Treaty of Salbai, which practically restored the *status quo*, though the Company were allowed to retain Salsette.

Madras was, at the same time, passing through a disastrous and discreditable epoch. Difficulties in relation to the hostile Powers of southern India were aggravated by the equivocal status of the presidency itself. Mohammad Ali, like the Subahdar of Bengal, was incapable of defending his own territories, and his dominion rested on the support of British arms; but, as Madras did not possess the executive and financial control of the Carnatic, he was left with a dangerous amount of power and responsibility. The attempt of the British Crown to maintain in Arcot during 1770–1 plenipotentiaries accredited to his Court proved an unhappy experiment, against which the Company vigorously protested on the ground that it hopelessly compromised their relations with the Nawáb. Mohammad Ali's corrupt and collusive financial transactions with the notorious Paul Benfield and other junior servants of the Company gave birth to the gigantic scandals known as "the Nawáb of Arcot's debts," which demoralised the whole internal government of the presidency. In the short period of seven years two Governors were expelled by the Court of Directors, and one suspended by Hastings, while a fourth, Lord Pigot, died in prison, where he had been confined by his own subordinates for the rather high-handed and unconstitutional measures he had taken against their corrupt policy. The result of these constant changes in the executive was a chaotic and contradictory policy, producing the most deplorable results. By 1780 the presidency had succeeded in manœuvring itself into a position of hostility to all the great Powers of the Dekhan. In that year Haidar Ali made his famous raid upon the Carnatic, which was immortalised in the oratory of Burke. An English force under Baillie was surrounded and utterly defeated after a gallant resistance. Munro, falsifying the reputation he had gained at Buxar, flung his heavy artillery into a tank at Conjeveram, and retreated to the suburbs of Madras.

Hastings now interfered drastically in the affairs of the presidency. He suspended the Governor and, appealing, not in vain, to the patriotism of Sir Eyre Coote, hurried him from Bengal with all available reinforcements to the scene of his former fame. The gallant old commander saved the English in southern India by the severe defeat he inflicted upon Haidar Ali at Porto Novo in July, 1781. An indecisive engagement at Pollilore was retrieved by another victory at Sholingar in September. The internal affairs of the presidency were reformed by Lord Macartney, who came out as Governor in June, 1781. Appointed by the Company from the ranks of the diplomatic service, he was in many respects a forerunner of Lord Cornwallis, and he introduced a standard of incorruptibility in pecuniary matters to which even the best of the Company's servants at this time were unable to attain. In administration he showed a vigour and independence of character which brought him into frequent collision with the Governor-General. In 1782 Tipu annihilated a British brigade under Braithwaite; but Coote won his last victory at Arni, and the signing of the Treaty of Salbai in May withdrew from Mysore the cooperation of the Maratha Powers.

Meanwhile, war had been declared against France in 1778, and Chandernagore and Pondicherry had been captured by the English. In the eclipse of British prestige in southern India the French saw a last chance of effective interference in the politics of the Dekhan. In 1782 a formidable French fleet with Bussy on board appeared off the Coromandel coast. Fortunately for the English the attempt was made a little too late. Pondicherry was already in their hands; there was no port of approach; and the military position on land had been retrieved. Suffren, the French admiral, was a naval commander of great genius; but in Sir Edward Hughes he met a worthy antagonist. The rival fleets inflicted great damage upon each other in five fiercely contested battles; but neither could gain complete command of the sea. When Bussy landed in 1783, he found the opportune moment had gone by. Haidar Ali had died in December of the foregoing year, worn out by his great activities and the ravages of a slow disease. Bussy himself was besieged by the English in Cuddalore, till the news of the Treaty of Versailles forced him to sever his connexion with Tipu. The son of Haidar Ali was however quite capable of continuing the war unaided. Eyre Coote died in April, 1783, and his successor in the command was a man without energy or genius. In March, 1784, by the Treaty of Mangalore, Tipu granted the English a Peace on terms of a mutual restoration of conquests. Such a conclusion of the war was far from being a glorious one, and Hastings severely censured Lord Macartney's conduct of the negotiations; but, when he looked back to the year 1780, in which he was called upon to face "a war, either actual or impending, in every quarter and with every Power in Hindustan," he had good reason for satisfaction. The armies of Mysore had been beaten back from the Carnatic; an understanding had been patched up with the Nizám; and a further breathing space had been won before the final and inevitable conflict with the Maratha confederacy.

During this time Hastings' path in Bengal had been anything but smooth. The long and costly wars begun by Madras and Bombay were supported mainly out of the revenues of Bengal. As a result, the Company's finances, which the Governor-General had placed on a sound footing at the beginning of his administration, proved even from 1778 unable to bear the strain imposed upon them. Casting about eagerly for relief, Hastings was led into that course of action in regard to the Rája of Benares and the Begams, or Princesses, of Oudh which formed two of the most serious charges against him at his trial. The circumstances were very briefly as follows. The sovereignty over Benares had passed by treaty in 1775 from the Nawáb Wazír of Oudh to the Company. On the outbreak of hostilities with France in 1778, Hastings held that he was justified in demanding from the Rája, Chait Singh, a special war contribution, in spite of a guarantee given by the English in the treaty that the annual revenue paid by him should not be increased. He obtained with difficulty sums of five lakhs of rupees in 1778 and 1779; in 1780 he ordered him to supply in addition 2000 cavalry. This Chait Singh refused to do, on the plea that it was beyond his power, and Hastings promptly determined to inflict upon him a fine of fifty lakhs as rebellious and contumacious. The Governor-General proceeded in person to Benares in 1781, and there denounced as " offensive in style and unsatisfactory in substance " a letter addressed to him by the Rája in mitigation of sentence, which certainly appears on impartial study to be neither the one nor the other, but rather to be couched in terms of almost abject submission. Though attended by only a weak escort, Hastings next ordered the arrest of the Rája in his own capital. Chait Singh quietly submitted; but his troops rose suddenly, massacred the English guard, and released him. Hastings was placed for a time in extreme peril, and it was only his extraordinary coolness and intrepidity that saved his life. The rising assumed alarming proportions, and serious fighting was necessary before the insurgents could be dispersed. The domains of Chait Singh were declared forfeited, and were transferred to his nephew in return for double the revenue formerly paid to Calcutta.

The Nawáb Wazír of Oudh had been for many years heavily in debt to the Company; but, while he was comparatively poor, his mother and grandmother, the famous Begams of Oudh, held large *jagirs*, or landed estates, and, on the strength of a rather doubtful will, the rich treasure valued at £2,000,000 left by Shuja-ud-daulá, which in the natural course of events should have been bequeathed to the ruling Nawáb. The latter, maintaining that he was unrighteously deprived of what was his due, suggested that he should pay his debts to the Company with the wealth of the Princesses, and that Hastings should help him to obtain it. Now, in 1775, on the earnest entreaty of the British resident at Lucknow, the widow of Shuja-ud-daulá had consented to pay a large sum to the Nawáb, on condition that the Bengal Government gave a guarantee that no further demands should be made upon her. Hastings at the time was strongly opposed to the giving of such a pledge, but had been overruled by his Council. The Nawáb now (1781) asked that the engagement with the Begam should no longer be considered binding, and Hastings consented, giving as his reason for a decision which certainly required justification, that the Begams had countenanced the rebellion of Chait Singh and had therefore forfeited anything of the nature of treaty rights with the British. Having once screwed himself to the point, Hastings urged the Nawáb Wazír, whose character was feeble and irresolute, to resume the *jagirs* and seize the treasure, though he stipulated that the Begams should receive ample pensions in compensation. British troops were marched to Fyzabad, for the Nawáb hung back when the crisis came, and the eunuchs who managed the Begams' affairs were compelled by imprisonment, deprivation of food, and other hardships, to disgorge the hoarded treasure. It has often been denied that anything in the way of "torture" took place; but a letter is in evidence from the British resident at Lucknow, stating that on several occasions the eunuchs were led forth for corporal punishment.

These transactions were properly condemned by the Court of Directors at the time. In both cases Hastings was driven to go back upon the treaty engagements of the Company. He contended, as to the business of Chait Singh, that the outbreak of the war with France justified the levy of a special subsidy, and he charged the Begams with complicity in the rising at Benares. But it was rightly felt that allegations of this kind might be advanced with fatal facility in the case of any treaties that the British found it inconvenient to keep. In his dealings with Chait Singh, Hastings showed an impatient ruthlessness which was alien to his kindly nature. The fine imposed by him was undoubtedly excessive. His own conduct in the matter was rash to the point of folly, and he seems for once to have been driven from his wonted serenity into a mood of petulance and vindictiveness. As for the case of the Begams, the evidence against them of any active part in the insurrection at Benares was extremely weak, and it cannot be said that British troops were worthily employed in aiding an Eastern sovereign to wrest money from his relatives and dependents, or in standing by while servants were maltreated, whose only fault was a too obstinate fidelity to the interests of their mistress. The Nawáb himself and the British resident at Lucknow faltered in the ugly work of coercion, and the reluctance of the latter to carry out the task imposed upon him called forth a severe reprimand from the Governor-General, who forbade him to allow any negotiations or forbearance "until the Begams are at the entire mercy

CH. XV.

37—2

of the Nawáb." Hastings' attitude throughout was that of one who willed the end, but did not wish to be held accountable for the means, or even to know too accurately what they were. The responsibility cannot be altogether thrust upon subordinate agents, and no special pleading, not even that of his able counsel at the trial, has quite availed to clear his reputation in this sinister business. Both the episodes therefore of the Rája of Benares and the Begams of Oudh merited an enquiry; to some extent they merited censure; but they did not warrant the ingenious distortions, the gross exaggerations, the malignant additions in the way of imputed motive and alleged corruption, with which they were overlaid by the managers of the impeachment.

The quarrel between the Council and the Supreme Court by 1779 became an open scandal, and all but produced a deadlock in the administration. In 1780 Hastings conciliated Impey by appointing him to the Presidency of the *Sadr Diwání Adálat* or Court of Appeal for the provincial Courts of Bengal, at a salary of £6500 revocable at the will of the Governor-General and Council. This action was loudly condemned at home, on the ground that to appoint the Chief Justice to a second judicial post under such terms was to run counter to the whole purpose of the Regulating Act, which aimed at making the Supreme Court independent of the executive. Impey seems not to have acted from corrupt motives; but he was hardly well advised in acceding to an arrangement which laid him open to the suspicion of having compromised his judicial independence for an increase of salary. He was recalled two years later by the Directors at the orders of Parliament, but the attempt to impeach him broke down. From Hastings' point of view the transaction had many advantages. It put an end to a wellnigh intolerable state of things, afforded Impey the opportunity to draw up a valuable Code of procedure, and anticipated the solution afterwards adopted of extending the appellate jurisdiction of the Supreme Court in Calcutta over the provincial Courts of the presidency.

Hastings spent eight months of the year 1784 in an extended tour through Benares and Oudh, where distress, partly the result of famine, partly of misgovernment, was everywhere rife. He proved his supreme administrative talents in a thorough-going reorganisation of the finances and internal affairs of these allied States, and in the autumn of the year returned to Calcutta, to find the news of Pitt's India Act awaiting him, with an account of the Minister's equivocal attitude towards himself. Hastings, who had survived the fierce hostility of his own colleagues, the censures of the Court of Directors, the condemnatory resolutions of Parliament, and one definite order for his recall, was destined after all to resign of his own accord the office he had held so long. Declaring that "fifty Burkes, Foxes, and Francises" could not have devised a worse measure, he quietly made the preparations for his departure, and sailed for home on February 8, 1785.

The government of the East India Company at this time might perhaps be described as an oligarchy tempered by recurrent periods of inquisitorial state inspection.   For the last seven years public attention had been fully occupied with the rebellion of the American Colonies and the war with France; but after 1780 the Indian question once more came prominently to the front.   Though the Company's privileges were extended for ten years, in 1781, as in 1772, both a Select and a Secret Committee were busy with their affairs.   The former investigated the relations between the Supreme Court and the Council in Bengal, the latter the causes of the Maratha War.   The voluminous Reports they presented were freely used as arsenals for weapons against the Company by party orators in Parliament.   Condemnatory resolutions were passed in the Commons against the Governors of Bombay and Madras.   The relentless enmity of Francis and the nobler anger of Burke were preparing to attack the man who had guided England's destinies in the East for the past nine years.   In the quick changes of the unstable Ministries at this time, the fate of Hastings often trembled in the balance.   The advent to power of Rockingham, Fox, and Burke, in 1782 brought a vote of censure in Parliament and the consent of the Directors to his recall; but their supersession by Shelburne's Ministry and the staunch support of the Court of Proprietors gave him a further respite.   The Coalition of Fox and North in 1783 was a political portent that boded ill both to the Company and their great servant, while at the same time the Directors were obliged openly to confess that the war had beggared them and to apply to the State for another loan of £1,000,000.   After a measure drafted by Dundas had been rejected, Fox introduced his India Bill.   It transferred all the political and military power of the Company to a Board of seven Commissioners to be nominated in the first instance by Parliament and afterwards by the Crown, and all its commercial powers to a subordinate body of nine assistant Directors, who were ultimately to be nominated by the holders of East India stock, though they too, in the first instance, were to be appointed by Parliament.   The feature of the Bill upon which the Opposition seized was the surrender of the immensely valuable patronage of India to the Ministry or the Crown, and Pitt thundered against it as the most desperate and alarming attempt at the exercise of tyranny that ever disgraced the annals of this or any other country.   Nevertheless, the Bill, being advocated with all the eloquence of its author and his coadjutor Burke, passed the Commons by large majorities, only to be strangled in the Lords, as Fox indignantly declared, by an infamous string of bed-chamber janissaries.   The truth was that George III, realising with his usual political shrewdness, that the Coalition, though all-powerful in Parliament, was highly unpopular in the country, had determined both to destroy the Bill and rid himself of advisers he intensely disliked.   He took measures to make his wishes known to the Lords; the Bill was thrown out; and the Ministry resigned. Pitt came into power and in 1784 carried his famous Act, which greatly extended the control of the State over the East India Company. While the patronage of the Company was left untouched, all civil, military, and revenue affairs were to be controlled by a Board consisting of the Chancellor of the Exchequer, one of the principal Secretaries of State, and four members of the Privy Council. A Secret Committee of three Directors was to be the channel through which important orders of the Board were to be transmitted to India. The Court of Proprietors lost the right to rescind, suspend, or revoke any resolution of the Directors which was approved by the Board. In India the chief government was placed in the hands of a Governor-General and Council of Three, and the Presidencies of Madras and Bombay were made subject to Bengal in all matters of diplomacy, revenue, and war.

Warren Hastings landed in England in June, 1785. The storm that was hanging over him did not break at once. In 1786, Burke on several occasions moved in the Commons for papers on various points of his administration. The attack upon Hastings in connexion with the Maratha War and the expedition against the Rohillas failed; but the House passed condemnatory resolutions on his transactions with Chait Singh and the Begams of Oudh. Pitt, who had defended Hastings on the first two of these counts, turned against him on the third. Much ingenuity has been wasted in the attempt to discover some recondite motive for this proceeding. In political matters the simplest motives are often those actually operative. Pitt was honourably desirous of preserving a judicial impartiality, and there is every reason to suppose, that when he read the evidence offered by the prosecution on the Benares charge, he was reluctantly driven to the conclusion that he could no longer stand in the way of a trial. On May 10, 1787, Burke formally impeached Hastings at the bar of the Lords. The trial began in Westminster Hall on February 13, 1788.

The articles of impeachment finally presented at the bar of the Lords were twenty in number, and differed in many respects from the original list of twenty-two, drawn up by Burke in 1786 for the consideration of the Commons. The indictment was clumsily drafted, and combined charges involving the highest criminality with others, which, if proved up to the hilt, hardly amounted to more than venial errors of judgment and policy. By far the greater number of the articles centred round the dealings of the late Governor-General with the allied and protected State of Oudh. Hastings was charged with tyranny and oppression in the case of the Rája of Benares, the spoliation of the Begams of Oudh, the fraudulent sale of contracts, the grant of pensions to friends and dependents from corrupt motives, the arbitrary settlement of the land revenues of Bengal, the removal of the treasury from Murshidábád to Calcutta, the violation of treaties made with the Nawáb Wazír of Oudh, compulsion put upon him to maintain an excessive number of troops, unnecessary interference in the internal affairs of his kingdom, and the confiscation of revenues and allowances due to his brothers and sisters.

Three of the episodes, which had given rise to the fiercest attacks upon Hastings in Parliament and in the pamphlet literature of the day, did not appear in the impeachment. The House of Commons had definitely acquitted him on the charges connected with the Rohilla campaign; and, in addition, neither the Maratha War, the subject of voluminous reports by the Secret Committee of 1781, nor the trial of Nuncomar, was included in the indictment. In his discursive conduct of the case for the prosecution, Burke was inclined to traverse the whole of Hastings' career in India, but acknowledged that he was debarred from commenting upon the Rohilla expedition, while he was censured by the House of Commons for having stated incidentally that the Governor-General had murdered Nuncomar by the hand of Sir Elijah Impey, on the ground that the condemnation and execution of Nuncomar had never been imputed as a charge.

Throughout the trial, there was an incessant wrangle on the question of the admissibility of evidence, between the eminent barristers conducting the defence and the managers of the impeachment, who were politicians and laymen in legal matters. Burke declared that the Lords were exempt from ordinary rules of procedure, and were bound only by the law and usage of Parliament. He claimed that an impeachment was a unique judicial process, designed to afford, in exceptional cases, exceptional facilities for investigation and enquiry. But Hastings' counsel obtained a decision that the rules of evidence of the ordinary Courts should be adopted, and they used to the full all the advantages which the technical forms of the Common Law permitted, or their own expert knowledge suggested, in order to shield their client and to hamper the conduct of the prosecution. Largely through disputes on this head, the trial was extended to so inordinate a length, that, in 1791, the Commons decided to abandon the greater part of the articles. Only the first, second, fourth, and sixth, with part of the seventh and fourteenth were retained. The first dealt with Chait Singh, the second with the Begams of Oudh, the fourth with contracts, and the remainder, which for greater convenience were consolidated into one, with the taking of bribes and presents. Upon these counts alone did the Commons offer evidence, and ultimately appeal to the verdict of the Lords.

The course and result of the impeachment are recorded in a later volume. The reputation of Warren Hastings has suffered curious changes. By the highest Court of judicature of his day he was acquitted; but on many counts the historical and literary verdict went against him for nearly a century. Modern research seems to have justified his acquittal on all the most serious charges; but the reaction in his favour has sometimes been carried too far. The impeachment

CH. XV.

was not only a piece of party tactics, nor was it due simply to the spite of Sir Philip Francis. The malignity of no man, however eminent, could have supported so vast a superstructure. It was upheld by nobler pillars—the high-motived though misdirected zeal of Burke, and Fox' devotion to the law of liberty.

There were many things in the administration of Warren Hastings that invited criticism, and some that deserved censure. It was well for the credit of the British name that his action in the case of Benares and Oudh should not crystallise into a tradition of British policy. It was well that the whole of his career should be scrutinised, and if the scrutiny was fair, his fame was bound to emerge justified, if not wholly triumphant, from the test. It was well that the humanitarian feelings quickening men's minds at the close of the eighteenth century should find expression in the field of England's relations with her Eastern dependencies, even though that expression was rhetorical, turgid, and over-elaborated. But it was not well that Hastings, who had on the whole played a great and splendid part, should be gibbeted as the modern Verres, and made year after year a target for Burke's scorching invective and Sheridan's theatrical calumny.

The managers of the impeachment (and this particularly applies to Burke) ruined their cause by the ferocity with which they conducted it. Had they been content with a temperate presentation of their charges, it is probable that, as was done in Clive's case, a qualified censure would have been passed on some of Hastings' acts, coupled with a generous recognition of his great services to his country. The machinery of an impeachment was a clumsy anachronism that defeated its own object. Many gave their votes for an acquittal, not because they believed there was nothing to reprobate, but because they deemed the long agony of the seven years' trial a more than adequate penalty for any errors of judgment on the part of the accused, who, whatever else he had done, had at least preserved India for England through a period of extreme peril and in the face of appalling difficulties.

No one has ever doubted the transcendent abilities of Warren Hastings. Even Francis paid a reluctant tribute to his high capacity. The leading traits of his character were an amazing industry, remarkable precision and clearness both of thought and expression, a serene equanimity, a dogged patience under misfortune that seems almost superhuman, a high and noble courage. Conjoined with these qualities there may be observed on occasion a certain note of unscrupulousness, a clear-eyed and rather cynical insight into the motive springs of human conduct, a steely relentlessness when his mind was once made up, and an unshakable and extremely provocative self-confidence in the rectitude of his conduct, even in cases where it was most open to criticism. Such a character forms a complete foil to the generous-souled and idealistic, but passionate and unbalanced temperament, of his great accuser. In doing justice to Hastings, it is unnecessary to disparage the motives of Burke. In so far as the latter was impeaching the vices inherent in the constitution of the Company, he was often victoriously in the right. The wrongs of India, as he himself declared, constantly preyed upon his peace, and haunted his imagination by night and day. One of his last letters contains an impassioned prayer that all he had ever said or written might be forgotten before his part in the impeachment of Warren Hastings. Right in his sincere dislike of many of the Governor-General's isolated acts, right in his profound distrust of some tendencies of his policy, right above all in his constant reiteration of the truth that the function delegated to the Company was a trust and to be rendered accountable, he allowed the strength of his feelings to carry him beyond the boundaries of taste and decency, and made the cardinal mistake of visiting the condemnation, justly incurred by the system, upon the head of the individual who was called upon to administer it. To his vivid and heated imagination, the Peers assembled in Westminster Hall were trying the cause of Asia in the presence of Europe, and the prisoner at the bar stood forth as "the grand delinquent of all India." He thus wholly missed the key to the character of his great antagonist, and failed to discern what to posterity is the most salient feature of Hastings' career, that though he committed faults and made mistakes, he was never influenced by a lower aim than what he conceived to be his duty to the Company, and the preservation at any cost of England's position in the East.

CH. XV.

CHAPTER XVI.

ITALY AND THE PAPACY.

ALTHOUGH the papal power itself was far too weak to affect the result of the War of the Spanish Succession, yet the attitude of Pope Clement XI as an Italian ruler had some importance, and he might have traded upon the ancient claim of the Papacy to feudal suzerainty over the Sicilies in order to obtain some temporal advantage. It was by the advice of Innocent XII that Charles II of Spain had made the Bourbon claimant his heir, and it was in accordance with the ancient papal tradition to prefer a French to an Imperial ruler of Naples. Besides, Louis XIV had of late years been militantly orthodox, warring perpetually against Huguenots and Jansenists. On the other hand, there had been little sympathy between the Papacy and the Empire since the Peace of Westphalia; the Papacy was naturally alarmed at the Habsburgs' obvious intention to reassert Imperial claims in Italy by means of the Spanish inheritance, and Austria's chief ally was William III, who represented the leading Protestant Powers. In 1700, the Curia had distinctly declared in favour of a French policy by electing Cardinal Albani, who had inspired Innocent's advice to Charles II, to the Papacy.

But Clement XI (as Albani now called himself), though learned, upright, intelligent, and an able politician, had not sufficient strength of character to carry through a bold and difficult policy. Alberoni said of him that "he changes with every changing breeze"; the Venetian Erizzo, that "his opinions and decisions are frequently at variance." He recognised Philip V as King of Spain, but, afraid of irrevocably offending Austria, refused him the Sicilian investiture, and declared himself neutral. As the investiture was also refused to Archduke Charles, the Emperor was not conciliated; by refusing investiture to either claimant, Clement practically renounced his suzerainty. Both parties carried on campaigns in the Papal States without any regard for the Pope's remonstrances. Clement did not resist until the Emperor forced the Duke of Parma to do him homage for his fiefs, over which the Church likewise claimed suzerainty; but in this question France had no interest in supporting the Papacy. The Austrian army occupied Comacchio as an ancient fief of the duchy of Modena, and advanced on Rome, unhindered by the

Pope's hastily raised levies of peasants. Clement was forced to treat, and ultimately to recognise the Archduke as King of Spain (1709); but Comacchio was not given back for sixteen years.

At Utrecht the interests and rights of the Papacy were totally disregarded; its feudal claims on Sicily and Parma were ignored. Afterwards, Clement made a desperate effort to restore its prestige by a new Crusade against the Turks; he induced Austria to join a new Holy League with himself and Venice, and persuaded Austria's enemies to promise neutrality during the war. At first there was much enthusiasm; smaller States and even Spain promised help; Clement fancied himself another Pius V, and dreamed of another Lepanto. But, even before the Allies had time to quarrel, Alberoni, having secured a Cardinal's hat by empty promises, turned his crusading fleet against Sardinia. Austria's attention was immediately diverted from the East, and Clement's dream vanished with the Peace of Passarowitz.

Victor Amadeus' Tacitean verdict on Clement—"he would always have been esteemed worthy of the Papacy if he had never obtained it"— might have been passed on his successors. Innocent XIII (1721), kind-hearted, but old and feeble, died, it was rumoured, of shame for having made Dubois a Cardinal. Benedict XIII (1724) was, said the traveller de Brosses, "*bonhomme, fort pieux, fort faible et fort sot.*" Amiably disposed and well-intentioned, he was ruled by his scandalous favourite, Cardinal Coscia, who trafficked in spiritual privileges; but Benedict would hear no complaints. When the Pope's death was announced at the opera, the people rushed out, crying, "Good; now we will go and burn Coscia!" Coscia was severely punished by Benedict's successor, Clement XII (1730). This Pope was a Corsini of Florence, who flooded Rome with Florentines, and, when old and blind, was ruled by domineering nephews. "Let them do as they like; they are masters," he cried. Clement's election had been the work of the *Zelanti* (zealot) party among the Cardinals, which, led by the dominating and terrible Cardinal Albani, Clement XI's nephew, was determined to fight against Jansenism and Liberalism.

The eighteenth century sovereigns envied the Church's wealth, and disliked her independence and privileges. It was hateful to them that the *imperium in imperio* which an independent self-jurisdiction and the right of self-taxation had obtained for the Church should be virtually exercised by a foreign Power, still formidable when it interfered in domestic affairs, though contemptible in politics. And popular movements, of which they were but partly conscious, irresistibly drove the sovereigns forward to attack the ecclesiastical position. These movements sprang from different sources and motives, but their strongest factor was Jansenism—the agitation for moderate Protestant reform, whose influence, beginning in France, extended to several other countries. In France it was really popular, and even affected the clergy. A few more daring and independent minds pushed heterodoxy to atheism; these were called, rather flatteringly, the "Philosophers," and their influence seriously menaced religion amongst the upper classes. Again, the lawyers, a compact and homogeneous body, almost a caste, were prejudiced by their professional feelings against a double jurisdiction. Different in motives and aims, these groups united against their common enemy. The "Philosophers" encouraged Jansenism as a menace to the Church; the French *Parlement* cherished it as a weapon in that campaign which, having begun with a vindication of the rights of the Gallican Church, now aimed at transferring the sovereignty over it from the Papacy to the State. In France, where all anti-clerical parties were strong, the first battles were fought. Clement XI, trusting to Louis XIV's orthodoxy, promulgated the Bull *Unigenitus*, which championed Jesuit theology against Jansenism so unwisely that it offended all Augustinian divines and moderate Catholics. Upon Louis' death there was a violent reaction; *Parlement* and people became more Jansenist, while the Court favoured the Philosophers. Anti-clericalism had grown immensely before Louis XV was old enough to exert his influence in favour of orthodoxy, and the *Parlement*, in its opposition to the Bull *Unigenitus*, dared to defy the royal authority. The Government vainly endeavoured to obtain peace by silencing the noisy controversialists.

Next to France, it was in Naples that anti-clericalism most flourished. No Jansenism existed there, and the movement hardly extended beyond the educated classes; but for centuries lawyers and officials had struggled against ecclesiastical privileges and jurisdiction. Clement's refusal of the investiture embittered the strife; the lawyers urged anti-papal reform upon the Government, and a group of anti-papal writers became prominent. The clerical party pitched as their scape-goat upon the historian, Giannone, and forced him to leave the country. But the city authorities pensioned him, and he found a refuge at Vienna, while his book, the *Istoria Civile*, though in itself neither powerful nor original, became the standard work for all Italian anti-clericals.

Accordingly, when the Infant Don Carlos conquered Naples (May, 1734), and Clement XII, for fear of the Emperor, refused him the investiture, he found his more influential and intelligent subjects eager that he should assert his independence of the Papacy by ignoring investiture and curtailing ecclesiastical power. They presented numerous petitions to this effect; and an eminent lawyer, Genovesi, propounded a scheme for ecclesiastical reform which would have suited Bonaparte. However, the Spanish Government, which had itself just completed a Concordat with the Pope, intervened, and the Pope was persuaded to grant the investiture (1738), and negotiations for a Neapolitan Concordat were begun.

In Sicily, there had already been a struggle about the *Monarchia*, the ancient royal tribunal which claimed supreme control over ecclesiastical affairs. The controversy was intensified when Victor Amadeus ascended the Sicilian throne without papal investiture. Clement XI, afraid to defy a great Power, thought that he could frighten Victor Amadeus, and declared the *Monarchia* abolished. The King and Piedmontese officials resisted firmly, but they actually had to hold in check the anti-ecclesiastical zeal of the Sicilian *Gran Corte*. Native enthusiasm soon cooled, and Victor Amadeus' loss of Sicily was partly due to clerical agitation among the lower classes.

In Piedmont, where the King was absolute, and the governing classes were his officials, the struggle lay wholly between the Monarchy and the Papacy, though Victor Amadeus was supported by the unquestioning loyalty of his subjects and by many of the clergy themselves. The Sicilian question was followed by a quarrel about the investiture of Sardinia, which Victor Amadeus declared unnecessary. Clement XI was irreconcilable; but the King sent the clever diplomat Ormea to Rome, to attempt an arrangement with the milder Benedict XIII. The Cardinals were set against any concessions, and Benedict was terribly afraid of them; but Ormea gained the Pope's confidence and the support of Coscia; and, after three years of intrigue, a favourable Concordat was made, and the Sardinian investiture dropped (1727). The *Zelanti* furiously declared that, though the Pope must die, the Sacred College was eternal, and, to prove their words true, elected Clement XII, on purpose to repudiate the Sardinian Concordat (1731). Charles Emmanuel III firmly continued his father's policy, though he obliged the Pope by treacherously arresting Giannone and imprisoning him for twelve years.

The Conclave of 1740 was fiercely contested between the *Zelanti* and the more moderate party, and the election of Benedict XIV (Lambertini) was a compromise. It was surprising that the *Zelanti* should have agreed to a candidate so unlike the typical Cardinal. Benedict was genial, friendly to everyone, and witty, a man who would turn an awkward situation with a jest—at times of a Rabelaisian flavour. Yet his private life was pure; he improved his States by good and economical administration; he was learned, especially in Canon Law. His chief interest was in literature, and he was a brilliant writer and conversationalist. His reign recalled the Renaissance days; he patronised literary men and societies; to encourage Roman art the Academy of St Luke was founded. The Catalogue of the Vatican MSS was begun, churches were restored, antiquities discovered, the Index modified, the Roman schools improved, even scientific professorships founded. Benedict's friends were Muratori, Noris, and Montfaucon; Hume, Montesquieu, and Frederick the Great joined in his praises. Voltaire dedicated *Mahomet* to him, and wrote him a flattering epitaph. Horace Walpole said "he was loved by Papists, esteemed by Protestants; a priest without insolence or interest, a Prince without favourites, a Pope without nephews." Conscious of his impotence to stem the tide of change and disintegration, he spent his energies on matters within his power, and hoped by ample concession in temporal affairs to improve the position of the Papacy. He wrote, " Princes are a better support to the Papacy than Prelates. With their aid I think myself invincible....I prefer to let the thunders of the Vatican rest; Christ would not call down fire from Heaven....Let us take care not to mistake passion for zeal, for this mistake has caused the greatest evils to religion." A series of Concordats and temporal concessions gained for Benedict himself general respect and admiration; but their ultimate result was to convince the anti-clericals that the Papacy was powerless and would concede any demand, while the zealous Church party was exasperated, and prepared for a violent reaction after Benedict's death. It was now indeed impossible to adjust the conflicting ideals of Church and State, of Catholic and anti-Catholic; moderate concessions would not satisfy Jansenists who wished for reform, nor the *Parlement,* which aimed at supreme control of the Church, nor the Philosophers, who wished to crush it altogether.

At first, however, Benedict's policy seemed to prosper. The Sardinian Concordat of 1727 had been in part his work; he now wrote to Ormea, "I have changed my rank, but not my heart nor my memory." Negotiations had already begun under Clement, and were now swiftly concluded (1742); the old Concordat was renewed, with some concessions on each side, and Sardinia thus obtained more ecclesiastical freedom than any Italian State excepting Venice. A Neapolitan Concordat was also soon concluded (1741); but it by no means satisfied Genovesi and the reforming party, though further changes were afterwards effected by the Government on its own authority. In reality the King was not in sympathy with the extreme party, nor was the populace, though a rumour that the Archbishop meant to introduce the Inquisition led to a riot. The clergy were still less satisfied; they continually evaded the Concordat, and excommunicated Magistrates for carrying out its provisions. Controversy was incessant, and attempts for another Concordat failed; so that, though on excellent terms with Charles, Benedict could not procure ecclesiastical peace for Naples.

To Spain Benedict conceded, amongst other matters, the appointment to nearly all Spanish benefices; thus the Government obtained a control over the secular clergy which proved very important at a later date. Venice, which had more ecclesiastical liberty than almost any State, had been for some time quiescent. In Benedict's reign, however, she published a decree infringing certain papal rights. Benedict protested, but to no effect. The situation of Tuscany was the exact opposite of that of Venice. No State had been so priest-ridden; the later Medici and their subjects were slaves to clerical domination. The range of ecclesiastical jurisdiction and privilege was extensive, and the clergy interfered in every department of life. The Grand Duke Francis could dare to be more independent, and began ecclesiastical reforms, which led to some friction with the Papacy, but not to a quarrel. Nor were there as yet serious difficulties with Austria. Benedict maintained neutrality in the War of Succession, and quietly disregarded d'Argenson's hectoring orders to oppose Francis' election as Emperor.

The greatest troubles still proceeded from France. Here society was atheistic; Madame de Pompadour exercised her authority against the Church; the Philosophers extended their influence by the publication of the *Encyclopédie.* Jansenism was highly popular; it was acquiring saints and miracles of its own. The Government wavered in face of whatever influence momentarily predominated; it claimed to subject the clergy to ordinary taxation, but withdrew before their firm opposition. The King was personally devout, but he was swayed by Mme de Pompadour. The storm broke, when the *Parlement* bullied and imprisoned priests for withholding the Sacrament from persons who had not confessed to authorised confessors, and who therefore might be tainted with Jansenism. The King forbade the *Parlement* to interfere, and, on its proving recalcitrant, banished it, but afterwards recalled it (1754). He ordered a cessation of controversy; but to this the *Parlement* would never submit. Bishops were fined and exiled; the King himself sent the Archbishop from Paris for obstinacy. Benedict was uncertain of the wisdom of interference; but the General Assembly of the clergy (1755) appealed to the Pope. After consultation with the Government, he issued a very moderate Encyclical, which, while proclaiming the Bull *Unigenitus* as a rule of faith, really waived the confession question. "Since infidelity progresses daily," he wrote, " we must rather ask whether men believe in God than whether they accept the Bull." Bernis attempted conciliation, but his Ministry ended too soon, and Benedict's moderation produced no ultimate good effects in France.

Towards the end of his reign the anti-papalists opened a new campaign. For nearly two hundred years the Jesuits had been the strongest champions of the Papacy. Their immense influence, especially in education, their discipline, devotion, intrepidity, above all their extraordinary cleverness, made them the most determined supporters of the Curia. Frederick of Prussia called them "the advanced sentinels of the Court of Rome." But they had now grown too confident in their own cunning, and were committing serious mistakes. Intrigue and greed of power had made them unpopular in France, and their system of morals was open to grave criticism on the part of the Jansenists. In Spain and Portugal the prosperity of their American settlements and trade provoked envy. They were identified with the uncompromising attitude of the Church, especially with the Bull *Unigenitus,* and were becoming rather a cause of weakness than of strength to the Papacy. Hence the anti-papalists now directed their attack against them rather than against the Papacy itself.

The moment was favourable, for several European Governments

were controlled by anti-papalist and Jansenist Ministers. Choiseul, indifferent to religion, was simply guided by expediency; but Roda and Aranda in Spain, Tanucci at Naples and Pombal in Portugal, were one and all enthusiasts. Pombal began by demanding an enquiry into the Jesuits' American trade; and Benedict, who disliked their worldly avocations, allowed Pombal's friend, Cardinal Saldanha, to hold the enquiry. Benedict could not have foreseen the violent hostility of Saldanha's report; but he died before it was issued, and his successor, Clement XIII (1758), had neither skill to avoid nor ability to master the approaching storm. Clement and his Minister Torrigiani had personal piety, courage and patience; but both were priests rather than politicians, and believed that the righteous must ultimately triumph, and that their trials could be overcome by passive endurance. Clement, elected by Jesuit influence, was convinced that their cause was that of the Church, and was prepared to submit to any humiliation rather than sacrifice them. But he could not effectually protect them, and thus only involved the Church in their misfortunes. As the Jesuits were always suspected of tolerating regicide, Pombal's next move was to discover a supposed Jesuit plot against the King's life. More than two hundred Jesuits were imprisoned; the rest were forcibly transhipped to the Papal States. When the Pope behaved meekly, Pombal picked a quarrel with the Nuncio, and so compassed a complete breach with the Papacy. Clement humbly craved for reconciliation, and the King and people were soon tired of the quarrel; but Pombal persisted.

The French *Parlement* was delighted to find a fresh object for attack, and tried to follow Pombal's lead. The French Jesuits had foolishly appealed to it against an unfavourable sentence in the law Courts, and the *Parlement* seized the opportunity to appoint a Commission to examine the Jesuits' Statutes. The King intervened half-heartedly, appointing a parallel Commission, which proposed, amongst other reforms, that the Jesuits should obey a French Vicar-General independent of Rome. The *Parlement* ignored its proceedings, and, wholly disregarding the royal authority, published a sweeping decree (1762), closing the Jesuit schools, confiscating their property and dissolving their foundations. In 1764 it banished all Jesuits except those who were willing to renounce their Order. Choiseul was not actively hostile to them, but prepared not to offend Mme de Pompadour on their account. Meanwhile, Clement's diplomacy was so formal, almost mysterious, that with him, as with Benedict XIV, friendly negotiation was impossible. As he and the Jesuit General Ricci scouted the proposals of the Royal Commission, the French Government made this the pretext for abandoning the Jesuits altogether. Thus the *Parlement* had its own way, and the King finally suppressed the Order in France (1764).

Charles III of Spain, in spite of his Jansenist Ministers, at first inclined towards the Jesuits, encouraging them to continue their work in

Paraguay, and sheltering some of the French exiles. But Charles, though pious, was an absolutist, and had an unshaken faith in his own rights. He was certain not to tolerate the Order for an instant, if convinced that its continuance in Spain was prejudicial to his authority. His Ministers accordingly declared the Jesuits responsible for some popular risings in 1766. Meanwhile, the Pope injured their cause, while involving himself in their unpopularity, by issuing a Bull, *Apostolicum Pascendi* (1765), which uncompromisingly proclaimed the innocence and merits of the Order. Charles appointed a Commission of lawyers, sure to be deeply prejudiced against the Jesuits, to report on their case; and, in 1767, he determined to suppress the Order in his dominions. Complete secrecy was preserved until, on an appointed day, all Jesuit establishments in Spain and its colonies were suddenly closed, and the Jesuits forcibly, though without discourtesy, shipped to Italy. Thus ended that interesting and successful experiment in the paternal government of savage races which the Order had conducted in Paraguay. The natives were told that they had been tyrannously ruled, but would now be free and possessors of their own land.

The Neapolitan Jesuits soon followed the Spanish. The Minister of Justice, Tanucci, had controlled his enmity reluctantly, until Spain unloosed his hands: when he drove the members of the Order across the border with brutal contumely. The sudden advent of so many exiles was very embarrassing to the papal Government. Many had been granted small pensions; but they arrived in great destitution, and the Roman clergy looked upon them with disfavour. Fearing lest Spain should threaten to withdraw their promised pensions, in order to obtain concessions from him, Clement refused admission to the Spanish Jesuits. Repelled from Civitá Vecchia, they suffered much hardship until Genoa gave them a refuge in Corsica. On the cession of the island to France, they were again expelled, and Clement had to allow them to come privately to the Papal States.

Hitherto no Power except the Bourbons had moved against the Jesuits; a clever politician would have used this circumstance, and in return for certain concessions partial toleration might have ultimately been obtained even from the Bourbons. If the Jesuits were nominally secularised, they would be permitted to return home, and might have gradually recovered their former position. But Ricci would listen to no such plan; "*Sint ut sunt,*" he said, "*aut non sint.*" The inevitable result was extinction.

Far from conciliating the Bourbons, Clement entered upon a new and quite unnecessary quarrel with them. Duke Ferdinand VI of Parma, or rather his Minister du Tillot, demanded the same concessions as Spain had received in her Concordat, and when Clement refused, took them without permission. The Pope might have disregarded the impertinences of this petty State; but, forgetting the solidarity of Bourbon interests, he issued a severe *monitorium* (1768), asserting his feudal claims over the duchy, and threatening the Duke and his Ministers with excommunication. The Duke retorted defiantly and expelled the Jesuits. All the Bourbons united to demand the withdrawal of the *monitorium*; and, when Clement, more courageous than wise, refused, France occupied Avignon, while Tanucci seized Benevento and Pontecorvo, the papal possessions in Naples, and threatened Castro, a former fief of Parma in the Papal States. Clement appealed to Maria Theresa; but she wished to marry her daughter to Ferdinand of Naples, and would not interfere. The Bourbons naturally, and no doubt rightly, blamed the Jesuits, to whose influence the Pope was entirely subject. Charles III formally demanded the entire dissolution of the Order; the other Bourbon Governments corroborated his demands; when Clement died (February, 1769).

To the next Conclave it practically fell to decide the fate of the Jesuits. The Powers had not recently taken much interest in papal elections; but on this occasion the Cardinals kept up a close communication with the ambassadors at Rome, who exercised direct, if not open, pressure upon the Conclave. The Cardinals dared not defy the Bourbons, yet the *Zelanti* struggled against electing a Pope pledged beforehand to destroy the Jesuits. Though Austria stood aloof, Joseph II happened to be then in Rome; the rules of the Conclave were relaxed, so that he might visit the Cardinals, to whom he gave plenty of informal advice, remarking, "A year would not be wasted in electing another Benedict XIV."

The intrigues of this Conclave are hard to unravel; the Jesuits afterwards declared that the election of Ganganelli was simoniacal, because he pledged himself, if elected, to abolish the Order. He was among the candidates approved by France; but no definite pledge of the kind can be proved. Indeed, Choiseul interfered when Spain wished to exact pledges from all candidates. Probably both parties thought that they might control Ganganelli, because of his known moderation, not to say pliability, of character. The new Pope, who took the name of Clement XIV, loved peace and justice; yet he was obliged to listen continually to the bitter complaints and malicious misrepresentations of the Jesuits and to the importunities and threats of the Bourbons' envoys. To gain time, and not to allow the Powers any fair ground for discontent, he made many concessions to their demands. The *monitorium* against Parma, though not formally revoked, was ignored; privileges were granted to Sardinia and Venice; Portugal was reconciled, to the delight of both King and people; Pombal behaved amicably, and his brother was created a Cardinal. Charles III also made concessions; while France appointed Bernis as ambassador, who gained Clement's confidence, and in his turn received a Cardinal's hat. Only Tanucci remained irreconcilable. Heedless of the reproofs of Charles III and Choiseul, he continued his violent anti-papal campaign, republishing the works of Giannone and Sarpi.

The contest as to the Jesuits continued for four years. Clement knew that he could not save them, nor had he much sympathy for them. He was a Franciscan and a Thomist, and had to suffer from their slanders. He called them "those men abandoned by God, who are about to undergo the consequences of their obstinacy." But he would not be forced to condemn them with unseemly haste, and without at least an appearance of judicial impartiality. He refused foreign troops to guard him against a real danger of assassination, and would not hear of bargaining on the basis of the restoration of Avignon. "I do not sell my decisions," he said. The Powers accused him of shuffling; and even Bernis complained of his reserve and inaccessibility. Nor was there any responsible Minister at the Vatican to bargain with, since the Pope dared not trust any Cardinal. The Curia was full of intrigue, even the Bourbon ambassadors mistrusting one another; Spain suspected France of lukewarmness, especially when Choiseul fell before Madame Du Barry, who favoured the Jesuits. Aiguillon, however, carried on the anti-Jesuit campaign.

But Clement's delay justified itself. The violence and duplicity of the Jesuits alienated their own friends, even Cardinal Albani; they were very unpopular in Rome, especially amongst the other clergy. By January, 1773, Clement had drafted a Bull for their suppression; it was modified to satisfy the scruples of Maria Theresa, and in August it was published. Early in 1774, Avignon, Benevento and Pontecorvo were restored to the Papacy; but many diplomatic forms had first to be gone through to make the bargain appear as a concession.

Most of the Powers granted pensions to ex-Jesuits, and allowed those who submitted to return home as secular priests; but the more refractory members of the Order refused even to acknowledge its dissolution. They heaped unmeasured obloquy upon the Pope; but the story spread by them of his madness is quite discredited; for, though his health soon began to fail, he could transact business until the end; but calumny probably shortened his life, and it is possible that he was poisoned. Bernis had to order French soldiers to protect his catafalque from insult.

So ended for a time the great Order of Ignatius Loyola. As Ranke observes, it had long survived its original function, the spread of the Counter-Reformation. It had been diverted to other ends—the contest with royal and national anti-ecclesiastical movements, with Jansenism and Rationalism. In spite of its influence on education, it had proved unequal to these struggles, and its unpopularity was injuring the papal cause. Yet the interests of the Jesuits and those of the Curia were so nearly identical that the fall of the Order was the heaviest blow which papal prestige had received since the Reformation. Philosophers, Jansenists and anti-papal statesmen exulted, and there followed within a few years tremendous ecclesiastical changes, some with the consent of the Pope, but many in defiance of his protests. The demands of the

Powers were not at all moderated by papal compliance on this occasion; they merely considered one success as a step towards others, and States, hitherto less aggressive, soon followed their example.

The Neapolitan nobility had appreciated the independence allowed them by the Austrian Government; but the populace remembered the strict hand kept by the Spanish Government over the nobles. They thought that an independent king would likewise keep the nobles in order, while giving Naples the advantages of a local Court. So Naples welcomed the Infant Don Carlos with many fireworks, and San Gennaro graciously signified his approval. Sicily, which had lately fought for Spain, was equally satisfied.

Charles III (Don Carlos) was young, good-looking, pleasant and well-meaning; he had fair abilities, and a careful education would have made him a good king. But Elisabeth Farnese intended to control Italy through Naples, and Naples by Ministers dependent upon herself, who encouraged her son's natural idleness and discouraged him from participation in the Government. His attendance at Council was almost formal; his time was spent in sport, especially hunting, at Church, at the theatre, in planning fine new estates and in stocking them with game. Hunting-lodges were built—it was in digging the foundations for the lodge at Portici that Herculaneum was discovered. Magnificent and costly palaces were begun at Capodimonte and Caserta; but both were unfinished when Don Carlos left Naples. For the city were built the huge theatre of San Carlo, some new streets and a mole. In 1738, more *fêtes* celebrated the King's marriage with Maria Theresa's niece, Maria Amalia of Saxony. Though only a child, she was clever, charming, and high-spirited, and joined enthusiastically in the King's sports, so that he was soon devoted to her. She wished for political power; but the Ministers, San Stefano and afterwards (1738) Montealegro di Salas, governed under the sole direction of Elisabeth Farnese. In foreign policy Naples had to follow Spain, and in 1741 sent its army to join Montemar in central Italy. Nevertheless the Neapolitan Government had declared itself neutral, and was disagreeably surprised when (August, 1742) an English fleet appeared off Naples, and threatened immediate bombardment if the Neapolitan troops were not withdrawn from the war. Di Salas, aware that Naples could not be defended, gave way, though the King wished to resist. Henceforth, however, more attention was paid to military preparations, and, when in 1744 Austria threatened invasion, an efficient Neapolitan army, commanded by the King, joined Gages' Spanish force in the Papal States, to oppose Lobkowitz' advance.

After much manœuvring on both sides about Velletri, Lobkowitz at last made a night attack and seized the town, Don Carlos himself narrowly escaping through a window. But while the Austrians were sacking Velletri, Gages reassembled his forces and expelled the invaders.

Afterwards the camps remained face to face, until in the autumn Lobkowitz slowly retired, Don Carlos following as far as Rome. His triumphant
return home made a great impression on the fickle Neapolitans, whose
loyalty would hardly have resisted an Austrian invasion. In fact there
was still a powerful and active Austrian party amongst the nobility.
They had persuaded Maria Theresa to attempt the reconquest of Naples,
and they promoted an Austrian propaganda amongst the people which
the Government severely repressed by a series of Commissions called
Giunte d'Inconfidenza, punishing many innocent as well as guilty persons.

In spite of his victory, Charles remained under Spanish domination
until Maria Amalia, weary of political insignificance, contrived to substitute for di Salas a less powerful Minister, Fogliani (1746), and the
death of Philip V ended the rule of Elisabeth Farnese. After this, Charles
seemed to acquire an unwonted sense of responsibility, developing a
policy of his own, and exercising control over his Ministers and even in
part over his wife, who had aspired to fill the place of his mother.
But her persistent meddling led to much court intrigue, and in 1755
Fogliani fell before her machinations. Henceforward, the King ruled
without a chief Minister through the Secretaries of Departments. One of
these was the clever Parmesan lawyer, Tanucci, who, from Minister of
Justice, now became Foreign Secretary.

Charles asserted his independence in refusing to sign the Treaty of
Aix, which implied that, if he succeeded to Spain, the Sicilies must be
ceded to his brother Philip. He did not hope to keep both, but intended
the Sicilies for his own younger son; and, when the Seven Years' War
began, France, anxious to secure the solidarity of the Bourbons, by the
Third Treaty of Versailles guaranteed the Sicilies to Charles' descendants.
Pitt also was bidding for his friendship, but the King shared Tanucci's
truly Tuscan hatred for Pitt's ally, Sardinia. Indeed, Naples and Sardinia were on the verge of a war over Piacenza, which, according to the
Treaty of Aix, Don Philip ought to cede to Sardinia if Charles succeeded
to Spain. France, however, intervened for peace, and Sardinia finally
accepted pecuniary compensation. Further to secure his son before
leaving Naples, Charles established good relations with Austria in a
treaty which guaranteed the succession to the Sicilies, in return for the
cession of the Presidi to Tuscany.

The death of Ferdinand VI (1759) made Charles King of Spain. As
his eldest son was an idiot, the second was heir to Spain, and the third,
Ferdinand, a child, was left at Naples with a Council of Regency, in
which Tanucci was supreme. So powerful was Tanucci's personality that
he was credited afterwards with having inspired and directed Charles'
policy from the first. But, until he became Foreign Secretary, his
Ministerial position was subordinate, and there is no evidence that
he exercised any special influence on the policy of the Government
outside his own office.

CH. XVI.

The Government had excellent intentions, but not sufficient strength of purpose to effect striking improvements. The Neapolitans, it has been said, were familiar with revolution, but could not understand or assimilate reform. The Government's action was continually hindered by the privileges of the nobles and clergy, the conservatism of the lawyers, and the prejudice, inertia and superstition of the populace. Some good reforms were effected, but they were few and not far-reaching. The chief were the ecclesiastical changes already mentioned, because in these matters public opinion assisted the Government. Ecclesiastical jurisdiction and immunities and rights of asylum were limited, and clerical property (about one-third of the whole kingdom) was taxed, though never beyond two per cent. of its value. Ecclesiastical censures on officials for the discharge of their duty were declared inoperative, and a limit was imposed to the number of Religious, which had reached one-fortieth of the population.

Thus but little progress could be made towards the most needful kind of reform, a change in the social system. The ancient "Grand Barons" had given way to a class of nobles, generally ignorant and idle, dissipated and extravagant, and devoid of political ability. Yet they possessed most of the land, and had feudal jurisdiction over four-fifths of the people. As the principal Estate in Parliament, they could withhold *donativi*, or voted taxes, and thus force the Government to abandon any unpopular reform. The municipality of Naples was mainly in their hands, and the control of the capital was of supreme importance for the kingdom at large. The Government diminished their authority by attracting them to the Court, where they spent more money on luxuries, and less on retinues of lawless feudal retainers. Austrian partisanship ruined many, and their place was taken by new creations from the official classes. Many titles were sold, and so too was membership of Charles' newly established knightly Order of San Gennaro. Thus rank decreased in social value, and "*È duca, ma non cavaliere*" was a popular saying. The lawyers, many of whom were of noble birth, held political power and filled the government offices. They formed a homogeneous, influential, and conservative body, including nearly all the talent of the nation. They usually opposed reform, especially in legal matters. A commercial middle class hardly existed; but the revenue officials, mostly Genoese, made fortunes by cheating both people and Government, and often bought land and titles. The city populace had been indulged with *festas* and cheap food by nervous Governments; it was lazy, turbulent, addicted to mendicancy; "*la plus abominable canaille, la plus dégoûtante vermine,*" de Brosses called it. The city was financially favoured at the expense of the provinces, and the upper classes at the expense of the lower; the unfortunate peasantry bore the weight of taxation, and were crushed between the nobles and government officials. Many lived on coarse grains and herbs, without salt or oil, and in the remote districts corn was unknown.   Misery drove many to brigandage; others joined the crowd of beggars in the city.   Genovesi, the noble Neapolitan seeker after reform, compared the people to savages, without civilisation or Christian morals.

The difficulties of fiscal reform were increased by the extravagances of the Court, which spent about five million francs annually, three times as much as that of Turin.   Building cost a nearly equal sum.   But the revenue was almost doubled, though the individual burden was actually rather diminished.   This was due in part to official economy, in part to ecclesiastical taxation, but mainly to economic reforms which increased the national wealth.   Many of the alienated customs were redeemed, and taxation was redistributed by means of a new *catasto* (valuation schedule).   By the old *catasto* land escaped lightly, while every kind of industry and labour was overburdened; the rich were exempted while the poor paid heavily.   Unfortunately, the new *catasto* perpetuated the worst faults of the old—the poll-tax, and the additional tax on every worker, which crippled industry and rewarded idleness.   It was therefore much less beneficial than had been hoped.   In spite, however, of economic fallacies, the Government really tried to increase the wealth of the country and its own revenue by rescuing trade from its disastrous condition. It was plundered by brigands within, by pirates without, and at the ports by Custom-house officials, who extorted what duties they pleased. The coinage was corrupt; laws against usury hindered the circulation of capital.   Manufactures hardly existed, exportation of natural products was narrowly limited; once, when a comet appeared, it was stopped altogether.   The *Giunta del Commercio*, acting on the advice of Vau-coulleur, a French economist, established a supreme magistracy of commerce, which was expected to work wonders.   It made commercial treaties, started and subsidised manufactures, reformed the coinage, and so forth.   But those who had battened upon the old abuses hated the new magistracy, and the nobles voted a *donativo* as a bribe to induce the Government to deprive it of its authority.   It had ventured to tolerate Jews; but, as the friars assured the King that it was for this reason he had no male heirs, the toleration was withdrawn.

In spite of the opposition of Barons and lawyers, Tanucci, as Minister of Justice, contrived to improve the judicial system; and no doubt the magistrates respected direct authority rather than that of a distant King.   Tanucci tried to check bribery, moderate the ferocity of criminal justice, impose limits on feudal tyranny, hasten procedure, subject the irresponsible magistrates to syndics, and punish the corrupt; but he had only partial success.   In imitation of Sardinia, an attempt was made to codify the law, which was in a hopeless confusion of Roman law, custom, royal and vice-regal edicts.   Unfortunately the codification was entrusted to a single incompetent lawyer, Cirillo, who had already made himself ridiculous by attacking Muratori.   His work could never be used; it contained many obsolete laws, and omitted whole sections of modern law, commercial, military, and so forth. The same fatuity appeared in every department of government. The Farnese collections, brought from Parma, were left in dirt and confusion; the royal architects wasted vast sums of money and did not complete their buildings. A pedant was appointed to describe the discoveries at Herculaneum, who diligently compiled vast tomes on the labours of Hercules, and prosecuted scholars who published actual descriptions of the antiquities.

Yet the Sicilies were certainly better off under Charles than they had been for many previous centuries. The Government was well-intentioned; its Ministers were personally upright; its direct supervision was valuable, and some real progress was made. Fair seasons and a long period of peace favoured prosperity, though much distress was caused by the terrific eruptions of Vesuvius and by earthquakes in 1738 and 1750. The King was popular, and the people fairly contented.

Tuscany, after two hundred years of stultifying Medicean government, needed reform as much as any Italian State. It was enslaved by ecclesiastical tyranny, and sunk in ignorance and superstition; for the Inquisition and the moral espionage of the friars had crushed its ancient intellectual qualities, whose last manifestation had been in the seventeenth century scientific school. The commercial prosperity, the old civic spirit and autonomy of the capital were dead; the place of the vigorous merchant nobles was taken by flaccid, dissipated courtiers. Trade was slack; unemployment and mendicancy, encouraged by "pious benefactions," prevailed. The provincial communes retained a measure of self-government, the peasantry, naturally more energetic, never sank to the level of the Neapolitans; but they were oppressed by tax-gatherers and feudal lords possessing rights to a multitude of "services," so that they were much in the position of medieval villeins, but without their customary rights. The prosperity of Livorno benefited only its principally foreign inhabitants, since it was cut off from the rest of the country by internal customs-barriers.

Reform had more apparent success in Tuscany than in Naples. The Tuscans, though not quite so lethargic and ignorant, were more pliable than the Neapolitans, and usually acquiesced in their ruler's dictates. The Grand Duke, Peter Leopold of Austria, son of Maria Theresa and brother of Joseph II, was of far more decided opinions and energetic character than Charles III, and was helped by excellent Ministers. The work of reform was begun under Francis of Lorraine (1737–65), by the Regency which governed for him, and especially by Richecourt, a Lorrainer, Minister of Finance and afterwards Governor (1747–57). He was, however, so despotic that he was at last overthrown by the able Tuscans whom he kept out of office; but his talents and ability effected some notable improvements. He checked certain feudal abuses, forbade the creation of new entails, and used the Emperor's authority to bring under control some almost independent Imperial feudatories. Judges approved by the Government were now to exercise feudal jurisdiction, and appeal was allowed from the feudal to the central Courts. Finance was burdened by the Medici debt; the country was already over-taxed, the customs mostly farmed out; nearly half the revenue had to be sent to the Emperor. Administrative economy, the unification of the public debt, and some commercial reforms and trade with Lombardy and Austria, slightly improved matters. Internal customs were lowered, and agriculture encouraged by permission to export a portion of its produce. But attempts to colonise the marshy and unhealthy Maremma district failed.

Conflict with the overweening clerical power was inevitable. The censorship of the Press was taken from the Inquisition, and its furious protests led to its temporary suppression and ultimate revival on the limited Venetian model. Clerical revenues were taxed, and a mortmain law passed which included large pecuniary bequests. Violent opposition followed, especially from the monks; but the firmness of the Government and the moderation of Benedict XIV prevented a quarrel.

In 1765 Tuscany became nominally autonomous under its youthful Grand Duke, Peter Leopold, in Italy called Leopold only. The Tuscans were pleased to have a sovereign of their own, and liked the pleasant, unassuming manners and the simple style of life of Leopold and his Spanish wife. The unpopular Minister, Botta Adorno, who had acted as Regent, was soon dismissed; but it was long before Leopold could shake off the control of his mother and brother. In spite of his protests, Joseph borrowed nearly all the money in the Tuscan Treasury. Joseph meant to be very kind: he wrote letters of affectionate advice, asked Leopold's opinion on his own policy, sometimes visited Tuscany, and treated Leopold's son as his own heir; but the Grand Duke resented all intrusion into his private affairs, and suspected evil motives in Joseph's well-meant interferences. The brothers were alike in their admiration of the new "philosophy," in their reforming notions, ecclesiastical tastes, love of symmetry, order, economy, efficiency, and of personally regulating minute details. But Leopold, as Botta remarked, "was more Jansenist than philosopher, and Joseph more philosopher than Jansenist." Leopold leaned more upon ministerial advice than did Joseph; he lacked Joseph's imperious self-confidence, but also his straightforwardness. Leopold was slow, timorous, cautious, and allowed his natural suspiciousness to grow into a painful obsession. He set spies upon his Ministers and Court, even upon his meanest subjects, and then spies upon the spies. "Let them deceive you sometimes," wrote Joseph, "rather than thus torment yourself constantly and vainly." Verri said of Leopold severely, but with truth, that "timid and tortuous, he was not upright like his brother, but was almost indecently false and immoral."

CH. XVI.

In the earlier part of his reign he had excellent Ministers, of whom the best was Pompeo Neri, Home Secretary, and then (1770) President of the Council of State, a prudent, logical, and far-sighted statesman, who planned Leopold's most successful measures. He had reformed municipal government for Lombardy, and gave Tuscany the benefit of his experience. Tavanti and Rucellai were good finance and ecclesiastical Ministers. After the deaths of Neri and Rucellai (1776 and 1778), the only able and intelligent Minister was Gianni. As Leopold grew more suspicious, he ceased to trust good advisers, and was deceived by bad. His jealousy induced him to prefer less capable men, some of whom he knew to be secretly scheming against his own policy. He ruled principally through the *Presidente del Buon Governo,* an inquisitorial and arbitrary official, with large fiscal, magisterial and disciplinary authority, who spied into the private affairs of the people, and kept them in a state of nervous apprehension. The police were so feared that even the soldiers mutinied against them.

Yet the one object of Leopold's life and interest was reform. Like Joseph he believed that only an autocratic government could effect this. The Government was frankly absolute, quite ignoring the last remaining constitutional authority, the Senate, which even the Medici had pretended to consult. Yet Leopold had abstract notions of educating the people by pamphlets and preaching, and, when they were sufficiently advanced, of granting a real Constitution, for which Gianni drew up an ideal scheme. More practical was Leopold's reconstruction of local administration, which he intended as a first step towards the establishment of popular institutions. The Medici had allowed a remnant of medieval local government to survive in the provinces, and there were voluntary leagues amongst the Communes for mutual protection against feudal tyranny. On the basis of these existing systems, Leopold drew up an organised scheme and set of statutes for communal self-government, which was gradually applied all over Tuscany and proved more successful than any of his other experiments, especially as a means for educating the people. Florence, which the Medici had utterly deprived of its autonomy, was the last to benefit by the new scheme.

In other directions, Leopold's secular reforms were necessarily more remedial than constructive. Great improvements were made in the judicial system by simplifying procedure, abolishing unnecessary tribunals, checking corruption, and especially by humanising the savage criminal law. Following Beccaria's advice, Leopold abolished torture, confiscation, and even the death-penalty.

Leopold could not put an end to feudalism; but he modified its worst effects by relaxing the entail law, protecting the peasantry, and limiting feudal jurisdiction. Rural servitude, with all its crushing burdens of wood-cutting, service, pasturage and so on, was gradually abolished; and, together with personal emancipation, Leopold assisted the emancipation of the land from its burdens of custom, entail and mortmain. The agrarian situation was further improved by unifying the land-tax, abolishing numerous vexatious regulations, magistracies and internal customs, which interfered with economic freedom, and permitting under certain circumstances the importation and exportation of corn. Before Leopold's reign famine was endemic, and the land-owners had no capital; at its close landed proprietors were able to invest largely in commercial undertakings, to their mutual profit. The morasses of the Val di Chiana were successfully drained and cultivated, though the Maremma was still a swamp. In reality the population was too scanty to make the cultivation of any but good land profitable. Industrial prosperity also increased with the abolition of the worst taxes and monopolies—especially those of town against country—the encouragement of new industries, and above all the abolition of the *Arti* and other ancient commercial tribunals, now mere forces of tyranny and reaction. But there was little foreign trade, and Leopold, with mistaken economy, put down the fleet which had at least partially protected it from pirates. Increased prosperity and administrative economy recovered the finances from the desperate condition in which Leopold found them. The alienated taxes were redeemed; and, by lowering the customs and the price of salt, contraband trade was checked and legitimate encouraged. In order to diminish the heavy national debt, the *Monti* (Government stock) were all incorporated into one fund, and the land-tax was applied for its redemption.

Yet Leopold never gained the real confidence of his subjects, whose conservatism credited him with an insensate mania for innovation. The feudal classes regretted their loss of privilege; the people resented the inquisitorial methods of the Government. Leopold was able to force reform upon them, but not to obtain their cooperation in it. They obeyed, but always unwillingly. Racial incompatibility made him seem a foreigner to them, and he was never really in sympathy with Italian sentiment. Most unpopular of all was the ecclesiastical policy which he regarded as the crown of his life's work. Joseph himself was not more enthusiastic; but while he, like a modern politician, aimed at separating the functions of Church and State, and preventing the former from infringing the rights and injuring the material interests of the latter, Leopold, like a sixteenth century Protestant, desired to reform the Church itself, so that it might advance the spiritual condition of his people. He believed himself "established by God as guardian and tutor of religion." His chief adviser, Scipione Ricci, Bishop of Pistoia and Prato, was practically a Jansenist; and so, in all but doctrinal matters, was Leopold.

In spite of the efforts of the Regency, Leopold found Tuscany behind most European States in the struggle for ecclesiastical freedom. He did not favour Concordats, believing that Rome generally profited by them, and preferred to make all changes on his own responsibility. Many of these followed the usual lines; a ducal *exequatur* was enforced, clerical taxation increased, the Inquisition suppressed, pecuniary payments to Rome strictly limited. Ecclesiastical jurisdiction was confined to purely spiritual matters, without power to impose temporal penalties; the Nuncio's Court was abolished, and appeals to Rome forbidden. The Curia's patronage to benefices with cure of souls was transferred to the Bishops, and the religious Orders were released from dependence upon Roman superiors, subjected to episcopal control, and no longer allowed to compete with parochial organisation. Superfluous and ill-conducted Houses were suppressed, and their revenues augmented the emoluments of poor benefices. To check mendicancy and indiscriminate charity, the number of begging friars was limited, while hospitals and other pious foundations were placed under lay control.

In his constructive moral and religious policy, however, Leopold departed from the ordinary course of the anti-ecclesiastical reformer. Here Ricci was his adviser, and in his own dioceses made experiments which the other more conservative and orthodox Bishops could not be induced to try. The most pressing necessity was a reform of the convents, especially those for women, which were mainly under the control of monks and friars and were in an utterly immoral condition. Their number was preposterous, because social conditions forced all women without dowries to take the veil. Ricci interfered in a flagrant case of immorality at Prato; and the Dominicans, who were really responsible, resisted furiously; but, finally, the Pope agreed to withdraw all nuns from their control. General improvements were effected by raising the age of profession, limiting the endowments which novices might bring to their convents, and providing occupation for the nuns by turning convents into schools. The parish priests, divided by an almost impassable gulf from the higher clergy of noble birth, were extremely poor and ignorant. Reform was initiated by placing patronage in the hands of the Bishops and the Grand Duke, by insisting on clerical residence, raising the emoluments of poorer benefices, and founding academies for clerical education. Meanwhile, provision was made for secular education by substituting lay for Jesuit schools and establishing girls' schools in convents; the condition of the Universities was also improved.

But what chiefly infuriated the ecclesiastical party was Leopold's interference in matters connected with worship: such as the prohibition of burials inside churches, the abolition of flagellation and of many unedifying local festivals, and of the innumerable "Confraternities" (guilds of a combined religious and social character) which fostered idleness, extravagance and political agitation. A single Confraternity was established in each parish; but the people generally refused to join it. Ricci celebrated Mass in Italian, and discouraged superstitious devotions; but his rumoured intention to remove the famous girdle of the Virgin from Prato as spurious caused a riot, in which his palace was sacked.

Leopold could not make reform popular; his explanatory pamphlets failed to touch the populace, into whose minds friars and ex-Jesuits instilled discontent. Hoping to enlist the Tuscan clergy on his side, he tried to revive the synodal system of church government. In 1786, a Diocesan Synod at Pistoia passed, under Ricci's influence, extraordinarily Liberal resolutions, even affirming the principles of the French "Four Articles of 1682"—including the propositions that the temporal power is independent of the spiritual, that a General Council is superior to a Pope, and that the Pope is not infallible, even in matters of faith. This Synod was in itself a remarkable assertion of the democratic ideal of church government. In 1787, Leopold called a General Assembly of the Tuscan Bishops; but even Ricci doubted the wisdom of this step. The Grand Duke drew up a programme for discussion, but refrained from any personal interference. The Assembly issued a few useful, if minor, disciplinary reforms, but was far too conservative and too much afraid of Roman censure to consider Leopold's sweeping proposals in any liberal spirit. He found that it was passing time in aimless discussion, and dismissed it. Though he might have expected the failure, it disappointed him greatly. But he was contemplating fresh efforts, when the death of his brother ended his activities in Tuscany.

His whole reign is extraordinarily interesting as a typical experiment in reform worked out by a personal autocrat in minute detail upon a small and homogeneous State. The scheme never bore fruit; it was destroyed, partly by popular reaction, partly by the power of the coming Revolution; we may doubt whether at that date it could possibly have been fruitful; but, while recognising its ultimate futility and the weaknesses of its author, we must admire his high ideals, industry, self-denial and perseverance, his grasp of the problems of his age, and his insight into modern methods of solving them.

Neither temptations nor threats could move Venice from her attitude of formal neutrality in Western politics; but her geographical position on the Austrian route into Italy threatened her independence, since she was obliged to grant passage to Austrian troops. She could not even obtain the inviolability of a neutral; the War of the Spanish Succession was partly fought within her territories, and in the later campaigns even her expensive army could not protect them from damage. The Peace of Utrecht surrounded her *terra firma* with Austrian dominions; even her command of the Adriatic was threatened when Austria held the Sicilies. The Holy League and Turkish War bound her to friendliness; but this tie was severed when Austria abandoned her interests, and in the Peace of Passarowitz acquiesced in her loss of the Morea. Venice therefore refused to renew the Holy League in 1735, and tried to hinder the efforts of Charles VI to develop an Adriatic and Mediterranean commerce. There were various border disputes, especially as to the patronage to the patriarchate of Aquileia, whose diocese embraced both Austrian and Venetian territory.

Venice really preserved her independence because the rival Great Powers would not permit each other to violate it. She had little vital force left to sustain her after her last gallant struggle in the Morea. To preserve the remains of her commerce, she was obliged, against her traditions, to make treaties with barbarous States. Once more the old spirit blazed up in her last Admiral, Angelo Emo, who, after immense difficulties, humbled Algiers and Tunis (1769, 1787). But her navy was really decaying together with her commercial marine. Her protective tariffs had driven away both Levantine and Mediterranean trade to the more open ports of Genoa, Ancona, Livorno and Trieste. New commercial treaties were useless, and her remaining Levantine ports were more expensive than profitable. The nobles had abandoned commerce; the people no longer loved a sea-faring life; ship-yards and arsenal were idle. Yet in the eighteenth century the Republic accomplished her last splendid building, the Murazzi, or great marble walls, five thousand metres long, which strengthened the shifting Lidi and protected the harbour. Internal industries were stagnant, and agriculture seriously burdened, though the Venetian provinces were the most prosperous in Italy. Yet much private wealth remained in Venice, and no signs of exhaustion or poverty appeared in its life of luxury and display, its feasts and carnivals, its theatres, concerts, and balls. In Goldoni's work, reflecting the life of the middle and lower classes, the Venetian theatre now reached its highest development. Still, strangers from every part flocked to share the gaieties of Venice, its life of amenity and licence, where everyone might enjoy himself to the utmost, sure of excellent police and sanitation, while there was no government interference with those who did not disturb the peace or try to meddle in politics. Yet amongst the nobles there was much discontent, which occasionally broke out in open agitation. Many were impoverished by gambling and debauchery, and lived miserably upon government allowances. Interbreeding, limitation of families, strict entails, and the custom of younger sons taking Orders, had so diminished the nobility that during this century the members of the Grand Council decreased from fourteen to seven hundred. An attempt to infuse new blood by ennobling good provincial families failed, since few would pay the sum demanded for the honour.

Discontented and dissolute nobles complained of the strict rule of the Inquisitors of State, and thought that they would find independence and prosperity if the Inquisitors' authority were restored to the Grand Council which had delegated it. Another party, imbued with new

Liberal ideas, desired more liberty and disliked the secret methods of the Inquisitors; a Moderate group wished to limit their power without crippling it. The wisest understood that the tyranny of the Inquisitors alone protected the State and citizens from the licence of the worst nobles and of ruffians of all classes.

In 1761 a particularly high-handed action of the Inquisitors caused the Grand Council to appoint a committee of *Correttori* to consider some modifications in their power. The *Correttori* presented two reports, one far more stringent than the other. The populace, which appreciated the Inquisitors, was delighted when the Grand Council adopted the milder report. But the discontented faction of nobles was unsatisfied, and became so turbulent that an order was issued for the early closing of the *cafés* in which its revolutionary theories were discussed. This, however, had soon to be rescinded. In 1779, a new committee of *Correttori* was appointed; its most popular member, Giorgio Pisani, played the part of a demagogue, and even dared to appeal to the sentiment of the populace. This was going too far, and the Grand Council acquiesced in his arrest by the Inquisitors and long imprisonment. The *Correttori* continued their work, and carried several minor reforms, but no substantial change was made in the Inquisitors' position.

All through the century the physical weakness and the political and moral decadence of Venice continued; yet the changes which accompanied her decay were so gradual that they can only be estimated by their ultimate results. Venice really existed on her past reputation and on the mutual jealousies which withheld her powerful neighbours from attacking her; but the whole artificial fabric of her structure, since it had no innate strength to support it from within, collapsed before the first sharp blow from without.

Genoa, unlike Venice, had no social attractions, and her citizens lived simply and soberly. Many were very wealthy, for her geographical position and comparatively moderate tariff enabled Genoa to retain more of her ancient commercial prosperity than Venice. Some were officials in Rome, with large shares in the *Monti* (papal Government stock); some, as bankers, merchants and revenue officers, controlled nearly all the finance of Naples. A narrow oligarchy still ruled the State. Once it seemed as if the people, still strenuous and patriotic, would displace their feeble rulers, but after the crisis the keys of the city were restored to the Senate, merely with a warning to take better care of them in future. Probably the popular leaders knew that foreign Powers which allowed the Republic to exist under an unenterprising Government would never permit her to make an experiment in democracy.

Genoa, like Venice, preserved her autonomy only because of the mutual jealousies of the Great Powers on either flank; for she was even weaker than Venice, and her geographical position as a gate of Italy was almost equally valuable. She, too, preferred neutrality and obscurity, but she did not altogether escape political trouble and danger. These were partly caused by her ancient territorial rivalry with Savoy and her position on the Riviera, which cut off that acquisitive Power from coastward expansion, partly by her possession of Corsica, always rebellious, and growing important, now that England and France were competing for the control of the western Mediterranean.

But Genoa's difficulties were also due to her own unwisdom in buying Finale from the Emperor at the moment when Savoy was bidding for it (1714). Finale was not a commodious port and its inhabitants were troublesome, but Savoy never forgave the interference. In the Treaty of Worms, Charles Emmanuel III obtained the cession of all Imperial rights upon Finale, which really meant that he might either purchase or conquer it if he could. Any additional outlet to the sea was valuable to Piedmont; but this clause in the treaty was really a serious political mistake. It confirmed the belief of the Italian States in Sardinia's insatiable ambition, and it drove Genoa to side with Sardinia's enemies. In 1745 she concluded the League of Aranjuez with France and Spain, who recklessly promised her all that she claimed from Sardinia, whether rightfully or no. Henceforward, the Bourbon armies were reinforced by Genoese troops, while a new route was opened for France into Italy, and another by which Maillebois' army could cooperate with the Spaniards under Gages. Thus they were able to conquer the south-west portion of Piedmont and besiege Alessandria, while Don Philip successfully invaded Lombardy and established himself at Parma and Milan. However, clever diplomacy and generalship extricated Sardinia from her critical position, and in 1746 Genoa, abandoned by both allies, was defenceless before Charles Emmanuel and the Austrian General, Botta Adorno, whose father, a Genoese, had been executed by the Republic. The feeble Senate submitted to Adorno without attempting resistance, surrendered the city gates, lodged his troops, and paid him huge sums of money. Meanwhile Charles Emmanuel occupied many Ri[v]ieran towns, including the coveted Finale. But Adorno was more concerned to extract money than to consolidate his military position; and in December the Genoese populace rose, seized arms from the Arsenal, and, without any assistance from their Government, drove the Austrians from the city. The neighbouring peasantry joined to complete the rout, and Genoa regained her independence.

Austria was eager to recover its prey, and Sardinia would not easily surrender its conquests. In 1747 they concluded a " treaty of Genoese Partition," and, helped by an English fleet, again attacked the town; but this time Genoa resisted bravely, and French ships contrived to bring help. A new Franco-Spanish invasion drove Charles Emmanuel to defend his own borders, and the siege was raised. The Peace of Aix-la-Chapelle (1748) ignored Charles Emmanuel's Rivieran ambitions.

and his subsequent efforts to obtain compensation there for Piacenza proved unsuccessful. But Genoa had demonstrated a vitality and a power to defend herself, hitherto unsuspected.

For a century and a half, Corsica had been nominally submissive, but not really tranquil. Genoa never learned wisdom by experience; the aim of her Government seemed to be to extort large taxes and provide offices for needy Genoese. The Corsicans were debarred from lucrative offices and professions; order was not enforced; the country districts were half savage and, since licenses to carry arms were cheap, were ravaged by interminable vendettas. In a population of two hundred thousand, there were nearly a thousand murders annually.

Famine and additional taxation caused a fresh revolt in 1729. The Corsicans mastered all but a few coast towns, proclaimed their independence, and created governors and a General Assembly. At Genoa's request, Austria sent troops, which obtained a temporary submission; but Genoa violated the conditions of peace, and the revolt broke out again. Internal dissensions and the difficulty of obtaining provisions and munitions caused the Corsicans to seek external aid; and in 1736 they elected Baron Theodore von Neuhof, a rich Westphalian adventurer, as King under constitutional limitations. It was a rather farcical sovereignty; and Theodore, though well intentioned, found the situation impossible. He spent his time and energies in travelling to Holland to procure food and war material for his straitened kingdom. He was finally frightened off by a French army which, at Genoa's appeal, succeeded in obtaining the partial submission of the Corsicans (1739). France had begun to realise the importance of Corsica in the Mediterranean, and, though not yet prepared to seize it herself, meant to acquire sufficient influence there to smooth the way for future annexation.

During the War of the Austrian Succession, English ships landed Rivarolo, a Corsican refugee, on the island, and the rebellion broke out afresh. England, Sardinia and Austria issued proclamations in favour of Corsican independence, and numerous foreign troops appeared on the island, but were withdrawn after the Treaty of Aix. In 1755, the Corsicans chose as their General Pasquale de' Paoli, the son of Giacinto, a former leader who had voluntarily retired to facilitate the settlement of 1739. A Constitution, extraordinarily modern for the eighteenth century, was drawn up; it established a really popular Government, and was loyally carried out by Paoli, who was President with large, but constitutional, powers. Order and justice were restored, assassinations became rare, taxation was low, material prosperity increased, the people were educated and civilised. Paoli corresponded with England, where his constitutional government was admired; but France was now determined to obtain Corsica in order to counterbalance the Mediterranean possessions of England. First, she obtained Genoa's permission for a military occupation, and then (1768) she bought the island outright. England was occupied with her American troubles; Sardinia dared not defy France; and Corsica only received irregular help in her last gallant struggle for liberty. The Corsicans fought furiously; Paoli showed brilliant generalship, and the French were defeated frequently; but ultimately their military superiority overwhelmed the scanty resources of the islanders. Assisted by some treacherous Corsicans, they at last utterly defeated Paoli at Pontenuovo (May, 1769). Rather than involve the people in useless sufferings, he and other leaders quitted the island, and the French were soon in complete possession. After a period of severity, they instituted a moderate government, which made the Corsicans fairly contented and prosperous. Paoli settled in England with a government pension; he became an honoured member of Samuel Johnson's circle, and lived peacefully, except when the French Revolution unfortunately tempted him back to Corsica (1790). He was received with enthusiasm and made President of the Department, but soon learned that the principles of Liberty were not to be extended to the subject province. Before long the Republic proclaimed him a traitor; and in 1794 he ceded the island to England, which held it for two years. Paoli died in England in 1807. One of the few heroic and romantic figures of the eighteenth century, he might, under more favourable circumstances, have been the Washington of Corsica. His period of rule, with its loyal effort after constitutional government and devoted patriotism, provokes more sympathy than any other episode in contemporary Italian history.

CHAPTER XVII.

SWITZERLAND FROM THE TREATY OF AARAU TO THE FRENCH REVOLUTION.

For two centuries Switzerland had ceased to play any part as a Great Power—since 1515, when in the battle of Marignano the Swiss had after their famous Italian campaigns been defeated by France with the help of Venice and forced to withdraw from Lombardy. Peace was made with France in 1516; and in 1521 an alliance followed which for Switzerland was to be the beginning of centuries of subjection, and which once more hired out the prowess and fame of her soldiers for the pay of foreign Powers. It was this French alliance and the foreign service of her sons which chiefly occupied Switzerland in her external relations during the eighteenth century, together with the maintenance of her neutrality and independence throughout the numerous great wars of that period. On the time of her greatest military glory there followed immediately the beginning of the Reformation, which occasioned two centuries of religious strife in Switzerland. But the wars of religion, as is shown below, came to a termination with the Treaty of Aarau (1712). The cleavage between Catholics and Protestants, indeed, continued for some decades, until the new compact with France in 1777; but it had changed in character and become purely a question of the balance of political power between the two sides. With the opening of the eighteenth century the period of religious wars had ended in Switzerland as in the rest of the Christian world. In their place class wars became more and more prominent until the outbreak of the great Revolution, which had been advancing on parallel lines with the general intellectual awakening (*Aufklärung*). Such are the characteristic notes of Swiss history in the eighteenth century: during which the French alliance, foreign military service, neutrality, the class wars, and the intellectual awakening, alike leave their impress upon the national life.

The alliance with France was for Switzerland the most important affair of the century before the great Revolution, and occupied those concerned during the greater part of the period in question. The preceding treaties with France, by which Switzerland entered into relations as an independent Power with a foreign State not included in the German Empire, were the result of the military prowess exhibited by the Swiss on an occasion of very ancient date in their history—the battle of St Jacob on the Birs in 1444. At the commencement of the connexion, however, in the course of the fifteenth century, the Swiss did not serve the purposes of France exclusively, but still pursued ends of their own. When, after Marignano, the Swiss again made peace with France, the French alliance of May 5, 1521, marks a complete change in Swiss policy. Switzerland had ceased to occupy a place among the Great Powers, and had fallen to the position of a recruiting-ground for French mercenaries. This state of things had been brought about by the propensity of the Swiss for foreign service, and by a greed of yearly subsidies to which their soldiers and statesmen alike had been accustomed by France. Under this curse they remained until the absolute upheaval of all ways of thought and political action in the great Revolution. After taking part in the numerous wars of France with Charles V (1521–44), the Swiss, themselves divided into two camps by the Reformation, were fighting against each other in the French religious wars (1562–90) both for the League and the Huguenots. But Henry IV, after putting an end to the French religious struggle, in 1602 further succeeded in once more uniting the Swiss of both confessions in a common alliance with France. This union, concluded for the lifetime of the King and of his son Louis XIII and for eight years after, endured until 1651. In 1663 was effected another alliance, the last before the period covered by the present volume; and it is with the renewal of this that we are now particularly concerned.

The reasons which once more brought about a general alliance with Switzerland differed to some extent from those of 1521. France had for some time past provoked bitter complaints from Switzerland, partly by employing, in violation of the agreement between them, Swiss troops for attacks on foreign countries, and partly by delaying payment of the yearly subsidy to the Governments and even the soldiers' pay. Moreover, the Treaty of Westphalia had by its recognition of Switzerland as a sovereign Power awakened a feeling of independence in the Swiss Governments which asserted itself as against France. It was, therefore, unanimously resolved by the Diet, in 1651 and 1652, that there should be no renewal of the alliance till these grievances had been redressed. In 1653 Solothurn was, nevertheless, persuaded to promise a renewal of the alliance with France; in 1654 Luzern followed suit, and in 1655 the remaining Catholic cantons. The Catholic districts, lacking both money and ways of earning it, were moved by the old passion for foreign service and its gains. Hereupon the Protestant cantons also turned back to France, but on political grounds—to avert the dangers of a one-sided combination between the Catholic cantons and France—the more readily as in the Third Religious War (1656), sometimes called the War of Rapperswyl or the First Vilmergen War, they had been overcome by the Catholic cantons unaided, and had no other ally of equal standing in view. Thus a new general alliance with France was concluded on September 24, 1663.

This alliance, like that of 1602, was concluded not only for the life of the reigning monarch (Louis XIV) but also for that of his son and for eight years after. But, before the King felt his end near, no member of his family remained to succeed him but his infant great-grandson, afterwards Louis XV. In order, therefore, that affairs might be left on a satisfactory footing for the King's successor, negotiations were opened in 1713 for a renewal of the alliance with the Swiss. In the meantime, however, the situation had changed in such a way that the Catholic cantons were quite ready for a renewal of the league, but not so the Protestant, notably Zurich and Bern. In the previous year, 1712, the Fourth and last Religious War in Switzerland had been waged, terminating in the Treaty of Aarau (August 11, 1712) between Zurich and Bern and the five Catholic cantons of Luzern, Uri, Schwyz, Unterwalden, and Zug. In this War, the Second Vilmergen War (which, like its predecessor in 1656, arose out of the dispute as to the relations of the county and abbacy of Toggenburg to the Empire), the wheel of fortune spun round: the Five Cantons were defeated by Zurich and Bern and were routed a second time by Bern alone ; and the supremacy of the victorious cantons was established in the Treaty of Aarau. Apart from other arrangements, the "free bailiwicks" (*freie Aemter*) of Aargau were ceded to Bern and Zurich, in order to secure the connexion between their territories, while the Catholic cantons were, with the exception of a small remainder, excluded from the resettlement. Bern was further admitted to a share in the control of the common prefectures (*Vogteien*) of Aargau and Thurgau, in order to establish the preponderance of the Protestants as governing cantons. Such treatment was unbearable to the Catholics, not so much on religious grounds as in view of the political disadvantage involved and, last but not least, because the lucrative sway over the "free bailiwicks" thus slipped from their hold. They therefore set to work again on their little separate leagues, but all to little avail. Then came the offer from France for the renewal of her alliance, very opportunely for the Catholic cantons if it could be renewed with them alone, so that they could obtain the powerful aid of France against their Protestant rivals. The French Court would really have preferred a general alliance which should also include the Protestants ; but the Protestants did not desire it, and the French ambassador in Switzerland, Du Luc, who regarded Zurich and Bern with detestation because of their obstinacy and arrogance, pushed the interests of the Catholic cantons, giving his Court to understand that the Protestants would soon join. But their hatred of France had increased since 1663, and now

CH. XVII.

they had in view a substitute for the French alliance. To the list of hardships inflicted by France were now added the curtailment of the privileges granted to the Swiss in France by earlier treaties, and the check imposed upon commerce; and, above all, the Protestants of Switzerland, as of every other country, were exasperated by the Revocation of the Edict of Nantes (1685). On the other hand, Bern had concluded a treaty of alliance with the States General in 1712; the Grisons had done the same in 1713; with England, too, the Protestant cantons were on a friendly footing; and there was even some talk of the Maritime Powers taking up again Cromwell's idea of uniting in one great Protestant league all the Protestant countries and communities of Europe. This made it all the easier for the Swiss Protestant cantons to give play to their natural dislike of France and refuse to league themselves with her. Thus the alliance which she desired was concluded with the Catholic cantons only, precisely as they had intended, but not without their having to submit to her supremacy. The fifth clause of the treaty concluded on May 5, 1715, contains a stipulation that in the event of disputes arising among the Catholics or between them and the Protestants, the King of France shall mediate, and eventually have the right of enforcing his will—much as in the later days of the Act of Mediation. There was, besides, a secret article or bond, the *Trücklibund*—a name given to it because it was enclosed in a tin capsule—and in course of time applied to the whole treaty. In this bond the King promised the restoration of Catholicism, that is to say, the restoration to the Catholic cantons of their recently forfeited prerogatives—the control of the free bailiwicks and their ascendancy over the Protestant cantons—in a word, the much-vext "Restitution"; the admission of Zurich and Bern to the alliance being made conditional on their consent to it. The whole ignominious treaty was kept secret, not only from the Protestants but even from the popular assemblies (*Landsgemeinden*) of the Catholic cantons. The supplementary agreement was concluded by the French ambassador absolutely without the King's knowledge, because in default of it no alliance at all might have been brought about with the Catholics.

Up to the time of the alliance between the Catholic cantons and France there had still been no settlement effected between the victorious Protestant cantons and the Abbot of St Gallen as to the Toggenburg, which was situate in his dominions. This was due to the fact that the Emperor took the part of the Abbot and the Catholics. The dangers generally besetting the Protestants had been greatly augmented by the Treaties of Rastatt and Baden (in Aargau) in 1714 between the Catholicising Louis XIV and the Catholic Emperor. In the case of this particular dispute of the Protestants with the Abbot, the Imperial Diet wished to intervene in favour of the Abbot as a Prince of the Empire— a proceeding contrary to Article VI of the Treaty of Westphalia. When the Catholics formed the alliance with France, however, the Emperor lost patience and ordered the Abbot to come to terms with Zurich and Bern; and after the death of that headstrong personage, a peace was finally concluded on the Toggenburg question (June 15, 1718).

On September 1 of the year 1715, in which he had concluded the alliance with the Catholic cantons, Louis XIV died. Two months previously Du Luc had been sent as ambassador to Vienna. But the policy of France was still to win over the Protestant cantons to the alliance. It was of great importance that a general alliance with the Swiss should be effected, not only in order to make the fullest use possible of them in the interests of France, but also to draw them away from the side of her opponents, the Emperor and the Maritime Powers. This was the great end pursued by all the succeeding French ambassadors to Switzerland; and, numerous as they were and various as were the principles advanced by them, not one of them attained this object until the occurrence of an event of European importance, the First Partition of Poland. This so terrified the Swiss that they yielded and sought protection from a like fate in a general alliance with France. Before this, on the occasion of the expiration, in 1723, of the Treaty of alliance of 1663, Basel opened negotiations on her own account, in order to propitiate France and the Catholic cantons, whom she had alike offended by favouring the enterprise of General Mercy in 1709. Further attempts were made in 1738, and in 1756, when Kaunitz, at that time ambassador in Paris, had effected an alliance between Austria and France against Frederick the Great, which increased the dangers threatening the Protestant cantons, while it furnished the five Catholic cantons with fresh hopes of restitution and led to a renewal of the " Borromean " League of the year 1586. Chavigny seized this moment to treat with the Zurich Burgomaster Heidegger; but the negotiations again fell through. In 1759 Zurich rejected an offer on the subject made by Roll, the *Schultheiss* of Solothurn. The last fruitless effort was made in 1762, after which there was for ten years no thought of renewing the French alliance. As one attempt succeeded another, the most various political principles were followed. The experience of 1663 seemed to teach that the Catholics could be won over by pecuniary considerations, and that the Protestants would follow of themselves for fear of being left to stand alone. So Du Luc (who was ambassador from 1708 to 1715) concluded; but his expectations were in part defeated because the Protestants had meanwhile gained the support of the Maritime Powers. Bonnac (ambassador from 1727 to 1737) had to try another expedient, namely that of winning over the smaller strongholds of the Reformed faith and abandoning Zurich and Bern; but this measure was prevented by the strong influence wielded by the two leading cantons over the rest. Bonnac expressed the opinion, in a memorandum to his Court in 1733, that the general alliance, useful as it would be, was not essential; a perpetual peace might be made to serve instead, as it had ten years before. But, for the next few years, during which France was involved in continual wars with Austria and Prussia—the Polish and Austrian Wars of Succession and the Silesian Wars—she required not only peace with Switzerland but direct assistance from her, which nothing short of an alliance could ensure, so that Bonnac's counsels of renunciation seemed merely a case of sour grapes. Mariane, chargé d'affaires, took a quite different line; he concentrated his efforts upon the two chief cantons, whose lead the lesser Protestant cantons always followed. But no plan was of any avail; each attempt broke down over the question of the Restitution, upon which France invariably insisted, and which Zurich and Bern would not accept at any price. Bonnac had, it is true, cancelled one part of the stipulation: Bremgarten and Mellingen were to be exempt from the Restitution so as to secure the territorial connexion between Zurich and Bern; but Heidegger would not even accede to this proposal. There was, however, nothing to prevent the Protestant districts from concluding with France an agreement as to the engagement of soldiers (*Militärkapitulation*), which they did on May 8, 1764.

With the year 1772 came the First Partition of Poland between Austria, Prussia, and Russia, which terrified the Swiss all the more, because at the time the conduct of the Emperor Joseph II had roused their mistrust, while it made the Protestants doubtful of Prussia also, whose King had hitherto been a good friend to them. Leopold I (1705) had revived the old Austrian designs on Switzerland; Joseph II followed in his steps and proved a dangerous neighbour to the Swiss; and there was a rumour that Austria and France had already planned a partition of Switzerland like that of Poland. The whole affair of the alliance of the two Powers, secured by Kaunitz' treaty and cemented by the marriage of Marie-Antoinette with the future King Louis XVI (1770), looked suspicious; and the Chancellor's journey through Switzerland in 1777, shortly before the conclusion of the French alliance with the Swiss, gave fresh cause for anxiety. The feeling aroused in Switzerland by the Partition of Poland was immediately turned to account by France; and in that very year she made fresh attempts to obtain a renewal of the alliance. Not till after the death of Louis XV, on May 10, 1774, and the accession of Louis XVI, who as a man of upright character dealt honestly with the Protestants, would they consent to come to terms. In 1776, for the first time for 113 years, a conference of all the cantons was held to consider an alliance with France, which led to the "Treaty of alliance between the Crown of France and the States of all Switzerland," concluded on May 28, 1777. The Protestants secured, first and foremost, that there should be no question of restitution, and, secondly, though the *Trücklibund* was not formally annulled, a clear statement in the preamble that by the Treaty all the States of the Confederation were united in one and the same alliance with France. The part of mediator, so humiliating to the Swiss, which had been assigned to France in the *Trücklibund*, she now abandoned; in return, it was agreed that the privileges of the Swiss in France, which were very unpopular there, should be considered in detail with a view to their revision or removal. For the rest, a perpetual peace was stipulated for, as in the alliance of 1663, and laid down as a treaty obligation. France had the right, in case of need, of raising any number of recruits not exceeding 6000 in Switzerland, beyond the number of Swiss soldiers agreed upon by capitulation. Neither country was to allow enemies of the other to pass through or to remain in her territory. Swiss neutrality must at all costs be maintained, as towards every Power. Geneva and Neuchâtel, despite the wishes of Switzerland, were not admitted as parties to this treaty—the former on account of the revolutionary tendency of Geneva politics even before the French Revolution, the latter as being a dependency of the King of Prussia.

Instead of France acting as mediator in the interest of the internal security of Switzerland, this was to be ensured by an agreement between the cantons themselves with regard to matters coming under the cognisance of the Federal law, the procedure in the event of disputes between Estates or relating to jurisdictions held in common, the preservation of security at home, and the administration of the Federal law. For this purpose, at the general meeting of the Diet in 1776 a so-called "Plan of Protection" (*Tuitionsplan*) for the French alliance was drafted, but in the end abandoned. Neither was anything gained by subsequent negotiations with France in regard to the question of privileges; so that Switzerland left off treating with her on the subject.

The alliance of 1777 was concluded for fifty years; in 1798, after the great Revolution, when the Helvetic Republic was set up and Switzerland came under the yoke of France, its place was taken, in widely different circumstances, by a fresh compact, likewise termed a treaty of alliance.

Foreign military service on the part of the Swiss dates from the beginning of the fourteenth century, that is to say, from the early days of the Swiss Confederation. Soldiers who travelled about from one foreign war to another were called *Reisläufer* (travellers). So early as 1319, soon after the battle of Morgarten, which laid the foundation of Swiss military glory, warlike men marched from the three original cantons of Switzerland to join in the battles of the valiant House of Visconti, which had risen to the mastery of Milan. In 1373 no less than 3000 Swiss entered the service of another Visconti of Milan. The military renown of the Swiss grew and increased, notably through the battles of Sempach and Näfels, the last great fights for liberty, in which they broke away from Austria and raised themselves to the rank of an independent Power on a footing of equality with Austria and other States. So much the more the soldiers of Switzerland were sought after by foreign rulers and took service under them. This increase of mercenary service gave rise to two evils which in time became disastrous—the fact that the Swiss occasionally found themselves fighting on opposite sides; and the system of yearly subsidies (*Pensionenwesen,* as it was later termed). The former result became increasingly difficult to avoid, as the military service of the Swiss grew and spread on all sides and their soldiers were in constant demand; so that influential intermediaries were continually being called in, to obtain satisfactory conditions or to outbid rival claimants. Still, it was a long time before the Swiss cantons took upon themselves this office of go-between. When Louis XI first drew them away from Germany to France and involved them in wider political issues, he turned their steps in this direction, in order that he might gain military rights over Switzerland. This came about by the Treaty of 1474, which affords the first example of a military capitulation; it was called an alliance, though, so far as the obligations on the Swiss were concerned, it was nothing more than a military capitulation binding them to furnish 6000 men—just as subsequent military capitulations were called alliances or unions down to that between Switzerland and France in 1764, which, for the first time so far as we are aware, is called a military capitulation. The Treaty of 1474 was followed by military capitulations of the cantons with various other Powers, often hostile to each other. Besides this foreign service regulated by treaty, there continued in practice that of the private mercenary, who fought for countries with which there was as yet no capitulation, so long as he could get his pay or more especially get higher pay than those in treaty service. The numbers of Swiss on foreign service accordingly became excessive; with their numbers the evils increased which are inseparable from any such relation, especially when complicated by the coexistence of different and mutually contrasting kinds of service. Besides the treaty troops there came to be irregular companies recruited without authorisation, not to mention the many who enlisted independently and were simply enrolled among the national troops of the foreign State. Among these last there were even vaga-bonds who had provided themselves with a uniform and a Swiss name. Thus, by the side of treaty service, *Reislaufen* developed into individual enlistment; and the entire practice, under the name of foreign service, contributed to drain Switzerland for wars in which the country had no concern. In the French wars against the Empire the Swiss were "Frenchmen" or "Imperialists"; in the French Religious Wars they were "Leaguers" or "Huguenots," and so forth; and thus it came to their having to fight against each other and to shed each other's blood. On the other hand, in addition to the yearly subventions payable by virtue of the capitulations to the canton, its Government, or the people, there was a continuous and increasing stream of payments and gratuities or every description on account of free companies and other levies. As the military capitulations succeeded one another, it was easy to include in their terms such unlawful payments, according as this or that party became predominant in the canton; while other receipts might in their turn be declared illicit, supposing it were desired to retain them in practice while abandoning them as obligatory by treaty.

But, the more general the prevalence of foreign military service, the more patent were its disadvantages: the country was sapped of its economic strength, especially of the labour required for agriculture; its youth were running wild; while avarice, idleness, luxury and self-indulgence grew, until finally the whole nation was possessed by an unhealthy spirit of discontent and demoralisation. The Diet had opposed foreign service so soon as it began to assume serious dimensions —even as early as 1460, when it was exclusively the affair of private individuals, and when capitulations were as yet unheard of; and measures were set on foot against general enlisting abroad. Subsequent decrees of the Diet on the subject, after military capitulations had become customary, were directed against "wild," *i.e.* promiscuous, foreign service, and "wild" pensions not authorised by capitulations. This form of foreign service and pensions had to be withstood, not only because it seemed unlawful, but because it was altogether without limit or restriction, and therefore all the more dangerous. The capitulations had at least introduced some law and order into foreign service; troops so engaged were put under special officers and special jurisdiction; they might not be broken up and sent on any service whatever, neither could they be sent oversea, nor employed for attack on other countries; and the agreements contained definite provisions as to the rates and recipients of the subsidies, which could be controlled accordingly. The Free Companies, on the contrary, were mustered and employed as the supreme authority thought fit; they must be ready to serve anywhere, for that was the purpose indicated by their name; it was naturally still easier to dispose as might seem best of the individual recruits. The "wild" pensions were infecting the whole country like a slow poison, perceptible only in its effects and perhaps not even then, since intrigues and opposition arose which proved unexpectedly traceable to the same hidden agency. The excrescences of foreign service at least were attacked in later decrees of the Diet, and when these had been removed there was less of foreign service and its evils. Such was notably the subject and spirit of the decrees of the Diet enacted after the Burgundian Wars and during the Italian campaigns, of which those of July 18, 1495, and July 23, 1503, are typical and on that account famous. This tendency can be traced further in the action of Zwingli, whose reforms bore not only upon religion, but first and foremost upon the question of foreign service; not till he had reformed this did he set about a reformation of the faith. His attack was, however, directed not only against promiscuous foreign service, but against the whole system of mercenary service and of subventions, even as settled by treaty; and, following his lead, those cantons which had adopted the Reformed faith abstained from such agreements, notably Zurich, also Bern, etc.; but the rest soon fell back

CH. XVII.

into their old ways. Nothing, not even the decrees of the Diet, was of permanent avail in the face of the universal, deep-seated system of self-subjection to the foreigner which had taken root in Switzerland and thriven on the glory of the Burgundian victories and the still greater renown of the Milanese campaigns. *Reislaufen* and illicit subsidies could not be abandoned for any length of time, because they were part and parcel of the whole system of foreign service and pensions, legalised or otherwise. If the one were permitted, how could the other be criminal? So these abuses sprang up again and flourished, until by the eighteenth century almost all foreign service was undertaken by capitulation. All interest, too, in foreign service culminated in the question of money. Originally, even the *Reislaufen* of individuals had been prompted by other interests, by skill and delight in warfare, although from the first money played an important part, as it was the poorer and remoter and the highland cantons which had mostly furnished the mercenaries. The wealthy Protestant towns might well preach against foreign service; but even they could never quite put a stop to it. The capitulations too were for some time largely directed by political interests, according to the existing bias in favour of one or the other of the belligerent foreign Powers: the Swiss came to terms with France and not with Burgundy against whom they wished to make war, although Burgundy was wealthier and able to pay a higher price. The cantons allied themselves with France or with the Empire according to their sympathies; and, in the French Religious Wars, with the Guises or the Huguenots according to the form of their faith. Thus, until the eighteenth century it was a question more or less of political considerations; but thenceforth military treaties were simply business transactions settled according to the price offered. So soon as the money interest was predominant and came to turn the scale in the conclusion of capitulations, fraud and corruption were the order of the day in carrying them out; promotion was for sale, the strength of the companies was overstated in order to pocket more pay, and so on. Before the eighteenth century foreign service had undergone another change in common with the general military system. After the Treaty of Westphalia absolutism developed, and with it came the establishment of standing armies. Hitherto, regiments had been drawn up and disbanded according to the contingencies of foreign war or of a period of war: those were the days of hired foot-soldiers (*Landsknechte*). Absolutism on the other hand required, to maintain its internal integrity and external independence, perpetually mobilised troops, like those of a standing army. Thus foreign service became constant. So early as 1497 the first standing Swiss guard of 100 men was formed; but this was simply a body-guard for the King, such as had been customary from ancient times: the other Swiss regiments were disbanded as occasion demanded. From the reign of Louis XIV onwards, however, these regiments, too, were permanent, although particular corps were occasionally discharged; and finally, the

Swiss Guard was merely the *élite* of the standing Swiss regiments. It ended gloriously (August 10, 1792) as a last witness to ancient Swiss loyalty and valour. The Swiss regiments of other monarchs thus also became standing armies.

Such is the note of Swiss foreign service in the eighteenth century: its conditions entirely regulated by capitulation, a business transaction pure and simple between rulers and ruled, and essentially a standing service. Still, it was France which, after having first introduced the Swiss to official foreign service, was chiefly instrumental in keeping them to it. The system had thus reached its zenith, and the returns for foreign regiments and annual subsidies their highest point: in 1748, 60,000 Swiss are stated to have been in the service of foreign Powers, and for 1761 and 1762 the expenditure of the French Government on subventions and bribes is given at 1,400,000 *livres* (= £55,416. 13*s.* 4*d.*). According to Waser, between 1474 and 1715 the Swiss sacrificed 700,000 men to France, receiving in return 1146 million *gulden* (= £95,500,000) in pay and pensions.

From a political point of view there can be but one verdict as to the system of which Swiss history offers so conspicuous an example—wholehearted condemnation. Even private military service cannot be approved; for all military service is the service of the State, and as such properly given only by the subjects of the country to which it is rendered. But in regard to capitulations the case is self-evident: they degrade an entire State to the position of a hireling soldier of another, and simply show that it has no work worth doing to offer its citizens and is incapable of making them fight its own battles. As Rudolf Reding, *Landammann* of Schwyz, said in the Diet of 1492, "a Swiss ought to have a hole" (*i.e.* way out); but it was for Switzerland herself to lead forth her sons in her own interests. Neither is the argument admissible that foreign service contributed to the safety of Switzerland; she would have been safe, and more than safe, had she known how to keep her sons together and turn their energies to her own account.

There was no reason why neutrality, after it had once been adopted by Switzerland, should not have been combined with foreign service—as the term neutrality was understood in those days. Swiss neutrality dates from the abandonment of independent warfare after the battle of Marignano, the effects of which were enhanced by the further defeats at Bicocca and Pavia, sustained shortly afterwards in the service of France. This occasion determined the character of the neutrality observed from that time: it simply involved abstention on the part of Switzerland from wars in her own right; but the Swiss forces were not required to desist from fighting in foreign services. There was consequently a continuance of capitulations and of *Reislaufen* according to a man's own choice; which latter was indeed forbidden, though not out of consideration for other States but as prejudicial to the nation itself. The capitulations, express agreements for assistance in foreign wars, increased to the exclusion of all other forms of foreign service. Switzerland held aloof from wars in her own right, although she defended herself from harm by means of foreign armies. Such was the character of Swiss neutrality from its origin throughout the early history of Switzerland. No other form of neutrality was required from her by the other Powers, all of which had their part in the Swiss capitulations and were only concerned to see that no exceptions were made in favour of their opponents. Although Switzerland took no part by means of armies of her own in the Thirty Years' War, this was not because such an abstention was required by the terms of her neutrality, but for reasons of policy (suggested by France, that is to say, Richelieu), inasmuch as her own neutrality and territorial immunity would otherwise have been risked, and there would have been danger of her own soil becoming the seat of war. Until the Treaty of Westphalia, moreover, it was even held to be compatible with the neutrality of Switzerland that she should allow friendly Powers to march through her territory for purposes of war, as was chiefly done in the case of French troops. Subsequently, however, after Gustavus Adolphus had nearly made war upon the Catholic cantons because they had granted a passage to Spanish troops, the interpretation of the term neutrality was altered, and Switzerland closed her territory to the passage of foreign armies. Foreign service, on the other hand, was still looked upon as permissible until last century, when it was in its turn forbidden as a breach of neutrality, which term now excludes all support, direct or indirect, of the military operations of a belligerent.

In its numerous wars of the eighteenth century in particular, an important part is played by the foreign service and neutrality of Switzerland; and on both heads important negotiations and transactions result from abuses and breaches, claims and questions. There were the three Wars of Succession—the Spanish, the Polish and the Austrian War (ending with the Treaty of Aix-la-Chapelle), and, following close on the last two, came the three Silesian Wars, including as the Third the Seven Years' War; so that throughout the whole century one war followed as it were on the heels of another, until the great Revolution broke out and along with it a general war of the nations. In the Wars of Succession it was chiefly France and Austria which were opposed to each other, with their respective allies, Spain, Sardinia, and the States General; in the Seven Years' War it was Austria, France, and the rest, against Prussia. Switzerland was constantly taking part on both sides by virtue of her foreign service—the Catholic cantons for the French, and the Protestant, notably Zurich and Bern, for the Emperor and the States General. Austria demanded, not only that the French regiments of Swiss should confine themselves to the defence of France, but that Switzerland should, in conformity with the standing agreement of 1511, herself undertake the defence of the Austrian territory indicated in its provisions;

but France merely conceded that her Swiss regiments should not be used against such territory, while constantly employing them to attack her enemies, and even sending regiments from the Protestant cantons as the case might be against the Emperor or Prussia. Questions incessantly arose in regard to the neutrality of Switzerland, to the protection of that country from molestation by the belligerents, whether in the north, on the Rhine, or in the War of the Spanish Succession in the south also, as against Sardinia; and Switzerland claimed neutrality not only for her own territory but also for the Austrian Forest Cantons and more remote territories and districts in the north and for Savoy in the south, inasmuch as the "security" of these neighbouring regions contributed to assure her own safety. The question of declaring Savoy neutral dates therefore from this time (actually from 1690). The cession of the Austrian Forest Cantons to Switzerland came frequently under discussion; Bern on one occasion (1734) treated with Austria on the subject; but no settlement was reached in either direction. Such were the main points on which the negotiations and transactions during these wars depended. In particular, the following instances may be cited. In the War of the Spanish Succession the neutrality of Switzerland was twice infringed: once, in 1702, by the French, when, in order to secure a passage over the Rhine, they occupied the Schusterinsel, including the part of it belonging to Basel; and, again, in 1709, by the Austrian General Mercy, who descended upon Alsace by way of Basel territory. In the latter case France and the Catholic cantons, already specially attached to her, were stirred against Basel for permitting the passage, and Basel thereupon strove to recover the goodwill of both by her intervention in favour of the French alliance. In the subsequent wars there were complaints in particular of abuses in the employment of Swiss regiments in the French service—by their being employed for purposes of attack, in the Wars of the Polish and Austrian Successions against Austria, and in the Seven Years' War against Prussia. In the latter instance, complaints were made not only by the enemy but by the Swiss themselves, *i.e.* by the Protestant cantons, which, in spite of having hitherto refused the alliance with France, nevertheless had soldiery in her service; but then Frederick II was regarded by them as the hero of the century and the inventor of a new art of war—especially by the Bernese, who had been among his godfathers. In 1774, another abuse was committed on the part of France—by her sending Swiss regiments oversea to Corsica to put down the struggle of the islanders for liberty; and this eventually led to the conclusion of the general alliance with France in 1777.

With the eighteenth century begins in Switzerland, as elsewhere, that long succession of conflicts between class and class which continued throughout the century until their culmination in the French Revolution, that historic class struggle. The way for this was prepared by a general

CH. XVII.

intellectual movement, the *Aufklärung* as it was termed, which made
its appearance in Switzerland also in the second half of the century.
The class conflicts were the result of the development of oligarchies, a
reaction against the suppression of the privileges acquired by particular
classes and families. This growth of oligarchies began with the Reformation, inasmuch as, in the first instance, public authority was concentrated
in the hands of the State at the expense of the Church, which was set aside,
and, again, as the tendency of the times was in the direction of absolutism
which the Reformation had thus far helped to foster. Switzerland was
specially exposed to this tendency, as being closely connected with other
countries by means of her foreign service, especially with France, whose
King Louis XIV had brought absolutism to its highest pitch. It was
through foreign service that the Swiss of higher rank, the sons of the
ruling families, came into touch with the life of foreign Courts, where
they learnt court ways, and that money and affluence came into the
influential circles in the various districts, bringing with them an arrogant
and exclusive tone. In this sense foreign service also had a bearing upon
the class conflicts. The development of oligarchical rule, which grew and
throve in a soil thus prepared for it, was carried out in concentric circles.
First came the suppression of the rights of dependencies—of the subject
territories and common prefectures (*Vogteien*)—and the concentration of
all rights and powers in the hands of the towns or governing cantons;
next, within that town or canton, followed the ruling out from among
the burghers of outsiders (*Hintersassen*) or resident aliens (*Beisassen*);
and their exclusion from any share in the government. Finally, individual families from among the burghers set themselves over the rest;
and thus begins the supremacy of certain families or the patriciate. In
Bern the patriciate had been handed down from early times in the shape
of government by the nobility; but in the other towns and cantons it
only grew up in the last period of old Switzerland; in any case, it had
reached its full development at the beginning of the eighteenth century,
so that this century stands out above its predecessor as the period of
the all-prevalent patriciate. In Freiburg only a legalised patriciate
existed, inasmuch as the group of families in power was defined by
a formal ordinance, whereas in other places it had arisen simply by
usurpation on the one side and voluntary submission on the other.
The entire development of oligarchical rule, from the suppression of the
rights of dependencies down to the establishment of the patriciate, was
effected, where the requisite preliminary conditions were in existence, in
three concentric circles, although these circles partly intersect in this way:
that a further concentration of authority begins before the last has been
quite completed. Thus, and to this extent, the dependencies, the outsiders
or resident aliens in the towns, and the citizens themselves, were in
succession suppressed, and it was the revolt of one or other of these
bodies or groups which constituted the class wars. There was an

impressive prelude to these struggles in the Swiss Peasants' War of 1653, when the districts round the towns of Luzern, Basel, Solothurn, and Bern rose in concert; but the defeat of the peasants was so complete that no further attempt was made until in the next century movements took place, independent but universal, now here and now there, incessant and constantly renewed. First of all in 1713, a year after the Second Vilmergen War and caused by it, came the rising of the burghers of the town of Zurich against the patriciate; then, from 1717 to 1729, the revolt at Wilchingen in the canton of Schaffhausen; 1719–32, the rising in Werdenberg, a dependency of Glarus; 1723, the attempt on the part of Davel to snatch Vaud from Bern; 1728–35, the struggle between the families of Schumacher and Zurlauben in Zug; 1732–5, that between the Wetters and Zellwegers in Ausserrhoden; 1749, Henzi's plot in Bern; 1755, the Val Leventina rising against Uri; 1757–70, the affair of the Schumachers and Meiers in Luzern; 1762–75, the Suter affair at Innerrhoden; 1764–8, that of the Pfeils against the Redings in Schwyz; 1766, that of Einsiedeln against Schwyz; 1781, that of Greyerz against Freiburg, and many others. Sometimes these were struggles of dependencies or subject territories against the town or ruling canton, sometimes of the burghers against the patriciate, or of one family against another for supremacy—"cock-fights" as these last were called—struggles of the Montagues and Capulets, the most selfish and therefore the most reprehensible of all social struggles. In Geneva, these party conflicts lasted for almost the whole of the eighteenth century. As these class wars in Switzerland were in general the precursors of the world-famed class war in France, so it was Geneva in particular from which the French, before they had yet emerged out of the sphere of theories, derived their examples of popular risings, of delibera-tive assemblies and imperious action on the part of private societies, and finally even a supply of agents versed in the art of insurrection.

Meanwhile the intellectual movement called the *Aufklärung* had communicated itself to Switzerland also—with the aid of literary and scientific men such as Bodmer and Breitinger, Gesner, Lavater, Johannes von Müller, Haller, and of societies like the Helvetic Society, founded in 1760, which entered upon a fresh lease of life and activity in the so-called "Regeneration," when the reaction of the Restoration had followed on the Revolution.

After the outbreak of the French Revolution, the class struggle began afresh in Switzerland, now stimulated by the example of France, in the agitation, rigorously repressed, at Stäfa, 1794–5; the object, however, was no longer to regain ancient popular rights, but to introduce the new "equality" and "fraternity" of the French. The struggle was again put down, until the great Revolution spread into Switzerland and brought about, in 1798, the complete overthrow of the Swiss Constitution by the establishment of the Helvetic Republic.

CHAPTER XVIII.

JOSEPH II.

JOSEPH II, the eldest son of Maria Theresa, since the death of Francis I in 1765 Emperor and co-regent with his mother in the Habsburg dominions, took up the reins of government in a spirit wholly deserving of praise. He was endowed by nature with an unrivalled zeal for hard work, and with great openness of mind: he claimed in addition to belong wholly to his own age, and held an exalted view of the responsibilities of his office. He had learnt history and the law of nations from Bartenstein, natural law and the economic sciences from Martini, tactics and strategy from Daun, Laudon, and Lacy.

Desirous of possessing a thorough knowledge of his dominions and of the principal countries of Europe, he undertook many journeys, primarily in quest of information. No pride of State attended him; he would put up at inns, and rarely showed himself at entertainments or spectacles, devoting the whole of his time to matters of real importance. In every town through which he passed, it was his care to enquire minutely into all that concerned the army, trade, industry, and charity, and in his thirst for comprehensive knowledge he plied with eager questions anyone who could furnish him with useful information. Thus he visited Hungary twice, in 1764 and 1768; the Banat of Temesvár in 1766; Rome and Italy twice, in 1769 and 1783; Bohemia and Moravia in 1772; Galicia in 1773; France twice, in 1777 and 1781; the Austrian Netherlands and the Republic of the United Provinces in 1781.

The dominions which were to be the scene of the young Emperor's activity were of the most heterogeneous character, endlessly subdivided and occupied by peoples separated from each other by every law of their being—by birth, language, tradition, and interests. These 250,000 square miles of land were in fact composed of territories rather contiguous than united, whose inhabitants displayed an infinitive diversity, and belonged to races not only different, but in many instances hostile: there were Germans, Magyars, Italians, Roumanians, Slavs, vying with each other in their subdivisions; and it might have been said with truth that, save for the Catholic religion professed by all but a small minority among them, they had nothing in common except the person of the Emperor and the service due to him. The task to which Joseph II was to devote all his energies would clearly be hard, and full of difficulties. It was inevitable that struggles should ensue, when the administration was shared by an eager and ambitious Prince, athirst for progress, and an autocratic Empress, who was jealous of her own power, no less ambitious but infinitely more prudent than her son, essentially conservative and distrustful of innovation. The temperaments of the two rulers were, in a word, mutually antipathetic, and with regard to certain definite aims they disagreed from the first.

Scarcely was Joseph installed when he declared war upon all expenses which were useless, or judged by him to be such, and sought to compass the conversion of the national debt. Besides this, he undertook a minute inspection of his frontiers and his troops, returning with the conviction that the military equipment of the Empire was inadequate and demanded considerable reinforcement, though this would entail great pecuniary sacrifices. The Chancellor, Kaunitz, who sided with the Empress, resisted the projected reforms, submitting that every increase in the public burdens would make itself felt by a perceptible decline in general prosperity. Moreover, unless the state coffers were to be completely exhausted, it would be impossible to keep continually under arms a body of troops sufficient to guarantee the safety of all the frontiers at once. They must content themselves with possessing a good standing army, and such facilities for recruiting as would ensure the speedy enlistment of the necessary additions. Any other course of action would involve the risk of paralysing industry and trade; moreover, such a widespread distribution of military forces would rouse uneasiness in the foreign Powers, and would be likely to result in diplomatic complications.

Nor were these the only points at issue between the co-regents. Joseph II, whose heart was in the system of centralisation, pronounced the State Conference to be ill-organised and the surveillance exercised by the superior authority a mere pretence; and he criticised in no measured terms the working of the office of Chancellor, the joint creation of the Empress and Kaunitz. Although in the end he was to succeed in bringing about certain reforms in these directions, he had first to encounter a stubborn and fierce resistance.

When the young Emperor visited Hungary and Bohemia, he was profoundly impressed by the wretched plight of the peasantry. He rightly attributed their deplorable condition to the unfair pressure of the seigniorial charges and to the ignorance of the people, and he wished to mitigate their serfdom, to lighten the feudal burdens imposed upon them, and to build schools. Maria Theresa eventually yielded to his representations, and issued, in 1773, a decree regarding feudal servitudes.

But the result of this proceeding was unfortunate: the peasants, imagining that their rulers wished to free them from all dues, and that the nobles were opposed to this measure and had gained to their side the ministers of State, rose in revolt. Bands of insurgents spread terror in the rural districts; the insurrection spread to Moravia, to Austrian Silesia, Styria, and Hungary, and was only quelled at last by a summary application of martial law. Kaunitz advocated the withdrawal of all concessions hitherto made, and the refusal of all favours to rebels; but the influence of Joseph carried the day, and the more crying abuses were suppressed.

The Emperor, again, was in favour of a complete remodelling of public education in a more secular spirit. "The State is no cloister," he said, "and we have, in good truth, no monks for our neighbours." It is not difficult to imagine how his mother's strict piety felt itself outraged by such sentiments. Later, the breach between the two was widened still further upon the question of religion, when, after the persecutions carried on against dissenters in Moravia, Joseph wrote to his mother, during the month of June, 1777: "I am more and more convinced of the soundness of my principles by these open avowals of irreligion in Moravia: once grant freedom of belief, and there will be but one religion—that of directing all the citizens equally towards the good of the State. On any other plan it will be impossible to save men's souls, and many bodies will be sacrificed which we need and might have used. Shall the power of man aspire to pass judgment on the mercy of God, to save men in their own despite, to make a law to rule over conscience? You who are temporal lords, if only the State be duly served, if the laws of nature and society meet with reverence and the Supreme Being fail not of honour—why should you seek a wider sphere of influence? Hearts may not be enlightened, save by the Holy Spirit, whose workings your laws can only disannul. Such, as your Majesty is well aware, is my creed: and the strength of my convictions will hold me to it as long as I live." Maria Theresa replied: "Without a supreme religion, tolerance and indifference are the very means whereby comes ruin and total overthrow. We ourselves should fare the worst." The contest grew so bitter that Joseph proposed to his mother that he should abdicate, and peace was only restored with the utmost difficulty.

In the sphere of external politics, too, harmony was far to seek. Poland had, for a long time past, maintained its position, not by its own strength, but simply through the feuds and jealousies of the neighbouring States. After the death of Augustus III, the kingdom passed (September 7, 1764) to Stanislaus Poniatowski, under the guardianship of the Russian ambassador Repnin. The policy of Russia was to resist all reforms which might tend to strengthen Poland, and to maintain the *liberum veto,* together with all the drawbacks of the ancient Constitution.

Again, Russia interfered on behalf of the non-Catholics, and, notwithstanding the fierce opposition of the nobles and clergy, she forced upon the country liberty of worship, and the admission of dissenters to all the public offices and the electoral assemblies. This conduct provoked a revolt, which was cruelly suppressed by the Russians. In 1768 their troops pursued some Polish insurgents into Turkish territory, and the Porte, in consequence, declared war on the Tsarina: and from this time onward the fortunes of Poland became intimately connected with the Turco-Russian question.

At this juncture, Kaunitz devised a plan which he thought very ingenious. Austria was to take the initiative in a coalition with Prussia and Turkey: this triple alliance would quickly get the better of Russia, and check the threatening growth of that Power. At the same time, Silesia would be won back, Frederick being allowed to take Courland and the grand duchy of Posen. Joseph II had little difficulty in exposing the chimerical nature of this arrangement. It savoured of childish folly to imagine that Frederick would give up Silesia in exchange for territories which were certainly larger, but at the same time far less necessary for the consolidation of his dominions: nor was it more likely that he would abandon at such a price the chief supporter of his policy. Baffled, but not disheartened, Kaunitz, who had already drawn the attention of Frederick to the dangers threatening the equilibrium of eastern Europe from the pretensions of Russia, tried to convince his sovereigns that war was to be preferred to the complete success of the Tsarina's troops in Turkey. If they could come to an agreement with Prussia, the entry of an Austro-Prussian army into Poland would force Catharine to make peace, without striking a blow. But Maria Theresa was afraid of war, and her son doubted the readiness of the Austrian army to take the field. His reply to his Chancellor accordingly ran: "Leave Russia and Turkey to come to blows; but let us reinforce our military strength, and, when the two rivals have weakened one another, the Porte will pay us highly for our help. Then, we will hold the Russians in check, if they encroach towards the Danube, and we will leave Frederick a free hand in Poland." After prolonged hesitation, Maria Theresa acquiesced in this opinion, and the negotiations resulted in the Convention of July, 1771, described below.

Frederick, for his part, could not acquiesce in the outrageous stipulations to which Russia demanded that the Turks should accede. The downfall of Turkey could involve no possible advantage to Prussia, and might even draw her, in the end, into war against Austria on behalf of Russia. Thus it was that he conceived the idea of partitioning Poland, by way of a solution of all these difficulties; for by this means the rapaciousness of all the claimants would be satisfied, with the additional advantage that the balance of power would be restored. Joseph II had already anticipated this step during the year 1768, when he had caused

CH. XVIII.

his troops to occupy the Polish district of Zips, taking his stand upon the doubtful mortgage of it to the Polish Crown in 1412. Maria Theresa disapproved of this course of action, and held very different views. Austria, in her opinion, should offer her mediation to win more favourable terms for Turkey; and the Empress fondly hoped to win Little Wallachia in return for these good offices. In this way the projected partition of Poland was resisted, and a blow was dealt at the influence of Prussia in Constantinople. But the Emperor and his Chancellor were opposed to such a plan, and the Tsarina, on her part, refusing to give it countenance, signed with Frederick II the secret Treaty of St Petersburg (February 17, 1772). It was thenceforth impossible to prevent either Russia from establishing her supremacy on the Black Sea, or the two allied Powers from seizing whatever part of Poland they coveted ; and Austria had no choice but to share in the dismemberment proposed by Prussia. Maria Theresa expostulated with sighs—"She is always in tears," said Frederick ; "yet she is always ready to take her share." She sent Kaunitz a note breathing trepidation and anguish : "When all my dominions were threatened and I knew not where I might bring forth my son in safety, I trusted in my right and in the help of God. But in this matter, where among other voices the voice of manifest right cries out against us to Heaven, I must acknowledge that never in my life have I suffered pangs like these, that I feel shame to show my face. Let the Prince bethink him what example we set to the world, when we prostitute our honour and our good name for a wretched fragment of Poland or Moldavia or Wallachia. I know well that I am weak and friendless, and for this reason I suffer events to take their course ; but my spirit is bitterly vexed."

The Treaty of August 5, 1772, gave to Prussia the whole basin of the lower Vistula with the exception of Danzig, about 20,000 square miles with 600,000 inhabitants, thus establishing continuity between the eastern provinces and the centre of the monarchy. Russia received White Russia with 1,600,000 inhabitants; Austria had for her share the Comitat of Zips, an important part of Red Russia, certain portions of Podolia and Volhynia, the southern part of Little Poland, more than two millions of subjects, and the northern slope of the Carpathians.

From the point of view of general politics, the partition of Poland linked the three Courts of the north in a complicity which for a long time involved a joint responsibility; for the rest, it substituted for the ancient right of nations the proclamation of brute force as supreme, of might as right.

Austria had for many a year cast longing glances in the direction of Bavaria. The marriage of Archduke Joseph with Princess Maria Josepha, sister of the childless Elector Maximilian Joseph, had been concluded mainly in order that the inheritance of the Elector might pass to the

House of Habsburg; but the Empress died, without issue, in 1767, and the cherished dream came to nothing. But hope was not yet abandoned. The inheritance of the Elector Maximilian Joseph of Bavaria had on his death (December 30, 1777) lapsed to the Elector Palatine (Charles Theodore of Sulzbach). Skilful negotiations, carried on under the seal of absolute secrecy, resulted, on January 15, 1778, in an agreement whereby the Elector, in exchange for advantageous settlements secured by Austria to his natural children, recognised the Austrian claim to Bavaria, thus sacrificing the interest of his heir presumptive, Duke Charles II of Zweibrücken-Birkenfeld, who was descended in collateral line from the Rudolfine branch of the House of Wittelsbach. The House of Austria thus acquired, without striking a blow, a German land, part of which carried the Habsburg monarchy into the heart of the Empire and brought its dominions in Germany near to its Italian possessions.

The agreement once signed, Kaunitz believed that the game was won. On the one hand, he reckoned on the French alliance; on the other, the attention of Russia was absorbed by the events in the Crimea, as was that of England by the insurrection of her colonies, and the King of Prussia, now grown old, could have no other preoccupation beyond keeping intact the conquests of his youth. The Chancellor was soon to see how grievously he had deceived himself. Vainly did Joseph II try to secure the support of Louis XVI by offering him a share of the Austrian Netherlands: seductive as the offer was, it could not outweigh the disadvantages which, from the point of view of France, must inevitably attend the extension of the Austrian power into the heart of Germany, and its acquisition of absolute control over the Empire and the highway into Italy.

Frederick had foreseen this attitude on the part of France; at the same time, he had persuaded the Tsarina that the least change in the Germanic Constitution would be prejudicial to the interests of Russia. Having no fears in this quarter, he occupied himself in winning over to his views the Duke of Zweibrücken-Birkenfeld. Austria had brought about the relinquishment of all claims on the part of the Elector Palatine; but the agreement of January 15, 1778, was not completely valid without the assent of the heir presumptive aforesaid. But, far from identifying himself with the intrigues of Austria, the young Prince, obeying the instigation of Frederick, disputed at the Diet the validity of the transfer. The King of Prussia was not slow to intervene. His attitude at first was that of peacemaker, and he had much to say in favour of a new arrangement: the Palatine House should give up to Austria two districts of Bavaria, on the Danube and on the Inn; Austria for her part should cede to the Elector the duchy of Limburg, with the small portion of Gelders which she then held, comprising the town of Ruremonde and certain villages. The Elector of

Saxony should have Mindelheim and Wiesensteig. Maria Theresa was to renounce the suzerain rights of Bohemia over the fiefs of the Upper Palatinate, Saxony, and the margravates of Franconia. These offers not being accepted, the negotiations were broken off, and war became a certain prospect.

The Cabinet of Vienna instantly put in a claim at Versailles for the military assistance stipulated in the Treaty of 1756. But the French Ministry refused the demand, on the ground that the possessions guaranteed to Maria Theresa by the Treaty cited were not now the ground of dispute. The present difference related to territories which had not been in question at the time when the alliance was concluded: the matter now at issue was thus no longer the protection of the Austrian dominions, but their extension, and the *casus foederis* could not therefore be said to arise. Besides these reasons, borrowed from the Treaty, France had others as to which she kept silence: was it not to be feared that the enlargement of Austria towards the upper Danube might tempt her to extend her sway towards the Rhine? Moreover, was it wise for France to involve herself in the difficulties of a continental war, when a maritime war was imminent and would tax her resources to the utmost? Would there not be a risk of reviving the Anglo-Prussian alliance? France accordingly remained neutral.

In July, 1778, Frederick II at the head of more than 100,000 men, entered Bohemia by the county of Glatz, occupied Nachod and advanced as far as the Elbe. Joseph II was awaiting him in a formidable position on the opposite bank, and for several months the two armies kept a watchful eye on one another, but made no important movement. It seemed as if the old King shrank from tempting Fortune again, while the young Emperor was afraid to expose to the hazard of a battle the soldierly reputation which was his cherished ambition. Whatever the explanation may be, he was content to show himself as a very calm and vigilant commander. This extraordinary campaign, in which some of the foremost generals of the age—Frederick II and Prince Henry, Lacy and Laudon—were brought together, came to an end in October, 1778, without a siege or engagement of any moment.

The war had filled the Empress with intense fear. Without her son's knowledge, she entered upon negotiations with Frederick II, and, when these proved fruitless, sought the mediation of France and Russia. France, absorbed in restoring the efficiency of her navy, and involved in a costly war with England, was all for peace; Russia, still preserving an unpleasant remembrance of the behaviour of Austria towards her during her disputes with the Porte, and recalling with gratitude, on the other hand, the intervention of Prussia in the same matter, was prepared to listen to the demands of Maria Theresa, but with the reservation that Frederick's interests must be consulted.

In a congress hereupon opened at Teschen, there were vehement discussions and much heated advocacy of the opposing claims, and more than once it seemed that the negotiations were in jeopardy. The news of the decisive peace concluded at Constantinople between the Sultan and the Tsarina gave a timely support to the efforts of diplomacy. Fearing that Russia, relieved from anxiety with regard to Turkey, might give military aid to the Prussians, Austria adopted a more conciliatory attitude, and the Conference came to an end on May 13, 1779.

The Treaty of Teschen bestowed upon Austria that part of the territory of Berghausen which lies between the Danube, the Inn, and the Salza—an acquisition offering the advantage of establishing direct communication between the archduchy of Austria and Tyrol. In exchange for this extension of their dominions, the Emperor and his mother gave up their claim to the inheritance of Bavaria, which remained in the hands of the Elector Palatine, with a reversion in favour of the Duke of Zweibrücken. They also bound themselves to further the eventual reunion of the margravates of Baireuth and Ansbach with the Prussian Crown. The consequences of this Treaty were of no small importance. The readjustment of the plan of alliance, the work on which Kaunitz prided himself so highly, did not, as a matter of fact, produce any of the important results for which its author had fondly hoped; the alliance with France brought no appreciable advantage to Austria. On the other hand, the Peace of Teschen revealed the growing influence of Russia. Joseph II was profoundly impressed; he noted the additional strength given to Prussia by the Russian support, and (finding himself, once again, at variance with his mother) he was disposed to shift the basis of the Austrian policy, moving it eastwards towards Russia rather than in the direction of France, and to renounce the traditional hostility between Vienna and St Petersburg. In fine, Russia had now for the first time made her voice heard in German affairs; Prussia had increased in strength; and Austria was doomed to fall into the second rank.

If the pretensions of Russia in the direction of the Vistula were alarming to Austria, that Power viewed with still more suspicion the steps taken by the Tsarina towards the provinces of the Danube, the natural outlet of the Austrian dominions into the Black Sea. In order to strengthen himself beforehand against the Muscovite encroachments, Joseph II negotiated a reconciliation with Prussia, in his celebrated interview with Frederick II at Neisse, in August, 1769. To this date we may trace back the first symptom of coolness in the Franco-Austrian alliance, and the first steps taken by Prussia to free herself from Russian influence. The two sovereigns met again at Neustadt, in September, 1770, when Turkey, disheartened by the calamity of Tchesmé, implored their joint mediation. It has already been indicated how closely this question was entangled with that of Poland; and these transactions, which are treated in another volume, need not be discussed here.

Kaunitz now negotiated an alliance with the Porte, with intent to protect the interests of the monarchy in the east. By the Convention of July 7, 1771, Austria bound herself to make common cause with Turkey, "to deliver her out of the hands of Russia by the means either of negotiations or of arms, and to cause to be restored all the fortresses, provinces and territories, which, being in the possession of the Sublime Porte, have been unlawfully seized by Russia." As the price of this alliance Turkey promised to pay a subsidy of 11,250,000 florins, to grant to Austrian subjects the most-favoured-nation terms as to trade and to give up the part of Wallachia between Transylvania, the Banat of Temesvár, the Danube, and the Aluta. But when (as has been seen) Austria came to terms with Russia about the partition of Poland, it became clear that the cause of Turkey could no longer be upheld otherwise than by diplomacy, the alternative of war being naturally excluded. Thugut showed his skill in bringing the Porte to acknowledge this; and he further offered to cancel the Treaty in question. The Sultan showed a conciliatory temper, and offered to abide by the concessions he had granted, if Austria succeeded in obtaining by her mediation a peace which would secure to him the Danubian Provinces and Crimean Tartary.

In the conferences held at Focktchany in August, 1772, the questions of secondary importance were settled with no great difficulty; but, since no agreement could be reached on the subject of the independence of the Tartars, the negotiations were broken off; and the efforts made to come to terms at Bucharest, in the following year, proved fruitless. The point at issue on this occasion was the right of navigation in the Black Sea, demanded by Russia, together with the cession of Kerch and of Yenikale. There was accordingly a fresh outbreak of war: the Russian army, defeated successively in the neighbourhood of Silistria and of Varna, had the greatest difficulty in recrossing the Danube. But in 1774 Rumyantseff succeeded in routing the Turkish army at Shumla, and the Porte, in face of this pressing danger, concluded, on July 21, 1774, the Treaty of Kutchuk-Kainardji. This was the first great treaty concluded between Russia and the Porte, "the foundation-stone of the lengthy transaction, varied by intervals of bloodshed, which was destined, after a century of endeavour, to bring the soldiers of the Tsar to the gates of Constantinople." It made Russia the protectress of the Mussulmans of the Crimea in the matter of political independence, and of the Christians of the Ottoman empire in that of religious liberty. Joseph II claimed, in return for his good offices, that the Bukowina should be given up to him: it was relinquished by the Turks on May 7, 1775. Austria thus acquired a strategic position of the first order, enabling her, at her choice, to support the Russians in a joint campaign, or to intimidate them, if the two Powers should happen to disagree.

By the death of Maria Theresa, on November 29, 1780, Joseph II became sole monarch of the Habsburg dominions. He now hoped to be able to carry out sweeping reforms in every direction. He was not, however, the originator of these reforms; their spirit was that of the eighteenth century, and similar endeavours are observable in almost every part of Europe. Reason must rule the world, the omnipotence of the State must be servant to reason. The State, acting in its own interest, must be the agent of reform. The programme of this "enlightened despotism" included the general distribution and equitable apportionment of taxation, uniformity of legislation, subordination of the Church to the State, abolition of annates and tithes, establishment of intellectual liberty, of tolerance in religion, of impartial justice for every man. All these boons must be the gift of a sovereign whose authority was beyond question, and who devoted himself wholly to his people's welfare. It was to the sovereigns only that the reformers looked for the realisation of their schemes.

All the statesmen of Austria were more or less imbued with these ideas, and not even Maria Theresa herself had entirely escaped their influence. Jealous as she was of her authority, and deeply devoted to the happiness of her subjects, she had been inspired by Kaunitz, van Swieten, Martini, Sonnenfels, and others, to encourage intellectual culture, to amend the penal laws, and to restrict the application of torture. At the same time she did not cease to regard the nobility and clergy as the mainstay of her power, while her son was not likely to be hampered by these conservative predilections. In his turn, he was led astray by a tendency to excessive theorising, and a failure to take sufficient account of tradition, time, and surroundings; and he was apt to fall into yet another mistake—that of believing the men whom he entrusted with the execution of his orders possessed of his own virtues, his own zeal and devotion to the public welfare. Thus he was destined to a cruel disillusionment, which embittered the last years of his life.

Joseph II always protested that he was not the enemy of the Church, and that it was his wish to remain a believing Christian. But he would not suffer the papal authority to intervene in his dominions; in his eyes, the nuncio was only the ambassador of a temporal sovereign. Without decisively advocating a transformation of the hierarchy, he wished to see the episcopal power more independent of Rome; his views on this question being closely allied to those of the Archbishops of Cologne, Trier, Mainz and Salzburg. He was presently to adopt more radical opinions; and he may even have thought of creating a national Church—of proceeding, that is, so far as schism.

Judging it inadmissible that citizens should be branded with inferiority by reason of their religious principles, the Emperor issued, in 1781, the Patent of Tolerance. In this, while proclaiming his firm resolve to protect and uphold with unvarying consistency the religion of the Catholic Church, he declared himself at the same time on the side of that civil tolerance, which, without enquiring into a man's belief, in each case considers only his worth as a citizen. In consequence, while the Catholic religion alone was to continue to enjoy the prerogative of public worship, in all the districts containing a fixed number of persons sufficient to defray the expenses of the Protestant or Greek form of worship, these sects were to be free to use their own service. Dissenters might build places of worship, on condition that these edifices should bear no outward resemblance to churches, and should have neither bells nor steeples; they should be capable of becoming citizens, and be admissible to trades and corporations, and to academic degrees; and the Emperor reserved to himself the right of admitting them, by special dispensation, to public offices. The freedom thus granted was, it is true, by no means untrammelled; and the condition of the Jews, in particular, was in no respect bettered. Nevertheless, this decree bore the stamp of a generous and lofty spirit; heresy was no longer an infringement of the law; honourable careers were opened to dissenters; and, if it be borne in mind that the Patent was the work of a Prince whose life had been spent in the austerely orthodox atmosphere of the Court of Austria, it must be pronounced a document of a singularly broad-minded type. Pope Pius VI was moved by this Patent to take a step unprecedented in the history of Christianity. In 1782 he repaired to Vienna, where he stayed for a considerable time. Received with all due honour, he frequently conversed with the Emperor on ecclesiastical questions, but without succeeding in his wishes; and the Patent remained in full force.

Disliking the cosmopolitan character of the religious Orders, Joseph II prescribed that they should no longer be subordinate to foreign Generals, and that they should be for the future entirely dependent on the Ordinary. Shortly afterwards, he declared his intention of completing the work of reform undertaken and left unfinished by the Council of Trent; and he suppressed all the contemplative Orders, which he condemned as useless, allowing only the Congregations occupied with the care of the sick and with teaching to remain. At the end of his reign, 700 out of 2000 convents had disappeared, and the number of monks had been diminished by 30,000. In the substitution of the episcopal authority just mentioned it is possible to trace the influence of Febronius. In spite of the refutations directed against them, the doctrines defended in the works of "Febronius" (Hontheim)—of which an account is given in a later volume—had long exercised a powerful influence in the ecclesiastical world of Germany, and many Austrian statesmen were deeply imbued with their teaching.

In opposition to this tradition it has recently been urged that the son of Maria Theresa cannot be regarded as a disciple of the theologian of Trier. The Emperor, according to this view, wished to subordinate the Church to the State, while Febronius urged the national Churches to emancipate themselves, not only from the Pope, but also from the temporal power. The truth is that Hontheim made his appeal to all Princes, to help him in protecting the episcopate against the encroachments of the Roman See. It seems certain that Joseph II did wish to see the Church subordinated to the State; but there are none the less unmistakable indications of the influence of Febronius in certain of the imperial reforms. We can still find its mark in the decrees bearing on dispensations in questions of marriage, and in the rule that the pontifical Bulls must be submitted to the *placet*, as well as in the prohibition of written sermons, and of exegetical discussion in the seminaries of the two Bulls *In Coena Domini* and *Unigenitus*, which define the prerogatives of the sovereign pontiff.

The Emperor's wish to restore the primitive simplicity of worship and to restrain the prevailing extravagance of display led him to interfere in the inner details of parochial life and church service, thus encroaching upon a domain not his own. He took no less interest in the education of the secular clergy. The work of instruction being much neglected in the diocesan seminaries, the Emperor desired that the secular branches of knowledge should be added to the courses of theological and canonical learning: and, judging that these studies would bear more fruit in centralised institutions than in independent schools, he issued a decree suppressing all the diocesan seminaries. These he replaced by five general seminaries, at Vienna, Pest, Freiburg, Louvain, and Pavia, together with several affiliated seminaries, playing the part of subsidiary institutions, at Grätz, Olmütz, Innsbruck, Prague, and Luxemburg. His ostensible aim was to provide the young priests with a solid, comprehensive, and liberal education, in conformity with all the latest results of science, and in touch with all the learning of the age. Care was taken to admit as masters in these establishments none but the "enlightened"; but, in choosing this staff, the Government was not invariably fortunate from the point of view of orthodoxy. The general seminaries were in fact placed under the authority of the State, and the education of the young clergy was entirely removed from the hands of the episcopate. Serious difficulties were thus to be expected.

The judicial system was certain to engage the Emperor's passion for reform. Already in 1753, Maria Theresa had established a committee called the Compilations Commission, whose work it was to draw up a new and very definite code, perfectly uniform in character. The young Emperor wished to complete his mother's work by simplifying the organisation of tribunals, establishing a uniform procedure, and equipping the Courts of justice with a body of men worthy of their task. In his view, judicial and political power ought to be kept entirely separate; he suppressed the greater number of the subordinate jurisdictions, as impotent and withal costly, and created a complete hierarchy of linked tribunals, descending from the High Court of Vienna to the judges in the rural districts, with a first instance, an appeal and a final revision, as in our own day. At the same time, the heavy fees payable by newly appointed magistrates and for written judgments were abolished, and the cost of obtaining justice was considerably lessened. To this substantial improvement of the judicial organisation Joseph II added an admirable reform of the penal laws. The principle of terror and vengeance, which lay at the foundation of the old legislation, was abandoned, and the idea of a social safeguard adopted in its stead. Inquisitional procedure and torture, already partially abolished by Maria Theresa, now disappeared entirely; the infliction of the death-penalty, hitherto indiscriminate, was restrained within reasonable limits, and all penalties were considerably lightened. The list of crimes no longer included magic, apostasy, and intermarriage between Christians and infidels. The Emperor had also ordered a revision of the civil laws, but he had not time to complete his work; he could only publish certain preparatory edicts, whereby marriage became a civil contract and the law of inheritance underwent some equitable modifications.

The condition of the peasants left much to be desired in more than one province, more especially the case in Moravia and Bohemia. In a report on the latter addressed to the Council of State in 1769, we read: "One cannot remark without amazement, without real terror and profound emotion, the state of utter misery in which the peasants languish under the crushing burdens imposed on them by their feudal lords." Joseph II visited the country, as we have seen, and returned in dismay. The peasants were almost entirely dependent upon the lord of the manor; they were not owners of the land, but simply held it in usufruct; they could not leave their lord's estate without his permission, or marry, or give to their children any profession but that of labourers; they were bound by a thousand forms of servitude, called *robot*. Maria Theresa had already commanded certain reforms; she had, in particular, defined the limits of statute labour and undertaken to transform feudal rights into dues payable in money. Joseph II carried on this work, abolishing serfdom in the Slav provinces, and securing to the peasants the right of owning land, of marrying according to their choice, and of changing their domicile at their own pleasure. He also increased considerably the powers of the offices of the "circles" (*Kreisämter*), so as almost to paralyse those of the feudal proprietors.

The young Emperor had been especially struck by the want of regularity and uniformity in the laws which governed his dominions, and it was his wish to divide the Empire into districts identical in administration. There were thirteen governments, divided into "circles," which in their turn were subdivided into urban and rural communities. The true basis of the organisation was the "circle," which was the unit in all that concerned the army, education, and finance. At the same time, the provincial Estates underwent a diminution of their power. They had already, under Maria Theresa, ceased to meet oftener than once in ten years; henceforth, they would not be assembled at all, unless by express summons of the Prince; their permanent representatives were in future to be assembled only for the voting of necessary subsidies; nor were they permitted even then to give any opinion as to the object of the requisition, but might only discuss ways and means. A similar system was to be adopted with regard to the towns, whose privileges were to be withdrawn or evaded, one by one; and steps were to be taken to substitute for the local governing bodies delegacies from the State.

During the earlier half of the eighteenth century, the Austrian Government was constantly involved in financial difficulties. The reason of this was not, however, as in France, the extravagance of the Court, the erection of ostentatious monuments, the lavish expenditure of the sovereigns on their favourites—the all but hopeless embarrassment of the administrators of the exchequer was due to the demands made upon them by the army. To defend so vast a territory and keep the peace among so many different peoples was a task necessitating an army of considerable strength, involving a proportionate cost to the country. This state of affairs had already caused grave anxiety to Maria Theresa, who, at the instigation of her husband, had caused the most rigorous economy to be observed in the management of the Court; then, with the aid of Chotek, a Čech nobleman who, in 1761, succeeded Haugwitz as Chancellor of Bohemia and Austria, she had introduced the principle of the twofold tax, on land and personalty, which affected all classes of the population. At the same time, she caused the harbour of Trieste to be reconstructed, and the roads and canals improved; scrupulous payment of the state interest raised the credit of the country, and the financial situation became more favourable. Joseph, who shared the views of the "Physiocrats," and dreamed of bringing the organisation of taxation into conformity with them, yet shrank from a radical reform, and established a provisional tax on land, calculated from the average revenue of ten years. At the same time, he set on foot the colossal enterprise of revising the register of landed property throughout the monarchy, and thus brought about a rearrangement of the scale of taxes, whereby, if an estate yielded an income of a hundred florins, seventy of these remained in the possession of the tenant, seventeen at most belonged to the feudal lord, and the remainder went into the state coffers. In addition to all this, the Emperor, as a true disciple of Colbert, imposed upon foreign products taxes so heavy that they were in some cases prohibitive. In matters of this kind his convictions differed from those of his Chancellor, Kaunitz, who, though in agreement with his master upon the principle of equality for purposes of taxation and upon the expediency of adopting the least expensive method of collecting the taxes, held that taxation should not be expected to meet more than the indispensable necessities of the State; while any alleviation of the public burdens must, in his view, presuppose an increase in the general prosperity

CH. XVIII.

and therefore in the wealth of the country. But Joseph, to whom the strengthening of the army was a matter of the most immediate concern, refused to sacrifice any possible source of income.

We pass once more to external events. The Treaty concluded on November 16, 1715, with a view to the establishment of a "Barrier" against the ambition of France, granted to the United Provinces the right of garrisoning seven fortified places in southern Belgium. The contingent of troops occupying these fortresses was to number, in time of peace, 35,000 men, of whom three-fifths were to be furnished by Austria and two-fifths by the Dutch Republic. All the expense—it might be 1,250,000 florins—was to be defrayed by Belgium. This Treaty had caused much dissatisfaction among the various populations, and the States of Flanders and Brabant had stubbornly objected; but during twenty-five years Charles VI had submitted to this condition, which impaired his sovereignty over the Netherlands. The War of the Austrian Succession had interrupted the observance of the Treaty; and in 1748, at the Conference of Aix-la-Chapelle, Kaunitz attempted to obtain its withdrawal, supporting himself by the plea that the greater number of the "Barrier" fortresses had been gradually dismantled after the French victories; and that their possession had therefore ceased to be a matter of any importance; moreover, they had yielded so easily to the attack of Maurice de Saxe, that all could see how idle were the precautions taken by the Dutch in their defence. Besides this very admissible reason, there was another, which the Austrian plenipotentiary did not mention: the fact, namely, that the circumstances had greatly changed. When the "Barrier" was established in 1715, Austria, England, and the United Provinces were just emerging from a long struggle with Louis XIV, their common enemy; their interests were identical, and they had all agreed without demur upon the means to be adopted in order to restrain the ambition of the conqueror. But since that time thirty years had passed away; in 1748, Holland had been the accomplice of England when the latter country betrayed the confidence of Austria, and Maria Theresa was pondering the advisability of disengaging herself from the Maritime Powers, in order to shift the basis of her policy in the direction of the French alliance. Under such conditions, for Austria to receive Dutch troops into the country could only be, to say the least, to expose herself to a highly inconvenient surveillance.

But the United Provinces, vaguely conscious of these new tendencies on the part of the Empress, insisted with considerable asperity on the observance of their right, and the only success achieved by Kaunitz was the suppression, in the new diplomatic contract, of the annual subsidy. This henceforth remained unpaid; there was no further attempt to save the fortresses from falling into decay, and the Republic, no longer setting any store by their preservation, left in the unprotected towns of Belgium the mere semblance of a garrison, exactly large enough to affirm a right which it did not please her to abandon openly. During the whole period of the occupation, difficulties were continually springing up in the towns of the Barrier between the national authorities and the Dutch commanders. Independently of the religious complications resulting from the presence of Protestant garrisons, incessant disputes arose between the Belgian magistrates and the Dutch officers—disputes that were often very serious in character, respecting the police, the chase, fishing, economic matters, and so forth, often involving the two Governments in grave anxiety. Joseph seized the opportunity of his journey to the Netherlands to examine the question for himself at close quarters. He was of opinion that the general condition of the Austrian monarchy did not warrant him in despatching to the Netherlands a body of troops boasting sufficient strength to resist a possible attack. Moreover, scarcely one of the fortresses was now in a condition to endure a siege, and there was reason to fear that an enemy would have no difficulty in establishing a position in one or more of them, and might, if it so chanced, thus find a substantial base from which to prolong the horrors of war. The restoration of the fortresses to efficiency would have demanded sacrifices which the state of the Treasury did not warrant; thus the wiser plan would be to keep in perfect condition only Antwerp and Luxemburg, as strategic positions of the first importance—and to dismantle the rest. Besides the considerable economic advantages which this proceeding afforded to the towns concerned, it also furnished a method of getting rid of the Dutch in the natural order of events. The Republic submitted; the Belgian forts were evacuated under the pretext of a change of garrison, and no fresh troops were sent to fill them, so that on April 18, 1782, there was not a single Dutch soldier left in Belgium. But a short time sufficed to allay the agitation caused in the United Provinces by the unexpected demands of the Emperor. The Minister of France accredited at the Hague wrote to his Government that the mass of the people were but little affected; but the statesmen could not accept the transaction with such philosophic resignation—on the contrary, there were many who nursed resentment on that score against the Court of Vienna, and held the suppression of the Barrier to be a cruel stab at the dignity of the nation.

When Spain, after a war of eighty years' duration, had been compelled to recognise the independence of the United Provinces and to give up to them certain prosperous colonies, the Treaty of Münster, sanctioning a state of things which had long been in existence, had closed the Scheldt to Belgian vessels and reserved the freedom of the river to the Dutch navy and mercantile marine. On a later occasion, the Convention of September 20, 1664, which went even further than this stipulation, so disastrous to the trade of Belgium, had ceded to the States General the fort of Liefkenshoeck, in Belgian territory. In this way, the fronting guns of Lillo and of Liefkenshoeck gave Holland the control over the two banks of the Scheldt all the way to the sea. The Government of the Hague, by way of asserting its power, stationed off Lillo a *nippel* to levy import and export duty on cargoes from Antwerp going to Saftingen or Doel, which were Belgian possessions, and found many ways of annoying the inhabitants along the banks. The Treaty of 1715 left this state of things unaltered, and at the Conference held at Aix-la-Chapelle in 1748, the Ministers of Maria Theresa, preoccupied with the question of the Barrier, seem not to have discussed the opening of the Scheldt.

In 1780, Antwerp could number no more than from 35,000 to 45,000 inhabitants, 12,000 of whom were beholden to the public charity. Such was the condition of affairs when, on December 20, 1780, England, annoyed at the refusal of the Republic to make common cause with her against the disaffection in America, declared war upon her former ally. To outwit her enemies, and to open new markets for British trade, the English Cabinet did not scruple to hint to the Viennese Government that they might take advantage of the occasion to restore the prosperity of Antwerp, by reopening the Scheldt. It was inevitable that these advances should be favourably regarded by the Emperor, who, in his eager ambition to raise his dominions to the rank of a maritime Power, could ill brook the humiliating dependence forced upon him so long as the chief river of the Netherlands was closed to vessels under his flag. He wrote to Kaunitz to point out to him the happy opportunity now at hand; but the Chancellor's reply was far from encouraging. He directed his master's attention to the inevitable risk of letting loose a general war, merely for the slender advantage "of enriching certain individuals of Antwerp." The proceedings of England, he wrote, were inspired by a momentary irritation against the States General, and to lend countenance to her interested projects would involve the risk of upsetting the existing system of alliances, which enabled Austria to defend herself at need against either Prussia or the Porte, without fear of being worsted. Clearly, Kaunitz could not admit that the particular advantage of the Netherlands balanced the general interests of the monarchy. During his journey in 1781, Joseph II received numerous petitions demanding the opening of the Scheldt. He revealed his intentions to no one; his language was always the same, and he said to the Minister of France what he said to the Burgomaster of Antwerp: that, so long as the Treaty of Münster remained in force, there could be no thought of restoring the freedom of the river. The truth is that the question was never out of his thoughts; but he was apparently scheming to obtain the support of France in carrying out his design, and therefore postponed to a more propitious moment the opening of negotiations or of a campaign with a view to the liberation of the Scheldt. The demands of Antwerp were premature; the occasion was not yet ripe; the best policy was to wait, and to discourage impatience by citing some treaty as a pretext for inaction. Two years later, circumstances seeming more favourable, the Emperor openly advanced his claims.

In 1783, an incident, in itself devoid of importance, marked the beginning of an affair which almost involved the European Powers in war, and which was not to be ended before two troubled years had passed. On October 17 the Dutch commander of the fort of Liefkens-hoeck permitted the burial of one of his soldiers in the Belgian cemetery of the disputed village of Doel. Some days afterwards, the bailiff, acting on the orders of the Government, caused the body to be exhumed and thrown into the moat of Liefkenshoeck. Almost at the same time, Joseph II delivered to the States General a veritable catalogue of territorial grievances laid at the door of the Republic, styled a "Summary of the Emperor's Claims." This document practically set forth that, if the United Provinces consented to open the Scheldt and allowed the Emperor to trade with India, he would abandon the question of the indivisible sovereignty of Maestricht. He added that he considered the Scheldt to be entirely open to the two riverain Powers, and that "if on the side of the Republic the least insult were offered to the Imperial flag, his Majesty would look upon it as a declaration of war and a formal act of hostility." The States General returned a stubborn refusal, and Joseph lost no time in carrying out his threat. Two ships of the Austrian navy were ordered to navigate the Scheldt, one in either direction. Their instructions were, not to allow themselves to be stopped, but to avoid violent measures. The brigantine *Louis* was stopped by gun-fire near Saftingen, the boundary of the territory of the Austrian Netherlands; the other could not get beyond Flushing (October, 1784). The Emperor instantly broke off all diplomatic relations. This naval demonstration on the part of Austria aroused an extraordinary agitation throughout the Netherlands, both north and south. In the United Provinces, opinion was unanimous in favour of urging the Government to defend, to the last gasp, the nation's rights and her honour. Nor was the struggle confined to a question of disputed frontiers, but it was raised immediately to higher ground : the point at issue was the freedom of seas and rivers, the opening of the Scheldt, claimed by the one State in the name of natural right, while the other opposed the claim with an appeal to treaties safeguarding its independence. Joseph II's violation of the Treaty of Münster, the work of the Great Powers, had the consequence of making the question of the Scheldt an international affair of the utmost gravity. It attracted the attention of the world at large and of legal specialists, as well as of politicians in every part of Europe, and innumerable dissertations for or against the Emperor's claims appeared in every language. Already before the naval incident, the Cabinet of Versailles had recommended moderation to the rival Powers. Even while they mobilised their troops and declared their resolution to resist to the death, the States General were well aware that they could not sustain without assistance the attack of the Imperial forces, and solicited the intervention of France. The Emperor on his side, while asserting that he was about to send out 80,000 men against the Republic, counted on the connivance of Louis XVI, his ally by blood as well as by policy, to defeat the Dutch without drawing a sword.

He was not slow to remind the Ministers of his brother-in-law of the services rendered to French trade by the port of Ostend during the American War, and he threw out a hint that Antwerp might prove equally useful. But France had many reasons, both political and commercial, for caution in her conduct towards the Republic; if Marie-Antoinette, at the instigation of Mercy, championed her brother's cause, she had Vergennes against her, supported by the whole Cabinet and by the King himself. French opinion was clear that Joseph II wished to annihilate the United Provinces, or at all events to make himself master of a great part of their dominions. We know the truth now, through the Emperor's correspondence: his real thought was that war was to be a last resort, to which he would not betake himself until all the resources of diplomacy had been exhausted. His ultimatum was merely a device to intimidate the enemy. France (of this he had proof) dreaded war, which would mean ruin for her already embarrassed finances; and, he argued, she would ensure peace by supporting his plans with regard to the Scheldt. Should his wishes on this point be met, he would make all the concessions compatible with his dignity in order to bring about a friendly understanding, and thus ward off the possibility of a campaign, so greatly dreaded by France. But he knew very well how to compensate himself for this conciliatory attitude. Louis XVI, delighted to have been able to escape the giving of armed assistance, would lend powerful help to his brother-in-law's project of exchanging the Austrian Netherlands for Bavaria—a scheme to which we shall return. Joseph II was soon to learn that he had deceived himself egregiously. It was true that France was anxious to avoid war at any price; but, contrary to the hopes of the Emperor, she succeeded in avoiding it without turning her back on the United Provinces and without facilitating the desired exchange.

Louis XVI had offered to mediate, and the offer was accepted. Joseph II lost no time in making an important concession: while his ultimatum demanded the opening of the Scheldt, under the penalty of an instant declaration of war, he had now an alternative to propose. The Dutch should either grant the freedom of the river or give up Maestricht and the contested districts in Flanders. But the French Ministry feared that the quarrel, if prolonged, would only incline the politicians of Holland towards an alliance with England—a result which would be greatly to the detriment of France in the event, always a possibility, of war with England. Further, the language employed by Vergennes lacked candour, and in action he lost his presence of mind.

The declaration of the mediating Power explicitly recognised the right of the Republic over the disputed river. The King proposed the resumption of negotiations, dealing with no questions other than those enumerated in the Emperor's "Summary"; any other course of action entailed the risk of disturbing the Powers. At the same time, two detachments of French troops took up their position, the one on the Rhine, the other on the frontier of Flanders. This was a severe blow to the Emperor. He felt that he could no longer persist in his claims to the Scheldt without exposing himself to a war which he would have to encounter without an ally. He put a good face, however, on a bad business; and, feeling that the slightest manifestation of vexation might jeopardise his yet unrevealed plan of the exchange of the Netherlands, he concealed his annoyance. "So long as we have still need of the Court of France," he wrote to Leopold, "we must swallow her humour and keep her in ignorance of our real opinions." He then suddenly showed himself much less exacting in his demands, furthering the cause of peace in accordance with the unconcealed sentiments of the Cabinet of Versailles, and calculating that the latter would evince its gratitude by helping him in the matter of Bavaria.

He did not, however, wish to expose his schemes in full daylight. His plan was rather to keep alive a wholesome fear by refusing to check the march of his troops towards the Netherlands; for such an attitude must, according to his reckoning, predispose France to facilitate the exchange, and thus remove the fear of war by destroying its very motive. In the light of this secret design of the Emperor, it becomes easy to understand the contradictions apparent in his policy—his persistent preparations for war going hand in hand with declarations of a singularly conciliatory nature. The first and principal concession had reference to the Scheldt: in the protocols of the Conference so complete a silence was maintained regarding this river, that Austria seemed to have abandoned the idea of making any further claim upon the right of navigating it, and to have resolved to restrict herself henceforth to territorial demands. On the other hand, Louis XVI took up a firm attitude towards the Republic, threatening to abandon her unless all her unreasonable pretensions were given up. Thus, at last, the disputants came to terms. The Scheldt remained closed; but the possession of the portion of the river between Saftingen and Antwerp was guaranteed to the Austrian Netherlands; and the States General were in consequence debarred from levying any toll there for the future, or in any way impeding trade; they were obliged to pull down certain forts and to give up others. The Emperor received ten million florins in exchange for the sovereignty of Maestricht, and the frontiers of Brabant and Limburg were readjusted, somewhat to his advantage. Such were the main stipulations of the Treaty concluded at Fontainebleau on November 8, 1785. From the point of view of modern ideas, the cause upheld by

Joseph II was that of liberty and justice. But, if the question be regarded strictly from its practical side, and all the circumstances taken into account, the Emperor must be held to have been wrong in wishing to decide, summarily and upon his own responsibility, a question of the most delicate nature, by refusing to recognise the existence of a particular clause in a solemn Treaty, to which all the Powers of Europe had pledged themselves and which Charles VI had in 1715 accepted without demur. Whether or not the son of Maria Theresa would have attained his end if he had betaken himself to negotiations with the various States which had given their signature to the act of 1648, it is impossible to say positively; but it is certain that the course which he actually pursued brought him into collision with the desperate energy of the Dutch, showed him his ally France ready to turn her weapons against him, and struck an humiliating blow at his self-respect. In the words of a recent writer, this Prince, who with all his faults can still stir sympathy because he was sincere, was inspired for the most part by excellent intentions and lawful motives; but the means adopted by him in order to realise his projects were generally maladroit and extravagant. If, however, the Treaty of Fontainebleau did not procure for the Belgians all the advantages they could have wished, and, if they saw themselves baulked of the hope which had for an instant been theirs, that the fetters which held and bound the port of Antwerp might be broken in pieces before their eyes, yet it is well at least to acknowledge that this was one of the most glorious treaties concluded for many years past by the sovereigns of the Netherlands with their neighbours. Flanders restored to the boundaries of 1664 and assured of the freedom of her rivers, the frontiers of Brabant, which included Antwerp, advanced towards the north; liberty gained to make regulations about the customs and trade according as the interest of the country should dictate, in opposition to the stipulations made at Münster; the humiliating treaties of 1715 and 1718 annulled and territory of considerable extent acquired beyond the Meuse—these were results of sufficient importance to fill the Belgians with gratitude towards the Imperial Government.

While negotiations were pending as to the freedom of the Scheldt, Joseph II had reverted to his schemes about Bavaria, though not without modifying them to a certain extent. His design now was to secure this country, which was marked off by well-defined boundaries and could easily be amalgamated with his own territory, thus rounding off the Austrian dominions and increasing his power of withstanding Frederick II, by ceding in exchange for it the Austrian Netherlands, which by reason of their remoteness were difficult to defend in the case of a possible attack, and which, in their extravagant particularism, were strenuously opposed to his views as a reformer. In this project the Emperor had

Catharine II for an ally, having induced her to believe that Austria could only cooperate seriously with the designs of Russia in the east, if she were secured, by the projected acquisition, against possible attack on the part of Prussia. The diplomacy of Russia played a very active part in the design; nor had Rumyantseff much difficulty in winning the ear of Charles Theodore. The Elector was old, cared but little for his new domains, and was not embarrassed by patriotic scruples. The territory of the Austrian Netherlands being the larger, the inequality was to be made good by the addition of Salzburg. The Elector was to receive the Netherlands under the designation of the kingdom of Burgundy, but curtailed by the transfer of the provinces of Limburg, Namur, and Luxemburg to the Archbishop of Salzburg in the way of compensation; the attempt was also to be made to secure to that prelate the prince-bishopric of Liége. Such was the gist of the secret treaty signed at Munich on January 15, 1785. But the acquiescence of the Duke of Zweibrücken, heir presumptive of Charles Theodore, had still to be obtained—and he was under Prussian influence. But Joseph II reckoned on the support of Russia and France. France, however, played him false; and the Tsarina, fearing that she would be drawn into a war against both France and Prussia, finally made her concurrence dependent on the consent of the Duke of Zweibrücken. The refusal of the Duke was emphatic; and the Emperor, perceiving that he had been utterly deceived and that success was out of the question, abandoned his project. Frederick II had in secret carried on an ardent campaign against him at the Courts of the Princes of the Empire, and had, as is related elsewhere, succeeded in gaining, on July 23, 1785, the signatures of fifteen German Governments to the *Fürstenbund*, an alliance of the Princes directed to the maintenance of the constitutional rights of the Empire; nor was any attempt made to conceal the intention of this league, which was opposition—if necessary armed opposition—to the projected exchange of Bavaria.

When Frederick II died on August 17, 1786, Joseph II mediated a reconciliation with Prussia, hoping to obliterate the traces of the bitter rivalry which had torn Germany asunder. He wrote to Kaunitz that the establishment of goodwill was not impossible, and might eventually secure to the two monarchies the lead in European politics; beyond a doubt, he added, an understanding of the kind could never have come to pass between Maria Theresa and Frederick, for the hostility which prevailed between them arose from causes too deeply rooted; but circumstances had now altered, many prejudices had disappeared, and this alliance between two peoples of the same race and of the same language was greatly to be desired. But the Chancellor, in his devotion to the system of which he had been the architect, maintained that there could be no sincere alliance between two Powers whose interests must always be mutually opposed, until one of them had been reduced to subordinate rank.　Austria would not have a free hand in the east until Prussia had been incapacitated from doing her any injury.　While the Emperor was occupied in this discussion with his Minister, the favourable opportunity was allowed to escape, and the futility of any attempt to bring about an alliance between the two Powers soon became apparent, when Frederick William II retained in office Hertzberg, the determined foe of Austrian influence.

It will be remembered that early in 1783 Austria and Russia had concluded an arrangement whereby the Tsarina was authorised to annex the Crimea and Kuban, and the Danube was opened to Russian ships. Catharine's dream was now to annihilate the domination of Turkey and to establish in its stead a Christian empire at Constantinople; and it seemed to her that, if this project were to be carried out, the Austrian alliance was indispensable.　There is strong evidence that she tried to purchase it, hinting at a readjustment of the frontiers towards Galicia and the Bukowina, together with the cession of part of Wallachia, and of Venetian Istria and Dalmatia.　Thanks to the assistance of Austria, Russia extended her borders considerably towards the Black Sea, making formidable arsenals of Kherson and Sevastopol, and Austrian mediation aided her in becoming mistress of Georgia (1783–5).　During the month of April, 1787, Joseph II met Catharine at Kherson, in an interview which was shortened by the news of the revolt of the Austrian Netherlands. A few weeks later, the Russian ambassador laid before the Divan the new demands of his sovereign.　He was answered by a counter-proposal involving the restoration by Russia of the Crimea.　When the diplomatist refused his signature on the plea that he was not empowered to give it, the Turkish Government threw him into prison.　Such a violation of the law of nations could not fail to provoke war, and, as is related elsewhere, a close alliance was concluded between St Petersburg and Vienna. Russia was but ill prepared, and the Turks displayed an unforeseen strength; and, though the Austrian army suffered no defeat, the results of the campaign of 1788, which is narrated elsewhere, were poor enough, if compared with the hopes which ushered it in.　Joseph II was not discouraged, however, and the Austro-Russian Treaty was renewed in 1789. The second campaign was more successful, and on September 29 Belgrade was taken by Laudon, who pursued his advantage as far as Bosnia.

The revolt of the Austrian Netherlands bore no resemblance to the contemporary insurrections in America and France, or to the Revolution in England a century before.　It was of an exceptional—possibly a unique—character, for in this case the sovereign was anxious for reform in the spirit of modern ideas, while the revolutionary party was conservative to the last degree.　The Belgian Provinces had been ruled from time immemorial by institutions, incongruous enough, retaining for the most part the methods of the Middle Ages.　Each Province formed a miniature State, with its own Constitution, its own representation, its own magistrates. To Joseph, who could not but be painfully impressed by the inner inconsistency of the Belgian institutions and laws, this time-honoured state of things seemed to demand radical alteration. To the mind of the young Emperor, no freedom was possible for a nation unless all the citizens enjoyed the same kind and the same amount of liberty; everything that he called "an abuse," or "antediluvian rubbish," he condemned, failing to understand the Belgian character, which Charles of Lorraine had appreciated so exactly. After the death of that Prince, Maria Theresa had entrusted the general government of the Netherlands to her daughter, Maria Christina, conjointly with her husband, Duke Albert of Saxe-Teschen, and Joseph II had confirmed the nomination.

From the beginning of his reign, edicts followed one another in rapid succession. First came, on November 12, 1781, the Patent of Tolerance, which aroused the most fiery opposition on the part of all the civil, judicial, and religious authorities; this appears, indeed, entirely natural, if the exclusive character of Catholicism, and the preponderating influence it had hitherto wielded, are borne in mind. Then followed, in rapid sequence, the Edict of November 28, 1781, rendering the monastic Orders entirely independent of all extraneous authority; that of December 5, 1781, forbidding any appeal to the Court of Rome for dispensations in questions of marriage; that of March 17, 1783, declaring the Emperor's intention of suppressing certain monasteries and devoting their revenues to a more useful purpose; and, finally, the Edict of November 24, 1783, forbidding assent to papal Bulls conferring benefices.

On February 11, 1786, Joseph II issued an order that the *Kermesse*, a local festival, should be celebrated on the same day in every commune. He was accused of wishing to disturb the ordinary customs and pleasures of the people—and this for no really advantageous purpose, but simply in order to gratify his passion for uniformity; the truth, however, is, that these festivals, when celebrated on different dates, used to attract huge crowds from the neighbouring districts, and meant for the working classes much expenditure on amusements, food and drink, even apart from the fact that they commonly ended in unseemly drunkenness and in vehement, even murderous, brawls. The dissatisfaction of the clergy reached its height upon the appearance of the Edict of October 16, 1786, establishing at Louvain one general seminary for the whole of the Netherlands. The Emperor, wishing the young candidates for the priesthood to be equipped with a thorough education and flawless morals, gave out that no man could be ordained a priest without having studied theology at Louvain for five years. It followed that the Belgian clergy, whose morality was for the most part unimpeachable, even if their learning left something to be desired, felt themselves greatly aggrieved by the unjust suspicion to which the Edict gave voice. They submitted, however, after lodging futile protests with the Government; only one prelate, the Bishop of Namur, refused to send his seminarists to Louvain. The professors for the new college were ill-chosen; some were accused of professing doctrines of doubtful orthodoxy, and others were the reverse of exemplary in conduct. Disturbances arose and became serious, so that the military had to be called in to restore order. The majority of the seminarists took refuge in flight, and but few remained at Louvain.

The reforms which have been described met with but a sorry reception; but the opposition only became really dangerous when Joseph II, after having dealt his blow at the religious institutions, threatened, by two patents issued on January 1, 1787, to disturb likewise the civil order. The first of these introduced radical changes into the administrative system: it substituted a single Council for the three collateral Councils and divided the Provinces into nine Circles, administered by as many *intendants,* who were invested with wide powers in matters of policy and finance. The States saw almost the whole management of affairs snatched from their grasp, leaving them practically nothing but the power of voting subsidies. Had this measure strengthened the action of the central power, it might have been advantageous to the public interest; but a grave mistake was made in granting undue authority to officials who were to all intents and purposes irresponsible. However that may be, it is never safe to introduce even the most admirable of innovations without employing the utmost discretion and tact, and neither of these qualities distinguished the Austrian rulers.

In his other declaration the Emperor suppressed all the civil tribunals, and established in their stead sixty-four tribunals of the first instance, two Councils of Appeal and a Supreme Council of Revision. Judged on its own merits, the new organisation was well conceived, and it introduced into the administration of justice an order and unity hitherto conspicuous by their absence. In fact, the system at present in force in Belgium is nothing but an imitation of the Josephine; but the reform was one which contradicted the spirit of the Constitution, since the judicial administration, like the Constitution itself, could not be remodelled, save by common consent of the Estates and the Crown. And, when it is added that the displaced magistrates were left without the indemnity to which they were lawfully entitled, it will be readily understood that the storm was not long in breaking. On April 29, 1787, the Estates of Brabant refused further payment of the ordinary subsidy—a resolution involving the suspension of taxes, until the edicts hostile to the Constitution should be revoked. In the other Provinces the Estates adopted a less radical attitude, contenting themselves with addressing vehement remonstrances to the Emperor. It is worthy of remark that these protests scarcely touched upon the religious reforms (which were apparently regarded, from that time forward, as an accomplished fact), but concerned themselves exclusively with the political aspect of the question.

The Governors-General, intimidated by the bold proceeding of the Estates of Brabant, and by the decision of the Judicial Council of that Province, declaring the institution of the tribunals of first instance to be illegal, and alarmed by the universal outburst of dissatisfaction, were in no haste to put the Emperor's wishes into execution. At the same time, Belgiojoso, the unpopular Minister, left the country. Meanwhile, the Emperor was travelling with the Tsarina in the Crimea, and during his absence Kaunitz replied to the report of the Governors, persuading them to wait quietly for the decision which the sovereign would make when he returned. But fears were entertained in Belgium of resentment on the part of Joseph II, and preparations for armed defence were set on foot. Henri van der Noot, an advocate practising before the Council of Brabant, an ambitious upstart not devoid of cleverness, published a violent pamphlet on the rights of the people of Brabant and the recent interference with their ancient Constitution, the *Joyeuse Entrée*; he enrolled volunteers under the banner of the *Serments*, a kind of citizen guard, whose function was to defend the town in case of need. This example was followed in the other Provinces, and there was no attempt to conceal the scheme of raising in this manner a national army to protect the threatened privileges. At the same time, the Estates of Brabant took secret measures to obtain the intervention of France. The Emperor, in his reply to his sister Christina, made no attempt to conceal his dissatisfaction, but consented to the temporary suspension of the edicts until he should have had the opportunity of consulting at Vienna with the deputies of all the Provinces. The result of these deliberations was that the patents of January 1, 1787, were definitely withdrawn; but the edicts bearing upon religious questions were left in force nevertheless.

A few months earlier, such a concession would have saved the whole situation; but the party of resistance had learnt its own strength, and would unquestionably lose no time in making demands of a more and more exacting nature. The clergy, now assured of the concurrence of the Estates, refused to accept the conciliatory measures adopted by the Government in the matter of the general seminary, and the Bishops utterly refused to cooperate in the administration of the odious innovations. The new Minister Plenipotentiary, Trautmannsdorff, who upheld a pacific policy, found his suggestions but coldly received at Vienna, and Joseph II associated him with the Governors-General in a charge of incompetence. The Emperor, indeed, entrusted the command of the troops to General d'Alton, and made him independent of the Minister— a serious mistake which could not but entail grave difficulties. The inopportune deployment of some troops caused an affray at Brussels in which some citizens were killed or wounded (January 22, 1788). A few days later, Antwerp was the scene of further deadly struggles, when d'Alton tried to close by force the episcopal seminaries of Malines and Antwerp. These disturbances were followed by illegal measures against

the newspapers and by arbitrary arrests of members of the Opposition
in the Estates, and all public meetings were forbidden. The hopes of a
reconciliation now became more and more doubtful; and, in November,
1789, the Estates of Brabant and Hainault refused to vote the subsidies.
Joseph II answered this manifestation of hostility by abolishing the *Joyeuse
Entrée*; at the same time he suppressed the "Permanent Deputation" of
the Estates, dismissed the members of the Council of Justice, and placed
Brabant under the jurisdiction of the Grand Council of Malines. Almost
at the same moment, the Archbishop of Malines condemned as heretical
the teaching of the General Seminary, and wild riots simultaneously
broke out in many parts of the country. Van der Noot, for his part,
convinced that it was impossible to succeed without foreign help, was
carrying on an intrigue with the Hague and Berlin. This short-sighted
politician imagined that the United Provinces and Prussia, being hostile
to Austria, would provide the malcontents with sufficient troops, and
ask in return merely a pecuniary indemnity. He traded on the uneasiness inspired in Berlin by the close alliance between the Courts of
St Petersburg and Vienna; and, on the other hand, he hinted to the
leading statesmen of the United Provinces that Austria would not be
slow to undertake the conquest of their territory. The violation of the
Barrier Treaty and the attempt to obtain the liberation of the Scheldt
had been (so he said) the first indications of a project to which the
Emperor would take the earliest possible opportunity of returning. He
counted on the fears thus aroused, to bring the two Governments into
active and effectual corroboration. There had arisen in the Austrian
Netherlands, besides the ultra-conservative party headed by van der
Noot, which included the mass of the people, an important body drawn
from the most cultured classes of the nation, directed by the lawyer
Vonck, and drawing its inspiration from French Liberal ideas. It would
not have been difficult for the Austrian Government to win to their side
these reforming spirits; but the blundering methods of their agents
drove the adherents of Vonck towards an alliance with the partisans of
van der Noot. A regiment of patriots was organised in the Dutch
territory; but d'Alton, failing to realise that this was a struggle in good
earnest, and thinking to inspire the Provinces with greater respect, took
the false step of dispersing his troops; and the patriots, under Colonel
van der Meerset, defeated the Austrian corps of Schroeder at Turnhout,
and seized Ghent. D'Alton, with incredible weakness and lack of
decision, retreated instantly to Luxemburg. His disgrace followed
forthwith; Joseph II entrusted his command to General Ferraris, and,
since the complications in the east prevented the despatch to Belgium
of an army strong enough to quell the revolt, he sent the Imperial Vice-
Chancellor, Philip von Cobenzl, to Brussels, with full powers to negotiate
an arrangement, having for its main clauses the reestablishment of
the *Joyeuse Entrée*, the suppression of the General Seminary, and an

unconditional amnesty. But the time had gone by; Cobenzl's mission failed of its desired effect, and in December, 1789, the States General proclaimed the deposition of Joseph II and the foundation of the Republic of the United States of Belgium. Only a short time was, however, to elapse before they split asunder into two irreconcilable parties—the *Statists* of van der Noot, on the one hand, and the Democrats of Vonck on the other. This schism was destined to bring about the downfall of the new Government.

Serious troubles had arisen in Hungary almost at the same moment as in Belgium. In Hungary, too, an unfavourable reception had been given to a series of religious reforms similar to those promulgated in the Netherlands—such as the diminution of the episcopal revenues, the prohibition of pluralism, the reorganisation of parochial administration, the establishment of new seminaries; certain innovations in the administrative system had also excited complaint; but, as they did not affect the Constitution, they had met with no violent opposition. The net result was, however, a widespread sense of uneasiness and apprehension, heightened by the fact that the Emperor was delaying his coronation; he was accordingly suspected of intentions inimical to the liberties of the people. The truth is that the Hungarian Constitution, based as it was entirely on privilege, was opposed to all the instincts of Joseph II. By the terms of this Constitution, all the rights belonged to the Magyars, the descendants of the ancient conquerors; the descendants of the conquered peoples, on the contrary, were literally kept in a state of slavery.

The Hungarian nobility, jealously attached to their privileges, which they regarded as reciprocally binding on the sovereign, thought to treat with him as one power with another, affecting to know him not as Emperor, but simply as King of Hungary. They could not feel more than a qualified sympathy with a prince whose levelling principles were well known to the whole world, and whose innovations were, one and all, regarded with suspicion. When in 1784 he prescribed the employment of German instead of Latin as the official language he was accused of wishing to Germanise the country; and this measure has been represented as the first step towards the introduction of German officials into the Hungarian administration of Hungary—a suspicion wholly unfounded, for throughout the reign of Joseph II all official posts were reserved for natives of the country. The real truth is that he aimed at centralising every institution; thus he introduced into Hungary the division into Circles, each with a Crown official at its head. There were other measures, too, which ruffled the nobles: the organisation of the Courts of justice in three grades, the abolition of serfdom, the revision of the register of property, the suppression of fiscal immunities. Yet the reforms did not prove so beneficial as their author had hoped, for the historic law that alterations for the better, if too abrupt, are perilous, was once more fulfilled. Violent disputes having arisen between feudal landowners and tenants, the latter sent to the Emperor delegates, who subsequently drew up a formal list of their claims. Joseph II, to whom insubordination was quite as hateful as servility, dismissed them harshly. The peasants rose in fury; a regular *Jacquerie* was organised, hundreds of castles fell a prey to the flames, and the landowners took up arms in brutal retaliation.

The Emperor restored order by putting forth an imposing array of military forces, but showed himself full of clemency towards the bewildered peasants, refusing to lend an ear to the grievances of the nobles. But the crisis was only deferred. When the imminence of war with Turkey forced the Government to demand subsidies and soldiers from Hungary, the request was met by the stipulation, as a preliminary condition, that the Diet should be convoked. And, when the Emperor was so ill-advised as to object that the circumstances were unfavourable, the ferment in men's minds reached such a pitch that Kaunitz exclaimed, "Here we have the story of Belgium over again." Beyond a doubt, the majority of the Hungarians were in favour of remaining united with Austria, while retaining their privileges; but one section of the nobility went further, and demanded the support of the King of Prussia. A revolution seemed inevitable; and, meanwhile, the condition of affairs outside the country was far from reassuring. Turkey and Prussia had just concluded an offensive and defensive alliance. From France, herself in revolution, nothing was to be hoped, while Russia was paralysed by Sweden. On February 4, 1790, Joseph II decreed that everything should be restored to the condition in which it had stood at the time of the death of Maria Theresa; the single reform of his to which he adhered was the abolition of serfdom. The fair dreams of his youth had vanished, and his days were numbered; he prepared himself bravely for death, and expired on February 10, 1790, charging the Belgians, with his last breath, with having failed to understand him.

The most conflicting judgments have been passed upon the character and actions of Joseph II. Historians have dealt with him as their political prejudices inclined them—while some exalt him to the skies, seeing in him the martyr of public ignorance and ingratitude, others pronounce him an unscrupulous seeker after fame, a savage despot, trampling under his feet all the feelings of his subjects. The truth may probably be found midway between these extreme opinions. The son of Maria Theresa cannot be pronounced impeccable—he was human: we have had occasion to observe that his reforms, if for the most part fundamentally just, were not introduced with the fitting discretion; but it is impossible to mistake either the purity of his intentions or that deep love for his fellow-men which was his inspiring motive. It must be remembered that the violent animosity aroused by him was due, above all, to the fact that his projects injuriously affected all privileged persons, of whatever class—and privileged persons are always hostile to any man who dares lay hands upon even the most questionable of their prerogatives. Most of his reforms have been put into practice since his day, under circumstances more favourable to their realisation, and there is scarcely one which has not triumphantly endured the test of time and experience.

A study of the foreign policy of Joseph II reveals the fact that he was ambitious; but his ambition might almost be called defensive in its nature. He judged, and rightly, that the configuration of his dominions exposed him to serious dangers; he aimed, in consequence, at consolidating his scattered domains, and at making them one compact whole, capable of sturdy resistance against possible attacks on the part of Prussia and Turkey; and the project of exchanging the Netherlands, which lay at a great distance from the centre of his monarchy, and uncomfortably near the enemies of Austria, had no other end in view. He has been accused of attempting to aggrandise himself at the expense of Prussia. His letters establish, on the contrary, that he lived in perpetual fear of the hostility of Frederick II, and that, but for the stubborn resistance of Kaunitz, he would have sought an opportunity of establishing friendly relations with his mother's ancient enemy; but, thwarted in this design, he was fain to turn to Russia, the only Power which he held capable of withstanding Prussia's growing strength.

Leopold II, successor to his brother Joseph, was imbued with the same ideas, but equipped with more discretion and tact. He had had no difficulty in carrying out, in his dominions of Tuscany, many of the reforms which in Austria caused so much trouble. He found a tottering throne, Belgium set free from allegiance, excitement still intense in Hungary, the capital of the Empire a prey to distraction, the conferences with Turkey broken off, war with Prussia on the point of being declared. He had need of all the skill and all the genius for conciliation which he displayed during his unfortunately brief reign, to extricate himself with honour from a situation so fraught with peril. Turning his attention first to Belgium, he repeated the propositions of Cobenzl, with the addition that the Estates should henceforth have the right to meet when they judged it desirable, and that the Emperor should not have the power to make new laws without their adhesion. The Congress of Brussels made no reply, but the offers made by the sovereign lent new bitterness to the party quarrels of the Belgians, and a struggle between the political factions became inevitable. The Emperor returned to the charge, promising that the whole constitutional system should remain as it had been under Maria Theresa, and that he would both grant a general amnesty and introduce into the organisation of the Estates, with their consent, such modifications as the public advantage should demand. This time he was not left without a reply. On November 21, 1790, the Belgian Estates elected Archduke Charles, the third son of Leopold, Hereditary Grand Duke, on condition that this dignity should never be merged in a sovereignty compelling the Grand Duke to reside elsewhere than in Belgium; for the nation attributed their calamities to the distance separating them from their Princes.

In the meantime, the Austrian army had invaded the Netherlands, and the forces of the States retired without an engagement. Their commander, the Prussian General Schönfeld, who on this occasion played a very equivocal part, had, on November 25, 1790, abandoned the important strategic position of Namur, and fled to France. On December 3 the Austrians entered Brussels. Van der Noot and the more compromised of the statesmen hastened to seek shelter abroad. Negotiations were opened at the Hague, and resulted on December 11 in a treaty which breathed the spirit of the proposals made by the Emperor at the time of his accession. The Government exacted no other revenge than that of forcing the Archbishop of Malines to sing a *Te Deum* at the Church of St Gudule at Brussels, and of compelling him to make a recantation which must have been a severe blow to his self-respect.

Leopold II turned next to Prussia. He knew, without sharing, the prejudices of Kaunitz against that Power, and, leaving the Chancellor outside the negotiations, he treated directly with Frederick William II. A conference was soon opened at Reichenbach, to determine the basis of a treaty of reconciliation; and shortly afterwards the Treaty of Sistova (August 4, 1791) put an end to hostilities between Austria and Turkey. The political horizon was thus unexpectedly swept clear of clouds, but the condition of France was causing anxiety to the whole of Europe. Leopold's caution in dealing with the Emigrants and their designs, and his general wish to defer any definite action against the existing *régime* in France, are described elsewhere. He consented, however, at last, to see Count d'Artois at Mantua on May 20, 1791, when, without consenting to make any definite promise, he spoke of a projected understanding with the other Powers; and, after the flight of Varennes, he had an interview with the King of Prussia at Pillnitz in Saxony, which resulted in the joint Declaration of August 27, 1791. They wished to enable the King of France to secure the foundations of a monarchical government, and had therefore "resolved to take prompt measures, with one consent, to attain the end desired by both." War was now inevitable, but Leopold died at the moment when the storm was about to break, on March 1, 1792.

CHAPTER XIX.

CATHARINE II.

"Happy the writer who a century hence shall tell the history of Catharine II!"—so Voltaire exclaimed in a letter to that monarch. No historian, however, has yet been found to give a really conclusive portrayal of her character in its whole bearing on the history of Russia; Bilbassoff's great work only reaches the year 1764. The task remains unfulfilled to which Voltaire refers—with flattering intent it is true—but at all events the Tsarina's memory has been cleared of a considerable amount of detail traceable to unauthentic anecdotes with which an interest not untinged by gossip and malice had surrounded it. Neither the cheap designation, "the Northern Semiramis," nor any comparison with Louis XIV, really goes to the root of this remarkable and complex character, which we are now able to survey as it passed through the history of the nation and the age to which it belonged.

Sophia Augusta Frederica, Princess of Anhalt-Zerbst, was born at Stettin on May 2, 1729[1]. Her father, Prince Christian August, was a Prussian officer, a somewhat commonplace man of the old-fashioned rigid Lutheran creed. The mother was Johanna Elizabeth, a princess of Holstein-Gottorp, a superficial, lively woman, fond of intrigue, and her husband's junior by many years; she was a sister of Prince Carl August, who died in St Petersburg as the betrothed of Elizabeth, afterwards Tsarina. The girl grew up amid the environment provided by a large commercial centre and an officer's household conducted on a far from brilliant scale. She was brought up strictly, but not very carefully, in the habits and traditions of the petty princesses then so numerous in Germany, only perhaps in circumstances modest below the average. Her journeys afforded her the best teaching she received; but at an early date she displayed a taste for reading. In no respect did she stand forth among her fellows, except that, even in her youth, she was supposed to have shown signs of a "serious, cold, calculating mind";

[1] All the dates in this chapter are N. S.

exhibiting little or nothing of that liveliness, mental activity, and passionate nature so strikingly evident in her as Tsarina.

The turning-point in her life was the invitation to St Petersburg from the Empress Elizabeth of Russia which reached her and her mother at Zerbst on January 1, 1744, followed by a letter from Frederick the Great clearly stating the object of the summons, namely, the proposed marriage of Princess Sophia to the Russian heir apparent, Peter Carl Ulrich of Holstein-Gottorp, the son of Anna Petrovna, Elizabeth's elder sister.

The circumstances which had led the Tsarina to take this step have been described in an earlier chapter. Mardefeld, Frederick II's ambassador at St Petersburg, had opposed the plan of marrying the destined successor to the throne to a Saxon princess; it was probably Podewils, the Prussian Minister, who first drew attention to the young Princess of Anhalt-Zerbst. Frederick strongly recommended her to Elizabeth, since as the daughter of one of his generals she was in his interest, while at the same time in her he had not to "sacrifice" a Prussian princess; but, in thus deciding the marriage question, the Empress in the main acted on her own judgment. It was in Sophia's favour that she was descended from a small princely house, an alliance with which could involve no difficulties for Russia; and that she was cousin to the Tsarevich through her mother.

Mother and daughter set out on January 10, 1744; the father giving them a great deal of advice which at a later date must have struck his daughter as singularly homely, precise and narrow. This girl of fifteen was entering upon an utterly unknown future and an absolutely strange world. She cannot have really experienced the feelings which in her Memoirs she describes as having animated her at that time; as a matter of fact, this record was not taken in hand till after 1780. It may be added that, though the Memoirs excited much and just surprise when published in London by Alexander Herzen in 1859, there can be no doubt as to their authenticity. Unfortunately, the extremely interesting evidence as to Catharine's character furnished in this work, one of the chief authorities for her biography, comes to an end with the close of 1759, and thus does not cover what is really its most interesting period. The Memoirs cannot of course be regarded as an unadulterated historical source; in spite of the almost unfeminine coldness of their tone, they are even more strongly biassed than is ordinarily the case with this class of writings. Facts and events are generally correctly narrated, but the opinions expressed are for the most part coloured by partisan feeling. Perhaps Catharine was calculating the effect on her son Paul and his wife; but, be that as it may, her tendency is to represent her marriage with Peter and her whole position as a martyrdom which at last became unbearable, and so to render the *coup d'état* intrinsically intelligible and justifiable.

No unreserved use can therefore be made of this source in any attempt to draw the character of the Prince to whom in 1744 the Princess of Anhalt was wedded. Peter was by no means half-witted, but had been very badly brought up, miseducated, and even physically neglected. In St Petersburg, too, all efforts to develop his powers were in vain; in the words of Solowjeff, "he displayed every symptom of mental backwardness; and resembled a grown-up child." He indulged without restraint in childish pastimes, yielded to common and low propensities, and was both mentally and morally of an inferior type. Moreover, he neither could nor would adapt himself to Russian ways and to the special circumstances of his position as Tsarevich. He remained a Lutheran at heart, and ridiculed the Orthodox faith and its usages. Even as a future Tsar he retained his pride in his rank as a German Prince and a lasting passionate and personal devotion to Frederick the Great, whose interests he served against those of his adopted country. In every respect he did precisely what he ought not to have done in his position, especially when the throne was so insecure.

After, at the end of August, 1745, he had married the Princess Sophia, the contrast between husband and wife was from the very outset made evident by the rapidity with which the Princess accommodated herself to her difficult position, though she was certainly not assisted in the matter by her tactless, intriguing mother. With an insight and judgment remarkable in one so young, she immediately perceived the course she must pursue to win her way in Russia: she must learn the language and adopt the Orthodox faith. Princess Sophia became the Grand Duchess Katharina Alexeievna. She had no longer any home in Germany nor any connexion with it, after her mother had been obliged to leave Russia and her father had died (March, 1747).

There was no question of an intimate relation with her husband, though she would have been prepared for it. He neglected her, absorbed in amusing himself with his soldiers, in carousals and amours, and making it clearer every day how ill-fitted he was to become the ruler of the Russian empire. Catharine's early years as Tsarevna were a lonely time for her, and she was jealously watched and guarded. Nevertheless, she lost neither her force and elasticity of mind nor her cheerfulness of disposition. Like Peter I, she was her own teacher; but he learnt practically, whereas she had to educate herself theoretically. She read a great deal, passing from novels to Voltaire, Bayle, Montesquieu, and then to the *Annals* of Tacitus and the early volumes of the *Encyclopédie*. Her reading developed that political sense which was so characteristic of her; she became imbued with ideas of enlightened absolutism, and her intellectual labours may be to some extent compared with those by which Frederick the Great as Crown Prince trained himself for the duties of King. During the years thus spent in serious work, as she recognised what manner of ruler her husband would make, she became at heart a Pretender by his side. In the outside world she deliberately sought popularity; she had to act a part and acted it consciously, calculating the while, mistress of herself.

But in the heavy atmosphere of the Russian Court there awoke in her at the same time a craving for the joys of life, hitherto latent within her passionate soul and vigorous nature. She had no family life with her husband; and her first child, Paul, had been taken from her by Elizabeth, delighted by the advent of an heir to the throne. After brief love passages with others, in 1759 the first favourite proper, Gregori Orloff, came on the scene. Husband and wife drifted further apart, and the "young Court" presented a sorry picture of discord.

But, politically also, Peter and Catharine belonged to opposite sides. The ambition which animated Catharine taught her that for her own sake she must be a Russian or at any rate appear such outwardly. Peter, on the other hand, seems to have set his Holstein interests before those of the Russian imperial Crown, not realising that it was precisely in the identification of himself with national aims that lay his one and only chance of the succession—and even so it was a very uncertain chance. Thus he was constantly outraging public feeling, and entered into the maze of politics without either thought or capacity, while Catharine assumed her part sagaciously and as one acting with mature and conscious judgment. It was soon evident that their ways could not lie together. Both were kept under close and constant supervision; Elizabeth's relations with Catharine were singularly lacking in confidence and kindness. The attention of high officers of State and foreign diplomats was claimed increasingly by the Grand Duchess as the Empress grew older, and as Peter's conduct strengthened the conviction that he would not reign for long. For ten years Catharine had stood alone at Court; now the several parties were drawing round her. Bestuzheff, hitherto her enemy, provided her ambition with a definite political aim, namely, the exclusion of Peter from the throne and her own regency during the minority of her son Paul. Catharine availed herself, too, of her credit with the English ambassador. There were two parties at Court whose object was to set aside Peter, and she had entered into secret relations with both, when she was brought into serious danger by the fall of Bestuzheff in February, 1758, already described elsewhere. But Bestuzheff had burnt all compromising correspondence, and Catharine escaped a great peril; in a dramatic scene she quieted the suspicions of the Empress, whose confidence was, however, forfeited by Bestuzheff.

Though Elizabeth was obliged to acknowledge openly that her nephew would not be competent to reign for any length of time, she did not alter the succession. For Catharine, too, the situation was becoming more critical, as it was anticipated that, on his accession, Peter would divorce her, pronounce Paul a bastard, and marry his mistress, Elizabeth Vorontsoff. Moreover, another claimant to the throne was still living in the person of Ivan Antonovich, imprisoned at Schlüsselburg. Thus it was altogether uncertain who would succeed, should Elizabeth die suddenly. Shortly before that event Princess Catharine Dashkoff, a sister of Elizabeth Vorontsoff, implored the Grand Duchess, of whom she was an enthusiastic partisan, to end the suspense by taking an extreme step—the purport of which was obvious. But Catharine refused, being apparently persuaded that there was no help for it if Peter meant to get rid of her. Hence, when Elizabeth died on January 5, 1762, his accession followed without any hindrance.

Peter III was now in a position to give practical expression to his veneration for Frederick the Great, and took immediate advantage of it by making peace with him, giving back all conquered territories, and freeing Prussia from the almost overwhelming pressure brought to bear on her by the coalition between Russia, Austria, and France. This was not in itself contrary to the interests of Russia. But the sudden change of front was regarded as an ignoble surrender of what had been won and a capitulation to the "mortal enemy"; and this charge was (according to one version at any rate) subsequently brought against Peter in the manifesto of July 9, 1762. Most other measures taken by him were of a similar nature and contributed to his ruin. His efforts at reform, for the most part well-meant, included the abolition of torture and capital punishment (the latter at all events for the nobility)—while the exemption of that Order from the obligation of service to the State was not justifiable and incited the peasants to revolt—and the secularisation of ecclesiastical property. But Peter's wild zeal for reform set everyone against him, as too many interests were threatened at once. Again, his endeavour to reduce the Guards to discipline by means of Prussian drill was well-intentioned. But, mainly because of the petty way in which it was introduced, this innovation roused against him the Guards and their officers, who were precisely the one element able to carry out a revolution effectively. Things grew still more serious as the Emperor became more and more possessed by the idea of engaging in war with Denmark for the sake of Schleswig—a war which must naturally find very little favour with the Guards and among the populace. He continued to wound Russian susceptibilities on all sides just as he had done when Tsarevich; and the increasing dissoluteness of his life rendered him more and more unfitted to rule, while he treated his wife with more brutality and ignominy than ever. Catharine bore every insult with perfect self-control, her immediate object being that the Russians should come to see in her the means of delivering them from the present tyranny and maladministration. The more imminent the danger became that Peter would drive her from the throne into a convent or Schlüsselburg, so as to be enabled to marry his mistress, the more assiduously Catharine added mesh to mesh in the net of conspiracy which finally brought about his downfall. All who desired a change thronged to her side; but she was astute enough to keep the several contributory currents distinct from each other, and to retain in her own hands the management of the whole. The several factions which were helping her—the Orloffs, Princess Dashkoff, Panin—at various times ascribed to themselves the leading part in the entire affair. As a matter of fact, Catharine alone directed its course, and her strongest allies were the brothers Orloff. Gregori Orloff, her passionately devoted lover, won over his brothers, first and foremost the sharp-witted Alexei; they in turn won over to the cause other officers and soldiers of the Guards, among whom there was enough hatred of the Tsar. Princess Dashkoff, in her Memoirs, attributes to herself a larger part in the revolution than she actually played; but she enlisted supporters among the aristocracy, in particular Nikita Panin, Paul's tutor.

From afar, Frederick the Great perceived that his satellite, the Tsar, would not long hold his own, and Peter was not left without admonitions from that quarter. Lulled, however, by a false sense of security he failed to notice how isolated his position was becoming, and how the tide had turned in the Tsarina's favour. The sword of divorce still hung over her; and, at the beginning of July, 1762, the catastrophe seemed on the point of overtaking her. Thus it came to pass that, on her side, the conspiracy broke out by which she saved herself and Russia; and, though the moment for action came sooner than had been expected, the several agencies ended by cooperating most successfully, little as they knew of each other's movements. Peter fell, and he alone; and an otherwise bloodless revolution, accomplished with the utmost ease, reached its terrible climax in the murder of the Tsar.

By a mere chance one of the accessories to the plot was arrested. The conspirators at once took decisive action, although nothing was prepared. In hot haste, Alexei Orloff fetched the Tsarina from Peterhof into the city of St Petersburg, on the night of July 8—9. Early in the morning of the 9th, she drove to the barracks of the Guards, who immediately swore allegiance to her. Then, in the Kasan cathedral, whither Panin had meanwhile taken the Tsarevich Paul, Catharine was proclaimed Autocrat. From the Winter Palace she issued a manifesto informing the people of the step. Peter had been dethroned, practically without opposition.

On the evening of the same day, the Guards marched from St Petersburg to Peterhof, where Peter had remained; what had been begun must be carried through. Catharine headed the march in person, wearing the uniform of the Guards and accompanied by a splendid suite. The brilliant personal qualities of this amazing woman were most strikingly evinced on this occasion and held everyone as it were spell-bound; political action was undistinguishable from romantic masquerade. Peter was perfectly helpless, and surrendered unconditionally; he agreed to the declaration of abdication sent him and was taken as a prisoner to the country seat of Ropscha. The military revolt against the reigning

Tsar had triumphed speedily and without bloodshed; as in 1741, it had been effected by the Guards, who had no intention of going to war on behalf of a foreign princess, and she succeeded in giving a national Russian significance to the enterprise. Disorderly and undisciplined behaviour on the part of the soldiery, which made the danger attaching to these revolts abundantly evident, was quickly put down by the firmness of Catharine and those around her. But a dark shadow was cast on the whole transaction, which had been so easy of accomplishment, by the murder of Peter at Ropscha on July 17. Catharine did not give the order for this deed; but the guilt of it nevertheless lies at her door. Alexei Orloff and several others were the actual perpetrators of the murder; but he would not have ventured so far unless he had been certain that Catharine would breathe more freely if this still dangerous rival were disposed of, and that they were carrying out Catharine's own secret wish. And Orloff's deed went unpunished.

Catharine had taken the lead in the revolution, and was now Autocrat of the Russias. For there was no question of her merely holding the regency during the minority of her son, as Panin had desired. She seized the reins in her own hands and held them till her death. Her innate fitness for personal rule was at once made manifest; with impressive calmness and self-control she at once commanded the situation; the kindly, grateful side of her character was seen in the nature of the rewards bestowed by her; and, from the very outset, she revealed that mental superiority, energy, and, above all, that mastery of the art of government, which make her reign appear truly great.

In the early years, Catharine's advisers as to foreign affairs were Panin and, to a less extent, Bestuzheff, who had been recalled. She did not, as was naturally expected, reverse Peter's sudden change of policy in regard to Prussia; she did not return unconditionally to Austria; for she was of opinion that Russia required peace, followed by a foreign policy independent of any foreign Power and calculated to serve no interests but her own. From 1725 to 1762, the influence of other Powers upon Russia had been continually on the increase; after 1762, Russia once more became an independent State. During the eighteen years of her life as Grand Duchess, Catharine had herself awakened and cultivated the natural gifts which she possessed; and now, as Tsarina, she boldly proceeded to deal with a problem which Peter I had left behind him and which had since been neglected, and worked out a solution of it in which the other Powers were obliged to concur. This problem was the Polish question.

After the revolution of 1762 the first problem which Catharine had to face was the attitude to be adopted towards Prussia. The Treaty of Hubertusburg, which terminated the Seven Years' War, was concluded without the participation of Russia, whose proffered mediation

Frederick had firmly refused. But only a year afterwards this neutral attitude towards Prussia had developed into an alliance which lasted till 1780. Catharine and Frederick recognised each other's intellectual calibre; in the pleasing personal correspondence carried on between them one can detect beneath all the courtly verbiage the conversation of two great personalities mutually congenial—that is to say, in their political capacity. It is a purely political correspondence, carried on for definite political ends by two writers gifted with *esprit*. Each delighted and vied with the other in manipulating with the utmost possible virtuosity the ingeniously graceful forms of the eighteenth century. What brought Frederick and Catharine together, and kept them together, in the first instance, for a decade and a half, consisted of very real political interests—in fact, of the community of interests between them in the matter of the kingdom of Poland.

Poland was drifting towards a doom, which had, even in this very form, been long since predicted. For the idea of a partition of Poland between the adjacent Powers did not originate with Catharine, Frederick, or Joseph II. It had been in the air earlier than that; Charles X Gustavus of Sweden had spoken of it to the Great Elector of Brandenburg; and, so early as 1662, John Casimir of Poland had actually foretold the details of the process: the Lithuanians were mostly in favour of the Muscovite; and after his death it could hardly be but that the latter would keep Lithuania, while the Emperor would get possession of Poland (*i.e.* Little Poland), in which case the Elector of Brandenburg might get a slice of Great Poland. The partition of Poland thus predicted, of which Catharine II must be considered the real author, must be differently judged from different points of view. The Poles anathematise it because it deprived them of their independent existence as a nation. The Cabinets of the Powers concerned have endeavoured to exonerate themselves from the blame of, at any rate, the initial step. Contemporaries, however, regarded Poland as a centre of religious intolerance and aristocratic tyranny, and they welcomed Catharine's action; Voltaire wrote in commendation of it, when she sent troops into Poland. But the root of the matter was that, since Brandenburg and Moscow had come to the fore, only a strong State could hold its ground between these two Powers. Poland was not a strong State, if State she could be called at all—and so she was overwhelmed. Out of this policy of the Eastern Powers, initiated by Catharine, arose the Polish question, which became an important political problem of the nineteenth century. The action of the Powers might obliterate the Polish kingdom, but it could not wipe out the Polish nation.

For various reasons, external and internal, which cannot be discussed here, Poland, though a powerful political community at the beginning of her history, had never become an actual State. The difficulty of building up a State was in this case enhanced by the fact that to the east and west Poland was practically without natural frontiers, while to the north and south such could not be acquired by the natural expansion of the nation, but must be won by conquest and subjugation of foreign races. The kingdom of Poland thus expended a great deal of strength on the struggle against the Turks in the south and south-east, thereby serving its own special purposes and a common European interest at the same time. But at home, instead of going through those stages in the development of political life which we denote by the terms mercantilism and absolutism, Poland came to a standstill at a lower stage, and her institutions were developed on that level and in a direction detrimental to the monarchy. King and Constitution succumbed to the idea of a Confederation, which Moltke aptly defined as the "legal organisation of revolution." By means of the Confederation, by the *pacta conventa* imposed by the nobility on the elective monarchy, and by their position in the central Diet (*Sejm*) and in the provincial Diets (*Sejmiki*), the nobles managed to prevent the several provinces from becoming welded together into a corporate whole and to identify the State with their own Order. Their interests alone were considered; no strong middle class arose; and the pressure on the peasants left them no longer capable of revolt, and at the same time devoid of all patriotic feeling. While the economic and political interests of the nobility were thus paramount, the security and independence of the nation had not been duly vindicated as towards other Powers. When the Powers concerned in the affairs of eastern Europe interfered more and more freely in Polish politics, there was no possibility either of resistance or of independence. By means of political and military pressure and of bribery, to which all classes of the nobility were susceptible, these Powers managed to influence the election of the King, so that after 1572 very few candidates who were not foreigners ascended the throne. The foreign Powers in question were: Austria, France, the Papacy, Sweden; subsequently, Brandenburg, Saxony; and, finally, Russia. The weakest of these, Saxony, had come into possession of the Polish throne, which from 1697 till 1763 had been held by Augustus the Strong and Augustus III. The rule of the latter had, however, been no rule at all. Belligerents had infringed on Polish territory with impunity. In the duchy of Courland, a fief of the Polish Crown, Russian influence established itself when, in 1737, Biren, the favourite of the Tsarina Anne, became Duke after the death of the last Duke of the House of Kettler. Poland herself had taken no part in the Seven Years' War; but she had had to submit to being utilised by Russia as a military base, while Frederick levied contributions and recruited soldiers on Polish soil. Poland was at Catharine's mercy when she ascended the throne and aggressively resumed the policy of expansion westwards, which Peter had actually begun, but of which the origin is really to be sought in the course which Muscovite history had for centuries followed. The turn of Courland came first; in 1763 Biren was restored, and the son of Augustus III of Poland was ousted from the dukedom which he had obtained in 1758. The fate of Courland was thus sealed, and the consummation made possible which in 1795 converted this Polish dependency into a Russian province. Henceforth, Russian influence was firmly established in Courland, a country of vital importance for the position of Russia on the Baltic coast, and containing the river Duna and the ports of Libau and Windau. Poland legally retained the overlordship; but as a matter of fact it had passed to Catharine, whose foreign policy thus achieved its first great success.

But the real Polish question, as Catharine and Frederick fully recognised, would be set in motion on the death of Augustus III. This event took place in October, 1763. Neither of the two sovereigns wished an Austrian Prince to succeed Augustus; Frederick was, on the whole, in favour of a *Piast, i.e.* a native Polish King; but Catharine was determined to utilise the election of the King for her own purpose in regard to Poland; the time had not yet come for the incorporation of Poland or part of it, but, at least, the influence of Russia should predominate in Warsaw. Her candidate for the throne was to serve this interest, and she had one ready to hand in Stanislaus Poniatowski. He had had a passing personal intimacy with Catharine, but was now to be ruthlessly employed as an instrument of her purposes. To ensure his election, she took advantage of the differences among the Polish nobility. For the nobles no longer formed a homogeneous body, even though the democratic equality supposed to exist within their circle was still marked with a ludicrous emphasis. The nobility was divided into the *Szlachta,* or lesser nobility, and a group of about one hundred families of grandees, among which sixteen or seventeen held a leading position. This small circle represented a brilliant aristocracy, possessed of the culture and manners of western Europe—that is to say, France. Around them were grouped in solid factions the dependent families of the *Szlachta,* which was again divided into a middle and an inferior stratum, the latter often of the poorest sort. The public life of Poland still consisted solely in the rivalry of these factions, following the selfish lead of the most influential families of grandees. Some patriotic ideas were still to be found, but they were always rendered ineffective by the prevailing selfishness, absence of all discipline, and habit of looking to foreign countries for assistance, financial and other. The most important family, called "the family" *par excellence,* were, as has been seen, the Czartoryskis, whose aim was actually to win the throne for their House. They formed the nucleus of the Russian party and favoured the election of Stanislaus Poniatowski, himself a member of their family.

Frederick and Catharine had a common interest, in the first instance, in the continuance of the present anarchy in Poland, since a strong well-regulated Polish State was contrary to the tendencies at work in their own monarchies. They accordingly insisted that "free" election, the *liberum veto*, and all the pomp of the Diet, should be kept up. Furthermore, however, a pretext was afforded them in the question of the "Dissidents," or "Dysunits," as the Polish Dissenters (Protestants and Greek Orthodox Catholics) were termed. Their position afforded Catharine a welcome opportunity of coming forward as the protectress of religious toleration for the Orthodox in Poland, while at the same time it increased her influence and facilitated an interference on her part, analogous to that which she had asserted on behalf of the Christians of the Balkans under Turkish rule. She proceeded resolutely, setting her diplomats, Kayserling and Repnin, to work in Warsaw, distributing money, and sending troops into Poland; she also concluded the alliance of 1764 with Frederick the Great, engaging him to move troops to the Polish frontier. She thus secured her end; and, on September 7, 1764, Stanislaus Poniatowski was elected King—as Catharine herself afterwards very truly remarked, "the candidate who had least right of all and must therefore feel more indebted to Russia than anyone else." This first election of a Polish King "made" by Russia was the second success of her foreign policy, the elections having been hitherto determined by Austria, France, and Brandenburg; and it might logically be expected that fortune would favour Russia still further.

Once safely on the throne, Stanislaus attempted to initiate reforms. He submitted a proposal to the Diet abolishing the *liberum veto*, at any rate in matters of finance; while the Czartoryskis had already brought forward schemes of reform at the "Diet of Convocation." But Russian and Prussian interests clashed with any honest effort to consolidate the State by means of reforms: and Stanislaus had to recognise in despair that it was now too late for any reform in Poland which should tend to strengthen the power of the Crown. Repnin, Catharine's ambassador at Warsaw, was instructed to prevent any alteration in the existing form of government. The fundamental evil lay in the *liberum veto*, which required unanimity in all resolutions; but the policy of Russia and Prussia required that this should be preserved as precluding the Diet from passing any constructive measures. Anarchy was still further increased under the pretext of protecting the Dissidents, for whom Russia claimed equal political rights with the Roman Catholics. When the King, backed by the Czartoryskis, refused to grant this demand, Repnin, availing himself of the feeling in the *Szlachta* against the supposed absolutist tendencies of the King, contrived the Confederation of Radom, in support of which Russian troops came on the scene. From 1767 to 1768 the Diet sat at Warsaw surrounded by Russian soldiers, and under this pressure consented to the removal of the regulations against members of other creeds, and to a compact by which Russia guaranteed the integrity of Poland and the maintenance of her Constitution. Catharine seemed already to be mistress of Poland; but she had bent the bow too far. Two days after the Diet had risen, was formed the Confederation of Bar (in Podolia) "*pro religione et libertate*," *i.e.* against all concessions to the Dissidents, absolutist reforms in the State, and any guarantee by Russia of the Polish Constitution. A terrible local war began between Russians and Confederates. The Confederation obtained the support of France, which sent money and officers, and of Austria. For some time, as has been seen, these two Powers had been agitating against Russia and Prussia in Constantinople; and now Turkey intervened on behalf of Poland and declared war against Russia (September, 1767). The Polish and Eastern questions were thus combined. It was a fatal step for Poland to have asked and received help from Turkey, thus abandoning her old historic hostility against the Porte, and committing an act of virtual self-surrender. For the amalgamation of the Polish and Eastern questions gave rise to an international tension which nothing short of the first partition of Poland could bring to a close, unless it were to find vent in a great European war.

In her ensuing war with Turkey, Catharine was successful, as will be related below. The conflicts of the Confederation, on the other hand, in which everyone operated on his own account, ended disastrously. Austria watched with growing resentment the triumphs of Russian arms, which threatened to annex the Danubian Principalities; and if, as seemed likely, a war broke out between Austria and Russia, Prussia, which was the ally of Russia and was already subsidising her, would be drawn into hostilities, which Frederick desired to avoid. Accordingly, as has been narrated elsewhere, he met Austria's advances by the interviews with Joseph II at Neisse and Neustadt, and sought to induce Catharine to relinquish her designs on the Crimea and the Danubian Principalities. With war on her hands against Turkey and against the Confederation of Bar, while Austria was assuming a threatening attitude, Catharine had to try at all costs to retain Prussia on her side. In order to impart a more personal note to her relations with Prussia, she therefore, so early as July 30, 1770, invited Prince Henry, Frederick's brother, who was then staying at Stockholm with his sister the Queen of Sweden, to pay a visit to St Petersburg. Unexpected as was the invitation, Prince Henry accepted it, and spent several months in the Russian capital. It was at one of the Tsarina's *soirées* that the question of the partition of Poland was first broached to the Prussian Prince on the part of Russia.

At the Russian Court there had hitherto been two conflicting opinions in regard to the fate of Poland, and as to how it could best be made to serve the interests of Russia. One view, advocated by Count Nikita Panin, the Foreign Minister, was in favour of Poland being brought into increasing dependence on Russia by continuous interference in her internal affairs, without any curtailment of her territory. The other view, advocated in particular by the War Minister, Count Zachary Chernuisheff, favoured the annexation of Poland. Now, in the summer of 1770, Austria had furnished a precedent for this course by the occupation of the Zips, to which she alleged herself to possess ancient rights. On the evening of January 8, 1771, Count Chernuisheff observed to Prince Henry on this subject: "Then, why not seize the bishopric of Ermeland? for, after all, everyone ought to have something"; and Catharine asked the Prince "And why should not everybody help himself likewise[1]?" The first hint as to the partition of Poland was conveyed in this conversation, which, quite in Catharine's way, touched seriously, though in a seemingly light and even jesting tone, on an important topic. The strongest argument in favour of such a line of action on the part of Russia was that, if she relinquished her schemes of extension along the lower Danube, which might compromise her with Austria and cost her the Prussian alliance, she ought to seek a compensation in Poland. Panin put this quite plainly to the Prussian ambassador, and King Frederick concurred. But Austria hereupon, in her turn, insisted on remaining in possession of those parts of Poland which she had appropriated; and Prussia's actual political position enabled her to demand something beyond Ermeland, viz., the German districts of Poland separating it from East Prussia. At the close of 1771, Catharine made a binding declaration to Frederick that she would give up the Danubian Principalities; and hereupon they struck a bargain about Poland. On February 17, 1772, the Russo-Prussian Treaty of Partition was signed at St Petersburg, and on August 5 Austria joined in this compact. Maria Theresa naturally had much more difficulty in taking part in this transaction, which was not essential to Austria from a politico-geographical point of view. Her son Joseph, in his eagerness for annexations, of course failed to see how the occupation of the Zips sufficed to involve Austria in all the consequences of this Polish policy, and how her share of Poland would only encumber her with territory which it was not to her interest to possess, and which did away with the former security of her north-eastern frontier.

The First Partition of Poland (August 5, 1772) deprived that country of about one-third of its territory and almost a third of its population. Prussia acquired Ermeland and what was called Royal Prussia (the West Prussia of the present day) with the exception of Danzig and Thorn. Austria obtained part of Little Poland (excepting Cracow) and the greater part of East Galicia, then called Red Russia. To Russia fell the strip of Livonia which had remained a Polish possession, with White Russia along the Duna and the Dnieper (the districts of Polozk, Vitebsk, Minsk, and Mstislavl). Whereas there was no historical justification for the extension of Austria, Prussia and Russia by the First Partition of Poland only took territories to which they could assert well-founded claims. For Polish Prussia had formerly been under German rule,

---

[1] "*Mais pourquoi pas s'emparer de l'évêché de Warmie? Car il faut, après tout, que chacun ait quelque chose.*" "*Mais pourquoi pas tout le monde se prendrait-il aussi?*"

and the districts taken by Russia were inhabited by Russian-speaking Greek Catholics. Catharine always maintained that she had taken no genuine Polish country; and there was some foundation for this statement, even when she repeated it after the Third Partition. The acquisition of White Russia, with its rigidly Russian and Orthodox population, even wore the appearance of a national act of liberation, though in point of fact it was nothing of the kind.

Catharine did not bring about the situation leading to the Partition of Poland which was really the beginning of its end; but she availed herself of that situation with so much skill and energy, that her action was designated as a masterpiece of political *finesse* by so experienced a statesman as Kaunitz. But the fact that the situation was not of her making had the further consequence that the whole of Poland did not fall into her hands, which was the final goal towards which the expansion of Russia might be and actually was directed. The Tsarina was on the horns of a dilemma: the maintenance of Polish integrity might in the end bring Poland under Russian influence, but Austria had already violated it. Unless Prussia stood firmly by her alliance with Russia, Austria would probably take up arms in favour of Turkey, while on the other hand any acquisition of Polish territory by Prussia would arouse the jealousy of Austria against that Power. Frederick the Great in his Memoirs correctly judged that the violation of the integrity of Poland was suddenly made to serve as an expedient for avoiding a great European war. Under the influence of his brother Henry, he thereupon adopted the suggestion emanating from St Petersburg, adroitly availing himself of it to effect a much-needed enlargement of his borders. By the occupation of the Zips Austria had made the first move, and it was therefore she who, as Frederick says, "did most to pave the way" for the Partition Treaty. But it was the fault of Poland herself that her own state organisation had been too weak to offer any resistance to the long-cherished aspirations of her two neighbours when these crystallised into action; and it was her fault, again, that her own ruling class, the nobility, itself helped to assure the success of this foreign encroachment.

Poland was not annihilated by the First Partition. Of course it was the death-blow to the conception of a Greater Poland "from sea to sea," *i.e.* from the Baltic to the Black Sea; this, however, was no true national ideal, but a mere scheme of aggression against peoples of different race. Nor can Poland, after 1772, be said to have been anything more than a Russian tributary State under the rule of the Russian ambassador at Warsaw, and in the hold of the Russian garrisons distributed throughout the country. But, even so, the nucleus of the State remained; and Poland might still have a future before her if she resolved on a reform of her home affairs. And such a reform was actually attempted with some show of zeal, while the part of the country which had fallen to Russia was energetically and judiciously brought into line with the Russian civil and ecclesiastical system by its Governor-General, Count Zachary Chernuisheff, in most of whose ideas and plans Catharine concurred.

The Partition by the three Powers was ratified by what was called the "Delegation Diet," which lasted from 1773 to 1775. Thus Poland was brought by persuasion, compulsion, and bribery to consent to the loss of one-third of her territory without striking a blow—a national surrender scarcely paralleled in history. The same Diet, however, at once adopted measures of reform and "cardinal rights," as they were termed, which, however, left untouched the weakest points in the Constitution, such as the election of the King and the *liberum veto*. The most important reforms were, first, the establishment of a "perpetual Council of State" (*Rada nieustająca*), under the presidency of the King, in which the executive power was vested when the Diet was not sitting, and, secondly, the appointment of an Education Commission endowed with the wealth of the expelled Order of Jesuits, which was to reform public instruction. These two bodies were the first central authorities exercising jurisdiction over Lithuania as well as Poland—for, by the Union of Lublin (1569), Lithuania had retained its separate administration, finances, and army. Though the Education Commission in particular did zealous and effective work for public instruction, no really far-reaching reforms were achieved till 1788, owing to the continuance of the intrigues and personal antagonisms and ambitions of the several factions. And the reforms planned by the King and his adherents were likewise crippled by the fact that the "cardinal rights" were under the guarantee of the partitioning Powers, which had no interest in any real reform and internal consolidation of Poland. It should be noted how the ideas of the *Aufklärung* gradually penetrated into the Polish world, in particular through the writings of Staszic and Kołłątaj, and prepared the way for still more widespread reforms—for example, the emancipation of the peasants. Altogether, these last years of the kingdom of Poland were a period of intellectual activity. Stanislaus loved and promoted art and literature; and many poets and writers, such as Krasicki, Naruszewicz, Niemcewicz and the two mentioned above, shed a glory as of sunset on the last years of the doomed country. Politically, Poland stood alone throughout the years which included the dissolution of the Russo-Prussian, and the formation of the Russo-Austrian, alliance. In 1787, Russia, conjointly with Austria, began her second Turkish War, and the question arose: which side would Poland take? Stanislaus inclined towards that of Russia, though there was little hope that she would concede anything in the matter of reforms, and much less that she would consent to the strengthening of the Polish army. Although desirous of getting possession of Danzig and Thorn, Prussia, being now hostile to Russia, had no objection to reforms in Poland, and she therefore proposed to Poland an alliance on these lines, which was negotiated by the Diet opened on October 6, 1788. This

CH. XIX.

famous "Four Years' Diet" began the last period of Polish independence, and accomplished reforms culminating in the Constitution of May 3, 1791. But no time was left for Poland to show whether she was capable of carrying through an organic change in the conditions of her public and social life. It is told elsewhere, how, in 1793 and 1795, Catharine completed what she had begun in 1772, and Poland fell out of the ranks of independent States. The Tsarina had taken skilful and unscrupulous advantage of the impotence and internal decay of Poland, and, though obliged to share the spoils with Prussia and Austria, contrived that the historic struggle carried on for centuries with Poland should end triumphantly for Russia. The Russian frontier was thus pushed forward into central Europe, while the position of the empire on the Baltic was at the same time brought into connexion with that which it held in regard to the Eastern question.

The antagonism between Russia and Turkey was, and remains to this day, partially due to the fact that the Turks are the successors of the Tartars. This antagonism is deep-rooted and quite exceptionally widespread among the Russians, and explains the sympathy inspired in them by an enduring sense of community of race and faith for the Christian subjects of Turkey. Furthermore, the actual situation of Turkey had prevented Russia from obtaining a natural frontier and sea-board in the south, and her European expansion in the south-west. Throughout the course of centuries this antagonism continued closely interwoven with that between Moscow and Poland. Peter I sought to dispose of this menace to Russian development by endeavouring, first of all, to turn the national and religious sympathies of the Balkan peninsula to Russia's account as against Turkey. This plan, as we know, failed absolutely. The Tsarina Anne then continued his projects in alliance with Austria. Their direct political objects are stated in an instruction of 1737: namely, incorporation of the region of the south Russian steppe, the conquest of the Crimea, the left bank of the Danube as Russia's southern frontier, the liberation of the two Danubian Principalities (Moldavia and Wallachia), in which of course Russian influence was henceforth to predominate. This programme once realised, Turkey would cease to be a dangerous enemy to Russia, which could then aim at putting an end to the very existence of a Turkey in Europe, and substituting for it any other sort of States—provided always that they were dependent on Russia, or, better still, under her direct rule. Catharine had in the main carried out the earlier programme; this later scheme she was unable to accomplish, but left as an inheritance to her successors. Antagonism to Turkey in Asia was not overlooked by her, but kept more in the background. Though in this quarter also she achieved successes towards the end of her life—such as, for instance, the establishment of a protectorate over Georgia (1783) and the war with Persia—their significance was merely incidental to her

Eastern policy: for the European side of the question was paramount. In this respect her reign brought about the important and lasting result that no solution of the question was conceivable either without Russia, or through Russia alone.

It has already been stated how Russia's first Turkish War (1768–74) was consequent upon the struggle against the Confederation of Bar. Catharine entered upon the War with confidence and courage, although the odds were heavy against her. Her throne was still far from secure; there were still internal crises to be overcome, and she had France and Austria against her in the conflict with Poland and Turkey. All this enhanced the importance of Prussian support. The Russian equipment left much to be desired; in particular, the war department and commissariat failed, as always in Russian wars. However, the Porte was still worse prepared, so that Frederick the Great ridiculed the War as a fight between the blind and the one-eyed. It proved a protracted affair; especially as Catharine had no competent generals except Peter Panin; and in him she placed no implicit trust.

The invasion of New Servia by the Tartars at the beginning of 1769 pointed to the necessity of settling accounts with them once for all. But this could only be accomplished if Russian territory were extended to the shores of the Black Sea. Catharine's hopes, however, soared beyond this —to naval operations on the waters of the Black Sea; to securing a free navigation of its waters; to the acquisition of the Caucasus; and, finally, to rousing the Greeks to a revolt against the Turks. Thus the daring expedition to the Black Sea which started from Kronstadt in 1770 was pursuing the ultimate and most ambitious aims of this Eastern policy. And, though no general rising of the Greeks took place, yet the expedition, which was commanded by Alexei Orloff, achieved the greatest naval victory at any time won by Russia. On July 5 and 7, 1770, the Turkish fleet was defeated off Scio and absolutely annihilated off Tchesmé— a victory comparable with Lepanto and Navarino. The Russians owed it rather to the admirals of English extraction (Greig and Elphinston) who were commanding under Orloff, than to that officer himself, who was comparatively ignorant of naval tactics. He reaped the greatest honours, however, as Catharine wisely always saw fit to confer higher rewards and more brilliant promotion on native Russians than on foreigners, though the latter were for the most part more capable, and were certainly indispensable when it came to gaining victories.

The land forces, too, were successful: in 1770, Bender, Ismail, Kilia, Akerman, Brailoff fell in succession, and, in the next year, Kerch, Eupatoria, Perekop, with the whole Crimean peninsula, were occupied. The other European Powers looked on with mingled feelings at these successes of the Russian arms. England was little affected by them, but was unwilling that Russia should secure the passage of the Bosphorus as a result of this War. France was more strongly opposed to the advance of

Russia; and Prussia, which was paying subsidies to Russia, was by no means pleased with the War in itself, and still less by Catharine's victories, which threatened to drag Prussia into a conflict with Austria. In the Peace of Belgrade in 1739, the Austrians had made away with the fair prospects of their own Eastern policy, while at the same time destroying the great and legitimate expectations of Russia; and now it was they on whom the Russian successes against the Porte pressed most heavily, and whose Balkan schemes were threatened. The state of tension between the Powers was fraught with possibilities of a European war; but a solution of the difficulty was found, as described above, by the First Partition of Poland among the Eastern Powers.

Meanwhile, the Russo-Turkish War was progressing. The first peace negotiations were abortive, and fresh Russian victories followed, the Turk proving as usual a far more obdurate foe than had been anticipated. Then, when Pugachoff's rising broke out at home in Russia, Catharine concluded a peace, which, although it did not fulfil all her high hopes, was nevertheless one of the most advantageous treaties ever made by a Russian sovereign. By this Treaty of Kutchuk-Kainardji of July 21, 1774, Russia obtained Azoff, Kerch, and Yenikale, which meant the control of the straits between the Sea of Azoff and the Black Sea, also Kinburn at the mouth of the Dnieper, and the steppe beyond it lying between the Bug and the Dnieper. The Treaty declared the independence of the Crimean Tartars—the first step towards their subjection to Russia. The Black Sea from which other nations were still excluded was thrown open to Russia, and her merchantmen were allowed to pass through the Bosphorus and the Dardanelles. Further, Great and Little Kabardia, parts, that is to say, of the Kuban and Terek district, became Russian; whereby a footing on the eastern shore of the Black Sea and in the Caucasus was secured, involving of course conflict with the Circassians. Articles 7 and 14, again, afforded Russia a pretext—not justified by the wording—for claiming protective rights over adherents of the Greek Church living in Turkey and so interfering in the internal affairs of that country. Henceforth, the Eastern policy of Russia could be based on the popular conception of her as the natural protectress of the Greek Christians. Thus, the Treaty of Kutchuk-Kainardji abundantly rewarded the immense sacrifices made by Russia for the war. But even so it was no final settlement of the vexed question. In the first place, Catharine did not relinquish those more ambitious schemes which, particularly after Potemkin's rise to favour, became almost reckless in their scope. She dreamed of breaking up Turkey in order to form a new Greek empire, which was destined for her second grandson, significantly named Constantine, while Moldavia, Wallachia, and Bessarabia were to constitute a kingdom of Dacia, to be ruled by an Orthodox Prince—Potemkin to wit. These fantastic and prodigious plans could only be realised by a yet greater war, in which Austria must side with Russia, for without the help of that Power, much less in opposition to it, Catharine's projects were futile. Now, the longer Catharine pursued this path, the further she drew away from Prussia and the nearer to Austria, for Joseph II's way of thinking met such notions half-way, even if they savoured of extravagance. He was prepared to fall in with Catharine's plans against Turkey, claiming for Austria by way of return Servia, Bosnia, Herzegovina and Dalmatia, while Venice was to receive the Morea, Candia, and Cyprus. So the eggs were carefully counted before they were hatched. Meanwhile, Frederick II felt certain that, so soon as there was any real question of a partition of Turkey, the interests of Austria and Russia would clash, in particular as to the lower Danube.

There was no mention of the Crimea in Catharine's scheme, for it was already regarded as the property of Russia, which it actually became in 1783, without any objection on the part of Joseph II. For this achievement Potemkin was decorated with the agnomen of "the Taurian," and raised to the rank of a Prince of the Holy Roman Empire. He had, however, performed no specially glorious feat. The internal discord always seething among the Tartars had been turned to account, and the subsequent annexation of their country had been accompanied by scenes of terror and butchery, which must not of course be laid at Catharine's door. She was pleased and elated by the conquest, declaring that she had come to Russia empty-handed but had won Tauria and Poland as her dowry. Now, at length, Russia had won a firm and sure southern frontier and respite from the races which had formerly borne her down by their numbers and had since constantly harassed her; these had now been brought beneath her sway or had migrated. The union of the Crimea with Russia at last put an end to the trade carried on thence for centuries in Russian slaves.

In France and Turkey, however, the annexation of the Crimea aroused considerable misgivings, and war once more seemed imminent. In face of this, Catharine contrived a singular demonstration, namely, the famous Tauric journey begun in January, 1787. She was accompanied by the Emperor Joseph II, and by a brilliant suite which included the Austrian, English, and French ambassadors. The expedition was largely a pleasure party, producing by its magnificent and often theatrical setting a perfectly incredible impression; but it was also a political move, intended to show off the wealth of Russia, the newly acquired steppe, the southern beauty of the Crimea, the rapid development of the recently founded towns, fortresses, and harbours. There was certainly a good deal of staging about all this; for Potemkin was, all of a sudden, to appear in the light of a splendid organiser and administrator, and there is justification for the proverbial use of the expression "Potemkin's villages" to signify sham splendour. The spectators, however, realised the significance of a naval port having arisen at Sevastopol from which Constantinople could be reached in two days; and it was felt far and near how vast a change the present Tsarina had wrought in the position of Russia in the Eastern question.

For this very reason Catharine's journey only increased the existing tension; and in August, 1787, war with Turkey broke out afresh. The immediate cause alleged by the Porte was the annexation of the Crimea; but it was further apprehended that the dependence of Georgia (since, in 1783, its sovereign, Irakli, had put himself under Russian protection) would ultimately involve the subjection of the whole Caucasus. Joseph recognised a *casus foederis* for Austria as the ally of Russia; and in February, 1788, he likewise declared war against Turkey, by which means the two Powers thought to accomplish its projected partition. Accordingly, a few years afterwards (1790), Prussia entered into an alliance with the Porte, and then with Poland, so that Prussia was henceforth opposed to Russia all along the line.

The year 1788 ended with a decisive victory for Russia in the capture of Ochakoff. Once again, there was some idea of a naval expedition to the Mediterranean to rouse the Greeks to insurrection. This renewed advance of the Russians was already causing great excitement in Europe, more especially in England. However, the fleet was not despatched, as it was needed elsewhere, Gustavus III of Sweden having declared war. Thus, despite her successes against Turkey, Catharine found herself in a precarious position, which was further aggravated by the death of Joseph and a change in the attitude of Austria. Thanks to her own skill and energy, she was able to extricate herself by means of the Treaty of Värälä with Sweden (1790) and that of Jassy with Turkey (January 9, 1792), thus avoiding the intervention of one of the European Powers. The Treaty of Jassy confirmed that of Kutchuk-Kainardji: the partition of Turkey had certainly not been effected, neither had the Greek empire and the kingdom of Dacia come into being. But the Dniester had become the boundary river of Russia, and the northern shore of the Black Sea to the confines of the Caucasus was now Russian. It remained for Catharine's successors to improve upon the position of Russia in Asia and to pursue her plan of utilising against Turkey the foothold afforded by the protectorship over the Greek Christians of that country. Sevastopol and Odessa (founded in 1794) remained the outward and visible signs of what Catharine had achieved in the East; henceforth Turkey had no longer any terrors for Russia.

The nature and results of Catharine's foreign policy will now have become sufficiently intelligible. Its gist was the consistent assertion of the strength of Russia in the interests of Russia; nor was it devoid of a Machiavellian note. Catharine never allowed her country to be taken in tow by another Power. To her, alliances and understandings were, simply and solely, means for increasing the strength of Russia with a view to securing for it the status of a really European Power.

And herein she was so successful, that, apart from the acquisition of territory, which in itself furthered her aims, she almost attained to the position of arbitress in the affairs of central Europe. She was able to avail herself of the strong antagonism between Prussia and Austria, siding now with one and now with the other, and thus dependent on neither. In the crisis created by the Bavarian War of Succession in 1778, both Powers sought her help at the same time; so that she could announce her intention to stand surety for the Constitution of Germany, thus assuming a *rôle* hitherto played by France. After the conclusion of the Treaty of Teschen, on which Russia had brought a decisive influence to bear, Frederick and Maria Theresa expressed their gratitude for her mediation—an indication of the change in the European status of Russia, even as compared with that reached under Peter. It was at Teschen that Catharine laid the foundation of the political influence exercised by Russia in Germany, and more especially in Prussia, which lasted far into the nineteenth century.

With England there were not as yet so many points of contact, since that Power had offered no special opposition to the Russian forward movement in the East. The change in the Russian relations with Prussia was, however, accompanied by a similar alienation of England, and, in the last years of Catharine's reign Pitt was definitely opposed to her in Eastern affairs. It was against England that the system of "Armed Neutrality" (1780) was directed, by means of which Catharine sought to secure the neutral flag in face of the English practices against neutral shipping in the war with the North American Colonies. The declaration marked an important advance in the theoretical development of maritime law, but could be of no practical avail against the naval strength of England.

With all her liking for French society and literature, Catharine's relations to France had always been rather cool; and, as to the Eastern question, France had sided against her, without, however, taking any leading part. But, despite her attitude towards the *Aufklärung*, she was adverse on principle to the French Revolution, just as she had been indignant at the American. For the same reason, she became, towards the close of her reign, more reactionary in her home policy. But, though she might express her views on the Revolution in France, she took care not to be drawn into the war for its suppression. On the contrary, she openly confessed that the War of the First Coalition appeared to her an excellent way of occupying the Courts of Vienna and Berlin, so as to leave her a free hand for her undertakings. In fact, however, she served the Revolution, inasmuch as her Polish and Eastern policy compelled the coalition directed against the West to turn its attention to the East, and thus hampered and crippled its action.

The results of Catharine's foreign policy were, as regards diplomacy, almost exclusively the work of the sovereign herself. Her ministers and ambassadors were her assistants ; of counsellors she had no need. Neither Nikita Panin nor Alexander Besborodko, her Foreign Ministers, held a position with her resembling that of Bestuzheff with the Tsarina Elizabeth or that of Kaunitz with Maria Theresa. Catharine, exactly like Frederick the Great, managed her foreign affairs herself, notably by dint of vigorous private correspondence with other crowned heads, Frederick II, Joseph II, Gustavus III of Sweden (her correspondence with Prince Henry of Prussia may likewise be included). Her literary correspondence with Grimm, Voltaire, and Diderot was of some political significance : she meant these *literati* to influence the public opinion of Europe by blowing the Russian trumpet ; and, herein too, she was highly successful. It is true that these letters betray an undercurrent of personal vanity on her part ; but she exhibits at the same time a marvellous versatility of mind and skill in dealing with political matters. Her letters prove her a woman of great political talent, by whom the privileges of her sex and position alike were utilised to the full for public ends, both in her correspondence and more especially in her conversation. She often tried to transact affairs of State under cover of social pleasures, delightful as these were to her in themselves. Nor must the influence of Potemkin on this essentially independent woman be over-estimated, though he was a favourite of hers and seemed preeminently trusted by her to play a leading part in public matters. It is certainly an exaggeration to divide her reign simply into the period before Potemkin (to *c.* 1774) and the time of his ascendancy. He may have imparted a rather more adventurous and fantastic tone to her Eastern schemes than would otherwise have belonged to them ; but they formed an organic part of Russia's historic development, and the political action of the Tsarina did not run out of all bounds in obedience to the wishes of this strange favourite. He did not dominate her ; anyone who seriously considers the two personalities must be convinced that such a supposition is psychologically inconceivable. When he took command of the troops in the second Turkish War, it was she who led and advised, and allowed herself to be disconcerted by no emergency, while his passive nature broke down utterly. It was her individual will which prompted and determined her foreign policy ; though it must of course be borne in mind that, while her statesmanship justly commands admiration by reason of its firmness, breadth and uniformity, the main lines of her foreign policy were defined for her with comparative clearness and simplicity, so soon as she had made up her mind to consult none but Russian interests. But, if the masterly conduct of foreign affairs in which lay the chief glory of this reign is entirely attributable to Catharine, at her door must also be laid the immense sacrifice of life and property imposed upon the Russian nation by that policy, to whose demands all home affairs, the material prosperity of her people, and their advance in civilisation, had always to remain subordinate and subservient.

From the first Catharine threw herself with great zeal into the tasks appertaining to absolute rule. She endeavoured to inform herself on every subject, read and wrote a vast amount with this end in view, and strove to be absolute monarch in home affairs as well as foreign. Her first task, indeed, was that of securing her own position. She had usurped the throne; and, although the *coup d'état* had easily raised her to it, a turn of the tide might just as easily bring her down. For the Guards had been demoralised by the *coup d'état*, and aspirants to Catharine's position were not far to seek. She confessed to having felt insecure on the throne till the middle of the seventies. At Court, the various factions were scheming against each other for the upper hand, as, for example, Princess Dashkoff against the Orloffs. Catharine owed the Crown mainly to the energetic support of the Orloffs, who consequently rose to the top, although Gregori, her actual favourite, was incapable of exerting any real influence on state affairs. For a time it seemed as if the Tsarina meant to legitimatise her relations with him by marriage; and this step was advised by Bestuzheff, though strongly opposed by Panin. But she can hardly have seriously contemplated it, as such a marriage could be of no service to her and must have involved her immediately in the petty rivalries of the various court cliques. For her, a stranger to Russia, it was even more important than it had been to the English Queen Elizabeth to be "wedded to her people." That Russians proper felt no very great enthusiasm for the German usurper became evident at the coronation, when the Moscow populace cheered her son Paul far more than they did the Tsarina herself. She had all the more need of emphasising her determination to be a Russian; and herein she was aided by the fact that no foreigner ever more thoroughly understood the character, often wholly mysterious, and the psychology of the Russian people. For instance, no German was ever one of her numerous favourites, or placed at the head of Cabinet or army, although in administrative and military affairs she could but ill dispense with the German element in her State. In this way she flattered the patriotic feeling which was intensified by the splendid successes of her foreign policy; and, in the end, she was accounted a genuine Russian, though she never was or could become such at heart.

At the outset of her reign she had to struggle against the opposition of the Orthodox clergy, which might have become exceedingly dangerous to her. As regards religion, she was heart and soul a child of the *Aufklärung*; but such convictions did not prevent her from clearly recognising the importance of the Greek Church, in which Old Russian opinion might find a support against her. She therefore pursued vigorously and successfully the ecclesiastical policy of Peter III, namely the secularisation of church lands. Archbishop Arseni Mazeievich of Rostoff became the representative of the opposition against her and her policy, which ended by openly questioning her right to the throne (1763

and 1767).   Catharine had to face a dangerous crisis, and came through
it successfully.   The common people associated various legends with
the person of the prelate who vanished into the dungeons of Reval;
evidently, he had elicited something of an echo among the masses, and
their attitude towards the new *régime* was by no means enthusiastic.
This disaffection and unrest might easily have found a tangible and
thus exceedingly dangerous centre.   Ivan Antonovich was still living in
Schlüsselburg, though almost reduced to idiocy by his long imprisonment, and any fresh revolutionary movement might well make use of
him as a rival for the throne.   It was, therefore, fortunate for Catharine
that he met his end in a wild attempt made for his liberation (1764).
In this case also Catharine has been accused of the trick of having
participated in the plan for her rival's release in order to effect his
removal.   She was, however, assuredly innocent of Ivan's murder; but
the rumour proves how insecure her position was thought.

The last genuine claimant was thus disposed of.   But all through the
reign there was a succession of false claimants.   Russia has always been
the classical land for the type; so that each instance of it must be
regarded as part of a problem in social pathology.   So far as Catharine's
reign is concerned, the murder of Peter III, Ivan's long imprisonment,
and the criminal proceedings against supposed revolutionary designs,
were shrouded in so much mystery as to excite the imagination of the
people, who were quite prepared to believe that it was not the real
Peter, Ivan, and so forth, that had been done away with.   Pseudo-
pretenders, often mere adventurers or robber-chiefs, were readily followed
by the Russian populace, who thus testified to a complicated series of
experiences that had impressed themselves upon it—bad government
and a barbarously arbitrary administration of justice; the miserable
social condition of the peasantry, oppressed by the conscription and by
a load of taxation imposed by authorities ruthlessly set upon finding
men and money; together with the instinctive hostility of the people to
non-Russian domination; the hatred nursed by the sectaries against
the persecution of their creed by the state Church; the remembrance
of their lost freedom cherished by the Cossacks; the hostility of the
"foreign" elements towards Russian nationalism; the repugnance to a
settled condition of things natural to a people which, after all, had not
as yet fully emerged from the nomadic state and still clung largely to
vagrant habits.   Amid these constant convulsions of the body politic the
pretender became in the end a mere accessory; the movements in question
were in fact social upheavals, with a national woof in the texture.   The
most formidable rising was Pugachoff's, of which Bibikoff, who had been
sent to quell it, wrote appositely: "Pugachoff matters little, but the
universal discontent much."

This rising of Pugachoff (1773–5), coinciding as it did with the
Turkish War, was the most serious internal crisis which Catharine had

to face during her reign. Jemelian Pugachoff, a Don Cossack, who could neither read nor write, came forward as Pretender, professing to be Peter III, who was not really dead at all. The wave of insurrection stirred up by him in the south-east rolled onwards amid terrible atrocities, and was swelled by all the currents of feeling noted above. It was at one and the same time a peasant revolt and a rising of Cossacks, Tartars, Chuvas, Bashkirs, and others, against the Russians. It lasted for a long time, until the insurgents, who were already threatening Moscow, were overthrown and Pugachoff was put to death. But the Pretender had almost been lost sight of in the horrors of the struggle and in the universal excitement. The rising was no longer a movement to dethrone the Tsarina, but a revolution—not a political revolution with definite political aims, but a social upheaval, a sort of *Jacquerie.* It became glaringly evident how unprepared and how unsound at heart was the State which at that very time succeeded in concluding the Treaty of Kutchuk-Kainardji. An appalling contrast was thus revealed between the outward splendour and the wild ferment of the interior, between the European form of the State and the Asiatic barbarity of the people.

After 1775 the Tsarina felt secure, even though the intrigues at Court had not ceased, nor the discontent among the people, especially in Moscow. To this was added her suspicion of her own son Paul. The relations between mother and son were not of the best; he reminded her of his father, like whom she considered him unfit to rule the empire. She intended accordingly to exclude him from the succession to the throne. From a legal point of view, the execution of this intention would not have amounted to an act of violence; for it had been provided by Peter I that every Tsar should appoint his successor. Catharine had her grandson Alexander in view as her successor and made a point of alienating him from his father; while Paul was kept away from the Court and from affairs of State, she won over Alexander and Constantine to herself. Thus, the same condition of things repeated itself which she had experienced as Tsarevna under Elizabeth; and the throne which Catharine had herself with difficulty secured was once more exposed to the risk of violent agitations. But her death intervened before the matter had been entirely settled according to her wishes; and Paul was able to ascend the throne without difficulty or opposition. In 1797, he reintroduced the law of succession by primogeniture, which continues in force in Russia at the present day.

Catharine, being a usurper, had to depend very specially on the support of the new bureaucracy created by Peter I in the order of precedence issued on February 4, 1722. Russia was henceforth in civil and military affairs under the sway of the agreement between the Tsar and this bureaucracy (the *Chin*), who were alike separated from the people by a broad line of cleavage. These allied authorities held the reins of government, each being deeply interested in the existence of the other; the vast subject mass of the people stood by, uncomprehending and apathetic like a sacrificial lamb, while its rulers brought about the new development of Russia as part of the European world. Far from reforming, Catharine rather intensified this relation, which possesses so enormous an importance for the history of Russia. The instruments of her policy were the officers, who commanded the soldiers drawn from the peasantry, and the bureaucracy, whose formal composition and organisation she altered to some extent, but without being able to change its character materially. It was the task of this bureaucracy to hold the resources of the country in readiness, so as to place them at the immediate disposal of the sole and absolute sovereign. Thus the whole administration absolutely and entirely centred in St Petersburg and the Tsarina.

In the first instance, she was environed by a number of Ministries, or Colleges, as Peter I had termed these central authorities founded by him. Of these only the Department for Foreign Affairs, the War Department, and the Admiralty, remained intact and of importance. The title of Chancellor, which was attached to the Ministry for Foreign Affairs, lapsed under Catharine: the Foreign Ministers (Panin and Besborodko), however, discharged the office of Chancellor, with the assistance of a Vice-Chancellor (Prince Alexander Galitsin, and afterwards Count Osterman). The other departments lost their *raison d'être* under Catharine and were abolished, their functions being transferred by her to the Boards constituted in the provinces. On the other hand an attempt was made by her to establish a central administration of revenue; but this was not systematically carried out. The head of this central financial administration was the Procurator-General, whose post, created by Peter in order to facilitate the relations between Tsar and Senate, became an exceedingly important one under Catharine: this official (since 1764 Prince Viasemski), as the head of the whole internal administration, took the lead in home affairs. No real importance was attained by the departmental organisations, which the central offices were to weld into a systematic whole, nor by the Senate, which had originated in Peter I's reign, nor yet by the Imperial Council, which Catharine had added in 1768, to meet the needs of the military administration in the Turkish War. For Catharine had herself so strong an interest in legislative and administrative matters, that she preferred to manage the various branches directly through the agency of persons on whom she could rely. In the main she was her own Minister, Chancellor, and Imperial Council.

The fundamental principle of administration in Russia was centralisation in the hands of the sovereign. Catharine was, however, shrewd enough to see that in her enormous empire such a centralisation was, as a matter of fact, impracticable, unless methodically supplemented by allowing the highest possible measure of independence to the administration of the provinces. In place, therefore, of the more or less chaotic conditions of local administration, she established (1775) a system of governorships on which the provincial administration of Russia at the present day is largely based. This reform, if tending overmuch towards regular uniformity, was at the same time of great importance. Its chief features were as follows: the unwieldy governmental districts then existing were to be split up into smaller districts of 300,000 to 400,000 inhabitants, which were further subdivided into circles of 20,000 to 30,000, but grouped together in large provinces under Governors-General. There was to be decentralisation, distribution of functions, and establishment of judicial and administrative Boards; while the population was to cooperate, organised in Estates, for purposes of local administration. The model for the main part of these changes was supplied by the German (Baltic) provinces, and during the two decades required for carrying them into effect the Tsarina was materially assisted by Count Johann Jakob Sievers, a Baltic nobleman, one of her leading officials. The idea was to have a local administration which would best serve the interests of people and State, whereas direction and control should rest with the central body. The framework was to consist of two governmental Boards (administrative and financial) under the Governor and Vice-Governor, with the Governor's Civil and Criminal Court. In addition, a number of authorities superintended justice, police, poor-relief, etc., which were to be elected by the people partially in the case of the provinces and entirely in that of the circles. By means of this comprehensive reform, Catharine wished to give self-government to the people as organised in Estates. But what was established was, of course, not "self-government" properly so called; for it is contradictory to the spirit of even the most enlightened despotism to permit any really independent participation of the people in government by means of elective bodies. Catharine looked upon the share taken by the Estates as a function of the State, and upon the officials elected by them as state officials; she allowed them a wide scope for activity, but not the conditions of any real autonomy, and much less the right of levying taxes. For these organs of the Estates were intended to carry out the will, not of the people, but of the sovereign, and to perform the tasks prescribed by her; since, according to the conception of enlightened despotism, the will of the sovereign must of necessity be the most rational. Yet even this concession in the direction of self-government was excessive in the eyes of the official classes. With the aid of the autocracy, conceived of as indicated, these new bodies were utilised by them in such a way as entirely to forfeit their character of organs of self-government. Such a course was rendered possible by the compact between Tsardom and *Chin* on the one hand, and by the immaturity of the population on the other. As a matter of fact, self-government did not ensue from the law of 1775, as might have been anticipated from its wording. The centre of gravity of the local administration lay in the

Governor or Governor-General as the case might be, who was virtually nothing more than the local representative of the central Government. Thus, this reform associated with Catharine's name failed to bring about so great an advance in the art of administration as ought to have ensued. A better distribution of functions between central and provincial authorities was achieved, and a general organisation of local government was effected which was a considerable improvement on the former state of affairs, although, it must be confessed, somewhat inelastic, and not altogether calculated to work smoothly. The law of 1775, however, failed to result in real self-government, and to shake the power of the bureaucracy; it did not give rise to that restraining force which alone could improve the character of the civil service. Catharine endeavoured to master every difficulty and to reform in every direction; she was the first sovereign since Peter the Great to travel about Russia, in order to form an idea of things for herself; but, owing to the enormous size of the country, the lack of means of communication, and the passive obstruction of the official classes, she was unable, in spite of all her great natural gifts and force of character, to accomplish a wholesale reform. She could not, single-handed, alter the character of the officials, who remained on the whole arbitrary, negligent, corrupt, and mercenary; and often she was herself only too prone to judge by appearances. Catharine's administrative reform manifests her eminence in a sphere of action usually closed to women; but at the same time it reveals the limitations imposed on an enlightened despotism even when represented by a sovereign of such brilliant gifts and so powerful a will.

If the nation was to be led up after this fashion to self-government, it needed to be already organised, or to become organised in one way or another, and in its several Estates, since it was in strict accordance with the system of Estates that this particular form of self-government was devised. The peasantry had from of old been organised in their traditional communities. Catharine's legislation tried to bring these into line for self-government. In the newly constituted bodies, few in number, which were to embrace all ranks of society, the peasantry were to be represented, and, where a special agency had been provided for each Estate, the peasants also were to have one of their own. But this only held good in respect of peasants belonging to the Crown; the vast majority were manorial peasants, who, being debarred from all rights conferred by this administrative reform, remained under the exclusive control of the landowners. But even this limited measure of self-government was shorn of all significance for the crown peasants, too, in consequence of the construction put upon it by the bureaucracy and of the low state of civilisation of the peasant population.

On the other hand, it was of some importance for the towns on which the municipal system promulgated in 1785 conferred a form of self-government based on a classification of their inhabitants (in guilds, companies, etc.). But, here again, self-government did not imply very much—for the simple reason that in Russia there existed as yet no middle class as such with its distinctive social aspirations. Thus, at bottom, in the towns also everything remained virtually dependent on the organs of the Government.

What amount of self-government the administrative reform of 1775 did bring about was, as a matter of fact, solely to the advantage of the nobility; this reform, coupled with the "Letter of Grace to the Nobility," of 1785, completed the process by which they became the privileged class. Not only did they enjoy unconditional, direct, and unrestrained power over their own peasantry, but the State was virtually, if indirectly, controlled by them as a bureaucracy, and through the medium of this so-called self-government. By the "Letter of Grace" the nobles were corporately organised as belonging to the several circles and provinces (with an assembly and a marshal of the order); this organisation, which continues in the main to the present day, was modelled on that of the Baltic provinces. The elections of the official functionaries of the Estates, instituted in 1775, took place according to the circles and provinces. The exemption of the nobility from state service, granted by Peter III, was continued by Catharine. The nobles enjoyed immunity from taxation, might not be subjected to corporal punishment, and so forth. They now possessed absolute power over their peasantry, but were responsible to the Government for the due performance of state obligations by their peasants, in the way of military service and payment of poll tax. Thus, the reform of 1775 had conceded no real self-government of a kind to educate the nation politically. The State was ruled by an absolute Tsar and a bureaucracy in the hands of the *Chin*, whose hierarchy remained. As a highly privileged class of landed proprietors and as a social order, the nobles had a great measure of power; it was from their ranks that the officials were mainly drawn, and they thus controlled administration and justice—but political importance they had none, more especially as the rank of a noble was easily attained, being conferred as a matter of course on anyone who reached a certain position in the table of precedence. The *Chin* and the landed proprietors were actual powers in the land; but the nobles constituted no country gentry, as such, in the Russia of the Tsars, corresponding to that which existed in western Europe. This development, the result of which was of vital importance for Russia, was definitively marked out by Catharine's legislation. Speaking generally, the whole reform aimed at an organically subdivided national life on a local basis; but it failed to achieve a result which presupposed a freedom incompatible with the absolutism of the Tsars and consequently not permitted by them.

This contrast between theory and practice is still more clearly apparent in Catharine's treatment of the peasant question and in her famous "Legislative Commission." This Commission, which sat from

1767 to 1768, seemed to be a move in the direction of legislation by the people themselves—the beginning, in other words, of a parliamentary system in Russia. It will therefore be easily understood that this step caused the greatest possible sensation in Europe and, since it was inconceivable that Russia could be transformed from an absolute monarchy into a State which had limited its own powers, was regarded, and ridiculed, as sheer comedy. As a matter of fact, the Commission was intended to be neither a parliament, nor even the germ of one.

Catharine had eagerly assumed the duties of a ruler, having prepared herself for them by her study of writings in French political philosophy. As an enthusiastic student of the new French school, she felt that an opportunity was now afforded her of introducing into Russia its liberal and humane doctrines, so fraught with blessings for the people. She was imbued with the conviction that a clear legal code and good laws were of paramount, indeed of all-important, value. Such laws as there were in Russia consisted of a confused mass of the most heterogeneous provisions; it had been recognised before Catharine's time that they required systematic codification, though this had not been accomplished. Catharine, a true child of the eighteenth century, was of opinion that it was necessary, in the first place, to establish fresh legal principles adapted to the age, with which the detailed regulations must be made to accord; this method of procedure would best remedy the deficiencies in the existing laws and render them what they had not been in the past —a really just expression of existing conditions. She undertook herself the task of establishing the general principles on which the legal code was to be drawn up; she even represented it to Voltaire as a simple matter to determine the general principles. The problem of working out the details according to these principles was confided to representatives of the people, so that the nation should have an opportunity of making known its wishes and needs in regard to the legislative settlement.

Catharine next proceeded, quite in private, to elaborate these general principles; and they were published in 1767 in the shape of her famous "Instruction (*Nakás*) to the commission appointed to prepare a draft for a new code." This remarkable document did not, however, appear in the form which she had originally given it, but previously underwent extensive modification at the hands of persons consulted by her. Catharine had herself felt, and her advisers had made it still clearer, that the general ideals of the *Aufklärung* in State and society, not practicable even in western Europe, were little adapted to Russian circumstances; "these are axioms fit to bring down stone walls," Count Nikita Panin had said of the Liberal views of the *Nakás* in its first form. With Catharine's authorisation it had been transformed and had received a thoroughly conservative tone; in particular its views on the condition and future of the peasantry were revised—it need hardly be said in what sense. Thus, here already, is observable the contradiction between theory and practice which permeates the whole work.

Even in this form, however, the *Nakás* is a book of great note and interest. It affords some insight into Catharine's social and political views in general. These are by no means original, since the work as a whole reveals but little independent thought. She herself confesses to wearing a great many borrowed plumes. Her sources were in the first place Montesquieu's *Esprit des Lois,* and, next, Beccaria's recent work *Dei delitti e delle pene* (Crime and Punishment), published in 1764. The several paragraphs offer general remarks on State and society rather than an enunciation of set legal principles; in fact, the book is a sort of legislative catechism. It is permeated by an optimism that delights in human progress, and is derived from ethics based on the law of nature; and it is instinct with the sense of responsibility proper to enlightened despotism, though these latter ideas are unable to blend quite harmoniously with the rest. "The people do not exist for the ruler, but the ruler for the people," and "the ruler is the source of all civil and political power"—here we have natural right and Tsarism in juxtaposition. The impression created by the book in Europe was deservedly great; but it was of course practically useless as a guide to the codification of Russian law.

If in this general design Catharine had not been able to mould all the principles and demands contained in it as she had desired, far more serious difficulties were encountered in the process of elaborating her suggestions into particular laws and adapting to them the existing legal material. Though the Commission appointed for this purpose was not intended to be a parliament, it was in point of fact the first representation of the whole nation since the *Semskie Sobory* of the sixteenth and seventeenth centuries, and was thus virtually a parliament—consisting of no less than 564 members elected by the people and embracing all ranks of society except the clergy, who were not represented as a class. The manorial peasants were of course only represented by their masters, whereas the crown peasants sent deputies. The total was made up of 161 representatives of the nobility, 208 of the towns, 79 from the peasantry, 54 from the Cossacks, 34 from "foreign" peoples as they were called—this representation of Samoyedes and Bashkirs was ridiculed abroad—and in addition 28 representatives of the Government. These class divisions exhibit the same feature in the system of representation as that which recurs in 1775 and again in 1785, and which is fundamentally opposed to the ideas of the *Aufklärung* and of the *Nakás* itself.

The elections went off smoothly, and on August 10, 1767, the Commission was opened in the audience-chamber at the Kremlin in Moscow. Out of three candidates nominated by Catharine, Bibikoff was chosen President, and he with the Procurator-General of Finance (Viasemski) conducted the proceedings, which passed off in a dignified and orderly fashion. The deputies displayed the natural eloquence and parliamentary ability innate in the Russian people. After the Tsarina's mandate had been read aloud, there followed the mandates of each electoral district to its deputy. These, nearly 1500 in number, together present an almost complete picture of the condition of the most widely divergent sections of the Russian people, and for this reason an exceptional historical interest attaches to them like that belonging to the *cahiers* of the French Revolution. With the Tsarina's *Nakás* for their guidance, and with the aid of these, of course entirely unsystematic, lists of popular requests, the Commission now had to compile a modern code out of the confused and incongruous mass of materials confronting them in the existing laws, over 10,000 in number. It is obvious that the task was an impossible one for this body of men. Catharine had sought to win the fame of a Justinian, underrating in happy ignorance the enormous difficulty of such a work. There was, as a matter of course, considerable difficulty about producing a systematic codification within a reasonable time through an assembly of such diverse social aims; and it was rendered insurmountable by the utter absence of all preparatory work, the unpractical and ill-defined distribution of the labours of the Commission and the incapacity of those responsible for its management. Not a single section of the future code was produced, nor, in the course of 200 sittings, were all the mandates of the deputies read out. At the end of 1767, the Commission was transferred to St Petersburg, and the sittings became less frequent. Then, on the outbreak of the Turkish War in 1768, many of the members were called away to serve in the army, and the Commission was adjourned, never to meet again. The sub-committees went on working for a time, till they too came to a quiet end. Catharine seems to have entirely forgotten the Commission after 1775. She must have realised that nothing was to be accomplished in this way, and so have determined to confine herself to legislation. But this interesting experiment was not in vain; although begun without any serious appreciation of its importance, it diffused, in Catharine's own words, " light and knowledge over the whole empire with which we have to deal and for which we have to provide." No Tsar had hitherto adopted this attitude towards the condition, wishes, and needs of the various strata of his people; the mandates of the deputies, the privileges of the nobility and of the merchants, the peasant question, and so forth, had been very amply discussed. Abundant proofs had been given of the class selfishness of the nobles, more especially of those of Moscow, who had a leader of weight in Prince Scherbatoff, yet had been the chief opponents of the demands advanced by him. The representatives of Little Russians and Cossacks, and those of the Baltic provinces, who, though in part not even able to speak Russian, had formed the most important element in the Commission, had brought to light their various special needs. The administration of justice, decentralisation, and self-government had been discussed. In a word, there was now in hand a mass of valuable information as to the temper and condition of the people. But the lofty designs formed by Catharine, when undertaking the reform of legislation, had produced no results but the administrative regulations of 1775 and the Letters of Grace of 1785; and even these documents had only in part the significance which at first sight they seem to possess.

The important point was, however, that the peasant question, in which Catharine had been interested even as Tsarevna, had thus before her death met with a treatment diametrically opposed to the fact that, in accordance with the ideas of the century, she was, as her own statements testify, in favour of the liberation of the serfs. Among her papers there are projects for the gradual abolition of serfdom by the emancipation of the peasants in cases of land changing hands. In the first edition of the *Nakás* a great deal was said about the necessity for ameliorating the condition of the peasantry and doing away with serfdom. When the St Petersburg Free Economic Society had announced as the subject of a prize essay the emancipation of the peasantry, the Tsarina promoted a widespread competition both in Russia and abroad; and the prize was awarded to an inhabitant of Aix-la-Chapelle, who advocated the emancipation of the peasants. She also allowed the "Legislative Commission" to discuss the question at considerable length and was ill-pleased when the majority supported the existing law. It appeared consistent and logical that the abolition of serfdom should go hand in hand with the exemption of the nobility from state service definitively established by the Letter of Grace of 1785. It seemed scandalous that advertisements should appear in the papers for the sale of peasants unattached to any land; this was slavery pure and simple—a term otherwise inapplicable to the relations between landowners and peasants, though sometimes used for purposes of agitation.

In spite of all this, however, serfdom continued to be censured in theory, whereas in practice the existing state of things was aggravated in the interests of the landowners. In the final printed version of the *Nakás* numerous Liberal expressions on the subject of the peasantry were suppressed under the influence of the current which had set in against reform. It was not, as the Slavophils maintained, the fault of the Tsarina or even of the Germans that nothing came of the emancipation of the peasants in Catharine's reign; the result must be laid at the door of the landed nobility, who in this matter proved too strong for the sovereign. She was on the horns of a dilemma: if she abandoned her compact with the dominant section of society and effected the emancipation of the serfs in spite of its opposition, could she in her still precarious position rely upon the wild and largely fluctuating masses let loose by her act of emancipation? Their constant convulsions and risings proved how insecure was her footing; for Pugachoff's revolt, the greatest and most dangerous, was by no means an isolated occurrence. The Tsarina must have seen she would have run too great a risk in carrying such a measure in opposition to the nobility; and thus she did not throw the whole force of her will into her theoretical scheme of emancipation. Hence her agrarian policy likewise bore a twofold character. She placed peasants in the towns which she founded and of which she made them free citizens. She changed the whole mass of peasantry formerly owned by the clergy from manorial into crown peasants—certainly a considerable advance for them. On the German peasant colonists who came into her dominions and were settled on the lower Volga, she bestowed an admirable legal and administrative system, which, in conjunction with the influence of schools and religious ministry, produced great prosperity in these settlements. On the other hand, by her enormous gifts of land and peasants to her favourites she vastly increased the number of peasants attached to private estates. Altogether, her administrative reform did not in the slightest degree affect the manorial serfs, as they were not represented on the " Legislative Commission." Despite all her vaunted enthusiasm for liberty, the rights of the landowners were increased under her *régime,* and villanage continued in the same form as before. Thus landowners, in addition to the right of sending their peasants to Siberia—which was already allowed— gained that of imposing on them forced labour for " insolence " towards their masters. A landed proprietor might send a peasant to serve in the army, whenever he pleased, without waiting for the regular recruiting time; and a peasant was actually forbidden to bring an action against his master. In short, the peasant seemed to be a mere chattel, a personal possession, a slave, and not a subject of the State. The sale of peasants unattached to the land was indeed forbidden, but it did not cease, any more than illicit traffic in peasants at recruiting time. In Little Russia serfdom was first introduced in this reign. Thus the economic interests of the nobility as a class outweighed the theoretical opinions and wishes of the Tsarina; and the patriarchal relation between the peasant and his master survived. It was not as a matter of course oppressive for the peasant, but it kept him entirely at the mercy of his master, whose one-sided interest in the services of his peasants, coupled with his own responsibility for the burdens imposed by the State, effectively checked all progress of civilisation among the peasants, who in so purely agricultural a country formed the enormous majority of its population. In fact, the condition of the peasantry under Catharine was deplorably wretched. This became alarmingly evident from the description of their condition in Radishcheff's *Journey from St Petersburg to Moscow* (1790), a simple, somewhat sentimental narrative in the style of Sterne. But the views of Catharine, upon whom the French Revolution in particular had exercised its effect, were no longer those of the authoress of the *Nakás,* with which the *Journey* was in perfect accord. The unfortunate writer was banished to Siberia as a revolutionary agitator.

At the same time, the burdens and sacrifices imposed by the Government weighed heavily upon these very peasants, who were treated as slaves, but who had to be regarded as subjects of the State and as citizens, at all events from the point of view of duties. In order to win her great successes abroad, Catharine strained the resources of the nation to the utmost, more than it could bear without detriment to its advance in civilisation. Her home policy was entirely subservient to her foreign policy, and no thorough-going reforms could be achieved because the claims of foreign affairs constantly intervened. This pressure, unavoidable in itself, but fatal to the internal progress of the nation, was due to Russia's recent political advance, and was a legacy from Peter the Great to Catharine, who in turn bequeathed it to her successors. The primary duty of the Government at home was the supply of men and money. The wars cost many lives, and the losses were even greater than in the case of other European States, by reason of the bad military administration, and the natural difficulties presented by the theatres of these wars. The annual expenditure during Catharine's reign rose from 17 to 70 or 80 million *roubles* (£2,408,000 to £9,917,000), almost exclusively for purposes of foreign policy—and this in a country whose population was far too low in proportion to its vast area, and where no surplus wealth was produced. Catharine succeeded in raising the importance of Russia abroad, but only by drawing upon the capital which the country possessed in the powers and resources of its people. She was unable to repress the unscrupulousness of the officials and the abuses connected with conscription, which rendered the popular burdens still harder to bear. Neither was it beneficial to the public health, that under her rule the proceeds of the state monopoly of spirits formed one-eighth of the whole revenue.

In her economic views and in the tendencies of her economic and commercial policy Catharine appears to have been a moderate Liberal, with physiocratic principles. In this respect she differed from Peter the Great who was a strong mercantilist; and, here again, she was a direct adherent of contemporary theories. She was therefore in favour of freedom of trade and manufacture and, instead of continuing to impose all sorts of regulations, removed many oppressive restrictions. Export duties were abolished, and the prohibition of the export of wheat was cancelled; all monopolies were abolished, and for a time the Empress actually allowed the unrestricted import and export of gold, which was contrary to all mercantilist theories. Industries were to be carried on freely; private works and factories might be founded without special permission from the authorities and were to be treated as private property; the benefit of free competition at home being thus recognised. In Catharine's commercial policy she consequently likewise adhered to moderate Liberal lines; in 1782, a Liberal tariff was put in force instead of that of 1767, which had still been mercantilist in character. In 1763, she appointed a "Trade Commission" to deal with all matters connected with trade; it was a sort of Ministry for Commerce of an advisory nature, which continued in force till 1796. The moderate Liberal views of the Empress prevailed in this body, which was under her sole super-intendence; hence, when the Tsarina veered round to protectionism in 1793, the Commission followed suit; for towards the end of her reign she relinquished her Liberal propensities on this head also. The unsatisfactory financial condition into which the empire was sinking deeper and deeper furnished the immediate pretext for a revision of the customs policy of which the new tariff of 1796 was the outcome; this did not, however, come into force, as the death of the Tsarina ensued and her successor rescinded the tariff.

But in general, too, Catharine's Liberalism in commercial and industrial matters was mainly a paper policy. In practice, political and fiscal interests were paramount all through, and her economic Liberalism only came into play where it directly contributed to these ends, or at all events did not run counter to them. If the natural law of the freedom of the individual is an essential element in the Physio-cratic conception, Russia could not have been further from following it. Despite free trade and the abolition of monopoly no part of Russia was ripe for a really free economic system, and the economic Liberalism of this enlightened Empress accordingly had little real meaning. Catharine's whole policy in regard to the internal welfare of Russia is fragmentary and spasmodic; it was not free from dilettantism and paid no due attention to detail; it suffered from the lack of an efficient executive and from the restrictions placed upon it by the Tsarina's foreign policy. Her memory is best perpetuated by her efforts for the improvement of the water-ways of the empire, in which Count Sievers vigorously supported her, and by the foundation of new towns, often rashly undertaken, and genuinely successful only in the case of Odessa.

What has been said of Catharine's economic policy is equally true of her course of action in regard to the education and the general advance-ment of her people, much as she prided herself on her entire legislative activity and liked to look at everything in the most favourable light. "It is clear," she says, "that education is at the root of all good and evil; a new race or new fathers and mothers must therefore, so to speak, be produced, by means of education in the first instance." She accordingly provided cadet corps for boys, boarding-schools for girls—the school for noblemen's daughters at Smolna was founded by her. There were to be national schools in the capital of each province and circle; and she intended to found new universities. But though her energy and that of her adviser Betzki call for commendation, no thorough-going reforms could be effected because of the want of resources and other drawbacks to which reference has been made. Nothing, therefore, came of the interest in learning which animated the Tsarina and of which she gave so many proofs. Recognition is also due to her efforts on behalf of the public health, in the engagement of medical men, the provision of hospitals, etc. She instituted an Imperial Medical Commission, and created a great sensation by being inoculated for the small-pox and thus helping to overcome the prejudices on that head. Thus her fields of activity were many and various; sometimes she moved prematurely, but always with a sense of her responsibility, and her methods were invariably shrewd and vigorous. But she met with insurmountable barriers in the vastness of her dominions, the low grade of culture of the population, and the incapacity and indolence of the administration; while the overwhelming demands of her foreign policy left to the merits and successes of her domestic rule a value nominal rather than substantial.

In religion Catharine was a child of the *Aufklärung*. She was, accordingly, tolerant towards sectaries and divergent forms of faith. In her ecclesiastical policy she was entirely guided by reasons of State; while admitting the importance of maintaining the Orthodox Church, she made it absolutely a state institution. In carrying out the secularisation of ecclesiastical property up to 1768, she deprived the clergy of all independent political significance, since in future they were the paid servants of the State. In this, she was following in the steps of Peter the Great; the very measures which he had adopted in regard to the old Boyars she was applying to the clergy—a move of singular importance for the Tsardom. She had to come to an understanding with the Roman Catholic Church, since large numbers professing that faith had become her subjects by the Partitions of Poland. She treated this difficult problem with her customary good sense and vigour; extending toleration to the Church of Rome, and establishing satisfactory relations with the Papacy, but at the same time rigidly maintaining however the supremacy of the State. She never dreamt of a concordat; and, when the Pope dissolved the Order of Jesus, she thanked the Fathers for the services which they had rendered to her ecclesiastical policy, giving them permission to found a noviciate so that the Order could continue in her country in spite of the Bull of dissolution. It was particularly in ecclesiastical matters that Catharine revealed her statesmanship and resolutely practical policy; and, in so far as matters of this kind could be decided by these qualities, she thoroughly mastered the situation—which can be said of but few monarchs. In ecclesiastical questions, however, statesmanship does not count for everything; it could wipe out neither the mistrust felt by the White Russian clergy towards the Jesuits, nor the loyal attachment to Rome; neither could it solve off-hand the problems suggested by these currents of feeling.

Was it, we may now proceed to ask, Catharine's aim to Russify her non-Russian subjects? On this point she expressed herself in no uncertain manner in the instructions which she drew up with her own hand for Prince Viasemski as Procurator-General of Finance: " Little

Russia, Livonia and Finland are administered according to the privileges confirmed to them. To break through these and annul them all at once would be extremely ill-advised. But to call them alien peoples and treat them on this basis would be worse than a mistake—it would be a serious blunder. These provinces, together with Smolensk, must be induced by the gentlest methods to consent to being Russified." These remarks, of course, do not apply to Poland; the Tsarina was not as yet confronted with the whole difficult problem of the treatment of Poland and of the position to be assigned to it within the Russian empire. But her Polish policy proved that she knew how to treat the Polish nobles and to attach them to herself. Her own words show her to have consciously favoured the creation of a centralised Great Russia—an ideal to which she was attracted, generally, by the levelling tendency inherent in absolutism, and, in particular, by her own position as Tsarina. But this ideal was to be realised without any forcible repression of foreign nationalities, whom she rather sought to weld into the Great Russian State by means of good government such as would arouse a sense of gratitude in them. Her willingness, in some cases, to allow the continuance of separate conditions of existence in particular provinces was simply and solely a matter of tactics. In her dealings with respect to the frontier lands she knew exactly how far she could go, how far from the point of view of the interests of Russia as a Great Power she must go, and where she was at liberty to stop. She was not inclined to grant to the Baltic Provinces a measure of political autonomy such as would be inimical to the position won by Russia on the Baltic, and she was ill-pleased at the manner in which the Baltic members of the Legislative Commission pleaded for the maintenance of separate conditions for their provinces. She intervened by introducing, in 1783, the establishment of Governors and the imposition of a poll tax on the peasants in the Baltic Provinces also; they were not to be allowed to develop in such a way as to be estranged from Russia. But she respected the privileges recognised by Peter the Great, and allowed the body of Knights (*Ritterschaft*) to retain their self-government, being much too wise and liberal not to see that the independent German culture of the Baltic Provinces was far ahead of that of the rest of Russia and, instead of becoming a danger, might serve as a model. By this policy she brought her non-Russian dominions into the right and necessary relation with the empire, while arousing in them an enthusiastic loyalty, which she turned to good account, towards herself and the dynasty. The Baltic countries indeed furnished her with a whole series of statesmen and officers; of eight men who held the important post of ambassador at Warsaw in her reign, four (or five) were Baltic nobles.

Her action in regard to the particular frontier land to which she attached primary importance in her dealings with Viasemski, if somewhat painful for those concerned, was equally right from the point of

view of the power of Russia as a whole. Catharine brought it to pass
that Little Russia ceased to be a frontier country. The Little Russians
regarded the Great Russians with aversion and detestation, the two
being distinct races and speaking different languages. They were united
with Moscow only by the common sovereignty established by the Treaty
of Pereyaslavl (1654) and they retained at their head a Hetman of their
own as an indication of their independence. Of primary importance to
Moscow were the Saporog Cossacks, who had settled on the far side of
the rapids of the Dnieper (hence the name) and whose free and warlike
community of Sich had constituted an outpost against the Tartars.
Without a close connexion with these, which had been endangered by
Charles XII in the days of Mazepa, the Russian route to the Black Sea
was insecure. But Catharine, who looked askance on the separate rights
and organisation of the Ukraine, and on the innate hostility of the Little
Russians towards the claims of Great Russia, desired, to begin with, the
abolition of the office of Hetman, which, without being dangerous in
itself, served to emphasise the independent position of Little Russia. It
was done away with in 1764 and a Little Russian Board under a Governor-
General was established in its place, which meant the substitution of a real
for a personal union. In 1775 followed the suppression of the Saporog
Cossack Constitution of Sich; the entire civil administration passed
into the hands of the imperial authorities, and the Cossacks thenceforth
ceased to exist as a distinct nationality. They survived, however, as a
distinct class, whose part it now became to serve Russia by securing the
annexation of the Crimea and the newly acquired position on the Black
Sea. In order to reconcile the landowners of Little Russia to her policy,
Catharine carried into effect a measure abrogating freedom of settlement
for Little Russian peasants; in 1783, she introduced serfdom into Little
Russia, where it did not as yet exist, although the local conditions were
of course ripe for its introduction. Naturally, Catharine's measures
could not bridge over the gulf fixed between Great Russians and Little
Russians; they rather tended to widen it. They were designed to
guarantee the predominance of the Russian Tsardom in the south, and,
so far as possible, to weld north and south together, and thereby to
assure its full value to the acquisition of the northern shore of the Black
Sea. This was of course no final solution of the Ukrainian problem,
which Catharine left it to her successors to achieve. She also bequeathed
to them the Polish question, which indeed she had created for Russia
by means of the Partitions; whereas the problem of the Ukraine she had
inherited from the past.

The Court of St Petersburg under Catharine owed its special significance to the fact that it was the seat of enlightened despotism, incarnate
in a woman of genius. She, and she alone, was the centre of it all; for
she had not been happy in her marriage and domestic life; indeed, her
relations to her son and his family were a repetition of what had been

her own lot as Grand Duchess. A growing mistrust and estrangement prevailed between Catharine and her son Paul, and the bearing of the Tsarina was at times the reverse of dignified towards the "young Court" at Gatschina, although, since her position had become strengthened, Paul was no longer to be regarded as a rival. A deep shadow was thus cast on the years of Paul's manhood, during which he was deprived of any sort of power and obliged to keep entirely aloof from public affairs. Paul had married, as his second wife, Maria Feodorovna (Sophia of Würtemberg), who proved a most devoted consort. (This marriage had been adroitly promoted by Prince Henry of Prussia, behind whom of course stood Frederick the Great.) Their life was further embittered by Catharine lavishing her whole affection upon her grandsons Alexander and Constantine, whom she sought to alienate from their parents, though without success, notwithstanding that she brought the whole weight of her general interest in educational matters to bear upon the training of these princes. Nor, as has been seen, did she achieve her purpose of making Alexander her successor to the throne in place of his father.

The cleavage within the family was maintained and aggravated by the uninterrupted succession of favourites who shared the Tsarina's political labours and obtruded themselves between her and the members of her family. Her son and grandson always remained aloof from this innermost circle of her life. Little need here be said about her systematic favouritism, which, of course, provided ample field for all manner of scandal and has often been exclusively emphasised to the exclusion of all else in delineations of her character. For, though the political influence of Potemkin, and subsequently of Plato Suboff, was undoubtedly great, not one of all her many favourites can be said to have ever dominated the Tsarina. Intellectually, she was the superior of every one of them, and she never allowed her heart to influence her against her better judgment. The material prosperity of Russia was, no doubt, seriously affected by the gross selfishness of these men, on whom their mistress heaped gifts and whom she enabled to enrich themselves at the public expense. None of them, however, exercised any political influence in the wider sense; whatever be the estimate formed of Catharine's rule and its results, to her alone belongs the praise or blame. Favouritism brought up both good and evil sides of her nature; in it she found vent both for that feminine capacity for self-devotion pent up within her and frustrated by her wretched marriage, and for unrestrained and unmitigated sensuality. She really loved Gregori Orloff, to whose devotion she owed her Crown, and Potemkin, who was indolent and utterly selfish in spite of all his great gifts, but whose strange individuality may have exercised upon this rationalist Princess the peculiar charm of the "Russian soul." These blemishes are inseparable from any portrait of Catharine; but they should not be allowed to overshadow all else.

The feminine element of Catharine's Court was very much in the background as compared with her male favourites, the single prominent exception being Princess Dashkoff, whose interesting Memoirs exhibit the impression produced by Catharine's personality upon those who were capable of understanding it. She was congenial to the Tsarina on account of her great intellectual interests and her virile qualities of energy and force of will. She played a unique part among the Russian ladies of that day; she was President of the Russian Academy of Sciences, and it was in no small degree due to her that its Dictionary was compiled. The Princess had stood beside Catharine in her hour of good fortune, when the *coup d'état* had been successful; but she was unable, chiefly through her own fault, to maintain herself in the position to which she aspired, and she certainly exerted no strong political influence upon her mistress.

The same remark applies more or less to the whole bevy of government officers, diplomats and generals gathered about the Tsarina—statesmen such as Nikita Panin and Besborodko, public officials such as Viasemski, Chernuisheff, Sievers, diplomats like Repnin, Vorontsoff, Dmitri Galitsin, generals like Alexander Galitsin, Peter Panin, Rumyantseff, Suvoroff. They were one and all, in varying degrees, the intelligent and energetic instruments of her will, but nothing further. She was extraordinarily skilful in training her officers and her army, and, above all, in drawing out diplomatic talent; and, if she was unable to secure like efficiency in her civil service, the fault was not entirely hers. But what is characteristic of her reign is that the circle of her Court supplied the entire body of persons with whom and through whom she carried on the task of government. The work of these generals and statesmen was in the main court service, and the whole national and political life of the country centred in the Court. And an amazingly brilliant centre it was. The excessive luxury which reigned everywhere at Court was the more obtrusive in character because unrestrained by any refinement of taste; indeed, there was often a frankly barbarous and oriental flavour about it. Far and wide in Europe admiration was aroused by the exotic splendour of the lavish entertainments of Catharine and her favourites. The extravagance which prevailed was boundless; but outside Russia hardly anyone noticed or knew how heavy a burden was thus laid upon the nation.

The general aspect and tone of the Court was thoroughly French; it was evident that the presiding genius was a lady of French culture, and no longer Peter the Great with his guard-room manners. A leading part was played in this brilliant society by foreigners, such, for example, as the French ambassador, Count Ségur, and that typical *rococo* courtier, Prince de Ligne, who lacked the capacity for becoming a commander or a statesman, but who was an elegant and an accomplished *causeur* such as Catharine loved to fence with in conversation, and with whom she long kept up a correspondence. For Russia it was of moment that the Court of St Petersburg thus imparted a French character to the members of the Russian nobility so far as they came into contact with it; and these were the men at the head of army and administration. Thus, a Russian Empress of German blood and French culture accomplished organically what Peter had begun externally, namely, the separation of the governing classes from the governed. The Russian nation consisted from the reign of Catharine of an upper stratum with foreign culture and manners and a bed-rock composed of those who adhered to the old mode of living. This upper stratum of society was heterogeneous in character, being a combination of the corrupt culture of the *ancien régime* with Russian barbarism; it was at the same time utterly degenerate in tendency. The immense danger to the whole nation involved in this line of development was lost to view in the dazzling splendour of the Court, which was at the same time a centre of intellectual life. Catharine introduced the *salon* into Russia, and allowed liberty of criticism there. Derschavin composed his odes in her honour. She encouraged Wisin, the "Russian Molière," to satirise society in his comedies. With her reign is associated the first bloom, as it were, of intellectual life; and in these endeavours the Tsarina bore an active part herself, besides promoting and encouraging them.

Catharine was a prolific writer, and delighted in her work. Reference has already been made to her political and literary correspondence (with Grimm, Voltaire, Diderot, d'Alembert). She displayed great talent in her letters, which were written not only with the direct intention of influencing public opinion in Europe, but from a real interest in the intellectual movement of her day, of which she was an enthusiastic disciple. The richness and versatility of her mind, the diversity of her interests, and her charming talent for *causerie* and witty banter, find full and delightful expression in her letters. She was keenly interested in literature, science, and art, and endeavoured often with considerable tact to play the *rôle* of a Maecenas. On the other hand, she probed for herself subtle questions of history, philology and political economy, wrote on these subjects, and stimulated research in them. She produced the *Nakás* and composed her Memoirs, besides contributing to a periodical edited by Princess Dashkoff, in which the Tsarina gave free play to her satirical gifts and caprices in a column reserved for her. More than this, she was a dramatic poet in her own right, whose works, in the last edition of them, fill four large volumes. Her plays were actually put on the stage, their authorship being concealed to a certain extent from the Russian public, but not from her foreign correspondents. Her writings (comedies, stories, librettos, proverbs) are no literary masterpieces—the comedies alone possessing interest; in these she satirises the freemasons, the Cagliostro craze, etc. Catharine herself regarded her literary efforts solely as a hobby; "I look upon my writings as play," she wrote to

Grimm. They certainly bear the stamp of dilettantism, and cannot, as to seriousness and depth, bear comparison with the literary productions of Frederick the Great. But they exhibit her mental freshness, wealth, and versatility, after a fashion assuredly unique among female sovereigns of modern times.

The older Catharine grew, the more reactionary she became on this head also. The surface splendour of her reign could not conceal its deep defects; criticism was excited; and she became more and more suspicious and severe, whenever she scented in Russian authors tendencies towards political and social reforms. Her reign furnishes a startling contrast between the patronage of literature and science at Court, on the one hand, and, on the other, the cruel treatment of Radishcheff and the persecution inflicted on Novikoff at Moscow. Catharine was in theory a disciple of the *Aufklärung*, and in practice an absolute monarch.

It would be difficult, indeed impossible, to characterise in a word so rich and varied a nature as Catharine's; but she might perhaps be described as a "political woman." For a woman, she had a singularly strong political sense and notable theoretical insight into the conditions of existence for a State and the duties of a monarch. Her policy was, therefore, a thoroughly practical policy in the selfish interests of Russia, devoid of all moral scruples or sentiment. There was no mystical side to her nature; she was entirely dominated by a clear, rationalist intelligence. In political matters, she was not affected in the slightest degree by her own feelings, nor did she allow herself to be confused by the flattery lavished upon her or diverted for a single moment from the pursuit of her political aims. At the same time, she never lost her grasp of the situation or her courage, so that this aspect of her character is absolutely masculine; Prince de Ligne was not without justification in saluting her as "*Cathérine le grand.*"

But this Princess, whose virile personality becomes especially manifest if she is compared with Maria Theresa, was, nevertheless, a thorough woman—not the virago of the Renaissance to which she has been likened, nor yet, despite her sins and shortcomings, an ordinary example of female frailty. There are many testimonies from which to choose; perhaps the best is the Diary of Chrapovitzki, her private secretary, which gives a true picture of Catharine as she really was and as she appeared in everyday life. It shows a woman full of merits and failings; bright and active, with sanguine temperament and very variable moods, sometimes arbitrary and often supremely vain, and with a strong propensity for praising and for being praised. Touches are not wanting of real womanly kindness and motherliness in her care of her grandsons or in her letters to a young lady at the *Fräuleinstift* (school for young ladies of the nobility). At close quarters, there is nothing majestic to be found in her. She had a feminine charm and lovableness of her own, the attraction of which was felt by all diplomatists who conversed with her, and of which she made good use for obtaining her own way. And this same imperial lady was so little able to curb her warm-blooded passions that her love affairs, especially as she grew older, became public scandals.

In dealing historically with an absolute ruler who regards the State and the personality of the sovereign as identical, it is not easy to differentiate precisely between what appertains to the one and to the other. No certain estimate can accordingly be formed as to the objective significance of Catharine's reign, and the problem remains unsolved by accepting as an adequate definition of her character and reign such a formula as " the search for glory, supplemented by self-indulgence." Catharine recognised the objective ends laid down by Peter the Great, and felt herself to be continuing the rule of that monarch, whom her heart revered as a hero and whom her reason bade her follow for practical purposes, foreign usurper though she was. She achieved so large a part of his design that there could be no ultimate turning back for the Russian nation, and that the policy of Russia was indissolubly bound up with European interests and questions. Under her, St Petersburg became the real capital of the empire. She brought about the union of the Baltic Provinces and Poland with Russia, thus securing a position for her country as a European Power. She changed the face of the Oriental question in the same way and definitely fixed the southern frontier of the empire. Thus, she acquired (according to Storch's estimate) over 500,000 square *versts* (= 219,704 square miles) of territory for her empire and an addition of nearly seven million subjects. Her policy was prompted not only by personal ambition, but by a sense of responsibility for her country and people. Under her, Russia fully developed into a European Power, whose prestige and sphere of influence abroad she increased enormously, while at home systematic centralisation had firmly established its authority. The direct gains and the general results of her reign were, therefore, enormous, and found unmistakable expression in the enhanced national confidence of Russia.

The Tsarina was hailed as standard-bearer of the *Aufklärung* and of liberty in Russia by contemporary writers generally, more especially those of France. Peter had not more than a simple instinctive sense of being a European, and had accordingly wished to make Europeans of his people, who had not yet passed beyond the Asiatic stage of civilisation; Catharine, on the other hand, was a European by birth and education and stood in close relation with the great intellectual movement of her time. But, amid the chorus of praise bestowed upon her, Europe easily overlooked the fact that this brilliant reign had achieved virtually nothing towards the advance of European civilisation among the mass of the Russian people. Her thirty-four years' reign is ostensibly the second and decisive stage in the historic process of " Europeanising " Russia begun by Peter I. As a matter of fact, she left it to her successors to solve the second part of the great problem with which Peter had begun to grapple, and to accomplish the internal metamorphosis of Russia into a European State. For it is a mistake to maintain that ideas of humanity and the rights of man came to Russia with Catharine; these conceptions, for which she professed such enthusiasm, had very little to do with the actual course of affairs in Russia. Moreover, this German Princess, with her cosmopolitan and rationalist views, was utterly alien to the nation, and in herself promoted the Germanisation of the Romanoffs and with it their estrangement from the Russian people. So much she achieved: that at the time of her death the upper class had the outward semblance of Europeans in the externals of life, in dress and speech, and, finally, in their ideals of culture. But the common people acclaimed Paul; they rebelled against this *régime* in Pugachoff's insurrection and in many other risings; they lived on in their old stolid barbarism, separated by a broad gulf from their sovereign and the upper strata. For them, the only result of this reign was that the institution of serfdom was developed to the full, and that the process of depriving the vast majority of Russians of all rights was thereby completed. Thus, the cleavage already existing between the ruling class and the people was further widened under Catharine, while the first beginnings of internal reform and of the reconciliation of conflicting elements attempted by her remained wholly barren. There are many points of resemblance between Catharine and Elizabeth Tudor, although the Tsarina was assuredly the more gifted of the pair. The likeness does not however hold good in this respect: it could not be said of the Tsarina, as it could of the English Queen, that the pulses of sovereign and people beat in unison. A great historical idea was the basis of Elizabeth's rule, whereas the necessary historical tasks which Catharine's policy had to perform implied only the announcement of an idea, but not the expression of it. Nevertheless, her reign with all its defects was one of the greatest in the annals of Russia, and she herself among the most notable monarchs of history—a Princess whose virtues far outweighed her shortcomings. She was, every inch, a "political being" unmatched by anyone of her sex in modern history, and yet at the same time a thorough woman and a great lady. She died on November 17, 1796.

CHAPTER XX.

FREDERICK THE GREAT AND HIS SUCCESSOR.

(1) HOME AND FOREIGN POLICY.
(1763–97.)

AFTER the Treaty of Hubertusburg, the King of Prussia found himself, diplomatically, in an exceedingly difficult position. There was no thought of dissolving the Austro-French alliance, for Vienna and Paris were united in the conviction that Frederick was only watching his opportunity to overthrow completely the Constitution of the Empire. Between the Courts of Versailles and Potsdam personal animosity ran so high that for years no renewal of diplomatic relations between France and Prussia could be brought about. Frederick hardly stood on a better footing with George III of England and Hanover than with Louis XV. In his capacity of Elector of Hanover more especially, George entertained the most violent feelings of antipathy against the King of Prussia, as the adversary of the existing distribution of power in Germany.

The bitter antagonism between Prussia and Austria, the cause of their seven years' conflict in arms, continued with but little abatement, despite the restoration of diplomatic relations between the two Courts. Prince Kaunitz speciously suggested to the Prussian chargé d'affaires in Vienna the possibility of agreeing upon a disarmament—say, on the lines that each Power should discharge seventy-five per cent. of the soldiers who had been in her service at the time of the Peace of Hubertusburg. Commissioners might be appointed to see that such an agreement was conscientiously carried out. Frederick, however, would have nothing to do with Kaunitz' plan of disarmament, observing that it savoured somewhat of the ideas of the Abbé de Saint-Pierre. In April, he entered into a defensive alliance with Russia. While Catharine II was openly undermining the Polish Republic, she was attacked by the Turks, who rightly surmised that it would be their turn next to be swallowed up by Russia. Throughout the Russo-Turkish War, which lasted six years, Frederick II had, according to the terms of his compact with the Tsarina, to pay her an annual subsidy of 400,000 *roubles*

(£72,000), which he could ill spare in drawing up his budget. On the other hand, the complication in south-eastern Europe was in so far to his advantage, that it led the Court of Vienna to incline more towards Prussia. At the end of August, 1769, the Emperor Joseph visited the King of Prussia at Neisse in Silesia; and Frederick returned the visit in September, 1770, spending a few days with Joseph at Neustadt in Moravia.

Meanwhile, at St Petersburg, King Frederick had proposed the partition of Poland, allotting to Austria eastern Galicia only (not western, which borders on Silesia). In order to forestall Prussia's prospective claims to this district, the Austrians in 1769 and 1770 occupied, as Frederick expressed it, "a region twenty miles long, from the county of Saros to the Silesian frontier." Their troops, instead of halting here, were spreading themselves slowly but surely over the whole of the south-west of Poland; and this fact induced the Tsarina at length to adopt Frederick's plan for the partition of Poland, which appeared to her a very critical step, and which she had opposed for some time. Frederick acquired West Prussia—the territorial link between East Prussia and the main body of the monarchy; and the increase in his revenues permitted of his raising the numbers of his standing army from 160,000 to 186,000 men. At the same time, he unintermittently continued his efforts for the acquisition of Saxony. In this he was now, as before, opposed by all the Powers, even by his ally Russia, who, in order to disturb his designs, made a new move by proposing that the Russo-Prussian alliance should be expanded into a great coalition of the north. In the first place, the Tsarina and he were to join with England and Hanover; and then, "as more passive members," Holland, the Scandinavian States, and "some German States like Saxony," were to be admitted to the coalition. But this insidious scheme was promptly rejected by Frederick.

At the close of 1777, a good opportunity appeared to offer itself to him for gaining possession of at least some parts of Saxony. The Elector Frederick Augustus III of Saxony, son of the sister of the late Elector Maximilian Joseph of Bavaria, laid claim to the freehold property left by his uncle, estates valued by him at several millions. The new Elector of Bavaria, Charles Theodore, who like his predecessor had no legitimate issue, but wished to provide for his bastards, was keenly interested in this property—much more so than in the electorate. In order to secure the protection of the head of the Empire against Saxony, Charles Theodore resigned part of Bavaria to the Emperor Joseph (January, 1778); but a protest against this dismemberment of the Bavarian electorate was raised by Duke Charles of Zweibrücken, who stood first in the succession to it. His cause and that of Frederick Augustus III were espoused by King Frederick; and, though formerly sworn enemies to each other, Prussia and Saxony formed an alliance against Austria. Sixty thousand Prussians under Prince Henry marched into Saxony, where they were joined by 21,000 Saxon troops;

CH. XX.

while the Prussian main army of 80,000 men, commanded by the King in person, concentrated in Silesia.

The Austrians, under the command of the Emperor Joseph and Laudon, mustered in Bohemia. They were greatly inferior in numbers to the Prussians; and, consequently, no strong hopes of victory were entertained on the Austrian side. The King of Prussia, however, had no desire to fight for the integrity of Bavaria, of which, indeed, he proved to be quite willing to allow Austria to annex a province. But, as the price of his consent, he demanded some compensation; and negotiations to that end were carried on under arms.

At this time, it seemed as if the line of Margraves of Ansbach-Baireuth would become extinct at no remote date—an event which actually happened in a few decades. This dynasty was a branch of the House of Brandenburg, which possessed an incontestable reversionary right to the south German principalities in question. The King of Prussia, accordingly, planned that homage should be done in Ansbach and Baireuth to the Elector Frederick Augustus III, whose right of succession there would thus be recognised. On the other hand, Lusatia, a considerable section of the Saxon dominions, was to swear allegiance to the King of Prussia, together with Wittenberg, the cradle of the Protestant faith, and other possessions of the House of Wettin on the right bank of the Elbe.

The Dresden Court did not reject these proposals, but demanded that, besides Ansbach and Baireuth, Prussia should secure to Saxony part of the Bavarian Upper Palatinate, or the bishopric of Bamberg, or Erfurt, which belonged to the Archbishop of Mainz. Once more, the Saxon statesmen sought protection against their new and highly dangerous ally at St Petersburg; Baron von Sacken, the Saxon ambassador to Catharine II, affirming that Russia might now play the "great and flattering part" which Louis XIV and his successors had in their time played in Germany. On the other hand, Saxony could in no wise depend upon Austria, the former champion of Saxon integrity against Frederick, but now prepared to let Prussia indemnify herself out of the possessions of the House of Wettin, provided that the Austrian dominions could be rounded off at the expense of the Wittelsbachs. By means of a compromise of this sort, it was confidently anticipated on the Austrian side that war with Prussia would be avoided. "The King's inclination to wage war is very slight," Joseph wrote from his headquarters to Vienna; "but his desire for Lusatia is all the stronger." The two German Great Powers could, however, arrive at no final settlement in the details of their plans of annexation. No adequate explanation has yet been offered of Frederick's special reasons for ultimately breaking off the negotiations carried on for months between himself and the Austrians, and declaring war. In any case, the political and military situation was very favourable to Prussia. Louis XVI declared himself neutral, because it was Austria who had virtually assumed the offensive; Russia was the ally of Prussia, who was actively supported by Saxony and morally by almost all the Princes of the Empire, apprehensive as they were, for the moment, of Joseph's territorial greed rather than of Frederick's. Altogether, therefore, the chances of the latter were far more promising in 1778 than they had been in 1756.

At the beginning of July, the main body of the Prussian army crossed the mountain range between Silesia and Bohemia at Nachod. But the invasion came to an immediate standstill. The main body of the Emperor's army stood on the Upper Elbe. It was commanded nominally by Joseph, but in reality by Lacy, who in the Seven Years' War had been quartermaster-general to Daun (now dead). The centre of the Austrian formation was Jaromircz, where a triple line of redoubts, extending the whole length of the river as far as Königgrätz, had been constructed and an immense amount of heavy artillery stationed. Austrian tactics had obviously profited by the experiences of the Seven Years' War, which had proved that defensive operations promised the Austrian army the best chances of success.

Once before—in 1758—Austrians and Prussians had been drawn up in the neighbourhood of Königgrätz, and had stood there face to face for weeks, without Frederick II venturing to attack his foes in their trenches. On the present occasion, he remained inactive for fully three months, from the middle of July to the middle of October, on the borderland between Bohemia and Silesia south of the Giant Mountains, never once attempting a serious engagement with the enemy. The statement that he did not really mean to make war, and merely wished to carry on "armed negotiations," is quite erroneous: on the contrary, he was, with a view to facilitating the negotiations, awaiting the opportunity for a "good battle."

While the main body of the Austrians lay facing towards Silesia, a smaller Imperial army, with Laudon at its head, was watching the passes leading from Saxony and Lusatia into Bohemia. Along this extensive frontier there were far too many passes for Laudon to be able to prevent the entry of Prussians and Saxons into Bohemia. His chance of covering the whole frontier line was rendered still more remote by the exceptional mobility and endurance of the Prussian troops; and Prince Henry, who was one of the most distinguished strategists of the age, succeeded in marching into Bohemia a few weeks after his royal brother. Descending by the right bank of the Elbe, he touched Bohemian soil at Hainspach, where the difficulties of crossing the mountains were enormous. However, the defiles once safely left behind, Prince Henry's chances were very promising, the Austrians being numerically far weaker. Laudon had to retreat beyond the Iser; but even in this position he could not hope to hold out long. By this time the whole fighting force of the Austrians had come between two fires; Prince Henry was advancing on their left wing and placing it in imminent danger of being outflanked, while their right was threatened by the Prussian main army.

On August 10 Prince Henry wrote to the King of Prussia that his operations would be in time if completed by the 20th or 22nd; after that, lack of forage would make it necessary for Prince Henry's force to retreat upon Lusatia. Frederick would not have been a great general if he had not determined to cooperate most vigorously with Henry during those precious ten or twelve days. He meant to attempt to cross the Elbe at Arnau and thus reach the Emperor Joseph's rear. The depression felt in the Austrian headquarters was profound. The King estimated the strength of his adversaries at Arnau and Hohenelbe at 30,000 men. "If fortune still favours the aged," he wrote to his brother, "I hope soon to defeat this corps." At Turnau he then expected to effect a junction with Prince Henry's army.

Frederick's preparations for action lasted till August 25, that is to say, beyond the term up to which Prince Henry had thought that he could procure fodder for his horses in the region of Niemes. However, this delay was of no consequence, for the Prince, a master of manœuvring operations, managed to hold out considerably longer in front of the Iser. But, on August 25, Frederick finally gave up his designs of attacking, recognising that the enemy's position at Hohenelbe was far too strong to be forced. After this, he made up his mind that the campaign was lost. For the rest, he had already a week earlier told his Foreign Minister, Count Finkenstein, that he felt no particular confidence in the success of the advance on Arnau, and that, should it fail, Russia alone could help him by creating a diversion which would set his army free.

The inevitable consequence of this ill success was that the Emperor Joseph, who had twice already sent reinforcements to Laudon during the seven weeks of Frederick's manœuvring in Bohemia, now despatched a third detachment to the Iser. Any action on the part of Prince Henry was thus out of the question; and both the Prussian armies thenceforth confined themselves to the "potato war"—that is, they consumed the resources of the enemy's country, till the cold weather set in and forced them to terminate their inglorious campaign by evacuating Bohemia. It was Moravia, not Bohemia which Frederick had originally intended to invade. If the main army of the Prussians had, nevertheless, entered Bohemia, this had been in consequence of Prince Henry's advice, whose plan of campaign, as the King extravagantly expressed it, seemed to him inspired by some divinity. But, though devised and prepared by two strategists of such eminence, the Bohemian invasion of 1778 had collapsed—just as that of 1757 had failed after brilliant initial successes. It is quite uncertain whether Frederick would have achieved any better result by an attack on Moravia. This, too, he had once before attempted under very favourable conditions (the Austrians having been almost annihilated at Leuthen in the preceding year); yet he had been obliged to abandon the siege of Olmütz without attaining his object. The strategy of Frederick's age was much stronger in the defensive than in the offensive. He had wrested Silesia from Austria at a time when Maria Theresa's reforms had not yet developed the Austrian military system, while a formidable coalition was threatening her monarchy. His subsequent campaigns, carried on for the purpose of occupying Austrian territory, whether directed against Bohemia or Moravia, ended without exception in failure.

Despite his sixty-six years, Frederick was still physically well fitted for war; in the recent campaign he had been in the saddle for many hours daily. But he felt little inclination for a renewal of military operations, after it had become evident that his Russian allies would not comply with his summons to attack Galicia. Prussia had declared war, not Austria; and, therefore, Catharine argued that her defensive alliance with Frederick did not bind her to give him military assistance. What weighed more with the Tsarina than this formal question was that she saw no reason for handing over Lusatia to the foremost military Power of eastern Europe and thus materially increasing its strength. Without an ally, however, an attack on the monarchy of the Habsburgs was hopeless, as the experience of the campaign of 1778 had proved. Frederick, therefore, consented to relinquish once more the attempt to acquire Saxon territory. In the Peace concluded at Teschen in May, 1779, through the mediation of France and Russia, Frederick Augustus III received 4,000,000 *thalers* (£600,000) from Charles Theodore in satisfaction of the Saxon claims to the freehold property of the late Elector Maximilian Joseph. There was no question at Teschen of any exchange of Saxon territory for the Ansbach-Baireuth lands of the House of Brandenburg; so that the Saxons had successfully disengaged themselves from the friendly demonstrations of their Prussian ally without being stifled in his embrace. The Elector of Saxony might regard it as a guarantee for the future that by the Treaty of Teschen Russia had secured protective rights over the Germanic Imperial Constitution, just as a similar authority had already been conceded to her in Poland and Sweden with regard to the Constitutions of those countries; and it had become more difficult than before for the King of Prussia to round off his monarchy at the expense of any Prince of the Empire.

The Austrians were justly dismayed, in 1778, by Frederick's unexpected declaration of war, and now fully realised that they were not strong enough to effect conquests against the King of Prussia's will. On the representations of France and Russia they, therefore, agreed to evacuate the regions of Bavaria which they had occupied, with the single exception of the Innviertel. This was a district of inconsiderable size; but the Prussian Foreign Minister, Ewald Friedrich von Hertzberg, implored his sovereign not to allow the principle of the integrity of Bavaria to be violated in even the smallest degree. To this Frederick replied that Hertzberg's ideas were excellent, but that political business could not be managed by ideas alone; the question was whether they could be carried out.

About this time, Frederick's alliance with the Tsarina began to give way. One of the first symptoms of a change in the policy of Russia, at once noticed by the King, was that the Tsarina did not reply personally to an autograph letter from him, but answered it through her private secretary. The Poles, whom Catharine treated as her *protégés*, complained incessantly at St Petersburg of the ruinous way in which Prussia had set herself to worry their only seaport, Danzig. Diplomatic explanations thus began between Potsdam and St Petersburg, which led to nothing. At Vienna, Kaunitz had been for some time under the correct impression that Frederick was aiming at the possession of Great Poland —that is to say, Danzig, Thorn, and the districts which now form the Prussian province of Posen. In Russia, Potemkin endeavoured to get at the bottom of King Frederick's plans by hinting to the Prussian ambassador at St Petersburg that Russia might find it expedient to join with Prussia in putting an end to the Polish State. Frederick replied by proposals at the Russian Court for admitting to the Russo-Prussian alliance the Ottoman empire, for which the Tsarina wished to substitute a Greek empire under her grandson Constantine. Catharine intervened all the more strongly on behalf of the ill-used Danzigers, while Frederick would not yield an inch.

The aged King found himself once more diplomatically isolated, when, in 1780, Catharine definitively deserted him, and concluded her alliance with Joseph against Turkey. But such was the admirably consolidated strength of his monarchy that he might at any time expect to secure new allies. When the Emperor Joseph, not content with the vista of Eastern conquests, resumed his policy of expansion within the Empire, the German States, whose independent sovereignty and very existence were threatened, rallied round the King of Prussia. Thus, in July, 1785, shortly before Frederick's death, was brought about the *Fürstenbund* (Confederation of Princes); the Archbishop of Mainz, the Elector of Saxony, George III as Elector of Hanover, with many other German Princes, both Protestant and Catholic, ranging themselves under the leadership of Prussia. Frederick the Great had often expressed his just contempt for the Constitution of the Teutonic Empire; but now, as against the actual designs of annexation cherished at Vienna, he, at the head of the *Fürstenbund*, powerfully represented the Protestant interest, and was hailed as the champion of universal freedom by German public opinion, which was mainly determined by the Protestants as the intellectually more alert moiety of the nation.

At the same time, Prussia's relations with France and England improved. Frederick now considered his position so favourable for new conquests in Poland that, of the European Governments, his alone was working against the preservation of the general peace. Among the representatives of the European Powers at the Golden Horn, the Prussian envoy alone tried to provoke the Turks to an armed resistance against the definitive establishment of Russian domination in the Crimea. Frederick was extremely dissatisfied when the Porte, instead, concluded the Treaty of Aïnali Kavak, by which the Kuban and the Crimea were ceded to Russia.

In the midst of the planning about Poland, Frederick the Great died, on August 17, 1786. He was succeeded by his nephew, Frederick William II, who was then approaching his forty-third year.

At midsummer, 1787, there ensued the declaration of war by the Porte against Russia, which the deceased King had so eagerly desired, Austria joining in the war in support of her ally, Russia. In his foreign policy Frederick William II was advised by Hertzberg, who (with Finkenstein) had directed the same department under Frederick II. In accordance with the late King's ideas, Hertzberg hoped to utilise the complication in the East to obtain possession of Danzig, Thorn, and Poland between the lower Vistula and the town of Posen. Now, to carry out a policy of this sort, some alliance was needful to Prussia, at that time isolated except for the *Fürstenbund*. The choice fell on England, whose King as Elector of Hanover belonged to that league. In order to gain over the Cabinet of St James' to his Polish policy, Frederick William, in the autumn of 1787, sent an army into Holland, where the party of the patriots, who were friendly to France, was oppressing the supporters of the Stadholder, William V of Orange, who were adherents of England. The intervention of Prussia in the Netherlands had a romantic as well as a political origin. The Princess of Orange (Wilhelmina), a sister of the King of Prussia, had been treated so disrespectfully by her political opponents that her royal brother felt himself bound to insist upon signal reparation. But the chief object of the Prussian Government remained the establishment of a close relation between Prussia and England; and this was actually attained by the despatch of 24,000 Prussian troops whose campaign, though almost bloodless, was thoroughly successful. At midsummer, 1788, the defensive Alliance of Berlin was concluded, by the secret articles of which Prussia and Great Britain undertook to act in concert with regard to the Eastern troubles, while, in the event of a war with the Tsarina, Frederick William might claim the assistance of the English fleet.

Frederick the Great had expressed to Finkenstein his intention, when Russia should have been exhausted by a few campaigns against the Turks, to begin preparations for war, and by threats of hostilities to bring about the Tsarina's acquiescence in his Polish policy. Seven years later, Frederick William II actually carried out this plan, except that the Prussian preparations were directed in the first instance against Austria—not against Russia, whose turn was to come afterwards. In May, 1790, a large Prussian army mustered in Silesia. In consequence of the reforms of Joseph II, the Austrian Netherlands had revolted against the Austrian Government, while the Hungarians refused to supply troops or render other services to the Emperor, and threatened rebellion. In face of these difficulties, Leopold II, who had ascended the Austrian throne on the death of his brother Joseph, had to agree, in June, 1790, to the Convention of Reichenbach with Prussia. The Austrians renounced the acquisition of Turkish territory, thus forfeiting the results of two exhausting campaigns on the Danube. Prussia had no objection to a slight readjustment of frontier at Turkey's expense; but the Convention of Reichenbach provided that the Cabinet of Berlin should in that case be likewise entitled to demand some compensation—which, of course, must be in Poland. It has been shown elsewhere how the Reichenbach Convention led to Prussia's participation in the Revolutionary Wars, and to the Second, as well as the Third, Partition of Poland.

The territorial acquisitions of Prussia between the close of the Seven Years' War and the death of Frederick William II increased her population from four and a half to nearly seven and a half millions, and the growth of the State in area was relatively even greater. The Prussian Government owed this remarkable expansion to negotiation rather than to force of arms, and the diplomatic prestige of Prussia was very largely due to the results of Frederick the Great's home policy. He laboured without intermission at the replenishment of his Treasury. This source had in time of war to supply him with the means for military operations which the Governments of western Europe raised by means of war loans; and to it the Prussians looked to save them from the necessity of carrying on war by the aid of foreign subsidies, like Austria, Russia, and the smaller States of Europe. After the Treaty of Hubertusburg, the Royal Exchequer still contained nominally $14\frac{1}{2}$ million *thalers* (£2,175,000); but this sum of money consisted largely of coin enormously depreciated in value, which Frederick had put in circulation during the war. Thirteen years later, all the bad money was withdrawn from the Treasury, and a reserve put by of $23\frac{1}{2}$ millions (£3,525,000) in coinage of full weight. At the death of Frederick the Great, the Exchequer contained 51 million *thalers* (£7,650,000), as against an annual revenue of barely 22 millions (£3,300,000). An English Government of the present day which should propose to lay by two and a third times the yearly revenue of the State would have to deposit £336,000,000. Frederick the Great had to pursue an unflinching, not to say oppressive, fiscal policy in order to save up out of the surplus of the yearly budget so huge a reserve, unparalleled in the history of the seventeenth and eighteenth centuries. As to the fiscal burdens of the country, the second half of his reign (1763 to 1786) compares very unfavourably in this respect with the first (1740 to 1763).

The reorganisation of the coinage system furnished the King with an early opportunity of applying inexorably the strictest principles of a one-sided fiscalism. After 1764 better money was again minted; but the debased coinage issued during the war was henceforth taken by the royal banks only at its actual (that is, at little more than twenty-five per cent. of its nominal) value. This sweeping measure was the culmination of pernicious manipulations which may be compared to the national bankruptcies of Louis XIV and Louis XV. During the war, fines and imprisonment, or corporal chastisement, had been unhesitatingly inflicted on persons refusing to accept money utterly debased; tradesmen had even been punished because they had in despair given up their business and closed their shops and stalls. The statement, that in 1764 Prussia returned to a standard of full weight in her coinage, can only be accepted with considerable qualification. For the reorganisation of the coinage in that year inundated the country with small coins, the standard of which was so greatly lowered by amalgamation with base metals, that a nominal three *thalers'* worth of this minor currency contained no greater proportion of silver than that required by law in two *thalers.* In the absence of a sufficient supply of larger coins, small change often had to be used even for the payment of large amounts. This unsound practice did much harm already in Frederick's time and still more under his successors, to whom he bequeathed, in the guise of a dead weight of base coin, the obligation of discharging a heavy debt, on which, to be sure, he had not been obliged to pay any interest.

The mints of the Prussian State were empowered to demand from the Jews, who bought up the old silver in the country, that they should supply every year a certain quantity of silver at considerably below the market price; it being left to them to shift the burden, if they could, on those who had to part with their family plate. This impost had been introduced by Frederick once before, and abandoned. On this occasion, when it was considerably increased and levied afresh from the Jews, it yielded no more than 23,000 *thalers* (£3450) per annum; but at this period of his reign the King found no duty too petty or too invidious. The revenue from stamp duties was more than quadrupled. Even street bands were obliged henceforth to take out stamped licenses. About the same time, the receipts from the salt monopoly were doubled by the introduction of the "salt conscription," as it was termed. In Europe the King of Prussia was called *le roi des lisières* (king of frontiers), on account of the scattered configuration of his kingdom. There was, consequently, an immense amount of smuggling. A great deal of smuggled salt, too, was consumed in Prussia. This was now effectively excluded by the minute regulations of the salt conscription, which obliged every household to purchase yearly a certain amount of fiscal salt for the consumption of human beings and cattle.

Frederick II gradually became more and more convinced that the best means of putting down smuggling and generally increasing his

CH. XX.

revenues was to appoint French revenue officers. The French official class, the pattern of all modern bureaucracies, was still superior to the Prussian in ability. In 1766, therefore, the King of Prussia appointed de Launay *Generalregisseur* (chief superintendent), at the head of his customs and excise administration; and, out of the 2000 posts in these branches of the public service, from 175 to 200 were filled by Frenchmen. The Postmaster-General (*Generalintendant der Post*) was likewise a Frenchman. An Italian trained in French financial administration organised a lottery. De Launay abolished the tax on rye-flour, and the duty on pork was at any rate not raised. Rye-bread and pork were the chief articles of food of the poor and of the soldiers, who had to live on their very scanty pay and the little they could earn when on leave.

Frederick II gave in his adhesion to no religious creed; yet, like his father, he possessed conscience, sense of duty and feeling for the masses. The soldiers idolised him, although flogging in the army was, if possible, even more common and more arbitrary under him than under his father. But, on the other hand, he cared for the material welfare of the private soldier, shielded him from many an injustice, and, altogether, used no empty phrase when he called himself the *roi des gueux*. In this spirit, he wished to distribute the burden of taxation more fairly than had hitherto been the case among the several classes; but his need of money was so pressing that the promptings of humanity were in the main abandoned. As not unfrequently happens, de Launay's financial reforms amounted in the end to little more than an increase of taxation. For, with the exception of pork, all kinds of meat, as well as beer, spirits and coffee, were subjected to heavy additional taxation. A monopoly was laid on tobacco. The prosperity of the people increased but slowly under Frederick II, as it had under his father; so that it was a very long time before his subjects were accustomed to the enhanced price of salt, tobacco, coffee, meat, beer, and wine, not to mention the increase in various other duties. Even six years after the imposition of the additional duties on meat and alcoholic liquors, we find a high official—no doubt reluctantly—urging their withdrawal upon the irascible King, who rarely brooked contradiction.

In 1779, Frederick II reckoned that the sources of revenue opened since 1763, apart from money drawn from West Prussia, were yielding nearly 3 million *thalers* (£450,000). The total public revenue at this time reached 21 millions a year (£3,150,000). The check on smuggling contributed to this thoroughly satisfactory result. The *Regie* (excise) introduced on the French model certificates of origin, cockets (*plombes*), etc., organised *brigades* of excise officers (*douaniers*), and set up offices for them on the frontiers. The whole system was new in Prussia; hitherto the whole of the customs had been levied at the gates of the towns. The native official class had been incapable of adapting to the primitive conditions obtaining in Prussia institutions which in western Europe were the outcome of a very highly developed political and economic situation. Consequently, Frederick retained de Launay for twenty years as *Generalregisseur*, and preserved the French element generally in his administration during the rest of his reign.

His departure from de Launay's advice in one matter of some fiscal importance is not likely to be forgotten. A coffee monopoly had been introduced, of which the King wished to take advantage (in order to protect beer-soup) so as to restrict greatly the consumption of coffee in his dominions. This (though he gave way to some extent) was the origin of the famous caricature ridiculing him as grinding coffee and trying to save the beans as they fell—which, when he noticed it on a street wall at Berlin as he rode past, he ordered to be "hung lower so that the people need not crane their necks to see it." Much in the same way, he had said on his accession, when he stopped the interference of the censorship with the non-political portion of the public journals: "Newspapers must not be worried if they are to be interesting." Such declarations, proceeding from such a source, acted as a ferment in the mental and political development of the contemporary world, England not excepted. Nevertheless, Frederick's stirring liberal utterances sprang from the liberalism of a despot—however "enlightened." "Pray do not tell me," said Lessing, "about your Berlin liberty of thought and writing: it merely consists in the liberty of circulating as many witticisms as you like against religion." The governing classes of the Prussian nation perceived no trace of practical Liberalism in the King. His conduct towards officers and civil servants was only too often cruel and capricious. After the Treaty of Hubertusburg, he required heavy pecuniary sacrifices even from the officers of the army, who in other respects constituted so highly privileged a body, and the necessity for filling his Treasury obliged him to lower the pay of the regimental commanders and captains. The income of the officers, most of whom were the sons of very poor noble families, ran short in the case of lieutenants, and was not sufficient for their needs till they obtained a company. Now, the lieutenants had lost this chance, while the captains in command of companies found their reduced pay inadequate.

The author of *Letters of an old Prussian Officer*, Kaltenborn, who entered the Prussian army in the course of the Seven Years' War, although he preserved no kindly remembrance of Frederick the Great, cannot but acknowledge a marked advance in refinement under his rule in the manners and tone of Prussian officers. The same judgment no doubt applies to their conceptions of the *point d'honneur*. The moral trustworthiness of military and civil officials, which is taken for granted in the best administered States of modern Europe, was in the eighteenth century only an idea in process of gradual evolution; and this moral purification was considerably impeded by Frederick's deference to fiscal considerations. It was one of the most painful consequences of the excessive and long-continued financial strain, that the corruptness of the officers, which had so greatly added to the burden of the "cantonment" system under Frederick William I, could not be extirpated under Frederick II. The officers of the army were, in the words of an ordinance of Frederick's, "the foremost class in the State." The middle and lower classes had practically no legal redress even against the worst excesses committed by officers. On the other hand, Frederick, in agreement with the extreme views of his father, held the civil servants as a class in far lower esteem than was their due. "Out of a hundred *Kriegsräthe*," he wrote, "one can always with a good conscience send ninety-nine to be hanged, since the chance is small of there being one honest man in the lot."

The hope of the Prussian bureaucracy proved vain, that the King would in time renounce his predilection for the countrymen of de Launay, and abandon the *Regie*, exasperated as he was by the corruptibility of a large number of its members. The moral defects of the foreign excise officials were regarded by Frederick with comparative leniency, because the Frenchmen brought him in money. As his father's son, he knew how to quell the latent opposition of the native Prussian officials to the French, more especially as very few of the Presidents, Directors and Councillors in the various War and Domains Offices throughout his dominions were men of property, or so much as had sources of income even in part independent of the Government.

The judges met with a treatment at the hands of the King no less harsh than that of the administrative officers. Arnold, a water-miller in the neighbourhood of Züllichau in the Neumark, did not pay his rent and was on two occasions condemned to eviction. He petitioned the King, maintaining that he could not pay, because a carp-pond made above his mill carried away the water needed for his business. The King took an interest in the maintenance of the country middle class which they gratefully appreciated. On this occasion, therefore, he, in Russian style, sent a colonel to report on the provincial judges. The colonel decided in favour of the miller. Hereupon, the King entertained no further doubt but that there existed a conspiracy of aristocrats between Arnold's landlord and the owner of the carp-pond, on the one side, and the Neumark judges, on the other, and twice ordered the case to be tried over again, the second time before the Supreme Court at Berlin. Both times Arnold was sentenced afresh to eviction—and rightly so, for a saw-mill situated between his property and the carp-pond was working excellently and not suffering from any shortage of water.

However Frederick II might warp or force justice, he required it to be strictly maintained by his magistrates. It seemed to him to be in this case outrageously disregarded. He determined to expose as secret enemies of public justice those persons who seemed to be thwarting his efforts for the preservation of the existing distribution of rural property. Orders were accordingly issued by the King's sovereign authority declaring that Arnold's sentence of eviction was revised, and that the carp-pond should be filled up. Two members of the Supreme Court were dismissed and thrown into prison. The High Chancellor of Justice, von Fürst, at an audience on the subject, ventured to express an independent opinion on some secondary point; but he was imperiously set aside: " Leave the room; your successor has been appointed."

It is evident that Frederick the Great closely resembled his father in temperament and character. In the military and administrative institutions of Frederick William I, he made no material change. Consequently, it was quite impossible for the middle classes to cherish any enthusiastic patriotism towards the State as built up on Frederick's lines. However conscientiously and judiciously he might govern, the system of the officers' State remained all too illiberal. The nobility, in their turn, were far from content, but the principle of chivalrous fidelity bound them to the throne. The personal relation between noblemen and king was one of the strongest of the invisible buttresses supporting the social edifice of Prussia, which rested on no common national basis. In recognition of his moral dependence on the nobility, Frederick favoured them in many ways. He did not scruple to assert that noblemen had more sense of honour than the *bourgeoisie.* Commissions in the army were reserved by him for the nobility, and commoners were only tolerated as officers in the artillery and in the garrison regiments. The purchase of manorial estates (*Rittergüter*) by commoners was forbidden.

The King entertained the opinion that each historic class had its definite calling, and that disorder arose when one invaded the sphere of another. He, therefore, opposed the attempts of the nobles to absorb peasant properties. After the Treaty of Hubertusburg, those peasants who had been ruined by the hostile invasions received from the King corn for consumption and for sowing, flour, bread, oxen, horses, sheep, pigs, cows. In the Neumark alone, where a large part of the population of the plains lived by wool-spinning and cloth-weaving, 68,866 sheep were distributed. For the rebuilding of farms and houses destroyed by fire the distressed peasants and burghers received timber free of charge from the royal forests, besides some ready money. Ten-thousand houses, barns and sheds were thus rebuilt with the aid of public funds. It is not known how much this *rétablissement* cost the King; in any case, immediately on the conclusion of peace millions of *thalers* were distributed among citizens, peasants, and noblemen also. These last had been plunged deep into debt by the war. A two years' respite (*moratorium*) was accorded to the landowners by the Courts; but the only result was, as the King expressed it in his *History,* to destroy completely the credit of the " first and most brilliant class of society." In order to assist the landed aristocracy, the King, from 1767 onwards, increased his extraordinary expenditure by nearly three million *thalers* (£450,000), which he allotted, partly as gifts and partly as a two per cent. loan, in Pomerania, Silesia and the Neumark.

CH. XX.

With this assistance, highly effectual in itself, a new departure in organisation was closely connected. In Silesia—for it was here that the organisation of agricultural credit began—the great landowners as a company issued shares paying interest. For money so invested the company was liable to the holders to the extent of the total property of its members. It then lent out to them the funds entrusted to it; they had, however, to mortgage their property to the *Landschaft*, that is, to the company of great landowners, mortgages being only accepted up to half the assessed value of each estate. The Silesian large landholders thus secured easy credit. To defray the initial cost of the arrangement, the King made over 200,000 *thalers* (£30,000) to the province at two per cent. When, six years afterwards, in 1776, representatives of the Estates of the Kurmark waited upon the King at Potsdam, he referred to the agricultural credit system of Silesia, and added: "You must imitate that; it answers capitally." The deputies objected that there might be another Thirty Years' War; when every single great landowner would be ruined by this general liability. The King replied: "You need not trouble about that; if the skies fall all the birds will be caught, and if the end of the world comes we shall all be bankrupt. And, even if a province were ruined, the King would have to come to the rescue, for he and his Estates are one." This encouraging speech of the sovereign had for its result the formation of the *Creditsocietät* (credit company) of the Kurmark and the Neumark, on a similar basis to that adopted in Silesia. To this undertaking also the King lent 200,000 *thalers* (£30,000) at a low rate of interest. In the same way, he assisted the Pomeranian nobles, who of their own accord asked him for an institution of agricultural credit. "I will gladly help you," he said, "for I love the Pomeranians like brothers; and they could not be loved better than I love them, for they are brave people who have at all times helped me in the defence of our country with their purses and their persons both in the field and at home." Frederick solved an important problem of true conservative policy by saving his nobles from usury even at the sacrifice of public money. Moreover, the mortgage banks instituted by him for the landed nobility spread all over Germany, and still flourish; whereas the differentiation of political rights according to birth, which he rigidly maintained, has in the main passed away.

In the matter of colonisation, again, Frederick followed in his father's footsteps; except that his chief exertions on this head concerned the Mark Brandenburg and Silesia instead of East Prussia. Colonisation was, nevertheless, likewise carried out very extensively in East and West Prussia, in Pomerania and in the duchy of Magdeburg. It is estimated that, during the course of his reign, the King settled 300,000 foreigners on specially privileged conditions. Even if that figure is an exaggeration, it is at all events certain that Frederick's colonisation policy very considerably increased moderate-sized and small rural holdings. Under

Frederick II, as under Frederick William I, large numbers of immigrants were settled on comparatively unproductive soil; the fertile portion of the royal domains was reserved for the farmers-general (*Generalpächter*), whose rents were, after 1763, raised more relentlessly than ever.

In almost all his provinces Frederick drained marshes, cut canals, cleared away virgin forests, cultivated estates running to waste; in these respects too he was following the example of his predecessors, but on a very much larger scale. If it was at all possible, foreign immigrants were settled on such reclaimed land. After the draining of the bog on the Warthe in the Neumark, the colonists settled there had to see for themselves to the clearing of their new homesteads and to bringing them under cultivation. There was certainly little of the free and independent life of the squatter in the conditions of existence of these people. As the townsfolk were under the *Steuerrath* (surveyor of taxes), so the rural colonists were under the *Amtmann* (crown bailiff)—the designation of the farmer-general as a vicarious representative of magisterial authority. The colonist, having almost invariably accepted benefits from the Government, was not at liberty to leave his holding again at pleasure, or had at all events to find a proper substitute. Colonists were also liable to forced labour. The King held liberal opinions on this point, and, instead of feudal services, imposed dues in money on the peasants newly settled on the crown lands. But, with regard again to the imposition of forced labour on those settled there from of old, the march of progress had to give way before considerations of finance. In 1748 Frederick had laid down the principle that peasants on crown lands should not render more than a four days a week statute service, personal and with their teams. After the Seven Years' War this concession was dropped, as it would have prevented the War and Domains Offices from demanding higher rents from the crown tenants.

The peasants in the service of the nobility—two-thirds of the total rural population—lived under still more unfavourable conditions than the crown lands peasantry. Their statute labour was for the most part unlimited. The King was not blind to the fact that the extreme poverty of the rustic population could only be remedied by the abolition of feudal services; but such fundamental reforms were hardly compatible with his conservative method of government. The Prussian peasant was induced by his forced labour to put no heart into his work. The French peasant, who, long before the Revolution, had ceased to be harassed to any considerable extent by the feudal system, was indefatigably industrious, and was constantly purchasing more land; whereas King Frederick could only with difficulty prevent the large estates from swallowing up the peasant properties. The Prussian landlords and bailiffs, on whom the patrimonial jurisdiction depended, practically possessed the right of inflicting corporal punishment on the peasants. A peasant had to get their consent to his marriage, and to give up his children to them as

servants for a number of years. Such things, if occurring at all in the
France of 1786, were sporadic phenomena. But, even if Prussia could not
bear comparison with the sphere of civilisation of western Europe, the
conditions prevailing in Frederick's monarchy had a strong attraction
for the subjects of many German Princes. It is true that in the years
of famine, from 1770 to 1774, when there were many deaths from privation in other parts of Germany, Prussia too suffered from exorbitant
corn prices; but the Government was able here to prevent the distress
from reaching the highest pitch. In innumerable instances, Frederick fed
communities or individuals at the cheapest possible rate, and seed corn
was often distributed by him gratuitously. Forty thousand Bohemians
and Saxons are said to have been driven by famine across the border,
where they found a new home under the wings of the Black Eagle. In
no country of Europe was the public corn supply at that time regulated
according to the principle of *laisser faire, laisser aller*; not even in
England. By means of prohibitions of exportation and importation, and
by the establishment of *dépôts* which bought at cheap and sold at dear
times, Frederick succeeded in keeping the price of corn at a moderate
level, except in quite abnormal years. In his testament of 1768 he
says: "With regard to the price of corn, it is incumbent on the ruler to
draw a hard and fast line, striking the mean between the interests of the
nobleman, the farmer of crown lands, and the peasant, on the one side,
and those of the soldier and the working man, on the other." This policy
was unquestionably right. Thoroughly adapted to the age in its whole
conception, it acted all the more advantageously, in that the Prussian
dépôts could command for their purchases not only the home market, but
also the neighbouring market of Poland, where corn was absurdly cheap.
It must not be forgotten that, here again, Frederick was merely carrying
on the work of his father. He added thirteen fresh *dépôts* to the seventeen left by Frederick William I.

Frederick II was more powerful at home than Louis XIV, and his
dominions were easier to supervise; consequently, economic conditions in
Prussia could be more effectually regulated from above than in France,
the model country of mercantilism. The Crown had a monopoly of salt,
coffee, and tobacco. The state institution of the *Seehandlung* (Board of
Maritime Trade) possessed a monopoly of sea-salt, and partially of wax.
The King was the chief corn-merchant in his realm; he owned a third
of the arable land. He was building great merchantmen at Stettin
for sale abroad. A government concern, endowed with monopoly rights,
purveyed firewood to Berlin and Potsdam; another was granted the sole
right of exporting timber from the state forests of the Kurmark and
the duchy of Magdeburg, together with a right of preemption as to
all timber from private forests destined for export. As regards mining,
in Upper Silesia lead-mines and blast-furnaces were worked in the
fiscal interest, and there was in Berlin a government iron *dépôt* for

the sale of Silesian iron. In the Westphalian county of Mark the iron industry, which was already highly prosperous, was at least restricted to ground forming part of the crown domains, and paid tithe. In this and in every other trade, no less minute and careful regulations were made under Frederick II than under Frederick William I. In order to supply efficient labour for the Silesian woollen trade, spinning-schools were established, and the agricultural labourers were not allowed by the authorities to marry, until they had given proof of their qualification as wool spinners. The tutelage exercised by the State over the domestic affairs of the citizens was extended to the most trivial matters. Thus, on the occasion of the proposed erection of a paper-mill, the King issued the following order: "In our land the bad habit is prevalent among maid-servants both in town and country of burning up rags for tinder to light the fires; an effort must be made to break them of this. The ragmen must therefore be provided with touch-wood to give to the maids in exchange for rags. They can light their fires just as well with that as with rags for tinder."

But Frederick II further resembled his predecessor in not merely extending a sort of police protection to those engaged in industries or trades, but also, in patriarchal fashion, assisted them with money and money's worth. He declared that of the 3,000,000 *thalers* (£450,000) yielded annually by the increased duties nothing should be expended for political purposes, but that the whole sum should be devoted to promoting the welfare of the country. And he fully redeemed his word. Between 1763 and 1786 he spent nearly 60,000,000 *thalers* (£9,000,000) in raising the economic condition of his people. He built factories in Berlin at a cost of 9,000,000 *thalers* (£1,350,000), and made them over to the manufacturers. This absorbed thrice the sum given or lent by the King to the nobles who had suffered damage through the Seven Years' War. One special feature of Frederick's mercantilism was the development of the silk and velvet industry from quite insignificant beginnings. Throughout the civilised world of that day, efforts were being made to set this industry on foot; but no Government strove with so much tenacity, intelligence and liberality as the Prussian to reach the unattainable height of the example given by Lyons. During his reign Frederick expended 2,000,000 *thalers* (£300,000) on the advancement of this trade. Of course, but a very small proportion of the raw material was obtained at home, and a government *dépôt* for raw silk ensured a regular supply for the mills at steady prices. Except for a few temporary crises, the manufacture of velvet and silk grew steadily in Prussia.

The King called the Silesian linen industry his "Peru." He said that in the linen-manufacturing districts he would permit no mining, not even for gold, lest the supply of wood should be diverted from the bleacheries. Recruits for filling up the gaps made by the Seven Years' War in the ranks of the weavers were sought abroad not less energetically than they were for the army. Every immigrant weaver received a loom as a free gift. Of course, he was not allowed to leave Prussia at his option, after he had once settled there and accepted benefits from the Government. The position of the linen weavers was most unfavourable in Prussia—as indeed all over Germany. The King was ignorant of those social ills which the eighteenth century in general was little capable of understanding. In his eyes, the salient point was that Silesian linen should reach the Spanish market at a low enough price to be able to undersell that manufactured across the frontier in France close by.

As in the case of the velvet and silk manufacturers and the weavers, Frederick assisted employers and employed alike in every trade with free gifts, pecuniary advances, indemnifications, premiums. "Let it be known," the King said to one of his Ministers, "that, if an economic enterprise is beyond the power of my subjects, it is my affair to defray the costs, and they have nothing further to do than to gather in the profits." Keen advocates of mercantilism affirmed that the flourishing condition of Prussian industry was due to the great circulation of money, as debased coins could not pass out of the country. This strange notion certainly failed to hit the mark; but, in point of fact, the means employed for securing the productiveness of Prussian industry, though efficacious, were two-edged. "I make use of prohibition as much as I can," the King said to de Launay. Prohibitions of importation, exportation, and transit followed one another in rapid succession after 1763. Soon after the Treaty of Hubertusburg the importation of pig-iron and raw steel from Austria was forbidden. At the same time, the export of Silesian wool to the Habsburg monarchy was stopped, as also the transit thither of Polish wool. The exportation of that commodity from the other provinces had been already prohibited by Frederick William I. The political economists of Vienna replied with the strongest countervailing measures. Austria forbade the importation of Prussian silk goods, woollen cloths and shawls, hats and stockings. After Prussia had also stopped the supply of wool from Silesia and Poland to the factories of the Saxon electorate, a still fiercer tariff war began on that frontier. A Dresden edict of 1765 prohibited outright all Prussian manufactures; and Prussia retaliated by an edict forbidding the importation from Electoral Saxony of all silk, cotton, woollen and linen goods, gold and silver plate of every sort, and china.

In 1768, rich strata of iron ore were discovered in Upper Silesia, a district hitherto of little account. Hereupon, the importation of iron from Sweden was forbidden. The iron-workers thought it impossible to do without Swedish iron, and, in order to teach them better, artillery experiments were made upon Swedish and Silesian iron. It was alleged that the native metal stood the test better than the foreign; but the Prussian Ordnance Office, which could of course procure import licenses, continued to use principally Swedish iron, and, for several years afterwards, the wrought-iron trade considered itself very heavily damaged by the prohibition.

The necessity of securing some return from the concerns carried on or subsidised by the State caused the system of prohibitions to be extended further and further; and this of course reacted very unfavourably on the development of trade. How much this branch of economic policy left to be desired, is clearly seen in the history of the origin of the Prussian Bank, the forerunner of the modern German *Reichsbank*. This institution was founded by Frederick the Great at Berlin in 1765; and a branch was started at Breslau, where it was lodged in the refectory of the Jesuits. This was done despite the protests of the reverend Fathers, whom Frederick took under his protection against the Pope, because they conducted the higher education of the Silesian Catholics free of charge—not that he otherwise entertained any special regard for the rights and property of the Order. Privy Councillor Wurmb, who took in hand the establishment of the Breslau branch of the Prussian Bank, soon recognised that the merchants of the Silesian capital were full of mistrust, and told the chief men among them that it would be folly for everyone to be afraid of bank-notes, and to try to get rid of them immediately on receiving them. This dread of paper money was in fact the crux of the matter. The commercial world had not forgotten the catastrophe produced by the fall in the standard value of money during the Seven Years' War. The Prussian Bank was started with 450,000 *thalers* (£67,500) cash in public money and the right to issue bank-notes up to 1,300,000 *thalers* (£195,000). The King further held out the prospect of making over to the Bank 8,000,000 *thalers* (£1,200,000) in cash out of the War Exchequer. The leading merchants of Breslau begged that a part of this sum might be put in circulation at once, but that the issue of paper money might be stopped; otherwise they would enter into no business transactions with the Bank. But their hand was forced, as that of the Jesuits had been; and twenty-one of the chief merchants of Breslau were obliged to open accounts with the Bank.

The centre of the linen industry of Silesia was Hirschberg. In their distrust of paper money, the merchants there gave up sending their bills to the capital of the province for discounting, and sent instead to Leipzig or Prague. The notes on the Prussian Bank continued to fall in value; and the Breslau merchants after all had their way in the main. Of the 1,300,000 *thalers* which the Bank, according to its patent of 1765, might issue in notes, only 580,000 had been set in circulation by 1806. In business and general dealings, Prussian paper money counted for so little as to warrant Mirabeau's gibe that no scoundrel had ever yet counterfeited a Berlin bank-note. King Frederick put a quite different interpretation from that anticipated by the Breslau merchants on his edict proposing to endow the Bank with 8,000,000 *thalers*. He caused, in the first instance, 900,000 *thalers* and then another

7,900,000, to be transferred from the Treasury to the Bank. But these 8,800,000 *thalers* were not invested, but merely deposited. The royal deposit was called *Fouragegelder* (forage moneys), in order to indicate that it still belonged to the War Exchequer.

The "forage moneys" constituted an apparent security for the voluntary and compulsory deposits of the general public flowing into the Bank. The compulsory deposits were due to a second edict, issued by Frederick in 1768, directing the authorities to invest in the Bank, at an interest of 3 per cent., all unemployed capital deposited with them belonging to widows, orphans, minors, institutions, hospitals, or charitable and educational foundations, unless such money could be placed in mortgages. This was a serious enactment from the moral point of view; and its economic expediency is also open to grave question. The trade of Prussia, hampered as it was by the system of monopolies and privileges and by tariff wars, could not profitably employ the capital which was to reach it through the medium of the Bank. The directors of the Bank looked round them in vain for an opportunity to make suitable investments. So they did the best they could, putting the money into tobacco shares, ships, and commodities. Under the two Kings who followed on Frederick II, the directors of the Bank found themselves driven further and further along this precipitous path. There was all the less chance of safeguarding the deposit-holders, when the avalanche of the Napoleonic invasion descended upon the kingdom of Prussia. At that time, all the possessions of widows and orphans, and the like, which through the Bank had been brought into an unnaturally close connexion with the State, were involved in its catastrophe. But, during Frederick's lifetime, all seemed safe; and the net profit from the Bank was continually increasing; in the year of the King's death the 450,000 *thalers* of initial capital paid over 50 per cent. This money had been earned by the many millions of voluntary and compulsory deposits. In spite of this, Frederick claimed the total profit of the Bank for the Exchequer. No reserve fund was started. The security of the creditors now as ever rested solely on the "forage moneys," for which the Bank had to pay the King 3 per cent. interest. On the other hand, the rate of interest to other depositors was soon lowered to 2 or 2½ per cent. The institution of this Bank was manifestly premature from an economic standpoint. All manner of coercive measures on the part of the Government, indeed, gradually accustomed the business world to having its transactions managed to a certain extent by the Bank; but this probably had no effect on trade, one way or the other. Thus, there was no palpable result from the foundation of the Prussian Bank beyond the creation of a new surplus in favour of the royal finances.

There was economic progress in Prussia under Frederick II, just as there had been under Frederick William I, though the figures of contemporary statistics, which should indicate a marked rise, are absolutely untrustworthy. It was no case of a rapid advance in material welfare either under Frederick the Great or under his father; but from certain facts it may be inferred that a certain improvement in the welfare of the people actually took place. Frederick the Great once complained to de Launay that luxury was so much on the increase that every servant-girl must now have a thread of silk in what she wore. The purchasing public can only have gratified fresh wants of this sort by means of additions which must have been made to the national wealth. What applies to silk must be also said of coffee, the consumption of which from 1750 onwards became a more and more general custom. As stated above, however, it must not be supposed that there was any very considerable increase in public prosperity between 1763 and 1786. The revenue from excise and customs yielded, between 1766 and 1786, a net increase in returns of 23,500,000 *thalers* (£3,525,000). The revenues from the province of West Prussia, not acquired till 1772, are not included in this sum. Thus the French revenue officials managed to raise on the average another million *thalers* per annum. This represents both the proceeds from increased taxes and the additional receipts due to increased purchasing power, which latter must therefore not be reckoned at too high a rate. For the Prussian body politic rested, after all, on a substructure of unfree peasantry, who, whenever the landlords and farmers-general required, had to furnish statute labour four days and more in the week; whose way of work was slack; and who, if they earned 55 *thalers* cash in the year, were only allowed 20 *thalers* and less for their own domestic purposes.

Shortly after Frederick's death Mirabeau's book *De la monarchie prussienne sous Frédéric le Grand* appeared in London. The author passes a crushing judgment on Frederick's economic policy, by applying the standard of those theories of political economy which had recently come to the fore in western Europe and eclipsed mercantilism. But, for the present, the English and French in practical politics applied the new doctrines only very cautiously and not even consistently, while in Prussia not only Frederick II but almost the whole body of his civil officers steadily adhered to mercantilist principles. The Prussian nation, which was far behind the nations of western Europe in almost every respect, seemed for a long time yet to require direction from above in economic matters.

"Mankind," Frederick complains in his testament of 1768, "move if you urge them on, and stop so soon as you leave off driving them. Nobody approves of habits and customs but those of his fathers. Men read little, and have no desire to learn how anything can be managed differently; and, as for me, who never did them anything but good, they think that I want to put a knife to their throats, so soon as there is any question of introducing a useful improvement, or indeed any change at all. In such cases I have relied on my honest purposes and my good conscience, and also on the information in my possession, and have calmly pursued my way." It has been shown that only too many changes ordered by the King put the fiscal knife to his subjects' throats; and it was no wonder that they cried out, forgetting in that perilous moment the economic blessings which beyond all doubt they likewise owed to him.

It was not merely by victorious battles and diplomatic skill, but also by his home policy, that Frederick the Great raised Prussia to the third place among the Powers of the world. As the champion of enlightenment he appears in a specially glorious light. In the Belgian possessions of Maria Theresa, from whose intolerant rule Frederick had freed the Protestants of Silesia, a *Bockreiter* ("gentleman of the road") was burnt alive, about 1780, because, when committing his highway robberies, he was said to have performed blasphemous ceremonies after the manner of the customs formerly imputed to the Templars. If, at the close of the eighteenth century, inhumanity, superstition, intolerance, and pseudo-science had to give way all over Europe, incalculable services for the victory of rationalism were rendered by the royal philosopher, who took the lead on the Continent in the abolition of torture. Where Voltaire is praised, Frederick must not be left unhonoured.

Frederick William II, the successor of Frederick the Great, was a gentle, kind-hearted man, who tried to do away with the innumerable hard and ugly corners in the State built up by his grandfather and his uncle. He raised the pay of captains and commanders of regiments, and also the salaries of civil officials. He abandoned the plan of constantly raising the rent paid by the farmers-general, abolished the monopolies on coffee and tobacco, and put an end to the *Regie,* sending all the French revenue officers back to their homes. The new ruler earned great popularity by this measure; for, just as the people of Prussia had before laid the chief blame for the debasement of the coinage on Frederick II's Jewish financiers, so the odium subsequently aroused by oppressive taxation attached mainly to the French.

The eleven years' reign of Frederick William II was economically a happy period. Customs and excise, the proceeds from which had grown so slowly under Frederick II, yielded a constantly ample and steadily increasing revenue, despite the fact that the vexatious methods of the French excisemen were a thing of the past. The causes of this material advance are to be sought in the fact, that, though Frederick William II carried on numerous campaigns in Holland, in Champagne, on the Rhine and in Poland, all these wars were fought outside Prussia, and consequently had no deleterious effects upon the economic conditions of the country. On the contrary, they stimulated trade, in accordance with Cobden's maxim that war is the greatest of all consumers. The expenditure on these wars was not defrayed by increased taxation, any more than Frederick the Great had augmented the taxes in the Seven Years' War. Such a step would have been quite irrational; for the non-noble classes in Prussia had so great a burden of taxation to bear, even in time of peace, that progress was but slow and difficult. Heavy war taxes would have crushed them. Thus, nothing remained then for Frederick William II but to pour out the 51 million *thalers* (£7,650,000) left by Frederick the Great, in order to meet the expenditure on military operations and armaments which preceded the Convention of Reichenbach. The whole of this sum was not expended at home, but a large part of it was; and the contraction of a public debt to the amount of 9½ million *thalers* (£1,425,000) which was, though with a good deal of trouble, floated abroad, brought foreign money into the country, and was thus more or less to the advantage of Prussian trade and industry. The "forage moneys" in the bank, were, in strict accordance with their designation, used up for military purposes together with the entire reserve in the Treasury, so that the private deposits were, together with the widows' and orphans' funds, the hospitals and charitable and educational endowments, left absolutely unsecured. But a more serious result of the political decadence of Prussia was the fact that, by the exhaustion of her Exchequer, she was degraded financially to the level of her rivals, Austria and Russia, who were not in a position to sustain great European wars without the aid of subsidies from England or France.

When Frederick made peace at Hubertusburg, there were still, after seven campaigns, over 14 million *thalers* (£2,100,000) in his Treasury. If he could have made territorial acquisitions, as his nephew did, without a great war, but at the cost of his whole treasure, he would probably have preferred to risk a war on a large scale, which would then have been self-supporting—just as the Seven Years' War was fought on the Prussian side by means of the resources of conquered Saxony, and, subsequently, the cost of Napoleon's war with England was squeezed out of subjugated Prussia.

Frederick's title to be called "the Great" is more than half due to his having made room in the world for the *Aufklärung*. But the "spirit of the world" did not cease to work; religious feeling and the historic sense began to stir in their turn, and to react against rationalism. At the head of this mighty host of opinion marched a troop of strange and repulsive figures. The Rosicrucian Order, which was widespread in the aristocratic circles of Germany, sought for the philosopher's stone, busied itself with alchemy and spiritualism, laboured at the preparation of a balm to make old people young and bring the dead to life again. The surgeon-general of the Prussian army, Theden, endeavoured to catch falling stars in order to distil the balm from this elemental matter. With alchemy, spiritualism, and the search for panaceas, bigotry was associated, and thus some very queer saints came to the front. Towards the end of his time as heir presumptive, Frederick William was persuaded that he had been cured of a large abscess in the thigh by the secret panacea and devoted care of the Rosicrucians. The heir to the crown hereupon entered the Order and received the name of Ormesus Magnus. When he came to the throne, Frederick William II directed his foreign policy chiefly according to the advice of a brother of the Order, Farferus, whose name in ordinary life was von Bischoffswerder, and who was adjutant-general to the King.

In his home policy, Frederick William relied to a large extent on another Rosicrucian, Minister von Wöllner. He was the son of a poor country clergyman, and, as private tutor in a wealthy noble family, had by his intelligence and eloquence secured the goodwill of the mother and the hand of the daughter. Frederick the Great, who desired that a caste-like distinction between classes should remain the basis of the Prussian State, was wroth at Wöllner's successful *coup*, and pronounced him " an intriguing and tricky parson." In any case, " Heliconus " was without reproach in his private life—something of a merit in the Berlin of that day. In other ways, the "Minister for the Lutheran Department" was not without his merits; but as to this we cannot here enter into further particulars. Wöllner owes his place in history solely to the *Religionsedict*, as it was called, which he drew up for the King, and which was promulgated by Frederick William II in the summer of 1788.

The censures of the *Religionsedict* on the teaching and conduct of the rationalistic clergy, university professors and schoolmasters cannot be termed altogether unwarranted, in view of the shallowness and indiscretion of many *aufgeklärte* preachers and teachers. On the other hand, Frederick William and his advisers exhibited a startling lack of appreciation of the intellectual achievements of the past century; for the edict threatened all who were not orthodox with removal from their pulpits and chairs. The Government also abrogated that freedom of speech and writing in regard to religious matters by which Prussia had under the late King set so glorious an example to the world. In this Frederick William II appealed to the example of his sober-minded grandfather, Frederick William I, in accordance with whose views he wished to restore the Christian religion in its original purity and authenticity, in order to check so far as he was able the immorality arising from infidelity and the perversion of the fundamental truths of religion.

The Rosicrucian Order imposed on its members among other obligations that of chastity, after the example of the Templars. Frederick William II attacked immorality in his *Religionsedict*, and, as a matter of fact, rationalism had tended to upset the moral views of many men and women. But the morality of the pious King himself was anything but strict. He carried on innumerable love-intrigues; his favourite mistress, Wilhelmine Enke, the sister of a ballet-dancer, was married to a groom of the chamber named Rietz, and enjoyed the favour of the King until his death. Frederick William's second consort, Princess Louisa of Hesse-Darmstadt, bore him four sons; but, in her lifetime, he contracted a morganatic marriage with one of her maids of honour, who was succeeded on her death by another of the Queen's ladies. Both these bigamous alliances were solemnised according to the rites of the Church by Zöllner, the rationalistic court chaplain.

The Rosicrucians, a medley of religious enthusiasts, hypocrites, and deceived deceivers, were hardly more virtuous in their everyday life than the rationalists. Their self-knowledge did not prevent them from taking their stand on the Edict and adopting violent measures in the name of true Christianity against the clergy, the teaching profession, the universities, and literature, "lest the mass of poor folk be handed over to the delusions of the teachers of the day, and millions of our good subjects by thus forfeiting the peace of their lives and the consolation of their death-beds, be made utterly miserable." Wöllner issued a rescript against Kant, in which the philosopher was charged with the perversion and degradation of many of the cardinal doctrines of Christianity and of Holy Scripture, and with thus violating his duty as a teacher of youth at the university. If such conduct should be repeated by him, he would most certainly have to take the consequences. "Heliconus" enjoyed a triumph; for Kant, old and desirous of quiet, almost entirely suspended his academic activity. But in other quarters the execution of the *Religionsedict* encountered the most tenacious opposition. In Prussia there existed at that time only the small beginnings of a cultured middle class in independent circumstances. Culture belonged almost exclusively to the official class. Trained as this body of men had been by Frederick the Great, it was, clergy and all, thoroughly permeated with rationalist views. This official class accordingly summoned up courage to defy the obscurantist Government. The judicial and administrative authorities took under their protection the persecuted literary adherents of the *Aufklärung*, as well as the rationalist clergy, professors and teachers. Moreover, the persecutors themselves proved to be not untouched by the humanitarian spirit of the age; and, when the rare event occurred of a clergyman losing his benefice, Frederick William ordered that he should be provided with some well-paid secular post. The Rosicrucians' attack on the *Aufklärung* dwindled away and, at the most, served to confirm Prussian society in its hostile attitude towards orthodoxy. The nucleus of that society, the official class, not merely earned the negative credit of having averted an unhealthy mysticism, but won a high positive title to fame in the sphere of legislation. The Prussian official class had been trained by two great Kings in the way, not always of justice, but of practical intelligence, insight and indefatigable zeal, and now bade fair to surpass its French prototype, and to become the most efficient bureaucratic body in the world.

This phase of the internal history of the country found expression in the codification of the common law of Prussia (*Allgemeines Preussisches Landrecht*). A different system of law prevailed in every province of the Prussian State, as it did in every German territory; and the general development of the law in Germany at large had been for centuries at a standstill. Frederick the Great had, therefore, commissioned von Carmer, the successor of von Fürst, who had been so brusquely dismissed from the High Chancellorship, to prepare a general code for the whole Prussian kingdom. Carmer surrounded himself with a staff of lawyers, of whom Privy Councillor Suarez was by far the most important. This Herculean task, which occupied ten years and was not interrupted by the change of sovereign, reached its conclusion in 1791. The code bore the stamp of the absolutist polity of officers, with its spirit of caste ; but on the other hand it was full of the tendencies of the *Aufklärung*. It may be noted, in this connexion, that Frederick the Great had removed from the Prussian code the application of torture, but not the infliction of cruel and barbarous additions to the punishment of death. Frederick William II laid it down that, though the death penalty could not be abolished, there must under no circumstances be any deliberate increase of the physical pain necessary in its application. But the King's gentleness of disposition was such that he was very imperfectly obeyed ; and almost half a century passed before Prussian justice absolutely ceased, in certain cases, to direct that the bones of criminals should be broken on the wheel. Carmer and Suarez even took over some of the French ideas of political liberty ; but the King, under the influence of the mystics, struck out most of these. Some remnants, however, survived ; and these, together with the whole spirit of the code, supplied the Prussian officials as a class with the force which enabled them to accomplish their development into an independent factor in the history of their country, instead of being as heretofore, merely an instrument in the hands of its Government. The *Allgemeine Landrecht* was a masterpiece as to both form and contents, and morally advanced the cause of rationalism throughout the whole of Germany. The first great codification of law since the time of Justinian was supplemented by the philosophy of Kant. Thus it was not only the body of military officers who in this State had laurels to show. When, in 1806, it was annihilated, the enlightened men among both its military and its civil servants joined hands, and, by means of the reforms of Stein and Hardenberg, succeeded in founding a new Prussia.

Although he permitted the Rosicrucians to exert a baneful influence over him, it cannot be said of Frederick William II that he was merely a tool in the hands of that sect. On the contrary, he often made important decisions repugnant to the mystics. To the women about him the King allowed no political influence at all. Despite his love of pleasure, he did not squander public money. He was not deterred by financial difficulties from considerably strengthening the army, herein acting like a true King of Prussia. Frederick William II died, in his fifty-third year, on November 16, 1797, just about the time when Napoleon Bonaparte was coming to the front in France.

(2) POLAND AND PRUSSIA.

(1763–91.)

The acquisition of Polish Prussia (the present province of West Prussia) had been described as a political necessity by Frederick the Great when still Crown Prince, and a glance at the map fully bears out this view. In the political testament of November 7, 1768, he pictures the time when this connecting link shall have been gained for his monarchy, and when, certain points along the Vistula having been fortified, it will at last have become possible to defend East Prussia effectively against any Russian aspirations. But, he adds, it is from Russia that the strongest opposition will come to the endeavours to annex Polish Prussia. His successors must, therefore, try to get possession of the country piecemeal, by means of negotiation based on Russia's urgent need, at any time, of Prussian support. It was a conjuncture of this kind which led to the First Partition of Poland. Russia was, then, at this time of vital importance to Prussia in respect both to her Eastern and to her general policy; because both of the tension between Prussia and the Western Powers, and of the enduring historic antagonism between Prussia and Austria. Though, after the murder of Peter III and the Treaty of Hubertusburg, the attitude of Russia towards Prussia had seemed, at the best, one of neutrality, the common interest of the two Powers in Polish affairs brought about relations between Frederick and Catharine which she wished to limit to an understanding as to Poland, but which he desired to expand into a general cooperation between them against Austria. The difficulty of bringing the Polish interregnum to a close in such a way as to suit Russian interests at length compelled Catharine to commit herself to an alliance which was more in those of Prussia than in her own. The compact was concluded on April 11, 1764, the two Powers undertaking to effect the election of Stanislaus Poniatowski. Should either of the signatories be attacked within his or her own frontiers by a hostile Power, the other was bound to furnish military assistance; if " subjects of the Polish nation should disturb the peace of the Republic and form a confederation against the lawful sovereign, the Tsarina and the King would advance their troops into Poland." In this treaty of alliance Russia guaranteed the possession of Silesia to Frederick; on the other hand, he was now bound to Russia, whatever consequences might arise from her own policy in regard to Poland; for both Powers further pledged themselves to maintain the Constitution and freedom of election in Poland and proposed a line of action in common in regard to the "Dissidents" (dissenters). It was to the advantage of Prussia that anarchy was kept up in Poland, and the pressure long exercised by that Power along the Prussian frontiers proportionately weakened. On the other hand, Prussia had nothing to gain from the Russian ascendancy in a kingdom so impotent as Poland, which implied the advance of the Russian empire to the Prussian frontier. There was thus an inherent inconsistency in the Prusso-Russian alliance, of which Frederick was fully aware; the position in which he had to carry on his Polish policy was one of constraint, but he made admirable use of it when the crisis of the Partition of Poland was reached.

With the election of Stanislaus Poniatowski Catharine had attained her object, and till 1768 she seemed to have become absolutely mistress of Poland. Her policy, however, led to the Confederation of Bar, and to the war which broke out in consequence between Turkey and Russia. A dangerous international tension arose, France and Austria in particular, as has been previously related, in their turn assuming a threatening attitude towards Catharine. Should a European war ensue, Frederick would be involved in it as a matter of course, and must stand or fall with Russia. In this event, he was resolved to fulfil his obligations towards Russia; but he told himself that he would then be fighting for ends which either had no bearing on Prussian interests or were directly opposed to them, and that it would therefore be better from his point of view if there were no war. He was also determined, if war there must be, to put in a claim for territorial compensation from Russia: here was the occasion indicated in the political testament which at this very time he was revising.

Frederick recognised the *casus foederis* and paid the stipulated subsidies to Russia for her Turkish War. At the same time, he endeavoured to effect a renewal of the alliance with Russia; but the modest condition which he laid down for such a renewal proves how slight was his expectation of acquiring West Prussia; for he merely asked that Russia should agree to a not very serious guarantee of a Prussian claim to the reversion of a certain territory within the Empire. Prince Henry, however, was already of opinion that this crisis would force Russia and Austria to consent to an acquisition of territory by Prussia at the expense of Poland. Now, so early as the beginning of 1769, Frederick had suggested to Panin a scheme of partition which was ostensibly put forward by the Saxon minister Count zu Lynar, but of which the real originator was the King himself. According to this plan, Russia, in return for the assistance rendered her against the Turks, was to offer to Austria the town of Lemberg with its surroundings and the Zips; to hand over to Prussia Polish Prussia, with Ermeland and protective rights over Danzig; and, by way of indemnity for the expenses of the war, take for herself whatever part of Poland would suit her. The significance of this suggestion should not, however, be overestimated. Frederick simply intended "Lynar's project" as a feeler; and it absolutely fell through when Panin replied with a quite different scheme, drily observing that, so far as Russia was concerned, she already possessed larger dominions than she could govern.

The negotiations for the renewal of the Prusso-Russian alliance dragged on so long that before their termination the meeting between Frederick and Joseph had taken place at Neisse (August 25-7, 1769). Inasmuch as this meeting indicated a *rapprochement* between the two Powers from whose inveterate antagonism Russia had much to gain, she was obliged once more to come to terms with Prussia. The alliance was extended till the end of March, 1780; but, of course, no mention was made in the treaty of a partition of Poland.

In the middle of the following year, 1770, the Porte called in the intervention of Prussia and Austria in her struggle with Russia. Frederick and Joseph met again, this time at Neustadt in Moravia; and, immediately afterwards, Frederick formally enquired of Catharine whether the mediation of Prussia and Austria in the war with Turkey would be agreeable to her, adding that Austria wished the Danubian Principalities to remain under Turkish domination. This turn of affairs placed Catharine in a difficult position: and it has been already related how, in July, 1770, she quite unexpectedly invited Prince Henry of Prussia to visit St Petersburg, in order that a personal note might be struck in the progress of her relations with Prussia. Henry arrived in St Petersburg on October 12 and remained there till the following February; and the intimacy then formed between him and the Tsarina was kept up by a correspondence of ten years' duration. But Henry was not, as has been surmised, the bearer of secret instructions for a treaty of partition of Poland. The correspondence between the two brothers shows that Frederick did not at that time wish "to interfere either in the peace (with Turkey) or in the affairs of Poland, but simply to watch the course of events"; and Henry's sole business was to induce moderation and compliance in the Court of St Petersburg. However, Catharine would not hear of any mediation by other Powers, and the terms of peace which she offered to the Porte seemed tantamount to a declaration of war against Austria. At the critical moment, a way of escape was provided by the occupation of a part of Poland by Austria. The famous brief conversation on the subject which took place between Catharine, Chernuisheff, and Henry at St Petersburg on January 8, 1771, set the ball rolling towards the partition of Poland as a solution of the problem. A tract of Polish territory was offered to Prussia on that occasion, Russia thus abandoning her principle of maintaining the integrity of Poland. But Frederick disapproved, because his acceptance at the moment seemed necessarily conditional upon his implication in war—and war there would apparently be, since Chernuisheff clearly meant the Danubian Principalities to fall to Russia's lot—a result which Austria would never tolerate. Frederick felt, too, that for so great a risk Ermeland was too small a gain. "My share is so slight," he writes to his brother on January 31, 1771, "that it would not make up for the tumult which it would arouse; but Polish Prussia would be worth the trouble, even if Danzig were not included, for we should then have the Vistula and free communication with the kingdom (*i.e.* East Prussia)— an important matter." Even in that event, Frederick wished to adhere to his plan of neutrality and, if need were, pay a sum of money for his strip of Poland. But Prince Henry, on his return, correctly summed up the situation: "You hold the balance between Austria and Russia; in the end Russia will have to give in and to grant you some advantage in return for those you secure her; when the Austrians see this, they will in their turn desire some advantage; so that each of the Powers, in seeking an advantage for itself, will agree to an arrangement beneficial to all three." Accordingly, lest by persisting in neutrality he should fall to the ground between two stools, Frederick made up his mind to enter into the suggestion made from St Petersburg. This suggestion itself was, therefore, by no means the result of an offensive policy against Poland on the part of Prussia, whose line of action was rather forced upon her by stress of circumstances. It is to Frederick's credit that he was able to turn this pressure to good account in the interests of his monarchy. Further developments were determined by Russia's stand-point, which Panin expressed quite frankly and which Frederick shared: if Russia had to forgo what she had gained by the war with Turkey, she must seek compensation elsewhere, namely, in Poland. Negotiations were carried on between Panin and Count Solms at St Petersburg. On the other hand, the opposition of Austria seemed to quell all hope that war between Russia and Austria could be averted by means of the plan for the partition of Poland, the origin and extension of which have just been described. It was only when Catharine, at the close of 1771, formally declared to Prussia that she would renounce all claim to the Danubian Principalities, and when both Powers thus came to terms about Poland, that Austria determined to participate in this solution of the question, distasteful as it was to Maria Theresa. On August 5, 1772, Austria entered into the Prusso-Russian Treaty of Partition of the previous February 17; and, as has been related above, the First Partition of Poland was concluded.

While the policy of Austria in the Polish question was artificial and showed no steady purpose, that of Frederick was clear, definite and tactically correct. He had, no doubt, now accepted a solution the effects of which were contrary to the traditional interests of Prussia; but his hand was forced in the matter and, in any event, the independence of Poland was doomed. He must not, therefore, be regarded as the author of the Partition of Poland, for which Catharine is responsible both in its general bearing and as a move in political tactics. The opposition in which he stood to Austria forced him to follow the Russian lead in this question. On the other hand, as Ranke shows, it was certainly due to his action that the scope of the Partition scheme was so enlarged as to bring about a readjustment of the balance of power in both north and east. Frederick's Polish policy was fraught with still more important results; inasmuch as it may be said to have largely contributed to the prevention of a violent crisis in the Eastern question and to the stoppage of Russia's advance on the Danube. Furthermore, it rendered impossible the sole domination of Russia in Poland. Russia's claim to the *dominium maris Baltici* was henceforth contested by a strong Power, Prussia, instead of by a weak one, Poland, and the lower Vistula became once more a German river. Finally, through Frederick's Polish policy the foundations were laid for an understanding between the two German Great Powers. These far-reaching results were, it is true, secured at the cost of Polish independence. But Germany, and more especially Prussia, had an inherent historical title to the parts of Poland allotted to her in 1772. They consisted in fact of ancient German territory which had never become thoroughly incorporated into the Polish community; so that " *regno redintegrato* " was an appropriate inscription for the medal struck to celebrate the allegiance of the newly acquired territory. Nowhere was there any opposition to the occupation, the Protestants in particular eagerly welcoming the new rule. The lands annexed by Prussia were, indeed, in a miserably neglected condition; but this did not lead Frederick to mistake the importance of what he had gained: "It is a very good bargain," he wrote to Prince Henry on June 12, 1772, "and very advantageous both financially and as regards the political position of the State"; and, on June 18, 1772: Prussia, he added, now controlled all the products and all the imports of Poland—an important point; but the chief gain was that the inhabitants of Prussia could never again be exposed to famine, since they had the corn supply in their own hands. Notwithstanding all the efforts made, however, her new commercial position could not attain to its full importance, so long as Danzig, the emporium of the Baltic corn trade, remained outside her frontier.

Frederick next set to work with great energy to raise this new part of his kingdom to the economic level of the rest of his dominions. In this task he found valuable and far-seeing assistants in Johann Friedrich von Domhardt, president of the Board of Domains, and Franz Balthasar Schönberg von Brenkenhof, the first administrator of the Netze district. But, as a matter of fact, Frederick was himself the real administrative head of this province of West Prussia, as the newly acquired territory was named. His policy was practical and most carefully thought out, and he pursued it steadily and with due moderation. The liberation of the peasants was at once proclaimed; the land was taken out of the hands of the Polish nobility, and German peasants and burghers were settled on it; a systematic administration of justice was introduced, and national schools were established—measures which brought the country into line with the order of things existing in the Prussian State.

The further development of the Prussian policy in regard to Poland was a matter of course, so long as the alliance with Russia held good;

CH. XX.

in this Prince Henry remained the intermediary, who corresponded with Catharine and paid a second visit to Russia. Notwithstanding the prolongation, in 1777, of the agreement between the two Powers to March 31, 1788, Russia's Eastern schemes led to her abandonment of the Prussian side for that of Austria, which momentous decision ranged Prussia in a triple alliance with the Maritime Powers against Austria and Russia. How entirely anti-Russian the policy of Prussia had now become was shown by the agreement with Turkey, concluded on January 30, 1790, and by that with Poland, which followed on March 29 of the same year. Prussia now took the side of reform in Poland, and in the end recognised the Constitution of May 3, 1791. Thus Frederick William II wholly reversed his predecessor's policy, and placed Prussia in a false position. Such an alliance was in itself unnatural : the most important provision of the Constitution of May 3, namely, the establishment of a hereditary succession to the Crown, ran counter to Prussian interests ; and they must likewise suffer if the new Constitution restored the union with the Saxon electorate, of which the cooperation of Frederick and Catharine had relieved Prussia. This preposterous agreement with Poland precluded the extension and adjustment of the Prussian frontier—at all events by the acquisition of Danzig and Thorn, on which Hertzberg had concentrated his diplomacy, even in the lifetime of Frederick the Great. Yet this end had to be reached, if the work of the Hohenzollerns was to reach its organic consummation.

CHAPTER XXI.

DENMARK UNDER THE BERNSTORFFS AND STRUENSEE.

BETWEEN 1730, when Frederick IV died, and 1784, when his great-grandson, afterwards Frederick VI, successfully claimed the regency, the part played by Denmark in the politics of Europe was but small. It is true that, in an age of great wars, she increased her commerce, her possessions overseas, and even her dominions in Europe, gaining prizes such as tempted other nations to fight. But it was by quiet astuteness and good fortune that these advantages were secured. The Oldenburg Kings, it seemed, had at last learned the limits of their power. The partial detachment of Denmark from the main current of European affairs, however, by no means robs her history of interest. In an age of absolute monarchies, she presents the spectacle of one entirely wielded by feeble Kings. Power soon fell to a series of remarkable Ministers, and Moltke, Bernstorff, Struensee, Guldberg, and the younger Bernstorff, furnish a demonstration, unique in its amplitude, of the range and possibilities of benevolent despotism.

Frederick IV, a monarch whose industry equalled his ambition, and who won a place beside Christian IV and Frederick III in the reverence of his people, perfected the machinery of despotism and simplified the foreign policy of Denmark. After the downfall of Charles XII, Sweden no longer dwarfed and menaced her neighbours. And, while traces of the past were evident both in the determination of Frederick and his successors to uphold the aristocracy which kept Sweden weak, and in their hope that fortune might once more place the three Crowns of Scandinavia on the head of an Oldenburg, the reconquest of Scania had ceased to be an aim of the Danish State. The rulers at Copenhagen now pursued clear dynastic ends on their own side of the Sound. They cherished, indeed, hopes of attaining to a vote standing earlier on the list than the thirty-fifth in the Imperial College of Princes, as well as of filling their coffers with French or English subsidies and with the profits of world-wide trade. But these aspirations were feeble and fitful in comparison with those which concerned the Duchies. To retain the lands in Schleswig which had been estreated from the House of Gottorp during the Northern War, and to acquire the Gottorp heritage in Holstein, were throughout these years the first aims of all who worked for the security of Denmark and the glory of her Kings.

Home affairs, on the other hand, confronted the monarchy with problems of greater diversity. During the two generations which had passed since the *coup d'état* of 1660, autocracy had fortified itself unchallenged. The old Danish nobles, though not numerous and apparently loyal, saw above them a Privy Council and an array of governmental Colleges or Boards, chiefly officered by foreigners imported and ennobled by the King. Besides the members of the central Government, the Services, and the Bench, the principal officers of local government were agents of the Crown. The citizens and the peasants were still as of old the faithful upholders of absolutism. The Church supplied a docile royal servant in every parish. The higher clergy, however deeply wounded by royal decrees, submitted to a Divine purpose which had made Saul and Jeroboam kings. The unquestioning loyalty of the free Norwegian peasants was paid, not to the Danes, but to the King of Denmark and Norway, and it was to him that the Duchies likewise owed allegiance. In an age in which loyalty was almost a religion, the King of Denmark was the cynosure of all his subjects. He alone could sway and reform the State.

In 1730 the area and political influence of Denmark were far greater than at the present day. The dominions of her King then included Norway, Schleswig, Oldenburg, Delmenhorst, and the royal portion of Holstein. This considerable area, it is true, nourished a somewhat scanty population. In 1769, when the first census was taken, the kingdom of Denmark numbered only some 825,000 souls, while the Norwegians numbered some 727,600, and the whole State little more than two millions. When compared with the resources of some other European nations, however, this number appeared respectable. Commanded by an autocrat, and endowed by nature with the elements of power at sea, it might easily become formidable.

After seventy years of absolutism, however, the social and economic structure of Denmark still showed grave defects. Although, in 1702, Frederick had abolished the worst form of serfdom (*Vornedskap*), so that the peasants of Zealand and Fünen were no longer the property of their lords, and although Norway was in great part peopled by small proprietors, agriculture, the staple industry of the State, remained primitive and unprogressive. The peasants were ignorant and poor. Great masses of them held their lands on condition of paying to their lord taxes which were commonly beyond their strength, and of performing labour services whose incidence was determined by him. The lord, who in many cases appointed the local judges, could with a fair prospect of impunity resort to brutal violence against his tenants. Apart from these evils, moreover, agriculture could hardly flourish, so long as the system of cultivation remained medieval in type. The peasants still yoked four or six horses to cumbrous wheeled ploughs, and feebly scratched the soil with wooden harrows. The villages still cultivated all their lands in common, each owner possessing strips of land scattered over the surface of vast open fields. The three-field system of tillage, with its wasteful monotony of corn-crops and fallow, had not yet given place to a wiser rotation. In Jutland great tracts of territory still lay waste, while throughout Denmark the nobles often found it no easy task to secure tenants for their vacant farms. Industry, confined to the towns and crippled by the gild system, was even more feeble than agriculture. An unprosperous nation, where the rural populace fed and clothed itself, offered no place for thriving towns. Copenhagen, which, with some 70,000 inhabitants, was more than five times as populous as any other Danish borough, could not rebuild itself after the great fire of 1728, until the King withdrew his ban against houses framed with timber. Some seaports, notably Bergen, Aalborg, Aarhuus, and Altona, showed signs of energy and progress; but even within their confines vigorous municipal life had not yet sprung up. The market towns, though numerous, were insignificant and poor.

Of the national temper it is hard to speak with confidence. The sacrifices exacted by the long Northern War had been bravely made. Ignorance, sluggishness, and good-humour seem to have characterised the common people. Foreign travellers, whose impressions were naturally formed chiefly in the capital, found the upper classes cold and dull. Critics, both native and foreign, derided their excessive greed for titles. "The world here," wrote Colonel Robert Keith in 1771, "is parcelled out into no less than nine classes, six of whom I must never encounter without horror. Yet my opera-glass tells me that numbers eight and nine beat us all hollow as to flesh and blood." The first three classes, which formed the Court, included no one of lower degree than an acting councillor of State, a colonel, or a commander. The King, as supreme disposer of the whole hierarchy, gave or sold rank as he pleased, thus by yet another method enhancing his own autocracy.

Of this heterogeneous and somewhat unprogressive State the Oldenburg dynasty was the conscience and the soul. Nothing was too distant or too trivial for the eye and ear of the King. It was he who appointed the organists in provincial churches, who gave or withheld permission to follow callings outside the gilds, and who licensed the unfortunate to beg. To him and to the Council, whose powers and functions he determined, men and women from the furthest confines of Norway presented their petitions for favours and for redress. His paternal activity embraced the affairs both of this world and of the next. By the "Sabbath Ordinance" of 1730 Frederick IV, a bigamist, doomed his subjects to observe Sundays and holy days with Judaic rigour. On these festivals work and amusements were alike forbidden, the town gates locked until four o'clock in the afternoon, and the people directed on pain of the pillory to attend church. This edict, and the absence of protest against it, illustrate the character of the autocracy which in the same year devolved upon Christian, Frederick's son.

Christian VI, a man of little ability, mean presence, and somewhat petty disposition, was to prove a humane, industrious, and thoroughly well-meaning King. He came to the throne permeated with the belief that by the exercise of his power he could make his people happy and good. Surrounding himself with Ministers of his own choosing, of whom the genial soldier Poul Vendelbo Löwenörn remained longest in power, he promptly swept away the most vexatious ordinances of his father. The taxes were reduced, the compulsory militia was abolished, the grant of trading monopoly to Copenhagen revoked, and the Sabbath Ordinance annulled. Unhappily for Denmark, however, Christian was tenacious only of dignity, industry, and good intentions. Lacking genius to divine the national needs, he did not supply its place by personal contact with the people or by choice of Danish counsellors. Himself German in speech, he had married, for her godliness, Sophia Magdalena of Baireuth. The Queen despised the Danes, but spent the revenue profusely. She demanded a new diadem, and thought it unqueenly to don a garment more than once. To this German lady and her mother the King gave a ready ear, while the court preacher and almost all his Ministers were German.

With so little security that Danish policy should be national, it is not surprising that, both in home and in foreign affairs, Christian failed to hold a steady course. Early in 1733, the peasants were once more subjected to military service which bound them to the soil. The new militia was only one-half as numerous as the old; but the provisions for maintaining it fixed by law made it far more onerous. Before the close of the reign peasants from nine to forty years of age were forbidden to quit their holdings without the permission of their lord, while it rested with him to determine which of them should compose the contingent due from his estate.

Attempts on the part of the Crown to regulate trade were numerous and violent. In 1732, the King founded an Asiatic Company. In the following year, the West India and Guinea Company was permitted to buy from France the island of St Croix. In 1735, a new department of State for Economy and Commerce was created, and in 1736 the Bank of Copenhagen was established. Foreign spinners and weavers were brought in and paid to manufacture a number of products for which purchasers could not be found. In order to nurture home industries, the ports of Denmark and southern Norway were closed against ships with certain freights, of which the chief was corn. In 1737, paternal interference reached its climax with the establishment of a royal store in the capital. Government secured funds for purchasing goods from the manufacturers, by forcing its pensioners to accept deferred orders for goods on the store in place of the payments due on account of their pensions.

The King's interference in the sphere of religion likewise savoured of the limitless autocracy which he claimed. He and his Queen were swayed by the pietism which at this time powerfully appealed to the deep feeling and traditional independent manhood of the North. The Copenhageners, thousands of whom had seen their homes destroyed by fire in 1728, listened willingly to the call to repentance. To Christian, however, the revival of religious life seemed attainable by a social reformation dictated by himself and by the increased activity of a state Church controlled by him. He closed theatres and dancing-halls, forbade masquerades, and banished actors. In 1735 he reenacted the Sabbath Ordinance, with reduced penalties and permission to do necessary harvest work on Sundays. In the next year he signalised the second centenary of the Danish Reformation by introducing the rite of Confirmation, and thus made further religious instruction compulsory for all his subjects. In 1737, to supplement his own unceasing supervision over all departments of religious life and thought, a General Board of Ecclesiastical Inspection was set up. Later in the reign the King, by means of edicts, waged war upon conventicles and sectaries. Unorthodox propagandists were banished from all Denmark with the exception of four towns.

The Puritan King who frowned upon amusements eagerly furthered every branch of education. Holberg ceased to be a playwright, and became a historian. In 1732 the University of Copenhagen was refounded, and the overwhelming preponderance of its theological faculty reduced, by means of favours shown to that of jurisprudence. Seven years later, the few secondary schools which Denmark possessed underwent drastic reform. Something was done to continue the work of Frederick IV in founding elementary schools. Towards the close of the reign, two societies for the promotion of Danish national learning and culture were founded with the countenance of the King.

To Christian VI succeeded in 1746 his son Frederick V, a Prince of glittering qualities, who took all hearts by storm, and in his reign of twenty years gained for Denmark the reputation of a fortunate and happy State. He proved himself at first too wise, and afterwards, perhaps, too indolent, to attempt by sweeping changes to gain his aim of pleasing all. Suavely disappointing the young courtiers who thought to rule in his name, and dismissing Count Frederick Danneskjold-Samsöe, the able but difficult Minister of Marine, he retained in the main the councillors and the policy of his father. Even the Sabbath Ordinance remained unrevoked. The accent of royalty was, however, changed. Social life, taking its tone from the King and his popular Queen Louise, became unaffected, genial and gay. Absolutism was put into commission.

The King's friend and Chief Marshal, Count Adam Gottlob Moltke, German by origin, but in patriotism a thorough Dane, took unofficially a very large share in the business of the State. Working with Johann Sigismund Schulin and his successor in foreign affairs, and in home affairs with the Council or the several high officials, Moltke gave his master leisure for the dissipation to which he gradually became a slave.

Even, however, after his degeneration had begun, Frederick V remained a force to be reckoned with. His German lieutenants served him with enthusiasm while he lived, and never ceased to extol him to each other after his death. Within the kingdom, the Council, a benevolent oligarchy, trod with measured pace in the paths of policy which were already familiar. To promote manufactures, shipping, and agriculture, and to remedy, when occasion offered, the defects in education, in the status of the peasants and in the organisation of the army, were plain duties. In foreign affairs, on the other hand, Denmark, after a quarter of a century of successful opportunism, had to face crises which imperilled her existence as a nation. In 1750 she lost Schulin, killed, as was believed, by the blunders of his physician. To find a competent successor, whether native or alien, was no easy task. Next year, however, the death of Frederick, Prince of Wales, removed a prior claim upon the future career of his friend, the Hanoverian Baron Johann Hartwig Ernst von Bernstorff, who, as chief secretary of the so-called German Chancery, was to guide Danish diplomacy and influence Danish life for nearly twenty years.

Bernstorff had already won renown by his skilful and zealous services to Denmark, notably at the Imperial Diet. During a six years' embassy at the Court of Louis XV he gained a European reputation and procured for Denmark the profitable Treaty of Alliance of April, 1746. From 1751 onwards, he was for twenty years settled at Copenhagen, and gained such eminence as to make credible the reputed epigram of Frederick the Great: "Denmark has her fleet and her Bernstorff." In some respects, however, he was to prove an indifferent consultant to the State. Prone to magnificence, and believing that, inasmuch as he abstained from gambling, he could not be extravagant, he influenced the King and Court in the direction of their natural inclinations. Luxury reigned and debt increased in time of peace. Bernstorff countenanced the costly efforts to create trade by laws and subsidies. Loving the French and loved by them, he clung to the common belief that France was still as preeminent in Europe as she had been in the days of Louis XIV. A North German Protestant, he was blind to the fact that leagues of small States based on religion were out of date. A disciple of Schulin, he did not perceive that the rise of Russia ought to change the policy of upholding oligarchic "freedom" at Stockholm in order to keep Sweden weak. He exposed his adopted country, moreover, to the undying hatred which Frederick of Prussia cherished against him and his House.

But, although posterity finds some qualification necessary to the national and international laudation of the "oracle of Denmark," the advent of Bernstorff must be pronounced to have been highly fortunate for the State. Not only did he diffuse through the administration an atmosphere of honesty, industry, and goodwill, but it was also through him that the ideas of France, England, and Germany were brought into the small and backward country which he served. Society and the arts also owed much to him. In Moltke and Bernstorff, it was said, Denmark possessed two Colberts. A strict Protectionist, Bernstorff was all for free trade in men of talent. Besides officials, he imported from France and Germany professors, divines, poets, sculptors, physicians, and men of science. Klopstock, Johann Andreas Cramer, "the German Bossuet," and his own nephew and successor Andreas Peter Bernstorff are but the chief in a crowd of these profitable allies. In his own department, Bernstorff made good use of the slender means at his disposal. Denmark possessed a fleet which was far from contemptible, but her war-chest stood empty, and her army, although more than 50,000 strong, consisted of unruly German mercenaries, supported by an ill-trained militia. Yet in 1758 Bernstorff was able to develop the French alliance into an arrangement by which France subsidised a Danish army and pledged herself with Austria to further that *mageskifte*, or exchange of Oldenburg and Delmenhorst for the dominions of the House of Gottorp in Schleswig-Holstein, which was long the lodestar of Danish policy. In 1756 Sweden became for a short time the ally of Denmark in armed neutrality; and ten years later the Swedish Crown Prince Gustavus was allowed to marry Sophia Magdalena, the daughter of Frederick V. Denmark, guided by Bernstorff, was almost the only State of northern Europe which held aloof from the Seven Years' War, while she succeeded in avoiding collision with England, the terror of maritime neutrals. Most delicate and dangerous of all were the relations with Russia.

The difficulties of Denmark with Russia had their root in the Holstein-Gottorp question. It was an axiom with the Gottorp Dukes that the confiscation of their possessions in Schleswig had been a direct breach of law. That view found support outside, notably from the Emperor. Frederick IV, on the other hand, offered nothing by way of compensation, and declared that he would defend his acquisition to the last drop of his blood. But the House of Holstein-Gottorp, powerless by itself, became formidable through marriages with the sister of Charles XII and the daughter of Peter the Great. Frederick IV and Christian VI therefore sedulously courted France and England, and strove to secure Schleswig by means of far-reaching alliances. For many years this policy proved successful. In 1742, however, Charles Peter Ulrich, the son of the dispossessed Charles Frederick, was declared heir to the throne of the Tsarina; and in the following year his cousin Adolphus Frederick was unanimously elected by the Swedish Diet to be the future successor of King Frederick I. The choice of Adolphus Frederick marked the triumph of the Tsarina's diplomacy over that of Christian VI, who all but declared war against Sweden in support of the candidature of Frederick his son.

In the course of the next few years, however, Denmark secured a better understanding with both Russia and Sweden. In 1750 Schulin procured a treaty by which Adolphus Frederick undertook that, if the inheritance of Holstein-Gottorp should ever fall to him, he would resign it to the King of Denmark in return for Oldenburg, Delmenhorst, and 200,000 dollars. Charles Peter Ulrich, now the husband of the future Catharine the Great, proved less amenable. For nearly twenty years he steadfastly refused to sell his birthright; and it seemed only too probable that, on the death of the Tsarina Elizabeth, he would employ the might of Russia to avenge the wrongs of his House. To avert this peril, Bernstorff tried every resource of diplomacy in vain. Through six campaigns of the Seven Years' War he had preserved the neutrality of Denmark. But in January, 1762, the Tsar, Peter III, became her foe. Denmark soon found herself, without a single ally, confronting the veteran hordes of Muscovy supported by Frederick the Great.

Peter III, however, changed the issue of the European struggle without harming his enemy. Neither her strong naval squadron nor the army of thirty thousand which her French Field-Marshal, Count Louis St Germain, led into Mecklenburg, was called upon to strike a blow for Denmark. The deposition of Peter III in July dissolved her peril. Less than three years later, in March, 1765, Catharine became the ally of Frederick V, and undertook, while the Duke of Schleswig-Holstein, her son Paul, was still a minor, to make such arrangements as would put an end to the Gottorp disputes.

When, in January, 1766, Frederick paid the penalty of his excesses by a premature death, his servants contemplated with pride the fruit of their labours at home and abroad. The realm had unquestionably advanced in agriculture, industry, commerce, and general organisation, and it was at peace with all the world. But two decades of power had produced in the Council a certain self-sufficiency. While reform was needed on all sides, and the public debt amounted to twenty million dollars, Bernstorff and his friends showed no desire to quicken their pace or to welcome the cooperation of other forces. It was not unnatural that others thought that the great King who ruled Prussia from his Cabinet should form a model for the future conduct of the Danish autocratic State.

The sceptre now fell into the unwilling hands of Frederick's son Christian VII, a youth not quite seventeen years of age. Under the stern and perhaps brutal governance of Privy Councillor Ditlev Reventlow, he had grown up in complete ignorance of the management of public or even of private affairs. He had never been free to spend a ducat or to open a letter by himself, and the companions provided for him had achieved his moral ruin. He possessed considerable ability and great, though fitful, ambition. During boyhood his memory and facility of speech had often roused admiration, and in early manhood his talents commanded unfeigned respect. His form was agile and graceful, and he retained for many years great insensibility to fatigue and no inconsiderable power of charming those who met him for the first time. But grave defects in his character soon made Danish patriots tremble. He lacked industry and tenacity, delighted in the misfortunes of others, proved himself a traitor to his friends and servants, and devoted his wild imagination to the invention of new forms of debauch. It is now confidently asserted that he was already in the grip of an inexorable mental disease (*dementia praecox*) which, advancing fitfully after the dawn of manhood, could not fail to reduce him to imbecility in the course of a few years. In that age, however, insanity was so little understood that the court physician could in 1786 attribute the King's malady to his premature assumption of the duties and freedom of a sovereign. From his accession to the year 1772, acts which betoken disease were attributed to youthful folly or to evil counsels, and the meek obedience of Denmark was often rendered to the scribbled mandates of a madman.

During the first four years of the reign, two of Christian's delusions formed the most potent influences in the history of the State. He believed that his own power and genius were incomparable, but that to attain perfection he must harden himself by physical excess. He delighted to show his power by cashiering officials who had been denounced either as serving him ill or as appropriating to themselves his proper glory. St Germain, the able organiser of the army, was removed from the Board of War. Moltke, long so omnipotent as to be nicknamed "King," was dismissed without a pension. Prince Charles of Hesse-Cassel received in 1766 the hand of Christian's sister and unbounded favour, only to be driven into retirement in the following year. Even Bernstorff lived in constant insecurity. At the same time Christian's resolute profligacy was endangering the repute of the monarchy and the life of the King. His ministers had therefore other inducements than their desire for the friendship of England, when they prevailed on him to make an early marriage. In November, 1766, he consented to espouse the sister of George III, Caroline Matilda, then fifteen years of age. The gay young Queen brightened the social life of the capital. In January, 1768, she gave the Crown an heir, the future Frederick VI.

Bernstorff remained in power, and his policy gained a notable triumph when, in April, 1767, the "Provisional Treaty of Exchange" was signed in Copenhagen. Renouncing for herself the Gottorp claims in Schleswig, Catharine undertook to use her good offices with her son Paul, when he should come of age, to follow the same course and also

promote the exchange of Ducal Holstein for Oldenburg and Delmenhorst. The negotiations for this Treaty had thrown a striking light
upon the political situation. Patriots may justly lament that the
policy of Denmark was decided by a diplomatic struggle at Copenhagen
between one Prussian and two Russian diplomatists and two soldiers
from France and Germany. Bernstorff, whose German origin was now
almost forgotten, had carried his point only by inciting Catharine and
her representatives to secure the dismissal of the King of Prussia's agents.
Thanks to the same powerful support, he was now created Count.
But Russian assistance was not rendered without payment. Under the
influence of the fear that Sweden, the common foe, would gain strength
by reform, the *entente* between Russia and Denmark soon developed into
a relation too closely resembling that of a patron and a client State.

Meanwhile, Christian VII was falling under the influence of the
companions of his orgies, particularly Count Conrad Holck and the
so-called *Slövlet* Katrine (Catharine of the Gaiters), who seemed on
the eve of becoming his official mistress. Holck gained for a time an
ascendancy so complete that Bernstorff pledged himself to support the
favourite on condition that he did not intrude into politics. It was he
who in November, 1767, banished the disinterested Swiss philosopher
Elias Solomon Francis Reverdil, formerly the King's tutor and now
his Cabinet Secretary. Court intrigues, lunatic outrages, and the overthrow of notables offensive to Russia, filled the history of Denmark,
until in 1768 the King announced his invincible determination to visit
foreign lands. Escorted by a train of more than fifty persons, among
whom Bernstorff seemed to English eyes the only man of sense and
virtue, he journeyed by way of Holstein and the Netherlands to England
and France. Here he went through a summer and autumn of festivities
with a show of enjoyment and with a regal bearing which in public
never gave way, while his disease was fast reducing him to senility. The
design of including Italy and St Petersburg in the tour was abandoned.
After his return in January, 1769, when his delighted subjects discovered
that the royal orgies had come to an end, Christian was at heart
indifferent to everything save what caused discomfort to himself.

Thus afflicted, the King came under the influence of a young German
doctor, John Frederick Struensee, who had accompanied him on his
journey in 1768. Struensee owed his post as royal physician, like
his previous success among the nobles of Holstein, to his own talent and
to his friendship with Count Schack Charles Rantzau-Ascheberg, a
brilliant adventurer, in whose revolt against the accepted rules of religion
and morality he shared. By treating the King with intelligence and
tact, Struensee gradually became indispensable to him. In what
degree Christian's astonishingly good behaviour while abroad was due to
Struensee's advice, it is impossible to determine. On his return to Copenhagen with the King, his modesty, handsome person, and talent for

pleasing, partially overcame the contempt which the arrogance of the Court deemed fitting towards a " pill-maker " and a pastor's son.   The Queen's prejudice against him melted away when he first restored her to health, and then achieved the miracle of bringing to her feet a husband who during eight months' absence had wellnigh ignored her existence. As Christian sank deeper into apathy, the Queen's influence over him and over the Court of Denmark grew, while Struensee became the confidant and director of the royal couple.   Often tormented by delusions and always regarding contempt for marriage as a mark of superiority, the King looked on with indifference while, during the year 1770, his wife became the paramour of his friend.   It was his complete and enduring conquest of the Queen that rendered possible the extraordinary empire over Denmark to which Struensee attained during 1770 and 1771, and the cascade of reforming edicts associated with his name.

From the nature of the case, the record of these years can hardly be free from uncertainty.   The King, whose brief decrees overthrew Ministers and created institutions, was at times unquestionably sane. Amid all his wayward fancies, he had long before aspired to become the benefactor of the people and to emancipate himself from the oligarchy of high officials.   That these results were now zealously sought after, that in this Struensee played a great part, and that he eventually used the lunatic King as a machine for registering his own decrees—are facts established beyond dispute.   His share in the government during 1770 and the first months of 1771, on the other hand, like the springs of his action and the sources of his information, may well provoke debate.

It was not until near the close of 1770 that Struensee began to be regarded as a person of importance.   He was notoriously the favourite of the Queen; but the Queen shunned politics and devoted herself to her lover and to her son.   To the world the King's reader and ex-physician seemed a humble member of a royalist clique, whose notables were Rantzau-Ascheberg, St Germain, and General Peter Elias Gähler. These men, apart from their personal grievances and aspirations, united in regarding the power of the Council as a usurpation.   They would have Denmark ruled like Prussia, by edicts framed in the Cabinet of the King.   Struensee they may well have regarded as one who might commend their designs to Christian and Matilda, acting thus as their useful and harmless ally.

The struggle between the old Government, of which Bernstorff was the centre, and its opponents was decided during the summer of 1770. The long seclusion of the King and Court on a visit to the Duchies, and the humiliation of the Danish arms in an attempt to coerce the Dey of Algiers, facilitated the triumph of Struensee and the Opposition. Enevold Brandt, a young votary of pleasure, once the comrade of Rantzau and Struensee in Altona, received a summons to the Court, from which he had been banished for attacking Holck. Despite the earnest and outspoken remonstrances of Bernstorff, who regarded the Treaty of Exchange as lost if a man proscribed by Catharine were favoured by Christian, the recall of Rantzau followed. Meanwhile Reventlow received a severe rebuff, and Holck, after witnessing the dismissal of his associates, found himself cashiered. These events foreshadowed the fall of Bernstorff, which took place in September. The veteran statesman received the blow with dignity, and from his retreat in northern Germany continued to serve Denmark to the utmost of his power. His successor as Minister for Foreign Affairs was Count Adolphus Sigfried Osten, an able diplomat whose appointment might, it was hoped, be not wholly unacceptable to Catharine without implicitly pledging Christian to remain her slave. Soon, however, the changes went far beyond the dismissal of high officials in favour of new men, and the rearrangement of offices so as to leave the oligarchy out in the cold. In December, 1770, the Council was abolished; and the secret Cabinet, in which the royal decrees were drafted, thus became the unrivalled centre of influence in the Government. At the same time Struensee succeeded an insignificant person in the Mastership of Requests—a confidential secretariate of little dignity but of enormous potential importance. Early in 1771, the King's disease made a notable advance, and it became more than ever necessary to screen him from his subjects. Brandt, the master of the revels in which the Court continued to indulge, became almost formally the King's keeper, and, in June, Reverdil received an unexpected invitation to return to Copenhagen. On his arrival, in September, he found the King in a pitiable condition, but still able to conceal his infirmity from some who saw him, and at times to act and speak with intelligence.

Meanwhile, Struensee had made more definite advances towards official power. During the first half of the year he had become master of the privy purses of the King and Queen, from which he and Brandt had each received a sum of 60,000 dollars. In July, he was declared Minister of the Cabinet, with power to write down the verbal orders of the King, to seal them with his cabinet seal, and to promulgate them as law. After July 15, 1771, cabinet orders were issued with the signature "By command of the King—Struensee." A week later, Christian and his stepmother Juliana Maria attended the christening of a little daughter whom the Queen had borne to Struensee, and both Struensee and Brandt were made Counts.

During the eleven months which had passed since the ideas of Struensee became dominant in the State, the nation had lived in a whirlwind of reform. Every Danish institution had been subjected to an examination in which popularity counted for little and antiquity for nothing. It was significant that Struensee knew little of history and never learned Danish. Often indeed the advice of a specialist, a board, or a commission, was sought; but there was no security that the cabinet order which swiftly followed on the first enquiry would do more than solve the questions at issue by the forcible application of what the Minister held to be enlightened principles.

The key-note of the new *régime* had been struck early in September, 1770, when cabinet orders, composed in German, struck at the abuse of rank and titles and abolished the censorship of the Press. Before the close of the year, while government by Cabinet was being organised, an elaborate scheme for the reception and education of some 2500 waifs received the force of law. These measures were but the pioneers of a host which followed in 1771. To give Denmark a benevolent despotism secure against bureaucratic restraint, to strike down privilege in every sphere of life, to abolish practices which outraged contemporary sentiment, and to maintain for every citizen the widest possible freedom to live the life which seemed good to him—such were the main motives of Struensee's profuse and hasty legislation. It is impossible to mention here more than a small number of the edicts which he poured forth from the royal Cabinet, or to indicate how far some of the more important can be shown to have had their origin outside his era or his brain. Although he had never been distinguished by industry and did not now withdraw from the gaieties of court life, he appears to have devised and constructed the great majority of the edicts by himself, with only such aid as a few private secretaries could afford. Working single-handed and with no predetermined plan, he saw tasks on every side and shrank from none of them. Reverdil, who is manifestly a witness of truth, learned from a friend that Struensee had declared to him that he would so reform the State as to leave no stone of it undisturbed.

The emancipation of the King, which for the moment implied the omnipotence of Reform, had been in great measure attained by the abolition of the Council. It was still further advanced by changes in the administrative system. In imitation of Prussian absolutism, the several Boards were taught complete subservience. Their staffs were ruthlessly reorganised, and their mutual relations rearranged; while they were compelled to rely upon written reports in place of personal access to the King. Their presidencies and other great posts held by nobles who might impair the royal autocracy were abolished. A great advance was made towards purifying the Civil Service from aristocratic jobbery and corruption. The Treasury, which received a great augmentation of importance, was filled with men of letters, including Professor Oeder, the advocate of peasant emancipation, and Charles Augustus, the elder brother of Struensee, a professor of mathematics from Liegnitz. It could not be expected that among the slow-moving Danes such changes, dictated by men unfamiliar with the existing machinery of government, would create in a moment a smooth and efficient administration. The old officials, however, yielded without a struggle, and their places were

CH. XXI.

filled by zealous dependents of the Crown. Some parts at least of public business were performed with unwonted and welcome despatch.

Benevolent despotism, however, could not attain perfection while the Crown was hampered by debt. Struensee, therefore, submitted a policy of harsh retrenchment for the gracious improvidence of the former Council. Although the amusements of the Court continued to be costly, its daily life departed far from the model of Versailles. Pensions were reduced or refused without mercy. The costly policy of buttressing the fabric of industry by subsidies was abandoned. The erection of superfluous churches was stopped. A reform of the University was planned by which the State would be spared large payments to the professors. The Guards were broken up. The higher posts in the Civil Service were abolished. As a new source of revenue, a public lottery was established, while the revenues of pious foundations were appropriated without scruple to public ends.

Struensee's war with privilege went far beyond the bounds of revenge upon the nobles, who had been wont to scorn the *bourgeois* and to secure for their own lackeys places under the Crown. In trade, in industry, in municipal government, and even in religion, vested interests were menaced or swept away. The free port of Copenhagen, the gild system of industry, and the governmental devices for securing well-filled churches, were equally objectionable to the new "enlightened" views, and severally suffered attack. The freedom of all Danish subjects and their equal treatment by the law seemed to be within measurable distance of attainment.

Power so unfettered made short work of abuses which survived from ages long gone by. Copenhagen was transformed into a well-ordered city. Throughout Denmark the scale of punishments became lighter. Torture for judicial purposes was abolished. So far as lay in the power of the law, the stigma of illegitimacy was removed. Parents might no longer consign their refractory children to gaol, or great nobles prevent the imprisonment of debtors.

Struensee's zeal for liberty embraced every section of the State. The cause of the serf was taken up in earnest. The number of holidays imposed by the Church upon the people was cut down, and the degrees enlarged within which marriages were lawful. The vindication of personal freedom was carried so far that the police were prohibited from entering any house in order to put down vice. Danish subjects were no longer forbidden to leave or enter towns by night, or, in many cases, to apply themselves, within or without the walls, to the calling of their choice.

Salutary and even admirable as were many of these reforms, they lost much of their value by the manner of their promulgation. It became more and more clear to the people that these changes expressed the will, not of an anointed King, but of an upstart and ungracious Minister. Struensee seldom appeared in public save with the King and Queen, and he was reputed to be the harsh gaoler of the one and the paramour of the other. "There was no Dane," declared Reverdil, "who did not regard it as a personal insult to be subjected to a power whose sole foundation was the scandal in the royal family." This power, moreover, was habitually exercised with studied indifference to the feelings of those whom it affected. To Christian Frederick Moltke, a son of the friend of Christian's father, the royal will was communicated in a missive of a type to which Danish officials had now to accustom themselves. "You are no longer my Grand Marshal. My circumstances do not permit me to keep one; I dismiss you without a pension." The government of Copenhagen was transformed and her cherished civic rights annihilated by careless edicts composed in German. In comparison with an "enlightened" principle, common convenience or opinion ranked as nothing. The poor of the capital found themselves prohibited from burying their dead by daylight, while the mass of the people regarded the extension of religious freedom as a conspiracy against religion.

As the summer waned, Struensee might well show signs of prostration brought on by many months of assiduous court life combined with unprecedented labours of State. Never widely beloved, he no longer possessed a single friend save the Queen. Even the good-humoured Brandt desired his overthrow. Many hated him for what he had already done, and more for what they believed that he might do in the future. In the meantime, the failure of two successive harvests had spread misery through the country; and, under Struensee's *régime,* no one could feel secure for a single day that a cabinet order would not threaten his means of living. The capital was in a ferment. Throughout the nation, in Norway and the Duchies no less than in the kingdom proper, all men of standing expected and longed for the deliverance of the King from the bondage in which he was supposed to live. The Press nourished sedition. Both within and without the confines of Denmark, the most fantastic crimes and designs were attributed to the Minister and the Queen. Struensee, who could not be wholly unconscious of the public hatred, wavered in his course, feigned a serenity which he did not feel, and suffered petty but notorious mutinies in the fleet and army to go unpunished. Thus encouraged and egged on by another adventurer, Colonel Magnus Beringskjold, Rantzau resolved to become the prime agent in bringing about a catastrophe which, since the summer of 1771, shrewd observers had deemed inevitable. Bernstorff and Moltke scouted any enterprise in which Rantzau was engaged. Among the officers, Danish and German, however, he found willing instruments. It was of still greater importance that the fear of popular revolt and the display of a forged proof of Struensee's intention to usurp the protectorship induced the Queen Dowager, Juliana Maria, her son, the Hereditary Prince Frederick, and his tutor, Ove Höegh Guldberg, to join in plotting a palace revolution.

CH. XXI.

In the early hours of January 17, 1772, Guldberg and a party of the conspirators woke the King from sleep. The terror inspired by their appearance, and the figment of a plot against his life, made Christian ready to sign whatever they put before him. At his stepmother's dictation, he wrote with his own hand the order for the imprisonment of his Queen. Meanwhile Struensee and Brandt were seized in the royal palace, and several of their adherents at home. Rantzau carried out with cynical brutality the deportation of the Queen to Kronborg, Hamlet's castle at the northern entrance to the Sound. The King's signature was, as usual, accepted as hallowing the most violent deeds. "Glorious, eventful night," wrote the historian Suhm, in an open letter to the King; "future Homers and Virgils shall sing thy praise. As long as Danish and Norwegian bravery shall live, so long shall the fame of Juliana and Frederick endure—but not increase, for that is impossible." Next day the King, cowering in fear, was driven in a gilded coach through his capital; while Rantzau and his accomplices, as it was believed, contrived that the rejoicings of the people at his liberation should end in a riot. Thus was the seal set upon the triumph of the revolution.

It remained for the King's deliverers, who promptly seized the reins of power, to make their work secure. To this end Struensee and Brandt were kept in irons while their papers were ransacked in search of proofs that they had aspired to dethrone the King. Nothing of the kind existed, and their accusers were therefore compelled to rely upon more general charges. Brandt had, under great provocation, actually bitten the King in the finger and beaten him with his fists, while Struensee could be charged with having broken the *Kongelov*, or fundamental law, by undermining the authority of the King and by issuing official papers which had not received the royal signature. Yet, as being here expressly authorised by a monarch whose omnipotence and whose sanity no one disputed, his proceedings could with difficulty be construed as high treason. But all hope for his escape vanished when, broken by five weeks' misery in a dungeon, he confessed to a criminal intimacy with the Queen. Jealously guarded by the victorious party, the King was hardly capable of interference, and the intercession of Catharine was soon to be proved unavailing. On April 6 an extraordinary tribunal decreed the royal divorce, and on the 25th Struensee and Brandt were sentenced to death. Three days later, in the presence of an enormous multitude, they were hewn to pieces on the scaffold. Their remains were for years exposed on wheels in the neighbourhood of Copenhagen.

Queen Matilda found a protector in the English Minister, Colonel Robert Murray Keith, who denounced war against Denmark, if she were in any way molested. His firmness (which George III instantly rewarded with the red riband of the Bath) saved her from a lifelong imprisonment in Aalborg Castle. At the end of May, having embraced her infant daughter for the last time, she passed into retirement at Celle. The vindictiveness of the King's half-brother Frederick, called the "Hereditary Prince," and his associates had cooled the ardent royalism of Copenhagen; and it completely alienated the unforgiving King of England.

If anything could have made the Danes regret Struensee, it might well have been the rule of his destroyers. The clique which had emancipated Christian VII possessed no common aim, save the overthrow of Struensee and the Queen. Devoid of policy, they made the King and the nation subservient to a cabal. They created, it is true, a Privy Council, and they were always careful to extort the King's signature before issuing their decrees. The deformed and contemptible Hereditary Prince strove to play the part of regent, and his mother to exercise the influence of a regnant queen. They made free use of the national resources to reward their fellow-conspirators. On Beringskjold and Rantzau, men of bad character, were showered offices, donations, and pensions. Colonel Köller was ennobled and eventually also received office and a pension. General Hans Henrik Eickstedt, a rough soldier, became a member of the Ministry and Governor of the Crown Prince. In talent and experience of affairs they were too deficient to dispense with men of merit. Osten remained in charge of foreign affairs, the incorruptible Joachim Otto Schack Rathlou was summoned to the Council, and Baron Henrik Karl Schimmelmann placed his great authority in commerce, taxation and finance at the service of the Crown. Bernstorff, however, was suffered to remain in exile. It became more and more apparent that the seat of power was to be found not in the Council but in the Court, and that the man who inspired the Court and carried out its wishes was Guldberg. For twelve years (1772–84) Denmark obeyed court decrees, signed by Christian VII, but drafted by the mentor of the Hereditary Prince.

The rise of Guldberg to high office had been a far slower process than that of Struensee. Preferring the reality to the appearance of power, he was not created a noble until 1777 or a Privy Councillor until 1780. But, by becoming ruler of Denmark through his influence over the royal family, he formed the true counterpart to the confidant of Christian and Caroline Matilda. In talent, character, and ideas, indeed, no two men could offer a sharper contrast. Guldberg was an incorruptible patriot. Hating foreigners and foreign ideas, he personified the reaction against the cosmopolitan humanitarianism of Struensee. Save in the Duchies, Danish became the language of government. It displaced German in the army. Instruction in German was denied to the Crown Prince. An Ordinance of May, 1775, enforced the study of the Danish language and literature in schools. In January, 1776, without the privity of the Council, an unalterable law was issued which provided that none but Danish nationals might in future hold offices of State. These measures sprang from the whole-hearted belief in the perfection of the old Danish system so far as social organisation and religion were concerned—a belief which inspired Guldberg's attempts to make Denmark retrace every step taken by her under Struensee's guidance.

To have created afresh the chaos of which his Court and City Tribunal and his Poor Law had made an end, would, however, have taxed fanaticism too heavily, and these institutions were suffered to remain. Queen Juliana Maria and her son, the "Hereditary Prince" Frederick, who stood above the nobles, and Guldberg, whose birth was humble, combined to enforce the eligibility of commoners to serve the State, and to develop the results of the principle once established. The lottery, which brought pecuniary profit, was undertaken by the State. The most flagrant perquisites and the worst scandals of patronage, by which offices fell to the mere lackeys of the great, were not revived. The Press continued to enjoy a freedom qualified by peremptory orders not to meddle with politics and by the personality of Guldberg, the vigilant defender of the faith. The spirit of his paternal government breathes in the notorious sentence passed in 1783 upon a flippant author. Not only was the edition of his book confiscated and a fine imposed, but the editor was sentenced "to be better instructed and convinced of his sin." To this end the Bishop was to have him cate-chised by a few priests and eventually instructed by a schoolmaster, unless one of the priests would undertake the task. Accused persons might once more be examined under torture. The University and the schools were, as of old, to devote themselves principally to the teaching of religion. Apart from some vexatious but trifling burdens, labour services again became due from the peasants to their lords. In September, 1774, a new army law carried ascription to the soil to its furthest limit. An augmented proportion of natives to mercenaries in both infantry and cavalry made the number of conscripts greater by almost one-half than under the law of 1764. They were now to serve for twelve years, and then to accept the holdings proffered by their lords or be liable to serve for six years more. While the clergy and the landed proprietors were thus propitiated, the manufacturers and merchants were not forgotten. The ports of southern Norway were again closed to foreign corn. Once more, millions were squandered on attempts to make Denmark an industrial country. By a natural sequence, the Government was led on to state factories, a state store, state-provided technical education, state-built trading ships, a state bank, and a heavy over-issue of inconvertible state paper. Thanks chiefly to the War of American Independence, Danish commerce flourished; but, when peace returned in 1783, the national debt stood higher than at the beginning of the reign.

In the domain of foreign affairs Guldberg enjoyed great and con-tinuous good fortune. The exiled Queen lived only long enough to strengthen the foundations of his power by the fear of her vengeance. She died at Celle in 1775, before the projects of her partisans had come to a head or her son, the Crown Prince Frederick, had ceased to be a child. In March, 1773, Andreas Peter Bernstorff, whose uncle had died two years before, consented to place his rare industry and unblemished character at the service of the State. He had been, in the words used by the elder Bernstorff in the constant correspondence carried on between them, the "dear and intimate friend" of his uncle; and, within a few months of his accession to office, he had gathered the coveted harvest which that statesman had sown and tended. Russia and Denmark, menaced alike by the monarchical power which Gustavus III seized in 1772, secretly allied themselves against Sweden, and on May 21, 1773 (N.S.), at Tsarskoye Selo, the Grand Duke Paul signed the Treaty of Exchange without any reservations. Henceforward, at the cost of Oldenburg and Delmenhorst, the King of Denmark might feel secure in his possession of the Duchies.

The Schleswig-Holstein question was, however, far from being solved by this transfer. The relation of the Duchies to Denmark proper had yet to be determined by time. It was significant that Caspar von Saldern, the domineering Holsteiner who represented Russia in the negotiations, had stipulated in 1767 that in future the officials employed in Schleswig-Holstein should have studied for two years in the University of Kiel. He was now able to insist that the "German Chancery," which administered the affairs of the Duchies, should receive a Director of its own, and that a Holstein noble should fill this post. Bernstorff, being duly qualified, received the first appointment to a post which the traditional hatred of the Gottorp Holsteiners against Denmark made one of no small difficulty.

In the first instance, however, the transfer of Denmark from the French to the Russian "system" brought many advantages. It could not fail to be a valuable safeguard against the conquest of Norway by Gustavus III, the fear of which had caused a hasty defensive armament in 1772. Bernstorff's efforts to check the political revival of Sweden profited little; but the course of events ran so strongly in favour of Denmark that in 1780 the two Scandinavian States found themselves leagued together in the First Armed Neutrality of the North. Of that important, though abortive, political transaction an account will be found in another volume of this *History*. It may be added here that the idea of a league between Russia and Denmark for the protection of the claims of neutrals had been suggested by Bernstorff to the Russian Government so early as 1778, in lieu of a Russian proposal for a joint convoy to guard navigation in the Arctic Seas. Catharine II, after rejecting the Danish counter-proposal, adopted it two years later, when, under the influence of Panin, she abandoned the project of a British alliance which Potemkin had been bribed to urge, extending the conception, however, from that of a Russo-Danish into that of a general league. Bernstorff, who at once fell in with the Tsarina's enlarged scheme, signing the treaty with Russia on July 9, 1780, anticipated the execution of it by declaring the Baltic closed to ships of war belonging to belligerents. He proved a staunch adherent, so long as it lasted, of the scheme of Armed Neutrality of which he is thus to be credited with the actual authorship.

So soon, however, as November, 1780, Bernstorff was suddenly dismissed from office. The reasons for this step can only be conjectured. It is said that Guldberg was incensed by a convention concluded by Bernstorff with the British Government just before Denmark joined the Armed Neutrality, which by limiting the definition of contraband weakened the force of the agreement with Russia; and it may be that Guldberg really feared lest his colleague's personal sympathy with England might jeopardise the Russian alliance. The two Ministers were equally antagonistic to each other on questions of domestic policy. Bernstorff's consistent endeavours to promote the emancipation of the peasantry were offensive to his chief, who looked upon such an issue as involving the ruin of the monarchy. Again, Guldberg was far from sharing Bernstorff's avowed anxiety for the maintenance of distinct administrative systems as lawfully established in each division of the tripartite monarchy, and in the Duchies in particular, with which ties of race and of intellectual culture closely connected him. As the elder Bernstorff was the friend of Klopstock, so the younger was the brother-in-law of the Stolbergs, the comrades of Goethe in the eager aspirations of his youth.

Under Andreas Peter Bernstorff's successor as Minister for Foreign Affairs, the Norwegian Baron Marcus Gerhard Rosenkrone, a pupil of Guldberg, fortune continued to favour Denmark. The action or inaction of the Dutch saved her from war with England in 1780, and three years later the easy triumph of Russia in the Crimea frustrated the design formed by Gustavus III of conquering Norway by a sudden descent on Copenhagen. The attempt of the Queen Dowager to yoke the Crown Prince to Prussia by marriage was foiled by his resistance.

Seldom, indeed, has a foolish and feeble Government, in a land which had been regarded as conquerable by an army of not more than fifteen thousand men, passed unscathed and even triumphant through a period so vexed. By its very feebleness and stupidity, the rule of Guldberg and the cabal procured indirect advantages for Denmark. During eight years it taught Bernstorff what to avoid, and then furnished him with the opportunity of studying from afar for more than three years the needs of his adopted country. The Crown Prince Frederick, moreover, grew towards manhood with a well-founded conviction, which every worthy Danish statesman shared, of his own mission to rescue and rule the State. For three years the plan of yet another seizure by force of the regency of the kingdom was debated and matured within and without its limits. An earlier attempt at carrying out the design was prevented, chiefly by the counsels of Bernstorff and other men of weight. Frederick of Prussia sent warning to the Court of Copenhagen. Yet, to the last moment, Guldberg and his patrons believed themselves indispensable and secure. At last, in April, 1784, when the long-deferred Confirmation of the Crown Prince Frederick had been held, and he was admitted for the first time to the Privy Council, he declared to his astonished relatives and their supporters that Bernstorff with three others ought to join the Council, and that government by the Cabinet should cease. An order to this effect immediately received the signature of the King, who then fled from the Council-chamber, pursued by his indignant brother, the Hereditary Prince. Meanwhile the young Crown Prince informed Guldberg and his associates that the King had no further need of their services. Having thus brought the meeting of the Council to an end, he succeeded in recapturing his father, who signed a rescript which made him practically Regent. The day closed with a ball in which both factions of the royal family took part. The victors, secure of the moral support of society and of the nation, treated the cabal with generosity, and the way was thus prepared for the beneficent sway of the younger Bernstorff.

Andreas Peter Bernstorff held office as Minister for Foreign Affairs and as President of the German Chancery from May, 1784, to his death in June, 1797—so that the greater part of this last and most important period of his activity as a statesman lies beyond the scope of the present volume. But it seems desirable to note, in a few concluding words, some of the chief features of a period of government to which Denmark long looked back with grateful recognition, while justly connecting its achievements with those of the even longer series of years (1751–70) during which the elder Bernstorff had controlled the affairs of the monarchy. The period from 1784 to 1797 was, first and foremost, a period of peace—with the exception of the brief conflict with Sweden, in which Denmark was reluctantly obliged to engage by her treaties of defensive alliance with Russia. In 1788, Gustavus III of Sweden having taken the opportunity of the recent outbreak of war between Turkey and Russia to declare war against the latter Power, a Danish army, under the command of Prince Charles of Hesse-Cassel (brother-in-law to King Christian VII) invaded Sweden from Norway, and seriously endangered Göteborg (October). But the Maritime Powers and Prussia assumed so menacing an attitude of " mediation " that Bernstorff hastened to conclude a truce with Sweden, and succeeded, by the exertion of much diplomatic skill, in inducing the Tsarina to consent that Denmark should remain neutral during the remainder of the War.

In the general European War which began in 1792 against Revolutionary France the same prudent statesmanship, as has been related elsewhere, preserved the neutrality of Denmark; nor did her great peace Minister live to see the final frustration of the efforts, which, both before and after the conclusion of the alliance between Denmark and Sweden for the protection of northern trade, on the lines of the Armed Neutrality, he had made to avoid any collision with the two chief maritime belligerents. Of these France was even more overbearing than Great Britain; but Bernstorff had been unable to make up his mind to side with the latter against the former.

The neutrality of Denmark—which was fated to come to so disastrous an end—had beyond doubt brought to the country an unprecedented prosperity, which was enhanced by the far-sighted intelligence displayed by several branches of the Administration of which Bernstorff was at once the head and the soul. In the earlier years of the Revolutionary War the mercantile dealings of Denmark with both the East and the West Indies, and in Mediterranean waters—where, in the year of Bernstorff's death, the honour of the Danish flag was vigorously asserted against the fleet of the Dey of Tripoli—were developed with extraordinary success; so that Denmark has been, without much exaggeration, described as having at this time shared with Great Britain and the United States the commerce of the world. That, however, in this as in other spheres of effort Bernstorff and those who were associated with him were animated by something more than the desire to advance the material interests of their country, is shown by the abolition—in 1792— of the African slave-trade within the Danish dominions—an example set, to her lasting glory, by Denmark to the other States of Europe.

At home, Bernstorff's Administration gave signal proofs of the same enlightened spirit. Like Struensee before him, he dispensed with the censorship of the Press; though (as has been noted elsewhere) he used the power of the Crown in order to punish attacks upon existing institutions by dismissal or banishment. But his chief and most beneficent reform—and that which was most directly instrumental in confining to certain literary and academical circles the sympathy shown towards the French Revolution within the limits of the Danish monarchy —was one of which the conception had constantly occupied the elder Bernstorff, and which he had carried out with remarkable success on the Zealand estate presented to him by the King. To split up the open fields, to create free hereditary holdings, and to determine exactly the villein services due, had long been the cherished aims of enlightened political thinkers. In spite of the attempts of the elder Bernstorff and of Struensee, the general condition of the Danish peasantry had sunk again; nor was it till the downfall of Guldberg that a sustained effort was made for its fundamental amelioration. In 1786, the Crown Prince on the advice of Bernstorff appointed for the purpose a Commission, of which the leading members were the Prime Minister's friends, Count Christian Ditlev Frederick Reventlow and Christian Colbjörnsen, who afterwards, as Procurator-General, won renown as the reformer of the administration of justice.   The first results of the Commission were two royal ordinances, which, in 1787, regulated the relations between the landlords and their peasant tenantry, greatly restricting the penal powers of the former.   In 1788, despite the opposition of men who predicted ruin for the army and navy and for agriculture, a third ordinance released the peasants from ascription to the soil, declaring the emancipation of those between fourteen and thirty-six years of age as from January 1, 1800, or from their discharge from the army, and that of the rest immediately.   Further ordinances removed the prohibition of the importation of foreign corn into Denmark and southern Norway, and made a great advance towards complete freedom of trade in cattle. A long series of enactments followed, whose design was to secure the legal rights of the peasants, to improve their education, to relieve them of a portion of the burdens, such as tithe, which still lay upon them, and to facilitate the acquisition by them of land.   Thus was gradually called into life that flourishing peasantry which became a main element in the national strength of Denmark.   In the Duchies, where the powerful landed nobility obstinately resisted analogous reforms, they in consequence progressed more slowly ; but Bernstorff was fortunately here possessed of special opportunities for asserting the influence of his personality. A Commission of nobles (*Ritterschaft*) was appointed in 1796 ; and in the following year it reported that the landed proprietors of the Duchies, with but a single exception, were in favour of the emancipation of the peasants.   Here, too, the triumph of Bernstorff's ideas was accordingly assured before his death in 1797, though the emancipation was not actually promulgated till some years later.   Thus the nephew had accomplished a work dear to the heart of his uncle and predecessor as well as to his own, and one which, more than any other of their services to the Danish monarchy, has enshrined their name in the hearts of its peoples.

CHAPTER XXII.

THE HATS AND CAPS AND GUSTAVUS III.
(1721-92.)

It was not the least of Sweden's misfortunes after the humiliating Peace of Nystad (August 30, 1721), that the Constitution which was to be the compensation for all her past sacrifices should contain within it the elements of most of her future calamities. Violently anti-monarchical, this Constitution was still anything but democratic. Theoretically, all power was vested in the people as represented by the *Riksdag*, or Diet, consisting of four distinct Orders or Estates—Nobles, Priests, Burgesses, and Peasants, deliberating apart. The conflicting interests and mutual jealousies of these four independent Orders made the work of legislation exceptionally difficult. No measure could, indeed, become law till it had obtained the assent of three at least of the four Estates; but this pro-vision, which seems to have been designed to protect the lower Orders against the nobility, produced far greater ills than those which it pro-fessed to cure. Thus, measures might be passed by a bare majority in three Estates when a real and substantial majority of all four Estates might be actually against it. Or, again, a dominant faction in any three of the Estates might enact laws highly detrimental to the interests of the remaining Estate; a danger the more to be apprehended as class distinctions in Sweden were very sharply defined. The nobility possessed the usual privileges of the Order. The head of each noble family had the right to sit in the *Riddarhus*; but most of these hereditary legislators derived a considerable income from the sale of their *fullmakts*, or proxies, to the highest bidder. The invidious and untranslatable epithet *ofrälse*[1] sharply distinguished the three lower Estates from the dominant and privileged class. Of the three, the clergy stood first in rank and reputation, being by far the best educated and the least servile body in the kingdom. Yet the hard-worked Swedish ministry was so poorly paid that the poorest gentleman rarely thought of the Church as a pro-fession. The Bishops, again, were not lords spiritual, as in England, but simply the first among equals in their own Order. The burgesses, again,

---

[1] *Ofrälse* is the negative of *frälse*, which means privileged, exempted.

were such in the most literal acceptation of the term, merchants and traders with the exclusive right of representing in the *Riksdag* the boroughs where they traded. The peasantry also could only be represented in the *Riksdag* by peasants. The peasant deputies were, however, generally excluded from the special committees in which the most intricate and important business of the session was done. Each Estate was ruled by its *Talman*, or Speaker, who was elected at the beginning of each Diet. The Speaker of the House of Nobles, called *Landsmarskalk*, or Marshal of the Diet, was always chairman when the four Orders met in congress. He also presided, by virtue of his office, in the *Hemliga Utskottet*, or "Secret Committee," consisting of 50 nobles, 25 priests, and 25 burgesses, which during the session of the *Riksdag* exercised not only the supreme executive, but also the supreme judicial and legislative, functions. It prepared all bills for the *Riksdag*, created and deposed the Ministers, controlled the foreign policy of the nation, and claimed and often exercised the right of superseding the ordinary Courts of justice. During the parliamentary recess, however, the executive remained in the hands of the *Råd* or Senate, now limited to 24 members. The King was obliged to select one of three candidates submitted to him by a committee of the three higher Orders, to fill up any vacancy in the *Råd*.

It is obvious that there was little room in this republican Constitution for a constitutional monarch in the ordinary sense of the word. The crowned puppet who possessed a casting-vote in the Senate, over which he presided, and who was allowed to create nobles at his coronation only, was rather an ornamental than an essential part of the machinery of government.

At first, this complicated system worked tolerably well beneath the firm but cautious control of Count Arvid Bernhard Horn, the Swedish Chancellor. In his anxiety to avoid embroiling his country abroad, Horn reversed the traditional foreign policy of Sweden by keeping France at a distance and drawing near to England. Thus, a twenty years' war was succeeded by a twenty years' peace, during which the nation recovered so rapidly from its wounds that it began to forget them. A new race of politicians was now springing up, whose ambition and martial ardour led them to undervalue the blessings of peace. Since 1719, when the influence of the few great territorial families had been all but extinguished in a *Riddarhus* of needy gentlemen who claimed to be their equals, the first Estate became the nursery, and afterwards the stronghold, of an Opposition which found its natural leaders in Count Carl Gyllenborg, Baron Daniel Niklas von Höpken, and Count Carl Gustav Tessin. Tessin, the son of Charles XI's great architect, Nicodemus Tessin, was the Admirable Crichton of the Opposition, and by far their ablest leader. These men and their followers were never weary of ridiculing the timid caution of the aged Count Horn, who sacrificed everything to perpetuate "an inglorious peace." They nicknamed his adherents "Night-caps" (a term subsequently softened into Caps), themselves adopting the sobriquet Hats. These epithets instantly caught the public fancy. The nickname "Night-cap" seemed exactly to suit the drowsy policy of old Horn, while the three-cornered hat, worn by officers and gentlemen, no less happily hit off the manly self-assertion of the Opposition. From 1738 onwards these party badges were in general use. The *Riksdag* of that year marked a turning-point in Swedish history. The Hats carried everything before them; Tessin won the *bâton* of Marshal of the Diet by an enormous majority; the Caps were almost totally excluded from the Secret Committee; and Count Horn was compelled to retire from a scene where, for three-and-thirty years, he had been absolutely dominant.

The foreign policy of the Hats was a return to the old historical alliance between France and Sweden. This alliance had, on the whole, been mutually advantageous to both States, so long as Sweden had remained a great and active military monarchy. When, however, she descended to her natural position as a second-rate Power, the French alliance became a luxury too costly for her straitened means. Horn had clearly perceived this, and his cautious neutrality was therefore the wisest statesmanship. But to the politicians who ousted Horn prosperity without glory was a worthless possession. They aimed at nothing less than restoring Sweden to her former proud position as a Great Power. France naturally hailed with satisfaction the rise of a faction which was content to be her armour-bearer in the north, and the rich golden streams which flowed continuously from Versailles to Stockholm during the next two generations were the political life-blood of the Hats. Yet no alliance was ever so mischievous or illusory. The hopeless blundering of the Hats upset all the calculations of their ally, and the millions lavished upon them were so many millions thrown away.

The first great blunder of this party was the hasty and ill-advised war with Russia. The European complications consequent upon the all but simultaneous deaths of the Emperor Charles VI and the Russian Empress Anne seemed to favour their adventurous schemes. Despite the frantic protests of the Caps, a project for the conquest of the Baltic provinces was rushed through the extraordinary *Riksdag* of 1740, and on July 20, 1741, war was formally declared against Russia. A month later the *Riksdag* was dissolved and the Hat *Landsmarskalk*, Carl Emil Lewenhaupt, set off for Finland to take command of the army. The humiliation of Russia, whose domestic embarrassments were notorious, was taken for granted, and it was confidently declared at Stockholm that, within six months' time, peace would be dictated at the gates of St Petersburg. But even the first blow was not struck till six months after the declaration of war, and, then, by the enemy who routed General Wrangel at Vilmanstrand and captured and destroyed that frontier fortress. Nothing was done on either side for six months more;

and then Lewenhaupt made "a tacit truce" with the Russians through the mediation of La Chétardie, the French Minister at St Petersburg. By the time this tacit truce had come to an end, the Swedish forces were so demoralised that the mere rumour of a hostile attack made them abandon everything and retire hastily to Helsingfors. Before the end of the year all Finland was in the hands of the Russians. The fleet, disabled from the first by a terrible epidemic, had become a huge floating hospital, and did nothing at all.

To face another *Riksdag*, with such a war as this upon their consciences, was an ordeal from which the Hats naturally shrank; but they had to meet it, and, to do them justice, they showed themselves better parliamentary than military strategists. A motion for an enquiry into the conduct of the War was skilfully evaded by obtaining precedence for the Succession question. (The Queen Consort, Ulrica Leonora, had died childless on November 24, 1741, and King Frederick who had succeeded her as sovereign on her abdication (February 29, 1720), was now an old man.) The Hats immediately opened negotiations with the new Russian Empress Elizabeth, who consented to restitute all Finland except the small portion of it eastwards of the river Kymmene, the original boundary between the two States, on condition that her cousin, Adolphus Frederick of Holstein-Gottorp, was elected successor to the Swedish throne. The Hats eagerly caught at the opportunity of recovering the grand duchy, and their own prestige along with it; and the Peace of Åbo, a singularly favourable compact in the circumstances (August 7, 1743), put an end to their first unlucky political speculation.

The new Crown Prince, Adolphus Frederick, was remotely connected with the ancient dynasty, his grandfather's grandmother having been the sister of the great Gustavus. Personally he was altogether insignificant, being chiefly remarkable as the father of Sweden's last great monarch and as the willing slave of a beautiful and talented, but haughty and imperious, consort. That consort was Louisa Ulrica, Frederick the Great's sister, whom Tessin, now Chancellor of Sweden, conducted with great pomp from Berlin to Stockholm, where (August 27, 1744) she was married to Adolphus Frederick and speedily gathered around her a brilliant circle. Her support became the prize for which both the factions contended; but all the French tastes and sympathies of the Voltairean Princess drew her towards the Hats, and from 1744 to 1750 the brilliant Tessin became the friend and confidant of the Crown Princess. The birth of her first-born son Gustavus (January 24, 1746), of whom Tessin was forthwith appointed Governor, seemed to be an additional bond of union between them. Louisa Ulrica now began to build the most extravagant hopes on the amity of a statesman who was at once the first Minister of the Crown and the leader of the dominant Hat party. Unfortunately, she ignored the fact that, for all his courtliness and complacency, a more determined foe of autocracy than Tessin never existed. Brought up in the belief that monarchy had been the bane of Sweden, he was firmly convinced that the Constitution of 1720 was the most perfect form of government devisable. The only authority he recognised was the *Riksdag*, from which he derived his power, and to which he was alone responsible. A collision, therefore, between a would-be autocrat like Louisa Ulrica and a virtual republican like Tessin was inevitable. It came in the course of 1750, when Tessin, justly alarmed at the *rapprochement* between Russia and Denmark, skilfully interposed with the scheme of a family alliance between the Swedish and Danish Courts, which Frederick V of Denmark eagerly welcomed. Tessin, thereupon, arranged a betrothal between his little pupil and the Danish Princess Royal, without even consulting the parents of the infant bridegroom. Now, the Danish Court had ever been the most bitter foe of the House of Holstein-Gottorp; the Danish King had even refused to recognise the right of Adolphus Frederick to the Crown of Sweden. To both the Crown Prince and his consort, therefore, the Danish match was monstrous. Both parents appealed to the Senate against the unnatural betrothal, but in vain. Adolphus Frederick was compelled to sign the detested contract, and to write the usual letters of congratulation.

For this Louisa Ulrica never forgave Tessin; and, when in March, 1751, the old King Frederick died, and Adolphus Frederick succeeded him, the situation became acute. The troubles of the new King began early. The Estates seemed bent upon going out of their way to mortify him. They forced upon him a new Chancellor, Count Anders Johan von Höpken, renowned as the most pregnant and incisive orator of the day; they disputed the King's right to appoint his own household or create peers; they declared that all state appointments were to go by seniority; they threatened to use a royal "name-stamp," if his Majesty refused to append his sign-manual to official documents. In 1756, an attempted revolution, planned by the Queen and a few devoted young noblemen, was easily and remorselessly crushed. The ringleaders, after being tortured, were beheaded, and, though the unhappy King did not, as he anticipated, "share the fate of Charles Stewart", he was humiliated as never monarch was humiliated before. The Estates stung him to the quick by means of an absolutely unique document which, ostensibly "an instruction" to the young Crown Prince's new Governor, was, in reality, a violent tirade against his royal father. Royalty had sunk low when "most humble and most dutiful subjects" could venture to remind their "most mighty and gracious King" that Kings in general are "the natural enemies of their subjects"; that "in free States" they merely "exist on sufferance"; that, because they are occasionally invested with pomp and dignity "more for the honour of the realm than for the sake of the person who may happen to occupy the chief place in the pageant," they must not therefore imagine that "they are more than men while other men are less than worms"; that, "as the glare and glitter of a Court" may tend to puff them up with the idea that they are made of finer stuff than their fellow-creatures, they would do well, occasionally, to visit the lowly hut of the peasant and there learn that it is because of the wasteful extravagance of a Court that the peasant's loaf is so light and his burdens are so heavy—and so on through a score of long-winded paragraphs. This "instruction" was solemnly presented to his Majesty by the Marshal of the Diet and the *Talmen* of the three lower Estates, and he was requested to give it with his own hand to the Prince's new Governor, Count Carl Fredrik Scheffer.

From 1756 to 1771 the most conspicuous figures in the political history of Sweden are Count Axel Fredrik af Fersen and Baron Carl Fredrik Pechlin. Fersen, the descendant of a branch of the Macpherson family which had been settled in Sweden for generations, was the worthiest Swedish nobleman of his day. He enjoys the honourable distinction of having been the purest of politicians at a time when the whole course of Swedish politics was tainted at its source. His abilities were considerable. As an orator in an age of orators he had few equals. He was also an admirable parliamentary tactician. The fatal defects of his character were a want of initiative, which made him useless in a crisis, and a dread of responsibility which caused him to decline, persistently, high offices to which he seemed to be born. Pechlin, a Holsteiner by descent, was the Henry Fox of Sweden. His whole career was an unbroken series of treacheries and treasons, and the easy effrontery with which this political chameleon changed his colours has rarely been surpassed. That Pechlin should have wielded such enormous influence as to receive the nickname of "General of the *Riksdag*," is significant of the foulness of the political atmosphere in which he flourished; but it is also a proof of the personal talents of the arch-renegade. Neither love of power nor love of money, but an ingrained passion for intrigue for its own sake, seems to have been the leading motive of his otherwise inexplicable conduct.

Fersen was a Hat by conviction, and his generous purse was always at the disposal of his party. Pechlin professed to be a Cap, and just then, after an eclipse of twenty-five years, the star of the Caps was once more in the ascendant. The game of their adversaries was, indeed, by this time nearly played out. Their last adventure (a heedless plunging into the Seven Years' War at the instigation of France) had utterly wrecked their resources. The French subsidies, which might have sufficed for a six weeks' demonstration (it was too generally assumed that the King of Prussia would give little trouble to a European coalition), proved quite inadequate, and, after five unsuccessful campaigns, the Hats were glad to make peace on a *status quo ante bellum* basis after throwing away £5,000,000 and 40,000 men. When the *Riksdag* met in 1760, the indignation against the Hat Cabinet was so violent that an impeachment of them seemed inevitable; but Pechlin, suddenly changing sides at the very moment of the Cap triumph, contrived to pull the Hats out of the mire by a combination of the most intricate and amazing intrigues; at the same time, however, involving everything in such inextricable confusion that the session was brought to a close by the mutual consent of both the exhausted factions. It had lasted twenty months, and its sole result was to bolster up the Hat Government for another four years.

But the day of reckoning could not be postponed for ever, and, when the Estates met again in 1765, the Caps came into power at last. Their leader Thure Rudbeck was elected Marshal of the Diet over Fersen by a large majority, and, out of the 100 seats in the Secret Committee, the Hats only succeeded in securing 10. The Caps at once struck at the weak point of their opponents by ordering a Budget report to be made; and it was speedily found that the whole financial system of the Hats had been based upon reckless improvidence and wilful misrepresentation, and that the only fruits of their long rule was a doubling of the National Debt, with such a depreciation of the note circulation that £15 in paper was worth only £5 in specie. This startling revelation led to a general retrenchment, carried into effect with a drastic thoroughness which has earned for this Parliament the name of the " Reduction *Riksdag.*" By this means the Caps succeeded in transferring £500,000 from the pockets of the merchants and landowners of the Hat party to the empty Treasury, considerably reducing the National Debt, and reestablishing some sort of equilibrium between revenue and expenditure.

The " Reduction *Riksdag*" rose in October, 1766, and with it the short-lived popularity of the Caps passed away. Their sweeping system of retrenchment had irritated everyone who had anything to lose, while the severity with which it had been applied had caused universal suffering. Nevertheless, their domestic policy was, in the main, a commendable attempt to grapple with abuses of long standing against which they had always protested. Their worst condemnation, from a statesman's point of view, was their short-sighted, suicidal, foreign policy.

Sweden at this time had still a voice in European affairs. Although no longer a first-class Power she was still the foremost among the second-class Powers, and the Swedish alliance, depreciated as it might be, was at any rate a marketable article. Her Pomeranian possessions afforded her an easy ingress into the very heart of the Empire, and her Finnish frontier was not many leagues from the Russian capital. A watchful neutrality which did not venture much beyond defensive alliances was therefore Sweden's safest policy, and this the older Caps had always recognised. But, when the Hats became the henchmen of France in the north, their opponents needed a protector strong enough to countervail the French influence; and so it came about that the younger Caps flung themselves into the arms of Russia, overlooking the fact that even a pacific union with Russia was far more to be feared than a martial alliance with France.   For France was too distant to be really dangerous.   She sought an ally in Sweden, and it was her endeavour to make that ally as strong as possible.   An alliance with Russia, on the other hand, meant absolute subservience, for Russia was deliberately aiming at the hegemony of the north.   These were the days of the famous " Northern Accord," the invention of Count Nikita Panin, Catharine II's political mentor from 1763 to 1781, which, although never fully carried out, profoundly affected the politics of northern and central Europe, and which was to attract Poland and Sweden within the orbit of Russia under much the same conditions.   Both Powers were to be kept strong enough to be serviceable, but not strong enough to be dangerous, to Russian interests. In each case the maintenance of a vicious Constitution under the express guarantee of Russia was to be the curb upon too ambitious a progress. This double arrangement first appears in the secret clauses of the Treaty of 1763, between Russia and Prussia, on the eve of the election of Stanislaus Poniatowski to the throne of Poland.   In 1766, the Caps were induced, by a secret understanding, to accept the Russian guarantee for the Swedish Constitution also.

Fortunately for Sweden, the Cap Government was of too brief duration to do much mischief.   An Order in Council issued by the Senate, declaring that all complaints against the measures of the last *Riksdag* should be punished with fine and imprisonment, brought matters to a head.   The King, secretly instigated by the Crown Prince Gustavus and the Hats, presented (February 9, 1768) a message to the Senate urging it to convoke the *Riksdag* instantly, as the only available means of finding relief for the great and growing distress of the nation under the new economical system.   The Senate, after a week's reflexion, informed his Majesty that it saw no reason for departing from the precept of the last *Riksdag*, which had fixed October, 1770, for the convocation of its successor.   On December 14, further encouraged by the arrival of the new French ambassador, de Modène, with a well-filled purse, the King, accompanied by the Crown Prince, once more urged the Senate to convoke an extraordinary *Riksdag*.   Upon their still refusing to comply with his request, he formally abdicated, at the same time forbidding the Senate to make use of his name in any of its resolutions. From December 15 to 21 Sweden was without a legal government. The capital was much disturbed.   Crowds of people surrounded the Palace, where the Senate passed the time in anxious deliberation, issuing orders which were no longer obeyed, the various Departments of State and the magistrates of Stockholm resolutely refusing to accept a name-stamp as a substitute for the royal sign-manual.   Still the Senate held out.   But, when the Treasury refused to part with a single dollar more, when Count Fersen, as Colonel of the Guards, appeared in the Council-chamber and declared he could no longer answer for the troops, the stubborn resistance of the Caps was, at last, broken.   On December 19 they resolved to convoke the Estates for April 19, 1769. On the 21st, Adolphus Frederick reappeared in the Council-chamber and resumed the Crown.

Both parties now prepared for the elections, which were to decide whether the nation preferred to be governed by a King or a name-stamp. On the eve of the contest there was a general assembly of the Hats at the French Embassy where de Modène provided them with 6,000,000 *livres*, but not till they had signed in his presence an undertaking to reform the Constitution in a monarchical sense. Still more energetic was Russia, on the other side. The Russian ambassador, Count Ivan Andreivich Osterman, scattered his *roubles* with a lavish hand; and so lost to all sense of patriotism were the Caps that they threatened all who dared to vote against them with the vengeance of the Russian Empress, and fixed Norrköping, instead of Stockholm, as the place of meeting for the *Riksdag*, because it was more accessible to the Russian fleet. But it soon became evident that the Caps were playing a losing game; and, when the *Riksdag* met at Norrköping, they found themselves in a minority in all four Estates. In the contest for the Marshalship of the Diet, the verdict of the last *Riksdag* was exactly reversed, Fersen, the Hat candidate, defeating the Cap leader Rudbeck by 234 votes, though Russia spent £11,500 to secure his election.

The first act of the *Riksdag* was to move a humble address of thanks to the King " because he had not shut his ears to the bitter cry of the nation." The Caps got short shrift; and the note which the Russian, Prussian and Danish ministers presented to the Estates, protesting, in menacing terms, against any reprisals on the part of the triumphant faction, only hastened the fall of the Government. The Cap Senate resigned *en masse*, to escape impeachment; and the *Riksdag* appointed an exclusively Hat administration. On June 1, the Reaction *Riksdag*, as it is generally called, removed to the capital; and the French ambassador and the Crown Prince hereupon called on the new Senators to redeem their promise as to a reform of the Constitution. But, when the Hats, towards the end of the session, reluctantly and half-heartedly, brought the matter forward, the *Riksdag* suddenly seemed to be stricken with paralysis. Impediments, not unwelcome to the party chiefs, multiplied at every step; and on January 30, 1770, the Reaction *Riksdag*, after a barren ten months' session, dissolved itself amidst the most chaotic confusion.

A little more than twelve months later (February 12, 1771), Adolphus Frederick expired. The suddenness of the catastrophe gave rise, at first, to sinister rumours; but the highly-spiced condiments with which the deceased monarch had overloaded a weak stomach constituted the only poison which killed him. The elections on the demise of the Crown resulted in a partial victory for the Caps, especially among the lower three Orders; but in the Estate of peasants their majority was very small, while the mass of the nobility was still dead against them. Nothing could be done, however, till the new King had returned from France, where (from February 4 to March 25) he had shone in the brilliant firmament of Parisian society as a star of the first magnitude. The charming young Prince had captivated hearts and minds alike by his grace, wit, and *savoir-faire.* Even Madame du Deffand was satisfied with him. In Sweden also his abilities were already generally recognised and inspired equal hope and fear. Everyone felt that with Gustavus a new and incalculable factor had entered into Swedish politics.

Gustavus III was born on January 24, 1746. All his Governors and tutors—and among them we find the most eminent statesmen and the most learned scholars of their day—were struck by the lad's extraordinary precocity, vivid imagination, and retentive memory. But an abhorrence of everything requiring sustained mental exertion, the disturbing interference of the factions, who repeatedly changed his tutors to suit the ever varying political atmosphere of the moment, and his own natural indolence, prevented him from making a proper use of the talents of his preceptors, as he himself in his memoirs frankly acknowledges. Another most curious feature in the child's character was his passion for the theatre. "No sooner has he seen a play," writes his second Governor, Count Scheffer, "than his memory absorbs the whole of it, often retaining long portions of the dialogue....Often, while he is being dressed and undressed, you may hear him solemnly declaim the monologues of queens and princesses." A love of dramatic display was, indeed, to characterise him throughout life. Somewhat later, we remark in him a careful cultivation of that natural charm of manner which was to make him so irresistibly fascinating. French he learnt from his very cradle, and with the literature of France he was intimately acquainted at a very early age. There was scarcely a French book of any note that he had not read before he was five-and-twenty. On the other hand, the Prince had next to no political education. The little he knew of state-craft he had picked up as best he could. The leading politicians of both parties looked askance at the keen-witted aspiring youth, and threw every possible obstacle in his way. The Estates even refused him permission to study the science of war in the army of his uncle, Frederick the Great, lest he should learn to undervalue the blessings of a free Constitution in that school of enlightened despotism. Thus, full of ambitious energy, yet constrained to stand in the background, Gustavus learnt betimes to weigh his words, disguise his thoughts, and keep a constant watch upon himself and others. He followed with the keenest interest the ever shifting course of events; carefully studied the characters of the politicians by whom those events were controlled, and resolved to seize the first opportunity for rescuing the monarchy from the constitutional bondage under which it languished. He took the first step in this direction, before he quitted France, by inducing Louis XV to pay, unconditionally, the outstanding Swedish subsidies, at the rate of 1½ million *livres* annually, commencing from January, 1772, and to send as ambassador to Stockholm Count de Vergennes, one of the great names of French diplomacy, to support him in the coming struggle with Russia and her partisans, which he already foresaw.

On June 6, 1771, Gustavus III entered his capital. A fortnight later, in full regalia, and with the silver sceptre of Gustavus Adolphus in his hand, he formally opened his first Parliament in a speech which awakened strange and deep emotions in all who heard it. It was the first time for more than a century that a Swedish King had addressed a Swedish *Riksdag* from the throne in its native language. After a touching allusion to his father's death the orator thus proceeded : " Born and bred among you, I have learned, from my tenderest youth, to love my country, and hold it the highest privilege to be born a Swede, the greatest honour to be the first citizen of a free people....I have seen many lands. I have studied the...institutions...of many peoples. I have found that neither the pomp and magnificence of monarchy, nor the most frugal economy, nor the most overflowing exchequer, can ensure content or prosperity where patriotism, where unity, is wanting. It rests with you to become the happiest nation in the world. Let this *Riksdag* be for ever memorable in our annals for the sacrifice of all party animosities, of all interested motives, to the common weal. So far as in me lies, I will contribute to reunite your diverging opinions, to reconcile your estranged affections, so that the nation may ever look back with gratitude on a Parliament on whose deliberations I now invoke the blessings of the Most High."

The determination of the royal peace-maker to reconcile the jarring factions was perfectly sincere. He began by inducing them to appoint a " Composition Committee" with a view to the formation of a coalition Ministry, which was to divide all offices of public emolument equally between the Hats and Caps. The scheme was frustrated by the preposterous demands of the Caps. Pechlin, who had now gone over to that party, seemed bent upon breaking up the Composition project altogether, and the King had to interfere to prevent a violent collision between him and Fersen. Still more dictatorial became the tone of the Caps when its nominees, after a severe struggle, were elected speakers of the three lower Estates. Crowds of deserters at once passed over into the ranks of the Caps, who forthwith endeavoured, under every imaginable pretext, to invalidate the elections of their opponents. In this way, they at last obtained a decisive majority in the lower three Orders.

It was now absolutely necessary to snatch the *Riddarhus* from the grasp of the triumphant Caps. If the first Estate were lost, all was lost. Yet lost it must be without money, and no money was forthcoming, the new French ambassador, much to the consternation of the royalists, having arrived (June 8) almost empty-handed. Gustavus saved the situation by borrowing £200,000 from the Dutch banking-house of Harneca on the sole security of the first instalment of the French subsidy, which was not due till January 1, 1772. With the aid of this bribing fund, he managed to secure the election of the royal nominee as Marshal of the Diet by 524 votes to 450. This, the first victory of the Court party, was more than neutralised, however, by the result of the elections to the Secret Committee, where the Caps triumphed in the lower Orders and obtained a majority in the Committee (54 to 46) sufficient to outvote their colleagues. This success cost Catharine II £40,000, and she considered it cheap at the price.

Gustavus now desired to terminate, as soon as possible, a *Riksdag* from which he had evidently little to hope and everything to fear. The Estates had been summoned ostensibly to bury his father and crown himself. One half of their work had, therefore, already been done. It only remained for them to prepare "the Royal Assurance," or Coronation Oath. They were shrewd enough to recognise that this was their trump card, and they determined to make the most of it. As finally presented to the King, it contained three new clauses which can only be described as subversive. The first of these clauses bound the King to reign in future "uninterruptedly," so as to make a future abdication impossible. The second bound him to abide by the decision, not "of the Estates of the Realm altogether" as heretofore, but simply "of the Estates of the Realm," *i.e.* a majority of the Estates. This clause was to enable the lower three Estates to rule without, and even in spite of, the first Estate. The third clause required his Majesty, in all cases of preferment, to be guided "solely" by merit. In all former coronation oaths the word "principally" had been used. This new clause aimed at the very root of oligarchical privilege, by placing "noble" and "non-noble" on precisely the same footing. Two things were evident from these radical propositions: the strife of Hats and Caps had lapsed into a still more ominous strife of classes, and the lower Orders were resolved to fight *à outrance* for their own hands.

All through the summer and autumn of 1771 the Estates were engaged in wrangling over the coronation oath. A well-meant attempt of the King, at the end of the year, to mediate between the Orders, as he had already mediated between the factions, only resulted in an unseemly collision between him and the *Talman* of the Estate of burgesses, Carl Fredrik Sebald. After the brief Christmas recess, the interminable discussion was renewed. Finally, on February 24, 1772, the first Estate, from sheer weariness, conceded, virtually, everything that the lower Estates demanded, though only by a majority of 32 in a House of 686 members. So late as February 11th Gustavus had resolved rather to resign his crown than sign the new coronation oath; on March 3 he signed it with cheerful alacrity, without even taking the trouble to read it. As a matter of fact, he was hesitating on the brink of a revolution. The jolt which finally impelled him to that desperate plunge was the violent dismissal of the Hat Senate, the last asylum of the monarchy and the gentry, on April 25, 1772.

The situation of the young King was now truly pitiable. He was little better than a hostage, for the maintenance of the existing anarchy, in the hands of Ministers who were the humble servants of the Russian Empress. He was completely isolated in the midst of three States—Russia, Prussia, and Denmark—which had bound themselves jointly by treaty to uphold the existing Swedish Constitution and treat any attempt to modify it, either from within or from without, as a *casus belli*. The time had arrived for Gustavus to translate his idea of a revolution into action.

Two men of determined character and infinite resource, Baron Jakob Magnus Sprengtporten, Colonel of the Nyland Dragoons in Finland, and ex-ranger Johan Kristoffer Toll, both of them having old scores to settle with the dominant Caps, were the prompters and original contrivers of the picturesque *coup d'état* which was to make Gustavus III a European celebrity. The scheme, matured shortly after the coronation (May 29, 1772), was two-fold. Sprengtporten undertook to cross over to Finland and seize Sveaborg, as a base for further operations, while Toll was to secure the Scanian fortress of Christianstadt as a *rendezvous* for the conspirators in Sweden. This done, Sprengtporten and Toll were to advance simultaneously against Stockholm from the east and south, overthrow the Government and establish a limited monarchy in its stead. So uncertain were the arch-conspirators of the fitness of Gustavus for so perilous an enterprise that they resolved to leave as little as possible to chance, by keeping him in the background till the last moment when, as Sprengtporten expressed it, "we must thrust a weapon into his hand and trust to him to use it." Nevertheless, fate decreed that Gustavus, after all, should play the leading part in the whole affair.

Sprengtporten and Toll, by sheer bluff, achieved all they set out to do. Then, contrary winds detained Sprengtporten in Finland, and, before Toll could assemble an army round Christianstadt, the Cap Senate at Stockholm was warned by the English minister, Sir John Goodrich, that a mysterious plot was afoot to overthrow the Government. The contingency so much dreaded by Sprengtporten had actually arrived: the King found himself isolated in the midst of his enemies. On the evening of August 18, Gustavus was secretly warned that the Government intended to arrest him within twelve hours. His resolution was at once taken. He would strike the decisive blow himself, without waiting for his confederates. All the officers in the capital whom he could trust were commanded to meet him, at 10 o'clock on the following morning, in the great square facing the Arsenal. Some two-hundred of them obeyed the summons; and forthwith he led them to the guard-room of the barracks where, in twenty minutes, he won over the Guards by a splendid speech, depicting in vivid colours the unhappy situation of Sweden. "If," cried he, in conclusion, "you will follow me as your forefathers followed Gustavus Vasa and Gustavus Adolphus, I will venture my life-blood for the safety and honour of my country." There was a brief pause; and then, with a single exception, they declared their willingness to follow him. Thereupon, after detaching a picket to arrest the Senate (it was holding a council at the Palace, and quietly submitted to be locked in), he dictated a new oath of allegiance in the guard-room, absolving the officers from their allegiance to the Estates, and binding them to obey solely their lawful King Gustavus III and defend him and the new Constitution which he promised to give them. The soldiers on the parade-ground followed the example of their officers, and received a ducat apiece, with six rounds of ammunition.

From the guard-room Gustavus, after occupying the Arsenal on his way, proceeded to the Artillery-yard, which he had fixed upon as his headquarters. Here he tied a white handkerchief round his left arm as a mark of recognition, and bade all his friends do the same. In less than an hour the whole city had donned the white handkerchief. All the gates of Stockholm were then closed; the fleet, anchored off the Skepperholm, was secured; and, after making a complete tour of the capital, the King returned to the Palace absolute master of the situation. On the evening of the 20th, heralds perambulated the city proclaiming that the Estates were to meet in the *Rikssaal* at four o'clock on the following day. Extraordinary and elaborate precautions were taken on this occasion. The principal thoroughfares were lined by battalions of the guard. The *Rikssaal* itself was surrounded by a park of artillery. One-hundred grenadiers stood behind the guns with lighted matches. On the 21st the terrified Riksdagsmen crept, by twos and threes, into their places, between rows of glittering bayonets. A few minutes after the Estates had assembled, the King, in full regalia, appeared, took his seat on the throne, and delivered that famous philippic which is one of the masterpieces of Swedish oratory. Not since Gustavus Vasa had trounced the Estates at the *Riksdag* of Västerås in 1527 had a Swedish parliament received such a reprimand from the Throne. There was a reproach in every eloquent sentence, a sting in every stately period. His audience were made to feel that the King regarded them as either dupes or traitors.

When Gustavus had finished speaking, he ordered that the new Constitution, his own handiwork, should be read to the Estates, and, without allowing them a moment for deliberation, demanded whether they would now solemnly engage to keep it inviolably. The Estates responded by a loud and unanimous "Yes!" thrice repeated. It was then signed and sealed by the four *Talmen*; and the King, reverently removing his crown, beckoned to Archdeacon Lütkeman to intone a *Te Deum*.

Briefly, the new Constitution restored to the Crown most of its ancient rights, and converted a weak and despotic republic into a strong and limited monarchy, in which the balance of power inclined, on the whole, to the side of the monarch. The King again became the source of promotion, the commander-in-chief of the forces, the sole medium of communication with foreign Powers. The appointment and dismissal of Ministers, including the Senators and the four *Talmen*, was transferred from the Estates to the Crown. The summoning and the dismissal of the *Riksdag* once more became royal prerogatives. The deliberations of the Estates were to be confined exclusively to the propositions which the King might think fit to lay before them. But these large powers were subject to many important checks. No new law could be imposed, no old law repealed, no offensive war undertaken, no extraordinary war subsidy levied, without the previous consent of the Estates. The Estates alone could tax themselves; they had the absolute charge of the Bank of Sweden, and the inalienable right of controlling the national expenditure. Moreover, the King pledged himself never to alter his own Constitution without the consent of the *Riksdag*, and never to quit the realm without the consent of the Senate. But, inasmuch as the Senators were henceforth to be appointed by the King and be responsible to him alone, a Senate in opposition to the Crown was barely conceivable. It is no reproach to Gustavus that eleven of the new Senators had been Hats and only five Caps, for both Hats and Caps had now ceased to exist. A proclamation forbade, peremptorily, the use of "those odious and abominable names" which had "smitten the land with the most hideous abuses ever known in a Christian community." Finally, the new Constitution introduced many salutary reforms. The Judges were made immovable. All extraordinary tribunals were declared to be unlawful. A Habeas Corpus Act was introduced. No special privileges were henceforth to be conferred on any one of the four Estates without the consent of the other three. The weak points of the Constitution were the vagueness of some of its paragraphs, which did not sufficiently define the limits between the prerogative and parliamentary privilege, and the hampering restraint upon the royal power as regards offensive warfare, which was to have serious consequences in the future. Diplomatically regarded, the Swedish Revolution was the first political triumph of France since 1740. It was, at the same time, a distinct rebuff to Russia. Panin always insisted that the *coup d'état* of 1772 was the one really serious *contretemps* of the reign of Catharine II, inasmuch as it destroyed the Russian influence in the extreme north. The Empress herself, when she first heard of it, regarded an immediate war

with Sweden as inevitable, and actually detached nine infantry regiments
from Rumyantseff's army on the Danube, and sent them to Pskoff in
view of an expected Swedish invasion.   But Gustavus was not prepared
at present to imperil his newly won position by any fresh adventures,
while Turkish and Polish complications were to tie the hands of
Catharine for many years to come.

Secure, at last, from foreign interference, the young monarch was
now free to throw himself, heart and soul, into that ambitious plan of
reform which was the necessary consequence of the Revolution and its
triumphant vindication.   A fairer and wider field of operation for an
ardent and capable reformer than that presented by Sweden in 1772 is
scarcely imaginable.   Half a century of misrule had dislocated the whole
machinery of government, given the licence of prescription to the worst
abuses, and brought the State to the very verge of financial and political
bankruptcy.   The first two measures of the new Government, the abolition of judicial torture and the establishment of the freedom of the
Press, showed that, at least, it had a liberal and progressive programme.
The regulation of the currency was the King's next care.   He began by
appointing a Commission of six experts to report on the subject.   After
three months of incessant labour, the Commission was ready with its
report, which deprecated as mischievous any attempt to redeem the notes
of the Bank of Sweden for many years to come.   Gustavus, ill pleased
with this report, asked the chairman whether it represented the
unanimous opinion of the Commission.   He replied that the junior
commissioner, Johan Liljencrantz, had alone refused to sign it.   The
King immediately asked Liljencrantz why he had withheld his signature.
He replied that he had done so, because he was persuaded that the
redemption of the enormous note currency, although a difficult, was by
no means an impossible, operation.   The upshot of it was that the
King resolved to give Liljencrantz' project a fair chance, and, when the
Senate twice refused to consent to it, Gustavus boldly took the matter
into his own hands, created a new Department of Finance, of which he
made Liljencrantz the first President, and ordered him to carry his
scheme into execution.   The result more than justified the King's
venture.   Favoured by a succession of good harvests, and assisted by
three loans from Holland, on unprecedently advantageous terms, Liljencrantz, despite the constant resistance of the Senate and the reiterated
protests and warnings of the Bank Directors, persisted in his endeavours
and, after six years of incessant labour, was able to lay before the
Riksdag of 1778 a national balance-sheet which has been well described
as "an artistic masterpiece in the highest finance."   Briefly, it was found
that the whole of the State's debt to the Bank, contracted during the
last fifty years, had been discharged, and there was a substantial surplus
in hand.   When the *Landsmarskalk*, in the name of the Finance Committee of the *Riksdag*, proceeded to thank the King for having restored

CH. XXII.

the national credit and reestablished the equilibrium of the finances, Gustavus beckoned to Liljencrantz to come forward and stand on his left, in order that "he who had done the work might also receive the praise."

Next to the finances, it was the judicature which most needed reformation, and here the King again took the initiative, though his labours were considerably lightened by the zeal and intelligence of Joachim Vilhelm Liliestråle, whom he discovered and employed as his first Vicar-General in civil and ecclesiastical matters. Liliestråle was instructed to make a thorough inquisition into the condition of the magistracy and the general administration of justice. He discovered, *inter alia*, that a very large percentage of the *Landshöfdingar*, or Lord Lieutenants of the counties, and their deputies were, practically, absentees; that charitable funds had been appropriated wholesale by their administrators; that many districts had been untaxed while other districts had been taxed ten times over during the same period; that scores of parsonages were in ruins; that in one diocese there had been no episcopal visitation for twelve years; that the rich see of Linköping had derived not the slightest spiritual benefit from its revenues for nearly a century. The maladministration of justice was found to be universal. The complaints brought against one of the two Supreme Courts, the *Göta Hofrätt*, were, in particular, so scandalous that the King felt bound to impeach the whole tribunal before the full Senate, under his personal presidency. The trial, which began on November 2, 1774, with open doors, lasted six weeks, and resulted in the disbenching of five of the eight judges, while the remaining three were heavily fined.

No less sweeping and drastic than his civil reforms were the military reforms of Gustavus III. And, certainly, the state of the national defences had never been so deplorable as when Gustavus ascended the throne. The military spirit which had predominated in Sweden under Charles XII had been succeeded by a mania for economy. Every penny spent on armaments was grudged and carped at. The standard of military education was lower than it had ever been. The officers spent three-quarters of their time on furlough; the men were very often not manœuvred from one year's end to another. The superior officers had no hold upon subalterns who were their accusers and judges in the *Riksdag*. Seniority was the sole title to promotion, and the various attempts to mitigate its mischievous consequences had only produced the monstrous "*accord*" arrangement, almost identical with the extinct British Purchase system. Officers wishing to retire were permitted to receive from their successors a certain bounty, or *accord*. The whole arrangement was transparently unmilitary, as an instance, of a kind by no means uncommon, will show. An officer who has, perhaps, vegetated through half a century of inglorious peace retires at last upon the *accord* paid to him by his successor. That successor is killed shortly afterwards on active service. Had he survived, he, too, in course of time, would have comfortably retired in turn on his *accord*; but death, by cutting him off on the battle-field, deprives him of his perquisite. Thus the officer dying in defence of his country fared worse than the officer who avoided the foe. The "*accord*" system was abolished by the Royal Decree of March 21, 1774; and, in the same year, a Commission of National Defence, ultimately presided over by Toll, from which all the new measures of army reform were to originate, was appointed by the King.

Even more indispensable to the security of Sweden than a strong army was a strong fleet. France expressly stipulated that three-quarters of her annual subsidies to Gustavus should be spent upon the Swedish navy. Something had already been done in this direction by the great naval engineer, August Ehrensvärd, who, recognising that Finland was Sweden's weak point, made the fortifying of the grand duchy against a Russian attack his main object. It was he who first hit upon the idea of building a *Skärgårdsflotta*, or galley flotilla, to ply among the shallow rock-studded waters of the Gulf of Finland, and, in case of a war with Russia, to cooperate with an invading army; while the *Orlogsflotta*, or man-of-war fleet, dealt with the enemy in the open sea. He was also the constructor of the gigantic fortress of Sveaborg, whose impregnable harbour was to serve as a refuge, in case of defeat, for the galley flotilla. Gustavus followed energetically in the footsteps of Ehrensvärd, by reforming the whole naval administration. The Admiralty was transferred from Karlskrona to Stockholm for better supervision. The building of new ships of war under the direction of Frederick Henry Chapman, the son of an English naval officer settled in Sweden, proceeded with extraordinary rapidity; and the superb docks at Karlskrona were completed by the architect Thunberg, who was ennobled for a piece of work comparable even to the works of Ehrensvärd. Nor was the galley flotilla overlooked. A plan for placing the whole of the *Skärgårdsflotta* on a war footing was elaborated by Admiral Henrik af Trolle, and carried out with masterly thoroughness.

Gustavus could now meet his people with perfect confidence. On October 19, 1778, the session of the first Parliament on the new model was opened. Gustavus laid before the Estates a clear and succinct account of the numerous reforms which had been carried out since the last *Riksdag*. If it had been impossible to find a remedy for every evil within so short a time, they were to recollect "that Kings are but men, and that time alone can heal the wounds which time has inflicted." The peroration exhorted to mutual confidence and concord. The session lasted till January 17, 1779, when the King dismissed the Riksdagsmen to their homes with every expression of goodwill.

Never had a Parliament been more obsequious, or a King more gracious. There was no room for a single "No" during the whole session. For the first time for fifty years, the course of Swedish politics had run smoothly and equably in its natural channel. Everyone, apparently, had come to the *Riksdag* of 1778 only to approve and applaud. There was scarcely a glimpse of a legitimate Parliamentary Opposition. One single party chief, the venerable Axel Fredrik af Fersen, had, indeed, warily raised his head, but only, as warily, to withdraw it. "I have reached the happiest stage of my career," wrote Gustavus to a friend. "My people are convinced that I desire nothing but to promote their welfare and establish their freedom on a firm basis." Nevertheless, this harmonious *Riksdag* had roughly shaken the popularity of Gustavus III. Short as the session had been, it was quite long enough to open the eyes of the deputies to the fact that their political supremacy had departed. They had changed places with the King. He was now indeed their sovereign lord, and the jealousy with which he guarded, the vigour with which he enforced, his prerogatives, plainly showed that he meant to remain such. Even the minority, who were prudent and patriotic enough to acquiesce in the change, by no means relished it. The inevitable explosion came eight years later, when Gustavus, very reluctantly and against his better judgment, but yielding to the urgent representations of Liljencrantz, who required the assistance of the Estates to balance the finances, and of Toll, whose scheme of military organisation was at a standstill for want of funds, summoned "that mutinous and ungrateful *Riksdag*" from which he subsequently dated all his misfortunes.

On May 6, 1786, the second Gustavan *Riksdag*, on the new model, was "blown in[1]." On the following day, Gustavus' new Vicar-General, Elis Schröderheim, read to the Houses a skilfully worded retrospect of all that had been done during the last eight years. The retrospect, after enumerating a whole series of successful economic and social reforms, dwelt with especial pride and satisfaction on the improved condition of the national defences. Since 1778, no fewer than 11 liners, 10 frigates, 7 sloops and a multitude of transport-vessels had been fully equipped, while 3 more liners and 3 frigates would be ready by the end of the current year. The new docks at Karlskrona, then the largest in the world, had also been completed; Finland had been provided with a more efficient galley flotilla; the principal fortresses had been put upon a war footing; the artillery had been reorganised; three large camps had been formed to promote military manoeuvres on a large scale. To enable him to continue as he had begun, the King requested the assent of the Estates to a number of propositions, or Bills, of which three only need be specified here. The first aimed at increasing the mobility of the army by commuting the transport obligations of the small landowners into small cash payments; the second desired the Estates to grant the usual subsidies until the next *Riksdag*, instead of for a fixed period; the

---

[1] To "blow in" and "blow out" (*i.e.* with trumpets) were the technical expressions for opening and closing the *Riksdag*.

third offered to surrender the government monopoly in the distillation of spirits (the single economic blunder, though a serious one, of Gustavus' reign) in return for an annual grant to the Crown of £140,000. All these propositions were either rejected outright or so attenuated as to be of little value. It at once became evident to Gustavus that nothing was to be done with a *Riksdag* which, already troublesome, might, at any moment, become dangerous. On July 5 he dissolved it, after an abortive session of two months.

If Gustavus III, at this point of his career, could have seen his way to retreat within the bounds of a strictly limited constitutional monarchy with honour and safety, he would doubtless have done so. But, in truth, such a retreat was scarcely possible. In 1772, the King had deliberately placed himself at the mercy of the Estates by not only relinquishing to them the power of the purse, but also by solemnly engaging not to engage in an offensive war without their consent. It has been well observed that to Russia her knowledge that her north-western frontier could not be attacked without the permission of the Swedish *Riksdag* was worth as much as an army corps. Even before 1786, Gustavus had begun to realise that circumstances might perhaps compel him to ride rough-shod over his own Constitution. As the lesser of two evils he finally resolved to curtail the liberty in order to secure the independence of the nation. But the passage from semi-constitutionalism to semi-absolutism was so cautious and gradual, legal forms were so carefully retained long after they had lost all their force, that very few people were really aware of the great change that was silently proceeding. The King's first care was to remove, dexterously, from the Administration all the friends of the old system, and surround his throne with men of his own way of thinking. Thus Liljencrantz, who was growing restive at the increasing extravagance of the Court, was superseded by the more pliant Eric Ruuth; and the office of Chancellor, after the death (1784) of its last holder, Count Philip Creutz, was left vacant, Gustavus considering that the dignity it conferred was too great for a subject. Toll was now the man on whom the King principally relied. That great administrator was the soul of the secret council of four, which practically ruled Sweden during the King's long continental tour (September, 1783, to July, 1784), and at the end of 1785 he was made War Minister. But, although the chief, Toll was by no means the only royal counsellor. It is about this time that we find very near to the King two clergymen whose rare political genius Gustavus himself had been the first to discover, and on whom he was to lean more and more as his former friends fell away from him; namely, Olaf Wallqvist, whom he created Bishop of Wexiö, and Carl Gustaf Nordin, who preferred, for the present, to remain a simple prebendary. With a nice discrimination of their respective characters, Gustavus employed the masterful and eloquent prelate to defend the royal measures in public, while the quiet self-effacing prebendary, whom Wallqvist feared and hated as a rival, was the King's secret, indispensable adviser whose opinion was always taken beforehand. Another invaluable coadjutor, by reason of his fine courage and absolute devotion, was the dashing royal favourite Gustaf Maurice Armfelt, whom Gustavus attached to his Court in 1782.

So early as 1784, Gustavus had made up his mind that a rupture with Russia was inevitable. On his return to Sweden, in 1785, he began to prepare for war, pushing on his preparations with the speed and secrecy of a conspiracy. Toll alone was privy to his master's designs, though both Wallqvist and Nordin suspected them. Secret negotiations were entered into with all the anti-Russian Courts simultaneously, and the results of these negotiations were communicated to Toll and Ruuth at a series of Cabinet Councils held during 1788, at which they were the only Ministers present. The apparently inextricable difficulties of Catharine II during her Second War with Turkey gave him his opportunity. After addressing an ultimatum to the Empress, in which he demanded the cession of Carelia and Livonia to Sweden, the restoration of the Crimea to Turkey (a Suedo-Turkish alliance had already been brought about by Great Britain and Prussia, and the first subsidy of piastres had reached Stockholm *viâ* Amsterdam and Hamburg), and the instant disbandment of the Russian forces on the Swedish frontier, he embarked for Finland on Midsummer day, arriving at Helsingfors on July 2, 1788.

Success seemed certain. The Empress was completely taken by surprise. Gustavus, at the head of a fine army of 40,000 men, was only thirty-six hours' sail from the inadequately garrisoned Russian capital. Fortunately for St Petersburg, the Russian fleet proved to be as strong as the Swedish, which it repulsed, after a fierce engagement, off the isle of Hogland (July 17), while a fortnight later the operations on land were paralysed by a sudden outbreak of mutiny in the Swedish camp at Hussula, in which Catharine saw the hand of Providence. The officers bluntly declared that they were weary of a war which was illegal, because it had never received the sanction of the Estates; and the King was compelled by them to recross the boundary river Kymmene and transfer his camp to Anjala, within Swedish territory. On August 11 the rebels sent an emissary to St Petersburg from Anjala, placing themselves formally beneath the protection of the Empress, on condition that Russian and Swedish Finland were erected into an autonomous State. The conspirators then proceeded to draw up a formal Act of Confederation, on the Polish model, which was subscribed, within a week, by no fewer than 113 officers. Gustavus, in the midst of wavering friends and open foes, had been powerless to check the progress of the mutiny. Yet honour forbade his flying from Finland; and to open negotiations with the Empress would, in the circumstances, have been tantamount to an act of political suicide. His one remaining hope was that the Danes might declare war against him. A Danish invasion would imperatively require his presence in Sweden and therefore justify his departure from Finland, and he was clear-sighted enough to perceive that such a contingency "would open the eyes of the Swedes to the reality of their danger and rally the people round the throne." When, therefore, the tidings reached him that the Danes, in pursuance of their treaty obligations with Russia, had actually declared war against Sweden, he exclaimed: "We are saved!" and set out at once for Stockholm, leaving his brother Charles, Duke of Sudermania, commander-in-chief in his stead.

Rarely has a King been in such evil case as Gustavus III when, at the end of August, 1788, he reappeared at Stockholm. The army was in open mutiny. The fleet was blockaded at Sveaborg. A Russian squadron held the Gulf of Bothnia. A combined Russo-Danish squadron swept the Cattegat. A Danish army, under the Prince of Hesse, had actually crossed the frontier and was advancing against Göteborg, in rank the second, in wealth the first, city in the kingdom. Confusion reigned in the capital, panic in the provinces. A perplexed Senate, a hostile nobility, a stupefied population were anxiously watching every movement of a defenceless King. His friends united in imploring him to summon a *Riksdag* instantly, as the one remaining means of salvation. But Gustavus saw much further than his counsellors. A *Riksdag* at that moment would have been uncontrollable, and he had been quick to recognise that the tide of public opinion had turned again, and was beginning to run very strongly in his favour. If only he could take this tide at its flood, it must inevitably carry him on to victory. His proper course was to appeal from a cowardly, treacherous, and disloyal army to the martial and patriotic instincts of the lower classes, and let the robust common-sense of the nation at large decide between him and deserters who negotiated with the enemy instead of fighting him. He would turn, first and foremost, as he himself finely expressed it, to "that portion of the people which has the right, by long prescription, to be the bulwark of the realm against the Danes"—to the peasantry of the Dales, as the rugged mining districts of Sweden were called. Theirs was the glory of having saved Sweden 250 years before at the call of Gustavus Vasa; they should now have the opportunity of saving her a second time under another Gustavus.

The King's friends contemplated with dismay the step he proposed to take. Even the sagacious Nordin considered the letting loose of a wild peasantry a most hazardous experiment. But Gustavus fearlessly took all the risks, and was rewarded with complete success. Into the romantic and dramatic details of this hardy adventure it is impossible to enter. Suffice it to say that Gustavus, at the head of his peasant levies, snatched Göteborg from the hands of the Danes at the last moment, and then, with the diplomatic support of Great Britain and Prussia (which, themselves on the point of a rupture with Russia, were deeply interested in the prolongation of the Russo-Swedish War), rid Sweden of the Danes altogether. Hugh Elliot, the British Minister at Copenhagen, took the initiative and conducted the negotiations with overwhelming energy. On November 6, 1788, the final convention for the evacuation of Sweden was drawn up at Uddevalla, the headquarters of the Prince of Hesse. A fortnight later, not a single Danish soldier remained on Swedish soil. And now, sure of his people, Gustavus no longer hesitated to convoke the Estates. On December 8 a royal proclamation, issued from Göteborg, summoned an extraordinary *Riksdag* to meet at Stockholm on January 26, 1789.

From the first the temper of the four Orders was unmistakable. Of the 950 gentlemen who sat in the *Riddarhus* during this *Riksdag*, more than 700 were *soi-disant* "patriots," *i.e.* defenders of the Anjala treason, whereas the lower three Orders were all for the King. Even of the clergy, among whom the Court was weakest, the Opposition could only count upon sixteen deputies out of fifty-two, while among the 112 burgesses and the 178 peasants there were not half-a-dozen anti-royalists. So sure, indeed, was the King of the burgesses and the peasants that he left them pretty much to themselves; but for the guidance of the Estate of Clergy, which Nordin had compared to ice which might be walked upon but must not be driven over, he reserved his most audacious coadjutor— Wallqvist.

Only the barest outlines of the dramatic history of this momentous *Riksdag* can here be adumbrated. On February 2 the session was opened by an eirenicon from the Throne. "My only enemies," concluded the orator, "are the enemies of my country." On the following day, the King proposed that a Committee of ways and means, for which he demanded urgency, should be appointed to provide the subsidies necessary "for the maintenance of the honour, safety and independence of the realm"—in other words, the continuation of the War. The lower three Estates proceeded at once to elect their committee-men; but the first Estate exhausted every means of obstruction to produce delay, and, when their Marshal refused to tolerate such tactics any longer, they insulted him so grossly that he appealed to the King for satisfaction. Meanwhile, as the whole machinery of legislation had come to a standstill, Gustavus resolved to expedite matters by a *coup de main*. On February 17 he summoned the four Estates in congress, and, after bitterly reproaching the nobility for their neglect of public business and their indecent treatment of their Marshal, he dismissed them from his presence till they had apologised to that dignitary. The nobility having withdrawn, cowed by his fulminating eloquence but sullenly mutinous, Gustavus invited the lower three Orders to appoint delegates to confer with him as to those privileges "which it was only just and right that all citizens should enjoy equally." In other words, he boldly bid for the support of the non-noble Estates by abolishing the peculiar privileges of the nobility.

The royal propositions were embodied in the famous " Act of Union and Security," the object of which was to substitute for the existing Constitution a more monarchical form of government. In brief, it invested the King with the supreme executive and legislative functions. The *Riksdag* was only to meet when he chose to summon it and was only to consider such propositions as he chose to lay before it. On the other hand, paragraphs 2 to 4 broke down the invidious distinction between noble and non-noble which had so long been the standing grievance of the *Ofrälse* Estates. Henceforth, commoners were to be eligible to all, or nearly all, the offices and dignities of the State; some of the vexatious exemptions of the nobility from public burdens were, at the same time, abolished. This revolutionary Act was accepted by the lower three Estates in another congress (February 20); but the first Estate, though depressed by the arrest and imprisonment of twenty-one of its leaders, including Fersen and Pechlin (February 21), rejected it (March 16) as unconstitutional. Nevertheless, on April 3, the Act of Union and Security, with some slight modifications, received the royal sanction.

The worst of the difficulties of Gustavus were now over. The lower three Estates after much debate (the peasants were particularly obstinate) consented to grant the King the necessary subsidies " till the following *Riksdag*," in other words indefinitely; but the utmost the first Estate would do was to grant them for two years. The opposition of the nobility had to be overcome somehow, as the consent of all four Estates was essential to the validity of a subsidy Bill. Gustavus got his way by a *ruse* as impudent as it was audacious. On April 27 he suddenly appeared in the *Riddarhus*, unattended, and seating himself in the presidential chair, " as the first nobleman in the land," solemnly declared that, if the first Estate persisted in refusing to grant him the new war-tax till the next *Riksdag*, he would not be responsible for the con-sequences. To the objection that those who had the right to grant subsidies had also the right to fix their amount and terminus, he replied that he was not there to dispute the rights of the nobility, but simply to desire them to acquiesce, on this unique occasion, in the decision of the three lower Estates for the welfare of their common country. He then formally put the question to the House, and, ignoring the greatly preponderating " Noes " with imperturbable composure pronounced that the " Ayes " had it, at the same time cordially thanking the *Riddarhus* for a consent which they had never given, but refusing to put the question to the vote. On the following day this stormy *Riksdag* was " blown out," to the intense relief of the King's friends, who expected every moment to hear of his assassination at the hands of some infuriated adherent of the oligarchical system.

The Revolution of 1789 converted Sweden from a limited into a semi-despotic Government. Yet, in the circumstances, the change was necessary, if only for a time. But for this fiercely debated act of authority, Sweden indisputably ran the risk of becoming a mere dependency of Russia. The Confederation of Anjala was as criminal and might easily have proved as fatal as the similar Confederation of Targowicz was to prove to Poland three years later. The King had, once for all, put a stop to the possible recurrence of any such treason in the future, and Catharine was obliged to leave the Finnish rebels to their fate and to fall back on the defensive. Two fresh campaigns in Finland, into the details of which we are here precluded from entering, finally convinced the Russian Empress that it would be safer henceforth to treat Gustavus as an ally rather than as a foe. Little more than a month after the King's crowning victory in the second battle of Svensksund (July 9-11, 1790), where the Russians lost 53 ships of war and 9500 men, peace was concluded at the little Finnish village of Värälä (August 14, 1790). Only eight months earlier, Catharine had haughtily declared that "the odious and revolting aggressiveness" of the King of Sweden would be forgiven "only if he testified his repentance" by agreeing to a peace confirming the Treaties of Åbo and Nystad, granting a general and unlimited amnesty to all rebels, and consenting to a guarantee by the *Riksdag* ("as it would be imprudent to confide in his good faith alone") for the observance of peace in future. The Peace of Värälä saved Sweden from any such humiliating concessions. The increasing difficulties of Catharine, and the shuffling conduct of Gustavus' allies, Great Britain and Prussia, had convinced both sovereigns of the necessity of adjusting their differences without any foreign intervention. On October 19, 1791, Gustavus went still further, and took the bold, but by no means imprudent, step of concluding an eight years' defensive alliance with the Empress, who thereupon bound herself to pay her new ally annual subsidies amounting to 300,000 *roubles*.

Mutual respect and, still more, a common antagonism to revolutionary France, united these two great rulers in their declining years. Gustavus now aimed at forming a league of Princes against the Jacobins : and every other consideration was subordinated to this end. His profound knowledge of popular assemblies enabled him, alone among contemporary sovereigns, accurately to gauge from the first the scope and bearing of the French Revolution. "The King of France has lost his throne, perhaps his life!" he exclaimed when the news reached him that Louis XVI had convoked the States General. The much belauded Necker he regarded, from the first, as a vainglorious charlatan. When the emigration began, Gustavus offered an asylum in his camp to the French Princes, and took up an unmistakably hostile attitude towards the new French Government. In the summer of 1789, he declared officially that he would never recognise any envoy accredited by the National Assembly, and on the substitution in October, 1790, of the tricolour for the historical white flag he forbade the display in his harbours of "the symbol of rampant demagogism in its most outrageous form." It was Gustavus who planned the flight of the royal family from France, the execution of which project he entrusted to his confidential agent Count Hans Axel af Fersen. At the last moment he himself came to Aix-la-Chapelle, so as to be close to the scene of action. Far from being daunted by the Varennes fiasco, he was more than ever resolved to restore the French monarchy. His first plan was for Monsieur to take the title of Regent, form a Ministry of his most uncompromising supporters, and invite all the European Powers to assist him in an armed intervention. But the imprisoned royal family—especially the Queen—were averse both from the proposed regency and from a foreign invasion. The more prudent of his own friends also warned Gustavus not to build too much on the representations of the *Émigrés*, and questioned the sincerity of the Emperor and the ability of the French Princes.

Gustavus' chief hope was now in his new ally, the Russian Empress. But Catharine, although she hated the French Revolution and all its works as energetically as Gustavus, agreed, nevertheless, with her shrewdest counsellor, Alexander Besborodko, that absolute neutrality, as regards France, was Russia's best policy. She had no objection, however, to give her dangerously restless "brother and cousin" something to do in the West, so that she herself might have "free elbow-room" in the Near East, and accordingly pretended to listen favourably to his new project of a coalition of Princes against Revolutionary France. She even contributed half a million *roubles* towards the expense of it. Gustavus proposed that France should be invaded simultaneously, at different points, by the Austrians, the Sardinians, the Spaniards, and the Princes of the Empire.

But the Emperor Leopold's strong dislike of the first coalition project of Gustavus proved its death-blow. Catharine also declined to move a step in the matter till the sentiments of all the other Powers had been ascertained. She insisted, too, on the neutrality of Great Britain and the cooperation of the Emperor as indispensable preliminaries. With equal coldness she regarded a subsequent proposal of an invasion of Normandy by 30,000 Swedish troops, while a Russo-Swedish fleet blockaded the mouth of the Seine and cut Paris off from all communication with the sea. Besborodko considered any such isolated attack as altogether impracticable, as no doubt it was.

The acknowledgment of the new Constitutional French Government by the Court of Vienna (Kaunitz' memorandum of November 12, 1791) put an end, for a time, to all "declarations," or "concerts," let alone warlike demonstrations. Gustavus alone remained immovably firm in his reactionary policy; but his projects became, in the circumstances, wilder and wilder. At the end of 1791 he proposed a convention between

Russia, Spain, and Sweden. The allies were to guarantee jointly the French King his full prerogatives, using force to that end if necessary ; they were to recall their Ministers from Paris ; refuse to receive the so-called national flag into their harbours ; and recognise Monsieur as Regent till the King had been set free. When Spain, which was to find the money for this adventure, refused to entertain it, Gustavus submitted to the Emperor a more modest programme, originally suggested by Marie-Antoinette. An armed Congress, under the protection of an army consisting of Austrian, Prussian, Russian and Swedish troops, was to be summoned to protect the territories of the minor German Princes bordering upon France and reestablish the balance of power in Europe. The Congress was to be held at a place sufficiently close to the French frontier to intimidate the Jacobins, and was to take action against them if necessary. But Leopold at once rejected the idea of an armed Congress, and neither Prussia nor Spain would move a step without him. Thus all the anti-revolutionary schemes of Gustavus (to which reference is made elsewhere) foundered against the obstinate indifference of the Great Powers.

But Gustavus' own course was now nearly run. After showing once more his unrivalled mastery over masses of men during the brief Gefle *Riksdag* (January 22—February 24, 1792), he fell a victim to a widespread aristocratic conspiracy. Shot in the back by Anckarström, at a midnight masquerade at the Stockholm Opera House on March 16, 1792, he expired on the 29th. Although he may fairly be charged with many foibles and extravagances, Gustavus III was, indisputably, one of the greatest sovereigns of the eighteenth century. Unfortunately, his genius never had full scope, and his opportunity came too late.

CHAPTER XXIII.

ENGLISH POLITICAL PHILOSOPHY IN THE SEVENTEENTH AND EIGHTEENTH CENTURIES.

In the troublous years 1640–60, the air was thick with political manifestos and schemes, each of which fell dismally to earth by some inherent defect. None went to the root of the matter as Hobbes did. Men took refuge in one despotic form after another; a single person, a Parliament, a single House; even the Independents who did see that one despotism was only replaced by another, had in their own despite to force men to be free. They had to enforce their liberty of the subject and liberty of tender consciences by parliamentary purgings and by the Major-Generals' swords. Through this welter of fogs and darkness the trenchant theory of the *Leviathan* cuts its ruthless way like a blast of the north wind. It is clear-sighted where others were blind; consistent where they were confused; single in aim where they were entangled in contradictions. The mid-seventeenth century was a great creative time, but creation had hardly got beyond the stage of chaos. Hobbes saw better than anyone from what quarters of the sky light was to come. Thus nothing is more characteristic of the Civil War than that, while it began in constitutional questions, it soon revealed itself as a great religious struggle. He sees that the deepest question for the State is its relation to religion. Again, the war began with an attempt to restore the pre-Tudor conception of sovereignty as a partnership between Crown and Parliament, and went on to a transfer of sovereignty from Crown to Parliament. He saw that the first step in political science was to define sovereignty. Again, the various proposals and schemes of accommodation from the Grand Remonstrance to the Humble Petition and Advice, were so many predestined failures because they tried to break up sovereign power into parcels, administrative, judicial, financial, military. He saw that it was inseparable and indivisible. The logic of events in seven short years had produced the army's manifesto of January 15, 1649, and so made visible the logical goal, the sovereignty of the people. In Hobbes the sovereign is not merely acting for the people; he and he alone is the people.

Taking all these documents as a whole, their moral is that constitutional forms are neither here nor there in comparison with a proper relation between government and the governed. This is what Hobbes would emphasise when he says that the power of sovereignty is the same whatever be the form of commonwealth, and prosperity comes not from the form of government but from the obedience and concord of the subjects.

Even if Hobbes were judged on his doctrine of sovereignty alone our debt to him would be immense. If he took it from Bodin, he took it by the right of better power to use it ; never was this fundamental part of political theory expressed so trenchantly and proved to such demonstration. The very term Sovereignty is the catchword of all the controversies of the seventeenth century. Was prerogative "intrinsical to sovereignty and entrusted to the king by God"? Or was it part of the law and within legal boundaries? In this discussion on the Petition of Right Wentworth had said: "Let us make what law we may, there must, nay there will, be a trust left in the Crown. *Salus populi suprema lex.*" But the lawyers would not see this. They had lately developed the idea of limits on sovereignty. Thus the word absolute in 1586 had meant an autonomous ruler ; but in 1607 Cowell argues that the King must be above Parliament or he is not absolute. For the idea of limitations came into collision with another idea becoming more and more clear-cut ; if sovereignty is by Divine right, how can it be limited ? And each holder of sovereign power was forced in practice to transcend limits ; not merely Stewart Kings but Long Parliaments and Protectors. Men had recourse to the theory of limitations only when the sovereign was not an expression of their own will.

There was evident need of some clear thinking, and the time was ripe for the true theory of sovereignty and the true grounds on which it is not amenable to legal limitations, namely, that it is not so much a personal ruler as a general will of the community. Hobbes has a real grasp of this true theory despite the form of "he," "him," "his" in which he speaks of the sovereign. The face is the face of a Stewart King but the voice is the voice of a Commonwealth. *Non est potestas super terram quae comparetur ei.* It is no man but "Leviathan our mortal God." And if he follows his age in this matter of personifying sovereignty, he avoids the worse error of basing sovereignty on insecure foundations. Where others trusted to Divine right alone, by which they meant a supposed deduction from Noah and Melchizedek, Hobbes drew his sovereignty first and independently from the principles of reason, and "from the principles of Nature only"; and left the proof "from supernatural revelations of the will of God, the prophetical ground" to Part III of his great work, with the dry prefatory remark that of four hundred prophets only Micaiah was a true one. Where others reserved a coordinate or even superior share of Divine right to another body, the Church, Hobbes will have no such dualism; no man can serve two masters, the civil sovereign is also the supreme pastor. God's law has two parts: the first is obedience, the second is obedience. The inviolable obligation of obedience; that is the note on which he closes.

The essential points of this theory are beyond question. That there must be in every State a sovereign power, illimitable, indivisible, unalienable; that the attempt to separate it, to set it up against itself, to create a " balance of powers" or a "mixed government," is chimerical; that denial of these essential points leads to a contradiction in terms. Thus if the objection be made that such sovereign power is a menace, *e.g.* to constitutional liberty or to religious independence, the objection falls pointless to the ground before these inherent attributes of sovereignty: they are inherent, not dependent on contract, but deducible from the thing in itself; not what suits our special party or sect, but what needs must be, is what Hobbes offers us, and his doctrine of sovereignty is wholly unaffected by the historicalness or unhistoricalness of his hypothesis of a social contract. Nor is his conception of sovereign power fairly open to the criticism that it is wholly taken up with sovereign rights and hardly alive to sovereign duties. In fact his " duties of the sovereign " (*Lev.* c. 30) constitutes a fair sketch of what we call the functions and sphere of the State. If he thought that it was rather the duties of the citizen which required emphasising at the time, would not this still be true in our day?

Not that his picture of sovereign power is wholly free from defects. He regards sovereign power only as mature and adult, and allows it no infancy or adolescence. Doubtless some form of judiciary existed long before legislation as such, and the earliest and longest period was the reign of custom. He does too often speak of a transfer of " the natural rights of all to everything"; and of the rights of the sovereign as derived from this transfer; it would be truer to say rights come from the community and grow with its growth. He is too ready also to throw sovereign and subject into antagonism; not the crushing of the individual, but his full evolution and realisation, is the aim of a true State, and it is to the development of individual judgment that we must look for a healthy national conscience. To this false antagonism Hobbes was led by his too ready identification of sovereignty with government; the State is viewed too much on its coercive side; and we feel that, when individuals' freedom to choose their own clothes and diet is represented as only precarious and dependent on the sovereign's silence, this does incomplete justice to one side of human life and undervalues individual freedom. We feel that the subjects would strike, and Hobbes has forgotten this practical limitation on sovereignty.

But however Hobbes may have over-emphasised a true theory, it was a very different matter when Locke's influence set a false theory in its place. Very convenient it was, certainly. Sovereignty limited, to

square with the Bill of Rights; revocable, that the nation might hold
over William and the Georges, the threat of a notice to quit; partible,
the very thing to suit the great Whig houses. But like some other
convenient fallacies, it led to more than inconvenience in the end, and
had to be corrected by more and more stress on " the omnipotence of
Parliament." The modern Parliament is not far from Hobbes' sovereign : according to the saying, it can do anything but make a woman
into a man; indeed it can do this also, as for franchise purposes and for
property law. The recent tendency to displace Parliament itself by the
Cabinet, carries the likeness still further; for the Cabinet is almost a
person, in Hobbes' sense.

Hobbes meant his theory of sovereignty to correct a current tyranno-
phobia. Our constitutional history had seemed to make the whole
object of politics to consist in putting the brake on the state machine,
and keeping the safety-valve open, not in providing for a good head of
steam. But we are coming to see that what we want is not less but
more central power, now that it is in the hands of the community.
Trusts, interests, tariffs, may be relied on to supply all and more than
all the desired friction and resistance. The more united and more
developed a people, the more active is its sovereign power; and the
modern sovereign power comes more and more to add the work of
legislation to its older executive and judicial work. The political
development of a people may be measured by the energy of its
legislative function. Modern civilisation depends on a true conception
of sovereignty. These various aphorisms from publicists are enough to
suggest the importance of Hobbes' doctrine of sovereignty.

"Temporal and spiritual are two words brought into the world to
make men see double, and mistake their lawful sovereign....A man
cannot obey two [masters, and a house divided against itself cannot
stand....Seeing there are no men on earth whose bodies are spiritual,
there can be no spiritual commonwealth among men that are yet in the
flesh....My kingdom is not of this world....Men's actions proceed from
their opinions...if the sovereign give away the government of doctrines,
men will be frighted into rebellion with the fear of spirits."

These sentences contain in essence the whole theory of Hobbes on
that eternal problem, the relation between Church and State, and they
are enough of themselves to show his originality and audacity, and to
explain the alarm inspired by " the atheist of Malmesbury."

"A church is a company of Christian men assembled at the command
of a sovereign." But what if the sovereign forbid us to believe in
Christ? Well, profession with the tongue is no more than a gesture,
and a Christian has the liberty allowed to Naaman to bow in the house
of Rimmon.

Does Hobbes then foresee the modern severance of the State from any one religious form, and general toleration of all forms? No: Hobbes would have said that he had made ample provision for conscience, when he rejected any inquisition into opinions, and only claimed to control their external expression; had he not said, "Faith is a gift of God which man can neither take nor give away"; and, "There ought to be no power over the consciences of men save the Word itself"? It is possible that he was the more willing to make these concessions from a conviction that they would not prove very expensive in the end; for he has all the Elizabethan sense of externalities in religion. Like the Tudor sovereign his aim is peace, and not persecution for a dogma. As things were then, Hobbes would have made everyone attend an episcopal state Church with a very Erastian service. But as things are now in a modern community, Hobbes would admit the public rites of all sects except such as preached some illegal doctrines, like Mormons; with the general and absolute provision that no dogma whatever was to be appealed to against a law of the State.

Here we have the very antipodes to all sacerdotalism, whether of Rome or Geneva. The very texts on which the champions of spiritual power relied are wrested out of their hands and turned against them. Was he making a *reductio ad absurdum* of the scriptural argument, to force men back on the argument from reason which he claimed to be irrefutably on his side? Or was it a politic condescension to the universal treatment of such topics at that time? Never was the argument from authority handled with such subtlety, such consummate special pleading, and such contemptuous confidence. Was he simply retaliating in kind upon his predecessors? or was he quite candid in his two surprising statements, that he has only taken each text in its plainest sense, and that he is only offering provisional interpretations until the sword shall have settled what is to be the authority on doctrines? At any rate he could have said to each antagonist in turn, "Hast thou appealed unto Scripture? To Scripture shalt thou go." And when they did go thither, they would find considerable surprises awaiting them under his exegesis.

There has always been in English history an undercurrent of the theory which the Civil War thus forced to the surface: *rex est vicarius Dei*. But even Henry VIII is a pale shadow beside the spiritual supremacy in which the *Leviathan* is enthroned. There are only two positions in history which rise to this height; the position of a Caliph, the vicegerent of Allah, with the book on his knees that contains all law as well as all religion and all morals; and the position of the Greek πόλις where heresy was treason where the State gods and no other were the citizens' gods, and the citizen must accept the State's standard of virtue.

In his recoil from spiritual tyranny and sacerdotal arrogance, Hobbes has overshot the mark. From stewards of the Divine mysteries, the

CH. XXIII.

clergy are reduced in his State to so many gramophones stocked with homilies on the rights of sovereignty. They are paid by results; for "the common people's minds are like clean paper fit to receive any imprint from public authority." Before such ultra-Erastianism the vicar of Bray himself would have revolted. The *Leviathan* would have had to face a general "strike" of the clergy, despite the drastic measures taken to tune "those operatories of enchantment, the Universities." Even for this the sovereign is prepared, for has he not proved his own right to preach, baptise, administer sacraments of himself? But of what sort would be the men who would take Orders under such a dispensation, and what would be the level of spirituality in a community whose pastors were reduced to such machines?

Nor would the atmosphere of the house of Rimmon be less stifling to the individual layman. Both politics and morals require a purer atmosphere above them from which to draw, and religion that gets reduced to law would end by being unable to secure even a legal obedience.

It would be difficult nowadays to accept Hobbes' summary treatment of cases of conscience. The modern State is too firmly based to seem to need such uncompromising procedure. It is a sound social instinct which treats the conscientious objector with respect, instead of summoning him in the name of the law to swallow his principles. Hobbes' policy is too much like sitting on the safety-valve. The fact is that he takes too external and materialist a view of men's actions. He looks too much to the community, and too much at one aspect of that, the coercive and governmental aspect. He bears no rival near the throne, and would crush the individual so as to make more of the community. But assuredly the conception which needs strengthening in modern England is the conception of social duty, that conception to which Hobbes gave so powerful if a somewhat one-sided expression.

When men were receiving orders from their consciences to refuse taxes, to resist military service, or even to keep their hats on in law courts, when they were receiving direct "revelations" how to vote or against whom to march, it was high time for some clear thinking and some trenchant speaking on these topics. Hobbes' immediate effect on the religious thought of his time was mainly in the direction of reaction. Instinctively all of whatever creed felt that here was the enemy. Hobbes' doctrines were denounced as pernicious to all nations, destructive of royal titles, an encouragement to usurpers, unhistorical, unscriptural, immoral; he arrogated to himself the position of a prophet or apostle, and made the Koran a Gospel, he was the boar that would root up the Lord's vineyard, an Epicurean, a Cromwellian, the foe of property, justice and order, conscience and religion; a fellow to Machiavelli, an atheist, a garbler of texts, an enemy to chartered companies, corporations, and trade, a slanderer of lawyers; he cannot believe his own books, he is bound by his own principles to recant all he has said; he denies the social nature of man and would dissolve all human relationships, conjugal, parental, political; he has cheated people into a vast opinion of himself as the prodigy of the age; he has said nothing new but only devises new words; he is the champion of evil living and has made Hell the bigness of a quartan ague; he has even quarrelled with the elements of Euclid. These prelates and chancellors were plainly very angry; Hobbes might well say, *Leviathan clerum totum mihi fecerat hostem.* It is noticeable that the chorus swells in the twenty years following the Restoration. "Hobbists" were not made up only, as one reverend critic declares, of "debauchees, fine gentlemen, and Don-friends who say Mr H. alone hath got to fundamentals," but included a great number of learned men from abroad, besides the poet Cowley, Richard Bathurst, President of Trinity College, Oxford, and Robert Blackburne, who in 1681 wrote the *Auctarium,* a life of Hobbes with some valuable additions. Foreign writers were more ready to acknowledge the merits of originality, acuteness, learning; the only merit the native critics would allow was a mastery of English.

He dealt a mortal blow at a method of reasoning which ever since St Augustine's day had cramped the advance of political science, the method of reasoning from texts. When a text can be found for everything, and every text can be stretched to cover any view, and when no one for all this hail of missiles is a penny the worse, the game ceases to be worth the candle. Sidney still relies partly on texts, but Locke drops the method as antiquated and inconclusive. Politics has at last shaken itself free from the medieval tradition, and every student of politics heaves a sigh of relief at parting with Noah and Nimrod, Melchizedek and Meroz.

Hobbes himself had laid down that the only ground besides Scripture was reason. Hobbes is therefore placed next to Lord Herbert of Cherbury as one of the founders of the School of English Deists.

A still more important influence of Hobbes was in the direction of Erastianism. He had made short work of the "power ecclesiastical," he had identified bishops with elders, and reduced their office to teaching, referred their appointment to the civil sovereign, and left their sustenance to voluntary contributions. All dogmas, except that of the Divinity of our Lord, he had declared unessential; the idea of life in another world than this earth, and the idea of a kingdom of God in opposition to earthly kingdoms, he had rejected. His analysis of good and evil into appetite and aversion, seemed to sap the foundations of morality. Above all, his caustic humour, his malicious insinuations, were still harder to bear. His whole tone and manner provoked more resentment than even his matter.

Charles II had applied to Hobbes the description of Ishmael, his hand against every man and every man's hand against him.

CH. XXIII.

No man ever had greater self-confidence than he, who was wont to say that, if he had read as much as other men, he should have known no more; whose first literary work was a translation of Thucydides to convict the ancient world out of its own mouth, by showing that its liberty was anarchy and demagogism; who set out at the age of 70 to demonstrate the squaring of the circle against all the great mathematicians—either all they or he himself must be mad, he said; and at the age of 76 began a treatise to confute Coke; who meets the criticism that the whole world is against him by the retort, "Though the whole world build their houses on the sand, it could not thence be inferred that so it ought to be."

It had been Papist influence which had got him as "the grand atheist" dismissed from the exiled Court in 1652. But his views were quite as distasteful to the Anglicans, and Clarendon had already told him that his book would be punished in every country in Europe. Most scathing of all were his sayings on conscience, saintship and inspiration, the shibboleths of Puritanism. He makes, it is true, a rather suspicious concession to Independency. But Presbytery, Prelacy, Papacy are joined in condemnation as the three successive "knots on Christian liberty." Politicians too would find him as elusive as the theologians did. Royalists hated his absolutism and his rejection of Divine Right, and his justification of *de facto* governments. Parliamentarians had "caressed" him on his return in 1652, but found that he made a disconcerting distinction between innocent subjects and guilty leaders.

"Civil philosophy is no older (I say it provoked and that my enemies may know how little they have wrought upon me) than my own book *De Cive* (1642)." No one as yet, Hobbes continues, had applied to civil philosophy the clear method of natural philosophy, the gate of which was first opened by Galileo, following Copernicus and Harvey. The universal law is motion. The new method will apply this law to the body politic. It will be deductive from a few axioms; demonstrative, like Euclid; rigorously abstract. Fortunately this "synthetic" method, deducing all politics and morals from geometrical first principles, is not long pursued. Men, he saw, would never let politics be reduced to mere mathematics. So after the geometry trumpet has been blown in a few flourishes, it is laid aside for the sake of "them that have not learned the first part of philosophy, namely geometry and physics," and they are allowed to "attain the principles of civil philosophy by the analytical method." This turns out to be a very old friend. It is the method we use in everyday life, to reduce a problem to its elements, and then see what these amount to when recompounded. All we have to do is to analyse terms into their ultimate constituents. Thus an unjust act is seen to mean an act against law; and law is resolved into the command of one that hath power; and power is derived from the wills of those that set it up, their object being peace; and that this is so, every man may know by simply looking into his own mind. We have thus got back to our first principle in politics, self-preservation, and then from this everything follows deductively by irresistible short steps as in a proposition of Euclid. This air of irresistible deduction is immensely assisted by Hobbes' inimitable style, its lucidity, its logical fearlessness, its terse felicity of phrase. No one ever realised so well what Machiavelli meant when he said, " Penetrate the actual verity of the thing itself, and be content with no mere imagination thereof." He sees everything in sharp outline. There is no haze, nor any perspective. The science of state ceases to be a mystery ; it has to drop what he calls its jargon. Politics become a matter in which any plain man can get to the bottom of it, if he will only think clearly and use his terms consistently. No new terminology is required. There is no need to call in the expert, whether lawyer or divine. We have politics set free from theology and from jurisprudence as from metaphysics. This was a great achievement. After a course of the treatises of that time, it is like emerging out of stale incense into the fresh air. It was the beginning of that literary tradition which has made political discussion a native atmosphere to Englishmen, and to which therefore indirectly we owe the successful working of our constitutional governments, our local institutions, the aptitude of our race for colonisation, and even the solid, almost too solid, qualities of our newspaper Press.

Such a mode of treatment was well suited for the pioneer stage of a new subject. The simplification which later enquirers find to be too simplified, is a necessary stage, the laying bare of the anatomy of the subject. The paradoxes which dazzle the eyes that would fain take a complete survey, had their value by startling the contemporaries out of their dogmatic slumbers. Even manifest one-sidedness effected a hearing for an unpopular side, and forced the orthodox champions to come out into the open.

The method of course has its defects. Civil philosophy cannot be modelled on natural philosophy, then in its infancy ; it can only be so, if ever, by wide and patient induction. But Hobbes had little patience, and no belief at all in this use of induction. In fact, here lies the first gap which a modern eye would note in him. There is no historical method about his line of reasoning, he is almost devoid of a historical sense. And yet here too he started a line of thought that he could not have foreseen. By his insistence on taking men as they are, studying their ordinary actions and motives, analysing the terms and thoughts of common life, he was already giving the lines for the historical method of the next century, as he had himself borrowed it from the century preceding. Are not the " false doctrines" which hamper sovereignty a reminiscence of Bacon's idols which hamper knowledge ? and does not the non-moral Prince of Machiavelli reappear in the *Leviathan,* none of whose acts can be called unjust? We may say that Hobbes founded a social science, but not the civil philosophy he conceived, and inaugurated a new method, but not the geometrical method he promised. Further, that abstract man which he set up, the political man, served also as model for another abstraction, destined to be of vast importance, the economic man. The state of nature, translated into economic terms, became a natural order of cut-throat competition. This "economic" man is less of a lay figure. Real men do sometimes act from economic motives alone; whereas social life can never be all deduced from the one motive of self-preservation. Economic motives again are measurable ("how much dost thee sympathise with the widow?"); whereas politics has no such instrument of science in its hands.

To us a written constitution, popular consent, and popular consultation, are familiar ideas. But their appearance as working realities was only made possible by the constructive energy evolved by the Civil War; they were products of the sword as much as of the pen. They came also from the convergence of various influences. Greek philosophy, Roman law, Teutonic custom, medieval readings of Scripture and history, combined to make the idea of contract irresistibly attractive. Feudalism was in essence and origin, contractual. By its code rebellion was often a duty. The very relation of God to man was fitted into this frame of contract or covenant. Jehovah had vouchsafed to make covenant with Noah and Abraham; the chosen people joined themselves in a covenant with Jehovah. This covenant had passed on to the new dispensation. Christians were under obligation to render dues to God as well as to Caesar. But, again, King David had made a covenant with the elders of Israel in Hebron before the Lord, and they anointed David King over Israel; it was easy to deduce that a King is unaccountable for his acts as King. When Kings were becoming each the head of his own Church, this accountability under a covenant was developed alongside, especially in Scotland, where the soil was so favourable to "un-kinging." The "band" was not less a band for being called a covenant. Scots history is a series of biographs illustrating the contractual groups, the revocable compact, the universal "diffidence" which is the seed-plot of society, the actual war or continual inclination thereto, even the "dissolute condition of masterless man." As Puritanism was the Reformation raised to the *n*th, the idea of obligations resting on a covenant with God developed into the doctrine of "tender consciences," and with the "Saints," into anarchy tempered only by revelations.

Of the various forms of Covenant, that of Covenant with God was too much identified with Scots who said "Gude Lard" and lived at free quarters; so that the Covenant of a King with his people came to have the greatest popular effect; this was the formula by which the mass of the nation salved their deposition of James II. Unfortunately, in this form the ruler's own consent seemed to be required to justify a breaking of the compact with him; and this consent could only be deduced from his surrender or his flight; hence the stress laid on Charles' surrender to the Scots, and the clumsy fiction that James II had abdicated.

But at the same time the idea of a covenant between all individuals gained ground with the thinkers; beginning with Hooker, it comes into more prominence with Milton and the Independents; or shedding its theological wrappings, emerges as a purely philosophic theory of society in Hobbes and in Locke.

When we come to the great name of Milton, we have to ask why his political writings count for so little. The answer lies partly in a certain hard aloofness there was about him, partly in his impracticability, as when he qualifies his Republicanism by confining representation to the *pars melior et sanior populi*, or when he sounds his clarion when his own side are already flying from the field. His origin of civil society is that which Hobbes had already given in the *De Cive*, but with the fall of man as a prior cause. He argues that tyrants are lawfully put to death, and rulers are trustees; the people may choose Kings or not, as they please.

His highest note is liberty; he would have no over-legislation, no muzzling of the Press, no state-fed Church, no bondage to ceremonies; the two enemies of religion are force and hire...Christ's kingdom is not of this world...force only produces hypocrites...religion means our faith and practice depending on God alone...was not a voice heard from Heaven on Constantine's donation saying, *Hodie venenum infunditur in ecclesiam?*

In the critical months, when Lambert and then Monck held the balance, Milton tried to make a coalition between the Army and the Council with Republicanism and liberty of conscience as fundamentals, and a remarkable system of decentralised local government; he would concede to the Harringtonians a rotation in the governing body, but would sift the elections to leave only the worthiest; "for by the trial of just battle long ago the people lost their right, and it is just that a less number compel a greater to retain their liberty rather than all be slaves." In trying to combine as he said, democracy with a true aristocracy, he, like Cromwell and like Rousseau, would force the people to be free. But he admits the case is hopeless, and that his pleadings for "the good old cause are the last words of expiring liberty"; that the nation is in a torrent sweeping over a precipice, and that like the prophet crying, O Earth, Earth, Earth, he is speaking only to trees and stones. The lingering hope, "Perhaps God may raise up of these stones some to be children of reviving liberty and lead them back from Egypt," was to be fulfilled, but not till a generation later.

An opponent who admires Milton's style, learning and wit, and

CH. XXIII.

refers to the applause given to his works, yet dismisses their practical proposals as "fanatic state-whimsies of a windmill brain." No doubt like other fanaticisms and "whimsies" they were swept into oblivion down the torrent; they cannot be shown to have germinated in a later age. He was like Cassandra; his oracles came too late; his *Tenure of Kings*, after Charles' execution; his *Defensio Secunda*, when Oliver was pledged to set up a state Church; his letter to Monck, in the weeks when that great man was getting "as drunk as a beast" at City companies' dinners; his second edition of the *Ready and Easy Way* was issued when Monck had already got Charles' letters in his pocket.

Violent, unpractical as Milton's tracts often are, they are never without a depth of thought and a magnificence of diction that make them not unworthy of him, and they have passages which are truly Miltonic. His mind has such an intensity and such a reach of vision, that he rises high out of the mere circumstances to the loftiest principles. He is a democrat who demands of the people to submit to the wisest and best men. to raise government beyond popular mutation, and to elevate civic duty into religion; and of religion he demands that it shall purge itself of all contact with material interest and all temptation to support itself by force. His tracts remain in some respects the most interesting, the most heroic of the countless productions of this prolific and heroic age. He is the best example of the stirring of men's souls to their very depths by the great issues of the time; the pitch of self-sacrifice to which they rose in devotion to their ideals, the foundations of the democratic movement in new religious conceptions.

Harrington had an influence somewhat beyond his real weight both in his own day and a century later. Not that Englishmen are apt to fall in love at first sight with Utopias. But the characteristic of Harrington's ideal kingdom is its almost prosaic practicability. His object is to drive home certain laws of politics. The first is the law of rotation, typified by the orange tree which bears leaves, blossom, and fruit, all at once. In the Senate and Representatives, in the great Councils of State, War, Trade, Religion, in all lesser offices, one-third retire yearly. It is the circulation of the blood in the body politic and is secured by the ballot "to which Venice owes her 1300 years' life."

The second law is that which prescribes a Commonwealth of God's making, not the mere work of man. In fact, England is a Commonwealth already. Popular election, even extending to jurors and militia officers, is to be the great remedy against "interests" such as that of the clergy, "those declared and inveterate enemies of popular power," or the lawyers, "armed with a private interest point-blank against the public."

The third law is the "Agrarian." This is founded on another great discovery. Power follows the balance of property, especially of landed property. Harrington's Agrarian means a Republic based on land, landed estate being the qualification for all offices, but that land divided equally among the sons and no estate allowed above £2000 a year. A territorial army, the officers of which are elected from the gentry of each county, will be a safeguard not a menace to liberty.

But there was to be a form of public national worship, such that all Christians could take part in it. Here was an attempt to reconcile the old conception of a State acknowledging a uniformity in worship, with the irresistible pressure from the growth of sects and from the force of events making for liberty of conscience. An impracticable attempt, all religious partisans will unite in calling it; but a bold attempt and a generous one.

It is a peculiar point in *Oceana* that the Senate alone can initiate, and the representatives alone legislate. For this, and for the further attempt to make an absolute incommunicable division between the functions of government, legislative, executive, judicial, we may blame that kaleidoscopic time and the longing to get peace between Army, Protector and Parliament by a mechanical device.

After much commendation of Harrington and some criticism, his acutest reviewer, Wren, with remarkable clearheadedness observes that the contention between *Leviathan* and *Oceana*, whether it is power or property that is the basis of society, is immaterial, as the one comes to the other; that though Harrington professes enmity to Hobbes, he has really "swallowed many of his notions," that it would be impossible to fix an agrarian limit; that the Rota is a false principle of keeping political wisdom in a perpetual nonage; that an absolute libration or balance of social forces is as chimerical as perpetual motion. To a modern mind the most fatal blots in Harrington's scheme are his excessive belief in political machinery; his weakening of the executive, and his hopeless dissociation of the different functions of government. His influence however from 1656 to 1660 can hardly be over-estimated. To men storm-tossed in the sweltering turmoil of that time, he seemed to offer close under their lee a vision of a blessed country, a land of ancient peace and religious tranquility. During the last three months (July 6 to October 13) of the restored Rump, Harrington's followers petitioned Parliament to start on his scheme at once; while nightly meetings of the Rota Club were held with very full meetings (September, 1659, to February, 1660), which found it "very taking doctrine," as Anthony Wood reports. "The greatest of the Parliament men," he goes on, "hated this rotation and balloting as being against their power"; nor could the Rota men carry it with the new Committee of Safety, when this took up again the old task of framing a constitution. With the advent of Monck the *Oceana* model fell to earth.

The permanent contributions it left to English political theory were in the direction of religious toleration, and the separation of functions of government. But Harrington's ideas had a remarkable renascence in the constitution of the United States of America, which adopted his principles of rotation in office, and residential qualification, his severance of the executive from the legislative body, his belief in machinery, his use of indirect and secondary electoral bodies, his spirit of extravagant optimism as to the working of popular government; "the people's interest being to choose good governors, they may be trusted to do so."

Yet there had been withal a strong aristocratic element in Harrington's republicanism; everything depended, he thought, on the natural aristocracy within a democracy being allowed to rule, and it was to secure this that he had insisted so much on a universal national education, and on complete liberty of individual religious opinions.

The Restoration period is superficially a reaction towards authority, conventionality, materialism; but this is rather the superficial than the real character of the period. On a deeper view it is a long pause, to allow of settlement and digestion, to allow a general infiltration of the great movements. Thus it was that the literary activity under the last two Stewarts was not one-fourth of that amazing output of the twenty years, 1640 to 1660. The great literary names are those of men who had grown up in the intenser atmosphere of the earlier time. The energy evoked by the great events of that earlier time, and by the searching controversies which laid bare the very foundations of politics and religion, now passed off into scientific enquiry, into industrial, commercial, and agricultural enterprise, into economic and financial speculation. Political writing represents only the eddies and coming to rest of the old currents of thought. The heart is gone out of journalism, and the new censorship and Press Acts were like calling in the military when the crowd had dispersed. Even the bitter anti-Puritanism of the first years of the reign dies out into mere cynicism and disgust as it realises that worse even than a rule of saints can be a "fatal brand and signature of nothing else but the impure" (Butler).

The first notes of a call to arms against militant Puritanism had been sounded even before by the foreign writers, Saumaise and More. Hudson, in 1647, had depicted kingship as accountable only to God, who has made a covenant with the people that they are to obey His representative. Sancroft, in 1652, had traced the troubles to "modern policies taken from Machiavel, Borgia, and other choice authors"; Heylin, to Calvin, when he laid down that magistrates of popular election can interpose to check a King's arbitrariness; which "all our later scribblers have turned into a maxim that we must procure the peace of Sion by the fall of Babylon." Wright, in 1656, had made a violent attack upon Presbyterian and Independent preachers; "these God Almighties of the pulpit" who called impudence "inspirations," and ignorance "the Holy Spirit"; preaching was a mere knack which any barber, shoemaker and tailor can pick up. The Chancellor in September, 1660, had said that religion was nowadays made the ground of all animosity, hatred, malice, and revenge, and godliness measured by morosity in manners and affectation in gesture; and a certain doctor of divinity dubbed "the Godly party" as a congregation of Satan. Others fell foul of the Barebones Parliament, "that sorry rebaptising conventicle of mechanical unqualified persons"; or the cry of "tender consciences" ("We were not allowed to have consciences at all, but only stomachs to swallow covenants and subscriptions"). Others ridiculed the hypocrites who make long prayers a preface to the devouring of widows' houses; or asked, Where are now your "Providences"? Heylin sketched the History of Puritanism, 1536 to 1647, especially the greed, opinionatedness, and rebellious humour of the Scots, with a bitterness that almost amounts to literary gift. The author of the *Rebels' Plea*, a criticism on Baxter, put the same views more ably and fairly; Who ever saw a copy of the social contract? Do not the writs show Parliament is called only to give advice? How can sovereignty be divided? *The Old English Puritan as no enemy to kingly power* is interesting as a temperate tract on the other side. As to unjust laws, he would submit passively, saying, "*Vincit qui patitur.*" "I appeal to all who witnessed their way of life."

Another moderate view is put in *The League illegal, or the Covenant examined*, which admits that if one side appealed to loyalty and conscience, the other could at least appeal to liberty and estate.

But the rising tide soon drowned such voices of sense and justice. Puritanism was not argued down but simply lived down. "It seemed as if virtue were forbid by law." "The streets are become like Sodom." "Drunkenness, swearing, and whoredom are now modish." These descriptions come from the scholar Evelyn, the Quaker Fox, and a royalist preacher respectively. Those "resolved villains," Harrison and Okey, had in their dying speeches prophesied a resurrection of "the good old cause," but they foresaw there was to be an inundation of Antichrist meantime.

The revival of the alliance between hierarchy and monarchy is celebrated by a rush of pamphlets in 1660. *The dignity of kingship asserted by G. S.* still has hesitations, and is anxious to prove that kingship will not necessarily bring episcopacy with it. But already in 1658 Heylin had gone further; the legislative power lies with the King alone, no part of sovereignty is invested in Parliament. And this rapidly became the dominant tone. *The sovereign authority of the people, and the natural liberty of free-born fellow-creatures* was "cant, the cant of our time" (Ford). One sermon boldly said, Disobedience is a sin, whether active or passive. Others were content to say, We can only refuse if the act is expressly forbidden by God's law; leaving in pleasing uncertainty who is to be judge whether such a case has arisen. The old tracts were reprinted exalting the kingly power all but to a level with the Deity, "Were not the King a God to man, one man would be a wolf to another."

The royal supremacy in ecclesiastical causes has to be asserted against the Presbyterians, says a preacher, as much as the existence of monarchy against the Independents, or the existence of laws against the Anabaptists, or the existence of religion itself against Atheists. The King is the Atlas of the moral world, says another; he beareth not the sword in vain, and this text becomes a pulpit commonplace against "Fifth Monarchists, Levellers, English Mammalukes, and Scottish enthusiasts." "The magistrate's halter scares more than the minister's hell."

In Mackenzie's *Jus Regium* (1684) a lawyer came to aid in beating the drum ecclesiastic, and proved the absolute power of monarchy from the law of God, the law of Nature, the law of Nations.

By 1684 Non-Resistance holds the field and thrusts contemptuously aside "those who argue that absolute obedience was only a duty in the earliest days of the Church, and who cover all up with Glory of God, Purity of Religion, Liberty of Conscience, Property of the Subject and so forth." It was certainly high time for the clergy to have a rude awakening; and a better man for the purpose could not have been imagined than James II.

"1680, origin of the Whig party" seems almost as fixed a point as "1066, Norman Conquest." But the Whigs were simply the country party formed that day in February, 1673, when Parliament by passing the Test Act and forcing the King to recall his Declaration of Indulgence, made the approximation to the Dissenters which ultimately brought about the Revolution. Whiggism has been not unjustly described as " Puritanism and water"; and its origin therefore goes far back. Thus the issue whether monarchy is of Divine Right or is from the people and conditioned by a pact, is clearly put between two disputants writing in 1643. In Selden's broad and reconciling mind, both aspects are found together; kingship is divine, and based on patriarchy; yet a King is a thing men make for their own sakes, granting him privileges on condition that he guards their liberties; the moment he neglects this, the privileges are forfeit, and he comes within the power of the law. A Parliamentarian but no Republican, a constitutionalist but not a pedant, a latitudinarian without being a Hobbist, monarchical without allowing irresponsibility, he combines already the features that make up the Whig of 1688. The same balance appears in an obscurer author (Ware); while Prerogative is a "tuber," privilege of Parliament may also mean corruption; the foundation of all government being the people, these may choose, change, or regulate their government and hold their ruler to an account. Or again, in a pamphlet of 1648, we seem already to be listening to the cool reasonableness of Locke; "nothing man more abhorreth than government without consent....Rulers are by God's will but are accountable to man, God creating the office, man setting its limits...good or ill government depends on administration far more than on outward form....The worst of government is far better than none at all....That the origin of government is the people, does not make democracy more 'natural' than any other form....We must remember all checks are only preventive of bad, not creative of good, government. For that we must look to a moral change, till then it will be all overturnings, over-turnings, overturnings, till the millennium." Another writer of 1658 remarks that tracing to the people the origin of political power, which had now become the chief maxim in politics, was as old as Hooker; and he harmonises the text "The powers that be are ordained of God," with the view that consent is both the constitutive and the conservative cause of government, by the argument that God's ordination is conveyed to the particular magistrate through the consent of the community. Baxter's reconciliation of liberty with obedience, in his *Holy Commonwealth,* is difficult to follow, because he tries to sit on two stools at once; the magistrate cannot compel men to believe and yet he has to restrain wicked beliefs, such as Popery, and such liberty as is the way to damna-tion. He holds the Whig doctrines of a mixed sovereignty between King, Lords, and Commons, a popular right to select the form of govern-ment, a social contract, in which the people reserved to themselves fundamental rights of which the legislators are the trustees, a nation's duty to preserve itself, the limits to Non-resistance.

But he has also the Whig scorn for "the ignorant and ungodly rabble, the Damn-me's," and for "men fetched from the dung-cart to make our laws, and from the alehouses and maypole to dispose of our religion, lives, and estates"; democracy, far from being God's will, is the worst of all government, for twenty elaborate reasons. He even goes further when he condemns juries ("it would often do as well to throw dice"), and Parliaments ("as such they are neither divine nor religious, Protestant nor just"), and a liberty which "would let in all the sensual gang." His system in fact is a "parity of civil magistrates and godly ministers," and sets up a hopeless delusion; "if the magistrate orders what is evil, we are not to obey"; as Hobbes said, "who is to judge what is 'evil'!"

One way and another it was hardly too much to claim that by 1660 "all good people agree that the people are under God the original of all just authority"; and the work of the last two Stewarts was to convert Cavaliers into such "good people"; for Harrington had shrewdly prophesied, "let the King return, and call a Parliament of the greatest Cavaliers, so they be men of estate, in seven years they will all turn Commonwealth men." By this he meant Republicans, and he was not far wrong, only that the Whigs found a way, as a preacher said in 1662, to balance prerogative of Kings, privilege of Parliament, and liberty of subject.

The one new idea that was contributed was the distinction between the King as sole executive and the King as partner in the legislation, as is expressed in Burnet's *Reflections*, 1687, "all men are born free, but they compact to form a government....The presumption is always for liberty....All Christians are bound to the constitution as fixed by the laws, and our laws secure property....But our laws also forbid resistance on any pretence; and it is a heavy imputation on our Church that we held these opinions as long as the Court and Crown have favoured us, yet as soon as the Court turns against us we change our principles...but Non-resistance is qualified by the need of liberty; that is, we must not resist the King for any ill administration but only if he tries to subvert the laws."

Expressed in another form, this was the justification of resistance as a last resort if the King was manifestly usurping sole legislative power, and this is how the whole Revolution came to turn on the Declaration of Indulgence. By this, as Burnet puts it a year later, and by his encroachment on corporations, the King is usurping the legislative, and this makes that extreme case when the ordinary submission enjoined by Scripture gives way to the duty of defence of religion and property. As in 1640, the constitutional theory had to stretch itself when the matter came to be the defence of religion; religious feeling is a torrent which creates its own new channels.

Cambridge University in 1686 set forth these propositions:
(1)   Kings are from God, their power is not from the people;
(2)   they are accountable to God alone;
(3)   theirs is a fundamental hereditary right.
These may be completed by two propositions from Filmer, another Royalist:
(4)   "Kings are as absolute as Adam over the creatures";
(5)   subjects are bound to absolute obedience, either active or passive, with patient suffering if we are well assured it is a case of obeying God rather than man, and do not pretend conscience for a cloak of stubbornness. Hobbes adds, "To obey the King who is God's lieutenant, is the same as to obey God...we shall have no peace till we have absolute obedience"; quoted by Hobbes from the *Whole Duty of Man*, as the best statement of the Royalist position.

Locke sums up the whole of "this short system of politics" thus: "princes have their power absolute and by Divine Right ever since Adam."

We cannot, with Macaulay, dismiss as a monstrous absurdity a theory which covered all Europe for two centuries, and was held as a passionate conviction by the majority of able and conscientious men. The theory was due to many converging influences. First: at the Reformation, the civil power became rival claimant with the Pope to represent God upon earth; and it had to counter the papal axioms of sovereignty of the people, right of resistance, accountability of Kings, by propositions the direct contrary. Secondly: in England, Wars of the Roses, risings of the Commons, French and Spanish threats, papal interferences, had led to a Tudor monarchy which Bodin could quote as a type of absolutism. Now James I put the finishing touch with his hereditary title ostentatiously, not based on election, and flouting two Acts of Parliament. Thirdly: England also borrowed from France, where monarchy was asserting itself against the Huguenot coalition of feudal, municipal, aristocratic privilege, and against Papist use of theories of social contract and limited monarchy. Fourthly: the theory which James had already expressed in his *True Law of Free Monarchy* throve fast in English air. Churchmen repaid James' " no bishop no King" with their *Appello Caesarem*, and Convocation in 1640 endorsed Sibthorpe's and Maynwaring's preaching, that to resist was to receive damnation. Publicists defined " absolute " as " above Parliament." English law, already " as favourable to Kings as any in the world," seemed to range itself on this side in cases such as Calvin's and Bate's, Darnel's or Hampden's. Chancery was a Court of absolute power, Bacon told James. The history of the word " Prerogative," from 1399 to 1689, covers a great growth in ideas.

The writer identified with Divine Right is Filmer. He had before 1653 written with acuteness and breadth on usury and witchcraft, on parliamentary claims, on the value of Aristotle's politics, on Hobbes and Milton, and on the patriarchal or patrimonial origin of kingship. He is very modern in his use of the Bible, not as an armoury but as a sociological document; in his application of a historical method in politics; in his emphasis on the naturalness of human society. What is at fault is not his claim of absolutism for the State, but the attempt to make monarchy the exclusive form of State; not his derivation of political power from a *Patria Potestas*, but his exclusion of other lines of argument, such as that from Utility; not his parallel of the State to a family, but his slurring over the difference between a State and a family. Moreover to argue that if government was natural it was therefore divine, was really to push the theological basis into the background; and opened a gap at which it was easy for his assailants to make entry. Thus Sidney and Locke are able first to make a very different picture of Adam and the patriarchs; and then triumphantly to ask, What has Adam to do with present day government? and finally to claim Divine sanction for any *de facto* government that answers the test of expediency and Utility. So in a sensible answer to Filmer by Tyrell, *Patriarcha non Monarcha*, it is evident how Filmer's book was at least the occasion of a new method of handling such topics. Tyrell sketches the practical evils that would result from a modern interpretation of absolutism in the hands of an English King; he then remarks that the same powers could have belonged to Oliver, once he had taken the Crown; and asks, How can that be specially Divine which is not for the people's happiness or good? Of history he justly says, History has at least as much to tell of bad rulers as of bad democracies; of scriptural analogies, we must not press too far the letter of such texts as "Resist not evil," "Swear not at all"; and of the whole patriarchal argument, that children's rights rest on an even weightier sanction than parents' rights over children.

The *Patriarcha* appeared at a crisis, early in 1680. Its pithy phrases seemed marvellously apt; such as, "Parliament at first contained no Commons, their privilege must therefore have come by growth, that is by royal grace:…Ecclesiastics, determined to put Kings below the Pope, made secure by putting the people above Kings." His trumpet gave no uncertain sound: "to deem the King bound by laws or by his own oath, is absurd, inconsistent with sovereignty, contrary both to law and to reason." No wonder "the pulpits owned him at once," as Locke puts it; for he popularised the abstractions of sovereignty by making them concrete and personal, and hitching them on to English constitutional history. Divine Right was one way of expressing obedience, orderliness, continuity; it made 1660 and 1689 bloodless revolutions, and saved the throne from a bastard in 1679. Much that it asserted remains true; that the State is divine and above legal limitations; that non-resistance is a duty; that the established succession is a fundamental law; finally, that a true concept of sovereignty is the most essential need in politics.

At the Revolution it was said of Algernon Sidney that "he being dead yet speaketh." But Sidney's *Discourses concerning Government* follow seriatim the arguments of Filmer's *Patriarcha*, who is declared not to have used one argument that was not false, nor cited one author whom he did not pervert; whose conclusions are wicked infamous brutal absurdities, and so on. This plan leads to repetitions. Ahab and Nero, Canute and Clovis, Mazarin and the Emperor Leopold, recur over and over again; and even the chronicle of monarchical scandals from the story of Uriah to the services rendered to the State by their Graces of Cl-v-l-d and P-ts-m-th, comes to pall at last.

But we have here a remarkable contribution to political literature. His range of learning and observation is extraordinarily wide. He throws aside masses of speculative lumber of his own day. His style has great vigour and great variety; he is especially a master of irony; "Filmer might plead his malice is against England and he hurts other countries only by accident: so Brinvilliers meant only to poison her own relations but had to put in the rest of the diners." "Protestantism and liberty will both flourish under a Popish prince taught that his will is law; look at the fatherly care of the Valois Kings to Huguenots, Philip's mercy to Indians and Netherlanders, the moderation of the dukes of Saxony, the gentleness of the two Maries, etc., etc."

Above all, his views are put trenchantly; a King who breaks the law ceases to be King; Parliament is as old as the nation itself; Parliaments are bound to be held annually, if not, a free people may assemble when they please; the people can judge, change, depose Kings. Such propositions hardly needed a Jeffreys to read constructive treason into them. But what cost Sidney his life were his scathing words on the " vermin of a Court " and the way titles were earned nowadays. He had been too stiff a Republican to bow to Cromwell, and his dying speech attested his fidelity to the " old Cause."

Much for which Locke got the sole credit had already been better expressed by Sidney. The state of nature, the surrender of rights, the inference that we can frame society as we will; that changes in the superstructure of government leave the foundations of society intact, and that a revolt of a whole people is not rebellion; many such and many other sentences show how much of the Lockian system Sidney already had struck out for himself. The continuity of thought between the two writers comes out even in small points, as the use of Bellarmin's argument, the citation from the Aragonese constitution, the handling of the text *Redde Caesari*, etc. Sometimes the argument is almost repeated verbatim; *e.g.* allegiance is such obedience as the law requires (Sidney); allegiance is nothing but an obedience according to law (Locke). We find more developed in Locke the theoretic basis of social contract (on which there is a gap in Sidney's manuscript), the division of functions of government, the relation of religion to politics, and the practical rules for future regulation of the constitution. Locke also is certainly more balanced, more reasonable, more respectable, than Sidney; he does not show, and he had no reason to show, the other's bitterness of tone. In Locke Independency is softened into general toleration; and Republicanism is watered down into constitutional monarchy.

English opinion has never been persuaded to declare war on monarchy, to give Parliament irremovability, to accentuate the collision between laws of God and laws of man, or to set up an aristocratic republic. The balance should be put into the hands of those who by birth and estates having the greatest interest, are superior to bribes from a Court, " so that the nobles should not be forced to unite with the Commons to make head against the Crown." This opens an abyss of bottomless Whiggery, and shows us that Sidney, like another and greater exile, would have had to be a party by himself.

The political literature of the last two decades of the seventeenth century all centres about the term Passive Obedience.

The Declaration of Indulgence in 1687 had in its Scottish form boldly claimed " that absolute power which all subjects are to obey without reserve," and Oxford in 1685 had professed obedience without limitations or restrictions. How to pass gracefully in three years from this theory to a practical duty of armed resistance, how to effect a right-about-face so startling, was an interesting question. Any doctrine that could bridge this *impasse* ought to be regarded with gratitude. We should not therefore too ruthlessly expose all that is glaring or even ridiculous about the dogma of Passive Obedience, as it rang from thousands of pulpits and was hammered out in hundreds of pamphlets in these ten years.

Passive Obedience was a sort of political postscript or proviso to the creed of Non-resistance.

It might seem that the Restoration victory had given Non-resistance a fresh sanction. So late as 1684 Bishop Parker was able to say, "Anyone who at any time on any pretence should offer any resistance to the Sovereign, must renounce Christ, the four Evangelists, the twelve Apostles, to join with Mahomet, Hildebrand, and the Kirk." This seems raving, but even so it was a natural revulsion from the still-remembered ravings of Fifth Monarchists. After all, it was only a too robust way of expressing the discovery of a new sanction for Non-resistance, the sanction of experience. This was even more convincing than the theoretic expediency and logical necessity on which Hobbes had relied for its sanction, or that on which Berkeley relied, namely deduction from those laws of nature which admit no exception, or the common lawyers' sanction, that taking arms against the King's person is a "traitorous position." All these sanctions blended in the theory of Non-resistance; and it was the clergy who clothed it in the garb of a divinely-ordered duty, and who in so doing did a good service.

Non-resistance even gained strength after the Restoration, by its being as useful a weapon against Dissenters as against Papists; the rabble defending the faith, like another Henry VIII, would have drawn both sets of rebels to execution upon one and the same hurdle. "The Jesuits are Rome's Fifth Monarchy men." "Presbytery jostles with Papacy for universal supremacy." "They believe in that monarchy for Rome and expect it soon." For what roused the seventeenth century fury of anti-Popery was not papal dogmas such as Transubstantiation, nor papal abuses such as indulgences, nor even Jesuit morality, but the papal claim of the deposing power and the Jesuit principle of Resistance. Non-resistance is not an absurdity, the "fiction of a time-serving hierarchy intent on Court favours." That its chief exponents were the clergy was natural, seeing that the roots of the theory go down to the deepest strata of religion; and besides being natural, the fact was of incalculable importance, seeing that, as a modern writer has observed, the obligation to obedience as a religious duty could most effectively be preached by a body of religious teachers. The question when, how, and how far men must obey, is of all others the question for their spiritual guides to face first. That they made it a rule absolute and without exception was also natural; had they done otherwise they would have been, as the author (A. Seller) of the *History of Passive Obedience* shows, false to their canons and homilies, their great divines, the Acts of Supremacy and Uniformity, their ordination vows, and their own interpretation of Scripture. That they bound up the indefeasible claim of government to our obedience with a supposed indefeasible right of a particular form of government, or even a particular dynasty, was unfortunate, but inevitable, till the events of 1689 had made a severance practicable, and the arguments of Locke had made that severance logical.

When the hope of civilisation lies in rehabilitating and reasserting the State, an undue emphasis on Resistance seems to throw over the State a shade of illegitimacy, even irreligiousness; and if pushed a little further, would lead us not only to the eighteenth century view of the State as a necessary evil, but right back to the medieval view of the State as a sort of kingdom of darkness, an anti-Church. "The private conscience is bound to submit to the public conscience, that is law." In the last resort the choice is between government and anarchy; "without a last resort, there can be no government" (Leslie). It was good that this should be put clearly by the clergy, and not left to Hobbes to preach; that the obligation should be accepted not merely *ob iram* but still more *ob conscientiam.* Nothing can do more to elevate the body of citizens than the feeling that they are, as Aristotle puts it, obeying the reason that is in the law and not merely the force that is behind the law.

The meaning of Passive Obedience and its connexion with Non-resistance is commonly misunderstood. The older writers had demanded Active Obedience; "nothing can excuse us from this, except the law of God or an utter impossibility," Sibthorpe had preached in his famous sermon. But Sanderson wrote after the Restoration that even in doubtful cases Active Obedience was our duty; and where another duty imperatively ordered non-action, this was still a sin. For it was easily seen how a merely Passive Obedience might slide into Active Resistance. But at any rate, if Active Obedience could not be guaranteed in every conceivable case, the balance was to be made up by the absolute inexorable undeviating obligation to an obedience that should at least be passive. This was held up as "the doctrine of the Cross"; the indispensable postulate of government; Parliament affirmed it as a principle of the constitution in 1661, and nearly passed a law in 1665 to impose it by oath.

If some ridiculed it as "a doctrine of the bowstring" and ridiculed as "old Lachrymists" those who would use no weapons against their sovereign but prayers and tears, there were many more who claimed it for the glory of the English Church. Oxford in 1683 publicly committed to the flames the works of Milton, Baxter, Goodwin, Owen, Johnson and others who put forth any of the following doctrines:—That authority is

CH. XXIII.

derived from the people; that there is a compact between a prince and his subjects; that the rights of tyrants are forfeited; that self-preservation is a fundamental law; that the New Testament allows resistance in defence of religion; that Passive Obedience is not obligatory if the prince's command is against the law.

Passive Obedience was a very happy discovery whereby "God's law," Non-resistance, might be brought into a practicable relation to actual life. In fact, Passive Obedience is the safety-valve which alone prevented an explosion. That theory had been "screwed up to the highest peg"; the pressure per square inch was dangerous. Passive Obedience not only allowed for "conscience," but for individual conscience. Resistance had only been allowed to corporate bodies both in Papist and in Huguenot theory. Each was an extravagant way of providing for cases of conscience; using a steam-hammer to crack a nut. Passive Obedience therefore provides an outlet for individual conscience that is capable of much more exact adjustment to the individual as well as infinitely less menacing to the State. The Church in some form was thus the protector and guardian of the individual's rights of private conscience.

The pamphlet literature, then, from the Exclusion Bill to the Bill of Rights may well turn on Passive Obedience. It was this doctrine which kept the gentry and middle class from following the *ignis fatuus* of Shaftesbury, and made possible the remarkable rally of the Crown in the last years of Charles II. It was this doctrine that left to the clergy a back-way out from that absolute Non-resistance to which James fondly imagined them pledged; and so imagining he plunged obstinately along his fatuous way. It was this doctrine which enabled the clergy to refuse to publish the Declaration of Indulgence; a doctrine "providing for revolt" as their detractors sneered, but only for revolt in the very last resort, when they saw that principle of submission to the State, which had been forged as a weapon against Rome, now perverted into a tool of Rome. Finally this doctrine made them hold out till a concurrence of conditions had appeared which never before or since had been combined in a revolution; till they could plead the will of God manifested first in practical unanimity of the whole nation; second in William's right of conquest, the more indisputable because bloodless; and third, above all, in James' "abdication" by his flight. Hence the importance attached to what seems to us this somewhat clumsy fiction of an abdication, and the dismay when the well-meaning fishermen of Sheerness, all unversed in metaphysics, dragged James back again for a while.

Even so, there was a high-minded group who could not stretch Passive Obedience to cover a transfer of allegiance. Had the Non-jurors not acted with scrupulous restraint, had the mass of the nation been more logical, the schism might have overthrown the new Constitution, and the Jacobite cause might have had a very different history.

The weak point in Passive Obedience is that it runs into Active Resistance; and modern malcontents have ingenuously illustrated this by calling themselves Passive Resisters.

As Hobbes said, they plead " Obey God rather than man ; that is, obey their interpretation of Scripture rather than the law's interpretation of it." " He that means his suffering to be taken for obedience, must not only not resist but also not fly nor hide. Law is a command : how do we obey it if we do not what it enjoins ? How can a thief hanged for breaking laws be said to be obeying them ? The only suffering that can be called obedience is voluntary suffering, that which we do not try to avoid."

" All the compact that is or needs be between the individuals that enter into or make up a Commonwealth is, barely agreeing to unite into one political society." In these words Locke has got almost completely the Contract idea in its true and profounder form; a contract of all individuals or rather of each with all, which imposes an obligation on each as one of a community, which tells each that he is part of a whole and cannot divest himself of his social relations, any more than of his other human qualities. The narrower conception of Contract as a pact between government on one side and individual citizens on the other, was a hereditary defect due to its descent from Roman and feudal lawyers. It was a very imperfect way of expressing the relation of a people to its rulers, and led to much of that confused thinking which makes seventeenth century political literature so indigestible, and which is reflected in the many confused attempts to represent the Crown as one of the three Estates, not to mention the consequent trouble required to get Stewart monarchical theory out of the way along with Stewart monarchs. The brains were out ; but the man would not die so long as he could plead either indefeasible Divine right or indefeasible original contract. But Locke put government in its proper position as a trustee for the ends for which society exists; now a trustee has great discretionary powers and great freedom from interference, but is also held strictly accountable, and under a properly drawn deed nothing is simpler than the appointment of new trustees. For after all, the ultimate trust remains in the people, in Locke's words; and this is the sovereign people, the irrevocable depositary of all powers.

While therefore what was valuable in the doctrine of sovereignty of the people was retained, that on the other side which was narrow and dangerous about the Contract theory could be got rid of; and England, refusing Divine right to any one form of government, set out on the path of vigorous and healthy criticism of its rulers. When the people place government in a new form and in new hands, this is not a reversion to an anarchical state of nature, but the wholesome exercise of an inalienable right and duty.

CH. XXIII.

Government is a trustee for the people. The practical working of this maxim in English politics has been manifold and far-reaching.

First: the inalienable rights with which mankind have been endowed by their Creator (Declaration of Independence, July 4, 1776); the bald citation of this declaration is suggestive enough of Locke's contribution to American Independence.

Second: when "estates, liberties, lives are in danger, and perhaps religion too," the limit is overpast, law ends, tyranny has begun, and resistance becomes a right, nay a duty. No doubt when Walpole found that a rational system of revenue collection was met by cries of "No slavery, no wooden shoes," or when the presence of Presbyterians in Parliament was met by the cry of "The Church in danger," the obstructive capacity of this doctrine was unduly prominent. But all the same it was a balance to the counter-theory of the omnipotence of Parliament, which was being developed by the coincidence of legal theory and historical facts, and that at a time when Parliament was pretty far from possessing those other attributes of wisdom and goodness which ought to be found along with omnipotence. A Parliament which was to a farcical degree non-representative, and of which it was only a slight exaggeration to say that every man had his price; and which was being told by lawyers that it could do everything but make a woman into a man, certainly had to be reminded of other writings which held that it could not tax without consent, nor punish but by legal process, nor elect its own members. It was impossible ever again to have the monarch standing over against the Commonwealth as an equal contracting party. "Absolute monarchy is inconsistent with civil society and is no form of government at all"; "Prerogative can be nothing but the people's permitting their rulers to do things where the law was silent." These are very different from the definitions current half a century earlier.

Third: Locke's people is not evoked just to give the initial push to the governmental machine and then retire to limbo. It is a people which actively chooses the form of government which it thinks fit, and every member of which is free at years of discretion to give his consent or withhold it; which perpetually retains a right of resistance, which is not to be called rebellion. The next hundred years seem to be giving a demonstration of these principles; they provide for an instalment of revolution every seven years.

Fourth: no one could be subjected to authority without his own consent; and as this consent is next to impossible ever to be had, this is "a doctrine which makes the mighty *Leviathan* not outlast the day it is born," unless some other doctrine comes to the rescue. Hence a rule that the majority must include the rest, is the only remedy against instantaneous dissolution; and therefore that the act of the majority is the act of the whole is a law both of Nature and of Reason.

Fifth: the trustee character of all governments entails important consequences as to the division of the functions of government into legislative, judicial, executive. To combine these functions in the same hands is a temptation too great for human frailty. This separation of the functions of government constitutes one of Locke's most permanent contributions to politics. It became an axiom with English politicians. Montesquieu canonised it: Blackstone made it part of the education of a gentleman. Even Hamilton dared not boldly throw it aside. In our English world it has tended to set up friction as to the political ideal, and suspicion as the proper attitude towards an executive. It has obscured the common ground that conjoins the different spheres of governmental action, and substituted an illusory theory of water-tight compartments. It has resisted the acknowledgment of a true doctrine of sovereignty as one and indivisible, and so delayed the advent of centralisation and efficiency. It has diverted attention from the real centres of gravity in our politics, the Cabinet and the questions asked in the House of Commons. Under the hallucination of this theory, the eighteenth century was haunted by three great bogies: the growth of a Cabinet system, the growth of a National Debt, the retention of a standing army; just the three things which guaranteed that government should not override the national will.

It is a suggestive fact that Locke's two treatises on Government were produced in 1689. For Locke was to serve as the Bible of the Revolution. It would have been infinitely worse for the nation had the choice seemed to be between reason, conscience, honour on one side, and mere material interests on the other; it would have made the era of the Georges a veritable " pudding-time " indeed.

To compare Locke with Hobbes in the matter of style would be cruel. Locke may have written " a treatise to which no other ancient or modern is comparable in influence " (Blakey); Hobbes may be " the author of a political and moral system which sears the heart " (Hallam); but he is the author of a style never equalled in English for combination of lucidity, terseness, pungency. Not that Locke always fails to reach the high standard of the seventeenth century in force of expression. His definitions are often pointed, suggestive, excellent; " Passive obedience was what Ulysses no doubt preached in Polyphemus' cave "; " Learning and religion shall be found out to justify all a monarch shall do to his subjects "; " Truth is the seed-plot of all the virtues "; " The people are more disposed to suffer than to right themselves by resistance "; " In most things 99-hundredths of the expense is the labour." This common sense raised to a point at which it becomes luminous is the light which he turns on to dispel many of the old difficulties that had haunted men; Divine Right, prerogative, paternal power, the natural equality of men, the coexistence of individual property and common, the coexistence of a stable society and free political criticism. It may

CH. XXIII.

even be said without paradox that Locke saved much of Hobbes by removing the exaggerations which by this time had put his writings out of circulation; for men were bound to recoil from such a chain of reasoning, however flawless the links, when they saw arbitrary imprisonment and cessation of Parliaments were pooh-poohed as mere "inconveniences," ship-money levied by precedents of Æthelred's reign was justified under threat of anarchy, the clergy were reduced to gramophones, and conscience diagnosed as a sort of indigestion.

But in this comparative estimate there is another side to the shield. Hobbes was far sounder in regard to a historical basis of the social contract. He dismisses the question rather cavalierly, "Whether there ever was a time when these things were generally so?" But at any rate his whole system stands independent of historical basis. Locke cannot help hankering after such a basis. What he contemptuously calls "the mighty objection," where are or ever were any men in such a state of Nature, he thus answers: first, that rulers of independent governments are in such a state: second, that all men remain in that state till they form a politic society. So, to the demand for instances of a social contract in history, he refers to the beginnings of Rome and Venice as evident matter of fact, not to mention "those who went away from Sparta with Palantus"; he refers also to men who still live "in troops with no government at all in Florida, Brazil, and many parts of America"; and sums up that all history gives either plain instances of foundation in contract or manifest traces of it; that in fact, all lawful governments began in this way; the only other origin being force. He is even bold enough to be confident that governments had at first a "golden age" of innocence and sincerity, when rulers were nursing fathers and subjects less vicious, and therefore there were no contests between rulers and people.

In many respects Locke gathered up and handed on to the next century those parts of the intellectual revolution of the seventeenth century which were destined to be most permanent. Thus he even exaggerates the claim of the individual, that "freedom" which had become almost a cant term; each of his works is a defence of the individual's liberty—religious liberty in the *Letters on Toleration*, political liberty in the *Treatises on Government*, and intellectual liberty in the *Essay*.

He, therefore, fully shares the seventeenth century impatience of all medieval and even of more recent authority: "we cannot see by another man's eyes," and "masters take men off the use of their own judgment." If Hobbes said that, had he read as many books as other men, he would have been as ignorant as they, Locke went further and said he had not read Hobbes. But this was to foster an English contempt for the "learning" belonging to a subject, an English confidence in "the plain man" and the light of Nature. This was so far a wholesome reaction from the wearisome parade of authorities legal and historical, the deadly monotony of Solon and Numa, Cicero and Ulpian, which reaches a climax in Prynne, who pours out whole dust-bins of such learning into his margins.

But to lay down that in our enquiry after knowledge it concerns us not what other men have thought, was a flagrant contempt of the historical method and a presumption that there is no such thing as evolution in politics, the practice or the theory. The fundamental axiom of modern political science tells us that the present is rooted in the past; and Burke's contention that there are no new principles to be found in ethics or politics, is hardly further from the truth on one side than is Locke's contention on the other.

Locke also represents a reaction from the extravagant use of the Bible in argumentation. Puritan Scripturalism had clothed everything in Bible language and referred every controversy to biblical decision, till even contemporaries had grown weary, after some fifty years of Jephthah and Meroz, Israel and Amalek.

The great tenet of religious toleration was put by Locke on many grounds and expressed in many ways. Religion is a man's private concern, his belief is part of himself, and he is the sole judge of the means to his own salvation. Persecution only creates hypocrites, while free opinion is the best guarantee of truth. Most ceremonies are indifferent : Christianity is simple; it is only theologians who have encrusted it with dogma. Sacerdotalism, ritual, orthodoxy, do not constitute Christianity if they are divorced from charity. Our attempts to express the truth of religion must always be imperfect and relative, and cannot amount to certainty. Each of these propositions may be found in writers anterior to Locke or in his contemporaries; but it was Locke who first combined them all and drove them home to his own generation; and thus it was through Locke that the eighteenth century gradually became possessed of Cromwell's sense that things spiritual can only be brought home by light and reason, Milton's confidence that truth will emerge victorious, Harrington's idea of a national worship supplemented by free private rites. In fact it was Locke who did most to make toleration the practice and comprehension the ideal of the most thoughtful men. Puritan opinion, whether Presbyterian or Independent, sharply divided religious from civil society without very clearly defining which was to ride in front, as Hobbes puts it; and to this division Locke had inclined in some of his earlier writings. But in his more settled view, this division was replaced by alliance and harmony; Church and State can be united if the Church be made broad enough and simple enough, and the State accepts the Christian basis. Thus religion and morality might be reunited, sectarianism would disappear with sacerdotalism; the Church would become the nation organised for goodness. A noble vision, but, " Who is to ride in front ? "

CH. XXIII.

Here however lies in outline the eighteenth century tendency to reduce religion to "cold morality," to emphasise the "reasonableness of Christianity," to make faith a balance of probabilities, and creeds a matter of individual choice.

Finally, Locke is the precursor of Bentham. To say so much is to indicate a great movement which, counting to the date when John Stuart Mill adopted Elijah's mantle, was dominant in English thought for 150 years. In Locke's ethics, rules of conduct are merely means to the happiness of the individual; in his politics, forms of government were merely means to the happiness of the governed; and in each case, the test is experience, how much happiness does each secure? This test even claims a Divine sanction; "at the right hand of God are pleasures for evermore; and that which we are condemned for is, not for seeking pleasure, but for preferring the momentary pleasures of this life to those joys which shall have no end." "God has by an inseparable connexion joined virtue and public happiness together; that which is for the public welfare is God's will." It is hardly possible to exaggerate the influence of this conception of utility; as Maine says, it made the good of the community take precedence of every other object, and there is no single law reform effected since 1817 which cannot be traced to it. It did more than suggest and stimulate reforms, for it supplied a ready test of all legislation; does this law demonstrably do good? Hitherto, the only question asked was, does it correspond with the law of God, the law of nature, the fundamental laws of the kingdom, or some such *à priori* standard? But now, does it do good? Can we prove this? Here we have in germ the whole modern science and art of legislation, the apparatus of commissions, blue books, statistics. The energy of legislation means the community vigorously adapting its environment; it is the measure of its civilisation.

In more than one respect Locke's Utilitarianism marks the transition from a heroic age to one more sober but more prosaic. But there is one respect that is very significant. Locke might be called the prophet of Property. Man has a property in his own person, and therefore in the work of his hands. It is his because he "hath mixed his labour with it, and thus removed it out of the common state." To preserve his property is man's right and privilege by the law of nature; to ensure the better preservation of it is the motive and origin of civil society. Property includes lives, liberties, estates. The supreme power of a Commonwealth cannot take a penny from a man without his consent. Violation of this right of property is a breach of trust, and justifies the institution of a new government. This is a profound truth; property is a necessary part of personality. Hobbes had denied any right of property as against the sovereign. Locke's view expresses another and equally necessary side of the truth.

Thus the head-lines of Locke's bequest to the eighteenth century are indicated by the words Individualism, Reason, Utility, Toleration, Property; all of which words might be summed up in the first of them. No wonder that the century witnesses in England the rise of a gospel of self-interest which made the wealth of a nation consist in setting the individual free; and in France that Titanic evolution of the pent-up force of the individual which made the French Revolution so epoch-making.

A long pause for digestion and assimilation—such is the main character of the reigns of William III and Anne. The assimilation was not a peaceful process; what the Revolution really did was to lay down the lines of settlement for the next generation to work out, not without dust and heat. The lines of force, then, along which the political writing and action of the period arranges itself, are the following. The first need to be satisfied is political stability. "We are all in the ship and must sink or swim together; that I don't like the crew, is no reason to sink the ship....I go along with every Ministry so long as they do not break in our laws and liberties." This sounds such common sense that we hardly realise how it had cost twenty-one years of bitter experience of strife since 1689 to bring it home even to so clear a mind as Defoe's. The next need was to accommodate new ideas to the old forms. Somehow, monarchical executive, a royal prerogative, an established Church, must learn to make room within themselves for theories of a sovereign people, a trusteeship of government, religious toleration. Such a task is always difficult; but to avoid a rupture with the past has always been the good fortune of English political progress; it has made change slow—perhaps too slow—but it has made it part of an ordered growth and saved us from the recourse to cataclysms. The next task which this period had to accomplish was to set party spirit in its proper place. Parties were violent because they were young; and they had to buy their own experience, to work out their own way to clearness and to a *modus vivendi*. It needed all the party agitations of the next twenty-five years to hammer home the philosophy which underlay the Revolution, to translate into practical terms the ideals put forth by Sidney and Locke. We must look indulgently even on Seymour and Sacheverell as the alarums which kept our unphilosophic race from turning aside too soon from those abstractions and those theorisings on sovereignty, obedience, government, toleration, to which they had had to give ear when seeking escape from Popery and James II.

Further, we ought to realise that only slowly in this period was the party system allowed its proper corrective—responsibility. None of the writers, none of the statesmen, saw the absurdity of having one party supreme in the legislature while the other retained its predominance in the administration. Tory majorities raved in the Commons, because they could not get at a Whig Ministry outside. This absurdity was due to the age being so possessed with the conviction that the three great functions of government were to be kept as separate and independent as possible. Such an elevation of the administration above the party system certainly gave more opportunities to the Crown, which could also make use of the balance and alternation between the two parties; and so far it was a good thing, for the Revolution had threatened to bring too great and too sudden a diminution of the central executive power. But the separation of functions also laid open this central power to all party rancour and violence. Therefore, one of the most important developments in practical politics during this period was the evolution of that constitutional creation, a parliamentary Ministry. All this provision of due scope for the party system had been ignored in Locke's scheme, and its full importance was not realised till Burke. Yet Locke's theory of the trustee character of government and his declaration in favour of representative reform required to be adjusted to the new facts involved in the formation of two great permanent parties. Instead of a water-tight separation between legislature and executive, what was wanted was a closer connexion between them, so that a great change in popular feeling should be reflected in both simultaneously. This is now done by the Cabinet at once being the executive organ and having a party majority in Parliament. The party warfare from the Revolution to the death of Anne was, therefore, not the mere venom and futility that it seems, but a necessary stage towards a great result.

Of Whig principles the most thorough-going exponent is Defoe. "Parliament has often harmed the country, but *vox populi* saved it"; and against a tyrannous legislature, traitorous factions, persecuting high-churchmen, he appealed to the Crown as the representative of the people. Unite these two elements as he wished them united, and you have the Patriot King—a conception very much in the air at the time, as may be seen from Burnet's epilogue to his *History*.

To political theory his chief contribution is his tract of 1701, *The Original Power of the Collective Body of the People of England*, which Chalmers pronounced to be equal to Locke in reasoning and superior in style. Defoe himself makes no secret of his debt to Locke, from whom he takes almost verbatim his four maxims: All government is to secure the property of the people; a government which acts ill ceases to be a government; no representatives can claim to be infallible; the legislature's enactments must be tested by reason. There always remains a supreme power; the division of functions into three streams implies a prior fountain; the fountain does not give up all its waters at once. He often quotes his own line, "then power retreats to its original."

The anti-Lockians are important rather as politicians and as pamphleteers than as affecting political theory save in the way of friction. The ablest of these literary Non-jurors, as Dr Johnson says, was Leslie. When Leslie attempts serious criticism, he hits, but not very hard, some obvious weak places; much of his writing, however, only amounts to lively and rather cheap banter: "if silence gives consent, none are so free as the Grand Signior's mutes"; "the Scripture is full of that Divine Right which they laugh at"; "they make God ordain government, but in no particular form at all." He feels, however, that the tide has turned against his party; "the Whigs' pamphlets are tenfold what ours are in number and tenfold in virulence." There is something hopeless, too, about his theory of Church and State, if indeed it amounts to a coherent theory at all. There are, he argues, two separate powers distinct *per se*, not merely by the subjects or cases over which the power is exerted, for there are none which do not come both under the heavenly and under the earthly power. Yet he also says: to call the one spiritual, the other temporal, and then to set Church and State fighting, and to ask who shall be the judge between them, is either malice or ignorance. Church and State are not incorporated but are, it appears, to be regarded as a federal union; there can be no collision so long as each keeps its own sphere. The fact is, the Non-jurors' cause was ruined logically by their practical English sense and compromise.

We must not make too much of Sacheverell and the High Church movement. "The high-bred high-fed high-fliers" rattled the drum ecclesiastic, but it was to cover a retreat or to disguise a losing cause. They contribute nothing to political theory beyond what they had already contributed in the preceding generation. The time was nearly ripe for Burke. All that was needed was someone to awaken the complacent and hard-shelled individualism of the day from its dogmatic slumbers. This awakener was Hume. But, short of originality in theory, Defoe contributed to political progress in almost every other direction. Much cant he laughed out of court; many prejudices he shamed into silence; on fallacies and misrepresentations his common sense came down like a sledge-hammer. The work he did in his numberless writings— some of them, such as the *True-born Englishman*, and the *Shortest Way with the Dissenters*, permanent in their historical importance—the work of writing single-handed the whole of the *Review*, even to the fictitious correspondence, was work of the first value; it was educating a nation into political sense and morality. It was Defoe who applied and popularised Locke, and drove home the philosopher's principles.

In the half-century between the Revolution and the fall of Walpole political life and the conflict of parties had become, as Bolingbroke says, a matter of men rather than measures. And this process went on under the first two Georges, as the Tories shed their October Club elements, as the Pretender came to be "renounced with one voice even by the common people," and as Walpole's jealousy threw all able men into the ranks of the opposition to himself.

Whatever Bolingbroke's faults, it is impossible to doubt the sincerity of his protests against political corruption. It runs through his whole life, his whole works, his private letters, and his private conduct. It raises his rhetoric to the genuine ring of eloquence. It gives him true insight and lifts him almost to a prophetic strain. He foresees a day when the offer of a bribe will be as great an affront as the offer of a blow. Sometimes, he is in despair in face of an evil which penetrates the whole frame of society. " Do you think you can banish corruption and reform the world? You might as well try to batter down the Minister's Norfolk palace with your head." But he goes on all the same, with indomitable energy and an amazing variety of attack, " to trace corruption through all its dark lurking holes."

Bolingbroke has been charged with having no remedy to propose beyond the downfall of his hated enemy. The charge is not quite fair; for he was vehement in urging penalties on electoral corruption, disfranchisement of rotten boroughs, exclusion of placemen from Parliament, full liberty of the Press; besides a total reversal of foreign policy and a more generous colonial policy. It is true, however, that constructiveness was not his strong point. Nor among all that brilliant literary group on the *Craftsman's* staff, was there anyone to be named in the same day with Walpole as a master of detail, a judge of measures, an authority in finance. Bolingbroke did, however, contribute to the *Craftsman* a certain unmistakable sincerity, even a touch of idealism. His aim was to supersede existing parties by the creation of a national party. Existing parties had become utterly unreal, more " factious " with avowed private interests. What was needed was a new conception of patriotism, the union of all in the service of the country.

It is quite true that the Patriots, once in office, were not very different from the jobbers they displaced. But for all that, a new idea, or an old idea with renewed vitality, had been definitely introduced into the arena. Of course, if what he meant was altogether to eliminate party and the party system from the world, no project could be more chimerical, and Macaulay would have had a perfect right to call it a childish scheme of using prerogative to break up parties and defy Parliament. But we may safely say that to call in prerogative to break up parties and defy Parliament was not his scheme.

In the first place, his definition of prerogative is precisely that which Locke and Sidney had substituted for the older royalist definition of an absolute prerogative overriding both law and popular will. The King was to be the most popular man in the nation, to represent the true voice of the people against a debased Parliament, if necessary. The absolute power (he says) that must be somewhere in every government, need not, and with us cannot, be lodged with the monarch alone. It is no weakness for Kings to be subject to limitations; omnipotence itself submits to such. " I neither dress up Kings as burlesque Jupiters nor strip them to a few tattered rags." A true King, a patriot King, in Britain may govern with power as extended as the most absolute monarch, but he must be a patriot, looking on his rights as a trust, and the people's rights as their property. Against the spirit and strength of the nation he must never attempt to govern so as to refuse to change his Ministers and his measures. As he will espouse no party, much less will he proscribe any. He will enlist no party, much less enlist himself in any. In other Constitutions a Prince may have influence independently of the people's: in ours he must acquire it by their affection. Those after me (he says) may live to see a patriot King at the head of a united people. This may be Utopian, and certainly is somewhat intangible. But at any rate it cannot be identified with George III's government by King's friends, and his rejection of the people's Minister in favour of one of "the vain carved things about a Court"; any more than George III himself can be identified with the ideal Prince educating his people out of their prejudices.

In the second place, Bolingbroke's scheme was not to break down party government, but to break down the abuse of party government when parties had sunk into "factions," that is, as he defines faction, a group pursuing private interests. He appeals to a national party, to be created; and the conception of such a national party has been a powerful idea at crises in a nation's life. He complains that the Hanoverian dynasty was from its first accession dipped in the party quarrels of the time; "the King is ours" was the victorious party's cry. What he wanted to form was a coalition of the best elements of either party. He grasped the central fact that there was then no real division of principle between the two parties, and that there was a wide ground which they had in common.

Bolingbroke's aim, the union of all in the service of the State, could not be achieved by his means, the elimination of party spirit and party rivalry, but by its elevation to a higher plane, by the discovery of real and worthy principles of party division, and by the elevation of certain fundamentals outside and above party strife. Foreign policy, naval predominance, have been practically elevated to this position in English politics. Similarly, the maintenance of the federation of the Empire is passing into the same agreed and unassailable position. It seems that civilised communities will tend to increase the number of these axiomatic and sacred subjects.

With Hume's *Essays on Political Questions,* we leave behind the stilted artificialities of Bolingbroke. At one stride we have reached a modern world. We move among ideas that are familiar to us, in a region of expediency and common sense, set forth in a style that the best standards of the nineteenth century cannot surpass for limpidity and ease. The worship of the Glorious Revolution has decidedly cooled, even when we make a liberal discount for Hume's own level-headed personality, the Scottish atmosphere in which he wrote, and his steady pruning of any "Whiggish shoots" in successive editions of his writings. Let obedience be the rule, he says, and resistance the exception; it is absurd to provide for and to propagate maxims of non-obedience. A real Revolution must be a terrible thing; we must not be misled by ours, for 1689 was not the "dissolution of society," but a mere change in the succession, and only in the regal part of that; besides, it was not the work of the ten millions but of the seven hundred who concluded for them. This coolness of judgment in Hume tends to take the form of a general scepticism, as when he questions current assumptions as to national character and the effects of climate and food, or ridicules the fashionable argument that all human actions are reducible to self-love. In the same spirit, he has a keen eye for the absurdities which passed for Roman history, and for the weak points in both the theories of Original Contract and of Divine Right; "a philosophic patriot under William or Anne would have found it hard to decide between the Stewarts and the Hanoverians." To his mind the balance hangs pretty even between the evils of monarchy and the evils of popular government. The one thing he holds in horror is religious enthusiasm, which he defines as a compound of hope, pride, presumption and a warm imagination, together with ignorance. He points out great advances made by modern politics, such as the balance of power, the government by laws, not men, the order, peace, and industry of societies. But, he notes, we have no standard book yet in political science. There will arise such a science, he thinks; but as yet "the world is too young to fix many general truths in politics"; "Machiavel was a great genius; but there is hardly any maxim in his *Prince* which subsequent experience has not entirely refuted." He offers in a scattered form some fundamental maxims, such as that all government rests ultimately on opinion, for mere force must be on the side of the governed; men obey a ruler because they believe it to be their interest and his right, and also from the secondary motives of fear and affection; to make property the foundation of government, as Harrington does, is therefore a very incomplete account; to say that forms of government are immaterial and that administration makes all in all, is against both reasoning and experience. The great aim of all government may be summed up as the support of the twelve judges, or in other words, the distribution of justice; "even the clergy so far as this world is concerned have no other use or object of their institution." In this last maxim we see that we have indeed passed away from medieval views of the paternal and religious duties of the State, and are ready for the *laissez-faire* view and the reduction of the State to a policeman. In this and in other ways Hume shows an insight that amounts to prophecy. He foresees the predominance of the House of Commons, the transformation of Britain into a virtual republic by the development of the delegate theory of membership of Parliament, the disappearance of the factitious distinction between wealth in land and wealth from trade, the rehabilitation of kingship as a constitutional monarchy, the increase of friction in our political machinery, the increase of taxation, the disappearance of slavery in the colonies as economically unprofitable. He predicts that France will become a great republic. Even his judgment, in 1742, that Jacobitism was dead, is not refuted but confirmed on any but the most superficial reading of the '45. The many changes made in the successive editions of his essays measure no doubt the author's own advance in monarchical sentiment; but also may be taken as pointing to a general movement of public opinion away from Whig principles; while the author himself justly claims to trace a general decay of authority, especially that of the clergy, and a general perception that popular government is in danger of turning out to be mob-rule. It is not well to make too much of errors in prevision, but it is certainly instructive to see that even a Hume may be a false prophet; our Constitution has not degenerated into an absolute monarchy, the standing army has not proved "a mortal distemper," nor has the National Debt destroyed the nation. Again, we should demur to the fixing of a near period for the dissolution of a body politic on the analogy of a natural body, and not regard the balance of power as so infallible a rule for international relations; we should hesitate to say that priests always have been and always will be foes to liberty; nor does a union between democracy and religious fanaticism seem likely to wreck society in our time. Hume himself is not exempt from the last infirmity of the theorists; he constructs an ideal commonwealth of his own; it is kindest to say nothing about it.

From the vantage-ground of Hume's final work we look back on 150 years of political theory. A very notable progress has been made in the rise of a historical sense. The great subject of the origin of government is handled on much sounder lines; it is seen to be a thing of slow growth; if consent is still justly taken as its basis, yet room is made for other secondary formations, such as habit; it is seen that most actual States have originated in conquest and have never been built on any formal or conscious consent; it is admitted that we owe allegiance by the mere fact of birth in this or that community, and that we are under an obligation to the constitution under which we are born; we are not to " propagate maxims of resistance," but to make obedience our rule and not hunt out exceptions and excuses from this primary duty. The relation of history to politics is estimated much more fairly; Rome and Sparta, France and Spain, are relegated to their proper place as illustrations. A true historical method is beginning to emerge. All this is a preparation for Burke. So too is the deep sense of the sacredness of established order. We have now for seventy years, he says, enjoyed settlement, with harmony between Prince and Parliament, with peace and order almost unbroken, trade, manufactures, agriculture, arts, and sciences all flourishing; there has been no such period in the history of mankind. Such a pæan shows us Hume as the precursor of Burke, as on other sides he is the precursor of Bentham, of Herbert Spencer, and of Maine.

CH. XXIII.

CHAPTER XXIV.

THE ROMANTIC MOVEMENT IN EUROPEAN LITERATURE.

DURING the latter half of the eighteenth century a fresh current swept through the literature of Europe. The spurious classicism of the Augustan age was everywhere shaken. Everywhere the stream set violently against the ideals of the last generation; it set, in the main, towards what we may loosely call Romance. New ideas thronged in from every side; new imaginative ideals began to shape themselves. This, if we consider the obstacles which stood in the way, is hardly less true of France than it is of England and of Germany; it is as true of Italy, of the Norse countries, of the Slavonic races, as it is of France. The term Romance, however, in this connexion must be interpreted with extreme laxity. And it will be well to indicate at the outset the various tendencies which it will here be taken to imply.

Thus, starting from the bare reaction against the purely intellectual outlook of the Augustan age, we are met, sooner or later, by tendencies so distinct, in some cases so conflicting, yet in the last resort so closely connected, as the following: the cry of long-stifled emotion and of "return to nature," in the most general sense which that phrase will bear; the utterance of individual personality; the renewed love of external nature, and the sense of a living bond between it and man; the reawakening of religion; the revival of humour; the return towards the medieval past; the craving for the remote and the supernatural; the reversion to the ideals of Greek poetry and the simplicity of Greek imagination. One tendency, the cult of realism, must be held entirely apart. For, though in some cases it worked hand in hand with the romantic impulse, it is manifestly of a different origin and sooner or later it was certain to assert itself in hostility more or less pronounced.

The germ of the whole movement, so far as it is to be brought into connexion with Romance, is to be found in the revolt of the emotions against the tyranny of intellect. "Reason" was the guiding star of the Augustan poets, of Pope hardly less than Boileau; and reason, on their lips, was apt to mean no more than common sense, the faculty which may be supposed to guide us in the affairs of daily life. Can we wonder that, after two generations, the world should have begun to question so distorted a view of poetry that a strong reaction should have set in, and that, for a time, something more than its rights should have been given to the element of emotion? It was in Britain that the reaction first declared itself—timidly in the poetry of Thomson (*Winter*, 1726); boldly in the novels of Richardson (1740–53) and in the resounding echo which they awakened through a large section of English society, particularly, as is well known, among cultivated women. It would be a shallow criticism which should find in *Pamela* and *Clarissa* nothing more than the strain of emotion, and ignore the deep knowledge of human character and motive, or the dramatic genius which gives to Richardson's fictions the force and vividness of reality. But the appeal to emotion was the first thing to strike his contemporaries; and in a sketch of the thought and temper of Europe it is the first thing to be recorded.

The influence of Richardson soon made itself felt upon the Continent; and nowhere more clearly, or more fruitfully, than in France. There, strongly as the classical tradition was entrenched, the new leaven was at once welcomed and appropriated by the two most original writers of the time. Diderot in the drama, Rousseau in the novel, gave it applications of which Richardson had never thought, a significance which lay entirely beyond his horizon. No one can read the two dramas of Diderot, or the discourses *Sur la Poésie dramatique* (1757–8) with which they are buttressed up, without feeling that a wholly new spirit is making its way into French literature; that, to an extent even greater than was realised by the dramatist, this spirit was fundamentally hostile to the classical tradition; and that its origin is to be traced to the literature of England and, above all, to the influence of Richardson, at that time its most celebrated representative. The same influence may be traced a few years earlier on the drama of Germany (Lessing's *Miss Sara Sampson*, 1755) and, a little later, on that of Spain (*El Delinquente honrado* by Jovellanos, 1774). In the latter case the emotional strain, which is here raised to the top note of intensity, may be drawn from the French rather than from the English. In the other cases the influence of Richardson, Lillo (the author of *The London Merchant*), and other British writers is direct, and it is openly proclaimed. Among the French, in particular, it gave rise to an entirely new type of play, something between comedy and tragedy, which came to be known as *le drame*. From Diderot onwards to the Revolution, the stream of *comédies larmoyantes* flowed almost unbroken. Sedaine in *Le Philosophe sans le savoir* (1765), Beaumarchais in *Les deux Amis* (1770), La Harpe in *Mélanie* (1770), Marie-Joseph Chénier in *Fénelon* (1793) carried on the tradition which had been founded by the zealous admirer of Richardson. The last two writers, indeed, definitely crossed the border line, in no case very clearly drawn, between *comédie larmoyante* and *tragédie bourgeoise*.

Far more fruitful was the influence of Rousseau; upon the novel in the first instance, then upon literature at large. Neither in form nor in substance could *La nouvelle Héloïse* (1761) have been written as it was but for the influence of Richardson, or again for that of Prévost (1728–40), whose later years were devoted to the translation of Richardson. But an entirely new strain comes into the novel with the appearance of Rousseau; the lyric note, and that sense of harmony between man and outward nature which led him to seek an appropriate setting for the passions that he paints, to interweave the woes of his heroine with a scene which seemed to reecho them from every rock and copse and impressed them indelibly upon the imagination of his readers. *Werther* (1774) in the literature of Germany, Foscolo's *Jacopo Ortis* (1800–2) in that of Italy, take up the double strain; and it is heard again and again throughout the literature of the following century. Few men have done more than Rousseau to widen the scope of the novel, or deepen its imaginative appeal.

The lyric note, which breaks through the prose of Rousseau, had been as much lacking to the poetry as to the prose of the Augustans; and its absence had inevitably been yet more disastrous. After a silence of two generations it is heard once more in the odes and dirges of Collins (1746); with far fuller and richer power in the early songs of Goethe (1770–86); and, yet later, in the magic of Blake (1783–94) and the ringing melodies of Burns (1786–96). There is no need, in this connexion, to point to the specifically Romantic elements in each of these poets. The mere fact that each was essentially a singer is sufficient for our purpose. For it is the revolt of the emotions against the dominance of intellect with which at the moment we are concerned; and the supreme expression of the emotions is to be found in song, in that field of poetry which, however hard it may be to define, the world instinctively recognises as lyric. The absence of such poetry is the worst blot upon the Augustan age; its presence, the first and chief glory of the age that followed.

From the lyric note it is a short step to the expression of individual personality. And, once more, the step was taken by Rousseau. The *Confessions*, the *Dialogues*, the *Rêveries*, all written between 1765 and 1778, are even now the supreme examples of the type. And no writings could more defiantly challenge the classical canons. Henceforth it could no longer be assumed that *le moi est haïssable* to all whose opinion is worth counting. And, within the next generation, the example of Rousseau was followed, with more or less of completeness, by men of tempers so different as Richter, Wordsworth, Alfieri, and even Goethe.

We pass to other, and yet more characteristic, aspects of the movement which changed the whole spirit of European literature and thought; to the impulse which drew men to seek return, at least in imagination, to simpler and more primitive conditions of life; to the renewed love of external nature and the sense of a living bond between it and man. And, here again, we are met by Rousseau. The former of these, the craving for a "return to nature," had already made itself felt in the earlier poetry of Gray, above all in the *Elegy*; under another form, it was soon to appear in *The deserted Village* and *The Vicar of Wakefield*. But it is in Rousseau that it takes the purest and most universal shape; and it is from him that it radiated through the whole literature of Europe. The writings which give the most complete expression to this craving are the two *Discourses* (1750, 1755) and *Émile* (1762). They sent an electric shock through Europe. And the eagerness with which they were welcomed showed that Rousseau had spoken the word in season—the word which all men had unconsciously been waiting to hear, but which none had had the insight to conceive or the courage to utter. The message of Rousseau has its negative and its positive side. In the first instance, it was a cry of indignant protest against the artificialities of an outworn civilisation; in this aspect it led to that revolt against convention which inspired so much of the best literature of the next three generations. The *Sturm und Drang* of Germany, much of what is most characteristic in the work of Wordsworth, Byron and Shelley, much of what is best in the romantic movement of France—all trace their origin to this source. And, though he would have indignantly denied it, there is a curious echo of it in the ideas which inspired the poetry of Blake. The political results of these memorable writings were still more startling; but, for the moment, they fall beyond our scope.

The positive side of Rousseau's influence is, however, yet more important. From the first *Discours* onwards it was manifest that he appealed from the intellect to the emotions; that he thrust aside the rationalist ideals of Voltaire and the Encyclopedists, as one-sided and barren; that, in his view, reason was constituted not merely by the logical faculties acting upon the material offered through the senses, but also and no less by the intuitive power in virtue of which man interprets the blinder and more mysterious promptings of his nature. This was to attack at its very foundation the philosophy of the eighteenth century— the philosophy which, from Locke onwards to Condillac, had been slowly shaping itself more and more precisely. It was also to apply a standard of human worth the very negation of that which, at the time when Rousseau wrote, was currently accepted. The whole body of opinion which had grown up under the artificial conditions of modern society— indeed, of society in all possible forms—was to be swept away. Man was to be taken "as he came from the hands of the Creator." This was nothing short of a revolution; and its significance was at once perceived both by friend and foe. D'Alembert was at first content to remonstrate with Rousseau as an erring, but well-meaning, brother (1751). But remonstrance was soon exchanged for anathema. Kant, on the other hand, dated the great change in the earlier history of his mind from the moment when he learned the lesson of the second *Discours*; and he compared the moral revolution wrought by Rousseau in his "discovery of the deep-hidden nature of man" to the intellectual revolution inaugurated by the discoveries of Newton (*Über das Gefühl des Schönen und Erhabenen*, 1765). With Kant we stand at the fountain-head of modern philosophy. And nothing could illustrate more clearly the significance of the ideas first proclaimed by Rousseau than the supreme value attached to them by a thinker so cautious and so profound.

The reawakening of the religious temper, so characteristic of this period and its literature, is closely connected with the point we have just treated and may conveniently be considered next. The religious revival, as was to be expected, had shown itself in the general life of Europe— nowhere more markedly than in England—before it found its way into literature. And it is probable that Pietism in Germany and the Evangelical movement in England did much to prepare the ground for the reception—perhaps even for the creation—of the new spirit which was just coming into poetry. In any case, it is impossible to overlook the contrast between the hard, the increasingly rationalist, strain of the earlier half of the century and the deep, at times impassioned, religion of its close. The first writer to show the change in a very marked degree is perhaps Rousseau; and, in this as in other respects, he stands in the sharpest possible opposition to Voltaire and the Encyclopedists. *Le Vicaire Savoyard*, which is the lasting monument of this side of his genius, was published, as part of *Émile*, in 1762; and throughout the remainder of the century the chillier vein, represented by Pope at the one end, by Diderot, Helvétius, and Holbach at the other, tends to sink more and more beneath the surface, the religious temper to assert itself more and more unmistakably. The latter appears in two widely different shapes. Under a vague form, merging into pantheism, it is found, to take only a few instances, in Rousseau, Goethe, and Wordsworth; under a distinctly Christian form, again to limit our examples, in Cowper and Chateaubriand. A more complete reversal of the current it is impossible to conceive. During the second third of the century an observer might well have been forgiven for thinking that the end of Christianity—nay, of religion itself in any form that was not either a popular superstition or a purely intellectual formula—was in sight. With the appearance of Rousseau the whole face of things was changed. The religious spirit had once more found voice; it once more spoke with conviction and therefore with authority; and a whole world of thought and imagination was unsealed. No mistake could be greater than to confine the results of this to the direct and avowed expression of the religious impulse. The indirect results, the results both upon speculative and imaginative thought, were yet more important. The whole bearing of man towards the world, and its appeal to his heart and reason, was altered. A new breath of spring had passed into his being; his sense of mystery was quickened; he read more deeply into his own inner life and that of nature; he saw the colour and the movement which form the outward reflexion of that life more vividly and therefore more truly. The whole force of the romantic awakening, as well as of the philosophical revolution, from Kant to Hegel, which went hand in hand with it, is closely connected with this change.

In their more specific application, in that craving for a "return to nature" with which, in part at least, they were bound up, these ideas may fairly be said to have inspired that which is of permanent value in the work of Herder; that which, *Faust* excepted (if indeed it be an exception), is most fruitful and characteristic in the earlier work of Goethe; the early dramas and lyrics of Schiller; the writings of Bernardin de Saint-Pierre and, to some extent, of Chateaubriand; above all, that part of Wordsworth's poetry which is concerned with human life—"the haunt and the main region of his song."

In close connexion with the "return to nature" in the region of human life and of human relations must be taken the renewed love of outward nature which so strongly marks the poetry of this period and distinguishes it so clearly from all that had gone before. The contrast here is not only with the poetry of the Augustan age; that is obvious enough. In a less, but still a very marked, degree it is with the poetry of all previous ages. And that in more ways than one. Not only do natural objects fill a much larger space in the poetry of this age than they had ever done before; but they are brought into a much closer and more living relation with the life of man; the inner harmony between man and nature is more keenly felt, and more truthfully suggested; the varying moods of nature are more lovingly studied; the subtle play of light and shade, of rest and changefulness, without is followed with all the more eagerness under the instinctive faith that these things are in part the reflexion, in part the moving cause, of joy or sorrow, of gloom or confidence, within. And we may trace an ever deepening sense of this bond between man and nature, as the period wears on.

In Thomson, with whom the movement may be said to take its rise, nature is, on the whole, a world apart from man, though rich in interest for him. And Thomson was followed almost immediately by Haller in Switzerland (1729); after an interval, by Bernis (1763) and other descriptive poets, from Saint-Lambert (1768) to Delille (1769–1806), in France. From Switzerland, with contributory aid from England, the new mood of description soon spread into Germany (Kleist's *Frühling*, 1749). It was in Germany, however, that the fashion received its first decisive check; from the hand of Lessing (1766). In England it held its ground much longer. From *The Traveller* (1764) to *The Task* (1785), from *The Task* to Wordsworth's *Descriptive Sketches* (1793), the succession is almost unbroken; though each one of these poems is both more subtle in description, and more abundant in elements which are not "pure description," than those of Thomson. Thus, while

CH. XXIV.

Thomson is commonly content to take nature in her more general aspects, in the broad and obvious changes wrought by the seasons, Goldsmith essays the harder task of seizing that which is distinctive of each different country; and, at least in the case of France and Holland, his cunning has assuredly not failed him. A like attempt, but with a less broad and more elusive landscape, is made by Cowper; and the subtlety with which he renders the rich pastures and winding reaches of the Ouse is a new thing in the poetry of Europe; though an anticipation of it may be found in the prose of Goethe, still more perhaps in that of Rousseau. And the tradition, with a yet deeper faculty of minute and distinctive observation, is carried yet further in the *Evening Walk*, if not in the *Descriptive Sketches*, of Wordsworth. Something of the same advance may be traced in the treatment of atmosphere, and of the magical effects of light and shade, of distinctness and haziness, which depend upon its changes. Here, however, the great step forward was taken much earlier; and, in this point, the *Ode to Evening* (1746) by Collins has probably never been surpassed; or, if surpassed at all, not until the advent of Shelley (*Euganean Hills*, 1818) and, a little later, of Hugo (*Les Orientales*, 1828); though it is only just to mention certain passages of Wordsworth (*e.g. A Night Piece* and the Moon above the mists of Snowdon in the *Prelude*) which, if less delicate in touch, are profoundly memorable as imaginative renderings of atmospheric effect.

More widespread, though not in itself more important, was the growing tendency to "moralise" nature, to weave a bond between her changing moods and those of man, to make her the mirror of his joys and sorrows, of his dejection and his gladness. Under a crude form, this tendency had from the first been latent in the descriptive poets of the period. In Thomson, still more in his French disciples, didactic and moralising passages are inserted at stated intervals among the landscapes and field sports which supply the chief source of inspiration. In Blair and Young, almost to the exclusion of natural description, they form the staple of the whole; and the influence of the latter, great in France, in Germany was immeasurable. It was Collins and Gray who took the first step in advance, who first sought in nature an appropriate background, or a mirror, for the moods and emotions of man. And the *Elegy*, which awoke several echoes both in France and Germany, is the most familiar record of this phase of imaginative feeling. To Gray, however, nature is merely a background for certain human figures and emotions; and the mood which she throws into relief is almost invariably that of melancholy—the mood which, traceable in the last resort to *Il Penseroso*, gave to the whole poetry of that day, above all in England, its prevailing character and discriminating effect. In Collins we find a yet more intense expression of the same mood. But he has more of variety and modulation, he moralises less, he holds the scales much more evenly between man and nature. Something of the same note, but with yet more of modulation, more power to give voice to varying passions, to make nature the echo of the most diverse moods of man, of his joy no less than of his sorrow, was soon to be struck by Rousseau, and after him by Goethe; at a yet later time by Burns, Wordsworth, and Coleridge. And, with each of these writers in succession, the moralising strain tends more and more to disappear, its place to be more and more taken by spontaneous feeling or passion, and nature to be accepted more and more for her own sake, for the readiness with which she takes up the life of man, with all its fleeting moods, into herself, or breathes her own spirit, with all its healing influences, into his. The former is the view presented in Coleridge's *Dejection*; the latter, it need hardly be said, is the prevailing note of Wordsworth. In Wordsworth, moreover, we catch a strain which had already made itself heard dimly in Rousseau, and again, more clearly, in Goethe; the conviction that, behind the "outward shows" of nature, man is able to penetrate to her spirit and, in doing so, to rise to a purer atmosphere, to win for himself "a foretaste, a dim earnest of the calm That nature breathes among the hills and groves." This is the religious strain, the pantheism, to which reference has been made above; the strain which reaches its highest intensity in Goethe and Wordsworth and, a few years later, in Shelley.

So far we have been concerned with the vaguer and less specific springs of the romantic current. We pass now to those which are more intimate and distinctive. And first, the return towards the past and, in particular, the medieval past. Among the least pleasant characteristics of the Augustan age was the contempt for all that was "barbarous" and "Gothic," which was then commonly professed and almost universally felt. In part, no doubt, this feeling rested on pure ignorance. But it is easy to see that, given the "legislation of Parnassus," the antipathy was inevitable; and that knowledge, had it under such circumstances been possible, would, in all probability, have served only to deepen it. It was equally natural that, when the tide began to turn against classicism, men should look to the ideas, the life, the poetry of the middle, and even the dark, ages for inspiration. Adventure, romance, strong and simple passion, the remote, the unfamiliar, the supernatural —all the elements that, on the whole, were conspicuously lacking to the Latin literature which supplied the core of the Augustan ideal, were here found, and found in a form which could hardly fail to captivate men just escaped from the tyranny of Boileau. The first step in this direction, intelligibly enough, was a revival of that interest in Spenser which indeed had never entirely died out. The *Faerie Queene* was full of the ideas and the matter of chivalry; but it was cast in a form moulded by the richest culture of the Renaissance and by a loving study of the great poets of antiquity. Romantic matter, clad in a form the beauty of which

CH. XXIV.

even the most hardened Augustan was scarcely able to deny, and which unquestionably bore marks of the study of Homer and Virgil, of Ariosto and Tasso—here was treasure-trove for those who were moving, not without many misgivings, from the false classicism to the true, from both together in the direction of Romance. The cult of Spenser, doubtless under a hybrid form, may be traced back as far as Prior (1706); but the first worthy memorial of it is *The Schoolmistress* of Shenstone (1741). This was closely followed by Thomson's *Castle of Indolence* in which the vein of mock-heroic, hitherto so often associated with the Spenserian revival, was markedly reduced; and with the appearance of this poem, which has caught the melody, if not the manner, of the original more fully than any subsequent production, the influence of Spenser may be said to have been fairly launched upon its way. It was the lifelong task of Thomas Warton to further it. It appears in the latest poem of Collins, perhaps even in his earlier work; and through Burns, possibly through Beattie also, it was handed down, now raised to a higher power, to the generation of Wordsworth and Byron, of Shelley and Keats.

Admiration for Spenser, however, was but the first step towards the medieval past. And, had the movement stopped there, it would have counted for little in England, for nothing at all upon the Continent. It was once more Gray who made the crucial advance; who opened the promised land, first of national tradition, then of primitive mythology, to the poetry of his generation. *The Bard*, which revealed the treasures of Celtic legend, was published in 1757; *The Descent of Odin*, which did the same service by Norse mythology, followed ten years later. Between these dates had appeared two works which were destined to have a far deeper and wider influence than that of Gray upon the imaginative life of Europe; Macpherson's *Ossian* (1760-3) and Percy's *Reliques* (1765). Round these two collections all in the Romantic movement that belongs to medievalism and much, perhaps most, of that which springs from the love of adventure or of tragic passion, much even of that which embodies the sense of mystery and of the supernatural, may be said to gather. But the fortunes of the two books were curiously different. "Ossian," discredited on antiquarian grounds in the country of his birth, had an unrivalled influence on the whole of Europe. Goethe, Herder, and Schiller in Germany, Napoleon and Chateaubriand in France, Cesarotti, Monti and Foscolo in Italy, Ozeroff in Russia, all drew largely from his inspiration. He was translated, either wholly or in part, by Goethe, Herder, and Cesarotti; by Turgot, Letourneur and Baour-Lormian; while in England, apart from second-rate writers, we have to wait till Byron before his influence showed itself—and, even then, only to a very limited extent. With the *Reliques* it was very different. On the Continent, except in Germany, their hour was long delayed; and, when it did come, came rather through the medium of such collections as Herder's *Stimmen der Völker in Liedern* (1778-9), or such ballads as those of Bürger,

Schiller, and Goethe, than by their own force or because they were widely
known and loved.　Even in their own country their effect was for a long
time much smaller than might have been expected.　They did, indeed,
call out an immediate response from Chatterton (1768).　But, with that
exception, their influence seems to have slept for a generation.　*The
Ancient Mariner* is the first marked and certain sign of its revival; and
they hardly came to their own until they fired and moulded the genius
of Scott.

If we ask what it was precisely that these two collections contributed
to the Romantic movement, the answer is not far to seek.　*Ossian*
appealed to the feeling for the wilder aspects of nature, to the craving
for the mysterious and supernatural, to the sense of " old, unhappy, far-
off things," of the tragedy which lies in the last struggles of a doomed
race; to emotions, that is, which were already in the air, but which were
immeasurably strengthened when they found themselves repeated in echoes
that came, or seemed to come, from the remote past.　The very defects
of Macpherson's *fantasia*, its vague imagery and anglicised rhetoric, were
rather in its favour than against it.　A literal transcript of Gaelic
originals would probably have fallen on deaf ears.　What he actually
gave was sufficiently unlike the poetry of the time to provoke interest
and curiosity, yet sufficiently like it not to bar out sympathy and
admiration.　And it is perhaps significant that the influence of *Ossian*
was greatest in translations of the translation, and, possibly, in those
Latin countries, France and Italy, where the Augustan tradition was
most firmly rooted.　The appeal of the *Reliques* was simpler and more
straightforward.　The love of action and adventure, the joy of battle
and of freedom unchecked by law, the instincts of courage and loyalty—
most of all, perhaps, the craving for strong and simple passion, for the
tragic note which had hardly been heard since the deaths of Milton and
Racine—all these things found expression in the *Reliques*; and, despite
Percy's alterations and adornments, they did so in a style which was
strikingly simple, rapid, and direct.　Can we wonder that, to ears jaded
by a century of Augustan reason and convention, these two collections,
alike in form and matter, should have come as an inspiration?

Three fields in particular were opened out, directly or indirectly, by
the *Reliques* and *Ossian*: the past, the distant and the supernatural.
And in each case the attraction was essentially romantic in quality.　Of
the return to the past—which, just because the Romantic impulse prevailed over all others, for our purposes means the Middle Ages, the ages
above all others of Romance—it only remains to say that, immediately
and in the first instance, it was carried out nowhere but in Germany.　In
France, if we except such forgotten writers as de Belloy and Lemierre,
it plays no considerable part until Chateaubriand, and no decisive one
till Hugo.　In Italy, it enters only with Manzoni; in the Norse countries,
with Oehlenschläger; in Russia, but under a strangely conventional

CH. XXIV.

form, with Ozeroff; while in England, if such subordinate writers as Horace Walpole and Mrs Radcliffe be excepted, there is little or no trace of it between Chatterton and Coleridge; nor does it reach its full importance until Scott. Much the same is true of the search for distant scenes, which may be regarded as a natural offshoot of the return towards the past. Here again, Germany led the way; Lessing's *Nathan*, a somewhat doubtful instance, and the later work of Herder (1798–1802) being perhaps the earliest examples. In English literature, apart from such experiments as *Vathek* (1782–6), there is nothing in this kind until *The Ancient Mariner* and *Kubla Khan* (1797–8); and, in spite of Southey's efforts, the exotic hardly became naturalised till the advent of Byron. In France, once more, the great innovator was Chateaubriand. And with the publication of *Atala* and *René* (1801–2) the quest of local colouring and unfamiliar scenery may be reckoned to have become as much part and parcel of the Romantic temper, as the worship of the past had been from the beginning. The cult of the Supernatural, lastly, was for a long time virtually confined to Germany. Bürger led the way (1774); and, with infinitely more of subtlety, he was followed by Goethe; not only in *Faust*, the beginnings of which must be put back at least so far as 1774, but also in ballads which rather render the workings of supernatural terror on the soul of man than the world of spirits in and for itself. And the same way, at a later time, was trodden by Coleridge. In British literature, Coleridge may almost be called the pioneer, as well as supreme master, of the Supernatural. The theme had been handled timidly by Collins, before the appearance of *Ossian* and the *Reliques*; it was treated vividly, yet with more than a touch of irony, by Burns. The full value was first given to it by *The Ancient Mariner*, which divides the interest almost equally between the terror of the Supernatural for its own sake and the dramatic appeal of "such emotions as would naturally accompany supernatural situations, supposing them to be real." After this poem and *Christabel* (1798–1800), the reign of the Supernatural was fairly established in England. And few were the poets of the next generation who did not, in some form or other, avail themselves of its magic; none, however, with the same confidence and exulting strength which had been shown by Coleridge. In France it can hardly be said to have ever taken root; and when it did appear, as in the earlier poetry of Lamartine, Hugo, and Vigny, did so rather under the symbolism of the Old Testament than under the forms which passed current in Germany and England. Nor was there any other country where it found a soil so congenial as in these.

Among the diverse characteristics of the literature of this period— and it is one which, except in the vaguest sense, has little or no relation to the Romantic spirit—is the reawakening of humour. The later Augustan age had been plentifully endowed with wit; the very name of

Voltaire is sufficient proof of that. But, except in England, it hardly gave birth to a single work of humour. Lesage and Marivaux, in very different ways, present the nearest approach to it elsewhere; and it will be felt at once that the latter at any rate is hardly, in our sense of the term, to be called a humourist at all. With Fielding the old tradition, the tradition which linked humour indissolubly with sympathy, is once more restored; and he passed on the torch to a long line of successors, including Burns in the field of poetry and ending, so far as our period is concerned, with Miss Austen and Scott in that of the novel. In Germany we may trace something of the same revival; who can deny the humour of Lessing, or the strangely different humour of Richter? Of other countries, if we except Diderot's *Le Neveu de Rameau*—and naturalism rather than humour for its own sake is the inspiration of that amazing portrait—the same thing can hardly be said. So that, once more, we are fain to recognise in Germany, and still more in England, the peculiar home of this form of creative energy during the period with which we are concerned.

From humour we not unnaturally pass to the strain of realism which marks this period and reappears, under a far more uncompromising shape, in the century that followed. The part it plays in shaping the thought and method of Diderot has already been noticed; and in him, there is little need to say, it is intimately connected with naturalism, as a philosophical creed. In the field of imaginative work, Diderot found a successor in Restif de la Bretonne (1776-93); and Restif, in his turn, points the way to certain sides—they are not the only, nor perhaps the most significant sides—of the genius of Balzac. The only other literature in which realism makes itself felt during our period is that of England. And here it is curiously different both in origin and character. It has nothing to do with theories of philosophy; and, at least in one instance, it is clearly bent to the purposes of the moralist. The two chief authors, Wordsworth excepted, in whom it is to be reckoned with are Miss Austen and Crabbe. In the former it hardly amounts to more than a resolute determination to paint only those sides of life which observation at first hand had made familiar, and it is guided by an instinct for unsparing selection which goes far to destroy its initial character. In the latter it approaches more nearly to realism, as commonly understood. It is a method of viewing both human life and outward nature; and, as in so many other cases, it goes hand in hand with a mood of remorseless pessimism. Yet, even here, a difference asserts itself. Crabbe, like Defoe, is essentially a moralist. His first object was to protest against the Arcadian pastoralism of Goldsmith and others, to shame rich and poor alike by stripping the tinsel off their vices and weaknesses. In the earlier poems of Wordsworth a tinge of realism is not to be denied; and, as with Crabbe, it is directed by a moral purpose. But behind the misery, which to Crabbe had seemed the inexpiable curse of poverty, Wordsworth hears "the still, sad music of humanity"; and in that music all "harsher" sounds were "chastened and subdued." And his realism is so closely pressed into the service of what has fitly been called the Renascence of Wonder that it has something of the effect of romance. After the *Lyrical Ballads* of 1798 it virtually fades out of his poetry altogether.

Perhaps the most curious of all the currents which go to swell the poetic achievement of this period, and certainly the most difficult to analyse, is the reversion to classicism which has left so deep a mark on the three great literatures of the time. Goethe and Schiller in Germany, André Chénier in France, Collins at certain angles of his poetry and, at a later time, Keats, Shelley, and Landor in England—all these present different phases of the tendency in question. That in all it was a reversion not to the Latin Classicism of the Augustans, but to Hellenism, is sufficiently obvious. And, so far, it was not only compatible with all that we understand by romance—that would naturally follow from the unquestionable fact that many of these writers were essentially romantic in temper—but actually went to swell its force. The plainest proof of this is probably to be found in the work of André Chénier, the least Romantic of the group. For, whatever may be the "true truth" about that great but extremely enigmatic figure, it cannot be denied that he was hailed as precursor by the Romantics of 1830, or that his influence upon the early, and some even of the later, work of Hugo—an influence which is by no means confined to matters of metrical form—was very great. In a negative sense, then, we are entitled to say that, in all these writers, the Hellenic strain represents a reaction, or a continued protest, against the Latin Classicism of the preceding period. How far that reaction had anything positively in common with the Romantic movement, it is more difficult to determine. It is probable that each case requires a separate answer. Thus, with Goethe and Schiller, there can be no doubt that Hellenism meant a conscious and deliberate protest against the excesses of Romanticism, as represented by the whole literature of *Sturm und Drang* and, consequently, by their own earlier productions. At the same time, it must be admitted that in the most characteristic of their Hellenic creations, in *Iphigenie* and *Die Braut von Messina*, the Romantic spirit in its nobler forms, in its inwardness or in its ardent passion, is not only present but does much to inspire the whole. The impulse of Chénier is more purely Greek. Of all modern poets he is perhaps the one who has come nearest to the unrefracted, impersonal, reflexion of the object before him, which we commonly recognise as the mark of Greek poetry and of Greek art in general. This at once puts a barrier between him and the Romantic writers who from Rousseau downwards, and in many cases of set purpose, fuse their material through and through with personal emotion. Yet, here again, it is probable that the poet, so far as outward conditions influenced him at all, was prompted by rebellion not so much against Romanticism as against the moralising and often conventional descriptions of the Augustans. And there are other sides of his genius, his craving for richness of colour and his subtle sense of life in the hidden processes of nature, which clearly stand in close relation to the inner spirit of Romance. With the English poets of the period no doubt of the same kind presents itself. In none of them does there seem to be any opposition between Hellenism and Romance. The former either enters as a controlling force, arranging material which is manifestly supplied by the latter, or it is itself subordinated to the latter, and does little more than yield subjects which the Romantic impulse moulds imperiously to its own purpose. The first statement would be true of Collins; the second, of Shelley and Keats. There is but one of Collins' poems in which the Hellenic, as distinct from the Pindaric, strain makes itself felt: the *Ode to Simplicity*. And, however Greek its inspiration, the whole poem is so interwoven with the promptings and memories of romance, that it should rather perhaps be taken as an instance of the readiness with which Hellenism lends itself to romantic purposes than of any inherent conflict between the one spirit and the other. The flowers, we may say, adapting a crucial verse of the Ode, are to be "culled" by Romance, though the hand, which "ranges their ordered hues," is that of Hellenism. With Shelley and Keats the case is clearer still. Both are apt to select subjects from the mythology or the legendary lore of Greece. But neither handles such subjects in the manner or spirit of the Greek poets. As both poets, however, fall beyond our period, we must content ourselves with one instance: the *Ode on a Grecian Urn*, where the antique figures, Greek as they are in form and posture, speak, it must be admitted, with a voice which comes from the inmost soul of romance.

This sketch began with the return to nature in the field of imaginative thought. It may fitly close with the return to nature in the field of speculation and politics. The fountain-head of the stream which sweeps in this direction, it need hardly be said, is to be found in Rousseau; not indeed in *Le Contrat Social* (1762), which is, in the main, the embodiment of a very different creed; but in *Émile* and, still more, in the second *Discours* (1755), which took the imagination of men captive and effectually shut their ears to the qualifications—we may almost say, the antagonistic doctrine—subsequently put forward by the writer. No writing of this, and few of any other, period can claim to have wielded a stronger or deeper influence than these. Witness the earlier phases of the French Revolution, on the one hand; the early work of Goethe and the whole literature of *Sturm und Drang*, upon the other. These, however, for different reasons fall beyond our limits. Nor is it possible to dwell upon the Jacobin dramas of Giovanni Pindemonte in Italy (1797–1800). It must suffice to pause for a moment on the corresponding movement —a movement too often neglected—in England. This reached its height in the very years of the revolutionary ferment across the water. It is to these years (1790–6) that belong the early, the distinctively Jacobin, writings of Wordsworth, Coleridge, and Southey; the glorification of "nature" as against "art" to be found in the novels of Godwin, Bage and Mrs Inchbald; and, above all, the *Political Justice* of Godwin (1793). If any one book can be said to embody the revolutionary spirit of these wild years, the years of the Jacobin crusade and the anti-Jacobin reaction, it is this strange medley of political, social, and philosophical nihilism which casts a spell over minds so different as those of Wordsworth and Shelley; while even a writer so little given to dreams as Madame de Staël was accused, absurdly enough, of using it as an arsenal of free-thinking ideas. Godwin's argument is full of confusions, and he was the last man in the world to carry uncompromising principles into action. But, as a symptom of the extent to which the revolutionary ferment had spread to other countries, and as the first of a long line of writings which have urged a reconstruction of the social fabric from top to bottom, his book is intensely significant. And the protest raised by *Political Justice* has never fallen entirely silent. Much of it is echoed, and echoed with a far purer note, in the earlier poetry first of Wordsworth, then of Shelley. And, from Saint-Simon onwards, it has become almost a commonplace of European literature and thought. The only other writer of these troubled years whom there is need to mention is Paine; the author of *The Rights of Man* (1791–2), a fiery and, in some points, a not altogether unmerited assault on Burke.

Burke, it need hardly be said, was the deadly enemy of the creed, so dear to the earlier romanticists, which exalted nature above society and found in a return to nature the only remedy for the ills of mankind. Yet, behind these differences, there was common ground on which he might have joined hands with his opponents; ground far deeper than that on which he met and fought them. In his conception of reason, in his belief that the purely logical and conscious elements of man's mind do not make the whole of it, that the instinctive, unconscious imaginative elements must be admitted as factors—nay, that they are, and ought to be, the determining factors of the whole—in all this he was at one with the ideas which lay at the very root of the Romantic movement, and which declared themselves more and more plainly as that movement gathered strength. It was this that secured the triumph of the imagination over the intellectual elements in the poetry of this and the succeeding age. It was this that cleared the way for the philosophical revolution which reached its height in the theories of Hegel. And of all this Burke, in his later and more significant writings (1790–7), is the precursor. This is true not only of his thought, but of the style in which it found appropriate expression. In passion, in richness of colouring, in his power of touching the deepest springs of thought and feeling, of passing without an effort from the homeliest effects to the highest and most imaginative, he reaches back to the great writers of the seventeenth century, and marks nothing short of a revolution in the history of English prose style.   And the effects of that revolution are not yet exhausted. On the writers of his own day it might be difficult to show that Burke exercised any considerable influence.   Yet echoes of his thought, and in a less degree of his style, make themselves dimly heard in the prose of Coleridge and Wordsworth; more clearly, unless appearances are altogether deceptive, in that of Joseph de Maistre (1796–1819).   And, if the question of direct influence be waived, it is certain that the author of *Le Pape* moves on the same plane as the author of the *Reflections,* and has a certain kinship with him in respect of style.

Of the other literary developments of the time—of the renewal of History by Gibbon, of the great work done by Lessing, Diderot, and others in criticism, of the new birth of philosophy associated with Kant and his successors—there is no room to speak.   In so great a wealth of material, it has been necessary to keep within the limits of literature, in the narrower sense.

(*Addendum to p.* 342.)

NAVAL OPERATIONS IN THE PERIOD OF THE SEVEN YEARS' WAR.

The failure of Washington (1754) and of Braddock (1755) to check the advance of the French on the Ohio obliged the British Government to despatch reinforcements to America. With the counter-preparations of the French for the defence of Canada the naval war really began. Boscawen was sent to intercept the French reinforcements off Louisburg (April, 1755); and, sighting the enemy in the mouth of the St Lawrence (June 10), he captured two vessels. The remainder eluded him in a fog and reached Quebec. In July, Hawke was ordered to cruise in the Bay of Biscay to prevent the union of the French Atlantic and Mediterranean fleets and the return of the American squadron to Brest. His instructions were extended to include the seizure of French merchantmen, and, in the course of three months, 300 vessels with 6000 sailors were brought into British ports. All this preceded the formal declaration of war. The French had good reason for delaying it: they were making secret preparations, which were not complete, for delivering a blow in the Mediterranean. The British Government failed to divine their object, and suspected that a descent on England or an expedition to America was intended. At last, Sir John Byng was despatched with ten sail of the line to prevent the Toulon squadron passing the Straits and to defend Minorca (April 6, 1756). At Gibraltar he learned that Port Mahon had already been surprised and invested. Arriving off Minorca, he found a French fleet equal to his own in numbers, and superior in weight and men. After an indecisive engagement, in which several of his vessels suffered considerable damage, he decided to leave Minorca to its fate and to withdraw for the protection of Gibraltar. There he was superseded by Hawke, and on his return home was court-martialled and sentenced to death for neglect of duty (January, 1757). In the existing temper of the country, discouraged by reports of disasters from America, the Government dared not pardon his excessive caution; although, had it shown more foresight and energy, he would never have been placed in difficulties which he had not the qualities of character to overcome. The surrender of Port Mahon, which followed (June 28), did not much change the situation. It was not for Minorca, but for America and India, that the War was being waged; and, while Great Britain possessed Gibraltar, the loss of Minorca did little to weaken her at the seats of war.

The ministerial changes in England, which gave Pitt a controlling voice in British policy, led to a concentration on a vigorous offensive against the French colonies, combined with the support of Frederick in the continental war by means of money subsidies, military operations, and naval diversions on the French coast. In America the British object was the conquest of Canada. The gateway to Canada was Louisburg, a powerful fortress on Cape Breton Isle, at once the first line of Canada's defence and a perpetual menace to New England. From Louisburg, the French carried on the cod-fishery, reinforced themselves in America, and harboured the privateers which, in time of war, preyed on British trade. In 1757, Quebec was to be assailed both by way of Lake Champlain and of the St Lawrence—from the latter direction by a force under the command of the Earl of Loudoun, whose first work was to be the capture of Louisburg. Vice-Admiral Holburne, with seventeen sail of the line, escorted the expedition from Halifax (July). But the French concentrated their squadrons for the defence of the island and had a superiority of one ship. In the circumstances, Holburne hesitated to attack, and the attempt was abandoned. The autumn of the same year saw another discouraging failure. In order to distract the French from their operations in America and Germany, an expedition against Rochefort was planned. Sir John Mordaunt commanded the troops, Hawke the accompanying fleet. But, ignorant of the locality, the generals failed to form a plan which promised success, and the force returned without having struck a blow.

In 1758, the attack on Louisburg was renewed. To ensure success, it was necessary to prevent the French from again concentrating a fleet for its defence. La Clue was waiting in Cartagena for reinforcements from Toulon, with which he hoped to pass the Straits and make for America. Osborne skilfully intercepted and dispersed the Toulon squadron (February), while Hawke attacked the French off the Île d'Aix (March) and prevented the formation of a fleet in the Biscay ports. At the same time, Boscawen with a large squadron covered the operations of Amherst and Wolfe; and in July the great fortress surrendered. Meanwhile, Frederick was urging the British Government to create a diversion in his favour by a descent on the enemy's coast. The temporary dispersal of the French fleets rendered this possible, and in May a force was collected in the Isle of Wight. Pitt's intention was to take and hold St Malo, and thus compel the French to withdraw troops from the Rhine to their northern coast. But, though St Malo was pillaged and Cherbourg attacked, no substantial result was achieved. On a second attempt in August, Cherbourg, "that most galling thorn in the side of British commerce," was taken, and the forts destroyed; but a third attempt on St Malo in September was repulsed with heavy loss. The incapacity or unwisdom of the commanders and the preparations of the French prevented these operations from succeeding, though as a diversion they contributed to the victories in America, where not only Louisburg, but also Forts Frontenac and Duquesne, fell to the British.

To the French it was now evident that, in the struggle for the mastery of the sea, Great Britain was gaining the upper hand, and that the loss of Louisburg—the first great blow dealt to them during the War—had exposed Canada to imminent danger. Only a vigorous counter-stroke at the heart of the enemy, which would affect his financial stability and prestige and distract him from distant enterprises, could change the aspect of affairs. In the latter part of 1758, they boldly designed the invasion of England. A force of 50,000 was to be landed in Essex, another of 12,000 in Scotland, and a raid was to be made on the Irish coast. Transports were prepared in the Biscay and Channel ports, while at Toulon and Brest fleets were equipped, which were to unite and clear the way for the expedition. Pitt, while preparing to resist the attack at home, did not stay his hand in the colonies; and his plans for the year included an attack on the French West Indies as well as the operations in Canada and India. Thus, in 1759, both sides assumed the offensive.

The first act in the great disaster which overwhelmed the grand design of the French was begun in the Mediterranean. Boscawen, who was watching Toulon, was compelled to withdraw to Gibraltar for repairs. La Clue, seizing his opportunity, came out with twelve sail of the line. On August 17 he was detected in the Straits by a British frigate. Boscawen immediately gave chase. During the night, La Clue's fleet divided, and five vessels took refuge in Cadiz. In the afternoon of the following day, the rear vessel of the remaining seven was overtaken and, after a desperate struggle, captured. Of the others, two escaped to the west, and four ran ashore between Lagos and Cape St Vincent, where the British, disregarding the neutrality of Portugal, destroyed two and captured two. This defeat deprived the French of any prospect of invading England, though they did not abandon the remainder of their plan. The second act was more prolonged, but in its issue more dramatic and decisive. In blockading the large fleet which was waiting in Brest, Hawke had a task which only his pertinacity could have carried through. His chief difficulties were to maintain his crews and ships in fighting condition and to hold his ground under all conditions of weather. He met the former by sending his ships, two or three at a time, to be cleaned and revictualled at Plymouth. But, with a westerly wind blowing, the blockading fleet was in danger of being driven on shore and was compelled to withdraw. Fortunately, the same conditions of weather made it impossible for the French to get out of port. Early in November, a tremendous gale drove the British fleet into Torbay, where it was detained for several days. Meanwhile, Bompart, returning from the West Indies, got into Brest, bringing battered ships but experienced sailors who were drafted into the waiting fleet. From him Conflans learnt of Hawke's absence, and accordingly determined to sail at once for Quiberon Bay, to overpower the frigates under Duff, which were cruising along the coast of southern Britanny, and to take up the troops at Morbihan. On the day of his departure from Brest (November 14), Hawke returned with twenty-three sail of the line and promptly started in pursuit. On the morning of the 20th, the French ships were sighted near Belle Isle. Conflans, surprised to find himself overtaken by a larger force, endeavoured to retreat into the Bay, trusting that the British would not venture on a stormy November afternoon to follow him into its treacherous waters. But Hawke bore down in pursuit, following the course of the French, and, within the contracted area of the Bay, among shoals and reefs, in the midst of a great storm, the Trafalgar of this War was fought. Seven of the French ships escaped into the Vilaine, nine to the Loire or to Rochefort, five were taken or destroyed. During the night two British ships struck on the rocks. It was the price of a crushing victory, which dispersed all fear of invasion and gave the command of the sea to Great Britain for the remainder of the War. Various fates befell the remnants of the great armament which had been prepared. Thurot, who escaped from Dunkirk with three ships, after visiting Sweden descended on the Irish coast early in 1760. He gained a small success at Carrickfergus, but was overtaken by Captain Eliot off the Isle of Man, and defeated and killed. Rodney destroyed the flat-bottomed boats at Havre; but the ships blockaded in the Vilaine slipped out one dark night and got safely into Brest; and, with similar good fortune, the division of La Clue's fleet in Cadiz escaped to Toulon (January, 1761).

During the remainder of the War, the British fleets maintained a grand blockade of the French coast from Dunkirk to Marseilles. They prevented the reunion of the scattered remnants of the French navy, covered the operations in Canada, paralysed French trade, and kept the coast towns in a constant state of alarm. At the same time, Great Britain achieved unparalleled success in the main undertakings which the containing naval operations covered. In 1759, Quebec fell to the brilliant genius of Wolfe; in the West Indies Guadeloupe was taken, in Africa Goree; in the East Indies much indecisive fighting ended in the withdrawal of the French fleet from Indian waters (October). In the following year the conquest of Canada was completed. Their command of the sea gave the colony into the hands of the British. The slender British garrison at Quebec, outnumbered, defeated, and besieged, depended on reinforcements. These arrived (May 18), while those of the French were intercepted off the coast of New Brunswick (June 14). Thus, Quebec was held and Montreal taken. Further successes followed. In June, 1761, Belle Isle was captured; in February, 1762, Rodney reduced the French sugar islands, first Martinique and afterwards St Lucia, Grenada, Tobago and St Vincent. When Spain joined in the War, her colonies became objects of attack; and she lost Havana (August) and Manila (October) with the whole Philippine group. Supreme on the sea, Great Britain concentrated on colonial conquest; and, though in the last years of the war she lost many merchant vessels to the French privateers, she gained her great object—empire in east and west, resulting from and resting upon maritime power.

CHAPTER I.

GREAT BRITAIN UNDER GEORGE I.

(1) THE HANOVERIAN SUCCESSION.

[*See also Bibliographies of Chapters II and IV in the present volume; also the Bibliographies of Chapter XIV, Section (2) and of Chapters XV and XXI in Vol. V.*]

I. BIBLIOGRAPHIES.

Loewe, V. Bibliographie der Hannoverschen und Braunschweigischen Geschichte. Posen. 1908.

[This exhaustive bibliography of the history of the House of Brunswick and its dominions supersedes the necessity of any others; references to earlier bibliographies will be found in it, as well as to the catalogues of important libraries, such as that of the late King George V of Hanover, and that of the Historische Verein für Niedersachsen at Hanover.]

See also Dahlmann-Waitz, Quellenkunde der Deutschen Geschichte, 7th edn., edited by E. Brandenburg, Leipzig, 1906.

In Loewe's Bibliography are also enumerated the various historical periodicals of this part of Germany, notably the

Zeitschrift des Historischen Vereins für Niedersachsen, Hanover, 1850, etc.; from 1892 with the supplementary title: Zugleich Organ d. Vereins für Gesch. d. Herzogthümer Bremen und Verden, und des Landes Hadeln (*In progress*),

and the Archives, Repertories and subsidiary publications of this and other Societies.

II. MANUSCRIPTS.

It is unlikely that any extant documentary evidence concerning the transactions connected with the Hanoverian Succession, or illustrating its antecedents and the personages who had part in bringing it about or obstructing it, remains unutilised, though not all of it may have been reproduced at length in print. The most important among the repositories of this ms. evidence are, of course, our own Record Office and the British Museum. In the former, Foreign Entry Books, 49, 217, and Germany (States), 164, may be specially noted; in the latter, eleven folio vols. of Hanover Correspondence, together with transcripts of the same, and a collection of documents made by Thomas Astle, intended as an appendix to the Hanover Papers, are preserved among the Stowe mss., the contents of which are fully described in the Catalogue of Stowe mss., London, 1895, Vol. i, pp. 287-321. For valuable guidance as to diplomatic personages see:

Chance, J. F. List of Diplomatic Representatives and Agents, England and North Germany, 1689-1727. Contributed to Notes on Diplomatic Relations between England and Germany. Ed. C. H. Firth. Oxford. 1907.

Next come the treasures, which for a long time seemed inexhaustible, of the Royal
Archives at Hanover ; as to which see

Bär, M.   Übersicht über die Bestände des K. Staatsarchivs zu Hannover.   (Mit-
theilungen der K. Preuss. Archiv-verwaltung, 3.)   Leipzig.   1900.

Cf. Bär, M.   Geschichte des K. Staatsarchivs zu Hannover.   (Mittheil. 2.)
Leipzig.   1900.

Of the Electress Sophia's vast correspondence preserved in the Hanover Archives
a large proportion has been printed.   (See the publications enumerated below.)   The
copy of the Act of Settlement brought to Hanover in 1701 is preserved there.   The
original patent of the same date conferring the Garter on the Elector (afterwards
King George I) is preserved in the Royal Public Library at Hanover, where the MSS.
connected with the transactions and prominent personages of the Succession period
are relatively few in number.   See

Bodemann, E.   Die Handschriften der K. öffentlichen Bibliothek zu Hannover.
Hanover.   1867.

For the history of the Hanoverian Succession the MS. material in the diplomatic
correspondences at Vienna (more especially Hoffmann's reports), the Hague (the
correspondence of Heinsius) and Paris (where Torcy's correspondence is of course
chiefly concerned with the other side) has been assiduously examined.   Among
English sources of importance for the history of the Succession the following have
been calendered for the Historical MSS. Commission :

Harley Letters and Papers, Vols. II and III, forming Vols. IV and V of the MSS. of the
Duke of Portland.   1897–9.

Shrewsbury Papers.   MSS. of the Duke of Buccleuch.   Vol. II.   Part I.   1903.

Stuart Papers, belonging to the King.   Vol. I.   1902.

III.   CONTEMPORARY LETTERS AND MEMOIRS.

Burnet, Gilbert, Bp. of Salisbury.   History of my own times.   Vols. V and VI.
Oxford.   1823.

——   A Memorial offered to the Princess Sophia, containing a Delineation of the
Policy of England.   (From the Hanover Archives.)   London.   1815.

Ernest Augustus (the younger), Duke.   Briefe an Johann Franz Diedrich von Wendt
aus den Jahren 1703–26.   Ed. by Count E. Kielmannsegg.   Leipzig.   1902.

Kemble, J. M.   State Papers and Correspondence, 1686–1707.   London.   1857.
[Contains letters of Leibniz.]

——   Zur Geschichte der Succession des Hauses Hannover in England.   (Contains
contemporary letters.)   In Zeitschr. d. hist. Ver. für Niedersachsen.   Hanover.
1852.

Leibniz, G.   Werke.   Ed. O. Klopp.   Series I.   Hanover.   1864, etc.

Vol. V.   Briefe und Berichte an den Herzog Ernst August.—Die Feststellung
der Primogenitur im Welfenhause.—Briefe und Berichte über d. Reise von
1678–9 bis zum Ende d. Aufenthalts in Wien.—Erster Aufenthalt in Wien.

Vol. VI.   Die neunte Kurwürde.—Personalien des Kürfursten Ernst August
von Braunschweig-Lüneburg.

Vols. VII–IX.   Correspondenz mit der Prinzessin Sophie, später Kürfurstin
von Braunschweig-Lüneburg.   1680–1714.

Vol. X.   Correspondenz mit Sophie Charlotte, Königin von Preussen.

Vol. XI.   Correspondenz mit Caroline geb. Prinzessin von Anspach.

——   Geschichtliche Aufsätze und Gedichte.   Ed. G. H. Pertz.   Hanover.   1847.

Marchmont Papers.—A selection from the papers of the Earls of Marchmont, in the
possession of Sir G. H. Rose, illustrative of events, 1685–1750.   Vol. III.
London.   1831.

Original Papers containing the Secret History of Great Britain from the Restoration to the Accession of the House of Hanover, arranged and published by James Macpherson. Section: Hanover Papers. Vol. II. London. 1775.

As to these Papers, which are copies of translations, extracts, or abstracts from a portion of the papers left by John de Robethon concerned with English domestic politics, see J. F. Chance, Corrections to James Macpherson's Original Papers in English Historical Review, vol. XIII, July, 1898.

Pauli, R. Aktenstücke zur Thronbesteigung des Welfenhauses in England. In Zeitschr. des hist. Vereins für Niedersachsen. Hanover. 1883.

Sophia, Electress.—Memoiren der Herzogin Sophie, nachmals Kurfürstin von Hannover. Hrsgbn. von A. Köcher. (Publicationen a. d. K. Preuss. Staatsarchiven. IV.) Leipzig. 1879.

—— The Electress Sophia. Quarterly Review. July, 1885.

—— Aus den Briefwechsel König Friedrichs I von Preussen u. der Kurfürstin Sophie von Hannover. (Aus den Briefwechsel König F. I und seiner Familie.) Ed. by E. Berner. (Quellen und Unters. z. G. d. H. Hohenzollern.) Berlin. 1901.

—— Aus den Briefen der Herzogin Elisabeth Charlotte von Orléans an die Kurfürstin Sophie von Hannover. Ed. E. Bodemann. 2 vols. Hanover. 1891.

—— Briefe an die Raugräfinnen und Raugrafen zu Pfalz. Ed. E. Bodemann. Publicationen a. d. K. Preuss. Staatsarchiven. XXXVII. Leipzig. 1888.

—— Briefe der Königin Sophie Charlotte von Preussen und der Kurfürstin Sophie von Hannover an hannoversche Diplomaten. Ed. R. Doebner. (Publicationen a. d. K. Preuss. Staatsarchiven. LXXIX.) Leipzig. 1905.

—— Briefe des Königs Friedrich I von Preussen und seines Sohnes des Kronprinzen Friedrich Wilhelm I an die Kurfürstin Sophie von Hanover. Ed. E. Bodemann. In Zeitschr. des hist. Vereins für Niedersachsen, 1899. Hanover.

—— Memoirs of Mary, Queen of England (1689–93), together with her letters and those of Kings James II and William III to the Electress Sophia of Hanover. Edited by R. Doebner. Leipzig. 1886.

Toland, John. Account of the Courts of Prussia and Hanover. London. 1705. German transl. Frankfort. 1706.

Wentworth Papers, the. Selected from the Correspondence of the Earl of Strafford. Edited by J. J. Cartwright. London. 1883.

IV. LATER WORKS.

A. WORKS REFERRING TO THE HANOVERIAN SUCCESSION.

Bodemann, E. Herzogin Sophie von Hannover. In Hist. Taschenbuch. Leipzig. 1887.

Chance, J. F. John de Robethon and the Robethon Papers. In English Historical Review. Vol. XIII, January. 1898. London.

Droysen, J. G. Geschichte der preussischen Politik. Part IV. Sections 1 and 2 (Frederick I and Frederick William I). Leipzig. 1867–9.

Erdmannsdörffer, B. Deutsche Geschichte vom westfälischen Frieden bis zum Regierungsantritt Friedrichs des Grossen. Vol. II. Berlin. 1893.

Favre, C. B. La diplomatie de Leibniz. Négociations et mémoires pour la succession d'Angleterre. In Revue d'histoire diplomatique, 1905, 1906, 1907. Paris.

Fester, R. Kurfürstin Sophie von Hannover. Hamburg. 1893.

Fischer, Kuno. Gottfried Wilhelm Leibniz. (Chapters VIII and IX.) 4th edn. Heidelberg. 1902.

Foxcroft, H. C. A Life of Bishop Burnet. II. England. 1674–1715. With an Introduction by C. H. Firth. Cambridge. 1907.

Guhrauer, Gottfried Wilhelm Freiherr von Leibnitz. 2 vols. Breslau. 1846.

Hallam, H. The Constitutional History of England. Vol. iii. 7th edn. London. 1854.

Halliday, A. A General History of the House of Guelph. With an appendix of authentic and original documents. London. 1821.

Havemann, W. Geschichte der Lande Braunschweig und Lüneburg. 3 vols. Göttingen. 1853–7.

Heinemann, O. von. Geschichte von Braunschweig und Hannover. Vol. iii. Gotha. 1892.

Klopp, O. Der Fall des Hauses Stuart und die Succession d. Hauses Hannover in Grossbritannien und Irland. 14 vols. Vienna. 1875–88.

    Meinardus, O. Die Succession d. Hauses Hannover in England und Leibniz. Ein Beitrag zur Kritik des Dr Onno Klopp. Oldenburg. 1878.

Köcher, A. Andreas Gottlieb Graf von Bernstorff (1649–1726). In Allgemeine Deutsche Biog. Vol. xlvi. Leipzig. 1902.

—— Sophie Kurfürstin von Hannover (1630–1714). In Allgemeine Deutsche Biog. Vol. xxxiv. Leipzig. 1892.

Michael, W. Englische Geschichte im 18. Jahrhundert. Vol. i, pp. 281–400, 403–59. Hamburg and Leipzig. 1896.

Pauli, R. Die Aussichten des Hauses Hannover auf den englischen Thron im Jahre 1711. In Pauli's Aufsätze zur englischen Geschichte. (New series.) Leipzig. 1883.

—— Confessionelle Bedenken bei der Thronbesteigung des Hauses Hannover in England. In Pauli's Aufsätze zur englischen Geschichte. (New series.) Leipzig. 1883.

Ranke, L. von. Englische Geschichte vornehmlich im xvii. Jahrhundert. 2nd edn. Vol. vii: Grundlegung und Bedingungen der hanoverschen Succession. Sämmtliche Werke. Leipzig. 1871, etc. Vol. xxi. English translation: Oxford. 1875, etc. Vol. vi.

Roscoe, E. S. Robert Harley, Earl of Oxford. A Study of Politics and Letters in the Age of Anne. London. 1902.

Salomon, F. Geschichte des letzten Ministeriums Königin Annas von England, 1710–4, und der englischen Thronfolgefrage. Gotha. 1894.

Schaumann, A. Georg I, Kurfürst von Hannover (1600–1727). In Allgemeine Deutsche Biog. Vol. viii. Leipzig. 1878.

—— Geschichte der Erwebung der Krone Grossbritanniens von Seiten des Hauses Hannover. Hanover. 1878.

—— Johann Caspar von Bothmer (1656–1732). In Allgemeine Deutsche Biog. Vol. iii. Leipzig. 1876.

—— Zwei Aufsätze zur Geschichte des Welfischen Hauses. In Zeitschr. des hist. Vereins für Niedersachsen, 1874–5. Hanover.

Schmidt, H. Die Kurfürstin Sophie von Hannover. With Appendix by A. Haupt: Die bildende Kunst in Hannover zur Zeit der Kurfürstin Sophie. No. v of Veröffentlichungen zur Niedersächsischen Geschichte. Hanover. 1899, etc.

Sichel, W. Bolingbroke and his Times. Vol. i. London. 1901.

Stanhope, Earl (Lord Mahon). History of England from the Peace of Utrecht to the Peace of Versailles, 1713–83. 3rd edn. Vol. i. London. 1853.

Thornton, P. M. The Brunswick Accession. London. 1887.

Vehse, F. Geschichte der Höfe des Hauses Braunschweig in Deutschland und England. Vol. i. (Gesch. d. deutschen Höfe seit d. Reformation. Vol. xviii.) Hamburg. 1853.

Ward, A. W. The Electress Sophia and the Hanoverian succession. Paris and London. 1903. 2nd edn. (revised). London. 1909.

—— The Electress Sophia and the Hanoverian succession. English Historical Review. Vol. i. London. 1886.

Ward, A. W. Great Britain and Hanover. Some aspects of the personal union. Oxford. 1899. German translation, by K. Woltereck. Hanover. 1906.

Weber, O. Der Friede von Utrecht. Verhandlungen zwischen England, Frankreich, dem Kaiser u. der Generalstaaten, 1710–3. Gotha. 1891.

Wright, Th. Caricature history of the Georges, or Annals of the House of Hanover. London. 1898.

Wyon, F. W. The History of Great Britain during the reign of Queen Anne. Vol. ii. London. 1876.

Böttger, H. Stammtafel der regierenden Fürsten des Welfenhauses und ihrer Vorfahren. Hanover. 1858.

Böttger, H. Die allmähliche Entstehung der jetzigen welfischen Lande. Zur Erläuterung der Stammtafel. 2nd edn. Hanover. 1859.

Guelph, Pedigree of the House of. Founded principally on L'Art de Vérifier les Dates. By W. A. Lindsay. Compiled for the Guelph Exhibition, 1891.

Stewart, Pedigree of the House of. Founded on the accounts printed in Wood's edition of Douglas' Peerage. By W. A. Lindsay. Compiled for the Stewart Exhibition, 1890.

B. Miscellaneous.

Beaucaire, H. de. Une mésalliance dans la maison de Brunswick (1665–1725). Éléonore Desmier d'Olbreuze, duchesse de Zell. Paris. 1884.

Bodemann, E. Neue Beiträge zur Geschichte der cellischen Herzogin Eleonore geb. d'Olbreuse. Zeitschr. des hist. Vereins für Niedersachsen, 1887. Hanover.

—— J. H. von Ilten. Nebst Anlagen: Briefe an Ilten. Zeitschr. des historischen Vereins für Niedersachsen, 1879. Hanover.

Chance, J. F. A Jacobite at the Court of Hanover. [On Lady Bellamont.] English Historical Review. July, 1896. London.

Deecken, Count von der. Beiträge zur hannoverschen Geschichte unter Georg Wilhelm, 1649–65. Vaterländ. Archiv d. histor. Vereins für Niedersachsen. Lüneburg and Hanover. 1839.

Greenwood, A. D. Queens of the House of Hanover. Vol. i. (Sophia Dorothea.) London. 1909.

Heimbürger, H. T. Georg Wilhelm Herzog von Braunschweig und Lüneburg Celle. 1852.

Köcher, A. Die letzte Herzogin von Celle. Preussische Jahrb. lxiv. Berlin. 1899.

—— Gesch. von Hannover und Braunschweig, 1648–1714. Vols. i and ii, 1648–68, have appeared so far. Leipzig. 1884, etc.

—— Sophie Dorothea, Prinzessin von Ahlden (1666–1726). Allgemeine Deutsche Biog. Vol. xxxiv. Leipzig. 1892.

Malortie, C. E. von. Beiträge zur Gesch. des braunschweig-lüneburgischen Hauses und Hofes. 7 parts. Hanover. 1860–84.

—— Beiträge zur braunschweig-lüneburg. Gesch. New Series. Vol. i. Hanover. 1879.

—— Der hanoversche Hof unter dem Kurfürsten Ernst August und der Kurfürstin Sophie. Hanover. 1847.

Meier, E. von. Hanoversche Verfassungs- und Verwaltungsgeschichte. 2 vols. Leipzig. 1898–9.

Rocholl, H. Die Braunschweig-Lüneburger im Feldzug d. Grossen Kurfürsten gegen Frankreich. Zeitschr. d. histor. Vereins für Niedersachsen, 1895. Hanover.

Spittler, C. T. Geschichte des Fürstenthums Hanover seit den Zeiten der Reformation bis zu Ende des 17. Jahrh. 2nd edn. 2 vols. Hanover. 1798.

Tytler, Sarah.   Six Royal Ladies of the House of Hanover.   London.   1898.
Wilkins, W. H.   The love of an uncrowned Queen.   Correspondence of Sophie
    Dorothea with Count Königsmarck.   London.   1900.
    Geerds, R.   Die Briefe der Herzogin von Ahlden, etc.   Beilage zur Allgemeinen
    Zeitung, No. 77.   Munich.   1902.
    Sophia Dorothea.   Edinburgh Review.   January, 1901.
    See also Appendix B to second edition of A. W. Ward, The Electress Sophia
    (*ante*, A).

(2) THE FOREIGN POLICY OF GEORGE I.

1714–21.

[*See also Bibliographies to Section* (1) *of the present Chapter, to Chapters II, VII,
VIII, 1, and X of the present volume, and to Chapters I and II of Vol. V.*]

I. BIBLIOGRAPHIES.

(This list is confined to bibliographies specially concerning affairs treated in this
Section and not given elsewhere.)

Allen, C. F.   Scandinavian bibliographies prefixed to Haandbog i Foedrelandets
    Historie.   Seventh edn.   Copenhagen.   1870.   And to the French translation by
    E. Beauvois.   Copenhagen.   1878.
Baden, G. L.   Dansk-Norsk historisk Bibliothek.   Odense.   1815.
Brunn, C.   Bibliotheca Danica.   Systematisk Fortegnelse over den Danske Literatur
    fra 1482 til 1830.   Vol. III.   Copenhagen.   1896.
Hidalgo, D.   Diccionario General de Bibliografía Española.   7 vols.   Madrid.
    1862–81.
Minzloff, R.   Pierre le Grand dans la littérature étrangère.   [Publié à l'occasion de
    l'anniversaire deux fois séculaire de la naissance de Pierre le Grand,] d'après les
    notes du Comte de Korff, etc.   St Petersburg.   1872.
Pirenne, H.   Bibliographie de l'histoire de la Belgique.   Ghent.   1893.   Second
    edn., Ghent.   1902.
Setterwall, K.   Svensk historisk Bibliografi, 1875–1900.   Stockholm.   1907.

II. MANUSCRIPT SOURCES.

British Museum.

Alberoni, Cardinal.   Unione de Scritture attenenti all' Em^mo Giulio Alberoni, fatto
    Cardinale li 12 Luglio, 1717, etc.   2 vols.   Add. 16481–2.   Sucessos de Alveroni,
    y diligencias de la Corte de España, en carta del duque de Parma de 21 de
    Marzo 1721.   Egerton, 361, f. 231.   Manifiesto de el Cardenal Jullio Alveroni.
    Carta escripta al Exmo Señor Cardenal Paoluzzi secretario de Estado de N. Señor.
    (March 1, 1721.)   Egerton, 361, f. 247.   (French translation from an Italian
    version, " Nouvelle Lettre," etc.   Amsterdam.   1721.)
Carteret Papers.   Official copies of Lord Carteret's despatches, etc., from Sweden,
    1719–20, and as Secretary of State, 1721–4.   Add. 22511–9 and 22523–4.
Dayrolle Papers.   Official diplomatic correspondence of James Dayrolle, British
    Resident at Geneva, 1715–7, and at The Hague, 1717–38.   Vols. I–IV (1706–
    38).   Add. 15866–9.   Letterbooks, Vols. II–IV (1715–38).   Add. 15876–8.

Gualterio Papers. Correspondence, chiefly of Cardinal F. A. Gualterio, Protector of the English Catholics at Rome, with all the principal Courts of Europe, Add. 20241–20583 B ; of which, 20241, correspondence with Clement XI, 1716–9 ; 20242, registers of drafts of secret letters, chiefly 1701–6 and 1716–7 ; 20243, copies of Papal briefs, etc. ; 20292–20310, Jacobite correspondence ; 20311–13, miscellaneous papers relating to England, 1701–23. Further Jacobite correspondence, Add. 31254–67.

Gyllenborg, Count. Deciphers of his intercepted (or seized) correspondence, 1716–7, Add. 32235, and of other like correspondence, French and Italian, 32307–8.

Histoire Politique du Siècle depuis 1648, jusqu'en 1748. Par l'éditeur du Testament Pol. du Cardinal Alberoni. The dedication is signed M. B. R., Lausanne, October 10, 1753. Add. 4207, No. 5.

Melcombe Papers. Original correspondence and papers of George Bubb, Envoy Extraordinary to Spain, 1714–8. 6 vols. Egerton 2170–5.

Monumenta Britannica ex autographis Romanorum Pontificum deprompta. Vol. xlviii. Add. 15398. (Includes important letters of Clement XI and other Popes, with other papers, relating to the Pretender. Transcripts.)

Newcastle Papers. Vol. i (1697–1723). Add. 32686.

Noailles, Card. de. Correspondence with the Pretender, 1714–22. Egerton 1677.

Norris, Admiral Sir John. Journals, letter-books, etc., 1715–21. Add. 28128–9, 28135, 28143–7, 28154–6.

Northern Pacification, The, 1719–20. Copies and drafts of papers concerning this and other subjects. Add. 4193.

Ormonde, James Butler, Duke of. Letter-book, concerning the projected Spanish invasion of 1719. Add. 33950. (Dickson, W. K. See under IV B below.)

Relazioni e scritture della Successione del Duca d' Angiò di Francia, etc. Vol. xviii includes a letter of the Marchese Grimaldi to Cardinal Acquaviva, August 9, 1717, on the invasion of Sardinia, with answers thereto. Add. 16468.

Robethon Papers. Miscellaneous correspondence and papers of Jean de Robethon, confidential secretary to George I. Vols. vi–xi, 1714–9. Stowe 227–32.

Rome, Newsletters from, 1719–24. Add. 8381.

Schaub Papers. Correspondence and papers of Sir Luke Schaub, 1714–23, mostly copies. Add. 4204.

—— Diplomatic correspondence, 1717–25. Add. 35837, iii.

Spanish correspondence, deciphers (6), 1719–20. Add. 32298.

Spanish War. (1) An Extract of the Masters Journalls of the Barfleur in relation to the Engagement with the Spanish Fleet by Sir George Byng, 1718. (2) An Account of Capt. Cavendish's Engagement with three Spanish Ships of Warr Anno 1719. Extracted from the Masters Journalls of the Ships concerned in that Expedition. Add. 5439, ff. 84, 90.

—— Losses sustained by Spanish Depredations at Sea and in Port in the years 1718, 1719, and 1720, etc. Add. 34335, f. 146.

Stanhope, General James. Letter-book (Hanover, etc.), July–Sept. 1716. Add. 22510.

—— Colonel W. Original despatches from Madrid, 1721. Add. 22520.

Sutton, Sir R., and others. Original despatches, etc., from Paris, 1721–2. Add. 22521–2.

Warrants (copies) for the payment of £130,000 to the Emperor, Jan. 2, 1718, and of £63,000 for the Queen of Sweden, Nov. 19, 1719. Add. 22616, ff. 178, 180.

Worsley, Henry. Original letters and despatches to him, when Ambassador to Portugal, 1714–21, with various papers, including a narrative of the battle of Cape Passaro. Add. 15936.

III. PRINTED ORIGINAL DOCUMENTS.

A. TREATIES AND STATE PAPERS.

Most of the Treaties, without, of course, the secret articles, were published in various languages immediately upon their conclusion. The originals of the British Treaties, and papers concerning them and others, may be consulted at the Public Record Office (State Papers Foreign, Treaties and Treaty Papers).

See specially:

Cantillo, A. del. Tratados, convenios y declaraciones de paz y de comercio que han hecho con las potencias estranjeras los monarcos españoles de la casa de Borbon. Desde el año de 1700 hasta el dia. Madrid. 1843.

Collection of Treaties, Alliances and Conventions, a, relating to the Security, Commerce, and Navigation of the British Dominions, made since His Majesty's Accession to the Crown. London (S. Buckley). 1717–8. (Latin, French, Spanish and English texts.)

Faber, A. (pseud.). Europäischer Staats-Cantzley, etc. (the title varies for each volume). Vols. xxii sqq. Frankfort and Leipzig. 1714 foll.

Falck, N. N. Sammlung der wichtigsten Urkunden welche auf das Staatsrecht der Herzogthümer Schleswig und Holstein Bezug haben. Kiel. 1847.

Garden, Comte de. Histoire générale des Traités de Paix et autres transactions principales entre toutes les puissances de l'Europe depuis la paix de Westphalie. Ouvrage comprenant les travaux de Koch, Schoell, etc., entièrement refondus et continués jusqu'à ce jour. Vols. i, iv, v. Paris. [1847.]

General Collection of Treatys of Peace and Commerce, Manifestos, Declarations of War, and other Publick Papers, a, from the end of the Reign of Queen Anne to the year 1731. Vol. iv (the titles of the other volumes differ). London. 1732.

Ghillany, F. W. Diplomatisches Handbuch. Sammlung der wichtigsten Europaeischen Friedenschluesse, Congressacten, und sonstigen Staatsurkunden vom Westphälischen Frieden bis auf die neueste Zeit. Parts i, ii. Nördlingen, 1855. *Bibl.*

[Harris, W., D.D.] A Complete Collection of all the Marine Treaties subsisting between Great Britain and France, Spain, etc. (1546–1763). London. 1779.

Hertslet, Sir E., C.B. Treaties and Tariffs regulating the trade between Great Britain and foreign nations, etc. Part v, Spain. London. 1878.

Höchst-gemüssigter Historischer-Acten-mässiger Bericht, von dem was vom Anfang der, im Monath Augusto 1713 angetretenen Regierung CARL LEOPOLD, Hertzogen zu Mecklenburg,......bis zu der, im Monath Martio und April 1719 ergangenen Kayserlichen Execution, von dem Fürstl. Mecklenburgischen MINISTERIO,......vorgenommen worden, etc. 1719. (886 *docs.*)

Martens, F. de. Recueil des Traités et Conventions conclus par la Russie avec les Puissances Étrangères. Vol. v, Germany (1656–1762). St Petersburg. 1880. Vol. ix (x), England (1710–1801), ibid. 1892. Vol. xiii, France (1717–1807), ibid. 1902.

Martens, G. F. de. Supplément au Recueil des principaux Traités,......précédé de Traités du xviiime siècle antérieurs à cet époque et qui se ne trouvent pas dans le Corps Universel Diplomatique de Mrs Dumont et Rousset et autres recueils généraux de traités. Vol. i. Göttingen. 1802.

Modée, G. R. Utdrag af de emellan Hans Konglige Majestät och Kronan Swerige å ena, och Utrikes Magter å andra sidan, sedan 1718 slutna Alliance-Traktater och Afhandlingar. Stockholm. 1761.

Noradounghian, G. Recueil d'Actes Internationaux de l'Empire Ottoman. Vol. i (1300–1789). Paris, Leipzig, Neuchâtel. 1897.

Sammlung verschiedener Berichte, auch Staatschriften, den Tod Karls des XII, die in Schweden hierauf erfolgten Veränderungen, und die Erhebung der Königin Ulricae Eleonorae auf den Schwedischen Thron, betreffend. Second edn. Freistadt (Jena). 1719.

Schleswig-Holstein. Texts of the French and English guarantees, June and July 1720. Archives diplomatiques (ed. Amyot). Année iv. Vol. i. Paris. 1860.

Testa, Baron I. de. Recueil des Traités de la Porte Ottomane avec les Puissances Étrangères, etc. Vol. ix. (Autriche, Vol. i.) Paris. 1898.

B. Letters, Despatches, etc.

Bosscha, P. De Geschiedenis van Oostelijk en Noordelijk Europa gedurende het merkwaardig tijdvark van 1687–1716. (Correspondence of Dutch Ministers, chiefly on Turkish affairs.) Zalt-Bommel. 1860.

Brefvexling mellan Konung Carl XII och Rådet (1714–5). Historiska handlingar, Kongligt Samfundet. Vols. xiv, xv. Stockholm. 1892–5.

Brunet, G. Correspondance complète de Madame Duchesse d'Orléans, née Princesse Palatine, Mère du Régent. Traduction entièrement nouvelle. 2 vols. Paris. 1857. Later editions, Paris, 1869 [1904].

Carlson, E. Kapten Jefferyes bref til Engelska regeringen från Bender och Adrianopel, 1711–4, från Stralsund 1714–5 (in English). Historiska handlingar. Vol. xvi, No. ii. Stockholm. 1897.

—— Konung Karl XII's egenhändiga Bref. Stockholm. 1893. German transl. by E. Mewius. Berlin. 1894.

Droysen, J. G. Eine Denkschrift Ilgen's [1716?]. Zur Politik von 1715 (correspondence). Das Journal des Feldzugs von 1715. Ein Bericht von Bonnet. (London, August 7/18, 1719). Lord Cadogan's Memorial und Graf Bothmer's Project von 1721 (as to a coalition against Peter the Great). Geschichte der preussischen Politik. Vol. iv. Part iv. Leipzig. 1870.

Elagin, S. Materialui dlya istorii russkago flota. Baltysky flota, 1702–25. 4 vols. St Petersburg. 1865–7.

[Gaspari, A. C.] Briefe Friedrichs IV, Königs in Dänemark. Urkunden und Materialien z. n. K. Gesch. und Staatsverwaltung Nordischer Reiche. Vol. i. [Hamburg?] 1786. [See especially letter of August 12, 1718, to Count Holsten-Holstenborg, with the answer, and drafts for treaties with Great Britain and Hanover.]

Gordon, Admiral Sir Thomas (of the Russian navy). Correspondence and papers of. 1716–40. Historical Manuscripts Commission. Report x. Part i, pp. 157–99. London. 1885.

Handlingar rörande Skandinaviens historia. Kongligt Samfundet, Vols. vi, viii, x, xii, xviii, xxi (Correspondence). Stockholm. 1816 sqq.

Hardwicke Miscellaneous State Papers. Vol. ii. No. ix. Lord Stair's Embassy in France, 1714, etc. (Stair's journal and correspondence, 1714–9.) 1778.

Lamberty, G. de. Mémoires pour servir à l'histoire du xviiie siècle. Vols. viii to xi, 1714–8; Vol. x including Treaties of 1718 to 1751. Amsterdam. 1734–6. (First edn., 1723.)

Critique by J. G. Droysen. Gesch. d. preuss. Politik. Vol. iv, Pt iv. Leipzig. 1870.

Letters which passed between Count Gyllenborg, the Barons Gortz, Sparre, and others, relating to the Design of raising a Rebellion in His Majesty's Dominions, to be supported by a Force from Sweden. Published by Authority. London. 1717. (French and English.) Also printed in Tindal's History, and Cobbett's

Parliamentary History.   Translations in various languages.   The originals at the Public Record Office, chiefly in State Papers, Foreign, Confidential I[A], I[B]. Decipers, British Museum.   Add. MSS. 32285, 32307–8.

Moe, B.   Actstykker til den norske Krigshistorie under Kong Frederik den Fjerde (1716–8).   Reprinted from the Milit. Tidsskrift, vols. XV–XVII.   3 parts. Christiania.   1838–40.

Privateers, The Ordinance of, 8–19 February 1715.   The Swedish text in G. Floder's Handlingar hörande til Konung Carl XII's historia, Part IV. Stockholm. 1826. French translation, and pamphlets concerning it, Lamberty, vol. IX.   Abstract, English Historical Review, vol. XVII, p. 70.

Russia.—Diplomatic correspondence, chiefly of French ministers in Russia, 1711–33. (French.) Sbornik, etc.   Vols. XXIV, XL, XLIX, LII, LVIII, LXIV, LXXV, LXXXI. Diplomatic correspondence of James Jefferyes and other English Ministers in Russia, 1711–40.   Ib. Vols. LXI, LXVI, LXXVI, LXXX, LXXXV.   Other Correspondence, etc.   Ib. Vols. III, V, XI, XV, XXV, XXXIV (2).   St Petersburg. –1893.

Theiner, A.   Monuments historiques relatifs aux règnes d'Alexis Michaélowitch, Féodor III et Pierre le Grand, Czars de Russie, extraits des Archives du Vatican et de Naples.   (Includes important despatches of the Papal Nuncio, 1715–25, about Russian doings in Courland, Poland, etc.)   Rome.   1859.

Townshend, Charles, Viscount.   Extracts from his correspondence.   Historical Manuscripts Commission.   Report XI, Part IV.   London.   1887.

Villebois, Sieur de.   Mémoires secrets pour servir à l'histoire de la Cour de Russie, sous les règnes de Pierre-le-Grand et de Catherine Ière.   Rédigés et publiés par le Comte Théophile Hallez.   Paris.   1858.

Wijnne, J. A.   Stukken rakende de Quadrupel Alliantie van 1718.   (Despatches of Dutch envoys, etc., Jan.–July 1720.)   Kroniek of Utrecht Historical Society, 27 Jaargang, 1871, 6th Ser., Pt II.   Utrecht.   1872.

C. PERIODICALS OTHER THAN NEWSPAPERS.

(The principal British newspaper of the time was the London Gazette, thrice weekly.)

The Annals of King George.   Year the first, to sixth, containing not only the affairs of Great Britain, but the general History of Europe during that time ; with an introduction in defence of His Majesty's title, etc.   6 vols.   London.   1716–21.

La Clef du Cabinet des Princes de l'Europe, ou Recueïl Historique et Politique sur les matières du tems.   (Monthly ; half-yearly volumes.)

Die Europäische Fama, welche den gegenwärtigen Zustand der vornehmsten Höfe entdeckt.   Parts I–CCCLX.   30 vols. [Leipzig.]   1702–35.

The Historical Register, containing an Impartial Relation of all Transactions Foreign and Domestick.   Vols. I. foll. (from 1716).   London.   1717 foll. Supplementary : Transactions…that happen'd during the first Seventeen Months of the Reign of King George.   2 vols.   London.   1724.

Lettres Historiques ; contenant ce qui se passe de plus important en Europe ; et les réflexions nécessaires sur ce sujet.   Monthly ; half-yearly volumes.   Vols. XLV sqq.   1714, etc.   The Hague ; from Vol. XLVIII, Amsterdam.   1692–1736.

IV. SECONDARY WORKS, CONTEMPORARY OR NEARLY CONTEMPORARY.

A. MEMOIRS AND JOURNALS.

[See also Bibliography to Section (1) *above and Chapter II.]*

Bonnac, Marquis de. Mémoire historique sur l'Ambassade de France à Constantinople, par le Marquis de Bonnac. Publ. par C. Schefer. (Société d'histoire diplomatique.) Paris. 1894. (*Docs.*)

Bruce, P. H. Memoirs of Peter Henry Bruce. Translated by himself (1753), from his original German, and published after his death. London. 1782.

Franclieu, Marquis de. Mémoires du Marquis de Franclieu (1630–1745). Ed. L. de Germon. (Société historique de Gascogne: Archives historiques de la Gascogne, Ser. II, fasc. i.) Paris and Auch. 1896. [Valuable for the Duke of Ormond's expedition of 1719.]

Galitzin (Golitsuin), Prince A., ed. La Russie au XVIIIe siècle. Mémoires inédits sur les règnes de Pierre le Grand, Catherine Ière et Pierre II. Paris. 1863.

Ker, John. The Memoirs of John Ker, of Kersland in North Britain. With an Account of the Rise and Progress of the Ostend Company in the Austrian Netherlands. Published by himself. 3 vols. London. 1726.

Le Dran. Mémoires sur les négociations entre la France et le Czar de la Grande Russie Pierre I (1719–24). Sbornik imp. russk. istor. obschtschestra, Vols. XL, XLIX, LII. St Petersburg. 1884–6. Prefaced in Vol. XXXIV (Appendix) by Traités d'entre la France et la Moscovie, 1613–1717; an essay chiefly consisting of Négociations entre la France et le Czar Pierre I. 1715–7. St Petersburg. 1881.

Peter the Great's Journal from 1698 to the conclusion of the Peace of Nystad. Ed. Prince M. Shcherbatov. 2 vols. St Petersburg. 1770–2. Complete translation, by H. L. C. Bacmeister and C. G. Arndt. 3 vols. Riga. 1774–6–84.

Pöllnitz, Baron de. Nouveaux Mémoires du Baron de Pöllnitz, contenant l'Histoire de sa vie, et la Relation de ses premiers voyages. 2 vols. Amsterdam. 1737.

B. HISTORIES AND PAMPHLETS.

[See also Bibliographies to Chapters II (1), *III, IV and V.]*

Account, an, of the rise of the War with Spain in 1718. London. 1740.

Alberoni, Cardinal. The Conduct of Card. Alberoni, with an Account of some Secret Transactions at the Spanish Court. London. 1720.

—— The History of Card. Alberoni, from his Birth to the year 1719. To which are added, Considerations upon the Present State of the Spanish Monarchy. Translated from the originals. London. 1719. [Perhaps a translation of the work attributed to J. Rousset de Missy, below.]

Bolingbroke, Viscount. Works. 8 vols. 1809. (Vols. I–III.)

Bothmer, Count. Memoiren d. Engl. Ministers Grafen Bothmer über die Quadrupelallianz von 1718. Ed. R. Doebner. Forsch. z. deutsch. Gesch. Vol. XXVI. Göttingen. 1886.

Colliber, S. Columna Rostrata, or, a Critical History of the English Sea-Affairs. London. 1727 and 1742.

[Corbett, T.] An Account (or, a True Account) of the Expedition of the British
Fleet to Sicily in the years 1718, 1719 and 1720, under the command of Sir
George Byng, Bart., etc. London. 1739. French translation : Relation
de l'expédition de la Flotte Angloise, 1718–20. The Hague. 1741.

De la Gardiska Archivet, ed. P. Wieselgren. Vol. XVI. (1) Fredrik, Prins af
Hessen. (2) Fredspunkter emellan Carl XII och Czar Petter I fundne i
Görtzens papper. (3) Ytterligare om K. Carl XII's död. (4) Drottning
Ulrika Eleanora d. y. (5) Riksdagen 1719. (6) Riksdagen 1720. (7) K.
Fredrik I. Lund. 1842.

[Defoe, D.] The History of the Wars of his late Majesty Charles XII, King
of Sweden, from his First Landing in Denmark to his Return from Turkey to
Pomerania. The Second Edition. With a Continuation to the Time of his
Death. By a Scots Gentleman in the Swedish service. London. 1720.

[Defoe, D.?] The case of the War in Italy stated : being a Serious Enquiry how
far Great-Britain is Engaged to Concern it Self in the Quarrel between the
Emperor and the King of Spain. London. 1718.

Die abgezogene Masque des Alandischen Friedens-Congresses...Eine Schrifft, in
welcher die Intriguen des Weltbekannten Barons von Görtz, und bisherigen
Absichten des Russischen Hofes wahrhafftig und deutlich entdecket werden.
A. d. Frantzös. und Holländ. ins Teutsche übersetzet. Hamburg. 1720.

Discussion universelle de tous les articles du Traité de la Barrière des Pais-Bas
entre sa Majesté Impériale et Catholique, Sa M. le Roy de la Grande Bretagne,
& Les Seigneurs États Généraux des Provinces Unies. Par le Sr. S***.
Cologne. [1716?]

Disquisitio Juris Naturalis et Gentium de justo Gyllenborgii et Goertzii, Sueciae
legatorum in Britannia et Confoederato Belgio, arresto. With German translation. Frankfort and Leipzig. 1717.

[Gyllenborg, Count C.] The Northern Crisis : or, Impartial reflections on the
policies of the Czar. Occasioned by van Stocken's Reasons for delaying the
descent upon Schonen (prefixed in transl.). 1716. French translation : La Crise
du Nord, etc. London. 1717.

[——] An English Merchant's Remarks upon a scandalous Jacobite paper published
in the Post Boy under the name of A Memorial presented to the Chancery of
Sweden by the Resident of Great Britain. London. 1716. French translation
in Lamberty. IX. 667.

Interest, the, of Great Britain with Relation to the Differences among the Northern
Potentates, consider'd.... (The dedication to Stanhope signed A. Boyer.)
London. 1716. [Defence of the policy of George I.]

Istoria del Cardinale Alberoni dal giorno della sua nascità fino alla metà dell' anno
1720. Seconda edizione. Amsterdam. 1720.

Klüver, H. H. Hans Heinrich Klüver's Beschreibung des Herzogthums Mecklenburg u. dazu geh. Länder. Parts IV, V (1713–29). Hamburg. 1739–40. (*Docs.*)

La Conduite des Cours de la Grande Bretagne et Espagne, ou Relation de ce qui
s'est passé entre ces deux Cours par rapport à la situation présente des affaires.
Amsterdam. 1719. Engl. tr. 1720.

Letter, a, to a Friend at the Hague, concerning the Danger of Europe, and
particularly of Great Britain, in case the Quadruple Alliance should not
succeed. (London, June 23, 1718.) London. 1718.

"Nestesuranoi, Ivan" (J. Rousset de Missy). Mémoires du Règne de Pierre le
Grand. Vols. III, IV. The Hague and Amsterdam. 1726. Later editions,
Amsterdam (4 vols.), 1728–30, and (5 vols.), 1740.
  Critique by J. G. Droysen. Geschichte der preussischen Politik. Vol. IV,
  Pt. IV. Leipzig. 1870.

Pfeffinger, Joh. Friderich (Königl. Gross-Britannischen Rath). Historie des

Braunschweig-Lüneburgischen Hauses, bis auf das Jahr 1733, etc. Part III. Hamburg. 1734.

Reasons for a War with France. The Second Edition. London. 1715. (Dunkirk and Mardyk, with Prior's memorial and the answer, and a general discussion.) An Argument against a War with France, wherein a late Pamphlet entitled "Reasons for a War," is...refuted, etc. 1715.

Reasons for the present Conduct of Sweden, in relation to the Trade in the Baltick, etc. London. 1715.

Reflections upon the Present State of affairs in France....In a Letter to the Right Honourable the E. of S——. London. 1715.

Relacion de lo sucedido en el regno de Sicilia por las armas de su Magestad. Barcelona. [1719.]

Relacion veridica del combate que el 11 Agosto 1718, huvo entre la Armada de España y la de Inglaterra en las Costas Orientales de Sicilia, y en la Canal de Malta. Madrid.

Rousset de Missy, J. Histoire du Cardinal Alberoni, trad. de l'Espagnol [which is untrue]. The Hague. 1719.
    Critique by J. G. Droysen, as above.

San Phelipe, Marqués de. Comentarios de la Guerra de España, e historia de su Rey Phelipe V el Animoso, desde el principio de su Reynado, hasta la Paz General del año 1725. Genoa [1790?]. French translation by L. L. Féderbe, Comte de Maudave. 4 vols. Amsterdam. 1756. Mutilated. German translation from this (not from the Spanish, as stated). Mittau, etc. 1772–7 (The principal source for the history of Philip V.)

Schmauss, J. J. Johann Jacob Schmaussens Einleitung zu der Staats-Wissenschaft, und Erleuterung des von ihm herausgegebenen Corporis Juris Gentium Academici und aller andern seit mehr als zweyen Seculis her geschossenen Bündnisse, Friedens- und Commercien-Tractaten. I, Sec. III (1700–40). Die Historie der Balance von Europa, der Barrière der Niederlande, der Oesterreichischen Sanctionis pragmaticae, etc. Leipzig, 1741. II, Sec. II (1700–43). Die Historie aller zwischen den Nordischen Potentzen, Dänemarck, Schweden, Russland, Poland und Preussen geschlossenen Tractaten in sich haltend. Leipzig. 1747.

Secret Memoirs of the New Treaty of Alliance with France; with some Characters of Persons. London. 1716.

Some Considerations upon his Majesty's Message; and the Dutchies of Bremen and Verden. In a Letter to the Worshipful Mr ——, Mayor of S——. To which is prefix'd, A Map of those Dutchies; and of the Rivers Elbe and Weser. (8 April, 1717.) London. 1717.

Stanhope, Earl. Memoirs of the Life and Actions of the Right Honourable James Earl Stanhope. With his Character, and a Poem occasion'd by his Death. London. 1721.

Struve, B. G. Mémoires pour servir à l'Histoire du Congrès de Cambrai, avec un Traité historique sur les Investitures de quelques États d'Italie. 1723.

—— Discurs vom Uhrsprung, Unterscheid und Gerechtsamen der Lande-Stände in Teutschland, insonderheit im Hertzogthum Mecklenburg; wobey die im Jahre 1715 zwischen dem reg. Hertzog Carl Leopold von Mecklenburg-Schwerin und der Mecklenburg. Ritter- und Landschafft enstandene Dispute erörtert werden. Hrsgbn. von C. G. J. [C. G. Jargow]. Hamburg. 1741.

Theatrum Europaeum. Theatri Europaei Zwantzigster Theil. 2 parts (1713–5). Frankfort. 1734. Jubilaeum Theatri Europaei. 2 parts (1716–8). Frankfort. 1738.

Townshend, Viscount. An Impartial Enquiry into the Conduct of the Right Honourable Charles Lord Viscount T——. London. 1717.

V. LATER WORKS.

A. GREAT BRITAIN.

[See also Bibliographies of Section 1 above and Chapters II and III.]

Acton, Lord. The Hanoverian Settlement. Lectures on Modern History, XVI. 1906.

Ballantyne, A. Lord Carteret, a political biography, 1690–1763. London. 1887.

Bussemaker, Th. De Triple-Alliantie van 1717. Bijdragen voor vaderlandsche Geschiedenis en Oudheidkunde. Series LV. Part II. The Hague. 1901.

Chance, J. F. George I and the Northern War. London. 1909.

Clowes, Sir W. L., and others. The Royal Navy. Vol. III (1714–92). London. 1898.

Colomb, Rear-Admiral Sir P. H. Naval warfare, its ruling principles and practice historically treated. 1891, etc.

Dickson, W. K. The Jacobite Attempt of 1719. (Publications of the Scottish History Society. Vol. XIX.) Edinburgh. 1895.

Leadam, I. S. The Political History of England, Vol. IX: from the Accession of Anne to the death of George II (1702–60). London. 1909.

Mahan, Capt. A. T. The Influence of Sea Power upon History. 1660–1783. Boston (Mass.). 1890, etc.

Mahon, Lord (Earl Stanhope). History of England from the peace of Utrecht to the peace of Versailles. (Vols. I and II.) London. 1853 and 1858.

Michael, W. Englische Geschichte im 18 Jahrh. Vol. I. Hamburg and Leipzig. 1896.

Weber, O. Die Quadrupel-Allianz vom Jahre 1718. Ein Beitrag zur Geschichte der Diplomatie im achtzehnten Jahrhundert. Vienna, etc. 1887.

Whitworth, Sir C. State of the Trade of Great Britain in its imports and exports, progressively from the year 1697. London. 1776.

B. THE NETHERLANDS.

[See also Bibliography of Chapters XIV 2 of Vol. V.]

Bussche, E. van den. Le Traité de la Barrière. Pourquoi l'art. 1 de la convention de 1718, sur les limites entre la Flandre et le territoire soumis aux États-Généraux ne fut point exécuté. "La Flandre, année 1880." Bruges. 1880.

Dollot, R. Les origines de la neutralité de la Belgique et le système de la Barrière, 1609–1830. Paris. 1902. (*Bibl. and Docs.*)

C. FRANCE, SPAIN AND ITALY.

[See also Bibliographies of Chapters IV and V.]

Armstrong, E. Alberoni and the Quadruple Alliance. The Scottish Review. Vol. XXIX. London. 1897.

—— Elizabeth Farnese. London. 1892.

Baraudon, A. Le Roi de Sicile Victor Amadée II et la Triple Alliance (1715–20). Annales de l'École Libre des Sciences Politiques, Vols. VI, VII. Paris. 1891–2.

—— La Maison de Savoie et la Triple Alliance (1713–22). Paris. 1896.

Bliard, P. Dubois, Cardinal et Premier Ministre. 2 vols. Paris. [1901.]

—— Dubois et l'Alliance de 1717. Revue des questions historiques. Vol. LXVIII. Paris. July. 1900.

Bossaud, A. Le Port de Dunkerque après le traité d'Utrecht. Ibid. Vol. XXX. Dunkirk. Paris. 1898.

Carutti, D. Storia del Regno di Vittorio Amadeo II (1675–1730). Turin. 1856.
2nd edn. Florence. 1863.

  Criticism on Carutti's works by S. Bersani, Storia del Cardinale Giulio
    Alberoni. Appendix. Piacenza. 1661.

Fantin, A. E. N. des Odoards. Histoire de France, depuis la mort de Louis XIV
jusqu'à la paix de Versailles de 1783. Vols. I, II (1715–35). Paris. 1789.

Fernandez Duro, C. Armada Española desde la Union de los Reinos de Castilla y
de Aragon. Vol. VI. Madrid. 1900.

Filon, C. A. D. L'Alliance Anglaise au dix-huitième siècle. Depuis la paix
d'Utrecht jusqu'à la guerre de la succession d'Autriche. (Mémoire lu à
l'Académie des Sciences Morales et Politiques.) Paris. 1860.

Flassan, G. de Raxis de. Histoire générale et raisonnée de la Diplomatie Française.
2nd edn. Vols IV, V (1679–1784). Paris and Strassburg. 1811.

Gaillard, G. H. Histoire de la rivalité de la France et de l'Espagne. Vol. VIII.
Paris. 1801.

La Rocca, L. La cessione del Regno di Sardegna alla Casa Sabauda. (Miscellanea
di Storia Patria. R. Deputazione sovra gli studi di Storia Patria, etc. 3rd
Series, Vol. X.) Turin. 1906. (*Bibl. and Docs.*)

Lavisse, E. Histoire de France. Vol. VIII, Part 2. (*To appear.*)

Legrelle, A. La Diplomatie française et la Succession d'Espagne. Vol. VI. La
Paix. (1710–25.) Second edn. Braine-le-Comte. 1899.

Martin, B. L. H. Histoire de France depuis les temps les plus reculés jusqu'en
1789. Fourth edn. Vol. XV. Paris. 1878.

  H. de l'Épinois. Critiques et réfutations. M. Henri Martin et son Histoire
    de France. Paris. 1872.

Ranke, L. von. Französische Geschichte, vornehmlich im sechszehnten und siebzehnten Jahrhundert. Vol. IV, Book XVII. Die Regentschaft und Cardinal
Fleury. Stuttgart and Tübingen. 1856. (Werke, Vol. XI. Leipzig. 1869.)

Schmidt, E. A. Geschichte von Frankreich. (Gesch. der europäischen Staaten.)
Vol. IV. Hamburg. 1848.

Wiesener, L. Le Régent, l'Abbé Dubois et les Anglais, d'après des sources
Britanniques. 3 vols. Paris. 1891–3–9. (*Docs.*)

D. THE EMPIRE AND THE GERMAN STATES.

[*See also Bibliography of Chapter VIII* 1.]

Beer, A. Zur Geschichte der Politik Karls VI. Historische Zeitschrift, Vol. LV.
Munich and Leipzig. 1866.

Droysen, J. G. Die Wiener Allianz vom 5 Januar 1719. Abhandlungen zur
neueren Geschichte. No. VII. Leipzig. 1876. Also in his Geschichte der
preussischen Politik. Vol. IV. Part IV. (Text of the treaty with notes
by Ilgen and Frederick William I.) Leipzig. 1870.

  Critique by W. Michael. Ein schwieriger diplomatischer Fall aus dem Jahre
    1719. Historische Zeitschrift, LXXXVIII. Part I. Munich. 1901.

—— Geschichte der preussischen Politik. Vol. IV. Parts II and IV. Leipzig.
1869–70. Second edn. 1872. Index to Vols. I to IV, by C. Gerstenberg. Leipzig.
1876.

Erdmannsdörffer, B. Deutsche Geschichte vom Westphalischen Frieden bis zum
Regierungsantritt Friedrichs des Grossen. 1648–1740. Vol. II. Berlin.
1893.

Franck, D. Alt- und Neues Mecklenburg. Vol. VI, Book XVII : Von Mecklenburgs
Zerrüttung in allen Ständen, etc. (1713–27). Güstrow and Leipzig. 1757.

Gottorp.—Gesch. d. Herzoglich Schleswig-Holstein-Gottorfischen Hofes und dessen vornehmsten Staats-Bedienten unter der Regierung Herzog Friedrichs IV und dessen Sohnes Herzog Carl Friedrichs. (1700–34.) Frankfort and Leipzig. 1774.

Graff, W. P. Die zweite Ehe des Herzogs Karl Leopold. Ein Kulturbild aus Mecklenburg im ersten Viertel des 18 Jahrhunderts. Jahrbücher des Vereins für Mecklenburgische Geschichte und Alterthumskunde, Jahrgang LX. Schwerin. 1895. (*Bibl.*)

Havemann, W. Geschichte der Lande Braunschweig und Lüneburg. Vol. II. Lüneburg. 1838. New edn. Vol. III. Göttingen. 1857.

Mailáth, Count J. Geschichte des östreichischen Kaiserstaates. (Gesch. der europäischen Staaten.) Vol. IV. Hamburg. 1848.

Matthias, C. Die Mecklenburger Frage in der ersten Hälfte des achtzehnten Jahrhunderts, und das Decret des Kaisers Karls VI vom 11 Mai 1728. Hallische Abhandlungen, 1885.

Menzel, K. A. Neuere Geschichte der Deutschen von der Reformation bis zur Bundesacte. Vol. X. Die Zeit Karls VI und die Anfänge Friedrichs II. Breslau. 1843 and 1854–5.

Möller, C. Geschichte Schleswig-Holsteins. Von der ältesten Zeit bis auf die Gegenwart. Vol. II. Hanover. 1865.

Pratje, J. H. Die Herzogthümer Bremen und Verden, ein Eigenthum des königlichen Grossbritannischen und Churfürstlichen Braunschweig-Lüneburg'schen Hauses. (Vermischte historische Sammlungen. Herausgegeben unter Leitung des vaterländischen Vereins zu Stade. Vol. I. No. XI.) Stade. 1842. (*Treaties and docs.*)

Prutz, H. Preussische Geschichte. Vol. II. Stuttgart. 1900.

Ranke, L. von. Neun Bücher Preussischer Geschichte. Vol. I (Book I). Berlin. 1847. Zwölf Bücher Preussischer Geschichte. Vol. III (Werke, Vol. XXVII). Leipzig. 1874. English tr. by Sir A. and Lady Duff Gordon. Vol. I. 1849.

Schleswig-Holstein.—Beseler, G. Die englisch-französische Garantie vom Jahre 1720. Berlin. 1864. *Docs.* Cf. Archives Diplomatiques (ed. Amyot), Année IV. Vol. I. Paris. 1864.

—— Thomsen, G. Om de Fransk-Engelske Garantie for Slesvig af 1720. (A. F. Krieger's Antislesvigholstenske Fragmenter, No. III.) Copenhagen. 1848. (*Correspondence and docs.*) German and French translations. Copenhagen. 1848.

E. SCANDINAVIA.

[See also Bibliographies of Chap. XIX of Vol. V and Chap. XXII of present Vol.]

Allen, C. F. Haandbog i Foedrelandets Historie. 7th edn., revised and improved, Copenhagen. 1870. (*Bibl.*) French translation by E. Beauvois. Copenhagen. 1878. (*Bibl.*)

Bäckström, P. O. Svenska flottans historia. Stockholm. 1884.

Baden, G. L. Danmarks Riges Historie. Vol. V. Copenhagen. 1832.

Bain, R. N. Scandinavia, a political history of Denmark, Norway and Sweden, from 1513 to 1900. (Cambridge Historical Series.) Cambridge. 1905.

Beskow, B. von. Friherre Georg Henrik von Görtz, statsman och statsoffer. Svenska Akad. Handlingar ifrån år 1796, Vol. XLIII. Stockholm. 1868.

Carlson, F. F. Om fredsunderhandlingarne åren 1709–18. Ett bidrag till Carl XII's historia. Stockholm. 1857.

Cedercreutz, Baron H. Sverige under Ulrica Eleonora och Fredric I, eller ifrån 1718 till 1751. Efter den, af framledne Hans Excellens Riks-Rådet, Herr Friherre Cedercreutz, forfattade handskrift. Ett inledande bihang till Skriften Tessin och Tessiniana. Stockholm. 1821.

Larsson, H. Grefve Karl Gyllenborg i London åren 1715–7. Ett bidrag till Sveriges yttre Politik under Karl XII's sista regeringsår. Gothenburg. 1891.

[Moser, F. C., Baron von.] Rettung der Ehre und Unschuld des Freyherrn von Schlitz, genannt von Goerz, etc. Mit xxx Beylagen. 1776. 2ᵈ enlarged edn. Hamburg. 1791. *Docs.*

Scherer, H. Der Sundzoll, seine Geschichte, sein jetziger Bestand, und seine staatsrechtlich-politische Lösung. Berlin. 1845.

Stavenow, L. Frihetstiden, 1713–72. Part iii of Sveriges historia intill tjugonde seklet. Ed. E. Hildebrand. Stockholm. 1903. German translation: Geschichte Schwedens, 1718–72, by C. Koch. (Geschichte Schwedens, Vol. vii. Gesch. d. europ. Staaten.) Gotha. 1908.

Syveton, G. L'erreur de Goertz. Revue d'histoire diplomatique. Vol. ix, No. iii. Vol. x, Nos. i, ii, iii, iv. Paris. 1895–6.

Woltmann, K. L. Freiherr von Görz, Freund Karls des Zwölften. Woltmann's Geschichte und Politik, Vols. i, ii. Berlin. 1800.

F. Russia, Turkey, etc.

[See also Bibliographies of Chaps. XVII and XIX of Vol. V and of Chap. XIX c of present Vol.]

Abeken, H. Der Eintritt der Türkei in die Europäische Politik des achtzehnten Jahrhunderts. Berlin. 1856.

Hartmann, K. J. Tsar Peter's Underhandlingar 1716 om Landgång i Skåne. Helsingfors. 1887. (*Critical bibl. and docs.*)

Herrmann, E. Geschichte des russischen Staates. (Geschichte der europäischen Staaten.) Vol. iv. Hamburg. 1849.

Popov, N. A. Materialui dlya istory morskago dyela pri Petrye Velikom', v' 1717–20 godakh'. (Materials for the history of naval affairs in the time of Peter the Great, in the years 1717–20.) Moscow. 1859.

Solov'ev, S. M. Istoria Rossy s' drevnyeishikh' vremen'. (History of Russia from the earliest times.) Vols. xvii, xviii. Moscow. 1867–8. "Second" edn. Vol. iv. St Petersburg. [1896.] *Docs.*

Stoerk, F. Das Greifswalder Bündniss zwischen Peter d. Gr. und Georg I vom 28/17 Oktober 1715. (Separatabdruck aus Pommersche Jahrbücher. Vol. ii.) Greifswald. 1901.

Uhlenbeck, C. C. Verslag aangaande een onderzoek in de archieven van Rusland ten bate der Nederlandsche Geschiedenis. Part iii. Het tijdperk van Koerákiens verblijf hier te land (1711–24). The Hague. 1891. (*Bibl.* by T. Cordt. *Docs.*)

Ustryalov, N. G. Russkaya Istoria. Vol. iii (1689–1762). St Petersburg. 1838. 5th edn. Vol. ii. St Petersburg. 1855. [Introduction and critical bibliography in Vol. i.]

Veselago, T. T. Ocherk' russkoi morskoi istorii. (Outline of Russian naval history, to 1725.) St Petersburg. 1875.

CHAPTER II.

THE AGE OF WALPOLE AND THE PELHAMS.

(1) GENERAL.

I. BIBLIOGRAPHIES.

Fortescue, G. K. Subject Index of the Modern Works added to the Library of the British Museum, 1881–1900. London. 1902; 1901–5; 1906.

For diplomatic matters, so far as they relate to France:

Monod, G. Bibliographie de l'histoire de France à 1789. Paris. 1888.

For English political history:

Leadam, I. S. Political History of England, 1702–62, pp. 503 sqq., supplies a good critical bibliography.

For all American and Colonial affairs:

The Literature of American History, by various writers. Ed. J. N. Larned, and supplements in subsequent years. London. 1902. A most valuable critical bibliography.

II. MANUSCRIPT SOURCES.

A. *Diplomacy and Foreign Affairs.*

References to the unpublished material in Hanover, Berlin, Vienna, the Hague, Madrid, Paris, and Edinburgh are given in the Bibliographies to Chapters I, III, IV and V. Unpublished documents dealing with Jacobite affairs are fully described in the Bibliography to Chapter III. So far as the English Records are concerned, the following is the unpublished material on which the present Chapter is based.

For the diplomatic history of the period:

British Museum. Stowe MSS. 246–7. Craggs Papers, being principally letters to James Craggs the younger, Secretary at War and Secretary of State, from Earl of Stair etc. (1711–20.)

Stowe MSS. 251, Townshend, Viscount. Transcripts of correspondence when at Hanover in 1723. [Mostly in Coxe's Memoirs of Sir R. Walpole. Vol. II. Appendix. London. 1798.]

Add. MSS. 32743–4. Correspondence of Newcastle, W. Stanhope, Horatio (Lord) Walpole, Viscount Townshend, etc. 1724–6. [Partly used by Coxe.]

Add. MSS. 32780–2. Correspondence of Newcastle and Waldegrave.

Add. MSS. 37444. Correspondence of Newcastle, Horatio (Lord) Walpole, Viscount Townshend etc. Important for the year 1725.

For the Spanish War and its causes, 1738–9 :

Add. MSS. 23802, f. 86, 23803, f. 121 ; Add. MSS. 32691–2 ; Add. MSS. 35406–7 *passim* ; Hardwicke Correspondence ; Add. MSS. 32800 ; Add. MSS. 33028 ; for a general detail of the South Sea Company's affairs v. Add. MSS. 33032, copy, ff. 218–28, ff. 277–82 ; the documents as to British Rights on the Mosquito Shore from 1672 onwards are transcribed in Stowe MSS. 256, ff. 305–17, and Add. MSS. 33117, ff. 25–37.

The papers at the Public Record Office, some of which are duplicated at the British Museum, exhibit a far fuller detail of the causes of the War ; see especially the following :

Public Record Office, State Papers Foreign, Spain, 109, 113, 118, 130, 131–4, the correspondence between Keene and Newcastle *passim* ; see also P.R.O., S.P.F., Spain, 224, for the reports of Consuls at Cadiz, Barcelona, etc. ; the proofs of Newcastle's duplicity as to the Counter Orders—described in the text—will be found in P.R.O., Admiralty Outletters. Vol. LV, pp. 194–8, 208, 230–5, 242–5, 270, 296, 304, 370, 389, 445 sqq.

British Museum. Stowe MSS. 256 ff., 282–304, shows the respective attitudes of Pitt and Keene towards Spain in 1757 and is interesting by way of comparison with 1739. This correspondence has been printed (apparently from copies) in Hist. MSS. Comm. Rep. X. App. 1, pp. 212–21.

At the British Museum other parts of the Newcastle and Hardwicke Correspondence than those mentioned supply materials of great value for the period, but the arrangement of both series, especially of the Hardwicke Papers, is too heterogeneous in character to permit of further specific reference. The Coxe Papers, Add. MSS. 9123–97, afford a vast mine of information, which has already been much used.

Besides these sources the Whitworth Papers, British Museum Add. MSS. 37361–97 [Charles Lord Whitworth was envoy at various Courts and Plenipotentiary at Cambray, 1722–5], will probably be found to contain materials of the most value. For English policy generally see B. Williams (below IV 2), who gives many MSS. references for the period 1721–31. For Spain see Baudrillart (below III A).

B. *Home Affairs.*

The Newcastle and Hardwicke Papers are again our chief source of information— but suffer even more from the defects above alluded to—viz. the miscellaneous and unchronological character of their arrangement. For this period as a whole the following volumes, which have been used in the preparation of this chapter, may be found useful. They contain many details on the party disputes and Ministerial intrigues of the period.

British Museum. Add. MSS. 32947 ; 32994–99 ; 35335 ; 35408 ; 35416 ; 35423–4 ; 35870.

The working of the Cabinet-system during the eighteenth century—a subject full of difficulty—is probably most fully illustrated by the following volumes at the Public Record Office :
Home Office Council Office. Vols. X, XVI, XIX, XX.
Home Office Secretaries Letter Books. Vol. XXVI.

III. PRINTED ORIGINAL DOCUMENTS AND CONTEMPORARY PUBLICATIONS.

A. *Diplomacy and Foreign Affairs.*

Baudrillart, A. (see above). (1) Rapport sur une Mission en Espagne aux Archives d'Alcala de Hénarès et de Simancas. (2) Ditto, aux Archives de Simancas (Part III). Correspondances diplomatiques après 1715. Archives des Missions Scientifiques et Littéraires. 3rd ser. Vol. XV. Paris. 1889. Further correspondence after 1724 in Nouvelles Archives des M. S. et L. Vol. VI. Paris. 1895.

Berwick, Duc de. Mémoires. Coll. Petitot. Vols. LXV–VI. Paris. 1828.

Recueil des instructions données aux Ambassadeurs et Ministres de la France, 1648–1789. Vol. XII, *bis* (Pt. 2). (1722–93.) Espagne. By A. Morel-Fatio and H. Léonardon. Paris. 1899.

Historical Manuscripts Commission Reports :

Townshend, Charles, Viscount. Extract from Correspondence. Rep. XI, Pt. 4. London. 1887.

Spanish Affairs, 1738–9, etc.

Trevor, Robert. Correspondence of, with Horatio, Lord Walpole. Earl of Buckinghamshire's Papers. Rep. XIV, Pt. 9, pp. 1–56. London. 1895.

Hare MSS., pp. 239–55. Rep. XIV, Pt. 9. London. 1895.

Stirling-Home-Drummond-Moray, C. H. S. Papers, pp. 170–99. Rep. X, App. 1. London. 1895.

Weston-Underwood. Papers of Edward Weston, pp. 199–314, 427–44, 452, 518. Rep. X, App. 1. London. 1885.

Pamphlets chiefly concerned with the Spanish War of 1739 :

For the Convention—Gordon's Appeal to the Unprejudiced concerning the Present Discontents ; Popular Prejudices against the Convention with Spain ; the Grand Question War or no War with Spain. London. 1739.

Those against are innumerable and nearly all of the same abusive and uncritical character. Review of all that passed between 1731–9 [by W. Pulteney], London, 1739, is typical. See as to further pamphlets and information Boyer's Pol. State of Great Britain, Vol. LVII, London, 1739, and Hertz, British Imperialism in the Eighteenth Century. London. 1908.

B. *Home Affairs.*

(1) *Periodicals.*

London Gazette (thrice weekly). Boyer, A. Political State of Great Britain. Vol. VIII sqq. London. 1714 sqq. The Historical Register. 2 vols. London. 1724. The Craftsman. London. 1726–7 sqq. Gentleman's Magazine, 1738 sqq. London. The Old Whig or the consistent Protestant. 2 vols. London. 1739.

For Newspapers :

Fox Bourne, H. R. English Newspapers. 2 vols. London. 1887.

(2) *Memoirs, Correspondence, and Papers; chiefly unofficial.*

[For Jacobite Papers, etc. see Bibliography to Chap. III.]

Ailesbury, Marquis of. Westmoreland MSS. Hist. MSS. Comm. Rep. X, App. Pt. 4, pp. 29–35. London. 1885.

Bath, Marquis of. Longleat MSS. Hist. MSS. Comm. Rep. XV. Vol. I, pp. 244–323. Vols. II and III. London. 1904–8.

Bedford, John Russell, fourth Duke of. Correspondence of. Ed. Lord J. Russell. 4 vols. London. 1842.

Bolingbroke, Viscount. Works. 8 vols. London. 1809.

Buccleuch and Queensberry, first Duke of. MSS. Hist. MSS. Comm. Rep. XV, App. Pt. 8. Vol. I, pp. 361–417. London. 1897.

Carlisle, Earl of. MSS. Hist. MSS. Comm. Rep. XV, App. Pt. 6, pp. 1–211. London. 1897.

Charlemart, Earl of. MSS. Vol. I. Hist. MSS. Comm. Rep. XII, App. Pt. 10. London. 1891.

Chatham Correspondence. 4 vols. Edd. W. S. Taylor and J. H. Pringle. London. 1838–40.

Chesterfield, Philip Dormer Stanhope, Earl. Miscellaneous Works. [Pamphlets etc.] Ed. M. Matz. London. 1777.

—— Letters to his Son. Ed. C. Strachey. 2 vols. London. 1901.

—— Letters to his godson and successor. Ed. Earl of Carnarvon. Oxford. 1890.

Cobbett's Parliamentary History. Vols. VII–XIV. London. 1811–2.

Cowper, Earl. Coke Papers. Hist. MSS. Comm. Rep. XII, App. Pt. 3, pp. 116–31. London. 1889.

—— Lord Chancellor. Private Diary. (Roxburghe Club.) London. 1833.

—— Mary, Countess of. Diary. Ed. S. Cowper. London. 1865.

Dodington, George Bubb, first Lord Melcombe. Diary (1749–61). Ed. H. P. Wyndham. 4th edn. London. 1823.

Du Cane, Lady. MSS. Hist. MSS. Comm. Rep. XV [Chiefly naval]. London. 1905.

Fortescue MSS. Dropmore Papers. Hist. MSS. Comm. Rep. XIII, pp. 1–142, App. Pt. 3. Vol. I. London. 1892.

Frankland-Russell-Astley, Mrs. Hist. MSS. Comm. Rep. XV, pp. 206 sqq. London. 1900.

(Glover, Richard.) Memoirs by a celebrated literary and political character (1742–57). New edn. London. 1815.

Grenville Papers. Ed. W. J. Smith. 4 vols. London. 1852–3.

Hardwicke, Philip, first Earl of. Miscellaneous State Papers. Vol. II. London. 1778.

Hervey, John, Lord. Memoirs of the Reign of George II to the death of Queen Caroline. Ed. J. W. Croker. 2 vols. London. 1848.

Kenyon, Lord. MSS. Hist. MSS. Comm. Rep. XIV, App. Pt. 4, pp. 455–94. London. 1894.

Ketton, R. W. MSS. Hist. MSS. Comm. Rep. XII, App. Pt. 9, pp. 196–209. London. 1891.

Leyborne Popham MSS. Hist. MSS. Comm. Rep. XV, pp. 253 sqq. London. 1899.

Lonsdale, Earl. MSS. Hist. MSS. Comm. Rep. XIII, App. Pt. 7, pp. 121–32. London. 1893.

Lothian, Marquess of. MSS. Drury Papers. Hist. MSS. Comm. Rep. XVI, pp. 148–65. London. 1905.

Lyttelton, George, first Lord. Works. 3rd edn. London. 1776.

Mar and Kellie, Earl of. MSS. Hist. MSS. Comm. Rep. XVI. London. 1904.

Marchmont, ninth Earl of. Papers. 3 vols. London. 1831.

Marlborough MSS. Hist. MSS. Comm. Rep. VIII, App. 1. London. 1881.

Montagu, Lady Mary Wortley. Letters of (1714–27). 2 vols. London. 1861.

Onslow, Earl of. MSS. Hist. MSS. Comm. Rep. XIV, App. Pt. 9, pp. 450–524. London. 1895.

Pelham, Henry. Memoirs of Life of. By Arch. W. Coxe. 2 vols. London. 1829.

Pope, Alexander. Poetical Works. Ed. A. W. Ward. London. 1869.

—— Letters of, to Atterbury when in the Tower. Ed. J. G. Nichols. Camden Misc. Vol. IV. London. 1859.

—— Letters of. Ed. M. Elwin. Vols. I–V. London. 1871.

Portland, Duke of. MSS. Hist. MSS. Comm. Rep. XIII, App. Pt. 2. Vol. II, pp. 255–314, 1893; Rep. XV, App. vol. V, pp. 506–669, 1899; vols. VI and VII (chiefly correspondence of Atterbury and Harley). 1901.

Pulteney, W. (Earl of Bath). Letters of. Mar and Kellie MSS. Hist. MSS. Comm. Rep. XVI, pp. 529 sqq. London. 1904.

—— English Hist. Rev. XIV, pp. 318 sqq.

Rogers, J. E. Thorold. Protests of the House of Lords. 2 vols. Oxford. 1875.

Somers Tracts, the. Vol. XIII. London. 1815.

Somerset, Frances, Duchess of. Correspondence of, with Henrietta Louisa Countess of Pomfret (1738–41). 3 vols. London. 1805.

Suffolk, Henrietta Howard, Countess of. Letters to and from her second husband. George Berkeley. Ed. J. W. Croker. 2 vols. London. 1824.

Sundon, Charlotte Clayton, Lady. Letters. Ed. Mrs Thompson. 2 vols. 1847.

Swift, Jonathan, Dean of St Patrick's. Prose Works of. Ed. Temple Scott. 12 vols. London. 1908.

Townshend, Charles, Visct. MSS. Hist. MSS. Comm. Rep. XI, Pt. 4. London. 1887.

Waldegrave, James, Earl. Memoirs. 1754–8. London. 1821.

Walpole, Horace, fourth Earl of Orford. Letters, complete, with Bibliography. Mrs Paget Toynbee. 16 vols. Oxford. 1903–5.

—— Memoirs of the Reign of King George II. Ed. Lord Holland. 3 vols. London. 1846.

—— Aedes Walpolianae. London. 1752. [Description of pictures at Houghton House.]

Walpole, Horatio, Lord. The Convention vindicated. London. 1739.

—— Interest of Great Britain steadily pursued. 3rd edn. London. 1743.

—— Answer to the later part of Bolingbroke's letters on History. London. 1763.

—— Memoirs of. By Archdeacon W. Coxe. 2nd edn. enlarged. London. 1808.

Walpole, Sir Robert, first Earl of Orford. A short History of the Parliament of 1713. London. 1713. [Pamphlet.]

—— Report from the Committee of Secrecy. London. 1715.

—— Observations on the Treaty, November 9, 1729. London. 1729.

—— General considerations concerning alteration and improvement of Publick Revenues; Letter on Duties on Wine and Tobacco. London. 1733.

—— Some considerations concerning the Public Funds, the Public Revenues and the Annual Supplies. London. 1735.

—— Memoirs of the Life and Administration of. By Archdeacon W. Coxe. 3 vols. London. 1798.

Wentworth Papers. [Correspondence, etc., of Lord Strafford, 1705–39.] Ed. J. J. Cartwright. London. 1883.

Whitefoord, Col. C. Caleb. Papers of, 1739–1810. Ed. W. A. S. Hewins. Oxford. 1898.

Williams, Sir C. Hanbury. Works. 3 vols. London. 1822. [Satires, etc., 1739–57.]

IV. SECONDARY WORKS.

(1) *General History of the Period.*

Brosch, M. Geschichte von England. Vol. III. (Gesch. d. europ. Staaten.) Gotha. 1893.

Cheyney, E. P. European background of American History. New York. 1904.

Heeren, A. H. L. Versuch einer historischen Entwickelung der Entstehung und des Wachsthums des Britischen Continental-Interesse. Hist. Werke. Vol. I. Göttingen. 1821. English translation. Oxford. 1836.

Knight, Charles. Pictorial History of England. Vol. IV. London. 1841.

Leadam, I. S. Political History of England (1702–60). Vol. IX. London. 1909.

Lecky, W. E. H. History of England in Eighteenth Century. Vols. I–III. London. 1897–9. Vol. VII, chap. XXI. London. 1899.

Michael, W. Englische Geschichte im Achtzehnten Jahrhundert. Vol. I. Hamburg and Leipzig. 1896.

Ranke, L. von. Englische Geschichte vornehmlich in sechzehnten und siebzehnten Jahrhundert. Sämmtl. Werke, Vol. VII. Leipzig. 1868. Eng. trans. Vol. v. Oxford. 1875.

Rapin, Thoyras de. History of England. The Continuation by N. Tindal to 1728. 2 vols. London. 1752.

Schlosser, F. C. History of the Eighteenth Century. English translation by D. Davison. Vols. I–II. London. 1843.

Smollett, T. History of England, 1688–1760. Vols. I–II. London. 1790. [Continuation of Hume.]

Stanhope, Philip H., fifth Earl. History of England, 1713–83. 7 vols. London. 1858.

(2) *Diplomacy (chiefly as to Relations of Spain and England).*

[*See also Bibliographies of Chaps. III and IV.*]

Armstrong, E. Elizabeth Farnese. London. 1892.

Baudrillart, A. Philippe V et la cour de France. Vols. III–IV. Paris. 1893.

Capefigue, J. B. H. R. Diplomatie de la France et de l'Espagne. Paris. 1846.

Clarke, E. Letters concerning the Spanish nation during 1760–1. London. 1763.

Coquelle, P. Les Projets de Descente en Angleterre. Paris. 1902. [Docs.]

Coxe, Archdeacon W. History of the Bourbon Kings of Spain (1700–88). 3 vols. London. 1813–5.

Filon, C. A. D. L'Alliance Anglaise aux dix-huitième siècle 1713–40. Académie des Sciences Morales et Politiques. Paris. 1860.

Hertz, G. B. British Imperialism in the Eighteenth Century. London. 1908.

Laughton, Sir J. K. Jenkins' Ear. English Hist. Review. Vol. IV, pp. 741–9. London. 1889.

Legrelle, A. La Diplomatie Française et la Succession d'Espagne. Vol. VI. (1710–25.) Second edn. Braine-le-Comte. 1899.

Seeley, Sir J. The House of Bourbon. English Hist. Review. Vol. I, pp. 86 sqq. London. 1886.

Temperley, H. W. V. The causes of the War of Jenkins' Ear. Trans. Royal Hist. Society. London. 1909.

Williams, B. The Foreign Policy of England under Walpole. English Historical Review, XV, 251, 479, 665; XVI, 67, 308, 439. [Deals only with the period 1721–31.]

(3) *Biographical and Miscellaneous.*

[*See also III B 2 ante.*]

Atterbury, Francis, Bishop of Rochester. Life. By Canon H. C. Beeching. London. 1909. [Docs.]

Besant, Sir Walter. London in the Eighteenth Century. London. 1902.

Bolingbroke, Henry St John, Viscount. Life. By T. Macknight. London. 1863.

—— Life and Times. By W. Sichel. London. 1902. [Docs.]

Carteret, John, Lord Granville. Life. By A. Ballantyne. London. 1887.

Chatham, William Pitt, Earl. Leben. By A. Ruville. 3 vols. Stuttgart and Berlin. 1905. English translation. 3 vols. London. 1907.

—— Life. By F. Thackeray. 2 vols. London. 1828. [Docs.]

Chesterfield, Philip D. Stanhope, fourth Earl. Life. W. Ernst. London. 1893. [Docs.]

Hardwicke, Philip, Lord. Life. By G. Harris. 3 vols. London. 1847. [Docs.]

Harley, Robert, Earl of Oxford. Life. By E. S. Roscoe. London. 1902.

Lloyd, E. M. The raising of the Highland Regiments in 1757. English Historical Review, XVII, pp. 452 sqq.

Lyttelton, George, 1st Lord. Life. By Sir R. J. Phillimore. London. 1845. [Docs.]

Nugent, Robert, Earl. Memoirs of (1741–60). By C. Nugent. London. 1898.

Shelburne, Marquis of Lansdowne. Life. By Lord E. Fitzmaurice. Vol. I. London. 1875. [Docs.]

Swift, Jonathan, Dean of St Patrick's. By Sir H. Craik. 2 vols. London. 1894.

Walpole, Sir Robert, first Earl of Orford. By A. C. Ewald. London. 1878.

—— By J. Morley. (Twelve English Statesmen.) London. 1889.

Ward, A. W. Great Britain and Hanover. Oxford. 1899.

(4) *Works illustrative of the History of Party Government and
Constitutional Theory.*

Blackstone, Sir Wm. Commentaries on the Laws of England. Book I. Vol. I.
9th edn. Ed. R. Burn. London. 1783.

Blauvelt, Mary T. Development of Cabinet Government. New York. 1902.

Brosch, M. Bolingbroke und die Whigs und Tories seiner Zeit. Frankfort. 1883.

Burnet, Gilbert (Bishop of Salisbury). Memorial to Princess Sophia. A delineation
of the constitution and policy of England. London. 1815.

Cowper, Earl, Lord Chancellor. An Impartial History of Parties. Memoir
delivered to George I on his accession. In Campbell's Lives of the Chancellors.
pp. 921-9. London. 1846.

Kent, C. B. Roylance. Early History of the Tories to 1702. London. 1909.
[Gives origin of Tory ideas.]

Montesquieu, Baron. L'Esprit des Lois. Book XI. Engl. tr. Vol. I. London. 1878.

Pike, L. O. Constitutional History of the House of Lords. London. 1894.

Political Disquisitions. 2 vols. London. 1774.

Porritt, E. and A. G. The Unreformed House of Commons. 2 vols. London. 1903.

Rapin, Thoyras de. Dissertation sur les Whigs et les Torys. The Hague. 1717.

Redlich, J. Procedure of the House of Commons. Translated from the German.
Ed. by Sir Courtenay Ilbert. 3 vols. London. 1908.

Todd, Alpheus. Parliamentary Government. Ed. Sir S. Walpole. 2 vols. London.
1892.

Torrens, W. M. History of Cabinets. 2 vols. London. 1894.

Wilkins, W. W. Political Ballads of Seventeenth and Eighteenth Centuries. 2 vols.
London. 1860.

Williams, B. Newcastle and the election of 1734. English Hist. Rev. Vol. XII,
pp. 448 sqq.

Winstanley, D. A. George III and his first Cabinet. English Historical Review.
Vol. XVII, pp. 678 sqq.

(5) *Financial, Economic and Colonial.*
[*See also Bibliography of Chap. VI.*]

American Manuscripts in Royal Inst. of Great Britain. Hist. MSS. Comm. Rep. XV.
Vol. I. London. 1904.

Ashley, W. J. Surveys Historic and Economic. Pp. 268-308. New York. 1900.

Beer, G. L. Commercial Policy of England towards the American Colonies. New
York. 1893.

—— British Colonial Policy, 1754-65. New York. 1907.

Bourne, E. G. Spain in America. New York. 1904.

Brisco, N. A. Economic Policy of Robert Walpole. Columbia University Press.
New York. 1907.

Brougham, H., Lord. Colonial Policy of the European Powers. 2 vols. Edinburgh.
1803.

Chalmers, G. Estimate of the comparative strength of Great Britain and losses of
her trade. London. 1782.

Channing, E. History of the United States, 1660-1760. Vol. II. New York. 1908.

Defoe, Daniel. The Complete English Tradesman. London. 1732.

—— An humble Proposal to the People of England for the encrease of their Trade.
London. 1729.

—— Plan of the English Commerce. London. 1737. Extracts in J. R. McCulloch's
Select Tracts on Commerce. London. 1859.

Davis. The Currency and Provincial Politics. Publications of Colonial Soc. of
Massachusetts. Vol. VI. Boston. 1900.

Dowell, S. History of Taxation. 4 vols. London. 1884.

Edwards, Bryan. History Civil and Commercial of British Colonies in West Indies. 5 vols. London. 1849.

Franklin, Benjamin. The interest of Great Britain considered with regard to her Colonies. London. 1761.

Gee, Joshua. The Trade and Navigation of Great Britain Considered [published 1729]. New edn. London. 1767.

Hertz, G. B. The old Colonial System. Manchester. 1905.

Hill, W. Colonial Tariffs. Quarterly Journal of Economics. vii, 78 sq.

Molasses Act of 1733. Parliamentary History. viii, 913, 992–1002, 1195–1200, 1261–66. London. 1811.

Moses, B. South America on the Eve of Emancipation. New York. 1908.

Pamphlets on British and West Indian aspects of the question.

    A—r—Z—h. Considerations on the Dispute now before the Commons. London. 1731.

    Comparison between British Sugar Colonies and New England as they relate to the interest of Great Britain. London. 1732.

    (Ashley, John.) Sugar Trade with incumbrances thereon laid open. London. 1734.

    Letter to the West India Merchants by a Fisherman. London. 1751. [On the New England side.]

Pitt, William, Earl of Chatham. Correspondence with Colonial Governors. Ed. Miss Kemball. London. 1907.

—— and the representation of the Colonies in the Imperial Parliament. By B. Williams. Eng. Hist. Rev. Vol. xxii, pp. 756–8. London. 1907.

Schmoller, G. The Mercantile System. Translated. New York. 1902.

Sinclair, Sir John. History of the Public Revenue. 3 vols. London. 1803.

Smith, Adam. Wealth of Nations. Vol. ii. Bk. iv, chap. vii. Ed. E. Cannan. London. 1904.

Somers Tracts. 13 vols. London. 1809–15.

Townshend mss. [full on American affairs]. Hist. mss. Comm. Rep. xi, Pt. 4. London. 1887.

Tucker, Josiah. Four Tracts on Political and Commercial Subjects. Gloucester. 1774.

Williams, W. M. J. The King's Revenue. London. 1908.

Zimmermann, A. Die Europäischen Kolonien. Berlin. 1896–1901.

(2) RELIGIOUS HISTORY.

I. Bibliographies.

Bibliography of the Works of John and Charles Wesley, arranged in chronological order, with notes. By R. Green. London. 1896. New edn. 1906.

A record of Methodist Literature, in two parts. By G. Osborn. London. 1869.

Anti-Methodist Publications during the Eighteenth Century, with notes. Being a list of all known books and pamphlets written in opposition to the Methodist Revival during the life of Wesley. By R. Green. London. 1902.

Useful short Bibliographical notes will be found in Overton and Relton's History of the English Church, 1714–1800. London. 1906. For fuller lists see Sir Leslie Stephen's Life and Thought in Eighteenth Century. Vol. i. London. 1902.

II. Manuscripts.

There are a number of manuscripts at the British Museum dealing with John Wesley, most of which have been published. Further material is also to be found in the City Road Chapel Museum and much information may be expected from the still unpublished parts of Wesley's journal and the various other ms. sources still in private hands or in the possession of societies. Much valuable material has, of late, been published by the Wesley Historical Society.

L. Tyerman's laborious volumes deal with the whole life of Wesley and of his family and friends, often from unpublished materials. Unfortunately his critical ability was by no means equal to his erudition. Thus, the history of John Wesley's marriage with Mrs Vazeille and of their subsequent relations is not treated by him with the requisite impartiality. Dr A. W. Stocks, himself a descendant of the Vazeille family, has inherited relics and traditions from them which show Mrs Vazeille's side of the question. He also possesses and has published in the Critic, N.S., Vol. IV, No. 85, of August 15, 1885, New York, U.S.A., an important letter from Mr Antony Vazeille (Mrs Vazeille's first husband) to his wife, which shows their harmonious relations. From another point of view, a valuable corrective of Tyerman is to be found in Hetty Wesley, by A. T. Quiller-Couch, London, 1903, a living if not always a too favourable presentment of the Wesley Family.

The notes and materials for a biography of William Law, privately printed—each copy with MS. notes by the author Christopher Walton—still await publication.

Materials for a biography of Archbishop Wake exist at Christ Church, Oxford. In general, nothing but the publication of diocesan records alone will throw light on the much debated question of parochial and clerical activity in this age. A good deal can be inferred from the charges of Bishops like Wake, Butler, and Gibson, delivered to the clergy of their dioceses; but the history of the Establishment during this period, and of Nonconformist bodies other than Wesleyan, can hardly be accurately written without a much more extensive research into unpublished materials than has yet been attempted. The first two numbers of the Transactions of the Baptist Historical Society—just published—reveal valuable sources of new materials.

III. The Established Church.

(A) *Papers and Works illustrative of General Conditions.*

Butler, Joseph, Bishop of Durham. Stanhope Memorials of. Ed. W. M. Egglestone. London. 1878.

—— Charge to Clergy of Diocese of Durham. London. 1751.

Gibson, Edmund, Bishop of London. Charges to Clergy of Lincoln. London. 1717.

—— Charges to the Clergy of London (1730). London. 1731; to the same (1741–2). London. 1742.

—— Some account of. By R. Smalbroke. London. 1749.

Hearne, Thomas. Works. Ed. P. Bliss. 3 vols. London. 1837.

Hurd, Richard, Bishop of Worcester. Correspondence with Bishop Warburton. London. 1809.

—— Memoirs of Life and Writings. By F. Kilvert. London. 1742.

—— Complete Works. London. 1811.

Lowth, Robert, Bishop of London. Letter to Warburton. 4th edn. London. 1766.

—— Memoirs of Life and Writings. By R. Laden. London. 1787.

Potter, John, Archbishop of Canterbury. Works. London. 1753.

Pyle, Dr E. Memoirs of a royal Chaplain, 1729–63. By A. Hartshorne. London. 1905.

Romaine, W. Life. By W. B. Cadogan. London. 1796.

Secker, Thomas, Archbishop of Canterbury. Works. (With Life.) 6 vols. London. 1825.

—— Review of life and character. By Bishop Porteus. London. 1797.

Sherlock, Thomas, Bishop of London. Works, with some account of his Life. By T. S. Hughes. 5 vols. London. 1830.

Somers Tracts. Vol. XIII. London. 1812.

Wake, William, Archbishop of Canterbury. State of English Church in Councils, Synods, Convocations, etc. London. 1703.

—— charge to the Clergy of Lincoln (1709). London. 1710.

Walker, S. Life of. By E. Sidney. London. 1835.

Wilson, Thomas, Bishop of Sodor and Man. Life and Works. By C. Cruttwell.
London. 1781.

—— Life. By H. Stowell. London. 1879. [First published 1788.]

—— Life and Works. By J. Keble. 7 vols. (Library of Anglo-Catholic Theology.)
London. 1863.

Woodward, J. Rise and Progress of the Religious Societies. 2nd edn. London. 1698.

(B) *Works by Churchmen dealing with religious controversy and thoughts.*

Berkeley, George, Bishop of Cloyne. Works and Life. Ed. A. C. Fraser. 4 vols.
Oxford. 1901.

Butler, Joseph, Bishop of Durham. Works. Ed. J. H. Bernard. 2 vols. London.
1900.

—— Remains hitherto unpublished. London. 1883.

Hervey, J. Meditations and Contemplations. Liverpool. 1814. With Memoir by
D. McNicoll. London. 1855.

—— Original Letters. Scarborough. 1829.

—— Herveiana : sketches of life and writings of J. H. By J. Cole. 2 pts.
Scarborough. 1822–3.

Hoadly, Benjamin, Bishop of Winchester. Works. 3 vols. London. 1773.

—— Answer to Convocation. London. 1718.

Warburton, William, Bishop of Gloucester. Works. London. 1811.

Byrom, John. Poems. Ed. A. W. Ward. 2 vols. Chetham Soc. Manchester. 1895.

Law, William. Works. 9 vols. London. 1753–76.

—— Ed. G. B. M[organ]. 9 vols. Privately printed. Canterbury. 1892–3.

Swift, Jonathan, Dean of St Patrick's. Prose Works. Ed. Temple Scott. London.
1908.

Whiston, William. Essays. London. 1713.

(C) *Constructive Deism.*

Addison, J. Evidences of the Christian Religion. London. 1721.

Berkeley, George, Bishop of Cloyne. Alciphron, or The Minute Philosopher.
London. 1732.

Leland, John. Answer to Morgan. London. 1737.

—— Answer to Tindal. London. 1740.

Locke, John. Works. 12th edn. London. 1824.

Morgan, Thomas. The Moral Philosopher. Pts. i–iii. London. 1737–40.

Tindal, M. Christianity as old as the Creation. London. 1730.

—— Reply to. By W. Law. Works. London. 1762.

Toland, J. J. Christianity not mysterious. London. 1696.

—— Vindicius Liberius. London. 1700.

—— Letters to Serena. London. 1704.

—— Adeisidaemon. London. 1709.

—— Nazarenus. London. 1718.

—— Tetradymus ; Pantheisticon. London. 1720.

(D) *Critical Deism.*

Blount, Charles. Anima Mundi. London. 1678–9.

—— Apollonius Tyanaeus. London. 1680.

—— Oracles of Reason. London. 1693.

Bolingbroke, Henry St John, Viscount. Works. 8 vols. London. 1809.
Collins, Anthony. Essay on Reason. London. 1707.
—— Priestcraft in Perfection. London. 1709.
—— Discourse on Freethinking. London. 1713; Reply to above Remarks on
Phileleutherus Lipsiensis. [Richard Bentley.] London. 1713. Part III. 1743.
—— Grounds and reasons of Christian Religion. London. 1724.
—— Scheme of Literal Prophecy. London. 1727.
Hume, David. Philosophical Works. Edd. T. H. Green and T. H. Grose. Oxford.
1874–5.
Middleton, Conyers. Miscellaneous Works. London. 1755.
Shaftesbury, A. A. Cooper, third Earl of. Life, Unpublished Letters, and Philo-
sophical Regimen of. Ed. B. Rand. London. 1900.

IV. SECONDARY WORKS.

(A) *General Histories of the Established Church and Dissenting Bodies.*

Abbey, C. J. and Overton, J. H. The English Church and its Bishops, 1700–1800.
2 vols. London. 1887.
Bogue, D. and J. Bennett. History of Dissenters, 1688–1808. 2 vols. London. 1833.
Dale, R. W. History of Congregationalism in England. London. 1908.
Lathbury, T. History of the Convocation of the Church of England. London. 1842.
Molesworth, Canon W. N. History of the Church of England from 1660. London.
1882.
New History of Methodism. Edd. W. J. Townsend, H. B. Workman, G. Eayrs.
2 vols. London. 1909.
Overton, Canon J. H. The English Church in the Eighteenth Century. 2 vols.
London. 1878. Abridged edn. London. 1887.
—— and F. Relton. The English Church (1714–1800). London. 1906.
Simon, J. S. Revival of Religion in England in the Eighteenth Century. London.
1907.
Skeats, H. S. History of the Free Churches. Ed. S. Miall. London. 1894.
Stevens, A. History of Methodism. 2 vols. London. 1873–4.
Stoughton, J. Religion in England, 1702–1800. London. 1878.

(B) *Works dealing with the History of Thought and Controversy.*

Atterbury, Francis, Bishop of Rochester. Life. By F. Williams. [Docs.] 2 vols.
London. 1869.
Berkeley, George, Bishop of Cloyne. Life. By A. C. Fraser. London. 1901.
Butler, Joseph, Bishop of Durham, Studies subsidiary to. By W. E. Gladstone.
Oxford. 1896.
—— T. Lorenz. Beitrag zur Lebensgeschichte von J. B. Berlin. 1900.
—— Weitere Beiträge zur Lebensgeschichte in den Jahren 1731–3. Berlin. 1901.
Farrar, H. S. Critical History of Free Thought. London. 1862.
Hunt, J. History of Religious Thought in England. 3 vols. London. 1870.
Hutton, W. H. Some Unpublished Letters of Nonjurors. Athenaeum, May 8, 1909.
Lathbury, T. History of the Non-Jurors. London. 1845.
Law, William. Life and Opinions of. Canon Overton. London. 1881.
—— Memorials of Birthplace and Residence. By "G. Moreton." London. 1895.
Lechler, G. V. Geschichte des Englischen Deismus. 2 Bde. Stuttgart and
Tübingen. 1841.
Mandeville, B. Works. London. 1772.
—— B. de M.'s Bienenfabel. By P. Goldbach. Halle. 1889. [Includes a Biblio-
graphy.]

Overton, Canon J. H.   The Non-Jurors.   London.   1902.

Pattison, Mark.   Essays.   Ed. H. Nettleship.   2 vols.   Oxford.   1889.

Robertson, J. M.   Pioneer Humanists.   London.   1907.

Stephen, Sir Leslie.   History of English Thought in the Eighteenth Century. 2 vols.   London.   1902.

Wake, Archbishop.   By J. H. Overton.   Lincoln Diocesan Magazine.   Lincoln. 1891.

—— and the Project of Union with the Gallican Church.   By J. H. Lupton.   London. 1896.

(C)   *Works exhibiting social conditions.*

Ashton, J.   The Fleet—its River, Prison, and Marriages.   London.   1888.

—— History of English Lotteries.   London.   1893.

Brown, J.   Estimate of the manners and principles of the times.   2 vols.   London. 1757.

—— Thoughts on Civil Liberty, licentiousness and faction.   Newcastle.   1765.

Buckle, H. T.   Introduction to History of Civilisation in England.   Ed. J. M. Robertson.   London.   1904.

Conway, B. K.   History of English Philanthropy.   London.   1905.

Defoe, D.   Tour through the whole island of Great Britain.   4 vols.   London.   1778. [1st edn. 1724.]

Kalm, Pehr.   Visit to England.   Translated by Joseph Lucas.   London.   1892.

Roberts, G.   Social History of the people of the Southern Counties in England in past Centuries.   London.   1856.

Rogers, Thorold.   Six Centuries of Work and Wages.   London.   1889.

Saussure, C. de.   Letters of.   A Foreign View of England under George I and II. English Translation : London.   1902.

Sydney, W. C.   England and the English in the Eighteenth Century.   2 vols. London.   1892.

Voltaire, F. M. A. de.   Letters concerning England.   English Translation : London. 1733.

—— Visit to England, 1726-9.   By A. Ballantyne.   London.   1893.

—— Montesquieu and Rousseau in England.   By J. Churton Collins.   London. 1908.

Watson, Bishop, Anecdotes of Life of.   By his son.   2 vols.   London.   1818.

Webb, S. and B.   English Local Government (1688-1834).   The Parish and the County.   3 vols.   London.   1906-8.

Wendeborn, G. F. A.   Reise durch einige westlichen und südlichen Provinzen Englands.   2 vols.   Hamburg.   1793.

Wright, T.   Caricature History of the Georges.   London.   1877.

(D)   *Works dealing with missionary effort etc.*

Anderson, J. S. M.   History of Church of England in Colonies and Foreign Dependencies of the British Empire.   3 vols.   London.   1856.

Canton, W.   History of British and Foreign Bible Society.   2 vols.   London.   1904.

Cross, A. L.   The Anglican Episcopate and the American Colonies.   Harvard Hist. Studies.   Vol. ix.   London.   1896.

Society for Propagation of Gospel.   Digest of Records, 1701-1892.   London.   1892.

Warneck, G.   History of the Protestant Missions.   Trans. by G. Robson.   Edinburgh and London.   1906.

Whites, W.   Memoirs of Protestant Episcopal Church in the United States.   Ed. B. F. de Costa.   London.   1880.

(E) *The Wesleyan and Welsh Revivals.*

(a) *General.*

Benson, J. Defence of the Methodists. London. 1793.
—— Apology for the Methodists. London. 1801.
Crowther, J. A Portraiture of Methodism. London. 1815.
Cudworth, W. Whitebrook, J. C. London. 1906. [A biography and vindication with reference to strictures of John Wesley.]
Dartmouth MSS. Hist. MSS. Comm. Rep. xv. App. Pt. 1. Vol. III. [Contains correspondence of John Newton.] London. 1896.
FitzGerald, W. B. The Roots of Methodism. (Handbook for the Wesley Guild.) London. 1903.
Fletcher, J. W., of Madeley. Works. 8 vols. London. 1836.
—— Wesley's Designated Successor. Life. By L. Tyerman. 1882. [Docs.]
Hall, Joseph. Memorials of Wesleyan Methodist Ministers and yearly death-roll, 1777–1840. London. 1876.
Harris, Howell. Memoirs of, with account of Calvinistic Methodists in Wales. By J. Bulmer. Haverfordwest. 1824.
Hervey, James. Theron and Aspasio. Wesley's Remarks on, with Hervey's Reply. London. 1755.
—— Life. By H. J. Hughes. London. 1892.
Huntingdon, Selina, Countess of. Two letters, pp. 209–11. In MSS. Mrs Frankland-Russell-Astley. Hist. MSS. Comm. Rep. xv. London. 1900.
—— Life and Times of. By a member of the Houses of Shirley and Hastings. 2 vols. London. 1844.
Jackson, T. Early Methodist Preachers. 6 vols. London. 1865; abridged edition of this, with notes, entitled Wesley's Veterans. By J. Telford. London. [Autobiographies of Wesley's principal helpers.] *In the press.*
Myles, W. Chronological History of the People called Methodists. London. 1813.
Nightingale, A. A Portraiture of Methodism. London. 1807.
—— Nightingale v. Stockdale. Report of Trial for Libel in connection with above. By Bartrum. London. 1809.
Stevens, A. B. History of Methodism. 3 vols. London. 1899.
Telford, J. Popular History of Methodism. London. 1899.
Warren and Stephens. Chronicles of Methodism. London. 1827.
Wesley, the Family of. Byrom and the Wesleys. By E. Hoole. London. 1864.
—— Hetty Wesley. By A. T. Quiller-Couch. London. 1908.
—— Memoirs of. By Adam Clarke. London. 1823.
—— Memorials of the Wesley Family. By G. J. Stevenson. London. 1876.
—— Oglethorpe and the Wesleys in America. By E. Hoole. London. 1863.
—— The Wesleys in Lincolnshire. By G. Lester. London. 1890.
Wesley, Charles. Early Journal. Ed. by J. Telford. (*To be published shortly.*)
—— Journal and Poetry of. By T. Jackson. London. 1862.
—— Life. By T. Jackson. 2 vols. London. 1841; abridged edn. 2 vols. London. 1848. [Docs.]
—— Life. By J. Telford. London. 1900.
—— and John. Poetical Works. Ed. G. Osborn. London. 1868.
Wesley, John. Conference Minutes: Wesleyan. Vol. I. (1744–98.) London. 1862.
—— Correspondence of, with S. Walker. Saturday Review, March 28. London. 1891.
—— Historical Society Publications. London. 1896 sqq.
—— Hymns, translation of German. By J. W. Ed. J. T. Hatfield. London. 1896.

Wesley, John. Works, etc. ; City Road Chapel and its Associations. By G. J. Stevenson. London. 1873.

—— Journal, October 14, 1735–7. Ed. Bishop E. R. Hendrix. New Orleans. 1901.

—— Journal. 4 vols. London. 1907. Standard edition. 6 vols. (*In process of publication.*)

—— Original letters of J. W. and his friends. Ed. J. Priestley. Birmingham. 1791.

—— Works. 32 vols. Bristol. 1771–4 ; 15 vols. London. 1856.

(β) *Centenary studies and publications.*

Homes, Haunts and friends of J. W. Centenary number of the Methodist Recorder. London. 1891.

Wesley Centenary Handbook, hymns, service, etc. London. 1891.

Wesley, the Living. By J. H. Rigg. Centenary edn. London. 1891. New edn. London. 1905.

—— The Man, his Teaching, and his Work. [Addresses and Sermons delivered in commemoration of the Centenary.] London. 1891.

Wesleyan studies by various writers from unpublished sources. London. 1903.

Wesley, John, and his successors. Centenary memorial. London. 1891.

(γ) *Biographies etc.*

Wesley, John, Essai dogmatique sur. By M. Haemmerlin. Colmar. 1857.

—— J. W., and George Whitefield in Scotland. By D. Butler. Edinburgh. 1898.

—— J. W. and the Evangelical Reaction of the Eighteenth Century. By Julia Wedgewood. London. 1870.

—— J. W.'s place in Church History. By D. O. Urlin. Edinburgh. 1870.

—— Life. By John Hampson. 3 vols. London. 1791.

—— Life. By Canon J. H. Overton. London. 1891.

—— Life. By F. J. Snell. Edinburgh. 1900.

—— Life. By J. Telford. New edn. London. 1906.

—— Life. By J. Whitehead. 2 vols. London. 1793–6.

—— Life and Times. By L. Tyerman. 3 vols. London. 1870. [Docs.]

—— Life and Works. By Matthieu Lelièvre. English Translation. London. 1900.

—— Life of, and use and progress of Methodism. By R. Southey. 3rd edn.
A. Knox. Notes by S. T. Coleridge. Ed. C. C. Southey. 2 vols. London. 1846.
Observations on Southey's Life of J. W. By R Watson. London. 1820.

—— The Oxford Methodists. By L. Tyerman. London. 1873. [Docs.]

—— Wesley et ses rapports avec les Français. By E. Gounelle. Paris. 1898.

Wesley, Samuel the elder, Life and Times of. By L. Tyerman. London. 1866.

—— Susanna. Life. By J. Kirk. London. 1864.

—— —— Life. By Eliza Clarke. London. 1886.

Whitefield, George. Account of. Gentleman's Magazine, pp. 150 sqq. London. 1734.

—— Eighteen Sermons. Ed A. Gifford. London. 1871.

—— Farewell Sermon at Moorfield, August 30, 1769. London. 1769.

—— Journals, with appreciations. Ed. W. Wale. London. 1905.

—— Life. By L. Tyerman. 2 vols. London. 1876. [Docs.]

—— Memoirs of the Life of. By J. Gillies. London. 1773. [Includes letters from John Wesley.]

Williams, H. W. Constitution and Polity of the Wesleyan Methodist Church. New edn. By D. J. Waller. London. 1898.

CHAPTER III.

JACOBITISM AND THE UNION.

A Bibliography of Jacobite history is appended to C. Sanford Terry's The Rising of 1745 (new edn. 1903).

I. MANUSCRIPTS.

In the P.R.O. are forty-six volumes of miscellaneous State Papers (Scotland), November, 1688—December 15, 1760; three volumes of "Church Books (Scotland)," May, 1724—May, 1760; eleven volumes of "Letter Book (Scotland)," September 8, 1713—May 7, 1725; twenty-eight volumes of "Warrant Book (Scotland)," August 15, 1670—September 14, 1714, and seven volumes of "Scottish Warrants," 1711-65. Besides the S.P., France, Spain, Sicily and Naples, Rome, Newsletters, and Foreign Entry Books, there are among the S.P., Tuscany, nine volumes of John Walton's despatches, 1730-57, and thirty-three volumes of Sir Horace Mann's despatches, 1737-79.

In the General Register House, Edinburgh, are several volumes of manuscripts relating to forfeited Jacobite estates, military orders and letters relating to the risings of 1715 and 1745 (State Papers, 338-65).

The British Museum contains a large and miscellaneous collection of Jacobite materials, chiefly among the Addit., Egerton, Gualterio, Hardwicke, Newcastle, and Stowe MSS. See a brief catalogue of them in C. Sanford Terry's Rising of 1745 (new edn. 1903, p. 306).

The Royal Library at Windsor Castle contains the large collection of Stuart Papers. They have been calendared to February, 1717, by F. H. Blackburne Daniell, for the Historical Manuscripts Commission (3 vols. London. 1902, 1904, 1907). The following volumes published by the Commission locate or print family archives of the post-Union and Jacobite period: Report I (1870); Rept. II (1871); Rept. III (1872); Rept. IV (1874); Rept. V (1876); Rept. VI (1877); Rept. VII (1879); Rept. VIII (1881); Rept. IX (1884); Rept. X, Pt. i (1885), Pt. iv (1885), Pt. vi (1887); Rept. XI, Pt. iv (1887), Pt. vii (1888); Rept. XII, Pt. viii (1891); Rept. XIII, Pt. vi (1893), Pt. vii (1893); Rept. XIV, Pt. iii (1894), Pt. iv (1894), Pt. ix (1895); Rept. XV, Pt. ii (1897), Pt. iv (1897), Pt. vi (1897); Portland MSS. vol. v (1899); Various Collections, vols. I, II (1901-3); Wedderburn MSS. (1902); Mar and Kellie MSS. (1904); Lady Du Cane's MSS. (1905). Sir William Fraser's reports upon the archives of Scottish families must also be noted.

In the French Archives des Affaires Étrangères there is much material bearing upon Jacobite projects and enterprises, 1707-60: in particular in Mémoires et Documents, Angleterre, tom. 24, 25, 52-4, 75-91, 93; ditto, Espagne, 238, 344; Correspondance Politique, Angleterre, 211-38, 241-3, 248-50, 252, 258, 260-4, 270-4, 279, 280, 283-5, 290, 294, 328, 332, 334, 338, 339, 344, 346, 349-51, 353, 354, 360, 364, 375-7, 380, 382-91, 417, 418, 420-2, 425, 441, 442; ditto (Supplément), Angleterre, 3-5, 7, 10.

The Spanish Archivo General de Simancas contains the correspondence of the Marqués de Villamayor with Cardinal Alberoni, 1717-9, of Cardinal Alberoni with the Marqués de San Felipe, 1717-9, of the Marqués Berrety Landy with Cardinal Alberoni, 1716-7, and of the Marqués de Monteleon with Cardinal Alberoni, 1717-9.

The relations of Charles XII of Sweden with the Jacobites are illuminated by the documents preserved in the Swedish Riksarkiv at Stockholm. The correspondence of Count Karl Gyllenborg, Swedish Minister at London, with Baron von Müllern, Minister of Foreign Affairs, February 26, 1715—September 5, 1717, and the letters of Baron Erik Sparre, Swedish Minister at Paris, to Gyllenborg, July 1, 1715—March 30, 1716, are among the Diplomatica Anglica. Sparre's correspondence with Charles XII and von Müllern, July 11, 1715—November 8, 1717, is among the Diplomatica Gallica. The Diplomatica Hollandica contain letters and documents relating to the arrest of Gyllenborg and Görtz, and the latter's letters written from prison at Arnhem in 1717 (published by T. Westrin in Historisk Tidsskrift, vol. XVIII, pp. 135-74. Stockholm. 1898). Görtz's letters to Charles XII, November 4, 1716—November 15, 1717, are in a separate volume.

II. CONTEMPORARY MATERIALS.

Historical Papers relating to the Jacobite Period, 1699-1750. Ed. J. Allardyce. 2 vols. (New Spalding Club.) Aberdeen. 1895-6.

Journal and Memoirs of the Marquis d'Argenson, 1694-1757. Ed. K. Wormeley. London. 1902.

Jacobite Correspondence of the Atholl Family during the Rebellion, 1745-6. (Abbotsford Club.) Edinburgh. 1840.

Chronicles of the Families of Atholl and Tullibardine. Collected and arranged by John seventh Duke of Atholl, K.T 4 vols. Edinburgh. 1896.

Berwick, James Duke of. Mémoires écrits par lui-même, avec une suite abrégée depuis 1716 jusqu'à sa mort en 1734. 2 vols. Paris. 1778.

Boston, Thomas. A general Account of my Life. London. 1908.

Broglie, J. V. A., Duc de. Le Secret du Roi: Correspondance secrète de Louis XV avec ses Agents diplomatiques, 1752-74. 2 vols. 4th edn. Paris. 1888.

Burt, Edward. Letters from a Gentleman in the North of Scotland. Fifth edn. 2 vols. London. 1818.

Cameron, Alan. Narrative: the End of the '15. Ed. C. Sanford Terry. Scott. Hist. Review. Vol. v. Glasgow. 1908.

State Papers and Letters addressed to William Carstares. Ed. Joseph M'Cormick. Edinburgh. 1774.

Les derniers Stuarts à Saint-Germain-en-Laye. Documents inédits et authentiques puisés aux Archives publiques et privées. Ed. Marquise Campana de Cavelli. 2 vols. Paris. 1871.

Jacobite Memoirs of the Rebellion of 1745. Ed. Robert Chambers. Edinburgh. 1834.

A full Collection of all the Proclamations and Orders published by the Authority of Charles Prince of Wales since his arrival in Edinburgh the 17th day of September till the 15th of October 1745. 2 pts. Glasgow. 1745-6.

Memoirs of the Life of Sir John Clerk of Penicuik. Ed. John M. Gray. (Scottish History Society.) Edinburgh. 1892.

The Cochrane Correspondence regarding the Affairs of Glasgow, 1745-6. Ed. James Dennistoun. (Maitland Club.) Glasgow. 1836.

Colin, J. Louis XV et les Jacobites: Le Projet de Débarquement en Angleterre de 1743-4. Paris. 1901.

The Report of the Proceedings and Opinion of the Board of General Officers on their Examination into the Conduct of Sir John Cope. London. 1749.

Cottin, P. Un Protégé de Bachaumont: Correspondance inédite du Marquis d'Éguilles, 1745–8. Paris. 1887.

Culloden Papers: comprising an extensive and interesting Correspondence from the year 1625 to 1748. London. 1815.

The Loch Lomond Expedition, 1715. Ed. James Dennistoun. Glasgow. 1834.

The Jacobite Attempt of 1719. Ed. William K. Dickson. (Scottish History Society.) Edinburgh. 1895.

Drummond, John. Memoirs of Sir Ewen Cameron of Locheill. (Abbotsford Club.) Edinburgh. 1842.

Elcho, David Lord. A short Account of the Affairs of Scotland in the Years 1744, 1745, 1746. Ed. the Hon. Evan Charteris. Edinburgh. 1907.

Forbes, Bishop Robert. The Lyon in Mourning. Ed. Henry Paton. 3 vols. (Scottish History Society.) Edinburgh. 1895–6.

The Gentleman's Magazine. Vols. xv, xvi. London. 1745–6.

The Stuart Papers. Ed. J. H. Glover. London. 1847.

Letters which passed between Count Gyllenborg, the Barons Görtz, Sparre, and Others. Edinburgh. 1717.

Home, John. The History of the Rebellion in the Year 1745. London. 1802.

Secret History of Colonel Hoocke's Negociations in Scotland in 1707. Edinburgh. 1760.

Correspondence of Colonel Nathaniel Hooke, 1703–7. Ed. William D. Macray. (Roxburghe Club.) 2 vols. London. 1870–1.

Johnstone, James, Chevalier de. Memoirs of the Rebellion in 1745 and 1746. London. 1820.

Handlingar rörande Skandinaviens Historia. Stockholm. 1822.

The Highlands of Scotland in 1750. Ed. Andrew Lang. Edinburgh. 1898.

Historisk Tidsskrift (pp. 135–74, 276–86). Stockholm. 1898. 1901. 1903.

Lockhart, George. Lockhart Papers. 2 vols. London. 1817.

The Decline of the last Stuarts. Ed. Lord Mahon. (Roxburghe Club.) London. 1843.

Analecta Scotica: Collections illustrative of the History of Scotland. Ed. James Maidment. 2 vols. Edinburgh. 1834–7.

The Argyle Papers. Ed. James Maidment. Edinburgh. 1834.

A Selection from the Papers of the Earls of Marchmont illustrative of Events from 1685 to 1750. 3 vols. London. 1831.

Maxwell of Kirkconnell, James. Narrative of Charles Prince of Wales' Expedition to Scotland in the Year 1745. (Maitland Club.) Edinburgh. 1841.

Scottish Forfeited Estates Papers, 1715–45. Ed. A. H. Millar. (Scottish History Society.) Edinburgh. 1909.

Memorials of John Murray of Broughton. Ed. Robert F. Bell. (Scottish History Society.) Edinburgh. 1898.

Papers about the Rebellions of 1715 and 1745. Ed. Henry Paton. (Miscellany of the Scottish History Society.) Edinburgh. 1893.

Patten, Robert. The History of the late Rebellion: with original Papers and Characters of the principal Noblemen and Gentlemen concern'd in it. London. 1717.

A true Account of the Proceedings at Perth; the Debates in the Secret Council there; with the Reasons and Causes of the suddain Breaking up of the Rebellion. Written by a Rebel. London. 1716.

Rae, Peter. The History of the late Rebellion (1715) rais'd against King George by the Friends of the Popish Pretender. Second edition. London. 1746.

Ramsay, John. Scotland and Scotsmen in the 18th Century. 2 vols. Edinburgh. 1888.

A Collection of original Letters and authentick Papers relating to the Rebellion of 1715. Edinburgh. 1730.

A Compleat History of the late Rebellion. London. 1716.

A List of Persons concerned in the Rebellion. Ed. the Earl of Roseberry and Walter Macleod. (Scottish History Society.) Edinburgh. 1890.

A Faithful Register of the late Rebellion. London. 1718.

Saint-Simon, Duc de. Mémoires complets et authentiques sur le Siècle de Louis XIV et la Régence. Ed. le Marquis de Saint-Simon. 21 vols. Paris. 1829–30.

Saxe, Maréchal de. Lettres et Mémoires relatifs aux Événements qui se sont passés depuis 1733 jusqu'en 1750. 5 vols. Paris. 1794.

The Scots Magazine. Vols. VII and VIII. Edinburgh. 1745–6.

A Collection of original Papers about the Scots Plot (1703). London. 1704.

Sinclair, John, Master of. Memoirs of the Insurrection in Scotland in 1715. (Abbotsford Club.) Edinburgh. 1858.

A complete Collection of State Trials. Vols. XV–XIX. London. 1812–3.

Statutes at Large. Vols. IV–VII. London. 1763–4.

The Albemarle Papers: being the Correspondence of William Anne second Earl of Albemarle, Commander-in-Chief in Scotland 1746–7, with an Appendix of Letters from Andrew Fletcher, Lord Justice-Clerk 1746–8. Ed. C. Sanford Terry. 2 vols. (New Spalding Club.) Aberdeen. 1902.

The Chevalier de St George and the Jacobite Movements in his Favour 1701–20. Ed. C. Sanford Terry. London. 1901.

The Rising of 1745: with a Bibliography of Jacobite History 1689–1788. Ed. C. Sanford Terry. New edn. London. 1903.

Thurot, François. Journal historique de la Campagne sur les Côtes d'Écosse et d'Irlande en 1757 et 1758. Dunkirk. 1760.

Wodrow, Robert. Analecta. (Maitland Club.) 4 vols. Edinburgh. 1842–3.

—— Correspondence. (Wodrow Society.) 3 vols. Edinburgh. 1842–3.

The Woodhouselee MS. Ed. A. F. Steuart. Edinburgh. 1907.

III. MODERN GENERAL WORKS.

Brown, P. Hume. History of Scotland. Vol. III. Cambridge. 1909.

Browne, J. A History of the Highlands and of the Highland Clans. 4 vols. Glasgow. 1838.

Burton, J. Hill. The History of Scotland to the Extinction of the last Jacobite Insurrection. Vol. VIII. Edinburgh. 1876.

Chambers, R. Domestic Annals of Scotland from the Revolution to the Rebellion of 1745. London. 1861.

Craik, Sir H. A Century of Scottish History. 2 vols. Edinburgh. 1901.

Cunningham, J. The Church History of Scotland. 2 vols. Edinburgh. 1859.

Graham, H. G. Social Life of Scotland in the 18th Century. 2 vols. London. 1899.

Grub, G. An Ecclesiastical History of Scotland. 4 vols. Edinburgh. 1861.

Lang, A. History of Scotland. Vol. IV. Edinburgh. 1907.

Mackerrow, J. History of the Secession Church. 2 vols. Edinburgh. 1839.

Mathieson, W. L. Scotland and the Union, 1695–1747. Glasgow. 1905.

Morren, N. Annals of the General Assembly of the Church of Scotland, 1739–52. 2 vols. Edinburgh. 1838–40.

Skinner, J. An Ecclesiastical History of Scotland. 2 vols. London. 1788.

Stephen, W. History of the Scottish Church. 2 vols. Edinburgh. 1894–6.

Stewart, D. Sketches of the Character, Manners, and present State of the Highlanders of Scotland. 2 vols. Edinburgh. 1822.

Struthers, J. The History of Scotland from the Union to 1748. 2 vols. Glasgow. 1827–8.

IV. MONOGRAPHS ON SPECIAL SUBJECTS.

Blaikie, W. B. Itinerary of Prince Charles Edward Stuart. (Scottish History Society.) Edinburgh. 1897.

Cadell, Sir R. Sir John Cope and the Rebellion of 1745. Edinburgh. 1898.

Chambers, R. History of the Rebellions in Scotland under the Viscount of Dundee and the Earl of Mar. Edinburgh. 1829.

—— History of the Rebellion in Scotland in 1745, 1746. 2 vols. Edinburgh. 1828.

Dixon, W. The Jacobite Episode in Scottish History. Edinburgh. 1874.

Doran, J. Mann and Manners at the Court of Florence 1740–86. London. 1876.

Ferguson, R. S. The Retreat of the Highlanders through Westmorland in 1745. Kendal. 1889.

Head, F. W. The fallen Stuarts. Cambridge Historical Essays. No. XII. Cambridge. 1901.

Kirsch, Peter Anton. Treibende Faktoren bei dem Schottischen Aufstande 1745–6 und Nachspiel desselben. In Historisches Jahrbuch, Vol. XXVII. Munich. 1906.

Lang, A. Pickle the Spy : or, The Incognito of Prince Charles. London. 1897.

—— The Companions of Pickle. London. 1898.

Lefèvre-Pontalis, G. Le Mission de Marquis d'Éguilles en Écosse auprès de Charles Édouard. In Annales de l'École des Sciences Politiques. Paris. 1887.

Macdonald, A. History of the Clan Donald. 3 vols. Inverness. 1896–1907.

Macgregor, A. G. M. History of the Clan Gregor. 2 vols. Edinburgh. 1898–1901.

A royalist Family, Irish and French (1689–1789), and Prince Charles Edward. Translated from the French by A. G. M. Macgregor. Edinburgh. 1904.

Mounsey, G. C. Carlisle in 1745. London. 1846.

Perthshire, a Military History of, 1660–1902. Ed. the Marchioness of Tullibardine. 2 vols. Perth. 1908.

Salomon, F. Geschichte des letzten Ministeriums Königin Annas von England, 1710–4. Gotha. 1894.

Thornton, P. M. The Stuart Dynasty : Short Studies of its Rise, Course, and early Exile. London. 1890.

V. BIOGRAPHIES AND MEMOIRS.

Biscoe, A. C. The Earls of Middleton. London. 1876.

Bissett, A. Memoirs and Papers of Sir Andrew Mitchell. 2 vols. London. 1850.

Burton, J. Hill. Lives of Simon Lord Lovat and Duncan Forbes of Culloden. London. 1847.

Campbell, R. The Life of John Duke of Argyle and Greenwich. London. 1745.

Carlyle, A. Autobiography. Edinburgh. 1860.

Dennistoun, J. Memoirs of Sir Robert Strange, Knt., and of Andrew Lumisden. 2 vols. London. 1855.

Dictionary of National Biography. 66 vols. London. 1885–1901.

Ewald, A. C. Life and Times of Prince Charles Stuart. New edn. London. 1904.

Forbin, Claude, Comte de. Mémoires. Amsterdam. 1730.

Graham, J. M. Annals and Correspondence of the Viscount and the first and second Earls of Stair. 2 vols. Edinburgh. 1875.

Haile, M. Queen Mary of Modena. London. 1905.

—— James Francis Edward : the Old Chevalier. London. 1907.

Jesse, J. H. Memoirs of the Pretenders and their Adherents. London. 1845.

Keith, Fieldmarshal James. Fragment of a Memoir, 1714–34. (Spalding Club.) Edinburgh. 1843.

Kelly, B. W. Life of Henry Benedict Stuart, Cardinal Duke of York. London. 1899.

—— The Conqueror of Culloden : being the Life and Times of William Augustus Duke of Cumberland, 1721–65. London. 1903.

Lang, A. Prince Charles Edward Stuart, the Young Chevalier. New edn. London. 1903.

—— and Shield, A. The King over the Water. [James III and VIII.] London. 1907.

Mackenzie, W. C. Simon Fraser, Lord Lovat: his Life and Times. London. 1908.

Maclachlan, A. N. C. William Augustus Duke of Cumberland : being a Sketch of his Military Life and Character. London. 1876.

Norie, W. Drummond. Life and Adventures of Prince Charles Edward Stuart. 4 vols. London. 1903–4.

Oliphant, T. L. K. The Jacobite Lairds of Gask. London. 1870.

Omond, G. W. T. The Lord Advocates of Scotland. 2 vols. Edinburgh. 1883.

—— The Arniston Memoirs. Edinburgh. 1887.

Rankin, R. The Marquis d'Argenson. London. 1901.

Roome, H. D. James Edward, the Old Pretender. Oxford. 1904.

Scott, Mrs Maxwell. The Youth of James III, 1688–1712. In Nineteenth Century. Vol. LV. London. 1904.

Shield, Alice. Henry Stuart, Cardinal of York, and his Times. London. 1908.

Story, R. H. William Carstares : a Character and Career of the revolutionary Epoch (1689–1715). London. 1874.

Terry, C. Sanford. The Young Pretender. London. 1903.

Thomson, K. Memoirs of the Jacobites of 1715 and 1745. 3 vols. London. 1845–6.

Vaughan, H. M. The last of the Royal Stuarts : Henry Stuart, Cardinal Duke of York. London. 1906.

Wolff, H. W. The Pretender at Bar-le-Duc. In Blackwood's Magazine. Vol. CLVI. Edinburgh. 1894.

Zévort, E. Le Marquis d'Argenson et le Ministère des Affaires Étrangères. Paris. 1880.

VI. MAPS AND PLANS.

A section entitled "Maps and Plans illustrating the Jacobite Risings" will be found at pp. 317–9 of C. Sanford Terry's The Rising of 1745 (edn. 1903). To those there mentioned should be added, a plan of Glenshiel in the Scottish Historical Review, vol. II, p. 416; of Prestonpans, Falkirk, and Culloden in Elcho's Short Account; of Culloden in Lang's History, vol. IV, p. 510. See also A. Smail's Side-Lights on the Forty-Five. (Edinburgh. 1903.)

CHAPTERS IV and V.

THE BOURBON GOVERNMENTS IN FRANCE AND SPAIN.
(1715–46.)

I. MANUSCRIPTS.

The principal sources for the diplomatic history of this period are to be found in the Public Record Office, the Archives du ministère des Affaires Étrangères, Paris, the Archivo histórico nacional de Madrid, to which the documents previously stored at Alcalá de Hénares have lately been removed. Much important correspondence is at Simancas. The Carte Farnesiane in the Archivio di Stato at Naples are valuable; and these are supplemented by correspondence and documents relating to Alberoni at the Collegio S. Lazaro, near Piacenza. The Venetian Relazioni, unfortunately not printed for the eighteenth century, are of much interest as taking an external point of view, and as throwing vivid light on the personalities at the Courts to which the ambassadors were accredited.

> See Flammermont, J. Rapport…sur les correspondances des Agents Diplomatiques Étrangers en France avant la Révolution conservées dans les Archives de Berlin, Dresde, Genève, Turin, Gênes, Florence, Naples, Simancas, Lisbonne, Londres, La Haye et Vienne. Nouvelles Archives des Missions Scientifiques et Littéraires. Vol. viii. Paris. 1896.
> Legg, L. G. Wickham. List of Diplomatic Representatives and Agents, England and France, 1689–1733. (Notes on the Diplomatic Relations of England and France, ed. C. H. Firth.) Oxford and London. 1909.

II. CONTEMPORARY OR NEARLY CONTEMPORARY AUTHORITIES
(IN PRINT).

A. MEMOIRS, CORRESPONDENCE ETC.

Alberoni, Card.—The Conduct of Cardinal Alberoni, with an Account of some Secret Transactions at the Spanish Court. London. 1720. [Untrustworthy.]

—— Armstrong, E. Letters of Alberoni to the Prince of Parma (from December, 1714). English Historical Review. Vol. v. London. 1890.

Antin, Duc de. Mémoires. Mélanges des Biblioph. Franç. Vol. ii. Paris. 1822.

Argenson, René Louis de Voyer, Marquis de. Journal et Mémoires. Ed. E. J. B. Rathéry. 9 vols. Paris. 1859–67.

Bacallar y Saña, Marques de San Felipe. Comentarios de la guerra de España hasta la paz general del año 1725. 4 vols. Genoa and Madrid. 1790–3.

Barbier, E. J. F. Chronique de la Régence et du Règne de Louis XV, 1718–63. 8 vols. Paris. 1857.

Belando, N. de. Historia Civil de España 1700–33. 3 vols. Madrid. 1744.

Bernis, Cardinal F. L. de Pierre de. Mémoires et Lettres, 1715–58. Ed. F. Masson. 2 vols. Paris. 1878.

Berwick, J. Fitzjames Duc de. Mémoires écrits par lui-même ; avec une suite abrégée depuis 1716, jusqu'à sa mort en 1734. Publ. par le Duc de Fitzjames. 2 vols. Paris. 1778–80. Engl. Transl. [by L. J. Hooke]. London. 1779.

Bois-Jourdain, M. de. Mélanges. 3 vols. Paris. 1807.

Bourgeois, E. Lettres intimes de L. M. Alberoni adressées au Comte I. Rocca. Paris. 1892.

Brancas, Duchesse de. Mémoires, suivies de la Correspondance de Mme de Chateauroux. Ed. E. Assé. Paris. 1890.

Brosses, C. de. L'Italie il y a cent ans, ou lettres écrites en 1739 et 1740. 2 vols. Paris. 1836.

Buvat, J. Journal de la Régence (1715–23). Ed. E. Campardon. 2 vols. Paris 1865.

Campo Raso, I. del. Memorias politicas y militares para servir de continuacion a los comentarios del Marques de San Felipe. 2 vols. Madrid. 1792.

Carutti, D. Relazione del Abbate Maro. Acad. R. di Torino. Series II, xix. Turin. 1861.

Dangeau, Marquis de. Journal. Vols. xvi–xviii (to 1720). Edd. E. Soulié and L. Dussieux. Paris. 1858–9.

[Defoe, Daniel.] The Case of the War in Italy stated. London. 1718.

Diguères, V. des. Lettres inédites de la reine Maria Leczinska et de la duchesse de Luynes au président Hénault. Paris. 1886.

Dorsanne, A. Journal contenant tout ce qui s'est passé à Rome et en France dans l'affaire de la Constitution Unigenitus. 2 vols. Rome. 1753.

Duclos, C. P. Mémoires secrètes sur le règne de Louis XIV, la Régence et le règne de Louis XV. Ed. J. F. Barrière. Paris. 1881.

Duport de Cheverny, Comte. Mémoires, 1731–87. Intr. et notes par R. de Crève-cœur. Paris. 1909.

Faur, M. Vie privée du Maréchal de Richelieu. 3 vols. Paris. 1803.

Feydeau de Marville, C. H. (Comte de Gien). Lettres du Ministre Maurepas à M. de Marville, lieutenant-général de police. Lettres de M. de Marville au Ministre Maurepas. (Soc. hist. de France.) Paris. 1896.

Foscarini, M. Storia Arcana. Arch. Stor. Ital. Vol. v. Florence. 1843.

Galluzzi, R. Istoria del Granducato di Toscana. 9 vols. Florence. 1781.

Hénault, le Président. Mémoires. Ed. Baron de Vigan. Paris. 1855.

L. M. D. M. [La Mothe, dit La Hode.] Vie de Philippe d'Orléans, Régent du Royaume. 2 vols. London. 1737.

Liria, Duke de. Diario del Viaje á Moscovia (1727–30). (Colección de Documentos ineditos para la historia de España. Vol. xciii.) Madrid. 1889.
　　A review of this work. Quarterly Review. January 1892.

Louis XV. Vie privée. [By Moufle d'Angerville.] 4 vols. London. 1791.

Louville, C. A. d'Allonville, Marquis de. Mémoires. 2 vols. Paris. 1818.

Luynes, Duc de. Mémoires sur la Cour de Louis XV, 1735–58. Edd. L. Dussieux and E. Soulié. 17 vols. Paris. 1860–5.

Manifeste sur les sujets de rupture entre la France et l'Espagne. Paris. 1719.

Marais, M. Journal et Mémoires sur la Régence et le règne de Louis XV, 1715–37. Ed. M. de Lescure. 4 vols. Paris. 1863.

Marmontel, J. F. Régence du Duc d'Orléans. Œuvres posthumes. 2 vols. Paris. 1805.

Massillon, J. B. Mémoires de la Minorité de Louis XV. Paris. 1792.

Maurepas, J. F. Phélypeaux de. Mémoires. 3rd edn. 4 vols. Paris. 1792.

—— Recueil dit de Maurepas. 6 vols. Leyden. 1865.

Montesquieu, C. de S., Baron de. Voyages. Ed. Baron A. de Montesquieu. 2 vols. Paris. 1896.

Montgon, C. A. de. Mémoires. 8 vols. Lausanne. 1753.

Morozzo della Bocca, E.   Lettere di Vittorio Amadeo II di Savoia, Re di Sicilia, a G. M. Conte di Morozzo, Marchese della Bocca, suo Ambasciatore a Madrid (1713–17).   (Miscellanea di Storia Patria.   Vol. xxvi.)   Turin.   1887.

Narbonne, P. (Premier Commissaire de police de la ville de Versailles).   Journal des règnes de Louis XIV et Louis XV, 1701–74.   Ed. J. A. Le Roi.   Paris and Versailles.   1866.

Noailles, Maréchal Duc de.—Millot, C. F. X.   Mémoires polit. et milit. pour servir à l'hist. de Louis XIV et Louis XV, composés sur les pièces recueill. par A.-M., D. de N.   Ed. G. T. Villenave.   Vol. iii.   Coll. Petitot.   ii, 72.   Paris.   1829.

Orléans, Elisabeth Charlotte, Duchess of.   See Bibliography to Vol. V, Chap. I.

Piossens, Chevalier de.   Mémoires de la Régence du Duc d'Orléans durant la minorité de Louis XV.   3 vols.   "The Hague" [Rouen].   1729 and 1730.   New enlarged edn, by N. Lenglet de Fresnoy.   5 vols.   Amsterdam.   1749.

Poggiali, C.   Memorie storiche della città di Piacenza.   Vol. xii.   Piacenza.   1766.

Poidebard, W.   Correspondance littéraire et anecdotique entre M. de Saint-Fonds et le Président Dugas.   Lyons.   1900.

Recueil des Instructions données aux ambassadeurs et ministres de France.
Naples et Parme.   Intr. et Notes de J. Reinach.   Paris.   1893.
Espagne.   Intr. et Notes de A. Morel-Fatio et H. Léonardon.   Vols. ii, iii.   Paris.   1899.
Savoie, Sardaigne et Mantoue.   Intr. et Notes du Comte Horric de Beaucaire.   Paris.   1899.

Relazioni diplomatiche della Corte di Savoia.   Francia.   Periodo iii.   Vols. i–iii (Biblioteca Storica Italiana.)   1886–8.

Richelieu, Duc de.   Mémoires historiques et anecdotiques.   6 vols.   Paris.   1829.

Ripperdá, Duke de.   Memoirs of the Duke de Ripperdá, containing a succinct account of...events...between 1715 and 1736.   London.   1740.   [Untrustworthy.]

Rousset, C.   Correspondance de Louis XV et du Maréchal de Noailles.   2 vols.   Paris.   1865.

Rousset de Missy, J.   Histoire du Cardinal Alberoni. [Pretended translation from the Spanish.]   The Hague, 1719.   Second edn, and Italian translation, 1720–1.

Saint-Simon, Duc de.   Mémoires.   Edd. A. Chéruel and A. Regnier.   21 vols.   Paris.   1873–86.   [From Vol. xi.]
—— Papiers inédits.   Lettres et dépêches sur l'ambassade d'Espagne.   Ed. E. Dumont.   Paris.   1889.
Picot, G.   Les papiers du Duc de Saint-Simon aux Archives des Affaires Étrangères.   (Compte Rendu de l'Acad. des Sc. Mor. et Pol.   New Series.   Vol. xiv.   Paris.   1880.)
Ranke, L. von.   Über die Memoiren des Duc von Saint-Simon.   Französ. Gesch.   Vol. v.   Sämmtl. Werke.   Vol. xii.   Leipzig.   1870.
Chéruel, A.   Saint-Simon et l'Abbé Dubois, leurs relations de 1718 à 1722.   Revue Historique.   Vol. i.   Paris.   1876.

Sévelinges, C. L. de.   Mémoires et correspondance du Cardinal Dubois.   Paris.   1815.

Tessé, Maréchal de.   Mémoires et Lettres.   2 vols.   Paris.   1806.
—— Madame de.   Souvenirs de Frouillay de Tessé, Marquise de Créquy, 1710–1802.   7 vols.   Paris.   1836.

(Toussaint, F. V.?)   Anecdotes curieuses de la Cour de France sous le règne de Louis XV.   Ed. P. Fould.   3rd edn.   Paris.   1908.

Ulloa, B. de.   Restablecimiento de las fábricas y comercio Español.   2 parts.   Madrid.   1749.

Ustariz, G. de.   Teórica y Práctica de Comercio y de Marina.   Madrid.   Editions of 1724, 1742 and 1757.

Van Hoey, A.   Lettres et négociations de M. Van Hoey pour servir à l'histoire de la vie du Cardinal de Fleury.   London.   1743.   Engl. Transl.   London.   1743.

Villa, A. R.   La Embajada del Barón de Ripperda en Viena.   Boletin de la R. Ac. de la Historia.   Vol. xxx.   Madrid.   1897.
——— Información del Marqués Beretti-Landy sobre antecedentes del Barón de Ripperda.   Ibid.   Vol. xxxi.   1897.
Villars, Maréchal L. H. Duc de.   Mémoires.   Ed. Marquis de Vogué.   Soc. Hist. France.   6 vols.   Paris.   1884–94.
    Vogüé, Marquis C. J. de.   Villars d'après sa correspondance et des documents inédits.   2 vols.   Paris.   1888.
Voltaire, F. Arouet de.   Précis du siècle de Louis XV.   Vol. xxii of Œuvres complètes.   Kehl.   1784–9.
——— Correspondance.   Vols. lii and liii of the same.

B.   Treaties.

The Collections of Dumont and Rousset, supplemented by G. F. de Martens, and especially by A. del Cantillo, Tratados, Convenios y declaraciónes de paz y de comercio, 1700–1842.   Madrid.   1843; G. de Lamberty, Mémoires pour servir à l'histoire du xviiime siècle.   Vol. x.   Amsterdam.   1736 (containing treaties from 1718–31); and L. Bittner, Chronologisches Verzeichniss der Oesterreichischen Staatsverträge.   Vol. i (to 1763).   Vienna.   1903.

C.   Periodicals.

Annual Register.   Gentleman's Magazine.   Gazette de France.   Mercure Historique et Politique contenant l'état présent de l'Europe.   (Engl. Translation: The Present State of Europe, to 1733.)   Recueil des Nouvelles ordinaires et extraordinaires (from 1714).   Gazette d'Hollande.   Gaceta de Madrid.

III.   SUBSIDIARY AUTHORITIES.

Altamira y Crevea, R.   Historia de España.   Vol. iv.   Barcelona.   1909.
Armstrong, E.   Elisabeth Farnese.   London.   1892.
——— Alberoni and the Quadruple Alliance.   Scottish Review.   Paisley.   January, 1897.
Arneth, A. Ritter von.   Prinz Eugen von Savoyen.   3 vols.   Vienna.   1869.
Aubertin, C.   L'esprit publique au dix-huitième siècle.   Paris.   1889, etc.
Baraudon, A.   La Maison de Savoie et la Triple Alliance, 1713–22.   Paris.   1896.
Barthélemy, E. M. Comte de.   Les filles du Régent.   2 vols.   Paris.   1874.
——— Mesdames de France, filles de Louis XV.   Paris.   1879.
——— Les Correspondants de la Marquise de Balleroy.   2 vols.   Paris.   1883.
Baudrillart, A.   Philippe V et La Cour de France.   5 vols.   Paris.   [The fullest and most important work on Franco-Spanish History in this period.]
——— Rapport sur une Mission en Espagne aux Archives d'Alcala de Hénarès et de Simancas.   Archives des Missions scientifiques et littéraires.   Sér. iii.   Vol. xv.   Paris.   1889.
——— Rapport sur une Mission en Espagne aux Archives de Simancas et d'Alcala de Hénarès en 1893.   Nouvelles Archives des Missions sc. et litt.   Vol. vi.   Paris.   1893.
Beauriez, L. de.   Une fille de France.   Paris.   1887.
Bersani, Abbé.   Storia del Cardinale Giulio Alberoni.   Piacenza.   1861.
Bianchi, G.   Giulio Alberoni e il suo secolo.   Piacenza.   1901.
Bliard, P.   Dubois, Cardinal et premier ministre.   Paris.   1901.
Bourgeois, E.   Alberoni, Madame des Ursins et la reine Elisabeth Farnèse.   Paris.   1891.
——— Le Secret du Régent et la politique de l'Abbé Dubois.   1716–8.   Paris.   1908.   [Triple and Quadruple Alliances.]

Boutry, M. Vicomte de. Une créature du Cardinal Dubois. Intrigues et missions diplomatiques du Cardinal de Tencin. Paris. 1902.

Boyé, P. Stanislas Leszcynski et le troisième traité de Vienne. Nancy. 1898.

Capefigue, J. B. H. R. Philippe d'Orléans, Régent de France. Paris. 1845.

—— Louis XV et la société du xviiime siècle. 4 vols. Paris. 1842.

—— Mesdemoiselles de Nesle et la jeunesse de Louis XV. Paris. 1864.

—— Diplomatie de la France et de l'Espagne depuis l'avènement de la Maison de Bourbon, 1698-1846. Paris. 1846.

Carré, H. La France sous Louis XV. Paris. 1891.

Carutti, D. Storia della Diplomazia nella Corte di Savoia. Vol. iv. Turin. 1880.

—— Storia del Regno di Vittorio Amedeo II. Florence. 1863.

—— Storia del Regno di Carlo Emanuele III. 2 vols. Turin. 1859.

Chevalier, E. Histoire de la Marine Française jusqu'au traité de paix de 1762. Paris. 1902.

Courcy, M. A. Marquis de. L'Espagne après la paix d'Utrecht. Paris. 1891.

Coxe, W. Memoirs of the Kings of Spain of the House of Bourbon. 3 vols. London. 1813-5.

Dalborno, C. Elisabetta Farnese. Atti della R. Acad. di Arcqueologia e Belle Arti. Vol. xiv. 1889-90.

Danvila y Burguero, A. Estudios españoles del siglo xviii.
    (1) Luisa Isabel de Orleans y Luis I. Madrid. 1902.
    (2) Fernando VI y Doña Barbara de Braganza. Madrid. 1905.

Danvila y Collado, M. Reinado de Carlos III. Vol. i. Madrid. 1892.

Desdevises du Dezert, G. L'Espagne de l'ancien régime. Paris. 1898.

Driault, E. Chauvelin. Rev. d'histoire diplomatique. No. i. 1893.

Duro, C. F. Armada española. 9 vols. Madrid. 1895-1903.

Duron, H. Philippe d'Orléans, Régent. Sa jeunesse. Mémoires de l'Acad. de Stanislas. Series v. Vol. xii. 1895.

Filon, C. A. O. L'Alliance Anglaise au xviiime siècle, depuis la paix d'Utrecht jusqu'à la Guerre de la Succ. d'Autriche. Mémoire lu à l'Acad. des Sc. Mor. et Pol. Paris. 1860.

Funck-Brentano, F. La Régence, 1715-23. Paris. 1909.

Gachard, M. Les Archives Farnésiennes à Naples. Bulletin de la Commission royale d'histoire. Vol. xi. Brussels. 1869.

Gauthier-Villars, H. Le mariage de Louis XV d'après des documents nouveaux. Paris. 1900.

Gay, C. Négociations relatives à l'établissement de la Maison de Bourbon sur le trône des Deux-Siciles (1701-36). Paris. 1853.

Haggard, Lieut.-Col. A. C. P. The Regent of the Roués. London. 1905.

—— The real Louis XV. 2 vols. London. 1906.

Haussonville, J. O. B. de Cléron, Comte de. Histoire de la réunion de la Lorraine à la France. 4 vols. Paris. 1880.

Hume, M. A. S. Spain; its greatness and decay. (Camb. Hist. Ser.) Cambridge. 1898.

Jobez, A. La France sous Louis XV. 6 vols. Paris. 1864-73.

Laborderie, A. de. Revue de Bretagne et de Vendée. 1857-8-9, 1868.

Lafuente, M. Historia general de España. Vol. xix. Madrid. 1857.

Lavisse, E. Histoire de France. Vol. viii. Pt. ii. Paris. 1909.

Lea, H. C. History of the Inquisition in Spain. 4 vols. New York. 1907.

Le Bègue de Serminy, Comte M. Les Brigandages Maritimes de l'Angleterre sous le règne de Louis XV. Revue des Questions Historiques. Paris. 1908. (i, ii.)

Legrelle, A. La Diplomatie Française et la Succession d'Espagne. Vol. ii. La Paix (1710-25). 2nd edn. Braine-le-Comte. 1899.

Lémontey, P. E. Histoire de la Régence et de la Minorité de Louis XV, jusqu'au ministère du Card. Fleury. 2 vols. Paris. 1832.

Lescure, M. de. Les maitresses du Régent. Paris. 1861.

Macanaz, M. Maldonado. Don Rafael Melchor Macanaz considerato como politico y como regalista. Madrid. 1886.

—— Articles on Alberoni. Revista de España. Madrid. 1884.

Marmontel, J. F. Régence du Duc d'Orléans. 2 vols. Paris. 1805.

Marquiset, A. La Duchesse de Fallary, 1697–1782. Paris. 1907.

Martin, H. Histoire de France. Vol. xv. Paris. 1864.

Michelet, J. Histoire de France. Vol. xvii. Paris. 1879.

Moore, G. Lives of Cardinal Alberoni, the Duke of Ripperda, and the Marquis of Pombal. 2 vols. London. 1806–19. [Untrustworthy.]

Noorden, C. von. Victor Amadeus II von Savoyen. In Historische Vorträge, hrsgbn. von W. Maurenbrecher. Leipzig. 1884.

Pajol, C. P. V. Comte de. Les guerres sous Louis XV. 7 vols. and Atlas. Paris. 1881–91.

Papa, V. L' Alberoni e la sua dipartita dalla Spagna. Turin. 1876.

Perez, L. Le Président Hénault et Mᵐᵉ du Deffand. 3rd edn. Paris. 1893.

Perkins, J. B. France under the Regency. London. 1892.

Professione, A. Il Ministero in Spagna e il Processo del Cardinale Giulio Alberoni. Turin. 1898.

Ranke, L. von. Französische Geschichte, vornehml. im xvi und xvii Jahrh. Vol. iv. Bk. xvii: Die Regentschaft und Card. Fleury. Sämmtl. Werke. Vol. xi. Leipzig. 1869.

Raynal, P. de. Le mariage d'un roi. Paris. 1887.

Reaulx, Marquise des. Le roi Stanislas et Maria Leczinska. Paris. 1895.

Rivière, H. La Marine française sous le règne de Louis XV. Paris. 1859.

Rulhière, C. C. de. Anecdotes sur le Maréchal de Richelieu. Paris. 1890.

Scelle, G. La Traité Négrière aux Indes de Castille. Vols. i, ii. Contrats et traités d'Assiente. Paris. 1906. [Vol. iii, not yet published, will treat of the period from 1715–50.]

Schipa, M. Il regno di Napoli al tempo di Carlo di Borbone. Naples. 1904.

Seilhac, Comte V. de. L'Abbé Dubois, premier Ministre de Louis XV. 2 vols. Paris. 1882.

Sempere, J. Historia del lujo y de las leyes suntuarias de España. Madrid. 1788.

Syveton, G. Une Cour et un Aventurier au xviiie siècle: le baron de Ripperda. Paris. 1896.

Thirion, H. La vie privée des financiers au dix-huitième siècle. Paris. 1895.

—— Madame de Prie, 1698–1727. Paris. 1905.

Vandal, A. Louis XV et Elisabeth de Russie. Paris. 1882.

—— Une ambassade française en Orient sous Louis XV. La Mission du Marquis de Villeneuve. 2nd edn. Paris.

Vernon, K. D. Italy, 1492–1792. (Cambridge Historical Series.) Cambridge. 1908.

Villa, A. R. Don Cenon de Somodevilla, Marqués de la Ensenada. Madrid. 1878.

—— Patiño y Campillo. Madrid. 1882.

Viollet, A. Histoire des Bourbons d'Espagne. Paris. 1843.

Weber, O. Die Quadrupel-Allianz vom Jahre 1718. Vienna. 1887.

Wiesener, L. Le régent, l'abbé Dubois et les Anglais d'après les sources britanniques. 3 vols. Paris. 1891–9.

Wilson, Lt.-Col. C. T. The Duke of Berwick, Marshal of France, 1702–34. London. 1883.

Wirminghaus, A. Zwei Spanische Mercantilisten: Geronimo de Ustariz un Bernardo de Ulloa. Halle. 1886.

Zevort, E. Le Marquis d'Argenson et le ministère des affaires étrangères du 18 nov. 1744 au 10 jan. 1747. Paris. 1880.

Zobi, A. Storia civile della Toscana, 1737–1848. Vol. i. Florence. 1850.

[*See also the Bibliographies to Chapters II* (1); *III; and Vol. V, Chapters I and II.*]

CHAPTER VI.

FINANCIAL EXPERIMENTS AND COLONIAL DEVELOPMENT.

[As to the general English and French history of the period see Bibliographies to Chapters I, 2; II; and IV. So far as concerns the colonies this Bibliography is confined to the British West Indies, West Africa, the Cape of Good Hope and the Slave Trade. For works relating to other parts of the colonial world reference should be made to the Bibliographies of Vol. VII, Chapters I and II, and Chapter III; Vol. IX, Chapter XXIII; Vol. X, Chapters VIII, X, and XXI.]

I. BIBLIOGRAPHIES.

Cunningham, W. Growth of English Industry and Commerce. Modern Times. Part II: Laissez Faire. Bibliographical Index. Cambridge. 1907.

Fairbridge, C. A. and Noble, J. Catalogue of Books relating to South Africa. Capetown. 1886.

Levasseur, E. Système de Law. Preface, with a description of the principal original documents. Paris. 1854.

Stevens, H. Catalogue of the American Books in the British Museum. London. 1866.

Theal, G. McC. History of South Africa under the Dutch East India Company. Vol. II. Appendix: Notes on Books. 2nd edn. London. 1897.

Winsor, J. Narrative and critical history of America. Vol. V. Editorial Notes, I, Law and the Mississippi Bubble. Vol. VIII. Bibliographical notes on the West Indies. London. 1889.

II. JOHN LAW AND THE MISSISSIPPI SCHEME.

A. CONTEMPORARY AUTHORITIES.

Barbier, E. J. F. Chronique de la Régence. 4 vols. Paris. 1857.

Buvat, J. Journal de la Régence. 1715–23. 2 vols. Paris. 1865.

Case of Mr Law truly stated, the. London. 1721.

Company of Mississippi, a full and impartial account of the...in French and English. London. 1720.

Defoe, D. The Chimera or the French way of paying National Debts laid open. London. 1720.

Duhautchamps, B. M. Histoire du Système des Finances pendant les années 1719 et 1720. 6 vols. The Hague. 1739. [Vols. V and VI contain a collection of Arrêts and Edicts relating to the System.]

—— Histoire du Visa. 4 vols. The Hague. 1743.

Dutot, C. de F. Réflexions politiques sur les finances et le commerce. 2 vols. The Hague. 1738. Reprinted in E. Daire's Économistes-Financiers. Paris. 1843.

Graham, J. M. Annals and Correspondence of the Viscount and the first and second Earls of Stair. 2 vols. Edinburgh and London. 1875.

Hardwicke, Philip Yorke, second Earl of. Miscellaneous State Papers. 1501–1726. Vol. II. London. 1778.

Kurtze Remarques über den...Mississipischen Actien-Handel in Paris, und andere grosse Unternehmungen des Heern Laws. Leipzig. 1720.

Law, John.

    Œuvres de Jean Law. Paris. 1790.

    Économistes-Financiers du XVIIIᵉ siècle. Law. E. Daire. Paris. 1843.

[These two collections of Law's works contain: Lettres sur le nouveau système des finances, published in the Mercure de France, Feb., Mar., Apr., May, 1720; Lettres sur les banques, 1715?; Mémoire sur l'usage des monnaies; Mémoires justificatifs, 1724; Mémoires sur les banques, 1715? and a French translation of the Money and Trade.]

    Letter, a, to Mr Law upon his arrival in Great Britain. London. 1721.

    Letter to Mr Law, a Second. London. 1721.

    Leven en caracter, het, van den Heer Jan Law. Amsterdam. 1722.

    Memoirs, life and character of the Great Mr Law, The. London. 1721.

    Money and Trade. Edinburgh. 1705. London. 1720.

    Observations on the New System of the Finances of France in two Letters by Mr Law. Trans. from the French. London. 1720.

    Secret, le, du Système de M. Law dévoilé en deux lettres écrites par un Duc et Pair de France et un Mylord Anglois. The Hague. 1721.

Melon, S. F. Essai politique sur le commerce. 1st edn. 1734. Reprinted in Daire's Économistes-Financiers.

Mémoire pour servir à justifier La Compagnie des Indes. 1720.

Montagu, Lady Mary Wortley, Letters of. Edited by Lord Wharncliffe. 2 vols. London. 1893.

Montesquieu, Charles de Secondat, Baron de. Lettres Persanes. *See* Œuvres of Montesquieu. 7 vols. Paris. 1769.

Paris-Duverney. Examen de Dutot's Réflexions politiques. 2 vols. The Hague. 1740.

Present State, the, of the French Revenues and Trade and of the Controversy betwixt the Parliament of Paris and Mr Law. London. 1720.

Saint-Simon, Mémoires du Duc de. Par M. Chéruel. Paris. 1856–8. Par A. de Boislisle. Paris. 1879– . (*In course of publication.*)

Tafereel, het groote, der Dwaasheid. Amsterdam (?). 1720.

Véron de Forbonnais, F. Recherches et considérations sur les finances de France. 1595–1721. 2 vols. Basle. 1758.

Villars, Mémoires du Maréchal de. 6 vols. Paris. 1884–1904.

B. Later Works.

Alexi, S. John Law und sein System. Berlin. 1885.

D'Avenel, Vicomte G. Histoire économique de la propriété, des salaires, et de tous les prix, 1200–1800. 4 vols. Paris. 1894.

Bailly, A. Histoire Financière de la France. Vol. II. Paris. 1830.

Blanc, L. Histoire de la Révolution Française. Vol. I. Paris. 1847.

Capefigue, J. B. H R. Histoire des grandes opérations financières. Vol. I. Les Fermiers Généraux depuis le XVIIIᵉ siècle. Paris. 1855.

Cochut, P. A. Law, son système et son époque. Paris. 1853. In English. London. 1856.

Courtois, A. Histoire de la Banque de France. Paris. 1875.

Daire, E. Économistes-Financiers du XVIIIᵉ siècle. Notice Historique sur Jean Law. Paris. 1843.

Davis, A. McFarland. Historical Study of Law's System. Boston. 1887. Reprinted from the American Quarterly Journal of Economics. Boston. April, 1887.

Heymann, J. Law und sein System. Munich. 1853.

Kurtzel, A. Geschichte der Law'schen Finanzoperation. Leipzig. 1846.

Lacretelle, J. C. D. de. Histoire de France pendant le dix-huitième siècle. 4th edn. Vol. I. Paris. 1819.

Lemontey, P. E. Histoire de la Régence et de la Minorité de Louis XV. 2 vols. Paris. 1832.

Levasseur, E. Recherches historiques sur le Système de Law. Paris. 1854.

Mackay, C. Memoirs of extraordinary popular delusions. 2nd edn. 2 vols. London. 1852.

Martin, H. Histoire de France. Vol. XVII. Paris. 1851.

Michelet, J. Histoire de France. Vol. XV. Paris. 1863.

Nicholson, J. S. Money and Monetary Problems. Essay on Law. 3rd edn. London. 1895.

Pereire, E. and I. Du Système de Law. (Essay, dated Nov. 1834, appended to Enquête sur la Banque de France. Depositions of MM. E. and I. Pereire.) Paris. 1866.

Russell, Lord John. History of the Principal States of Europe from the Peace of Utrecht. Vol. II. London. 1826.

Steuart, Sir J. An Inquiry into the Principles of Political Economy. London. 1767.

Thiers, A. Notice sur Law et son Système in the Dictionnaire de la Conversation. Vol. XXXV. London. 1837.

Vallée, Oscar de. Le Duc d'Orléans et le Chancelier Daguesseau. Paris. 1860.

Wood, J. P. A Sketch of the Life of John Law of Lauriston. Edinburgh and London. 1791.

—— Life of John Law of Lauriston. Edinburgh. 1824.

III. THE SOUTH SEA SCHEME.

A. Contemporary Authorities.

Account, an, of the Loans of the South Sea. 1722.

Account, an, of the Subscriptions of the South Sea Company. 1722.

Advantages...to the Public and to the South Sea Company by the execution of the South Sea Scheme. London. 1728.

Aislabie's second speech on his defence in the House of Lords, Mr. London. 1721.

American trade before and since the establishment of the South Sea Company. London. 1739.

Answer to a Calumny (Asiento Trade). London. 1728.

Argument, an, to show the disadvantage...from obliging the South Sea Company to fix what capital stock they will give for the annuities. London. 1720.

Barbier, S. An expedient to pay the public debts. London. 1719.

Battle of the Bubbles. By a Stander-by. London. 1720.

Bubblers Mirrour or England's Folly, the. 1720.

Case, the, of Contracts for the Third and Fourth Subscriptions. London. 1720.

Case, the, of the Annuitants stated. London. 1720.

Case, the, of the Bank Contract. London. 1735.

Case, the, of the Borrowers on the South Sea Loans stated. London. 1721.

Case, the, of the Right Hon. John Aislabie, Esq. London. 1721.

Case, the, of Sir Robert Chaplin, Bart., one of the late Directors of the South Sea Company. London. 1721.

Collection, a, of the Several Petitions of the Counties, Boroughs, etc., presented to the House of Commons complaining of the Great Miseries...occasioned by the...South Sea Company. London. 1721.

Comparison, a, between the Proposals of the Bank and the South Sea Company. London. 1720.

Considerations on the present state of the nation as to public credit. London. 1720.

Considerations recommending to the proprietors of South Sea Stock the proposals for engrafting part of that Company's funds into the stock of the Bank and East India Companies. London. 1722.

Critical History of the Administration of Sir Robert Walpole. London. 1743.

Davenant, C. Dissertation on the Plantation Trade. Political and Commercial Works, ed. Sir C. Whitworth. Vol. II. London. 1771. Also in Select Dissertations on Colonies and Plantations. London. 1775.

Defence of the observations on the Assiento Trade. London. 1728.

Defoe, D. The Anatomy of Exchange-Alley. London. 1719.

Detection, a, of the whole management of the South Sea Company. London. 1721.

Dialogue, a, concerning Sir Humphry Mackworth's proposal...for relief of the South Sea Company. London. 1720.

Elking, H. A view of the Greenland trade and whale fishery. London. 1722.

Essay, an, for discharging the debts of the nation...and the South Sea Scheme considered. London. 1720.

Essay, an, for establishing a new Parliament money. London. 1720.

Examination, an, and explanation of the South Sea Company's Scheme. London. 1720.

Hutcheson, A. An abstract of all the Public Debts remaining due Michaelmas 1722. London. 1723.

—— A Collection of Treatises relating to the National Debts and Funds. London. 1720.

—— A True State of the South Sea Scheme as it was first formed. London. 1722?

Index Rerum et Vocabulorum (Lists of subscribers). London. 1722.

Journals of the House of Commons. Vol. XIX.

Letter, a, to a conscientious man...demonstrating the fallaciousness of the South Sea Scheme. London. 1720.

Letter, a, to a member of Parliament concerning the South Sea Company. London. 1720.

Mackworth, Sir H. An answer to several queries relating to the proposals. London. 1720.

—— A proposal for payment of the Public Debts, for relief of the South Sea Company. London. 1720.

Midriff, Sir J. Observations on the Spleen and Vapours. London. 1721.

Milner, J. Three letters relating to the South Sea Company and the Bank. London. 1720.

New Year's gift for the Directors, a. London. 1721.

Observations on the Assiento Trade. London. 1728.

Pangs of Credit, the. By an orphan annuitant. London. 1722.

Parliamentary History. Vol. VII. London. 1811.

Philips, E. An Appeal to Common Sense. London. 1720. Part II. London. 1721.

Proceedings of the House of Lords in relation to the late Directors of the South Sea Company. London. 1722.

Proposals for restoring credit. London. 1721.

Rise, the, of the Stocks the Ruin of the People. London. 1721.

Several Reports, the, of the Committee of Secrecy. 2 vols. London. 1721.

Shaw, W. A. Select Tracts and Documents illustrative of English Monetary History, 1626–1730. London. 1896.

South Sea Scheme, the, examined. London. 1720.

South Sea Scheme, the, detected. London. 1720.

Speech, the, of the Right Hon. John Aislabie, Esq., upon his defence. London. 1721.

State of the nation. Appendix. The Assiento. London. 1725.

Steele, Sir R. The Crisis of Property. London. 1720.

Steele, Sir R. A nation a family. London. 1720.

Stevens, Captain J. The Rule established in Spain for the Trade in the West Indies. Translated from the Spanish. London. 1712?

Stiptick, a, for a bleeding nation. London. 1721.

Templeman, D. The Secret History of the late Directors of the South Sea Company containing a particular Account of their conduct with regard to the Assiento Commerce. London. 1735.

Time Bargains tried by the Rules of Equity. London. 1720.

True state, a, of public credit. London. 1721.

True state, a, of the contracts relating to the Third Money Subscription. London. 1721.

View, a, of the Coasts, Countries and Islands within the limits of the South Sea Company (with map). London. 1711.

B. Later Works.

Andréadès, A. Essai sur la fondation et l'histoire de la Banque d'Angleterre, 1694– 1844. Paris. 1901.

Bastable, C. F. Public Finance. 3rd edn. London. 1903.

Brisco, N. A. The Economic Policy of Robert Walpole. Columbia Univ. Studies. Vol. xxvii. No. 1. New York. 1907.

Burton, J. H. History of the Reign of Queen Anne. 3 vols. Edinburgh and London. 1880.

Coxe, W. Memoirs of the Life and Administration of Sir Robert Walpole. 3 vols. London. 1798.

Doubleday, T. A Financial, Monetary and Statistical History of England, 1688– 1847. London. 1847.

Francis, J. Chronicles and Characters of the Stock Exchange. London. 1855.

—— History of the Bank of England. Vol. i. London. 1847.

Gibbon, E. Memoirs of Life and Writings. Vol. i. London. 1796.

Hamilton, R. An Inquiry concerning the National Debt of Great Britain. 3rd edn. Edinburgh. 1818.

Lecky, W. E. H. History of England in the Eighteenth Century. 8 vols. London. 1883–90.

Mahon, Lord. History of England from the Peace of Utrecht to the Peace of Aix- la-Chapelle. 3 vols. London. 1837.

McCarthy, J. History of the Four Georges. 4 vols. London. 1884.

Michael, W. Der Südseeschwindel vom Jahre 1720. Stuttgart. 1908.

Rapin-Thoyras, Paul de. Histoire d'Angleterre. Vol. xiii. The Hague. 1736.

Rogers, J. E. T. Industrial and Commercial History of England. 2 vols. London. 1902.

Sinclair, Sir J. History of the Public Revenue of the British Empire. 3rd edn. 3 vols. London. 1803–4.

Willson, B. The Great Company. 2 vols. London. 1900.

Wright, T. Caricature History of the Georges. London. 1863.

IV. THE COLONIES.

A. Contemporary Authorities.

Abridgement of minutes of evidence taken before Committee of the whole House (Slave Trade). 1789.

Abstract of the evidence before a Select Committee of the House of Commons in 1790 and 1791 on the part of the petitioners for the abolition of the Slave Trade. London. 1791.

Account of the European Settlement in America. Revised by Edmund Burke. 2 vols. London. 1757.

African Trade, the great pillar and support of the British Plantation Trade in America, The. London. 1745.

Appeal, an, to the Candour and Justice of the people of England on behalf of the West India merchants and planters. London. 1792.

Barrow, Sir J. An account of travels into the interior of Southern Africa, in the years 1797 and 1798. 2 vols. London. 1801–4.

Benezet, A. A description of Guinea...with an enquiry into the rise and progress of the Slave Trade. London. 1788.

Calendar of Home Office Papers, 1760–75. 4 vols. London. 1878–99.

Calendar of Treasury Books and Papers, 1728–45. 5 vols. London. 1897–1903.

Calendar of Treasury Papers, 1714–28. 2 vols. London. 1883, 1889.

Case of the Sugar Colonies, the. London. 1792.

Clarkson, T. Essay on the Slavery and Commerce of the Human Species. London. 1786.

—— History of the Abolition of the African Slave Trade. London. 1839.

Comparative importance of our acquisitions from France in America. London. 1762.

Considerations on the present peace as far as it is relative to the Colonies and the African Trade. London. 1763.

Considerations relating to an additional duty on sugar. London. 1747.

Cook, Captain J. A Voyage to the Pacific Ocean. Vol. i. London. 1784.

Country, a, Gentleman's reasons for voting against Mr Wilberforce's motion. London. 1792.

Danvers, F. C. Report on the Records of the India Office. Vol. i. Part i. London. 1887.

Foot, J. A defence of the Planters in the West Indies. London. 1792.

Gisborne, T. Remarks on the late decision of the House of Commons respecting the abolition of the Slave Trade. London. 1792.

Hippisley, J. Essays, relating to the African Trade. London. 1764.

Houston, J. Account of the Coast of Guinea. London. 1725.

Hughes, G. Natural History of Barbados. London. 1750.

Importance of effectually supporting the Royal African Company. 2nd edn. (with useful map). London. 1745.

Importance of the Sugar Colonies to Great Britain. London. 1731.

Janisch, H. R. Extracts from the St Helena Records, 1673–1835. St Helena. 1885.

Johnson, Captain C. A General History of the Pirates. London. 1724.

Koch, C. G. de, and Schoell, M. S. F. Histoire Abrégée des Traités de Paix. 15 vols. Paris. 1817–8.

Kolbe, P. Description du Cap de Bonne-Espérance...tirée des Mémoires de Mr Pierre Kolbe. 3 vols. Amsterdam. 1743.

Labat, J. B. Nouveau Voyage aux isles d'Amérique. 6 vols. Paris. 1722.

Leguat, F. Voyage of. Hakluyt Society Publications. 2 vols. London. 1891.

Leibbrandt, H. C. V. Précis of the Archives of the Cape of Good Hope. 18 vols. published. Capetown. 1896– .

Meredith, H. An Account of the Gold Coast of Africa, with a brief history of the African Company. London. 1812.

Miscellaneous, a, essay, concerning the course pursued by Great Britain in the affairs of her colonies. London. 1755.

Moodie, D. The Record or A Series of Official Papers relative to the condition and treatment of the Native Tribes of South Africa. Capetown. 1838.

Mun, T. England's Treasure by Foreign Trade. London. 1713.

Papers relative to Codrington College, Barbados, 1709–1826. London. 1828.

Postlethwayt, M. The Importance of the African Expedition. London. 1758.

Pownall, T. The Administration of the Colonies. 3rd edn. London. 1766.

Present state of the British and French trade to Africa and America compared. London. 1745.

Ramsay, J. Essay on the Treatment and Conversion of the African Slaves in the British Sugar Colonies. London. 1784.

—— Objections to the abolition of the Slave Trade with answers. London. 1788.

Raynal, G. T. F. Philosophical and Political History of the Settlements and Trade of Europeans in the East and West Indies. Trans. from the French by J. Justamond. 4 vols. London. 1776.

Remarks upon a book entitled the Present State of the Sugar Colonies. London. 1731.

Report of the Privy Council on Trade to Africa, with appendices. 1789.

Representation of the Board of Trade relating to...His Majesty's Plantations in America. London. 1733–4.

Sharp, G. A representation of the injustice and dangerous tendency of tolerating slavery in England. London. 1769.

Sparmann, A. A Voyage to the Cape of Good Hope, 1772–6. Translated from the Swedish. 2 vols. Perth. 1789.

State of the Island of Jamaica. London. 1726.

Stavorinus, J. S. Voyages to the East Indies. Translated from the Dutch. 3 vols. London. 1798.

Substance of Report of the Directors of the Sierra Leone Company. London. 1792.

Thunberg, C. P. Voyages au Japon par le Cap de Bonne-Espérance. Translated into French. 4 vols. Paris. 1796.

Wadstrom, C. B. Observations on the Slave Trade and a description of some parts of the coast of Guinea. London. 1789.

—— An essay on Colonisation particularly applied to the Western Coast of Africa. 2 parts. London. 1794.

Wesley, J. Thoughts upon slavery. London. 1774.

Wilberforce, W. The Abolition of the Slave Trade. London. 1807.

—— Letter to the Prince of Talleyrand Périgord on the Slave Trade 1814. Printed in the Pamphleteer. Vol. v. London. 1815.

B. Later Works.

(1) *The West Indies.*

Atwood, T. History of Dominica. London. 1791.

Beckford, W. A descriptive account of Jamaica. 2 vols. London. 1790.

—— Situation of negroes in Jamaica. London. 1788.

Borde, P. G. L. Histoire de l'ile de la Trinidad. 1498–1797. Paris. 1876.

Breen, H. H. St Lucia. London. 1844.

Bridges, G. W. Annals of Jamaica. 2 vols. London. 1828.

Dallas, R. C. History of the Maroons. 2 vols. London. 1803.

Edwards, Bryan. History of the British Colonies in the West Indies. 5 vols. London. 1819.

—— Historical Survey of St Domingo. London. 1801.

Gardner, W. J. History of Jamaica. London. 1873.

Godet, T. L. Bermuda. London. 1860.

Joseph, E. L. History of Trinidad. 1498–1837. Trinidad. 1838.

Long, E. History of Jamaica. 3 vols. London. 1774.

Lucas, C. P. Historical Geography of the British Colonies. West Indies. Vol. II. 2nd edn. Oxford. 1905.

Ogilvy, J. An account of Bermuda, past and present. Hamilton, Bermuda. 1883.

Oliver, V. L. History of Antigua. 3 vols. London. 1894–9.

Pezuela, J. de la. Ensayo histórico de la Isla de Cuba. New York. 1842.

Schomburgk, Sir R. H.   History of Barbados.   London.   1848.
Southey, Captain T.   Chronological History of the West Indies.   3 vols.   London.   1827.
Stephen, Sir G.   Anti-Slavery Recollections.   London.   1854.
Williams, W. F.   Historical and statistical account of the Bermudas.   London.   1848.
Woodcock, H. I.   History of Tobago.   Ayr.   1867.

(2) *Africa.*

Bandinel, J.   Some account of the Trade in Slaves from Africa as connected with Europe and America.   London.   1842.
Brooke, T. H.   History of St Helena.   2nd edn.   London.   1824.
Carey, H. C.   Slave Trade, Domestic and Foreign.   London.   1853.
Cochin, A.   L'Abolition de l'Esclavage.   Paris.   1861.
Johnston, Sir H. H.   Colonization of Africa.   Cambridge.   1905.
Lucas, C. P.   Historical Geography of the British Colonies.   Vol. III.   West Africa. 2nd edn.   Oxford.   1900.   Vol. IV.   South and East Africa.   2 parts.   Oxford.   1898.
Melliss, J. C.   St Helena.   London.   1875.
Moodie, J. W. D.   Ten Years in South Africa.   London.   1835.
Owen, R. D.   The Wrong of Slavery, The Right of Emancipation.   Philadelphia.   1864.
Percival, Captain R.   An Account of the Cape of Good Hope.   London.   1804.
Theal, G. McC.   Chronicles of Cape Commanders 1652–91.   Contains also four papers relating to a later period and notes on English, Dutch and French books published before 1796 which refer to S. Africa.   Capetown.   1882.
——   History of South Africa, 1652–1795.   2 vols.   London.   1897.
Thomson, J.   Mungo Park and the Niger.   London.   1890.
Trotter, A. F.   Old Cape Colony from 1652 to 1806.   Westminster.   1903.

(3) *General Works on Commerce and Colonisation.*

Anderson, A.   History of Commerce.   4 vols.   London.   1787–9.
Beer, G. L.   Commercial Policy of England towards the American Colonies.   New York.   1893.
——   British Colonial Policy, 1754–65.   New York.   1907.
Bonnassieux, P.   Les Grandes Compagnies le Commerce.   Paris.   1892.
Brougham, H., Lord.   Colonial Policy of the European Powers.   2 vols.   Edinburgh.   1803.
Cawston, G., and Keane, A. H.   Early Chartered Companies.   London.   1906.
Cunningham, W.   Growth of English Industry and Commerce.   Modern Times.   Cambridge.   1907.
Egerton, H. E.   History of Colonial Policy.   London.   1898.
Heeren, A. H. L.   History of the Political System of Europe and its Colonies.   London.   1864.
Howison, J.   European Colonies.   2 vols.   London.   1834.
Leroy Beaulieu, P.   De la Colonisation chez les peuples modernes.   5th edn.   2 vols.   Paris.   1902.
Levi, L.   History of British Commerce, 1763–1870.   London.   1872.
Macpherson, D.   Annals of Commerce.   4 vols.   London.   1805.
McCulloch, J. R.   Dictionary of Commerce.   London.   1880.
Martin, R. M.   British Colonies.   6 vols.   London and New York.   1851–7.
Merivale, H.   Lecture on Colonies and Colonization.   2nd edn.   London.   1861.
Payne, E. J.   European Colonies.   London.   1890.
Playfair, W.   Commercial and Political Atlas.   London.   1786.
Postlethwayt, M.   Universal Dictionary of Trade and Commerce.   2 vols.   London.   1774.
Smith, A.   Wealth of Nations.   Ed. J. E. T. Rogers.   2 vols.   London.   1869.

CHAPTER VII.

POLAND UNDER THE SAXON KINGS.

[Works in the Polish language are marked (P.); works in the Russian (R.).]

I. BIBLIOGRAPHY.

Finkel, L. Bibliography of Polish History. Lemberg. 1891–1906. (*P.*)

II. ORIGINAL DOCUMENTS.

Catharine II. Works. Edited by A. N. Pypin. Vols. i–xii. St Petersburg. 1901 sqq. (*R.* and *French.*)

E. N. Documents relating to the Moscovite rule in Poland from 1734. Cracow. 1904. (*P.*)

Journal (Sbornik) of the Imperial Russian Historical Society. St Petersburg. 1867 sqq. (*R.*, *French* and *German.*)

Korwin, S. Materials for the history of the last century of the Polish Republic. Cracow. 1890. (*P.*)

Kurakin, J. A. The eighteenth century. Moscow. 1904 sqq. (*R.* and *French.*) [A collection of historical documents.]

Moszczynski, A. Memoirs relating to the history of Poland in the last years of the reign of Augustus III. Cracow. 1888. (*P.*)

Peter the Great. Papers and correspondence. St Petersburg. 1887 sqq. (*R.*)

Raczynski, E. Picture of the Polaks and of Poland in the eighteenth century. 19 vols. Posen. 1840–4. (*P.*)

Radziwill, Prince C. S. Correspondence, 1744–90. Cracow. 1898. (*P.*)

—— Letters, 1751–90. Warsaw. 1906. (*P.*)

Sapieha, family of. Archivum Domus Sapiehanæ. Lemberg. 1892 sqq. (*Latin* and *P.*)

Solov'eff, S. M. History of Russia. Vols. xviii–xx. St Petersburg. 1895 sqq. (*R.*)

Stanislaus II Poniatowski. Mémoires secrets et inédits. Leipzig. 1862.

III. CONTEMPORARY OR NEARLY CONTEMPORARY WRITINGS.

A. Augustus II.

Augustus II. Beschreibung was zu Krakau vor und nach der Krönung Frederici Augusti vorgezogen. [Dresden? 1697.] Italian version. Rome. 1698.

—— Manifest zur Unterstützung der freyen Wahl eines Königes in Pohlen, 1697. [1697.]

—— Relation aus dem Königreich Polen...anno 1697. [Dresden?] 1697.

B. Augustus III.

Augustus III. Das mit Cron und Scepter beschafftigte Pohlen, oder eigentliche Nachricht wie es bey die Wahl eines neuen Königs in Pohlen pfleget geschehen zu werden. Dresden. 1733.

—— De prospera electione Regis Poloniae...1733 peracta. [1733.]

—— Drey Schreiben die jetzige Confoederaten in Pohlen betreffende. Warsaw. 1741.

—— Gründlichste Nachricht von der rechtmässigen Wahl Augusts des III zum Könige von Pohlen. Dresden. 1734.

—— Historische und politische Betrachtungen über die gegenwärtigen pohlnischen Begebenheiten. Leipzig. 1733–4.

—— Pacta conventa Augusti III commentario perpetuo illustrata a G. Lengvich. Leipzig. 1763.

Justin, J. H. La vie et le caractère de M. le Comte de Brühl. [Frankfort?] 1760.

C. Stanislaus Leszczynski.

Manstein, C. H. von. Mémoires sur la Russie, 1727 jusqu'à 1740. Amsterdam. 1771. New edn. Paris. 1860. English versions: London. 1770 and 1773.

Potocki, T. Lettera a sua Santità Papa Clemente XII [on the election of Stanislaus Leszczynski as King of Poland]. 1733.

—— Manifeste [10 October, 1733, vindicating the election of Stanislaus I]. [Rome?] 1833. (*Fr.* and *Ital.*)

—— Schreiben an den König Stanislaum [on the affairs of Poland]. Königsberg. 1735.

Stanislaus I Leszczynski. Œuvres. Paris. 1763.

—— Commerce de lettres au sujet de la Diète d'élection et des proclamations de Stanislas Leszczynski et de l'Électeur de Saxe. 1734.

—— Declaratio nullitatis electionis Stanislai facta...14 Sept. 1733. [1733.]

—— Histoire de Stanislas I. [By de C***.] Frankfort. 1740. English edition: London. 1741.

—— Lettre du Roi de Pologne où il raconte la manière dont il est sorti de Dantsic, etc. The Hague. [1734.] English version: London, same date.

—— Relation exacte de ce qui s'est passé au sujet de l'élection du Comte Stanislas Leszczynski. [Warsaw. 1733.]

—— The free opinion of King Stanislaus. [A political pamphlet published from the original text by A. Rembourki.] Warsaw. 1903. (*P.*)

—— The true and cogent reasons which induced the Confederated Poles to disapprove the pretended election of Stanislaus Leszczynski. London. 1734.

—— Universaux publiés au nom du Roy de Pologne. [Rome? 1733?] (*French and Italian.*)

Tarlo, A. Excerptum literarum ad P. Clementem XII [asking for his support of the election of Stanislaus Leszczynski]. [Rome?] 1734. (*Latin* and *Italian.*)

Tarlo, J. Epistola in risposta al Conte Poniatowski che lo consigliava a sottomettersi all' Elettore de Sassonia. [Rome? 1734?]

IV. LATER WORKS.

A. General.

Gawronsky, F. History of the Polish and Cossack Guerrilla bands in the eighteenth century. Lemberg. 1899. (*P.*)

Heyking, C. H. Aus Polens und Kurlands letzten Tagen. Berlin. 1897.

Roepell, R.   Polen um die Mitte des xviii Jahrhunderts.   Gotha.   1874.
Sokolowski, A.   Illustrated History of Poland.   Vol. iii.   Vienna.   1896–1900.   (*P.*)
Szymanowski, O. K.   Beiträge zur Geschichte des Adels in Polen.   Zurich.   1834.
Titoff, T. J.   The Russian Orthodox Church in Poland in the seventeenth and
    eighteenth centuries.   Kieff.   1905.   (*R.*)

B.   Augustus II.

Augustus II.   History of the reign of Augustus II from the death of John III to the
    invasion of Charles XII.   Posen.   1856.   (*P.*)
Bastard, L. de.   Négociations de l'Abbé Polignac en Pologne concernant l'élection
    du Prince de Conti comme Roi de Pologne.   Auxerre.   1864.
Chomentowski, W.   The family of the Hetman Jablonowski.   Warsaw.   1880.   (*P.*)
Conradi, M.   Lebens- und Regierungs-Geschichte Augusti II.   Leipzig.   1797.
Haake, P.   König August der Starke.   Munich.   1902.
—— Die Wahl Augusts des Starken.   Historische Vierteljahrsheft.   Jahrg. xvii.
    Freiburg i. B.   1906.
Hallendorff, C.   Konung Augusts politik åren 1700–1.   Upsala.   1898.
Jarochowski, K.   History of the reign of Augustus II from the intervention of
    Charles XII to the election of Stanislaus Leszczynski.   Posen.   1874.   (*P.*)
—— History of the reign of Augustus II from the election of Stanislaus Leszczynski
    to the battle of Pultawa.   Posen.   1890.   (*P.*)
Otwinowski, E.   History of Poland under Augustus II from 1697 to 1728.   Cracow.
    1849.   (*P.*)
Theiner, A.   Geschichte der Rückkehr der regierenden Häuser Braunschweig u.
    Sachsen in den Schooss d. Kathol. Kirche im 18. Jahrh.   Einsiedeln.   1843.
    [With documents.]
Wagner, G.   Die Beziehungen Augusts des Starken zu seinen Ständen.   1694–1700.
    Leipzig.   1903.
Waliszewski, K.   Marysienka.   Paris.   1898.   English edition.   London, same year.

C.   War of the Polish Succession, 1733–4.

Bain, R. N.   The Pupils of Peter the Great.   Chap. vi.   London.   1897.
Bantuish-Kamensky.   Biographies of the Russian Generalissimos.   St Petersburg.
    1840.   (*R.*)
Des Reaux, Marchioness.   Le Roi Stanislas et Marie Leszczynski.   Paris.   1895.
Halem, G. A. von.   Lebensbeschreibung des Feldmarschalls B. C. Grafen von
    Münnich.   Oldenburg.   1803.   French version : Paris.   1807.
Mono Rajavamsa Siddhi, Prince of Siam.   The War of the Polish Succession.
    Oxford.   1901.

D.   Augustus III and the Czartoryscy.

Adelung, J. C.   Leben und Character des Grafens von Brühl.   Göttingen.   1760–4.
    English version.   London.   [1765 ?]
Dembicky, L.   Pulawy.   Vol. i.   Lemberg.   1887.
Kitowecz, J.   The history of manners and customs in the reign of Augustus III.
    Lemberg.   1883.   (*P.*)
Kollontaj, H.   The state of enlightenment during the last years of the reign of
    Augustus III, 1750–60.   Posen.   1840.   (*P.*)
Krawshar, A.   The feud of Konopki with the city of Thorn, 1742–56.   Cracow.
    1895.   (*P.*)

[*See also Bibliographies to Chaps. V and VIII.*]

CHAPTER VIII.

THE WAR OF THE AUSTRIAN SUCCESSION.

(1) THE PRAGMATIC SANCTION.

I. CONTEMPORARY AUTHORITIES AND DOCUMENTS.

Chronologisches Verzeichniss der österreich. Staatsverträge. I. Die öst. Staatsv. von 1526–1723. Von L. Bittner. Vienna. 1903.

Hœfler, L. Der Congress von Soissons nach den Instructionen des Kaiserlichen Cabinets. Vienna. 1876.

Instructions données aux ambassadeurs de France. Autriche. Edited by A. Sorel. Paris. 1890.

Oesterreichische Staatsverträge mit England. Bearb. von A. F. Pribram. Vol. I. 1526–1748. Innsbruck. 1907.

Preussische Staatschriften a. d. Regierungszeit Friedrichs II. Vol. I. 1740–5. Vol. II. 1746–56. Bearb. von R. Koser. Publ. by the Berlin Academy. Berlin. 1877–85.

Rousset, C. Recueil Historique d'actes, négociations etc. depuis la paix d'Utrecht jusqu'en 1748. The Hague. 1752.

II. LATER WORKS.

Aragon, M. La Compagnie d'Ostende et le Grand Commerce en Belgique au début du xviiime siècle. Annales des Sciences Politiques. Paris. March, 1901.

Arneth, A. Ritter von. Eugen von Savoyen. Allgemeine Deutsche Biographie. Vol. vi. Leipzig. 1877.

—— Karl VI, römisch-deutscher Kaiser. Allgemeine Deutsche Biographie. Vol. xv. Leipzig. 1882.

—— Prinz Eugen. Vol. iii. Vienna. 1864.

Bachmann, A. Die Pragmatische Sanction und die Erbfolgeordnung Leopold I's. Vienna. 1894.

Beer, A. Zur Geschichte der Politik Karl's VI. Historische Zeitschrift. 1886.

Broglie, Duc de. Le cardinal de Fleury et la Pragmatique impériale. Revue Historique. Paris. 1882.

Dullinger, J. Die Handels-Kompagnieen Oesterreichs nach dem Oriente u. nach Ostindien in der ersten Hälfte der 18. Jahrh. Part ii. Zeitschr. für Sozial- u. Wirthschaftsgesch. Vol. vii. Part i. Weimar. 1899.

Elvert, C. de. Zur Oesterreichischen Verwaltungsgeschichte. Brünn. 1886.

Erdmannsdörffer, B. Deutsche Geschichte 1648–1740. (Allg. Gesch. in Einzeldarst.) Vol. ii. Berlin. 1881.

Flassan, G. de R. de. Histoire de la diplomatie Française. Vol. v. Paris. 1811.

Förster, F. Die Höfe und Cabinette Europes im 18. Jahrh. Vols. I and II (with documents). Potsdam. 1835. [Charles VI and his government.]

Haussonville, Comte de. La Réunion de la Lorraine à la France. Vol. IV. Paris. 1860.

Hertz, G. B. England and the Ostend Company. English Historical Review. Vol. XXII. April, 1907.

Huisman, M. La Belgique Commerciale sous l'Empereur Charles VI. La Compagnie d'Ostende. Brussels and Paris. 1902.

Philipp, A. August der Starke und die pragmatische Sanktion. (Leipziger histor. Abh. II.) Leipzig. 1908.

Stefanović-Vilovsky, T. Ritter von. Belgrad unter der Regierung Kaiser Karls VI, 1717–39. Vienna. 1908.

(2) PRUSSIA UNDER FREDERICK WILLIAM I.

I. SOURCES.

Acta Borussica. Denkmäler der Preussischen Staatsverwaltung im 18. Jahrhundert. Hrsgbn. von der Königlichen Akademie der Wissenschaften in Berlin. Vols. I–XVI. Berlin. 1892, etc.

II. GENERAL.

Koser, R. König Friedrich der Grosse. Vol. I. 3rd edn. Stuttgart and Berlin. 1904.

Ranke, L. von. Zwölf Bücher Preussischer Geschichte. Books V and VI. Sämmtl. Werke. Vols. XXVII, XXVIII. Leipzig. 1874.

III. BIOGRAPHICAL.

Koser, R. Friedrich der Grosse als Kronprinz. Stuttgart. 1886.

Lavisse, E. La jeunesse du grand Frédéric. Paris. 1891.

Linnebach, R. König Friedrich Wilhelm I und Fürst Leopold I zu Anhalt-Dessau. Berlin. 1907.

IV. PUBLIC ECONOMY, ADMINISTRATION ETC.

Beheim-Schwarzbach, M. Hohenzollernsche Colonisationen. Leipzig. 1874.

Riedel, A. F. Der brandenburgisch-preussische Staatshaushalt in den beiden letzten Jahrhunderten. Berlin. 1866.

Schmoller, G. Umrisse und Untersuchungen zur Verfassungs-, Verwaltungs- und Wirthschaftsgeschichte besonders des Preussischen Staates im 17. und 18. Jahrhundert. Leipzig. 1898.

V. ARMY.

Lehmann, M. Werbung, Wehrpflicht und Beurlaubung im Heere Friedrich Wilhelms I. Historische Zeitschrift. Vol. LXVII.

Schultz, W. von. Die preussischen Werbungen unter Friedrich Wilhelm I und Friedrich dem Grossen bis zum Beginn des Siebenjährigen Krieges, mit besonderer Berücksichtigung Mecklenburg-Schwerins. Dargestellt nach den Acten des Grossherzoglichen Geh. und Hauptarchivs zu Schwerin. Schwerin. 1887.

VI. ECCLESIASTICAL AFFAIRS.

Pariset, G. L'état et les églises en Prusse sous Frédéric Guillaume I. Paris. 1897.

(3) THE WAR IN GERMANY AND THE NETHERLANDS.

I. Documents and Contemporary Authorities.

[Unpublished documents are marked *.]

Argenson, Marquis de. Mémoires. Published by the Société de l'Histoire de France. Paris. 1859–67.

Beer, A. Holland und der Oesterreichische Erbfolgekrieg. Archiv für Oesterreichische Geschichte. Vol. XLVI. Vienna.

—— Die Friede von Aachen. Archiv für Œsterreichische Geschichte. Vol. XLVII. Vienna.

*Belleisle, Duc de. Mémoires. 5 vols. In Bibliothèque Nationale, Paris.

Charles VII.—Correspondenz Karls VII mit Graf von Seinsheim. Edited by K. T. von Heigel. Munich. 1878.

—— Tagebuch Kaisers Karl VII. Edited by K. T. von Heigel. Munich. 1883.

Chevrier, F. A. Vie politique et militaire du Maréchal duc de Belleisle. The Hague. 1752.

Croy-Sobre, Prince de. Mémoires. Nouvelle Revue rétrospective. Paris. 1894.

Espagnac, Baron de. Journal Historique de la campagne en 1746. The Hague. 1747.

—— Campagne de l'armée du roi en 1747. The Hague. 1747.

—— Journal des campagnes du roi, 1744–7. Liége. 1748.

—— Histoire de Maurice, Comte de Saxe. Paris. 1775.

Frederick II. Histoire de mon temps. (2nd edn.) Berlin. 1775.

—— Politische Correspondenz. Berlin. 1879 etc.

Gentleman's Magazine. 1743–8. [Especially 1743 for Dettingen.]

Grimoard, Comte de. Lettres et Mémoires du Maréchal de Saxe. Paris. 1794.

Historical Manuscripts Commission. Chequers Court MSS. XVIth Report. 1900.

—— Montagu House MSS. XVIth Report. 1899.

—— Trevor MSS. XIVth Report. 1896.

—— Stopford Sackville MSS. Vol. I. XVIth Report. 1904.

—— Weston Underwood MSS. Xth Report. 1896.

Instructions aux Ambassadeurs de la France. Autriche. Edited by A. Sorel. Paris. 1890.

—— Bavière, etc. Edited by A. Lebon. Paris. 1899.

Löwendahl, Marshal de.—Leben und Thaten des Grafen von Löwendahl. Leipzig. 1749.

Louis XV. Correspondance avec le Maréchal de Noailles. Edited by C. Rousset. Paris. 1865.

Mamillon. Histoire de la dernière guerre de Bohême. Amsterdam. 1750.

*Military Auxiliary Expeditions. Public Record Office. London. [Despatches of Cumberland, Ligonier, etc.]

Moser, J. J. Staathistorie Deutschlands unter Kaiser Karl VII. Jena. 1748.

Noailles, Duc de. Mémoires. Edited by Abbé Millot. Collection Michaud et Poujoulat. 3rd series. Vol. X. Coll. Petitot. Vols. LXXI–LXXIV. Paris. 1828–9.

Podewils, Count von. Berichte über den Wiener Hof 1747–8. Vienna. 1850.

Ranft. Leben und Thaten des berühmten Grafen, Moritz von Sachsen. Leipzig. 1746.

Remarks on the Military Operations of the English and French Armies in 1747. London. 1760.

Rolt, R. Historical Memoirs of the Duke of Cumberland. London. 1767.

Spon, Baron de. Mémoires pour servir à l'histoire de l'Europe de 1740 à 1748. Amsterdam. 1749.

Valori, Louis, Marquis de. Mémoires. Paris. 1820.

Van Hoey, A. Lettres et négociations 1743–4. London. 1743.

Vitzthum, Count. Maurice comte de Saxe et Marie-Josèphe de Saxe dauphine de France. Lettres et documents inédits des archives de Dresde. Leipzig. 1867.

Walpole, Horace (Earl of Orford). Letters. Vols. ɪ and ɪɪ. Oxford. 1903.

II. Later Works.

Arneth, A. Ritter von. Maria Theresa. Vols. ɪ–ɪɪɪ. Vienna. 1868–79.

Arvers, A. Guerre de la succession d'Autriche. Paris. 1893.

Ballantyne, A. Lord Carteret. A political biography. London. 1887.

Brackenbury, Colonel C. B. Frederick II. (Military Biographies.) London. 1884.

Bright, J. F. Maria Theresa. (Foreign Statesmen Series.) London. 1897.

Broglie, Duc de. Frédéric II et Marie Thérèse. Paris. 1884.

——— Frédéric II et Louis XV. Paris. 1887.

——— Marie Thérèse Impératrice. Paris. 1890.

——— Maurice de Saxe et le Marquis d'Argenson. Paris. 1893.

——— La Paix d'Aix la Chapelle. Paris. 1895.

Campbell-Maclachlan, A. N. William Augustus, Duke of Cumberland. London. 1876.

Coxe, W. House of Austria. 2 vols. London. 1810.

——— Life of Sir R. Walpole. 3 vols. London. 1798.

——— Memoirs of the Administration of Henry Pelham. 2 vols. London. 1829.

Droysen, J. G. Geschichte der Preussischen Politik. Vols. xɪ and xɪɪ. Berlin. 1855.

Faesch, G. R. Geschichte der Oesterreichischen Erbfolgekrieges von 1740–8. Dresden. 1787.

Fortescue, J. W. History of the British Army. Vol. ɪɪ. London. 1897.

Grünhagen, C. Geschichte des ersten Schlesischen Krieges. Berlin. 1881.

Harris, C. Life of Lord Hardwicke. London. 1847.

Heigel, C. T. von. Karl VII, römisch-deutscher Kaiser. Allgemeine Deutsche Biographie. Vol. xv. Leipzig. 1882.

——— Der Œsterreichische Erbfolgestreit und die Kaiserwahl Karl's VII. Nördlingen. 1877.

Jobez, A. La France sous Louis XV. Paris. 1864–73.

Lacretelle, J. C. D. de. Histoire de France pendant le xvɪɪɪe siècle. Paris. 1830.

Lecky, W. E. H. History of England in the xvɪɪɪth century. Vol. ɪɪ. London. 1878.

Mahon, Lord (Earl Stanhope). History of England, 1713–83. 5th edition. Vol. ɪɪɪ. London. 1858.

Martin, H. Histoire de France. Vol. xv. (4th edition.) Paris. 1855–60.

O'Callaghan, J. C. The Irish Brigades in the Service of France. Glasgow. 1870.

Ogle, A. The Marquis d'Argenson. London. 1893.

Oncken, W. Das Zeitalter Friedrich's der Grossen. 2 vols. (Allg. Gesch. in Einzeldarst.) Berlin. 1880–2.

Pajol, Comte de. Les Guerres sous Louis XV. Vol. ɪɪ (Germany). Vol. ɪɪɪ (Flanders and Italy). Paris. 1881–7.

Ranke, L. von. Friedrich II. Allgemeine Deutsche Biographie. Vol. vɪɪ. Leipzig. 1878.

——— Zwölf Bücher Preussischer Geschichte. Sämmtl. Werke. Vols. xxv–xxɪx. Leipzig. 1874.

Raumer, F. von. König Friedrich II und seine Zeit. (1740–69.) Leipzig. 1836.

Saint-René Taillandier. Maurice de Saxe. Paris. 1865.

Sinéty, Marquis de. Vie du Maréchal de Löwendahl. Paris. 1867.

Skrine, F. H. Fontenoy. London. 1906.

Townshend, Colonel C. V. F.   Life of Marquess Townshend.   London.   1901.
Tuttle, H.   History of Prussia, 1740–56.   London.   1888.
Ward, A. W.   England and Hanover.   Oxford.   1899.
Weber, O. von.   Moritz, Graf von Sachsen.   1853.
Wolf, A.   Oesterreich unter Maria Theresa.   Berlin.   1884.
Zévort, E.   Le Marquis d'Argenson et le ministère des affaires étrangères, 1744–7.
   Paris.   1880.

(4) ITALY.

I. Contemporary Authorities, Documents etc.

Costa de Beauregard, Marquis C. A. de.   Mémoires historiques sur la maison royale
   de Savoie jusqu'à 1796.   3 vols.   Turin.   1816.
Grosley, P. J.   Mémoires sur les campagnes d'Italie en 1745 et 1746.   Amsterdam.
   1777.
Instructions données aux ambassadeurs de France.   Naples et Parme.   Edited by
   J. Reinach.   Paris.   1893.
—— Savoie.   Edited by Count Horrich de Beaucaire.   Paris.   1899.
Mailly, Chevalier de.   Histoire de la république de Gênes jusqu'à présent.   Paris.
   1742.
Mecatti, G. M.   Diario della guerra d' Italia.   Naples.   1748.
—— Guerra di Genova.   Naples.   1749.
Muratori, L. A.   Annali d' Italia.   Vol. xii.   Monaco.   1764.
Pezay, Marquis de.   Histoire des campagnes du Maréchal de Maillebois en Italie
   pendant les années 1745–6.   Paris.   1775.
Recueil des traités et conventions diplomatiques concernant l'Autriche et l'Italie
   (1703–1859).   Paris.   1859.
Traités publics de la maison de Savoie avec les puissances étrangères depuis la paix
   de Cateau-Cambrésis.   Turin.   1854.

II. Later Works.

Armstrong, E.   Elizabeth Farnese.   London.   1892.
Ayala, D. de.   Memorie Storico-militari dal 1734 al 1815.   Naples.   1835.
Carutti, D.   Storia del regno di Carlo Emmanuele III.   Turin.   1859.
Dumas, A.   Borboni di Napoli.   Naples.   1864–7.
Morris, H.   Opérations militaires dans les Alpes pendant la guerre de succession
   d'Autriche.   Paris.   1886.
Perrero, D.   La casa di Savoia negli Studi diplomatici del duca di Broglie.   1888.
Pinelli, F. A.   Storia militare del Piemonte.   Turin.   1863.
Saluces, Comte A. de.   Histoire militaire du Piémont.   Turin.   1818.

(5) THE NAVAL WAR.

I. Documents and Contemporary Works.

[Unpublished documents are marked *.]

*Admiralty Papers.   Secretary's Letters at Public Record Office, London.
—— Ships' Logs at Public Record Office, London.
Ducane mss.   Historical mss. Commission.   xvith Report.   1905.
Gentleman's Magazine, 1744–8.   [Esp. for the Matthews-Lestock controversy.]
(Lestock, Vice-Admiral.)   Defence to Court Martial.   1746.

Matthews, Admiral.   Authentic Letters from...relating to the expedition to the Mediterranean.   1745.
—— Original Letters and Papers between Admiral Matthews and Vice-Admiral Lestock.   1744.

II.   Later Works.

Beatson, R.   Naval and Military Memoirs.   Vol. I.   2nd edn.   London.   1804.

Burrows, Montagu, Captain.   Life of Lord Hawke.   2nd edn.   London.   1896.

Chevalier, E., Captain.   Histoire de la Marine Française jusqu'au traité de paix de 1763.   Paris.   1902.

Colomb, P. H., Admiral.   Naval Warfare.   2nd edn.   London.   1895.

Guérin, L.   Histoire Maritime de la France.   Paris.   1849.

Lacour-Gruyet, G.   La Marine Française sous le règne de Louis XV.   Paris.   1902.

Laird Clowes, Sir W.   History of the Royal Navy.   Vol. III.   London.   1898.

Mahan, A. T., Captain, U.S.N.   Influence of Sea Power upon History.   London.   1889 (and later editions).
—— Types of Naval Officers.   London.   1902.

Troude, O.   Batailles Navales de la France.   Paris.   1867.

[See also Bibliographies to Chapters II, V, XI, XII.]

CHAPTER IX.

THE SEVEN YEARS' WAR.

I. ORIGINAL AUTHORITIES.

Frederick II. Politische Correspondenz Friedrichs des Grossen. Vols. xii and following. Berlin. 1884, etc.
—— Histoire de la Guerre de Sept Ans. Œuvres de Frédéric le Grand. Vols. iv and v. Berlin. 1847.
Preussische Staatschriften a. d. Regierungszeit Friedrichs II. Vol. iii : Der Beginn des Siebenjähr. Krieges. Bearb. von O. Krauske. Publ. by the Berlin Academy. Berlin. 1892.
Preussische u. österreichische Acten zur Vorgeschichte d. Siebenj. Krieges. Bearb. von G. B. Volz u. G. Küntzel. Public. a. d. k. preuss. Staatsarchiven. Vol. lxxiv. Leipzig. 1899.

An original Journal of the Seven Years' War by Count St Paul, with plans of battles, of which the portion to be published covers the first two years of the war, will shortly appear.

II. GENERAL.

Arneth, Ritter A. von. Maria Theresia und der Siebenjährige Krieg. 2 vols. Vienna. 1875.
Daniels, E. Ferdinand von Braunschweig. Preussische Jahrbücher. Vols. lxxvii–lxxxii.
Delbrück, H. Über die Verschiedenheit der Strategie Friedrichs und Napoleons. In Historische und politische Aufsätze. 2nd edn. Berlin. 1907.
Lloyd, General. History of the late War in Germany. 2 vols. London. 1766–90. Tr. Continued by G. F. von Tempelhoff under the title of Geschichte des Siebenjährigen Krieges. 6 vols. Berlin. 1783–1801.
Masslowski. The Seven Years' War from the Russian point of view. 3 vols. (In Russian.) German Translation, by A. von Drygalski. Berlin. 1889–93.
Prussian General Staff.—Preussisches Generalstabswerk über den Siebenjährigen Krieg. 6 vols. Berlin. 1901.
Schäfer, A. Geschichte des Siebenjährigen Krieges. 2 vols. in 3 parts. Berlin. 1867–74.
Waddington, R. La Guerre de Sept Ans. Histoire diplomatique et militaire. Vols. i–iv. Paris. 1899–1907.

III. THE ORIGIN OF THE WAR.

Daniels, E.　Friedrich der Grosse und Maria Theresia am Vorabend des Siebenjährigen Krieges.　Preussische Jahrbücher.　Vol. c.

Delbrück, H.　Der Ursprung des Siebenjährigen Krieges.　In Erinnerungen,
Aufsätze und Reden.　Berlin.　1905.

Koser, H.　Zum Ursprung des Siebenjährigen Krieges.　Hist. Zeitschr. LXXIV–VII.

Lehmann, M.　Friedrich der Grosse und der Ursprung des Siebenjährigen Krieges.
Leipzig.　1894.

Mitchell, Sir Andrew.　Ueber den Ausbruch des Siebenjähr. Krieges.　Aus M.'s
ungedruckten Memoiren mitgeth. von L. von Ranke.　Sämmtl. Werke.　Vols.
LI, LII.　Leipzig.　1888.

Naudé, A.　Beiträge zur Entstehungsgeschichte des Siebenjähr. Krieges.　Repr.
from Forschungen zur Brandenb. u. Preuss. Gesch.　VIII, 2; IX, 1.　Leipzig.
1895–6.　[Contains a bibliography of the publications referring to the controversy up to date.]

(Vitzthum von Eckstädt, Count C. F.)　Die Geheimnisse des Sächsischen Cabinets.
2 vols.　Stuttgart.　1866.

IV.　PARTICULAR MILITARY OPERATIONS.

(In chronological order.)

Grawe, C.　Die Entwickelung des preussischen Feldzugsplans im Frühjahr 1757.
Berlin.　1903.

Gerber, P.　Die Schlacht bei Leuthen am 5 Dezember 1757.　Berlin.　1901.

Immich, M.　Die Schlacht bei Zorndorf am 25 August 1758.　Berlin.　1893.

Mollvo, L.　Die Capitulation von Maxen am 21 Nov. 1759.　(Diss.) Marburg.　1893.

Daniels, E.　Zur Schlacht von Torgau am 3 November 1760.　Berlin.　1886.

[*See also Bibliographies to Chapters X, XI, XIII* (II), *XIX.*]

CHAPTER X.

RUSSIA UNDER ANNE AND ELIZABETH.

[*Works in the Russian language are marked* (R.), *works in Polish* (P.).]

I. BIBLIOGRAPHIES.

The following systematic descriptions of, or guides or indexes to, Russian historical periodical publications may be consulted (all of them are *R.*): Ruskaya Starina (Russian Historical Review), St Petersburg, 1885–9; Istorichesky Vyestnik (Historical Messenger), St Petersburg, 1891; Russky Arkhiv (Russian Archives), Moscow,1892; Sbornik and Chteniia Imp. Russk. Istoritsch. Obschtschestra (Magazine or Journal, and Readings, of the Imperial Russian Historical Society), Moscow, 1883 and 1889.

See also:

Ikonnikoff, V. Essay towards a Russian Historiography. Moscow. 1889. (*R.*)
Mezhoff, V. Russian historical bibliography. St Petersburg. 1881. (*R.*) Bibliographie des livres russes d'histoire. St Petersburg. 1892–3.

II. COLLECTIONS OF ORIGINAL DOCUMENTS.

Bestuzheff, Count Alexis. Letters of Count A. Bestuzheff to Count M. Vorontsoff, 1744–60. Vorontsoff Archives. Vols. I, II. Moscow. 1870 sqq. (*R.*)
Botta, Marquis de. Letters relating to the conspiracy of the Marquis de Botta. Vorontsoff Arch. Vol. II. Moscow. 1870 sqq. (*R.* and *French.*)
Catharine II. Early correspondence, 1744–58. Sbornik. Vol. VII. St Petersburg. 1881 sqq. (*French.*)
Dickens, Guy. Despatches from St Petersburg. Record Office, For. State Pap. Russia.
Elizabeth, Empress of Russia. From the papers of the Elizabethan Ministerial Conference. Vorontsoff Archives. Vol. III. Moscow. 1870 sqq.
Elizabeth, Princess of Zerbst. Relation [of her residence in Russia, 1744–5]. Sbornik. Vol. VII. St Petersburg. 1881 sqq.
Filippoff, A. N. Papers of the Cabinet of Ministers of the Empress Anne. St Petersburg. 1898. (*R.*)
Finch, Edward. Despatches from Russia, 1740–2. Sbornik. Vols. LXXXV and XCI. St Petersburg. 1881 sqq.
Frederick II of Prussia. Politische Correspondenz, 1740–62. Vols. I–XX. Berlin. 1879–1900.

Geffroy, M. A.   Recueil des instructions données aux ambassadeurs de France depuis les traités de Westphalie.   Paris.   1884.

Hanbury Williams, Sir.   Despatches from Russia, 1755–8.   Record Office, Foreign State Papers, Russia.

Herrmann, E.   Diplomatic documents relating to the history of Russia from 1721 to 1744 from the Saxon archives.   Sbornik.   Vols. III, V and VI.   St Petersburg.   1868–71.   (*R. and German.*)

—— Diplomatic documents relating to the history of Russia from 1721 to 1744 from the Berlin archives.   Sbornik.   Vol. XV.   St Petersburg.   1875.

Hyndford, John, Earl of.   Despatches from the Russian Court, 1746–8.   Record Office, Foreign State Papers, Russia.   Also in Sbornik.   Vol. CIII.   St Petersburg.   1881 sqq.

Kurakin, J. A., Prince.   The Eighteenth Century.   Moscow.   1904 sqq.   [A collection of diplomatic documents in R. and French.]

La Chétardie, J. J. Trotti, Marquis de.   Despatches, 1740–2.   Vols. LXXXVI, XCII, XCVI, and C.   St Petersburg.   1893–7.   (*French.*)

—— The affair of the Marquis de la Chétardie.   Vorontsoff Archives.   Vol. I.   Moscow.   1870, etc.   (*R. and French.*)

Mardefeld, Baron G. von.   Relationen [of affairs in Russia, 1721–38].   Sbornik.   Vol. XV.   St Petersburg.   1875.   (*German.*)

—— Despatches from Russia, 1739–48.   Record Office, Foreign State Papers, Russia.   (*German.*)

Münnich, B. C. von, Count.   Reports issued from 1736 to 1739.   Issued by Russian General Staff.   Vol. X.   St Petersburg.   1892 sqq.   (*R. and German.*)

—— The Stavukhani Campaign.   General orders, etc.   Issued by Russian General Staff.   Vol. II.   St Petersburg.   1892 sqq.   (*R. and German.*)

—— Tagebuch, 1735–9.   Leipzig.   1843.

Nepluyeff, J. J.   Despatches from Constantinople, 1725–40.   St Petersburg.   1893.   (*R.*)

Rondeau, Claudius.   Despatches from Russia, 1728–39.   Collections of Russ. Hist. Soc.   Vols. LXVI, LXXVI, and LXXX.   St Petersburg.   1889–92.

Russian Government in Poland, from 1734, Documents relating to the doings of the.   Cracow.   1904.   (*P.*)

Shuvaloff, J. J.   From the papers of A. A. Shuvaloff, 1756–61.   Sbornik.   Vol. IX.   St Petersburg.   1881, etc.   (*R.*)

Tyrawley, Viscount.   Despatches from Russia.   Record Office, Foreign State Papers, Russia.

Wych, Sir Cyril.   Despatches from Russia.   Record Office, Foreign State Papers, Russia.

III.   CONTEMPORARY OR NEARLY CONTEMPORARY WRITINGS.

Bolotoff, A.   Mémoires, 1738–90.   St Petersburg.   1871.   (*R.*)

Copia Schreibens von Sʳ Russisch Kays. Maj. an Sᵉ Königliche Majestät in Preussen wegen die Schlesischen Sachen [dated 16 Dec., 1740].   1741.

Manstein, Baron C. H. von.   Mémoires historiques sur la Russie, 1727–44.   Amsterdam.   1771.   English editions.   London.   1770 and 1856.

Rondeau, Mrs.   Letters from a lady who resided some years [1728–40] in Russia.   London.   1777.

Thoughts, deliberate, on the system of our late treaties with Hesse-Cassel and Russia in regard to Hanover.   London.   1756.

Ursachen, die, des unglücklichen Gefolges des gegenwärtigen Krieges mit Frankreich auf Seiten Englands und die nachtheiligen Folgen der Allianzen des letztern mit Russland, etc. Gotha. 1757.

View, an impartial, of the conduct of the M......ry in regard to the engagements entered into with Russia, etc. London. 1756.

Vorontsoff, Prince A. R. Notes sur ma vie. Vorontsoff Archives. Vol. v. Moscow. 1870, etc.

Zustand, der gegenwärtige, des russischen Monarchie, etc. Erfurt. 1749.

IV. MONOGRAPHS AND LATER WORKS.

Bain, R. N. The Daughter of Peter the Great. London. 1899.
—— Peter III. London. 1902.
—— The Pupils of Peter the Great. London. 1897.

Bantuish-Kamensky, D. N. Biographies of the Russian Generalissimos. St Petersburg. 1840. (*R.*)

Danielson, J. R. Die nordische Frage in den Jahren 1746–51. Helsingfors. 1888.

Dolgoruki, Prince K. Count A. J. Osterman. St Petersburg. 1841. (*R.*)

Genishta, V. J. and Borisevich, A. T. History of the 30th Ingrion dragoon regiment from 1704. St Petersburg. 1904 sqq.

Halem, G. A. von. Lebensbeschreibung des Feldmarschalls B. C. Grafen von Münnich. Oldenburg. 1803. French edition: Paris. 1807.

Herrmann, E. Geschichte des russischen Staates. Vols. iv and v. (Gesch. d. europ. Staaten.) Hamburg. 1849–53.

Karge, P. Die russisch-österreichische Allianz von 1746. Göttingen. 1887.

Kochulinsky, A. A. Count Osterman and the proposed partition of Turkey, 1735–9. Odessa. 1899. (*R.*)

Kostomaroff, N. J. Russische Geschichte in Biographien. (German Translation.) Leipzig. 1889, etc.

Masslowski, Colonel. Der Siebenjährige Krieg nach russischer Darstellung. Berlin. 1888–92.

—— Zur Geschichte der russisch-österreichische Kooperation im Feldzüge von 1759. Hannover. 1888.

Panchulidzeff, S. History of the Russian Horse Guards from 1724, etc. St Petersburg. 1899–1901. (*R.*)

Rambaud, A. N. Histoire de la Russie. Paris. 1878. E. Tr. by L. B. Lang. 2 vols. London. 1879.

Shchepkin, E. Lectures on Russian history in the eighteenth century. St Petersburg. 1905. (*R.*)

Solovieff, S. M. History of Russia. Vols. xviii–xxii. St Petersburg. 1895, etc. (*R.*)

Titlinoff, B. V. The Government of the Empress Anne and its relations with the Orthodox Church. Wilna. 1905. (*R.*)

Vandal, A. Une ambassade française en Orient sous Louis XV. La mission du Marquis de Villeneuve, 1728–41. Paris. 1887.

—— Louis XV et Élisabeth de Russie. Paris. 1892.

Vasilchikoff, A. A., Prince. The Family of the Razumovskies. Moscow. 1868. (*R.*)

Waliszewski, K. La Dernière des Romanoffs. Paris. 1902.

—— L'Héritage de Pierre le Grand. Paris. 1900.

CHAPTER XI.

THE REVERSAL OF ALLIANCES AND THE FAMILY COMPACT.

I. MANUSCRIPTS.

The chief manuscript collections to be consulted for this chapter are: *In Paris:* Archives du Ministère des Affaires Étrangères; 1° Correspondance politique (Angleterre, Allemagne, Autriche-Hongrie, Espagne, Prusse, Russie, Saxe, Suède, etc....); 2° Mémoires et documents.—Archives nationales: Correspondance secrète de Louis XV avec de Broglie, Tercier, etc.—Bibliothèque nationale, département des manuscrits: Correspondance officielle et privée de Choiseul et de Bernis.—Ibid. Papiers de Béliardi.—*In London:* British Museum: Addit. MSS. Newcastle Papers. —*In Berlin:* Königliches geheimes Staatsarchiv.—*In Vienna:* Kaiserliches und Königliches Haus- Hof- und Staatsarchiv.—*In Spain:* Archivo histórico nacional and Archivo general de Simancas.

II. PRINTED DOCUMENTS.

Aranda, Count. Correspondencia diplomatica del Conde de Aranda embajador cerca del rey de Polonia 1760-2. (Coleccion de documentos ineditos para la historia de España, vol. CVIII, CIX.) 2 vols. Madrid. 1893-4.

Broglie, A., Duc de. Le Secret du Roi. Correspondance secrète de Louis XV avec ses agents diplomatiques 1752-74. Paris. 1878.

Brühl, Count. Des Grafen Brühl Korrespondenz mit dem Freiherrn von Riedesel. Beitrag zur Geschichte des Siebenjährigen Krieges 1760-2. Edited by M. von Eelking. Leipzig. 1854.

Frederick II. Politische Korrespondenz Friedrichs des Grossen. 32 vols. Berlin. 1879. (*In progress.*)

Hertzberg, Count E. F. von. Recueil des déductions, manifestes, déclarations, traités et autres actes et écrits publics qui ont été rédigés et publiés pour la Cour de Prusse, depuis l'année 1756 jusqu'à l'année 1790. 3 vols. Berlin. 1790-5.

Kaunitz, Prince. Correspondance secrète entre le comte W. A. Kaunitz-Rietberg, ambassadeur impérial à Paris, et le baron Ignaz de Koch, secrétaire de l'impératrice Marie-Thérèse, 1750-2. Paris. 1899.

Louis XV.—Boutaric, E. Correspondance inédite de Louis XV. Paris. 1886.

—— Correspondance de Louis XV et du maréchal de Noailles. 2 vols. Paris. 1865.

—— Political and confidential Correspondence of Louis XV. 3 vols. New York. 1803.

Recueil des instructions données aux ambassadeurs et ministres de France depuis les traités de Westphalie jusqu'à la Révolution française. Paris. (*In progress.*) Autriche, par A. Sorel ; Bavière, Palatinat et Deux-Ponts, par A. Lebon ; Suède et Danemark, par A. Geffroy ; Naples et Parme, par J. Reinach ; Russie, par A. Rambaud ; Pologne, par L. Farges ; Espagne, par Morel-Fatio et Léonardon ; Prusse, par A. Waddington.

(Vitzthum von Eckstädt, Count.) Die Geheimnisse des Sächsischen Cabinets. 2 vols. Stuttgart. 1866.

III. CONTEMPORARY LETTERS AND MEMOIRS.

A. FRANCE.

Aguesseau, Chancelier de. Lettres. 2 vols. Paris. 1823.

Argenson, Marquis de. Journal et mémoires, publiés par Rathery. 9 vols. Paris. 1859–67.

Barbier (Avocat). Journal historique et anecdotique du règne de Louis XV. 8 vols. Paris. 1857.

Bernis, Cardinal de. Mémoires et lettres. 2 vols. Paris. 1878.

—— Correspondance avec Pâris-Duverney (1752–69). 2 vols. Paris and London. 1790.

Broglie, V. F., Duc de. Correspondance inédite, pour servir à l'histoire de la Guerre de Sept Ans, 1759 à 1761. 4 vols. Paris. 1903–5.

Chansonnier historique du xviiie Siècle. Recueil de chansons, vaudevilles, sonnets, épigrammes...Publié par Émile Raunié. 10 vols. Paris. 1879–84.

Choiseul, Duc de. Mémoires écrits par lui-même et imprimés sous ses yeux en 1778 (par Soulavie). 2 vols. Paris. 1790.

—— Choiseul à Rome (1754–7). Lettres et mémoires inédits, publiés par le Vicomte Maurice Boutry. Paris. 1895.

—— Mémoires (1719–85). Paris. 1904.

Collé, C. Journal et Mémoires (1748–72). 3 vols. Paris. 1868.

—— Correspondance inédite. Paris. 1864.

Correspondance de plusieurs personnages illustres de la Cour de Louis XV depuis les années 1745 jusques et y compris 1774. 2 vols. Paris. 1808.

Croÿ, Duc de. Mémoires inédits sur les Cours de Louis XV et de Louis XVI, publiés par le Vicomte de Grouchy et P. Cottin. 4 vols. Paris. 1906–7.

Des Cars, Duc. Mémoires. Paris. 1890.

Duclos, C. P. Mémoires Secrets. 2 vols. Paris. 1791.

Du Deffand, Mme. Correspondance complète avec ses amis, Hénault, Montesquieu, Voltaire. Publiée par M. de Lescure. 2 vols. Paris. 1885.

—— Correspondance complète avec la Duchesse de Choiseul, l'abbé Barthélemy et M. Craufurt, publiée par M. le Marquis de Saint-Aulaire. 3 vols. Paris. 1867.

Dufort, Comte de Cheverny. Mémoires. 2 vols. Paris. 1886.

Du Hausset, Mme. Mémoires. Brussels. 1825.

Esterhazy, Count V. L. Mémoires (1757–97), avec une introduction par E. Daudet. Paris. 1905.

Grimm, Raynal and Meister. Correspondance littéraire, philosophique, et critique. 16 vols. Paris. 1877–87.

Hénault, President. Mémoires. Paris. 1854.

Lauzun, Duc de. Mémoires. 2 vols. Paris. 1822.

Lemoine, J. Sous Louis le Bien-Aimé. Correspondance amoureuse et militaire d'un officier pendant la Guerre de Sept Ans. Paris. 1905.

Lévy, President. Journal historique ou fastes du règne de Louis XV, surnommé le Bien-Aimé. 2 vols. Paris. 1766.

Luynes, Duc de. Mémoires. 17 vols. Paris. 1860–5.

Maria Theresia. Briefwechsel zwischen Kaiserin Maria Theresia u. Kurfürstin Maria Antonin von Sachsen. Ed. W. Lippert. Leipzig. 1909.

Marie Leczynska. Lettres inédites au Président Hénault. Paris. 1886.

Marmontel, J.-F. Mémoires. 6 vols. Paris. 1804–5.

Martange, N. B. de. Correspondance inédite, 1756–82. Paris. 1898.

Maurepas, Comte de. Mémoires, par Soulavie. 4 vols. Paris. 1792.

Mémoires secrets pour servir à l'histoire de la République des lettres depuis 1762 jusqu'à nos jours. 36 vols. London. 1777–89.

Mirabeau, Comte de. Mémoires du Ministère du duc d'Aiguillon et de son commandement en Bretagne. Paris. 1792.

Montalembert, Marquis de. Correspondance de M. le Marquis de Montalembert, employé par le roi de France à l'armée Suédoise (1757–61). London. 1777.

Montbarrey, Prince de. Mémoires (1732–96). 3 vols. Paris. 1826–7.

Morellet, Abbé. Mémoires sur le xviii⁰ siècle et sur la Révolution. 2 vols. Paris. 1821–3.

Narbonne, P. Journal des règnes de Louis XIV et de Louis XV (1701–74). Paris. 1866.

Nivernais, Duc de. Œuvres posthumes. 2 vols. Paris. 1807.

Pompadour, Mᵐᵉ de. Correspondance. Paris. 1878.

Richelieu, Duc de. Correspondance particulière historique du Maréchal duc de Richelieu en 1756, 1757 et 1758 avec M. Pâris-Duverney. 2 vols. London and Paris. 1789.

Soulavie, J.-L. G. Mémoires historiques et anecdotiques sur la Cour de France pendant la faveur de la Marquise de Pompadour. Paris. 1802.

—— Mémoires du Maréchal de Richelieu. 9 vols. Paris. 1790–3. [Dubious.]

Terrai, Abbé. Mémoires rédigés par Coquereau. London. 1776.

Thévenot, A. Correspondance inédite du prince François-Xavier de Saxe. Paris. 1875.

Tilly, Comte A. de. Mémoires. Paris. 1853.

Toussaint, F. V. Anecdotes de la Cour de France sous le règne de Louis XV, texte original publié par P. Fould. 2 vols. Paris. 1905.

Valori, Marquis de. Mémoires des négociations du Marquis de Valori, ambassadeur de France à la Cour de Berlin, accompagnés d'un recueil de lettres de Frédéric le Grand. 2 vols. Paris. 1820.

Vitzthum von Eckstädt, Count. Maurice comte de Saxe et Marie-Josèphe de Saxe, dauphine de France. Lettres et documents inédits. Leipzig. 1867.

Voltaire. Œuvres, édit. Beuchot. 72 vols. Paris. 1834.

B. Great Britain.

Buckinghamshire, Earl of. The Despatches and Correspondence of John, second Earl of Buckinghamshire, ambassador to the Court of Catherine II of Russia, 1762–5. London. 1900.

Chatham, William Pitt, Earl of. Correspondence. 2 vols. London. 1838.

Lord, W. F. The Counts of St Paul: Correspondence of H. Saint Paul, British minister at Versailles, 1772–6. Kingston. 1904.

Mitchell, Sir A. Memoirs and papers. 2 vols. London. 1850.

C. Prussia.

Frederick II. Briefe zwischen Friedrich II und Katharina von Russland. St Petersburg. 1877.

—— Briefwechsel Friedrichs des Grossen mit Grumbkow und Maupertuis 1731–59. Leipzig. 1898.

—— Œuvres de Frédéric le Grand. 30 vols. Berlin. 1846–56.

Frederick II. Originalbriefe K. Friedrichs II im Kriegsarchiv zu Wien 1759–60. Vienna. 1882.

Henckel v. Donnersmarck, Count L. A. Briefe der Brüder Friedrichs des Grossen. Berlin. 1877.

Krauel, R. Briefwechsel zwischen Heinrich Prinz von Preussen und Katharina II von Russland. Berlin. 1903.

Preussische Staatsschriften aus der Regierungszeit Königs Friedrichs II, herausgegeben v. J. G. Droysen, M. Duncker und H. v. Sybel. 3 vols. Berlin. 1877–92.

IV. SECONDARY WORKS.

A. GENERAL.

Bourgeois, E. Manuel de politique étrangère. 2 vols. Paris. 1901.

Brunner, S. Der Humor in der Diplomatie und Regierungskunde des 18. Jahrhunderts. 2 vols. Vienna. 1872.

Duncker, M. Die Bildung der Koalition des Jahres 1756. Preussische Jahrbücher. Vol. xlix.

Fain, Baron. Politique de tous les cabinets de l'Europe pendant les guerres de Louis XV et de Louis XVI. 3 vols. Paris. 1801.

Masslowski. Der Siebenjährige Krieg. 3 vols. Berlin. 1888–93.

Mémoire historique sur la négociation de la France et de l'Angleterre depuis le 26 mars 1761 jusqu'au 20 septembre de la même année. Paris. 1761.

Naudé, A. Beiträge zur Entstehungs-Geschichte des Siebenjährigen Krieges. 2 vols. Leipzig. 1895–6.

Raumer, F. V. Europa vom Ende des Siebenjährigen bis zum Ende des Amerikan-Krieges (1763–83). 5 vols. Berlin. 1839.

Schaefer, A. Geschichte des Siebenjährigen Krieges. 2 vols. Berlin. 1867–74.

Ségur, L. P. Politique de tous les cabinets de l'Europe pendant les règnes de Louis XV et de Louis XVI. 3 vols. Paris. 1801.

Sorel, A. La Question d'Orient au xviii⁰ siècle. Paris. 1889.

Stuhr, P. F. Forschungen und Erläuterungen über Hauptpunckte der Geschichte des Siebenjährigen Krieges. 2 vols. Hamburg. 1842.

Waddington, R. Louis XV et le Renversement des Alliances. Préliminaires de la Guerre de Sept Ans (1754–6). Paris. 1896.

—— La Guerre de Sept Ans. Histoire diplomatique et militaire. Vol. i : Les Débuts. Vol. ii : Crefeld et Zorndorf. Vol. iii : Minden, Kunersdorf. Vol. iv : Torgau, Pacte de famille. 4 vols. Paris. 1899–1903. (*In course of publication.*)

B. FRANCE.

Aubertin, Charles. L'Esprit public au xviii⁰ siècle. Paris. 1873.

Babeau, Albert. Le village sous l'ancien régime. Paris. 1882.

—— La ville sous l'ancien régime. Paris. 1884.

—— La vie rurale dans l'ancienne France. Paris. 1885.

Barthélemy, E. M., Count de. Histoire des relations de la France et du Danemark, 1751–70. Copenhagen. 1887.

Bastard d'Estang, Vicomte de. Les Parlements de France. 2 vols. Paris. 1857.

Bersot, P. E. Études sur le xviii⁰ siècle. Paris. 1855.

Bonhomme, Honoré. Louis XV et sa famille. Paris. 1873.

Bourguet. Le Duc de Choiseul et l'alliance espagnole. Paris. 1906.

Broc, Vicomte de. La France sous l'ancien régime. 2 vols. Paris. 1887–9.

Broglie, A., Duc de. Frédéric II et Louis XV. Paris. 1885.
—— L'Alliance autrichienne, 1756. Paris. 1897.
—— La paix d'Aix la Chapelle, 1748. Paris. 1895.
—— Voltaire avant et pendant la Guerre de Sept Ans. Paris. 1898.
Calmettes, Pierre. Choiseul et Voltaire. Paris. 1902.
Campardon, E. Madame de Pompadour à la Cour de Louis XV. Paris. 1867.
Carné, Count de. La monarchie française au xviiie siècle. Paris. 1859.
Carré, H. La France sous Louis XV. Paris. (s. d.)
—— La Chalotais et le duc d'Aiguillon. Correspondance du chevalier de Fontette. Paris. 1893.
Crétineau-Joly, J. A. M. Histoire religieuse, politique et littéraire de la compagnie de Jésus. 6 vols. Paris. 1845–6.
Daubigny, E. T. Choiseul et la France d'outre-mer après le traité de Paris. Étude sur la politique coloniale au xviiie siècle. Paris. 1892.
Des Réaux, Marquise. Le Roi Stanislas et Marie Leczynska. Paris. 1895.
Douglas, R. B. Life and times of Madame du Barry. London. 1896.
Faguet, E. La politique comparée de Montesquieu, Rousseau et Voltaire. Paris. 1902.
Flammermont, J. Le chancelier Maupeou et les parlements. Paris. 1884.
—— Rapport sur les correspondances des agents diplomatiques étrangers en France avant la Révolution. Paris. 1896.
Fleury, M. Louis XV et les petites maîtresses. Paris. 1899.
Ford, J. L. The Story of du Barry. New York. 1902.
Goncourt, E. and J. de. Madame de Pompadour. Paris. 1888.
Hamont, T. La Fin d'un empire français aux Indes sous Louis XV. Lally-Tollendal. Paris. 1887.
Jobez, A. La France sous Louis XV. 6 vols. Paris. 1864–73.
Koser, K., and Küntzel, G. Aus der Korrespondenz der französischen Gesandtschaft zu Berlin 1752–66. Forschungen zur Brand. und Preuss. Geschichte. Vols. vi and xii.
La Trémoille, C. L., Duc de. Mon grand-père, P. F. Walsh, à la Cour de Louis XV et à la Cour de Louis XVI (1767–89). Paris. 1904.
Lion, H. Le Président Hénault (1685–1770). Paris. 1903.
Luçay, Count de. Les Secrétaires d'État depuis leur institution jusqu'à la mort de Louis XV. Paris. 1881.
Marion, Marcel. La Bretagne et le duc d'Aiguillon. Paris. 1898.
Maugras, G. La fin d'une société. Le duc de Lauzun et la Cour intime de Louis XV (1747–74). Paris. 1893.
—— Le duc et la duchesse de Choiseul, leur vie intime et leur temps, 1755–70. Paris. 1902.
—— La disgrâce du duc et de la duchesse de Choiseul. Paris. 1905.
Mention, L. Le comte de Saint Germain et ses réformes. Paris. 1884.
Moufle d'Angerville. Vie privée de Louis XV. 4 vols. London. 1788.
Nolhac, P. de. Études sur la Cour de France. Louis XV et Madame de Pompadour. Paris. 1904.
—— Louis XV et Marie Leczinska. Paris. 1902.
Pérey, L. Le Duc de Nivernais. Paris. 1891.
—— Le Président Hénault et Mme du Deffand. Paris. 1893.
Pocquet, B. Le Pouvoir absolu et l'Esprit provincial. Le duc d'Aiguillon et La Chalotais. 2 vols. Paris. 1900.
Rankin, L. The Marquis d'Argenson. London. 1901.
Remontrances du Parlement de Paris au xviiie siècle, publiées par J. Flammermont. Paris. 1888.
Rocquain, F. L'esprit révolutionnaire avant la Révolution, 1715–89. Paris. 1878.

Sage, H.   Dom Philippe de Bourbon, infant des Espagnes, duc de Parme, et Louise-Élisabeth, fille aînée de Louis XV.   Paris.   1904.

Schaefer, A.   Das Ende der Preuss.-Französ. Alliance im Jahre 1756.   Historische Zeitschrift.   Vol. xiv.

Sénac de Meilhan.   Le gouvernement, les mœurs et les conditions en France avant la Révolution, avec introduction et notes par H. de Lescure.   Paris.   1862.

Soulange-Bodin, André.   La diplomatie de Louis XV et le pacte de famille.   Paris. 1894.

Stryienski, C.   La Mère des trois derniers Bourbons, Marie Josèphe de Saxe, et la Cour de Louis XV.   Paris.   1902.

—— Le Gendre de Louis XV, Don Philippe, infant d'Espagne et duc de Parme. Paris.   1904.

Vandal, A.   Louis XV et Élisabeth de Russie.   Paris.   1882.

Vatel, C.   Histoire de Madame du Barry.   3 vols.   Paris.   1882–3.

Villiers de Terrage, M.   Les dernières années de la Louisiane française.   Paris.   1903.

Williams, H. N.   Madame de Pompadour.   London.   1902.

—— Madame du Barry.   London.   1904.

Zorn de Bulach, A. J., Baron.   L'ambassade du Prince Louis de Rohan à la Cour de Vienne, 1771–4.   Strassburg.   1901.

C.   Great Britain.

Annual Register, the, 1758 sqq.

Burrows, Montagu.   Life of Edward, Lord Hawke, with account of origin of the English wars in the reign of George II, and the state of the Navy at that period. 1883.

Chatham, William Pitt, Earl of.   Anecdotes...of the principal events of his time, with his speeches....   3 vols.   London.   1810.

Corbett, J.   England in the Seven Years' War.   2 vols.   London.   1908.

Green, W. D.   William Pitt, Earl of Chatham.   London.   1902.

Innes, A. D.   Britain and her Rivals in the Eighteenth Century, 1712–89.   London. 1895.

Kelley, B. W.   The Conqueror of Culloden, life and times of William Augustus, Duke of Cumberland.   London.   1903.

Lecky, W. E. H.   History of England in the Eighteenth Century.   7 vols.   London. 1892.

Mahan, Capt.   The Influence of Sea Power upon History.   1889.

McCarthy, J.   History of the Four Georges and of William IV.   2 vols.   London.   1905.

Ruville, A. von.   W. Pitt, Graf von Chatham.   3 vols.   Stuttgart.   1905.

—— W. Pitt und Graf Bute.   Berlin.   1895.

—— Die Auflösung des Preussischen-Englischen Bündnisses im Jahre 1762.   Berlin. 1892.

Skohorne, B. C.   Our Hanoverian Kings.   London.   1884.

Thackeray, F.   History of the Earl of Chatham.   2 vols.   London.   1827.

Walpole, H.   Memoirs of the Reign of George the Third.   4 vols.   London.   1894.

D.   Prussia and Germany.

Bitterauf, T.   Die Kurbayrische Politik im Siebenjährigen Kriege.   Munich.   1901.

Bourdeau.   Le Grand Frédéric.   2 vols.   Paris.   1900–2.

Heussel, A.   Friedrichs des Grossen Annäherung an England 1755 und die Sendung des Herzogs von Nivernais nach Berlin.   Giessen.   1897.

Hoffmann, W.   Die Politik des Fürstbischofs von Würzburg und Bamberg, A. F. Grafen von Seinsheim, 1756–63.   Munich.   1903.

Klopp, O.   Der König Friedrich und seine Politik.   Schaffhausen.   1867.

Koser, R.   König Friedrich der Grosse.   2 vols.   Stuttgart.   1893–1903.

Lehmann, M.   Friedrich der Grosse und der Ursprung des Siebenjährigen Krieges. Leipzig.   1894.

Longman, F. W.   Frederick the Great and the Seven Years' War.   London.   1881.

Mendelssohn-Bartholdy, K.   Friedrich der Grosse und Polen.   Auszüge aus der Korrespondenz mit den Gesandten in Warschau und Petersburg 1762–6. Forschungen zur Deutsch. Geschichte.   Vol. ix.

Naudé, A.   Friedrichs des Grossen Angriffspläne gegen Oesterreich im Siebenjährigen Kriege.   Marburg.   1893.

Oncken, W.   Das Zeitalter Friedrichs des Grossen.   2 vols.   Allg. Gesch. in Einzeld. Berlin.   1880–2.

Paul-Dubois, L.   Frédéric le Grand, d'après sa correspondance politique.   Paris. 1903.

Ranke, L. von.   Zur Geschichte von Oesterreich und Preussen zwischen den Friedensschlüssen von Aachen und Hubertsburg.   Sämmtliche Werke, Vol. xxx. Leipzig.   1875.

Raumer, F. V.   König Friedrich II und seine Zeit (1760–9).   Leipzig.   1836.

Reddaway, W. F.   Frederick the Great and the rise of Prussia.   London.   1904.

Schöning, K. W. von.   Der Siebenjährige Krieg...nach der Originalkorrespondenz Friedrichs des Grossen mit dem Prinzen Heinrich und seine Generalen. Potsdam.   3 vols.   1851–2.

Volz, G. B.   Kriegführung und Politik Königs Friedrichs des Grossen in den ersten Jahren des Siebenjährigen Krieges.   Berlin.   1896.

Wagner, F.   Friedrichs des Grossen Beziehungen zu Frankreich und der Beginn des Siebenjährigen Krieges.   Hamburg.   1896.

E.   Austria-Hungary.

Arneth, A. von.   Geschichte Maria Theresia's.   10 vols.   Vienna.   1863–79.

—— Biographie des Fürsten Kaunitz.   Vienna.   1899.

Bermann, M.   Maria Theresia und Kaiser Josef II.   Vienna.   1881.

Broglie, A., Duc de.   Marie-Thérèse impératrice.   2 vols.   Paris.   1888.

Hennequin de Villermont, A. C.   Marie-Thérèse, 1717–80.   2 vols.   Paris.   1895.

Pérey, Lucien.   Charles de Lorraine et la Cour de Bruxelles sous le règne de Marie-Thérèse.   Paris.   1903.

Wolf, A.   Oesterreich unter Maria Theresia, Josef II und Leopold II, 1740–92. Vienna.   1883.

F.   Miscellaneous.

Danvila y Collado, M.   Reinado de Carlos III.   6 vols.   Madrid.   1907.

Elias, K.   Die Preussisch-russischen Beziehungen von der Thronbesteigung Peters III bis zum Abschluss des Preussisch-russischen Bündnisses vom 11. April, 1764.   Göttingen.   1900.

Masslowski.   Zur Geschichte der Russisch-österreichischen Kooperation, 1759. Hanover.   1888.

Rambaud, A.   Russes et Prussiens.   Guerre de Sept Ans.   Paris.   1895.

Rousseau, F.   Règne de Charles III, roi d'Espagne (1759–88).   2 vols.   Paris.   1907.

Volz, G. B., and Küntzel, G.   Preussische und österreichische Akten zur Vorgeschichte des Siebenjährigen Krieges.   Leipzig.   1899.

Waliszewski, K.   Le Roman d'une impératrice.   Paris.   1897.

CHAPTER XII.

SPAIN AND PORTUGAL, 1746–94.

(1) SPAIN UNDER FERDINAND VI AND CHARLES III.

A. Contemporary Authorities.

Angelis, Pedro de. Relaçion histórica de los sucesos de la rebelion de José Gabriel Tupae Amaru en las provincias del Perú el año de 1780....Coleccion de obras y documentos relativos à la historia...de las Provincias del Rio de la Plata. Vol. v. Buenos Ayres. 1831.

Aribau, B. C. Obras originales del Conde de Florida Blanca y escritos referentes à su persona. Bibl. de autores Españoles. Vol. lix. Madrid. 1899.

Becatini, Francisco. Storia del regno di Carlo III. Venice. 1790.

Bourgoing, J. F. de. Tableau de l'Espagne moderne. 2 vols. Paris. 1797.

Campomanes, Pedro Rodriguez, Count of. Cartas politico-económicas escritas...al Conde de Lerena, precedidas de una introduccion y de la biografia del autor. Madrid. 1878.

Clarke, E. D. (Chaplain to the Ambassador, Lord Bristol). Letters concerning the Spanish nation. London. 1763.

Crillon, Louis de Berton, Duc de. Mémoires militaires. Paris. 1791.

Dalrymple, William (Lieut.-Colonel). Travels through Spain and Portugal in 1774, with account of the Spanish expedition against Algiers, 1775. London. 1777.

Drinkwater, John. A history of the late siege of Gibraltar. London. 1785.

Fernan-Nuñez, C. J. Gutierrez de los Rios, Count of (Ambassador at Lisbon, Paris, etc.). Vida de Carlos III con la biografia del autor, notas y appendices por A. Morel-Fatio y A. Paz y Melia. 2 vols. Madrid. 1896.

Fernando, Manuel. Diario de lo ocurrido en el sitio de Gibraltar. Madrid. 1787.

Florida-Blanca, Joseph Moniño, Count of. Gobierno del Señor Rey Carlos III ...dada á luz por A. Muriel. Madrid. 1839.

Jovellanos, G. de. Obras publicados por D. Candido Nocedal. 3 vols. Madrid. 1903.

Lopez de Ayalá, Ignacio. Historia de Gibraltar. Madrid. 1782.

Malmesbury, first Earl of. Diaries and correspondence of. London. 1844.

Spain, a new account of the inhabitants, trade and government of. London. 1762.

Swinburne, Henry. Travels through Spain in 1775 and 1776. London. 1787.

B. Later Works.

Colmeiro, Manuel. Historia de la Economia Politica en España. Madrid. 1866.
Costa, Joaquin. Collectivismo agrario en España. Madrid. 1898.
Coterelo y Mori. Iriarte y su epoca. Madrid. 1897.
—— Don Ramon de la Cruz y sus obras. Madrid. 1899.
Coxe, William, Archdeacon of Wilts. Memoirs of the Kings of Spain of the House of Bourbon (1700–88). 5 vols. London. 1815. [Most valuable because of the copious extracts from diplomatic correspondence and other contemporary documents.]
Danvila y Collado, Manuel. Reinado de Carlos III. 6 vols. Madrid. 1892, etc. [These volumes, which form part of the Hist. Gen. de España, by members of the Real Acad. de Hist. under the direction of A. Canovas del Castillo, are thorough and detailed in their treatment. The elaborate and signally complete series of references in foot-notes to the original sources in the various Archives of the Kingdom forms a special feature.]
Ferrer del Rio, Antonio. Historia del Reinado de Carlos III. 4 vols. Madrid. 1856.
—— Coleccion de los articulos en la "Esperanza" sobre la historia del Reinado de Carlos III, escrito por. Madrid. 1859.
Haebler, C. Maria Josefa Amalia, Königin von Spanien. Dresden. 1893.
Lafuente, M. Historia General de España. Vols. xix to xxi. Madrid. 1850–62. [Contains many original documents.]
Lavalle, J. A. de. Don Pablo de Olavide. Lima. 1885.
Leguina, H. de. El P. Rávago, confesor de Fernando VI. Estudio biografico. Madrid. 1876.
Macanaz, M. R. de. España y Francia en el siglo xviii. Madrid. 1876.
Rodriguez Villa, A. El marques de la Ensenada. Madrid. 1876.
—— Patiño y Campillo. Madrid. 1882.
Rosseeuw Saint-Hilaire, E. F. A. Histoire d'Espagne. Vols. xii and xiii. Madrid. 1893–5.
Rousseau, François. Règne de Charles III d'Espagne (1759–88). 2 vols. Paris. 1907. [For Franco-Spanish relations in particular.]
Stryienski, C. Le Gendre de Louis XV, Don Philippe, Infant d'Espagne et duc de Parme. Paris. 1904.

(2) EXPULSION OF THE JESUITS FROM PORTUGAL AND SPAIN.

Azevedo, J. L. de. Os Jesuitas no Grão-Pará. Lisbon. 1902.
Brabo, J. Coleccion de documentos relativos à la expulsion de los Jesuitas de la Republica Argentina y del Paraguay, en el reinado de Carlos III. Madrid. 1872.
Carayon, P. Charles III et les Jésuites de ses États d'Europe et d'Amérique en 1767. Paris. 1868.
Causa Jesuitica de Portugal, o documentos autenticos, bulas, leyes reales, despachos de la Secretaria de estado y otras piezas originales. (Tr. from Portuguese.) Madrid. 1768.
Crétineau-Joly, J. A. M. Clément XIV et les Jésuites. Paris. 1847.
Garay, Blas. El Comunismo de las misiones de la Compania de Jesus en el Paraguay. Madrid. 1797.
Menezes, C. J. de. Os Jesuitas e o Marques de Pombal. Oporto. 1893.
Murr, Gottlieb von. Geschichte der Jesuiten in Portugal unter der Staatsverwaltung der Marquis von Pombal. 2 vols. Nuremberg. 1788.

Opperman, H. A. Pombal und die Jesuiten. Hanover. 1845.

Pombal, Choiseul et d'Aranda...un précis historique de ce qui s'est passé en Portugal, en France et en Espagne à l'occasion des Jésuites. Documents historiques. 3 vols. Paris. 1827.

Recueil de pièces qui n'avoient pas encore paru en France concernant le procès des Jésuites et de leurs complices en Portugal. Paris. 1761.

S. J. C. M. (Pombal). Relação abreviada da republica que os religiosos Jesuitas das Provincias de Portugal e Hespanha estabelecerão nos dominios ultramarinos das duas monarchias.... Paris. 1758.

(3) PORTUGAL.

A. CONTEMPORARY AUTHORITIES.

Administration du Marquis de Pombal. 4 vols. Amsterdam. 1787.
Anecdotes du ministère de Pombal. Warsaw. 1781.
Cartas e outras obras selectas do Marques de Pombal. 3 vols. Lisbon. 1820–4.
Memoirs of the Court of Portugal and of the administration of the Count d'Oeyras (from a series of original letters written in French). London. 1765.
Vita de Seb. G. de Carvalho (Marchese di Pombal). 4 vols. Siena. 1782.

B. LATER WRITERS.

Billot, A. Pombal et les Tavora. Revue Bleue. September, 1839.
Coelho, J. M. Latino. Historia de Portugal desde os fins do XVII seculo até 1814. Lisbon. 1874.
Duhr, B. (S. J.). Pombal, sein Charakter u. seine Politik. Freiburg i. B. 1891.
Gomez, F. L. Le Marquis de Pombal. Paris. 1869.
Luz Soriano, J. P. da. Historia do reino de Dom Jozé I. Lisbon. 1866.
Olfers, J. F. M. von. Über den Mordversuch gegen den König Joseph von Portugal an 3 September, 1758. Berlin. 1839.
Oliveira Martins, J. P. Historia de Portugal. 2 vols. Lisbon. 1901.
Processos celebres do Marquez de Pombal. Factos curiosos e escandalosos de sua epoca. Lisbon. 1882.
Schäfer, H. Geschichte von Portugal. 5 vols. (Gesch. d. europ. Staaten.) Hamburg u. Gotha. 1874.
Silva, L. A. Rebello da. Historia de Portugal nos seculos XVII e XVIII. 5 vols. Lisbon. 1860–71.
Smith, John, Count of Carnota. Memoirs of the Marquess of Pombal with extracts from his writings and despatches. 2 vols. London. 1843. [The author was private secretary to Marshal the Duke of Saldanha.]
Stephens, H. Morse. Portugal. (Story of Nations Series.) London. 1891.

[As to the expulsion of the Jesuits, cf. Bibliography to Chapter XVI, II D.]

(4) BRAZIL.

Galanti, P. R. M. Compendio da historia do Brazil. 4 vols. São Paulo. 1905.
Mello Moraes, A. J. Brazil historico. 4 vols. Rio de Janeiro. 1839.
Oliveira Martins, J. P. O Brazil e as Colonias Portuguezas. Lisbon. 1888.
Southey, R. History of Brazil. 3 vols. London. 1810.
Varnhagen, F. A. Historia General de Brazil. 3 vols. Madrid. 1854–7.

CHAPTER XIII.

GREAT BRITAIN.

(1756–93.)

A good critical bibliography of the years 1760–1801 will be found in W. Hunt's Political History of England, vol. x (see below). For the history of Ireland in this period see Bibliography to Chapter xiv. For the history of the American Colonies and the United States in this period see Bibliographies to Vol. vii, General, and Chapters ii, iii, iv, v, vi, and vii. For the history of India see Bibliography to Chapter xv. For the history of the Seven Years' War in Germany and the diplomatic history of the period, see Bibliographies to Chapters ix and xi.

I. GENERAL HISTORIES.

(Covering more than one section of this Chapter[1].)

Adolphus, J. The History of England, from the Accession to the decease of King George III. 7 vols. London. 1840–5.

Almon, J. Anecdotes of Eminent Persons of the Present Age. 3 vols. London. 1797.

Annual Register, the. (Commencing in 1758.) London. 1758 sqq. [The earliest volumes are edited by Edmund Burke.]

Bancroft, G. History of the United States of America. 6 vols. London. 1876.

Bisset, R. History of the reign of George III to the termination of the late War. 6 vols. London. 1803.

Brosch, M. Geschichte von England. Vols. viii, ix. (Gesch. d. europ. Staaten.) Gotha. 1893–5.

Channing, E. History of the United States. Vol. ii. New York. 1908.

Clowes, Sir W. L. The Royal Navy. 7 vols. London. 1897–1903.

Cust, Sir E. Annals of the Wars. 5 vols. London. 1858–60.

Fortescue, J. W. History of the British Army. Part I. 2 vols. London. 1899.

Hunt, W. History of England from the Accession of George III to the close of Pitt's first Administration. Political History of England. Vol. x. London. 1905.

Hunter, Sir W. W. The Indian Empire. New edn. London. 1893.

Laughton, Sir J. K. Studies in Navy History. London. 1887.

Leadam, I. S. History of England, 1702–60. (Political History of England, Vol. ix.) London. 1909.

Lecky, W. E. H. History of England in the Eighteenth Century. New edn. 7 vols. London. 1892.

---

[1] Works bearing more especially upon one of the three sections of this chapter are entered under the Bibliography of that section only.

Macpherson, D. Annals of Commerce. 4 vols. London. 1805.

Mahan, A. T. Influence of Sea Power upon History, 1660–1783. London. 1889 (and later editions).

Mahon, Lord (Earl Stanhope). History of England, from the Peace of Utrecht to the Peace of Versailles, 1713–83. New edn. 7 vols. London. 1836–54.

Marks, M. A. M. England and America, 1763–83. 2 vols. London. 1907.

Massey, W. A History of England during the Reign of George III. 4 vols. London. 1855–63.

May, Sir T. E. (Lord Farnborough). The Constitutional History of England since the accession of George III. 3rd edn. 3 vols. London. 1871.

Mill, James. History of British India. 9 vols. London. 1840–8.

Parliamentary History, the. Vols. xiv–xxx. London. 1813–17.

Plowden, F. Historical Review of the State of Ireland from the invasion of Henry II to the Union. 2 vols. London. 1803.

Seeley, Sir J. R. The Expansion of England. London. 1900.

Torrens, W. M. History of Cabinets. From the Union with Scotland to the Acquisition of Canada and Bengal. 2 vols. London. 1894.

See also, *passim*, The Dictionary of National Biography, edited by Sir Leslie Stephen and Sidney Lee. London. 1885–1900 ; and especially the articles on William Pitt the elder and the younger.

II. WILLIAM PITT THE ELDER.

A. Sources.

1. *Manuscript.*

Among the ms. sources for the history of this period the documents of the Record Office as a matter of course stand first, furnishing the chief material for the history of the foreign and the colonial policy of Great Britain as well as for the internal history of the country, during Pitt's great Administration. Of special importance are the diplomatic correspondences in State Papers, Foreign, and the State Papers, Colonial; also the Admiralty Records. The Home Office Records are calendared from 1760 to 1775. Lastly, the practice which prevailed in the eighteenth century in England as elsewhere, of opening the correspondences of the ambassadors of foreign States in the Post and having them transcribed so far as possible, led to the accumulation of a large number of "Intercepted Despatches," which are preserved in the section State Papers, Foreign, Confidential. They fill 27 vols. for the years 1756–63 only.

An important supplement to all these documents is to be found in the Chatham or Pringle Manuscripts, which were bequeathed to the Record Office by the late Admiral Pringle, and contain the correspondence of both the elder and the younger William Pitt. To judge from the use to which they have been already put by several enquirers (H. Hall, A. von Ruville, J. S. Corbett), they possess the very highest importance not only for the family history of the elder Pitt, but also for the home and foreign policy of his Administration. A selection of the most interesting pieces was printed in the Chatham Correspondence, edited by W. S. Taylor and J. H. Pringle. 4 vols. London. 1838–40.

In the British Museum the great collection of the Newcastle Papers is of exceptional value for this period as well as for the preceding decades. Of other manuscript collections it must suffice to mention here the Hardwicke Papers and the Mitchell Papers. From the latter A. Bisset's work, mentioned below, contains valuable extracts. The papers of Lord Egremont, which are valuable for the peace negotiations of 1761–3, are in the possession of the Marquis of Lansdowne and have been used by J. S. Corbett (see II, below).

Among the great Continental Archives the Berlin Secret Archives of State may probably be regarded as of the greatest importance, inasmuch as Prussia was the ally of Great Britain in the Seven Years' War. A. Schaefer in his History of the Seven Years' War was the first to use the material of these Archives in comprehensive fashion; the most interesting portions of it, more especially the Political Correspondence of Frederick the Great, have since appeared in print. Other historians, such as R. Koser and A. von Ruville, have also in the meantime utilised the documents of these Archives for their works on this period. The Archives of Paris and Vienna, though containing much of value, in accordance with the nature of the relations between the Austrian and French Governments, on the one hand, and the British, on the other, during the Seven Years' War possess only a secondary significance. A. von Arneth's narrative is based mainly on the material at Vienna, and the works of R. Waddington on that furnished by the Archives Étrangères at Paris.

2. *Printed Memoirs and Correspondence; Contemporary Speeches and Pamphlets.*

Acten. Preussische und Oesterreichische Acten zur Vorgeschichte des Siebenjährigen Krieges. Edd. G. B. Volz and G. Küntzel. (Publ. a. d. preuss. Staatsarch. 74.) Leipzig. 1899.

Almon, J. Anecdotes of the Life of the Earl of Chatham. London. 1793.

Annual Register, the. 1758 sqq. [The earliest volumes edited by Edmund Burke.]

Barham, Charles Lord. Letters and Papers of, 1758–1813. Ed. Sir J. K. Laughton.
    I. Navy Records Society. London. 1907.

Bedford, fourth Duke of. Correspondence. With an introduction by Lord John Russell. London. 1842–6.

Bisset, A. Memoirs and Papers of Sir Andrew Mitchell. 2 vols. London. 1850.

Byng, Admiral John, Trial of. Dublin. 1757.

—— A Candid Examination of the Court-Martial of Admiral Byng in a letter to the gentlemen of the Navy. By an old sea officer.

—— An exact copy of a letter from Admiral Byng to the Right Hon. W—— P——, Esq.

Calendars of Home Office Papers of the Reign of George III. Ed. T. Redington. Vol. I (1760–5). 1878.

Chatham, Earl of.—Authentic Memoirs of the Right Hon. the late Earl of Chatham. 1778.

—— The Speeches of the Right Hon. the Earl of Chatham with a biographical Memoir. 1848.

—— Pitt, W. Correspondence of. Edd. W. S. Taylor and J. H. Pringle. 4 vols. London. 1838–40.

—— —— Correspondence of, when Secretary of State with Colonial Governors and Military and Naval Commissioners in America. Ed., for the Club of The Colonial Dames of America, by Gertrude Selwyn Kimball. 1906.

Choiseul, Duc de. Mémoires de. [See Bibl. to Chapter XI, III A.]

Clarke, E. Letters concerning the Spanish Nation during 1760–1. London. 1763.

Fighting Instructions, 1530–1816. Ed. J. S. Corbett. Navy Records Society. London. 1905.

Frederick the Great.—Histoire de la Guerre de Sept Ans. (Œuvres IV, v.) Berlin, 1847.

—— Politische Correspondenz. Vols. XI–XXI. Berlin. 1883–94.

Grafton, A. H., third Duke of. Autobiography and political Correspondence. Ed. Sir W. R. Anson. London. 1898.

Grenville Papers, the, being the Correspondence of Rich. Grenville, Earl Temple, and George Grenville, their Friends and Contemporaries. Ed. W. T. Smith. 4 vols. 1852.

Louis XV, Correspondance de, et du Maréchal de Noailles. 2 vols. Paris. 1865.

Parliamentary History of England. Vols. xiv–xvi. 1813.

Recueil des Instructions données aux Ambassadeurs et Ministres de France depuis les traités de Westphalie jusqu'à la Révolution française. xvi: Prusse, avec une introd. et notes par A. Waddington. Paris. 1901. xii *bis*: Espagne. Vol. iii. (1722–93.) Par A. Morel-Fatio et H. Léonardon. Paris. 1899.

Rockingham, Marquis of. Memoirs of, and his Contemporaries. By G. Thomas, Earl of Albemarle. 2 vols. London. 1852.

Round mss. Hist. mss. Comm. Rep. xiv. App. Pt. ix, pp. 291 sqq. London. 1895.

Stopford-Sackville mss. Hist. mss. Comm. Rep. xv. London. 1904.

Townshend, Marquis, mss. Hist. mss. Comm. Rep. xi, Pt. 4, pp. 294–328. London. 1887.

Walpole, Horace. Letters. Ed. Mrs Paget Toynbee, with Bibliography. 16 vols. Oxford. 1903–5.

—— Memoirs of the last ten years of the Reign of George II. 2 vols. London. 1822.

—— Memoirs of the Reign of George III. Ed. Sir Denis Le Marchant. 4 vols. London. 1845.

Weston-Underwood mss. Hist. mss. Comm. Rep. x. App. Pt. 1. London. 1885.

II. Secondary Works.

Barthélemy, Comte E. de. Le traité de Paris. Revue des questions historiques. Vol. xliii. Paris. 1888.

Beer, A. Zur Geschichte des Jahres 1756. Mitteilungen des Instituts für Oester. Gesch. xvii.

Beer, G. L. British Colonial Policy, 1754–65. New York. 1907.

—— Commercial Policy of England towards the Colonies. New York. 1893.

Bourguet, A. Études sur la Politique étrangère du Duc de Choiseul. Paris. 1907.

Bourinot, J. G. Canada under British Rule. Cambridge. 1900.

Bourne, E. G. Spain in America. New York. 1904.

Bradley, A. G. The Fight with France for North America. Westminster. 1902.

Carlyle, T. History of Friedrich II of Prussia called Frederick the Great. 6 vols. London. 1858–65.

Coquelle, P. Les Projets de Descente en Angleterre. Paris. 1902. [Docs.]

Corbett, J. S. England in the Seven Years' War. A study in combined strategy. 2 vols. London. 1907.

Coxe, W. Memoirs of the Pelham Administration. 2 vols. London. 1829.

Droysen, T. G. Geschichte der preussischen Politik. Vol. v, Pt. 4. Leipzig. 1886.

Duncker, M. Die Bildung der Koalition des Jahres 1756. (Sitzungsberichte der Akad.) Berlin. 1882.

—— Preussen und England im Siebenjährigen Kriege. (Abhandlungen z. neueren Gesch.) Leipzig. 1887.

Fitzmaurice, Lord. Life of William, Earl of Shelburne. 3 vols. London. 1875.

Fortescue, J. W. A History of the British Army. Vol. ii. London. 1899.

Germiny, Comte M. de. Les brigandages maritimes de l'Angleterre sous le règne de Louis XV. Revue des questions historiques. 1908.

Godwin, W. History of the Life of William Pitt, Earl of Chatham. 1783.

Grant, W. L. La Mission de M. de Bussy à Londres en 1761. Revue d'Hist. Diplom. xx. Paris. 1906.

—— Pitt's Theory of Empire. Queen's Review. Kingston (Canada). July—Sept. 1908.

Hall, H.   Chatham's colonial policy.   American Historical Review, July, 1900.
——   Pitt and the Family Compact.   Quarterly Review, October, 1899.
——   Was Pitt a Prophet?   Contemporary Review.   October, 1896.
  See also papers on Pitt by the same writer in Athenæum, May 12, 1900, April 19 and July 12, 1902.
Harris, G.   Life of the Earl of Hardwicke.   3 vols.   London.   1847.
Harrison, F.   Chatham.   (Twelve English Statesmen.)   London.   1906.
——   Chatham.   Address.   Hist. Soc. Transactions.   1909.
Hertz, G. B.   The Old Colonial System.   Manchester.   1905.
Heussel, A.   Friedrichs des Grossen Annäherung an England 1755 und die Sendung des Herzogs v. Nivernais nach Berlin.   (Giessener Studien.)   Giessen.   1896.
Hotblack, Kate.   The Peace of Paris 1763.   Transactions Royal Hist. Soc.   3rd ser.   Vol. II.   London.   1908.
Hunt, W.   Pitt's retirement from office, 5 Oct. 1761.   English Historical Review, 1906, pp. 119 sqq.
Immich, M.   Geschichte des Europäischen Staatensystems von 1660 bis 1789.   Munich and Berlin.   1905.
Jesse, J. H.   Memoirs of the Life and Reign of King George III.   London.   1867.
Koser, R.   König Friedrich der Grosse.   2 vols.   Stuttgart.   1893–1903.
Lloyd, E. M.   The Raising of the Highland Regiments in 1757.   Engl. Hist. Rev. 1902, pp. 466 sqq.
Lucas, Sir C. P.   History of Canada to 1812.   London.   1909.
Luckwaldt, F.   Die Westminsterkonvention.   Preussische Jahrbücher.   Vol. LXXX.
Macaulay, Lord.   Essays.   William Pitt, Earl of Chatham.   The Earl of Chatham.   Frederic the Great.   3 vols.   London.   1843.
Mace, W. H.   Des älteren Pitt Beziehungen zur amerikanischen Revolution.   Jena.   1897.
Masson, F.   Le Cardinal de Bernis depuis son ministère.   Paris.   1884.
Michael, W.   Die englischen Koalitionsentwürfe des Jahres 1743.   Forschungen zur Brand. u. Preuss. Gesch.   I.   1888.
Moses, B.   South America on the eve of Emancipation.   New York and London.   1908.
Oncken, W.   Das Zeitalter Friedrichs des Grossen.   2 vols.   Berlin.   1880–2.
Preuss, T. D. E.   Friedrich der Grosse.   Eine Lebensgeschichte.   4 vols., with Urkundenbuch.   Berlin.   1832–4.
Ranke, L. von.   Französische Geschichte, vornehmlich im 16. u. 17. Jahrhundert.   Sämmtliche Werke.   Vols. VIII–XIII.   Leipzig.   1868–70.
——   Englische Geschichte, vornehmlich im 17. Jahrhundert.   Sämmtliche Werke.   Vols. XIV–XXII.   Leipzig.   1870.   English transl.   6 vols.   Oxford.   1875.
——   Friedrich II, König von Preussen.   Sämmtliche Werke.   Vols. LI, LII.   Leipzig, 1888.
——   Der Ursprung des Siebenjährigen Krieges.   Sämmtliche Werke.   Vol. XXX.   Leipzig.   1875.
Raumer, F. von.   König Friedrich II u. seine Zeit (1740–69).   Nach den gesandtschaftlichen Berichten im Brit. Mus. u. Reicharchive.   (Beiträge z. neuer. Gesch. II.)   Leipzig.   1836.
Ruville, A. von.   William Pitt, Graf von Chatham.   3 vols.   Stuttgart and Berlin.   1905.   Engl. transl., with preface by H. E. Egerton.   London.   1907.
——   William Pitt (Chatham) und Graf Bute.   Berlin.   1895.
——   Die Auflösung des preussisch-englischen Bündnisses im Jahre 1762.   Berlin.   1892.
  Michael, W.   Göttingische Gelehrte Anzeigen 1894.   No. 4.
  Ruville, A. von.   Friedrich der Grosse und Bute.   Eine Erwiderung.   Deutsche Zeitschr. f. Geschichtswiss.   1894.   XII.
Salomon, F.   William Pitt.   Vol. I.   Leipzig.   1901.

Strieder, J. Kritische Forschungen zur Oesterreichischen Politik (1748–56). (Leipziger Histor. Abh. 2.) Leipzig. 1906.

Temperley, H. W. V. Pitt's retirement from office, 5 Oct. 1761. English Historical Review, 1906, pp. 327 sqq.

Thackeray, F. A History of William Pitt, Earl of Chatham. 2 vols. London. 1827.

Waddington, R. Louis XV et le renversement des alliances. Paris. 1896.

—— La guerre de sept ans. Vols. I–IV. Paris. 1899–1907.

Ward, A. W. Great Britain and Hanover. (Ford Lectures.) Oxford. 1899.

Williams, B. William Pitt and the representation of the Colonies in the Imperial Parliament. Eng. Hist. Rev. Vol. XXII, pp. 756 sqq. London. 1907.

Winstanley, D. A. George III and his first Cabinet. Engl. Hist. Review. Vol. XVII, pp. 678 ff. London. 1902.

Winter, G. Friedrich der Grosse. (Geisteshelden.) 3 vols. Berlin. 1906.

III. THE KING'S FRIENDS.

A. Sources.

1. *Manuscript.*

British Museum. Conway Papers, Addit. MSS. 17497–8. George III, Letters of, Egerton MS. 982. Gunning Papers, Egerton MSS. 2696–2706. Hardwicke Papers, Addit. MSS. 35352–915. Mitchell Papers, Addit. MSS. 6819–36. Newcastle Papers, Addit. MSS. 32901–33002 and 33023–5. Wilkes Papers, Addit. MSS. 22131–2 and 30883–5.

Record Office. *See Section II, 1 above.*

Lansdowne House. Viry Papers, seen by kind permission of the Marquis of Lansdowne.

2. *Printed Documents; Contemporary Letters, Memoirs, etc.*

Almon, J. History of the late Minority, 1762–5. London. 1766.

—— Political Register. 11 vols. London. 1767–72.

—— Review of Lord Bute's Administration. London. 1763.

Annual Register. Vols. III–XXVII. London. 1761–83.

Bath MSS. Longleat Papers. Hist. MSS. Comm. Rep. XV. London. 1904.

Bedford, fourth Duke of. Correspondence. Ed. Lord John Russell. 3 vols. 1842–6.

Cavendish, Sir H. Debates of the House of Commons during the Thirteenth Parliament of Great Britain, 1768–71. With Memoir by W. Dowdeswell, and Journal of the fourth Duke of Bedford, 1766–70. 2 vols. London. 1841.

Changes in the Ministry, 1765–7. Edited from Newcastle MS. 33003 by Miss Bateson for Royal Historical Society. (Camden Ser.) London. 1898.

Cumberland, Richard. Memoirs. 2 vols. London. 1807.

Dartmouth MSS. Vols. II and III. Hist. MSS. Comm. Rep. XIV. App. Pt. 10. London. 1895.

Dodington, George Bubb (Baron Melcombe). Diary, 1748–61. London. 1785. 4th edn. 1809

Du Cane, Lady, MSS. Hist. MSS. Comm. Rep. XV. London. 1905.

Elizabeth, Princess, daughter of George III and Landgravine of Hesse-Homburg. Ed. P. C. Yorke. London. 1898.

Éon de Beaumont, Chevalier de. Lettres, Mémoires, etc. The Hague. 1764.

Frederick the Great. Politische Correspondenz. Vols. XIX–XXII. Berlin. 1892–5.

Garden, Comte de. Histoire Générale des Traités de Paix. Vols. IV, V. Paris, n. d.

George III. Correspondence with Lord North. 1768–83. Ed. W. B. Donne. 2 vols. London. 1867.

Gibbon, Edward. Autobiographies. Intr. by John, Earl of Sheffield. Ed. J. Murray. London. 1896.

Glover, Richard. Memoirs, 1742–57. London. 1814.

Grenville Papers. Ed. W. J. Smith. 4 vols. London. 1852–3.

Historical MSS. Commission, Reports of. Vols. III–XV. Appendices, and Reports on MSS. of Mrs Stopford Sackville, American MSS. in Royal Institution, and MSS. of the Marquess of Lothian. London. 1872–1905.

Junius. Letters of. Ed. J. M. Good. London. 1814.

Leeds, Francis, fifth Duke of. Political Memoranda. Ed. O. Browning. (Camden Soc.) London. 1884.

Lennox, Lady Sarah. Life and Letters, 1745–1826. Ed. Countess of Ilchester and Lord Stavordale. 2 vols. 1904.

Macfarlan, R. History of the first ten years of the reign of George III. 2nd edn. London. 1783.

McCulloch, H. Miscellaneous Representations to the Earl of Bute relative to our concerns in America (1761). Ed. W. A. Shaw. London. 1906. [The original project for taxing the Colonies.]

Montagu, Lady Mary Wortley. Letters and Works. Ed. Lord Wharncliffe. 3rd edn by W. M. Thomas. 3 vols. London. 1861.

Mure, W. Selections from the Family Papers preserved at Caldwell. (Maitland Club.) 3 vols. Glasgow. 1853–4.

Phillimore, Sir R. J. Memoirs and Correspondence of George Lord Lyttelton. 2 vols. London. 1845.

Rose, G. Diaries and Correspondence. Ed. L. V. Harcourt. 2 vols. London. 1860.

Selwyn, George. Letters and Life. Ed. E. S. Roscoe and H. Clergue. London. 1899.

—— Letters *passim.* Savile Foljambe Papers. Hist. MSS. Comm. Rep. xv, Pt. 5. London. 1897.

—— Title and Letters, 1745–1826. 2 vols. 1904.

Waldegrave, James, second Earl. Memoir from 1754 to 1758. London. 1821.

Walpole, Horace (Earl of Orford). Memoirs of the reign of King George III. Ed. Sir Denis Le Marchant; rev. G. F. Russell Barker. 4 vols. London. 1894.

—— Letters. Ed. Mrs Paget Toynbee. 16 vols. Oxford. 1903–5. [Bibliography.]

—— Journal of the reign of George III, 1771–83. Ed. J. Doran. 2 vols. London. 1859.

Weston Underwood MSS. Hist. MSS. Comm. Rep. x. App. Pt. I, pp. 321–427. London. 1885.

Wraxall, Sir N. W. Historical and Posthumous Memoirs, 1772–84. Ed. H. B. Wheatley. 5 vols. London. 1884.

B. Later Works.

Albemarle, Earl of. Memoirs of the Marquis of Rockingham and his contemporaries. 2 vols. London. 1852.

Almon, John. Anecdotes of the Life of Chatham. London. 1796, 1810.

Barrington, Shute. Political Life of Viscount Barrington. London. 1814.

Buckingham and Chandos, second Duke of. Memoirs of the Court and Cabinets of George III. 4 vols. London. 1853–5.

Buckinghamshire, John, second Earl of. Papers, 1762–5. Ed. A. D'Arcy Collier for the Royal Historical Society. 1900.

—— Papers, etc. in Lothian MSS. Hist. MSS. Comm. London. 1905.

Campbell, Lord. Lives of the Chancellors. 8 vols. London. 1845–69.

Choiseul-Stainville, Duc de. Mémoire Historique sur la négociation de la France et de l'Angleterre depuis le 26 mars 1761 jusqu'au 20 septembre de la même année. Leipzig. 1761.

Elliot, G. F. Stewart. The Border Elliots and the Family of Minto. Edinburgh. 1897.

Elliot, Sir Gilbert [Earl of Minto]. Memoir by the Countess of Minto. 3 vols. Edinburgh. 1874. [Docs.]

Family Compact, the. Quarterly Review. Vol. cxc, No. 380, Art. iii. London. 1899.

Gaillardet, F. Mémoires du Chevalier d'Éon. 3 vols. Brussels. 1837.

Harris, G. Life of Lord Chancellor Hardwicke. 3 vols. London. 1847. [Docs.]

Hertz, G. B. Diplomacy as to Falkland Isles, 1770. In British Imperialism, pp. 110–49. London. 1908.

Hotblack, Kate. The Peace of Paris, 1763. Transactions of the Royal Historical Society. 3rd ser. Vol. ii. London. 1908.

Jesse, J. H. George Selwyn and his contemporaries. 4 vols. London. 1843–4, 1882.

—— Memoirs of the Life and Reign of George III. 3 vols. London. 1867.

Nicholls, J. Recollections and Reflections as connected with public affairs during the reign of George III. 2 vols. London. 1820–2.

Ruville, A. von. William Pitt (Chatham) und Graf Bute. Ein Beitrag zur inneren Geschichte Englands unter Georg III. Berlin. 1895.

—— William Pitt, Graf von Chatham. 3 vols. Stuttgart and Berlin. 1905.

Sheffield, John, Lord. Observations on the Commerce of the American States. London. 1784.

Stanhope, Earl. Life of William Pitt. 4 vols. London. 1861–2. [Docs.]

Townshend, Charles. Life. By Percy Fitzgerald. London. 1866.

Tucker, Josiah. Four Tracts on Political and Commercial Subjects. Gloucester. 1774.

—— Series of Answers to certain Popular Objections against separating from the Rebellious Colonies. Gloucester. 1776.

Traité, le, de Paris entre la France et Angleterre (1763). Revue des Questions Historiques. Vol. xliii. Paris. 1888.

Trevelyan, Sir G. O., Bart. Early History of C. J. Fox. London. 1881, 1908.

Wiffen, J. H. Historical Memoirs of the House of Russell. 2 vols. London. 1833.

C. The Wilkes Affair.

Complete Collection of the Genuine Papers, Letters, etc., in the case of John Wilkes. Paris. 1767.

Howell, T. B. State Trials. Vol. xix, 982–1175, 1382–1418.

Kidgell, J. Genuine and Succinct Narrative of a Libel entitled An Essay on Woman. London. 1763.

Lloyd, C. Defence of the Majority in the Question relating to General Warrants. London. 1764.

Rae, W. Fraser. Wilkes, Sheridan, Fox: the Opposition under George III. London. 1874.

Stephens, A. Memoirs of J. Horne Tooke. 2 vols. London. 1813.

Townshend, C. Defence of the Minority on the Question relating to General Warrants. London. 1764.

Warburton, William, Bishop of Gloucester. Works. Supplement by F. Kilvert, pp. 223–32. London. 1841.

Wilkes, J. Correspondence and Memoirs. Ed. J. Almon. 5 vols. London. 1805.

Wright, T. Caricature History of the Georges. London. 1869.

See also the following newspapers for the years during which the controversy raged: Monitor, Auditor, Briton, North Briton, Public Advertiser, St James' Chronicle.

See also Section A above; and article on Wilkes in Dictionary of National Biography.

D. Naval and Military Affairs.

Barrow, Sir J.   Life of Richard, Earl Howe.   London.   1838.

Beatson, R.   Naval and Military Memoirs.   6 vols.   London.   1804.

Burrows, Montagu.   Life of Edward, Lord Hawke.   London.   1883.

Chevalier, E.   Histoire de la Marine Française pendant la guerre de l'Indépendance Américaine.   Paris.   1877.

Edwards, Bryan.   History of the British Colonies in the West Indies.   3 vols.   London.   1807.

Keppel, T.   Life of Augustus, Viscount Keppel.   2 vols.   London.   1842.

Laughton, Sir J. K.   Articles on naval commanders and John Montagu, fourth Earl of Sandwich, in Dictionary of National Biography.

Leboucher, O. G.   Histoire de la dernière Guerre entre la Grande-Bretagne et les États-Unis, la France, l'Espagne et la Hollande.   Paris.   1787.

Manners, W. E.   Life of John Manners, Marquis of Granby.   London.   1899.   [Docs.]

Montero y Vidal.   Historia de Filipinas.   Madrid.   1887.

Mundy, G. B.   Life and Correspondence of Admiral Lord Rodney.   2 vols.   London.   1830.

Valdés, A. J.   Historia de la Isla de Cuba y en especial de la Habana.   Havannah.   1780.   Reprinted in Los tres primeros Historiadores de la Isla de Cuba, etc   3 vols.   Havannah.   1876–7.

IV. ROCKINGHAM, SHELBURNE AND THE YOUNGER WILLIAM PITT.

A. Sources.

1. *Manuscript.*

The following Historical mss. Commission Reports indicate manuscript sources of special value for this period :

10th Report, Appendix, Pt. vi.   Abergavenny mss.   Lord Braye's mss.   London.   1887.   12th Report, Appendix, Pt. ix.   Ketton mss. ; Donoughmore mss.   London.   1891.   12th Report, Appendix, Pt. x, 1745–83.   Charlemont Papers.   London.   1891.   13th Report, Appendix, Pt. iii, 1782–90.   Fortescue Papers.   Vol. i.   London.   1892.   14th Report, Appendix, Pt. i.   Rutland Papers.   Vol. iii.   London.   1894.   14th Report, Appendix, Pt. iv.   Kenyon mss.   London.   1894.   14th Report, Appendix, Pt. v.   Fortescue Papers.   Vol. ii.   1791 to 1793.   London.   1896.   15th Report, Appendix, Pt. v, 1781–9.   Foljambe Papers.   London.   1897.   15th Report, Appendix, Pt. vi, 1782–93.   Carlisle Papers.   London.   1897.   15th Report, Appendix, Pt. vii.   Ailesbury mss, pp. 237–306.   London.   1898.   Stopford-Sackville mss.   London.   1904.   Lothian Papers, Earl of Buckinghamshire's Papers (1905).   American mss., Royal Institution Papers (1906).   Vol. ii.

2. *Printed Memoirs, Correspondence, etc.*

Auckland, Lord.   Journal and Correspondence.   Ed. Bishop of Bath and Wells.   4 vols.   London.   1861–2.

Buckingham and Chandos, Duke of.   Memoirs of Courts and Cabinets of George III.   2 vols.   London.   1853.

Burges, J. Bland, Under-Secretary for Foreign Affairs.   Letters, Correspondence and Life.   Ed. J. Hutton.   London.   1885.   [Docs.]

Burke, Edmund.   Works.   New edn.   6 vols.   London.   1826.

—— Memoir of Life and Character.   By J. Prior.   3rd edn.   London.   1839.

—— Memoir.   By T. Macknight.   3 vols.   London.   1858–60.

—— Correspondence.   Edd. Earl Fitzwilliam and General Sir R. Bourke.   4 vols.   1844.

Burke, Edmund. Correspondence of Burke with Dr F. Lawrence. London. 1827.

Cornwallis, Marquis. Correspondence. Ed. C. Ross. 3 vols. London. 1859.

Eldon, Earl of. Public and Private Life of. By Horace Twiss. 3 vols. London. 1844.

Fox, Charles James. Memorials and Correspondence. Ed. Lord John Russell. 4 vols. London. 1853.

—— Life. By Lord John Russell. 3 vols. London. 1859-67.

—— Speeches. 6 vols. London. 1815.

George III. Memoirs of the Life and Reign of. By J. Heneage Jesse. 3 vols. London. 1867.

—— Correspondence with Lord North, 1768 to 1783. Ed. W Bodham Donne. 2 vols. London. 1867

Gibbon, Edward. Memoirs of my Life and Writings. Ed. G. Birkbeck Hill. London. 1900.

—— Private Letters of, 1753-94. Ed. R. E. Prothero. 2 vols. London. 1896.

Grafton, A. H., third Duke of. Autobiography and Political Correspondence. Ed. Sir W. Anson. London. 1898.

Keith, Sir R. M. Memoirs. Ed. Mrs Smyth. 2 vols. London. 1849. [Docs.]

Leeds, Francis, fifth Duke of. Political Memoranda. Ed. O. Browning. London. 1884.

Lennox, Lady Sarah. Life and Letters, 1745-1826. Ed. Countess of Ilchester and Lord Stavordale. 2 vols. London. 1904.

Mackintosh, Sir James. Memoirs. By his son R. J. Mackintosh. 2 vols. London. 1835.

Malmesbury, Earl of. Diaries and Correspondence. Ed. the third Earl of Malmesbury. 4 vols. London. 1844.

Pitt, William (the younger). Life. By John Gifford. 6 vols. London. 1809.

—— Life. By Bishop William Tomline. 3 vols. 1821.

—— Life of. By Earl Stanhope. 4 vols. London. 1861-2.

—— Correspondence with Charles, Duke of Rutland, 1781-7. Ed. John, Duke of Rutland. Edinburgh. 1890.

—— Correspondence with the Rev. C. Wyvill. Newcastle. 1796.

—— Speeches. 4 vols. London. 1806.

—— Some Chapters of his Life and Times. By Lord Ashbourne. 2nd edn. London. 1898.

Rockingham, Marquis of. Memoirs of. Ed. the Earl of Albemarle. 2 vols. London. 1852.

Rose, George. Diaries and Correspondence. Ed. L. V. Harcourt. 2 vols. London. 1860.

Sheridan, R. B. Speeches. London. 1853.

Wilberforce, William. Life. By Robert Wilberforce and Samuel Wilberforce. 5 vols. London. 1839.

—— Private Papers of. Ed. A. M. Wilberforce. London. 1897.

Windham, William. Diary, 1784-1810. Ed. Mrs H. Baring. London. 1866.

—— Speeches. Ed. T. Amyot. 3 vols. London. 1812.

Wraxall, Sir N. W. Historical Memoirs of his own time. 4 vols. London. 1836.

For American affairs the Revolutionary Diplomatic Correspondence of the United States should be consulted. The whole course of the Peace negotiations, 1781-3, is to be traced from day to day in this valuable publication, edited under the direction of Congress, by Francis Wharton. New edition, 6 vols., by J. B. Moore, Washington, 1889. See also The Literature of American History by various writers. Ed. J. N. James, London, 1902 ; a valuable bibliography.

See also:

 Correspondence and Public Papers of John Jay. Edited by Henry P. Johnston.
  4 vols. New York. 1890–3. [Especially Vol. ii.]

 Documents relating to the Constitutional History of Canada. Canadian
  Archives, 1759–91. Edd. A. Short and G. Doughty. Ottawa. 1907.

B. Secondary Works.

Browning, O. The Flight to Varennes, and other historical essays. London. 1892.

Burke, Edmund. Works. New edition. 16 vols. London. 1826.

Butenval, Comte C. A. Précis du Traité de Commerce, 1786. Paris. 1869.

Clarkson, S. History of the Rise, Progress and Accomplishment of the Abolition
 of the African Slave Trade. 2nd edn. London. 1839.

Coquelle, P. L'Alliance Franco-Hollandaise. 1735–88. 2 vols. Paris. 1902.
 [Docs.]

Fitzmaurice, Lord. Life of the Earl of Shelburne. 3 vols. London. 1875.

Hammond, J. L. Le B. Charles James Fox, a Political Study. London. 1903.

Harris, W. History of the Radical Party in Parliament. London. 1885.

Howard, John. The State and the Prisons. London. 1792.

Kent, C. B. R. The English Radicals, a historical sketch. London. 1899.

Lewis, Sir George Cornewall. Essays on the administrations of Great Britain from
 1783 to 1830. Ed. Sir Edmund Head, Bart. London. 1864.

Macaulay, Lord. Life of Pitt. Miscellaneous Works. Vol. ii. London. 1860.

Minto, Countess of. Hugh Elliot. A Memoir. Edinburgh. 1868.

Morley, John (Viscount Morley of Blackburn). Burke, a Study. London. 1893.

Political Disquisitions. London. 1774.

Porritt, E. and A. G. The Unreformed House of Commons. 2 vols. Cambridge.
 1903.

Rae, W. Fraser. Life of Richard Brinsley Sheridan. 2 vols. London. 1896.

Rose, Dr J. H. Great Britain and the Dutch Question, 1787–8. American
 Historical Review. Vol. xiv. No. 2. New York. Jan. 1909.

—— The Mission of William Grenville to the Hague and Versailles, 1787.
 English Historical Review. Vol. xxiv. London. April, 1909.

Rosebery, Lord. Life of Pitt. London. 1891.

Ryerson, A. E. Loyalists in America and their times. 2 vols. Toronto. 1880.

Salisbury, Marquis of. Stanhope's Life of Pitt. Essays from the Quarterly Review.
 London. 1905.

Seeley, Sir J. R. The Expansion of England. Two courses of Lectures at Cambridge.
 London. 1900.

Smith, Edward. The Story of the English Jacobins. London. 1881.

Stirling, A. M. W. Coke of Norfolk [Coke, T. W., Earl of Leicester] and his
 Friends. 2 vols. London. 1908.

Van Tyne, C. H. The Loyalists in the American Revolution. New York. 1902.

Wilkins, W. H. George IV and Mrs Fitzherbert. 2 vols. London. 1905.

CHAPTER XIV.

IRELAND FROM 1700–89.

I. ORIGINAL SOURCES.

In addition to the State Papers, Ireland, preserved in the Record Office, Fetter Lane, comprising Vols. 363–465, and covering the period 1702 to 1779, after which date the permission of the Home Secretary is required for their inspection, the chief sources of information are as follows:

1. The Correspondence of Archbishop King (1696–1727) in 14 vols. preserved in the Library of Trinity College, Dublin (N. i. 7–9, and N. iii. 1–11), of which considerable use was made by Bishop Mant in his History of the Church of Ireland. Vol. ii. London. 1840.

2. The Correspondence of Edward Southwell (Secretary of State for Ireland, 1702–30) with Dr Marmaduke Coghill, preserved in the British Museum, Additional mss. 21,122–3. Other Southwell mss. were acquired by the Public Record Office, Dublin, in 1898. (Cf. Thirtieth Report of the Deputy Keeper of Public Records in Ireland. App. i. pp. 44–58.)

3. The Newcastle Correspondence in the British Museum, Additional mss. 32,637—32,738 ("Home Correspondence"), constitutes a perfect mine of information for the affairs of Ireland from 1724–67. Some of Archbishop Stone's letters in this collection have been printed by C. Litton Falkiner in the English Historical Review, Vol. xx.

4. The Pelham Correspondence, likewise in the British Museum, including the correspondence of Thomas Pelham (Secretary to the Lord Lieutenant 1783–4 and 1795–8). Additional mss. 33,100—33,105.

5. The Documents preserved in the Public Record Office, Dublin, falling into four main groups, viz.:

(a) British Departmental Correspondence (1683–1758), being the communications and letters from the Official Departments in England to the Irish Government. There is a ms. Calendar of this series.

(b) Irish Departmental Correspondence (1685–1797), being the communications from the Irish Government to the Official Departments in England.

(c) Irish Civil Correspondence, called "Country Letters," in 97 vols. (1685–1827); chiefly interesting for the period 1700–60, as containing information on the state of the country, details respecting the Whiteboys, Wildgeese, Rapparees, murders, abductions, etc. It was from these Letters that Froude wrote the most romantic chapters in his History of the English in Ireland.

(d) A Collection of State Papers (1786–1808), in 51 cartons; forming a connecting link between the Departmental Correspondence and the series of modern State Papers, beginning in 1821.

6. Other sources of information are noticed below under Reports of the Historical mss. Commission; but attention may be directed to the following minor items:

(a) Additional ms. 6117, ff. 1–186, containing Bishop Synge's letters to Archbishop Wake (1703–26).

(b) Egerton MS. 77: list of Converts and Protestant Settlers, 1660–1772.

(c) Egerton MS. 201: some original private correspondence.

(d) Egerton MS. 917, with some letters from King to Southwell (from the Southwell Collection).

(e) Lansdowne MS. 242, containing some miscellaneous papers relating to Ireland during the period.

(f) A Collection of Law Reports (1697–1793), and the Converts' Roll, preserved in the Public Record Office, Dublin.

The magnificent series of contemporary pamphlets, unfortunately still uncatalogued, is contained in the Haliday Collection, in the Royal Irish Academy, Dublin. A catalogue of the Bradshaw Collection of Irish books and pamphlets in the Cambridge University Library, many of which belong to the eighteenth century, is being prepared for publication.

II. CONTEMPORARY AUTHORITIES, INCLUDING PAMPHLETS.

Abernethy, J. Scarce and valuable Tracts. London. 1751.

Abstract, an, of the...Protestant and Popish families in...Ireland, etc. Dublin. 1736.

Account, an, of the Charity Schools in Ireland. Dublin. 1730.

Account, an, of the Progress of Charles Coote, Esq. [against the Oakboys]. Dublin. 1763.

Account, the Settled: or, a Balance struck between the Irish Propositions...and the English Resolutions. Dublin. 1785.

Address, an, from a noble Lord to the People of Ireland. [Dublin?] 1770.

Address, an, to the Independent Members of the House of Commons...on... establishing a Regency. Dublin. 1789.

Alarm, an, to the unprejudiced and well-minded Protestants...upon...the White Boys. Cork. 1762.

Albemarle, Earl of. Memoirs of the Marquis of Rockingham. London. 1852.

Answer, an, to...A Vindication of Marriage, etc. Dublin. 1704.

Answer, an, to a late proposal for uniting the Kingdoms of Great Britain and Ireland. Dublin. 1751.

Answer, an, to...A free and candid Inquiry, etc. Dublin. 1753.

Answer, an, to...the Proceedings of the House of Commons in rejecting the altered Money Bill...vindicated. Dublin. 1774.

Answer, an, to the Observations on the Mutiny Bill. Dublin. 1781.

Answer, an, to the Reply to the supposed Treasury Pamphlet, "The Proposed System of Trade...explained." London. 1785.

Apology, an, of the French Refugees...in Ireland. Dublin. 1712.

Argument, an, upon the Woollen Manufacture...demonstrating that Ireland must be...employed therein. London. 1737.

Arrangement, the, with Ireland considered. London. 1785.

Astraea, or a letter on the abuses in the administration of justice in Ireland. Dublin. 1788.

Attempt, an, to prove that a free and open trade...would be...advantageous to both Kingdoms. Exeter. 1753.

Auckland, Lord (W. Eden). Considerations submitted to the People of Ireland on their present condition, etc. Dublin. 1781.

Authenticus (*pseud.*). A defence of the Protestant Clergy in the South of Ireland in answer to Mr Grattan. Dublin. 1788.

Baratariana. Fugitive Political Pieces published during the Administration of Lord Townshend. Dublin. 1777.

Barrow, Sir J. Life and Writings of Lord Macartney. London. 1807.

Bedford, Correspondence of John, Duke of. (1742–70.) 3 vols. London. 1842.

Beresford, Correspondence of the Rt. Hon. J. 2 vols. London. 1854.

Berkeley, G. (Bishop of Cloyne). Works. Ed. G. N. Wright. 2 vols. London. 1843. Ed. A. C. Fraser. 4 vols. Oxford. 1871.

Both sides of the Gutter : or, the Humours of the Regency. London. 1789.

Boulter, H. (Archbishop of Dublin). Letters to several Ministers of State. 2 vols. Dublin. 1770.

Brief Review, a, of the Incorporated Society for promoting English Protestant Schools. Dublin. 1748.

Brooke, H. The Tryal of the Cause of the Roman Catholics, etc. Dublin. 1761.

[Browne, Sir J.] An Essay on Trade in general and on that of Ireland in particular. Dublin. 1728.

[——] A scheme of the money matters of Ireland, etc. Dublin. 1729.

Buckingham, Duke of. Memoirs of the Courts and Cabinets of George III. 4 vols. London. 1853.

Burdy, S. Life of the Rev. P. Skelton. London. 1792.

Burke, E. Works and Correspondence. 8 vols. London. 1852. (Bohn's Lib.) 6 vols. London. 1886.

—— Letters, Speeches and Tracts on Irish Affairs. Ed. M. Arnold. London. 1881.

[Burke, E.?] A reply to the Treasury pamphlet...."The proposed system of trade with Ireland explained." London. 1785.

Bush, J. Hibernia Curiosa. London. 1769.

Caldwell, Sir J. Examination whether it is expedient to enable Papists to take Real Securities. Dublin. 1764.

—— Debates on the affairs of Ireland in 1763 and 1764. 2 vols. London. 1766.

—— Proposal for employing children, etc. Dublin. 1771.

—— Inquiry into the Restrictions on the Trade of Ireland. Dublin. 1779.

[Campbell, T.] A Philosophical Survey of the South of Ireland. London. 1777. Dublin. 1778.

Candid Inquiry, a, into the late Riots in Munster. Dublin. 1767.

Candid Review, a, of Mr Pitt's Twenty Resolutions. London. 1785.

Case, the, fairly stated relative to an Act lately passed against the exportation of corn. (6 Geo. III, c. 18.) Dublin. 1766.

Case, the, of the Roman Catholics of Ireland. 1755.

Cavendish, Sir H. A Statement of the Public Accounts of Ireland. London. 1791.

Cavendish, W. (Duke of Devonshire). Letters which passed in Great Britain relative to the Absentee Tax. Dublin. 1773.

Chatham, William Pitt, Earl of, Correspondence of. 4 vols. London. 1838.

Chesterfield, Earl of. Letters. 5 vols. London. 1779.

—— Miscellaneous Works. 2 vols. London. 1777.

Clarendon, R. V. A Sketch of the Revenue and Finances of Ireland. London. 1791.

Collection, a, of tracts concerning the present state of Ireland. London. 1729.

Commercial Resolutions, the,...vindicated. London. 1785.

Comparative View, a, of the Public Burdens of Great Britain and Ireland. London. Dublin. 1779.

Complete Investigation, a, of Mr Eden's Treaty. Dublin. 1787.

Conduct, the, of the Dissenters of Ireland, etc. Dublin. 1712.

Conduct, the, of the Purse of Ireland. London. 1714.

Considerations...in answer to...Observations on the Mutiny Bill. Dublin. 1781.

Considerations on agriculture, etc. Dublin. 1730.

Considerations on the late Bill for payment of the remainder of the National Debt. Dublin. 1754.

Considerations on the present calamities of this Kingdom, etc. Dublin. 1760.

CH. XIV.

Considerations on the expediency...of frequent new Parliaments in Ireland. Dublin. 1766.

Considerations on the independency of Ireland, etc. London. 1779.

Considerations on the revenues of Ireland, etc. London. 1757.

Considerations on..."Seasonable Remarks," etc. and "An Essay on Trade in general," etc. London. 1728.

Considerations on the Political and Commercial Circumstances of Great Britain and Ireland. London. 1787.

Constitution, the, of Ireland, and Poynings' Laws explained. Dublin. 1770.

Counter-Appeal, a, to the people of Ireland. Dublin. 1749.

C[ourtie]rs, the, Apology...for their conduct this S-s-n of P-r-l-nt. Dublin. 1754.

Cox, Sir R. The present State of his Majesty's Revenue, etc. Dublin. 1762.

[Cox, Sir R.?] Previous promises inconsistent with a free Parliament, etc. Dublin. 1760.

Cox, W. (Archdeacon). Memoirs of the Life and Administration of Sir R. Walpole. 3 vols. London. 1798.

—— Memoirs of the Pelham Administration. London. 1829.

Crawford, W. History of Ireland. 2 vols. Strabane. 1783.

Crommelin, L. Essay towards improving the Hempen and Flaxen Manufacture of Ireland. Dublin. 1734.

Crumpe, S. Essay on the best means of providing employment for the People. London. 1793.

Curry, J. An Inquiry into the Causes of the late Riots in Munster. Dublin. 1766.

—— Historical and Critical Review of the Civil Wars in Ireland. Dublin. 1786.

Defence, a, of the Opposition with respect to their conduct on Irish Affairs, etc. Dublin. 1785.

Defence, a, of the...People of Ireland in their...refusal of Mr Wood's copper money. Dublin. 1724.

Delany, P. Account of the Laws in force for encouraging the residence of the parochial clergy. Dublin. 1723.

Delany, Mrs, Autobiography and Correspondence of. Ed. Lady Llanover. London. 1861.

Derrick, S. Letters written from Leverpoole...Dublin, etc. Dublin. 1767.

"Dionysius." A Letter from Dionysius to the renowned Triumvirate, etc. Dublin. 1754.

Dissertation, a, on the enlargement of Tillage and erecting of Public Granaries. Dublin. 1741.

Dissertation, a, on the present Bounty Laws for the encouragement of agriculture in Ireland. Dublin. 1780.

"Drapier, M. B." A Letter...occasioned by...Thoughts on the Affairs of Ireland. Dublin. 1754.

Dobbs, A. An Essay on the Trade...of Ireland. Dublin. 1729.

Dobbs, F. History of Irish Affairs from Oct. 12, 1779 to Sept. 15, 1782. Dublin. 1782.

—— Concise View of History and Prophecy. Dublin. 1800.

Dublin Spy, the. Dublin. 1753–4.

Dublin University Magazine (The). 1836. Dublin. 1833, etc.

Dunton, J. Some account of my Conversation in Ireland. London. 1699.

Eden, W. See Auckland, Lord.

Enquiry, an, how far it might be expedient...to permit the importation of Irish Cattle. London. 1743.

Enquiry, an, into the policy of the Penal Laws, etc. London and Dublin. 1775.

Enquiry, an, into the...Progress of the linen manufacture in Ireland. Dublin. 1757.

Enquiry, an, into the causes of Popular Discontents in Ireland. London. 1804.

Essay, an, concerning the establishment of a National Bank in Ireland. London. 1774.

Essay, an, on the Trade of Ireland, by the author of Seasonable Remarks. Dublin. 1729.

Essay, an, on the ancient and modern state of Ireland, etc. Dublin. 1759.

Essay, an, on the Character and Conduct of...Lord Viscount Townshend. London. 1771.

Few Thoughts, a, on the present posture of affairs in Ireland. Dublin. 1755.

Few Words, a, of advice to the Friends of Ireland, etc. Dublin. 1755.

Finishing Stroke, the. Dublin. 1754.

First Lines, the, of Ireland's Interest in the year 1780. Dublin. 1779.

Flood, H. A Letter...on the expediency...of the present Association...in favour of our own manufactures. Dublin. 1779.

Flood, H. W. Memoirs of the Life of Henry Flood. Dublin. 1838.

Forman, C. A Defence of the Courage of the Irish Nation. Dublin. 1735.

Four Letters, originally written in French, relating to...Ireland. Dublin. 1739.

Fox, C. G. Memorials and Correspondence. Ed. Lord John Russell. 3 vols. London. 1853.

Free and candid Inquiry, a,...addressed to...a Person of Distinction in the North from a Gentleman in Town. Dublin. 1753.

[French, R.] The Constitution of Ireland and Poynings' Laws explained. Dublin. 1770.

Full Account, a, of the present dispute...between the Prerogatives of the Crown and the Rights of the People. London and Dublin. 1754.

Gilbert, Sir J. T. Calendar of Ancient Records of Dublin. 11 vols. Dublin. 1889–1904.

Grattan, H. Speeches. 4 vols. London. 1822.

—— Miscellaneous Works. London. 1822.

—— Observations on the Mutiny Bill. Dublin. 1781.

—— junr. Memoirs of the Life and Times of Henry Grattan. 5 vols. London. 1839–46.

[Gray, J.] A plan for finally settling the Government of Ireland upon Constitutional principles. London and Dublin. 1785.

Grazier's Advocate, the, or Free Thoughts of Wool. Dublin. 1742.

Grenville Papers, the. Ed. W. J. Smith. 4 vols. London. 1852.

Groans, the, of Ireland, etc. Dublin. 1741.

Guatimozin's [i.e. F. Jebb] Letters on the Present State of Ireland. London. 1779.

Harcourt Papers, the. Ed. E. W. Harcourt. 14 vols. London. 1880–1905.

Hardy, F. Memoirs of the Earl of Charlemont. 2 vols. London. 1810.

Hiberniae Notitia: or a List of the present officers in Church and State, etc. London. 1723.

Hibernia pacata [relating to the events of 1753]. Dublin. 1754.

Historical Essay, an, upon the loyalty of Presbyterians...in answer...to...The Conduct of the Dissenters. Dublin. 1713.

Historical MSS. Commission:

> Report II, pp. 65–8. Puleston MSS.; with letters from Lord Barrymore, 1732–46. See also Rep. XV, App. 7, pp. 307–43.
>
> Report II, p. 99. Torrens MSS., pointing at certain Parliamentary Reports (1776–89), in 37 vols., now in the Library of Congress, Washington. Cf. Eng. Hist. Review, XXIV, pp. 104–6.
>
> Report II, p. 103. Willes MSS. (Baron Willes' Letters, 1757–68).
>
> Report III, pp. 432–4. Howard's Parliamentary History of Ireland.
>
> Report VI, p. 236. Lansdowne MSS. (Correspondence of Earl Shelburne relating to Ireland).

Report VIII, p. 73 sqq. Portsmouth MSS. (Sir Isaac Newton's letters on Wood's Coinage, etc.).

Report VIII, pp. 174–208. Emly MSS. (Correspondence of E. S. Pery, Speaker of the House of Commons), cont. in Rep. XIV, App. 9, pp. 155–99.

Report VIII, pp. 441–92. O'Conor (Charles) of Balanagare MSS. (Roman Catholic agitation).

Report IX (Pt. III), pp. 34–67. Stopford Sackville MSS. (Irish Affairs, 1731–83).

Report XII, App. 10; XIII, App. 8. Charlemont MSS. 2 vols.

Report XII, App. 9. Donoughmore MSS. (Letters of J. Hely Hutchinson).

Report XII, App. 9. Smith (P. V.) MSS. (Letters on the Commercial Treaty).

Report XIII, App. 3. Fortescue MSS. Vol. I (Correspondence of Lord Temple, afterwards Marquis of Buckingham).

Report XIV, App. 1. Rutland MSS. Vol. III (Correspondence of the Duke of Rutland during his viceroyalty).

Report XV, App. 6. Carlisle MSS.

History, the, of the Proceedings and Debates of the Volunteer Delegates...on the subject of Parliamentary Reform. Dublin. 1784.

History of the Ministerial Conduct of the Chief Governors of Ireland...from...1688 to...1753. London. 1754.

Hitchcock, R. An historical view of the Irish Stage. 2 vols. Dublin. 1788–94.

Howard, G. E. A treatise of the Exchequer and revenue of Ireland. 2 vols. Dublin. 1776.

—— A Letter to the Publick on the present posture of Affairs. Dublin. 1754.

—— A short Account of his Majesty's hereditary Revenue. 2nd edn. with additions. Dublin. 1754.

—— Some questions upon the Legislative Constitution of Ireland. Dublin. 1770.

Humble Address, an, to the nobility, etc. [against a Union]. Dublin. 1751.

Humble Proposal, an, for...promoting Christian Knowledge among the poor natives of...Ireland. Dublin. 1730.

Hunt, W. The Irish Parliament, 1775. London. 1907.

Hutchinson, J. H. Commercial Restraints of Ireland. Dublin. 1779. Ed. W. G. Carroll. Dublin. 1882.

Impartial Thoughts on a Free Trade to Ireland. London. 1779.

Insula Sacra et Libera. A list of members...who voted for and against the altered Money Bill. London. 1753.

Intelligencer, the. [Swift and Sheridan.] Dublin. 1729. 2nd edn. London. 1730.

Irish Monitor, the. (April.) 2 vols. Dublin. 1879.

Journals of the House of Commons, Ireland.

Judgements, the, of God upon Ireland. Dublin. 1741.

Junius. Grand Council upon the Affairs of Ireland.

Knox, A. Essays on the Political Circumstances of Ireland. London. 1799.

[Knox, W.] Considerations on the State of Ireland. Dublin. 1778.

Laffan, J. Political Arithmetic of the Population...of Ireland. Dublin. 1785.

[Langrishe, Sir H.] Considerations on the Dependencies of Great Britain. Dublin. 1789.

Lascelles, R. Liber Munerum Publicorum Hiberniae. 2 vols. London. 1824–30.

Legal Considerations on the Regency as...it regards Ireland. London. 1789.

[Leland, J.] The case fairly stated: or an inquiry how far the clause...for discharging the...National Debt...would have affected the liberties of the People. Dublin. 1754.

Letter from a Prime Serjeant to a High Priest. Dublin. 1754.

Letter, a, from a Member of the House of Commons of Ireland to a gentleman of the Long Robe in England, etc. London and Dublin. 1720.

Letter, a,...containing some remarks on..."A free and candid Inquiry," etc. Dublin. 1756.

Letter, a, from a Munster Layman...on the disturbances in the South. Dublin. 1787.

Letter, a, of advice to the I—sh Members. Dublin. 1753.

Letter, a, to Henry Flood on the State of the Representation in Ireland. Belfast. 1783.

Letter, a, to the Protestant Dissenters of Ireland. Dublin. 1745.

Letter, a, to the People of Ireland...on the effects of a Union. London. 1780.

Letter, a, to the People of Ireland on the...Fisheries. Dublin. 1775.

Letter, a [second and third]...on the subject of Tythes. Dublin. 1773.

Letter, a,...relative to our present feuds and jealousies. Dublin. 1775.

Letter, a, upon...taxing the estates of Absentees. Dublin. 1773.

Letters from a country gentleman...to his Grace the Lord Primate. Dublin. 1741.

Letters of a Dungannon and Munster Delegate [on] Parliamentary Reform. Dublin. 1784.

Life, character and parliamentary conduct of...H. Boyle [Earl of Shannon]. Dublin. 1754.

List, a, of the Members...who voted on the question previous to the expulsion of A. J. Nevill, Esq. London. 1753.

[Lodge, J.] The usage of holding Parliaments and passing Bills of Supply. Dublin and London. 1770.

Long History, a, of a certain Session of a certain Parliament in a certain Kingdom, in 1713. Dublin. 1714.

Lucas, C. Works. 2 vols. London. 1751.

Luckombe, P. A Tour through Ireland. London. 1780.

[Macartney, Lord.] An Account of Ireland in 1733. London. 1733.

[MacBride, J.] A Vindication of marriage as solemnized by Presbyterians, etc. Dublin. 1702.

MacGeoghegan, Abbé. Histoire d'Irlande. 3 vols. Amsterdam. 1758-63.

[Macnally, L.] The Claims of Ireland...vindicated. London. 1782.

Madden, S. Proposal for the general encouragement of learning in Dublin College. Dublin. 1732.

—— Reflections and resolutions proper for the Gentlemen of Ireland, etc. Dublin. 1738. Reprinted. Dublin. 1816.

Management, the, of the Revenue, etc. Dublin. 1758.

Maxims relative to the present state of Ireland, 1757. Dublin. 1757.

[Maxwell, H.] An Essay upon an Union of Ireland with England. Dublin. 1704.

McAulay, A. Enquiry into the legality of Pensions on the Irish Establishment. London. 1763.

Method, a, to prevent...the running of wool from Ireland to France. London. 1745.

M[olesworth], R. L. V., Lord. Some considerations for promoting Agriculture, etc. Dublin. 1723.

"Molineux." Some Thoughts on the Bill for the relief of tenants holding leases for lives. Dublin. 1780.

Moran, P. F. (Cardinal). Spicilegium Ossoriense. 3 vols. London. 1874-8. Vol. III.

Mountmorres, Lord. Impartial Reflections upon...the Trade between Great Britain and Ireland. London. 1785.

Mullala, J. View of Irish Affairs since the Revolution. Dublin. 1795.

[Nevill, A. J.] Some Hints on Trade, Money and Credit. Dublin. 1762.

Newenham, T. Statistical and Historical Inquiry into the Progress...of Population in Ireland. London. 1805.

CH. XIV.

Newenham, T. View of the Natural, Political and Commercial Circumstances of Ireland. London. 1809.

Nicholson, E. A Method of Charity Schools in Ireland. Dublin. 1712.

O'Brien, Sir L. The Resolutions of England and Ireland relative to Commercial Intercourse. Dublin. 1785.

—— A gleam of Comfort to this distracted Empire. London. 1785.

Observations on raising the value of money, etc. Dublin. 1718.

Observations on, and a short history of, Irish Banks and Bankers, by a Gentleman in Trade. Dublin. 1760.

Observations made by the Commissioners...of the Barracks throughout Ireland. Dublin. 1760.

Observations on the Popery Laws. Dublin. 1771.

Observations on the Finances and Trade of Ireland. Dublin. 1775.

O'Conor, M. The dangers of Popery to the present Government examined. Dublin. 1761.

Office, the, and power of a judge in Ireland...explained. Dublin. 1756.

O'Leary, A. Six Tracts on Historical and Religious Questions. Dublin. 1781.

Parliamentary Register, the. [Irish Parliamentary Debates.] 15 vols. Dublin. 1784–95.

Patriot Miscellany: or a Collection of Essays relative to the political contests in Ireland during the administration of the Duke of Dorset. 2 vols. Dublin. 1756.

Patriot Queries, occasioned by a late libel..."Querie to the People of Ireland." Dublin. 1754.

Pedlar's Letter, the, to the Bishops and Clergy of Ireland. Dublin. 1760.

[Pery, E. S.] Letters from an Armenian in Ireland (1756). London. 1757.

Pococke, R. (Bishop of Meath). Tour in Ireland in 1752. Ed. G. T. Stokes. Dublin. 1891.

Prescription Sacred: or reasons for opposing...tythes of agistment. Dublin. 1736.

Present Politics, the, of Ireland. London. 1786.

Present State, the, of Ireland considered. Dublin. 1780.

Present State, the, of Religion in Ireland. London. 1712?

Prior, T. A List of the Absentees of Ireland, etc. Dublin. 1729.

—— Observations on Coin in general, etc. Dublin. 1729.

—— An Essay to encourage...the Linen Manufacture...by Premiums. Dublin. 1749.

Proceeding, the, of the House of Commons...in rejecting the altered Money Bill... vindicated. Dublin. 1754.

Proceedings relative to the Ulster Assembly of Volunteers. Belfast. 1783.

Property inviolable: or some remarks upon..."Prescription Sacred." Dublin. 1736.

Proposal, a, for lessening the excessive price of Bread Corn. Dublin. 1741.

Proposal, a, for uniting the Kingdoms of Great Britain and Ireland. London. 1751.

Proposals humbly offered to Parliament for the restoration of cash and public credit to Ireland. Dublin. 1760.

Proposed System, the, of Trade with Ireland explained. Dublin. 1785.

Protestant Interest, the, considered, etc. Dublin. 1757.

Queries relating to the new Half-Pence. Dublin. 1737.

Queries relative to...some of the present laws of Ireland. 2nd edn. Dublin. 1761.

Question, a, to be considered previous to the rejection of the Bill for paying off the National Debt, etc. Dublin. 1754.

R., T. Original Letters :...to the Rt. Hon. H. Flood. [London.] 1820.

Radcliffe, S. A serious Inquiry whether a toleration of Popery should be enacted. Dublin. 1727.

Reasons...against...reducing the Interest of Money. Dublin. 1765.

Reasons why we should not lower the coins now current in this Kingdom, etc. Dublin. 1729.

Reflections on the National Debt, with reasons for reducing the legal Interest, etc. Dublin. 1731.

Remarks on..." Considerations on the late Bill for payment," etc. Dublin. 1754.

Representation, a, of the present state of Religion...agreed to by both Houses of Convocation. Dublin. 1712.

Resolutions, the, of the House of Commons...relating to the Lord Chancellor Phipps, examined, etc. London. 1714.

Richardson, J. Seanmora ar na priom phoncibh na chreideamh. London. 1711.

—— A Proposal for the Conversion of the Popish natives of Ireland. Dublin. 1712.

—— The Folly of Pilgrimages in Ireland. Dublin. 1727.

—— Short History of the attempts to convert the Popish natives of Ireland. London. 1712. 2nd edn. 1713.

[Robinson, C.] Considerations on the late Bill for payment of the...National Debt, etc. Dublin. 1754.

[Rose, G.] The proposed system of trade with Ireland explained. ["Treasury pamphlet."] London. 1785.

R-y-l Mistake, the: or, a Catechism for the I—sh Parliament. London. 1753.

Rutty, J. History of the Quakers in Ireland. Dublin. 1751. 2nd edn. 1800.

Rutland, Duke of. Correspondence between W. Pitt and Charles, Duke of Rutland (1781–7). London. 1890.

S., T. Impartial Thoughts on a Free Trade to...Ireland. London. 1789.

Seasonable Advice to the Friends of Ireland on the present Crisis. Dublin. 1755.

Seasonable Advice to the People of Ireland during the recent recess. Dublin. 1780.

Second Letter, a, to a gentleman of the long robe in Great Britain. Dublin. 1720.

Secret History, the, of the two last memorable S-ss-ons of Parliament. Dublin. 1754.

Secret History, the, and Memoirs of the Barracks of Ireland. London. 1747.

Seward, W. W. Rights of the People asserted. Dublin. 1783.

—— Collectanea Politica. 3 vols. Dublin. 1801–4.

Sheffield, Lord. Observations on the Trade of Ireland. London. 1785.

Short Account, a, of the reasons of the intended alteration of the value of the coins current in this Kingdom. Dublin. 1729.

Short, a, and easy method of preventing the clandestine exportation of wool, etc. London. 1745.

Short History, a, of the Opposition to the present time, etc. Dublin. 1796.

Short Revue, a, of the several pamphlets...on the subject of Coin, etc. Dublin. 1730.

Short Tour, a: or, an impartial and accurate Description of the county Clare. 1779.

Short View, a, of the Proposals...for a final adjustment of the Commercial System, etc. London. 1785.

Simon, J. Historical Account of Irish Coins. Dublin. 1749.

Skelton, P. Complete Works (with Burdy's Life). 6 vols. London. 1824.

Sketch, a, of the history of two Acts...2nd and 8th of Queen Anne, to prevent the further growth of Popery. London. 1778.

Smith, J. Memoirs of Wool. London. 1747.

Some Arguments for limiting the duration of Parliaments. Dublin. 1764.

Some Considerations on the Laws which incapacitate Papists from purchasing lands. Dublin. 1739.

Some Facts...relative to the fate of the late Linen Bill. Dublin. 1753.

Some farther account of the...Disputes in Ireland about Farthings, etc.　London. 1724.

Some hints for the better promoting of the laws in this Kingdom, etc.　Dublin. 1766.

Some important frauds...in trade...laid open.　London.　1746.

Some observations on the circumstances of Ireland.　[? Dublin.　1769.]

Some observations relative to the late Bill for paying off...the National Debt of Ireland.　2nd edn.　Dublin.　1754.

Some proposals humbly offered...for the advancement of Learning.　Dublin.　1707.

Some thoughts...towards an Union, etc.　London.　1708.

Some thoughts on the general improvement of Ireland, etc.　Dublin.　1758.

Some thoughts on the...Linen manufacture, etc.　Dublin.　1739.

Some thoughts on the tillage of Ireland, etc.　London.　1737.

State of the different Interests in the House of Commons, etc.

State, a, of the Public Revenues and Expence, 1751–69.　Dublin.　1769.

State, the, of Ireland laid open, etc.　London.　1745.

Statutes at Large.　(Ireland.)　8 vols.　Dublin.　1765.　20 vols.　Dublin.　1786–1801.

Stephenson, R.　An inquiry into the state and progress of the Linen Manufacture of Ireland.　Dublin.　1757.

Stevens, R.　Inquiry into the abuses of the Chartered Schools in Ireland.　1817.

Strictures on "Considerations submitted to the People of Ireland," etc.　Dublin. 1781.

Swift (Dean).　Works.　Ed. Sir W. Scott.　19 vols.　London.　1824.

—— Prose Works.　Ed. Temple.　(Bohn's Lib.)　8 vols.　London.　1897.

[Swift, Dean?]　Schemes from Ireland, for the benefit of the body natural, ecclesiastical and politick.　London.　1732.

Synge, E. (Archbishop of Tuam).　A Defence of the Established Church...in answer to..."A Vindication of Marriage," etc.　Dublin.　1705.

—— An account of the Charity Schools in Ireland.　Dublin.　1719.　Another edition under the title: Methods of erecting...Charity Schools.　Dublin.　1721.

Taaffe, Viscount.　Observations on Affairs of Ireland.　Dublin.　1766.

Temple, Sir W.　Works.　(Essay on the Advancement of Trade.)　Vol. iii. London.　1754.

Thoughts, English and Irish, on the Pension List of Ireland.　London.　1770.

Thoughts on the Affairs of Ireland, etc.　London.　1754.

Thoughts on...the establishment of a National Bank in Ireland.　London.　1780.

Thoughts on the establishment of new manufactures in Ireland.　Dublin.　1783.

To all the good people of Ireland, friendly and seasonable Advice.　Dublin.　1755.

Tour, a, through Ireland by two English Gentlemen.　London.　1748.

Townshend, Marquis.　Meditations upon a late Excursion in Ireland.　1767.

Trant, D.　Observations on the late Proceedings in the Parliament of Ireland on the question of a Regency.　Dublin.　1789.

Tribune, the.　Ed. P. Delany.　Dublin.　1729.

Tucker, J.　Reflections on the Present Matters in Dispute between Great Britain and Ireland.　London.　1785.

Twiss, R.　A Tour in Ireland in 1775.　Dublin.　1776.

Ulster Journal of Archaeology, the.　9 vols.　Belfast.　1853–61.　Vol. i: The French Settlers in Ireland.　Vol. iii: Contributions towards a History of Irish Commerce.

Universal Advertiser, the.　Dublin.　1753, etc.

Usurpations, the, of England the chief sources of the Miseries of Ireland.　London. 1780.

Utility, the, of an Union between Great Britain and Ireland.　London.　1787.

View, a, of the present State of Ireland, etc.　London.　1780.

Wallace, T.   An Essay on the Manufactures of Ireland.   Dublin.   1798.

Walpole, H.   Memoirs of the reign of George II.   London.   1846.

—— Memoirs of George III.   Ed. Barker.   London.

—— Journals of the reign of George III.   Ed. Doran.   London.   1859.

—— Letters.   Ed. P. Cunningham.   London.   1857–9.

Webber, S.   Short Account of...our Woollen Manufacturies, etc.   London.   1739.

Wesley, J.   Journals.   4 vols.   London.   1827.

Woodfall, W.   Debate in the Irish House of Commons (Aug. 12, 1785).   Dublin.   1785.

Woodward, R. (Bishop of Cloyne).   A Scheme for establishing Poor-Houses in... Ireland.   Dublin.   1768.

—— Present State of the Church of Ireland, etc.   Dublin.   1787.

Wraxall, Sir N. W.   Historical and Posthumous Memoirs.   5 vols.   London.   1884.

Young, A.   A Tour in Ireland (1776–9).   London.   1780.   Ed. A. W. Hutton. (Bohn's Lib.)   2 vols.   London.   1892.

III. LATER AUTHORITIES.

Agnew, D. C. A.   Protestant Exiles from France.   2 vols.   Edinburgh.   **1871.**

Ashbourne, Lord.   Pitt: Some Chapters of his Life and Times.   London.   1898.

Ball, J. T.   Historical Review of the Legislative Systems...in Ireland.   Dublin.   1382.

Barrington, Sir J.   Rise and Fall of the Irish Nation.   Dublin.   1843.

Bellesheim, A.   Geschichte der katholischen Kirche in Irland.   3 vols.   Mainz.   1891.

Benn, G.   History of the town of Belfast.   2 vols.   London.   1877–80.

Bonn, M. J.   Die englische Kolonisation in Irland.   2 vols.   Berlin.   1906.

Brenan, M. J.   Ecclesiastical History of Ireland.   2 vols.   Dublin.   1840.

Buckley, M. B.   Life and Writings of A. O'Leary.   Dublin.   1868.

Cairnes, J. E.   Political Essays.   London.   1873.

Collins, C.   Jonathan Swift, a Biographical and Critical Study.   London.   1893.

Craik, Sir H.   Life of Swift.   London.   1885.

Croker, C.   Researches in the South of Ireland.   London.   1824.

Cumberland, R.   Memoirs by himself.   London.   1806.

D'Alton, E. A.   History of Ireland.   London.   1906.

Dunlop, R.   Life of H. Grattan.   London.   1889.

England, T. R.   Life of A. O'Leary.   London.   1822.

Falkiner, C. Litton.   Studies in Irish History and Biography.   London.   1902.

Fitzmaurice, Lord.   Life of the Earl of Shelburne.   London.   1875.

Fraser, A. C.   Life of Bishop Berkeley.   Edinburgh.   1881.

Froude, J. A.   The English in Ireland.   3 vols.   London.   1895.

Hassencamp, R.   Geschichte Irlands.   Leipzig.   1886.

Hickson, M.   Old Kerry Records.   London.   1872.

Ingram, T. D.   Critical Examination of Irish History.   2 vols.   London.   1900.

Killen, W. D.   Ecclesiastical History of Ireland.   London.   1875.

Lecky, W. E. H.   Leaders of Public Opinion in Ireland.   New edn.   2 vols. London.   1903.

—— History of England in the Eighteenth Century.   8 vols.   London.   1877–90. The Irish portion published separately under the title of: History of Ireland in the Eighteenth Century.   5 vols.   London.   1892.

Lewis, Sir G. C.   Essay on Local Disturbances in Ireland.   London.   1836.

Lindsay, J.   The Coinage of Ireland, etc.   London.   1839.

Madden, R. R.   History of the Penal Laws.   London.   1847.

—— History of Irish Periodical Literature.   2 vols.   London.   1867.

Mant, R. (Bishop of Down). History of the Church of Ireland. 2 vols. London. 1840.

McNeven, T. History of the Volunteers of 1782. Dublin. 1845.

Macpherson, D. Annals of Commerce. London. 1805.

Monck-Mason, W. History of St Patrick's Cathedral. Dublin. 1820.

Morley, J. Life of Burke. (E. M. L.) London. 1879.

Murray, A. E. History of the Commercial and Financial Relations between England and Ireland. London. 1903.

Nicholls, Sir G. History of the Irish Poor Law. London. 1856.

O'Callaghan, J. C. History of the Irish Brigades in the Service of France. Dublin. 1854.

O'Conor, M. Military History of the Irish Nation. Dublin. 1845.

O'Flanagan, J. R. Lives of the Lord Chancellors of Ireland. London. 1870.

Parnell, Sir H. History of the Penal Laws. London. 1822.

Plowden, F. Historical Review of the State of Ireland. 3 vols. London. 1803.

—— History of Ireland to the Union. 2 vols. London. 1812.

Porter, G. R. Progress of the Nation. 3 vols. London. 1836-43.

Prior, Sir J. Memoir of the Life of E. Burke. London. 1824.

Reid, J. S. History of the Presbyterian Church in Ireland. 3 vols. Belfast. 1867.

Ruding, R. Annals of the Coinage. 3 vols. London. 1840.

Smiles, S. The Huguenots in England and Ireland. London. 1867.

Smyth, C. J. Law Officers of Ireland. London. 1839.

Smyth, G. L. Ireland, Historical and Statistical. 3 vols. London. 1844.

Stanhope, Earl. Life of William Pitt. 4 vols. London. 1862.

Stephen, Sir L. Life of Swift. (English Men of Letters.) London. 1882.

Studies in Irish History (1649-1775). Ed. B. O'Brien. Dublin. 1903.

Two Centuries of Irish History, 1691-1870. London. 1888. 2nd edn. enlarged. London. 1907.

Wakefield, E. Account of Ireland, Statistical and Political. 2 vols. London. 1812.

Wiffen, J. H. Memoirs of the House of Russell. 2 vols. London. 1833.

Wyse, T. History of the Catholic Association. 2 vols. London. 1829.

CHAPTER XV.

INDIA.

I. THE MOGHUL EMPIRE.

A. CONTEMPORARY MEMOIRS AND HISTORIES OF PRIMARY IMPORTANCE.

Abdulkurreem, Khojeh. The Memoirs of, who accompanied Nadir Shah, on his return from Hindostan to Persia. Translated from the original Persian, by F. Gladwin. Calcutta. 1788.

Abul Fazl. Ain-i-Akbari. Translated from the original Persian: Vol. ɪ by H. Blochmann, Vols. ɪɪ and ɪɪɪ by H. S. Jarrett. 3 vols. Calcutta. 1873, 1891, 1894.

Baber. Memoirs of Zehir-ed-Din Muhammed Baber, Emperor of Hindustan. Translated by J. Leyden and W. Erskine. London. 1826.

—— Mémoires de. Translated by A. P. de Courteille. 2 vols. Paris. 1871.

Elliot, Sir H. M. The History of India as told by its own Historians. Edited and continued by J. Dowson. 8 vols. London. 1867–77.

Ferishta. History of the Dekkan from the first Mahummedan Conquests. Translated by J. Scott. 2 vols. Shrewsbury. 1794.

Hosain Khan. Letters of Aurangzeb. Bombay. 1889.

Jahangueir. Memoirs of the Emperor. Written by Himself. Translated by Major D. Price. London. 1829. Reprint. Calcutta. 1904.

Jouher. The Tezkereh al Vakiat, or Private Memoirs of the Emperor Humayun. Translated by Major Charles Stewart. London. 1832. Reprint. Calcutta. 1904.

Manucci, N. Storia do Mogor. 1653–1708. Ed. and translated by W. Irvine. Indian Texts Series. 3 vols. Calcutta. 1907.

Mirza Muhammad Haidar. Tarikh-i-Rashidi. Translated and edited by E. Denison Ross and N. Elias. London. 1895.

B. EARLY EUROPEAN TRAVELS, VOYAGES AND NARRATIVES.

Bernier, F. Histoire de la dernière Révolution des États du Grand Mogol... Paris. 1670.

—— Travels in the Mogul Empire, A.D. 1656–68. Ed. by A. Constable. London. 1891.

Careri, Gemelli de. Voyage du Tour du Monde. Traduit de l'Italien. Par M. L. N. Vol. ɪɪɪ. 6 vols. Paris. 1727.

Fryer, John. A New Account of East India and Persia in eight letters, being nine years Travels, begun 1672 and finished 1681... London. 1698.

Hawkins, Sir R.   The observations of, in his voyage into the South Sea in 1593...
The Hawkins Voyages...   Ed. by C. R. Markham.   Hakluyt Society (Series I,
vol. LVII).   London.   1878.

Mandelslo, J. A. de.   The Voyages and Travels of, into the East Indies.   Begun
in...1638 and finish'd in 1640.   Rendered into English by John Davies.
London.   1662.

Ovington, F. A.   A voyage to Suratt in the year 1689.   London.   1696.

Roe, Sir Thomas.   Journal of his Embassy to the Great Mogul, 1615–9.   Ed. from
the contemporary records, by W. Foster.   2 vols.   Hakluyt Society (Series II,
vols. I and II).   London.   1899.

Tavernier, J. B.   Les Six Voyages de Jean Baptiste Tavernier...   2 vols.   Paris.
1676.

Terry, Edward.   A Voyage to East India.   London.   1655.

Valle, Pietro della.   Viaggi di.   2 vols.   Rome.   1662–3.

C.   EARLY WORKS OF SECONDARY IMPORTANCE.

Catrou, François.   Histoire Générale de l'Empire du Mogol...   Paris.   1715.

Dow, Alexander.   The History of Hindostan.   Translated from the Persian.   3 vols.
London.   1770.

Francklin, W.   A History of the reign of Shah-Aulum.   London.   1798.

Fraser, J.   The History of Nadir Shah.   London.   1770.

Gholam-Hossein-Khan.   Sëir Mutaqharin.   Translated from the Persian.   3 vols.
Calcutta.   1789.

Gladwin, F.   The History of Hindostan during the reigns of Jehangir, Shahjehan,
and Aurungzeb.   Calcutta.   1788.

Jones, Sir William.   The history of the life of Nader Shah, King of Persia.
London.   1773.

La Croix, P. de.   Histoire de Timur-Bec.   4 vols.   Delft.   1723.

Orme, Robert.   Historical Fragments of the Mogul Empire...   2 vols.   London.
1782.

D.   LATER WORKS.

Caldecott, R. M.   The Life of Baber.   London.   1844.

Duff, James Grant.   A History of the Mahrattas.   3 vols.   London.   1826.

Elphinstone, Mountstuart.   The History of India, The Hindu and Mahometan
Periods.   With notes and additions by E. B. Cowell.   London.   1905.

Erskine, W.   A History of India under the reigns of the first two sovereigns of the
House of Taimur, Baber and Humayun.   2 vols.   London.   1854.

Holden, E. S.   The Mogul Emperors of Hindustan.   New York.   1895.

Irvine, W.   The Army of the Indian Moghuls.   London.   1903.

Keene, H. G.   A Sketch of the History of Hindustan...   London.   1885.

—— The Moghul Empire.   London.   1866.

—— The Fall of the Moghul Empire.   London.   1876.

MacGregor, W. L.   The History of the Sikhs.   2 vols.   London.   1846.

Malcolm, Sir J.   A Sketch of the Sikhs.   London.   1812.

Noer, F. A., Count of.   The Emperor Akbar.   Translated by A. S. Beveridge.
2 vols.   Calcutta.   1890.

Owen, S. J.   India on the eve of the British Conquest.   London.   1872.

Poole, S. L.   History of the Moghul Emperors of Hindustan, illustrated by their
coins.   Westminster.   1892.

Poole, S. L.   Babar.   Rulers of India Series.   Oxford.   1899.
—— Aurangzib.   Rulers of India Series.   Oxford.   1896.
Stewart, Charles.   The History of Bengal.   London.   1813.
Thomas, E.   The chronicles of the Pathan Kings of Delhi.   London.   1871.
—— The Revenue Resources of the Mughal Empire...1593–1707.   London.   1871.
Tod, James.   Annals and Antiquities of Rajast'han or the Central and Southern Rajpoot States of India.   2 vols.   London.   1829–32.
Wilks, Mark.   Historical Sketches of the South of India in an attempt to trace the History of Mysoor.   3 vols.   London.   1810–7.

II. INDIA, 1720–85.

A. THE ENGLISH IN INDIA.

(1) UNPUBLISHED MATERIAL.

The India Office contains a great volume of MS. Records consisting of the Court Minutes of the East India Company, copies of Despatches to the Presidencies of Bengal, Bombay, and Madras, Letters received from the various settlements in India, and the Consultations, Ledgers, and Proceedings of the Presidential Councils. There may be also mentioned the Orme Papers, Collections of Charters, Treaties, and Parchment records, Dutch records, including transcripts from the Hague, the series known as Home Miscellaneous, and records collected under the heading of The French in India, especially the Collections numbered 2, 3, and 4.

The Record Offices of Bengal, Bombay, and Madras also contain an immense amount of material, much of which is being gradually calendared and printed by the Government of India.

The Public Record Office contains collections of Miscellaneous Correspondence under the title Colonial Office Records, East Indies, and there are some further papers among the Treasury Records.

Among the many MSS. in the British Museum may be mentioned Clive's correspondence with the Duke of Newcastle, the official and private correspondence and papers of Warren Hastings, papers relating to his Impeachment and Trial, and various letters of Mrs Hastings.

The Clive papers are in the possession of the Earl of Powis.

The Letters and Diaries of Warren Hastings are in the Victoria Hall, Calcutta.

(2) RECORD PUBLICATIONS.

Forrest, G. W.   Selections from the Letters, Despatches, and other State Papers preserved in the Bombay Secretariat.   Home Series.   Bombay.   1887.
—— —— Maratha Series.   Bombay.   1885.
—— Selections from the Letters, Despatches, and other State Papers preserved in the Foreign Department of the Government of India.   1772–85.   3 vols.   Calcutta.   1890.
Hill, S. C.   Bengal in 1756–7.   Indian Records Series.   3 vols.   London.   1905.
Long, J.   Selections from Unpublished Records of Government for the years 1748–67.   Calcutta.   1869.
Wheeler, J. T.   Madras in the Olden Time.   3 vols.   Madras.   1861.
Wilson, C. R.   The early annals of the English in Bengal.   2 vols.   Calcutta.   1895–1900.
—— Old Fort William in Bengal.   Indian Records Series.   2 vols.   London.   1906.

(3) Treaties, Parliamentary Reports, Debates, Speeches etc.

A Collection of Treaties, Engagements and Sunnuds relating to India and neighbouring countries. Ed. by Sir C. Aitchison. 9 vols. and Index volume. Calcutta. 1892.

Bond, E. A. Speeches of the Managers and Counsel in the Trial of Warren Hastings. 4 vols. London. 1859-61.

Hansard's Parliamentary History. Vols. viii sqq. London. 1812, etc.

History of the Trial of Warren Hastings, containing the whole of the proceedings and debates in both Houses of Parliament... 1796.

Journals of the House of Commons.

Journals of the House of Lords.

Minutes of the Evidence taken at the Trial of Warren Hastings. London. 1788-94.

Reports (i-v) of the Select Committee of the House of Commons. May 26, 1772-June 18, 1773.

Reports (i-ix) of the Committee of Secrecy appointed by the House of Commons. Dec. 7, 1772-June 30, 1773.

Reports (i-vi) of the Committee of Secrecy on the causes of the war in the Carnatic. 1781-2.

Reports (i-xi) of the Select Committee on the administration of Justice in Bengal, Behar, and Orissa. 1782-3.

(4) Contemporary Works and Pamphlets.

Advantages of Peace and Commerce with some remarks on the East India Trade. London. 1729.

Authentic and faithful history of that arch-pyrate, Angria. London. 1756.

Bolts, W. Considerations on India Affairs. 3 vols. London. 1772-5.

Broome, Ralph. A comparative review of the administration of Mr Hastings and Mr Dundas. London. 1791.

Cambridge, R. O. An account of the war in India between the English and French on the coast of Coromandel. London. 1761.

Caraccioli, C. The life of Robert, Lord Clive. 4 vols. London. 1775.

Comparative view, a, of the Dutch, French, and English East India Companies. 1770.

Complete History of the War in India, a. London. 1761.

Debates in the Asiatic Assembly. London. 1767.

Downing, Clement. A compendious history of the Indian wars with an account of the rise, progress, and forces of Angria the pyrate... London. 1737.

Essay, an, on the East India trade and its importance to the kingdom. London. 1770.

Five letters from a free merchant in Bengal to Warren Hastings. London. 1783.

Fullarton, W. A view of the English interests in India and an account of the military operations in the southern parts of the peninsula. London. 1788.

Hamilton, C. An historical relation of the origin, progress, and final dissolution of the government of the Rohilla Afghans. London. 1787.

Hastings, Warren. A narrative of the Insurrection which happened in the Zemeendary of Benares. Calcutta. 1782.

—— Memoirs relative to the state of India. London. 1786.

—— Letters of, to his wife. Ed. by S. C. Grier. London. 1905.

Holwell, J. Z. Narrative of the deplorable deaths of the English gentlemen and others who were suffocated in the Black Hole... London. 1758.

Holwell, J. Z. Interesting historical events... London. 1765.

Ives, Edward. A voyage from England to India. London. 1773.

Johnstone, J. A letter to the Proprietors of East India stock. London. 1766.

—— Thoughts on our acquisitions in the East Indies particularly respecting Bengal. 1771.

Letter, a, to a Proprietor of the East India Company. London. 1750.

Letters of Albanicus to the people of England on the partiality and injustice of the charges brought against Warren Hastings. London. 1786.

Letters from Simpkin the Second...containing an humble description of the trial of Warren Hastings. London. 1792.

Macpherson, J. The history and management of the East India Company. London. 1779.

Moodie, J. Remarks on the most important military operations...on the western side of Hindoostan in 1783–4. 1788.

Munro, Innes. A narrative of the military operations on the Coromandel Coast. London. 1789.

Narrative, a, of the transactions of the British squadrons in the East Indies... comprehending a particular account of the loss of Madras... By an officer who serv'd in those squadrons. London. 1751.

Oakes, H. An authentic narrative of the treatment of the English by Tippoo Saib. 1785.

Observations on the present state of the East India Company and on the measures to be pursued for ensuring its permanency and augmenting its commerce. London. 1771.

Origin, the, and authentic narrative of the present Maratha war and also the late Rohilla war in 1773 and 1774. London. 1781.

Original papers relative to the disturbances in Bengal. 2 vols. London. 1765.

Orme, Robert. A history of the military transactions of the British nation in Indostan. 2 vols. London. 1778.

Pigot, Lord, a defence of. London. 1776.

Proposals for relieving the sufferers of the South Sea Company, for the benefit of that of East India. 1721.

Robson, F. The life of Hyder Ali. London. 1786.

Rous, G. The restoration of the King of Tanjore considered. 3 vols. 1777.

Scheme, a, for raising £3,200,000 for the service of the Government by redeeming the fund and trade now enjoyed by the East India Company... 1730.

Scrafton, Luke. Reflections on the Government of Indostan. London. 1763.

Some considerations on the nature and importance of the East India trade. London. 1728.

Some thoughts on the present state of our trade to India. By a merchant of London. 1754.

Stanhope, P. D. Genuine memoirs of Asiaticus. London. 1785.

Sulivan, R. J. An analysis of the political history of India. London. 1779.

Thompson, H. F. The intrigues of a Nabob. 1780.

Tierney, G. The real situation of the East India Company. London. 1787.

Vansittart, H. A narrative of the transactions in Bengal. 3 vols. London. 1766.

Verelst, H. A view of the rise, progress and present state of the English government in Bengal... London. 1772.

Vindication, a, of Mr Holwell's character. London. 1764.

Other contemporary pamphlets, too numerous to detail, may be found in the many bound volumes of "India Office Tracts," in the Library of the India Office, Whitehall.

(5) General Works.

Auber, Peter. Rise and Progress of the British Power in India. 2 vols. London. 1837.

Dictionary of National Biography. Articles on Clive, Warren Hastings, Francis, Barwell, Impey, and *passim.* London. 1885–1900.

Elphinstone, M. Rise of the British Power in the East. Ed. by Sir Edward Colebrooke. London. 1887.

Kaye, J. W. The Administration of the East India Company. London. 1853.

Lecky, W. E. H. History of England in the Eighteenth Century. 7 vols. London. 1892.

Lyall, Sir A. C. The Rise and Expansion of the British Dominion in India. London. 1906.

Macpherson, D. Annals of Commerce. 4 vols. London. 1805.

—— European Commerce with India. London. 1812.

Mahan, A. T. The influence of Sea-Power upon History, 1660–1783. London. 1889.

Mahon, Lord (Earl of Stanhope). The Rise of our Indian Empire. London. 1858.

Marlès, J. L. de. Histoire Générale de l'Inde, ancienne et moderne. 6 vols. Paris. 1828.

Marshman, J. C. The History of India. 3 vols. London. 1867.

Martineau, Harriet. The History of British Rule in India. London. 1857.

Mill, James. The History of British India. Ed. with notes and continuations by H. H. Wilson. 10 vols. London. 1858.

Penhoen, B. de. Histoire de la conquête et la fondation de l'empire Anglais dans l'Inde. 6 vols. Paris. 1840–1.

Thornton, E. The History of the British Empire in India. London. 1858.

Willson, Beckles. Ledger and Sword. 2 vols. London. 1903.

(6) Special Works, mainly Biographical.

(a) *Clive and his Contemporaries.*

Arbuthnot, Sir A. J. Lord Clive. London. 1889.

Biddulph, J. Stringer Lawrence. London. 1901.

Broome, A. History of the rise and progress of the Bengal army. Calcutta. 1850.

Dalton, C. Memoir of Captain Dalton, Defender of Trichinopoly. London. 1836.

Gleig, G. R. The Life of Robert, Lord Clive. 3 vols. London. 1836.

Grant, R. A Sketch of the history of the East India Company from the first formation to the passing of the Regulating Act of 1773. London. 1813.

Macaulay, Lord. Critical and Historical Essays. The Essay on Clive. London. 1869.

Malcolm, Sir John. The life of Robert, Lord Clive. 3 vols. London. 1836.

Stewart, Charles. The History of Bengal. London. 1813.

Wilson, Sir Charles. Clive. London. 1890.

(b) *Warren Hastings and his Contemporaries.*

Beveridge, Henry. The trial of Maharaja Nanda Kumar. Calcutta. 1886.

Biovès, Achille. Les Anglais dans l'Inde. Warren Hastings. Paris. 1904.

Busteed, H. E. Echoes from Old Calcutta. London. 1908.

Gleig, G. R. Memoirs of the life of…Warren Hastings. 3 vols. London. 1841.

Impey, E. B. Memoirs of Sir Elijah Impey. London. 1846.

Kirkpatrick, W. Select letters of Tippoo Sultan. London. 1811.

Lawson, Sir C. The private life of Warren Hastings. London. 1895.

Lyall, Sir A. C. Warren Hastings. London. 1902.

Macartney, Earl of. Some account of the public life and a selection from the unpublished writings of the. By J. Barrow. 2 vols. London. 1807.

Macaulay, Lord. Critical and Historical Essays. The Essay on Warren Hastings. London. 1869.

Malleson, G. B. Life of Warren Hastings. London. 1894.

Parkes, J., and Merivale, Herbert. Memoirs of Sir Philip Francis with correspondence and journals. 2 vols. London. 1867.

Stephen, Sir J. F. The story of Nuncomar and the Impeachment of Sir Elijah Impey. 2 vols. 1885.

Stewart, C. Memoirs of Hyder Ali and Tippoo Sultan. Cambridge. 1809.

Strachey, Sir John. Hastings and the Rohilla war. Oxford. 1892.

Trotter, L. J. Warren Hastings. Oxford. 1894.

B. THE FRENCH IN INDIA.

(1) Unpublished Material.

There exists a great quantity of unpublished material, which has hitherto remained comparatively unexplored, in the French Foreign Office, Colonial Office, Bibliothèque de l'arsenal, Bibliothèque Nationale and elsewhere. For a more detailed description see the Bibliographies given by Prosper Cultru in his Dupleix (Paris, 1904), and Henri Weber in his La Compagnie Française des Indes (Paris, 1904).

(2) Contemporary Works, Memoirs etc.

Ananda Ranga Pillai, Private Diary of, 1736–61. Ed. by Sir J. F. Price. Madras. 1904.

Anandarangappoulé, Extraits du Journal de. Ed. by J. Vinson. Paris. 1894.

Bussy, le Sieur de. Mémoires, Lettres, etc. Paris. 1764.

Dupleix, J. F. Mémoire...contre la compagnie des Indes avec les pièces justificatives. Paris. 1769.

—— Réponse...à la lettre du Sieur Godeheu. Paris. 1763.

Godeheu. Lettre à M. Dupleix. Mémoire à consulter. Paris. 1760.

Guyon, Abbé. Histoire des Indes Orientales. Paris. 1744.

Harris, J. A history of the French East India Company. Navigantium atque Itinerantium bibliotheca. Vol. I. 1744.

Histoire du Siège de Pondichéry sous le gouvernement de M. Dupleix. Brussels. 1766.

Labourdonnais, Mémoire pour le Sieur de, avec les pièces justificatives. Paris. 1751.

—— B.-F. Mahé de. Mémoires historiques recueillis et publiés par son petit-fils. Paris. 1827.

Lally, Count de [Baron de Tollendal]. Memoirs of. London. 1766.

Lally-Tollendal, Marquis de. Plaidoyer du Comte de Lally-Tollendal, Curateur à la mémoire du feu Comte de Lally, son père. Rouen. 1780.

Lauraguais, Count de. Mémoire sur la compagnie des Indes, dans lequel on établit les droits et les intérêts des Actionnaires en réponse aux compilations de M. l'abbé Morellet. Paris. 1770.

Morellet, Abbé. Mémoire sur la situation actuelle de la compagnie des Indes. Paris. 1769.

—— Examen de la Réponse de M. N. au mémoire de M. l'Abbé Morellet... Paris. 1769.

Necker, J. Mémoire en réponse à celui de M. l'Abbé Morellet sur la compagnie des Indes. Paris. 1769.

Suffren, P. A. de. Journal de bord dans l'Inde 1781-4. Paris. 1888.

Voltaire, F. M. A. de. Fragments sur l'Inde, sur le Général Lalli et sur le Comte de Morangiés. 1773.

(3) Later Works and General Histories.

Barbé, E. Le nabab René Madec. Histoire diplomatique des projets de la France sur le Bengale et le Pendjab. Paris. 1894.

Cultru, Prosper. Dupleix, ses plans politiques ; sa disgrace. Paris. 1901.

Fosses, Castonnet des. Dupleix, ses dernières luttes dans l'Inde. 1889.

Guet, J. Origines de l'Inde française. Jan Begum. Paris. 1892.

Hamont, Tibulle. La fin d'un Empire français aux Indes sous Louis XV. Lally-Tollendal. Paris. 1887.

Hennequin, T. F. G. Essai historique sur la vie et les campagnes du Bailli de Suffren. Paris. 1824.

Herpin, E. Mahé de la Bourdonnais et la compagnie des Indes. Saint-Brieuc. 1905.

Hill, S. C. Three Frenchmen in Bengal, or the commercial ruin of the French Settlements in 1757. London. 1903.

Lescure, M. Précis historique sur les établissements français de l'Inde. Pondicherry. 1864.

Malleson, G. B. The history of the French in India. London. 1893.

—— Final French struggles in India. London. 1884.

Martin, Henri. Histoire de France. 19 vols. Paris. 1855-60.

Roux, J. S. Le Bailli de Suffren dans l'Inde. Marseilles. 1862.

Saint-Priest, A. G. de. La perte de l'Inde sous Louis XV. Paris. 1845.

Sismondi, J. C. L. de. Histoire des Français depuis l'origine jusqu'en 1789. 31 vols. Paris. 1821-44.

Weber, Henri. La Compagnie française des Indes. Paris. 1904.

CHAPTER XVI.

ITALY AND THE PAPACY.

I. GENERAL ITALIAN HISTORY.

A. Contemporary Annals, Letters etc.

Brosses, C. de. Lettres historiques et critiques sur l'Italie. Paris. 1799.
Dupaty, C. M. G. B. M. Lettres sur l'Italie. Rome. 1789. English translation by J. Pavoleri. London. 1789.
Goethe, J. W. von. Tagebücher und Briefe Goethes aus Italien an Frau von Stein und Herder. Weimar. 1886.
Montesquieu, C. de S. Voyages de Montesquieu. Paris. 1894.
Muratori, L. A. Annali d' Italia (to 1749). Milan. 1818–21.

B. Later Works.

(1) Political History.

Botta, C. Storia d' Italia continuata da quella del Guicciardini sino al 1789. Paris. 1832.
Cantù, C. Storia di Cento Anni (1750–1850). Florence. 1851.
—— Storia degli Italiani. Turin. 1855–6.
Coppi, A. Annali d' Italia (1750–1845). Rome. 1824–61.
Cosci, A. Le Preponderanze Straniere. Milan. 1879.
Denina, C. G. M. Delle Rivoluzioni d' Italia. Milan. 1820.
Ferrari, J. Histoire des Révolutions d'Italie. Paris. 1858.
Franchetti, A. Storia d' Italia dopo il 1789. Milan. 1880.
Leo, H. Geschichte von Italien. Vol. v. (Gesch. d. europ. Staaten.) Hamburg. 1832.
Quinet, Edgar. Les Révolutions d'Italie. Paris. 1848.

(2) Social, Economic, Constitutional or History.

Bielfeld, J. F. von. Institutions politiques. Vol. iii. Leyden. 1767–72.
Custodi, P. Scrittori classici Italiani di Economia Politica. Milan. 1803–16.
Schlopis, F. Storia della Legislazione Italiana. Vol. ii. Turin. 1863.
Schwartzkopf, A. von. Beiträge zur Geschichte der national-ökonomischen Studien in Italien im 17. und 18. Jahrhundert. Strassburg. 1873. [A compendium of Custodi's work.]
Sorel, A. L'Europe et la Révolution Française. Paris. 1887.
Vita Italiana, la, nel Settecento: Conferenze tenute a Firenze nel 1895. Edd. Fratelli Trèves. Milan. 1895.

CH. XVI.

II. THE PAPACY.

A. Documents.

Acta hist. eccles. 24 vols. Weimar. 1736–58.
Acta hist. eccles. nova. 12 vols. Weimar. 1758–73.
Acta hist. eccles. nostri temporis. 12 vols. Weimar. 1774–87.
Arrêts du 6 août 1761 et du 6 août 1762. (50 pp. of Recueil Isambert.)
Bull. romani continuatio. Rome. 1835, etc.
Chauvelin, Abbé. Discours sur les constitutions des Jésuites. Paris. 1761.
La Chalotais. Compte rendu des constitutions des Jésuites. Rennes. 1762.
Roussel de la Tour, Abbé Goujet, Dom Clémencet, etc. Extraits des assertions dangéreuses et pernicieuses que les Jésuites ont enseignées. Paris. 1762.

B. Contemporary Histories, Biographies, Memoirs.

Bonamicus, P. De Claris Pontificarum Epistolarum Scriptoribus ad Clementem XIV. Rome. 1770.
Borgia, A. Benedicti XIII Vita. Rome. 1752.
Caraccioli, L. A. de. La Vie du Pape Benoît XIV, Prosper Lambertini. Paris. 1783.
—— La Vie du Pape Clément XIV. Paris. 1775.
Clemente XIV. Lettere e altre Opere. Milan. 1841.
Einem, J. A. C. von. Versuch einer vollständigen Kirchengeschichte des Achtzehnten Jahrhunderts. Leipzig. 1776–8.
Fabroni, A. De Vita et Rebus Gestis Clementis XII Commentarius. Rome. 1760.
—— Vita di Benedetto XIV. Rome. 1787.
Gallethius, P. A. Memorie per servire alla Storia della Vita del Cardinale Passionei. Rome. 1762.
Kraus, F. X. Lettere di Benedetto XIV col Diario del Conclave di 1740. 2nd edition. Freiburg i. B. 1888.
Lafiteau, P. F. Histoire de la Constitution Unigenitus. Avignon. 1766.
Orsi, G. A. Storia degli ultimi quattro Secoli della Chiesa. Rome. 1788–97.
Saint-Simon, Rouvroy, L. de, Duc de. Mémoires. Vols. xvi, xvii, xix. Paris. 1829.
Schubart, C. F. Leben des Papstes Clemens XIV. Göttingen. 1774.
Theiner, A. Clementis XIV Epistolae et Brevia Selectiora. Paris. 1852.
Zanelli, A. Il Conclave per l' Elezione di Clemente XII. Archivio della R. Società Romana di Storia Patria. Vol. xiii.

C. Later Works.

(1) Political History (general).

Brosch, M. Geschichte des Kirchenstaates. (Gesch. d. europ. Staaten.) 2 vols. Gotha. 1880–2.
Capefigue, B. H. R. L'Église pendant les quatre derniers Siècles. Paris. 1854–8.
Crouzay-Crétet, P. de. L'Église et l'État, ou les deux Puissances au xviiie Siècle (1715–89). Paris. 1894.
Funk, F. X. Lehrbuch der Kirchengeschichte. Paderborn. 1898.
Hagenbach, K. R. Kirchengeschichte des 18. und 19. Jahrhunderts. Vol. i. Leipzig. 1848–9.
Henrion, Baron M. A. R. Histoire générale de l'Église pendant les xviiie et xixe siècles. Vol. i. Paris. 1840.
Lanfrey, P. Histoire politique des Papes. Paris. 1860.
Mamiani, T. Del Papato nei tre ultimi Secoli. Milan. 1885.

Picot, M.   Mémoires pour servir à l'histoire ecclésiastique pendant le xviiie siècle.   Paris.   1853.

Ranke, L. von.   Gesch. d. Röm. Päpste.   Vol. xxxviii of Sämmtl. Werke. Leipzig.   1879, etc.   History of the Popes.   Engl. Tr.   London.   1847.

Rattinger, D.   Der Papst und die Kirchenstadt.   Freiburg i. B.   1866.

(2) Biographies, Monographs etc.

Arneth, Ritter A. von.   Geschichte Maria Theresias.   Vienna.   1863–77.

Clement XI.   Archivio della R. Società Romana di Storia Patria.   Vols. xxi, xxii, xxiii.

Coppi, A.   Discorso sulle Finanze dello Stato Pontificio dal Secolo 16° al Principio del 19°.   Rome.   1855.

Förster, J.   Eine Papstwahl vor hundert Jahren.   Eine Erinnerung aus dem Jahre 1769.   Berlin.   1869.

Götting, C. F.   Ein verrückter Papst?   Ganganelli.   Berlin.   1886.

Masson, F.   Le Cardinal de Bernis depuis son Ministère.   Paris.   1884.

Ravignan, P. de.   Clément XIII et Clément XIV.   Paris.   1854.

Reumont, A. von.   Ganganelli, Papst Clemens XIV, seine Briefe und seine Zeit. Berlin.   1847.

Sforza, G.   Episodi della Storia di Roma nel Secolo xviii.   Archivio Storico Italiano.   Series iv, Vols. xix, xx.

Silvagni, D.   La Corte e la Società Romana nei Secoli xviii e xix.   Vol. i. Florence.   1882.

Theiner, A.   Histoire du Pontificat de Clément XIV.   Paris.   1852.

Ugolini, F.   Review of Theiner's History of Clement XIV.   Archivio Storico Italiano.   Series ii, Vol. iv.

Uschner, C.   Clemens XIV.   Ein Lebens- und Karakterbild.   Berlin.   1866.

D. The Suppression of the Jesuits.

Bertolini, F.   Clemente XIV e la Soppressione dei Gesuiti.   Nuova Antologia. Nov. 1886.

Chevalier, M.   Pombal.   Revue des Deux Mondes.   Paris.   Sept. 1870.

Crétineau-Joly, J.   Clément XIV et les Jésuites.   Paris.   1847.

Dubois, l'Abbé J. A.   Letters on the State of Christianity in India (for the Jesuit Missions).   London.   1823.

Du Hamel du Breuil.   Un Ministre Philosophe: Pombal.   Revue Historique. Paris.   Sept. 1895.   Jan. 1896.

Duhr, Father, S. J.   Pombal, sein Charakter und seine Politik.   (Stimmen aus Maria-Laach.)   Freiburg i. B.   1891.

Gomes, F. L.   Le Marquis de Pombal.   Paris.   1869.

Guignard, A, Comte de Saint-Priest.   Histoire de la Chute des Jésuites au xviiie Siècle.   Paris.   1844.

Murr, G. von.   Geschichte der Jesuiten in Portugal unter Pombal.   Nürnberg. 1787.

Olfers, J. M. von.   L'Attentat du 3 Sept., 1758.   Recherches historiques.   Berlin. 1839.

Rousseau, F.   Charles III de Bourbon.   Paris.   1907.

Sforza, G.   Il Conclave di Papa Ganganelli e la Soppressione dei Gesuiti.   Archivio Storico Italiano.   Series v, Vol. xx.

Theiner, A.   Processo a carico del P. F. Pisani e dei suoi Confratelli della Compagnia di Gesù, compilato per Ordine di S.S. Clemente XIV, da servire di Continuazione alla Storia del suo Pontificato....   Florence.   1854.

III. NAPLES AND SICILY.

A. DOCUMENTS.

Many unpublished documents are still to be found at Naples, especially in the Biblioteca Nazionale and in the Library of the Società Napolitana di Storia Patria, in the Archivio di Stato di Napoli, the Municipio di Napoli and the Casa de' Duchi di Maddaloni.

B. CONTEMPORARY HISTORIES, TRAVELS, LETTERS.

Bazzoni, A. Carteggio dell' Abate F. Galiani col Marchese Tanucci. Series III, Vols. IX, etc. : and Series IV, Vols. I–IV.

Becatini, F. Storia del Regno di Carlo III di Borbone. Venice. 1790.

Bonamicus, P. J. De Rebus ad Velitras gestis Commentarius. Leyden. 1749. Italian translation by D. N. Zehender. Naples. 1802.

Carignani, G. Carteggio diplomatico tra il Marchese B. Tanucci e il Principe Albertini. Archivio Storico per le Provincie Napolitane. Vols. III, IV.

Duclos, C. Voyage en Italie (1769). Paris. 1791.

Galiani, C. Diario della guerra di Velletri. Archivio Storico per le Provincie Napolitane. Vol. XXX.

Lande, M. de la. Voyage en Italie (1765). Geneva. 1790.

Marzo, G. di. Diario della Città di Palermo dal Secolo XVI al XIX. Vol. IX. Palermo. 1871.

Nicolini, F. Lettere inedite di B. Tanucci al F. Galiani. Archivio Storico per le Provincie Napolitane. Vols. XVIII, XXX and XXXI.

Onofri, P. Elogio estemporaneo per la gloriosa Memoria di Carlo III. Naples. 1803.

Orloff, Count Grégoire. Mémoires historiques, politiques et littéraires sur le Royaume de Naples. Paris. 1819–21.

Patrizi, S. Vita di Niccolo Fragianni. Translated by F. Palermo. Archivio Storico Italiano. Series II, Vol. I.

Pecchia, C. Storia civile e politica del Regno di Napoli. Naples. 1783. [A continuation of Giannone's history.]

Reinach, J. Recueil des Instructions données aux Ambassadeurs de France : Naples and Parma. Paris. 1893.

Swinburne, H. Travels in the Two Sicilies. London. 1873.

C. LATER WORKS.

(1) GENERAL POLITICAL HISTORY.

Blasi, G. E. di. Storia civile del Regno di Sicilia. Palermo. 1811–21.

Calà Ulloa, P. Di Bernardo Tanucci e dei suoi Tempi. Naples. 1875.

—— Intorno alla Storia del Reame di Napoli di Pietro Colletta, annotamenti.... Naples. 1877.

See also Review of the above in Archivio Storico per le Provincie Napolitane. Vol. III.

Carignani, G. Il Partito Austriaco nel Regno di Napoli al 1744. Archivio Storico per le Provincie Napolitane. Vol. VI.

—— Il Tempo di Carlo III, Re del Regno delle due Sicilie. Naples. 1865.

Collado, M. Danvila y. Reinado de Carlos III. Madrid. 1892.

Colletta, P. Storia del Reame di Napoli del 1734 al 1825. New edition, with notes, etc., by C. Manfroni. Milan. 1905.

Dumas, A. I Borboni di Napoli. Naples. 1864–7.

Gregorio, Rosario di. Considerazioni sulla Storia della Sicilia dai Normanni a noi. Palermo. 1805–10.

La Lumia, I. Storie Siciliane. Vol. IV. Palermo. 1881, etc.

Lanza, P. Considerazioni sulla Storia di Sicilia dal 1532 al 1789, quale Commento al Botta. Palermo. 1836.

Pozzo, L. del. Cronica civile e militare delle due Sicilie sotto la Dinastia Borbonica dal 1734 in poi. Naples. 1857.

Schipa, M. Il Regno di Napoli al Tempo di Carlo di Borbone. Naples. 1904.

(2) CONSTITUTIONAL, LEGAL, ECCLESIASTICAL ETC. AND MONOGRAPHS.

Ayala, M. de. Memorie Storico-militari dal 1734 al 1815. Naples. 1835.

Bianchini, L. Storia delle Finanze del Regno di Napoli. Palermo. 1839.

—— Della Storia economico-civile della Sicilia. Palermo. 1841.

Cagnazzi, L. di S. Saggio sulla Popolazione del Regno di Puglia. Naples. 1820–39.

Cesarini, Sforza. Le Guerre di Velletri. Rome. 1891.

Fornari, T. Delle Teorie economiche delle Provincie Napolitane dal 1735 al 1830. Milan. 1888.

Guerrieri, G. La Terra d' Otranto nel 1734. Trani. 1901.

Lomonasco, G. Del Foro Napolitano. Naples. 1884.

Maresca, B. La Marina Napolitana nel Secolo XVIII. Naples. 1902.

Palmieri, N. Saggio storico e politico sulla Costituzione del Regno di Sicilia fino al 1816. Lausanne. 1847.

Pascal, C. Vita ed Opere dell' Abate Galiani. Naples. 1885.

Pasquali, G. Le due Battaglie di Velletri. Velletri. 1891.

Racioppi, G. Antonio Genovesi. Naples. 1871.

Reinach, J. La Campagna del anno 1742. Rivista Militare Italiana. 1879.

Sariis, A. de. Codice delle Leggi del Regno di Napoli. Naples. 1792–7.

Scaduto, F. Stato e Chiesa nelle due Sicilie. Palermo. 1887.

Schipa, M. Il Muratori e la Cultura Napolitana del suo Tempo. Naples. 1902.

IV. TUSCANY.

A. DOCUMENTS.

There are still a certain number of unpublished documents in the Biblioteca Nazionale; but very many are printed in the works mentioned below, especially in the Atti dell' Assemblea degli Archivescovi e Vescovi, etc., in the Memorie di Scipione de' Ricci and in Cantini's Legislazione Toscana. Other valuable collections are Statuta Populi et Communis Florentiae. Freiburg i. B. 1815; and Bandi e Ordini da osservarsi nel Granducato di Toscana...pubblicati dal di XII Luglio 1737... raccolti...coll' ordine successivo dei tempi.... Florence. 1747–1848.

Atti dell' Assemblea degli Archivescovi e Vescovi della Toscana tenuta in Firenze nell' Anno 1787. Florence. 1787–8.

Atti e Decreti del Concilio Diocesano di Pistoja dell' Anno MDCCLXXXVI. Pistoia. 1788. Republished by C. M. F. in Il Vescovo Scipione de' Ricci e le Riforme Religiosi in Toscana sotto il Regno di Leopoldo I. Florence. 1865, which also contains De Potter's Life of Ricci (see C (2) below).

Cantini, L. Legislazione Toscana raccolta e illustrata. Florence. 1800–8.

Gianni, F. M. La Costituzione Toscana immaginata dal Gran Duca Pietro Leopoldo. Italy. 1847. [Written in 1805 by Leopold's Minister Gianni.]

Governo della Toscana sotto il Regno di S. M. il Re Leopoldo II.   Florence.   1790.
[Published by Cambiagi, the Grand Duke's printer, by Leopold's orders.]

B. Contemporary Memoirs, Biographies etc.

Arneth, Ritter A. von.   Marie Antoinette, Joseph II und Leopold II.   Ihr Briefwechsel.   Leipzig.   1866.
—— Joseph II und Leopold von Toscana.   Ihr Briefwechsel (1781–90).   Vienna.
1872.
Bourgoing, Baron J. F. de.   Mémoires historiques et philosophiques sur Pius VI et
son Pontificat.   Paris.   1799.
Huber, A.   Die Politik Kaiser Josephs II, beurtheilt von seinem Bruder Leopold
von Toscana.   Innsbruck.   1877.
Rastrelli, M.   Memorie di M. R. per servire alla Vita di Leopoldo II.   "Italy."
1792.   [Contains Leopold's Diary.]
Remigio Pupares (L. Beccatini).   Vita pubblica e privata di Pietro Leopoldo d' Austria.
Siena.   1797.
Ricci, S. de'.   Memorie di Scipione de' Ricci, Vescovo di Prato e Pistoja, scritti da
lui medesimo e pubblicati con documenti da A. Gelli.   Florence.   1865.
Tanzini, R.   Istoria dell' Assemblea degli Archivescovi e Vescovi della Toscana
tenuta in Firenze l' Anno MDCCLXXXVII.   Florence.   1788.
Wolf, A.   Marie Cristine und Leopold II.   Ihr Briefwechsel (1781–92).   Vienna.
1867.

C. Later Works.

(1) Political Histories.

Baldasseroni, G.   Leopoldo II Granduca di Toscana e i suoi Tempi.   Florence.   1871.
Délécluse, E. J.   Florence et ses Vicissitudes.   Paris.   1837.
Hirsch, F.   Leopold II als Grossherzog von Toskana.   Munich.   1878.
Reumont, A. von.   Geschichte Toskanas.   (Gesch. d. europ. Staaten.)   Vol. II.
Gotha.   1876.
Zobi, A.   Storia civile della Toscana dal 1737 al 1848.   Florence.   1850.
　　X....   Review of the above.   Archivio Storico Italiano.   Series II, Vol. I.

(2) Ecclesiastical History.

Apologia delle Leggi di Giurisdizione, Amministrazione e Polizia Ecclesiastica,
pubblicate in Toscana sotto il Regno di Leopoldo I.   Florence.   1858.
Potter, L. J. A. de.   Vie de Scipion de' Ricci.   Paris.   1826.   (See Section A
above.)
Scaduto, F.   Stato e Chiesa sotto Leopoldo I.   Florence.   1885.
Venturi, G. A.   Il Vescovo de' Ricci e la Corte Romana fino al Sinodo di Pistoja.
Florence.   1885.
—— Review of Scaduto's "Stato e Chiesa sotto Leopoldo I."   Archivio Storico
Italiano.   Series IV, Vol. XVI.
—— Le Controversie del Granduca Leopoldo I di Toscana e del Vescovo Scipione
de' Ricci con la Corte Romana.   Archivio Storico Italiano.   Series V, Vol. VIII.

(3) Constitutional etc. Memoirs.

Capponi, G.   Scritti editi e inediti.   [Pp. 347, etc.]   Florence.   1877.
Doran, J.   Mann and Manners at the Court of Florence (1740–86).   Founded on
the Letters of Horace Mann to Horace Walpole.   London.   1876.
Guasti, C.   Giuseppe Silvestri, etc.   Vol. I.   Prato.   1874.

Malaspina, A. G., last Marquis of Mulazzo. Il Granduca di Toscana Pietro Leopoldo a Pontremoli nel 1786. Edited by C. Cumati. Pontremoli. 1894.

Reumont, A. von. Giuseppe II, Pietro Leopoldo e la Toscana. Archivio Storico Italiano. Series III, Vol. XXIV.

—— Saggi di Storia e Letteratura. Florence. 1880.

Rigobon, P. La Contabilità di Stato nella Repubblica di Firenze e nel Granducato di Toscana. Girgenti. 1892.

Rocchi, G. Pompeo Neri. Archivio Storico Italiano. Ser. III, Vol. XXIV.

Tabarrini, M. Studii di Critica Storica. Florence. 1876.

Zimmermann, J. Das Verfassungsprojekt des Grossherzogs Peter Leopold von Toskana. Heidelberg. 1901.

Zobi, A. Memorie economico-politiche, o sia dei Danni arrecati dall' Austria alla Toscana dal 1737 al 1859. Florence. 1860.

Zuccagni-Orlandini, A. Ricerche statistiche del Granducato di Toscana. Florence. 1848-53.

V. VENICE.

A. Contemporary Histories and Memoirs.

Bazzoni, A. Le Annotazioni degli Inquisitori di Stato di Venezia. Archivio Storico Italiano. Ser. III, Vols. XI and XII.

Diedo, G. Storia della Repubblica di Venezia dalla fondazione sin' al anno 1747. Venice. 1751.

Goldoni, C. Mémoires pour servir à l'Histoire de sa Vie et à celle de son Théâtre. Paris. 1822.

Laugier, Abbé M. A. Histoire de la République de Venise. Paris. 1768.

Marin, C. A. Storia civile e politica del Commercio de' Veneziani. Venice. 1798.

Sagredo, A. Leggi Ecclesiastiche dei Veneziani spettanti alla pubblica Economia. Archivio Storico Italiano. Series III, Vol. VI.

B. Later Works.

(1) Political Histories.

Bonnal, E. Chute d'une République; Venise. Paris. 1885.

Dandolo, G. La Caduta della Repubblica di Venezia e i suoi ultimi anni. Venice. 1855-9.

Daru, P. A. N. B. Histoire de la République de Venise. Paris. 1819.

Mutinelli, F. Memorie storiche degli ultimi cinquant' anni della Repubblica Veneta. Venice. 1854.

Romanin, S. Storia documentata di Venezia. Venice. 1853-61.

X.... Review of the histories of Venice by Mutinelli and Dandolo. Archivio Storico Italiano. Series II, Vol. III.

(2) Monographs.

Cecchetti, B. Una delle Cause della Caduta della Repubblica Veneta. Venice. 1887.

Molmenti, P. G. La Storia di Venezia nella vita privata. Turin. 1880.

—— La Dogaressa di Venezia. Turin. 1884.

—— Venezia. Nuovi Studi di Storia e d' Arte. Florence. 1897.

Morpurgo, E. Marco Foscarini e Venezia nel Secolo XVIII. Florence. 1880.

VI. GENOA.

A. Contemporary Histories and Monographs.

Brequigny, L. G. Oudard-Feudrix de. Histoire des Révolutions de Gênes depuis son Établissement jusqu'à la Conclusion de la Paix de 1748. Paris. 1750.

Della Storia di Genova dal Trattato di Worms fino alla Pace di Aquisgrana. Leyden. 1750.

Lettera scritta ad un Amico in Roma circa lo Scacciamento de' Tedeschi dalla Città di Genova (1746). Edited by C. M. Archivio Storico Italiano. Series I, Appendix, Vol. v.

Mecatti, G. M. Guerra di Genova. Naples. 1749.

B. Later Works.

Histories.

Canale, M. G. Storia civile, commerciale e letteraria dei Genovesi dalle Origine all' Anno 1797. Genoa. 1845.

Varese, C. Storia della Repubblica di Genova dalla sua Origine sino al 1814. Genoa. 1838.

Vincens, E. Histoire de la République de Gènes. Paris. 1842.

C. Corsica.

(1) Contemporary Works.

Cambiagi, Abate G. Istoria del Regno di Corsica. Livorno. 1770.

Paoli, General.—Lettere di Pasquale de' Paoli. Edited by N. Tommaseo. Archivio Storico Italiano. Series I, Vol. xi.

—— Lettere inedite di Pasquale de' Paoli. Edited by G. Livi. Archivio Storico Italiano. Series v, Vols. v and vi.

(2) Later Works.

Buttafuoco, A. S. L. F. de. Fragments pour servir à l'Histoire de Corse de 1764 à 1769. Bastia. 1859.

Gregorovius, F. Wanderings in Corsica, its History and its Heroes. Translated by A. Muir. Edinburgh. 1855.

Varnhagen von Ense, K. A. Il Re Teodoro di Corsica. (Biographische Denkmale.) Berlin. 1824–30.

Viale, S. Delle Mutazioni dei Regimenti Politici in Corsica. Archivio Storico Italiano. Series II, Vol. xiv, Pt. 1.

CHAPTER XVII.

SWITZERLAND FROM THE TREATY OF AARAU TO THE REVOLUTION.

I. GENERAL.

Eidgenössische Abschiede, especially Vols. VI, 2 ; VII, 1 and 2 ; VIII.

Escher, H. Article Eidgenossenschaft in Ersch and Gruber's Encyklopädie. Sec. I, Part XXXII. Leipzig. 1839.

—— Geschichte der Schweiz. Eidgenossenschaft. Vol. III. Zurich. 1857.

Meyer von Knonau, L. Handbuch der Geschichte der Schweiz. Eidgenossenschaft. Zurich. 1826–9. 2nd edn. 1843.

Müller, Johannes von. Geschichte Schweizerischer Eidgenossenschaft. Vols. X, XI and XII. Edited by L. Vulliemin and C. Monnard. Zurich. 1845–8.

II. THE ALLIANCE WITH FRANCE.

Akten (Manualien) der Geheimen Räte der Städte und anderer Orte. Correspondance des ambassadeurs de France. Cantonal Archives of State.

Balthasar, F. U. Anmerkungen über den Bund von 1715. (Manuscript.)

Bonnac, J. L. Mémoire sur le renouvellement de l'alliance. 1733. Archives des Affaires Étrangères. Paris.

Du Luc, F. C. Denkschrift über die Schweiz, 1715. German Transl. in Schweiz. Museum. Aarau. 1816. (Part IV, pp. 610 sqq.)

Instructions laissées par Bonnac à Mariane. 1736. Archives, etc.

Inventaire sommaire des Archives du Département des Affaires Étrangères. Paris. 1892. [For the despatches and correspondences of the French ambassadors in Switzerland.]

Mémoire pour servir d'instruction au sieur Chevalier de Beauteville. 1763. Archives, etc.

Mémoire pour servir d'instruction au sieur de Courteille. 1738. Archives, etc.

Meyer von Knonau, G. Die Beschwörung des französischen Bündnisses zu Solothurn, 1777. Neujahrsblatt der Stadtbibliothek Zürich. Zurich. 1870.

Rott, E. Inventaire sommaire des documents relatifs à l'histoire de Suisse, conservés dans les archives et bibliothèques de Paris. Parts I–V. Publié par ordre du conseil fédéral suisse. Bern. 1882–94.

Vogel, F. A. Privilèges des Suisses. Paris. 1731.

Zellweger, J. K. Geschichte der diplomatischen Verhältnisse der Schweiz mit Frankreich von 1698–1784. St Gallen and Bern. 1848–9.

III. FOREIGN SERVICE AND NEUTRALITY.

Balthasar, F. U. Transgressionen der Franzosen, etc. (Manuscript.)

Chavigny, T. C. Mémoire sur...les troupes suisses, etc. Solothurn. 1755.

Fieffée, E. Histoire des troupes étrangères au service de France. 2 parts. Paris. 1854. German translation. Munich. 1856–60.

Girard, F. Histoire abrégée des officiers suisses qui se sont distingués aux services étrangers. Fribourg. 1781.

Maag, A. Geschichte der Schweizertruppen im Kriege Napoleons, etc. Biel. 1892, etc.

May, de Romainmotier. Histoire militaire de la Suisse, etc. Lausanne. 1788.

Morell, C. Die Schweizerregimenter in Frankreich 1789–92. St Gallen. 1858.

Mülinen, W. F. von. Geschichte der Schweizersöldner, etc. Bern. 1887.

Rodt, V. Geschichte des berner Kriegswesens. Bern. 1831–4.

Rudolf, J. M. Geschichte der Feldzüge und des Kriegsdienstes der Schweizer im Ausland. Baden. 1847.

Schwarz, F. Die Schweizerregimenter im französischen Diensten, etc. Basel. 1882.

Schweizer, P. Geschichte der schweiz. Neutralität. Frauenfeld. 1893–5.

Soldats Suisses au service étranger. Collective work by Rilliet, Cramer, Mayer and others. Geneva. 1907, etc.

Zurlauben, F. von. Histoire militaire des Suisses au service de la France. Paris. 1751.

IV. CLASS CONFLICTS AND THE *AUFKLÄRUNG*.

Schollenberger, J. Geschichte der schweiz. Politik. Frauenfeld. 1906. (Vol. i, pp. 434–5.)

CHAPTER XVIII.

JOSEPH II.

I. MANUSCRIPTS.

The most important unpublished material for the history of the reign of Joseph II is to be found in the following Archives, under the heads specified in each case:

Vienna: Kaiserlich Königliches Archiv: (1) Diplomatische Correspondenz (Diplomatic Correspondence); (2) Vorträge der Staats- und Reichskanzlei an den Kaiser (Oral Reports to the Emperor of the State and Imperial Chanceries); (3) Weisungen (Instructions); (4) Berichte (Reports); (5) Staatsrat (Council of State); (6) Kriegsacten; (7) Friedensacten (War and Peace documents); (8) Hungarica; (9) Belgica.

Paris: Archives du Ministère des affaires étrangères à Paris: Correspondance (1) de Vienne; (2) de Bruxelles; (3) de Hollande.

Brussels: Archives générales du Royaume: (1) Chancellerie autrichienne des Pas-Bas; (2) Conseil privé; (3) Conseil des Finances; (4) Secrétairerie d'État et de Guerre; (5) Conseil de Brabant; (6) Correspondance des Gouverneurs généraux avec la Cour de Vienne; (7) Conseil du Gouvernement général; (8) Archives des États Belgiques Unis.

The Hague: Archives du Royaume: (1) Archives of the States General of the United Provinces; (2) Registers van de Acten; (3) Commissie Boeken (Committee Books); (4) Registers van Instructien; (5) Liassen (Files): Ordinary Letters, Brussels; Ordinary Letters, Vienna; Secret Letters, Brussels; Secret Letters, Vienna; (6) Registers der uitgaende missiven van de Hooghmogende Heeren Staten Generael der Vereenigde Nederlanden (Despatches from the States General); (7) Registers of ordinary Resolutions; Registers of secret Resolutions; (8) Vredehandelingen (Peace Negotiations): Utrecht, 1713; Barrier, 1713 and 1718; Fontainebleau, 1785.

II. CONTEMPORARY AUTHORITIES.

Arneth, Ritter A. von. Maria Theresia und Josei II. Ihre Correspondenz. 3 vols. Vienna. 1867.
—— Marie Antoinette, Josef II und Leopold II. Ihr Briefwechsel. Vienna. 1866.
—— Joseph II und Leopold von Toscana. Ihr Briefwechsel von 1781–90. 2 vols. Vienna. 1872.
—— Joseph II und Katharina von Russland. Ihr Briefwechsel. Vienna. 1869.

Arneth, Ritter A. von, and Flammermont, J. Correspondance secrète du comte de Mercy Argenteau avec l'Empereur Joseph II et le prince de Kaunitz. 2 vols. Paris. 1890–1.

Bacourt, A. de. Correspondance entre le comte de Mirabeau et le comte de La Marck. Brussels. 1871.

Beer, A. Josef II, Leopold II und Kaunitz. Ihr Briefwechsel. Vienna. 1873.

Brünner, S. Correspondances intimes de l'Empereur Joseph II avec son ami le comte de Cobenzl et son premier ministre le prince de Kaunitz. Mayence. 1871.

Calvi, F. Lettere dell' Imperatore dei Romani eletto Giuseppe di Absburgo-Loreno, al S. A. di Belgiojoso-Este. Milan. 1878.

Feller, F. X. de. Recueil des représentations, protestations et réclamations de tous les ordres de citoyens dans les Pays-Bas catholiques au sujet des infractions faites à la constitution, aux privilèges, coutumes et usages de la nation et des provinces respectives. 17 vols. Brussels. 1787–90.

Gachard, L. Inventaire des archives des Chambres des comptes, précédé d'une notice historique sur ces anciennes institutions. 3 vols. Brussels. 1837.

—— Documents politiques et diplomatiques sur la Révolution belge de 1790. Brussels. 1834.

—— Lettre de Joseph II sur les troubles des Pays-Bas. Bulletin de la Commission royale d'histoire, 3e série, xiv. Brussels.

—— Lettres de l'archiduchesse Marie-Christine et du duc Albert de Saxe-Teschen à Joseph II, sur leur arrivée aux Pays-Bas. Analectes historiques, i–iv. Brussels.

—— Lettres écrites par les souverains des Pays-Bas aux États de ces provinces depuis Philippe II jusqu'à François II. Bulletin de la Commission royale d'histoire, 2e série, ii. Brussels.

—— Rapport adressé au chancelier de cour et d'État, prince de Kaunitz, par le baron de Martini sur les événements qui empêchèrent la mise en activité des nouveaux tribunaux aux Pays-Bas en 1782. Bulletin de la Commission royale d'histoire, 2e série, viii. Brussels.

Gachard, Piot-Delecourt. Recueil des anciennes lois et ordonnances de la Belgique, Pays-Bas autrichiens. 11 vols. Brussels. 1860, 1906.

Galesloot, L. Chronique des événements les plus remarquables arrivés à Bruxelles de 1780 à 1827. 2 vols. Collection de Mémoires relatifs à l'histoire de Belgique. Brussels. 1870.

Gérard, P. Ferdinand Rapedius de Berg. Mémoires et documents pour servir à l'histoire de la Révolution brabançonne. 2 vols. Brussels. 1842–3.

Historisch-politische Nachrichten von den Oesterreichischen Niederlanden, auf Befehl seiner Majestät des Kaisers herausgegeben. Gera. 1789.

Jaubert, A. Mémoires pour servir à la justification de feu S.E. le Général d'Alton et à l'histoire secrète de la Révolution brabançonne. Brussels. 1790.

Liste chronologique des édits et ordonnances des Pays-Bas autrichiens de 1715 à 1794. 3 vols. Brussels. 1858.

Murray, Comte de. Essai sur l'administration de S.E. le comte de Murray, commandant général dans les Pays-Bas autrichiens en 1787. Brussels. 1791.

—— Mémoire pour servir de réponse aux faux allégués qui se trouvent énoncés à son égard dans un imprimé qui a pour titre: Notes que M. le comte de Trauttmansdorff a remises au cabinet de Vienne pour sa justification. Brussels. 1791.

Noot, H. van der. Mémoire sur les droits du peuple brabançon et les atteintes y portées au nom de Sa Majesté l'Empereur et Roi, depuis quelques années, présenté à l'Assemblée générale des États de ladite province, le 23 avril 1787. Brussels. 1787.

Relation et protocole de Messieurs les Députés des États de la province de Flandre à Vienne. Messager des Sciences historiques de Belgique. Brussels. 1843.

Rendorp, A. Mémoires. 2 vols. Amsterdam. 1792.

Schlitter, H. Briefe und Denkschriften zur Vorgeschichte der Belgischen Revolu-tion. Vienna. 1900.

—— Kaunitz, Philipp Cobenzl und Spielmann. Ihr Briefwechsel. Vienna. 1899.

—— Geheime Correspondenz Josephs II mit seinem Minister in den Oesterreich-ischen Niederlanden Ferdinand Grafen Trauttmansdorff. 1787–9. Vienna. 1902.

Sorel, A. Recueil des instructions aux ambassadeurs et ministres de France depuis les traités de Westphalie jusqu'à la Révolution française. Autriche. Paris. 1884.

Spiegel, L. P. J. van de. Résumé des négociations qui accompagnèrent la révolution des Pays-Bas autrichiens. Amsterdam. 1841.

Trauttmansdorff, Prince F. von. Fragmens pour servir à l'histoire des événements qui se sont passés aux Pays-Bas depuis la fin de 1787 jusqu'à 1789. Amsterdam. 1792.

Vonck. Abrégé historique sur l'état du Brabant. Lille. 1791.

Wolf, A. Leopold II und Marie Christine. Ihr Briefwechsel (1781–92). Vienna. 1867.

III. SECONDARY WORKS.

A. GENERAL.

Beer, A. Die orientalische Politik Oesterreichs seit 1774. Prag. 1883.

Beidtel, J. Geschichte der Oesterreichischen Staatsverwaltung, 1740–8. Hrsgbn. von A. Huber. 2 vols. Innsbruck. 1896–7.

Borchgrave, Baron E. de. Histoire des rapports de droit public qui existèrent entre les provinces belges et l'empire d'Allemagne depuis le démembrement de la monarchie carolingienne jusqu'à l'incorporation de la Belgique à la République française. Mémoires couronnés de l'Académie royale de Belgique. Coll. in 4to. Vol. xxxvi. Brussels.

Borgnet, A. Histoire des Belges à la fin du dix-huitième siècle. 2 vols. Brussels. 1861–2.

Daudet, E. Histoire de l'émigration. 3 vols. Paris. 1889–96.

Forster, G. Ansichten vom Niederrhein. Leipzig. 1868.

Gachard, L. J. Histoire de la Belgique au commencement du xviiie siècle. Brussels. 1879.

Gerlache, Baron de. Histoire du royaume des Pays-Bas. 3 vols. Brussels. 1842.

Hubert, E. Étude sur la condition des protestants en Belgique depuis Charles-quint jusqu'à Joseph II. Brussels. 1882.

Janssens, J. H. Histoire des Pays-Bas depuis les temps anciens jusqu'à la création du royaume des Pays-Bas en 1815. 3 vols. Brussels. 1840.

Lüschin von Ebengreuth, A. Oesterreichische Reichsgeschichte. Geschichte der Staatsbildung, der Rechtsquellen, und des Rechts. Bamberg. 1896.

Marczali, H. Hungary in the time of Joseph II. 3 vols. Budapest. 1885–8. English Transl. by A. B. Yolland. (*Preparing for publication.*)

Neny, Comte de. Mémoires historiques et politiques sur les Pays-Bas autrichiens et sur la constitution tant interne qu'externe des provinces qui la composent. 2 vols. Brussels. 1784.

Poullet, E. Les constitutions nationales belges de l'ancien régime à l'époque de l'invasion française de 1794. Mémoires couronnés de l'académie royale de Belgique. Coll. in 8vo. Vol. xxvi. Brussels.

Praet, J. van. Les Pays-Bas autrichiens. Leur révolution au point de vue rétrospectif et européen. Vol. iii of Essais sur l'histoire des trois derniers siècles. Brussels. 1884.

Ranke, L. von. Die deutschen Mächte und der Fürstenbund. Deutsche Geschichte von 1780–90. 2 vols. Leipzig. 1871–2. Sämmtliche Werke. Vols. xxxi–ii.

Rückelingen, L. Mothot van. Geschiedenis der Oostenrijksche Nederlanden. 5 vols. Antwerp. 1876–80.

Schlitter, H. Die Regierung Josefs II in den Oesterreichischen Niederlanden. Vol. i. Vienna. 1900. [Vol. ii not yet published.]

Seidler, G. Studien zur Geschichte und Dogmatik des Oesterreichischen Staatsrechtes. Vienna. 1894.

Shaw, J. Sketches of the History of the Austrian Netherlands. London. 1786.

Sorel, A. La question d'Orient au xviiie siècle. Paris. 1880.

Wolf, A. Oesterreich unter Maria Theresia, Josef II und Leopold II. Berlin. 1882.

B. Monographs, Biographies etc.

Arendt, W. A. Ueber Verfassung und Geschichte der Städte in Belgien seit dem Aufgange des xvii Jahrhunderts bis zur Einverleibung des Landes in die französische Republik. Raumer's Hist. Taschenbuch. Vol. vi. Leipzig. 1845.

—— Die brabantische Revolution. 1789–90. Raumer's Hist. Taschenbuch. Vol. iv. Leipzig. 1843.

Arneth, Ritter A. von. Biographie des Fürsten Kaunitz. Ein Fragment. Vienna. 1899.

Borgnet, A. Lettres sur la Révolution brabançonne. Brussels. 1834.

Bright, T. F. Joseph II. London. 1897.

Brunner, S. Die theologische Dienerschaft am Hofe Josefs II. Vienna. 1868.

—— Die Mysterien der Aufklärung in Oesterreich. 1700–1800. Mainz. 1869.

Cornova, J. Leben Josefs II Römischer Kaisers. Prague. 1902.

Delplace, L. Joseph II et la Révolution brabançonne. Bruges. 1891.

Derival. Le voyageur dans les Pays-Bas autrichiens. Lettres sur l'état actuel de ce pays. 6 vols. Amsterdam. 1782–3.

Dohm, C. W. von. Denkwürdigkeiten meiner Zeit oder Beiträge zur Geschichte vom letzten Viertel des xviii und vom Anfange des xix Jahrhunderts. 1778–1806. Hanover. 1815.

Fournier, A. Josef der Zweite. Leipzig. 1885.

Francotte, H. Essai historique sur la propagande des Encyclopédistes français dans la principauté de Liège. Mémoires couronnés de l'Académie royale de Belgique. Coll. in 8vo. Vol. xxx. 1879.

Friedberg, E. Die Grenzen zwischen Staat und Kirche und die Garantien gegen deren Verletzung. Tübingen. 1872.

Gaillard, A. Histoire du Conseil de Brabant. 3 vols. Brussels. 1898–1903.

Galesloot, L. La commune de Louvain, ses troubles et ses émeutes au xviie et au xviiie siècle. Louvain. 1871.

Geier, F. Die Durchführung der kirchlichen Reformen Josephs II im vorderösterreichischen Breisgau. (Kirchenrechtl. Abhandlungen, hrsgbn. von U. Steetz, xvi and xvii.) Stuttgart. 1905.

Geisler, A. F. Skizzen aus den Karakter und Handlungen Josefs II izt regierenden Kaisers der Deutschen. 1783–91. Halle. 1825.

Gigl, A. Kaiser Josef II und Herr Ottokar Lorenz. Vienna. 1863.

Gräffer. Josefinische Curiosa. Vienna. 1848.

Gross-Hoffinger, A. J. Lebens- und Regierungsgeschichte Josefs des Zweiten, und Gemälde seiner Zeit. Stuttgart. 1842.

—— Geschichte Josefs des Zweiten. Leipzig. 1847.

Huber, F. X. Geschichte Josefs II. 2 vols. Vienna. 1792.

Hubert, E. Le voyage de l'empereur Joseph II dans les Pays-Bas autrichiens. Mémoires de l'Acad. royale de Belgique. Coll. in 4to. Vol. lviii. Brussels. 1900.

Hubert, E. Les finances des Pays-Bas à l'avènement de Joseph II. Bulletin de la Commission royale d'histoire, 5ᵉ série, IX. Brussels. 1899.

—— Les garnisons de la Barrière dans les Pays-Bas autrichiens. Mémoires de l'Académie royale de Belgique. Coll. in 4to. Vol. LXII. Brussels. 1902.

Jäger, A. Kaiser Josef II und Leopold II. Reform und Gegenreform. Vienna. 1869.

Juste, T. Histoire du règne de l'empereur Joseph II et de la révolution belge de 1790. 2 vols. Brussels. 1884.

Karajan, T. G. von. Maria-Theresia und Josef II während der Mitregenschaft. Vienna. 1865.

Kuntziger, J. Essai historique sur la propagande des Encyclopédistes français en Belgique dans la seconde moitié du XVIIIᵉ siècle. Mémoires couronnés de l'Académie royale de Belgique. Coll. in 8vo. Vol. XXX. Brussels. 1879.

—— Febronius et le Fébronianisme. Étude historique sur le mouvement réformateur provoqué dans l'église catholique au XVIIIᵉ siècle par Febronius (J. N. de Hontheim, évêque suffragant de Trèves). Mémoires couronnés de l'Académie royale de Belgique. Coll. in 8vo. Vol. XLIV. Brussels. 1893.

Lorenz, O. Josef II und die belgische Revolution, nach den Papieren des General-Gouverneurs Grafen Murray. Vienna. 1862.

Lustkandl, W. Die Josephinische Ideen und ihr Erfolg. Vienna. 1881.

Maasburg, M. F. Geschichte der obersten Justizstelle in Wien. 1749–1848. Prague. 1891.

Magnette, F. Joseph II et la liberté de l'Escaut. Mémoires de l'Académie royale de Belgique. Coll. in 8vo. Vol. LV. Brussels. 1897.

Menzel, K A. Deutsche Geschichte unter Josef II und Friedrich II. Breslau. 1847.

Meyer, O. Febronius, Weihbischof J. N. von Hontheim, und sein Widerruf. Tübingen. 1880.

Nosinich, J. Kaiser Josef II als Staatsmann und Feldherr. Oesterreichs Politik in den Jahren 1763–90. Vienna. 1882.

Paganel, C. Histoire de Joseph II, empereur d'Allemagne. Paris. 1843.

Pezzel, J. Charakteristik Josefs des Zweiten. Eine historisch-biographische Skizze. Vienna. 1803.

Pichler, C. Die Beziehungen zwischen Oesterreich und Frankreich innerhalb der Jahre 1780–90. Znaym. 1898.

Poullet, E. Histoire du droit pénal dans le duché de Brabant depuis l'avènement de Charles-quint jusqu'à la réunion de la Belgique à la France, à la fin du XVIIIᵉ siècle. 2 vols. Mémoires couronnés de l'Académie royale de Belgique. Coll. in 4to. Vols. XXXV, XXXVI. Brussels.

Professione, A. Anton-Felice Zondadari e Bartolomeo Pacca. Milan. 1899.

Ramshorn, K. Kaiser Josef II und seine Zeit. Leipzig. 1845.

Ritter, K. Kaiser Josef II und seine kirchlichen Reformen. Regensburg. 1867.

Robaulx de Soumoy, A. L. P. de. Considérations sur le gouvernement des Pays-Bas par Liévin-Étienne van der Noot. Collection de mémoires relatifs à l'histoire de Belgique. Brussels. 1872.

Schlitter, H. Die Reise des Papstes Pius VI nach Wien und sein Aufenthalt daselbst. Ein Beitrag zur Geschichte der Beziehungen Josefs II zur römischen Curie. Fontes rerum Austriacarum. Part II, Vol. XLVII. Vienna. 1892.

—— Pius VI und Josef II von der Rückkehr des Papstes nach Rom bis zum Abschlusse des Concordats. Fontes rerum Austriacarum, Part II, Vol. XLVII. Vienna. 1894.

Theiner, A. Der Cardinal Johann Heinrich, Graf von Frankenberg, Erzbischof von Mecheln, Primas von Belgien, und sein Kampf für die Freiheit der Kirche und die bischöflichen Seminarien unter Kaiser Josef II. Freiburg i. B. 1850.

Verhaegen, A. Les cinquante dernières années de l'Université de Louvain. Brussels. 1884.

—— Le Cardinal de Frankenberg, archevêque de Molines (1726–1804). Bruges. 1889.

Wappler, A. Geschichte der theologischen Facultät der K. K. Universität zu Wien. Vienna. 1884.

Wolf, A. Marie-Christine, Erzherzogin von Oesterreich. 2 vols. Vienna. 1863.

—— Die Aufhebung der Klöster in Innerösterreich. Vienna. 1871.

—— Die Verhältnisse der Protestanten in Oesterreich unter der Kaiserin Maria Theresia und das Toleranz Patent. Raumer's Hist. Taschenbuch. Leipzig. 1878.

—— Kaiser Josef II und die Oesterreichischen Generalseminarien. Raumer's Hist. Taschenbuch. Leipzig. 1878.

Wolf, P. Ph. Geschichte der Veränderungen in dem religiösen, kirchlichen und wissenschaftlichen Zustände der Oesterreichischen Staaten unter der Regierung Josefs II. Vienna. 1795.

Wolfsgrüber, C. Christoph Anton Cardinal Migazzi, Fürstbischof von Wien. Saalzau. 1891.

Wuttke, H. Der Kampf der Freiheitsmänner und der Geistlichen in Belgien in den letzten Jahrzehnten des vorigen Jahrhunderts. Raumer's Hist. Taschenbuch. Leipzig. 1864.

Zieglauer, F. von. Die politische Reformbewegung in Siebenbürgen in der Zeit Josefs II und Leopold II. Vienna. 1881.

[*See also Bibliographies to Chapters XIX, XX.*]

CHAPTER XIX.

CATHARINE II.

[Works in the Russian language are marked (R.), *works in Polish* (P.).]

BIBLIOGRAPHY.

A complete bibliography of Catharine II and her reign is Bilbassoff, B. von, Katharina II, Kaiserin von Russland im Urteile der Weltliteratur, authorised German Translation from the Russian. Berlin. 1897. Vol. i comprises the bibliographical literature to the death of Catharine; Vol. ii that since her death (1797–1896).

I. GENERAL.

A. ORIGINAL AUTHORITIES.

Sbornik imperatorskawo russkawo istoritscheskawo obschtschestra (Journal of the Imperial Russian Historical Society, St Petersburg, from 1867 (R.)), contains in a large proportion of its volumes, numbering 129 up to the present date, important materials for the history of Catharine II, more especially her political correspondence, that of N. Panin, etc. The same remark applies to the Archives of Prince Voronzoff. Moscow, from 1870. (R.)

Catharine II. Works. Edited by A. Smirdin. 3 vols. St Petersburg. 1849–50. (R.)
—— Works. Edited on the basis of the original mss., with explanatory notes, by A. N. Pypin. 5 vols. St Petersburg. 1901–3. (R.)
—— Mémoires de l'Impératrice Catherine II, écrits par elle-même. Précédés d'une préface par A. Herzen. London. 1859.
—— Diary of A. W. Chrapowitzki, January 18, 1782—September 17, 1793. Edited by N. Barsukow. Moscow. 1901. (R.)
—— Correspondence with Frederick II. Sbornik. Vol. xx.
—— Joseph II und Katharina von Russland. Ihr Briefwechsel. Hrsgbn. von A. von Arneth. Vienna. 1869.
—— Leopold II, Franz II und Katharina II. Ihre Correspondenz. Hrsgbn. von A. Beer. Leipzig. 1874.
—— Correspondence with Grimm. Sbornik. Vols. xxiii, xxxiii, xliv.
—— Letters to Prince Charles Joseph de Ligne. Sbornik. Vols. xxiv, xxvii.
—— Letters to Voltaire. Sbornik. Vol. xxvii.
—— Correspondence with the Grand Duke Paul and the Grand Duchess Maria Feodorovna. Ruskaya Starina. viii.
—— Correspondence with Potemkin. Ruskaya Starina. 1876.

Eighteenth Century, The. Historical Journal edited by Peter Bartenew. 4 vols.
Moscow. 1869. (R.)

Masson, C. F. P. Mémoires secrètes sur la Russie, et particulièrement sur la
fin du règne de Catherine II et sur celui de Paul I. 2nd edn. 3 vols. London.
1802. (Anon.)

Rambaud, A. Recueil des instructions données aux ambassadeurs et ministres de
France. Russie. 2 vols. Paris. 1890.

Ségur, Comte L. Ph. de. Mémoires ou souvenirs et anecdotes. 3 vols. Paris.
1825.

B. Later Works.

Barsukoff, A. Prince Grigori Grigorjewitsch Orlow. Russky Arkhiv. 1873. (R.)

Bernhardi, T. von. Geschichte Russlands und der europ. Politik in den Jahren
1814-31. Vol. II, 2. (Staatengesch. d. neuesten Zeit.) Leipzig. 1875

Blum, K. L. Ein russischer Staatsmann. Denkwürdigkeiten des Grafen Sievers.
4 vols. Leipzig. 1864.

Brückner, A. Katharina II. Berlin. 1883.

——— Potemkin. St Petersburg. 1891. (R.)

Caro, I. Katharina II von Russland. In Vorträge und Essays. Gotha. 1906.

Castera, I. H. Histoire de Catherine II, Impératrice de Russie. 4 vols. Paris. 1880.

Denina, Ch. Pierre-le-Grand, traduit par J. F. André, avec des notes relatives aux
calomnies répandues dans divers ouvrages français contre l'Impératrice
Catherine II. Paris. 1809.

Geismann, P. A. and Dubowski, A. J. Count P. I. Panin, 1721-89. St Petersburg.
1896. (R.)

Herrmann, E. Geschichte des russischen Staates. Vol. V-VII. (Gesch. d. europ.
Staaten.) Hamburg and Gotha. 1853, 60, 66.

Larivière, C. de. Catherine la grande d'après sa correspondance. Paris. 1895.

Morane, P. Paul Ier de Russie avant l'avènement. Paris. 1907.

Otscharkoff, W. W. G. A. Potemkin. St Petersburg. 1892. (R.)

Petruschewskij, Generalissimus Suworow. 3 vols. St Petersburg. 1884. (R.)

Potemkin, Prince G. A. Papers 1774-93. 2 vols. St Petersburg. 1893-5. (R.)

Samoilow, Count A. N. Leben und Taten des Gen. Feldmarschalles Fürst G. A.
Potemkin. Russky Arkhiv. 1867. (R.)

Schiemann, T. Geschichte Russlands unter Kaiser Nikolaus I. Vol. I, chap. I.
Berlin. 1904.

Solowjoff, S. Geschichte Russlands von den ältesten Zeiten. Vol. XXV-XXIX.
Moscow. 1875-9. (R.)

Sybel, H. von. Katharina II von Russland. In Kleine historische Schriften.
Vol. I. 3rd edn. Stuttgart. 1880.

Tooke, W. History of Russia in the reign of Catharine II. 4th edn. 3 vols.
London. 1800.

Waliszewski, K. Le Roman d'une Impératrice. 14th edn. Paris. 1902.

——— Autour d'un Trône. 3rd edn. Paris. 1894.

II. PERIOD TO 1762.

Bain, R. N. Peter III, Emperor of Russia. London. 1902.

Biographie Peters III. [By G. A. W. Helbig.] 2 vols. Tübingen. 1809.

Rulhière, C. C. de. Histoire ou anecdotes pour la révolution de Russie en l'année
1762. Paris. 1797.

Saldern, C. von. Histoire de la vie de Pierre III, Empereur de toutes les Russies.
Metz. 1802.

III. POLAND.

A. Original Authority.

Angeberg, Count de. Recueil des traités, conventions et actes diplomatiques concernant la Pologne 1762–1862. Paris. 1862.

B. Later Works.

Alkar, Książę. Repniní Polska w pierwszem czteroleciu Stanisława Augusta. 2 vols. Cracow. 1896. (P.)

Andreae, F. Preussische und russische Politik in Polen von der taurischen Reise Katharinas II (Januar 1787) bis zur Abwendung Friedrich Wilhelms II von den Hertzbergschen Plänen (August 1789). (Diss.) Berlin. 1905.

Askenazy, S. Die letzte polnische Königswahl. (Diss.) Göttingen. 1894.

Beer, A. Die erste Theilung Polens. 3 vols. Vienna. 1873.

Brückner, A. Geschichte der polnischen Literatur. Leipzig. 1901.

Brüggen, E. von der. Polens Auflösung. Leipzig. 1878.

Kalinka, V. Der vierjährige polnische Reichstag 1788 bis 1791. 2 vols. Berlin. 1896–8.

Karejeff, N. The Fall of Poland in historical literature. St Petersburg. 1888. (R.)

—— Polish Reforms in the 18th century. Wjestnik Jewropy V. 1889. (R.)

Korzon, T. Dzieje wewnętrzne Polski za Stanisława Augusta. 2nd edn. 6 vols. Warsaw. 1897. (P.)

Kostomaroff, N. J. Die letzten Jahre der Republik Polen. 2 vols. St Petersburg. 1886. (R.)

Kraszewski, J. J. Polska w czasie trzech rozbiorow. Posen. 1873. (P.)

Kutrzeba, St. Historya ustroju Polski w zarysie. Lemberg. 1905. (P.)

Lelewel, J. Histoire de Pologne. 2 vols. Paris. 1844.

—— Panowanie Króla polskiego Stanisława Augusta. 6th edn. Brussels. 1847. (P.)

Smitt, F. de. Frédéric II, Catherine et le partage de Pologne. Paris. 1861.

Solowjoff, S. M. Geschichte des Falls von Polen. Gotha. 1865.

Sorel, A. La question d'Orient au XVIIIme siècle, le partage de la Pologne et le Traité de Kainardji. 3rd edn. Paris. 1902.

Waliszewski, K. Walka stronnictw i programów politycznych przed upadkiem Rzeczypospolitej. Cracow. 1887. (P.)

—— Polska i Europa w drugiej połowie XVIII stuleciu. Cracow. 1890. (P.)

IV. THE EASTERN QUESTION AND GENERAL FOREIGN POLICY.

A. Original Authorities.

Dubrowin, N. The Union of the Crimea with Russia. Rescripts, letters, relations and reports. 4 vols. St Petersburg. 1885–9. (R.)

Martens, F. de. Recueil des traités et conventions conclus par la Russie avec les puissances étrangères. Vols. II, VI, IX, XIII. St Petersburg. 1875–1902.

Noradounghian, G. Recueil d'Actes internationaux de l'empire Ottoman. Vols. I and II. Paris. 1897–1900.

B. Later Works.

Bergbohm, K. Die bewaffnete Neutralität, 1780–3. Berlin. 1834.

Brückner, A. The War of Russia against Sweden. St Petersburg. 1869. (R.)

Grot, I. K. Catharine II and Gustavus III. St Petersburg. 1877. (R.)

Hammer-Purgstall, J. Frhr. von. Geschichte der Chane der Krim. Vienna. 1856.

Petroff. The War of Russia against Turkey and the Polish Confederates, 1769–74. 5 vols. St Petersburg. 1866–74. (R.)

—— The Second Turkish War, 1787–91. 2 vols. St Petersburg. 1880. (R.)

Reimann, E. Neuere Geschichte des preussischen Staates seit 1763. (Gesch. d. europ. Staaten.) 2 vols. Gotha. 1882–3.

Schiemann, T. Geschichte Russlands unter Kaiser Nikolaus I. Vol. i, chap. viii. Berlin. 1904.

Schlözer, K. von. Friedrich der Grosse und Katharina II. Berlin. 1859.

Sorel, A. La question d'Orient au xviiie siècle, le partage de la Pologne et le traité de Kainardji. 3rd edn. Paris. 1902.

—— Catherine II et la Révolution Française. In Essais d'histoire et de critique. Paris. 1883.

Tschetschulin. The foreign policy of Russia at the beginning of the reign of Catharine II. St Petersburg. 1896. (R.)

Zinkeisen, J. W. Geschichte des osmanischen Reiches in Europa. Vols. v, vi. (Gesch. d. europ. Staaten.) Gotha. 1857–9.

V. HOME AFFAIRS.

A. Original Authorities.

Archives of the Imperial Council. I. 2 vols. St Petersburg. 1869. (R.)

Bibikoff, A. Memoirs. Moscow. 1817. (R.)

Instruction de Sa Maj. Impér. Katherine II pour la Commission chargée de dresser le projet d'un nouveau code de loix (!). St Petersburg. 1893. L. Panteljeew éditeur. (In Russian and French.)

Acts of the Legislative Commission. Sbornik. Vols. iv, viii, xiv, xxxii.

Complete Collection of the Laws of the Russian Empire, since the year 1649. Vols. xvi–xxiii. St Petersburg. 1830, etc. (R.)

B. Later Works.

Andrejewski. Governors-General, Wojewodes and Governors. St Petersburg. 1864. (R.)

Annalen der Regierung Katharina II, Kaiserin von Russland. (Hrsgbn. von H. Storch.) Vol. i: Gesetzgebung. Leipzig. 1798.

Bienemann, F. Die Statthalterschaftszeit in Liv- und Estland (1783–96). Leipzig. 1886.

Danewski. History of the Origin and Growth of the Imperial Council. St Petersburg. 1859. (R.)

Eckardt, J. Livland im 18. Jahrhundert. Leipzig. 1876.

—— Die baltischen Provinzen Russlands. Leipzig. 1868.

Engelmann, J. Die Leibeigenschaft in Russland. Leipzig. 1884.

Firsoff, N. Die Regierung und die Gesellschaft in ihren Beziehungen zum Aussenhandel Russlands während der Regierung Katharinas II. (R.)

Gradowski, A. D. The higher Administration of Russia in the 18th century and the Governors-General. St Petersburg. 1866. (R.)

Hruschewskij, M. Outlines of the History of the People of the Ukraine. 2nd edn. St Petersburg. 1906. (R.)

Ikonnikoff, W. S. Arsenij Mazjeewitsch. Historical-biographical Sketch. Ruskaya Starina. 1879. (R.)

Lappo-Danilewski, A. Die russische Handelskommission von 1763–96. In Beiträge zur russischen Geschichte, hrsgbn. von O. Hötzsch. Berlin. 1907.

Lappo-Danilewski, A. Sketch of the domestic policy of Catharine II. St Petersburg. 1898. (R.)

Lehtonen, U. L. Die polnischen Provinzen Russlands unter Katharina II in den Jahren 1772–82. Berlin. 1907.

Mordowzeff. Pretenders and robbers. 2 vols. St Petersburg. 1867. (R.)

Pachman, S. W. History of the Codification of the Civil Law. St Petersburg. 1876. (R.)

Romanowitsch-Slawatinskij. The nobility in Russia from the beginning of the 18th century to the abolition of Serfdom. St Petersburg. 1870. (R.)

Semjewski, W. J. The Peasant Question in Russia in the 18th and in the first half of the 19th century. St Petersburg. 1888. (R.)

—— The Peasants during the reign of Catharine II. 2nd edn. 2 vols. St Petersburg. 1901–3. (R.)

Storch, H. Historisch-statistisches Gemälde des Russischen Reiches am Ende des 18. Jahrh. und unter der Regierung Katharina II. Vol. vi. Riga. 1797.

Tugan-Baranowski, M. Russian manufactories in the past and the present. 2nd edn. St Petersburg. 1900. (R.)

Wittscheffsky, V. Russlands Handels-, Zoll- und Industriepolitik von Peter dem Grossen bis auf die Gegenwart. Berlin. 1905.

VI. PERSONAL SURROUNDINGS AND INTELLECTUAL ACTIVITIES.

A. ORIGINAL AUTHORITIES.

Daschkoff, Princess. Memoirs of the history of the Empress Catharine II. Original French Text in Archives of Prince Voronzoff, vol. xxi. Moscow. 1881. German version, with introduction by A. Herzen. 2 vols. Hamburg. 1857. English translation by Mrs W. Bradford. 2 vols. London. 1840.

Derschawin, G. R. Works. Edited by J. K. Grot. 9 vols. St Petersburg. 1864–83. (R.)

Radischtschew, A. N. Reise von Petersburg nach Moskau. 1790. (R.) Ausgaben. London. 1858. Leipzig. 1876. St Petersburg (?). 1868.

Wisin, D. J. First complete collection of Works. St Petersburg. 1888. (R.)

B. LATER WORKS.

Adelung, F. Katharinens der Grossen Verdienste um die Vergleichung der Sprachenkunde. St Petersburg. 1815.

Andreae, Fr. Bemerkungen zu den Briefen der Kaiserin Katharina II von Russland an Charles Joseph Prince de Ligne. In Beiträge zur russischen Geschichte. Edited by O. Hötzsch. Berlin. 1907.

Bilbassoff, B. von. Prince de Ligne in Russia. Ruskaya Starina. Vols. lxxiii, lxxiv. St Petersburg. 1892. (R.)

Brückner, A. Geschichte der russischen Literatur. Leipzig. 1905.

Grot, J. K. Catharine II in her correspondence with Grimm. 2 vols. St Petersburg. 1879, 1884. (R.)

Helwig, G. A. W. Russische Günstlinge. Tübingen. 1809.

Otscharkoff, W. W. Princess K. R. Daschkow. St Petersburg. 1893. (R.)

Tourneux, M. Diderot et Catherine II. Paris. 1899.

[*See also Bibliographies to Chapters XVIII and XX.*]

CHAPTER XX.

FREDERICK II AND HIS SUCCESSOR.

(1) HOME AND FOREIGN AFFAIRS.

I. GENERAL.

Arneth, Ritter A. von. Maria Theresias letzte Regierungszeit. 1763–80. Vol. IV. Vienna. 1879.

Koser, R. König Friedrich der Grosse. Vol. II, Part 2. 3rd edn. Stuttgart. 1905.

Philippson, M. Geschichte des preussischen Staatswesens vom Tode Friedrichs des Grossen bis zu den Freiheitskriegen. 2 vols. Leipzig. 1880–2.

Ranke, L. von. Die Deutschen Mächte und der Fürstenbund. Deutsche Geschichte von 1780 bis 1790. 2 vols. Sämmtl. Werke. Vols. XXXI, XXXII. Leipzig. 1871–2.

Reimann, E. Neuere Geschichte des preussischen Staats. Vols. II and III. (Gesch. der europ. Staaten.) Gotha. 1888.

II. MONOGRAPHS.

Beer, A. Zur Geschichte des bairischen Erbfolgeskrieges. Historische Zeitschrift. Vol. XXXV.

—— Die Sendung Thuguts in das preussische Hauptquartier und der Friede zu Teschen. Histor. Zeitschrift. Vol XXXVIII.

Krauel, R. Graf Hertzberg als Minister Friedrich Wilhelms III. Berlin. 1899.

Naudé, A. Der preussische Staatsschatz unter König Friedrich Wilhelm II und seine Erschöpfung. Beiträge zur preussischen Finanzgeschichte im 18. Jahrhundert. Part I. Forschungen zur Brandenburgischen und Preussischen Geschichte. Vol. V.

Poschinger, H. von. Bankwesen und Bankpolitik in Preussen. Vol. I. Berlin. 1878.

Ruffert, B. Die Zusammenkunft Friedrichs d. Gr. mit Joseph II zu Neisse in J. 1769. (Rpt. from 37. Bericht d. Neisser Philomathie.) Neisse, 1918.

Sorel, A. La décadence de la Prusse après Frédéric II. Revue des Deux Mondes. Vol. LV. Paris. 1883.

Ziekursch, J. Aus der Entwicklungsgeschichte der preussischen Bureaucratie im fridericianischen Schlesien. Preussische Jahrbücher. Vol. XXXI. Berlin.

(2) POLAND AND PRUSSIA.

Angeberg, Count de. Recueil des traités, conventions et actes diplomatiques concernant la Pologne 1762–1862. Paris. 1862.

Arneth, Ritter A. von. Geschichte Maria Theresias. Vol. VIII. Vienna. 1877.

Bailleu, P. Graf Hertzberg. Historische Zeitschrift. Vol. XLII. Munich. 1879.

Beer, A. Die erste Theilung Polens. 3 vols. Vienna. 1873.

—— Friedrich II und van Swieten. Leipzig. 1874.

Brüggen, E. von der. Polens Auflösung. Leipzig. 1878.

Duncker, M. Die Besitzergreifung von Westpreussen. In Aus der Zeit Friedrichs des Grossen und Friedrich Wilhelms III. Leipzig. 1876.

Frederick II. Politische Correspondenz. Vols. xxiii–xxxii. Berlin. 1896–1908.

—— Œuvres. Vol. vi. Berlin. 1847.

[Görtz, J. E., Count de.] Mémoires et actes authentiques relatifs aux négotiations qui ont précédé le partage de la Pologne. Weimar. 1810.

Heigel, K. T. von. Deutsche Geschichte vom Tode Friedrichs des Grossen bis zur Auflösung des alten Reiches. Vol. i. Stuttgart. 1899.

Joachim, E. Johann Friedrich von Domhardt. Berlin. 1899.

Kalinka, V. Der vierjährige polnische Reichstag 1788 bis 1791. 2 vols. Berlin. 1896, 1898.

Koser, R. König Friedrich der Grosse. Vol. ii, chap. viii, 3, 4. 3rd edn. Stuttgart. 1905.

—— Aus der Vorgeschichte der ersten Theilung Polens. Sitzungsberichte der K. Preuss. Akademie der Wissenschaften. xiii. 1908.

Krauel, R. Prinz Heinrich von Preussen als Politiker. Berlin. 1902.

—— Briefwechsel zwischen Heinrich Prinz von Preussen und Katharina II von Russland. Berlin. 1903.

Martens, F. de. Recueil des traités et conventions conclus par la Russie avec les puissances étrangères. Vols. ii and vi. St Petersburg. 1875, 1883.

Preuss, A. T. Ewald Friedrich Graf von Hertzberg. Berlin. 1908.

Reimann, E. Neuere Geschichte des preussischen Staates seit 1763. Vols. i and ii. (Gesch. d. europ. Staaten.) Gotha. 1882–8.

Schlözer, K. von. Friedrich der Grosse und Katharina II. Berlin. 1859.

Smitt, F. de. Frédéric II, Catherine et le partage de Pologne. Paris. 1861.

Solowjow, S. M. Geschichte des Falls von Polen. Gotha. 1865.

Sybel, H. von. Die erste Theilung Polens. In Kleine Historische Schriften. Vol. iii. Stuttgart. 1880.

Wittichen, P. Die polnische Politik Preussens 1788–90. Göttingen. 1899.

[*See also Bibliographies to Chapters XVIII, XIX.*]

CHAPTER XXI.

DENMARK UNDER THE BERNSTORFFS AND STRUENSEE.

I. MANUSCRIPTS AND BIBLIOGRAPHIES.

The disposition of the mass of unpublished material preserved in the national archives at Copenhagen and Christiania is indicated in the Danmark-Norges Historie of Professor Edvard Holm.   Many private collections in Northern Germany have been examined by Dr Aage Friis and their contents described in his Bernstorffsche Papiere, and Bernstorff og Guldberg.

For printed books reference may be made to C. W. Bruun's Bibliotheca Danica (1482–1830), 4 vols., Copenhagen, 1872–1902, to the yearly bibliographies of the Danish Historical Society published in the Historisk Tidsskrift (Copenhagen, 1840, etc.), and to the French edition of C. F. Allen's History, mentioned below.

II. CONTEMPORARY AUTHORITIES.

Aarsberetninger fra det Kongelige Geheimearchiv indeholdende Bidrag til dansk Historie af utrykte Kilder. Ed. C. F. Wegener. 7 vols. Copenhagen. 1852–83.

Aktstykker til Oplysning om Stavnsbaandets Historie. Ed. J. A. Fridericia. Copenhagen. 1888.

Almanak, Dansk Historisk, udgiven af Det Kongelige Videnskabernes Societet. Copenhagen. 1760–82.

Baden, T. Beskrivelse over den paa Godset Bernstorff ivaerksatte nye Indretning i Landbruget. Copenhagen. 1774.

Bernstorff, Count J. H. E. Correspondance ministérielle du comte J. H. E. Bernstorff 1751–70. Ed. P. Vedel. Copenhagen. 1882.

Bernstorffs, the. Bernstorffsche Papiere. Ausgewählte Briefe und Aufzeichnungen die Familie Bernstorff betreffend aus der Zeit 1732 bis 1835. Ed. A. Friis. Copenhagen and Christiania. Vol. i, 1904. Vol. ii, 1907.

Biehl, C. D. Charlotte Dorothea Biehl's Breve om Kong Christian VII. Ed. L. T. A. Bobé. Copenhagen. 1901.

Brown, J. The Northern Courts, containing original memoirs of the sovereigns of Sweden and Denmark since 1766. 2 vols. London. 1818.

Documents rélatifs à l'histoire de la Russie. Vol. xiii. St Petersburg.

Eggers, C. U. D. von. Denkwürdigkeiten aus dem Leben des Königlich Dänischen Staatsministers Andreas Petrus Grafen von Bernstorff. Part ii: Diplomatische Actenstücke. Copenhagen. 1800.

(Falckenskiold, S. O.?) Authentische und höchstmerkwürdige Aufklärungen über die Geschichte der Grafen Struensee und Brandt, aus dem französischen Manuscript eines hohen Ungenannten zum erstenmal übersetzt und gedruckt. "Germanien" (Kempten). 1788.

Falckenskiold, S. O. Mémoires de M. de Falckenskiold, officier général au service de S. M. le roi de Dannemarck. Ed. P. Secretan. Paris. 1826.

Frederick II. Politische Correspondenz Friedr. d. Grossen. Vol. i–xxx. Berlin. 1879–1905.

Gaspari, A. C. Urkunden und Materialien zur nähern Kenntniss der Geschichte und Staatsverwaltung Nordischer Reiche. 3 vols. Hamburg. 1786–90.

Guldberg, O. H. Tale til sine Landsmaend ved Anledning af Hans Kongelige Höjhed vor naadigste Kronprinses Konfirmation. Copenhagen. 1765.

Hesse-Cassel, Charles, Landgrave of. Mémoires de mon Temps. Copenhagen. 1861. Translated into German, with introduction by K. Bernhardi. Cassel. 1866.

Holberg, L. Danmarks og Norges gejstlige og verdslige Stat. 3rd edition. Copenhagen. 1762.

Jessen, E. J. Det Kongerige Norge, fremstillet efter dets naturlige og borgerlige Tilstand. 1763.

Jörgensen, A. D. Regeringsskiftet 14 April, 1784. Fremstillinger og Aktstykker udgivne af de under Kultusministeriet samlede Arkiver. Copenhagen. 1888.

Keith, Sir Robert Murray. Memoirs and Correspondence. Ed. Mrs Gillespie Smyth. 2 vols. London. 1849.

Lütken, O. D. Undersögninger angaaende Statens almindelige Oeconomie. 2 vols. Sorö. 1760.

Lynar, Count R. F. Hinterlassene Staatsschriften. Hamburg. 1793.

Möller, J. Mnemosyne, eller samling af faedrenelandske Minder. 4 vols. Copenhagen. 1830–3.

Münter, B. (the elder) and Hee, J. Bekehrungsgeschichte der vormaligen beyden Grafen Johann Friedrich Struensee...von Hrn. D. Balthasar Münter und Enewold Brandt...von Hrn. Probst Jörgen Hee. 3rd edition. Copenhagen and Leipzig. 1773. (Translated into English, French, German, etc., various dates.)

Nyerup, R. (editor). Lüxdorphiana, eller Bidrag til den danske Literairhistorie, uddragne af B. W. Lüxdorphs efterladte Samlinger. Copenhagen. 1791. [Miscellaneous documents.]

Pontoppidan, E. Prokantsler Erik Pontoppidans Levnetsbeskrivelse og hans Dagbok fra en Reise i Norge i Aaret 1749. Ed. N. E. Hofman (Bang). Odense. 1874.

—— E. (and others). Den Danske Atlas eller Kongeriget Dannemark, etc. 7 vols. Copenhagen. 1763–81.

Reventlow Papers. Efterladte Papirer fra den Reventlowske Familiekreds. Ed. L. T. A. Bobé. 7 vols. Copenhagen. 1895, etc.

Reverdil, E. S. F. Struensée et la cour de Copenhague 1760–72. Mémoires de Reverdil. Ed. A. Roger. Paris. 1858. Danish translation. Copenhagen. 1859.

—— Lettres sur le Danemarc. 2 vols. Geneva. 1764.

Roque, B. Les délices du Danemark. Copenhagen. 1747. Danish translation.

Samlinger, Danske, for Historie, Topographi, Personal- og Literatur-historie. 12 vols. Copenhagen. 1865–79.

Schriften, die in Sachen der Grafen Struensee und Brandt herausgegeben sind. Copenhagen. 1772.

Struensee. Mémoires authentiques et intéressans du histoire des comtes Struensée et Brandt. Copenhagen and Brussels. 1789.

—— Mémoires pour servir à la connoissance de l'état actuel du royaume de Danemarck. (Translated from the German by M. de Schirach.) 1785.

Suhm, P. F. Samlade Skrifter. Ed. N. Nyerup. 15 vols. Copenhagen. 1788–99.

Tractater, Danske, 1751–1800. Udgivet par Udenrigsministeriets Foranstaltning. Copenhagen. 1882.

Treschow. Bidrag til Grev Frederik Danneskjold Samsöes Levnetsbeskrivelse. Copenhagen. 1796.

Wraxall, Sir N. W. Posthumous Memoirs of his own time. London.

Yves, Marquis L. de. Geheime Hof- und Staats-Geschichte des Königreichs Dänemark in den Zeiten nach der Struenseeischen Revolution. "Germanien." 1790.

III. SECONDARY WORKS.

Allen, C. F.   Haandbog i Faedrelandets Historie, med stadig Henblik paa Folkets og Statens indre Udvikling.   7th edition.   Copenhagen.   1870.   German translation by N. Falck.   2nd edition.   Kiel.   1846.   French translation by E. Beauvoise.   Copenhagen.   1878.

Barthélemy, Count E. M. de.   Histoire des relations de la France et du Danemarck sous la ministère du Comte de Bernstorff 1751–70.   Copenhagen.   1887.

Bergbohm, C.   Die bewaffnete Neutralität 1780–3.   Eine Entwickelungsphase des Völkerrechts im Seekriege.   Berlin.   1884.

Blangstrup, C.   Christian VII og Caroline Mathilde.   2nd edition.   Copenhagen 1891.

Bremer, J.   Geschichte Schleswig-Holsteins bis zum Jahre 1848.   Kiel.   1864.

Bricka, C. F., Steenstrup, J. and Laursen, L.   Dansk biografisk Lexikon.   19 vols.   Copenhagen.   1906.

Bruun, C.   Kjöbenhavn.   3 vols.   Copenhagen.   1887–1901.

Christiansen, C. (of Hörsholm).   Hörsholms Historie fra 1305 til 1875.   Copenhagen.   1879.

——— V.   Christian den VII's Sindssygdom.   Copenhagen and Christiania.   1906.

Danielson, J. R.   Die nordische Frage in den Jahren 1746–51.   Helsingfors.   1888.

Danmarks Riges Historie.   Vol. v; by Professor E. Holm.   Copenhagen.   n.d.

Fauchille, P.   La diplomatie française et la ligue des neutres de 1780.   Paris.   1893.

Fjelstrup, A.   Skilsmisseprocessen imellem Kong Kristian VII og Dronning Karoline Matilde.   Copenhagen.   1908.   [Documents.]

Flamand, L. J.   Christian den syvendes Hof, eller Struensee og Caroline Mathilde.   Copenhagen.   1854.   [Documents.]

Friis, A.   Andreas Peter Bernstorff og Ove Höegh Guldberg.   Copenhagen.   1899.

———   Bernstorfferne og Danmark.   Vol. i.   Copenhagen.   1903.   Also, in German : Die Bernstorffs.   Vol. i.   Leipzig.   1905.

Garde, H. G.   Efterretninger om den Danske og Norske Sömagt.   4 vols.   Copenhagen.   1832–5.

———   Den dansk-norske Sömagts Historie 1700–1814.   Copenhagen.   1852.

Giessing, H. P.   Struensee og Guldberg, eller tvende Revolutioner ved Hoffet i Kjöbenhavn.   Copenhagen.   1849.

———   Kong Frederik VI's Regierings-historie.   2 vols.   Copenhagen.   1850.   German edition.   Kiel.   1851.

Hanssen, G.   Die Aufhebung der Leibeigenschaft und die Umgestaltung der gutsherrlichbauerlichen Verhältnisse überhaupt in den Herzogthümern Schleswig und Holstein.   St Petersburg.   1861.

Hansen, V. F.   Stavnsbaandslösningen og Landboreformerne set fra Nationalökonomiens Standpunkt.   2 vols.   Copenhagen.   1888.

Helweg, L.   Den Danske Kirkes Historie efter Reformationen.   5 vols.   Copenhagen.   1851–5.

Holm, E.   Om det Syn paa Kongemagt, Folk og Borgerlig Frihed, der udviklede sig i den dansk-norske Stat 1746–70.   Copenhagen.   1883.

———   Danmark-Norges Historie fra den store nordiske Krigs Slutning til Rigernes Adskillelse (1720–1814).   Copenhagen.   1890, etc.

———   Danmark-Norges indre Historie 1660–1720.   2 vols.   Copenhagen.   1885–6.

———   Nogle Hovedtraek af Trykkefrihedstidens Historie 1770–3.   Copenhagen.   1885.

Höst, J. K.   Geheimekabinetsminister Grev Johann Friedrich Struensee og hans Ministerium.   3 vols. (with documents).   Copenhagen.   1824.   German translation.   2 vols.   Copenhagen.   1826–7.

Ingerslev, V. Danmarks Laeger og Laegevaesen fra de aeldste Tiden indtil aar 1800. 2 vols. Copenhagen. 1871–3.

Jenssen-Tusch, G. F. von. Die Verschwörung gegen die Königin Caroline Mathilde von Dänemark, geb. Prinzessin von Grossbritannien und Irland, und die Grafen Struensee und Brandt. Leipzig. 1864. [With documents.]

Kayser, R. Deutsches Leben in Dänemark. Preussische Jahrbücher, xxi, 2. Berlin. 1908.

Kjaer, S. Fra Stavnsbaandets Dage. Optegnelser efter Tingböger. Copenhagen. 1888.

Koch, H. L. S. P. Kong Christian den sjettes Historie. Copenhagen. 1886.

Lorentzen, K. Graf Johann Hartwig Ernst von Bernstorff. Graf Andreas Peter von Bernstorff. In Allgemeine deutsche Biographie. Vol. ii. Leipzig. 1875.

Möller, H. L. Kong Christian den Sjette og Grev Kristian Ernst af Stolberg-Wernigerode. Copenhagen. 1889.

Nilsson, N. O. J. Danmarks uppträdande i den svenska tronföljarefragan åren 1739–43. Efter handlingar i K. Danska Geheimearkivet och Svenska Riksarkivet. Malmö. 1875.

Raumer, F. von. Beiträge zur neueren Geschichte aus dem britischen und französischen Reichsarchive. iii, i : Europa vom Ende des siebenjährigen bis zum Ende des amerikanischen Krieges (1763–83). Leipzig. 1839.

Rawert, O. J. Danmarks industrielle Forhold fra de aeldste Tider indtil 1848. Copenhagen. 1850.

Reedtz, H. C. de. Répertoire...des traités conclus par la couronne de Dannemarck, ...jusqu'à 1800. Göttingen. 1826.

Stolpe, P. M. Dagspressen i Danmark, dens Vilkaar og Personer indtil Midten af det attende Aarhundrede. 4 vols. Copenhagen. 1878–82.

Trier, H. Revolutionen i Raadstuen, April 1771. Aktstykker fra Struensee-Tiden verdrörende Staden Kjöbenhavn's Styrelse. Copenhagen. 1905.

Vaupell, O. F. von. Den Danske Haers Historie til Nutiden og den Norske Haers Historie indtil 1814. 2 vols. Copenhagen. 1872–6.

Vedel, P. Den äldre Grev Bernstorffs Ministerium. Inledning til Correspondance ministérielle du comte J. H. E. Bernstorff. Copenhagen. 1882.

—— S. Den Dansk-Norske Höiesterets Historie under Enevaelden fra 1661 indtil 1790. Copenhagen. 1888.

Ward, A. W. Caroline Matilda. Dictionary of National Biography. Vol. ix. London. 1887. [With bibliography.]

Wilkins, W. H. A Queen of Tears, Caroline Matilda, Queen of Denmark and Norway. 2 vols. London. 1904. [With extracts from English State Papers.]

Wittich, K. Struensee. Leipzig. 1879. [With critical bibliography.] Danish translation by C. Blangstrup, with extracts from the Saxon ambassadorial despatches. Copenhagen. 1887.

See also numerous articles in the following periodical publications:
  Danske Magasin—Historisk Tidsskrift—Nyt historisk Tidsskrift—Musaeum—Norsk historisk Tidsskrift—Oekonomisk Magasin—Zeitschrift der Gesellschaft für Schleswig-Holstein-Lauenburgische Geschichte.

CHAPTER XXII.

SWEDEN FROM 1720-92.

I. BIBLIOGRAPHIES.

Alphabetisk register öfver handlingar rörande Skandinavenska Historia. Stockholm. 1865.
Catalogus der Geschiedenis-Skandinavie. The Hague. 1904.
Historisk Tidsskrift. Innehållsöfversikt, 1881-90. Stockholm. 1891.
Setterwall, K. Förteckning öfver Acta Sverica i Calendars of State Papers. Stockholm. 1889 sqq.

II. ORIGINAL DOCUMENTS.

Adlerbeth, G. C. Anteckningar. Örebro. 1856-7.
Björnstjerna, Count M. F. F. de. Mémoires posthumes du Comte de Stedingk. Paris. 1844-7.
Bordes de Folliquy, G. L. A. de. Journal de la campagne de Suède et de Danemark, 1789. Caen. 1904.
Bouillé, F. C. A. de, Marquis. Mémoires. Paris. 1859.
British Museum MSS. Add. 28,066 [relating to Gustavus III's naval victories over the Russian fleet]. (*In English.*)
Ehrensvärd, G. J., Baron. Dagboksanteckningar, 1776-84. Stockholm. 1878.
Engeström, J. von. Historiska anteckningar. Stockholm. 1877.
Engeström, Baron Lars von. Minnen och Anteckningar. Stockholm. 1876.
Fersen, Count Oxel Fredrick. Historiska skrifter. Stockholm. 1867-72.
Gustavus III and Russia. Journal (Sbornik) of the Imperial Russian Historical Society. Vols. XIII, XIX, XXIII. St Petersburg. 1881, etc.
—— Bref till C. A. Wachmeister och U. G. Franc. Örebro. 1860.
—— Bref till G. M. Armfelt. Stockholm. 1883. (*In French.*)
—— Discours, le 26 avril 1774, lors de la délibération sur l'établissement de la liberté de la Presse. Lausanne. 1775.
—— Efterlemnade papper. Stockholm. 1893.
—— Lettre à M. le Baron Staël de Holstein. Paris. 1791. [Relates to the treatment of King Louis XVI.]
—— Tal till Riksens-Ständer, 25 Jan. 1771. Stockholm. 1773.
—— Tal till Riksens-Ständer, 23 Juni 1786. Stockholm. [1786.]
—— Tal till Riksens-Ständer, 2 Feb. 1789. Stockholm. [1789.]
—— Tal hållit på Riks Salen, 17 Feb. 1789, i alla Fyra Ståndens närraro. Stockholm. [1789.]
—— Tal hållit til Riksens-Ständer, 28 April, 1789. Stockholm. [1789.]

Hamilton, Count A. M. Anecdoter till svenska historien under Gustaf III:s regering. Stockholm. 1901.

Hedwig, Elizabeth Charlotte, Consort of Charles XIII, King of Sweden. Dagbok. Stockholm. 1902.

Höpken, A. J. von, Count. Skrifter i urval utgifna af C. Silfverstolpe. Stockholm. 1890 sqq.

Khrapovitsky, A. V. Diary. St Petersburg. 1874. (*In Russian.*)

Liljencrantz, J., Count. Anteckningar. St Petersburg. 1878.

Louis XV, King of France. Correspondance secrète inédite. Ed. E. Bontaric. Paris. 1866.

Schröderheim, E. Anteckningar. Örebro. 1851.

—— Bref. Stockholm. 1900.

Schück, J. H. E. Ur Nils von Rosensteins brefsamling. Stockholm. 1905.

Silfverstolpe, C. Historiskt Bibliothek. Stockholm. 1875, etc.

Staël-Holstein, Baron E. M. de. Correspondance diplomatique, 1783–99. Ed. Leruzon le Duc. Paris. 1881.

Tessin, Count C. G. Dagbok. Stockholm. 1824.

III. CONTEMPORARY OR NEARLY CONTEMPORARY NARRATIVES.

Berattelse om den seger Svenska Arméens Flotta under Thergens eget höge Befäl den 9–10 Juli 1790 wunnit öfwer den Ryska Skärgårds Flottan. Stockholm. 1790.

Gustavus III. Letters of the Swedish Court written chiefly in the early part of the reign of Gustavus III. London. 1819.

Louisa Ulrica, Queen. Luise Ulrike, die schwedische Schwester Friedrichs des Grossen. Ungedruckte Briefe, etc. Hrsgbn. von F. Arnheim. Vol. I. (1726–46.) Gotha. 1909.

Michelessi, D. Lettre sur la Révolution arrivée en Suède le 19 août 1772. Stockholm. 1773.

Nassau-Siegen, Prince Charles Henry Nicholas Otho of. Extrait de la campagne du Prince de Nassau-Siegen contre les armées Suédoises en 1789. [Paris? 1790.]

—— Lettre à Sa Majesté le Roi de Suède et réfutation de la relation qui lui est attribuée de la bataille navale du 13 août 1789, etc. St Petersburg. 1789.

Sheridan, C. L. A history of the late Revolution in Sweden. London. 1778.

Sierakowski, Count. Histoire de l'assassinat de Gustave III. Paris. 1797.

Ståhlberg, G. An history of the late Revolution in Sweden, 19 of August, 1772. Edinburgh. 1776.

State Papers relating to the change of the Constitution of Sweden. London. 1772.

Tessin, Count C. G. Letters to a young Prince from his Governor. London. 1755.

Thomas, D. H. Versuch über Schwedens Geschichte und dermalige Staatsveränderung. Stralsund. 1780.

IV. LATER WORKS.

A. The Hats and Caps.

Arnheim, F. Die Memoiren der Königin Ulrike Luise. Halle. 1888.

Beskow, B., Baron. Minne af K. G. Tessin. Stockholm. 1864.

Botin, A. af. Svenska Folkets Historia. Stockholm. 1789–92.

Cedercreutz, H., Baron. Sverige under Ulrika Eleonora och Fredrik. Stockholm. 1821.

Danielson, J. R.   Die nordische Frage in den Jahren 1746-51.   Helsingfors.   1888.
Fryxell, A.   Berättelser ur Svenska Historien.   Stockholm.   1831, etc.
Geijer, E. G.   Teckning af Frihetstiden.   Stockholm.   1839.
Holm, E.   Danmarks-Norges Historie, 1720-1814.   Copenhagen.   1902.
Jansson, H.   Sveriges accession till Hannoverska Alliansen, 1725-7.   Stockholm.   1893.
Schybergson, M. G.   Riksdagsmanndvalen i Åbo under Frihetstiden.   Helsingfors.   1891.
Stavenow, L.   Geschichte Schwedens, 1718-72.   German transl. by C. Roch.   Vol. vii of Gesch. Schwedens.   (Gesch. d. europ. Staaten.)   Gotha.   1908.
Svedelius, W. E.   Minne af Grefve Arvid Horn.   Stockholm.   1879.
Sveriges Historia.   Vol. iv.   Stockholm.   1877-81.
Tengberg, N. A.   Bidrag till historien om Sveriges Krig med Ryssland åren 1741-3.   Lund.   1857-60.
—— Om Frihetstiden.   Stockholm.   1867.
Tengberg, R.   Sverige under Partitidhvarvet.   Stockholm.   1879.
Tessin, Count C. G.   Tessin och Tessiniana.   Stockholm.   1819.

B.   Gustavus III.

(1)   *General.*

Ahnfelt, A.   Ur svenska hofvets lif.   Stockholm.   1880-3.   German edition.   Stuttgart.   1887.
Bain, R. N.   Gustavus III and his contemporaries.   London.   1894.
Beskow, Baron Bron.   Minne af K. Gjörwell.   Stockholm.   1863.
—— Om Gustaf III såsom Konung och menniska.   Stockholm.   1860-9.   French edition.   Stockholm.   1868.
Fryxell, A.   Berättelser ur Svenska Historien.   Stockholm.   1831, etc.
Gustavus III.   Geschichte Gustavs des Dritten.   Frankfurt.   1810.
Holm, E.   Danmark-Norges Historie, 1720-1814.   Copenhagen.   1902.
Leuss, H.   Gustav III.   In Gekrönte Sanginiker.   Berlin.   1906.
Malmström, C. G.   Sveriges politiska historia.   Stockholm.   1893-1901.
Odhner, C. T.   Sveriges politiska historia under Gustaf III:s regering.   Stockholm.   1885, etc.
Schartaus, J.   Hemliga handlingar rörande till Sveriges historia efter Konung Gustaf III:s anträde till regeringen.   Stockholm.   1821.
Schinkel, B. von.   Minnen ur Sveriges nyare historia.   Stockholm.   1855-83.
Schück, J. H. E.   Gustaf III.   Stockholm.   1904.
Sveriges Historia.   Vol. iv.   Stockholm.   1877-81.
Tegnér, E.   G. M. Armfelt.   Stockholm.   1883-7.
Toll, J. C., Count.   Biografisk teckning.   Stockholm.   1849-50.
Wirsén, C. D. af.   Minne af Grefve J. G. Oxenstjerna.   Stockholm.   1885.

(2)   *Domestic Policy.*

Herrmann, E.   Gustav III und die politischen Partieen Schwedens im xviii Jahrhundert.   Leipzig.   1856.
Rosengren, J.   Om O. Wallqvist såsom biskop och eforus.   Vesiö.   1901.
Tengberg, N. A.   Konung Gustaf III:s första regerungstid.   Lund.   1871.
Tham, W.   Konung Gustaf III och Riketsständer.   Stockholm.   1866.
Wallqvist, O.   Minnen och bref.   Stockholm.   1878.

(3) Foreign Policy.

Armaillé, M. C. A. de.   La Comtesse d'Egmont d'après ses lettres inédites à Gustave III.   (1771–3.)   Paris.   1890.

Bonneville de Marsangy, L.   Le Comte de Vergennes, son ambassade en Suède.   (1771–4.)   Paris.   1898.

Broglie, J. V. A., Duc de.   Le Secret du Roi.   Vol. ii.   Paris.   1878.

Gregorevich, N. I.   Chancellor Prince A. Bezborodko.   St Petersburg.   1879–81.   (*In Russian.*)

Hjelt, A. J.   Sveriges ställning till Udlandet efter 1772.   Helsingfors.   1887.

Koersner, P. V.   Gustaf III:s yttre politik under tiden närmast före ryska Krigens utbrotta, 1786–9.   Falun.   1882.

Nielsen, Y.   Gustaf den III:s norske Politik.   Christiania.   1877.

Odhner, C. T.   Minne af Grefve U. Scheffer.   Stockholm.   1892.

(4) The Russian and Danish Wars.

Backström, P.   Svenska flottans historia.   Stockholm.   1884.

Barrow, J.   Life and correspondence of Sir W. S. Smith.   London.   1848.

Grot, Y. K.   Catherine II and Gustavus III.   St Petersburg.   1834.   (*In Russian.*)

Kynynmond, E. E. E. E. M., Countess of Minto.   Memoirs of the Right Hon. Hugh Elliot.   Edinburgh.   1868.

Markell, J.   Anteckningar rörande Finska Arméens Krigshistoria.   Stockholm.   1870.

—— Öfversigt af svenska krigens historia.   Stockholm.   1890.

Odhner, C. T.   Razumovski's not den 18 Juin 1788.   Stockholm.   1897.

(5) The French Revolution.

Åkeson, N.   Gustaf III:s förhållanden till Franska Revolutionen.   Lund.   1885.

Cruewell, G. A.   Die Beziehungen Gustafs III zur Königin Marie Antoinette von Frankreich.   Berlin.   1897.

Daudet, E.   Histoire de l'Émigration.   Vol. iii.   Coblentz.   Paris.   1890.

Fersen, Count Hans A. von.   Le Comte de Fersen et la Cour de France.   Paris.   1877–8.   English edition.   London.   1902.

Flach, F. F.   Grefve Hans Axel von Fersen.   Stockholm.   1896.

Geffroy, M. A.   Gustave III et la Cour de France.   Paris.   1867.

Odhner, C. T.   Gustaf III och Katarina II efter Freden i Värälä.   Stockholm.   1895.

Reumont, A. von.   König Gustav III in Aachen...1791.   Aix.   1880.

Schartau, J.   Bidrag till Konung Gustaf III:s historia innehållande hans tillärnade Expedition mot Frankrike, 1792.   Stockholm.   1826.

(6) The Gefle Diet and the assassination.

Ahngrist, J. A.   Riksdagen i Gefle, 1792.   Upsala.   1895.

Bain, R. N.   Assassination of Gustavus III of Sweden.   Eng. Hist. Review.   ii, 543.

Gustavus III.   Historia om Konung Gustafs mord.   Stockholm.   1843.

—— An account of the death of the late King of Sweden.   London.   1792.

—— Historiska anteckningar om de aristokratiska stämplingarne i Sverige under Konung Gustaf III, samt om dennes olycklige dödssätt.   Stockholm.   1821.

Lehndorf-Bandels, A. A. L.   Gustavs Tod.   Hamburg.   1793.

Nervo, Baron G. de.   Gustave III et Anckarström.   Paris.   1876.

CHAPTER XXIII.

POLITICAL PHILOSOPHY FROM HOBBES TO BURKE.

From the mass of pamphlets, sermons, fly-sheets, etc., especially in the British Museum (King's Tracts, Thomason Collection) and in the Bodleian Library (Ashmole, Bartholomew, Godwin, Gough, Lincoln, Rawlinson, Wood and other Collections), the few that follow are here singled out as presenting some distinctive features*. See R. Watt, Bibliotheca Britannica, for list and authors of many pamphlets.

A briefe discourse...on government. 1648. [Thorough good sense.]

Acton, Lord. Historical Essays and Studies. Edited by J. N. Figgis and R. V. Laurence. 1907.

—— The History of Freedom, and other Essays. Edited by J. N. Figgis and R. V. Laurence. 1907.

Alarm, a, to Corporations. 1659.

Anabaptists' Petition, the, from Maidstone gaol. 1660.

Austin, J. Jurisprudence. Ed. R. Campbell. 1835.

A winding sheet for the Good Old Cause. 1659.

A word to the purpose. 1659. [Anticipating Locke.]

Bacon, N. An Historical Discovery of the Uniformity of the Government of England. 1647. 5th edn. 1760. [Largely by Selden.]

Bagshaw, E. De monarchia absoluta. 1659. [An attack on Hobbes, etc.; a typical College Essay.]

Baron, R. A cordial for low spirits. 1751. [Re-edited by a republican.]

—— The pillars of priestcraft shaken. 1752.

Berkeley, G., Bishop of Cloyne. A discourse of passive obedience. 1709.

Blackburne, R. Thomæ Hobbes vita, et Auctarium. [Carolopoli.] 1681.

Blakey, R. History of political literature. 1855.

Bluntschli, J. C. Geschichte der Politik. Munich. 1867.

Bolingbroke, Viscount. Miscellaneous Works. 4 vols. Edinburgh. 1773. (Esp. Letter to Windham, Dissertation on Parties, Letter on History, Patriot King.)

Borgeaud, E. The rise of modern democracy. Transl. by Mrs Birkbeck Hill. 1894.

Bosanquet, B. The philosophical theory of the State. 1899.

Bramhall, J. A warning to the church of England. 1706.

—— Castigations of Mr Hobbes. 1658.

British Museum Subject Catalogue. Article: Government. 1836–1906.

Brown, Jethro. Austinian Theory of Law. 1906.

Bryce, J. Studies in History and Jurisprudence. Oxford. 1901.

Buhle, J. G. Histoire de la philosophie moderne. Translated by A. J. L. Jourdan. 6 vols. Paris. 1816.

* The place of publication is London, where not otherwise noted.

Burnet, G., Bishop of Salisbury. An enquiry into the measure of submission, etc. 1688.
—— Papers. 1689.
—— A history of his own time. 1815.
Butler, Samuel. Hudibras. Ed. Z. Grey. 2 vols. 1744.
Censure, the, of the Rota upon Mr Milton's book. [A typical Royalist squib.] 1660.
Chadwick, W. Life and times of D. Defoe. 1859. [Vigorous, violent, very useful.]
Christus Dei the Lord's Anointed. 1643.
Clapham, J. Obedience to magistrates. 1683.
Clarendon, Earl of. A brief view of errors in Mr Hobbes' Leviathan. Oxford. 1676.
Clark, E. C. Practical jurisprudence. 1883.
Clodius, J. De ratione status. 1659.
Collins, J. Churton. Bolingbroke and Voltaire. 1886.
Covel, W. A declaration unto the Parliament. 1659. [An extraordinary manifesto from a Leveller.]
Croftow, Z. The fastening of Peter's fetters or the Covenant vindicated. 1660.
Davenant, C. True picture of a modern Whig. 6th edn. 1701.
Defoe, D. Works. Ed. W. Hazlitt. Especially, The Original Power of the People 1701, Shortest Way with Dissenters 1702, The Review, etc. 1704–13. 1843.
Dryden, John. Poetical Works. Ed. G. Saintsbury. Vols. ix and x. Edinburgh 1844–5.
Du Moulin, Peter. Regii Sanguinis Clamor. With dedicatory epistle by A. Morus (Moir). The Hague. 1652.
Dunning, W. A. A history of political theories (Columbia series). New York. 1905.
Eachard, J. Mr Hobbes' State of Nature considered. Two dialogues. 1672–4.
England's monarchy, etc. 1660. [Eulogy of British constitution.]
Feak, C. Mr Tillinghast's eight last sermons. The banner of Truth displayed. 1647. [Manifestoes of the Fifth Monarchy men.]
Figgis, J. N. The divine right of Kings. Cambridge. 1896.
Filmer, R. The freeholder's grand inquest. 1647. Republished 1679.
—— Observations concerning the original of government. 1652. Republished 1679.
—— Patriarcha. Republished 1679.
—— The power of Kings. 1648. Republished 1679.
Firth, C. H. The Clarke Papers. Camden Soc. Publ. 2 vols. 1891–4.
Ford, S. The loyal subject's indignation. 1660. [A good royalist argument.]
Forset, E. A comparative discourse of bodies natural and politique. 1606. [The source of much of Hobbes.]
Gardiner, S. R. Constitutional documents. Oxford. 1889.
Gee, F. The right and original of the civil magistrate. 1658. [Able and thoughtful.]
Gierke, O. Althusius. Breslau. 1903.
Gooch, G. P. English democratic ideas in the seventeenth century. Cambridge. 1898.
Graham, W. English Political Philosophy. 1899.
Green, T. H. Principles of Political Obligation. 1885.
G. S. The dignity of kingship asserted, against J. M(ilton). 1660.
Hall, J. Treatise against Monarchy. 1651. [Able and interesting: the author died at 29.]
Hallam, H. Constitutional History of England. 8th edn. 3 vols. 1855.
Harrington, J. The art of lawgiving. 1659. [A popular abstract of the Oceana.]
—— The Rota, or Model of a free state. 1660. [The last manifesto of his party in February, 1660.]
—— Works. Ed. J. Toland. 2nd edn. 1737.
Herriott, F. I. Temple on Government. (Philadelphia. 1893?)
Heylin, P. The stumbling-block of rebellion. 1658.

Heylin, P. Aerius redivivus. [A bitter anti-Puritan history.] 1670–2.

Hoadly, B. Works. 1773. [Especially. The original of Civil Government, 1709, and the sermon on the Kingdom of Christ, 1717.]

Hobbes, T. Works. Ed. W. Molesworth. 11 vols. 1839–45.

Howes, J. Sermon against Atheists, Independents, Presbyterians, Anabaptists. [1670?]

Hudson, M. The Divine Right of Government. 1647.

Hume, D. Essays. Ed. T. H. Green and T. H. Grose. 1875.

Hunton, P. Treatise on Monarchy. 1643. Reprinted 1689.

Janet, P. Histoire de la Science politique. Paris. 1887.

J. H. A briefe admonition, etc. 1659.

Johnson, S. Julian the Apostate. 1686.

League Illegal, the, or the Covenant examined. 1657.

Lee, Wm. Defoe. 1869.

Leslie, C. A view of the times 1702–9. (The Rehearsal.) 6 vols. 2nd edn. 1750.

—— Cassandra (But I hope not). 1704. 2nd edn. 1750.

L'Estrange, R. Apology. 1660. [A racy account of events 1658–60, and an answer to a number of contemporary pamphlets.]

Letter, a, on Dr Lake. 1690. [Acute review of Passive Obedience.]

Lilburne, J. England's new chains. 1649.

—— Legall Liberties of the People. 1649.

—— Agreement of the People. 1649 [*i.e.* 1650].

Locke, J. Works. Ed. Bp Law. 1777.

Loewe, J. H. Bramhall's Verhältniss zu Hobbes. Abhandl. k. böhm. Gesellsch. Prag, vii, 1. 4. Prague. 1885–6.

Long, T. The impiety of an absolute toleration. 1662.

Lowde, J. Reasonableness of the Christian Religion. 1684.

Lucy, W. Observations on Mr Hobbes his Leviathan. 1663.

Mackenzie, Sir G. Jus Regium. 1684. [Scottish point of view.]

Maine, H. Ancient Law. Ed. Sir F. Pollock. 1906. [Criticism of Hobbes and Locke.]

—— Early Institutions. Ed. Sir F. Pollock. 1875. [Criticism of Hobbes and Locke.]

Marvell, A. The Rehearsal transprosed. 1672. [Witty attack on Bp Parker.]

Masson, D. Milton's Life and Times. 6 vols. Cambridge. 1859–94.

Mayer, K. T. Hobbes. Freiburg i. B. 1884.

Michel, H. L'Idée de l'État. Paris. 1896. [Reaction from Laissez-faire.]

Milton, J. Especially tenure of Kings. 1649. Treatise of Civil Power. 1659.

Minto, W. Daniel Defoe. (English Men of Letters.) 1879.

Miserere cleri. 1668. [Assize sermon at Exeter; a curious picture of clergy.]

Nalson, J. On monarchy. 1678.

—— Foxes and Firebrands. 2 parts. 1680–2. ["Quakers are Friars disguised."]

—— The common interest of king and people. 1678.

Needham, M. Excellencie of a free state. 1656.

Neville, H. Plato redivivus. 2nd edn. 1681. 4th edn. 1763.

Old English Puritan, the. 1660. [A good defence.]

Parker, S. Ecclesiastical Polity. 1670.

—— A defence of the Ecclesiastical Polity. 1671.

—— History of his own time. 1682.

—— Religion and loyalty. 1684. [Climax of Non-resistance.]

Perry, G. Student's Church History. 1884.

Pollock, Sir F. History of the Science of Politics. 1890.

Prynne, W. The sword of Christian magistracy. 1647.

—— The Good Old Cause anatomised. 1659.

Ranke, L. von. Sämmtliche Werke. Vol. xxiv. Leipzig. 1872. [On division of functions.]

Rebel's plea, the, or Mr Baxter's judgment. 1660. [A vigorous attack.]

Regicides, the dying speeches of the. [1660?]

Ritchie, D. G. Natural Rights. 1895.

Rively, B. A sermon against Fifth Monarchists, English Mamelukes, Scotch Enthusiasts. 1679.

Sadler, J. Olbia the new island. 1660.

—— Rights of the kingdom. 1649. [Anti-royalist argument from law and history.]

Salmond, J. W. Jurisprudence. 1902.

Sancroft, Abp. W. Modern policies taken from Machiavel, etc. 1652.

Savile, G., Ld Halifax. The character of a trimmer (in Miscellanies). 1699–1700.

Seasonable reflections on...Passive Obedience. 1690. [Good sense well expressed.]

Selden, W. Table Talk. Oxford. 1892. [Often reprinted.]

Seller, A. A history of passive obedience. 1689.

Sexby, E. Killing no murder. [1657?]

Sherlock, T. Works. 1730. [Especially Answer to Hoadley, etc. 1718.]

Sichel, W. Bolingbroke and his times, and The sequel. 1901.

Sidgwick, H. Elements of Politics. 1891.

Sidney, A. Works. Ed. J. Robertson. 1772.

Sidney redivivus. 1689.

South, R. Peculiar care of providence for kings. 1675.

Sprigge, W. A modest plea for an equal Commonwealth. 1659. [A vigorous Independent pamphlet.]

Stephen, Sir Leslie. Hobbes. (English Men of Letters.) 1904.

—— English Thought in the eighteenth century. 2 vols. 1876.

Stillingfleet, Bp E. Works, etc. Ed. R. Bentley. 1707–10. [Especially the Irenicon of 1659.]

Stubbe, H. An essay in defence of the Good Old Cause. 1659. [A witty defence of democracy against Baxter.]

—— A letter to an officer, etc. 1659.

Swift, J. Works. 1752–4.

Taylor, Jeremy. A liberty of prophecying. 1657.

Temple, Sir W. Essay on Government. 1672.

[Tenison, T.] The creed of Mr Hobbes examined. 2nd edn. 1672. [Lively and graphic.]

Tomkins, A. The rebels' plea. 1660. [An attack on Baxter, and anticipation of Locke.]

Tönnies, F. Hobbes, Leben u. Lehre. Breslau. 1896.

Trenchard, J. and Gordon, T. A collection of tracts. 1751. [Whig tracts, 1697–1730.]

Tucker, J. A treatise on Locke, etc. 1781.

Tyrrell, J. Patriarcha non monarcha. 1681. [The copy in the Bodleian Library has copious notes by the author.]

Votiva Tabula. 1660. [A sermon on Barebone's Parliament.]

Warburton, W. Works. 1811. [Especially Alliance between Church and State, 1736.]

Ware, J. The priviledges of the people. 1648.

Whewell, W. History of moral philosophy. Cambridge. 1862.

Williams, Roger. The bloody tenent of persecution. 1644.

Wren, M. Considerations on Mr H.'s Oceana. 1657.

—— Monarchy asserted. 1660. [Shrewd and caustic criticism of Harrington.]

Wright, A. Five sermons in five different ways. 1656. [Against "these God-Almighties of the pulpit."]

CHAPTER XXIV.

THE ROMANTIC MOVEMENT IN EUROPEAN LITERATURE.

I. GENERAL LITERARY HISTORY AND CRITICISM.

Hettner, H. Litteraturgeschichte des achtzehnten Jahrhunderts. 6 vols. 4th edn.
Brunswick. 1893–4.
Periods of European Literature. Ed. G. Saintsbury. Vol. ix. The Mid-eighteenth
century. By J. H. Miller. Vol. x. The Romantic Revolt. By C. E. Vaughan.
Edinburgh. 1902–7.
Sainte-Beuve, C. A. Causeries du Lundi. Vols. i–xv. Paris. 1857–62.
See also: Dictionary of National Biography. London. 1885–1901; Biographie
Universelle. Paris. 1811–62; Nouvelle Biographie Générale. Paris. 1853–66;
Allgemeine Deutsche Biographie. Leipzig. 1875–1905.

II. LITERATURES OF PARTICULAR COUNTRIES.

A. ENGLAND.

(1) *General and Collective History and Criticism.*

Chambers' Encyclopædia of English Literature. Ed. D. Patrick. Vols. ii and iii.
London. 1903.
Courthope, W. J. History of English Poetry. Vol. v. London. 1903.
English Men of Letters. Burke, J. Morley; Fanny Burney, A. Dobson; Coleridge,
H. D. Traill; Cowper, Goldwin Smith; Crabbe, A. Ainger; Maria Edgeworth,
E. Lawless; Fielding, A. Dobson; Gibbon, J. C. Morison; Gray, E. Gosse;
Johnson, L. Stephen; Lamb, A. Ainger; Richardson, A. Dobson; Scott,
R. H. Hutton; Southey, E. Dowden; Sterne, H. D. Traill; James Thomson,
G. C. Macaulay; Wordsworth, F. W. H. Myers. London. 1878, etc.
Handbooks of English Literature: T. Seccombe, The Age of Johnson; C. H. Herford,
The Age of Wordsworth. London. 1897–1900.
Stephen, Sir L. Hours in a Library. 3 vols. London. 1892.
—— English Literature and Society in the Eighteenth Century. London. 1904.
Taine, H. Histoire de la Littérature anglaise. Vol. iv. Paris. 1873.

(2) *Particular Writers.*

(a) *Editions of Works.*

Blake, W. Works Poetic, Symbolic, and Critical. Edd. E. J. Ellis and W. B. Yeats.
3 vols. London. 1893.
—— Poetical Works. Ed. J. Sampson. Oxford. 1905.
Burns, R. The poetry of. Edd. W. E. Henley and T. F. Henderson. 4 vols.
Edinburgh. 1896–7.
Coleridge, S. T. Poetical Works. Ed. J. D. Campbell. London. 1893.
—— Letters. Ed. E. H. Coleridge. 2 vols. London. 1895.
—— Anima Poetae. Ed. E. H. Coleridge. London. 1895.
Lillo, G. The London Merchant and Fatal Curiosity. With introd. by A. W. Ward.
(Belles-Lettres Series.) Boston and London. 1906.
Richardson, Samuel. Works. With pref. chapter by Sir L. Stephen. 12 vols.
London. 1883.
Scott, Sir W. Miscellaneous Prose Works. 28 vols. Edinburgh. 1837–40.

Scott, Sir W. Poetical Works. Ed. J. G. Lockhart. 12 vols. Edinburgh. 1833–4.
—— Waverley Novels. 25 vols. Edinburgh. 1870–1.
Wordsworth, W. Poetical Works. Ed. J. Morley. London. 1888.
—— Prose Works. Ed. A. B. Grosart. 3 vols. London. 1876.

(b) Biography and Criticism.

Blake, W.—Berger, P. Poitiers. 1907.
—— Life, by A. Gilchrist. 2 vols. London. 1863. [Vol. II: Selections by D. G. Rossetti.]
—— Swinburne, A. C. London. 1868.
Burns, R.—Angellier, A. 2 vols. Paris. 1893.
Coleridge, S. T.—Brandl, A. S. T. Coleridge und die englische Romantik. Berlin. 1886. Engl. transl. London. 1887.
Cowper, W.—Life and Letters by R. Southey. 7 vols. London. 1835–6.
Johnson, S. Lives of the Poets. Ed. G. Birkbeck Hill. 3 vols. Oxford. 1905.
—— Boswell, J. Life of Johnson. Ed. G. Birkbeck Hill. 6 vols. Oxford. 1887.
Scott, Sir W.—Lockhart, J. G. Life of Scott. 7 vols. Edinburgh. 1837.
Wordsworth, W.—Legouis, E. La jeunesse de Wordsworth. Paris. 1896. Engl. transl. London. 1897.
—— Raleigh, W London. 1903.
—— Dorothy. Journals. Ed. W. Knight. London. 1897.

B. FRANCE.

(1) History and Criticism, General and Collective.

Brunetière, F. Études critiques. 8 vols. Paris. 1902–7.
Caro, E. M. La fin du 18me siècle. 2 vols. Paris. 1881.
Faguet, E. Dix-huitième Siècle. Paris. 1890.
Julleville, Petit de (Editor). Histoire de la langue et de la littérature française. Vols. VI, VII. Paris. 1898–9.
Jusserand, J. J. Shakespeare en France sous l'ancien régime. Paris. 1898. Engl. Tr. London. 1899.
Sainte-Beuve, C. A. Portraits de Femmes. Paris. 1876.
—— Portraits littéraires. 3 vols. Paris. 1862–4.

(2) Particular Writers.

(a) Editions of Works.

Chateaubriand, F. R. de. Mémoires d'Outre-tombe. 12 vols. Paris. 1849–50.
Diderot, D. Œuvres complètes. 20 vols. Paris. 1875–7.
Grimm, Baron F. M. von. Correspondance littéraire. 17 vols. Paris. 1813–4.
Rousseau, J. J. Œuvres complètes. Ed. G. Streckeisen-Moulton. 8 vols. Paris. 1856–7.
—— Œuvres et Correspondance inédites. Paris. 1861.
Voltaire, F. M. A. de. Œuvres complètes. 70 vols. Kehl. 1785–9.

(b) Biography and Criticism.

Chénier, A.—Becq de Fouquières, L. Lettres critiques sur la vie, les œuvres, les manuscrits de A. Chénier. Paris. 1881.
Diderot, D.—Morley, John (Viscount Morley). Diderot and the Encyclopædists. 2 vols. London. 1891.
—— Reinach, J. Diderot. Paris. 1894.
Rousseau, J. J.—Épinay, Madame de. Mémoires. 3 vols. Paris. 1818.
   Macdonald, F. Jean-Jacques Rousseau. 2 vols. London. 1906. [Designed to destroy the credit of the above. If the case has been established, the Life of Rousseau, from 1756, must be re-written.]
—— Morley, John (Viscount Morley). Rousseau. 2 vols. London. 1873.
—— Musset-Pathay, V. D. Œuvres inédites de J. J. Rousseau. Paris. 1825.
—— Schmidt, Erich. Richardson, Rousseau und Goethe. Jena. 1875.

Rousseau, J. J.—Streckeisen-Moulton, G. Rousseau, ses amis et ses ennemis. Paris. 1865.

—— Texte, J. J. J. Rousseau et les origines du cosmopolitisme littér. Paris. 1895.

Voltaire, F. M. A. de.—Champion, E. Voltaire, études critiques. Paris. 1897.

—— Condorcet, M. J. Vie de Voltaire. London. 1791.

—— Desnoiresterres, G. Voltaire et la société française au 18me siècle. Paris. 1871–6.

—— Morley, John (Viscount Morley). Voltaire. London. 1874.

C. GERMANY.
(1) *General History and Criticism.*

Haym, R. Die romantische Schule. Berlin. 1870.

Hettner, H. Die romantische Schule in ihrem inneren Zusammenhang mit Goethe und Schiller. Brunswick. 1850.

Robertson, J. M. History of German literature. London. 1892.

Sauer, R. Stürmer und Dränger. 3 vols. Berlin and Stuttgart. 1883.

Scherer, W. Geschichte der deutschen Litteratur. 17th edn. Strassburg. 1894.

Schmidt, Julian. Geschichte des geistigen Lebens in Deutschland von Leibnitz bis auf Lessing's Tod. 2 vols. Leipzig. 1862–4.

—— Gesch. der deutschen Litt. seit Lessing's Tod. 5th edn. 3 vols. Leipzig. 1866–7.

(2) *Particular Writers.*
(a) *Editions of Works.*

Goethe, J. W. von. Werke. Weimar edn. Part I. Vols. I–L. Weimar. 1887, etc.

Herder, J. G. von. Sämmtliche Werke. Ed. B. Suphan. Vols. I–XXXIII. Berlin. 1877, etc.

Lessing, G. E. Sämmtliche Schriften. Ed. K. Lachmann. 3rd edn, by F. Muncker. Vols. I–XX. Berlin and Leipzig. 1886–1906. (*In progress.*)

Schiller, J. C. F. von. Sämmtliche Werke. With Introductions by K. Goedeke. 16 vols. Stuttgart. 1893–4.

(b) *Biography and Criticism.*

Goethe, J. W. von.—Bernays, M. Der junge Goethe. 3 vols. Leipzig. 1875.

—— Bielschowsky, A. Goethe, sein Leben u. seine Werke. Munich. 1896–1904.

—— Lewes, G. H. Life of Goethe. 3rd edn. London. 1882.

Herder, J. G. von.—Haym, R. Herder nach seinem Leben und seinen Werken dargestellt. 2 vols. Berlin. 1877–85.

Lessing, G. E.—Fischer, Kuno. Lessing als Reformator der deutschen Litteratur. Stuttgart. 1881.

Schiller, J. C. F. von.—Fischer, K. Schiller-Schriften. 2 vols. Heidelberg. 1891–2.

D. OTHER COUNTRIES.

Brückner, A. Geschichte der russischen Litteratur. Leipzig. 1905.

Fitzmaurice-Kelly, J. History of Spanish Literature. London. 1898.

Hansen, P. Illustr. Dansk Litteratur-Historie. 2nd edn. 3 vols. Copenhagen. 1902.

Pypin, A. N. Russkoi Literatury. 2nd edn. 4 vols. St Petersburg. 1902–3.

—— and Spasovič, V. D. Geschichte der slavischen Litteraturen. German transl. 3 vols. Leipzig. 1880.

Reinhardstoettner, R. von. Portugiesische Literaturgeschichte. (Sammlung Göschen.) Leipzig. 1904.

Storia letteraria d' Italia scritta da una Società di Professori. 10 vols. Milan. 1900–6.

Ten Brink, J. Geschiedenis der nederlandsche Letterkunde. Amsterdam. 1897.

Ticknor, G. History of Spanish literature. 6th edn. 3 vols. London. 1882.

CHRONOLOGICAL TABLE

OF

LEADING EVENTS MENTIONED IN THIS VOLUME.

1525 Bábar founds Moghul Empire in India.
1651 Hobbes' *Leviathan* published.
1654 Final acquisition of Brazil by Portugal.
1656 Harrington's *Oceana* published.
1657–1707 Reign of Aurungzeb in India.
1663 Renewal of Franco-Swiss alliance of 1602.
1668 Triple Alliance.
1680 Filmer's *Patriarcha* published.
1683 Siege of Vienna.
1689 Bill of Rights. Locke's *On Toleration* published.
1696 Frederick Augustus, Elector of Saxony, elected King Augustus II of Poland.
1701 June. Act of Settlement.
    August. Grand Alliance completed.
    September. Death of James II. Louis XIV recognises "James III."
1702 March. Death of William III. Accession of Anne.
1703 Methuen Treaty between England and Portugal.
1704 Act of Security (Scotland) receives Royal Assent.
1707 May. Act of Union of England and Scotland comes into force.
1710 South Sea Company established.
1712 Toleration Act (Scotland). Patronage restored in Scotland.
    Second Vilmergen War in Switzerland.
1713 February. Accession of Frederick William I of Prussia.
    Peace of Utrecht.
1714 June. Death of Electress Sophia.
    August. Death of Anne. Accession of George I.
    Marriage of Philip V with Elisabeth Farnese.
1715 April. Third Dutch Barrier Treaty signed.
    September. Death of Louis XIV. Accession of Louis XV. Regency of
        Orleans. Jacobite rising in Scotland.
    December. Commercial Treaty between Spain and Great Britain.
    Bremen and Verden ceded to Hanover by Denmark.
1716 February. Commercial Treaty between Great Britain and the Dutch.
    May. Law founds his Bank in France.
    June. Treaty of Westminster.
    Septennial Act.   Turkish conquest of Morea.
1717 January. Triple Alliance. Breach between Great Britain and Sweden.
    August. Louisiana Company founded by Law.
    Alberoni conquers Sardinia.
    Victory of Prince Eugene over the Turks at Belgrade.
    Congress of Passarowitz meets.
1718 Quadruple Alliance.

1718 July. Peace of Passarowitz.
    August. Spanish fleet destroyed off Cape Passaro by Byng.
        „ Cellamare's plot discovered. Franco-British invasion of Spain.
    November. Death of Charles XII.
    December. Great Britain declares war on Spain.
1719 January. France declares war on Spain.   First Treaty of Vienna.
    November. Treaty of Stockholm.
    December. Fall of Alberoni.
    Act empowering English Parliament to legislate for Ireland.
1720 Spain, Denmark, and Poland accede to Quadruple Alliance.
    Collapse of Law's System. Plague at Marseilles.
    August. Height of South Sea mania.
    Pragmatic Sanction recognised by Austrian Estates.
1721 March. Treaty of Madrid. Acceded to by Great Britain (June).
    August. Peace of Nystad.
1722 Walpole First Lord of Treasury. "Atterbury's" plot.
1723 December. Death of Duke of Orleans.
1724 January. Abdication of Philip V.
        „ Congress of Cambray meets.
    April. First *Drapier's Letter.*
    August. Death of Don Luis. Philip V reascends Spanish throne.
1725 April. Treaty of Vienna.
    September. Treaty of Herrenhausen.
        „ Marriage of Louis XV with Maria Leszczynska.
    November. Secret Austro-Spanish marriage treaty negotiated by Ripperdá.
1726 Denmark and Sweden join Herrenhausen Alliance.
    September. Hozier blockades Portobello.
    October. Treaty of Wusterhausen.
    Fleury First Minister of France.   Foundation of Monte Video.
1727 February. Spain declares war against England.
    May. Peace preliminaries signed at Paris.
    First Indemnity Act for Nonconformists.
1728 March. Convention of the Pardo. Congress of Soissons meets (June).
1729 Methodist movement begins at Oxford.
    September. Birth of the Dauphin.
    November. Treaty of Seville. End of Ostend Company.
1730 May. Accession of Tsarina Anne.
    Death of Frederick IV of Denmark. Accession of Christian VI.
1731 January. Spain denounces Treaty of Seville.
        „ England and Holland guarantee Pragmatic Sanction.
        „ Death of Antonio Farnese, Duke of Parma.
    March. Treaty of Vienna. Acceded to by Spain (July).
1732 Don Carlos Duke of Parma.
1733 Second election of Stanislaus Leszczynski. Polish Succession War begins.
    May. Spain attacks Austrian Italy. Battle of Bitonto.
    September. Treaty of Turin.
    November. Treaty of the Escurial (First *Pacte de Famille*).
    Walpole's Excise Act withdrawn. Molasses Act.
1735 January. S. Leszczynski abdicates. Augustus III recognised King of Poland.
    Preliminaries of Vienna signed.
    Don Carlos crowned King of the Two Sicilies.
    Russo-Turkish War begins.   Porteous riots in Edinburgh.
1737 Fall of Chauvelin.
1738–72 Strife of the *Caps* and *Hats* in Sweden.
1738 January. Convention of the Pardo.

1738 Third Treaty of Vienna.
1739 Vienna Treaty acceded to by Sardinia (February), Spain and Naples (June).
September. Peace of Belgrade. Peace of Constantinople.
October. War between Spain and Great Britain declared.
December. Vernon takes Portobello.
1740 May. Death of Frederick William I of Prussia. Accession of Frederick II.
October. Death of Tsarina Anne. Accession of Ivan VI.
  „   Death of Charles VI. Austrian Succession War begins.
December. Frederick II invades Silesia.
1741 April. Battle of Mollwitz.   June. Treaty of Breslau.
July. Sweden declares war on Russia. Battle of Vilmanstrand.
October. Convention of Klein-Schnellendorf.
December. Frederick II invades Moravia. Accession of Tsarina Elizabeth.
Siege of Cartagena de las Indias.
1742 Fall of Walpole.
May. Battle of Chotusitz.
Austro-Spanish hostilities begin in Italy.
1743 January. Death of Fleury.
February. Battle of Campo Santo.
June. Preliminaries of Breslau. Battle of Dettingen.
July. Peace of Berlin.
August. Peace of Åbo.
October. Treaty of Fontainebleau (Second *Pacte de Famille*).
December. Belleisle's retreat from Prague.
1744 May. Union of Frankfort. Frederick II invades Bohemia
War between Great Britain and France declared.
1745 January. Death of Charles Albert of Bavaria.
March. Treaty of Füssen.
May. Battle of Fontenoy.
June. Austro-Russian Alliance.
July. Jacobite rising.
December. Charles Edward retreats from Derby.
  „   Battle of Kesselsdorf. Saxony accedes to Convention of Hanover.
Treaty of Dresden between Austria and Prussia.
1746 January–March. Sardinian alliance with France.
February. Marshal Saxe takes Brussels.
  „   Death of Christian VI of Denmark. Accession of Frederick V.
April. Alliance of Denmark and France.   Battle of Culloden.
June. Cape Breton taken by the British.
July. Death of Philip V of Spain. Accession of Ferdinand VI.
August. Battle of Roucoux.
September. Madras taken by the French.
1747 May. William IV proclaimed Stadholder.
July. Battle of Lauffeldt. Battle of Exilles.
1748 Bergen-op-Zoom taken by the French.
Treaties of Aix-la-Chapelle signed by France and Great Britain (April) and
  by Spain (October).
1749 October. Treaty of Aquisgran.
  „   Treaty of Madrid.
Dupleix secures French control of the Carnatic.
Bolingbroke's *Idea of a Patriot King* published.
1750 Colonial Manufactures Prohibition Bill.   Rousseau's first *Discours*.
1751 Sieges of Trichinopoly and Arcot.
1752 June. Treaty of Aranjuez.
1754 Representatives of the English North American colonies meet at Albany.

1755 July. Braddock's disaster before Fort Duquesne.

September. Anglo-Russian Convention of St Petersburg (ratified Feb. 1756).

November. Earthquake of Lisbon.   Newcastle-Fox Ministry.

1756 January. Convention of Westminster.

May. Treaty of Versailles. Minorca taken by French.

„ War declared by England against France.

June. Calcutta seized by Siráj-ud-daulá.

August. Frederick II invades Saxony. Battle of Lobositz.

December. Russia accedes to Treaty of Versailles.

Acadia cleared of French settlers. French take Oswego.

1757 Newcastle-Pitt Ministry.

Jan.–Feb. Clive takes Calcutta, Hooghly and Chandernagore.

February. Austro-Russian Convention.

May. Second Treaty of Versailles.

June. Battle of Plassey.

Battles of Prague (May), Kolin (June), Hastenbeck (July), Gross-Jägerndorf (August); Convention of Klosterzeven (September); battles of Rossbach and Breslau (November), Leuthen (December).

1758 April. First annual convention between Great Britain and Prussia.

June. Louisburg taken by British. Clive Governor of Bengal.

Battles of Zorndorf (August), Hochkirch (October).

November. Choiseul Foreign Minister of France.

1759 March–May. Third Treaty of Paris completed.

Battles of Kay, Minden and Quebec (July), Kunersdorf (August), Quiberon Bay (Nov.).

August. Death of Ferdinand VI of Spain. Accession of Charles III.

Jesuits expelled from Portugal and Brazil.

1760 Battle of Landshut (June). Fall of Glatz. Battle of Liegnitz (July).

October. Russian occupation of Berlin.

„ Death of George II. Accession of George III.

November. Battle of Torgau.

1761 Spanish invasion of Portugal.

August. Treaty of San Ildefonso (Third *Pacte de Famille*).

October. Fall of Pitt.

1762 January. War declared against Spain by Great Britain.

„ Death of Tsarina Elizabeth. Accession of Peter III.

May. Prussia makes peace with Russia and Sweden.

„ Spanish invasion of Portugal.

June. Russo-Prussian Alliance. Accession of Catharine II.

British capture of Martinique (February), Havana (June), Manila (October).

Battles of Wilhelmsthal (June), Freiberg (October).

November. Preliminaries of Fontainebleau signed.

Rousseau's *Émile* published.

1763 February. Peace of Hubertusburg. Peace of Paris.

April. Resignation of Bute. Proceedings against Wilkes begin.

First Whiteboy outbreaks in Ireland.

1764 September. Stanislaus Poniatowski elected King of Poland.

Jesuits expelled from France.   Battle of Buxar.

1765 Clive's second governorship of Bengal begins.

March. Stamp Act.

August. Death of Emperor Francis I. Accession of Joseph II.

1766 Stamp Act repealed. Chatham-Grafton Ministry formed.

Lorraine annexed to France.

1767 Jesuits expelled from Spain.

Provisional Treaty of Exchange of Copenhagen.

1768 Purchase of Corsica from Genoa by France.

1768 Confederation of Bar. Russian invasion of Poland.
      Turkey declares war on Russia.
      Nullum Tempus Act.
1769 January. Letters of Junius begin.
      February. Wilkes expelled from House of Commons.
      August. Interview of Joseph II with Frederick II at Neisse.
1770 January. North's Ministry begins. Burke's *Thoughts on the Present Discontents*.
         „   Spanish attack on English settlement in the Falkland Isles.
      May. Marriage of the Dauphin Louis with Marie-Antoinette.
      August. Destruction of Turkish fleet by Russians at Tchesmé.
      December. Fall of Choiseul.
1771 January. Exile of the *Parlement* of Paris.
      Death of Adolphus Frederick of Sweden. Accession of Gustavus III.
      First Roman Catholic Relief Act (Ireland).
      Russian occupation of the Crimea.
1772 February. Secret Treaty of St Petersburg.
      August. First Partition of Poland.
      Royal Marriage Act.
      Coup d'état of Gustavus III in Sweden. Catastrophe of Struensee in Denmark.
         Ministry of Guldberg begins.
1773 Alliance of France and Sweden.
      August. Suppression of the Jesuit Order.
      North's Regulating Act for India. Warren Hastings Governor-General.
      Insurrection of Pugachoff in Russia.
1774 Boston Riot. Boston Port Act.
      May. Louis XV succeeded by Louis XVI. Turgot Finance Minister (Aug.).
      July. Battle of Shumla. Peace of Kutchuk-Kainardji.
1775 Skirmishes at Lexington (April), and Bunker Hill (June).
      July. Spanish attack on Algiers.
1776 Spanish attack on Sacramento.
      Prohibitory Act against American commerce.
      American Declaration of Independence.
1777 February. Joseph I of Portugal succeeded by Maria I. Fall of Pombal.
      June. Necker Director-General of French Finances.
      December. Death of Elector Maximilian Joseph of Bavaria.
1778-84 War with Haidar Ali in India.
1778 February. Treaty of Paris between France and America.
      March. Treaty of the Pardo between Spain and Portugal.
      July. Bavarian Succession War begins.
      September. Dutch-American Treaty of Amity and Commerce.
      Savile's Roman Catholic Relief Act.
1779 May. Peace of Teschen.
      June. Spain declares war on England. Siege of Gibraltar begins.
      December. English restrictions on Irish trade abolished.
1780 January. Rodney relieves Gibraltar.
      February. First Armed Neutrality mooted.
      November. Death of Maria Theresa. Joseph II sole Emperor.
      December. Great Britain declares war on the Dutch.
      Austro-Russian Alliance against Turkey.
1781 Rodney takes Dutch West Indian Islands.
      De Grasse takes Tobago and blockades Chesapeake Bay.
      June. Joseph II issues Patent of Tolerance.
      July. Battle of Porto Novo (July); battle of Dogger Bank (August).
      October. Capitulation of Yorktown.
      November. Joseph II abolishes serfdom.

1782   February.   Minorca and West Indian Islands taken by French.
      March.   Pius VI visits Vienna.   Peruvian rebellion against Spain suppressed.
      April.   Evacuation of the Barrier fortresses.
        ,,   Rodney defeats de Grasse in the West Indies.
        ,,   Grattan's Declaration of Rights.   Irish legislative independence.
      August–September.   French victorious in the East Indies.
      October.   Howe relieves Gibraltar.
      November.   Preliminaries of Peace accepted by Great Britain and America.
1783   September.   Peace of Versailles.
      December.   Fox' India Bill rejected by House of Lords.   Fall of North.
1784–97   Ministry of Andreas Bernstorff in Denmark.
1784   January.   Peace between Great Britain and the United States ratified.
      Pitt's India Act.
1785   February.   Return of Warren Hastings.
      July.   Formation of *Fürstenbund.*
      Sweden declares war on Russia.   Naval battle off Hogland (July).
      Denmark attacks Sweden.
      November.   Barrier Treaty of 1715 abrogated by Treaty of Fontainebleau.
1786   August.   Frederick II of Prussia succeeded by Frederick William II.
      September.   Commercial Treaty between Great Britain and France.
1787   Trial of Warren Hastings begins (ends 1795).
      Disturbances in Austrian Netherlands.
      Prussian troops invade Holland.   Austria and Russia declare war on Turkey.
1788   April.   Anglo-Dutch defensive alliance.
      July.   Suedo-Russian War.
      August.   Anglo-Prussian defensive alliance of Berlin.
      October.   Last Polish (Four Years') Diet meets.
      November.   Convention of Uddevalla.
      December.   Death of Charles III of Spain.   Accession of Charles IV.
        ,,   Ochakoff taken by Russians.
1789   January.   Regency debates.
      December.   Republic declared in Belgium.
      Insurrection threatened in Hungary.
      Swedish Act of Union and Security.
1790   February.   Emperor Joseph II succeeded by Leopold II.
      June.   Convention of Reichenbach.
      July.   Nootka Sound dispute between Great Britain and Spain settled.
      August.   Peace of Värälä between Russia and Sweden.
      Burke's *Reflections on the French Revolution.*
1791–2   Paine's *Rights of Man* published.
1791   Act to relieve Roman Catholics in England.   (Ireland, 1792, Scotland, 1793.)
      Quebec Government Act.
      Formation of the *London Corresponding Society.*
      May.   Polish Constitution announced.
1792   January.   Treaty of Jassy.
      February.   Tipu Sultan defeated at Seringapatam.
      March.   Death of Emperor Leopold II.   Accession of Francis II.
        ,,   Assassination of Gustavus III of Sweden.
      April.   France declares war on the Emperor.   Fox' Libel Act.
1793   January.   Execution of Louis XVI.
      February.   France declares war against Great Britain and Holland.
      British conquests from French in India.
1796   Death of Tsarina Catharine II.   Accession of Paul.
1797   Frederick William II of Prussia succeeded by Frederick William III.
1798   Proclamation of Helvetic Republic.

INDEX OF NAMES

CAMBRIDGE: PRINTED BY W. LEWIS AT THE UNIVERSITY PRESS

8718

D
208
C17
vol.6

THE CAMBRIDGE MODERN HISTORY.